S0-ARG-063

San Diego County

streetguide

We want to hear from you!
Give us your feedback at:
http://randmcnally.com/contact

SUSTAINABLE FORESTRY INITIATIVE   Certified Sourcing
www.sfiprogram.org
SFI-00507

The paper used inside this book is manufactured using an elemental chlorine-free method and is sourced from forests that are managed responsibly through forest certification programs such as the Sustainable Forestry Initiative.®

RAND M°NALLY   GMJohnsonmaps.com

If you have a comment, suggestion, or even a compliment, please email us at consumeraffairs@RandMcNally.com
Or write to:
Rand McNally Consumer Affairs
P.O. Box 7600
Chicago, IL 60680-9915

Contents
Contenidos

Introduction
Introducción

Maps
Mapas

Lists and Indexes
Lista e índices

Legend
Leyenda

Interstate highway
Autopista Federal

Interstate (business) highway
Ruta Comerciál de Autopista Federal

U.S. highway
Carretera Federal

State highway
Carretera Estatal

Secondary state highway/county highway
Carretera Secundaria Estatal, o del Condado

Mexican highway
Carretera Mexicana

Exit number
Número de salida

Carpool lane
Caril de alta ocupación

Freeway
Autopista

Freeway (proposed)
Autopista (propuesto)

Toll highway, toll plaza
Autopista de cuota, caseta de cobro

Ramp
Acceso y salida

Highway
Carretera

Primary road
Ruta mayor

Secondary road
Ruta secundaria

Minor road
Calle menor

Unpaved road
Calle sin pavimentar

Restricted road
Calle con acceso restringida

Walkway or trail
Camino peatonál

One-way road
Circulación

Gate, lock, barricade
Portal, bloquéo, barricada

Park and ride
Estacionamiento de tránsito

Rest area
Baños

Service area
Gasolina y servicios

Bus station
Estación del autobús

Railroad, station
Ferrocarril, estación

Metrolink/Coaster/Sprinter station
Estación Metrolink/Coaster/Sprinter

Metro rail station
Estación del Metro

Tramway, trolley
Tranvía

Transit line
Metro

Ferry
Transbordador

Waterway
Vía marina navegable

River/creek/shoreline
Río/arroyo/orilla

Levee
Dique

Dry lake
Lago seco

Dam
Presa

International boundary
Frontera Internacionál

State/provincial boundary
Frontera estatal o Provincial

County boundary
Límite del condado

Military installation boundary
Limite de base militar

Township/range boundary, section corner
Límite de terrenos públicos

Postal code boundary
Límite de código postál

12345 **Postal code**
Código postál

1200 **Block number**
Número de cuadra

Building footprint
Edificio

Border crossing/port of entry
Aduana

City/town/village hall or other government building
Ayúntamiento

Courthouse
Oficina de justicia

Fire station
Estación de bomberos

Golf course
Campo de golf

Hospital
Hospitál

Information/visitor center/welcome center
Información turística

Library
Biblioteca

Museum
Muséo

Police/sheriff, etc.
Policía

Post office
Correo

School
Escuela

University or college
Universidad o colegio

Theater/performing arts center
Teatro

Other point of interest
Punto de interés

Using Your Street Guide

The PageFinder™ Map

> Turn to the PageFinder™ Map. Each of the small squares outlined on this map represents a different map page in the Street Guide.

> Locate the specific part of the Street Guide coverage area that you're interested in.

> Note the appropriate map page number. Turn to that map page. Rural areas are sometimes published at multiple scales. Wherever available, select the map page represented on the PageFinder™ by the smaller square - these map pages offer the best available map scale for that area.

The Index

> The Street Guide includes separate indexes for streets, schools, parks, shopping centers, golf courses, and other points of interest.

> In the street listings, information is presented in the following order: block number, city, map page number and grid reference.

> A grid reference is a letter-number combination (B6 for example) that tells you precisely where to find a particular street or point of interest on a map. For index entries including a "See Page" reference, first locate the bracketed map page number, and then locate the desired feature using the particular page-grid information listed in the index.

STREET			
Block	City	Map#	Grid
Hidden Springs Rd			
32400	SBdC	**3762**	**F2**
33100	SBdC	**3682**	**F7**
(See Page 3592)			

The Maps

> Each map is divided into a grid formed by rows and columns. These rows and columns correspond to letters and numbers running horizontally and vertically along the edges of the map.

> To use a grid reference from the index, search horizontally within the appropriate row and vertically within the appropriate column. The destination can be found within the grid square where the row and column meet.

> Adjacent map pages are indicated by numbers that appear at the top, bottom, and sides of each map.

> The legend explains symbols that appear on the maps.

Como usar su Street Guide

El PageFinder™ Map

• Refiérese al PageFinder™ Map. Cada una de las cuadras enumeradas en este mapa representan una página de mapa distinta de este guía.

• Identifica el área del mapa PageFinder™ que le interesa.

• Hágase cuenta del número en la cuadra representada. Ese número es la página del guía donde se representa el mapa de esa área.

• Las áreas rurales son publicadas a veces en múltiples escalas. Dondequiera que este disponible, selecciona el cuadrado más pequeño en el PageFinder™ para encontrar la página de mapa con la mejor escala disponible para aquella área.

El Índice

• Esta guía incluye índices para calles, escuelas, parques, centros de comercio, campos de golf, y otros lugares de interés.

• En el índice de calles, información esta representada en forma de: nombre de la calle, número de la cuadra, página, y cuadrícula.

• La cuadrícula es una combinación de letra y números (por ejemplo "B6") que le indica precisamente donde se halla una calle o punto de interés en la página del mapa indicado. Para las entradas de índice incluyendo una referencia de la "See Page", primero localice el número de la página de mapa entre paréntesis, y entonces sitúa la característica deseada que utiliza la información particular de página-cuadrícula en la lista del índice.

Los Mapas

• Cada mapa está dividido en una cuadrícula de columnas y filas. Estas columnas y filas corresponden a las letras y números que se encuentran por las orillas del mapa.

• Para localizar una cuadrícula representada en el índice, busca la letra de la columna y el número de la fila por las orillas del mapa indicado y sigue la fila y la columna hasta que se encuentren. La calle o punto de interés que busca se encontrará en la cuadra donde la fila y la columna se encuentren.

• Los mapas de continuación se encontrarán en las páginas indicadas por las orillas de los mapas.

• La leyenda explica la mayoría de los símbolos representados en los mapas.

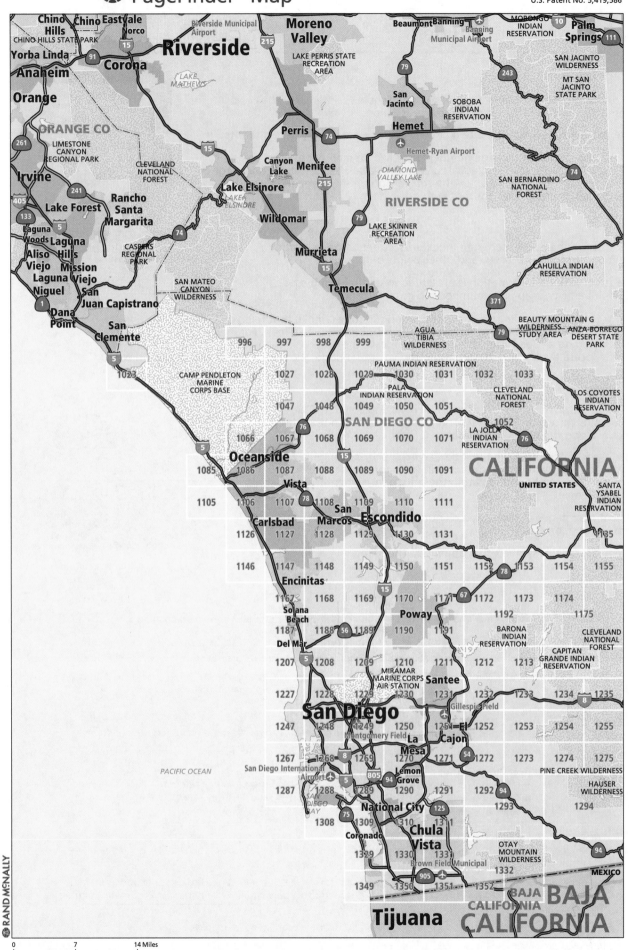

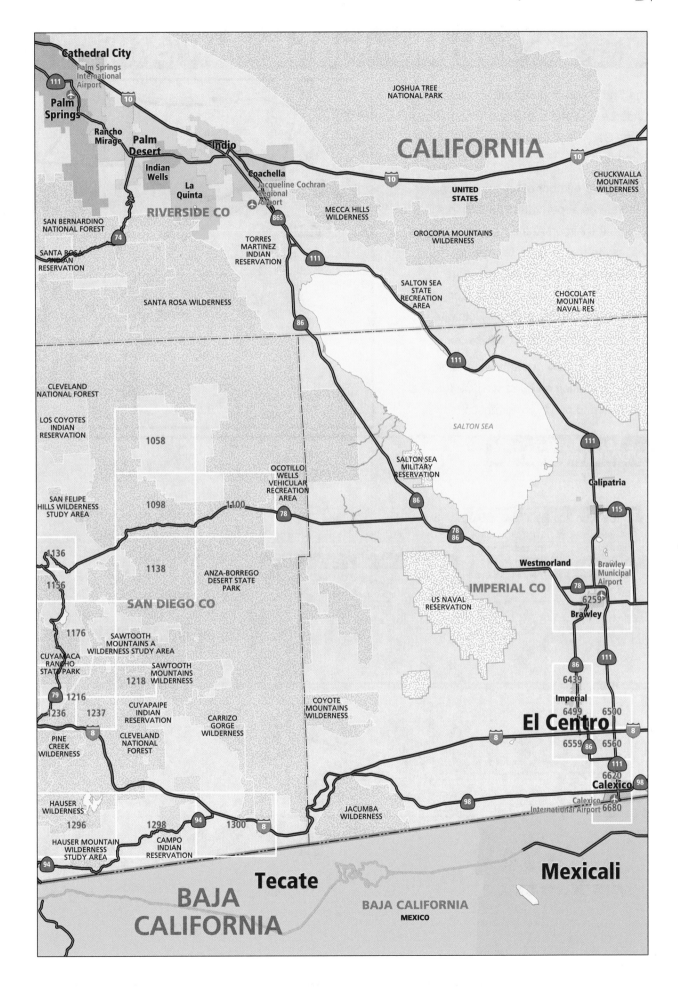

Cathedral City

Palm Springs
International
Airport

111

Palm Springs

Rancho Mirage

Palm Desert

Indio

10

Indian Wells

La Quinta

Coachella

Jacqueline Cochran Regional Airport

RIVERSIDE CO

86S

JOSHUA TREE NATIONAL PARK

CALIFORNIA

10

CHUCKWALLA MOUNTAINS WILDERNESS

UNITED STATES

MECCA HILLS WILDERNESS

SAN BERNARDINO NATIONAL FOREST

74

TORRES MARTINEZ INDIAN RESERVATION

OROCOPIA MOUNTAINS WILDERNESS

SANTA ROSA INDIAN RESERVATION

111

SANTA ROSA WILDERNESS

SALTON SEA STATE RECREATION AREA

CHOCOLATE MOUNTAIN NAVAL RES

86

CLEVELAND NATIONAL FOREST

LOS COYOTES INDIAN RESERVATION

1058

111

SALTON SEA

OCOTILLO WELLS VEHICULAR RECREATION AREA

SALTON SEA MILITARY RESERVATION

Calipatria

111

SAN FELIPE HILLS WILDERNESS STUDY AREA

1098

1100

78

86

115

1136

1138

ANZA-BORREGO DESERT STATE PARK

78
86

US NAVAL RESERVATION

Westmorland

Brawley Municipal Airport

78

1156

SAN DIEGO CO

IMPERIAL CO

6259

Brawley

1176

SAWTOOTH MOUNTAINS A WILDERNESS STUDY AREA

CUYAMACA RANCHO STATE PARK

SAWTOOTH MOUNTAINS WILDERNESS

1218

COYOTE MOUNTAINS WILDERNESS

86

111

6439

79

1216

CUYAPAIPE INDIAN RESERVATION

CARRIZO GORGE WILDERNESS

Imperial

6499

6500

1236

1237

8

PINE CREEK WILDERNESS

CLEVELAND NATIONAL FOREST

El Centro

8

6559

86

6560

111

HAUSER WILDERNESS

1296

1298

94

1300

8

JACUMBA WILDERNESS

98

6620

Calexico

98

HAUSER MOUNTAIN WILDERNESS STUDY AREA

CAMPO INDIAN RESERVATION

Calexico International Airport

6680

94

Tecate

Mexicali

BAJA CALIFORNIA

BAJA CALIFORNIA

MEXICO

San Diego International Airport (SAN)

The San Diego Airport, also known as Linderbergh Field is a public airport operated by the San Diego County Regional Airport Authority.

There are a number of parking options for visitors. The airport offers parking lots located outside the Airport Authority Administration Offices, Terminal 1 and Terminal 2. The parking lots in front of Terminal 2 are assigned for short term parking. Long term parking is available at all SAN lots offering shuttle services to the terminals.

Call 619.400.2404 or visit www.san.org for more information on current airline terminal locations and parking information.

REFER TO MAP PAGE AND GRID 1288 F1

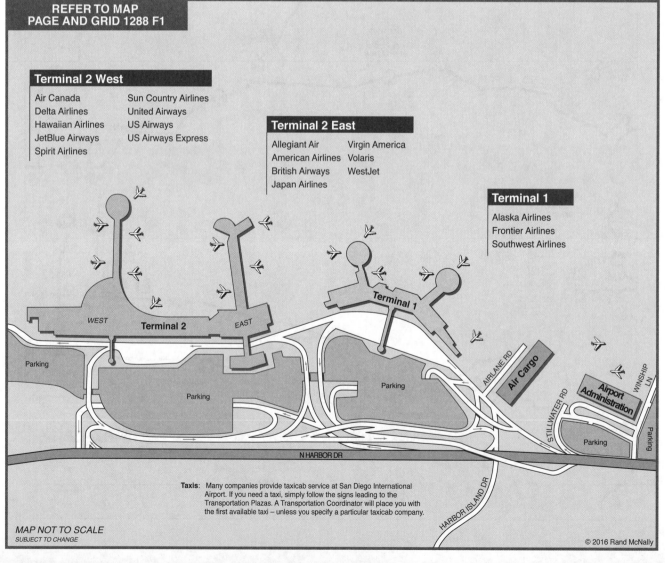

Terminal 2 West

Air Canada	Sun Country Airlines
Delta Airlines	United Airways
Hawaiian Airlines	US Airways
JetBlue Airways	US Airways Express
Spirit Airlines	

Terminal 2 East

Allegiant Air	Virgin America
American Airlines	Volaris
British Airways	WestJet
Japan Airlines	

Terminal 1

Alaska Airlines
Frontier Airlines
Southwest Airlines

Taxis: Many companies provide taxicab service at San Diego International Airport. If you need a taxi, simply follow the signs leading to the Transportation Plazas. A Transportation Coordinator will place you with the first available taxi – unless you specify a particular taxicab company.

MAP NOT TO SCALE
SUBJECT TO CHANGE

© 2016 Rand McNally

SAN DIEGO COUNTY REGIONAL
BUS, TROLLEY, TRAIN, FERRY, AND TAXI INFORMATION

TRANSIT, TRAFFIC, AND COMMUTE INFORMATION

Call 511 from any phone or visit www.511sd.com for all transportation service information including public transit routes and fares, traffic updates and emergency roadside assistance.

- For **MTS Bus, Rapid and Trolley** route, schedule and fare information, visit www.sdmts.com.
- For **NCTD COASTER, SPRINTER** and **BREEZE** route, schedule and fare information, visit www.gonctd.com.

To speak to a Transit Information Specialist:

(English/Español), call 619-233-3004, open 5:30 a.m. to 8:30 p.m. Monday through Friday, and 7 a.m. to 7 p.m. Saturday and Sunday. Holiday hours vary. TTY/TDD for persons with hearing impairments: 619-234-5005 or toll-free 1-888-722-4889. Have departure and destination points, as well as the date and time of travel.

Bus and Rail Station and Park & Ride Locations

See Points of Interest index under Transportation for Trolley, SPRINTER and COASTER station and bus Transit Center locations; see under Park & Ride for park & ride lot locations.

Regional Transit Map (RTM)

Download the RTM and other maps and route timetables at www.sdmts.com, under 'Schedules and Real Time.' You can also send a written request with your name and address to the MTS Marketing Department at 1255 Imperial Avenue, Suite 1000, San Diego, California 92101-7490.

METROPOLITAN TRANSIT SYSTEM (MTS)

 MTS Trolley - The Trolley's UC San Diego Blue, Orange and Green Lines provide daily service and stop at 53 stations in Downtown San Diego, Mission Valley, East County and South Bay, and serve major destinations like the Convention Center, Old Town, San Diego State University and the US Border crossing at San Ysidro.

 MTS Bus - MTS buses serve the metropolitan area including the International Airport (Route 992), schools, colleges and universities; employment, medical and shopping centers; and major attractions including the San Diego Zoo (Route 7, Rapid 215), Balboa Park (Routes 3, 7, 120 and Rapid 215), SeaWorld (Route 9) and area beaches.

NORTH COUNTY TRANSIT DISTRICT (NCTD)

NCTD COASTER – Trains serve eight stations between the Oceanside Transit Center and San Diego's Santa Fe Depot. There are 11 round-trip trains on weekdays and four on weekends.

NCTD SPRINTER - SPRINTER operates daily service serving 15 stations between the Oceanside and Escondido Transit Centers including stations at Palomar College and Cal State University San Marcos.

NCTD BREEZE - BREEZE buses travel throughout San Diego's north county serving coastal cities from Del Mar to Oceanside, the Camp Pendleton Marine Base, and the inland cities of Vista, San Marcos and Escondido, as well as popular destinations like Plaza Camino Real and Mira Costa College.

FARES

All passengers six years and older must have a valid fare when onboard (one-way fares do not include transfers). Monthly, 1-Day, and multi-day passes are sold on Compass Cards. There is a $2 charge for a Compass Card upon initial purchase. Cards are reloadable and last about five years with proper care. Use exact change (bills and coins) to purchase a one-way or Day Pass on the bus. Ticket vending machines accept credit and debit cards, and cash.

Where to Buy: Adult Compass Cards, monthly passes, multi-day passes and one-way fares can be purchased at any Trolley, COASTER or SPRINTER ticket vending machine with credit or debit cards, or cash (most vending machines give up to $5 in change). Adult Compass Cards can also be purchased online at www.511sd.com/compass, at any Albertsons grocery store, select Vons grocery stores, select community outlets and at all Transit Stores.

Youth and Senior/Disabled/Medicare Compass Cards must be purchased in person with proper identification at a Transit Store or Albertsons/Vons grocery store. All Compass Cards can be reloaded at all locations. Riders can reload also reload a Regional 1-Day Pass on a Compass Card on most MTS buses.

Mobile Application: Beginning late summer 2016, all MTS and NCTD fare passes will be available on a mobile app. Please visit sdmts.com for more information.

Kids Ride Free: Every Saturday and Sunday, two children 12 & under can ride free when accompanied by a paying adult (18+).

Regional and *RegionPlus* Day Passes: The Regional Day Pass ($5 with Compass Card) is valid on all MTS Trolley lines, regular Rapid routes, most MTS bus routes, and NCTD SPRINTER and BREEZE routes. The RegionPlus Day Pass ($12 with Compass Card) is valid for the COASTER, MTS Rapid Express, and all other bus and rail routes.

Area Transit Stores sell passes and provide information and route timetables:
- 12th & Imperial Transit Center in downtown San Diego, Monday-Friday, 9 a.m. - 5 p.m.
- Oceanside Transit Center, Monday-Friday, 7 a.m. to 7 p.m.
- Vista Transit Center, Monday- Friday, 8 a.m. to 5 p.m.
- Escondido Transit Center, Monday- Friday, 7 a.m. – 7 p.m.

ACCESSIBLE SERVICE and ADA CERTIFICATION

All MTS and NCTD bus and rail routes offer accessible service for riders in wheelchairs using lift equipped or low-floor vehicles. In compliance with the Americans with Disabilities Act (ADA), customers who cannot reach or ride fixed-route bus and rail routes due to mobility impairment, and who are certified, can use MTS Access or NCTD LIFT. To schedule a trip on MTS Access, call 1-888-517-9627 or 1-800-921-9664. To schedule a trip on NCTD LIFT, call 1-760-726-1111.

QUALCOMM STADIUM

The MTS Green Line Trolley provides direct, daily service to the Qualcomm Stadium Station. For major Qualcomm events, MTS Trolley offers enhanced service. COASTER and select AMTRAK trains provide service to the Old Town Transit Center and connect to the Trolley's Green Line.

PETCO PARK

All Trolley Lines and several MTS bus routes provide direct, daily service to PETCO Park (next to the 12th & Imperial Transit Center). From North County, COASTER and AMTRAK passengers should disembark at to the Santa Fe Depot and transfer to the Trolley's Green or Orange Line.

FLAGSHIP CORONADO FERRY - The Flagship Coronado Ferry operates daily between Coronado and San Diego, 9 a.m. to 9:30 p.m. (10:30 p.m. on Friday and Saturday), leaving San Diego on the hour and Coronado on the half-hour. A one-way fare is $4.25; bicycles are FREE. For more information, call 619-234-4111.

AMTRAK - Currently, 11 AMTRAK trains operate between San Diego and Los Angeles. Trains stop at three San Diego County Stations: Santa Fe Depot in Downtown San Diego; Solana Beach; and Oceanside Transit Center. Select trains also stop at the Old Town Transit Center. For information, call 1-800-USA-RAIL (1-800-872-7245), or visit www.amtrak.com.

METROLINK - Weekday morning and afternoon rush hour, rail service from Oceanside Transit Center to 54 Orange, Los Angeles, San Bernardino, Riverside and Ventura County stations. For information,call 1-800-371-LINK, or go to www.metrolink-trains.com.

TAXIS - San Diego's taxicab stands are located throughout Downtown, and at major hotels, attractions, employment, recreation and shopping centers. The meter displays the fare. Fare includes a flat "flag drop" charge, plus a per-mile and/or per-hour waiting time charge. All cabs leaving the International Airport charge a uniform rate of fare. Fares for all cab trips in the metropolitan area of San Diego vary from company to company, but cannot exceed a fixed amount set by MTS. To comment on service, call 619-235-2650.

This information is provided by the Metropolitan Transit System (MTS), North County Transit District (NCTD), and San Deigo Association of Governments (SANDAG)

EXISTING HIGH-OCCUPANCY VEHICLE (HOV) LANES SUMMARY

Route Description	Direction	Miles	Occupancy	Days & Hours Of Operation
Interstate 15 (I-15): SR 78 to SR 163	Southbound	20	2+*	FULL-TIME
Interstate 15 (I-15): SR 163 to SR 78	Northbound	20	2+*	FULL-TIME
I-5: I-805 to Via De La Valle	Northbound	6	2+	FULL-TIME
I-5: Via De La Valle to I-5/I-805 Interchange	Southbound	4	2+	FULL-TIME
I-805: at I-5/I-805 Interchange	Northbound	1/2	2+	FULL-TIME

*Single Occupancy Vehicles (SOV) may use the I-15 Express Lanes for a fee with a valid FasTrak transponder. Visit 511sd.com/fastrak for more information.

MOTORIST AID IN THE SAN DIEGO REGION

SANDAG operates the highway call box program and Freeway Service Patrol (FSP) in San Diego County. The roving fleet of FSP tow trucks and pickup trucks provide free roadside assistance (a gallon of gas, a "jump-start," tire change, or water for the radiator) to stranded motorists on weekdays from 5:30 to 9:30 a.m. and 3 to 7 p.m. To request motorist aid, call 511 and say "Roadside Assistance" or use one of 1,275 mobile call boxes throughout the region. For more information, visit www.511sd.com.

Downtown
San Diego
Mapa del Centro

1 in. = 1400 ft.

0   0.25   0.5

miles

Note: This grid references this map only

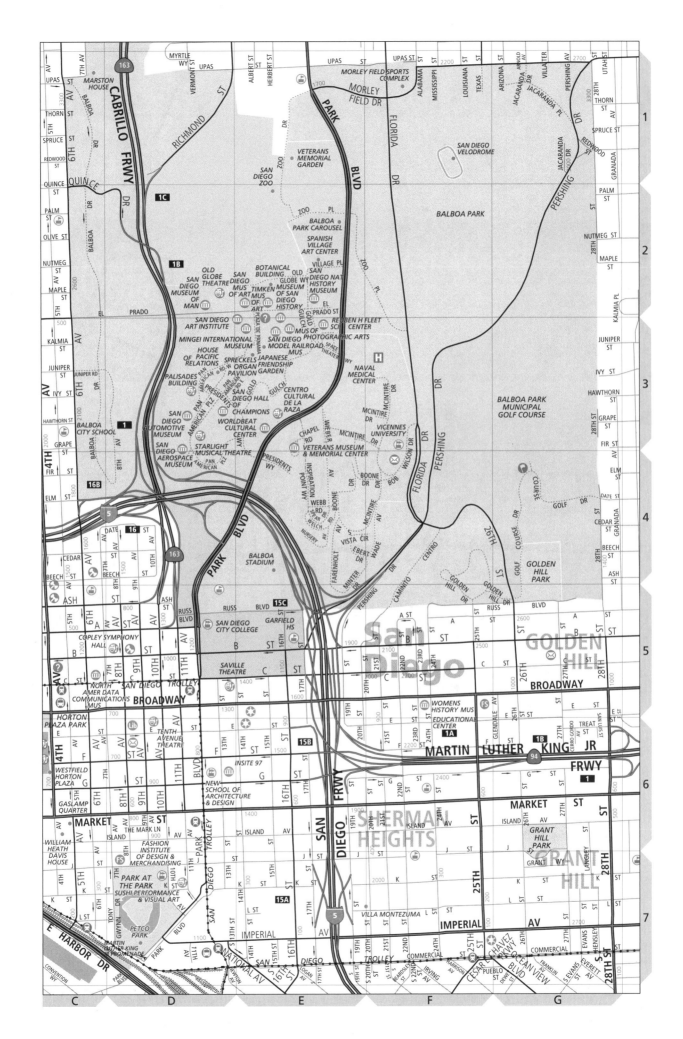

SAN DIEGO COUNTY FREEWAY ACCESS MAP

ORANGE COUNTY

RIVERSIDE COUNTY

OCEANSIDE

CRISTIANITOS RD (1023)
BASILONE RD (1023)
LAS PULGAS RD (408)
HARBOR DR (1085)
VANDEGRIFT BLVD (1085)
N COAST HWY (1085)
MISSION AV (1086)
SAN LUIS REY MISSION EXWY (1085) 76

OCEANSIDE BLVD (1106)
CALIFORNIA ST (1106)
CASSIDY ST (1106)
VISTA WY (1106)

CARLSBAD

LAS FLORES DR (1106)
CARLSBAD VILLAGE DR (1106)
TAMARACK AV (1106)
CANNON RD (1126)
PALOMAR AIRPORT RD (1126)
POINSETTIA LN (1126)
LA COSTA AV (1147)
LEUCADIA BLVD (1147)
ENCINITAS BLVD (1147)
SANTA FE DR (1167)
BIRMINGHAM DR (1167)
MANCHESTER AV (1167)
LOMAS SANTA FE DR (1187)
VIA DE LA VALLE (1187)

VISTA

JEFFERSON ST (1106)
EL CAMINO REAL (1106)
COLLEGE BLVD (1107)
PLAZA DR (1107)
EMERALD DR (1107)
MELROSE DR (1087)
VISTA VILLAGE DR (1087)
SUNSET DR (1107)
ESCONDIDO AV (1107)

SAN MARCOS

MAR VISTA DR (1107)
SYCAMORE AV (1108)
RANCHO SANTA FE RD (1108)
LAS POSAS RD (1108)
W SAN MARCOS BLVD (1108)
TWIN OAKS VALLEY RD (1128)
BARHAM DR (1109)
E BARHAM DR (1129)
RANCHEROS DR (1109)
NORDAHL RD (1129)

ESCONDIDO

CENTRE CITY PKWY (1129)
BROADWAY (1129)
LINCOLN PARKWAY (1129)

RAINBOW VALLEY BLVD W (998)
MISSION RD (1028)
OLD HWY 395 (1028)
PALA RD (1048) 76
OLD HWY 395 (1068)
CHAMPAGNE BLVD (1068)
GOPHER CANYON RD (1068)
OLD CASTLE RD (1068)
DEER SPRINGS RD (1089)
MOUNTAIN MEADOW RD (1089)
CENTRE CITY PKWY (1109)
EL NORTE PKWY (1109)

VALLEY PKWY (1129)
AUTO PARK WY (1129)
W 9TH AV (1129)
CITRACADO PKWY (1129)
FELICITA RD (1129)
S CENTRE CITY PKWY (1150)
VIA RANCHO PKWY (1150)
POMERADO RD (1150)
W BERNARDO DR (1150)
RANCHO BERNARDO RD (1170)
BERNARDO CENTER DR (1170)
CAMINO DEL NORTE (1169)
CARMEL MTN RD (1189)

POWAY

TED WILLIAMS PKWY (1189)
SABRE SPRINGS PKWY - CARPOOL ONLY
RANCHO PENASQUITOS BLVD (1189)
POWAY RD (1189)
MERCY RD (1189)
SCRIPPS POWAY PKWY (1189)
MIRA MESA BLVD (1209)

MIRA MESA

CARMEL MTN RD (1189)
RANCHO PENASQUITOS BLVD (1189)
CARMEL MTN RD (1189)
BLACK MTN RD (1189)
CAMINO DEL SUR (1189)
CONVOY ST (1229)

CARROLL CANYON RD (1209)
MIRAMAR RD (1209)
POMERADO RD (1209)
MIRAMAR WY (1229)

DEL MAR

DEL MAR HEIGHTS RD (1187)
CARMEL VALLEY RD (1207)
SORRENTO VALLEY RD (1207)
CARMEL MOUNTAIN RD (1208)

ENCINITAS

CARMEL VALLEY RD (1188)
CARMEL COUNTRY RD (1188)
CARMEL CREEK RD (1188)
EL CAMINO REAL (1208)

SORRENTO VALLEY RD (1208)
ROSELLE ST (1208)
GENESEE AV (1208)
LA JOLLA VILLAGE DR (1228)
NOBEL DR (1228)
GILMAN DR (1228)
LA JOLLA PKWY (1228)

SORRENTO VALLEY RD (1208)
GOVERNOR DR (1229)
NOBLE DR (1228)
MIRAMAR RD (1229)
LA JOLLA VILLAGE DR (1228)
MIRA MESA BLVD (1229)

GENESEE AV (1228)
REGENTS RD (1228)
LA JOLLA PKWY (1228)

MISSION BAY DR (1248)
BALBOA AV (1248)
GARNET AV (1248)

KEARNY VILLA RD (1229)
CLAIREMONT MESA BLVD (1249)
BALBOA AV (1249)
MERCURY ST (1249)
KEARNY VILLA RD (1249)
ARMOUR ST (1249)
CLAIREMONT MESA BLVD (1248)
BALBOA AV (1248)

MESA COLLEGE DR (1249)
KEARNY VILLA RD (1229)
DEARNY VILLA (1249)
DEARNA RIDGE RD (1249)
MURPHY CYN (1249)
AERO DR (1249)

CLAIREMONT MESA BLVD (1249)
BALBOASANTA (1249)
TIERRA (1249)
BLVD (1249)
MURRAY RIDGE RD (1249)
FRIARS RD (1249)

GENESEE AV (1228)
REGENTS RD (1228)
LA JOLLA PKWY (1228)

SANTEE

MAGNOLIA AV (1231)
CUYAMACA ST (1231)
FANITA DR (1231)
MAST BLVD (1230)
SANTO RD (1229)

WINTER GARDENS BLVD (1231)
WOODSIDE AV (1231)
RIVERFORD RD (1231)
WOODSIDE AV (1231)
PROSPECT AV (1231)
BRADLEY AV (1251)
FLETCHER PKWY (1251)
BROADWAY (1251)

MISSION GORGE
MISSION (1231)
RD (1231)
ROSSIDE DR (1251)
GOLLEO DR (1251)
NAVAJO PKWY
FLETCHER (1251)
AMAYA DR (1251)

EL CAJON

JOHNSON AV (1251)
W MAIN ST (1251)
EL CAJON BLVD (1251)
SEVERIN DR (1251)
FUERTE DR (1271)

MAGNOLIA AV (1251)

LA MESA

LA MESA BLVD (1271)
GROSSMONT CTR DR (1271)
JACKSON DR (1270)
EL CAJON BLVD (1270)
SPRING ST (1270)
FLETCHER PARKWAY (1270)
ALVARADO RD (1270)
LAKE MURRAY BLVD (1270)
COLLEGE AV (1270)
WARING RD (1270)
MISSION GORGE RD (1269)
FAIRMOUNT AV (1269)

CLAIREMONT MESA BLVD (1229)

CARRIZO GORGE RD (1300) 94
RIBBONWOOD RD (1298)
CRESTWOOD RD (430)
CAMERON INT RD (430)
SHEEPHEAD MTN RD (430)
OLD BUCKMAN SPRING RD (430)
SUNRISE HWY 80 (430)
OLD HWY 80 (430)
PINE VALLEY RD (1237) 79
JAPATUL VALLEY RD (1235)
WILLOWS RD (1235)
ALPINE BLVD (1234)
TAVERN RD (1233)
ALPINE BLVD (1234)
DUNBAR LN (1233)
LAKE JENNINGS PARK RD (1232)
LOS COCHES RD (1252)
GREENFIELD DR (1252)
E MAIN ST (1252)
2ND ST (1251)
MOLLISON AV (1251)

PACIFIC OCEAN

LEMON GROVE

CHULA VISTA

NATIONAL CITY

IMPERIAL BEACH

CORONADO

U.S.A.
MÉXICO

© Rand McNally

AVOCADO BLVD (1271)
CALAVO DR (1271)
CAMPO RD (1271)
SWEETWATER SPRINGS BLVD (1271)
KENWOOD DR (1271)
BANCROFT DR (1271)
BROADWAY (1271)
SPRING ST (1270)

GROSSMONT BLVD (1271)
LEMON AV (1271)
BROADWAY (1270)
SPRING ST (1271)
CAMPO RD (1271)

JAMACHA BLVD (1291)

E. JAMACHA RD (1290)
PARADISE VALLEY RD (1291)
ELKELTON BLVD

BRIARWOOD RD (1290)
WOODMAN ST (1310)
REO DR (1310)
PLAZA BONITA CTR WY (1310)

SAN MIGUEL RD (291)
SAN MIGUEL RD (1311)
SAN MIGUEL RANCH RD (1311)
MT MIGUEL RD (1311)
OTAY LAKES RD (1311)
H ST (311)
H ST (311)
OTAY LAKES RD (1311)

OLYMPIC PKWY (1311)
BIRCH RD (1331)
OTAY MESA RD (1352)
SIEMPRE VIVA RD (1352)

LA MEDIA RD (1351)
BRITANNIA BLVD (1351)
CALIENTE AV (1351)
OTAY MESA RD (1350)

GROVE ST (1270)
LEMON GROVE AV (1270)
WAITE DR (1270)
MASSACHUSETTS AV (1270)
COLLEGE AV (1270)
BROADWAY (1270)
COLLEGE GROVE WY (1270)
FEDERAL BLVD (1290)
BAYVIEW HTS WY (1290)
KELTON RD (1290)
EUCLID AV (1290)
49TH ST (1290)
47TH ST (1289)
HOME AV (1289)

MARKET ST (1289)
IMPERIAL AV (1289)
47TH ST (1289)
43RD ST (1289)

ADAMS AV (1269)
EL CAJON BLVD (1269)
UNIVERSITY AV (1289)
HOME AV (1289)

HOME AV (1289)
MARKET ST (1289)

HOME AV (1289)

IMPERIAL AV (1289)

OCEAN VIEW BLVD (1289)

PALM AV (1289)
PLAZA BLVD (1310)
SWEETWATER RD (1310)

BONITA RD (1310)
H ST (1310)
TELEGRAPH CANYON RD (1310)
L ST (1330)
ORANGE AV (1330)
MAIN ST (1330)
PALM AV (1330)

HIGHLAND AV (1310)
4TH AV (1310)
NATIONAL CITY BLVD (1309)
BROADWAY (1309)

PICADOR BL (1350)
SMYTHE AV (1350)
BEYER BLVD (1350)

SAN YSIDRO BLVD (1350)

DAIRY MART RD (1350)
SAN YSIDRO BLVD (1350)
VIA DE SAN YSIDRO (1350)

PICADOR BL (1350)
PALM AV (1350)
CORONADO AV (1350)
TOCAYO AV (1350)

PALOMAR ST (1330)
L ST (1330)
H ST (1330)
INDUSTRIAL BL (1330)
E ST (1309)

MESA COLLEGE DR (1249)
GENESEE AV (1249)
FRIARS RD (1269)

MISSION CENTER RD (1269)
MADISON AV (1269)
EL CAJON BLVD (1269)
BOUNDARY ST (1269)
UNIVERSITY AV (1269)
NORTH PARK WY (1269)

CAMINO DEL RIO N (1269)
QUALCOMM WY (1269)
TEXAS ST (1269)

WASHINGTON ST (1269)
UNIVERSITY AV (1269)
ROBINSON AV (1269)
RICHMOND ST (1269)
QUINCE DR (1269)
PARK BLVD (1289)

6TH AV (1269)

BROADWAY (1289)
32ND ST (1289)
28TH ST (1289)
25TH ST (1289)
19TH ST (1289)

MILES OF CARS AV (1309)
CIVIC CENTER DR (1309)
PLAZA BLVD (1309)
HARBOR DR (1309)

MAIN ST (1289)
DIVISION ST (1309)

28TH AV (1289)
NATIONAL AV (1289)
BOSTON AV (1289)
WABASH BLVD

CESAR E CHAVEZ PKWY (1289)

IMPERIAL AV (1289)
J ST (1289)
G ST (1289)
F ST (1289)
E ST (1289)
17TH ST (1289)

HOTEL CIR (1268)
TAYLOR ST (1268)
LINDA VISTA RD (1268)
MORENA BL (1268)
CM DL RIO W (1268)

PERSHING DR (1289)
PARK BLVD (1289)
B ST (1289)
C ST (1289)
D ST (1289)
E ST (1289)
F ST (1289)
ASH ST (1289)

MOORE ST (1268)
OLD TOWN AV (1268)
WASHINGTON ST (1268)
KETTNER BLVD (AIRPORT)

INDIA ST (1268)
PACIFIC HWY (1268)
HAWTHORN ST (1289)
GRAPE ST (1289)
BRANT ST (1289)
FRONT ST (1289)
CEDAR ST (1289)
1ST AV (1289)
5TH AV (1289)
6TH AV (1289)

MISSION BAY DR (1248)
CLAIREMONT DR (1248)
TECOLOTE RD (1268)
SEA WORLD DR (1268)
ROSECRANS ST (1268)
CM DL RIO W (1268)

MIDWAY DR (1268)
W MISSION BAY DR (1268)
SUNSET CLIFFS BLVD (1268)
NIMITZ BLVD (1268)

94
125
125
54
805
15
15
8
163
94
5
8
805
15
905
805
5
75
905

10.8
3.9
6.5
6.5
3
2.5
6
5
7
3.5
1.5
3
1
1
1
2
2
1.5
2.5
3
2.5
4
2
2
3
2
2
1.5
6
3
7
2
2
1
6.5
1.5
1

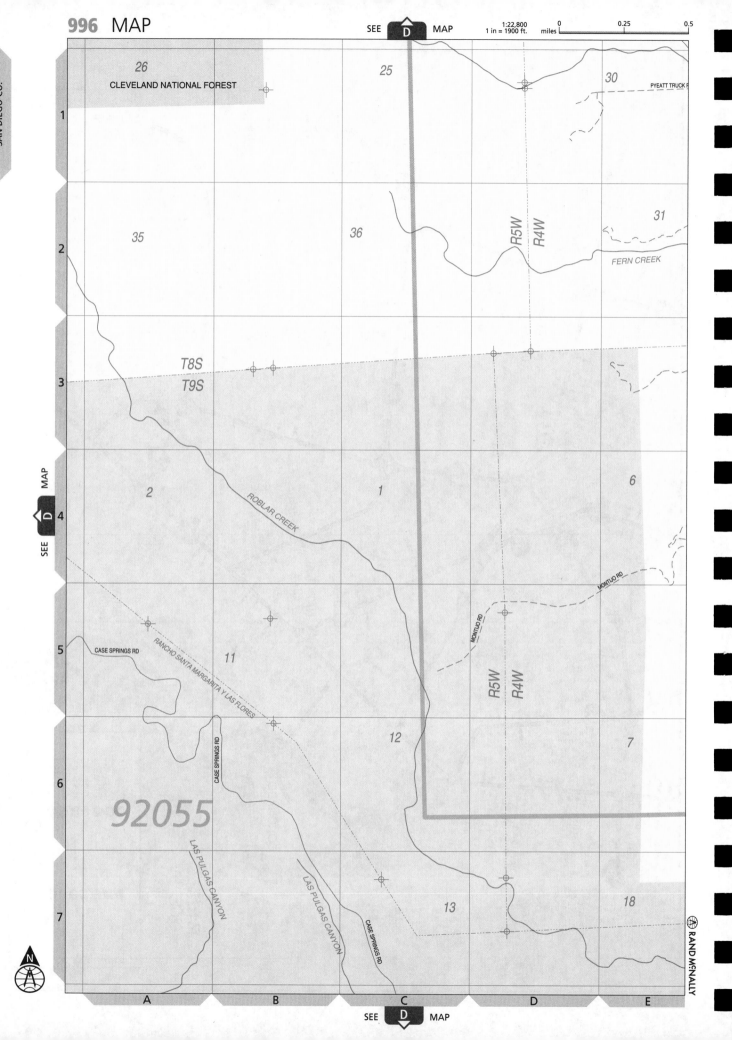

SAN DIEGO CO.

SEE **D** MAP

1:22,800
1 in = 1900 ft.   miles   0   0.25   0.5

26   CLEVELAND NATIONAL FOREST

25

30   PYEATT TRUCK

1

35   36   R5W R4W   31

FERN CREEK

2

T8S
T9S

3

SEE **D** MAP

2   1   6

4

ROBLAR CREEK

MONTIJO RD   MONTIJO RD

5   CASE SPRINGS RD   RANCHO SANTA MARGARITA Y LAS FLORES   11   R5W R4W

92055   CASE SPRINGS RD   12   7

6

LAS PULGAS CANYON   LAS PULGAS CANYON   CASE SPRINGS RD   13   18

7

N

A   B   C   D   E

SEE **D** MAP

RAND McNALLY

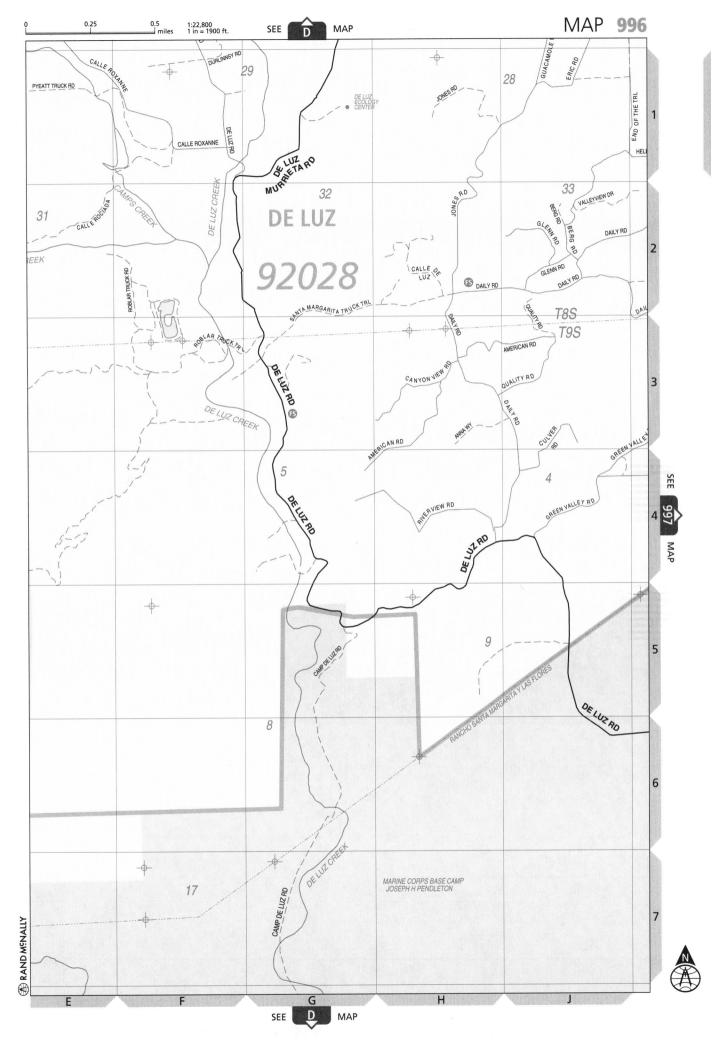

MAP **996**

SAN DIEGO CO.

SEE D MAP

0   0.25   0.5   1:22,800
         miles   1 in = 1900 ft.

DURLINNSY RD

CALLE ROXANNE

29

DE LUZ
ECOLOGY
CENTER

JONES RD

28

GUACAMOLE

ERIC RD

END OF THE TRL

PYEATT TRUCK RD

CALLE ROXANNE

DE LUZ RD

DE LUZ
MURRIETA RD

32

DE LUZ

HELE

1

33

VALLEYVIEW DR

CAMPS CREEK

DE LUZ CREEK

31

CALLE ROCIADA

JONES RD

BERG RD

GLENN RD

BERG RD

DAILY RD

2

CREEK

ROBLAR TRUCK RD

92028

CALLE DE
LUZ

FS

DAILY RD

GLENN RD

DAILY RD

SANTA MARGARITA TRUCK TRL

QUALITY RD

T8S

DAIL

ROBLAR TRUCK TRL

DE LUZ RD

DE LUZ CREEK

FS

DAILY RD

AMERICAN RD

T9S

CANYON VIEW RD

QUALITY RD

3

DE LUZ RD

5

AMERICAN RD

ANNA WY

DAILY RD

CULVER
RD

GREEN VALLEY

DE LUZ RD

4

RIVERVIEW RD

GREEN VALLEY RD

SEE

997

MAP

4

DE LUZ RD

5

CAMP DE LUZ RD

9

RANCHO SANTA MARGARITA Y LAS FLORES

DE LUZ RD

8

6

CAMP DE LUZ RD

DE LUZ CREEK

17

MARINE CORPS BASE CAMP
JOSEPH H PENDLETON

7

RAND McNALLY

E   F   G   H   J

SEE D MAP

N

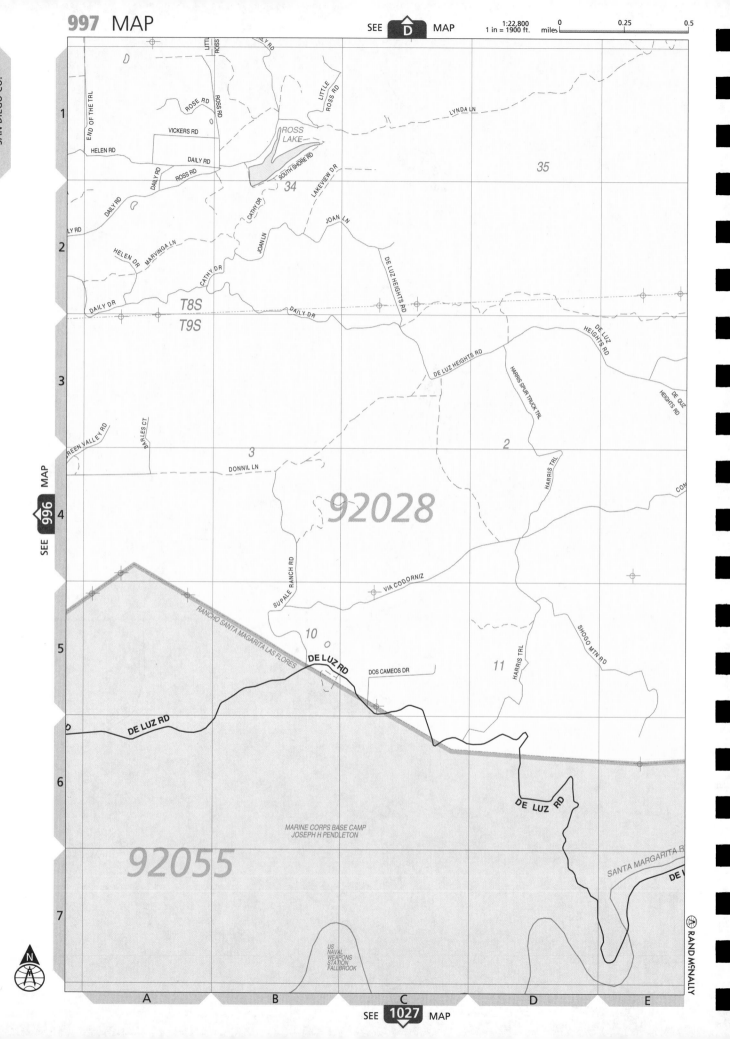

SAN DIEGO CO.

1:22,800
1 in = 1900 ft.   miles

0   0.25   0.5

END OF THE TRL

D

LITTLE ROSS RD

ROSS RD

ROSE RD

ROSS RD

LITTLE ROSS RD

LYNDA LN

VICKERS RD

HELEN RD

DAILY RD

DAILY RD

ROSS RD

ROSS LAKE

SOUTH SHORE RD

LAKEVIEW DR

35

34

DAILY RD

CATHY DR

JOAN LN

JOAN LN

DE LUZ HEIGHTS RD

HELEN DR

MARVINGA LN

CATHY DR

DAILY DR

DAILY DR

T8S
T9S

DE LUZ HEIGHTS RD

DE LUZ HEIGHTS RD

DE LUZ HEIGHTS RD

HARRIS SPUR TRUCK TRL

DE LUZ HEIGHTS RD

GREEN VALLEY RD

BAR-LES CT

DONNIL LN

3

2

HARRIS TRL

DE LUZ HEIGHTS RD

CON

92028

SUPALE RANCH RD

VIA CODORNIZ

RANCHO SANTA MARGARITA LAS FLORES

10

DE LUZ RD

DOS CAMEOS DR

11

HARRIS TRL

SHOGO MTN RD

DE LUZ RD

DE LUZ RD

DE LUZ RD

MARINE CORPS BASE CAMP
JOSEPH H PENDLETON

92055

SANTA MARGARITA R

DE L

US
NAVAL
WEAPONS
STATION
FALLBROOK

N

RAND McNALLY

A   B   C   D   E

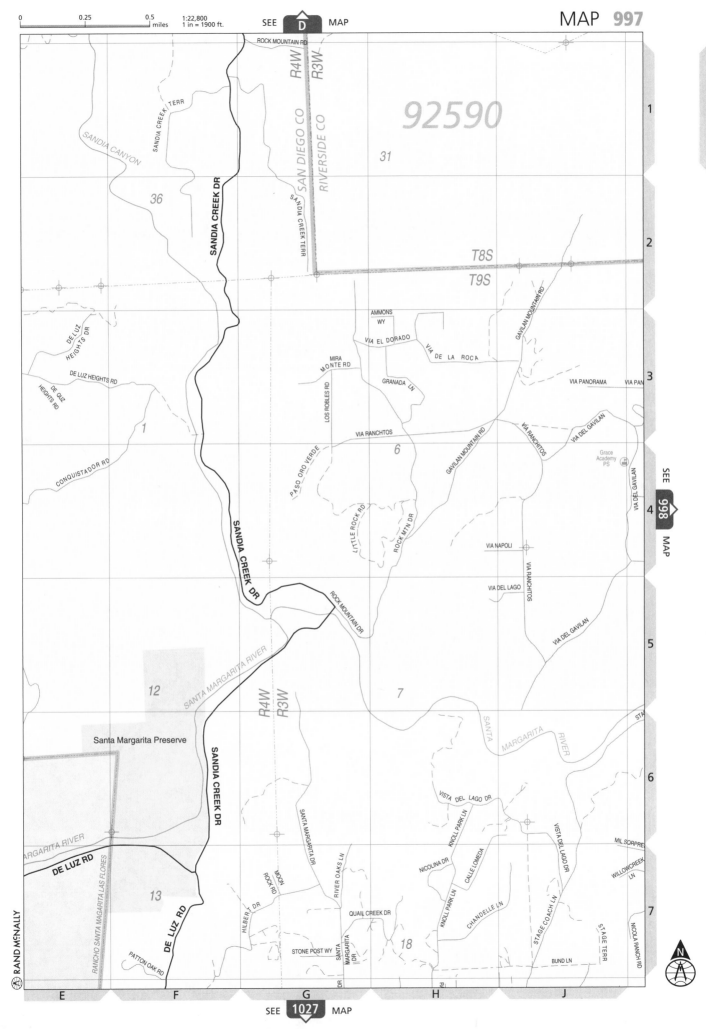

MAP **997**

SEE **D** MAP

0   0.25   0.5 miles
1:22,800
1 in = 1900 ft.

ROCK MOUNTAIN RD

R4W R3W

92590

31

SAN DIEGO CO
RIVERSIDE CO

SANDIA CANYON

SANDIA CREEK TERR

SANDIA CREEK DR

SANDIA CREEK TERR

36

T8S
T9S

DE LUZ HEIGHTS DR

DE LUZ HEIGHTS RD

DE LUZ HEIGHTS RD

AMMONS WY

VIA EL DORADO

VIA DE LA ROCA

GAVILAN MOUNTAIN RD

MIRA MONTE RD

LOS ROBLES RD

GRANADA LN

VIA PANORAMA

VIA PAN

1

PASO ORO VERDE

VIA RANCHTOS

6

GAVILAN MOUNTAIN RD

VIA RANCHITOS

VIA DEL GAVILAN

Grace Academy PS

VIA DEL GAVILAN

SEE **998** MAP

CONQUISTADOR RD

LITTLE ROCK RD

ROCK MTN DR

VIA NAPOLI

VIA RANCHITOS

VIA DEL LAGO

VIA DEL GAVILAN

SANDIA CREEK DR

ROCK MOUNTAIN DR

SANTA MARGARITA RIVER

12

R4W R3W

7

SANTA MARGARITA RIVER

STA

Santa Margarita Preserve

SANDIA CREEK DR

VISTA DEL LAGO DR

KNOLL PARK LN

MIL SORPRE

MARGARITA RIVER

DE LUZ RD

RANCHO SANTA MARGARITA LAS FLORES

SANTA MARGARITA DR

RIVER OAKS LN

NICOLINA DR

KNOLL PARK LN

CALLE LOMEDA

VISTA DEL LAGO DR

CHANDELLE LN

STAGE COACH LN

WILLOWCREEK LN

13

DE LUZ RD

HILBERT DR

MOON ROCK RD

QUAIL CREEK DR

STAGE TERR

NICOLA RANCH RD

PATTON OAK RD

STONE POST WY

SANTA MARGARITA DR

18

BUND LN

E   F   G   H   J

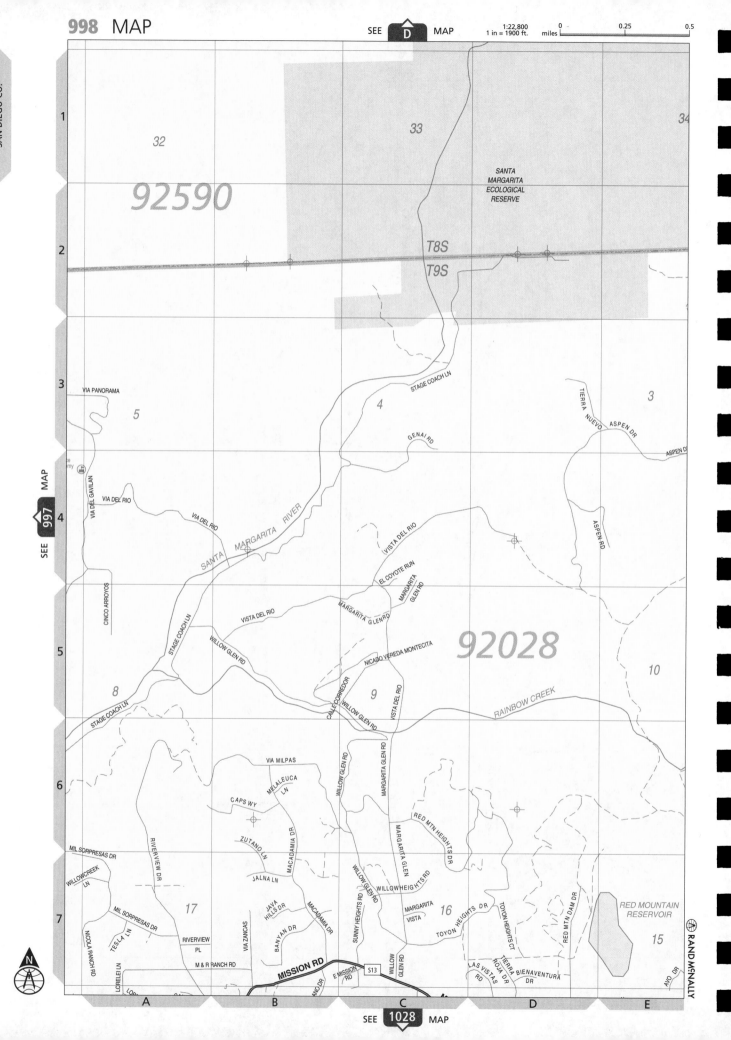

SEE D MAP

SAN DIEGO CO.

1:22,800
1 in = 1900 ft.   miles   0   0.25   0.5

92590

32

33

34

SANTA
MARGARITA
ECOLOGICAL
RESERVE

T8S
T9S

VIA PANORAMA

STAGE COACH LN

4

3

5

GENAI RD

TIERRA NUEVO

ASPEN DR

ASPEN D

SEE 997 MAP

VIA DEL GAVILAN

VIA DEL RIO

VIA DEL RIO

SANTA MARGARITA RIVER

VISTA DEL RIO

ASPEN RD

CINCO ARROYOS

STAGE COACH LN

VISTA DEL RIO

WILLOW GLEN RD

EL COYOTE RUN

MARGARITA GLEN RD

MARGARITA GLEN RD

92028

10

8

NICADO VEREDA MONTECITA

CALLE CORREDOR

9

WILLOW GLEN RD

VISTA DEL RIO

RAINBOW CREEK

STAGE COACH LN

VIA MILPAS

MELALEUCA LN

WILLOW GLEN RD

MARGARITA GLEN RD

RED MTN HEIGHTS DR

CAPS WY

RIVERVIEW DR

ZUTANO LN

MACADAMIA DR

MARGARITA GLEN

MIL SORPRESAS DR

JALNA LN

WILLOW GLEN RD

WILLOW HEIGHTS RD

RED MTN DAM DR

RED MOUNTAIN
RESERVOIR

WILLOWCREEK LN

JAVA HILLS DR

MACADAMIA DR

SUNNY HEIGHTS RD

MARGARITA
VISTA

16

TOYON HEIGHTS DR

TOYON HEIGHTS CT

15

17

MIL SORPRESAS DR

NICOLA RANCH RD

TESLA LN

RIVERVIEW PL

VIA ZANCAS

BANYAN DR

TOYON HEIGHTS DR

TIERRA ROJA DR

AVO DR

LORELEI LN

M & R RANCH RD

MISSION RD

E MISSION RD

S13

WILLOW GLEN RD

LAS VISTAS RD

BIENAVENTURA DR

RAND MCNALLY

N

A   B   C   D   E

SEE 1028 MAP

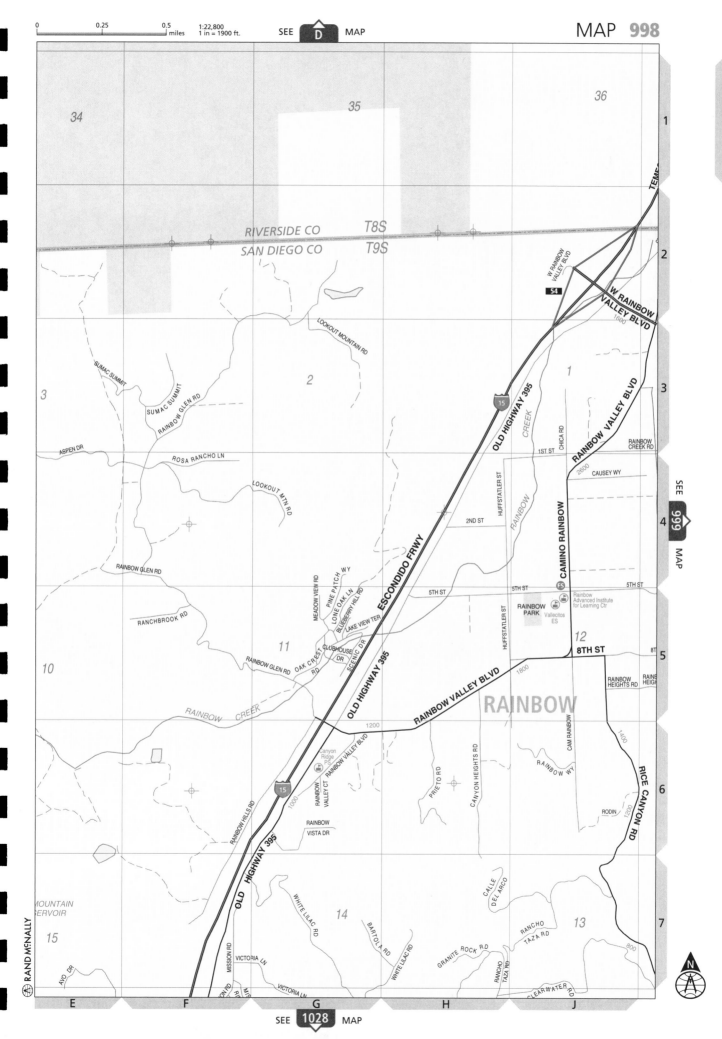

MAP 998

SAN DIEGO CO.

0   0.25   0.5
miles
1:22,800
1 in = 1900 ft.

SEE D MAP

SEE 999 MAP

SEE 1028 MAP

RIVERSIDE CO   T8S
SAN DIEGO CO   T9S

34   35   36

1

2

W RAINBOW VALLEY BLVD
W RAINBOW VALLEY BLVD
54

SUMAC SUMMIT
SUMAC SUMMIT
RAINBOW GLEN RD

LOOKOUT MOUNTAIN RD

3   2   3

ASPEN DR
ROSA RANCHO LN

OLD HIGHWAY 395
CREEK

1

CHICA RD
1ST ST
RAINBOW VALLEY BLVD
RAINBOW CREEK RD
2600   CAUSEY WY

LOOKOUT MTN RD

HUFFSTATLER ST
2ND ST
RAINBOW
CAMINO RAINBOW

4

RAINBOW GLEN RD

MEADOW VIEW RD
PINE PATCH WY
LONE OAK LN
BLUEBERRY HILL RD
LAKE VIEW TER
5TH ST   5TH ST   5TH ST
FS
Rainbow Advanced Institute for Learning Ctr
RAINBOW PARK
Vallecitos ES

RANCHBROOK RD

ESCONDIDO FRWY

HUFFSTATLER ST

12
8TH ST   8T

RAINBOW GLEN RD
OAK CREST RD
CLUBHOUSE DR
SCENIC DR
11

10   1800

RAINBOW   CREEK

OLD HIGHWAY 395
RAINBOW VALLEY BLVD
RAINBOW VALLEY BLVD

RAINBOW HEIGHTS RD
RAINE HEIGH

5

RAINBOW
CAM RAINBOW
RAINBOW WY
1400

1200

RICE CANYON RD

15
RAINBOW HILLS RD

Canyon Ridge PS
RAINBOW VALLEY CT
RAINBOW VALLEY BLVD

PRIETO RD
CANYON HEIGHTS RD

RODIN   1200

6

RAINBOW VISTA DR

OLD HIGHWAY 395

800

MOUNTAIN RESERVOIR

15

AVO DR
MISSION RD
VICTORIA LN
VICTORIA LN

WHITE LILAC RD
14
BARTOLA RD
WHITE LILAC RD
GRANITE ROCK RD

CALLE DEL ARCO
RANCHO TAZA RD
RANCHO TAZA RD
13

CLEARWATER RD

7

N

E   F   G   H   J

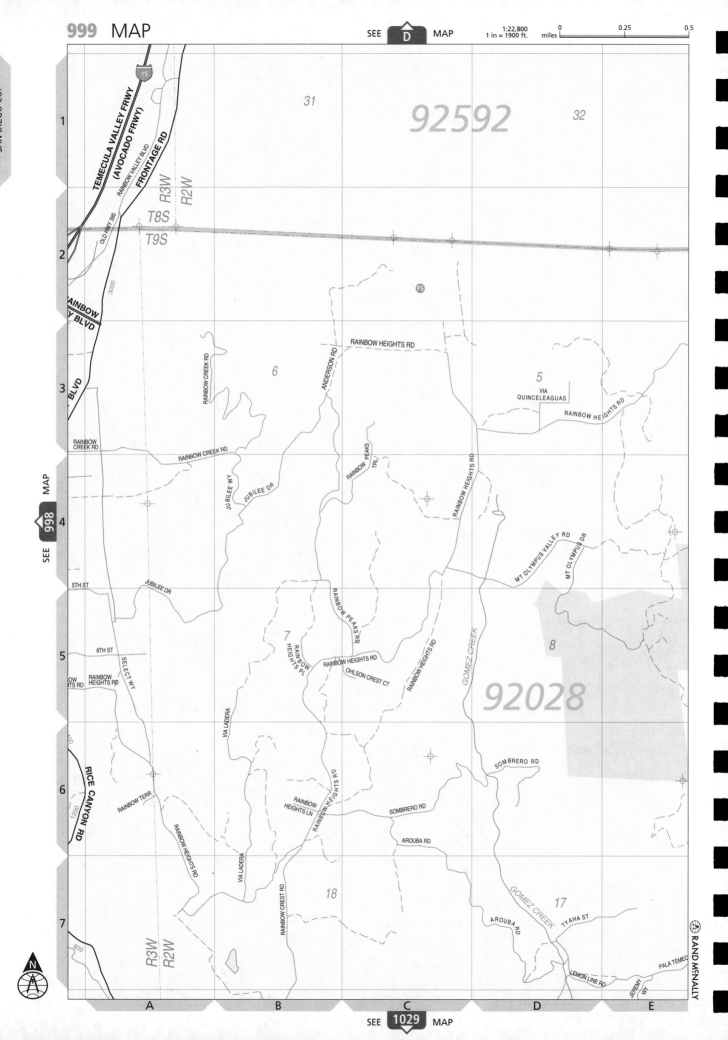

1:22,800
1 in = 1900 ft.

miles

0   0.25   0.5

SAN DIEGO CO.

31

92592

32

TEMECULA VALLEY FRWY
(AVOCADO FRWY)

RAINBOW VALLEY BLVD

FRONTAGE RD

R3W
R2W

T8S
T9S

OLD HWY 395

3000

RAINBOW VALLEY BLVD

BLVD

FS

RAINBOW HEIGHTS RD

RAINBOW CREEK RD

ANDERSON RD

6

5

VIA
QUINCELEAGUAS

RAINBOW HEIGHTS RD

RAINBOW
CREEK RD

RAINBOW CREEK RD

JUBILEE WY

JUBILEE DR

RAINBOW PEAKS TRL

RAINBOW HEIGHTS RD

SEE 998 MAP

MT OLYMPUS VALLEY RD

MT OLYMPUS DR

5TH ST

JUBILEE DR

RAINBOW PEAKS RD

GOMEZ CREEK

7

8

8TH ST

SELECT WY

RAINBOW HEIGHTS PL

RAINBOW HEIGHTS RD

OHLSON CREST CT

RAINBOW HEIGHTS RD

92028

OW TS RD

RAINBOW HEIGHTS RD

VIA LADERA

SOMBRERO RD

RICE CANYON RD

1200

RAINBOW TERR

RAINBOW HEIGHTS RD

RAINBOW HEIGHTS LN

RAINBOW HEIGHTS RD

SOMBRERO RD

AROUBA RD

VIA LADERA

RAINBOW CREST RD

18

GOMEZ CREEK

17

800

R3W
R2W

AROUBA RD

TYAHA ST

LEMON LINE RD

JEREMY WY

PALA TEMEC

N

A   B   C   D   E

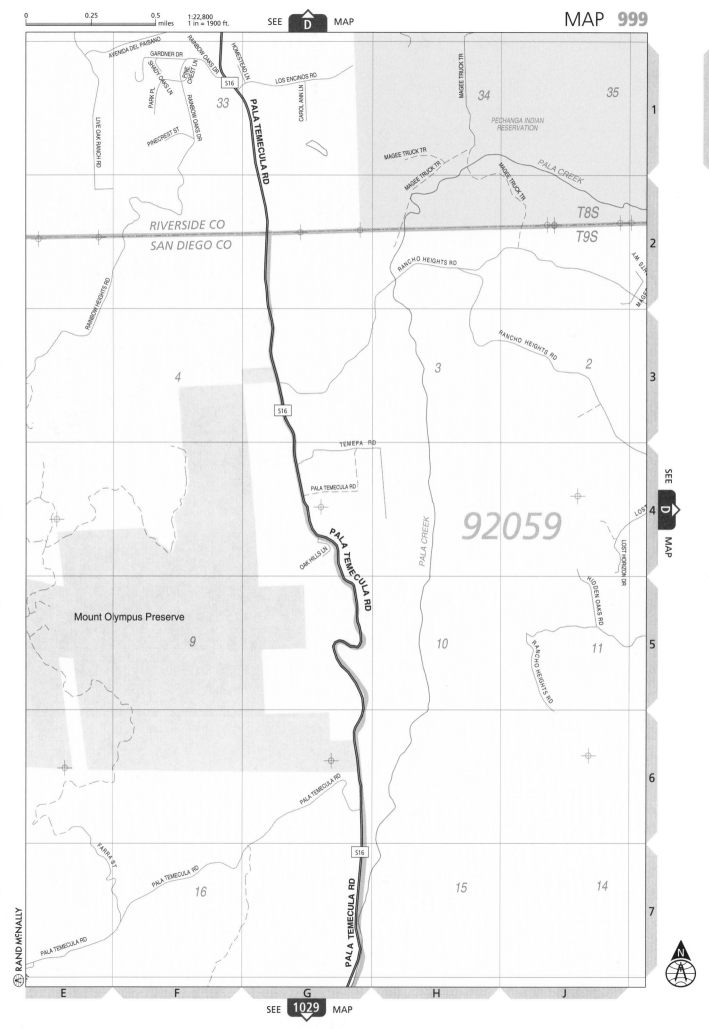

MAP 999

0   0.25   0.5
miles   1:22,800
1 in = 1900 ft.

SEE **D** MAP

AVENIDA DEL PAISANO

GARDNER DR

SHADY OAKS LN

PINE CREST LN

RAINBOW OAKS DR

HOMESTEAD LN

S16

LOS ENCINOS RD

PARK PL

RAINBOW OAKS DR

PINECREST ST

33

CAROL ANN LN

PALA TEMECULA RD

MAGEE TRUCK TR

34

35

PECHANGA INDIAN
RESERVATION

LIVE OAK RANCH RD

MAGEE TRUCK TR

MAGEE TRUCK TR

MAGEE TRUCK TR

MAGEE TRUCK TR

PALA CREEK

T8S

1

RIVERSIDE CO

SAN DIEGO CO

RANCHO HEIGHTS RD

T9S

2

RAINBOW HEIGHTS RD

MAGEE HTS WY

4

S16

3

RANCHO HEIGHTS RD

2

3

TEMEPA RD

PALA TEMECULA RD

92059

SEE **D** MAP

LOST

4

OAK HILLS LN

PALA TEMECULA RD

PALA CREEK

LOST HORIZON DR

Mount Olympus Preserve

9

10

HIDDEN OAKS RD

11

5

RANCHO HEIGHTS RD

PALA TEMECULA RD

6

FARRA ST

PALA TEMECULA RD

16

S16

PALA TEMECULA RD

15

14

7

PALA TEMECULA RD

PALA TEMECULA RD

RAND McNALLY

E   F   G   H   J

SEE 1029 MAP

N

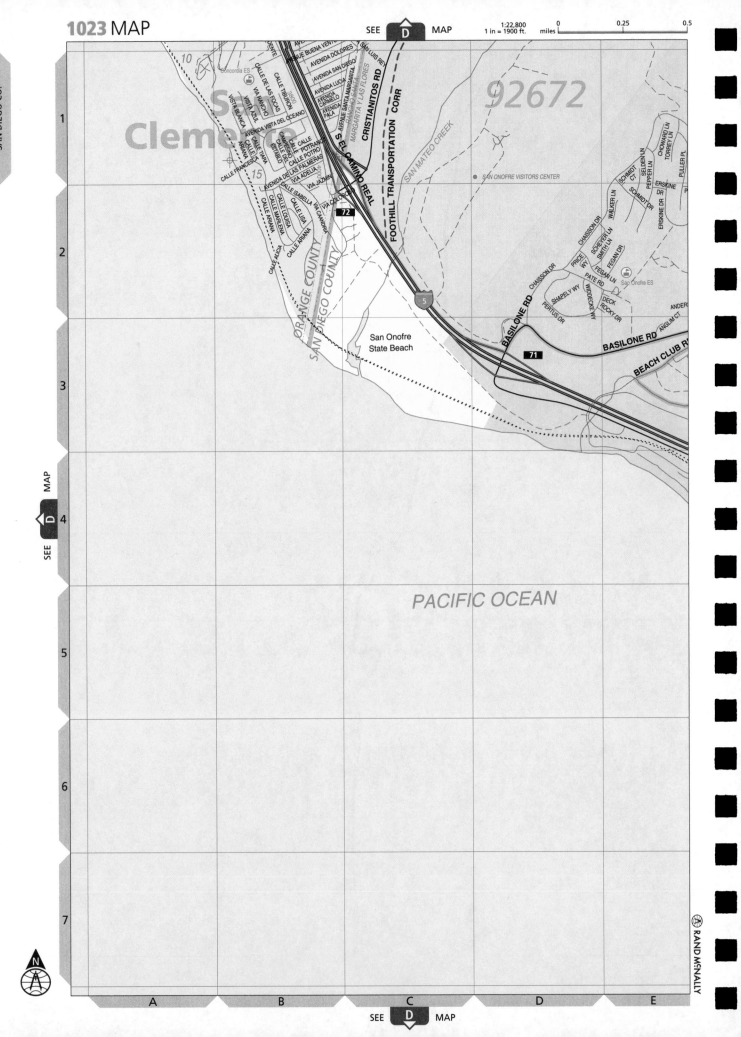

SAN DIEGO CO.

SEE **D** MAP

1:22,800
1 in = 1900 ft.

0   0.25   0.5
miles

92672

San Clemente

Concordia ES

10

15

3800

3600

AVENIDA BUENA VENTURA
AVENIDA SAN DIEGO
AVENIDA DOLORES
AVENIDA LUCIA
AVENIDA SAN DIEGO
AVENIDA CARMELO
AVENIDA PALA
SAN LUIS REY
AVENIDA SANTA MARGARITA
RANCHO SANTA MARGARITA Y LAS FLORES
CRISTIANITOS RD
S EL CAMINO REAL

CALLE DE LAS ROCAS
VIA RANCHO
VISTA AZUL
VISTA BLANCA
CALLE TIBURON
CAMPESINO
CALLE TIARA
CALLE ORO
CALLE POTRANCA
CALLE POTRO
CALLE PALMERAS
AVENIDA VISTA DEL OCEANO
CALLE FRANCESCA
CALLE ARIANA
CALLE MARLENA
CALLE LOUISA
CALLE LISA
CALLE ARIANA
CALLE ALICA
AVENIDA DE LAS PALMERAS
CALLE ISABELLA
VIA CANDRIA
VIA JAZMIN
VIA COLORES
VIA ADELIA

72

FOOTHILL TRANSPORTATION CORR

SAN MATEO CREEK

● SAN ONOFRE VISITORS CENTER

5

ORANGE COUNTY
SAN DIEGO COUNTY

San Onofre
State Beach

71

San Onofre ES

CHAISSON DR
WALKER LN
SCHMIDT CT
SELDEN LN
PEPPER LN
SCHMIDT DR
CHOWARD LN
TORREY LN
ERSKINE DR
PULLER PL
CHAISSON DR
PRICE WY
SCHEYER LN
SMITH LN
PATE RD
FEGAN LN
FEGAN DR
SHAPELY WY
WIDDECKE WY
DECK
ROCKY DR
FERTUS DR
ANDER
BASILONE RD
ANGLIM CT
BASILONE RD
BEACH CLUB R

MAP
SEE **D** 4

PACIFIC OCEAN

N

RAND McNALLY

SEE **D** MAP

A   B   C   D   E

1
2
3
4
5
6
7

MAP **1023**

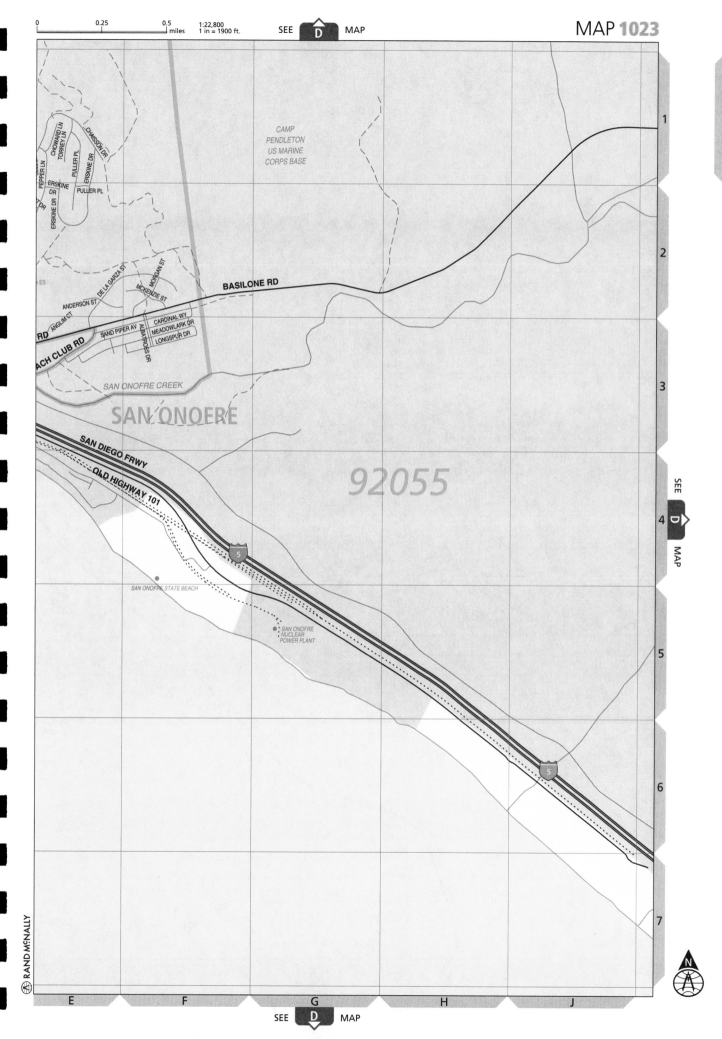

0   0.25   0.5   1:22,800
miles   1 in = 1900 ft.

SEE D MAP

1

CAMP
PENDLETON
US MARINE
CORPS BASE

2

CHOWARD LN
TORREY LN
CHASSON DR
PULLER PL
PEPPER LN
ERSKINE DR
ERSKINE DR
PULLER PL

BASILONE RD

e ES

ANDERSON ST
DE LA GARZA ST
MORGAN ST
MCKENZIE ST
ANGLIM CT
SAND PIPER AV
CARDINAL WY
MEADOWLARK DR
LONGSPUR DR
ALBATROSS DR
ACH CLUB RD
RD

SAN ONOFRE CREEK

3

SAN ONOFRE

SAN DIEGO FRWY
OLD HIGHWAY 101

92055

SEE D MAP

4

5

SAN ONOFRE STATE BEACH

SAN ONOFRE
NUCLEAR
POWER PLANT

5

6

5

7

RAND MᶜNALLY

E   F   G   H   J

SEE D MAP

N

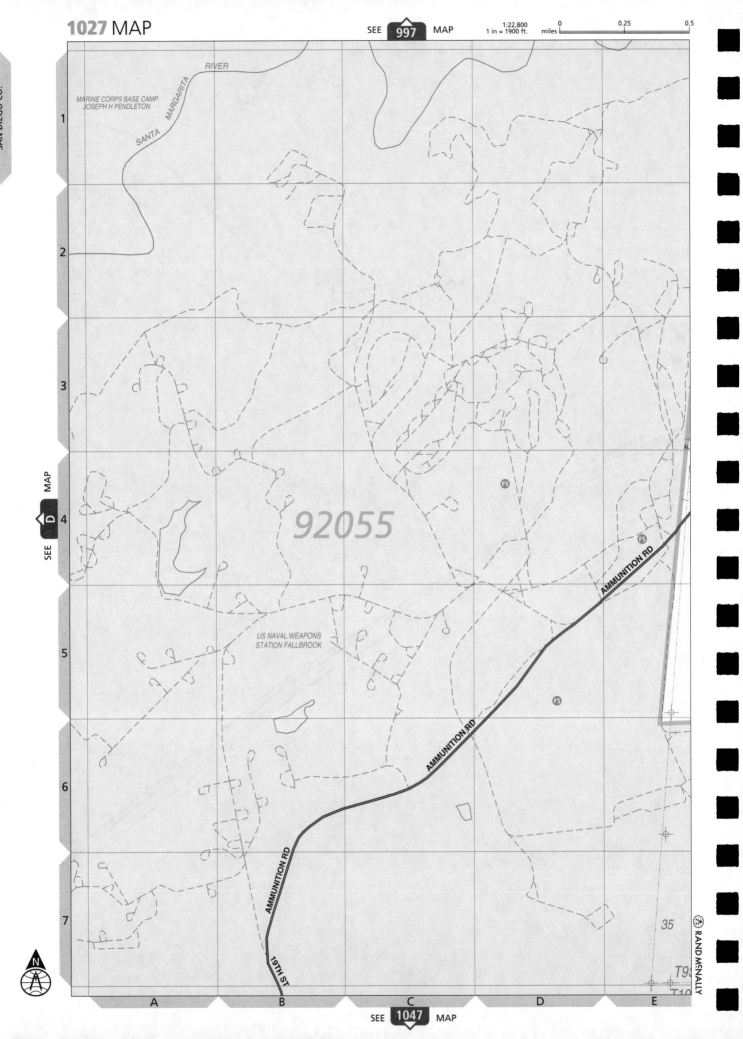

SEE 997 MAP

1:22,800
1 in = 1900 ft.

miles 0   0.25   0.5

SAN DIEGO CO.

SANTA MARGARITA RIVER

MARINE CORPS BASE CAMP
JOSEPH H PENDLETON

1

2

3

SEE D MAP

92055

4

US NAVAL WEAPONS
STATION FALLBROOK

5

6

AMMUNITION RD

AMMUNITION RD

AMMUNITION RD

19TH ST

7

35

T9
T10

N

RAND McNALLY

A   B   C   D   E

SEE 1047 MAP

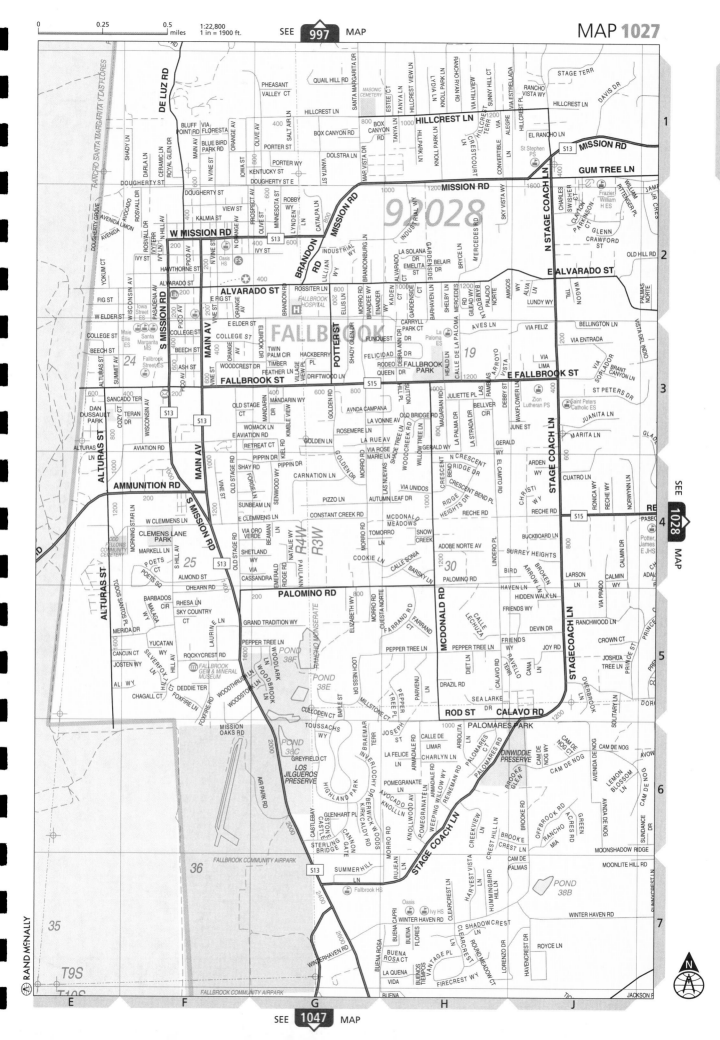

MAP 1027

SAN DIEGO CO.

FALLBROOK

92028

SEE 1028 MAP

RAND MCNALLY

N

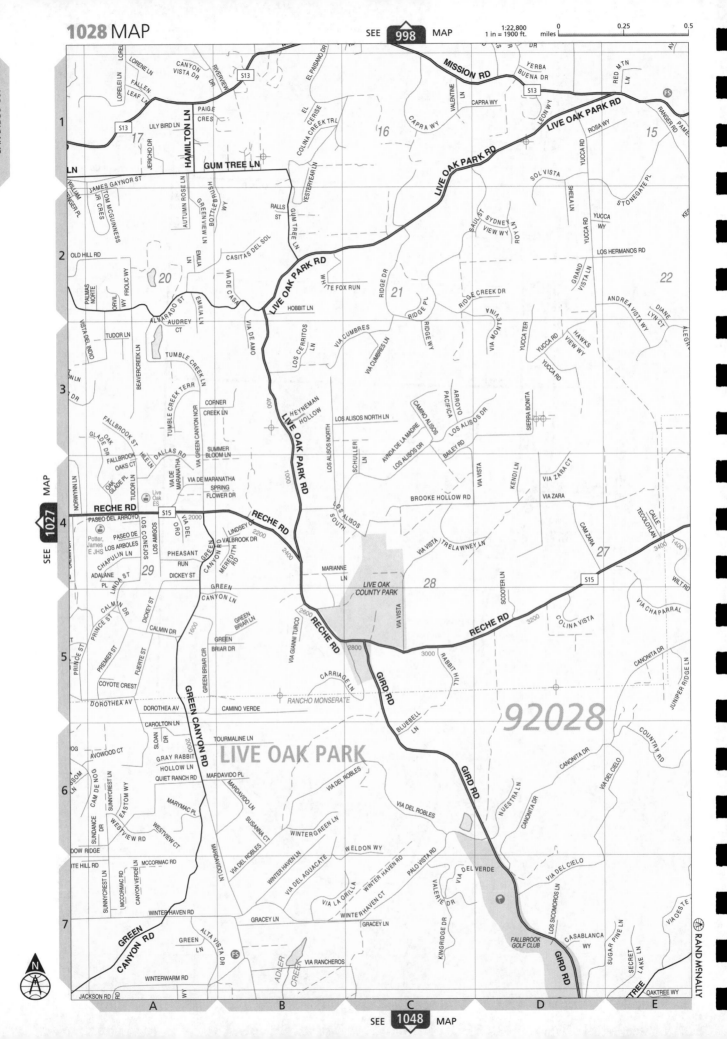

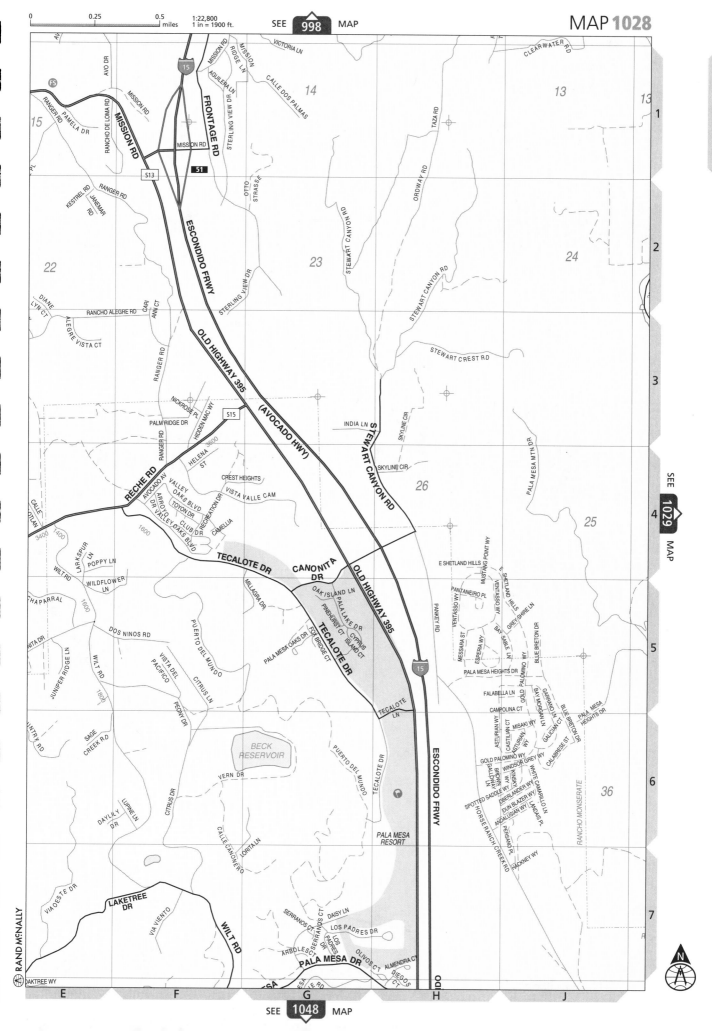

MAP **1028**

SAN DIEGO CO.

SEE 1029 MAP

0   0.25   0.5
miles
1:22,800
1 in = 1900 ft.

RAND McNALLY

N

15
51
S13
S15

14
13
13
15
22
23
24
26
25
36

MISSION RD
AVO DR
PAMELA DR
RANGER RD
RANCHO DE LOMA RD
MISSION RD
VICTORIA LN
MISSION RD
RIDGE LN
MISSION
AGUILERA LN
STERLING VIEW DR
CALLE DOS PALMAS
CLEARWATER RD
FS
RANGER RD
KESTREL RD
JANEMAR RD
RANCHO ALEGRE RD
CARI ANN CT
RANGER RD
DIANE LYN CT
ALEGRE VISTA CT
FRONTAGE RD
ESCONDIDO FRWY
OLD HIGHWAY 395
(AVOCADO HWY)
STERLING VIEW DR
OTTO STRASSE
TAZA RD
ORDWAY RD
STEWART CANYON RD
STEWART CANYON RD
STEWART CREST RD
INDIA LN
SKYLINE CIR
SKYLINE CIR
STEWART CANYON RD
PALA MESA MTN DR
NICKROSE PL
HIDDEN MAC WY
PALM RIDGE DR
RANGER RD
HELENA ST
3600
CREST HEIGHTS
VISTA VALLE CAM
RECHE RD
AVOCADO AV
VALLEY OAKS BLVD
ARROYO DR
TOYON DR
CLUB DR
RECREATION DR
CAMELLIA
VALLEY OAKS BLVD
CALLE OTLAN
3400
1400
1600
LARKSPUR LN
POPPY LN
WILT RD
WILDFLOWER LN
CHAPARRAL
1600
ANITA DR
DOS NINOS RD
JUNIPER RIDGE LN
WILT RD
1800
VISTA DEL PACIFICO
CITRUS LN
PUERTO DEL MUNDO
PEONY DR
TECALOTE DR
CANONITA DR
MILLAGRA DR
OAK ISLAND LN
PALA LAKE DR
PINEHURST CT
CYPRUS
ISLAND CT
TECALOTE DR
PALA MESA OAKS DR
FOX BRIDGE CT
OLD HIGHWAY 395
15
E SHETLAND HILLS
MUSTANG POINT WY
PANTANEIRO PL
VENTASSO WY
E SHETLAND HILLS
MESSARA ST
ESPERIA WY
BAY SABLE LN
GREY SHIRE LN
BLUE BRETON DR
GOLD PALOMINO WY
PALA MESA HEIGHTS DR
FALABELLA LN
GARRANO LN
BAY MORGAN LN
BLUE BRETON DR
PALA MESA HEIGHTS DR
CAMPOLINA CT
ASTURIAN WY
CASTILIAN CT
MISAKI WY
ASTURIAN WY
GALICIAN CT
CALABRESE ST
GOLD PALOMINO WY
WINDSOR GREY WY
WHITE CAMARILLO LN
BROWN GALLOWAY LN
KNABSKI WY
OBERLANDER WY
DUN BLAZER WY
ANDALUSIAN WY
LANDAIS PL
PERSANO PL
SPOTTED SADDLE WY
HORSE RANCH CREEK RD
HACKNEY WY
RANCHO MONSERATE
PANKEY RD
BECK RESERVOIR
VERN DR
SAGE CREEK RD
CITRUS DR
DAYLILY DR
LUPINE LN
COUNTRY RD
CALLE CANONERO
LORITA LN
PUERTO DEL MUNDO
TECALOTE DR
TECALOTE DR
TECALOTE LN
PALA MESA RESORT
ESCONDIDO FRWY
LAKETREE DR
VIA OESTE DR
VIA VIENTO
WILT RD
OAKTREE WY
SERRANOS CT
SERRANOS CT
DAISY LN
LOS PADRES DR
ARBOLES CT
LOS PADRES
SERRANOS CT
OLIVOS CT
ALMENDRA CT
DIEGOS CT
PALA MESA DR
MESA
E   F   G   H   J

1
2
3
4
5
6
7

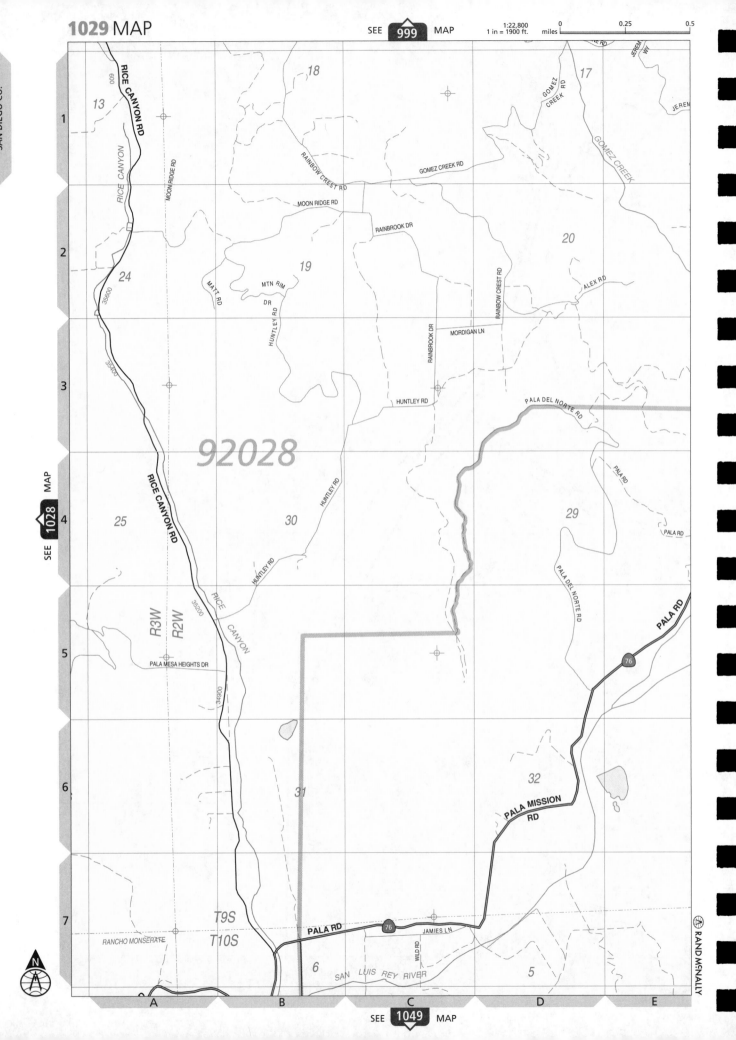

SAN DIEGO CO.

SEE **999** MAP

1:22,800
1 in = 1900 ft.

miles 0   0.25   0.5

SEE **1028** MAP

RICE CANYON RD

RICE CANYON

13

18

GOMEZ CREEK RD

17

JEREM WY

JEREM

RAINBOW CREST RD

GOMEZ CREEK RD

GOMEZ CREEK

MOON RIDGE RD

MOON RIDGE RD

RAINBROOK DR

20

24

19

MATT RD

MTN RIM DR

HUNTLEY RD

RAINBOW CREST RD

RAINBROOK DR

ALEX RD

MORDIGAN LN

HUNTLEY RD

HUNTLEY RD

PALA DEL NORTE RD

92028

RICE CANYON RD

25

R3W R2W

RICE CANYON

HUNTLEY RD

HUNTLEY RD

30

29

PALA RD

PALA RD

PALA DEL NORTE RD

PALA RD

PALA MESA HEIGHTS DR

31

32

PALA MISSION RD

76

PALA RD

RANCHO MONSERATE

T9S
T10S

PALA RD

76

JAMIES LN

WILD RD

SAN LUIS REY RIVER

6

5

A   B   C   D   E

1   2   3   4   5   6   7

N

RAND McNALLY

SEE **1049** MAP

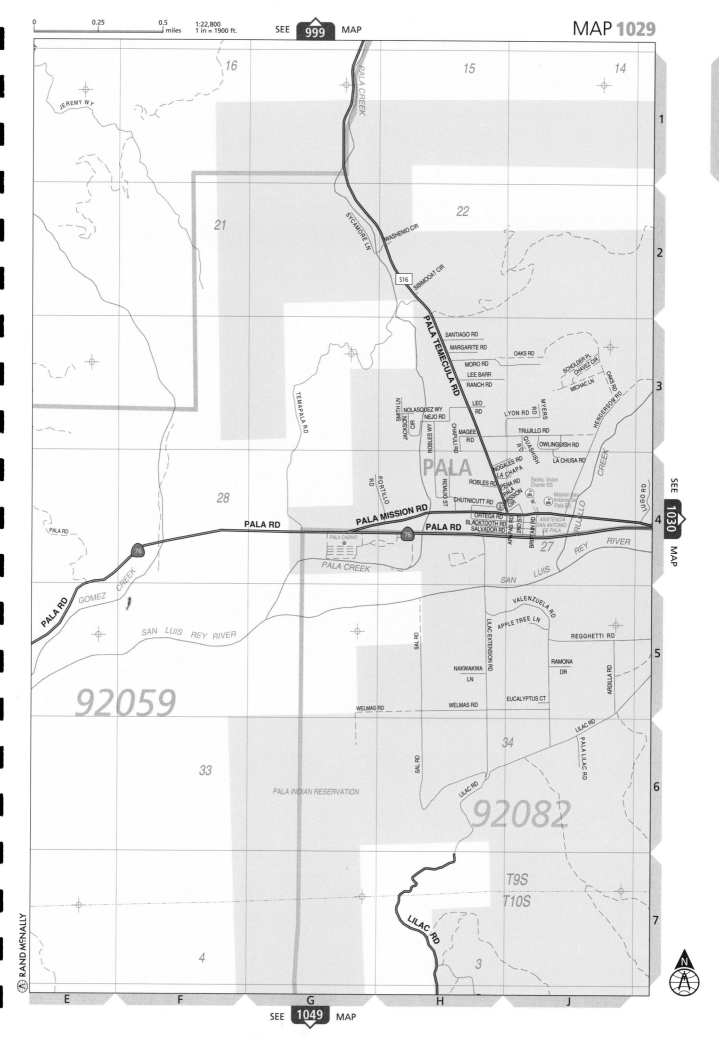

MAP 1029

0   0.25   0.5
miles
1:22,800
1 in = 1900 ft.

SEE 999 MAP

16   15   14

1

JEREMY WY

PALA CREEK

21   22

2

SYCAMORE LN

WASHENIO CIR

S16

SIBIMOOAT CIR

PALA TEMECULA RD

SANTIAGO RD
MARGARITE RD
OAKS RD
MORO RD   SCHOLDER PL
LEE BARR   CHAVEZ CIR   OAKS RD
RANCH RD   MICHAC LN   HENDERSON RD

3

TEMAPALA RD

SMITH LN
NOLASQUEZ WY   LEO RD   MYERS RD
JACKSON CIR   NEJO RD   LYON RD   TRUJILLO RD
ROBLES WY   MAGEE RD   QUASHISH RD   OWLINGUISH RD
CHAPULI RD   RD   LA CHUSA RD

PALA

RD   NOGALES RD   CREEK
PORTILLO   LA CHAPA
REMIJIO ST   ROBLES RD   PENA RD   Banks, Vivian
28   CHUTNICUTT RD   PALA   Charter ES
MISSION   Mission San
CIR   Antonio Del
Pala ES

LUGO RD

SEE 1030 MAP

ORTEGA RD
PALA RD   PALA MISSION RD   BLACKTOOTH RD   ASISTENCIA
SALVADOR RD   SAN ANTONIO
PALA RD   PALA RD   DE PALA   4

APPAS RD   27
2ND ST
BRITTAIN RD

PALA RD   76   PALA CASINO

SAN   LUIS   REY   RIVER

GOMEZ CREEK   PALA CREEK

76   PALA RD

SAN LUIS REY RIVER

VALENZUELA RD

APPLE TREE LN

SAL RD   LILAC EXTENSION RD   REGGHETTI RD   5

92059   NAKWAKWA   RAMONA
LN   DR   ARDILLA RD

WELMAS RD   WELMAS RD   EUCALYPTUS CT

LILAC RD

33   34   PALA LILAC RD   6

PALA INDIAN RESERVATION   92082

LILAC RD

T9S
T10S   7

LILAC RD

RAND MCNALLY

E   F   G   H   J

SEE 1049 MAP

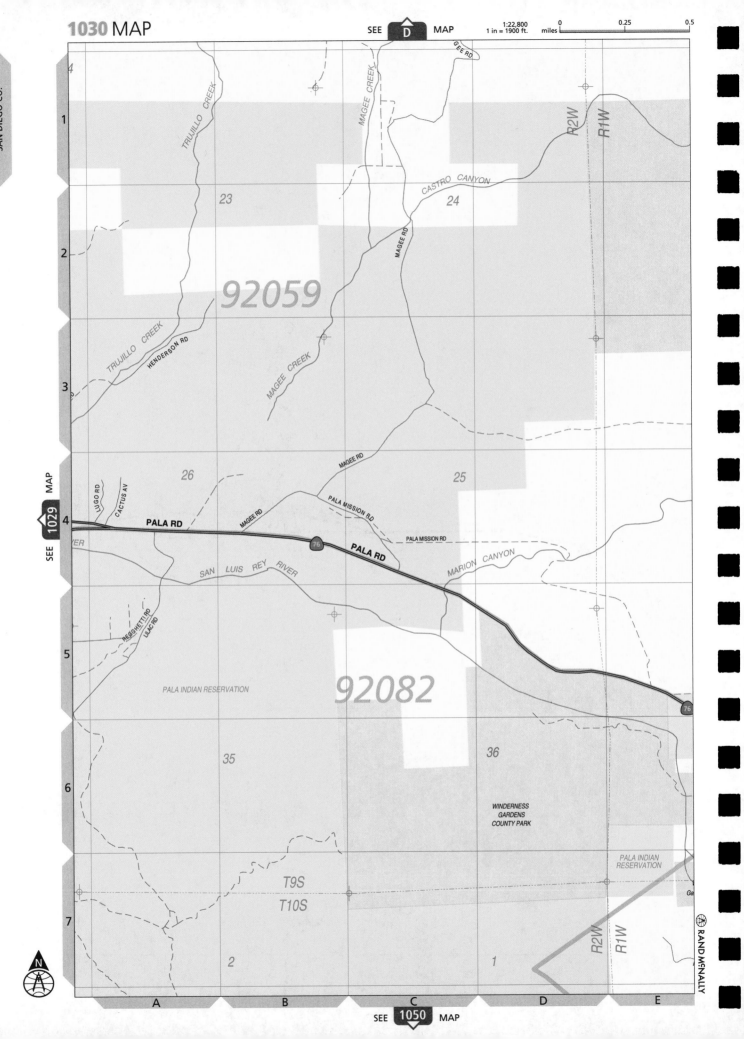

SAN DIEGO CO.

SEE **D** MAP

1:22,800
1 in = 1900 ft.

miles 0   0.25   0.5

4

TRUJILLO CREEK

MAGEE CREEK

GEE RD

1

R2W

R1W

23

CASTRO CANYON

24

MAGEE RD

2

92059

TRUJILLO CREEK

HENDERSON RD

MAGEE CREEK

3

26

MAGEE RD

25

LUGO RD

CACTUS AV

SEE **1029** MAP

PALA RD

MAGEE RD

PALA MISSION RD

4

PALA MISSION RD

75

PALA RD

MARION CANYON

VER

SAN LUIS REY RIVER

RESGHETTI RD

LILAC RD

5

92082

PALA INDIAN RESERVATION

76

35

36

6

WINDERNESS
GARDENS
COUNTY PARK

PALA INDIAN
RESERVATION

T9S

T10S

Ga

7

R2W

R1W

RAND McNALLY

N

2

1

A   B   C   D   E

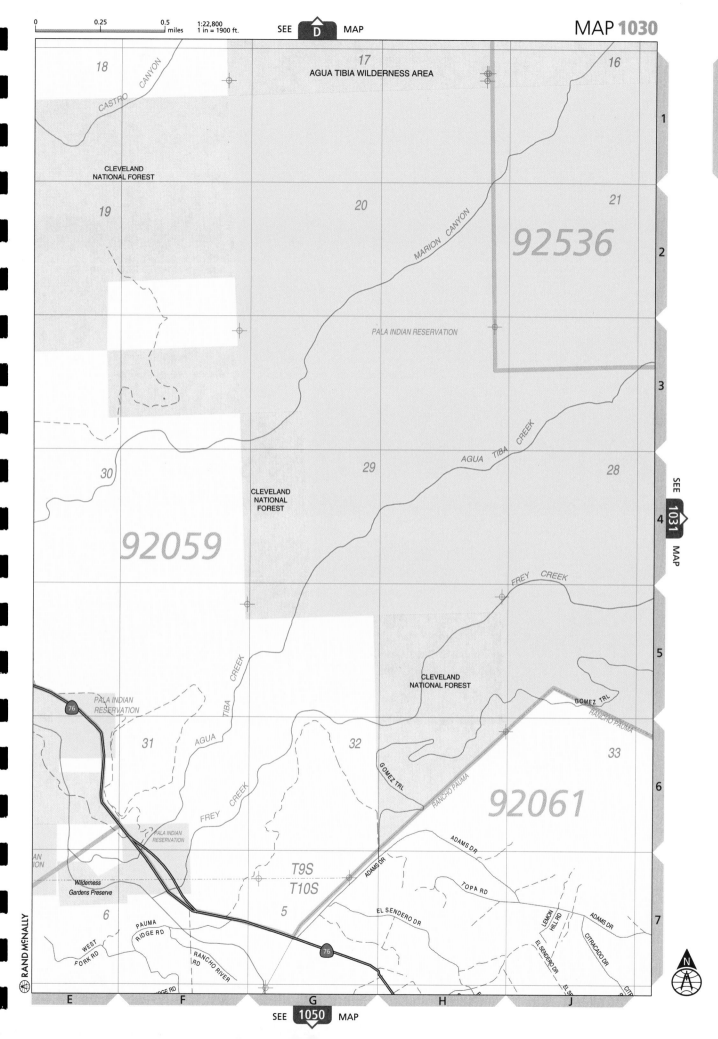

MAP **1030**

SEE D MAP

0   0.25   0.5
miles
1:22,800
1 in = 1900 ft.

18

17
AGUA TIBIA WILDERNESS AREA

16

1

CLEVELAND
NATIONAL FOREST

19

20

92536

MARION CANYON

21

2

PALA INDIAN RESERVATION

3

AGUA TIBA CREEK

30

29

CLEVELAND
NATIONAL
FOREST

28

SEE 1031 MAP

92059

FREY CREEK

4

AGUA TIBA CREEK

5

CLEVELAND
NATIONAL FOREST

76

PALA INDIAN
RESERVATION

GOMEZ TRL

RANCHO PAUMA

31

AGUA

32

GOMEZ TRL

RANCHO PAUMA

33

6

92061

FREY CREEK

FREY CREEK

PALA INDIAN
RESERVATION

ADAMS DR

ADAMS DR

AN
ION

Wilderness
Gardens Preserve

T9S
T10S

TOPA RD

7

6

5

EL SENDERO DR

PAUMA
RIDGE RD

76

ADAMS DR

LEMON
HILL RD

WEST
FORK RD

RANCHO RIVER
RD

EL SENDERO DR

CITRACADO DR

EL S

RAND MCNALLY

RIDGE RD

E   F   G   H   J

N

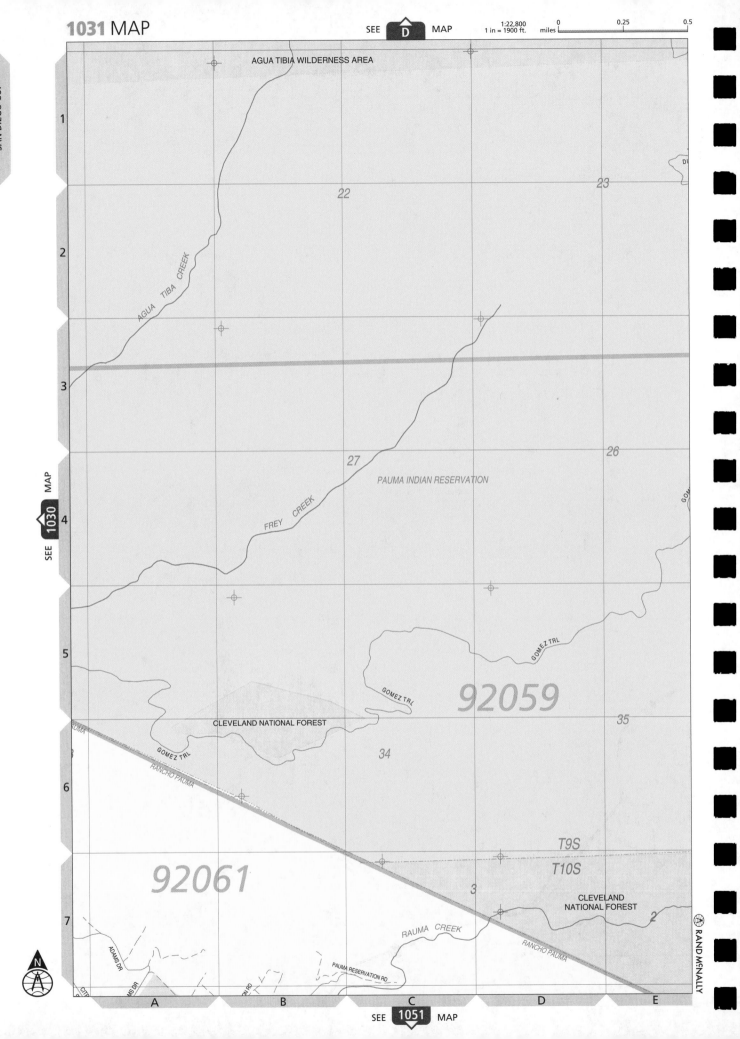

SEE **D** MAP

1:22,800
1 in = 1900 ft.   miles   0   0.25   0.5

SAN DIEGO CO.

AGUA TIBIA WILDERNESS AREA

1

22

23

2

AGUA TIBIA CREEK

3

SEE **1030** MAP

27

PAUMA INDIAN RESERVATION

26

4

FREY CREEK

GOMEZ

5

GOMEZ TRL

92059

GOMEZ TRL

CLEVELAND NATIONAL FOREST

35

GOMEZ TRL

34

6

RANCHO PAUMA

T9S

T10S

92061

3

CLEVELAND
NATIONAL FOREST

7

RAUMA CREEK

RANCHO PAUMA

2

ADAMS DR

PAUMA RESERVATION RD

RAND McNALLY

A   B   C   D   E

SEE **1051** MAP

SAN DIEGO CO.

0.25   0.5 miles
1:22,800
1 in = 1900 ft.

PALOMAR DIVIDE TRUCK TRL

24

R1W R1E

19

92536

GOMEZ TRL

25

30

PALOMAR DIVIDE TRUCK TRL

GOMEZ TRL

CLEVELAND
NATIONAL FOREST

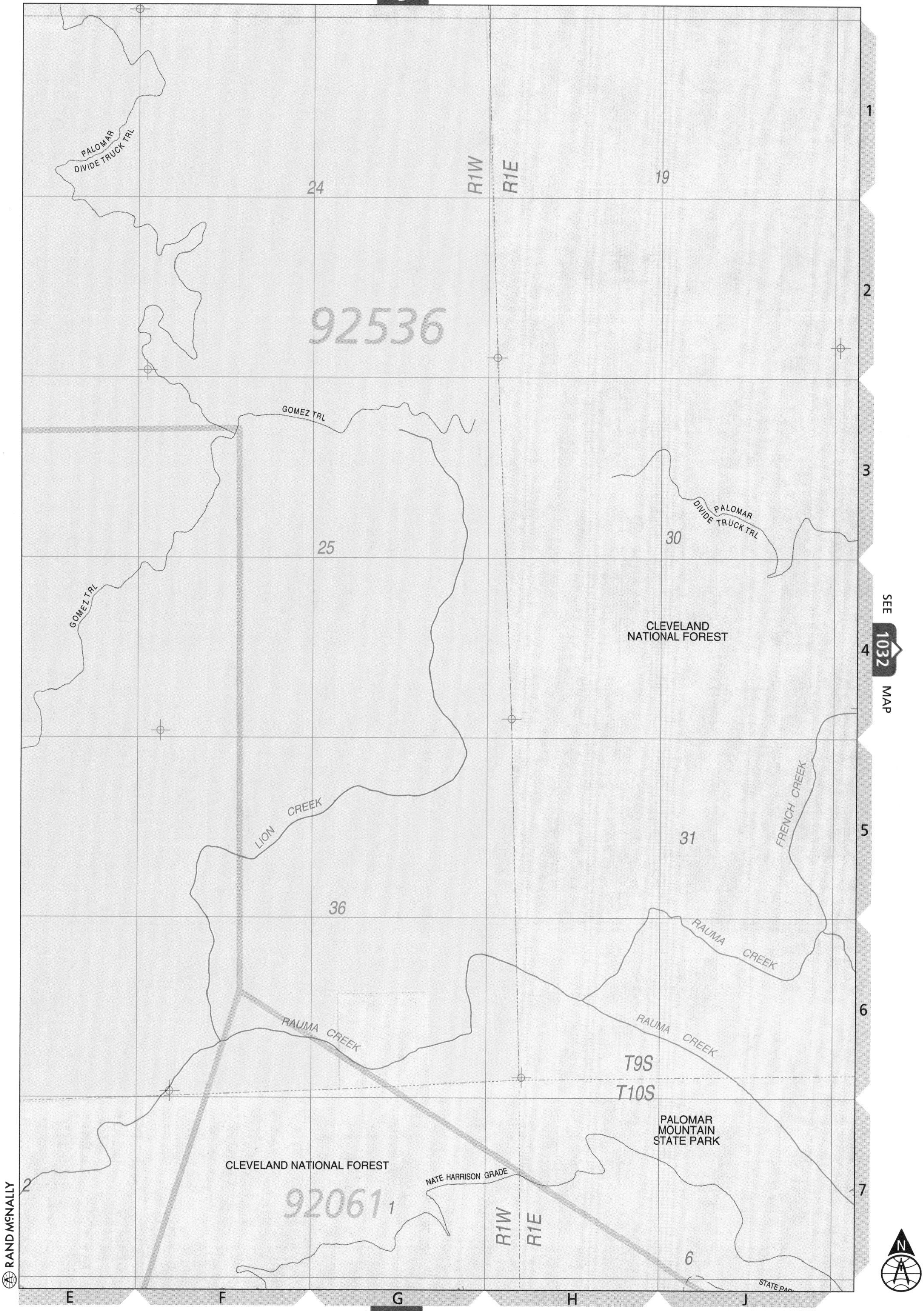

SEE 1032 MAP

FRENCH CREEK

LION CREEK

31

36

RAUMA CREEK

RAUMA CREEK

RAUMA CREEK

T9S
T10S

PALOMAR
MOUNTAIN
STATE PARK

2

CLEVELAND NATIONAL FOREST

92061

NATE HARRISON GRADE

R1W R1E

6

STATE PARK

RAND M°NALLY

E   F   G   H   J

1 2 3 4 5 6 7

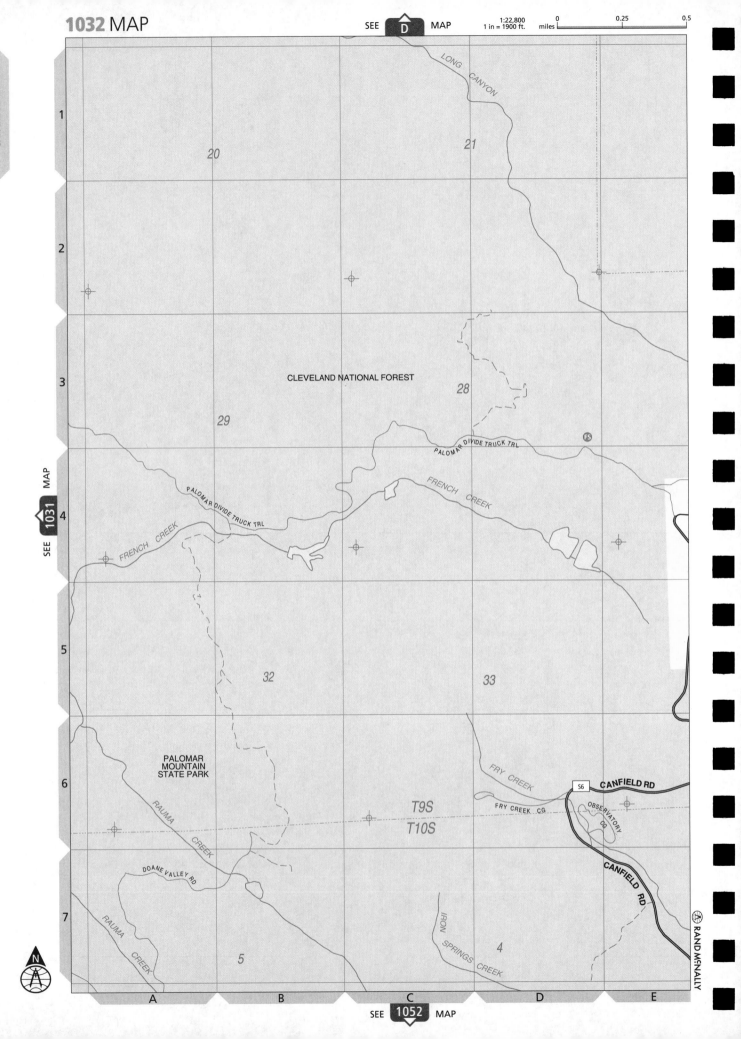

SAN DIEGO CO.

SEE **D** MAP

1:22,800
1 in = 1900 ft.

miles   0   0.25   0.5

LONG CANYON

1

20   21

2

3   CLEVELAND NATIONAL FOREST

28

29   FS

PALOMAR DIVIDE TRUCK TRL

FRENCH CREEK

SEE **1031** MAP

PALOMAR DIVIDE TRUCK TRL

4

FRENCH CREEK

5

32   33

FRY CREEK

PALOMAR
MOUNTAIN
STATE PARK

6   S6 CANFIELD RD

RAUMA CREEK   T9S   FRY CREEK CG   OBSERVATORY
                     T10S   CG

DOANE VALLEY RD   CANFIELD RD

7
RAUMA CREEK   5   IRON SPRINGS CREEK   4

N

A   B   C   D   E

SEE **1052** MAP

RAND MⁿNALLY

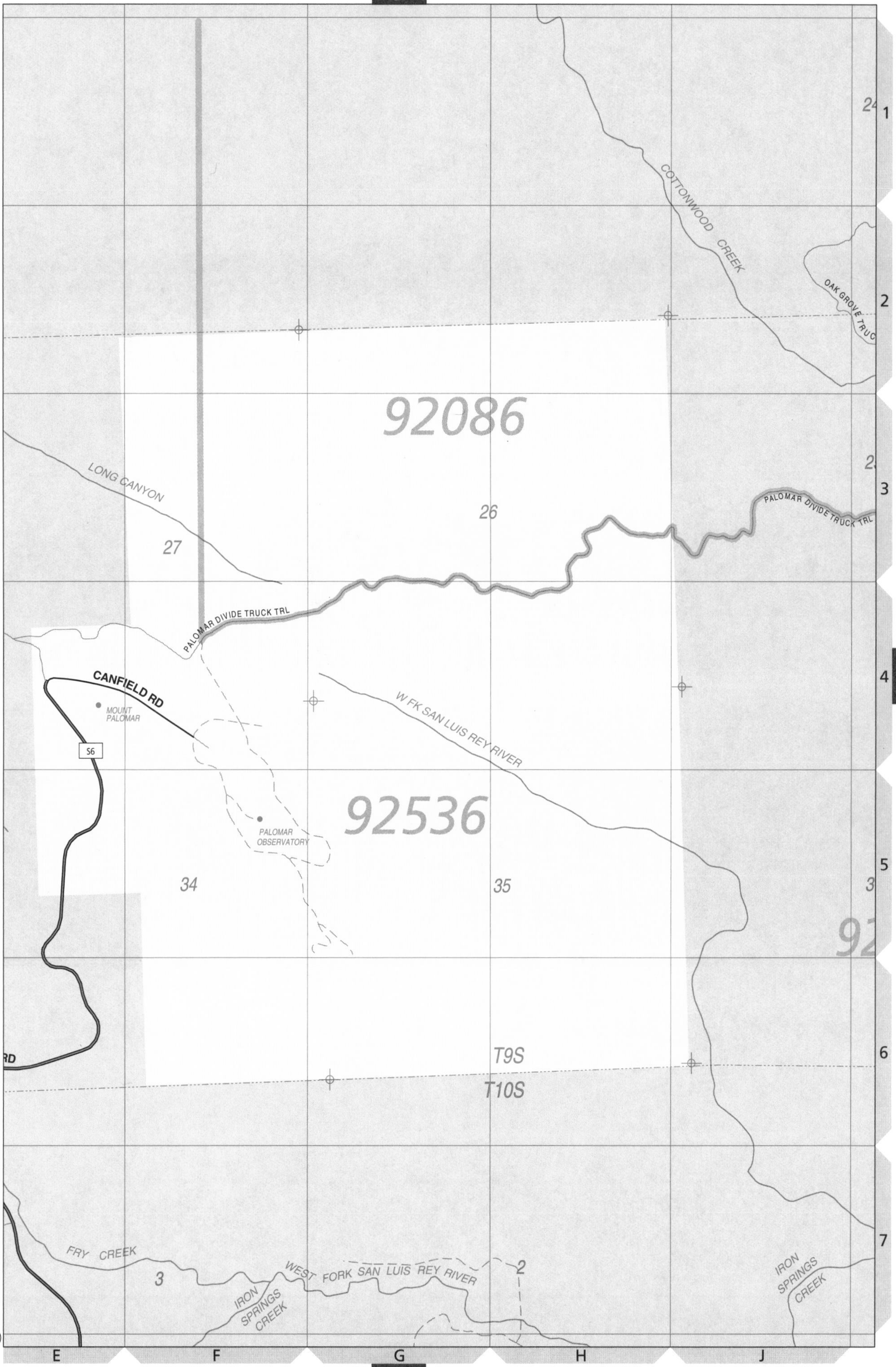

MAP **1032**

SEE D MAP

0   0.25   0.5
miles
1:22,800
1 in = 1900 ft.

24   1

COTTONWOOD CREEK

OAK GROVE TRC

2

92086

2   3

LONG CANYON

PALOMAR DIVIDE TRUCK TRL

26

27

PALOMAR DIVIDE TRUCK TRL

SEE 1033 MAP

CANFIELD RD

MOUNT PALOMAR

W FK SAN LUIS REY RIVER

4

S6

92536

PALOMAR OBSERVATORY

34

35

5   3

92

RD

T9S

6

T10S

7

FRY CREEK

3

IRON SPRINGS CREEK

WEST FORK SAN LUIS REY RIVER

2

IRON SPRINGS CREEK

RAND MCNALLY

E   F   G   H   J

N

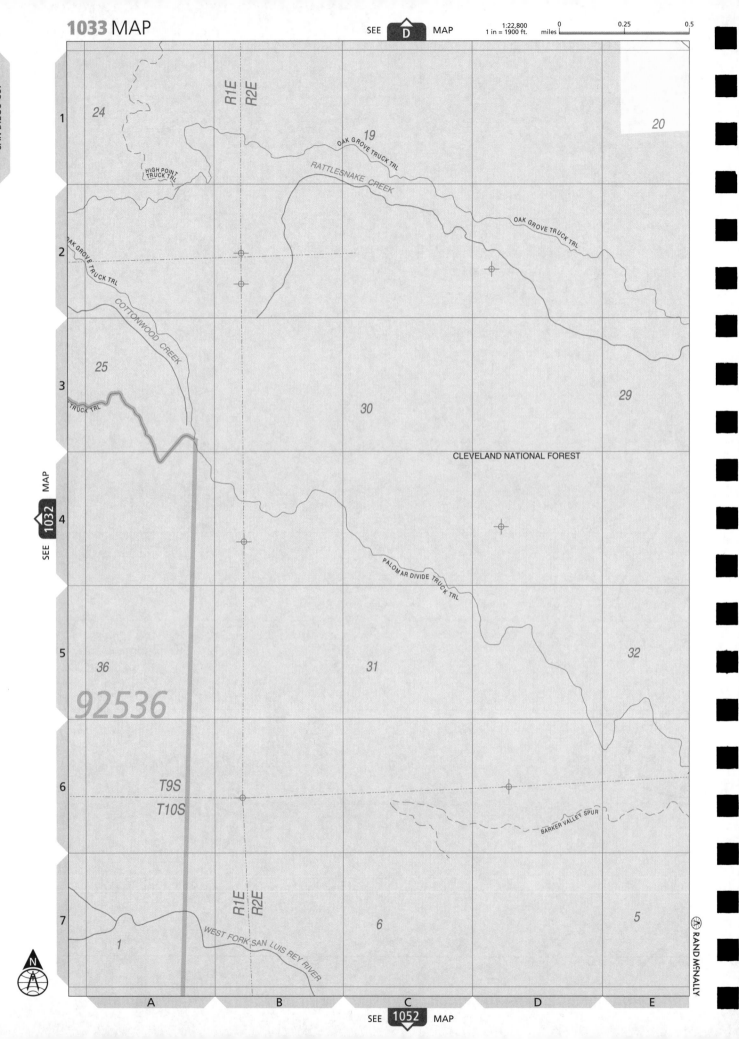

SEE D MAP

1:22,800
1 in = 1900 ft.   miles   0   0.25   0.5

SAN DIEGO CO.

R1E R2E

24

19

OAK GROVE TRUCK TRL

HIGH POINT
TRUCK TRL

RATTLESNAKE CREEK

OAK GROVE TRUCK TRL

20

OAK GROVE TRUCK TRL

COTTONWOOD CREEK

25

TRUCK TRL

30

29

CLEVELAND NATIONAL FOREST

SEE 1032 MAP

PALOMAR DIVIDE TRUCK TRL

36

92536

31

32

T9S
T10S

BARKER VALLEY SPUR

6

R1E R2E

7

1

WEST FORK SAN LUIS REY RIVER

5

N

A   B   C   D   E

SEE 1052 MAP

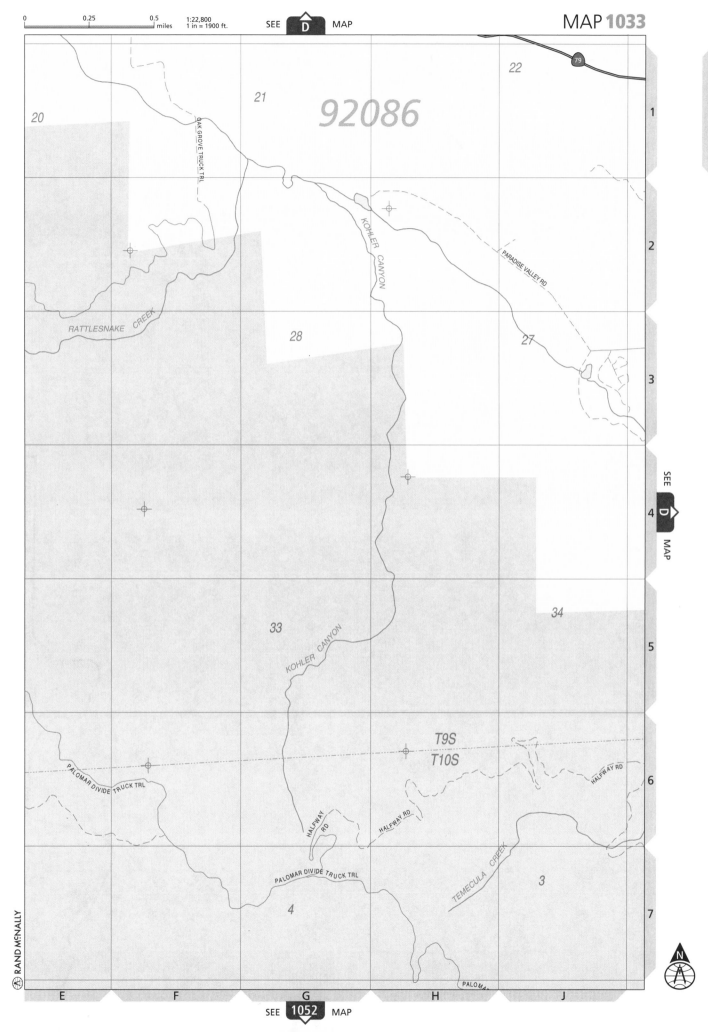

MAP **1033**

SAN DIEGO CO.

0   0.25   0.5
├──┼──┼──┤ miles
1:22,800
1 in = 1900 ft.

SEE D MAP

92086

20

21

22

79

OAK GROVE TRUCK TRL

KOHLER CANYON

PARADISE VALLEY RD

RATTLESNAKE   CREEK

28

27

1

2

3

SEE D MAP

4

34

33

KOHLER CANYON

5

T9S
T10S

PALOMAR DIVIDE TRUCK TRL

HALFWAY RD

HALFWAY RD

HALFWAY RD

6

PALOMAR DIVIDE TRUCK TRL

HALFWAY RD

TEMECULA CREEK

3

4

7

PALOMAR

RAND McNALLY

E   F   G   H   J

N

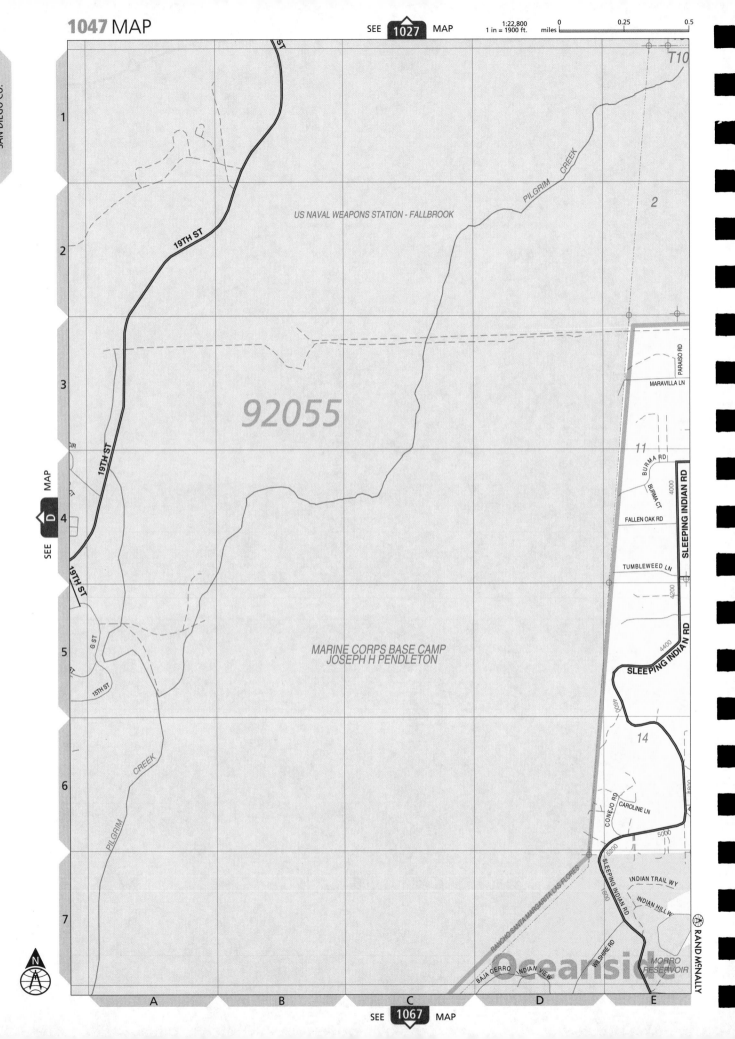

SAN DIEGO CO.

T10

19TH ST

US NAVAL WEAPONS STATION - FALLBROOK

PILGRIM CREEK

2

PARAISO RD

MARAVILLA LN

92055

11

BURMA RD

BURMA CT

4000

FALLEN OAK RD

SLEEPING INDIAN RD

TUMBLEWEED LN

4200

19TH ST

SEE D MAP

SLEEPING INDIAN RD

4400

MARINE CORPS BASE CAMP
JOSEPH H PENDLETON

4400

G ST

15TH ST

4600

14

PILGRIM CREEK

CONEJO RD

CAROLINE LN

4800

5000

5200

SLEEPING INDIAN RD

INDIAN TRAIL WY

RANCHO SANTA MARGARITA LAS FLORES

4800

INDIAN HILL WY

Oceanside

BAJA CERRO   INDIAN VIEW

WILSHIRE RD

MORRO RESERVOIR

RAND McNALLY

N

A   B   C   D   E

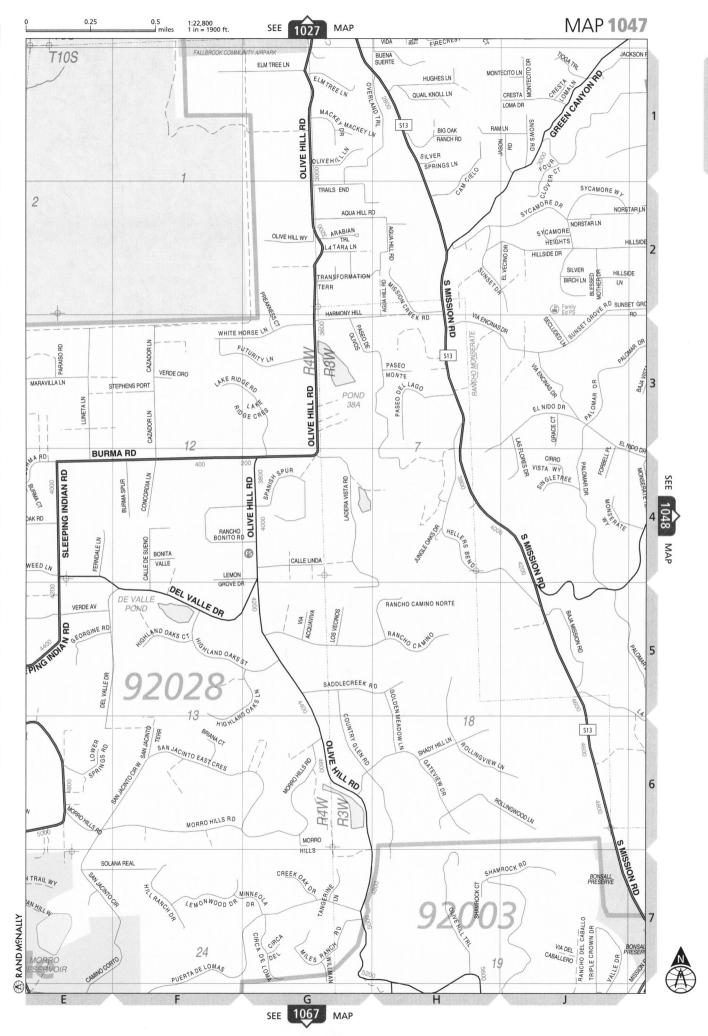

MAP **1047**

SAN DIEGO CO.

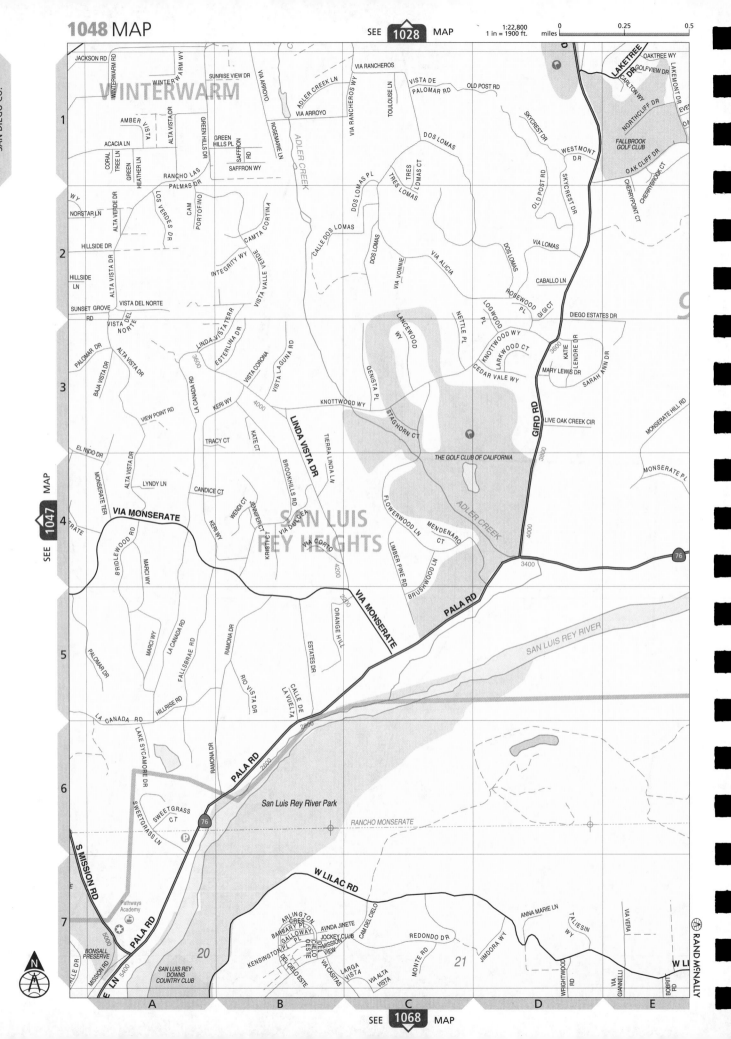

1:22,800
1 in = 1900 ft.

miles 0   0.25   0.5

SAN DIEGO CO.

WINTERWARM

SEE △ **1047** MAP

SAN LUIS
REY HEIGHTS

THE GOLF CLUB OF CALIFORNIA

ADLER CREEK

SAN LUIS REY RIVER

PALA RD

San Luis Rey River Park

RANCHO MONSERATE

S MISSION RD

PALA RD

Pathways
Academy

BONSALL
PRESERVE

20

SAN LUIS REY
DOWNS
COUNTRY CLUB

W LILAC RD

21

RAND McNALLY

A   B   C   D   E

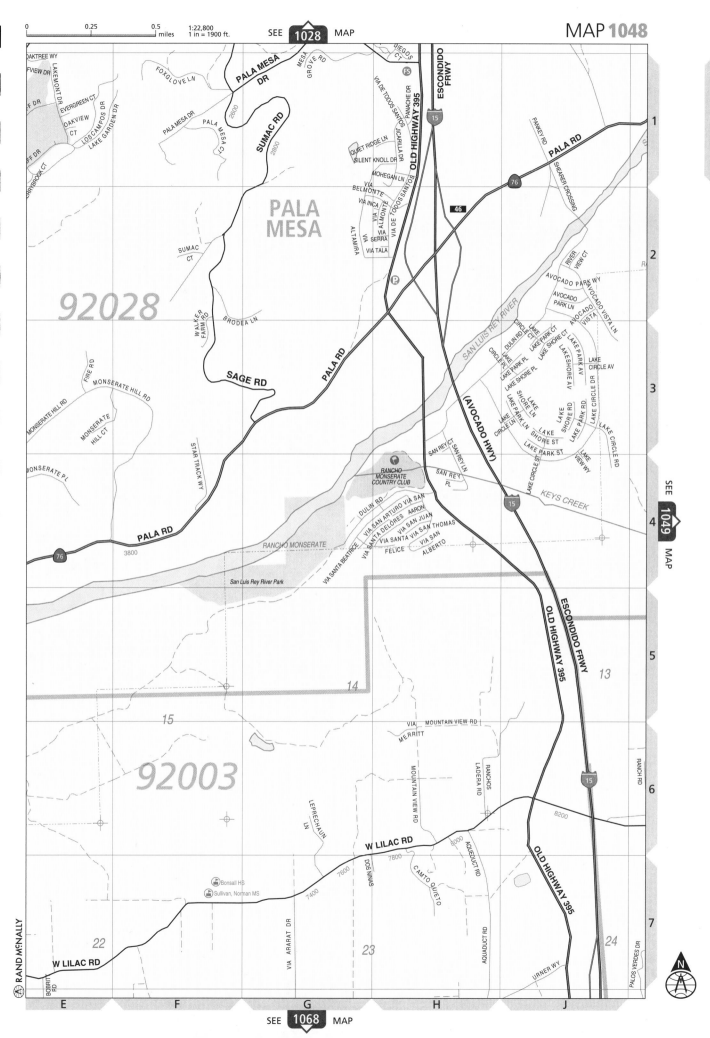

MAP **1048**

SAN DIEGO CO.

0   0.25   0.5
miles
1:22,800
1 in = 1900 ft.

OAKTREE WY
FVIEW DR
F DR
LAKEMONT DR
EVERGREEN CT
OAKVIEW CT
LOS CAMPOS DR
LAKE GARDEN DR
CRANBROOK CT
CRANBROOK CT
FF DR

FOXGLOVE LN
PALA MESA DR
PALA MESA CT
PALA MESA DR
SUMAC RD
2600
2800

MESA GROVE RD
DIEGOS CT
FS
VIA DE TODOS SANTOS
PANACHE DR
JICARILLA DR
QUIET RIDGE LN
SILENT KNOLL DR
MOHEGAN LN
VIA BELMONTE
VIA INCA
VIA ALMONTE
VIA SERRA
VIA TALA
ALTAMIRA
OLD HIGHWAY 395
VIA DE TODOS SANTOS
ESCONDIDO FRWY
15

PALA RD
PANKEY RD
SHEARER CROSSING
76
46

PALA MESA

92028

SUMAC CT
WALKER FARM RD
BRODEA LN
SAGE RD
PALA RD

SAN LUIS REY RIVER
RIVER VIEW CT
AVOCADO PARK WY
AVOCADO PARK LN
AVOCADO VISTA LN
AVOCADO VISTA
LAKE PARK CT
LAKE SHORE CT
LAKE PARK AV
LAKESHORE AV
LAKE CIRCLE AV
DULIN RD LP CT
LAKE PARK PL
CIRCLE PL
LAKE SHORE PL
LAKE SHORE RD
LAKE PARK RD
LAKE CIRCLE DR
LAKE SHORE LN
LAKE CIRCLE LN
LAKE PARK LN
LAKE SHORE ST
LAKE SHORE
LAKE PARK ST
LAKE CIRCLE ST
LAKE VIEW WY
LAKE CIRCLE RD

FIRE RD
MONSERATE HILL RD
MONSERATE HILL RD
MONSERATE HILL CT
MONSERATE PL
MONSERATE HILL RD
STAR TRACK WY

P
RANCHO MONSERATE COUNTRY CLUB
SAN REY CT
SAN REY LN
SAN REY PL
(AVOCADO HWY)
15
KEYS CREEK

PALA RD
76
3800

DULIN RD
VIA SAN ARTURO
VIA SANTA DELORES
VIA SAN AARON
VIA SANTA BEATRICE
VIA SANTA VIA SAN JUAN
FELICE
VIA SAN THOMAS
VIA SAN ALBERTO
RANCHO MONSERATE
San Luis Rey River Park

SEE ⬡1049 MAP

OLD HIGHWAY 395
ESCONDIDO FRWY

14
15
13

92003

VIA MOUNTAIN VIEW RD
VIA MERRITT
MOUNTAIN VIEW RD
LADERA RD
RANCHOS
15
RANCH RD

8200

LEPRECHAUN LN
W LILAC RD
DOS NIÑAS
C AMTO QUIETO
AQUEDUCT RD
OLD HIGHWAY 395

8000
7800
7600
7400

Bonsall HS
Sullivan, Norman MS

VIA ARARAT DR

22
23
24

W LILAC RD
BOBBITT RD
AQUADUCT RD
URNER WY
PALOS VERDES DR

RAND McNALLY

N

E   F   G   H   J

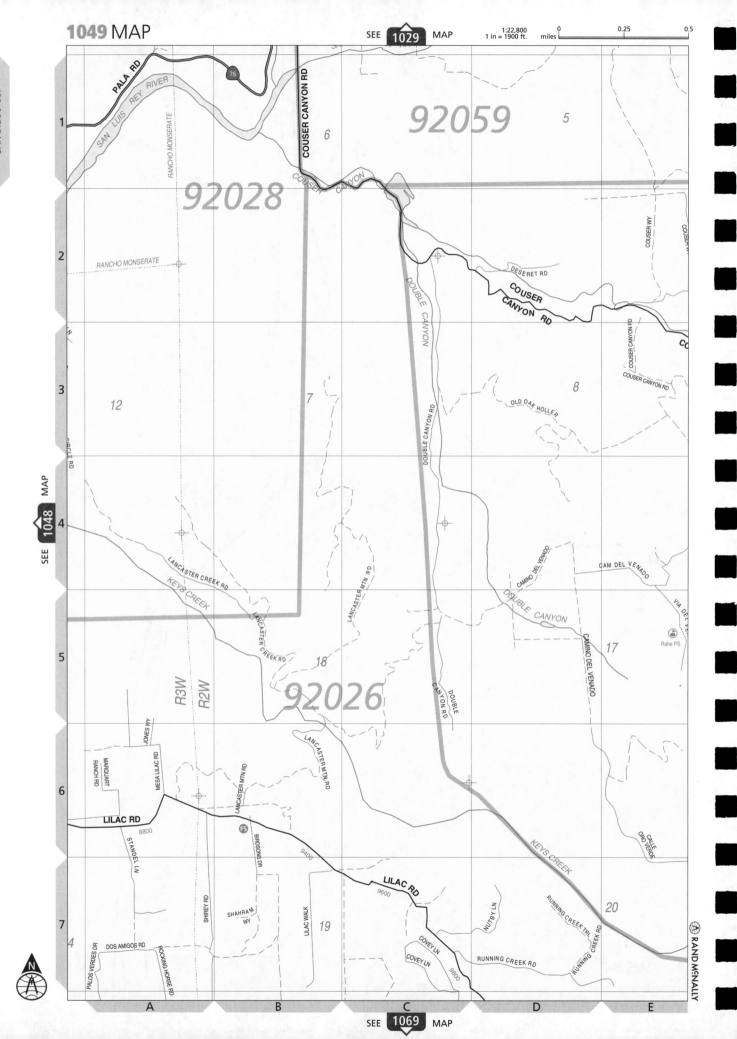

SEE 1029 MAP

1:22,800
1 in = 1900 ft.
miles
0   0.25   0.5

SAN DIEGO CO.

PALA RD

SAN LUIS REY RIVER

76

RANCHO MONSERATE

COUSER CANYON RD

92059

6

5

1

92028

COUSER CANYON

DESERET RD

COUSER CANYON RD

2

RANCHO MONSERATE

DOUBLE CANYON

COUSER WY

COUSER CANYON RD

COUSER CANYON RD

CO

CIRCLE RD

12

7

DOUBLE CANYON RD

OLD OAK HOLLER

8

3

SEE 1048 MAP

4

LANCASTER CREEK RD

KEYS CREEK

LANCASTER MTN RD

CAMINO DEL VENADO

CAM DEL VENADO

VIA DEL VE

R3W R2W

LANCASTER CREEK RD

DOUBLE CANYON

Rahe PS

17

5

18

92026

DOUBLE CANYON RD

CAMINO DEL VENADO

JONES WY

MARQUART RANCH RD

MESA LILAC RD

LANCASTER MTN RD

LANCASTER MTN RD

KEYS CREEK

CALLE ORO VERDE

6

LILAC RD

8800

STANDEL LN

FS

BIRDSONG DR

9400

RUNNING CREEK TRL

20

SHIREY RD

LILAC RD

9600

NUTBY LN

RUNNING CREEK RD

7

4

PALOS VERDES DR

DOS AMIGOS RD

ROCKING HORSE RD

SHAHRAM WY

LILAC WALK

19

COVEY LN

COVEY LN

9800

RUNNING CREEK RD

RUNNING CREEK RD

RAND McNALLY

A   B   C   D   E

SEE 1069 MAP

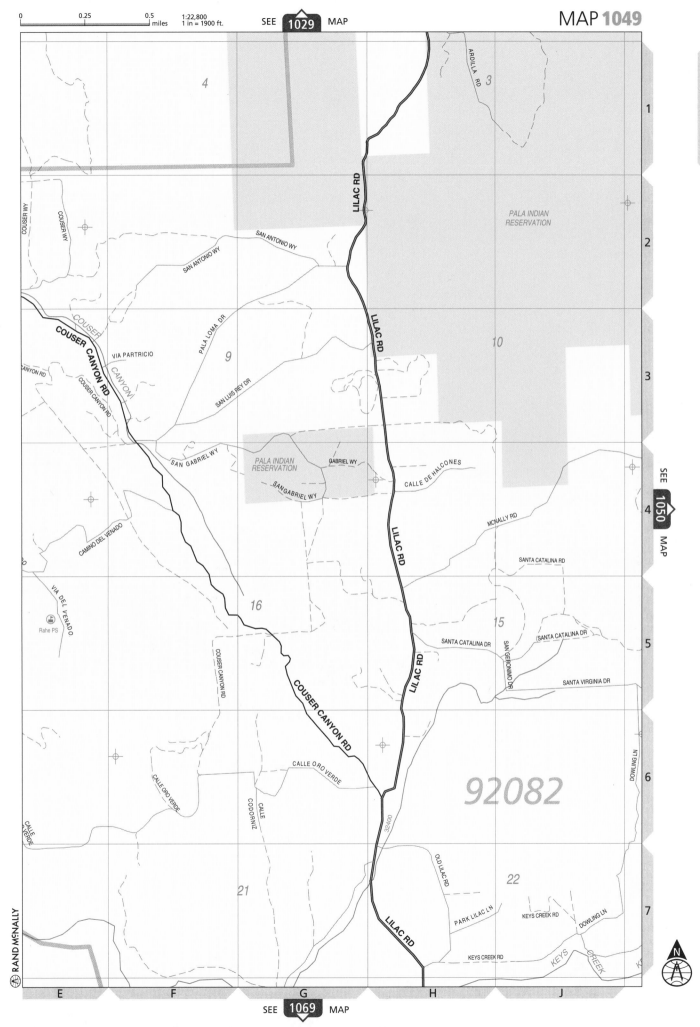

MAP **1049**

SAN DIEGO CO.

SEE **1029** MAP

SEE **1050** MAP

SEE **1069** MAP

0   0.25   0.5
miles
1:22,800
1 in = 1900 ft.

4

3

ARDILLA RD

1

LILAC RD

PALA INDIAN
RESERVATION

2

COUSER WY

COUSER WY

SAN ANTONIO WY

SAN ANTONIO WY

COUSER CANYON RD

COUSER
CANYON

CANYON RD

VIA PARTRICIO

COUSER CANYON RD

PALA LOMA DR

9

SAN LUIS REY DR

LILAC RD

10

3

SAN GABRIEL WY

PALA INDIAN
RESERVATION

GABRIEL WY

CALLE DE HALCONES

SANGABRIEL WY

LILAC RD

MCNALLY RD

4

CAMINO DEL VENADO

SANTA CATALINA RD

VIA DEL VENADO

Rahe PS

16

COUSER CANYON RD

15

SANTA CATALINA DR

SANTA CATALINA DR

SAN GERONIMO DR

SANTA VIRGINIA DR

LILAC RD

5

COUSER CANYON RD

DOWLING LN

CALLE ORO VERDE

92082

6

CALLE ORO VERDE

CALLE
CODORNIZ

32400

21

22

OLD LILAC RD

LILAC RD

PARK LILAC LN

KEYS CREEK RD

DOWLING LN

7

CALLE
VERDE

RAND MºNALLY

KEYS CREEK RD

KEYS CREEK

N

E   F   G   H   J

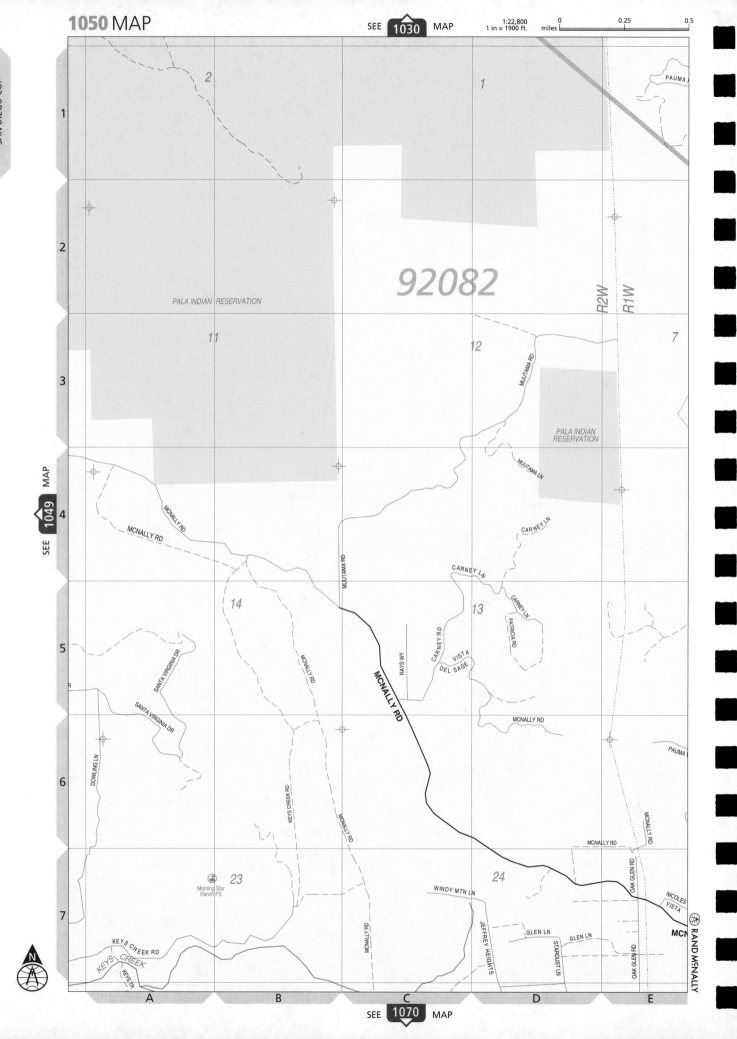

SEE 1030 MAP

1:22,800
1 in = 1900 ft.

0   0.25   0.5
miles

SAN DIEGO CO.

PAUMA

2

1

92082

PALA INDIAN RESERVATION

R2W   R1W

11

12

7

MUUTAMA RD

PALA INDIAN
RESERVATION

MUUTAMA LN

SEE 1049 MAP

MCNALLY RD

MCNALLY RD

CARNEY LN

CARNEY LN

MUUTAMA RD

CARNEY LN

14

13

CARNEY LN

PATRICIA RD

SANTA VIRGINIA DR

MCNALLY RD

MCNALLY RD

RAYS WY

CARNEY RD

VISTA
DEL SAGE

MCNALLY RD

SANTA VIRGINIA DR

DOWLING LN

KEYS CREEK RD

MCNALLY RD

PAUMA

MCNALLY RD

MCNALLY RD

OAK GLEN RD

NICOLES
VISTA

23

Morning Star
Ranch PS

24

WINDY MTN LN

MCNALLY RD

JEFFREY HEIGHTS

GLEN LN

GLEN LN

STARDUST LN

OAK GLEN RD

MCN

RAND McNALLY

KEYS CREEK RD

KEYS CREEK

KEYS TR

A   B   C   D   E

SEE 1070 MAP

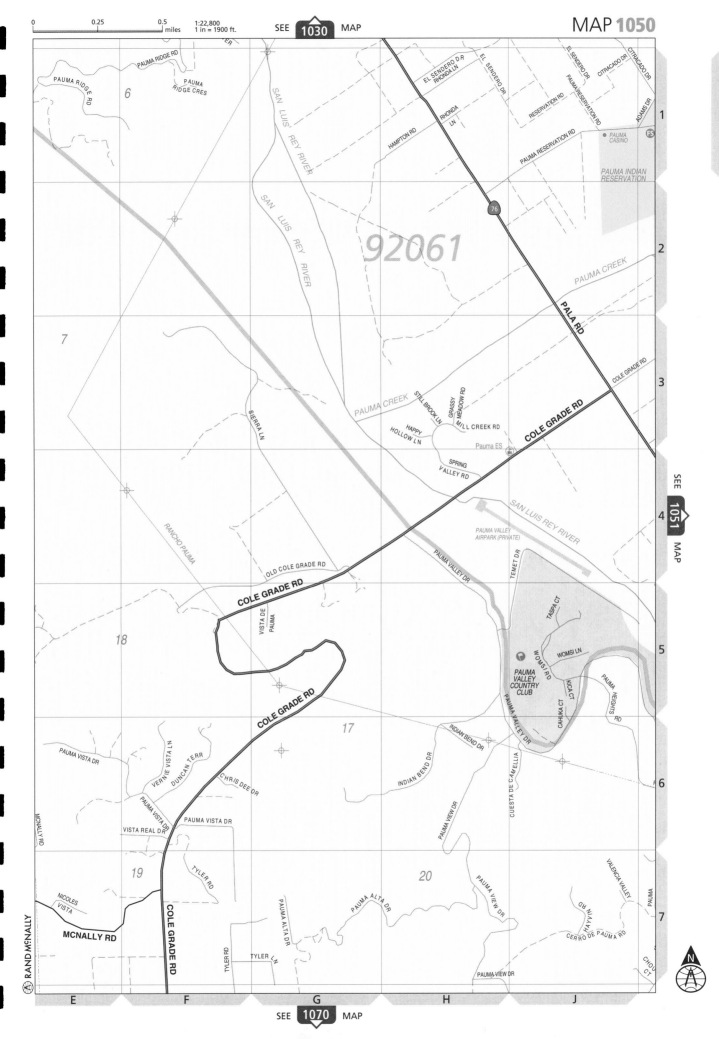

MAP **1050**

SAN DIEGO CO.

SEE 1030 MAP

SEE 1051 MAP

SEE 1070 MAP

0   0.25   0.5
miles
1:22,800
1 in = 1900 ft.

92061

PAUMA RIDGE RD
PAUMA RIDGE CRES
PAUMA RIDGE RD
6

SAN LUIS REY RIVER
SAN LUIS REY RIVER

EL SENDERO DR
RHONDA LN
EL SENDERO DR
EL SENDERO DR
CITRACADO DR
CITRACADO DR
ADAMS DR
RESERVATION RD
PAUMA RESERVATION RD
PAUMA RESERVATION RD
HAMPTON RD
RHONDA LN
PAUMA CASINO
FS
1

PAUMA INDIAN
RESERVATION

76

PALA RD

PAUMA CREEK
2

COLE GRADE RD
COLE GRADE RD
3

PAUMA CREEK
STILL BROOK LN
GRASSY MEADOW RD
MILL CREEK RD
HAPPY HOLLOW LN
Pauma ES
SPRING VALLEY RD

7

SIERRA LN

SAN LUIS REY RIVER
4

RANCHO PAUMA

PAUMA VALLEY AIRPARK (PRIVATE)
PAUMA VALLEY DR
TEMET DR
TASPA CT

OLD COLE GRADE RD
COLE GRADE RD
VISTA DE PAUMA

18

WOMSI RD
WOMSI LN
PAUMA VALLEY COUNTRY CLUB
KICA CT
CAHUILA CT
PAUMA HEIGHTS RD
5

COLE GRADE RD
17
INDIAN BEND DR
INDIAN BEND DR
PAUMA VALLEY DR
CUESTA DE CAMELLIA

PAUMA VISTA DR
VERNIE VISTA LN
DUNCAN TERR
CHRIS DEE DR
6

PAUMA VISTA DR
PAUMA VISTA DR
VISTA REAL DR
INDIAN BEND DR
PAUMA VIEW DR

MCNALLY RD
19
TYLER RD
PAUMA ALTA DR
20
PAUMA VIEW DR
VALENCIA VALLEY
PAUMA
7

NICOLES VISTA
MCNALLY RD
COLE GRADE RD
TYLER RD
TYLER LN
PAUMA ALTA DR
PAUMA VIEW DR
CERRO DE PAUMA RD
HANJAJU RD
CHOU CT

RAND MCNALLY

E   F   G   H   J

N

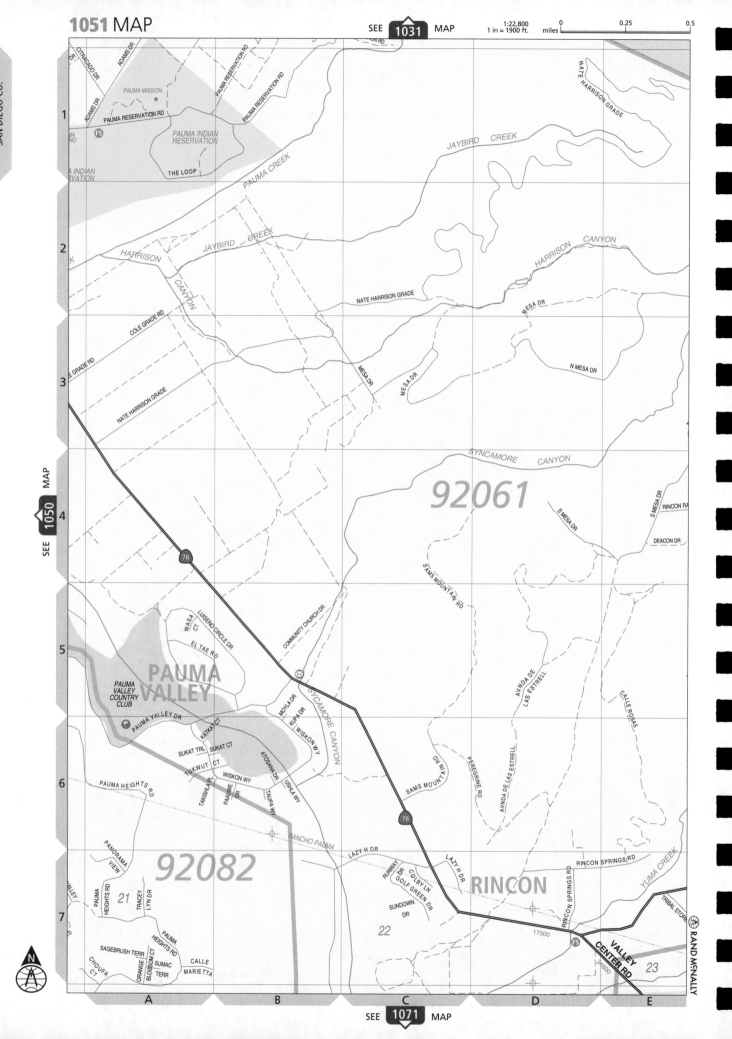

SAN DIEGO CO.

SEE ⌂ 1031 MAP

1:22,800
1 in = 1900 ft.

0   0.25   0.5
miles

SEE ◁ 1050 MAP

CITRACADO DR
ADAMS DR
ADAMS DR
ADAMS DR

PAUMA MISSION

PAUMA RESERVATION RD
PAUMA RESERVATION RD
PAUMA RESERVATION RD

NATE HARRISON GRADE

FS

PAUMA INDIAN
RESERVATION

JAYBIRD   CREEK

THE LOOP

PAUMA CREEK

A INDIAN
RVATION

HARRISON

JAYBIRD   CREEK

HARRISON   CANYON

CANYON

NATE HARRISON GRADE

MESA DR

COLE GRADE RD

N MESA DR

GRADE RD

NATE HARRISON GRADE

MESA DR

MESA DR

SYCAMORE   CANYON

S MESA DR

RINCON R

92061

S MESA DR

DEACON DR

76

SAMS MOUNTAIN RD

WASA CT

LUISENO CIRCLE DR

COMMUNITY CHURCH DR

EL TAE RD

AVNDA DE LAS ESTRELL

CALLE ROSAS

**PAUMA
VALLEY**

PAUMA
VALLEY
COUNTRY
CLUB

MOYLA DR

KUPA DR

SYCAMORE CANYON

PAUMA VALLEY DR

KATKAI CT

WISKON WY

ATOSANA DR

USHLA WY

AVNDA DE LAS ESTRELL

PEREGRINE RD

SUKAT TRL   SUKAT CT

TUKWUT CT

SAMS MOUNTAIN RD

PAUMA HEIGHTS RD

TAKISHLA PL

WISKON WY

PAUWE DR

TAUPA WY

76

RANCHO PAUMA

LAZY H DR

RINCON SPRINGS RD

YUMA CREEK

PANORAMA
VIEW

LAZY H DR

RINCON SPRINGS RD

92082

RUNWAY DR

COLBY LN

GOLF GREEN DR

RINCON

PAUMA HEIGHTS RD

TRACEY LYN DR

21

SUNDOWN DR

22

17000

TRIBAL STORE

PAUMA HEIGHTS RD

FS

SAGEBRUSH TERR

ORANGE BLOSSOM CT

SUMAC TERR

CALLE MARIETTA

**VALLEY
CENTER RD**

23

CHOUFA CT

24800

RAND McNALLY

N

A   B   C   D   E

SEE ▽ 1071 MAP

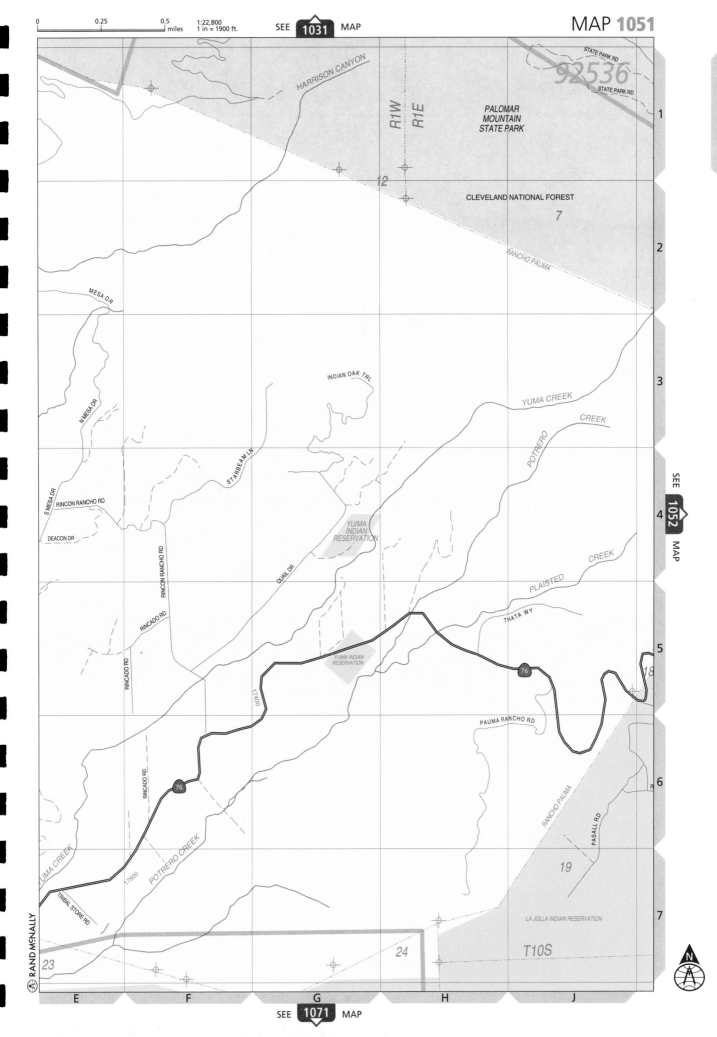

MAP **1051**

0   0.25   0.5
miles
1:22,800
1 in = 1900 ft.

SEE **1031** MAP

92536

HARRISON CANYON

STATE PARK RD
STATE PARK RD

R1W
R1E

PALOMAR
MOUNTAIN
STATE PARK

1

12

CLEVELAND NATIONAL FOREST

7

2

RANCHO PAUMA

MESA DR

3

INDIAN OAK TRL

YUMA CREEK

CREEK

N MESA DR

POTRERO

SEE
1052
MAP

STARBEAM LN

YUIMA
INDIAN
RESERVATION

S MESA DR

RINCON RANCHO RD

4

DEACON DR

QUAIL DR

CREEK

PLAISTED

THATA WY

RINCON RANCHO RD

RINCADO RD

YUIMA INDIAN
RESERVATION

76

18

5

RINCADO RD

17400

PAUMA RANCHO RD

RINCADO RD

76

6

RANCHO PAUMA

R

PASALL RD

POTRERO CREEK

UMA CREEK

19

17800

TRIBAL STORE RD

LA JOLLA INDIAN RESERVATION

7

RAND MCNALLY

23

24

T10S

N

E   F   G   H   J

SEE **1071** MAP

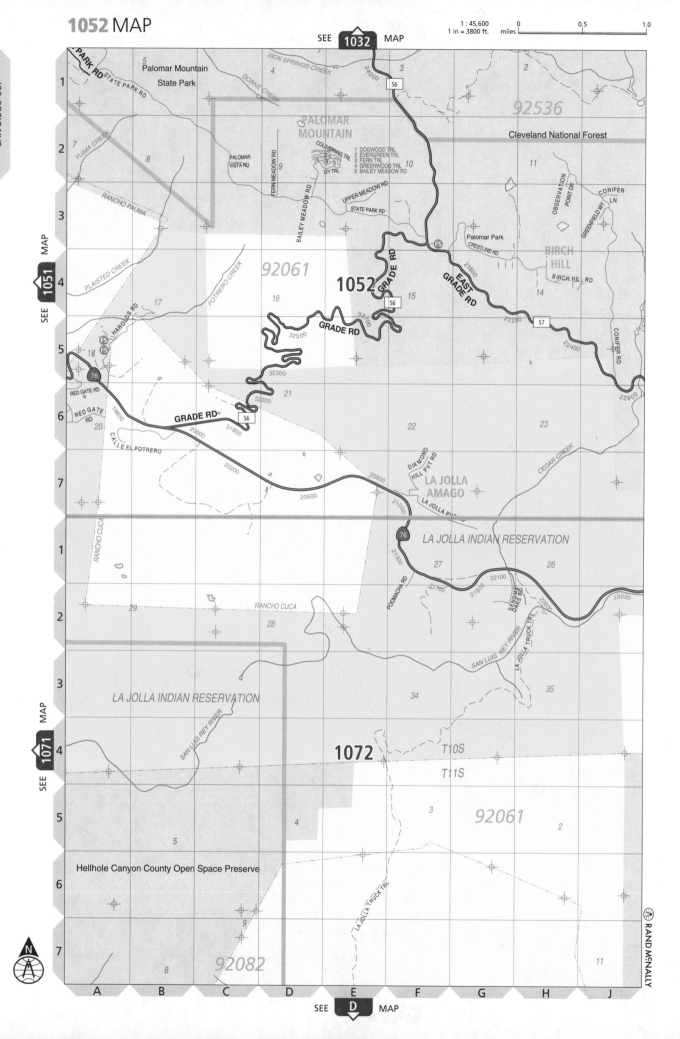

1052 MAP

1 : 45,600
1 in = 3800 ft.   miles   0   0.5   1.0

SEE 1032 MAP

PARK RD
STATE PARK RD

Palomar Mountain
State Park

IRON SPRINGS CREEK

34000

S6

92536

Cleveland National Forest

PALOMAR
MOUNTAIN

YUJIMA CREEK

DOANE CREEK

FERN MEADOW RD

PALOMAR
VISTA RD

COLD SPRING TRL
IVY TRL

1 DOGWOOD TRL
2 EVERGREEN TRL
3 FERN TRL
4 GREENWOOD TRL
5 BAILEY MEADOW RD

OBSERVATION
POINT DR

CONIFER
LN

GREENFIELD WY

RANCHO PAUMA

BAILEY MEADOW RD

UPPER MEADOW RD

STATE PARK RD

GRADE RD

FS

Palomar Park
CRESTLINE RD

BIRCH
HILL

BIRCH HILL RD

SEE 1051 MAP

PLAISTED CREEK

92061

POTRERO CREEK

1052

GRADE RD

S6

15

EAST
GRADE RD

21800

22200   S7

22400

CONIFER RD

HAROLDS RD

GRADE RD

32700

32500

32300

FS FS

18

76

RED GATE RD

RED GATE
RD

20

19800

CALLE EL POTRERO

GRADE RD

32000

S6

31800

20000

20200

20500

21

32300

22

20800

21000

23

22600

DIAMOND
HILL PVT RD

LA JOLLA
AMAGO

LA JOLLA PVT RD

CEDAR CREEK

76

LA JOLLA INDIAN RESERVATION

RANCHO CUCA

29

28

RANCHO CUCA

POOMACHA RD

27

21300

21700

21900

22100

26

SENGME
OAKS RD

22360

23000

SAN LUIS REY RIVER

LA JOLLA TRUCK TRL

LA JOLLA INDIAN RESERVATION

SAN LUIS REY RIVER

34

35

SEE 1071 MAP

1072

T10S

T11S

92061

3

4

2

5

Hellhole Canyon County Open Space Preserve

LA JOLLA TRUCK TRL

9

92082

8

11

N

RAND McNALLY

A   B   C   D   E   F   G   H   J

SEE D MAP

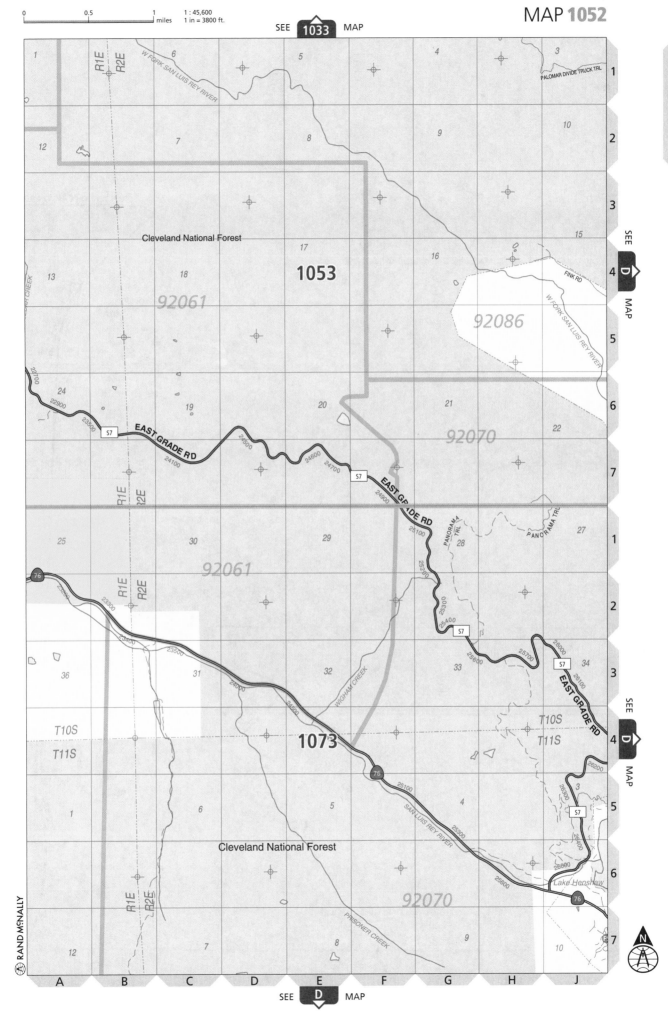

MAP **1052**

1 : 45,600
1 in = 3800 ft.

SEE 1033 MAP

SAN DIEGO CO.

Cleveland National Forest

1053

92061

92086

EAST GRADE RD

92070

92061

PANORAMA TRL

EAST GRADE RD

T10S
T11S

WIGHAM CREEK

1073

SAN LUIS REY RIVER

T10S
T11S

EAST GRADE RD

92070

Cleveland National Forest

PRISONER CREEK

Lake Henshaw

SEE D MAP

RAND McNALLY

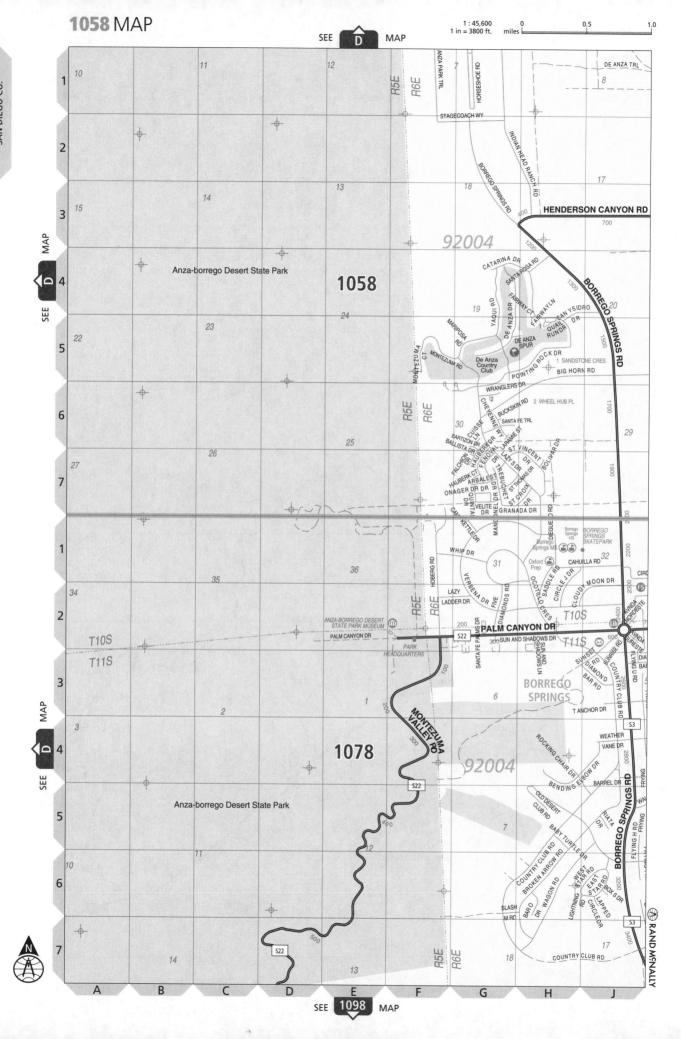

1 : 45,600
1 in = 3800 ft.

miles   0   0.5   1.0

SAN DIEGO CO.

SEE **D** MAP

R5E R6E

ANZA PARK TRL

HORSESHOE RD

STAGECOACH WY

DE ANZA TRL

INDIAN HEAD RANCH RD

BORREGO SPRINGS RD

HENDERSON CANYON RD

92004

1058

Anza-borrego Desert State Park

CATARINA DR
SANTA ROSA RD
FAIRWAY CT
DE ANZA DR
YAQUI RD
MARIPOSA RD
MONTEZUMA CT
MONTEZUMA RD
De Anza Spur
De Anza Country Club
SAN YSIDRO DR
QUAIL RUN DR
SANDSTONE CRES
POINTING ROCK DR
BIG HORN RD
WRANGLERS DR
CHEYENNE WY
BUCKSKIN DR
WHEEL HUB PL
CUISSE LN
BARTIZON DR
SANTA FE TRL
BALLISTA DR
FALCHION
HAUBERK CT
HAUBERK DR
FENOVAL DR
LACY ST
ST VINCENT ST
BOLIVAR DR
ARBALEST
ONAGER DR
QUINTAIN DR
ST THOMAS DR
ST CROIX DR
VELITE DR
GRANADA DR

R5E R6E

CAM. KETTLE DR
MANCONEL DR
DIEGUE RD

Borrego Springs MS
Borrego Springs HS
BORREGO SPRINGS SKATEPARK
WHIP DR
HOBERG RD
Oxford Prep
SADDLE RD
CAHUILLA RD
OCOTILLO CRES
CIRCLE J DR
CLOUDY MOON DR
LAZY LADDER DR
VERBENA DR
FIVE DIAMONDS RD

T10S

R5E R6E

Anza-Borrego Desert State Park Museum
PALM CANYON DR
Park Headquarters
PALM CANYON DR
S22
SANTA FE PALMS DR
SUN AND SHADOWS DR
SUN AND SHADOWS LN
SUNSET RD
SUNRISE RD

T10S
T11S

T11S

BORREGO SPRINGS

COUNTRY CLUB RD

DIAMOND D
BAR RD
T ANCHOR DR
S3
ROCKING CHAIR DR
WEATHER VANE DR
BENDING ELBOW DR
BARREL DR

MONTEZUMA VALLEY RD

1078

92004

S22

Anza-borrego Desert State Park

OLD DESERT CLUB RD
BABY TURTLE DR
RIATA DR

BORREGO SPRINGS RD

FLYING H RD
FRYING

COUNTRY CLUB RD
BROKEN ARROW RD
WEST STAR RD
EAST STAR RD
BOX SD DR
LIGHTNING RD
LAPPED CIRCLE DR
SLASH M RD
BAR O DR
WAGON RD
EAST CIRCLE DR
S3

RAND McNALLY

COUNTRY CLUB RD

N

A   B   C   D   E   F   G   H   J

1 2 3 4 5 6 7

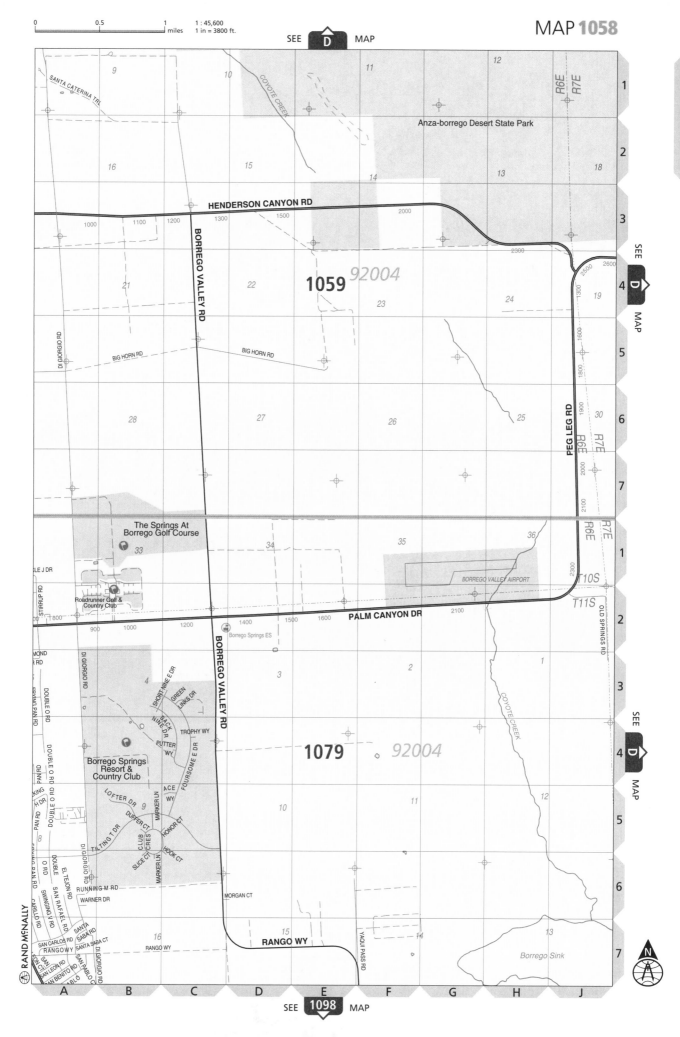

MAP **1058**

SAN DIEGO CO.

0   0.5   1
miles
1 : 45,600
1 in = 3800 ft.

SEE **D** MAP

9   10   11   12

R6E R7E

1

SANTA CATERINA TRL

Anza-borrego Desert State Park

16   15   14   13   18   2

COYOTE CREEK

HENDERSON CANYON RD   2000   3

1000   1100   1200   1300   1500   2300   2600   2500

BORREGO VALLEY RD

1059 92004   1300   19   4   SEE **D** MAP

21   22   23   24   1600   5

BIG HORN RD   BIG HORN RD   1800

28   27   26   25   1900   30   6

PEG LEG RD   2000   R6E R7E

2100   7

R6E R7E

The Springs At Borrego Golf Course   2300   T10S   1

33   34   35   36

DOUBLE J DR   Borrego Valley Airport

STIRRUP RD   T11S

Roadrunner Golf & Country Club   PALM CANYON DR   2

1800   900   1000   1200   1400   1500   1600   2100

DIAMOND RD   DI GIORGIO RD   Borrego Springs ES   OLD SPRINGS RD

3   2   1   3

4

SHORT NINE E DR   GREEN LINKS DR

BACK NINE DR   TROPHY WY

PUTTER WY   FOURSOME E DR

1079 92004   4   SEE **D** MAP

DOUBLE O RD   PAN RD

FRYING PAN RD   Borrego Springs Resort & Country Club   ACE WY

10   11   12

LOFTER DR   MARKER LN

PAN RD   9   DUFFER CT   HONOR CT   5

PAN RD   8   TILTING T DR   CLUB CT CRES

DI GIORGIO RD   SLICE CT   MARKER LN   HOOK CT

EL TEJON RD   RUNNING M RD

DOUBLE O RD   SAN RAFAEL RD   WARNER DR   MORGAN CT   6

SWINGING V RD

CARILLO RD

SAN CARLOS RD   SANTA SABA RD   16   15   14   13

SANTA SABA CT   YAQUI PASS RD   Borrego Sink

RANGO WY   SAN BENITO RD   RANGO WY   **RANGO WY**   7

SAN LEON RD   SAN PABLO RD

RAND MCNALLY

A   B   C   D   E   F   G   H   J

SEE **1098** MAP

N

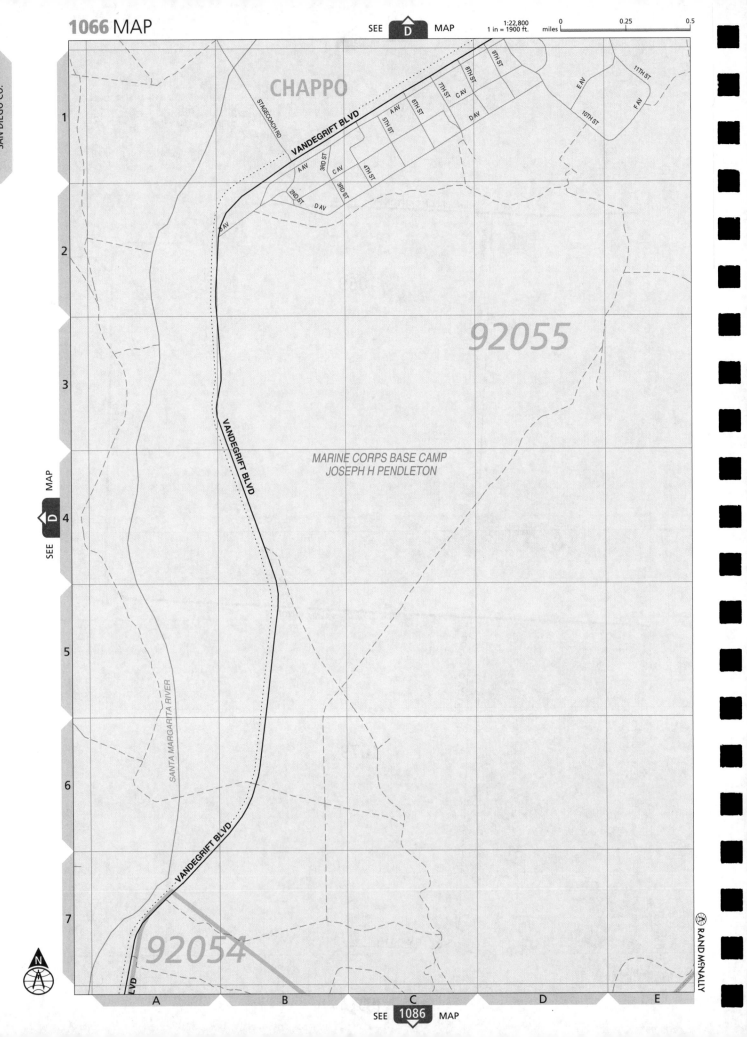

SEE D MAP

1:22,800
1 in = 1900 ft.

miles 0 ___ 0.25 ___ 0.5

SAN DIEGO CO.

CHAPPO

STAGECOACH RD

VANDEGRIFT BLVD

A AV
3RD ST
C AV
2ND ST
D AV
3RD ST
4TH ST
5TH ST
A AV
6TH ST
7TH ST
C AV
D AV
8TH ST
9TH ST
E AV
10TH ST
11TH ST
F AV

92055

VANDEGRIFT BLVD

MARINE CORPS BASE CAMP
JOSEPH H PENDLETON

SEE D MAP

SANTA MARGARITA RIVER

VANDEGRIFT BLVD

VANDEGRIFT BLVD

92054

N

A B C D E

SEE 1086 MAP

RAND McNALLY

MAP 1066

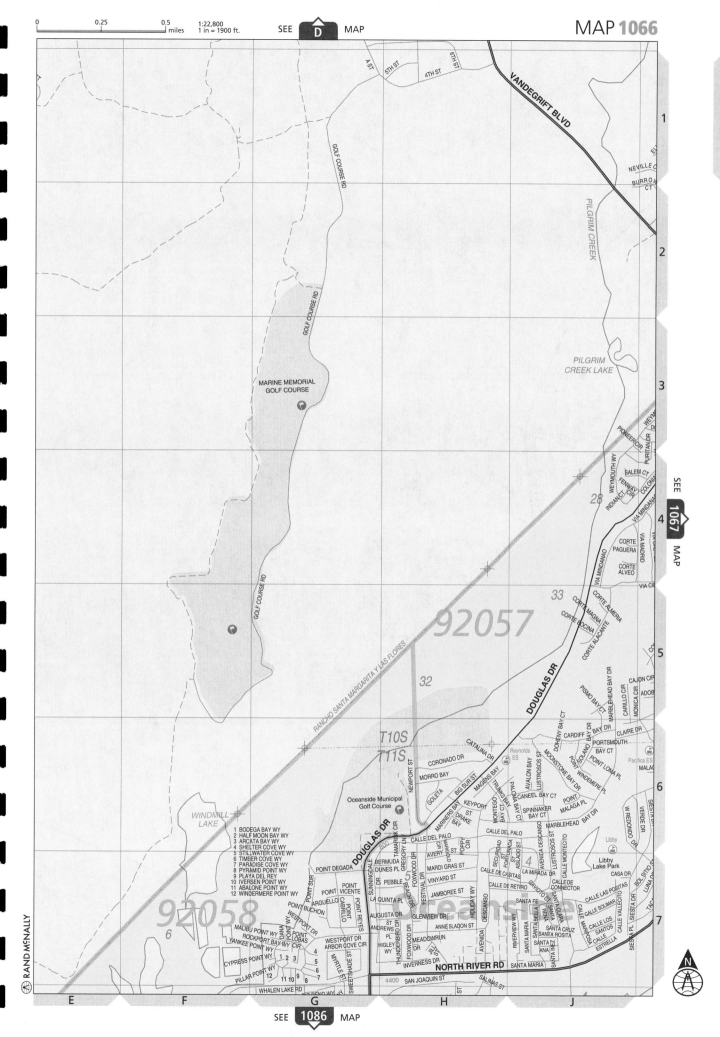

0   0.25   0.5
miles
1:22,800
1 in = 1900 ft.

SEE D MAP

SEE 1067 MAP

VANDEGRIFT BLVD

NEVILLE C

BURRO K CT

PILGRIM CREEK

PILGRIM CREEK LAKE

A ST
5TH ST
4TH ST
6TH ST

GOLF COURSE RD

MARINE MEMORIAL
GOLF COURSE

GOLF COURSE RD

RANCHO SANTA MARGARITA Y LAS FLORES

92057

28

33

32

T10S
T11S

WINDMILL
LAKE

PIONEER CIR
PURITAN DR
WEYMOUTH WY
SALEM CT
FENWAY ST
INDIAN CT CIR
COLONY

VIA MINDANAO
CORTE PAGUERA
VIA MADRID
CORTE ALVEO
VIA CIR

CORTE ALMERIA
CORTE MAGNA
CORTE BOCINA
CORTE ALICANTE

MARBLEHEAD BAY DR
PISMO BAY CT
CARILLO CIR
MONICA CIR
ADOB
CAJON CIR

DOUGLAS DR

CARDIFF
DOHENY BAY CT
SOLANO BAY CT
PORTSMOUTH
BAY CT
CLAIRE DR
POINT WINDEMERE PL
POINT LOMA PL
MALAG

Reynolds ES
Pacifica ES

CATALINA DR
CORONADO DR
MORRO BAY
NEWPORT ST
GOLETA
BIG SUR ST
MAGENS BAY
AVALON BAY
LUSTROSOS ST
MOONSTONE BAY DR

MARINERS BAY
KEYPORT ST
TRUMS BAY
MONTEGO BAY
PALOMA BAY CT
CANEEL BAY CT
SPINNAKER BAY CT
POINT MALAGA PL
MARBLEHEAD BAY DR

Oceanside Municipal
Golf Course

DRAKE BAY

Libby
Libby Lake Park

1 BODEGA BAY WY
2 HALF MOON BAY WY
3 ARCATA BAY WY
4 SHELTER COVE WY
5 STILLWATER COVE WY
6 TIMBER COVE WY
7 PARADISE COVE WY
8 PYRAMID POINT WY
9 PLAYA DEL REY
10 IVERSEN POINT WY
11 ABALONE POINT WY
12 WINDERMERE POINT WY

DOUGLAS DR

POINT DEGADA
POINT SUR
POINT LOBAS
POINT BUCHON
ARGUELLO
POINT VICENTE
POINT REYES
POINT CABRILLO

SUNNINGDALE
BERMUDA DR
DUNES PL
PEBBLE
GREGORY LN
TAMARIK CIR
FOXWOOD DR
FESTIVAL DR
FOXWOOD DR
LA QUINTA PL
AUGUSTA DR
ANDREWS PL

CALLE DEL PALO
CALLE DEL PALO
AVERY
POPPY CIR
MARDI GRAS ST
VINYARD ST
JAMBOREE ST
CALLE DE CASITAS
CALLE DE RETIRO
GLENVIEW DR

SECURIDAD
LA FORTUNA
ASILADO ST
AVENIDA DESCANSO
LUSTROSOS ST
CALLE MONTECITO
CALLE DE CONNECTOR
GAVOTO CT
SANTA FE
SANTA MARIA
SANTA BELLA
SANTA CLARA
SANTA CRUZ
SANTA ROSITA
RIVERVIEW WY
SANTA ANA
SANTA INEZ

LA MIRADA DR
CASA DR

VERDE DR
SIESTA DR
REDONDO W

SOL SITIO S
LUNA DR

CALLE LAS POSITAS
CALLE SOLIMAR
CALLE MAR
CALLE LOS SANTOS
CALLE ESTRELLA
CALLE VALLECITO
SIESTA PL

92058
6

MALIBU POINT WY
ROCKPORT BAY WY
YANKEE POINT WY
CYPRESS POINT WY
PILLAR POINT WY
12 11 10 9 8

WESTPORT DR
POINT
DANA CIR

WESTPORT DR
ARBOR COVE CIR
SWEETSHADE ST
MYRTLE ST
WHALEN LAKE RD
BEND WY

Oceanside

HOLIDAY WY
MEADOWRUN DR
HIGLEY WY
THUNDERBIRD DR
FOXWOOD DR
INVERNESS DR
JILL

ANNE SLADON ST
AVENIDA

NORTH RIVER RD
4400
SAN JOAQUIN ST
SALINAS ST
SANTA MARIA

SOL SITIO S

RAND M?NALLY

SEE 1086 MAP

E   F   G   H   J

N

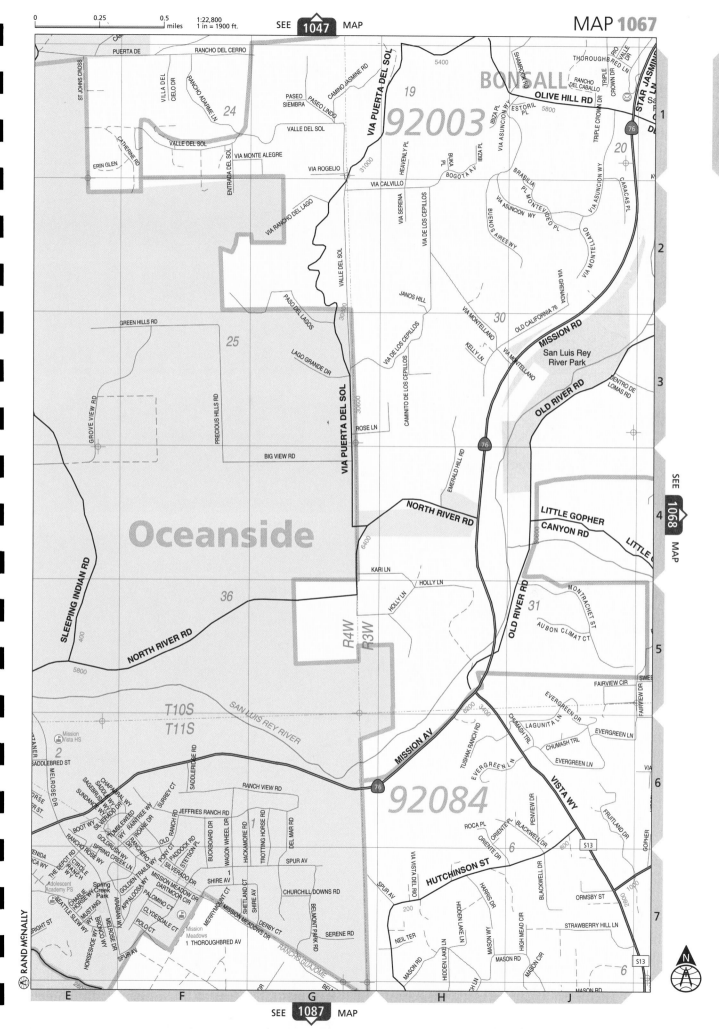

MAP **1067**

SAN DIEGO CO.

SEE **1047** MAP

BONSALL

92003

Oceanside

San Luis Rey River Park

SEE **1068** MAP

92084

SEE **1087** MAP

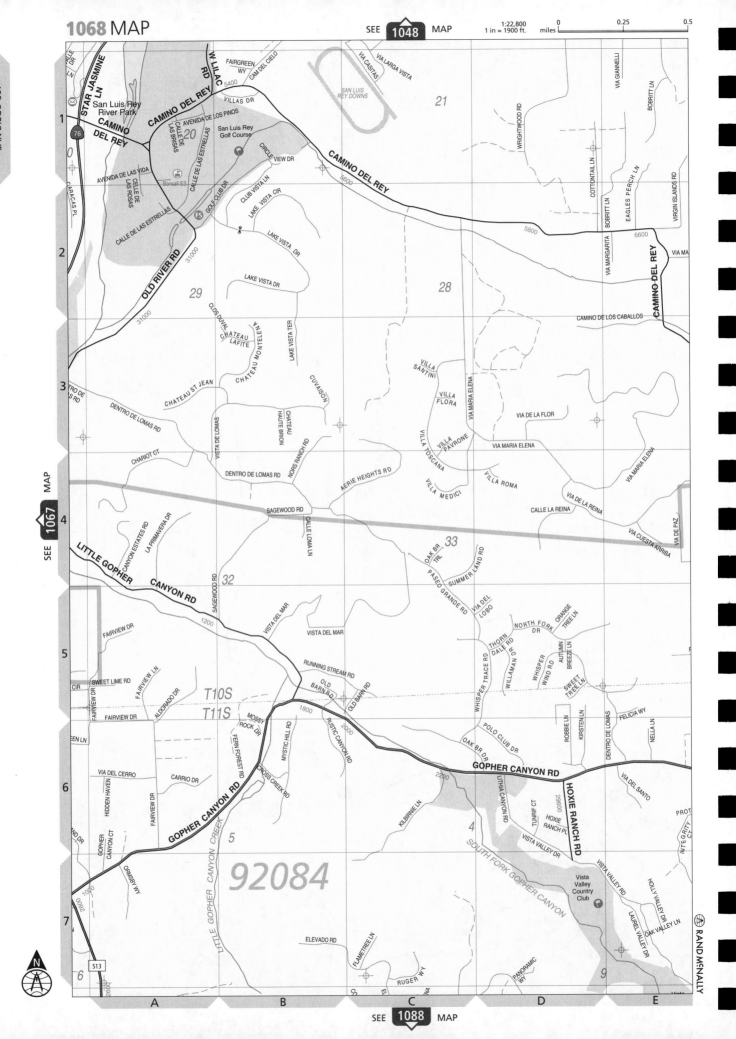

SEE ◢1048◣ MAP

1:22,800
1 in = 1900 ft.

miles   0   0.25   0.5

SAN DIEGO CO.

SEE ◢1067◣ MAP

RAND McNALLY

92084

A   B   C   D   E

MAP **1068**

SAN DIEGO CO.

SEE **1048** MAP

SEE **1069** MAP

SEE **1088** MAP

0   0.25   0.5 miles
1:22,800
1 in = 1900 ft.

RAND MCNALLY

92003

92026

BOBRITT LN

22

MT ARARAT WY

NIRA LN

23

MAR MA RY CRES

MOUNTAIN WY

VIA URNER

VIA URNER WY

AQUADUCT RD

24

1

Academia De Talar PS

CALLE DE TALAR

VIRGIN ISLANDS RD

VIA MARIPOSA CT

VIA MARIPOSA NORTE

AFTON FARMES LN

N RANCHO AMIGOS RD

RANCHO AMIGOS RD

RANCHO AMIGOS RD

43

CAMINO DEL REY

VIA MARIPOSA

27

VIA MARIPOSA SUR

RANCHO AMIGOS RD

26

RANCHO AMIGOS RD

25

2

31000

(AVOCADOW HWY)

OLD HIGHWAY 395

FRONTIER RD

NELSON WY

31400

7200

7200

CALLE JOYA

AQUADUCT RD

15

3

VIA DE LA REINA

EAGLE MOUNTAIN RD

MOOSA CANYON

CAMINO DEL REY

7400

VIA DE PAZ

DISNEY LN

LUIS REY HEIGHTS RD

7800

ESCONDIDO FRWY

36

VIA CANTAMAR

CAPTAIN'S CT

4

SRTA ARRIBA

KELLYN LN

CALLE DE LAS PIEDRAS

PICO RD

34

35

LUIS REY HEIGHTS RD

AVENIDA MIL FLORES

CAMINO DE LAS LOMAS

PAKAMA LN

BRUNS RD

T10S
T11S

OLD HIGHWAY 395

29600

CIRCLE R DR

CIRCLE R COURSE LN

CIRCLE R CREEK LN

5

CIRCLE R VALLEY LN

CIRCLE VIEW

SOUTH-WIND LN

DISNEY LN

PICO RD

AVOHILL DR

WILD ACRES RD

41

NELLA LN

JENNY LN

MARGALE LN

REZA CT

HAWKHILL RD

GRAMMER RD

4000

GOPHER CANYON RD

4200

CASTLE CREEK LN

Castle Creek Country Club

OLD CASTLE RD

6

8600

TWIN OAKS VALLEY RD

Gopher Canyon Reserve

VALLEY OF THE KING RD

VALLEY OF THE KING RD

CASTLEGARDEN CT

3800

EL PASEO

HOLLYHILL RD

2

LEISURE LN

INDIAN HILL RD

PROTEA VISTA TERR

INTEGRITY CT

3

TAREK TER

HOLLY VALLEY DR

PROTEA VISTA DR

W TWIN OAKS VALLEY RD

SILVERLEAF LN

EL PASEO

SILVERLEAF LN

15

CHAMPAGNE BLVD

29000

OAK VALLEY LN

10

11

12

7

E   F   G   H   J

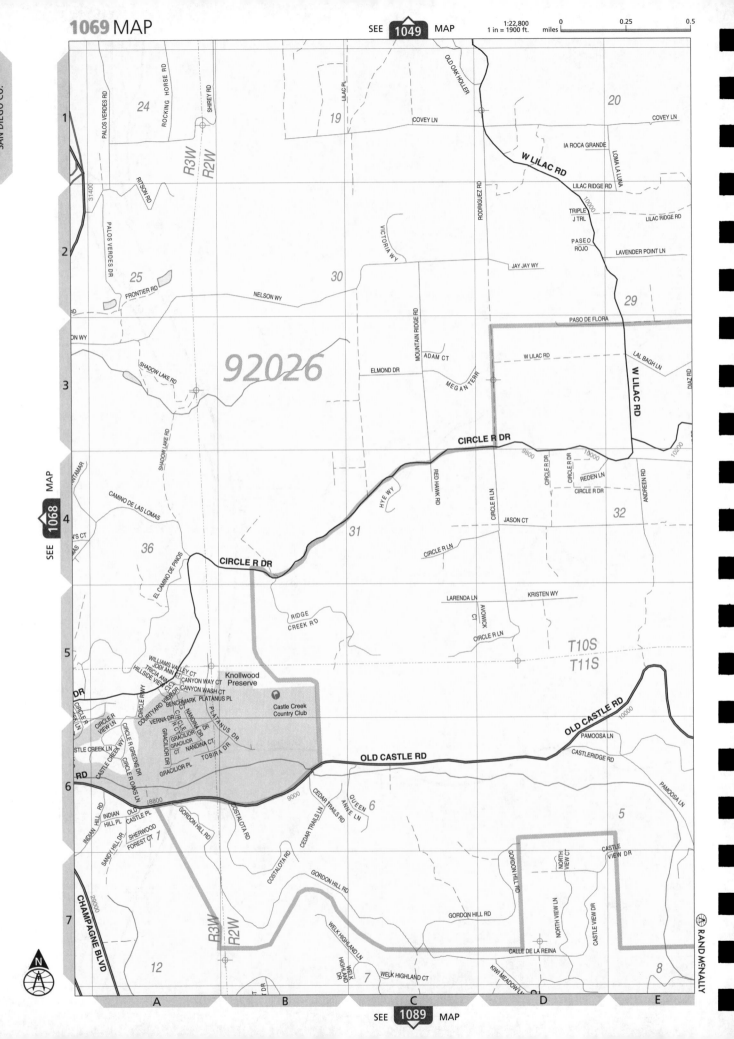

SAN DIEGO CO.

SEE 1049 MAP

1:22,800
1 in = 1900 ft.
miles
0   0.25   0.5

92026

SEE 1068 MAP

SEE 1089 MAP

RAND McNALLY

PALOS VERDES RD
ROCKING HORSE RD
SHIREY RD
24
19
20
OLD OAK HOLLER
COVEY LN
COVEY LN
W LILAC RD
IA ROCA GRANDE
LOMA LA LUNA
LILAC RIDGE RD
TRIPLE J TRL
LILAC RIDGE RD
RITSON RD
R3W R2W
RODRIGUEZ RD
PASEO ROJO
LAVENDER POINT LN
VICTORIA WY
JAY JAY WY
PALOS VERDES DR
25
FRONTIER RD
NELSON WY
30
29
PASO DE FLORA
SHADOW LAKE RD
MOUNTAIN RIDGE RD
ADAM CT
ELMOND DR
W LILAC RD
LAL BAGH LN
MEGAN TERR
W LILAC RD
DIAZ RD
CIRCLE R DR
SHADOW LAKE RD
CIRCLE R DR
CIRCLE R DR
REDEN LN
CIRCLE R DR
ANDREEN RD
MATAMAR
CAMINO DE LAS LOMAS
HYE WY
RED HAWK RD
CIRCLE R LN
JASON CT
32
'S CT
31
CIRCLE R LN
36
EL CAMINO DE PINOS
LARENDA LN
KRISTEN WY
AVOWICK
CT
RIDGE CREEK RD
CIRCLE R LN
T10S
T11S
WILLIAMS VALLEY CT
JODI ANN CT
TRICIA ANN CT
CANYON WAY CT
Knollwood Preserve
HILLSIDE VIEW CT
CANYON WASH CT
DR
CIRCLE RWY
COURTYARD VIEW DR
BENCHMARK
PLATANUS PL
Castle Creek Country Club
OLD CASTLE RD
CIRCLE R VIEW LN
VERNA DR
NANDINA DR
PLATANUS DR
PAMOOSA LN
GRACILIOR DR
GRACILIOR CT
NANDINA CT
CASTLERIDGE RD
STLE CREEK LN
CASTLE CREEK WY
CIRCLE R GREENS DR
GRACILIOR PL
TOBIRA DR
OLD CASTLE RD
RD
CIRCLE R OAKS LN
8800
GORDON HILL RD
COSTALOTA RD
CEDAR TRAILS LN
QUEEN ANNE LN
6
PAMOOSA LN
INDIAN HILL RD
INDIAN HILL PL
OLD CASTLE PL
SANDY HILL DR
SHERWOOD FOREST CT
1
CEDAR TRAILS RD
5
GORDON HILL RD
COSTALOTA RD
GORDON HILL RD
NORTH VIEW CT
CASTLE VIEW DR
CHAMPAGNE BLVD
12
R3W R2W
7
WELK HIGHLAND LN
WELK HIGHLAND DR
WELK HIGHLAND CT
GORDON HILL RD
NORTH VIEW LN
CALLE DE LA REINA
KIWI MEADOW LN
CASTLE VIEW DR
8

A   B   C   D   E

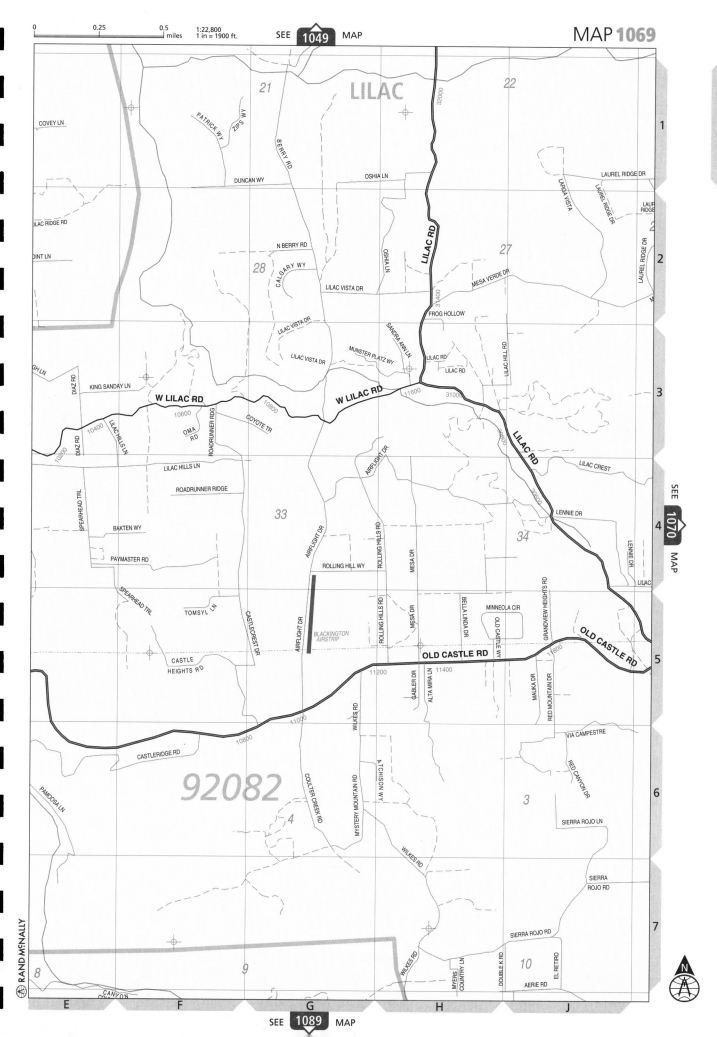

MAP 1069

0   0.25   0.5
⊢——⊢——⊢ miles
1:22,800
1 in = 1900 ft.

LILAC

21   22
32000

COVEY LN

PATRICK WY

ZIP'S WY

BERRY RD

DUNCAN WY   OSHIA LN

1

LILAC RIDGE RD   LAUREL RIDGE DR

LAUREL RIDGE DR

LARGA VISTA

LAUR RIDGE

DINT LN   N BERRY RD

28   CALGARY WY

OSHIA LN

LILAC RD

27   2

MESA VERDE DR

LAUREL RIDGE DR

2

LILAC VISTA DR

31400   FROG HOLLOW

LILAC VISTA DR   SANDRA ANN LN

LILAC HILL RD

GH LN   DIAZ RD   MUNSTER PLATZ WY   LILAC RD

LILAC RD

3

KING SANDAY LN   W LILAC RD   W LILAC RD   11600   31000

10600   LILAC RD

W LILAC RD   10800   ROADRUNNER RDG   COYOTE TR   LILAC CREST

10400   OMA RD

10200   DIAZ RD   LILAC HILLS LN   LILAC HILLS LN   AIRFLIGHT DR

30600   LENNIE DR

SEE 1070 MAP

ROADRUNNER RIDGE

SPEARHEAD TRL   33   34   4

BAKTEN WY   ROLLING HILLS RD   LENNIE DR

PAYMASTER RD   AIRFLIGHT DR   ROLLING HILL WY   MESA DR   LILAC

SPEARHEAD TRL   TOMSYL LN   ROLLING HILLS RD   MESA DR   BELLA LINDA DR   MINNEOLA CIR   GRANDVIEW HEIGHTS RD   OLD CASTLE RD

CASTLECREST DR   BLACKINGTON AIRSTRIP   OLD CASTLE WY

CASTLE HEIGHTS RD   OLD CASTLE RD   5

AIRFLIGHT DR   11200   GABLER DR   ALTA MIRA LN   11400   MAUKA DR   RED MOUNTAIN DR   11800

WILKES RD   VIA CAMPESTRE

11000   10800   CASTLERIDGE RD   RED CANYON DR

PAMOOSA LN   92082   COULTER CREEK RD   MYSTERY MOUNTAIN RD   ATCHISON WY   A   3   6

4   SIERRA ROJO LN

WILKES RD   SIERRA ROJO RD

7

SIERRA ROJO RD

8   9   WILKES RD   MYERS COUNTRY LN   DOUBLE K RD   10   EL RETIRO

CANYON   AERIE RD

RAND McNALLY

E   F   G   H   J

N

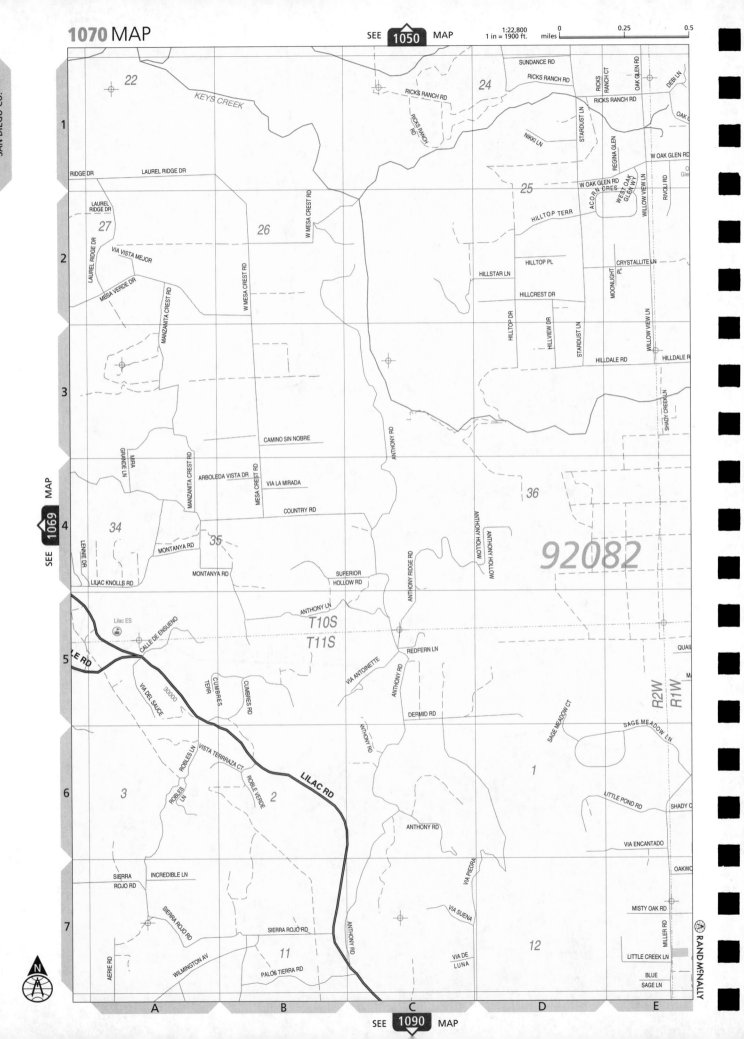

1:22,800
1 in = 1900 ft. miles

0   0.25   0.5

SAN DIEGO CO.

22

KEYS CREEK

SUNDANCE RD
RICKS RANCH RD
RICKS RANCH RD
RICKS RANCH RD
RICKS RANCH RD
24
RICKS RANCH RD
RICKS RANCH RD
OAK GLEN RD
DEBI LN
OAK G

1

NIKKI LN
STARDUST LN
REGINA GLEN
W OAK GLEN RD
Glen

RIDGE DR
LAUREL RIDGE DR

25
W OAK GLEN RD
ACORN CRES
WEST OAK GLEN WY
WILLOW VIEW LN
RIVOLI RD

LAUREL RIDGE DR
27
VIA VISTA MEJOR
MESA VERDE DR
26
W MESA CREST RD
HILLTOP TERR
HILLSTAR LN
HILLTOP PL
MOONLIGHT PL
CRYSTALLITE LN

2

LAUREL RIDGE DR
MANZANITA CREST RD
W MESA CREST RD
HILLCREST DR
HILLTOP DR
HILLVIEW DR
STARDUST LN
WILLOW VIEW LN

HILLDALE RD
HILLDALE R

3

CAMINO SIN NOBRE
ANTHONY RD
SHADY CREEK LN

MIRA GRANDE LN
MANZANITA CREST RD
ARBOLEDA VISTA DR
MESA CREST RD
VIA LA MIRADA
36

COUNTRY RD

92082

4

34
MONTANYA RD
35
ANTHONY RIDGE RD
ANTHONY HOLLOW
ANTHONY HOLLOW

LENNIE DR
MONTANYA RD
SUPERIOR HOLLOW RD

LILAC KNOLLS RD

ANTHONY LN
T10S
T11S

Lilac ES
CALLE DE ENSUENO
REDFERN LN
QUAIL

LE RD

5

VIA DEL SAUCE
30000
CUMBRES TERR
CUMBRES RD
VIA ANTOINETTE
ANTHONY RD

R2W
R1W

M

DERMID RD
SAGE MEADOW CT
SAGE MEADOW LN

ROBLES LN
VISTA TERRAZA CT.
ROBLE VERDE
ANTHONY RD

6

3
ROBLES LN
2
LILAC RD
1
LITTLE POND RD
SHADY C

ANTHONY RD
VIA ENCANTADO

SIERRA ROJO RD
INCREDIBLE LN
VIA PIEDRA
OAKWO

SIERRA ROJO RD
VIA SUENA
MISTY OAK RD

7

AERIE RD
WILMINGTON AV
SIERRA ROJO RD
11
PALOS TIERRA RD
ANTHONY RD
VIA DE LUNA
12
MILLER RD
LITTLE CREEK LN

BLUE SAGE LN

A   B   C   D   E

SEE 1069 MAP

RAND McNALLY

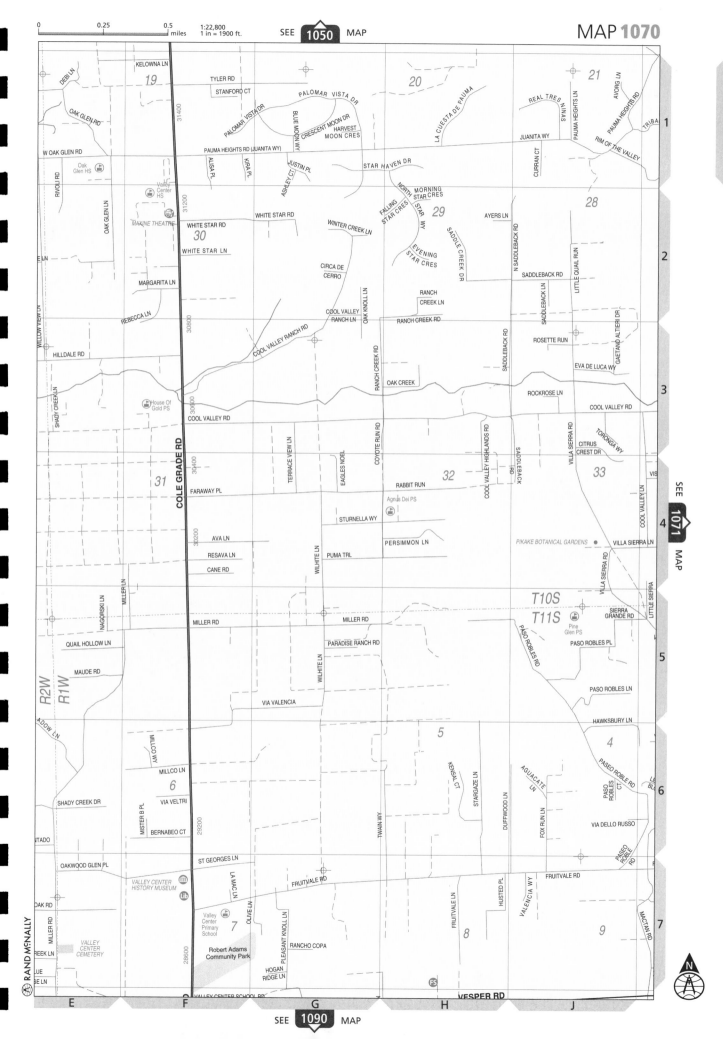

SAN DIEGO CO.

0   0.25   0.5 miles
1:22,800
1 in = 1900 ft.

KELOWNA LN
DEBI LN
19
TYLER RD
STANFORD CT
PALOMAR VISTA DR
OAK GLEN RD
PALOMAR VISTA DR
BLUE MOON WY
CRESCENT MOON DR
HARVEST MOON CRES
PAUMA HEIGHTS RD (JUANITA WY)
W OAK GLEN RD
RIVOLI RD
Oak Glen HS
ALISA PL
KIRA PL
JUSTIN PL
ASHLEY CT
STAR HAVEN DR
Valley Center HS
OAK GLEN LN
Maxine Theatre
WHITE STAR RD
WHITE STAR RD
30
WINTER CREEK LN
WHITE STAR LN
E LN
MARGARITA LN
CIRCA DE CERRO
REBECCA LN
COOL VALLEY RANCH RD
WILLOW VIEW LN
COOL VALLEY RANCH LN
OAK KNOLL LN
RANCH CREEK LN
HILLDALE RD
COOL VALLEY RANCH RD
RANCH CREEK RD
RANCH CREEK RD
SHADY CREEK LN
OAK CREEK
House Of Gold PS
COOL VALLEY RD
COLE GRADE RD
COOL VALLEY RD
31
TERRACE VIEW LN
COYOTE RUN RD
EAGLES NOEL
FARAWAY PL
32
RABBIT RUN
Agnus Dei PS
AVA LN
STURNELLA WY
RESAVA LN
PERSIMMON LN
CANE RD
WILHITE LN
PUMA TRL
MILLER LN
NAGORSKI LN
MILLER RD
MILLER RD
QUAIL HOLLOW LN
PARADISE RANCH RD
WILHITE LN
R2W R1W
MAUDE RD
VIA VALENCIA
ADOW LN
MILLCO WY
MILLCO LN
6
SHADY CREEK DR
VIA VELTRI
MISTER B PL
BERNABEO CT
OAKWOOD GLEN PL
ST GEORGES LN
Valley Center History Museum
LA MAC LN
OLIVE LN
FRUITVALE RD
OAK RD
MILLER RD
Valley Center Primary School
7
RANCHO COPA
PLEASANT KNOLL LN
VALLEY CENTER CEMETERY
Robert Adams Community Park
HOGAN RIDGE LN
CREEK LN
BLUE
SE LN
VALLEY CENTER SCHOOL RD

20
21
AVORG LN
REAL TRES NINAS
PAUMA HEIGHTS LN
PAUMA HEIGHTS RD
LA CUESTA DE PAUMA
JUANITA WY
TRIBA L
RIM OF THE VALLEY
CURRAN CT
1
STAR HAVEN DR
MORNING STAR CRES
28
NORTH STAR CRES
FALLING STAR CRES
MORNING STAR WY
AYERS LN
N SADDLEBACK RD
29
SADDLE CREEK DR
EVENING STAR CRES
LITTLE QUAIL RUN
2
SADDLEBACK RD
SADDLEBACK LN
RANCH CREEK LN
GAETANO ALTIERI DR
SADDLEBACK RD
ROSETTE RUN
EVA DE LUCA WY
ROCKROSE LN
3
COOL VALLEY RD
COOL VALLEY HIGHLANDS RD
VILLA SIERRA RD
TORONGA WY
CITRUS CREST DR
SADDLEBACK RD
33
VIS
COOL VALLEY LN
SEE 1071 MAP
Pikake Botanical Gardens
VILLA SIERRA LN
VILLA SIERRA RD
4
LITTLE SIERRA
T10S
T11S
SIERRA GRANDE RD
Pine Glen PS
PASO ROBLES RD
PASO ROBLES PL
5
PASO ROBLES LN
HAWKSBURY LN
5
4
PASEO ROBLE RD
KENSAL CT
STARGAZE LN
DUFFWOOD LN
AGUACATE LN
PASEO ROBLE CT
PASO ROBLES
LA BLU
6
VIA DELLO RUSSO
TWAIN WY
FOX RUN LN
PASEO ROBLE RD
FRUITVALE RD
FRUITVALE LN
HUSTED PL
VALENCIA WY
FRUITVALE RD
R
8
9
MACTAN RD
7

RAND McNALLY

E   F   G   H   J

N

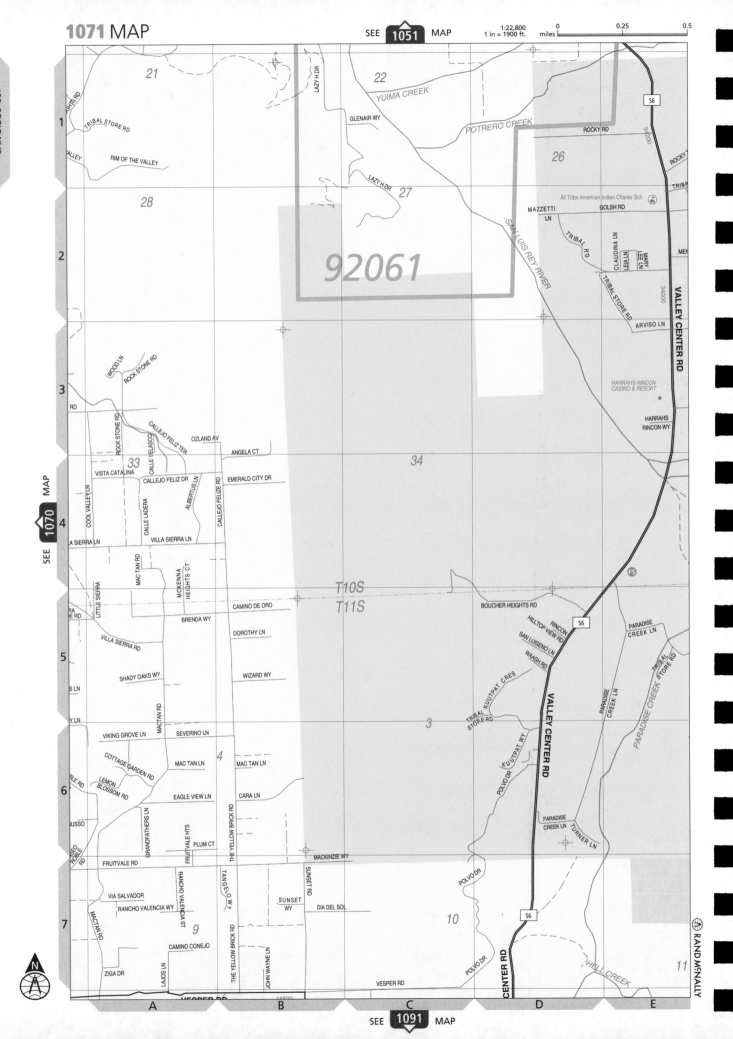

SEE 1051 MAP

1:22,800
1 in = 1900 ft.

miles 0   0.25   0.5

SAN DIEGO CO.

21

22

YUIMA CREEK

POTRERO CREEK

LAZY H DR

GLENAIR WY

ROCKY RD

S6

ROCKY T

TRIBAL STORE RD

RIM OF THE VALLEY

VALLEY

1

26

LAZY H DR

27

All Tribe American Indian Charter Sch

TRIBA

28

2

92061

MAZZETTI LN

GOLSH RD

CLAUDINA LN

TRIBAL RD

LEIA LN

MARY LEE LN

MEN

34000

SAN LUIS REY RIVER

TRIBAL STORE RD

ARVISO LN

VALLEY CENTER RD

WOOD LN

ROCK STONE RD

3

RD

ROCK STONE RD

CALLEJO FELIZ TER

OZLAND AV

ANGELA CT

HARRAHS RINCON CASINO & RESORT

HARRAHS RINCON WY

VISTA CATALINA

33

CALLE VELASCO

CALLEJO FELIZ DR

EMERALD CITY DR

34

COOL VALLEY LN

CALLE LADERA

ALBERTUS LN

CALLEJO FELIZE

4

LA SIERRA LN

VILLA SIERRA LN

SEE 1070 MAP

MAC TAN RD

MCKENNA HEIGHTS CT

LITTLE SIERRA

CAMINO DE ORO

T10S

T11S

BOUCHER HEIGHTS RD

FS

RA E RD

BRENDA WY

DOROTHY LN

RINCON

HILLTOP VIEW RD

S6

PARADISE CREEK LN

VILLA SIERRA RD

SAN LUISENO LN

5

S LN

SHADY OAKS WY

WIZARD WY

WAASH RD

PARADISE CREEK LN

TRIBAL STORE RD

Y LN

MACTAN RD

3

TRIBAL STORE RD

KUUTPAT CRES

VALLEY CENTER RD

PARADISE CREEK STORE RD

VIKING GROVE LN

SEVERINO LN

POLVO DR

KUUTPAT WY

COTTAGE GARDEN RD

MAC TAN LN

4

MAC TAN LN

CARA LN

6

LE RD

LEMON BLOSSOM RD

EAGLE VIEW LN

PARADISE CREEK LN

TURNER LN

USSO

GRANDFATHERS LN

FRUITVALE HTS

PLUM CT

THE YELLOW BRICK RD

MACKINZIE WY

SO BLE RD

FRUITVALE RD

POLVO DR

VIA SALVADOR

RANCHO VALENCIA ST

TANGELO WY

SUNSET RD

SUNSET WY

DIA DEL SOL

10

S6

7

RANCHO VALENCIA WY

9

CAMINO CONEJO

THE YELLOW BRICK RD

JOHN WAYNE LN

MACTAN RD

LAJOS LN

ZIGA DR

VESPER RD

VESPER RD

CENTER RD

POLVO DR

HELL CREEK

11

N

A   B   C   D   E

RAND McNALLY

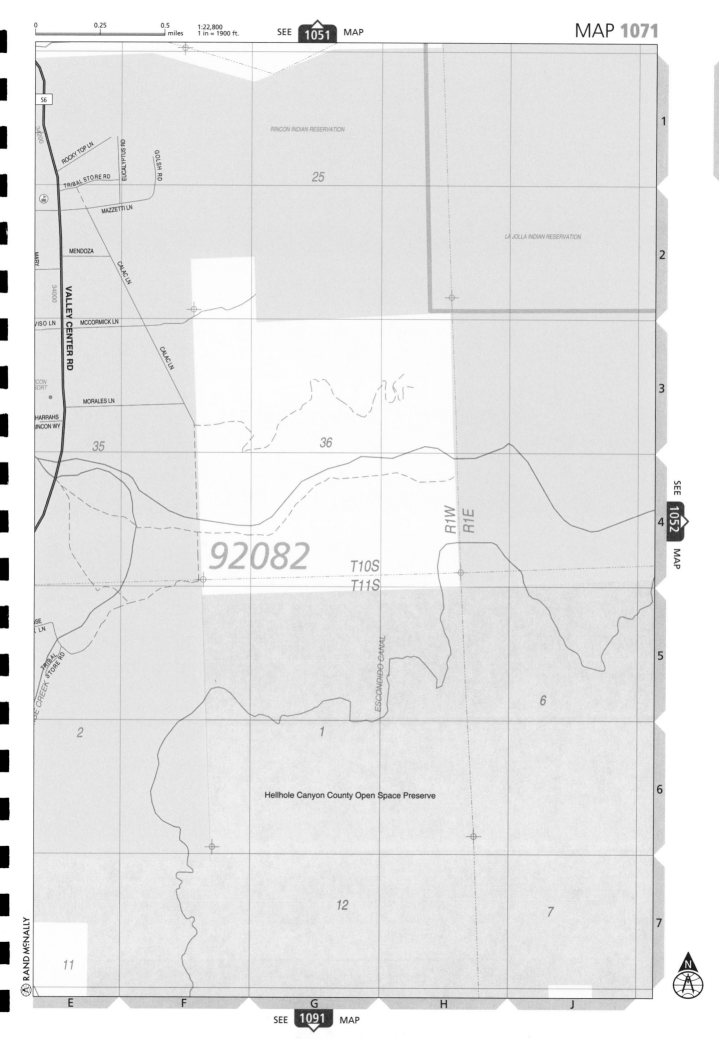

MAP **1071**

SAN DIEGO CO.

SEE **1051** MAP

SEE **1052** MAP

0
0.25
0.5
miles
1:22,800
1 in = 1900 ft.

S6

RINCON INDIAN RESERVATION

LA JOLLA INDIAN RESERVATION

25

ROCKY TOP LN
TRIBAL STORE RD
EUCALYPTUS RD
GOLSH RD
MAZZETTI LN

MENDOZA

VALLEY CENTER RD

MARY

34000
34200

CALAC LN

VISO LN
MCCORMICK LN

CALAC LN

RICON RESORT

MORALES LN

HARRAHS
RINCON WY

35

36

R1W
R1E

92082

T10S
T11S

ESCONDIDO CANAL

6

SE CREEK TRIBAL STORE RD

2

1

Hellhole Canyon County Open Space Preserve

12

7

11

RAND MCNALLY

E
F
G
H
J

1
2
3
4
5
6
7

N

1085 MAP

SEE D MAP

1:22,800
1 in = 1900 ft.

miles 0   0.25   0.5

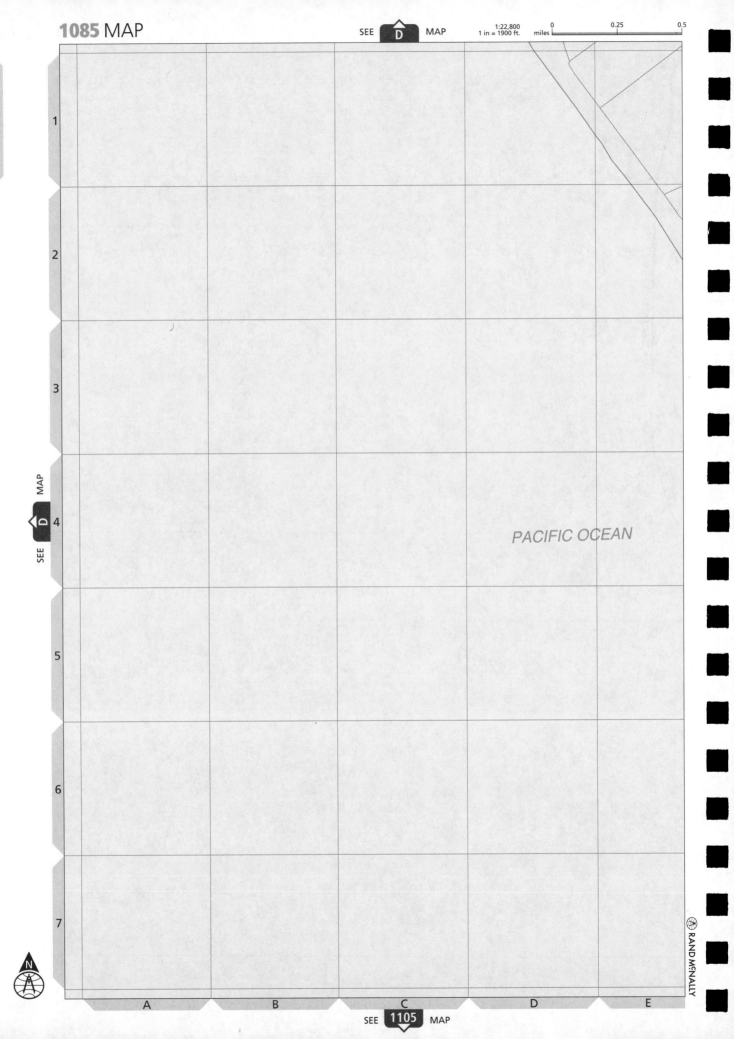

SEE D MAP

PACIFIC OCEAN

A   B   C   D   E

1
2
3
4
5
6
7

N

SEE 1105 MAP

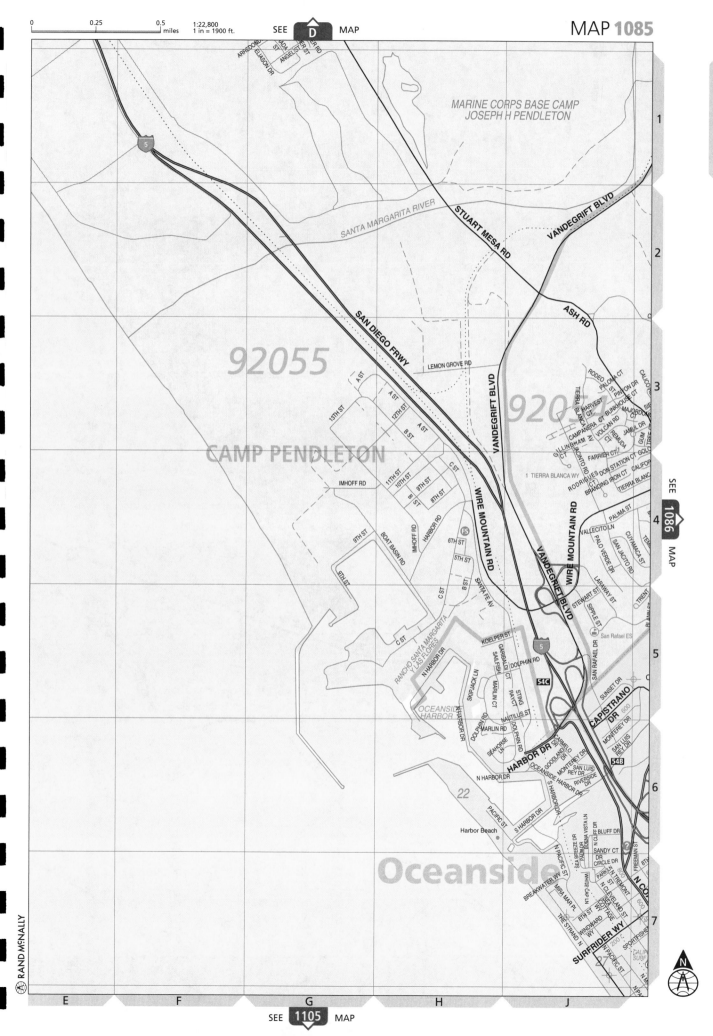

MAP **1085**

SAN DIEGO CO.

0 0.25 0.5 miles 1:22,800 1 in = 1900 ft.

SEE D MAP

MARINE CORPS BASE CAMP
JOSEPH H PENDLETON

STUART MESA RD

VANDEGRIFT BLVD

SANTA MARGARITA RIVER

ASH RD

SAN DIEGO FRWY

92055

LEMON GROVE RD

VANDEGRIFT BLVD

92057

CAMP PENDLETON

A ST
A ST
13TH ST
12TH ST
B ST
A ST
11TH ST
10TH ST
9TH ST
B ST
8TH ST
IMHOFF RD
C ST
IMHOFF RD
HARBOR RD
WIRE MOUNTAIN RD
6TH ST
9TH ST
BOAT BASIN RD
5TH ST
C ST
9TH ST
B ST
SANTA FE AV
C ST

WIRE MOUNTAIN RD

VANDEGRIFT BLVD

RANCHO SANTA MARGARITA
Y LAS FLORES

N HARBOR RD

KOELPER ST
GARIBALDI CT
SAILFISH
DOLPHIN RD
SKIPJACK LN
STING RAY CT
MARLIN CT
NAUTILUS ST
DOLPHIN LN
MARLIN RD
DOLPHIN RD
SEAHORSE LN
HARBOR DR
N HARBOR RD
S HARBOR DR
N HARBOR DR

OCEANSIDE
HARBOR

CAPISTRANO DR
SUNSET DR
MONTEREY DR
SAN LUIS REY DR
CARMELO
GOODLAND DR
MONTEREY DR
SAN LUIS REY DR
RIVERSIDE DR
OCEANSIDE HARBOR DR

54C
54B

San Rafael ES
SAN RAFAEL DR
STEWART ST
SIPPLE ST
LARAWAY ST
TRENT

PALIMA ST
VALLECITO LN
PALO VERDE DR
CUYAMACA ST
SAN JACINTO RD

RODEO DR
PALOMA CT
PINYON DR
CALICO
HARVEST CT
TIERRA BLANCA CT
BUNKHOUSE CT
MAJORDOMO
CAMPANERA CT
VOLCAN RD
BREMADA
WILLINGHAM CT
JAMUL CT
SAN JACINTO RD
FARRIER CT
GUM
GOLD
1 TIERRA BLANCA WY
RODRIGUES DON STATION CT
BRANDING IRON CT
TIERRA BLANCA
CALIFOR

SEE 1086 MAP

22

PACIFIC ST

Harbor Beach

Oceanside

SEA BREEZE DR
N CLIFF DR
PALM DR
BUENA VISTA LN
BLUFF DR
SANDY CT
DR
CIRCLE DR
N TREMONT
PAPRILIN
N CLEVELAND ST
FREEMAN ST
N CO
BREAKWATER WY
MIRA MAR PL
N PACIFIC ST
WHITE CAP LN
8TH ST
N TREMONT
WINDWARD
THE STRAND N
N PACIFIC ST
SURFRIDER WY
SPORTFISHE
27

RAND MCNALLY

N

E   F   G   H   J

SEE 1105 MAP

SEE ▢ 1066 ▢ MAP

1:22,800
1 in = 1900 ft.

miles   0   0.25   0.5

SAN DIEGO CO.

SEE ▢ 1085 ▢ MAP

MARINE CORPS BASE
CAMP PENDLETON

92055

92054

92058

HUBBERT LAKE

PRINCE OF PEACE
ABBEY
BENEDICTINE
MONASTERY

OCEANSIDE MUNICIPAL AIRPORT

Santa
Margarita ES

CARNES RD

Capistrano
Park

North
Terrace ES

Rafael ES

SAN LUIS REY RIVER

SAN LUIS REY MISSION EXWY

AIRPORT RD

Jefferson MS

Burgener, Clair
Academy

Mission
ES

Laurel ES

Balderama
Park

Woman's
Club Park

Center City Golf Course

Oceanside
HS

Oceanside
HIST MUSEUM

OCEANSIDE MUSEUM

Recreational
Park

OCEANS
ELEVEN
CASINO

SHOW
PALACE

Buddy
Todd
Park

California
SURF MUSEUM

Capistrano
Valley

SEE ▢ 1106 ▢ MAP

N

RAND McNALLY

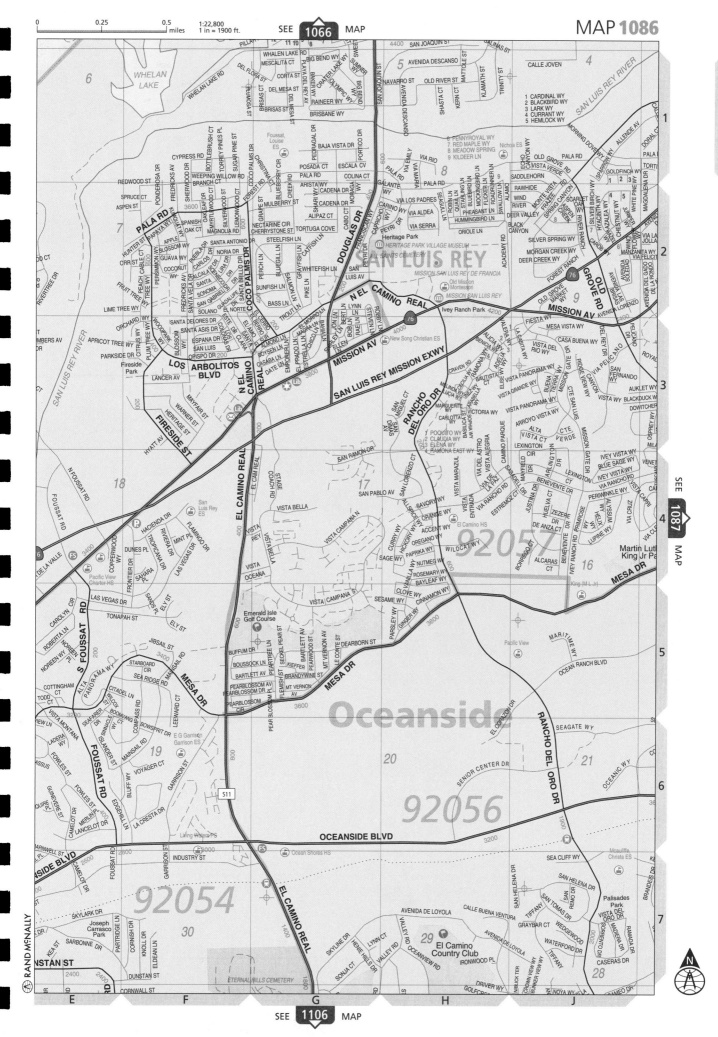

MAP 1086

SAN DIEGO CO.

SEE 1066 MAP

SEE 1087 MAP

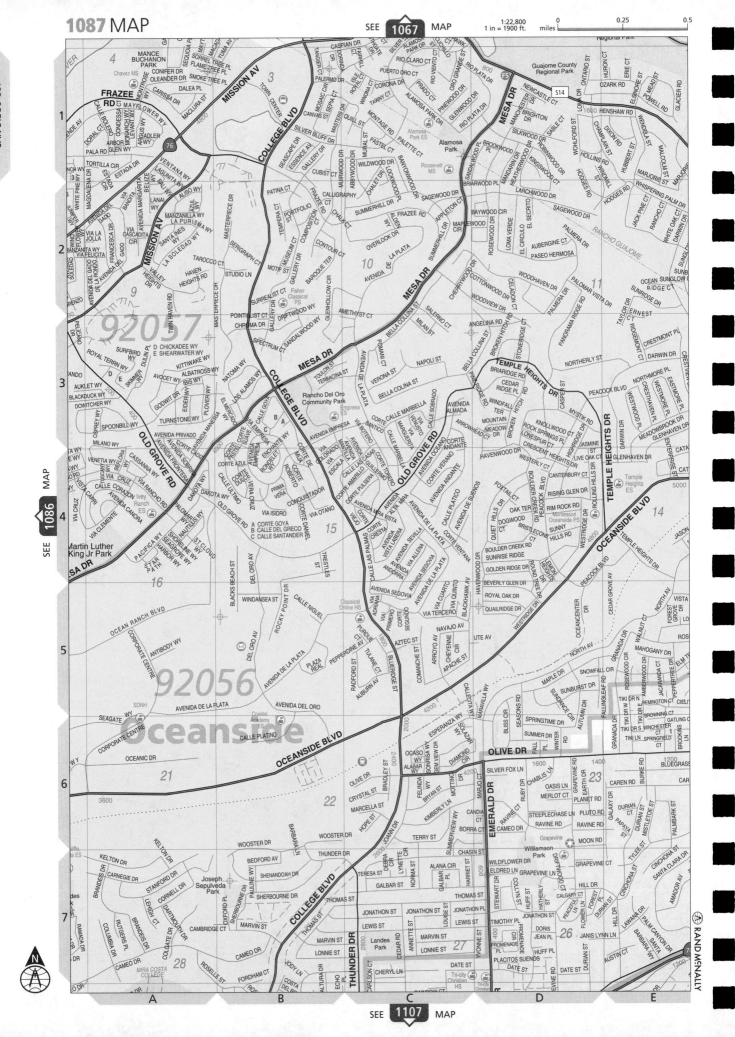

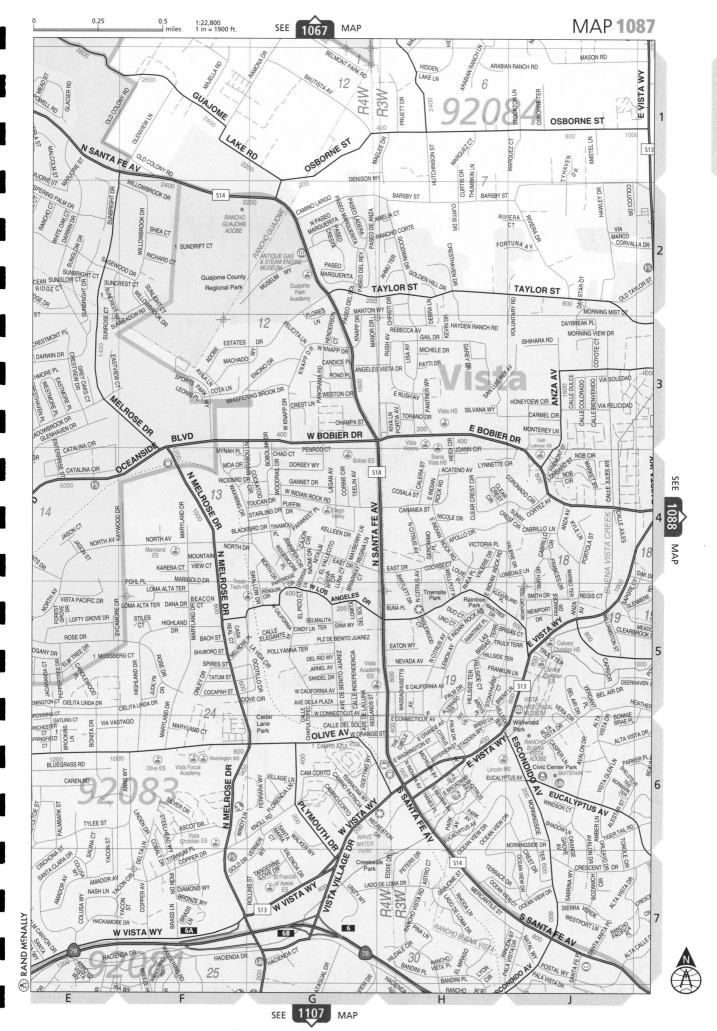

MAP 1087

SAN DIEGO CO.

0   0.25   0.5
miles   1:22,800
1 in = 1900 ft.

92084

92083

92081

SEE 1088 MAP

RAND M°NALLY

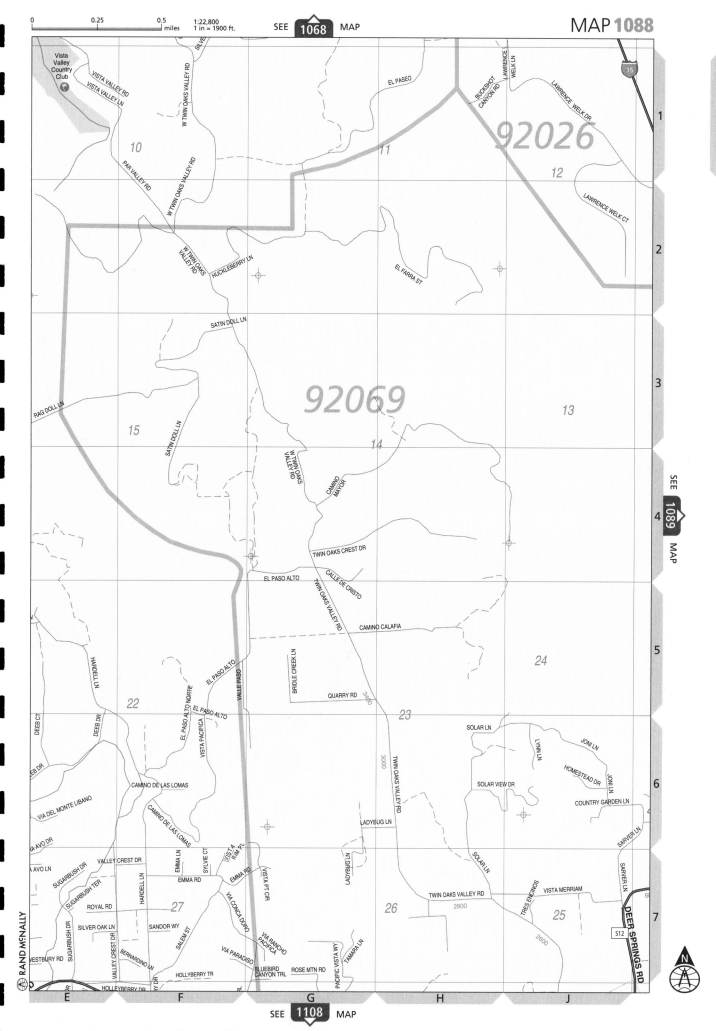

MAP **1088**

SAN DIEGO CO.

0   0.25   0.5
|___|___|___| miles
1:22,800
1 in = 1900 ft.

SEE 1068 MAP

Vista Valley Country Club

92026

92069

VISTA VALLEY RD
VISTA VALLEY LN
W TWIN OAKS VALLEY RD
PAR VALLEY RD
W TWIN OAKS VALLEY RD
HUCKLEBERRY LN
SATIN DOLL LN
RAG DOLL LN
SATIN DOLL LN
W TWIN OAKS VALLEY RD
EL PASO
EL PASO ALTO
HARDELL LN
DEEB CT
DEEB DR
DEEB DR
EL PASO ALTO NORTE
EL PASO ALTO
VISTA PACIFICA
VALLE PASO
CAMINO DE LAS LOMAS
VIA DEL MONTE LIBANO
CAMINO DE LAS LOMAS
BRIDLE CREEK LN
QUARRY RD
EL PASO ALTO
TWIN OAKS CREST DR
CALLE DE CRISTO
TWIN OAKS VALLEY RD
CAMINO CALAFIA
CAMINO MAYOR
EL PASO
EL PASO ALTO
VISTA RIM PL
SUGARBUSH DR
SUGARBUSH TER
VALLEY CREST DR
EMMA LN
SYLVIE CT
VISTA PT CIR
HARDELL LN
EMMA RD
EMMA RD
VIA CONCA DORO
SILVER OAK LN
ROYAL RD
SANDOR WY
SALEM ST
VALLEY CREST DR
BERNARDINO LN
VIA RANCHO PACIFICA
VIA PARADISO
HOLLYBERRY TR
BLUEBIRD CANYON TRL
ROSE MTN RD
PACIFIC VISTA WY
TAMARA LN
LADYBUG LN
LADYBUG LN
SOLAR LN
SOLAR VIEW DR
SOLAR LN
TWIN OAKS VALLEY RD
LYNN LN
JONI LN
HOMESTEAD DR
JONI LN
COUNTRY GARDEN LN
SARVER LN
SARVER LN
VISTA MERRIAM
TRES ENCINOS
BUCKSHOT CANYON RD
LAWRENCE WELK LN
LAWRENCE WELK DR
LAWRENCE WELK CT
EL FARRA ST
WESTBURY RD
HOLLEYBERRY DR
AVO DR
AVO LN
DEER SPRINGS RD

92026
92069

10
11
12
13
14
15
22
23
24
25
26
27

3400
3000
2800
2600

512
64

1
2
3
4
5
6
7

SEE 1089 MAP

SAN DIEGO CO.

RAND MⁿNALLY

SEE 1108 MAP

E   F   G   H   J

N

1:22,800
1 in = 1900 ft.

miles 0   0.25   0.5

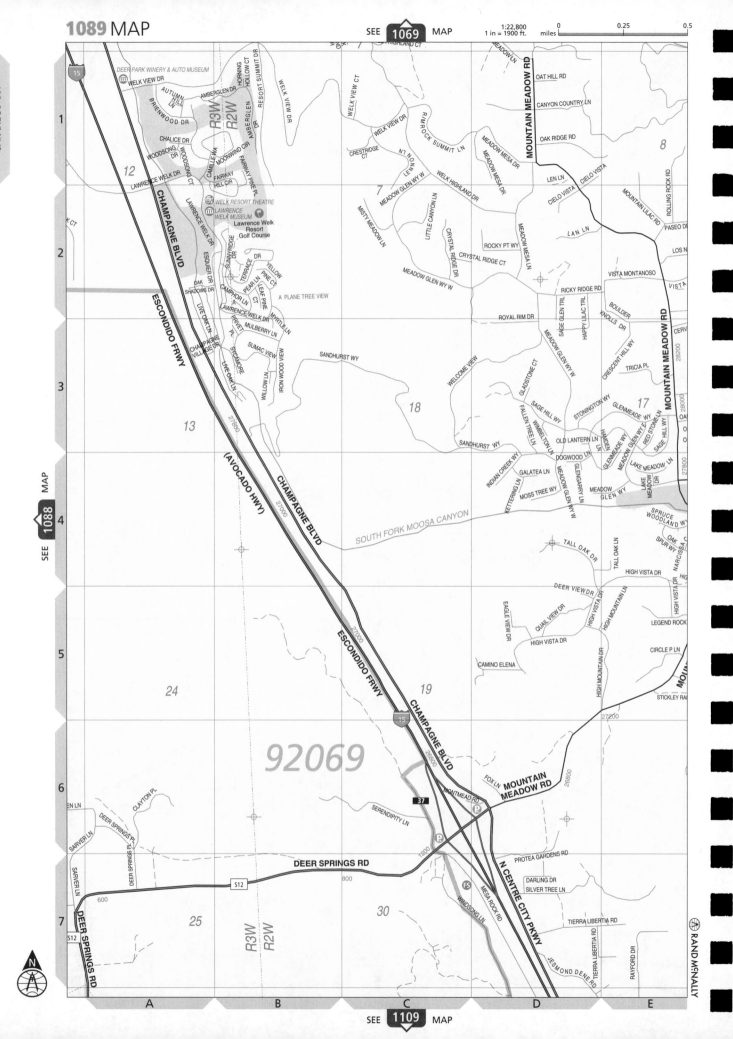

SAN DIEGO CO.

SEE △ 1088 MAP

RAND M≌NALLY

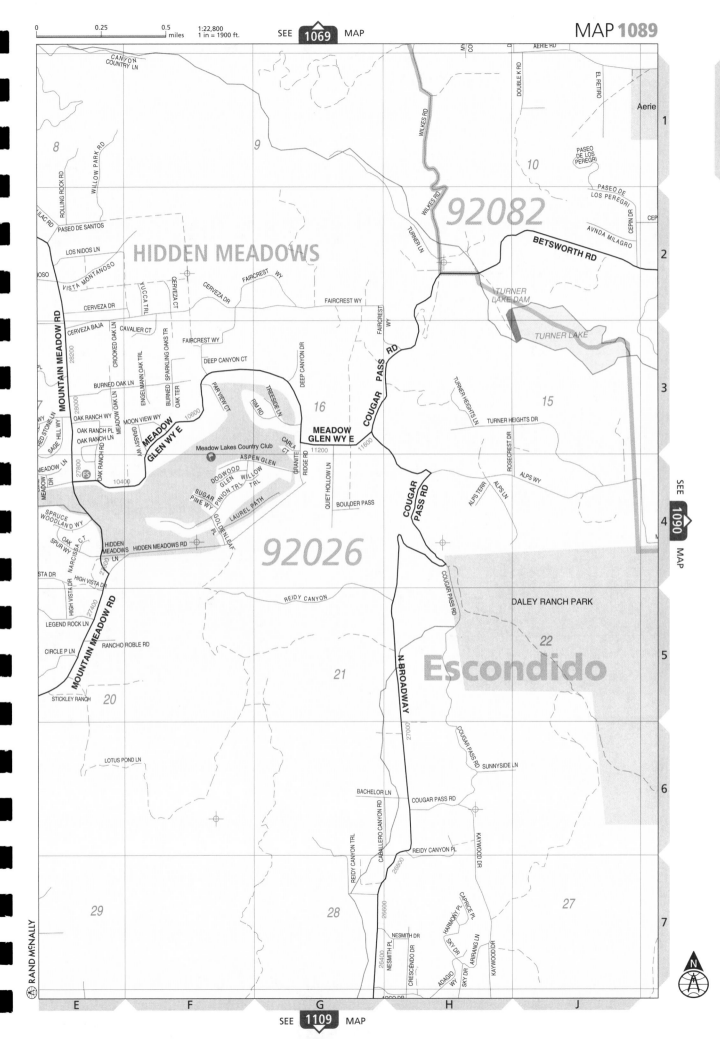

MAP **1089**

SAN DIEGO CO.

0   0.25   0.5
|_____|_____| miles
1:22,800
1 in = 1900 ft.

SEE **1069** MAP

1

CANYON COUNTRY LN

8

9

10

AERIE RD

DOUBLE K RD

EL RETIRO

Aerie

PASEO DE LOS PEREGRI

WILLOW PARK RD

ROLLING ROCK RD

LILAC RD

PASEO DE SANTOS

LOS NIDOS LN

VISTA MONTANOSO

HIDDEN MEADOWS

92082

WILKES RD

TURNER LN

PASEO DE LOS PEREGRI

CEPIN DR

CEP

AVNDA MILAGRO

BETSWORTH RD

2

CERVEZA DR

YUCCA TRL

CERVEZA CT

CERVEZA DR

FAIRCREST WY

FAIRCREST WY

FAIRCREST WY

TURNER LAKE DAM

TURNER LAKE

MOUNTAIN MEADOW RD

CERVEZA BAJA

CAVALIER CT

CROOKED OAK LN

BURNED OAK LN

ENGELMANN OAK TRL

SPARKLING OAKS TR

DEEP CANYON CT

DEEP CANYON DR

16

FAIRCREST WY

COUGAR PASS RD

15

TURNER HEIGHTS LN

TURNER HEIGHTS DR

3

28200

28000

OAK RANCH WY

MEADOW OAK LN

BURNED OAK TER

PAR VIEW CT

TREESIDE LN

RIM RD

MEADOW GLEN WY E

MEADOW GLEN WY E

10600

ROSECREST DR

ALPS WY

RED STONE LN

SAGE HILL WY

OAK RANCH PL
OAK RANCH LN

MOON VIEW WY

GRASSY WY

OAK RANCH RD

27800

FS

Meadow Lakes Country Club

CARLA CT

GRANITE

RIDGE RD

11200

11600

ALPS TERR

ALPS LN

ASPEN GLEN

MEADOW LN

MEADOW DR

10400

DOGWOOD GLEN

PINION TRL

WILLOW TRL

SUGAR PINE WY

LAUREL PATH

GOLDEN LEAF PL

QUIET HOLLOW LN

BOULDER PASS

COUGAR PASS RD

SEE **1090** MAP

4

SPRUCE WOODLAND WY

OAK SPUR WY

NARCISSA CT

HIDDEN MEADOWS LN

2900

HIDDEN MEADOWS RD

92026

VISTA DR

HIGH VISTA DR

HIGH VISTA DR

27400

LEGEND ROCK LN

CIRCLE P LN

RANCHO ROBLE RD

MOUNTAIN MEADOW RD

REIDY CANYON

COUGAR PASS RD

DALEY RANCH PARK

22

Escondido

5

STICKLEY RANCH

20

21

N. BROADWAY

27000

COUGAR PASS RD

SUNNYSIDE LN

LOTUS POND LN

BACHELOR LN

COUGAR PASS RD

6

REIDY CANYON TRL

CABALLERO CANYON RD

REIDY CANYON PL

KAYWOOD DR

26800

29

28

27

26600

26400

NESMITH PL

NESMITH DR

CRESCENDO DR

HARMONY PL

CAPRICE PL

SKY DR

ARIRANG LN

KAYWOOD DR

ADAGIO WY

SKY DR

7

ADGO DR

® RAND McNALLY

N

E   F   G   H   J

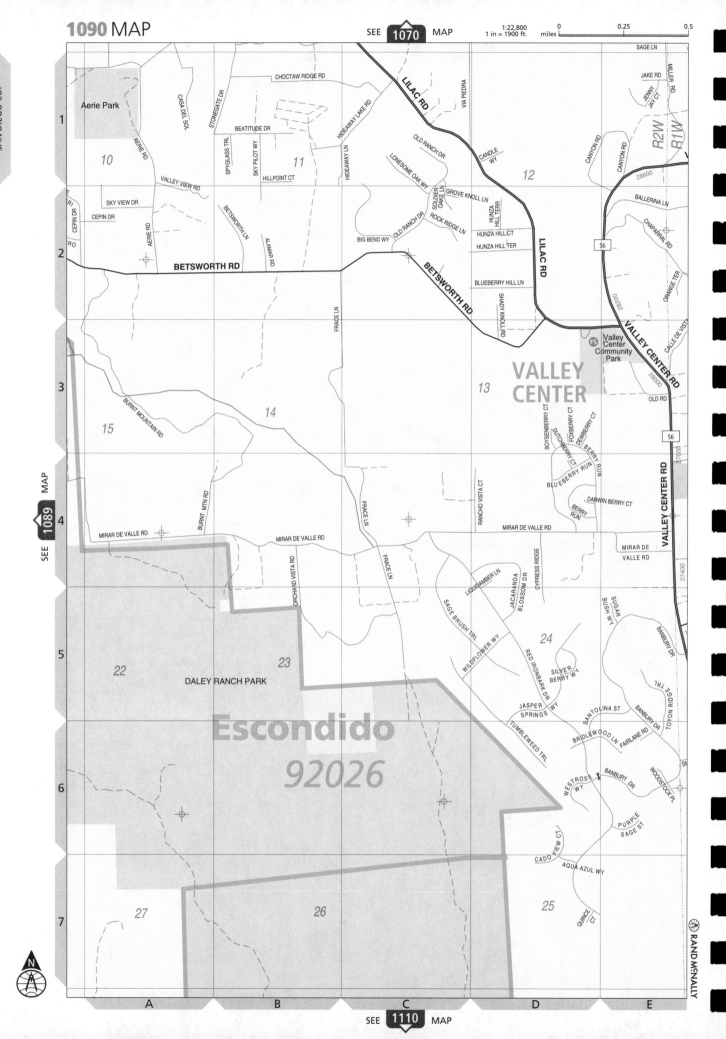

SEE ⬆ 1070 MAP

1:22,800
1 in = 1900 ft.

miles 0   0.25   0.5

SAN DIEGO CO.

SAGE LN

Aerie Park

CASA DEL SOL

CHOCTAW RIDGE RD

STONEGATE DR

BEATITUDE DR

SPYGLASS TRL

SKY PILOT WY

HILLPOINT CT

HIDEAWAY LAKE RD

HIDEAWAY LN

LILAC RD

VIA PIEDRA

JAKE RD

MILLER RD

JENNY JAY CT

R2W R1W

1

10

11

12

AERIE RD

VALLEY VIEW RD

OLD RANCH DR

CANDLE WY

CANYON RD

CANYON RD

28600

SKY VIEW DR

CEPIN DR

CEPIN DR

AERIE RD

BETSWORTH LN

ALAMAR RD

LONESOME OAK WY

SOLDIER OAKS LN

GROVE KNOLL LN

ROCK RIDGE LN

HUNZA HILL TERR

HUNZA HILL CT

LILAC RD

BALLERINA LN

CHAPARRAL RD

ORANGE TER

2

BETSWORTH RD

BIG BEND WY

OLD RANCH DR

HUNZA HILL TER

S6

BLUEBERRY HILL LN

BETSWORTH RD

SHADY KNOLL RD

VALLEY CENTER RD

CALLE DE VISTA

28000

FRACE LN

FS Valley Center Community Park

VALLEY CENTER

3

15

14

13

BURNT MOUNTAIN RD

OLD RD

S6

BOYSENBERRY CT

DUTCHBERRY CT

FOXBERRY CT

DEWBERRY CT

BERRY RUN

BLUEBERRY RUN

DARWIN BERRY CT

BERRY RUN

VALLEY CENTER RD

27600

4

BURNT MTN RD

FRACE LN

RANCHO VISTA CT

MIRAR DE VALLE RD

MIRAR DE VALLE RD

MIRAR DE VALLE RD

FRACE LN

MIRAR DE VALLE RD

27400

ORCHARD VISTA RD

FRACE LN

LIQUIDAMBER LN

JACARANDA BLOSSOM DR

CYPRESS RIDGE

SUGAR BUSH WY

BANBURY DR

5

22

23

SAGE BRUSH TRL

WILDFLOWER WY

RED IRONBARK DR

24

SILVER BERRY WY

TOYON RIDGE TRL

DALEY RANCH PARK

JASPER SPRINGS

SANTOLINA ST

BANBURY DR

Escondido

TUMBLEWEED TRL

BRIDLEWOOD LN

FAIRLANE RD

6

92026

WESTROSE WY

BANBURY DR

WOODSTOCK PL

PURPLE SAGE ST

CADO VIEW CT

AQUA AZUL WY

7

27

26

25

QUINCE CT

SEE ⬇ 1110 MAP

A   B   C   D   E

SEE ◀ 1089 MAP

N

RAND MCNALLY

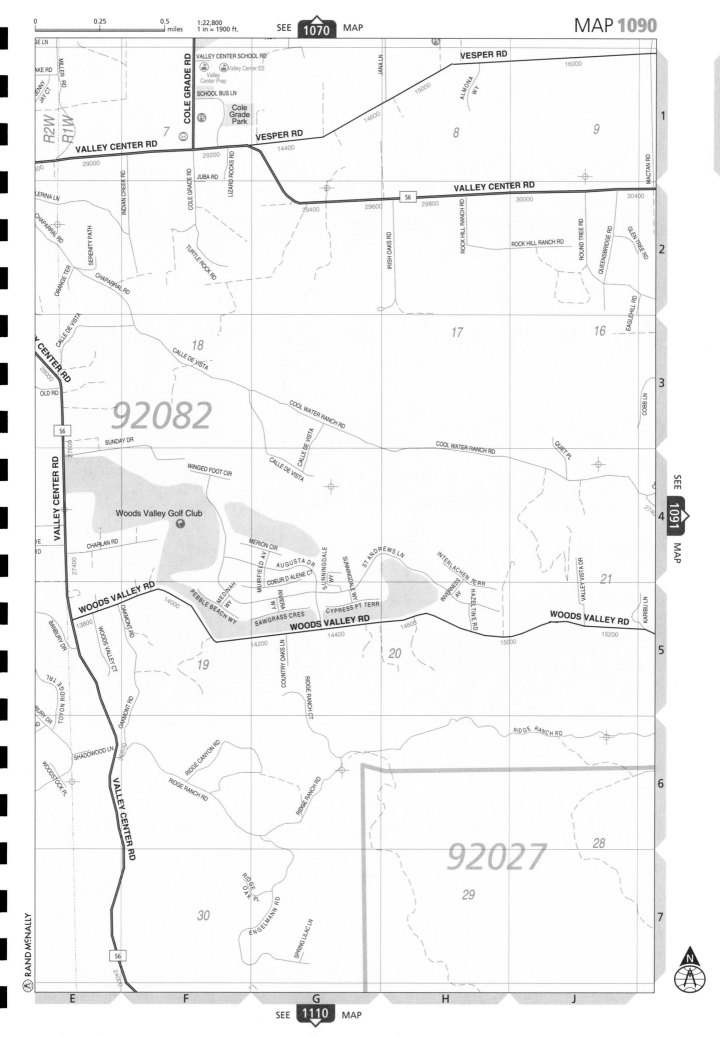

SAN DIEGO CO.

SE LN
LAKE RD
MILLER RD
DENNY
JAY CT
VALLEY CENTER SCHOOL RD
COLE GRADE RD
Valley Center ES
Valley Center Prep
SCHOOL BUS LN
Cole Grade Park
FS

VESPER RD
16000
JANA LN
ALMONA WY
15000
14600
9
8
1

R2W
R1W
7
VALLEY CENTER RD
29000
29200
VESPER RD
14400
JUBA RD
COLE GRADE RD
INDIAN CREEK RD
LIZARD ROCKS RD
29400
29600
S6
29800
VALLEY CENTER RD
30000
30400
MACTAN RD

LERINA LN
CHAPARRAL RD
SERENITY PATH
TURTLE ROCK RD
ORANGE TER
CHAPARRAL RD
IRISH OAKS RD
ROCK HILL RANCH RD
ROCK HILL RANCH RD
ROUND TREE RD
QUEENSBRIDGE RD
GLEN TREE RD
EAGLEHILL RD
2

CALLE DE VISTA
CENTER RD
26000
18
CALLE DE VISTA
17
16
COBB LN
3

OLD RD
S6
COOL WATER RANCH RD
CALLE DE VISTA
92082
SUNDAY DR
27800
WINGED FOOT CIR
CALLE DE VISTA
COOL WATER RANCH RD
QUIET PL
SEE 1091 MAP

Woods Valley Golf Club
CHARLAN RD
27400
MERION CIR
MURFIELD AV
AUGUSTA DR
COEUR D ALENE CT
SUNNINGDALE WY
ST ANDREWS LN
INTERLACHEN TERR
INVERNESS AV
HAZELTINE RD
VALLEY VISTA DR
21
4

WOODS VALLEY RD
14000
BANBURY DR
13800
WOODS VALLEY CT
OAKMONT RD
PEBBLE BEACH WY
MEDINAH WY
RIVIERA WY
SAWGRASS CRES
CYPRESS PT TERR
WOODS VALLEY RD
14200
14400
14600
15000
WOODS VALLEY RD
15200
KARIBU LN
5

TOYON RIDGE TRL
BURY DR
19
COUNTRY OAKS LN
RIDGE RANCH CT
20
RIDGE RANCH RD

SHADOWOOD LN
26000
RIDGE CANYON RD
RIDGE RANCH RD
RIDGE RANCH RD
RIDGE RANCH RD
RIDGE RANCH RD
6

WOODSTOCK PL
VALLEY CENTER RD
24000
S6
30
RIDGE OAK PL
ENGELMANN RD
SPRING LILAC LN
92027
29
28
7

RAND McNALLY

E
F
G
H
J

N

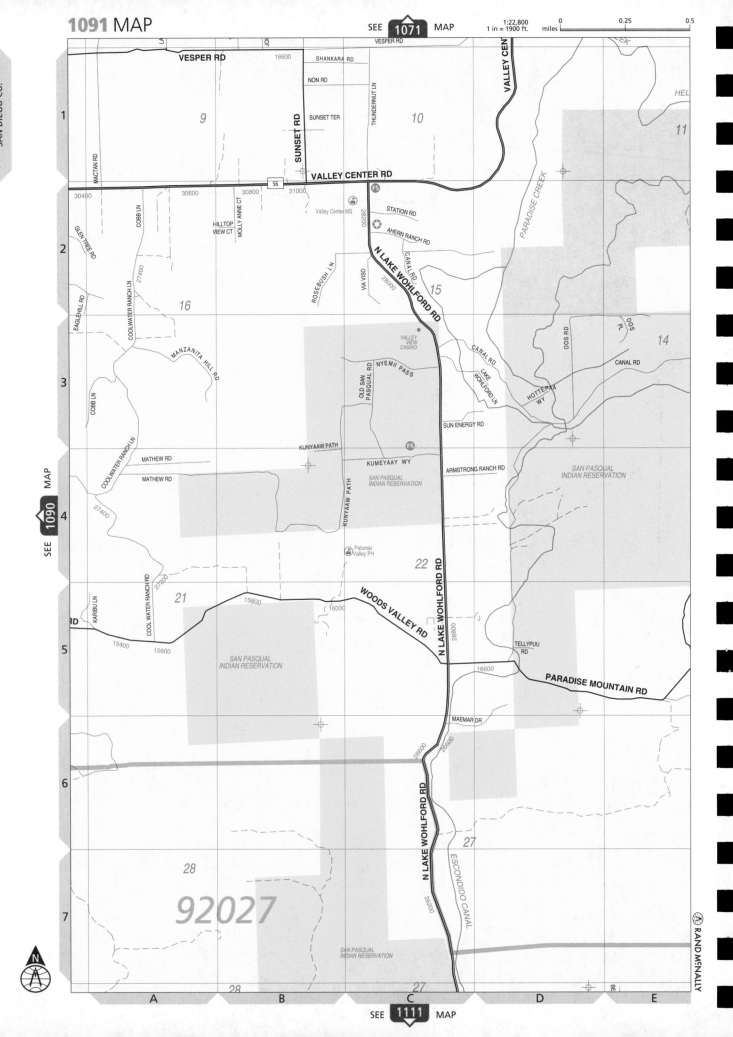

SEE 1071 MAP

1:22,800
1 in = 1900 ft.

miles

0   0.25   0.5

SAN DIEGO CO.

VESPER RD

SHANKARA RD

NON RD

SUNSET TER

THUNDERNUT LN

VESPER RD

VALLEY CEN

16600

9

SUNSET RD

10

11

HEL

MACTAN RD

S6

VALLEY CENTER RD

PARADISE CREEK

1

30400   30600   30800   31000

Valley Center MS

STATION RD

FS

GLEN TREE RD

COBB LN

HILLTOP VIEW CT

MOLLY ANNE CT

AHERN RANCH RD

2

27400

COOLWATER RANCH LN

ROSEBUSH LN

VIA VISO

N LAKE WOHLFORD RD

CANAL RD

15

28000

26200

EAGLEHILL RD

16

CANAL RD

OOS RD

OOS PL

14

MANZANITA HILL RD

VALLEY VIEW CASINO

NYEMII PASS

LAKE WOHLFORD LN

CANAL RD

3

COBB LN

OLD SAN PASQUAL RD

HOTTEPAA WY

COOLWATER RANCH LN

KUNYAAW PATH

FS

SUN ENERGY RD

MATHEW RD

KUMEYAAY WY

ARMSTRONG RANCH RD

SAN PASQUAL INDIAN RESERVATION

SEE 1090 MAP

MATHEW RD

KUNYAAW PATH

SAN PASQUAL INDIAN RESERVATION

4

27400

Palomar Valley PH

22

N LAKE WOHLFORD RD

KARIBU LN

21

15800

16000

WOODS VALLEY RD

26800

TELLYPUU RD

5

RD

COOL WATER RANCH RD

27200

15400   15600

SAN PASQUAL INDIAN RESERVATION

16600

PARADISE MOUNTAIN RD

MAEMAR DR

6

26500

26600

28

27

N LAKE WOHLFORD RD

ESCONDIDO CANAL

7

92027

26200

SAN PASQUAL INDIAN RESERVATION

28

27

BE

A   B   C   D   E

N

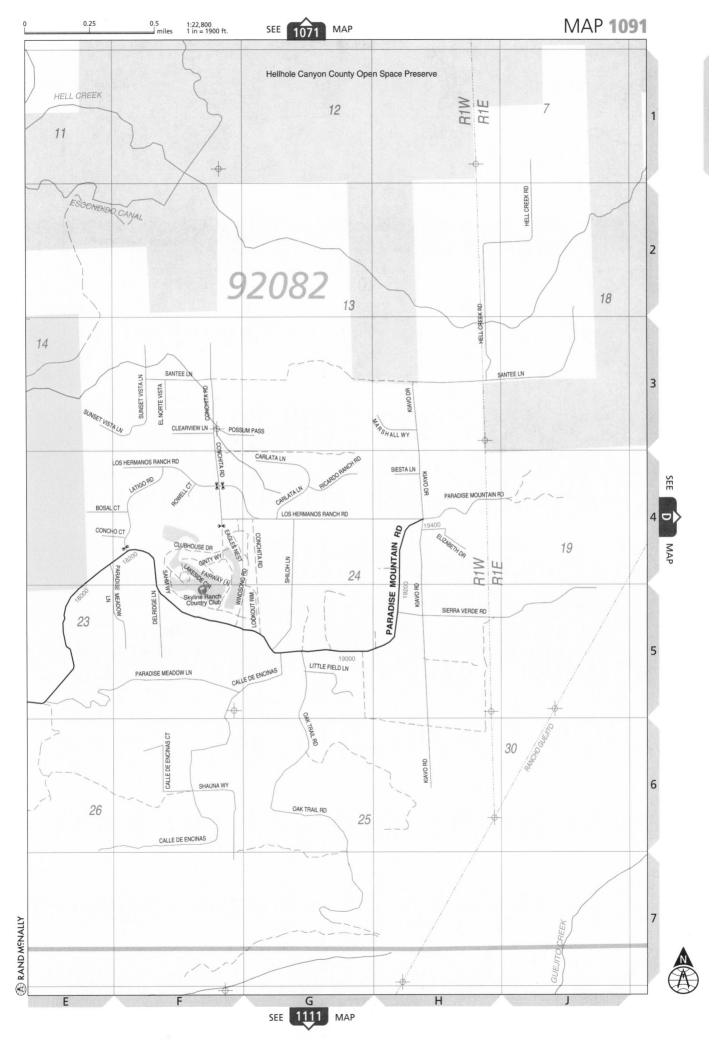

MAP **1091**

0   0.25   0.5
|___|___|___| miles
1:22,800
1 in = 1900 ft.

SEE **1071** MAP

SAN DIEGO CO.

Hellhole Canyon County Open Space Preserve

HELL CREEK

11

12

R1W R1E

7

HELL CREEK RD

1

ESCONDIDO CANAL

2

92082

13

18

HELL CREEK RD

SANTEE LN

14

SANTEE LN

KIAVO DR

3

SUNSET VISTA LN

SUNSET VISTA LN

EL NORTE VISTA

CONCHITA RD

CLEARVIEW LN   POSSUM PASS

CARLATA LN

MARSHALL WY

SEE
D
MAP

LOS HERMANOS RANCH RD

RICARDO RANCH RD

SIESTA LN

PARADISE MOUNTAIN RD

LATIGO RD

ROWELL CT

CARLATA LN

KIAVO DR

BOSAL CT

LOS HERMANOS RANCH RD

19400

ELIZABETH DR

19

R1W R1E

CONCHO CT

CLUBHOUSE DR

EAGLES NEST

CONCHITA RD

SHILOH LN

24

PARADISE MOUNTAIN RD

19200

KIAVO RD

18200

GINTY WY

FAIRWAY LN

WINDSONG RD

18000

PARADISE MEADOW LN

SHAWS

DELRIDGE LN

LAKESIDE CIR

LOOKOUT RIM

Skyline Ranch
Country Club

SIERRA VERDE RD

23

4

PARADISE MEADOW LN

CALLE DE ENCINAS

LITTLE FIELD LN

19000

5

CALLE DE ENCINAS CT

OAK TRAIL RD

KIAVO RD

30

RANCHO GUEJITO

6

SHAUNA WY

26

OAK TRAIL RD

25

CALLE DE ENCINAS

GUEJITO CREEK

7

RAND MºNALLY

E   F   G   H   J

N

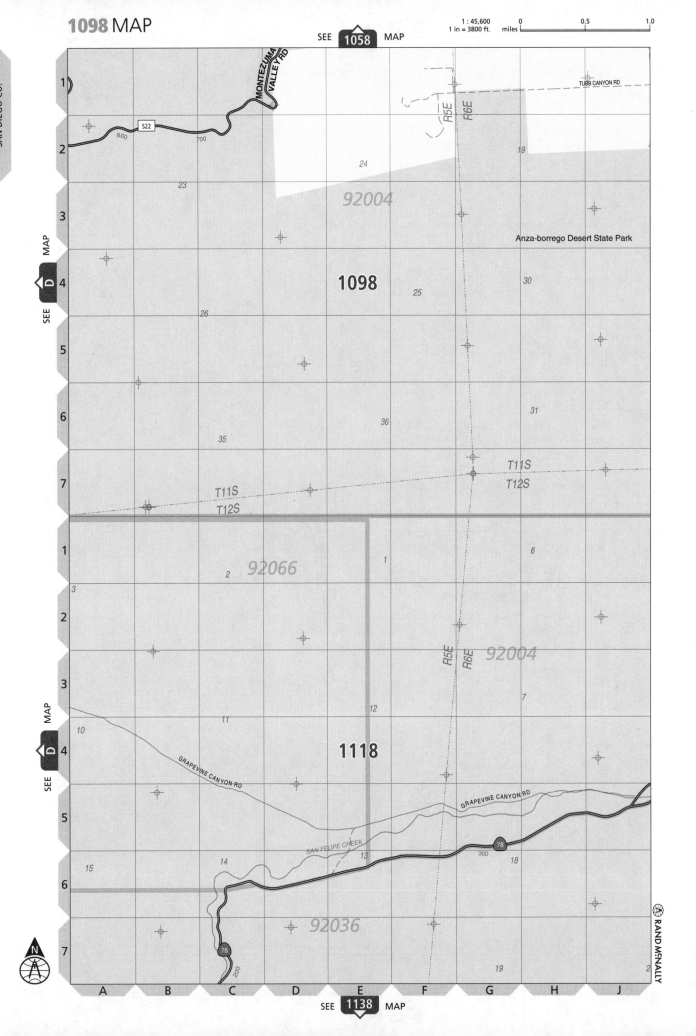

SAN DIEGO CO.

1 : 45,600
1 in = 3800 ft.   miles

0   0.5   1.0

SEE 1058 MAP

TUBB CANYON RD

R5E R6E

24

92004

23

Anza-borrego Desert State Park

1098

25

30

26

36

31

35

T11S
T12S

T11S
T12S

92066

2

1

6

3

11

10

92004

12

7

1118

GRAPEVINE CANYON RD

GRAPEVINE CANYON RD

R5E R6E

SAN FELIPE CREEK

13

78

300

18

15

14

92036

19

SEE 1138 MAP

S22

800 700

MONTEZUMA VALLEY RD

RAND McNALLY

N

A B C D E F G H J

1 2 3 4 5 6 7

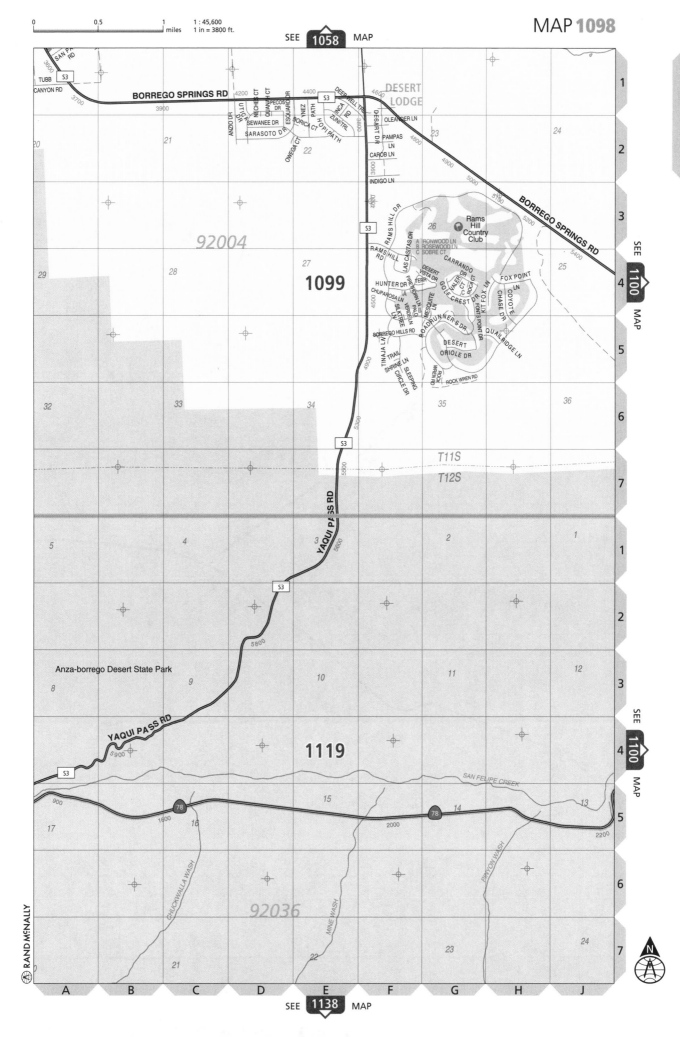

MAP **1098**

SAN DIEGO CO.

SEE [1058] MAP

0   0.5   1
miles

1 : 45,600
1 in = 3800 ft.

TUBB
CANYON RD

SAN PA
RD

S3

BORREGO SPRINGS RD

3600
3700
3900
4200

NECHES CT
QUANAH CT
SPECOS DR

UTICA DR
ANZIO DR
SEWANEE DR
SARASOTO DR
ESQUADRO DR
BORICA CT
OMEGA CT
YNEZ
PATH
HOPI PATH
INCA RD
ZUNI TRL
DESERT DR
DEER HILL TRL
S3
4400
4600
OLEANDER LN
PAMPAS LN
CAROB LN
INDIGO LN

DESERT
LODGE

4800
4900
5000
5100
5200
5400

BORREGO SPRINGS RD

92004

1099

S3

RAMS HILL DR
RAMS HILL RD
LAS CASITAS DR
HUNTER DR
CHUPAROSA LN
SILKTREE LN
FIRE THORN LN
VERBENA LN
DESERT VISTA DR
TERR
GOLF CREST DR
VALERI CT
CARRANDO
ROCA CT
KIT FOX LN
MESQUITE LN
PALO
FONTS POINT DR
FOX POINT
COYOTE LN
CHASE DR
QUAILRIDGE LN

A IRONWOOD LN
B ROSEWOOD LN
C SOBRE CT

Rams Hill Country Club

26
25

ROADRUNNER'S DR

BORREGO HILLS RD
TINAJA LN
TRAIL
SHRINE LN
SLEEPING
CIRCLE DR

DESERT ORIOLE DR
ROCK WREN RD

ROCK WREN RD

20   21   22

29   28   27

32   33   34   35   36

SEE [1100] MAP

4400
4500
4800
5300
5500

T11S
T12S

YAQUI PASS RD

5600

5   4   3   2   1

S3

5800

Anza-borrego Desert State Park

8   9   10   11   12

YAQUI PASS RD

5900

1119

S3

SAN FELIPE CREEK

900   1600   78   2000   78   2200

17   16   15   14   13

CHUCKWALLA WASH
MINE WASH
PINYON WASH

92036

21   22   23   24

RAND MCNALLY

N

A   B   C   D   E   F   G   H   J

1   2   3   4   5   6   7

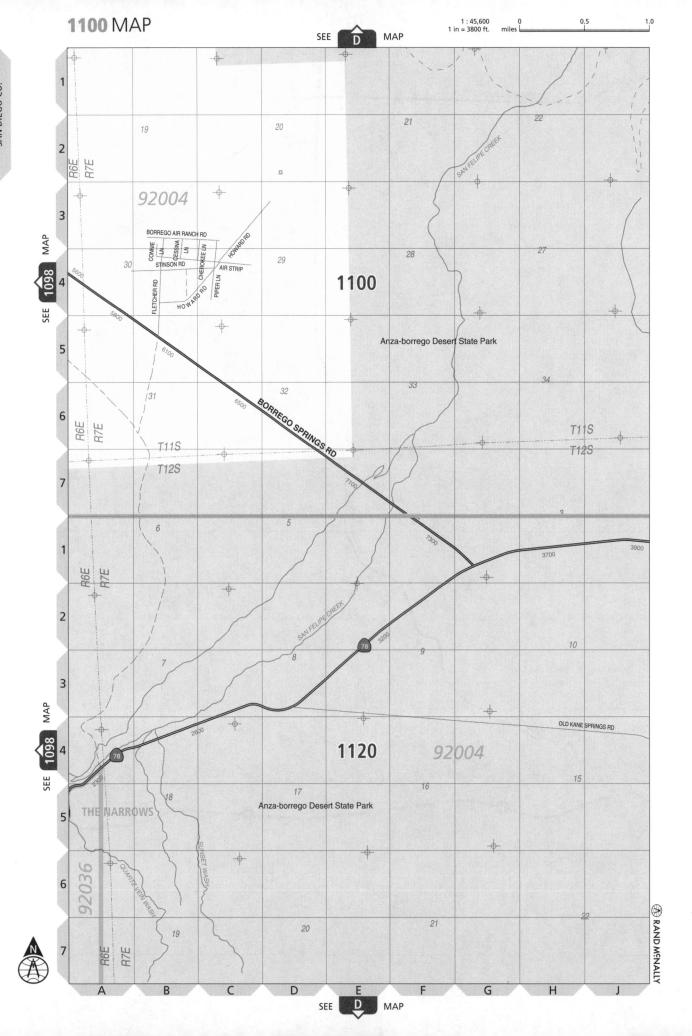

SAN DIEGO CO.

1 : 45,600
1 in = 3800 ft.   miles

0   0.5   1.0

SEE ▲ D MAP

R6E
R7E

1

19

20

21

22

SAN FELIPE CREEK

2

92004

SEE ◇ 1098 MAP

3

BORREGO AIR RANCH RD

CONNIE LN   CESSNA LN   CHEROKEE LN   HOWARD RD

STINSON RD   AIR STRIP

FLETCHER RD   HOWARD RD   PIPER LN

30

29

28

27

5600

4

1100

5900

5

6100

Anza-borrego Desert State Park

31

6500

32

33

34

BORREGO SPRINGS RD

6

R6E
R7E

T11S

T11S

T12S

T12S

7

7100

7

SEE ◇ 1098 MAP

6

5

7300

3

1

3700

3900

R6E
R7E

2

SAN FELIPE CREEK

7

8

78 3200

9

10

3

OLD KANE SPRINGS RD

2600

4

1120

92004

78

THE NARROWS

2300

18

17

16

15

5

Anza-borrego Desert State Park

92036

QUARTZ VEIN WASH

SUNSET WASH

6

19

20

21

22

R6E
R7E

N

7

A   B   C   D   E   F   G   H   J

SEE ▽ D MAP

RAND McNALLY

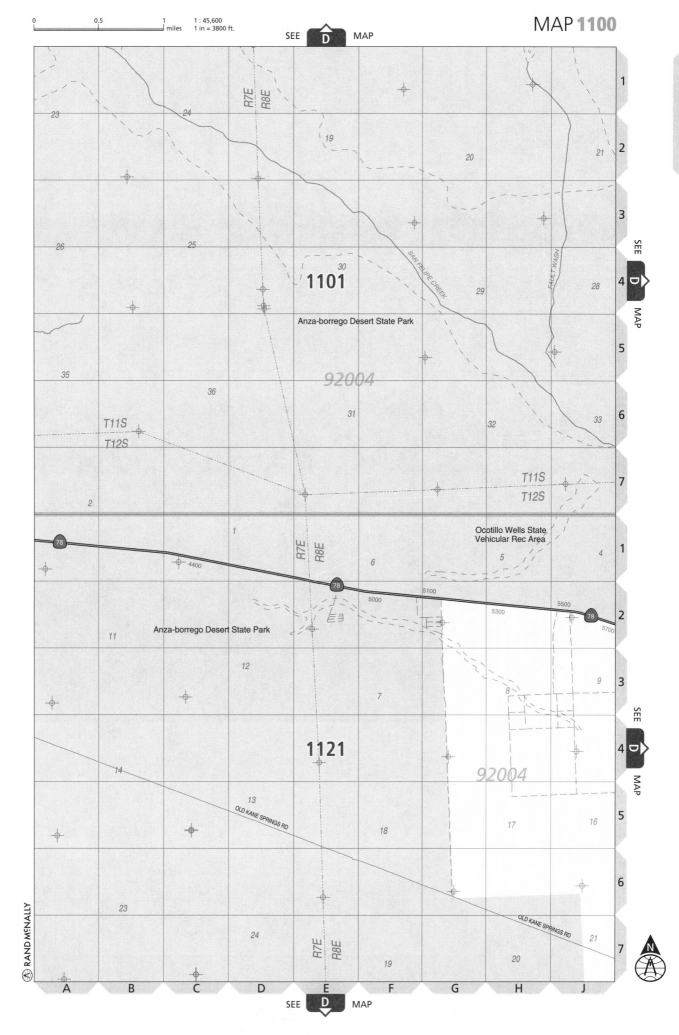

MAP **1100**

0   0.5   1   1 : 45,600
miles   1 in = 3800 ft.

SAN DIEGO CO.

R7E
R8E

23

24

19

20

21

1

2

26

25

30

1101

Anza-borrego Desert State Park

SAN FELIPE CREEK

29

FAULT WASH

28

SEE **D** MAP

3

4

35

36

92004

31

32

33

5

6

T11S
T12S

2

T11S
T12S

7

1

Ocotillo Wells State
Vehicular Rec Area

R7E
R8E

78

6

5

4

1

4400

78

5000

5100

5300

5500
5700

78

2

11

Anza-borrego Desert State Park

12

9

7

8

3

1121

92004

SEE **D** MAP

4

14

13

OLD KANE SPRINGS RD

18

17

16

5

23

24

R7E
R8E

OLD KANE SPRINGS RD

6

19

20

21

7

A   B   C   D   E   F   G   H   J

RAND McNALLY

N

SEE 1085 MAP

1:22,800
1 in = 1900 ft.

miles   0   0.25   0.5

SAN DIEGO CO.

SEE D MAP

PACIFIC OCEAN

A   B   C   D   E

1

2

3

4

5

6

7

N

RAND M°NALLY

SEE D MAP

Oceanside
92054

0   0.25   0.5   1:22,800
miles   1 in = 1900 ft.

1

2

3

PACIFIC OCEAN

SEE 1106 MAP

4

5

6

7

RAND MCNALLY

E   F   G   H   J

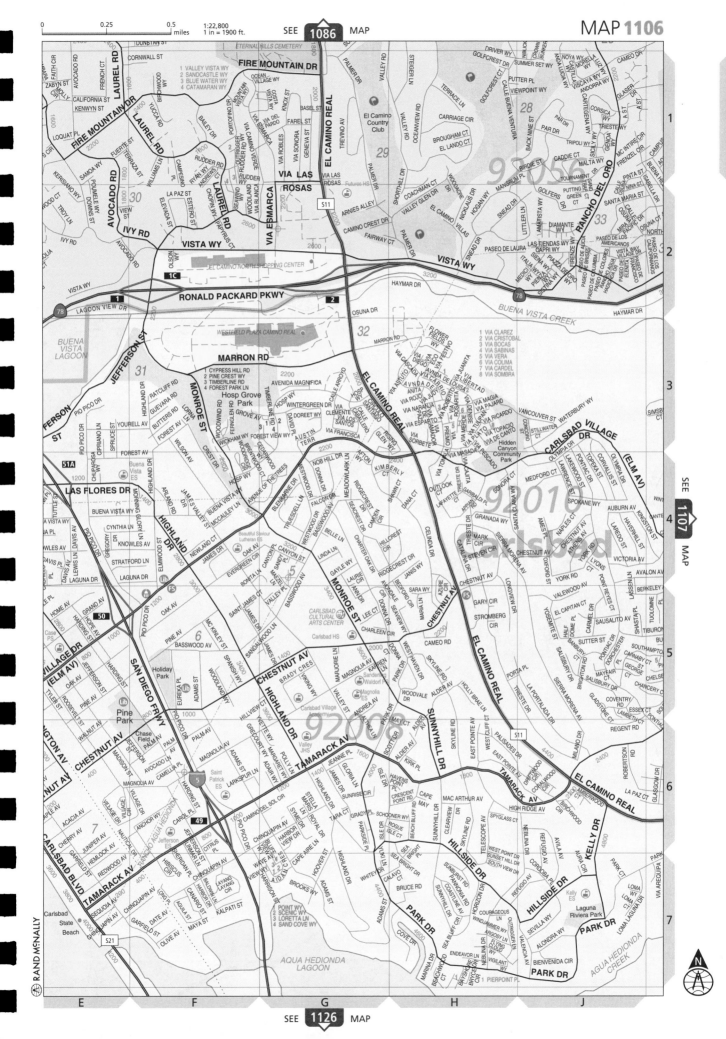

MAP 1106

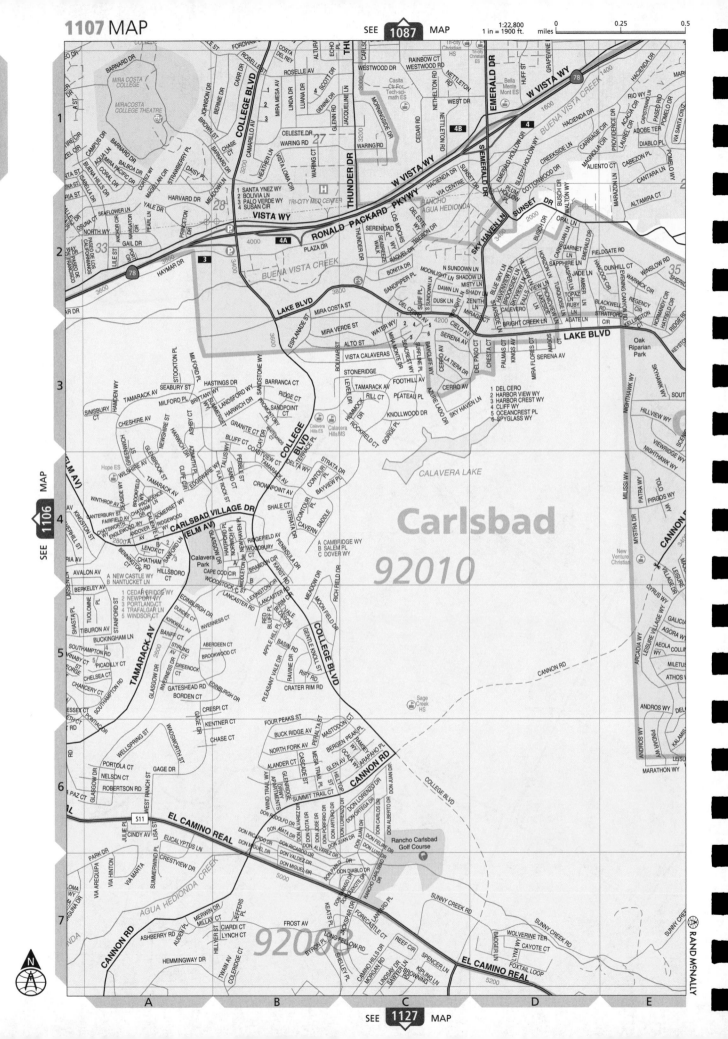

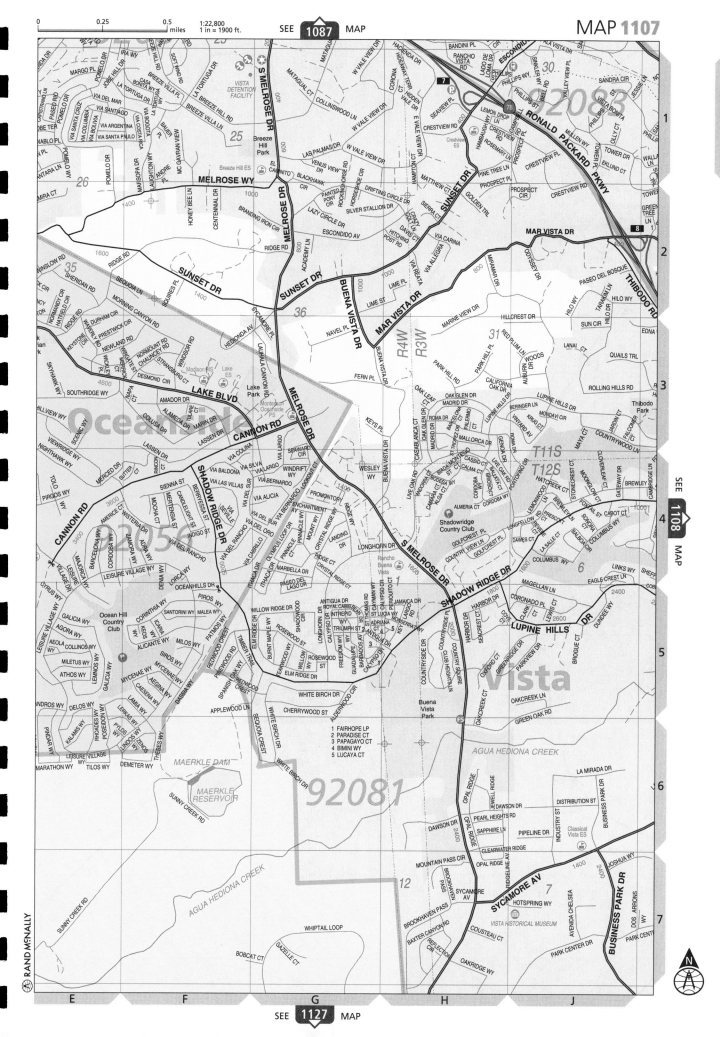

MAP 1107

SAN DIEGO CO.

SEE 1108 MAP

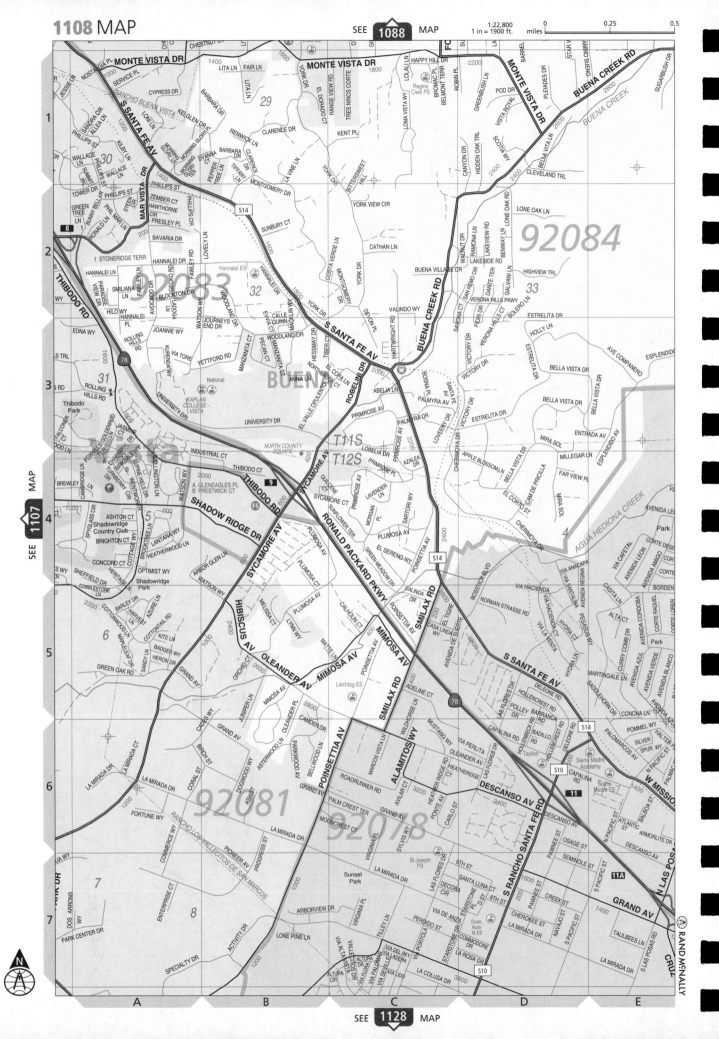

SEE 1088 MAP

1:22,800
1 in = 1900 ft.

miles   0   0.25   0.5

SAN DIEGO CO.

92084

92083

BUEN

VISTA

92081   92078

SEE 1107 MAP

N

RAND MCNALLY

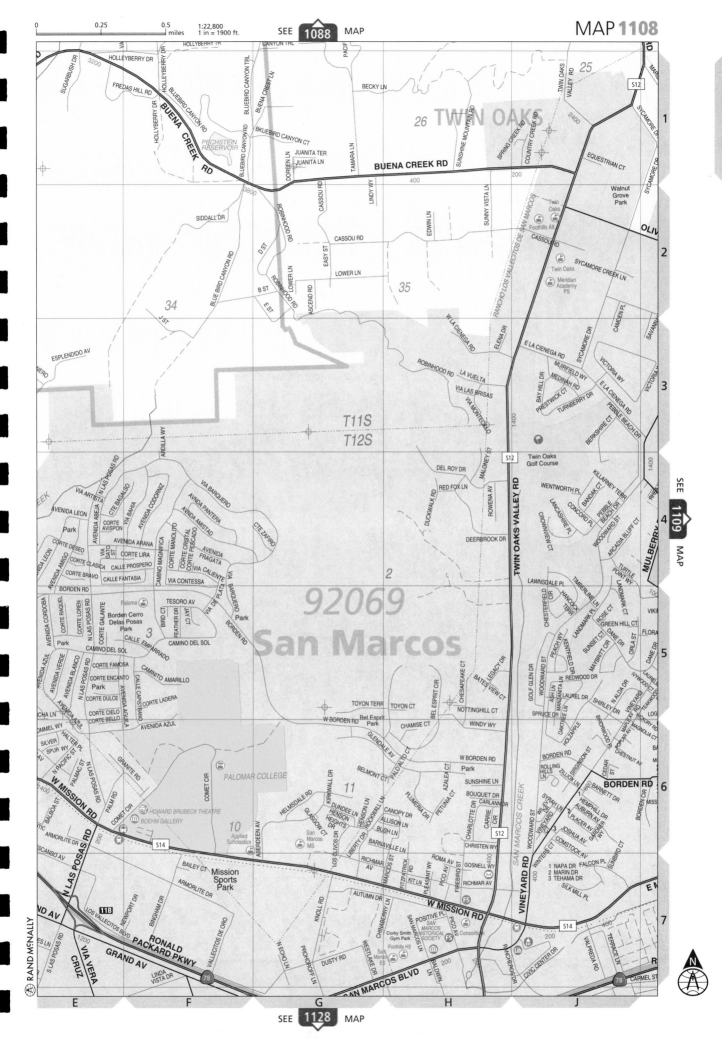

MAP **1108**

SAN DIEGO CO.

SEE ⬇ **1128** MAP

92069
San Marcos

SEE 1089 MAP

1:22,800
1 in = 1900 ft.

miles   0   0.25   0.5

SAN DIEGO CO.

SEE 1108 MAP

RAND McNALLY

A   B   C   D   E

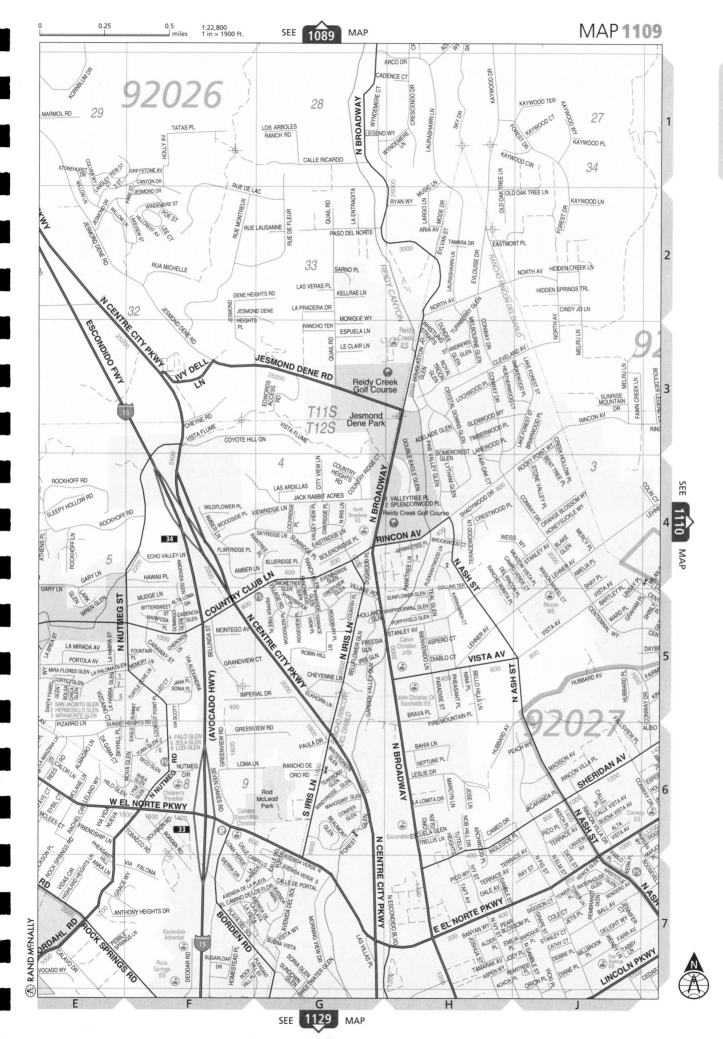

1:22,800
1 in = 1900 ft.

0   0.25   0.5
miles

27

26

25

DALEY RANCH PARK

34

35

36

92026

SEE **1109** MAP

T11S
T12S

RINCON AV

BOULDER LEGEND LN

FAWN CREEK LN

RINCON AV

COLIN CT

LEHNER AV

Dixon Lake Recreation Area

DIXON RESERVOIR

Mayflower Dog Pa

3

1 BULLRUSH GLEN
2 NORMANDY GLEN

LA HONDA DR

DUBLIN LN

GLASGOW LN

1600

STEVENS PL

MACNAUGHTON LN

FIRETHORN GLEN
BUCKSKIN GLEN
MAVERICK GLEN

MADRONE
GLEN

VISTA VERDE WY

ALAMEDA GN

SEDONA GN

AUDUBON GLEN

VINTAGE PL

2

TRIJULLO TERR

BRIDGE LN

DIPPON LN

Escondido

MURCOTT WY

BUQUI LIME LN

RANGPUR
CT

BURNET DR

CHA

MILAN GN

LORETO GLEN
CENTURY WY

GILMORE WY

CHARLOTTA WY

CENTENNIAL WY

ROSADA GLEN

SHERIDAN PL

FIESTA GLEN

SKYVIEW
GLEN

ZACHARY GLEN

CAMPO PL

HERMANS

VIA HONDITA

A STONEYBRAE WY
B FORTUNELLA CT
C ALTA CAMINO CT

A
B
C

STONEYBRAE PL

EL NORTE HILLS PL

12

GRAHAM PL

SHINLY

LAURA DR

JEREMY LN

ERINS PL

DREW
GLEN

ENTRADA
GLEN

JAFFA CT

PONDEROSA CT

EAGLES NEST GLN

SPRINGIME WY

RED ALDER PL

PRAIRIESTONE

NORTE VILLA WY

FIELDBROOK PL

DIMAIO WY

OAKWOOD
CREEK
WY

OAKSTONE CREEK PL

OAKWOOD CREEK PL

BERKSHIRE
PL

JACK CREEK PL

JACKS CREEK RD

KEY LIME

MORNING WALK CT

ROSEGLEN CT

DAYBREAK PL

FAIRMOUNT PL

CARRIZO PL

ALANA

APACHE
GLEN

TIMBER
WY

SKYVIEW
GLEN

ACORN GLEN

WOODLAND GLEN

GREENWAY
RISE

DREW RD

PUEBLO GLEN

LA HONDA DR

HONEYBELL LN

MINNEOLA CT

E WASHINGTON AV

KINGS WY

TIBIDABO DR

RIMROCK DR

MIMOSA CT

ALTA VISTA WY

NIGHTINGALE PL

E EL NORTE PKWY

11

RED
BLUSH RD

E MISSION

HAMLIN
CT

**E EL NORTE
PKWY**

STAR

PUMELO

CAMERON PL

2800

CONWAY DR

ESPERANZA WY

DOLORE PL

STANLEY WY

VISTA VERDE WY

SHERIDAN AV

DAISY ST

PAULA WY

GALE ST

BELKNAP WY

KINGS RD

PADDY

STANLEY WY

ASCENSION
Evangelical

E LINCOLN AV

PAULA ST

MARK AV

LEE ST

STEWART

FOOTBRIDGE

HOLLY AV

RUBY CT

JONATHON

AMYS PL

O'BRIAN PL

TROVITA CT

ALTA MEADOW LN

MALIBU PL

JUSTIN WY

DERRINGER PL

IONA CT

GEISE CT

ALBERT CT

WANEK RD

AMOR
PL

HOLLYHOCK AV

ALPINE

MARJORIE AV

1600

STANLEY WY

THOMAS WY

DONALD WY

IRIS WY

GOLDENROD ST

FERN ST

ERICA ST

FERN ST

VIRGINIA ST

MEDFORD

MAYWOOD AV

WALTON AV

HILLWARD ST

PITMAN ST

KIMBERLY PL

LINDA CT

CAMPBELL AV

WHITE OAK PL

MYRTLE WOOD

LAS BR
DR

PECA

ROSA CT

SOLEDAD CT

ANAME

MON

CONWAY DR

ALPINE

AMALFI PL

PEDRO ROSENO AV

CLEO CT

CLEO CT

VIA LOMITA

CAMELLIA ST

DAISY ST

1800

DAISY ST

MATTHEW

VIA VENETO

CACTUS

WILSON PL

TAYLOR PL

JEFFERSON AV

E WASHINGTON AV

E MISSION AV

N CITRUS ST

IVY

GLEN
MEADOW

CONWAY GLEN

DEVONSHIRE GLEN

ASHBURTON GLEN

NANTUCKET

MANTLAKE

HAWTHORN GLEN

2600

E VALLEY PKWY

FALCONER RD

BELFAST GLEN

BEAR VALLEY PKWY

GRANGER AV

SORRENTO

MANZANITA AV

KENT AV

CONWAY AV

VIEW POINTE AV

BRIDGEPORT ST

Escondido
Christian School

Rose
City

ERICA ST

FERN ST

DAISY ST

ERICA ST

GOLDENROD ST

BEGONIA ST

CAMELLIA ST

600

HOLLY AV

BOXWOOD
GLEN

E WEATHERBY AV

SWANSEA GLEN

CAMDEN GLEN

S6

WORCESTER
GLEN

ORLEANS

DARDANELLE

ENCANTO GN

N HAYDEN DR

2400

JODY

El Norte
Park

SIGGSON AV

HOOVER ST

MARJORIE AV

KENT AV

STANLEY WY

HARDING ST

MAGNOLIA AV

YORK AV

E LINCOLN AV

PEARL PL

SUMAC WY

OLEANDER PL

ASTER ST

1600

BEGONIA ST

DAISY ST

CAMELLIA ST

2000

INDIAN

JEFFERSON AV

E VALLEY PKWY

N CITRUS AV

200

SAPPHIRE GN

OPAL GN

CRESSEN GN

AUBURN GN

FIELDCREST GN

MEADOWLARK LN

DANIEL

ALGIERS LN

JED
RD

LO CAS

ADOREE GN

HEATHER PL

ORLEANS AV

RAND McNALLY

N NASH ST

N ROSE ST

N MIDWAY DR

E LINCOLN AV

Pioneer
ES

KERN PL

ROOSEVELT ST

ARMSTRONG ST

HOOVER ST

SANTA MARTHA GLEN

AWAN GLEN

MAGNOLIA AV

YORK AV

BUCHANAN ST

RONDA PL

MILLS PL

WILSON ST

WABASH ST

MILLS ST

ASTER ST

JEFFERSON AV

CROFTON ST

BECONIA ST

ANIZA PL

DAWN PL

1800

Escondido
Charter HS

Heritage K-8
Charter ES

P

S6

Lib

P

QUARRY GLEN

SAPPHIRE GN

OBSIDIAN GN

DIAMOND GN

AGATE

ONYX GN

TOPAZ

VILLA

N NASH ST

LN PKWY

JENNIFER

ABBY
WY

BEVERLY WY

CEDAR WY

MILANE LN

SANDER
CT

MONTROS

GROVE PARK

MC KINLEY AV

TAYLOR PL

JEFFERSON AV

THO WINH

1600

ASTER ST

Washington
Park

ESCONDIDO CREEK

PALOMAR
COLLEGE

DIAMOND GN

A   B   C   D   E

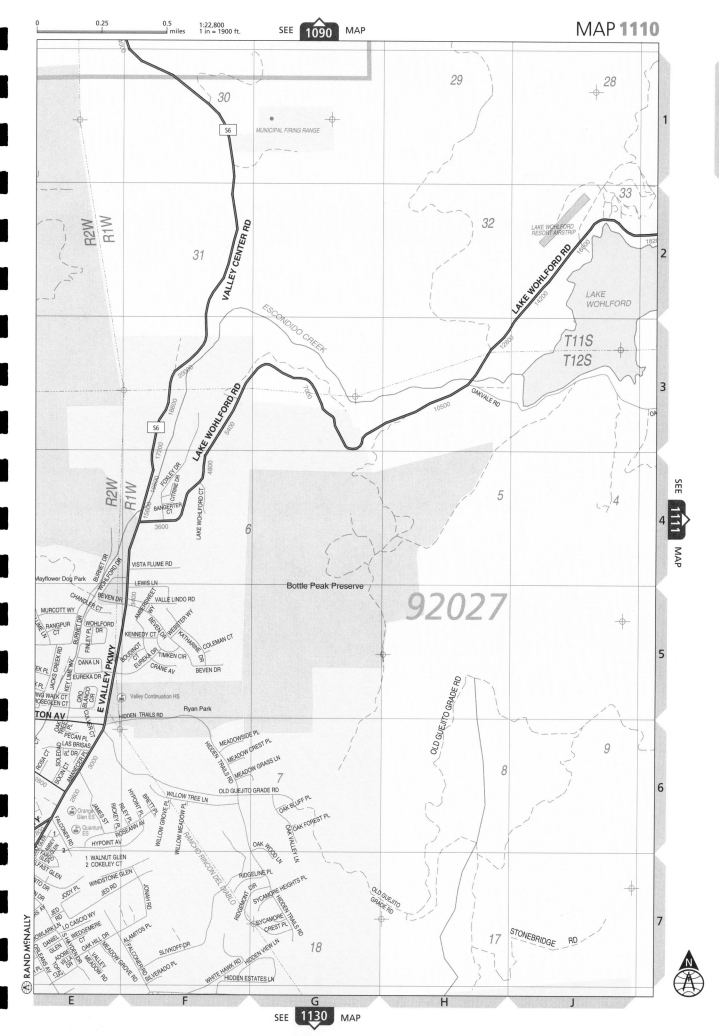

MAP 1110

SAN DIEGO CO.

0   0.25   0.5
miles
1:22,800
1 in = 1900 ft.

29   28

30

S6

MUNICIPAL FIRING RANGE

R2W R1W

31

32

33

LAKE WOHLFORD RESORT AIRSTRIP

VALLEY CENTER RD

LAKE WOHLFORD RD
16600   1820

14200

LAKE
WOHLFORD

ESCONDIDO CREEK

12800

T11S
T12S

20000

S6

18600

LAKE WOHLFORD RD

7000

OAKVALE RD

10500

3
OA

17200

5400

4800

R2W R1W

FOXLEY DR

CITRINE DR

BANGERTER CT

15600
16600

LAKE WOHLFORD CT

3600

5   4

6

SEE 1111 MAP

BURNET DR

WOHLFORD DR

VISTA FLUME RD

Mayflower Dog Park

LEWIS LN

Bottle Peak Preserve

92027

BEVEN DR

CHANDLER CT

VALLE LINDO RD

MURCOTT WY

3400

AMBERSWEET WY

RANGPUR CT

LIME LN

WOHLFORD DR

BURNET DR

FINLEY PL

KENNEDY CT

BEVEN DR

WEBSTER WY

KATHARINE DR

COLEMAN CT

JACKS CREEK RD

KEY LIME WY

DANA LN

EUREKA DR

BOUDINOT CT

EUREKA DR

TIMKEN CIR

CRANE AV

BEVEN DR

5

ING WALK CT

ROSEGLEN CT

ORO BLANCO CIR

E VALLEY PKWY

Valley Continuation HS

TON AV

OAK CREEK PL

HIDDEN TRAILS RD

Ryan Park

PECAN PL

LAS BRISAS

PL DR

ROSA CT

SOCIN CT

SOLEDAD

3000

2800

ANANECER PL

MEADOWSIDE PL

HIDDEN TRAILS RD

MEADOW CREST PL

MEADOW GRASS LN

7

8   9

6

WILLOW TREE LN

BRETT PL

HYPOINT PL

RILEY PL

RICKEY PL

JAMES ST

Orange Glen ES

Quantum ES

ROSEANN AV

HYPOINT AV

OLD GUEJITO GRADE RD

WILLOW GROVE PL

WILLOW MEADOW PL

OAK BLUFF PL

OAK FOREST PL

OAK VALLEY LN

OLD GUEJITO GRADE RD

FALCONER RD

1
2

1 WALNUT GLEN
2 COKELEY CT

OAK WOOD LN

RANCHO RINCON DEL DIABLO

WINDSTONE GLEN

JODY PL

JED RD

JONAH RD

RIDGELINE PL

SYCAMORE HEIGHTS PL

RIDGEMONT CIR

HIDDEN TRAILS RD

OLD GUEJITO GRADE RD

7

JED RD

LO CASCIO WY

DANIEL

WEDGEMERE CT

OAK HILL DR

MEADOW GROVE RD

ALAMITOS PL

FALCONERO RD

SYCAMORE CREST PL

17

STONEBRIDGE RD

LOWLARK LN

GLEN

HAVENDAIR DR

VILLA

SLIVKOFF DR

SILVERADO PL

WHITE HAWK RD

HIDDEN VIEW LN

18

ORLEANS CT

MEADOW RD

MEADOW RD

HIDDEN ESTATES LN

RAND MCNALLY

E   F   G   H   J

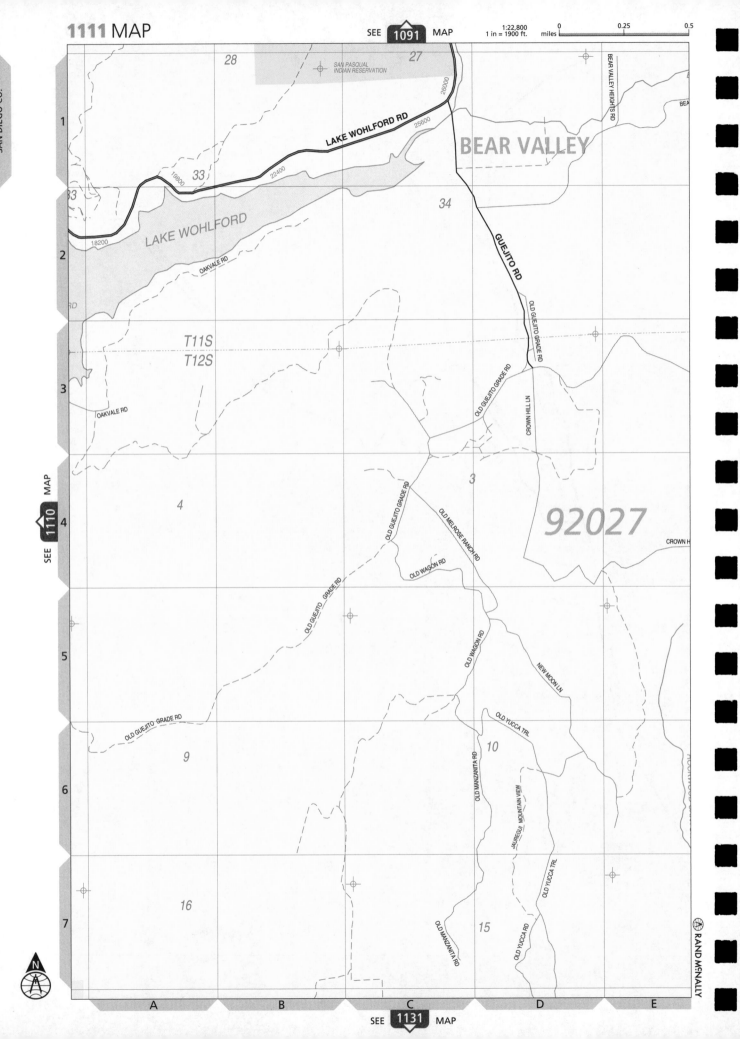

SEE 1091 MAP

1:22,800
1 in = 1900 ft.

miles
0   0.25   0.5

SAN DIEGO CO.

28

27

SAN PASQUAL
INDIAN RESERVATION

LAKE WOHLFORD RD

25600

26000

BEAR VALLEY HEIGHTS RD

BEAR

1

BEAR VALLEY

33

22400

19800

33

18200

LAKE WOHLFORD

34

GUEJITO RD

2

OAKVALE RD

RD

T11S
T12S

OLD GUEJITO GRADE RD

3

OAKVALE RD

OLD GUEJITO GRADE RD

CROWN HILL LN

3

SEE 1110 MAP

4

92027

OLD GUEJITO GRADE RD

OLD MELROSE RANCH RD

CROWN H

OLD WAGON RD

OLD GUEJITO GRADE RD

5

OLD WAGON RD

NEW MOON LN

OLD YUCCA TRL

OLD GUEJITO GRADE RD

9

OLD MANZANITA RD

10

JAUREGUI MOUNTAIN VIEW

6

16

OLD YUCCA TRL

OLD YUCCA TRL

7

15

OLD MANZANITA RD

OLD YUCCA RD

N

RAND McNALLY

A   B   C   D   E

SEE 1131 MAP

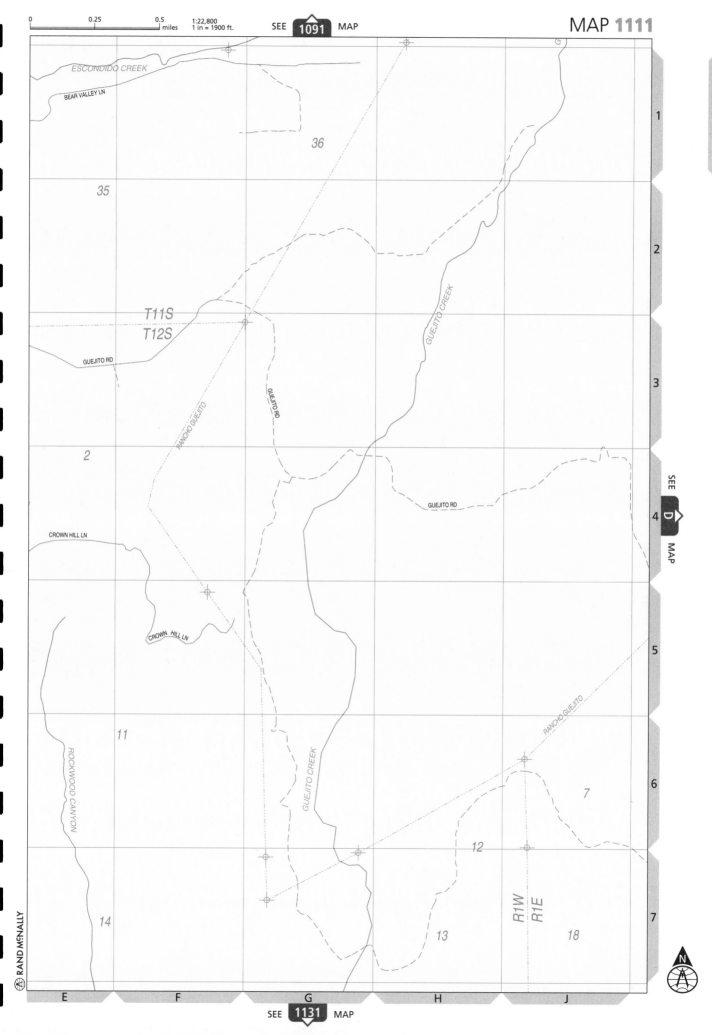

MAP **1111**

SAN DIEGO CO.

0   0.25   0.5
miles
1:22,800
1 in = 1900 ft.

ESCONDIDO CREEK

BEAR VALLEY LN

36

35

T11S
T12S

GUEJITO RD

GUEJITO RD

GUEJITO CREEK

RANCHO GUEJITO

2

GUEJITO RD

CROWN HILL LN

CROWN HILL LN

11

ROCKWOOD CANYON

RANCHO GUEJITO

GUEJITO CREEK

7

12

R1W
R1E

14

13

18

SEE D MAP

1
2
3
4
5
6
7

E   F   G   H   J

RAND M^CNALLY

N

1:22,800
1 in = 1900 ft.   miles

0   0.25   0.5

1

2

3

PACIFIC OCEAN

SEE D MAP

4

5

6

7

A   B   C   D   E

RAND McNALLY

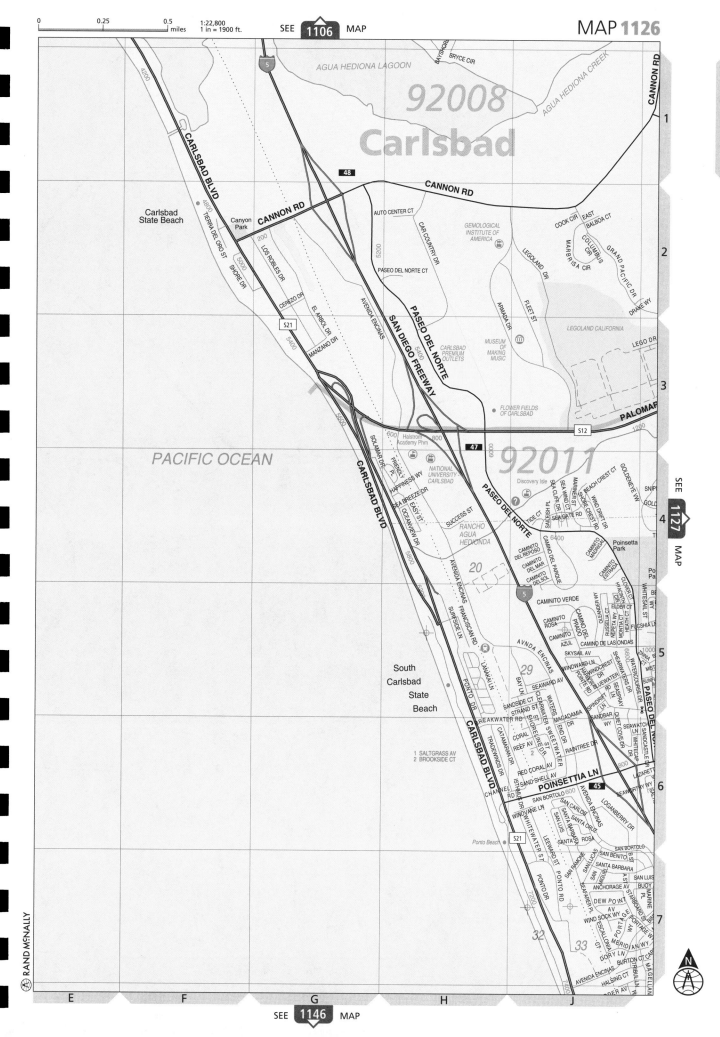

MAP **1126**

SAN DIEGO CO.

0   0.25   0.5
miles
1:22,800
1 in = 1900 ft.

AGUA HEDIONA LAGOON
AGUA HEDIONA CREEK

BAYSHORE
BRYCE CIR

CANNON RD

92008
Carlsbad

CANNON RD

48

CANNON RD

CARLSBAD BLVD

Carlsbad
State Beach

Canyon
Park

CANNON RD

AUTO CENTER CT

CAR COUNTRY DR

GEMOLOGICAL
INSTITUTE OF
AMERICA

COOK CIR   EAST
BALBOA CT

COLUMBUS
CIR

MARBRISA CIR

GRAND PACIFIC DR

LEGOLAND DR

DRAKE WY

TIERRA DEL ORO ST

4800

200

5000

LOS ROBLES DR

SHORE DR

S21

CEREZO DR

EL ARBOL DR

5400

MANZANO DR

AVENIDA ENCINAS

PASEO DEL NORTE CT

PASEO DEL NORTE

SAN DIEGO FREEWAY

5200

5000

ARMADA DR

FLEET ST

MUSEUM
OF
MAKING
MUSIC

LEGOLAND CALIFORNIA

LEGO DR

CARLSBAD
PREMIUM
OUTLETS

FLOWER FIELDS
OF CARLSBAD

PALOMAR

S12

1200

PACIFIC OCEAN

5600

SOLAMAR DR

FRIENDLY PL

HAPPINESS WY

SEA BREEZE DR

EASY ST

OCEANVIEW DR

SUCCESS ST

600   Halstrom   800
Academy Phm

NATIONAL
UNIVERSITY
CARLSBAD

6000

92011

Discovery Isle

?

PASEO DEL NORTE

47

MARINER ST

SEA WIND CT

SEA CLIFF DR

TIDE CT

SEAGATE RD

SEA CREST CT

SHORE CREST RD

WIND DRIFT RD

BEACH CREST CT

GOLDENEYE WY

SNIPI

GOLD

CARLSBAD BLVD

RANCHO
AGUA
HEDIONDA

20

AVENIDA ENCINAS

FRANCISCAN RD

SURFSIDE LN

CAMINITO
DEL REPOSO

CAMINITO
DEL MAR

CAMINITO
DELSOL

CAMINITO DEL PARQUE

6400

CAMINITO
MADRELA

CAMINITO
ESTRELLA

Poinsetta
Park

CAMINITO VERDE

5

CAMINITO
ROSA

CAMINITO
AZUL

CAMINO DEL PRADO

CLOVER CT

HYACINTH WY

GLENRIDGE WY

ELDER CT

RUSSELIA CT

NEPETA WY

JASMINE LN

WHITESAIL ST

FUCHSIA LN

Po
Pa

1000

CAMINO DE LAS ONDAS

SKYSAIL AV

AVNDA ENCINAS

WINDWARD LN

WINDCREST
DR

PONTE RD

SHEARWATERS DR

WATERCOURSE DR

600

SANDERLING

SUNF

SEAL

MIST

South
Carlsbad
State
Beach

29

BAY LN

SEAWARD AV

WATERS
END
DR

FARMER RD

HARBOR

BLUEWATER

SPINDRIFT
LN

SEASPRAY

QUIET COVE DR

SEAWATCH LN

WHITECAP

SANDCASTLE LN

PASEO DEL NOR

PONTO DR

LANIKAI LN

SANDSIDE CT

STRAND ST

CORAL

REEF AV

CLEARWATER ST

SHORELINE DR

SWEETWATER
ST

MAGADAMIA
DR

SANDBAR
WY

RED CORAL AV

SAND SHELL AV

1   SALTGRASS AV
2   BROOKSIDE CT

1

2

BREAKWATER RD

CATAMARAN DR

TRADEWINDS DR

CARLSBAD BLVD

CHANNEL

RD

ISTMUS

SEAWARD WY

POINSETTIA LN

SEAWORTHY WY

45

LIZARETT

800

Ponto Beach

S21

WINDVANE LN

WHITEWATER ST

SAN BORTOLO   600

SAN CARLOS

SAN LUIS

AVENIDA ENCINAS

SANTA CRUZ

SANTA BARBARA

SANTA ROSA

LOGANBERRY DR

LEEWARD ST

SAN BORTOLO

B ST

SAN BENITO

SANTA BARBARA

SAN LUCAS

SAN RAMONE

SAN

HIGBEE

PONTO DR

A ST

SAN LUIS

ANCHORAGE AV

BUOY

SEAFARER PL

DEW POINT
AV

MARINE
PL

STARBOARD PL

PORTAGE WY

ESCALONIA
CT

MERIDIAN WY

DORY LN

BURTON CT

TRIBUNAL

32

33

PORTAGE

WIND SOCK WY

AVENIDA ENCINAS

HALSING CT

MAGELLAN

DER AV

7200

RAND McNALLY

E   F   G   H   J

N

SEE ◁ **1127** MAP ▷

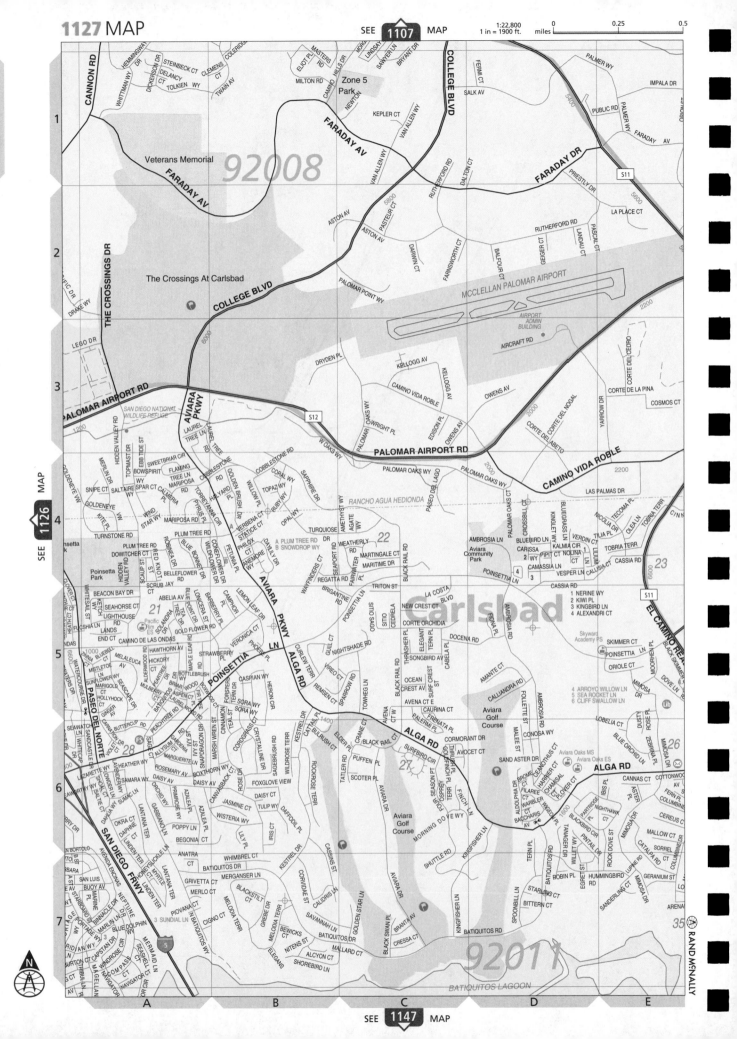

SAN DIEGO CO.

1:22,800
1 in = 1900 ft.

0   0.25   0.5
miles

92008

Veterans Memorial

FARADAY AV

The Crossings At Carlsbad

COLLEGE BLVD

MCCLELLAN PALOMAR AIRPORT

AIRPORT ADMIN BUILDING

AIRCRAFT RD

PALOMAR AIRPORT RD

AVIARA PKWY

San Diego National Wildlife Refuge

PALOMAR AIRPORT RD

CAMINO VIDA ROBLE

Carlsbad

AVIARA PKWY

POINSETTIA LN

ALGA RD

Poinsetta Park

Aviara Community Park

1 NERINE WY
2 KIWI PL
3 KINGBIRD LN
4 ALEXANDRI CT

Aviara Golf Course

Aviara Golf Course

4 ARROYO WILLOW LN
5 SEA ROCKET LN
6 CLIFF SWALLOW LN

ALGA RD

Aviara Oaks MS
Aviara Oaks ES

SAN DIEGO FRWY

PASEO DEL NORTE

92011

BATIQUITOS LAGOON

EL CAMINO REAL

35

RAND MCNALLY

A   B   C   D   E

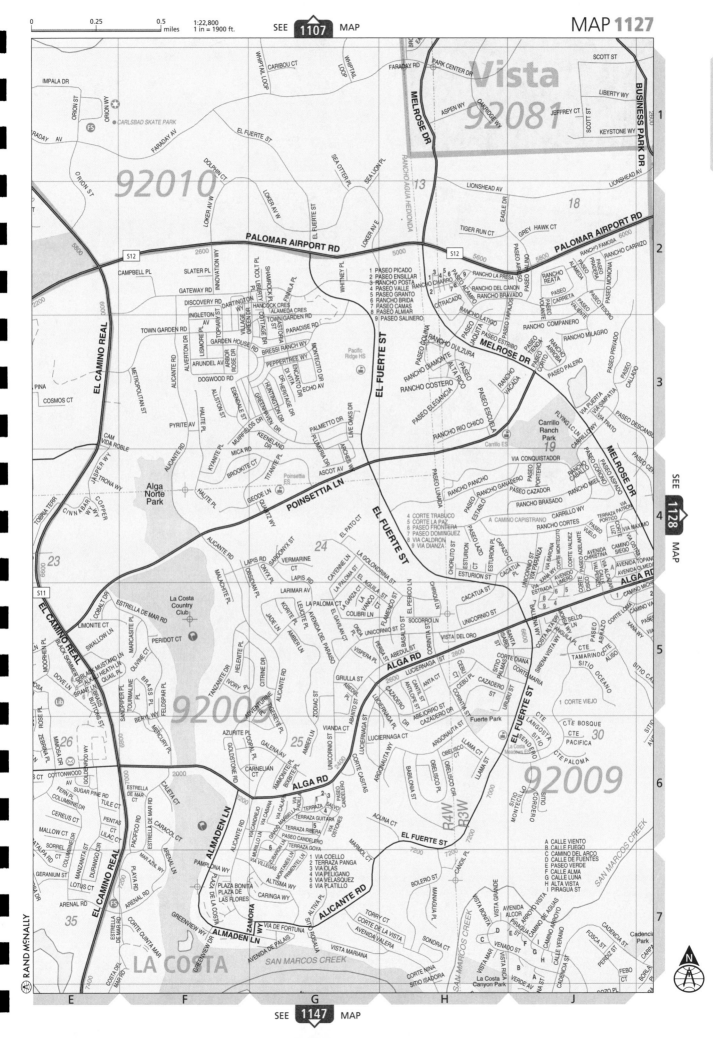

MAP **1127**

1:22,800
1 in = 1900 ft.

Vista
92081

92010

92009

92009

La Costa
Country Club

Alga
Norte
Park

Alga Norte Park

La Costa

Carrillo
Ranch
Park
19

Fuerte Park

La Costa
Canyon Park

RAND McNALLY

PALOMAR AIRPORT RD

MELROSE DR

EL CAMINO REAL

EL FUERTE ST

POINSETTIA LN

ALGA RD

ALMADEN LN

ALICANTE RD

1 PASEO PICADO
2 PASEO ENSILLAR
3 RANCHO POSTA
4 PASEO VALLE
5 PASEO GRANTO
6 RANCHO BRIDA
7 PASEO CAMAS
8 PASEO ALMIAR
9 PASEO SALINERO

4 CORTE TRABUCO
5 CORTE LA PAZ
6 PASEO FRONTERA
7 PASEO DOMINGUEZ
8 VIA CALDRON
9 VIA DIANZA

1 CORTE VIEJO

1 VIA COELLO
2 TERRAZA PANGA
3 VIA OLAS
4 VIA PELIGANO
5 VIA VELASQUEZ
6 VIA PLATILLO

A CALLE VIENTO
B CALLE FUEGO
C CAMINO DEL ARCO
D CALLE DE FUENTES
E PASEO VERDE
F CALLE ALMA
G CALLE LUNA
H ALTA VISTA
I PIRAGUA ST

Pacific
Ridge HS

Carlsbad Skate Park

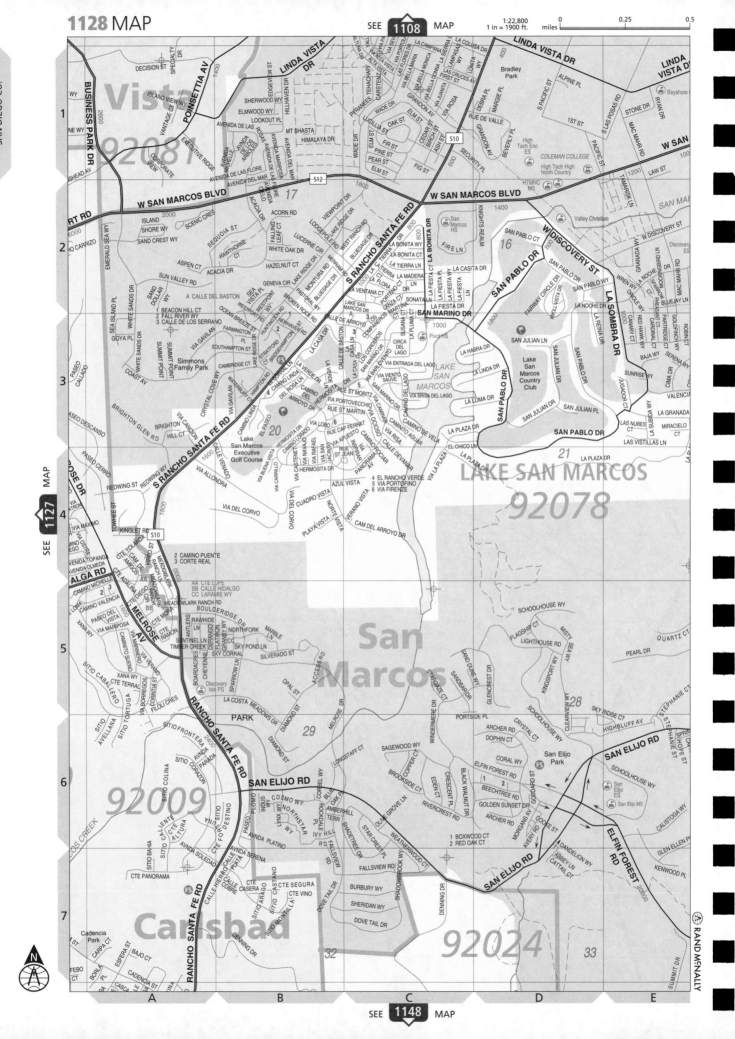

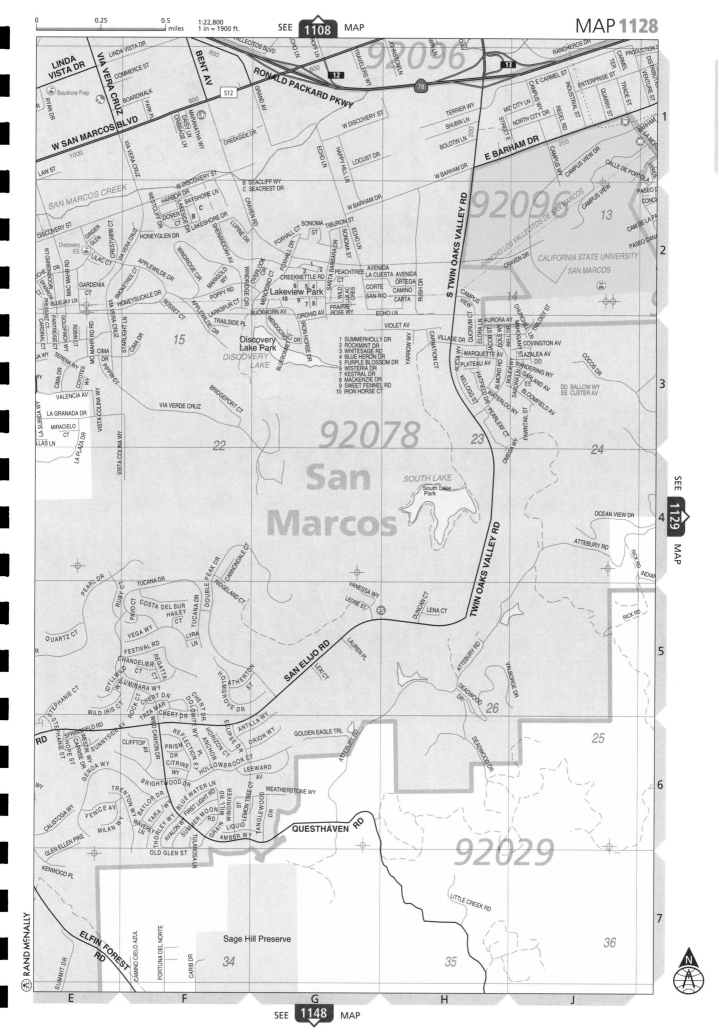

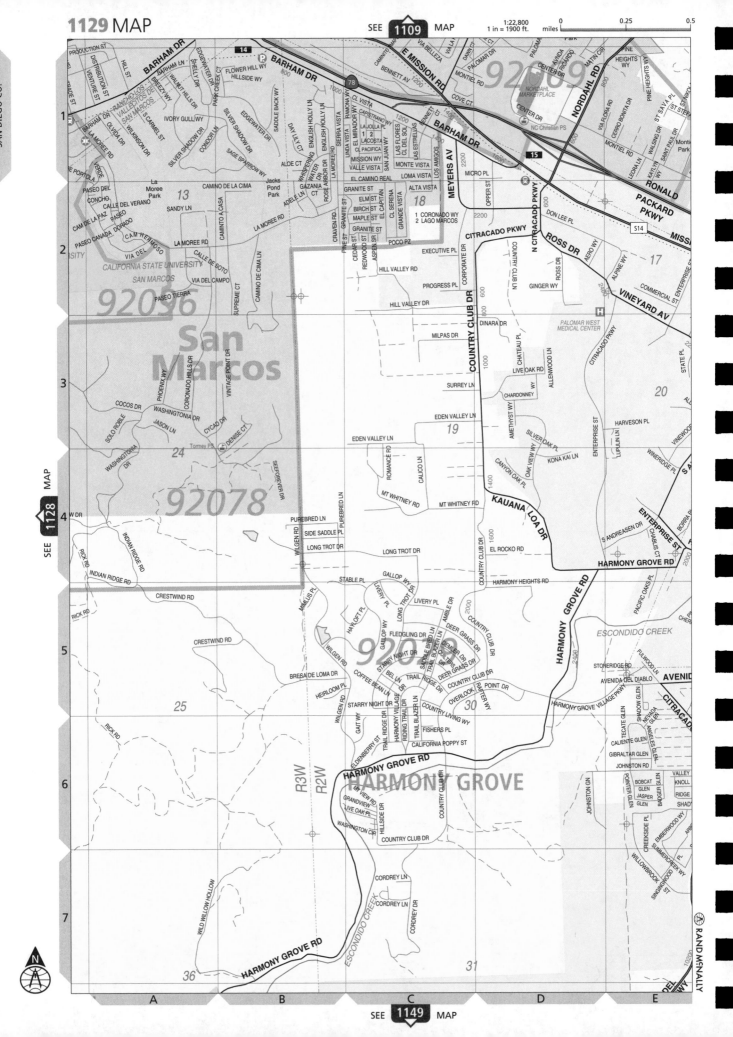

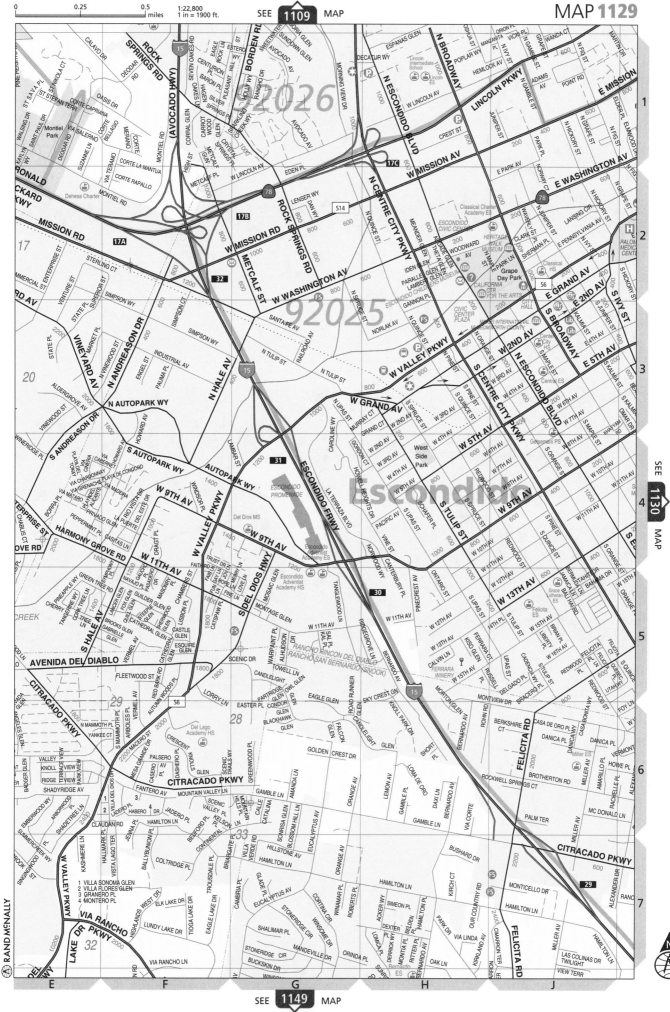

MAP 1129

SAN DIEGO CO.

SEE 1130 MAP

RAND McNALLY

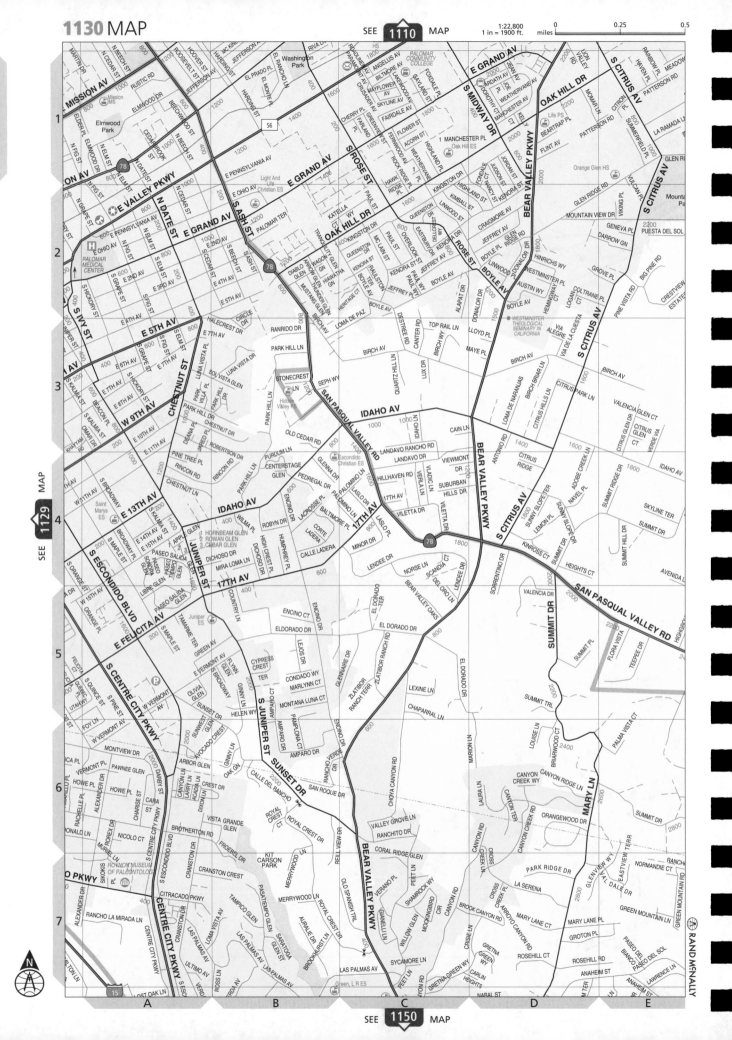

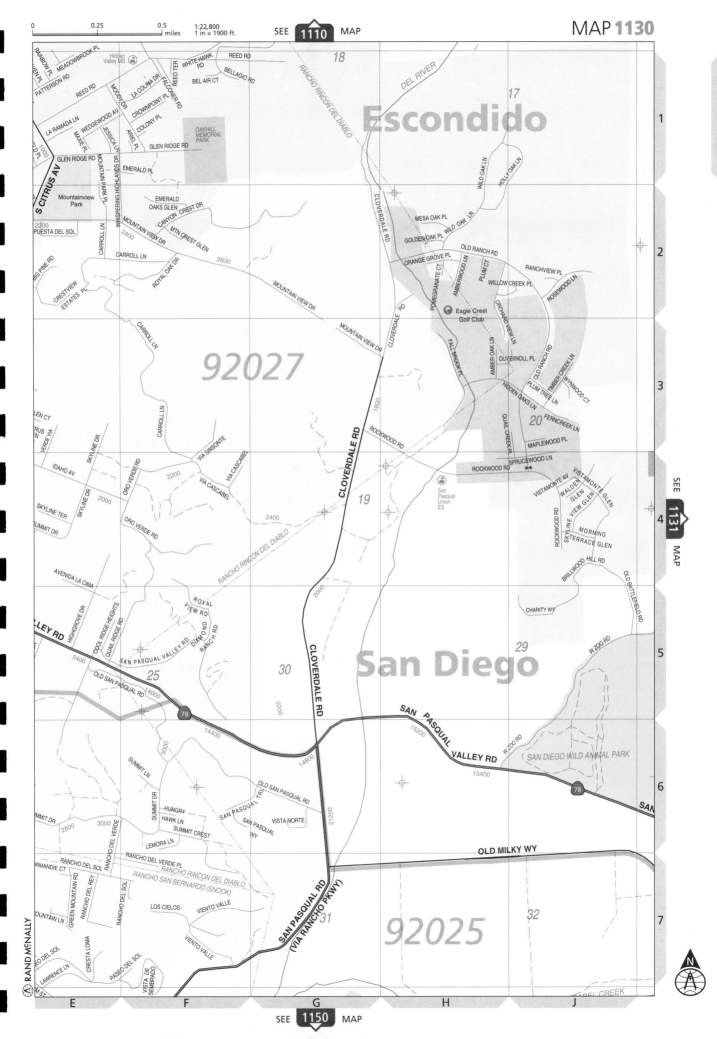

MAP **1130**

SAN DIEGO CO.

0   0.25   0.5
miles
1:22,800
1 in = 1900 ft.

18

17

Escondido

DEL RIVER

WILD OAK LN

HOLLY OAK LN

1

2

MESA OAK PL

GOLDEN OAK PL

WILD OAK LN

OLD RANCH RD

RANCHVIEW PL

ORANGE GROVE PL

AMBERWOOD LN

PLUM CT

WILLOW CREEK PL

ROSEWOOD LN

POMEGRANATE CT

Eagle Crest Golf Club

ORCHARD VIEW LN

AMBER OAK LN

OLIVE KNOLL PL

OLD RANCH RD

TIMBER CREEK LN

WYNWOOD CT

92027

HIDDEN OAKS LN

PLUM TREE LN

FERNCREEK LN

20

QUAIL CREEK PL

MAPLEWOOD PL

3

ROCKWOOD RD

SPRUCEWOOD LN

VISTAMONTE AV

VISTAMONTE GLEN

San Pasqual Union ES

ROCKWOOD RD

WALDEN GLEN

SKYLINE VIEW GLEN

ROCKWOOD RD

MORNING TERRACE GLEN

4

S CITRUS AV

RAINBOW PL

MEADOWBROOK PL

Hidden Valley MS

REED TER

WHITE HAWK RD

REED RD

REED RD

BEL AIR CT

BELLAGIO RD

RANCHO RINCON DEL DIABLO

PATTERSON RD

REED RD

LA COLINA DR

FALCONER RD

MOODY DR

CROWNPOINT PL

OAKHILL MEMORIAL PARK

LA RAMADA LN

WEDGEWOOD AV

MAXIE PL

JESSICA LN

ARIEL PL

COLONY PL

GLEN RIDGE RD

GLEN RIDGE RD

EMERALD PL

Mountainview Park

MOUNTAIN PARK PL

WHISPERING HIGHLANDS DR

EMERALD OAKS GLEN

CANYON CREST DR

PUESTA DEL SOL

CARROLL LN

MOUNTAIN VIEW DR

MTN CREST GLEN

CARROLL LN

MOUNTAIN VIEW DR

CLOVERDALE RD

MOUNTAIN VIEW DR

BIG PINE RD

CRESTVIEW ESTATES PL

ROYAL OAK DR

CARROLL LN

MOUNTAIN VIEW DR

CLOVERDALE RD

GLEN CT

CITRUS VIA GLEN

SKYLINE DR

VIA SINSONTE

VIA CASCABEL

ROCKWOOD RD

IDAHO AV

ORO VERDE RD

VIA CASCABEL

SKYLINE DR

SKYLINE TER

ORO VERDE RD

CLOVERDALE RD

19

SUMMIT DR

AVENIDA LA CIMA

ROYAL VIEW RD

CHARITY WY

BRILLWOOD HILL RD

OLD BATTLEFIELD RD

5

VALLEY RD

HIGHGROVE DR

COOL RIDGE HEIGHTS

QUAIL RIDGE RD

DIAMOND RANCH RD

SAN PASQUAL VALLEY RD

25

OLD SAN PASQUAL RD

30

CLOVERDALE RD

San Diego

29

W ZOO RD

SAN PASQUAL VALLEY RD

W ZOO RD

San Diego Wild Animal Park

78

78

SAN

6

SUMMIT LN

SUMMIT DR

HUNGRY HAWK LN

SUMMIT CREST

LEMORA LN

OLD SAN PASQUAL RD

SAN PASQUAL TRL

SAN PASQUAL WY

VISTA NORTE

OLD MILKY WY

RANCHO DEL SOL

RANCHO DEL VERDE PL

RANCHO DEL VERDE

RANCHO DEL SOL

RANCHO RINCON DEL DIABLO

RANCHO SAN BERNARDO (SNOOK)

NORMANDIE CT

GREEN MOUNTAIN RD

RANCHO DEL REY

RANCHO DEL SOL

LOS CIELOS

VIENTO VALLE

SAN PASQUAL RD (VIA RANCHO PKWY)

31

92025

32

7

MOUNTAIN LN

CRESTA LOMA

PASEO DEL SOL

VIENTO VALLE

VISTA DE SEMBRADO

LAWRENCE LN

PASEO DEL SOL

RAND MCNALLY

CREEK

E   F   G   H   J

N

SEE 1111 MAP

1:22,800
1 in = 1900 ft.

miles

0   0.25   0.5

16

15

OLD WAGON RD

OLD YUCCA TRL

ROCKWOOD RD

BARELIA RD

22

92027

21

ROCKWOOD RD

SEE 1130 MAP

Escondido

ROCKWOOD RD

COPPER CANYON RD

ROCKWOOD RD

OLD BATTLEFIELD RD

ROCKWOOD RD

27

ROCKWOOD CANYON

28

San Diego

29

SAN DIEGO WILD ANIMAL PARK

RK

SAN PASQUAL

SAN DIEGO
ARCHAEOLOGICAL
CENTER

SAN PASQUAL VALLEY RD

SAN PASQUAL VALLEY RD

SANTA YSABELL CREEK

SAN PASQUAL
BATTLEFIELD STATE
HISTORIC PARK

OLD MILKY WY

78

34

92025

33

YSABEL CREEK RD

32

BANDY CANYON RD

RAND McNALLY

K

A   B   C   D   E

SEE 1151 MAP

MAP **1131**

SAN DIEGO CO.

0 0.25 0.5 miles
1:22,800
1 in = 1900 ft.

14

13

18

1

GUEJITO CREEK

23

24

19

R1W
R1E

2

3

ROCKWOOD CANYON

San Pasqual Trails
Open Space

25

30

SEE
D
MAP

4

26

5

SAN PASQUAL CEMETERY

78

31

6

BANDY CANYON RD

SAN PASQUAL VALLEY RD

SANTA YSABEL CREEK

35

ACADEMY RD

36

SAN PASQUAL VALLEY RD

FS
San Pasqual
Academy

78

R1W
R1E

19000

7

RAND M?NALLY

92065

T12S

E   F   G   H   J

N

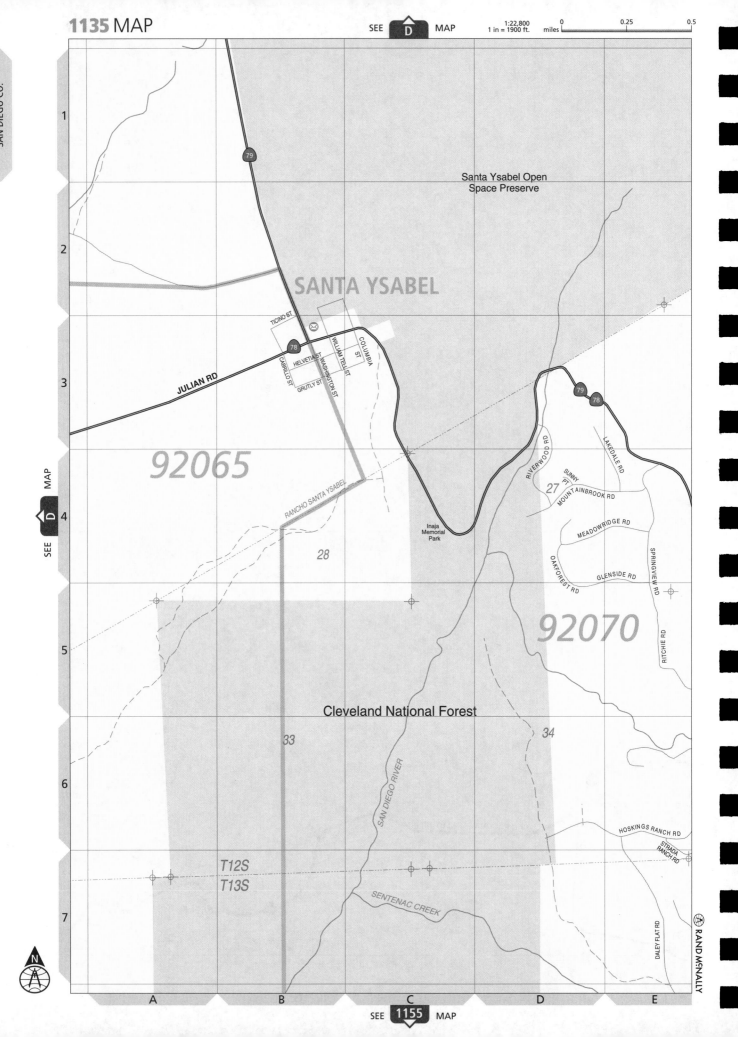

SEE **D** MAP

1:22,800
1 in = 1900 ft.

0   0.25   0.5
miles

SAN DIEGO CO.

1

2

79

Santa Ysabel Open
Space Preserve

SANTA YSABEL

TICINO ST

78

CABRILLO ST

HELVETIA ST

WILLIAM TELL ST

COLUMBIA ST

WASHINGTON ST

GRUTLY ST

3

JULIAN RD

79

78

92065

RANCHO SANTA YSABEL

RIVERWOOD RD

SUNNY PT

27

MOUNTAINBROOK RD

LAKEDALE RD

4

SEE **D** MAP

28

Inaja
Memorial
Park

MEADOWRIDGE RD

OAKFOREST RD

GLENSIDE RD

SPRINGVIEW RD

92070

5

RITCHIE RD

Cleveland National Forest

33

SAN DIEGO RIVER

34

6

HOSKINGS RANCH RD

STRADA RANCH RD

T12S
T13S

7

SENTENAC CREEK

DALEY FLAT RD

N

RAND McNALLY

A   B   C   D   E

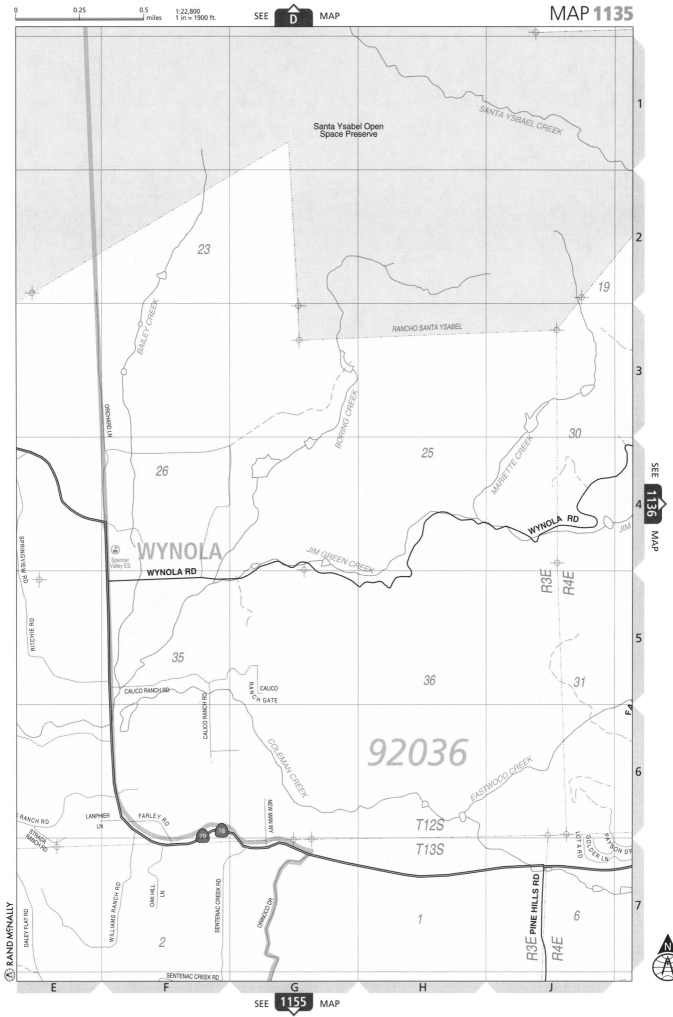

0 0.25 0.5
miles

1:22,800
1 in = 1900 ft.

SAN DIEGO CO.

Santa Ysabel Open
Space Preserve

SANTA YSBAEL CREEK

23

BAILEY CREEK

ORCHARD LN

19

RANCHO SANTA YSABEL

26

BORING CREEK

25

MARIETTE CREEK

30

SEE **1136** MAP

WYNOLA RD

JIM

SPRINGVIEW RD

WYNOLA

Spencer
Valley ES

WYNOLA RD

JIM GREEN CREEK

R3E

R4E

RITCHIE RD

35

36

31

CALICO RANCH RD

CALICO
RANCH GATE

CALICO RANCH RD

COLEMAN CREEK

92036

EASTWOOD CREEK

RANCH RD

LANPHIER
LN

FARLEY RD

NEW MAN WY

79 78

T12S

T13S

LOTA RD

GOLDER LN

PAYSON DR

STRADA
RANCH RD

WILLIAMS RANCH RD

OAK HILL
LN

SENTENAC CREEK RD

ORINOCO DR

PINE HILLS RD

DALEY FLAT RD

2

1

R3E

R4E

6

RAND MCNALLY

SENTENAC CREEK RD

E F G H J

N

SAN DIEGO CO.

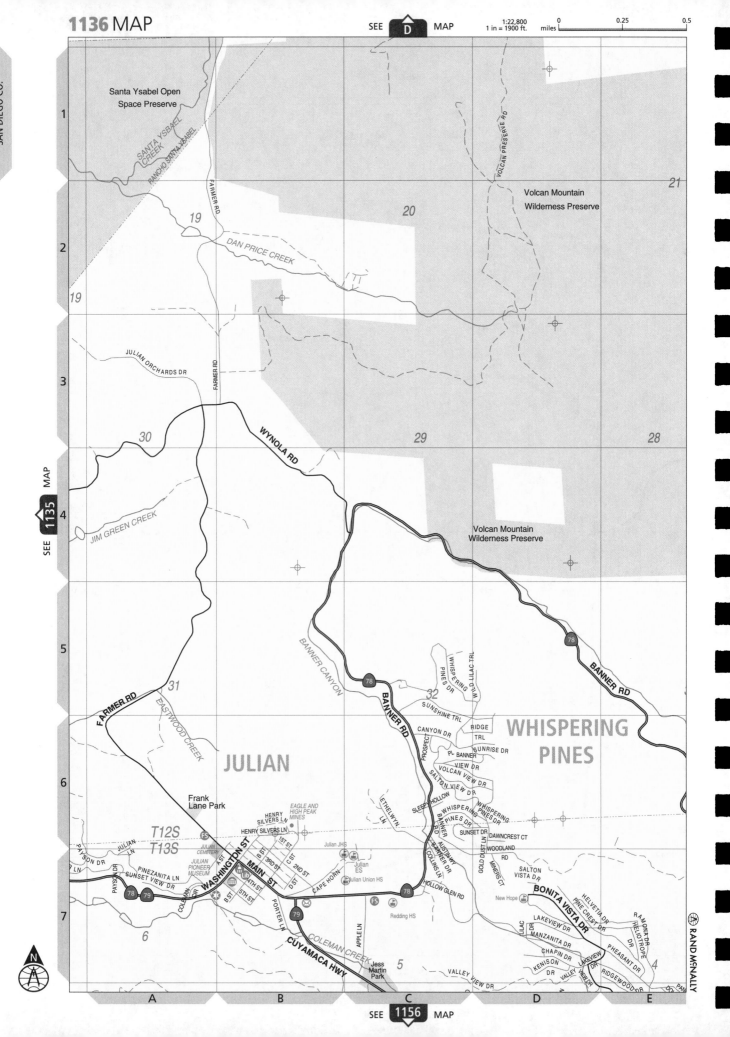

1:22,800
1 in = 1900 ft.

0   0.25   0.5
miles

1

Santa Ysabel Open
Space Preserve

SANTA YSABEL CREEK

RANCHO SANTA YSABEL

FARMER RD

19

VOLCAN PRESERVE RD

21

20

Volcan Mountain
Wilderness Preserve

2

DAN PRICE CREEK

19

3

JULIAN ORCHARDS DR

FARMER RD

30

WYNOLA RD

29

28

SEE **1135** MAP

4

JIM GREEN CREEK

Volcan Mountain
Wilderness Preserve

5

BANNER CANYON

78

78

BANNER RD

WHISPERING
PINES DR

WILD LILAC TRL

32

SUNSHINE TRL

BANNER RD

FARMER RD

31

EASTWOOD CREEK

JULIAN

CANYON DR

RIDGE
TRL

**WHISPERING
PINES**

PROSPECT

BANNER
VIEW DR

PL

GUNRISE DR

VOLCAN VIEW DR

6

Frank
Lane Park

T12S
T13S

HENRY
SILVERS LN

EAGLE AND
HIGH PEAK
MINES

SALTON VIEW DR

ETHELWYN
LN

SLEEPY HOLLOW

BANNER

WHISPERING
PINES DR

WHISPERING
PINES DR

WOODLAND
RD

SUNSET DR

DAWNCREST CT

GOLD DUST LN

MINERS CT

HENRY SILVERS LN

JULIAN
CEMETERY

PAYSON DR

JULIAN
LN

PINEZANITA LN

SUNSET VIEW DR

WASHINGTON ST

MAIN ST

B ST

C ST

1ST ST

3RD ST

2ND ST

D ST

Julian JHS

Julian
ES

CAPE HORN

AUSTIN HWY

COLLINS LN

BANNER RD

SALTON
VISTA DR

BONITA VISTA DR

HELVETIA DR

PINE CREST DR

RAMONA DR

HELIOTROPE

New Hope

LN

78

79

COLEMAN DR

A ST

4TH ST

5TH ST

B ST

PORTER LN

Julian Union HS

78

HOLLOW GLEN RD

FS

Redding HS

LILAC

LAKEVIEW DR

MANZANITA DR

CHAPIN DR

KENISON
DR

PHEASANT DR

VALLEY VIEW DR

LAKEVIEW DR

RIDGEWOOD DR

4

7

JULIAN
PIONEER
MUSEUM

6

79

APPLE LN

COLEMAN CREEK

CUYAMACA HWY

Jess
Martin
Park

5

VALLEY VIEW DR

N

RAND MCNALLY

A   B   C   D   E

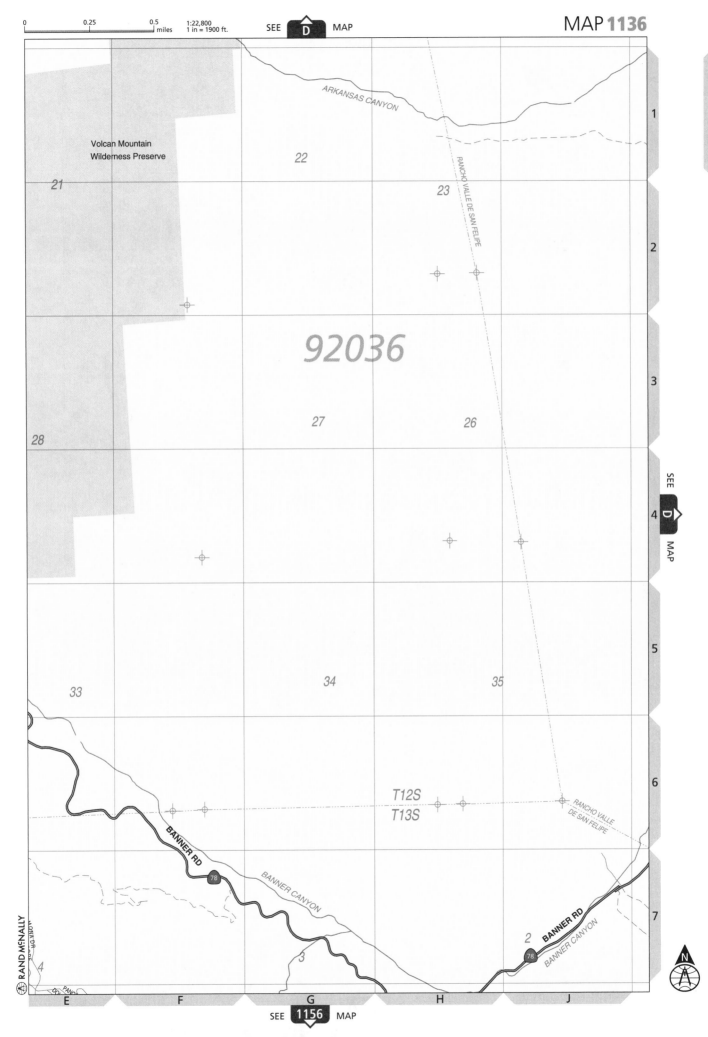

MAP **1136**

SAN DIEGO CO.

0   0.25   0.5 miles   1:22,800
1 in = 1900 ft.

SEE D MAP

ARKANSAS CANYON

Volcan Mountain
Wilderness Preserve

21

22

23

RANCHO VALLE DE SAN FELIPE

1

2

92036

3

28

27

26

SEE D MAP

4

5

33

34

35

6

T12S
T13S

RANCHO VALLE
DE SAN FELIPE

BANNER RD

78

BANNER CANYON

7

2
78

BANNER RD

BANNER CANYON

RAND MCNALLY

4

3

E   F   G   H   J

SEE 1156 MAP

N

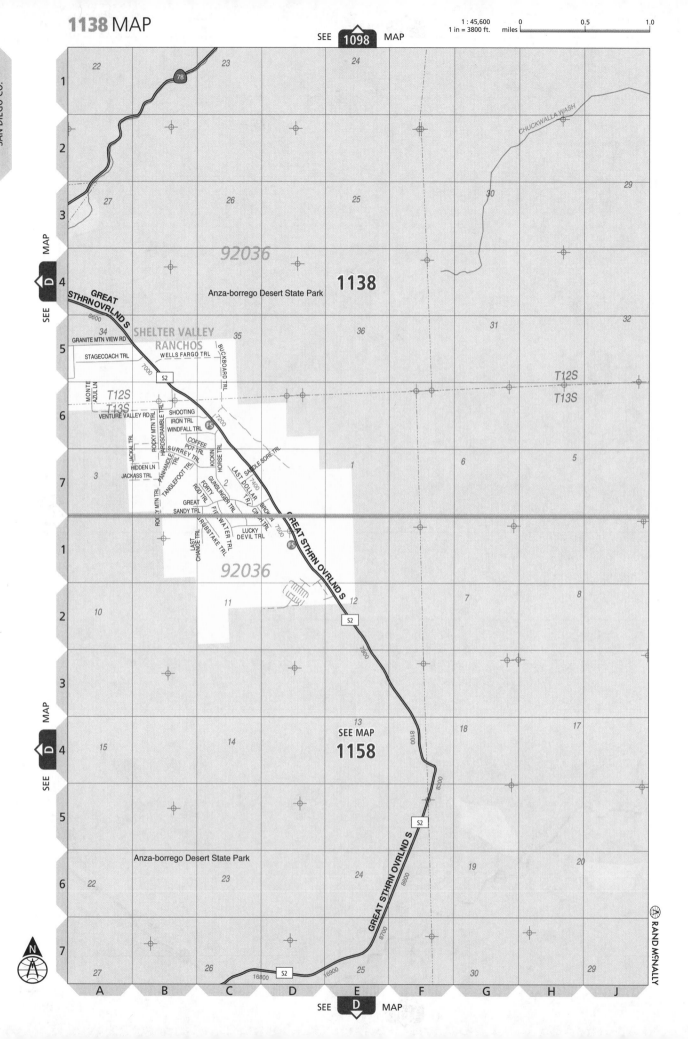

SAN DIEGO CO.

1 : 45,600
1 in = 3800 ft.

miles 0   0.5   1.0

SEE 1098 MAP

22   23   24

78

CHUCKWALLA WASH

27   26   25   30   29

SEE D MAP

92036

1138

Anza-borrego Desert State Park

GREAT STHRN OVRLND S

8600

34   SHELTER VALLEY RANCHOS   35   36   31   32

GRANITE MTN VIEW RD

STAGECOACH TRL   WELLS FARGO TRL   BUCKBOARD TRL

7000   S2   T12S   T13S

MONTE AZUL LN

T12S   T13S

VENTURE VALLEY RD   SHOOTING   IRON TRL   WINDFALL TRL   FS

7200

ROCKY MTN TRL   HARDSCRAMBLE TRL   COFFEE POT TRL   SURREY TRL   KICKIN   HORSE TRL   SADDLE SORE TRL

JACKXL TRL   HIDDEN LN   JACKASS TRL   3   PANHANDLE TRL   TANGLEFOOT TRL   FORTY   ROD TRL   GUNSLINGER TRL   LAST DOLLAR   7400   2   BROWN   1   6   5

ROCKY MTN TRL   GREAT SANDY TRL   FIFE WATER TRL   CH 1 TRL   7500

LAST CHANCE TRL   GRUBSTAKE TRL   LUCKY DEVIL TRL   GREAT STHRN OVRLND S   FS

92036   11   12   7   8

SEE D MAP

10   S2   7600

15   14   13   SEE MAP   18   17

8100   **1158**

8300

Anza-borrego Desert State Park   S2

22   23   24   19   20

8600

GREAT STHRN OVRLND S

8700

27   26   16800   S2   16900   25   30   29

N

RAND MCNALLY

A   B   C   D   E   F   G   H   J

SEE D MAP

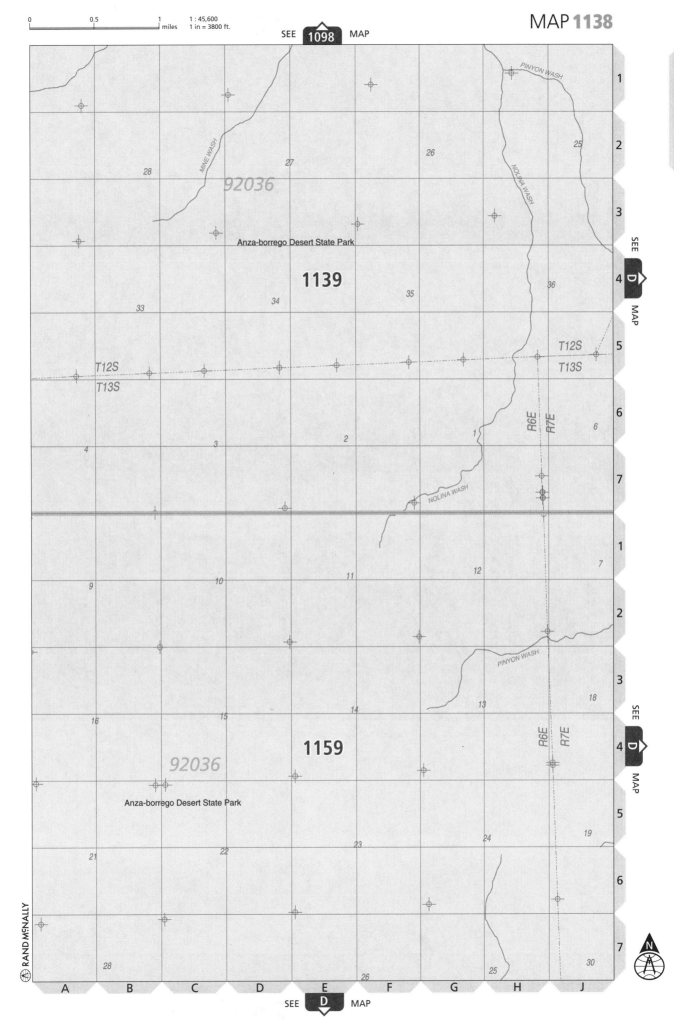

MAP **1138**

SAN DIEGO CO.

0   0.5   1
miles
1 : 45,600
1 in = 3800 ft.

SEE **1098** MAP

PINYON WASH

MINE WASH

92036

28

27

26

25

MOLINA WASH

Anza-borrego Desert State Park

1139

33

34

35

36

SEE **D** MAP

T12S
T13S

T12S
T13S

R6E
R7E

4

3

2

1

6

NOLINA WASH

9

10

11

12

7

16

15

14

13

18

SEE **D** MAP

1159

92036

R6E
R7E

Anza-borrego Desert State Park

PINYON WASH

21

22

23

24

19

RAND M?NALLY

28

26

25

30

N

A

B

C

D

E

F

G

H

J

SEE **D** MAP

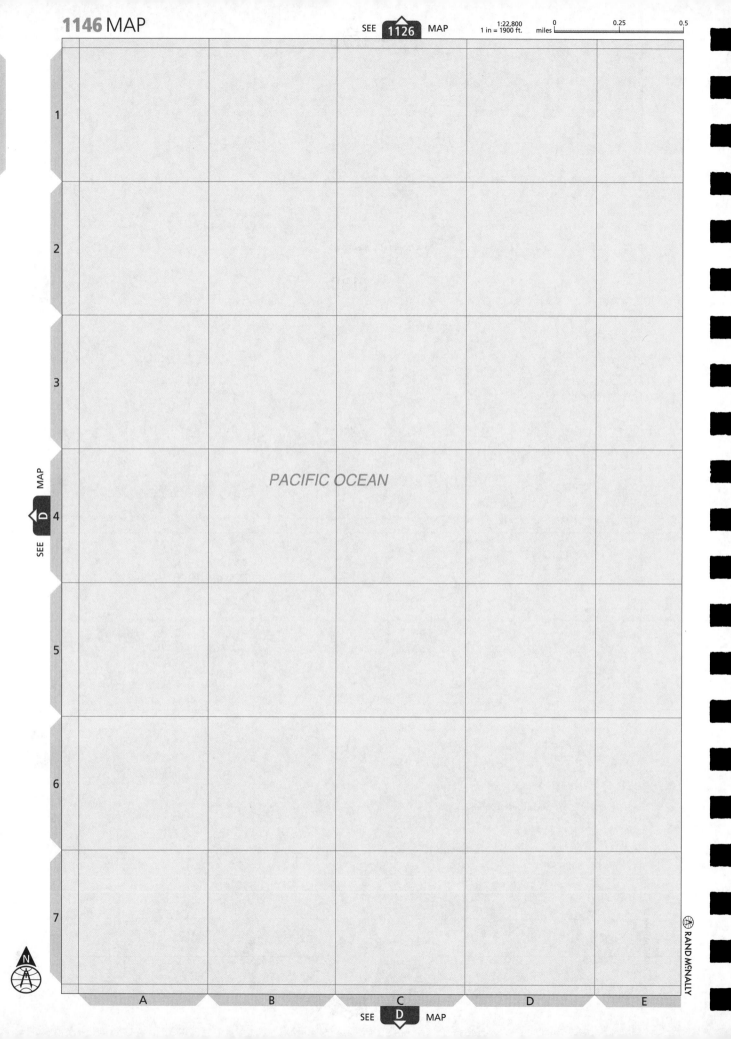

SEE 1126 MAP

1:22,800
1 in = 1900 ft.   miles   0   0.25   0.5

SAN DIEGO CO.

PACIFIC OCEAN

SEE D MAP

N

RAND McNALLY

SEE D MAP

A   B   C   D   E

MAP **1146**

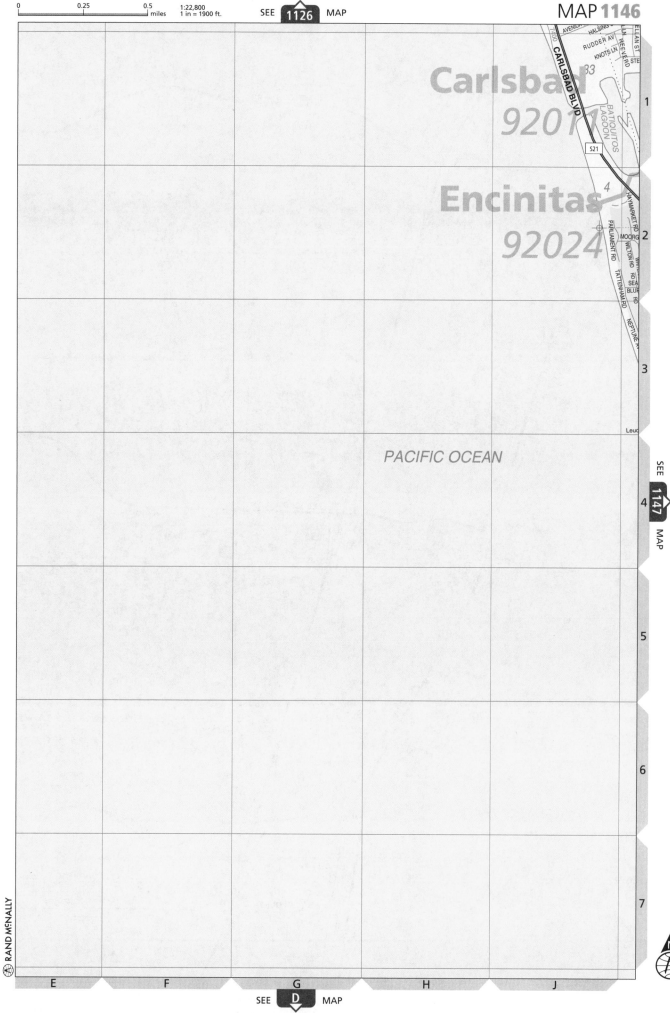

SEE 1126 MAP

0   0.25   0.5
miles
1:22,800
1 in = 1900 ft.

Carlsbad
92011

Encinitas
92024

PACIFIC OCEAN

SEE 1147 MAP

RAND M°NALLY

SEE D MAP

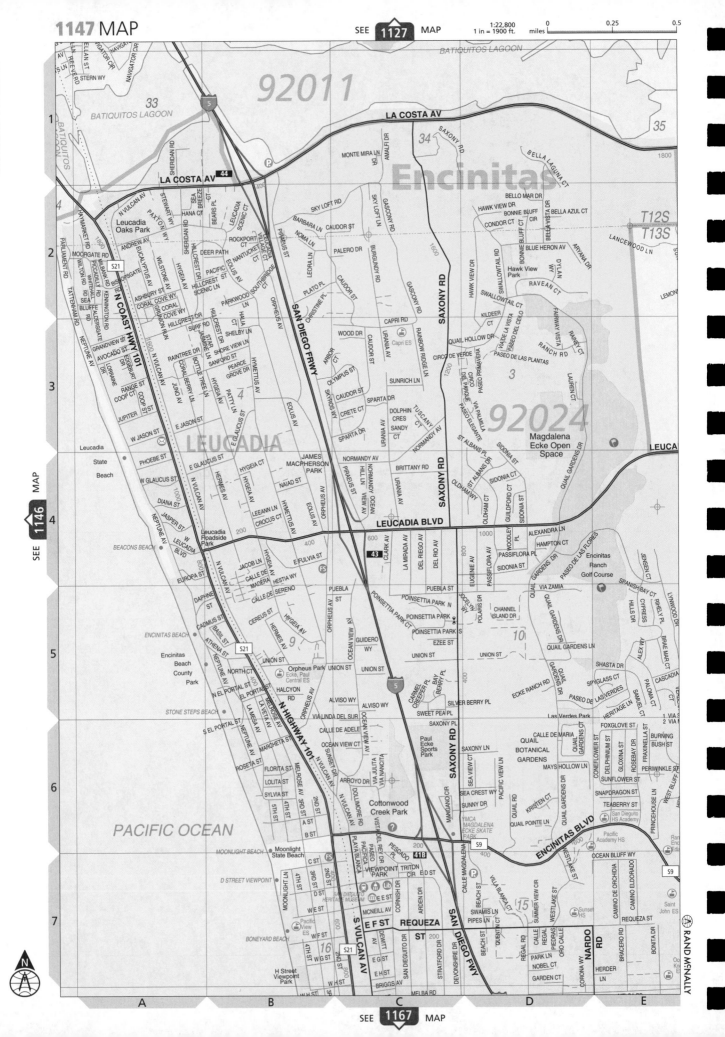

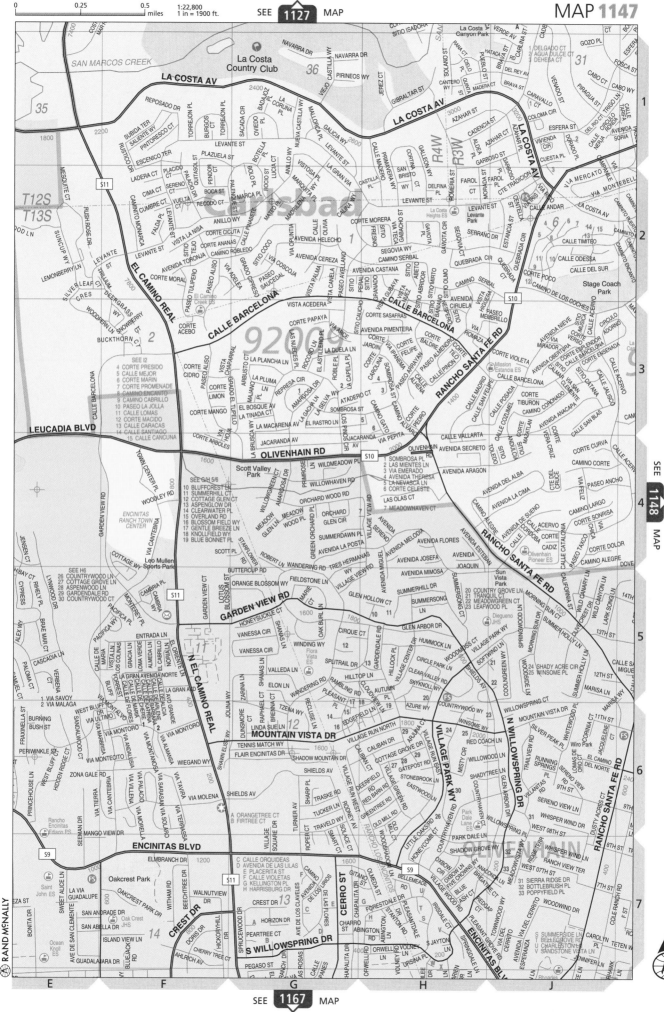

MAP 1147

SEE 1127 MAP

0   0.25   0.5
miles
1:22,800
1 in = 1900 ft.

La Costa
Country Club

San Marcos Creek

LA COSTA AV

Carlsbad

92009

LEUCADIA BLVD

OLIVENHAIN RD

SEE I2
4 CORTE PRESIDO
5 CALLE MEJOR
6 CORTE MARIN
7 CORTE PROMENADE
8 CAMINO ENCANTO
9 CAMINO CABRILLO
10 PASEO LA JOLLA
11 CALLE LOMAS
12 CORTE MACIDO
13 CALLE CARACAS
14 CALLE SANTIAGO
15 CALLE CANCUNA

SEE G/H 5/6
10 BLUFFCREST LN
11 SUMMERHILL CT
12 COTTAGE GLEN CT
13 ASPENGLOW DR
14 CLEARWATER PL
15 OVERLAND RD
16 BLOSSOM FIELD WY
17 GENTLE BREEZE WY
18 KNOLLFIELD WY
19 BLUE BONNET PL

SEE H6
26 COUNTRYWOOD LN
27 COTTAGE GROVE LN
28 ASPENWOOD LN
29 GARDENALE RD
30 COUNTRYWOOD CT

GARDEN VIEW RD

MOUNTAIN VISTA DR

N EL CAMINO REAL

ENCINITAS BLVD

CREST DR

S WILLOWSPRING DR

RANCHO SANTA FE RD

N WILLOWSPRING DR

VILLAGE PARK WY

LA COSTA AV

CALLE BARCELONA

RANCHO SANTA FE RD

1 SOMBROSA PL
2 LAS MIENTES LN
3 VIA EMERADO
4 AVENIDA THERESA
5 LA NEVASCA LN
6 CORTE CELESTE

7 MEADOWHAVEN CT

20 COUNTRY GROVE LN
21 TRANQUIL LN
22 MEADOWGREEN CT
23 LEAFWOOD PL

24 SHADY ACRE CIR
25 WINSOME PL

31 SIERRA RIDGE DR
32 BOTTLEBRUSH PL
33 POPPYFIELD PL

RAND McNALLY

SEE 1148 MAP

E   F   G   H   J

1

2

3

4

5

6

7

SEE 1167 MAP

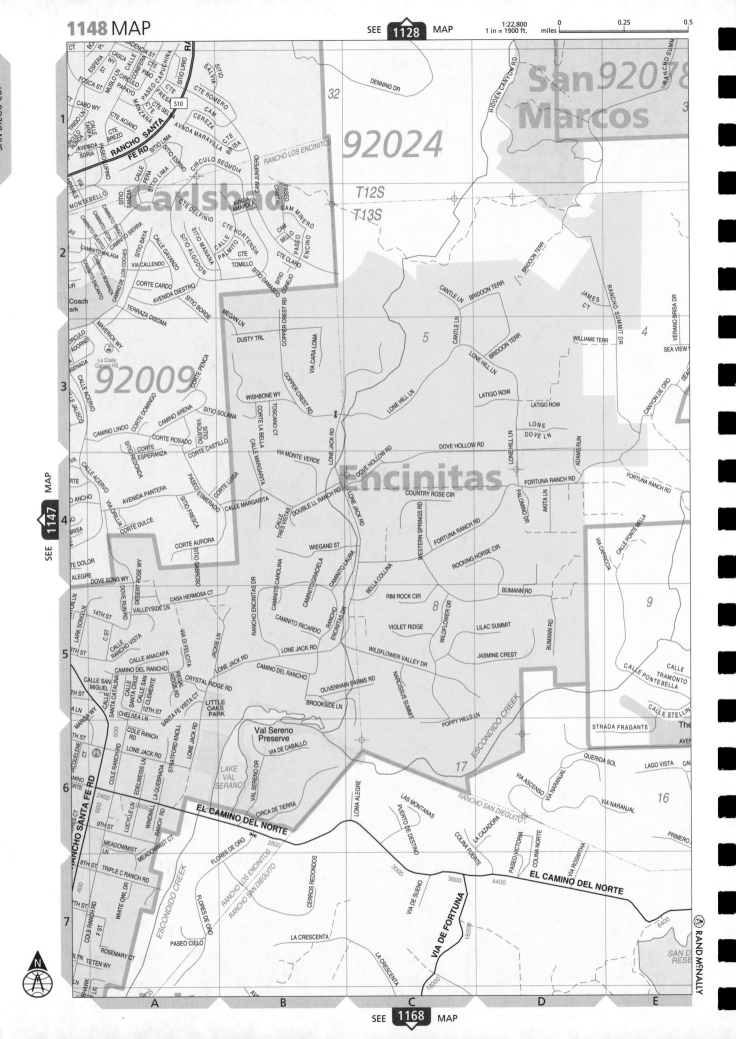

SEE **1128** MAP

1:22,800
1 in = 1900 ft.

miles   0   0.25   0.5

San Marcos
92078
92024
92009
Carlsbad
Encinitas

SEE 1147 MAP

T12S
T13S

DENNING DR

RANCHO SANTA FE RD

510

La Costa Canyon HS

Coach Park

Val Sereno Preserve

Little Oaks Park

Lake Val Serano

Escondido Creek

EL CAMINO DEL NORTE

VIA DE FORTUNA

RANCHO LOS ENCINITOS
RANCHO SAN DIEGUITO

RANCHO SAN DIEGUITO

32
5
4
8
9
17
16

A   B   C   D   E

1   2   3   4   5   6   7

SEE **1168** MAP

N

RAND McNALLY

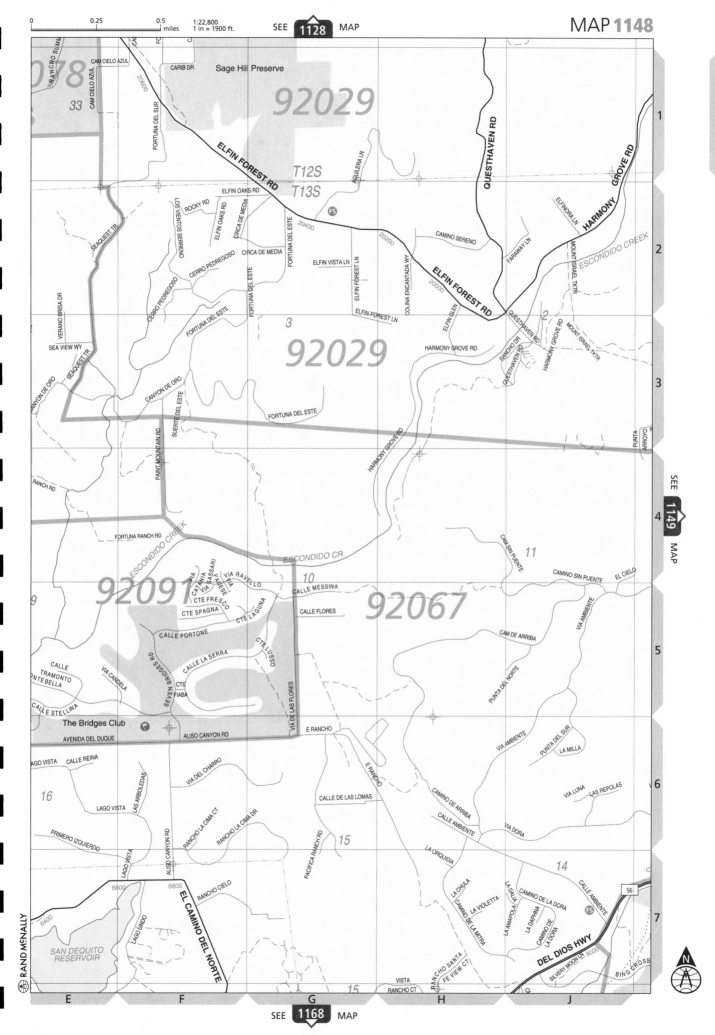

MAP **1148**

SAN DIEGO CO.

SEE **1128** MAP

0   0.25   0.5   miles   1:22,800
1 in = 1900 ft.

92029

Sage Hill Preserve

CAM CIELO AZUL
CARIB DR
CAM CIELO AZUL

RANCHO SUMMIT
33

QUESTHAVEN RD

HARMONY GROVE RD

1

ELFIN FOREST RD

FORTUNA DEL SUR

AGUILERA LN

T12S
T13S

ELFIN OAKS RD

ELFINORA LN

ESCONDIDO CREEK

2

LOS SIENTOS SERRENO
ROCKY RD
ELFIN OAKS RD
CIRCA DE MEDIA
FORTUNA DEL ESTE

20400
FS

CAMINO SERENO

FARAWAY LN

MOUNT ISRAEL TKTR

SEAQUEST TR

CERRO PEDREGOSO
CIRCA DE MEDIA
FORTUNA DEL ESTE

20200

ELFIN VISTA LN
ELFIN FOREST LN

COLINA ENCANTADA WY

ELFIN FOREST RD

20000

QUESTHAVEN RD

2

MOUNT ISRAEL TKTR

VERANO BRISA DR

CERRO PEDREGOSO

ELFIN FOREST LN

ELFIN GLEN

HARMONY GROVE RD

RANCHO DR

HARMONY GROVE RD

SEA VIEW WY
SEAQUEST TR

3

92029

QUESTHAVEN RD

3

CANYON DE ORO

CANYON DE ORO

SUERTE DEL ESTE

FORTUNA DEL ESTE

FORTUNA DEL ESTE

HARMONY GROVE RD

PUNTA ARROYO

CANYON DE ORO

PAINT MOUNTAIN RD

HARMONY GROVE RD

SEE **1149** MAP

4

RANCH RD

FORTUNA RANCH RD

ESCONDIDO CREEK

ESCONDIDO CR

11

CAM SIN PUENTE

CAMINO SIN PUENTE
EL CIELO

92091

VIA CATNIA
VIA SASSARI
VIA ARESE
VIA RAVELLO
CTE FRESCO
CTE SPAGNA
CTE LAGUNA

CALLE MESSINA

10

CALLE FLORES

92067

CAM DE ARRIBA

VIA AMBIENTE

5

CALLE PORTONE

CALLE LA SERRA

CTE LUSSO

PUNTA DEL NORTE

CALLE
TRAMONTO
MONTE BELLA

VIA CANDELA

SEVEN BRIDGES RD

CTE FIABA

VIA DE LAS FLORES

CALLE STELLINA

The Bridges Club

AVENIDA DEL DUQUE

ALISO CANYON RD

E RANCHO

PUNTA DEL SUR

LA MILLA

VIA AMBIENTE

LAGO VISTA
CALLE REINA

LAS ARBOLEDAS

VIA DEL CHAPRO

E RANCHO

CAMINO DE ARRIBA

VIA LUNA
LAS REPOLAS

6

16

LAGO VISTA

CALLE DE LAS LOMAS

CALLE AMBIENTE

VIA DORA

PRIMERO IZQUIERDO

LAGO VISTA

ALISO CANYON RD

RANCHO LA CIMA CT
RANCHO LA CIMA DR

PACIFICA RANCH RD

15

LA ORQUIDIA

14

CALLE AMBIENTE

S6

RANCHO CIELO

EL CAMINO DEL NORTE

RANCHO LA CIMA

LA CHULA
LA VIOLETTA
LA DALIA
CAMINO DE LA DORA

LA AMAPOLA
CAMINO DE LA MITRA
LA DAPHNA
CAMINO DE LA DORA

CALLE AMBIENTE

FS

6600
6800

LAGO LINDO

LAGO LINDO

6400

SAN DEQUITO
RESERVOIR

RANCHO SANTA
FE VIEW CT

DEL DIOS HWY

8000

VISTA
RANCHO CT

15

SILVERY MOON LN

BING CROSB

RAND MCNALLY

E   F   G   H   J

SEE **1168** MAP

N

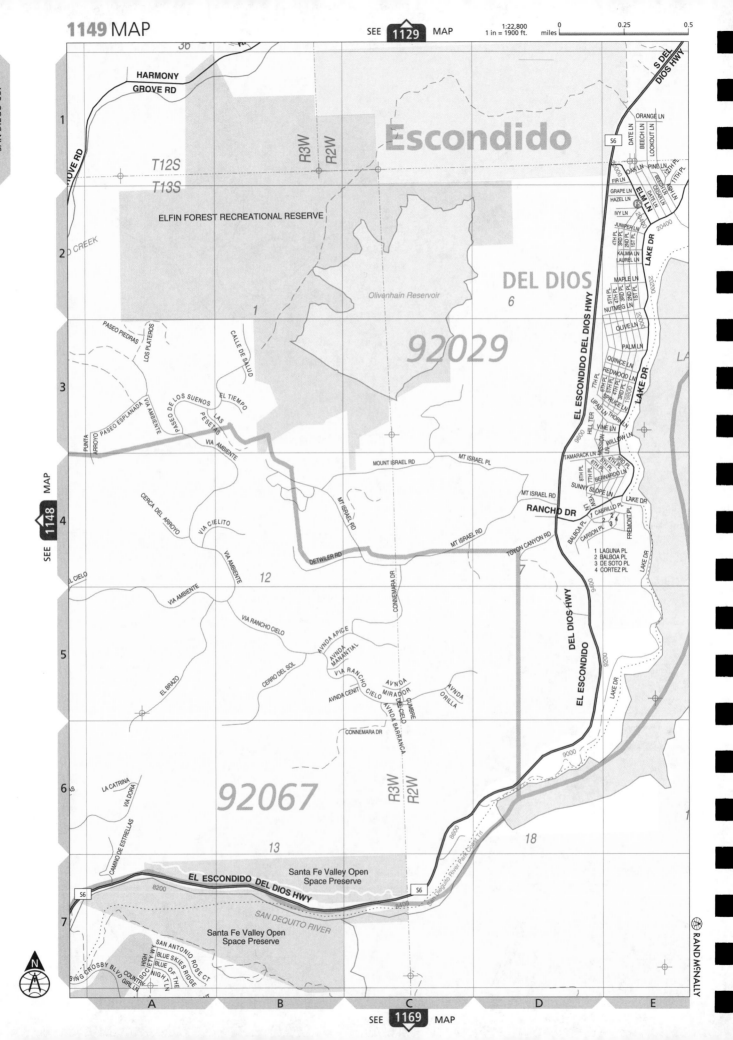

SEE 1129 MAP

1:22,800
1 in = 1900 ft.
miles
0   0.25   0.5

SAN DIEGO CO.

HARMONY
GROVE RD

GROVE RD

36

S DEL
DIOS HWY

ORANGE LN

S6

DATE LN
BEECH LN
LOOKOUT LN

1

Escondido

R3W R2W

T12S

T13S

OAK LN
PINE LN
FIR LN
BEECH LN
CEDAR LN
13TH PL
ASH LN
17TH PL

ELFIN FOREST RECREATIONAL RESERVE

GRAPE LN
HAZEL LN
IVY LN

ELM LN
DATE LN
24400

CREEK

JUNIPER LN
4TH PL
3RD PL
2ND PL
1ST PL

LAKE DR

20400

2

Olivenhain Reservoir

DEL DIOS

6

KALMIA LN
LAUREL LN

PASEO PIEDRAS

LOS PLATEROS

CALLE DE SALUD

92029

MAPLE LN
5TH PL
4TH PL
3RD PL
2ND PL
1ST PL

20200

NUTMEG LN

VIA AMBIENTE

EL TIEMPO

OLIVE LN

20000

3

VIA DE LOS SUENOS
PASEO ESPLANADA

LAS
PESETAS

PALM LN

QUINCE LN
7TH PL
6TH PL
5TH PL
4TH PL
REDWOOD LN
SPRUCE LN
18800

PUNTA
ARROYO

VIA AMBIENTE

EL ESCONDIDO DEL DIOS HWY

UPAS LN
THORN LN
VINE LN
WILLOW LN

HILL TER
9600
MISSION
1ST PL
3RD PL

LAKE DR

LA

CERCA DEL ARROYO

MT ISRAEL RD

MOUNT ISRAEL RD

MT ISRAEL PL

TAMARACK LN

8TH PL
6TH PL

4

VIA CIELITO

MT ISRAEL RD

SUNNY SLOPE LN

BERNARDO LN

LAKE DR

RANCHO DR

7TH PL
8TH PL
KEW

CABRILLO PL

FREMONT PL

EL CIELO

VIA AMBIENTE

DETWILER RD

MT ISRAEL RD

TOYON CANYON RD

7

BALBOA PL
CARSON PL

1
2
3
4

LAKE DR

12

1 LAGUNA PL
2 BALBOA PL
3 DE SOTO PL
4 CORTEZ PL

VIA AMBIENTE

DEL DIOS HWY

5

VIA RANCHO CIELO

AVNDA APICE

AVNDA
MANANTIAL

EL ESCONDIDO

9400

CERRO DEL SOL

VIA RANCHO CIELO

AVNDA
MIRADOR

AVNDA
ORILLA

9200

EL BRAZO

AVNDA CENIT

CUMBRE
AVNDA DEL CIELO

AVNDA BARRANCA

CONNEMARA DR

9000

LA CATRINA

CONNEMARA DR

6

92067

R3W
R2W

VIA DORA

18

8600

1

CAMINO DE ESTRELLAS

13

San Dieguito River Park Coast T11

EL ESCONDIDO DEL DIOS HWY

S6

Santa Fe Valley Open
Space Preserve

S6

8200

8400

7

SAN DEQUITO RIVER

Santa Fe Valley Open
Space Preserve

SAN ANTONIO ROSE CT

BLUE SKIES RIDGE

HIGH SOCIETY HWY
NIGH LN
BLUE OF THE
BING CROSBY BLVD
COUNTRY
GIRL LN

RAND McNALLY

A   B   C   D   E

SEE 1169 MAP

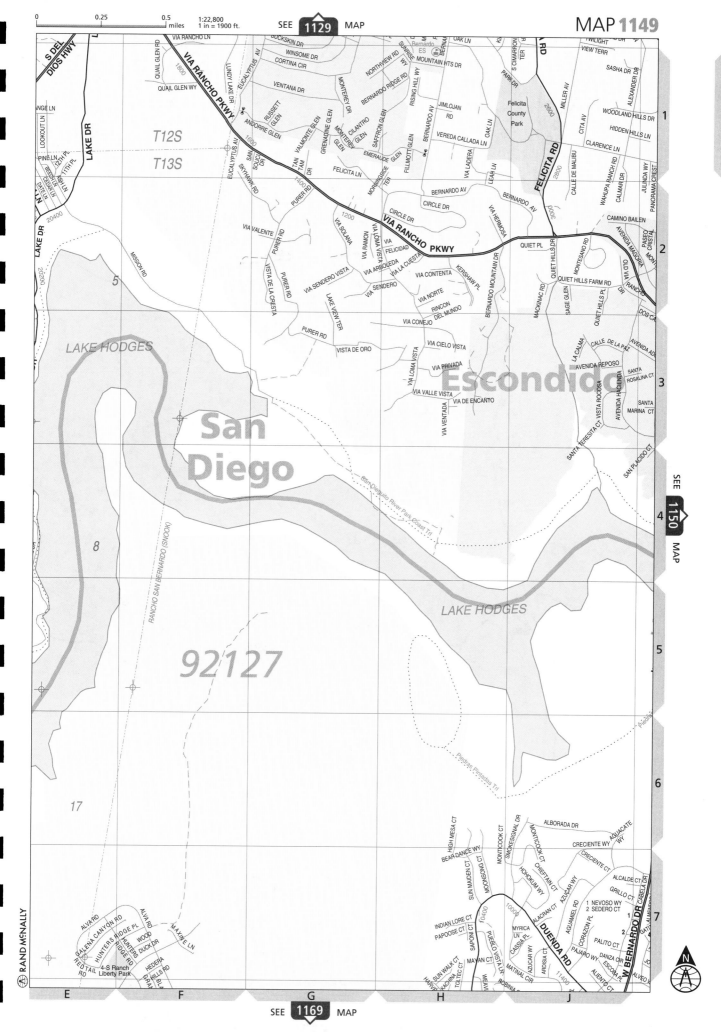

MAP 1149

SEE 1129 MAP

SAN DIEGO CO.

Escondido

San Diego

92127

LAKE HODGES

LAKE HODGES

Felicita County Park

SEE 1150 MAP

RAND McNALLY

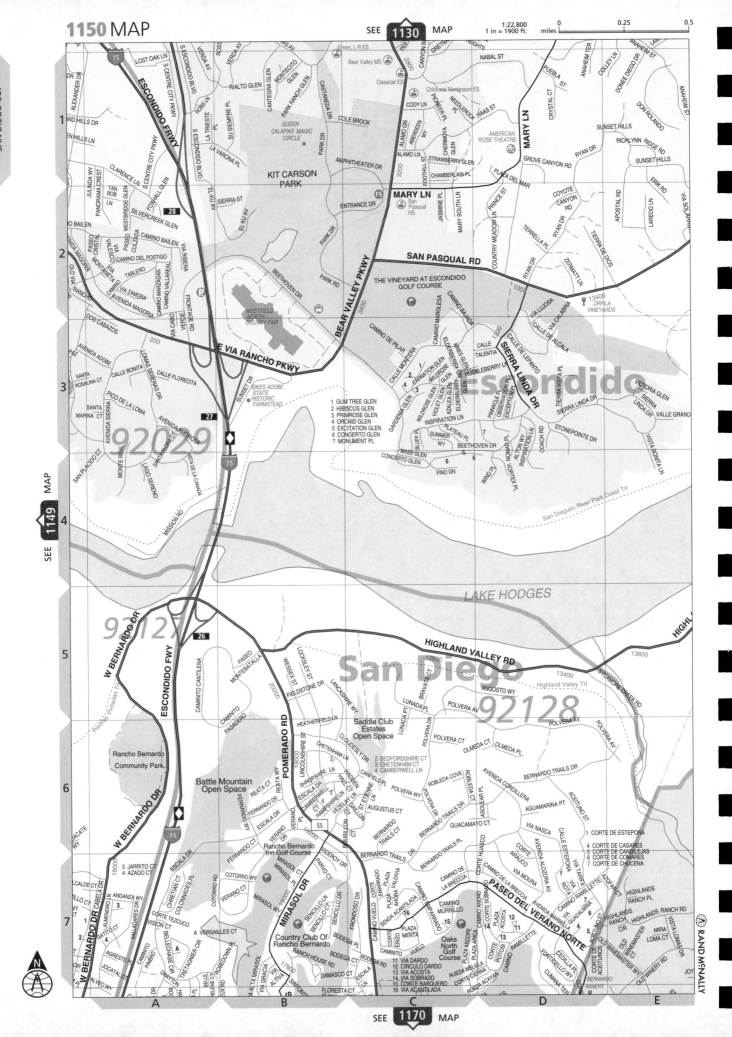

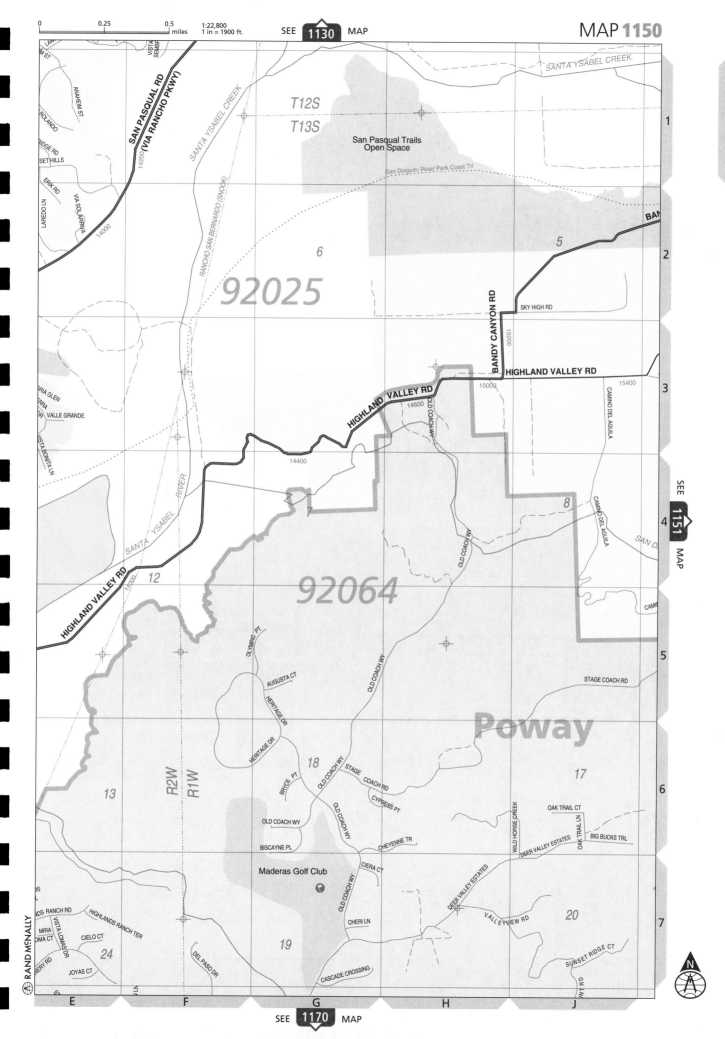

MAP **1150**

SAN DIEGO CO.

0   0.25   0.5
miles
1:22,800
1 in = 1900 ft.

Santa Ysabel Creek

T12S
T13S

San Pasqual Trails
Open Space

San Dieguito River Park Coast Trl

BANDY CANYON RD

SKY HIGH RD

BAN

5

6

92025

14200

14000

VIA SOLARRIVA

LAREDO LN

ERIK RD

RIDGE RD
SET HILLS

ROLANDO

ANAHEIM ST

LAW
M ST

VISTA
SEMBF

SAN PASQUAL RD
(VIA RANCHO PKWY)

RANCHO SAN BERNARDO (SNOOK)

SANTA YSABEL CREEK

HIGHLAND VALLEY RD

HIGHLAND VALLEY RD

15000

15400

15200

14600

OLD COACH HWY

14400

8

CAMINO DEL AGUILA

CAMINO DEL AGUILA

SAN D

CAMIN

1

2

3

4

5

6

7

92064

HIGHLAND VALLEY RD

14500L

12

OLYMPIC PT

AUGUSTA CT

HERITAGE DR

HERITAGE DR

BRYCE PT

OLD COACH WY

STAGE COACH RD

CYPRESS PT

OLD COACH WY

OLD COACH WY

BISCAYNE PL

CHEYENNE TR

CIERA CT

Maderas Golf Club

OLD COACH WY

CHERI LN

18

19

13

R2W
R1W

24

CASCADE CROSSING

DEL PASO DR

HIGHLANDS RANCH TER

NDS RANCH RD

MIRA
OMA CT

VISTA LOMAS DR

CIELO CT

JOYAS CT

NERY RD

OS

LN

T S

Poway

STAGE COACH RD

STAGE COACH RD

17

WILD HORSE CREEK

DEER VALLEY ESTATES

OAK TRAIL CT

OAK TRAIL LN

BIG BUCKS TRL

DEER VALLEY ESTATES

VALLEYVIEW RD

20

SUNSET RIDGE CT

NT RD

RAND M?NALLY

N

E   F   G   H   J

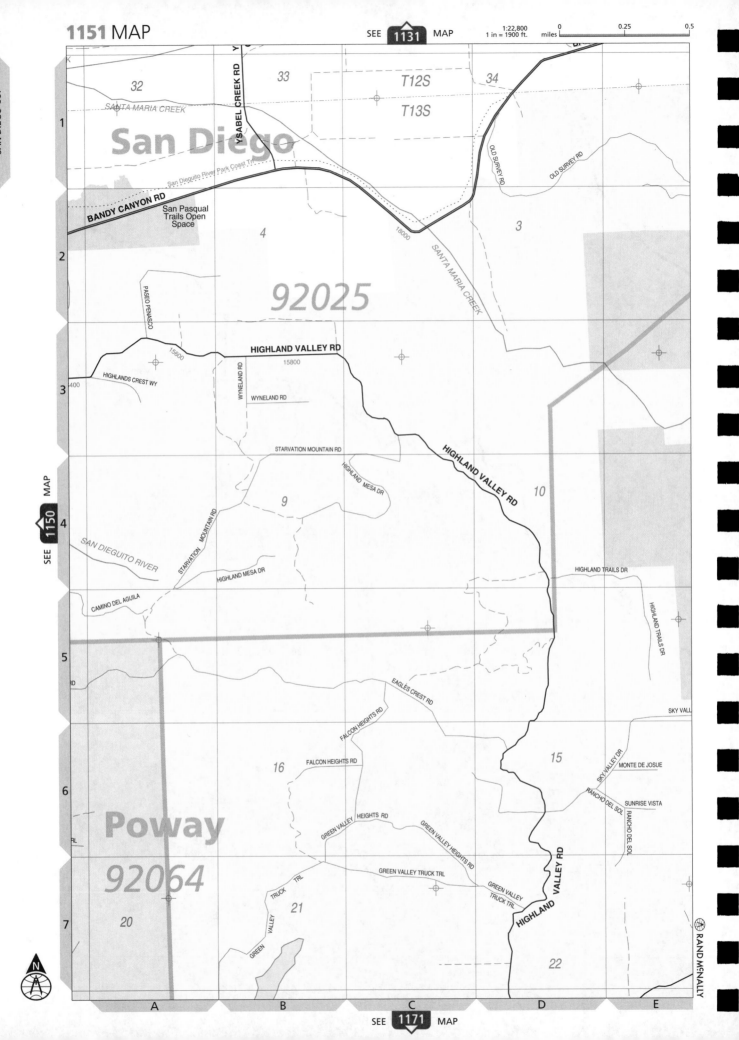

SEE 1131 MAP

1:22,800
1 in = 1900 ft.

0   0.25   0.5
miles

SAN DIEGO CO.

32

SANTA MARIA CREEK

33

T12S

T13S

34

1

YSABEL CREEK RD

OLD SURVEY RD

OLD SURVEY RD

San Dieguito River Park Coast Trl

San Diego

BANDY CANYON RD

San Pasqual
Trails Open
Space

4

3

18000

SANTA MARIA CREEK

2

92025

PASEO PENASCO

15600

HIGHLAND VALLEY RD

15800

WYNELAND RD

3

.400

HIGHLANDS CREST WY

WYNELAND RD

STARVATION MOUNTAIN RD

HIGHLAND MESA DR

HIGHLAND VALLEY RD

9

10

4

SAN DIEGUITO RIVER

STARVATION MOUNTAIN RD

HIGHLAND MESA DR

HIGHLAND TRAILS DR

CAMINO DEL AGUILA

HIGHLAND TRAILS DR

5

RD

EAGLES CREST RD

SKY VALL

FALCON HEIGHTS RD

16

FALCON HEIGHTS RD

15

SKY VALLEY DR

MONTE DE JOSUE

6

Poway

RANCHO DEL SOL

SUNRISE VISTA

GREEN VALLEY HEIGHTS RD

GREEN VALLEY HEIGHTS RD

RANCHO DEL SOL

92064

RL

GREEN VALLEY TRUCK TRL

GREEN VALLEY
TRUCK TRL

HIGHLAND VALLEY RD

20

GREEN VALLEY TRUCK TRL

21

7

22

RAND McNALLY

N

A   B   C   D   E

SEE 1171 MAP

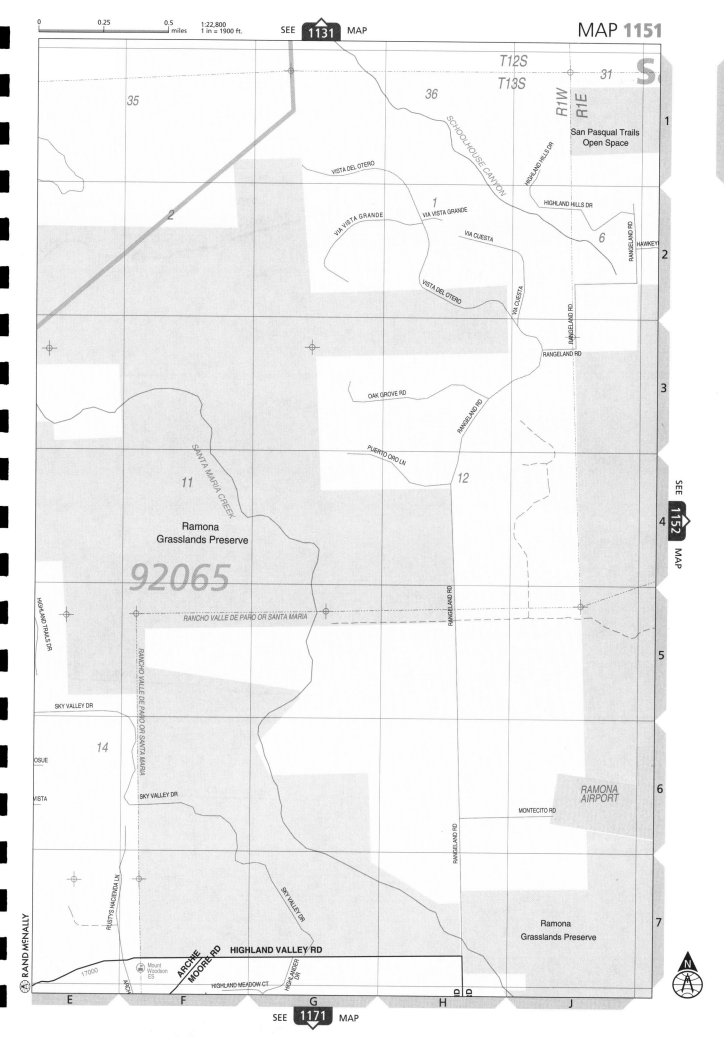

MAP **1151**

SEE 1131 MAP

SAN DIEGO CO.

0   0.25   0.5
miles   1:22,800
1 in = 1900 ft.

T12S
T13S
35
36
31

R1W
R1E

S

San Pasqual Trails
Open Space

1

VISTA DEL OTERO

SCHOOLHOUSE CANYON

HIGHLAND HILLS DR

HIGHLAND HILLS DR

2

VIA VISTA GRANDE
1   VIA VISTA GRANDE

VIA CUESTA

6

RANGELAND RD

HAWKEY

2

VISTA DEL OTERO

VIA CUESTA

RANGELAND RD

RANGELAND RD

3

OAK GROVE RD

RANGELAND RD

SANTA MARIA CREEK

PUERTO ORO LN

11   12

SEE 1152 MAP

Ramona
Grasslands Preserve

4

92065

HIGHLAND TRAILS DR

RANCHO VALLE DE PARO OR SANTA MARIA

RANGELAND RD

5

RANCHO VALLE DE PARO OR SANTA MARIA

SKY VALLEY DR

14

RAMONA
AIRPORT

6

OSUE

SKY VALLEY DR

VISTA

SKY VALLEY DR

RANGELAND RD

MONTECITO RD

RUSTY'S HACIENDA LN

SKY VALLEY DR

Ramona
Grasslands Preserve

7

RAND McNALLY

ARCHE MOORE RD   **HIGHLAND VALLEY RD**

17000   Mount
Woodson
ES

ARCH

HIGHLAND MEADOW CT

HIGHLANDER DR

E   F   G   H   J

N

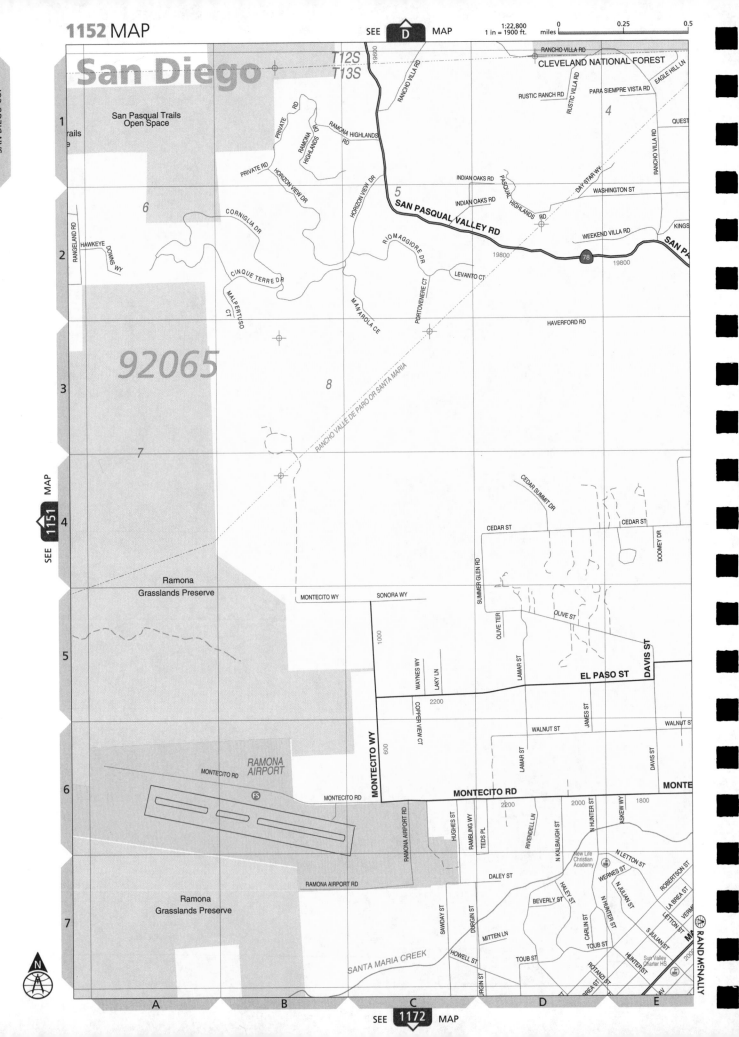

SEE **D** MAP

1:22,800
1 in = 1900 ft.

miles   0   0.25   0.5

SAN DIEGO CO.

San Diego

T12S
T13S

CLEVELAND NATIONAL FOREST

San Pasqual Trails
Open Space

RANCHO VILLA RD

RUSTIC RANCH RD

RANCHO VILLA RD

RUSTIC VILLA RD

PARA SIEMPRE VISTA RD

EAGLE HILL LN

QUEST

4

rails
e

1

6

RAMONA HIGHLANDS RD

RAMONA HIGHLANDS RD

PRIVATE RD

PRIVATE RD

HORIZON VIEW DR

HORIZON VIEW DR

INDIAN OAKS RD

INDIAN OAKS RD

PASQUAL HIGHLANDS RD

DAY STAR WY

WASHINGTON ST

RANCHO VILLA RD

19600

5

SAN PASQUAL VALLEY RD

CORNIGLIA DR

RANGELAND RD

HAWKEYE DOWNS WY

2

WEEKEND VILLA RD

KINGS

SAN PA

CINQUE TERRE DR

RIO MAGGIORE DR

LEVANTO CT

19800

78

19800

SAN PA

MALPERTUSO CT

MANAROLA CE

PORTOVENERE CT

HAVERFORD RD

92065

8

3

7

RANCHO VALLE DE PARO OR SANTA MARIA

CEDAR SUMMIT DR

SEE **1151** MAP

CEDAR ST

CEDAR ST

DOOMEY DR

4

SUMMER GLEN RD

Ramona
Grasslands Preserve

MONTECITO WY

SONORA WY

OLIVE TER

OLIVE ST

5

1000

WAYNES WY

LAKY LN

LAMAR ST

EL PASO ST

DAVIS ST

2200

COPPER VIEW CT

WALNUT ST

JAMES ST

WALNUT ST

MONTECITO WY

600

LAMAR ST

DAVIS ST

RAMONA
AIRPORT

6

MONTECITO RD

FS

MONTECITO RD

RAMONA AIRPORT RD

MONTECITO RD

MONTE

HUGHES ST

2200

2000

ASKEW WY

1800

MONTE

RAMBLING WY

TEDS PL

RIVENDELL LN

N KALBAUGH ST

N HUNTER ST

New Life
Christian
Academy

N LETTON ST

RAMONA AIRPORT RD

DALEY ST

WERNES ST

ROBERTSON ST

Ramona
Grasslands Preserve

7

SAWDAY ST

DURGIN ST

BEVERLY ST

HALEY ST

N HUNTER ST

N JULIAN ST

CARLIN ST

LA BREA ST

LETTON ST

VERM

MITTEN LN

TOUB ST

S JULIAN ST

HUNTER ST

MA

SANTA MARIA CREEK

HOWELL ST

URGIN ST

TOUB ST

ROTANZI ST

REA ST

Sun Valley
Charter HS

2000

RAND McNALLY

N

A   B   C   D   E

SEE **1172** MAP

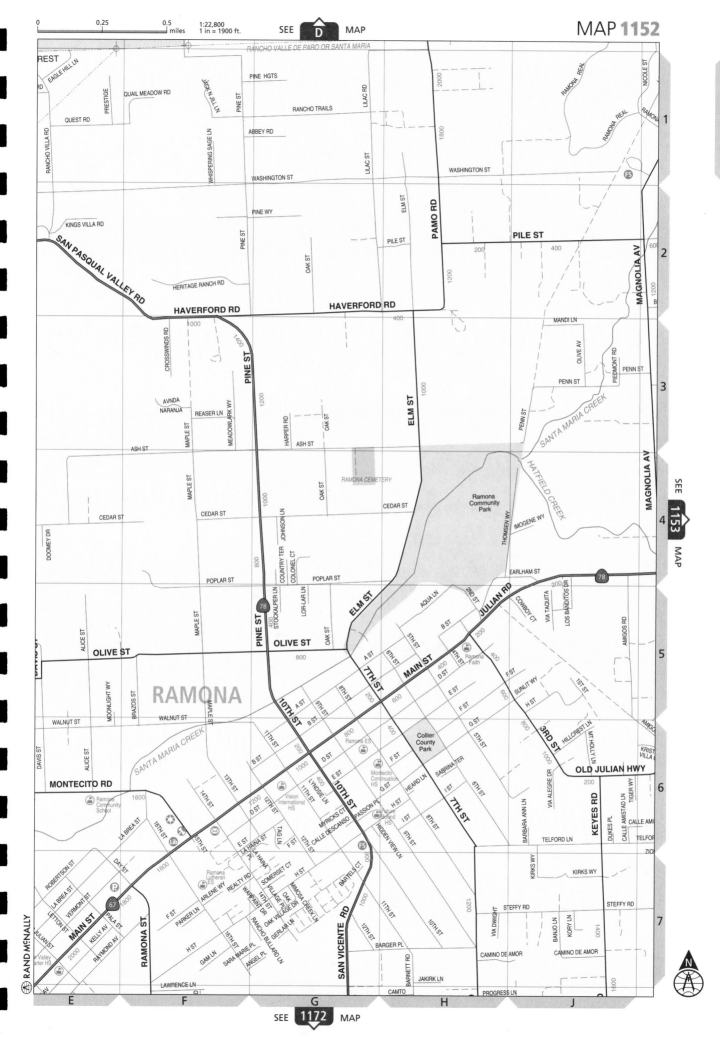

MAP 1152
SAN DIEGO CO.

SEE **D** MAP

0   0.25   0.5 miles
1:22,800
1 in = 1900 ft.

SEE **1153** MAP

REST

RANCHO VALLE DE PARO OR SANTA MARIA

EAGLE HILL LN
PRESTIGE
QUAIL MEADOW RD
QUEST RD
RANCHO VILLA RD
KINGS VILLA RD

PINE HGTS
PINE ST
RANCHO TRAILS
LILAC RD
ABBEY RD
N. TILL'N NOSH
WHISPERING SAGE LN
PINE WY
LILAC ST
PINE ST
WASHINGTON ST

PAMO RD
ELM ST
PILE ST
OAK ST

RAMONA REAL
RAMONA REAL
NICOLE ST
RAMONA

WASHINGTON ST

PILE ST
200   400   600
B
MAGNOLIA AV
1200

SAN PASQUAL VALLEY RD

HERITAGE RANCH RD

HAVERFORD RD   HAVERFORD RD
400

1200

MANDI LN
OLIVE AV
PENN ST
PIEDMONT RD
PENN ST

CROSSWINDS RD
1000
PINE ST
1400
AVNDA NARANJA
REASER LN
MEADOWLARK WY
MAPLE ST
HARPER RD
OAK ST
ASH ST
PENN ST

1200
1000

SANTA MARIA CREEK

ASH ST   ASH ST

MAGNOLIA AV

MAPLE ST

RAMONA CEMETERY

OAK ST

ELM ST

HATFIELD CREEK

DOOMEY DR
CEDAR ST   CEDAR ST   CEDAR ST
Ramona Community Park

THOMSEN WY
IMOGENE WY

800

COUNTRY TER
JOHNSON LN
COLONEL CT
POPLAR ST   POPLAR ST

EARLHAM ST
200
78

MAPLE ST
LOR-LAR LN
STOCKALPER LN
400
78
PINE ST
ELM ST
AQUA LN
2ND ST
JULIAN RD
COWBOY CT
VIA TAQUITA
LOS BANDITOS DR
AMIGOS RD

OLIVE ST   OLIVE ST
800
OAK ST
B ST
5TH ST
6TH ST
200
F ST
1ST ST
AMIGO

ALICE ST
7TH ST
A ST
MAIN ST
4TH ST
Ramona Faith
SUNLIT WY
H ST

RAMONA
MOONLIGHT WY
BRAZOS ST
A ST
8TH ST
9TH ST
200
D ST
E ST
F ST
600
800
3RD ST
HILLCREST LN
MT HOLLY LN
KRIST VILLA

WALNUT ST
WALNUT ST
MAPLE ST
B ST
D ST
F ST
G ST
5TH ST
OLD JULIAN HWY
200

DAVIS ST
ALICE ST
11TH ST
Ramona ES
400
Collier County Park
HEARD LN
SABRINA TER
6TH ST
KEYES RD
DUKES PL
CALLE AMISTAD LN
TIGER WY
TELFOR

MONTECITO RD
13TH ST
B ST
D ST
Montecito Continuation HS
G ST
1ST ST
BARBARA ANN LN
VIA ALEGRE DR
CALLE AMI

1600
Ramona Community School
14TH ST
12TH ST
D ST
Vision International HS
E ST
F ST
Future Ground
H ST
7TH ST
1000
TELFORD LN
ZIO

LA BREA ST
16TH ST
15TH ST
LYNDSIE LN
MYRICKS CT
CALLE DESCANSO
PASSION PL
HIDDEN VIEW LN
8TH ST
1200
KIRKS WY
KIRKS WY

ROBERTSON ST
LA BREA ST
VERMONT ST
DAY ST
F ST
PARKER LN
ARLENE WY
LA HAINA ST
LA HAINA ST
SOMERSET CT
14TH ST
OAK VILLAGE PL
MIMOSA CREEK LN
H ST
1ST ST
9TH ST
VIA DWIGHT
STEFFY RD
STEFFY RD
BANJO LN
KORY LN

JULIAN ST
LETTON ST
MAIN ST
PALA ST
KELLY AV
RAMOND AV
RAMONA ST
1800
57
Ramona Lutheran ES
REALTY RD
WARPAINT DR
RANCHO OAK VILLAGE DR
RANCHO BULLARD LN
GERLAH LN
SAN VICENTE RD
11TH ST
12TH ST
BARGER PL
CAMINO DE AMOR
CAMINO DE AMOR
1400

2000
Valley Charter HS
H ST
16TH ST
F ST
GAM LN
SARA MARIE PL
ANGEL PL
1000
10TH ST
BARNETT RD
JAKIRK LN
PROGRESS LN
1600

LAWRENCE LN
CAMTO
AV

E   F   G   H   J

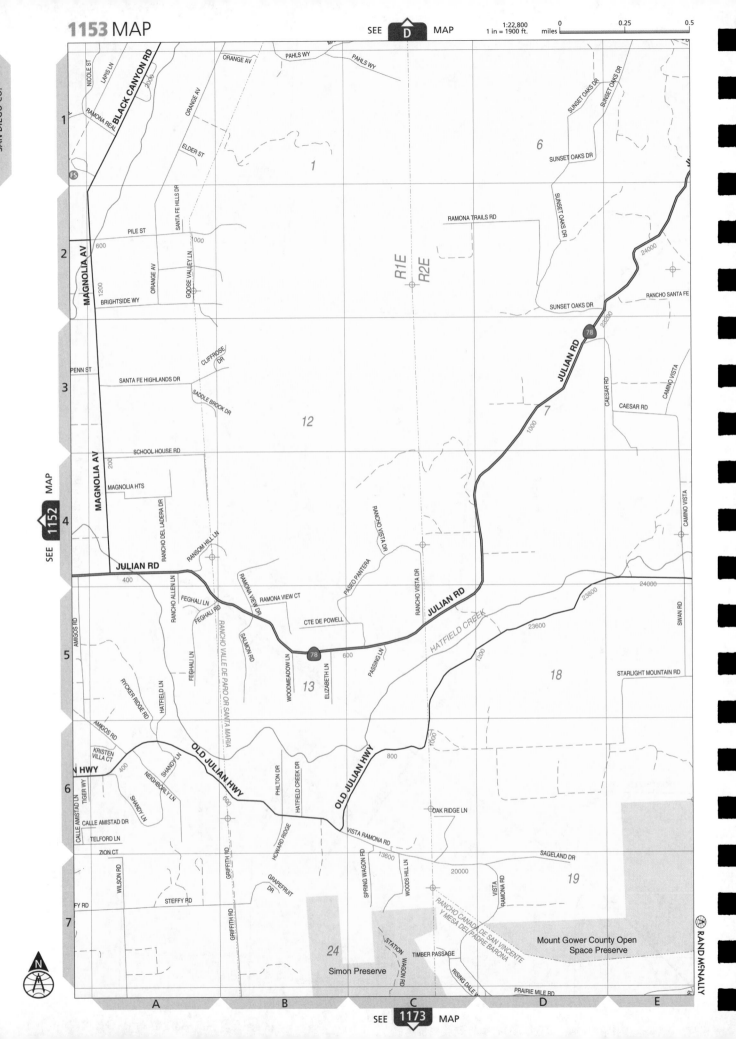

SAN DIEGO CO.

1:22,800
1 in = 1900 ft.

miles 0   0.25   0.5

BLACK CANYON RD

NICOLE ST
LAPIS LN
RAMONA REAL

ORANGE AV
PAHLS WY
PAHLS WY

2006

1

ELDER ST

SANTA FE HILLS DR

6

SUNSET OAKS DR
SUNSET OAKS DR

PILE ST

600

000

RAMONA TRAILS RD

SUNSET OAKS DR

SUNSET OAKS DR

24000

MAGNOLIA AV

2

ORANGE AV

GOOSE VALLEY LN

1200

BRIGHTSIDE WY

R1E   R2E

SUNSET OAKS DR

RANCHO SANTA FE

PENN ST

CLIFFROSE DR

SANTA FE HIGHLANDS DR

SADDLE BROOK DR

3

JULIAN RD

78

22600

CAESAR RD

CAMINO VISTA

CAESAR RD

1000

7

SCHOOL HOUSE RD

200

12

MAGNOLIA AV

MAGNOLIA HTS

RANCHO DEL LADERA DR

RANCHO VISTA DR

CAMINO VISTA

SEE **1152** MAP

4

RANSOM HILL LN

PASSO PANTERA

RANCHO VISTA DR

JULIAN RD

JULIAN RD

400

RANCHO ALLEN LN

FEGHALI LN

FEGHALI RD

RAMONA VIEW DR

RAMONA VIEW CT

CTE DE POWELL

RANCHO VISTA DR

24000

AMIGOS RD

FEGHALI LN

RANCHO VALLE DE PARO OR SANTA MARIA

SALMON RD

WOODMEADOW LN

78

600

PASSING LN

HATFIELD CREEK

23800

23600

1200

18

STARLIGHT MOUNTAIN RD

SWAN RD

5

RYCKER RIDGE RD

HATFIELD LN

13

ELIZABETH LN

AMIGOS RD

KRISTEN VILLA CT

OLD JULIAN HWY

PHILTON DR

HATFIELD CREEK DR

OLD JULIAN HWY

800

1000

N HWY

400

SHANDY LN

NEIGHBORLY LN

6

TIGER WY

CALLE AMISTAD LN

SHANDY LN

CALLE AMISTAD DR

660

HOWARD RIDGE

VISTA RAMONA RD

OAK RIDGE LN

1000

TELFORD LN

ZION CT

GRIFFITH RD

GRAPEFRUIT DR

SPRING WAGON RD

13600

WOODS HILL LN

20000

SAGELAND DR

VISTA RAMONA RD

19

WILSON RD

FY RD

STEFFY RD

GRIFFITH RD

7

24

STATION

TIMBER PASSAGE

WAGON RD

RANCHO CANADA DE SAN VINCENTE Y MESA DEL PADRE BARONA

RISING DALE

Mount Gower County Open Space Preserve

Simon Preserve

PRAIRIE MILE RD

RAND McNALLY

A   B   C   D   E

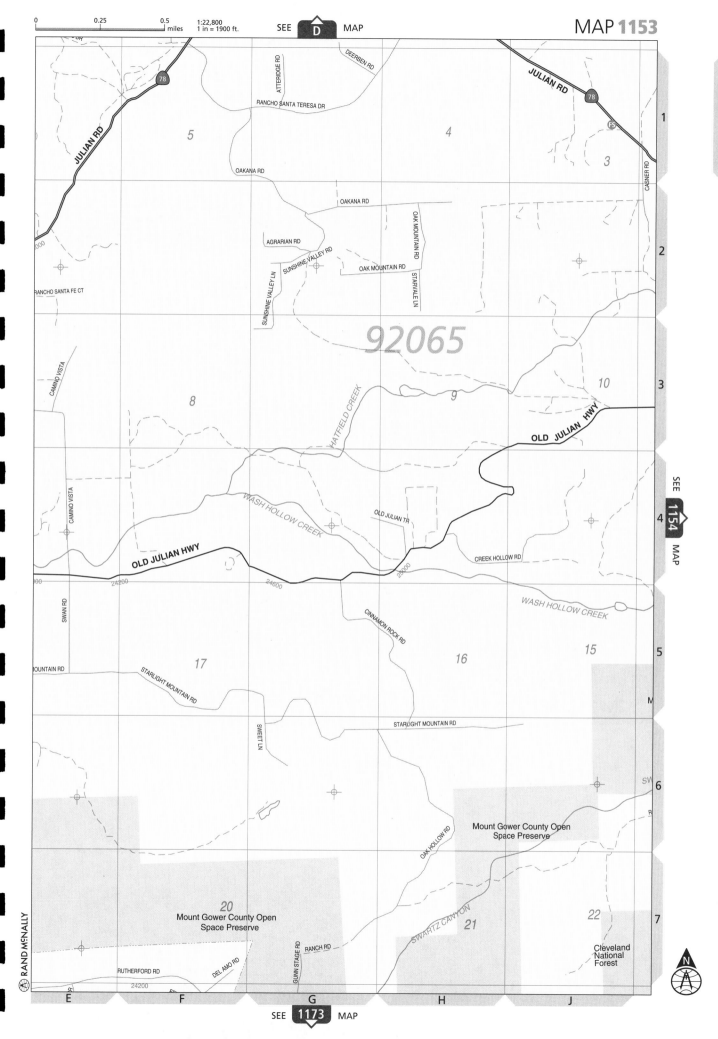

MAP **1153**

SAN DIEGO CO.

0   0.25   0.5
miles
1:22,800
1 in = 1900 ft.

SEE D MAP

SEE 1154 MAP

SEE 1173 MAP

JULIAN RD
78
DR
ATTERIDGE RD
DEERBEN RD
RANCHO SANTA TERESA DR
JULIAN RD
78
FS
CASNER RD

5
4
3

OAKANA RD
OAKANA RD
OAK MOUNTAIN RD
AGRARIAN RD
SUNSHINE VALLEY RD
OAK MOUNTAIN RD
STARVALE LN
SUNSHINE VALLEY LN

92065

RANCHO SANTA FE CT

CAMINO VISTA

HATFIELD CREEK

8
9
10

OLD JULIAN HWY

CAMINO VISTA

WASH HOLLOW CREEK
OLD JULIAN TR
CREEK HOLLOW RD

OLD JULIAN HWY
24200
24600
24000

WASH HOLLOW CREEK

SWAN RD

CINNAMON ROCK RD

17
16
15

STARLIGHT MOUNTAIN RD
MOUNTAIN RD

SWEET LN
STARLIGHT MOUNTAIN RD

Mount Gower County Open
Space Preserve

OAK HOLLOW RD

20
Mount Gower County Open
Space Preserve

SWARTZ CANYON
21
22

Cleveland
National
Forest

RUTHERFORD RD
DEL AMO RD
GUNN STAGE RD
RANCH RD
24200

RAND MCNALLY

E   F   G   H   J

1   2   3   4   5   M   6   R   SW   7

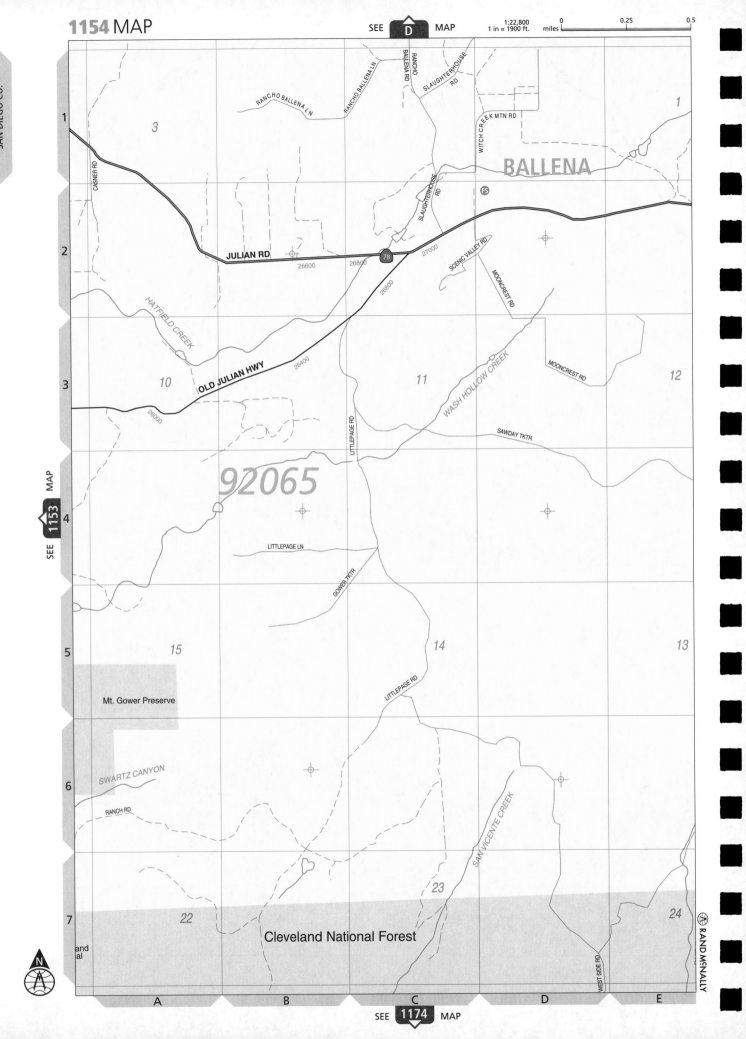

SAN DIEGO CO.

SEE D MAP

1:22,800
1 in = 1900 ft.

miles 0   0.25   0.5

BALLENA

RANCHO BALLENA LN
RANCHO BALLENA LN
RANCHO BALLENA RD
SLAUGHTERHOUSE RD
WITCH CREEK MTN RD

1

3

CASNER RD

SLAUGHTERHOUSE RD

F5

JULIAN RD

2

26600   26800   27000

28800

SCENIC VALLEY RD

MOONCREST RD

HATFIELD CREEK

OLD JULIAN HWY

26400

10

11

WASH HOLLOW CREEK

MOONCREST RD

12

26000

LITTLEPAGE RD

SAWDAY TKTR

92065

SEE 1153 MAP

4

LITTLEPAGE LN

GOWER TKTR

15

14

13

Mt. Gower Preserve

5

SWARTZ CANYON

LITTLEPAGE RD

RANCH RD

6

SAN VICENTE CREEK

23

22

24

7

Cleveland National Forest

and
al

WEST SIDE RD

N

RAND McNALLY

A   B   C   D   E

SEE 1174 MAP

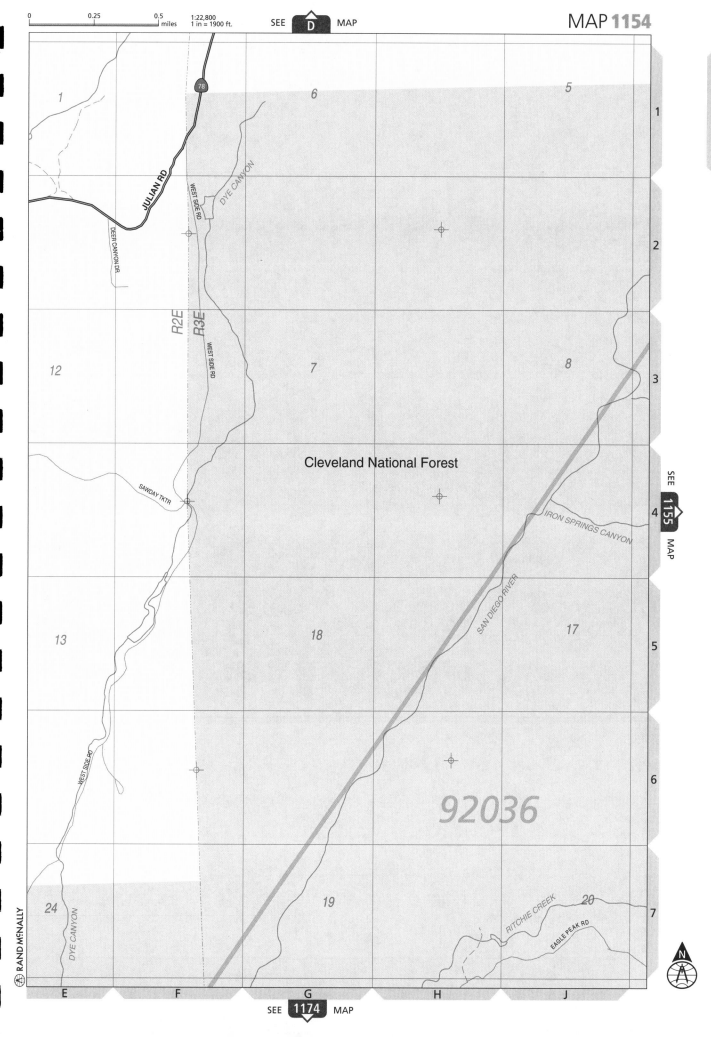

MAP **1154**

SAN DIEGO CO.

0   0.25   0.5
miles
1:22,800
1 in = 1900 ft.

SEE D MAP

1

6

5

1

JULIAN RD

WEST SIDE RD

DYE CANYON

DEER CANYON DR

2

R2E

R3E

WEST SIDE RD

12

7

8

3

Cleveland National Forest

SAWDAY TKTR

IRON SPRINGS CANYON

SEE 1155 MAP

4

SAN DIEGO RIVER

13

18

17

5

WEST SIDE RD

6

92036

24

DYE CANYON

19

RITCHIE CREEK

20

7

EAGLE PEAK RD

RAND MCNALLY

E   F   G   H   J

SEE 1174 MAP

N

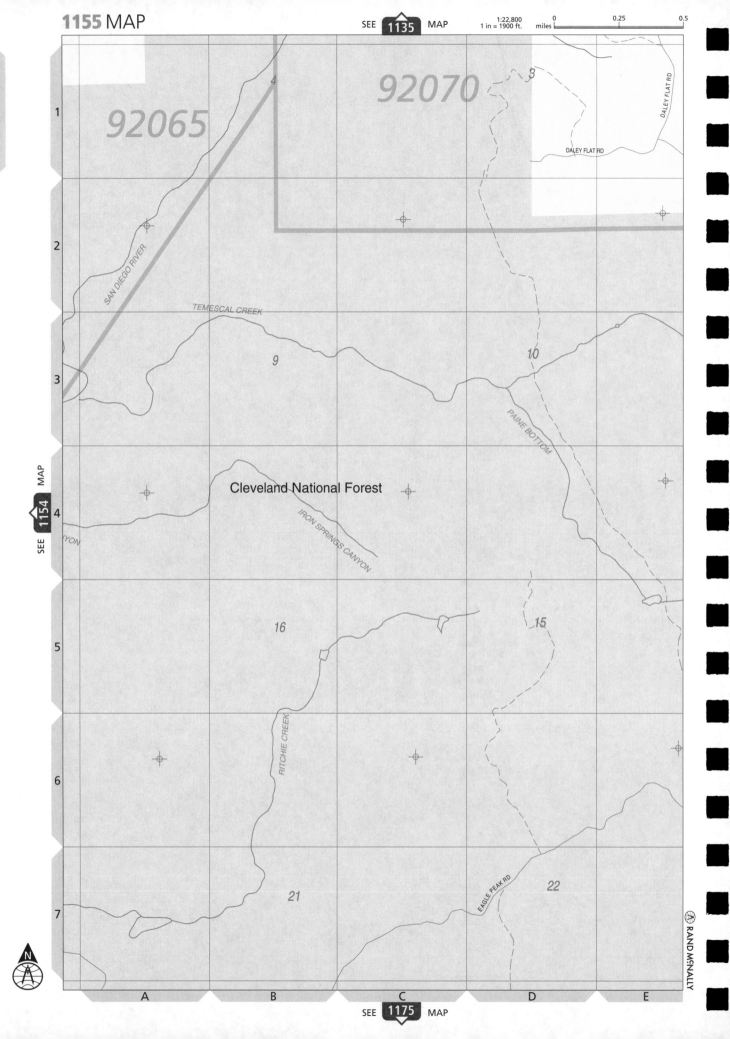

1:22,800
1 in = 1900 ft.

miles 0   0.25   0.5

SAN DIEGO CO.

92065

92070

DALEY FLAT RD

DALEY FLAT RD

SAN DIEGO RIVER

TEMESCAL CREEK

9

10

PAINE BOTTOM

SEE 1154 MAP

Cleveland National Forest

IRON SPRINGS CANYON

16

15

RITCHIE CREEK

21

22

EAGLE PEAK RD

N

A   B   C   D   E

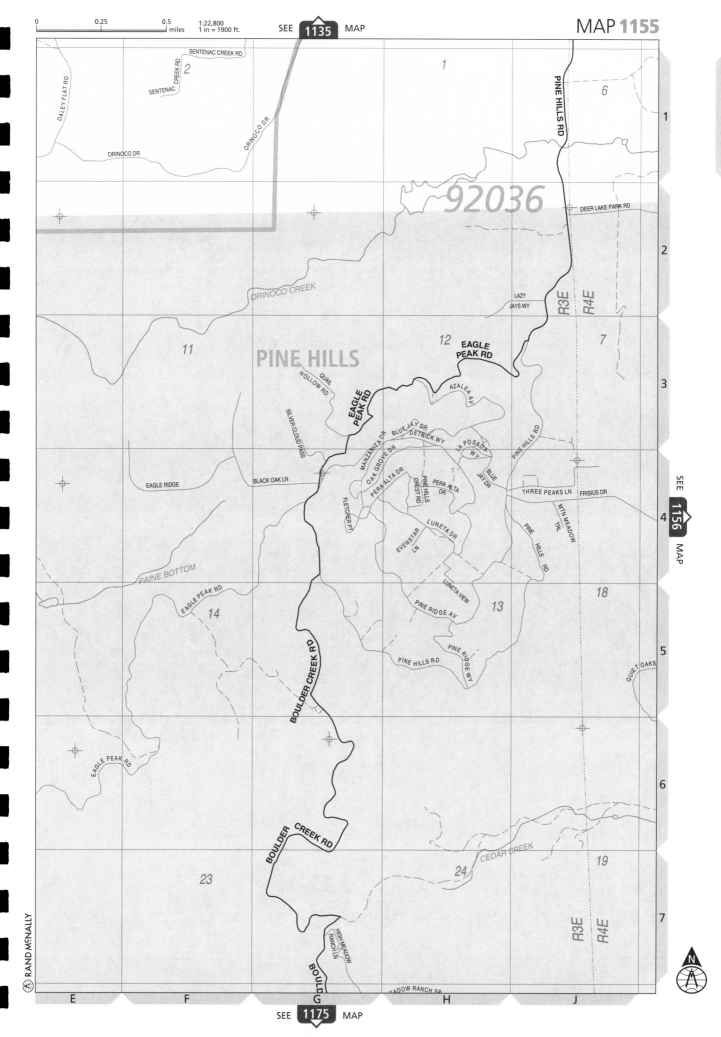

MAP **1155**

SAN DIEGO CO.

0 0.25 0.5
miles
1:22,800
1 in = 1900 ft.

SEE 1135 MAP

SENTENAC CREEK RD

DALEY FLAT RD

SENTENAC CREEK RD

2

ORINOCO DR

ORINOCO DR

1

6

PINE HILLS RD

92036

DEER LAKE PARK RD

ORINOCO CREEK

LAZY JAYS WY

R3E R4E

11

12

PINE HILLS

EAGLE PEAK RD

7

QUAIL HOLLOW RD

EAGLE PEAK RD

AZALEA AV

SILVER CLOUD PASS

MANZANITA DR

BLUE JAY DR

DETRICK WY

LA POSADA WY

PINE HILLS RD

EAGLE RIDGE

BLACK OAK LN

OAK GROVE DR

PERA ALTA DR

PINE HILLS CREST RD

PERA ALTA DR

BLUE JAY DR

THREE PEAKS LN

FRISIUS DR

SEE 1156 MAP

FLETCHER PT

EVENSTAR LN

LUNETA DR

MTN MEADOW TRL

PINE HILLS RD

PAINE BOTTOM

EAGLE PEAK RD

LUNETA VIEW

13

18

14

PINE RIDGE AV

PINE RIDGE WY

QUIET OAKS

BOULDER CREEK RD

PINE HILLS RD

EAGLE PEAK RD

BOULDER CREEK RD

CEDAR CREEK

23

24

19

R3E R4E

BOULDER

HIGH MEADOW RANCH LN

MEADOW RANCH SP

RAND McNALLY

E F G H J

SEE 1175 MAP

N

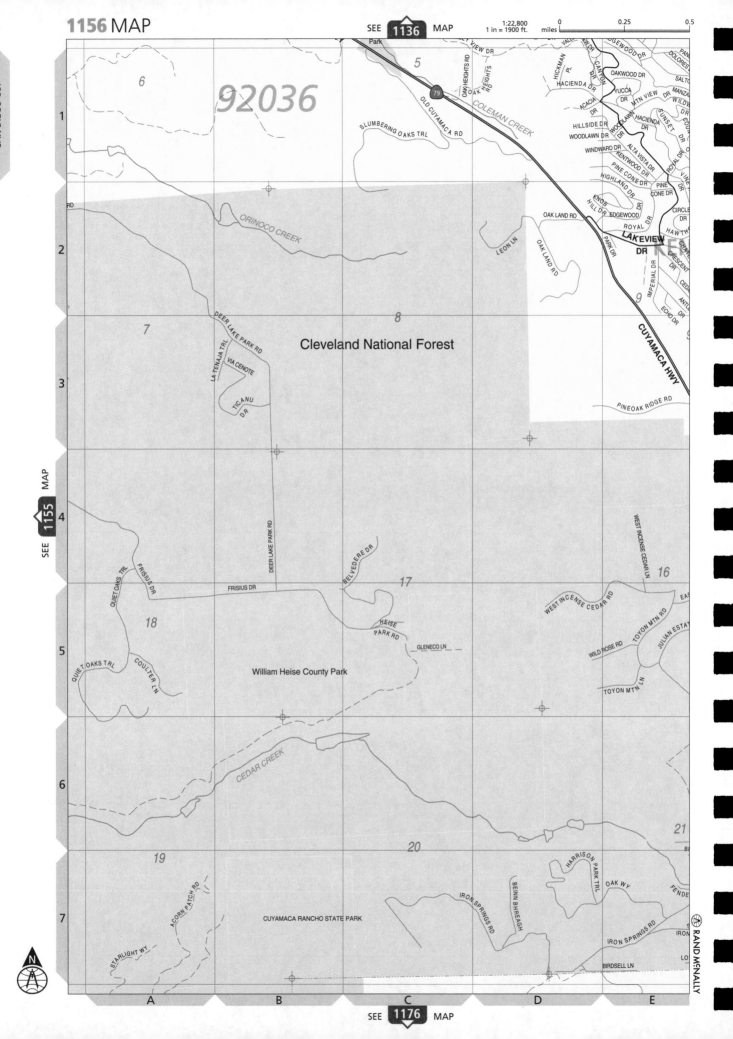

SAN DIEGO CO.

1:22,800
1 in = 1900 ft.

miles 0 0.25 0.5

92036

Cleveland National Forest

ORINOCO CREEK

SLUMBERING OAKS TRL

OLD CUYAMACA RD

COLEMAN CREEK

79

CUYAMACA HWY

OAK HEIGHTS RD
OAK HEIGHTS RD

VALLEY VIEW DR
HICKMAN PL
OAKWOOD DR
DOLORES
PANA
SALTO
HACIENDA DR
YUCCA DR
MTN VIEW DR
MANZA
WILDW
ACACIA DR
SUNSET DR
FOUR
HILLSIDE DR
WOODLAWN DR
HACIENDA DR
WOODLAWN DR
WINDWARD DR
ALTA VISTA DR
KENTWOOD DR
PINE CONE DR
PINE CONE DR
VINE
HIGHLAND DR
CIRCLE DR
KNOB HILL DR
EDGEWOOD
ROYAL DR
HAWTH
OAK LAND RD
EDGEWOOD DR
LAKEVIEW DR
IMPERIAL DR
CRESCENT DR
CEDA
ANTL
ECHO DR

LEON LN

OAK LAND RD

PARK DR

9

PINEOAK RIDGE RD

DEER LAKE PARK RD

LA TENAJA TRL

VIA CENOTE

TICANU DR

7

DEER LAKE PARK RD

8

FRISIUS DR

QUIET OAKS TRL

FRISIUS DR

FRISIUS DR

BELVEDERE DR

17

WEST INCENSE CEDAR LN

16

WEST INCENSE CEDAR RD

18

HEISE PARK RD

GLENECO LN

WILD ROSE RD

TOYON MTN RD

JULIAN ESTA

EAS

COULTER LN

William Heise County Park

TOYON MTN LN

QUIET OAKS TRL

CEDAR CREEK

6

19

ACORN PATCH RD

CUYAMACA RANCHO STATE PARK

20

IRON SPRINGS RD

BEINN BHREAGH

HARRISON PARK TRL

OAK WY

21

B

FENDE

IRON SPRINGS RD

IRON

LO

STARLIGHT WY

BIRDSELL LN

RAND MCNALLY

N

A B C D E

SEE 1155 MAP

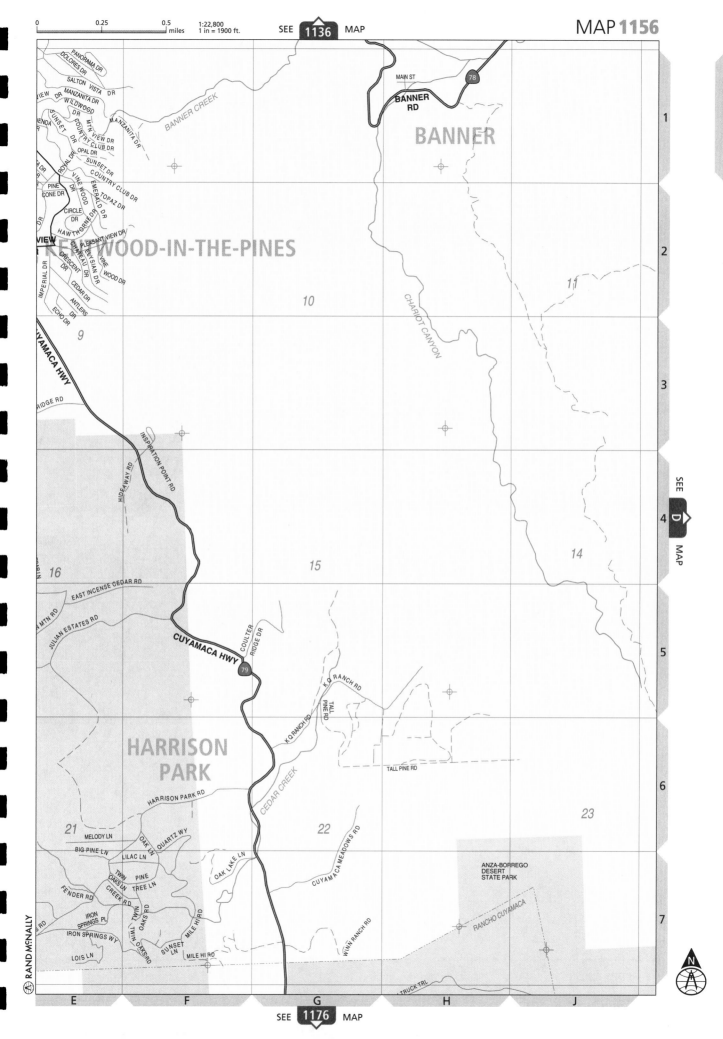

MAP **1156**

SAN DIEGO CO.

0   0.25   0.5
miles
1:22,800
1 in = 1900 ft.

BANNER CREEK

MAIN ST

78

BANNER
RD

BANNER

1

KEN WOOD-IN-THE-PINES

PANORAMA DR
DOLORES DR
SALTON VISTA DR
VIEW DR
MANZANITA DR
WILDWOOD DR
MANZANITA DR
SUNSET DR
HACIENDA DR
ROYAL DR
MTN VIEW DR
COUNTRY CLUB DR
OPAL DR
SUNSET DR
COUNTRY CLUB DR
VINE WOOD
EMERALD DR
TOPAZ DR
PINE CONE DR
HAWTHORNE DR
CIRCLE DR
VIEW
PLEASANT VIEW DR
CHATEAU DR
ELYSIAN DR
VINE WOOD DR
IMPERIAL DR
CRESCENT DR
CEDAR DR
ANTLERS DR
ECHO DR

2

10

11

CHARIOT CANYON

9

CUYAMACA HWY

RIDGE RD

3

INSPIRATION POINT RD

HIDEAWAY RD

SEE ▷ D MAP

4

16

15

14

EAST INCENSE CEDAR RD

MTN RD

JULIAN ESTATES RD

CUYAMACA HWY

COULTER RIDGE DR

79

5

K Q RANCH RD

TALL PINE RD

K Q RANCH RD

HARRISON
PARK

CEDAR CREEK

TALL PINE RD

6

23

21

MELODY LN
OAK LN
QUARTZ WY
BIG PINE LN
LILAC LN
TWIN OAKS LN
PINE TREE LN
FENDER RD
CREEK RD
TWIN OAKS RD
IRON SPRINGS PL
MILE HI RD
SUNSET LN
IRON SPRINGS WY
RD
LOIS LN
MILE HI RD

22

OAK LAKE LN

CUYAMACA MEADOWS RD

WINN RANCH RD

ANZA-BORREGO
DESERT
STATE PARK

RANCHO CUYAMACA

7

TRUCK TRL

RAND M°NALLY

E   F   G   H   J

N

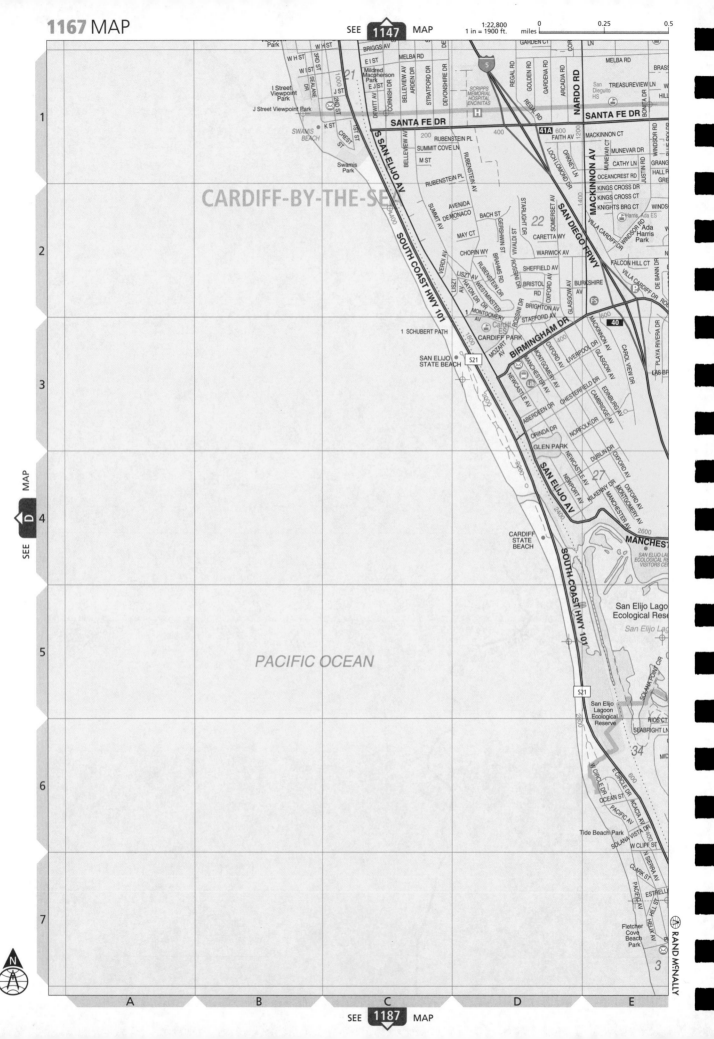

1:22,800
1 in = 1900 ft.

miles 0   0.25   0.5

SAN DIEGO CO.

CARDIFF-BY-THE-SEA

PACIFIC OCEAN

SEE D MAP

RAND McNALLY

A   B   C   D   E

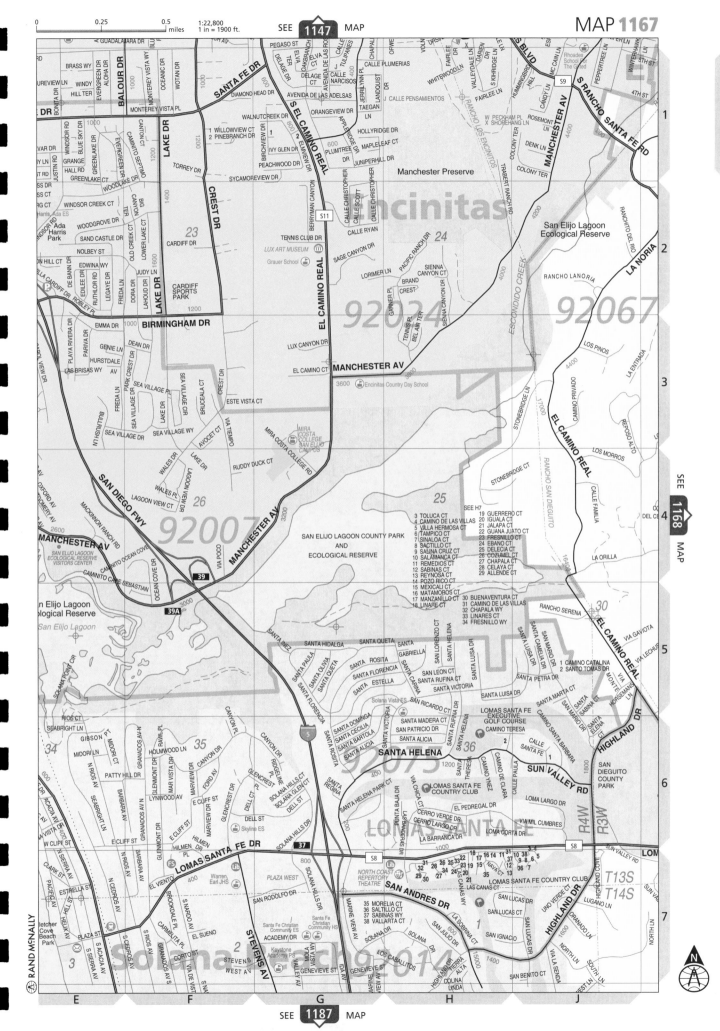

MAP **1167**

SEE ▷ 1168 MAP

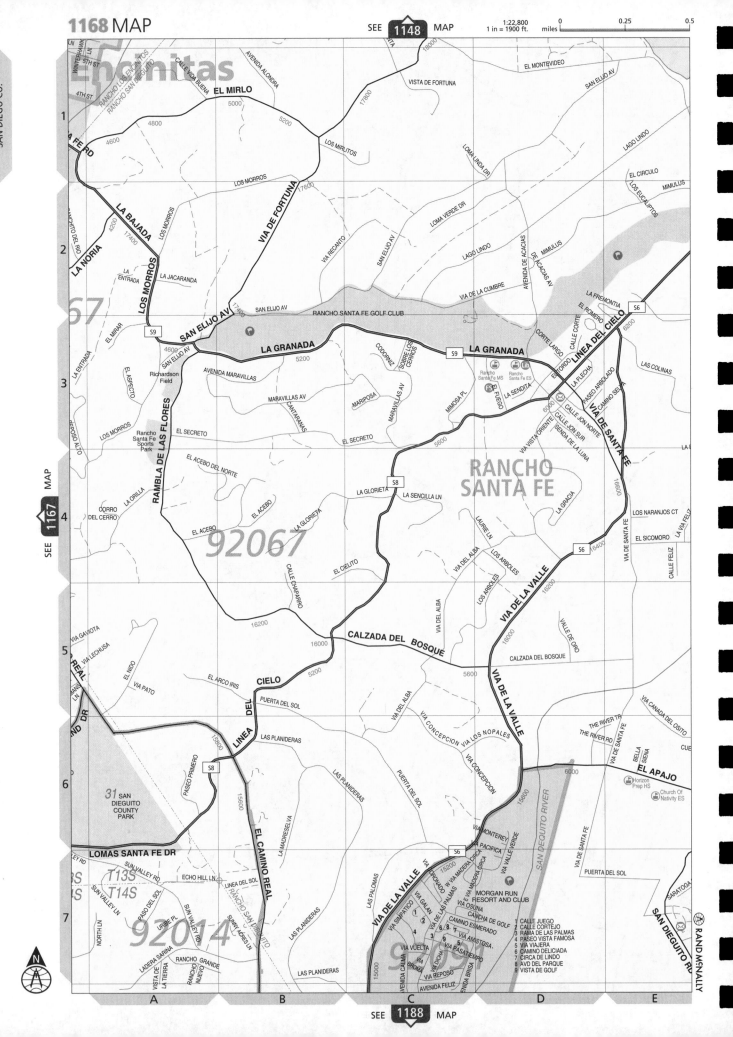

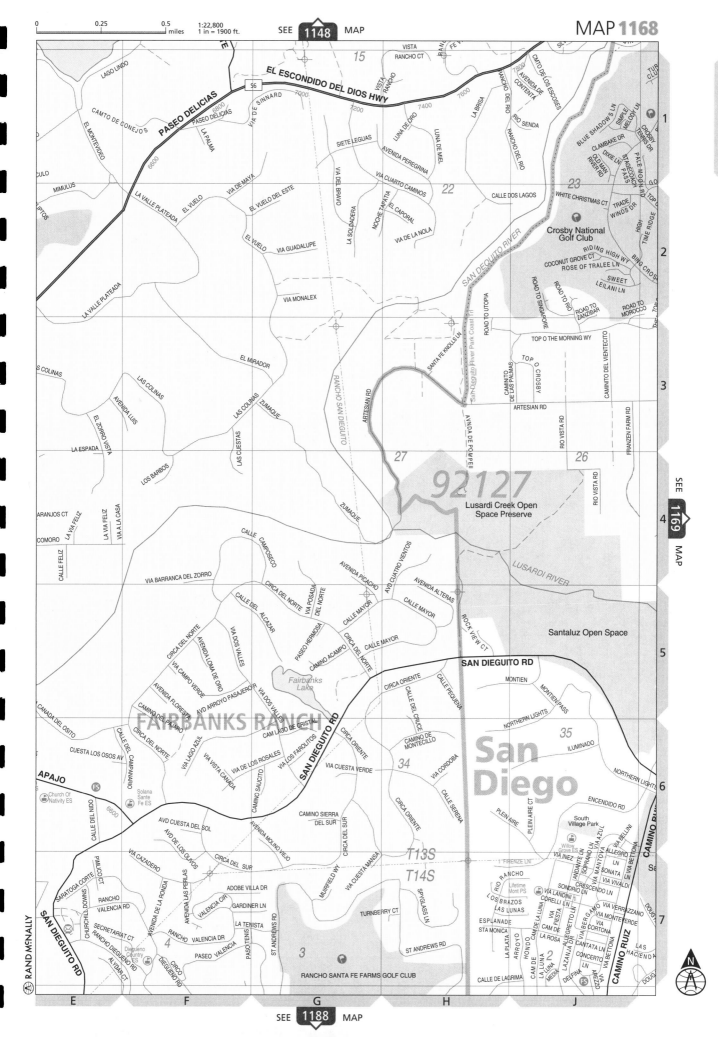

MAP 1168

SAN DIEGO CO.

SEE 1148 MAP

SEE 1169 MAP

92127

San Diego

FAIRBANKS RANCH

Crosby National Golf Club

Lusardi Creek Open Space Preserve

Santaluz Open Space

Rancho Santa Fe Farms Golf Club

RAND McNALLY

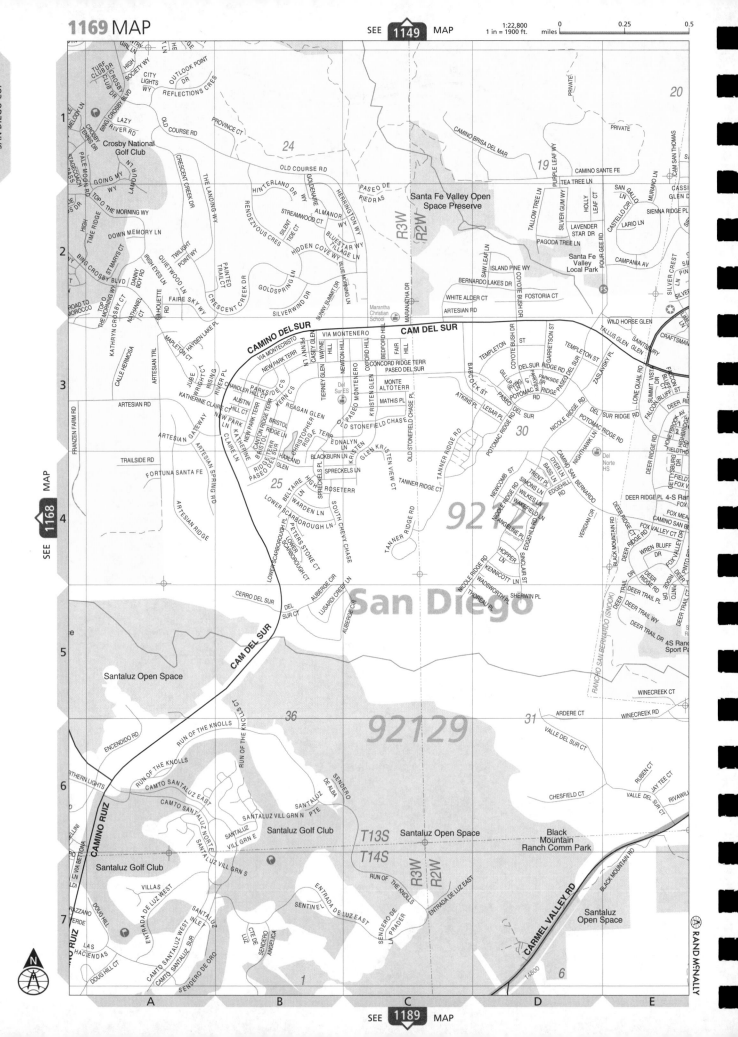

San Diego

92127

92129

Crosby National Golf Club

Santa Fe Valley Open Space Preserve

Santa Fe Valley Local Park

Santaluz Open Space

Santaluz Golf Club

Santaluz Open Space

Santaluz Golf Club

Santaluz Open Space

Black Mountain Ranch Comm Park

SEE ◄ **1168** MAP

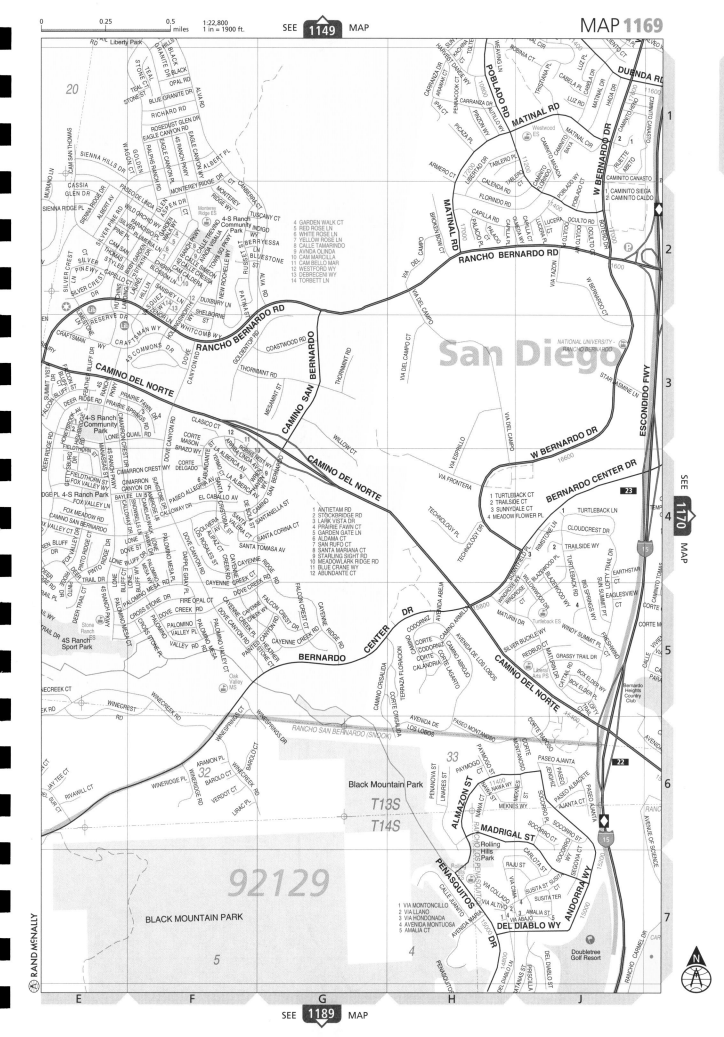

MAP 1169

SEE 1149 MAP

SEE 1170 MAP

SEE 1189 MAP

SAN DIEGO CO.

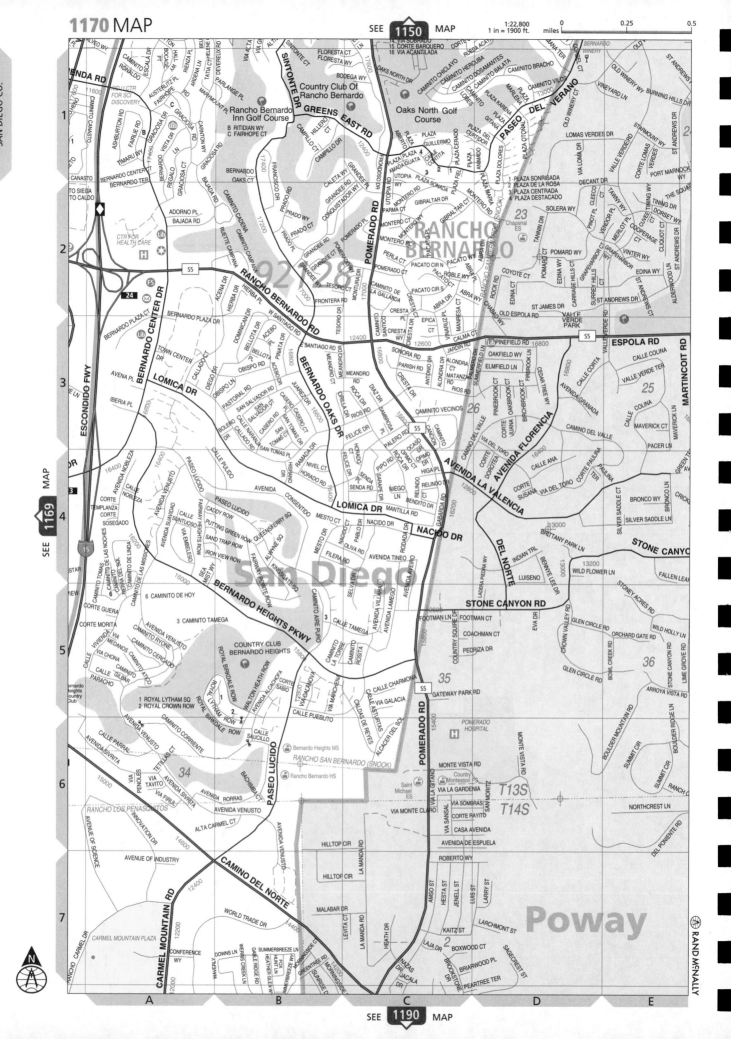

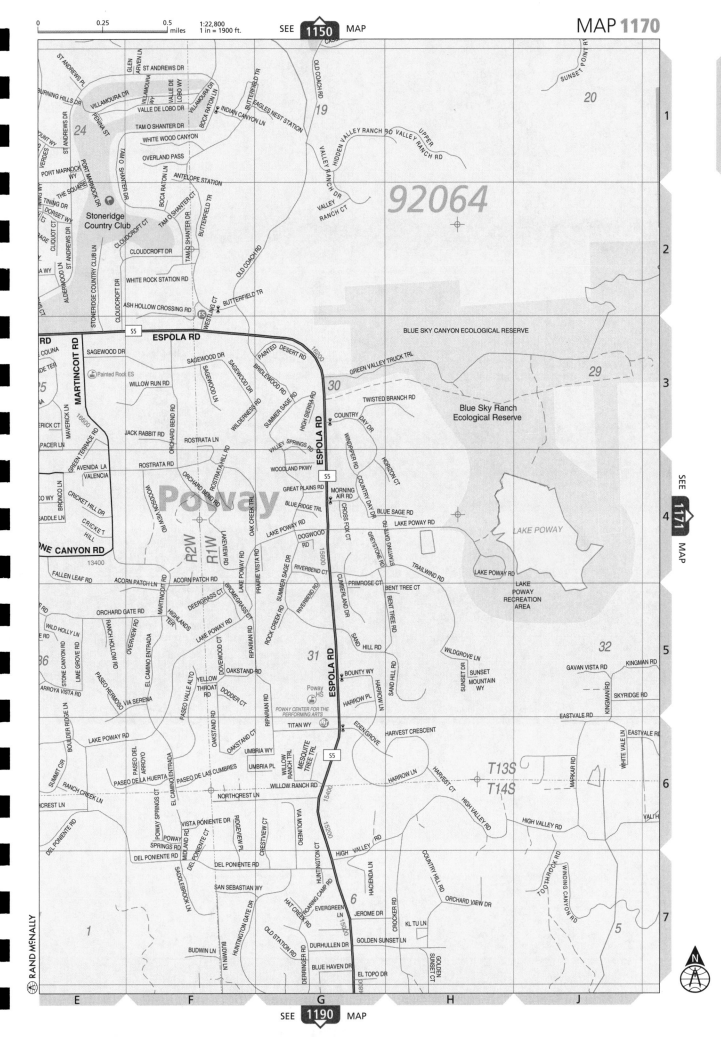

MAP 1170

SAN DIEGO CO.

92064

Poway

Stoneridge Country Club

Blue Sky Canyon Ecological Reserve

Blue Sky Ranch Ecological Reserve

Lake Poway

LAKE POWAY RECREATION AREA

SEE 1171 MAP

RAND McNALLY

0   0.25   0.5 miles   1:22,800   1 in = 1900 ft.

Roads and labels (partial listing):
St Andrews Pl, St Andrews Dr, Glen Arven Ln, Villamoura Dr, Valle De Lobo Wy, Burning Hills Dr, Villamoura Dr, Valle De Lobo Dr, Villamoura Ln, Boca Raton Ln, Indian Canyon Ln, Butterfield Tr, Eagles Nest Station, Old Coach Rd, Cason Dr, Sunset Point Wy, Tam O Shanter Dr, White Wood Canyon, Overland Pass, Antelope Station, Valley Ranch Dr, Hidden Valley Ranch Rd, Upper Valley Ranch Rd, Port Marnock Wy, St Andrews Dr, Cloudcroft Ct, Boca Raton Ln, Tam O Shanter Ct, Butterfield Tr, Valley Ranch Ct, Cloudcroft Dr, Tam O Shanter Ct, White Rock Station Rd, Old Coach Rd, Butterfield Tr, Cloudcroft Dr, Ash Hollow Crossing Rd, Westling Ct, Espola Rd, Martincoit Rd, Espola Rd, Sagewood Dr, Painted Desert Rd, Green Valley Truck Trl, Painted Rock ES, Sagewood Dr, Sagewood Ln, Bridlewood Rd, Willow Run Rd, Wilderness Rd, Summer Sage Rd, High Sierra Rd, Country Day Dr, Twisted Branch Rd, Jack Rabbit Rd, Orchard Bend Rd, Rostrata Ln, Rostrata Hill Rd, Valley Springs Rd, Windpiper Rd, Rostrata Rd, Woodland Pkwy, Horizon Ct, Great Plains Rd, Morning Air Rd, Blue Sage Rd, Cross Fox Ct, Blue Ridge Trl, Lake Poway Rd, Oak Creek Trl, Dogwood Rd, Greystone Rd, Stirling Gate Rd, Lake Poway Rd, Lakeview Rd, Prairie Vista Rd, Summer Sage Dr, Riverbend Ct, Trailwind Rd, Bent Tree Ct, Acorn Patch Ln, Acorn Patch Rd, Deergrass Ct, Bromegrass Ct, Riparian Rd, Rock Creek Rd, Riverbend Rd, Cumberland Dr, Primrose Ct, Bent Tree Rd, Fallen Leaf Rd, Orchard Gate Rd, Highlands Ter, Lake Poway Rd, Sand Hill Rd, Wildgrove Ln, Gavan Vista Rd, Kingman Rd, Wild Holly Ln, Overview Rd, El Camino Entrada, Dovewood Ct, Oakstand Rd, Bounty Wy, Sand Hill Rd, Sunset Dr, Sunset Mountain Wy, Kingman Rd, Skyridge Rd, Stone Canyon Rd, Lime Grove Rd, Yellow Throat Rd, Dodder Ct, Poway HS, Harrow Pl, Harrow Ln, Eastvale Rd, Arroya Vista Rd, Paseo Hermoso, Via Serena, Oakstand Rd, Titan Wy, Eden Grove, Harvest Crescent, White Vale Ln, Eastvale Rd, Boulder Ridge Ln, Paseo Del Arroyo, El Camino Entrada, Oakstand Ct, Umbria Wy, Markar Rd, Summit Cir, Ranch Creek Ln, Paseo De La Huerta, Paseo De Las Cumbres, Umbria Pl, Willow Ranch Trl, Mesquite Tree Trl, Harrow Ln, Harvest Ct, High Valley Rd, Del Poniente Rd, Northcrest Ln, Willow Ranch Rd, High Valley Rd, Poway Springs Ct, Vista Poniente Dr, Ridgeview Pl, Crestview Ct, Via Monticino, High Valley Rd, Poway Springs Rd, Midland Rd, Del Poniente Ct, Del Poniente Rd, Huntington Ct, San Sebastian Wy, Hacienda Ln, Country Hill Rd, Orchard View Dr, Winding Canyon Rd, Huntington Gate Dr, Hat Creek Rd, Roaring Camp Rd, Evergreen Ln, Jerome Dr, Crocker Rd, KL Tu Ln, Budwin Ln, Old Station Rd, Durhullen Dr, Golden Sunset Ln, Golden Sunset Ct, Derringer Rd, Blue Haven Dr, El Topo Dr

T13S / T14S

N

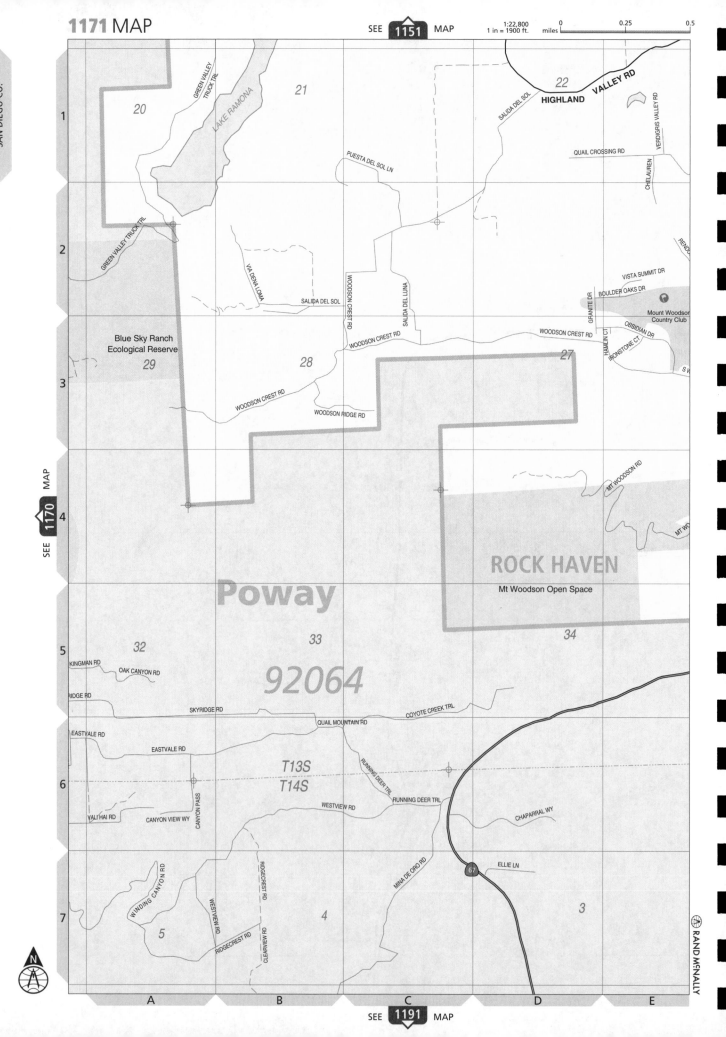

SEE 1151 MAP

1:22,800
1 in = 1900 ft.   miles   0   0.25   0.5

SAN DIEGO CO.

20

21

22   HIGHLAND   VALLEY RD

GREEN VALLEY TRUCK TRL

LAKE RAMONA

SALIDA DEL SOL

VERDIGRIS VALLEY RD

PUESTA DEL SOL LN

QUAIL CROSSING RD

CHELAUREN

1

2

GREEN VALLEY TRUCK TRL

VIA DENA LOMA

WOODSON CREST RD

SALIDA DEL SOL

SALIDA DEL LUNA

VISTA SUMMIT DR

BOULDER OAKS DR

GRANITE DR

RENDO

Blue Sky Ranch
Ecological Reserve

29

28

WOODSON CREST RD

WOODSON CREST RD

27

Mount Woodson
Country Club

HAMLIN CT

OBSIDIAN DR

IRONSTONE CT

S W

3

WOODSON CREST RD

WOODSON RIDGE RD

SEE 1170 MAP

MT WOODSON RD

MT WO

4

Poway

ROCK HAVEN

Mt Woodson Open Space

32

33

34

5

KINGMAN RD

OAK CANYON RD

92064

RIDGE RD

SKYRIDGE RD

COYOTE CREEK TRL

EASTVALE RD

QUAIL MOUNTAIN RD

EASTVALE RD

T13S
T14S

RUNNING DEER TRL

6

CANYON PASS

VALI HAI RD

CANYON VIEW WY

WESTVIEW RD

RUNNING DEER TRL

CHAPARRAL WY

WINDING CANYON RD

WESTVIEW RD

RIDGECREST RD

MINA DE ORO RD

67

ELLIE LN

3

7

5

RIDGECREST RD

CLEARVIEW RD

4

N

RAND McNALLY

A   B   C   D   E

SEE 1191 MAP

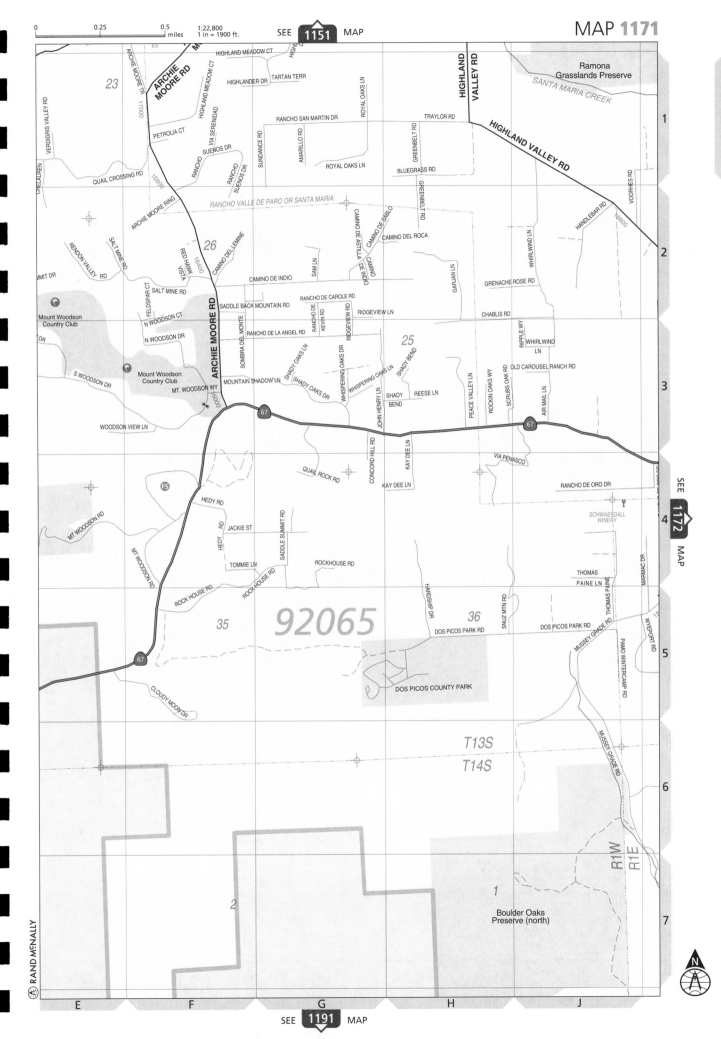

MAP **1171**

SAN DIEGO CO.

0   0.25   0.5
miles
1:22,800
1 in = 1900 ft.

SEE 1151 MAP

Ramona
Grasslands Preserve
SANTA MARIA CREEK

23
ARCHIE MOORE RD
ARCHIE MOORE TR
17000

HIGHLAND MEADOW CT
HIGHLAND MEADOW CT
HIGHLANDER DR   TARTAN TERR
HIGHLAND

HIGHLAND VALLEY RD
HIGHLAND VALLEY RD

VERDIGRIS VALLEY RD

RANCHO SAN MARTIN DR
ROYAL OAKS LN
TRAYLOR RD

PETROLIA CT

SUNDANCE RD
AMARILLO RD
ROYAL OAKS LN
GREENBELT RD
BLUEGRASS RD

CHELAUREN
QUAIL CROSSING RD
16800

VOORHES RD

RANCHO SUENOS DR
RANCHO SUENOS DR
VIA SERENIDAD
RANCHO

RANCHO VALLE DE PARO OR SANTA MARIA
GREENBELT RD

1

ARCHIE MOORE RING
16400

26
CAMINO DEL LEMINE
CAMINO DE ASTILLA
CAMINO DE SABLO
CAMINO DEL ROCA
CAMINO

HANDLEBAR RD
18800

WHIRLWIND LN

2

RENDON VALLEY RD
SALT MINE RD
RED HAWK VISTA

SAM LN
CAMINO DE INDIO
GARIAN LN
GRENACHE ROSE RD

SUMMIT DR
CAMINO DE INDIO

FELDSPAR CT
N WOODSON CT
SALT MINE RD

SADDLE BACK MOUNTAIN RD
RANCHO DE CAROLE RD
RANCHO DE KEVIN RD
RIDGEVIEW RD
RIDGEVIEW LN
CHABLIS RD

RIPPLE WY
WHIRLWIND LN

Mount Woodson
Country Club

N WOODSON DR
N WOODSON DR

SOMBRA DEL MONTE
RANCHO DE LA ANGEL RD

25
SHADY BEND

OLD CAROUSEL RANCH RD

DR
Mount Woodson
Country Club
MT. WOODSON WY

S WOODSON DR

MOUNTAIN SHADOW LN
SHADY OAKS LN
SHADY OAKS DR
WHISPERING OAKS DR
WHISPERING OAKS LN
SHADY BEND
SHADY BEND   REESE LN

PEACE VALLEY LN
ROCKIN OAKS WY
SCRUBS OAK RD
AIR MAIL LN

67
67

WOODSON VIEW LN
JOHN HENRY LN

VIA PENASCO

MT WOODSON RD

FS

QUAIL ROCK RD
KAY DEE LN

KAY DEE LN

RANCHO DE ORO DR

SCHWAESDALL WINERY

SEE 1172 MAP

3

HEDY RD

CONCORD HILL RD

JACKIE ST
HEDY RD
SADDLE SUMMIT RD

4

TOMMIE LN
ROCKHOUSE RD

MARMAC DR

THOMAS PAINE LN

MT WOODSON RD

ROCK HOUSE RD
ROCK HOUSE RD

35
92065
36

HARDSHIP DR
DOS PICOS PARK RD
SNUZ MTN RD
DOS PICOS PARK RD

THOMAS PAINE

WYEPORT RD
15

MUSSEY GRADE RD
PAMO WINTERCAMP RD

67

DOS PICOS COUNTY PARK

5

CLOUDY MOON DR

T13S
T14S

MUSSEY GRADE RD

6

R1W
R1E

2

1
Boulder Oaks
Preserve (north)

7

RAND M\NALLY

E   F   G   H   J

N

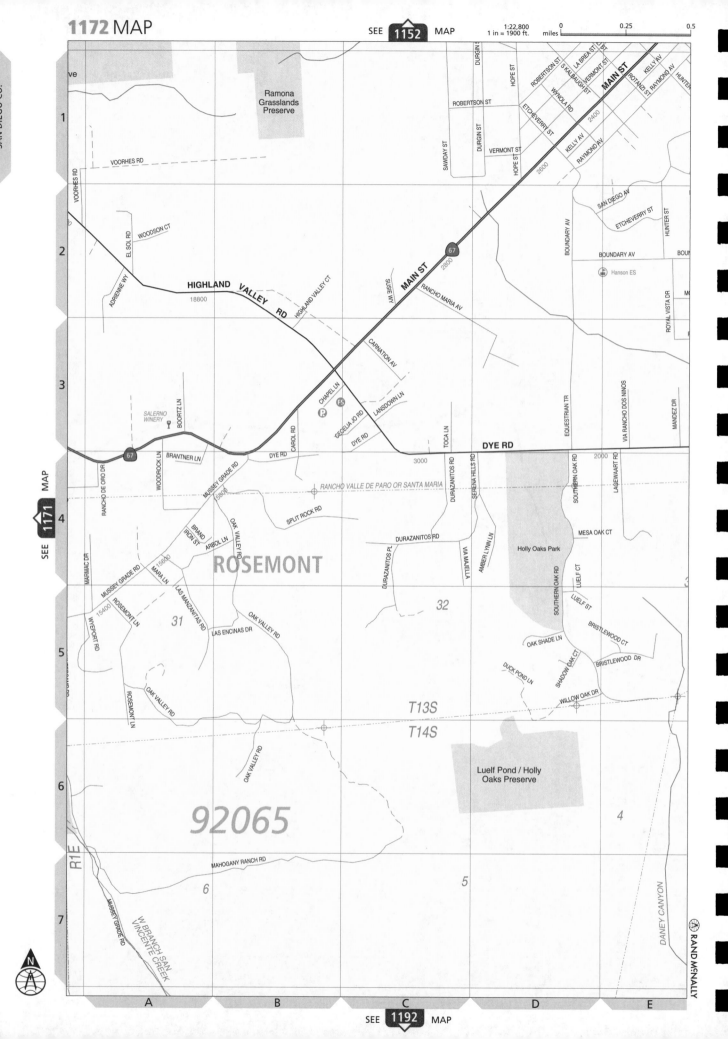

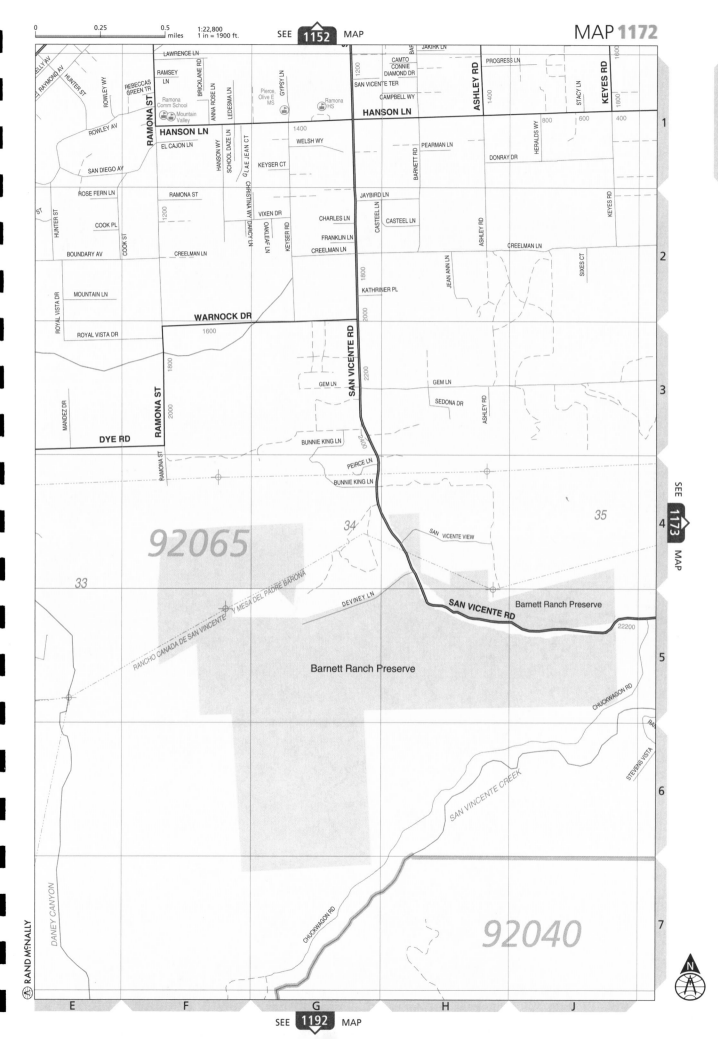

0   0.25   0.5
miles
1:22,800
1 in = 1900 ft.

LAWRENCE LN

RAMSEY LN

RELLY AV

RAYMOND RD

HUNTER ST

ROWLEY WY

REBECCAS GREEN TR

RAMONA ST

BRICKLANE RD

ANNA ROSE LN

LEDESMA LN

GYPSY LN

Pierce, Olive E MS

JAKIRK LN

CAMTO
CONNIE
DIAMOND DR

SAN VICENTE TER

CAMPBELL WY

PROGRESS LN

ASHLEY RD

KEYES RD

STACY LN

Ramona Comm School

Mountain Valley

Ramona HS

HANSON LN

HANSON LN

1400

1200

1400

800   600   400

ROWLEY AV

EL CAJON LN

HANSON LN

HANSON WY

SCHOOL DAZE LN

GL AE JEAN CT

WELSH WY

BARNETT RD

PEARMAN LN

HERALDS WY

DONRAY DR

1600

1800

SAN DIEGO AV

KEYSER CT

CHRISTINA WY

ROSE FERN LN

RAMONA ST

VIXEN DR

DARCY LN

CHARLES LN

JAYBIRD LN

CASTEEL LN

CASTEEL LN

KEYES RD

HUNTER ST

1200

COOK PL

OAKLEAF LN

KEYSER RD

FRANKLIN LN

CREELMAN LN

CREELMAN LN

ASHLEY RD

CREELMAN LN

SIXES CT

ST

BOUNDARY AV

CREELMAN LN

1800

JEAN ANN LN

2

MOUNTAIN LN

KATHRINER PL

ROYAL VISTA DR

ROYAL VISTA DR

WARNOCK DR

1600

SAN VICENTE RD

1800

2000

2200

GEM LN

GEM LN

SEDONA DR

ASHLEY RD

3

MANDEZ DR

RAMONA ST

2000

DYE RD

RAMONA ST

1800

2400

BUNNIE KING LN

PEIRCE LN

BUNNIE KING LN

SAN VICENTE VIEW

35

SEE 1173 MAP

92065

34

4

33

RANCHO CANADA DE SAN VINCENTE Y MESA DEL PADRE BARONA

DEVINEY LN

SAN VICENTE RD

Barnett Ranch Preserve

22200

Barnett Ranch Preserve

CHUCKWAGON RD

5

RAN

STEVENS VISTA

SAN VINCENTE CREEK

6

DANEY CANYON

CHUCKWAGON RD

92040

7

E   F   G   H   J

N

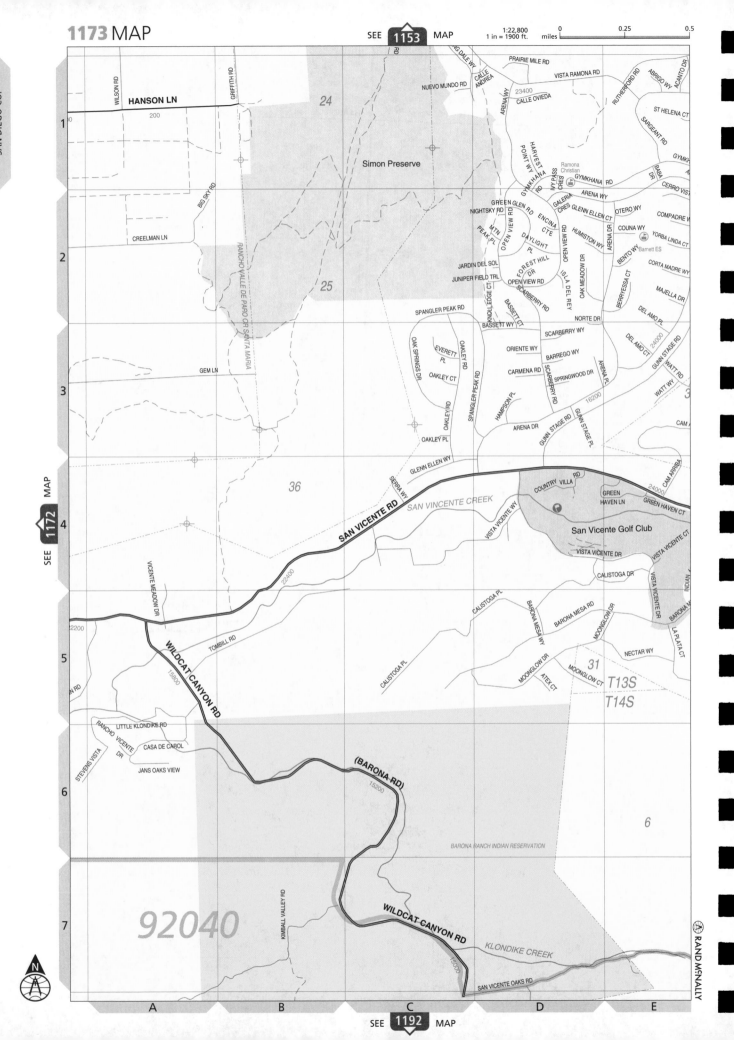

1:22,800
1 in = 1900 ft.

0   0.25   0.5
miles

SAN DIEGO CO.

HANSON LN

WILSON RD

GRIFFITH RD

200

24

Simon Preserve

NUEVO MUNDO RD

PRAIRIE MILE RD

VISTA RAMONA RD

CALLE ANDREA

23400

CALLE OVIEDA

ARENA WY

RUTHERFORD RD

ABRIGO WY

ACANITO DR

ST HELENA CT

SARGEANT RD

GYMKH

HARVEST POINT WY

IVY PASS CRES

Ramona Christian

GYMKHANA RD

CERRO VISTA

BABA DR

A

GYMKHANA RD

ARENA WY

CRESELMAN LN

BIG SKY RD

GREEN GLEN RD

NIGHTSKY RD

GLEN RD

ENCINA CTE

GALERIA CRES

GLENN ELLEN CT

OTERO WY

COMPADRE W

RANCHO VALLE DE PARO OR SANTA MARIA

MTN PEAK PL

OPEN VIEW RD

DAYLIGHT PL

HUMISTON WY

ARENA DR

COUNA WY

YORBA LINDA CT

Barnett ES

CORTA MADRE WY

2

25

JARDIN DEL SOL

JUNIPER FIELD TRL

FOREST HILL DR

OPEN VIEW RD

OPEN VIEW RD

ISLA DEL REY

OAK MEADOW DR

BENTO WY

BERRYESSA CT

MAJELLA DR

DEL AMO PL

KNOLLEDGE CT

SCARBERRY RD

BASSETT CT

NORTE DR

SPANGLER PEAK RD

BASSETT WY

SCARBERRY WY

DEL AMO PL

24000

GUNN STAGE RD

OAK SPRINGS DR

EVERETT PL

OAKLEY PL

ORIENTE WY

BARREGO WY

ARENA PL

GUNN WATT RD

OAKLEY CT

CARMENA RD

SCARBERRY RD

SPRINGWOOD DR

WATT WY

3

36

OAKLEY RD

SPANGLER PEAK RD

HAMPTON PL

ARENA DR

GUNN STAGE RD

GUNN STAGE PL

16200

CAM A

OAKLEY PL

GLENN ELLEN WY

24000

CAM ARRIBA

SIERRA WY

COUNTRY VILLA RD

GREEN HAVEN LN

GREEN HAVEN CT

SAN VICENTE RD

SAN VINCENTE CREEK

SEE ⌂ 1172 MAP

4

San Vicente Golf Club

VISTA VICENTE WY

VISTA VICENTE DR

VISTA VICENTE CT

VISTA VICENTE DR

BARONA

VICENTE MEADOW DR

22400

CALISTOGA DR

CALISTOGA PL

BARONA MESA RD

MOONGLOW DR

LA PLATA CT

WILDCAT CANYON RD

TOMBILL RD

22200

BARONA MESA WY

NECTAR WY

5

15890

CALISTOGA PL

MOONGLOW DR

MOONGLOW CT

31

T13S

N RD

ATEX CT

T14S

LITTLE KLONDIKE RD

RANCHO VICENTE DR

CASA DE CAROL

STEVENS VISTA

JANS OAKS VIEW

6

(BARONA RD)

15200

6

BARONA RANCH INDIAN RESERVATION

KIMBALL VALLEY RD

7

92040

WILDCAT CANYON RD

KLONDIKE CREEK

15200

SAN VICENTE OAKS RD

N

RAND McNALLY

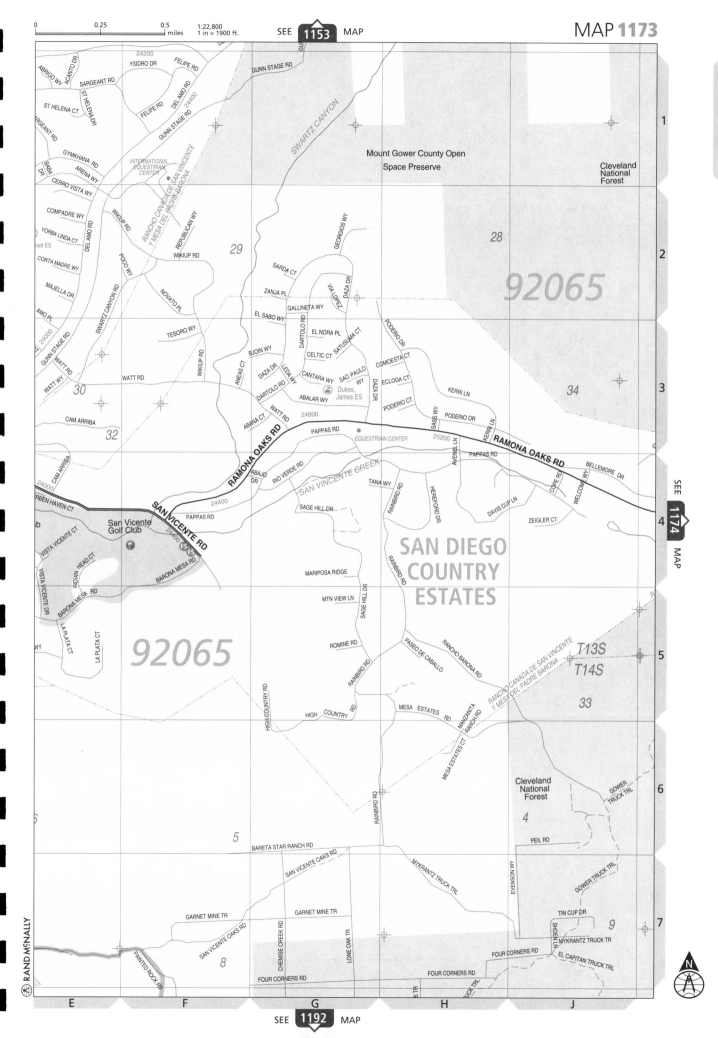

MAP **1173**

SAN DIEGO CO.

SEE 1153 MAP

0   0.25   0.5
miles
1:22,800
1 in = 1900 ft.

Mount Gower County Open
Space Preserve

Cleveland
National
Forest

92065

92065

SAN DIEGO
COUNTRY
ESTATES

Cleveland
National
Forest

SEE 1174 MAP

RAND McNALLY

E   F   G   H   J

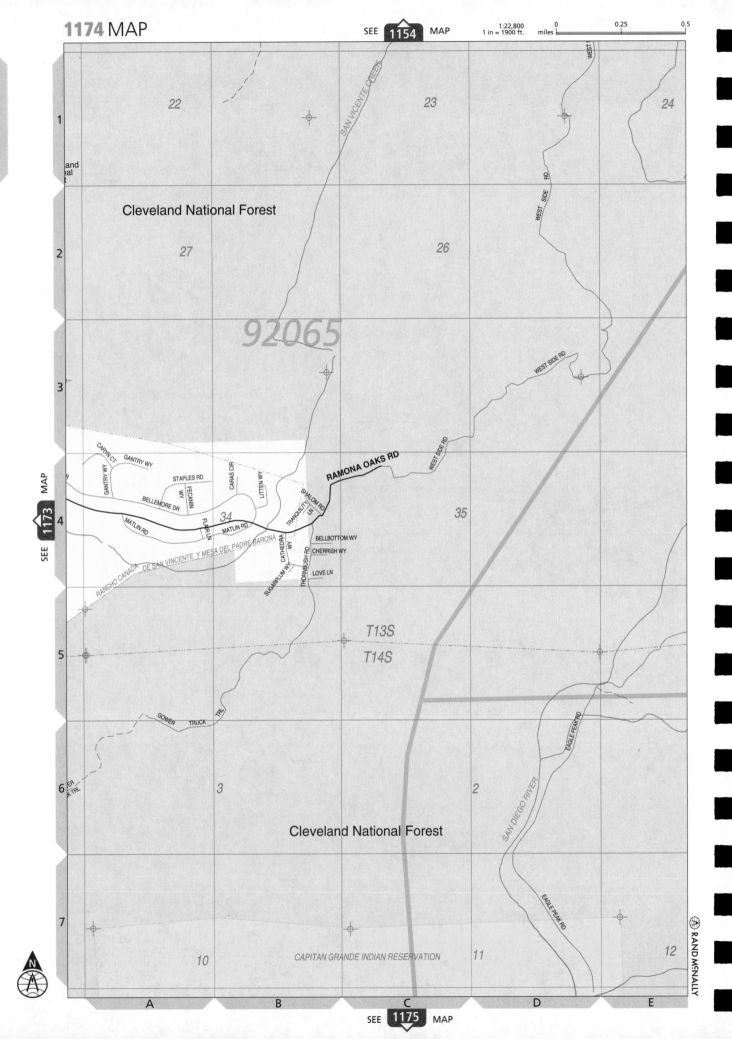

1:22,800
1 in = 1900 ft.

miles 0   0.25   0.5

SAN DIEGO CO.

Cleveland National Forest

22

23

24

27

26

92065

WEST SIDE RD

WEST SIDE RD

WEST SIDE RD

CARYN CT
GANTRY WY
GANTRY WY
STAPLES RD
FECANIN WY
BELLEMORE DR
CARAS CIR
LITTEN WY
RAMONA OAKS RD
SHALOM RD
TRANQUILITY LN
MATLIN RD
FLAIR LN
MATLIN RD
35

RANCHO CANADA DE SAN VINCENTE Y MESA DEL PADRE BARONA

34

SUGARPLUM WY
CATHEDRA WY
THORNBUSH RD
BELLBOTTOM WY
CHERRISH WY
LOVE LN

T13S
T14S

GOWER TRUCK TRL

ER K TRL

3

2

Cleveland National Forest

SAN DIEGO RIVER

EAGLE PEAK RD

EAGLE PEAK RD

7

10

11

12

CAPITAN GRANDE INDIAN RESERVATION

A   B   C   D   E

SEE 1173 MAP

RAND McNALLY

MAP **1174**

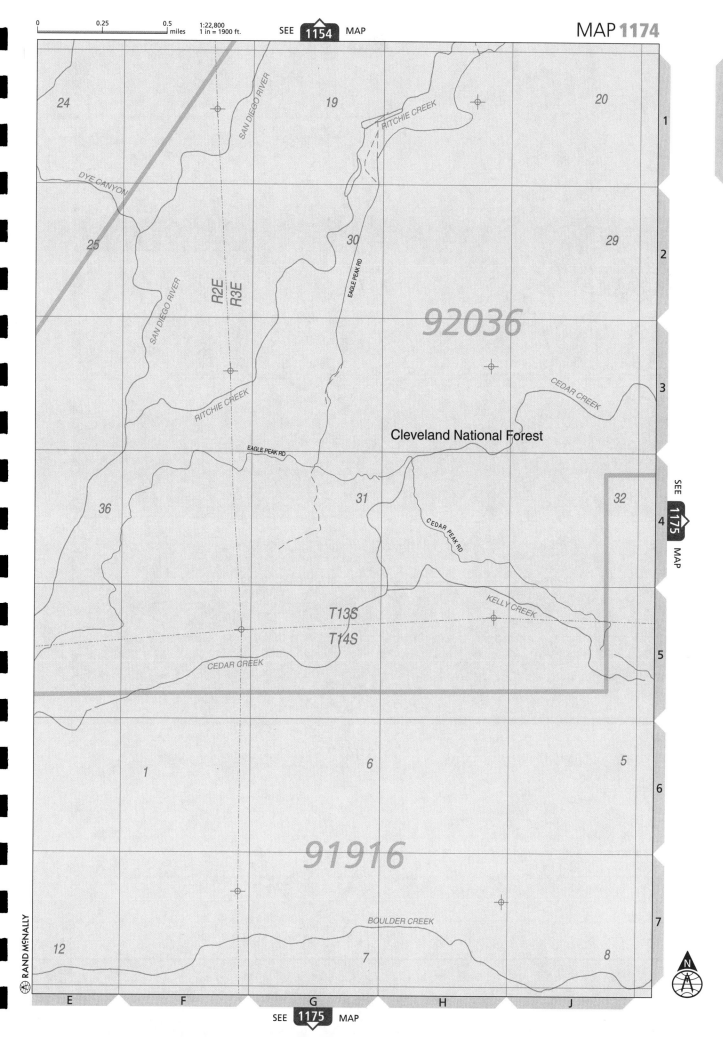

0   0.25   0.5
miles
1:22,800
1 in = 1900 ft.

SEE 1154 MAP

24

25

DYE CANYON

SAN DIEGO RIVER

R2E
R3E

RITCHIE CREEK

SAN DIEGO RIVER

19

RITCHIE CREEK

30

EAGLE PEAK RD

92036

CEDAR CREEK

20

29

1

2

3

Cleveland National Forest

EAGLE PEAK RD

36

31

CEDAR PEAK RD

32

KELLY CREEK

SEE 1175 MAP

4

T13S

T14S

CEDAR CREEK

5

1

6

5

6

91916

BOULDER CREEK

7

12

7

8

⊕ RAND M?NALLY

E   F   G   H   J

SEE 1175 MAP

1175 MAP

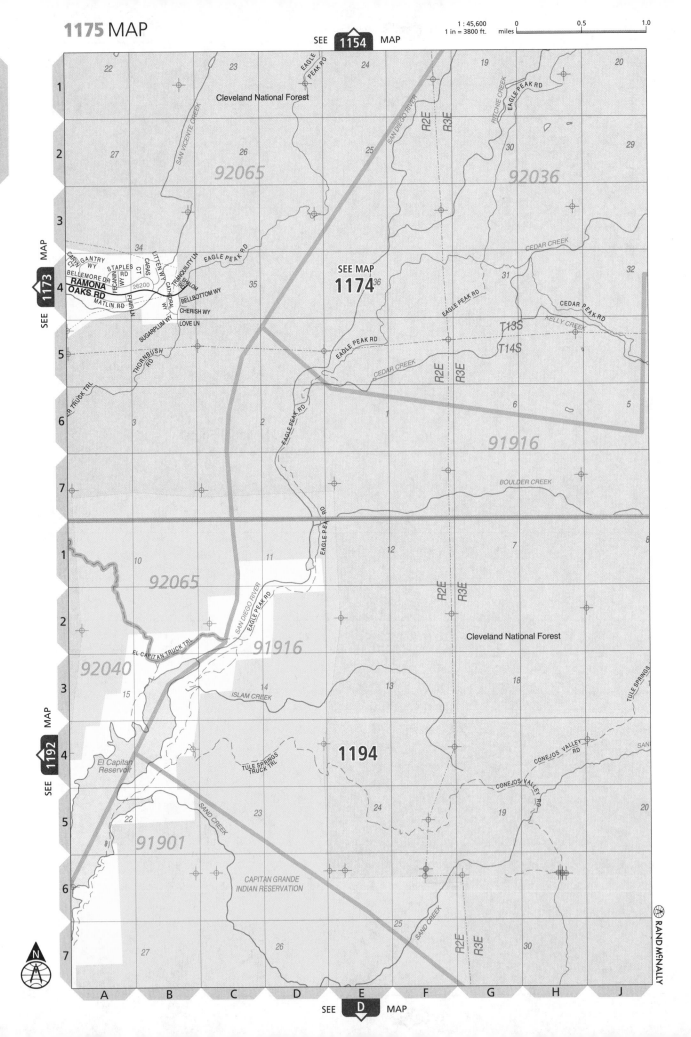

Cleveland National Forest

92065

92036

SEE MAP
1174

SEE 1173 MAP

GANTRY WY
BELLEMORE DR
RAMONA OAKS RD
STAPLES RD
CARAS CT
LITTEN WY
CATHEDRAL WY
TRANQUILITY LN
EAGLE PEAK RD
MATLIN RD
SUGARPLUM WY
CHERISH WY
BELLBOTTOM WY
SHALOM
LOVE LN
26200
THORNBUSH RD

EAGLE PEAK RD

CEDAR CREEK

CEDAR PEAK RD

KELLY CREEK

T13S
T14S

R2E
R3E

CEDAR CREEK

EAGLE PEAK RD

91916

BOULDER CREEK

EAGLE PEAK RD

92065

SAN DIEGO RIVER
EAGLE PEAK RD

91916

92040

EL CAPITAN TRUCK TRL

ISLAM CREEK

R2E
R3E

Cleveland National Forest

TULE SPRINGS

1194

El Capitan Reservoir

TULE SPRINGS TRUCK TRL

CONEJOS VALLEY RD

CONEJOS VALLEY RD

SAND CREEK

91901

CAPITAN GRANDE INDIAN RESERVATION

SAND CREEK

R2E
R3E

RAND MCNALLY

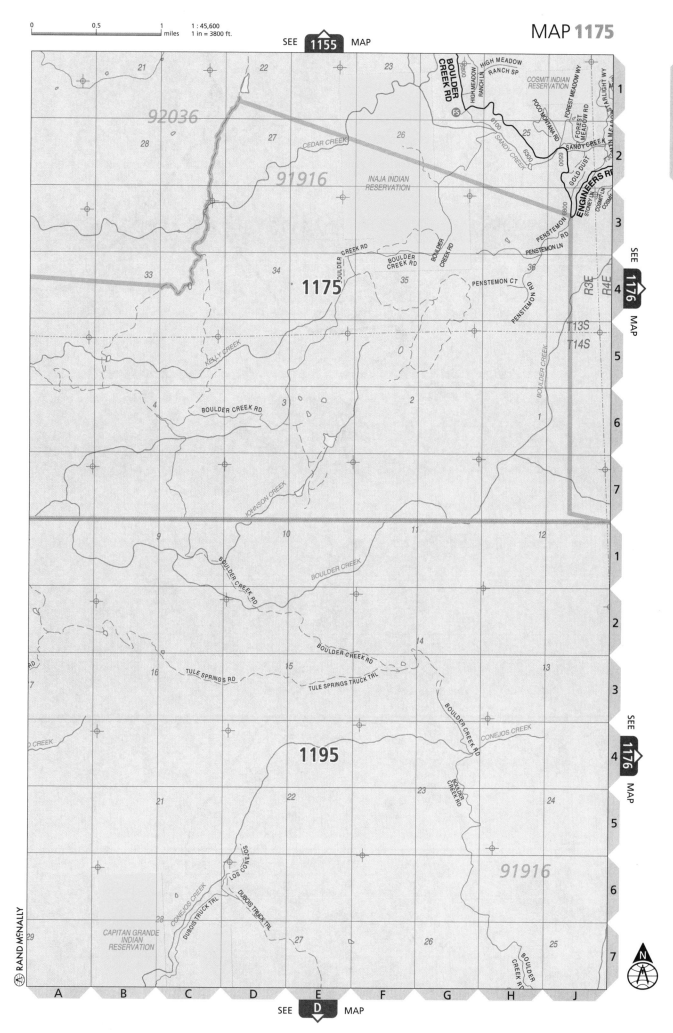

MAP **1175**

SAN DIEGO CO.

1 : 45,600
1 in = 3800 ft.

0   0.5   1
miles

SEE **1155** MAP

92036

91916

BOULDER CREEK RD

COSMIT INDIAN RESERVATION

HIGH MEADOW RANCH LN

HIGH MEADOW RANCH SP

HIGHMEADOW

FOREST MEADOW WY

STARLIGHT WY

POCO MONTANA RD

FOREST MEADOW RD

SANDY CREEK

GOLD DUST

ENGINEERS RD

COSMIT LN

CEDAR CREEK

INAJA INDIAN RESERVATION

PENSTEMON RD

PENSTEMON LN

BOULDER CREEK RD

BOULDER CREEK RD

PENSTEMON CT

PENSTEMON RD

R3E R4E

1175

T13S
T14S

BOULDER CREEK

KELLY CREEK

BOULDER CREEK RD

JOHNSON CREEK

SEE **1176** MAP

BOULDER CREEK

BOULDER CREEK RD

TULE SPRINGS RD

TULE SPRINGS TRUCK TRL

BOULDER CREEK RD

BOULDER CREEK RD

CONEJOS CREEK

1195

BOULDER CREEK RD

SEE **1176** MAP

CREEK

91916

CONEJOS CREEK

LOS CONEJOS

DUBOIS TRUCK TRL

DUBOIS TRUCK TRL

CONEJOS TRUCK TRL

CAPITAN GRANDE INDIAN RESERVATION

BOULDER CREEK RD

RAND McNALLY

SEE **D** MAP

21 22 23
28 27 26 25
33 34 35 36
4   3   2   1
9   10 11 12
16 15 14 13
21 22 23 24
28 27 26 25
29

A B C D E F G H J

1 2 3 4 5 6 7
1 2 3 4 5 6 7

N

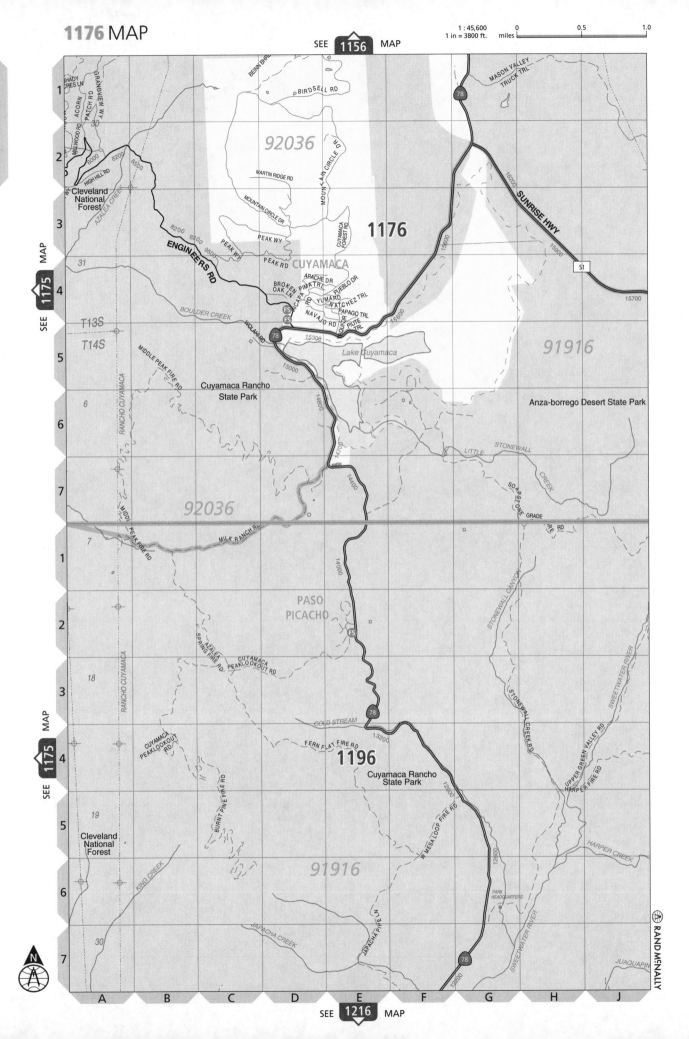

SAN DIEGO CO.

1 : 45,600
1 in = 3800 ft.

miles   0   0.5   1.0

SEE **1156** MAP

SHADY CRES LN
GRANDVIEW WY
ACORN PATCH RD
MILLWOOD RD
30
HIGH HILL RD
8000
8200
8500

Cleveland National Forest

AZALEA CREEK

BENN BIRD

BIRDSELL RD

MARTIN RIDGE RD

MOUNTAIN CIRCLE DR

92036

MOUNTAIN CIRCLE DR

PEAK WY

1176

8200
8200
9500
PEAK WH
PEAK RD

ENGINEERS RD

CUYAMACA FOREST RD

CUYAMACA

78

MASON VALLEY TRUCK TRL

16200

SUNRISE HWY

15600

15900

S1

15700

31

APACHE DR
PIMA TRL
PUEBLO DR
BROKEN OAK LN
YUMA RD
NATCHEZ TRL
PAPAGO TRL
QUINO RD
NAVAJO RD
PIUTE TRL

CAPA RD

FS
FS

WOLAHI RD

78

15300

15600

BOULDER CREEK

T13S
T14S

Lake Cuyamaca

91916

MIDDLE PEAK FIRE RD

RANCHO CUYAMACA

Cuyamaca Rancho State Park

6

15000

14800

14700

14400

Anza-borrego Desert State Park

LITTLE STONEWALL

SOAPSTONE GRADE

CREEK

RIE RD

92036

MIDDLE PEAK FIRE RD

MILK RANCH RD

7

14000

PASO PICACHO

AZALEA SPRING FIRE RD

CUYAMACA PEAKLOOKOUT RD

FS

18

RANCHO CUYAMACA

14000

STONEWALL CANYON

STONEWALL CREEK RD

SWEETWATER RIVER

CUYAMACA PEAKLOOKOUT RD

COLD STREAM

78

13200

FERN FLAT FIRE RD

1196

Cuyamaca Rancho State Park

UPPER GREEN VALLEY RD

HARPER FIRE RD

BURNT PINE FIRE RD

19

12800

W MESA LOOP FIRE RD

12600

HARPER CREEK

Cleveland National Forest

91916

KING CREEK

30

JAPACHA CREEK

JAPACHA PIPE LN

PARK HEADQUARTERS

SWEETWATER RIVER

78

12200

JUAQUAPIN

SEE **1175** MAP

SEE **1175** MAP

SEE **1216** MAP

RAND McNALLY

N

A B C D E F G H J

1 2 3 4 5 6 7

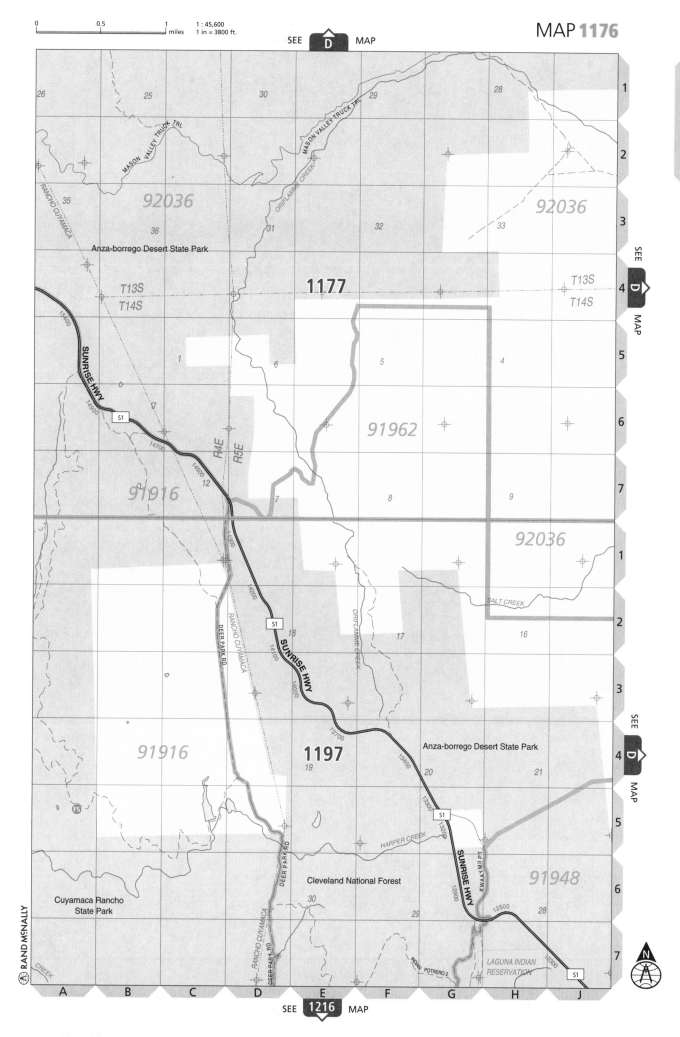

MAP **1176**

SAN DIEGO CO.

0   0.5   1   1 : 45,600
miles   1 in = 3800 ft.

SEE D MAP

26   25   30   29   28   1

2

MASON VALLEY TRUCK TRL

MASON VALLEY TRUCK TRL

RANCHO CUYAMACA

ORIFLAMME CREEK

92036   35   36   31   32   33   **92036**   3

Anza-borrego Desert State Park

T13S   T13S   SEE D MAP
T14S   **1177**   T14S   4

15400   1   6   5   4   5

SUNRISE HWY

14900   S1   **91962**   6

14700

14500

R4E   R5E

12   7   8   9   7

91916   14300

92036   1

SALT CREEK

14200   S1   2

RANCHO CUYAMACA   18   17   16

DEER PARK RD   14100   ORIFLAMME CREEK

SUNRISE HWY   14000   3

13700   SEE D MAP

Anza-borrego Desert State Park   4

91916   **1197**   13400   20   21
19   13300   S1

FS   HARPER CREEK   13200   5

SUNRISE HWY

KWAA'YMII PT.

Cleveland National Forest   12500   **91948**   6

Cuyamaca Rancho
State Park   30   29   12500   28

DEER PARK RD

RANCHO CUYAMACA   DEER PARK RD

INDIAN POTRERO 2   LAGUNA INDIAN
RESERVATION   12300

CREEK   S1   7

RAND M?NALLY

A   B   C   D   E   F   G   H   J

SEE **1216** MAP

N

1187 MAP

SEE 1167 MAP

1:22,800
1 in = 1900 ft.

miles
0   0.25   0.5

SAN DIEGO CO.

PACIFIC OCEAN

North Se

DEL MA

NO
Del Mar
Beach

1 OCEAN SU
2 PACIFIC SU
3 BEACH FRO

S HELIX AV

SEE D MAP

N

SEE 1207 MAP

RAND MCNALLY

A   B   C   D   E

1   2   3   4   5   6   7

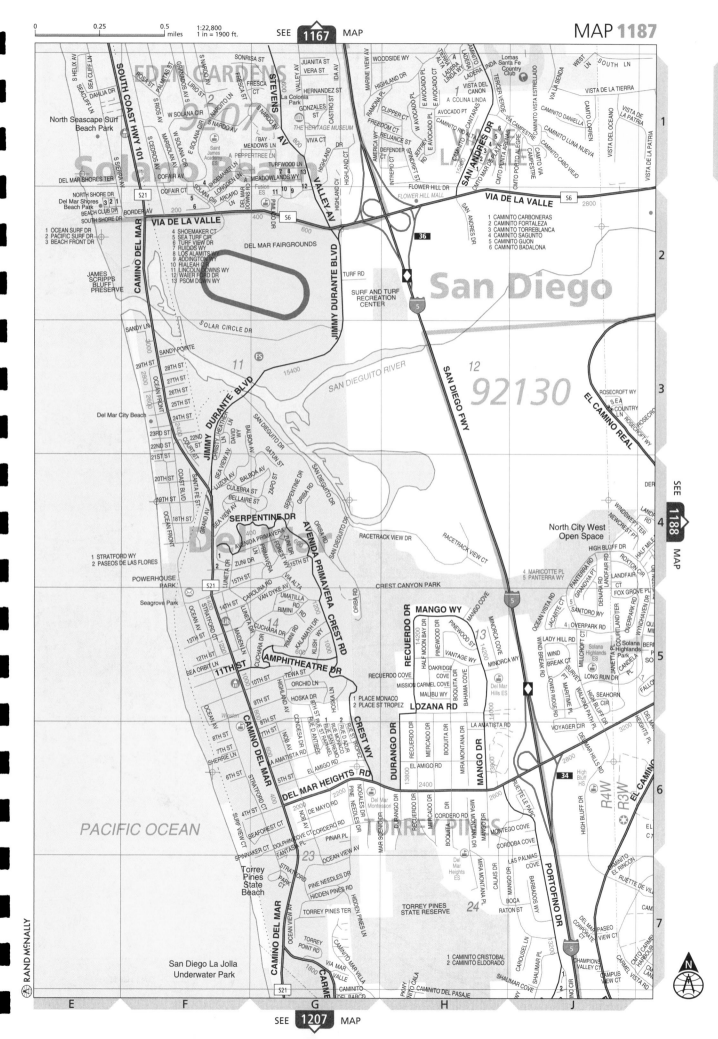

MAP 1187

SAN DIEGO CO.

SEE 1167 MAP

0   0.25   0.5
miles
1:22,800
1 in = 1900 ft.

EDEN GARDENS
92075

Solana Beach

S HELIX AV
S SEA CLIFF LN
S RIOS AV
PALMITAS ST
S SIERRA AV
S CLIFF FLORES LN
DAHLIA DR
ROSA ST
GRANADOS AV
S NARDO AV
NARDITO LN
W SOLANA CIR
S NARDO AV
SONRISA ST
LIRIO ST
FRESCA CT
JUANITA ST
VERA AV
VALLEY AV
IDA AV
WOODSIDE WY
MARINE VIEW AV
HIGHLAND DR
RAMONA AV
TIERRA ALTA
LADERA LN
LADERA LINDA
WEST LN
SOUTH LN
Lomas Santa Fe Country Club

North Seascape Surf Beach Park

W SOLANA CIR
S CEDROS AV
STEVENS AV
La Colonia Park
HERNANDEZ DR
CASTRO ST
GONZALES ST
THE HERITAGE MUSEUM
AVOCADO PL
W AVOCADO PL
E AVOCADO PL
A COLINA LINDA
VISTA DEL CANON
TERCER VERDE
CAMINITO DANIELLA
CAMINITO LUNA NUEVA
VISTA DE LA PATRIA

Saint James Academy
PEPPERTREE LN
TURFWOOD LN
MEADOWLANDS WY
Fusion ES
BAY MEADOWS LN
SHOEMAKER LN
LONGDEN LN
SOLANA CIR
AMERICA WY
FREEDOM CT
RELIANCE ST
DEFENDER CT
SAN ANDRES DR
VIA LA CAMPESTRE
CAMTO VIA CAMPESTRE
CAMTO CABO VIEJO

DEL MAR SHORES TER
COFAIR AV
COFAIR CT
ARCARO DR
DEL MAR DOWNS RD
PIMLICO DR
INTREPID CT
SPINDRIFT ST
JEFFREY
FLOWER HILL DR
FLOWER HILL MALL
VISTA DE LA TIERRA
VISTA DEL OCEANO
CAMTO LORREN
VISTA DE LA PATRIA

NORTH SHORE DR
Del Mar Shores Beach Park
3 2 1
BEACH CLUB DR
SOUTH SHORE DR
BORDER AV

VIA DE LA VALLE
VIA DE LA VALLE
S6
SAN ANDRES DR
2800

1 OCEAN SURF DR
2 PACIFIC SURF DR
3 BEACH FRONT DR

4 SHOEMAKER CT
5 SEA TURF CIR
6 TURF VIEW DR
7 RUIDOS WY
8 LOS ALAMITOS WY
9 ADDINGTON WY
10 HIALEAH WY
11 LINCOLN DOWNS WY
12 WATER FORD DR
13 PSOM DOWN WY

1 CAMINITO CARBONERAS
2 CAMINITO FORTALEZA
3 CAMINITO TORREBLANCA
4 CAMINITO SAGUNTO
5 CAMINITO GIJON
6 CAMINITO BADALONA

CAMINO DEL MAR

JAMES SCRIPPS BLUFF PRESERVE

DEL MAR FAIRGROUNDS

JIMMY DURANTE BLVD

TURF RD
SURF AND TURF RECREATION CENTER
36
5
San Diego

SANDY LN
SOLAR CIRCLE DR
11
FS
15400
SAN DIEGUITO RIVER
San Dieguito River
12
92130
EL CAMINO REAL
ROSECROFT WY
SEA COUNTRY
ROSECROFT

SANDY POINTE
29TH ST
28TH ST
27TH ST
26TH ST
25TH ST
24TH ST
23RD ST
22ND ST
21ST ST
20TH ST
19TH ST
18TH ST
OCEAN FRONT
3000
2800
2600
2400
Del Mar City Beach
JIMMY DURANTE BLVD
CHRISTY LN
HEATHER LN
DAVID AV
BALBOA AV
SAN DIEGUITO DR
SAN DIEGUITO DR
ORIBA DR
SEA VIEW AV
LUZON AV
CULEBRA ST
BELLAIRE ST
ZAPO ST
SERPENTINE DR
COAST BLVD
SANTA FE AV
GRAND AV
GATUN ST
RACETRACK VIEW DR
RACETRACK VIEW CT
North City West Open Space
WINDSWEPT TER
NEWCREST PT
LANDF
DER
SEE 1188 MAP

SERPENTINE DR
Del Mar
AVENIDA PRIMAVERA
CREST RD
400
AVENIDA PRIMAVERA
ZUNI DR
LUNETA DR
ZUNI DR
FOREST LN
VIA ALTA
ORIBA DR
4 MARICOTTE PL
5 PANTERRA WY
HIGH BLUFF DR
PANTERRA RD
ROXTON CIR
LANDFAIR
LANDFAIR CT
FOX GROVE PL
HALF MILE
1 STRATFORD WY
2 PASEOS DE LAS FLORES
POWERHOUSE PARK
S21
CAROLINA RD
VAN DYKE AV
UMATILLA ST
RIMINI
CREST CANYON PARK
OCEAN VISTA RD
GRANDVIA PT
DENARA RD
SANTORO WY
OVERPARK CT
WYNDHAVEN CT
QU
MIL

Seagrove Park
OCEAN AV
14TH ST
15TH ST
STRATFORD CT
KALAMATH DR
RIMINI RD
KLISH WY
1200
1000
MANGO COVE
MANGO WY
MINORCA COVE
MINORCA COVE
JACARTE CT
4 OVERPARK RD
OVERPARK RD

14
Lib
13TH ST
CUCHARA DR
MAIDEN LN
RECUERDO DR
14200
MANGO WY
13
14200
MANGO DR
LADY HILL RD
MILLCROFT CT
Solana Highlands ES
Solana Highlands Park
BER
CANDELA
FALLO

12TH ST
SEA ORBIT LN
11TH ST
AMPHITHEATRE DR
TEWA ST
ORCHID LN
HIGHLAND AV
HOSKA DR
HOSKA LN
HALF MOON BAY DR
PINEWOOD DR
PINEWOOD DR
VANTAGE WY
OAKRIDGE COVE
RECUERDO COVE
MISSION CARMEL COVE
MALIBU WY
BOQUITA DR
BAHAMA COVE
Del Mar Hills ES
WIND BREAK CT
WIND BREAK CT
LONG RUN DR
SURVEY PT
MARITIME PT
LOWER RIDGE RD
WALKING PATH PL
SEAHORN
HIGH BLUFF DR

10TH ST
9TH ST
8TH ST
NOB AV
CONDESA DR
RUE D AZUR
RUE MONACO
RUE DE ANTIBES
RUE ST RAPHAEL
RUE SANTINO
RUE ST TROPEZ
1 PLACE MONACO
2 PLACE ST TROPEZ
LOZANA RD
RECUERDO DR
MERCADO DR
BOQUITA DR
LA AMATISTA RD
MIRA MONTANA DR
VOYAGER CIR
DEL MAR HEIGHTS RD

CAMINO DEL MAR
8TH ST
7TH ST
SHERRIE LN
6TH ST
A AMATISTA DR
EL AMIGO RD
STRATFORD CT
DEL MAR HEIGHTS RD
DURANGO DR
EL AMIGO RD
13800
2400
RECUERDO DR
MERCADO DR
MIRA MONTANA DR
MANGO DR
2600
34
High Bluff HS
HIGH BLUFF DR
R4W
R3W
EL CAMINO

PACIFIC OCEAN
5TH ST
4TH ST
NOB AV
DE MAYO RD
SEAFOREST CT
SURF VIEW CT
NOGALES RD
PINE NEEDLES DR
Del Mar Montessori
CORDERO RD
PINAR PL
MAR SQ
MERCADO DR
CORDERO RD
MONTEGO COVE
CORDOBA COVE
Del Mar Heights ES
LAS PALMAS COVE
CALAIS DR
MANGO DR
BOCA RATON ST
BARBADOS WY
PORTOFINO DR
RUETTE LE PARC
Del Mar Corporate Ct
PASEO VIEW CT

23
SPINNAKER CT
FANTASIA PL
DOLPHIN COVE
OCEAN VIEW AV
Torrey Pines State Beach
STRATFORD PARK CT
PINE NEEDLES DR
HIDDEN PINES RD
TORREY PINES
24
Del Mar Heights ES
TORREY PINES STATE RESERVE
MIRA MONTANA PL

San Diego La Jolla Underwater Park
CAMINO DEL MAR
OCEAN VIEW AV
TORREY PINES TER
HIDDEN PINES LN
TORREY PINES STATE RESERVE
CAMINITO EL RINCON
RUETTE DE VILL
CAM

TORREY POINT RD
VIA MAR VILLA
CARME
VIA MAR VALLE
CAMINITO DEL BARCO
CAMINITO DEL PASAJE
PKWY INTO CALA
SHALIMAR COVE
CAROUSEL LN
SHALIMAR COVE
NO CIR
CHAMPIONS VALLEY CT
CAMPUS VIEW CT
CMTO CARMEL HARBOUR
S21
1 CAMINITO CRISTOBAL
2 CAMINITO ELDORADO
5

E   F   G   H   J

1   2   3   4   5   6   7

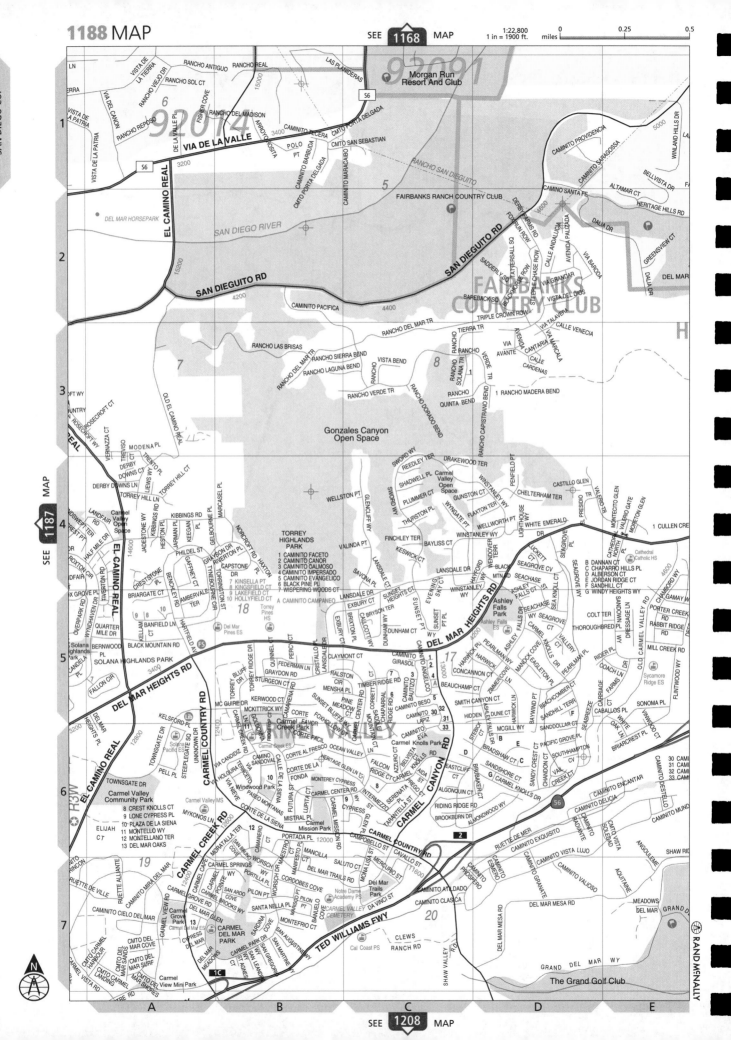

SEE 1168 MAP

1:22,800
1 in = 1900 ft.

SAN DIEGO CO.

SEE 1187 MAP

92091

92074

Morgan Run Resort And Club

VISTA DE LA TIERRA
RANCHO ANTIGUO
RANCHO REAL
LAS PLANDERAS

VISTA VIEJO DR
RANCHO SOL CT

6

VISTA DEL CANON
RANCHO REPOSO
FISHER COVE
RANCHO DEL MADISON
ARROYO COSTA
CAMINITO TECERA
CMTO PORTA DELGADA
CMTO SAN SEBASTIAN

VIA DE LA VALLE

POLO PT
CAMINITO BARBUDA
CMTO PORTA DELGADA
CAMINITO MARACAIBO

1

EL CAMINO REAL

DE LA VALLE

FAIRBANKS RANCH COUNTRY CLUB

CAMINO SANTA FE

CAMINITO PROVIDENCIA
CAMINITO SARAGOSSA
WINLAND HILLS DR

ALTAMAR CT
BELLVISTA DR
HERITAGE HILLS RD

5

DEL MAR HORSEPARK

SAN DIEGO RIVER

SAN DIEGUITO RD

SADDERLY SQ
TATTERSALL SQ
BLACKHORSE
STEEPLE CHASE ROW
FORELIN ROW
DERBY
ARMS RD

CALLE ANDALUCIA
AVENIDA PALIZADA
VIA GRANDAR
VIA BARODA

DALIA DR
GREENSVIEW DR
GREENSVIEW CT

2

SAN DIEGUITO RD

SAN DIEGUITO RD

CAMINITO PACIFICA

RANCHO DEL MAR TR

TRIPLE CROWN ROW

VISTA DEL DIOS

VIA TALAVERA
CALLE VENECIA

DEL MAR HTS

FAIRBANKS COUNTRY CLUB

H

RANCHO LAS BRISAS

RANCHO SIERRA BEND
RANCHO DEL MAR TR
RANCHO LAGUNA BEND

VISTA BEND
RANCHO
RANCHO SOLANA TR

RANCHO TIERRA TR

AVENIDA
VIA AVANTE
CANTARIA
CALLE CARDENAS
VIA MARCALA

7

RANCHO VERDE TR

RANCHO
QUINTA BEND

RANCHO DORADO BEND

8

RANCHO VERDE TR

1

RANCHO MADERA BEND

3

Gonzales Canyon Open Space

CROFT WY
ROSECROFT CT
ROSECROFT WY
OLD EL CAMINO REAL

MODENA PL

SWORD WY
REEDLEY TER
DRAKEWOOD TER

CASTILLO GLEN

VERNAZZA CT
TREVISO
TRENTO PL

SHADWELL PL

Carmel Valley Open Space

WINSTANLEY WY
PENFIELD PT
CHELTERHAM TER

VALERIO TER
MONTECITO GLEN
EL PRESIDIO

REAL

DERBY DOWNS CT
MVIEWS WY
TORREY HILL CT

GLENCLIFF WY

PLUMMER PT
GUNSTON CT

FLAXTON TER
WHITE EMERALD

CATHEDRAL NORTH
Cathedral Catholic HS

1 CULLEN CRE

DERBY DOWNS LN
TORREY HILL LN

WELLSTON PT

SWORD WY
THURSTON PL

WYNGATE PT
WELLWORTH WY

LIGHTHOUSE WY
WENDOVER TERR

4

LANDFAIR
ANDSWELTER

JADESTONE WY
KIBBINGS WY
KIBBINGS RD

MARCASEL PL
GELBOURNE PL

Carmel Valley Open Space

TORREY HIGHLANDS PARK

VALINDA PT

FINCHLEY TER

BAYLISS CT

WINSTANLEY WY

B DANNAN CT
C CHAPARRO HILLS PL
D ALBERSON CT
E JORDAN RIDGE CT
F SANDHILL CT
G WINDY HEIGHTS WY

ROXTON CT
RDFAIR

HESTON PL
JARMAN CT
GRAYSON CT
RIVERTON PL
HAXTON
TORRINGTON ST

1 Caminito Faceto
2 Caminito Canor
3 Caminito Dalmoso
4 Caminito Impersado
5 Caminito Evangelico
6 Black Pine Pl
7 Wispering Woods Ct

KESWICK CT

SAVONA PL

LANSDALE DR

LANSDALE DR

EVENING SKY CT
HAYFORD
BLACK MTN RD
LUCKETT

SEAGROVE PL
SEAGROVE CV

COLT TER

PORTER CREEK

IX GROVE PL
OVERPARK RD
WYNDHAVEN DR

CREST STONE
BRIARGATE CT
GAFFNEY CT
AMBERVALE TER
BENCHLEY RD

CAPSTONE DR

7 KINSELLA PT
8 KINGSFIELD CT
9 LAKEFIELD CT
10 HOLLYFIELD CT

A CAMINITO CAMPANEO

EXBURY PL

SUNSET HEIGHTS CT

WINSTANLEY WY

DEL MAR HEIGHTS RD

ASHLEY
SEACHASE ST
SEAGROVE WY
SEACHASE

CARMEL VALLEY RD

GAMAY W
CHAMORD WY

RABBIT RIDGE RD

QUARTER MILE DR

KELLAM CT
BANFIELD LN
HARTFIELD AV

18
Torrey Pines HS
Del Mar Pines ES

EXBURY DR

BRIXTON PL
CALLCOTT WY

DUNHAM CT

SUNSET
PT PL

ASHLEY FALLS DR

ASHLEY FALLS PARK
Ashley Falls ES

MANOCK COVE
SEA KNOLL CT

CARMEL KNOLLS DR

THOROUGHBRED PL
DRESSAGE LN

MILL CREEK RD
OLD CARMEL VALLEY RD

5

BERNWOOD PL
Solana Highlands Park
CANDELA PL

BLACK MOUNTAIN RD
Solana Highlands Park

FALLON CIR

DEL MAR HEIGHTS RD

TORREY RIDGE DR
TORREY BLUFF DR
GRAYDON RD

QUINNELL LN
FEDERMAN LN
CRISTALLO PL

CLAYMONT CT

17

CAMINITO GIRASOL
CAMINITO ANGELICO

1
2
A

HARWICK
PEARLMAN WY
HARWICK PL

COLT TER
EAGLETON PL

CARRIAGE
CABALLOS PL

SONOMA PL
Sycamore Ridge ES

RIDER RD
COACH LN
WHITE OAK LN

FLINTWOOD WY

FALLON CIR

DEL MAR HEIGHTS PL

MC GUIRE DR
CARMEL CREEK RD

STURGEON CT
RALSTON CIR
TIMBER RIDGE RD

CAMINITO BAUTIZO

CONCANNON CT
ZIMMER CT

BEACHCOMBER CT

SEABREEZE
WYNWOOD CT

TOWNSGATE DR
Solana Pacific ES

KELSFORD PL

KERWOOD CT
MCKITTRICK WY

MENSHA DR
PINE MEADOW WY

CAMINITO CORBETT
CHAPARRAL RD

CAMINITO BESO

BEAUCHAMP CT
SMITH CANYON CT

HIDDEN

MAND COVE
MCGILL WY
BAYWIND PT

SANDDOLLAR CT

BRIARCREST PL

30 CAMI
31 CAMI
32 CAMI
33 CAMI

STEEPLEGATE CT
PELL PL

KELLAM

CARMEL CREEK RD

CORTE FACIL

RIDGETOP DR

FOXHOLLOW CT

CAMINITO
LAPIZ

30
31
33

32

STEBICK CT

SANDY CREST CT
CHANDON CT

CAMINITO MUND

Carmel Creek Park

CARMEL CENTER RD

CAMINITO EVA

30

CARMEL KNOLLS DR

PACIFIC GROVE PL
SOUTHAMPTON
CV

EL CAMINO REAL

R3W

TOWNSGATE DR

Carmel Valley Community Park

8 CREST KNOLLS CT
9 LONE CYPRESS PL
10 PLAZA DE LA SIENA
11 MONTELLO WY
12 MONTELLANO TER
13 DEL MAR OAKS

UNKNOWN DR

VIA CANDIDIZ
VIA HOLGURA

CAMINO SANDOVAL

Windwood Park

CORTE DE LA SIENA

CAMEL VALLEY

10

11

CALLE DE LA SIENA

CORTE AL FRESCO
OCEAN VALLEY LN

CARMEL VALLEY RD

HERITAGE GLEN LN

FALCON
AZZURO RD
BELVIST
EVA

FONDA

Carmel Knolls Park

KADA

6

CARMEL CANYON RD

CARMEL

BRADSHAW CT
BRUBAKER CT
G CARMEL KNOLLS DR

EASTCLIFF
VAIL CREEK CT

ALGONQUIN CT

ALMONDWOOD WY

56

CAMINITO ENCANTAR
CAMINITO DELICIA
CAMINITO DESTELLO

ELIJAH CT

Carmel Valley MS
MYKONOS LN

CORTE DE LA SIENA

CAMARERO

12

PASEO MONTANA
FUTURA CT
MISTRAL PL
LUPITI CT

Carmel Mission Park

INTERMEZZO
SERENATA
WY

TARANTELLA ST

MISSION RD

RIDING RIDGE RD
BROOKBURN WY

2

RUETTE DE MER

CAMINITO EXQUISITO

CAMINITO PROSPERO
CAMINITO ESMERO

CMTO VISTA SOLEAD

SHAW RID

19

RUETTE DE VILLE
RUETTE ALLIANTE

CARMEL MIRA DEL MAR
CARMEL VIEW RD
MORATALLA TER
CARMEL CAPE
CARMEL SPRINGS WY

SAN BRUNO CT
CARMEL POINTE
WORSCH WY
PORTILLA PL
PILON PT
PILON WY

MAESTRO
MANIFESTO ST
CORDOBES COVE

PORTADA PL

12000

MANCILLA

MOLINA

CAMPOBELLO ST

SALUTO CT
MERCURIO ST

DEL MAR TRAILS RD

CAVALLO ST

CARMEL COUNTRY RD

11600

Notre Dame Academy PS

Del Mar Trails Park

CAMINITO ATILDADO

CAMINITO GRANATE
CAMINITO VISTA LUJO

CAMINITO VALIOSO

CAMINITO MUND

ANGOULEME
AQUITAINE

SHAW RID

CAMINITO CIELO DEL MAR

CARMEL GROVE RD

SAN ARDO COVE
CARMEL BROOKS WY

SANTA NELLA PL

MONTEFRIO CT

DA VINCI ST

Carmel Valley Cemetery

CAMINITO CLASICA

20

DEL MAR MESA RD

MEADOWS
GRAND DR

13
Carmel Grove Park
Carmel Del Mar ES

CARMEL DEL MAR PARK

CMTO DEL MAR COVE
CMTO DEL MAR SANDS
CMTO CARMEL HARBOUR

CMTO DEL MAR SURF

CARMEL DEL MAR GLEN

CYPRESS

BANUELO COVE

SAN AUGUSTINE ST

SARDINA COVE

CARMEL PARK DR

SAN MARTINE

SAN GREGORIO

DEL MAR MEADOWS

ST LEAND

ST AGNES

7

CMTO CARMEL SHORES
CMTO CARMEL LANDING
CARMEL VISTA RD

Carmel View Mini Park

1C

Cal Coast PS

CLEWS RANCH RD

SHAW VALLEY

GRAND DEL MAR WY

The Grand Golf Club

N

RAND McNALLY

SEE 1208 MAP

A   B   C   D   E

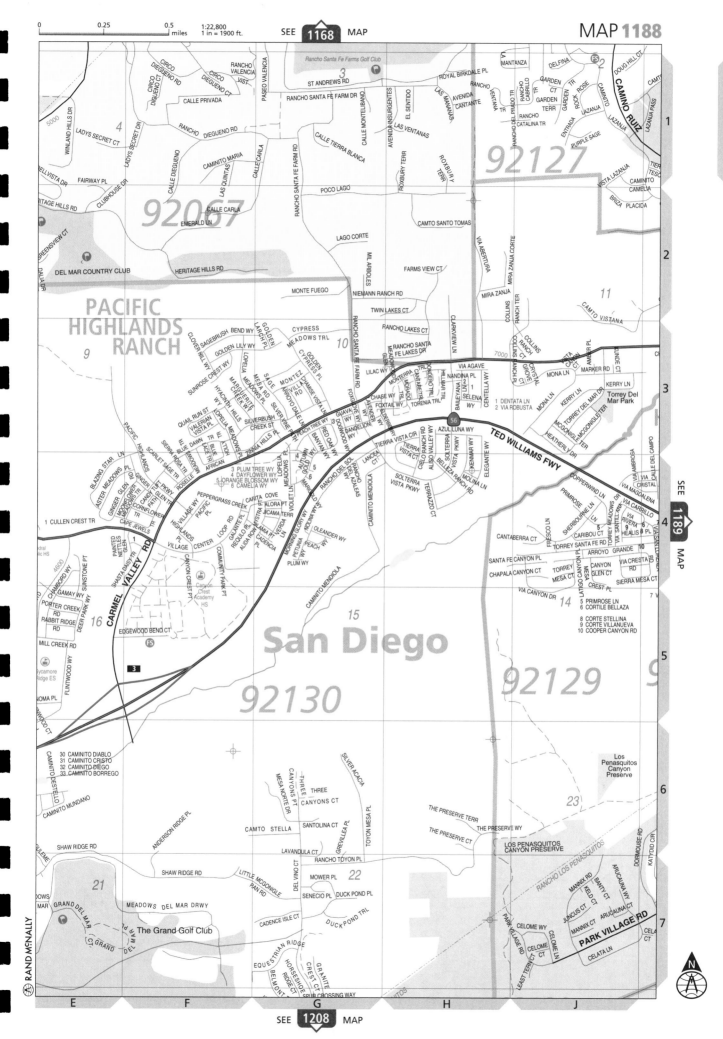

MAP 1188

SAN DIEGO CO.

SEE 1189 MAP

PACIFIC HIGHLANDS RANCH

San Diego

92130

92127

92067

92129

CARMEL VALLEY RD

TED WILLIAMS FWY

Rancho Santa Fe Farms Golf Club

Del Mar Country Club

The Grand Golf Club

Los Penasquitos Canyon Preserve

PARK VILLAGE RD

RAND McNALLY

0   0.25   0.5 miles   1:22,800   1 in = 1900 ft.

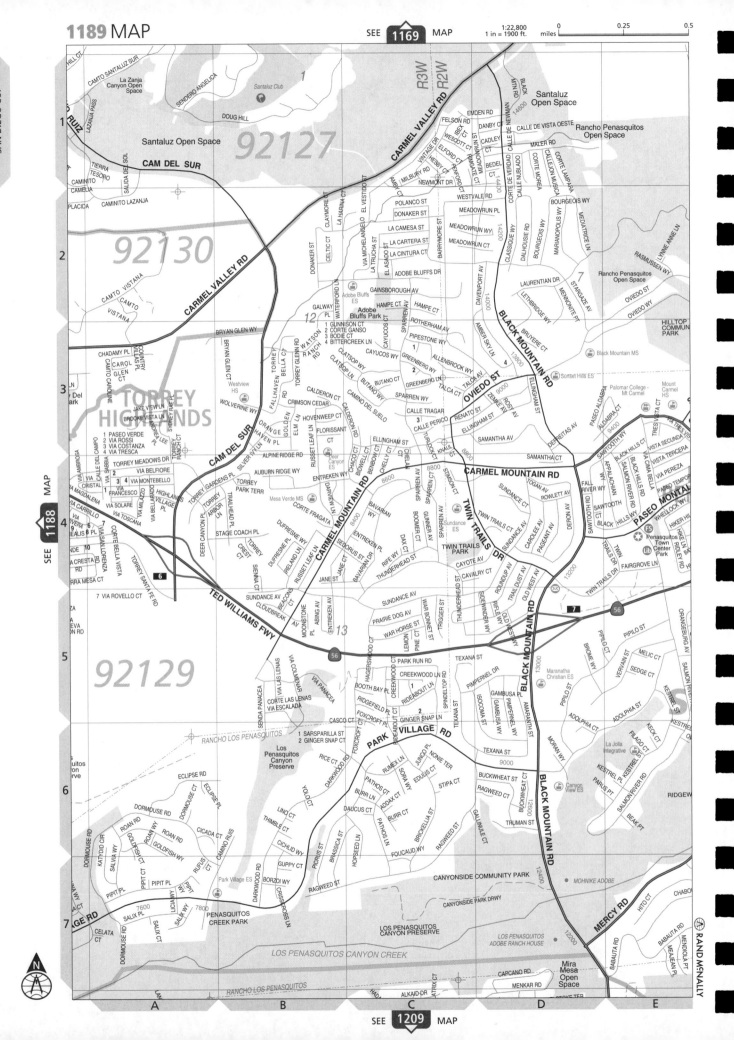

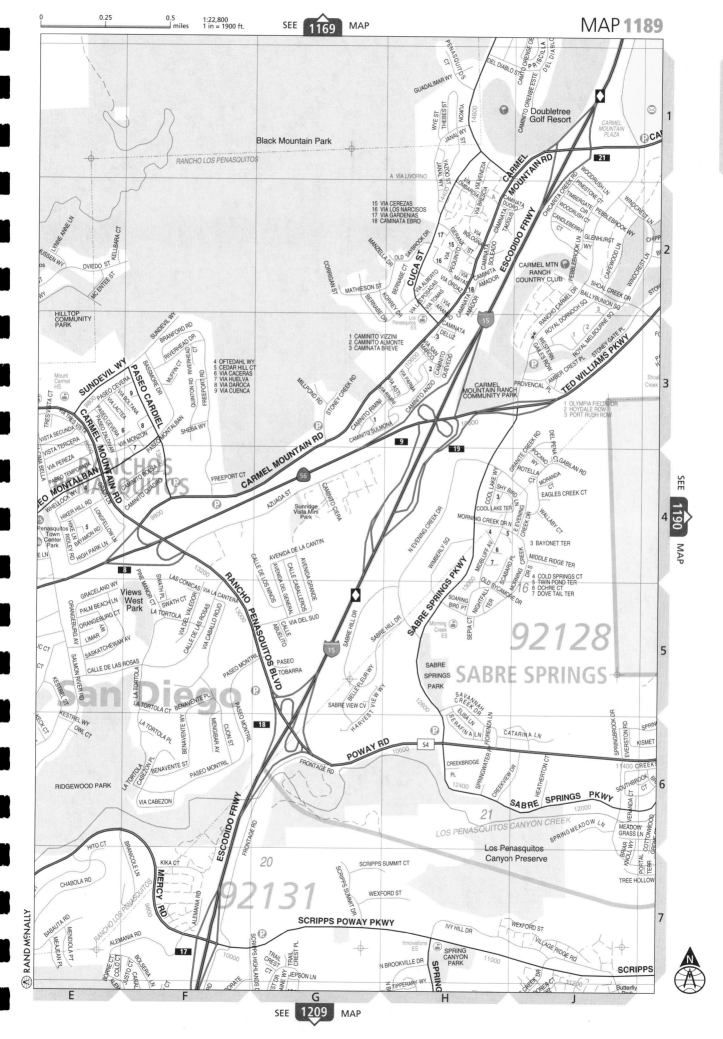

MAP 1189

SAN DIEGO CO.

1:22,800
1 in = 1900 ft.
0   0.25   0.5 miles

Black Mountain Park

RANCHO LOS PENASQUITOS

15 VIA CEREZAS
16 VIA LOS NARCISOS
17 VIA GARDENIAS
18 CAMINATA EBRO

Doubletree
Golf Resort

CARMEL MOUNTAIN RD

ESCODIDO FRWY

Carmel Mtn
Ranch Country Club

Carmel Mountain Ranch
Community Park

1 CAMINITO VIZZINI
2 CAMINITO ALMONTE
3 CAMINATA BREVE

4 OFTEDAHL WY
5 CEDAR HILL CT
6 VIA CACERAS
7 VIA HUELVA
8 VIA DAROCA
9 VIA CUENCA

HILLTOP
COMMUNITY
PARK

SUNDEVIL WY

PASEO CARDIEL

Mount
Carmel HS

CARMEL MOUNTAIN RD

RANCHOS
PENASQUITOS

PASEO MONTALBAN

Penasquitos
Town Center
Park

CARMEL MOUNTAIN RD

56

Sunridge
Vista Mini
Park

Views
West Park

RANCHO PENASQUITOS BLVD

8

18

TED WILLIAMS PKWY

1 OLYMPIA FIELD
2 HOYDALE ROW
3 PORT RUSH ROW

9

19

3 BAYONET TER

MIDDLE RIDGE TER

4 COLD SPRINGS CT
5 TWIN POND TER
6 OCHRE CT
7 DOVE TAIL TER

SABRE SPRINGS PKWY

92128
SABRE SPRINGS

SABRE
SPRINGS
PARK

SABRE HILL DR

RIDGEWOOD PARK

ESCODIDO FRWY

POWAY RD

S4

SABRE SPRINGS PKWY

Los Penasquitos
Canyon Preserve

LOS PENASQUITOS CANYON CREEK

21

MERCY RD

92131

SCRIPPS POWAY PKWY

Spring
Canyon Park

Innovations
ES

SCRIPPS

20

RAND MCNALLY

N

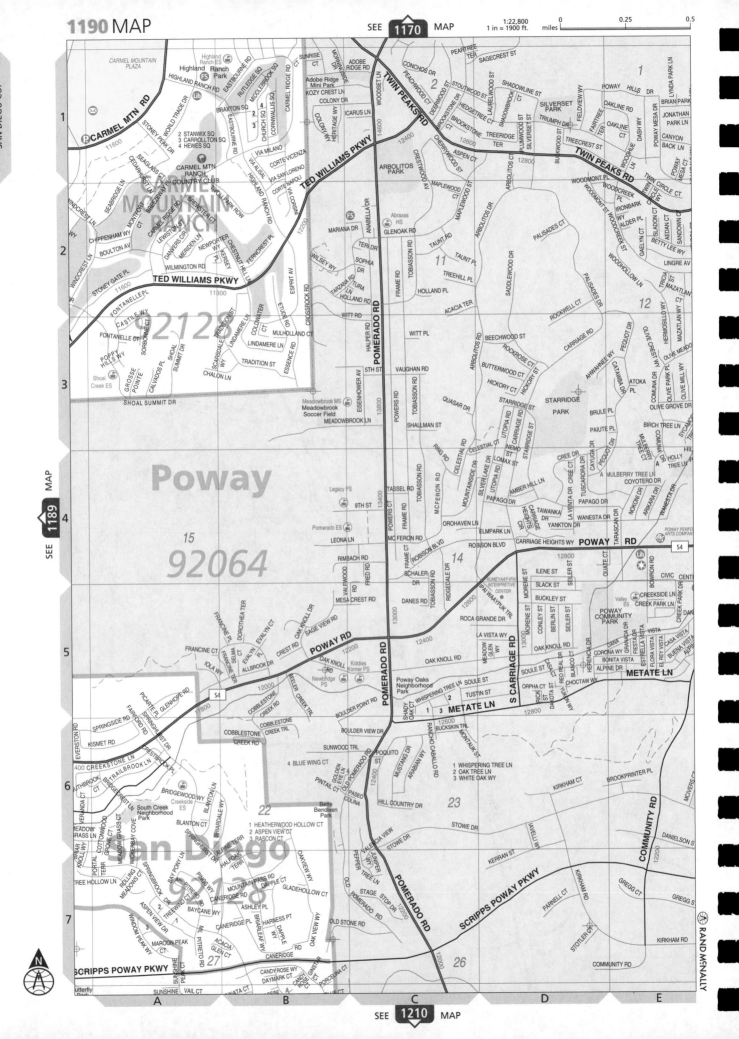

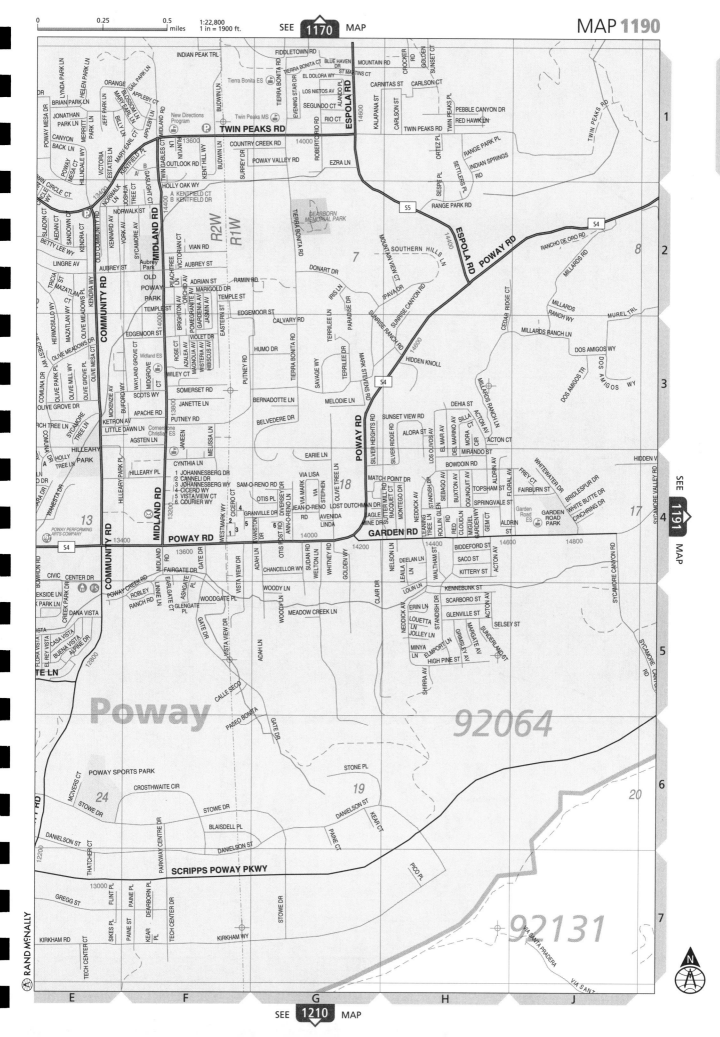

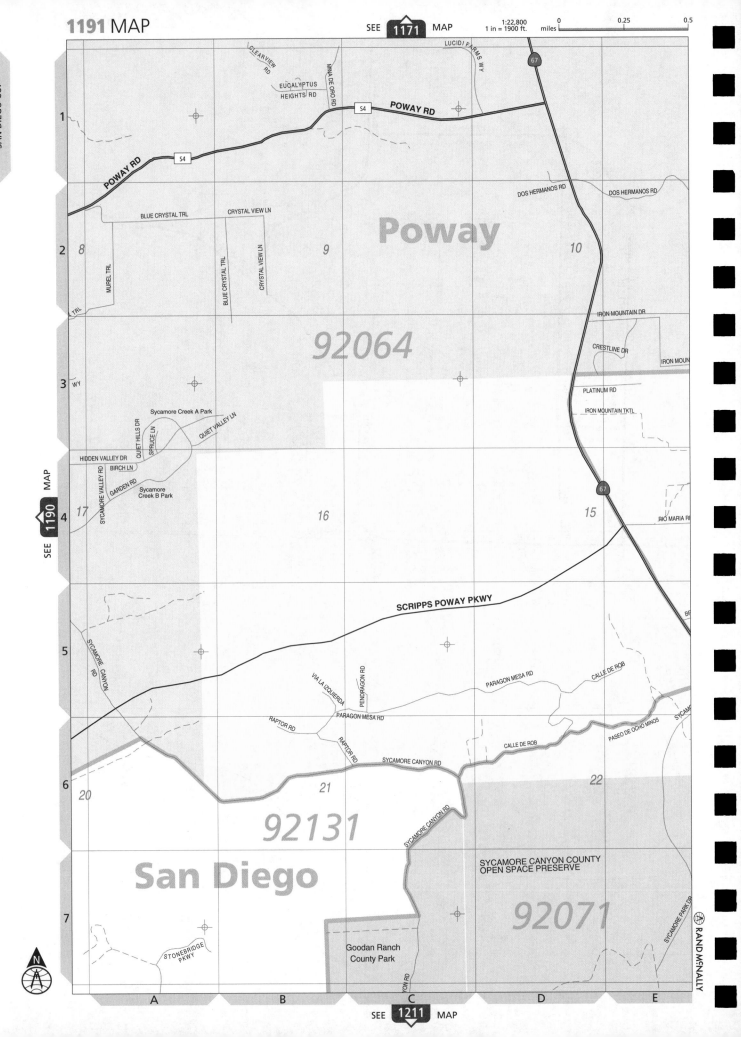

SEE ⌂ 1171 MAP

1:22,800
1 in = 1900 ft.

miles   0   0.25   0.5

SAN DIEGO CO.

CLEARVIEW RD

EUCALYPTUS
HEIGHTS RD

MNA DE ORO RD

LUCID/ FARMS WY

67

S4   POWAY RD

1

POWAY RD   S4

DOS HERMANOS RD   DOS HERMANOS RD

BLUE CRYSTAL TRL   CRYSTAL VIEW LN

MUREL TRL

BLUE CRYSTAL TRL

CRYSTAL VIEW LN

CRYSTAL VIEW LN

Poway

2   8   9   10

L TRL

IRON MOUNTAIN DR

92064

CRESTLINE DR

IRON MOUN

3   WY   PLATINUM RD

IRON MOUNTAIN TKTL

Sycamore Creek A Park

QUIET VALLEY LN

QUIET HILLS DR

SPRUCE LN

HIDDEN VALLEY DR

SYCAMORE VALLEY RD

BIRCH LN

GARDEN RD

Sycamore
Creek B Park

67

SEE ⌂ 1190 MAP

4   17   16   15

RIO MARIA R

SCRIPPS POWAY PKWY

SYCAMORE CANYON RD

VIA LA IZQUIERDA

PENDRAGON RD

PARAGON MESA RD   CALLE DE ROB

5   PARAGON MESA RD

RAPTOR RD   PARAGON MESA RD

CALLE DE ROB   PASEO DE OCHO MINOS   SYCAMO

RAPTOR RD

SYCAMORE CANYON RD   CALLE DE ROB

BR

6   20   21   22

92131

SYCAMORE CANYON RD

SYCAMORE CANYON COUNTY
OPEN SPACE PRESERVE

San Diego

92071

7   SYCAMORE PARK DR

STONEBRIDGE
PKWY

Goodan Ranch
County Park

YON RD

N

A   B   C   D   E

SEE ⌂ 1211 MAP

RAND MCNALLY

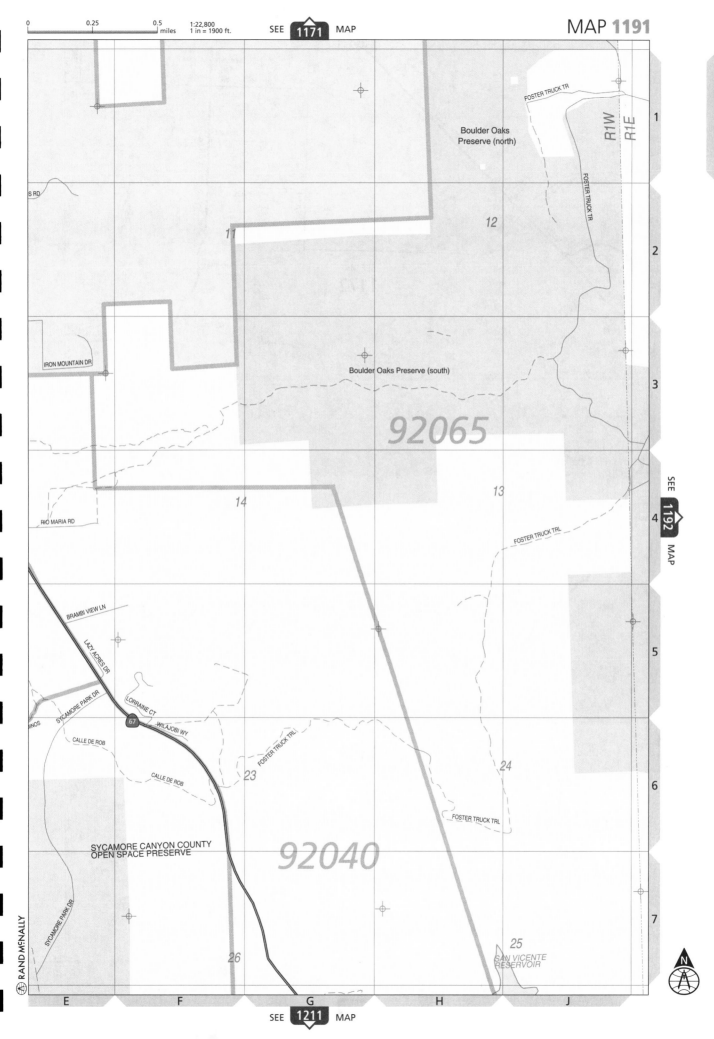

MAP **1191**

SAN DIEGO CO.

SEE **1171** MAP

0   0.25   0.5
miles   1:22,800
1 in = 1900 ft.

R1W | R1E

1

2

FOSTER TRUCK TR

Boulder Oaks
Preserve (north)

FOSTER TRUCK TR

S RD

11

12

IRON MOUNTAIN DR

Boulder Oaks Preserve (south)

3

92065

SEE **1192** MAP

RIO MARIA RD

14

13

FOSTER TRUCK TRL

4

BRAMBI VIEW LN

LAZY ACRES DR

5

SYCAMORE PARK DR

LORRAINE CT

67

WILAJOBI WY

MINOS

CALLE DE ROB

CALLE DE ROB

FOSTER TRUCK TRL

23

24

6

FOSTER TRUCK TRL

SYCAMORE CANYON COUNTY
OPEN SPACE PRESERVE

92040

SYCAMORE PARK DR

7

26

25

SAN VICENTE
RESERVOIR

RAND MᶜNALLY

E | F | G | H | J

SEE **1211** MAP

N

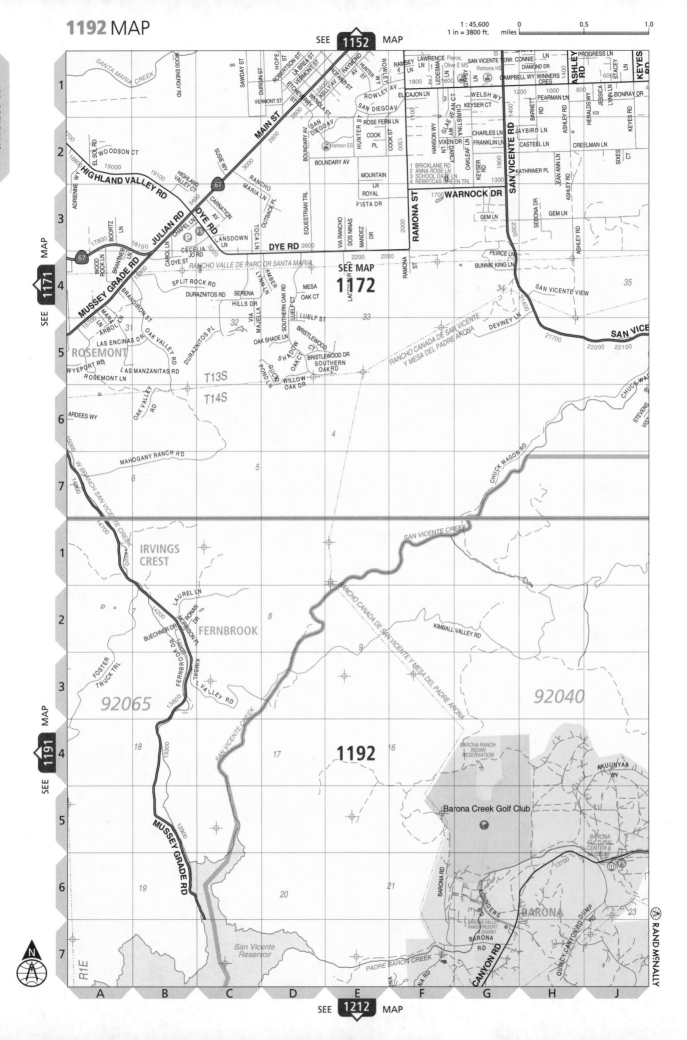

1192 MAP

SAN DIEGO CO.

1:45,600
1 in = 3800 ft.

miles 0   0.5   1.0

SEE 1152 MAP

SEE 1171 MAP

SEE 1191 MAP

SEE 1212 MAP

RAND McNALLY

SANTA MARIA CREEK

HIGHLAND VALLEY RD

MAIN ST

JULIAN RD

DYE RD

MUSSEY GRADE RD

ROSEMONT

RAMONA ST

SAN VICENTE RD

WARNOCK DR

SEE MAP 1172

SAN VICENTE RD

IRVINGS CREST

FERNBROOK

CHUCK WAGON RD

SAN VICENTE CREEK

KIMBALL VALLEY RD

92065

92040

1192

BARONA RANCH INDIAN RESERVATION

Barona Creek Golf Club

MUSSEY GRADE RD

CANYON RD

BARONA

San Vicente Reservoir

PADRE BARON CREEK

N

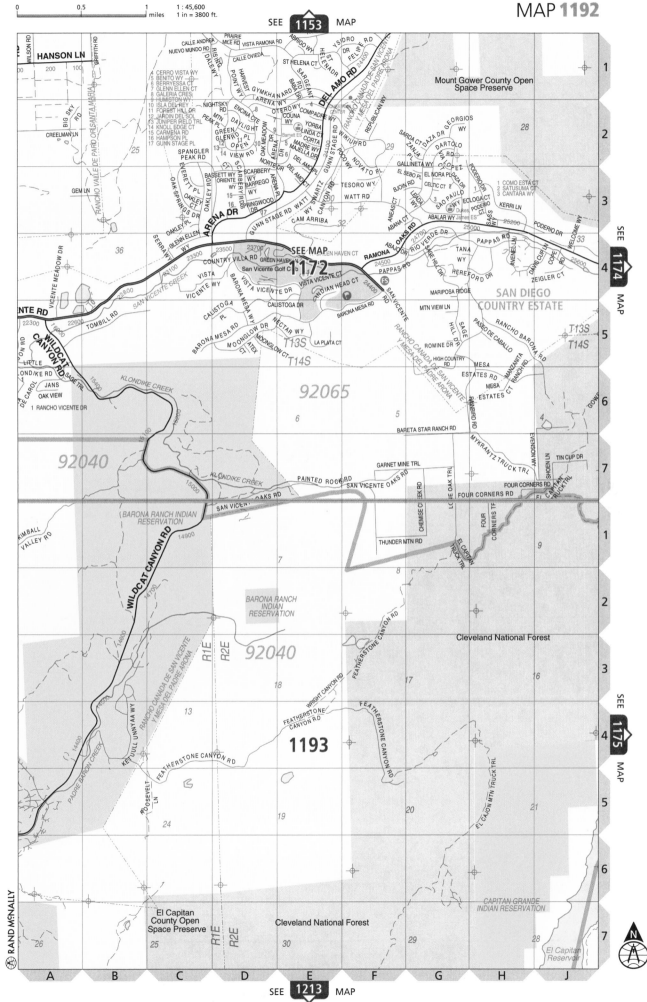

MAP **1192**

SAN DIEGO CO.

1 : 45,600
1 in = 3800 ft.

0   0.5   1
miles

SEE 1153 MAP

HANSON LN

WILSON RD
GRIFFITH RD
CALLE ANDREA
NUEVO MUNDO RD
PRAIRIE MILE WY
VISTA RAMONA RD
ABRIGO WY
YSIDRO DR
FELIPE RD
ST HELENA CT
ST HELENA DR
CERRO VISTA WY
4 BENITO WY
5 BERRYESSA CT
6 GLENN ELLEN CT
7 GALERIA CRES
8 HUMISTON WY
9 ISLA DEL REY
10 FOREST HILL DR
11 JARDIN DEL SOL
12 JUNIPER FIELD TRL
13 KNOLL EDGE CT
14 CARIMENA RD
15 HAMPSON PL
17 GUNN STAGE PL

BIG SKY RD
CREELMAN LN

DEL AMO RD

RANCHO CAÑADA DE SAN VICENTE
Y MESA DEL PADRE ARONA

Mount Gower County Open
Space Preserve

SAN DIEGO
COUNTRY ESTATE

SPANGLER PEAK RD

ARENA DR

OAK SPRINGS DR
OAKLEY RD
GLENN ELLEN WY
SERRA WY

GUNN STAGE RD

COUNTRY VILLA RD
SAN VICENTE CREEK
VICENTE MEADOW DR

VICENTE RD

WILDCAT
CANYON RD

TOMBILL RD

KLONDIKE CREEK

92040

92065

BARONA RANCH INDIAN
RESERVATION

WILDCAT CANYON RD

KIMBALL VALLEY RD

BARONA RANCH
INDIAN
RESERVATION

92040

R1E   R2E

Cleveland National Forest

1193

SAN VICENTE OAKS RD

FEATHERSTONE CANYON RD

WRIGHT CANYON RD

FEATHERSTONE CANYON RD

ROOSEVELT LN

El Capitan
County Open
Space Preserve

R1E   R2E

Cleveland National Forest

CAPITAN GRANDE
INDIAN RESERVATION

El Capitan
Reservoir

SEE 1174 MAP

SEE 1175 MAP

SEE 1213 MAP

RAND M:NALLY

A   B   C   D   E   F   G   H   J

1 2 3 4 5 6 7

SEE 1187 MAP

1:22,800
1 in = 1900 ft.   miles   0   0.25   0.5

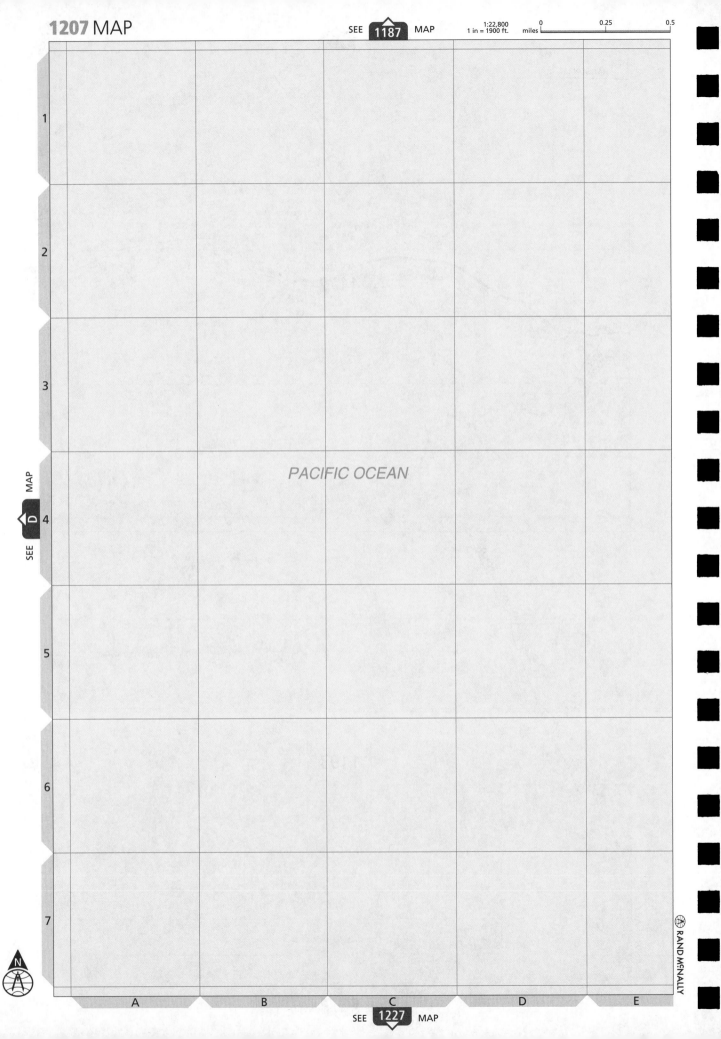

PACIFIC OCEAN

SEE D MAP

SEE 1227 MAP

RAND McNALLY

A   B   C   D   E

1   2   3   4   5   6   7

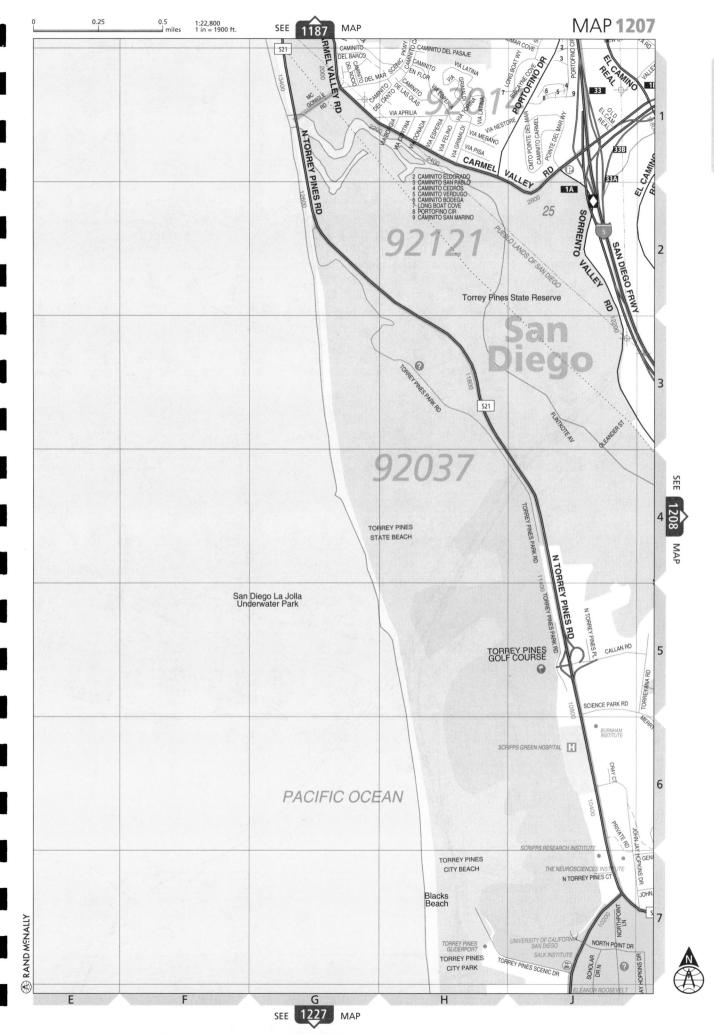

MAP 1207

0   0.25   0.5
miles
1:22,800
1 in = 1900 ft.

SEE 1187 MAP

92012

CARMEL VALLEY RD

N TORREY PINES RD

MC GONIGLE RD

CAMINITO DEL BARCO
CAMINITO DEL ROCIO
CAMINITO DEL MAR SCENIC
EN FLOR
CAMINITO DEL CANTO DE LAS OLAS

VIA ALBORGHA
VIA CRETINA
VIA MONDONADA

VIA APRILIA
VIA ESPERIA
VIA FELINO
VIA GRIMALDI
VIA MERANO
VIA PISA

CAMINITO DEL PASAJE
CAMINITO DEL MAR SCENIC
VIA LATINA
VIA LATINA
VIA GRIMALDI
VIA NESTORE

CARMEL VALLEY RD

BISCAYNE COVE
LONG BOAT WY
PORTOFINO CIR
POINTE DEL MAR
CMTO POINTE DEL MAR
POINTE DEL MAR WY
CAMINITO CARMEL

EL CAMINO REAL
33
33B
OLD EL CAM REAL

PORTOFINO DR

SORRENTO VALLEY RD

SAN DIEGO FRWY

EL CAMINO REAL

2 CAMINITO ELDORADO
3 CAMINITO SAN PABLO
4 CAMINITO CEDROS
5 CAMINITO VERDUGO
6 CAMINITO BODEGA
7 LONG BOAT COVE
8 PORTOFINO CIR
9 CAMINITO SAN MARINO

1A

33A

5

25

92121

PUEBLO LANDS OF SAN DIEGO

Torrey Pines State Reserve

San
Diego

TORREY PINES PARK RD

92037

S21

FLINTKOTE AV

OLEANDER ST

TORREY PINES
STATE BEACH

SEE 1208 MAP

San Diego La Jolla
Underwater Park

TORREY PINES PARK RD

N TORREY PINES RD

N TORREY PINES PL

CALLAN RD

TORREY PINES
GOLF COURSE

TORREYANA RD

SCIENCE PARK RD

MERRY

BURNHAM
INSTITUTE

SCRIPPS GREEN HOSPITAL H

CRAY CT

PACIFIC OCEAN

PRIVATE RD

JOHN JAY HOPKINS DR

SCRIPPS RESEARCH INSTITUTE

JOHN

TORREY PINES
CITY BEACH

THE NEUROSCIENCES INSTITUTE
N TORREY PINES CT

Blacks
Beach

NORTHPOINT LN

JOHN

S

TORREY PINES
GLIDERPORT

UNIVERSITY OF CALIFORNIA
SAN DIEGO
SALK INSTITUTE

NORTH POINT DR

TORREY PINES
CITY PARK

TORREY PINES SCENIC DR

SCHOLAR DR

JAY HOPKINS DR

ELEANOR ROOSEVELT

E   F   G   H   J

SEE 1227 MAP

1   2   3   4   5   6   7

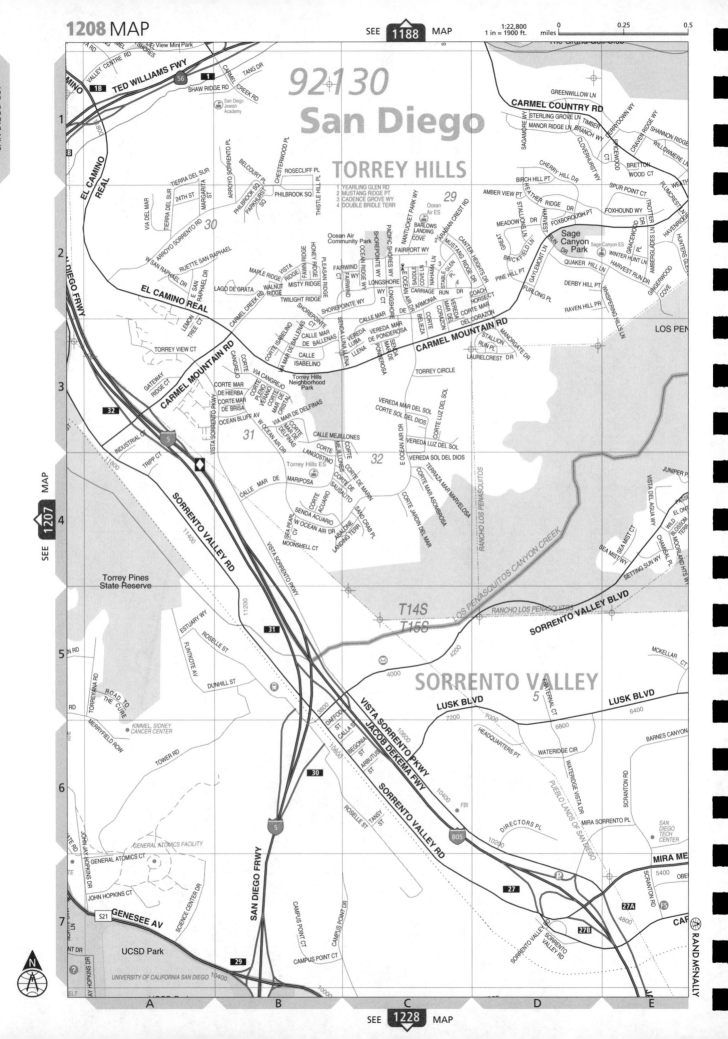

SEE △ 1188 MAP

1:22,800
1 in = 1900 ft.

0   0.25   0.5
miles

SAN DIEGO CO.

92130
San Diego

TORREY HILLS

1 YEARLING GLEN RD
2 MUSTANG RIDGE PT
3 CADENCE GROVE WY
4 DOUBLE BRIDLE TERR

SEE ◁ 1207 MAP

SORRENTO VALLEY

Torrey Pines
State Reserve

Kimmel, Sidney
Cancer Center

General Atomics Facility

LUSK BLVD

LUSK BLVD

MIRA ME

GENESEE AV

UCSD Park

UNIVERSITY OF CALIFORNIA SAN DIEGO

SEE ▽ 1228 MAP

A   B   C   D   E

RAND McNALLY

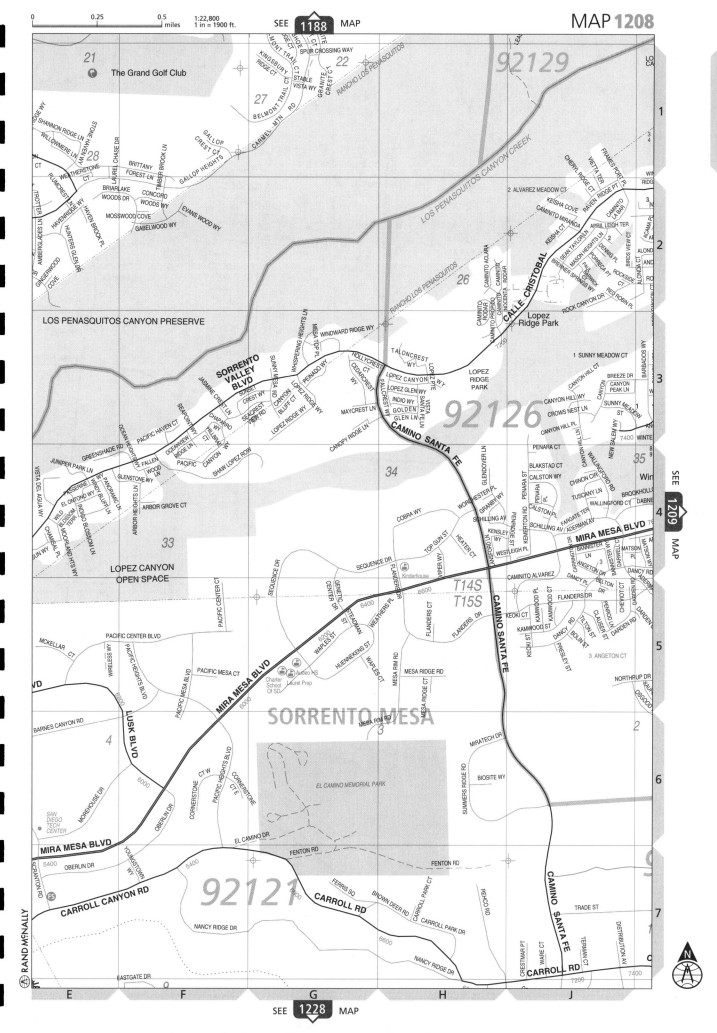

MAP **1208**

SAN DIEGO CO.

0   0.25   0.5
miles
1:22,800
1 in = 1900 ft.

21
The Grand Golf Club
27
92129

SPUR CROSSING WAY
MONT TRAIL CT
KINGSBURY RIDGE CT
STABLE
CREST CT
GRANITE
VISTA WY
Rancho Los Peñasquitos
22

SHANNON RIDGE LN
WILLOWMERE LN
STONE HAVEN
28
WEATHERSTONE CT
PLUMCREST
HAVENRIDGE WY
TROTTER LN
GINGERWOOD COVE
HUNTERS GLEN DR
AMBROSE WY
BRIARLAKE WOODS DR
MOSSWOOD COVE
CONCORD WOODS WY
GABELWOOD WY
LAUREL CHASE DR
BRITTANY FOREST LN
TIMBER BROOK LN
GALLOP CREST CT
GALLOP HEIGHTS
EVANS WOOD WY
CARMEL MTN RD
BELMONT TRAIL WY
HAVEN BROOK PL

92129
LOS PEÑASQUITOS CANYON CREEK
LOS PEÑASQUITOS CANYON PRESERVE

CHERYL RIDGE CT
VIETA TER
RAVEN RIDGE PT
CAMINITO LA BAR
2 ALVAREZ MEADOW CT
KEISHA COVE
CAMINITO MIRANDA
SEAN TAYLOR LN
MASON HEIGHTS LN
DENNIG PL
APRIL LEIGH TER
BIRDS VIEW CT
BRENNER SPRINGS WY
POBRECA PT
PARDWICK
PAUL BRAVE WY
RED ROBIN PL
ROCKSIDE
ALONDA CT
ACAMA PL
ROCK CANYON DR

CALLE CRISTOBAL
KEISHA CT
CAMINITO ACLARA
CAMINITO RODAR
CAMINITO PROPIO
CAMINITO INOCENTA RODAR
CAMINITO RODAR
Lopez Ridge Park
26
Rancho Los Peñasquitos
7200

1 SUNNY MEADOW CT
BARBADOS WY
LOPEZ RIDGE PARK
CANYON HILL LN
BREEZE DR
CANYON PEAK LN
CANYON HILL WY
CROWS NEST LN
SUNNY MEADOW ST
CANYON HILL PL
NEW SALEM WY
7400 WINTE

SORRENTO VALLEY BLVD
WHISPERING HEIGHTS LN
MESA TOP PL
WINDWARD RIDGE WY
TALONCREST
HOLLYCREST CT
CEDARCREST WY
LOPEZ CANYON WY
LOPEZ RIDGE WY
LOPEZ GLEN WY
INDIO WY
GOLDEN GLEN LN
VISTA SANTA FE LN
LOPEZ PTE
MAYCREST LN
FALLCREST WY

JASMINE CREST LN
SUNNY MESA RD
SUNSET CREST WY
SEACREST VIEW RD
CHAPARRO WY
PEINADO WY
CANYON BLUFF CT
LOPEZ RIDGE WY
CANOPY RIDGE LN

92126

CAMINO SANTA FE

GREENSHADE RD
SEAPOINT WY
OCEAN HEIGHTS WY
PACIFIC HAVEN CT
OCEANVIEW RIDGE LN
HILBRAE CT
PACIFIC CANYON WY
SHAW LOPEZ ROW

JUNIPER PARK LN
FALLEN WOOD LN
GLENSTONE WY
ARBOR HEIGHTS LN
ARBOR GROVE CT

34

GLENDOVER LN
WORCHESTER LN
GRANBY WY
PENARA ST
BLAKSTAD CT
CALSTON WY
CHINON CIR
TUSCANY LN
WALLINGFORD RD
BROOKHOLLO
Win

VISTA DEL AGUA WY
PRASERINE WY
WINDY BLUFF LN
PANORAMIC LN
EL ONTONO WY
INDIGO BLOSSOM LN
WILD BLOSSOM TERR
MCLOORLAND LN
CHAMISAL PL
SUN WY

33
LOPEZ CANYON OPEN SPACE

COBRA WY
TOP GUN ST
HEATER CT
SCHILLING AV
KENSLEY WY
WESTLEIGH PL
PENARA RD
PENARA PL
CALSTON PL
SCHILLING AV
FARGATE TER
ADERMAN AV
KEMERTON RD
PEBRIDGE LN
ANSFORD LN

MIRA MESA BLVD
CAMINITO ALVAREZ
CARRINGTON DR
BANNISTER LN
3
ANGETON DR
DARWELL PL
MATSON WY
DANCY RD
BELTON CT
FLANDERS DR
CHEVIOT CT
PENROD PL
CLAUSER ST
DARDEN RD
ADERM

SEQUENCE DR
GENETIC CENTER DR
STEADMAN ST
WEATHERS PL
VIPER WY
Kinderhouse
FLANDERS DR
FLANDERS CT
FLANDERS DR
KEOKI CT
KAMWOOD PL
KAMWOOD CT
KAMWOOD ST
KEOKI ST
DANCY RD
TILTON ST
BOLIN ST
PRESLEY ST
3 ANGETON CT
DARDEN RD

6400
6600
T14S
T15S
CAMINO SANTA FE

PACIFIC CENTER CT
SEQUENCE DR
PACIFIC CENTER BLVD
WAPLES ST
HUENNEKENS ST
WAPLES CT
MESA RIM RD
MESA RIDGE RD
MESA RIDGE CT

MCKELLAR CT
WIRELESS WY
PACIFIC HEIGHTS BLVD
PACIFIC MESA CT
PACIFIC MESA BLVD
Audeo HS
Laurel Prep
Charter School Of SD.

MIRA MESA BLVD
6200
6000

NORTHRUP DR
2
MIRATECH DR
BIOSITE WY

LUSK BLVD
4
BARNES CANYON RD
MOREHOUSE DR
OBERLIN DR
San Diego Tech Center

SORRENTO MESA
3
MESA RIM RD

CORNERSTONE CT W
PACIFIC HEIGHTS BLVD
CORNERSTONE CT E
EL CAMINO DR
El Camino Memorial Park
FENTON RD
FENTON RD
SUMMERS RIDGE RD

BLVD
MIRA MESA BLVD
5400
OBERLIN DR
YOUNGSTOWN WY
SCRANTON RD
5400
CARROLL CANYON RD
92121
NANCY RIDGE DR
FERRIS SQ
BROWN DEER RD
CARROLL RD
CARROLL PARK CT
CARROLL PARK DR
REHCO RD
CAMINO SANTA FE
CRESTMAR PT
WARE CT
TRADE ST
TERMAN CT
DISTRIBUTION AV
NANCY RIDGE DR
EASTGATE DR
CARROLL RD
7200
7400

RAND McNALLY

35
1
2
3
4
5
6
7

E   F   G   H   J

SEE ▷ **1209** MAP

N

1:22,800
1 in = 1900 ft.

0   0.25   0.5
miles

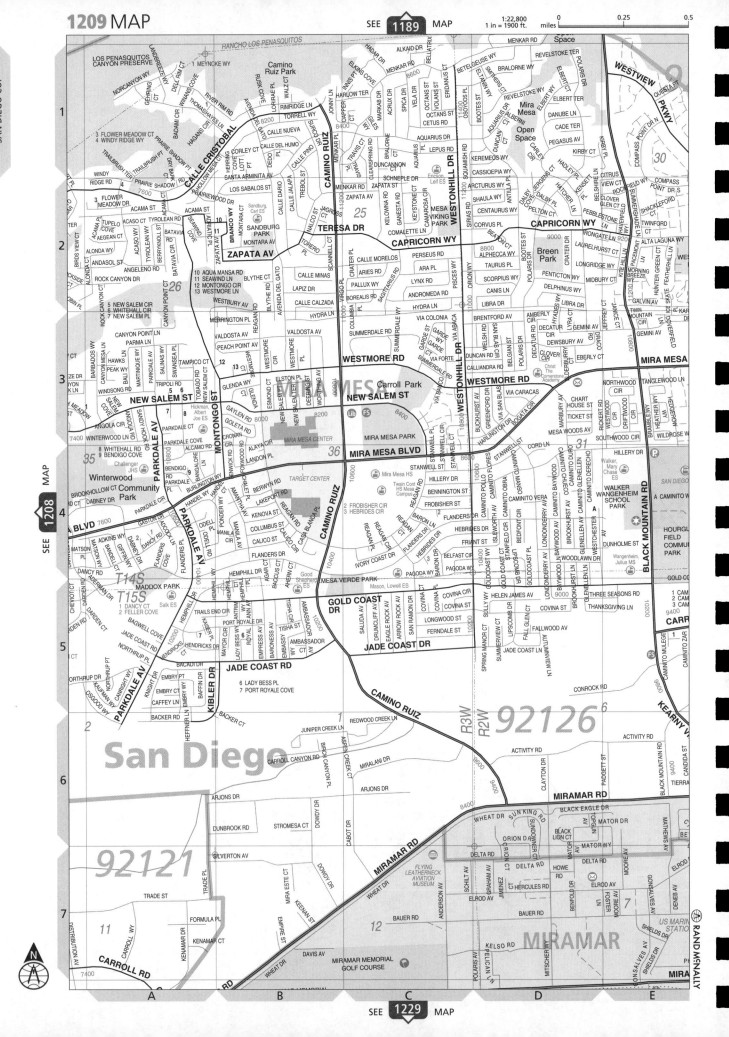

SAN DIEGO CO.

SEE 1208 MAP

San Diego

92126

92121

MIRAMAR

RAND McNALLY

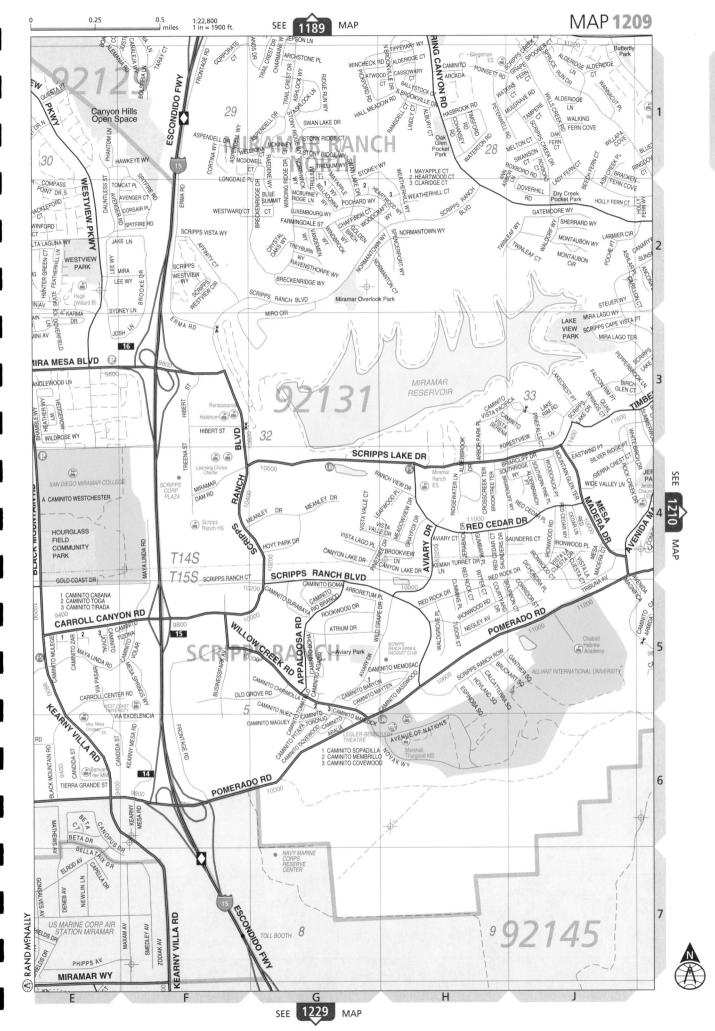

MAP **1209**

92129

Canyon Hills Open Space

ESCONDIDO FWY

MIRAMAR RANCH NORTH

92131

MIRAMAR RESERVOIR

WESTVIEW PKWY

WESTVIEW PARK

WESTVIEW PKWY

Hage (Willard B)

MIRA MESA BLVD

SCRIPPS RANCH BLVD

Miramar Overlook Park

LAKE VIEW PARK

SCRIPPS RANCH BLVD

SCRIPPS LAKE DR

San Diego Miramar College

SCRIPPS CORP PLAZA

MIRAMAR DAM RD

Scripps Ranch HS

Miramar Ranch ES

RED CEDAR DR

MESA MADERA DR

AVENIDA

HOURGLASS FIELD COMMUNITY PARK

T14S
T15S

GOLD COAST DR

SCRIPPS RANCH CT

AVIARY DR

POMERADO RD

1 CAMINITO CABANA
2 CAMINITO TOGA
3 CAMINITO TIRADA

CARROLL CANYON RD

SCRIPPS RANCH BLVD

WILLOW CREEK RD

APPALOOSA RD

SCRIPPS RANCH

Aviary Park

Scripps Ranch Swim & Racquet Club

Chabad Hebrew Academy

Scripps Ranch Row

ALLIANT INTERNATIONAL UNIVERSITY

CARROLL CENTER RD

KEARNY VILLA RD

West Coast University

OLD GROVE RD

Legler-Bensough Theatre

AVENUE OF NATIONS

Marshall, Thurgood MS

1 CAMINITO SOPADILLA
2 CAMINITO MEMBRILLO
3 CAMINITO COVEWOOD

POMERADO RD

KEARNY VILLA RD

TIERRA GRANDE ST

Banyan Tree MM

Mira Mesa Christian ES

POMERADO RD

NAVY MARINE CORPS RESERVE CENTER

92145

US MARINE CORP AIR STATION MIRAMAR

ESCONDIDO FWY

TOLL BOOTH

MIRAMAR WY

E   F   G   H   J

1   2   3   4   5   6   7

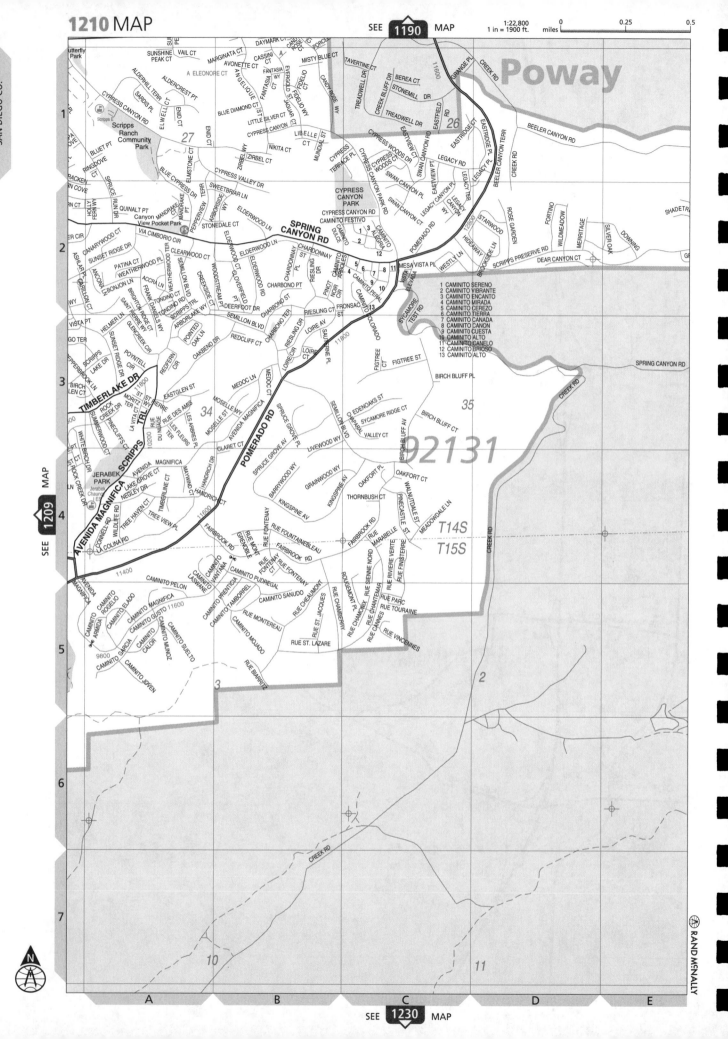

SEE **1190** MAP

1:22,800
1 in = 1900 ft.

0   0.25   0.5
miles

Poway

SAN DIEGO CO.

Butterfly Park

SUNSHINE PEAK CT
VAIL CT
DAYMARK CT
MARGINATA CT
A ELEONORE CT
AVONETTE CT
CASSINI CT
FANTASIA WY
FIDELIO WY
EVERGOLD WY
PORCELAIN
MISTY BLUE CT
CANDY ROSE WY

ALDERHILL TERR
ALDERCREST PT
SARDIS PL
ENID CT
EL WELL CT
CYPRESS CANYON RD
Scripps E
Scripps Ranch Community Park
BLUE DIAMOND CT
LITTLE SILVER CT
JAGUAR CT
CYPRESS CANYON
NIKITA CT
ZIRBEL CT
ZIRBEL WY

TAVERTINE CT
TREADWELL DR
CREEK BLUFF DR
BEREA CT
STONEMILL DR
TREADWELL DR
GRANGE PL
CREEK RD
11600
EASTFIELD RD
26
EASTRIDGE CT
EASTRIDGE PL
EASTRIDGE RD
BEELER CANYON RD

1

27

PA COVE
BLUET PT
RINGDOVE
CRACKEN
ON COVE
RN CT
HOLLY
MW HW
SPRUCE RUN DR
QUINALT PT
MANDRAKE
MANDRAKE CT
Canyon View Pocket Park
ABBORSIDE WY
PEPPERVIEW TERR
ELDERWOOD LN
STONEDALE CT

CYPRESS CANYON RD
LIBELLE
MUNDIAL ST
CYPRESS TERRACE PL
CYPRESS WOODS DR
CYPRESS CANYON PARK RD
CYPRESS WOODS CT

SWAN CANYON RD
SWAN CANYON PL
EASTVIEW PT
EASTVIEW CT
LEGACY RD
LEGACY TERR
LEGACY PL

CYPRESS CANYON PARK

ER CIR
CANARYWOOD CT
SUNSET RIDGE DR
VIA CIMBORIO CIR
CLEARWOOD CT
ELDERWOOD LN

2

SPRING CANYON RD

CAMINITO FESTIVO
CAMINITO DULCE
1
2
12
CAMINITO ALEGRIA

POMERADO RD

STARWOOD
ROSE GARDEN
FORTINO
WILDMEADOW
MERRITAGE
SILVER OAK
DOWNING
SHADETR

ASHLAR PL
PATINA CT
WEATHERWOOD PL
CARRILLON CT
BONJON LN
ANCONE LN
ACCRA LN
FRANK DANIELS WY
TONDINO CT
TONDINO RD
SEMILLON BLVD
GLOVERFIELD
CREEKSIDE CT
WOODSTREAM PT
CHARDONNAY PL
CHARBONO PT
RIESLING DR
PINOT NOIR CIR
CAMINITO PERLA
CAMINITO ARBOLES
5
4
3
6
7
8
9
10
11
12
WESTLY LN
HIDEAWAY
BROOKSIDE LN
SCRIPPS PRESERVE RD
DEAR CANYON CT

MESA VISTA PL
VISTA ELEVADA

1 CAMINITO SERENO
2 CAMINITO VIBRANTE
3 CAMINITO ENCANTO
4 CAMINITO MIRADA
5 CAMINITO CEREZO
6 CAMINITO TIERRA
7 CAMINITO CANADA
8 CAMINITO CANON
9 CAMINITO CUESTA
10 CAMINITO ALTO
11 CAMINITO CANELO
12 CAMINITO BRIOSO
13 CAMINITO ALTO

VISTA PT
GO TER
BRIGHTON RIDGE CT
SAINT PIERRE CT
HELMER LN
POINTED OAK LN
SCRIPPS TRL
DEERFOOT DR
ARBORLAKE WY
SEMILLON BLVD
CHARBONO ST
CHARBONO TER
REDCLIFF CT
RIESLING DR
LOIRE AV
LOIRE CT
FRONSAC ST
SAUTERNE PL
CAMINITO COLORADO
13

PEPPERBROOK LN
SCRIPPS LAKE DR
SUNSET RIDGE DR
POYNTELL CIR
GLENCREEK CIR
REDFERN CT
OAKBEND DR
LOIRE DR

FIGTREE CT
FIGTREE ST
SPRING CANYON RD

3

BIRCH GLEN CT
TIMBERLAKE DR
ROCK CREEK DR
PINECLIFFS CT
1ST WY
MORITZ CT
LA SIERRE
SCRIPPS TRL
EASTGLEN ST
MEDOC LN
MEDOC CT
MOSELLE ST
AVENIDA MAGNIFICA

11800

34

RUE DU NUAGE
RUE DES AMIS
LES ARBRES PL
LES FLEURS
CLARET CT
POMERADO RD
SPRUCE GROVE PL
SEMILLON BLVD
O EDENOAKS ST
CHAPRAL
SYCAMORE RIDGE CT
VALLEY CT
BIRCH BLUFF AV
BIRCH BLUFF CT
BIRCH BLUFF PL

35

CREEK RD

92131

WHITE BIRCH DR
SUMMERWOOD CT
ROCK CREEK DR
SP CT
JERABEK PARK
Jerabek Chaung
ES
LAKE GROVE CT
AVENIDA MAGNIFICA
AVENIDA MAGNIFICA
NEGLEY DR
MAYWIND CT
HANDRICH DR
HANDRICH CT

SPRUCE GROVE AV
BARRYWOOD WY
GRAINWOOD WY
KINGSPINE AV
KINGSPINE AV
LIVEWOOD WY
OAKFORT PL
OAKFORT CT
THORNBUSH CT
WALNUTDALE ST
PINECASTLE ST
MEADOWDALE LN

4

SEE **1209** MAP

WILDLIFE RD
TREE HAVEN CT
TIMBERLINE CT
TREE VIEW PL
LA COLINA RD
FAIRBROOK RD
FAIRBROOK RD
RUE MONT GRENOBLE
RUE FONTENAY
RUE FONTAINEBLEAU
FAIRBROOK RD
RUE FONTENAY
RUE FONTENAY
RUE MARABELLE
RUE FINISTERRE
RUE FINISTERRE

T14S
T15S

11600

AVENIDA MAGNIFICA
11400

CAMINITO PELON
CAMINITO VENTANA
CAMINITO LASWANE
CAMINITO PUDREGAL
RUE SIENNE NORD
RUE RIVIERE VERTE
RUE CHANTEMAR
RUE PARC
RUE TOURAINE

CAMINITO PRENTICIA
CAMINITO TAMBORREL
CAMINITO SANUDO
RUE MONTEREAU
RUE CHEAUMONT
RUE CHAMONIX
ROUGEMONT PL
RUE SIENNE NORD
RUE CANNES

AVENIDA MAGNIFICA
CAMINITO ROGELIO
CAMINITO ELADO
CAMINITO MAGNIFICA
CAMINITO GUSTO
11600
CAMINITO ARMIDA
CAMINITO GARCIA
CAMINITO CALOR
CAMINITO MUNOZ
CAMINITO SUELTO
RUE ST. JACQUES
RUE ST. LAZARE
RUE CHAMBERRY
RUE VINCENNES

5

9800
CAMINITO JOVEN
RUE BIARRITZ

3

2

6

7

10

11

A   B   C   D   E

N

RAND MCNALLY

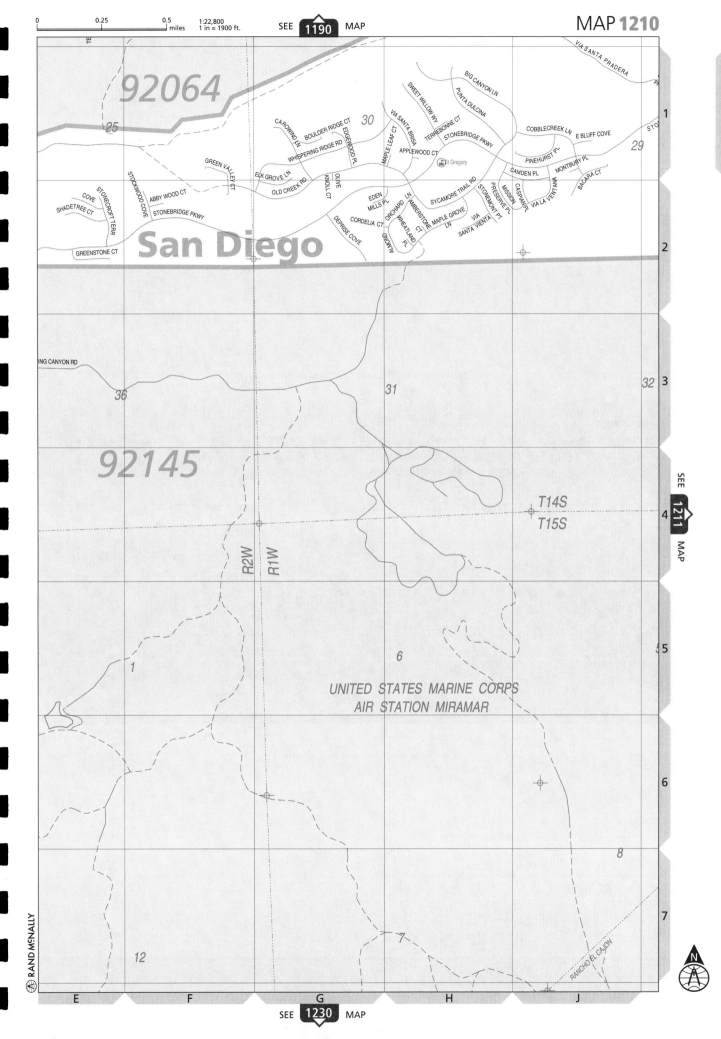

MAP **1210**

SEE 1190 MAP

SAN DIEGO CO.

0   0.25   0.5
miles
1:22,800
1 in = 1900 ft.

92064

25

30

VIA SANTA PRADERA

BIG CANYON LN

SWEET WILLOW WY

PUNTA DULCINA

CAROWIND LN

BOULDER RIDGE CT

TERREBONNE CT

VIA SANTA BRISA

STONEBRIDGE PKWY

COBBLECREEK LN

E BLUFF COVE

WHISPERING RIDGE RD

EDGEWOOD PL

MAPLE LEAF CT

APPLEWOOD CT

STO

29

GREEN VALLEY CT

ELK GROVE LN

OLIVE KNOLL CT

St Gregory

PINEHURST PL

CAMDEN PL

MONTBURY PL

COVE

STONECROFT TERR

STOCKWOOD COVE

ABBY WOOD CT

OLD CREEK RD

EDEN MILLS PL

ORCHARD LN

SYCAMORE TRAIL RD

CASPIAN PL

VIA LA VENTANA

BACARA CT

SHADETREE CT

STONEBRIDGE PKWY

DEPRISE COVE

CORDELIA CT

ALMOND

WHEATLAND PL

LAMBERSTONE LN

MAPLE GROVE LN

VIA SANTA VIENTA

STONEMONT PT

MISSION

PRESERVE PL

GREENSTONE CT

San Diego

ING CANYON RD

36

31

32

92145

T14S
T15S

SEE 1211 MAP

R2W
R1W

6

1

UNITED STATES MARINE CORPS
AIR STATION MIRAMAR

8

7

12

7

RANCHO EL CAJON

RAND MⁿNALLY

E   F   G   H   J

SEE 1230 MAP

N

1
2
3
4
5
6
7

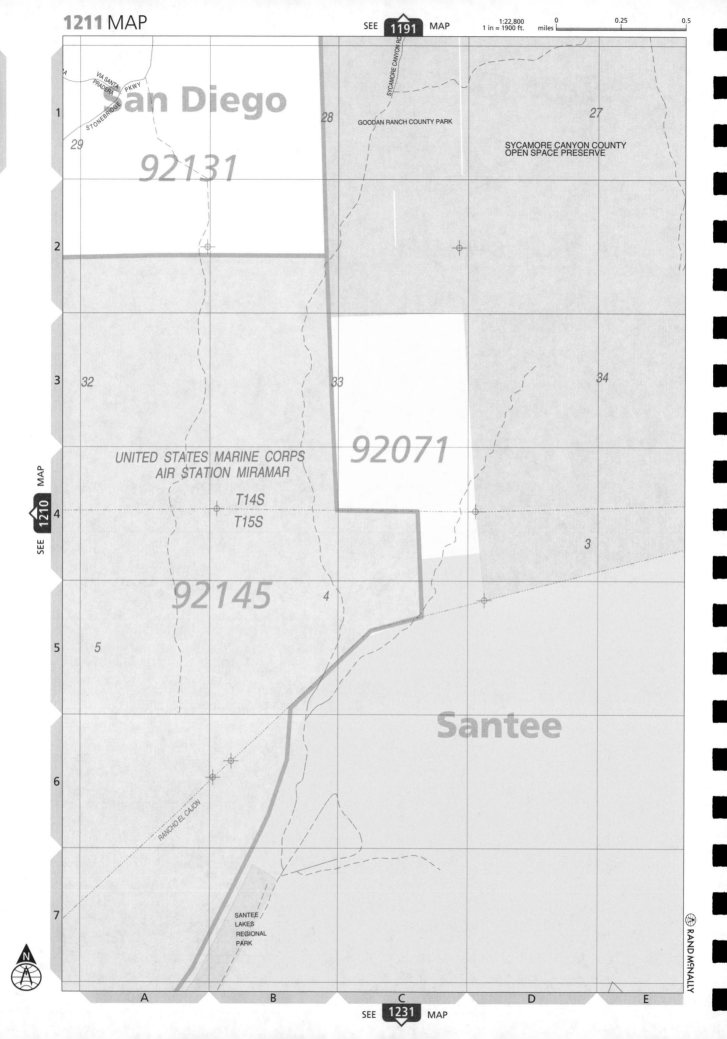

SAN DIEGO CO.

SEE 1191 MAP

1:22,800
1 in = 1900 ft.

miles 0   0.25   0.5

VIA SANTA PRADERA

STONEBRIDGE PKWY

San Diego

92131

29

28

27

GOODAN RANCH COUNTY PARK

SYCAMORE CANYON RD

SYCAMORE CANYON COUNTY
OPEN SPACE PRESERVE

32

33

34

92071

UNITED STATES MARINE CORPS
AIR STATION MIRAMAR

T14S
T15S

SEE 1210 MAP

92145

3

4

5

Santee

RANCHO EL CAJON

SANTEE
LAKES
REGIONAL
PARK

N

SEE 1231 MAP

RAND McNALLY

A   B   C   D   E

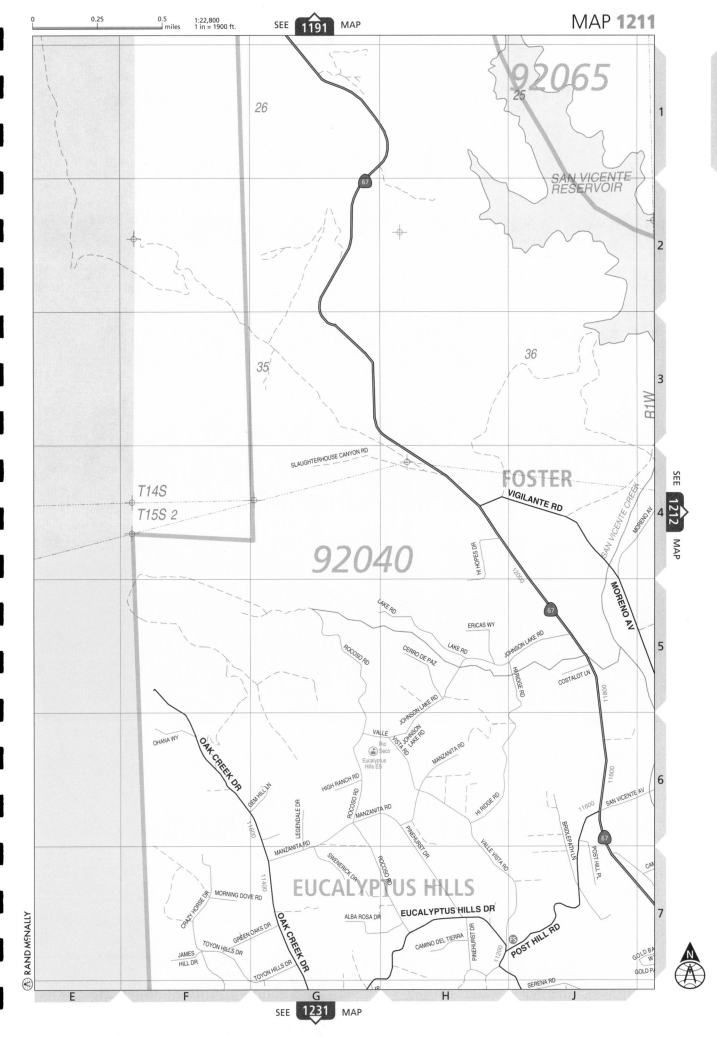

MAP **1211**

SAN DIEGO CO.

0   0.25   0.5
miles   1:22,800
1 in = 1900 ft.

SEE 1191 MAP

92065

25

SAN VICENTE
RESERVOIR

26

67

35

36

R1W

SLAUGHTERHOUSE CANYON RD

FOSTER

SEE 1212 MAP

VIGILANTE RD

T14S
T15S 2

92040

HI HOPES DR

12000

MORENO AV

67

MORENO AV

SAN VICENTE CREEK

LAKE RD

ERICAS WY

LAKE RD

JOHNSON LAKE RD

COSTALOT LN

ROCOSO RD

CERRO DE PAZ

11800

HI RIDGE RD

JOHNSON LAKE RD

OHANA WY

OAK CREEK DR

GEM HILL LN

VALLE

Rio
Seco

Eucalyptus
Hills ES

JOHNSON
LAKE RD

VISTA RD

MANZANITA RD

11600

HIGH RANCH RD

ROCOSO RD

LEGENDALE DR

MANZANITA RD

HI RIDGE RD

11600

SAN VICENTE AV

11600

MANZANITA RD

SWENERICK DR

ROCOSO RD

PINEHURST DR

VALLE VISTA RD

BRIDLEPATH LN

POST HILL PL.

67

CRAZY HORSE DR

MORNING DOVE RD

11400

EUCALYPTUS HILLS

ALBA ROSA DR

EUCALYPTUS HILLS DR

CAM

GREEN OAKS DR

OAK CREEK DR

TOYON HILLS DR

JAMES
HILL DR

TOYON HILLS DR

CAMINO DEL TIERRA

PINEHURST DR

11200

POST HILL RD

67

GOLD BA
WY

GOLD PA

SERENA RD

RAND McNALLY

E   F   G   H   J

SEE 1231 MAP

N

1   2   3   4   5   6   7

1:22,800
1 in = 1900 ft.

miles   0   0.25   0.5

SAN DIEGO CO.

92065

30

29

SAN VICENTE
RESERVOIR

OAK OASIS COUNTY OPEN SPACE PRESERVE

San Diego

LAKE VICENTE DR

YERBA VALLEY WY

VICENTE VIEW DR

MORENO AV

R1W
R1E

31

YERBA VALLEY WY

32

MUTH VALLEY RD

BUENA VIDA RD

YERBA VALLEY RD

VICENTE CREEK

MUTH VALLEY RD

GOLDEN EAGLE RD

GENESIS ST

MUTH VALLEY RD

T14S
T15S

WHIPTAIL CT

RACCOON CT

MOUNTAIN LION RD

MOUNTAIN LION RD

MUTH VALLEY RD

92040

RANCHO EL CAJON

OPOSSUM CT

MOUNTAIN RANCHES RD

HIGH MEADOW RD

MOUNTAIN LION RD

BADGER CT

WILDCAT CANYON RD

6

SQUIRREL RD

MOUNTAIN QUAIL CT

REDTAIL HAWK CT

5

RENO AV

MOUNTAIN RD

HORNED OWL RD

MOUNTAIN RD

MOUNTAIN LION RD

SPARROW HAWK CT

MORENO AV

VICENTE AV

SAN VICENTE AV

TOPO LN

ROCKY LN

8

CRADLE MOUNTAIN LN

MIDRANCH LN

ROCKY LN

CAMINO RIO

SANTA MARIA AV

SAN VICENTE CR

TOPO LN

ACADIA WY

MARY LN

67

ACADIA WY

11200

GOLD BAR
WY

GOLD PAN

MINE SHAFT

LOUIS A STELZER COUNTY PARK

GOLD PAN ALLLEY

GOLD BAR WY

WILDCAT CANYON RD

FILLBROOK DR

WOOD ST

N

RAND MCNALLY

A   B   C   D   E

MAP **1212**

SAN DIEGO CO.

0   0.25   0.5
miles
1:22,800
1 in = 1900 ft.

SEE **1192** MAP

DE SAN VINCENTE

RANCHO CANADA
Y MESA DEL
PADRE BARONA

28

OLD BARONA RD

WILDCAT CANYON RD

Silverwood
Wildlife Sanctuary

27

BARONA RANCH
INDIAN
RESERVATION

2

1

2

Oak Oasis County Open
Space Preserve

BLUE SKY RANCH RD

34

El Capitan County Open Space Preserve

33

3

PATA RANCH RD

12200

92040

T14S
T15S

SEE **1213** MAP

4

VALLEY RD

WILDCAT CANYON RD

3

4

MARGUERITE CANYON RD

5

RANCHO EL CAJON

SAN DIEGO RIVER

PATA VIEW DR

WILLOW RD

MOUNTAIN VALLEY PL

YUCC

9

MARGUERITE CANYON RD

GOLDA ODESSA LN

HAZY MEADOW LN

6

WILLOW RD

WILLOW RD

WILLOW RD EXT

EL MONTE RD

7

WILLOW RD EXT

SAN DIEGO RIVER

15400

92021

E

F

G

H

J

RAND McNALLY

N

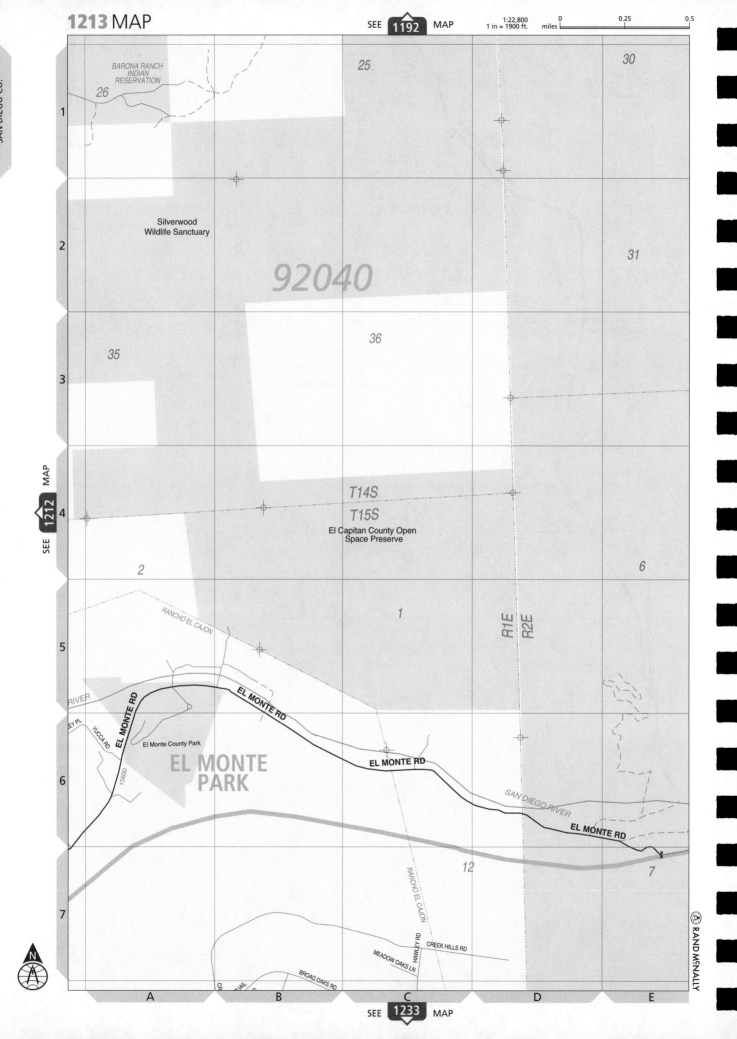

SAN DIEGO CO.

SEE 1192 MAP

1:22,800
1 in = 1900 ft.

0   0.25   0.5
miles

BARONA RANCH
INDIAN
RESERVATION

26

25

30

1

Silverwood
Wildlife Sanctuary

2

92040

31

35

36

3

SEE 1212 MAP

T14S

T15S
El Capitan County Open
Space Preserve

4

2

6

1

R1E
R2E

RANCHO EL CAJON

5

RIVER

EL MONTE RD

EL MONTE RD

EL MONTE RD

EL MONTE RD

YUCCA RD

EY PL

15600

El Monte County Park

**EL MONTE
PARK**

SAN DIEGO RIVER

EL MONTE RD

6

7

12

RANCHO EL CAJON

CREEK HILLS RD

HAWLEY RD

MEADOW OAKS LN

BROAD OAKS RD

7

N

A   B   C   D   E

SEE 1233 MAP

RAND McNALLY

0   0.25   0.5   1:22,800
└────┴────┴────┘ miles   1 in = 1900 ft.

SEE 1292 MAP

29   28

CAPITAN GRANDE
INDIAN RESERVATION

CAPITAN
RESERVOIR

Cleveland National Forest

32   33

T14S
T15S

5   4

CAPITAN
RESERVOIR

SEE
D
MAP

San Diego

EL CAPITAN DAM

EL CAPITAN RESERVOIR

Cleveland National Forest

8   9

EL MONTE RD

92021   **91901**

Cleveland National Forest

7

ANDERSON TRUCK TRL

E   F   G   H   J

1
2
3
4
5
6
7

N

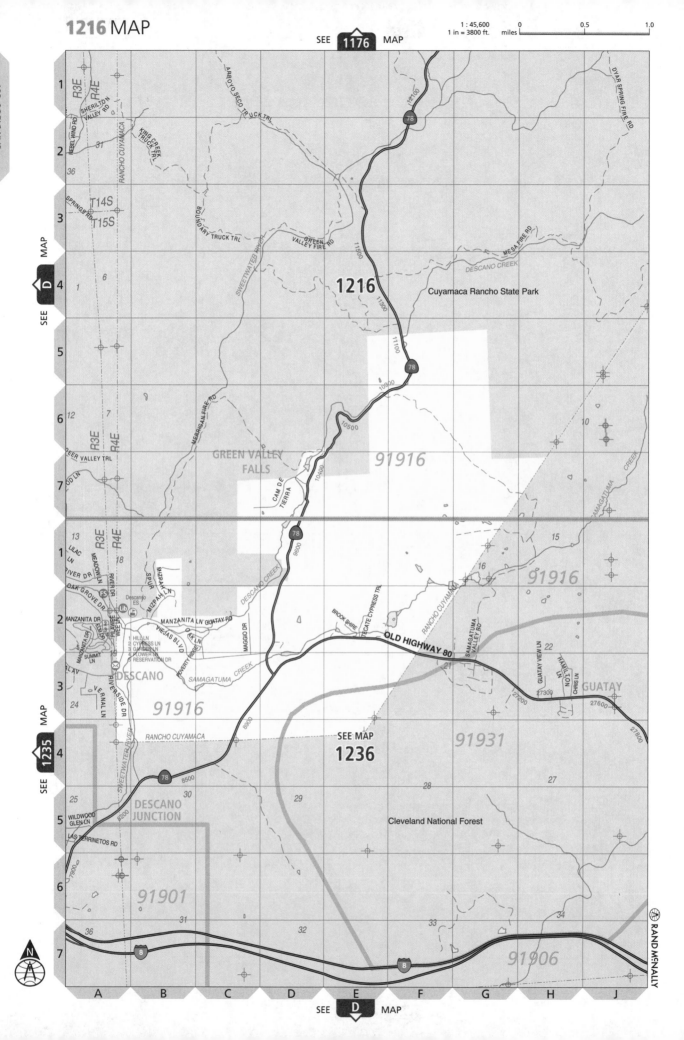

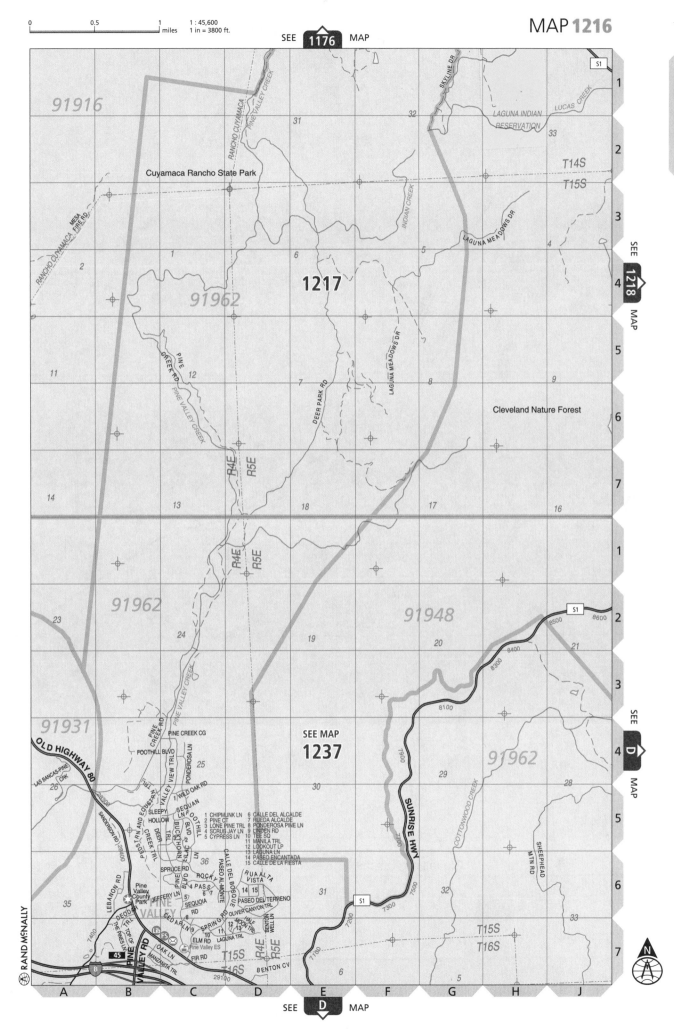

MAP 1216

SAN DIEGO CO.

0   0.5   1 miles
1 : 45,600
1 in = 3800 ft.

SEE 1176 MAP

S1

91916

SKYLINE DR

LUCAS CREEK

LAGUNA INDIAN RESERVATION

33

Cuyamaca Rancho State Park

31

32

T14S
T15S

INDIAN CREEK

LAGUNA MEADOWS DR

5

4

SEE 1218 MAP

1217

91962

RANCHO CUYAMACA

PINE VALLEY CREEK

MESA FIRE RD

RANCHO CUYAMACA FIRE RD

PINE CREEK RD

PINE VALLEY CREEK

6

DEER PARK RD

LAGUNA MEADOWS DR

Cleveland Nature Forest

11   12   7   8   9

14   13   18   17   16

R4E R5E

R4E R5E

91962

23   24   19   20   21

S1
8500   8600

8400

8300

91948

91931

OLD HIGHWAY 80

LAS BANCAS-PINE CRK

26

PINE CREEK RD

PINE CREEK CG

Foothill BLVD

25

30

SEE MAP
1237

8100

29   28

91962

SUNRISE HWY

COTTONWOOD CREEK

7900

SEE D MAP

SANDERSON RD 28400

PINE VALLEY CREEK

WILD OAK RD

SEQUAN

PONDEROSA LN

PINE VALLEY VIEW TRL

SLEEPY HOLLOW

FOOTHILL BLVD

DEER CREEK TRL

BUCKTHORN

1 CHIPMUNK LN   6 CALLE DEL ALCALDE
2 PINE CT   7 RUEDA ALCALDE
3 LONE PINE TRL   8 PONDEROSA PINE LN
4 SCRUB JAY LN   9 LINDEN RD
5 CYPRESS LN   10 TEE SQ
                   11 MANILA TRL
                   12 LOOKOUT LP
                   13 LAGUNA LN
                   14 PASEO ENCANTADA
                   15 CALLE DE LA FIESTA

36

CALLE DEL BOSQUE

PASEO AL MONTE

RU ALTA VISTA

31   32   33

7800

7700

7600

7500

7400   SPRUCE RD

ROCKY PASS

LEBANON RD

Pine Valley County Park

DEODAR

TOP OF THE PINES LN

PINE VALLEY RD

35

JEFFERY LN

PINE DR

CEDAR LN

SEQUOIA RD

8 9

5

SPRING RD

ELM RD

OAK LN

Pine Valley ES

FIR RD

MANZANITA TRL

29100

14 15

PASEO DEL TERRENO

OLIVER CANYON TRL

LAGUNA TRL

MOON TRL

BENTON WELL LN

BENTON CV

PINE VALLEY

45

8

S1
7300
7200
7100

8300

7900

7800

T15S
T16S

RAND MCNALLY

A   B   C   D   E   F   G   H   J

T15S
T16S

R4E R5E

6

SEE D MAP

N

SEE MAP

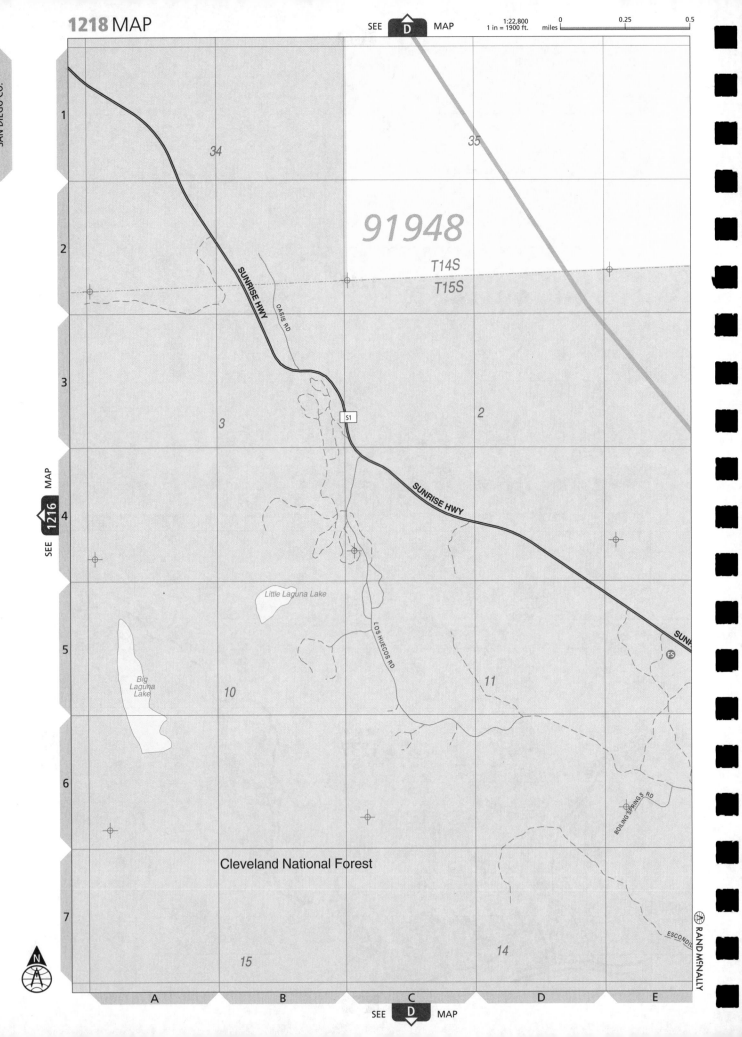

SAN DIEGO CO.

SEE **D** MAP

1:22,800
1 in = 1900 ft.

miles 0 0.25 0.5

34

35

91948

T14S
T15S

SUNRISE HWY

OASIS RD

3

S1

2

SUNRISE HWY

SEE **1216** MAP

Little Laguna Lake

LOS HUECOS RD

Big
Laguna
Lake

10

11

FS

SUNR

Cleveland National Forest

BOILING SPRINGS RD

14

15

ESCONDI

N

RAND McNALLY

A B C D E

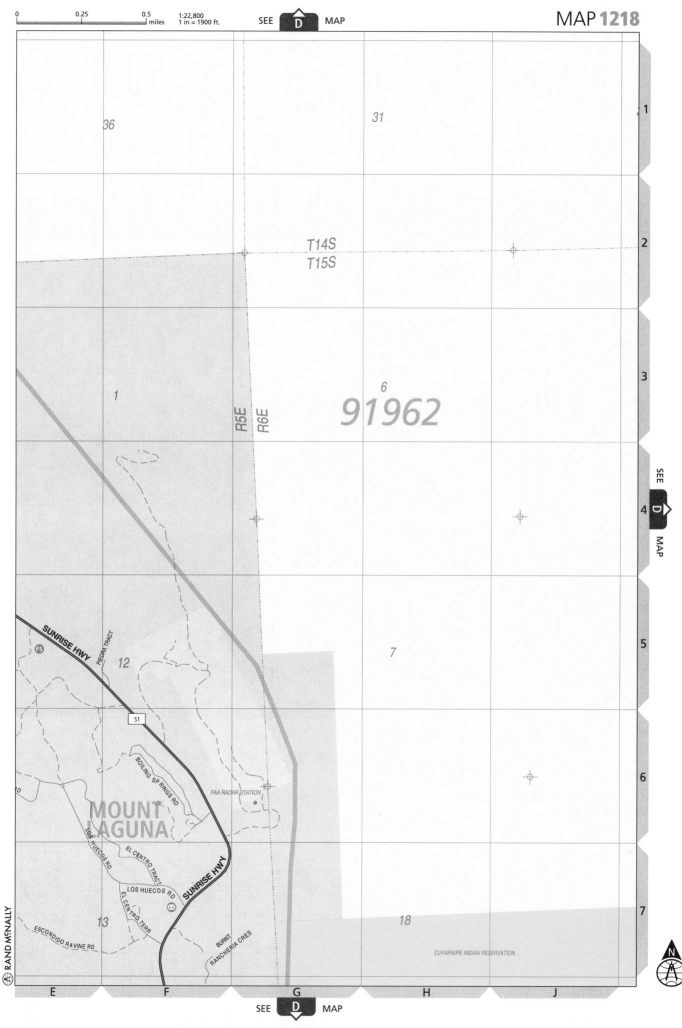

MAP **1218**

SAN DIEGO CO.

0   0.25   0.5
miles
1:22,800
1 in = 1900 ft.

SEE ▲D MAP

36

31

T14S
T15S

1

R5E
R6E

6
91962

SEE
▷D
MAP

SUNRISE HWY
FS
PIEDRA TRACT
12
S1

7

BOILING SP RINGS RD
FAA RADAR STATION

**MOUNT
LAGUNA**

LOS HUECOS RD
EL CENTRO TRACT
SUNRISE HWY

EL CENTRO TERR
LOS HUECOS RD

13

ESCONDIDO RAVINE RD

BURNT
RANCHERIA CRES

18

CUYAPAIPE INDIAN RESERVATION

RAND McNALLY

E   F   G   H   J

SEE ▼D MAP

1 2 3 4 5 6 7

N

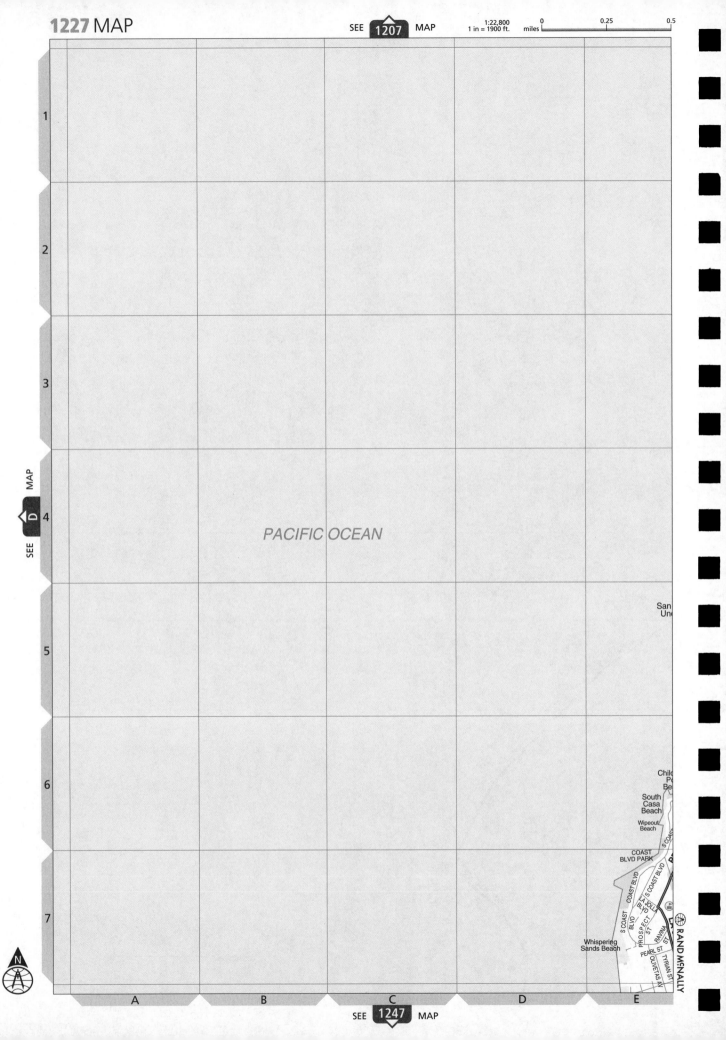

1:22,800
1 in = 1900 ft.
miles

0   0.25   0.5

SAN DIEGO CO.

PACIFIC OCEAN

SEE D MAP

San
Un

Chil
P
Be

South
Casa
Beach

Wipeout
Beach

COAST
BLVD PARK

S COAST
COAST BLVD
BLVD
S COAST BLVD
JOLL
ST
PROSPECT ST
RAVINA

S COAST
BLVD

Whispering
Sands Beach

PEARL ST

TYRIAN ST

OLIVETAS AV

RAND McNALLY

N

A   B   C   D   E

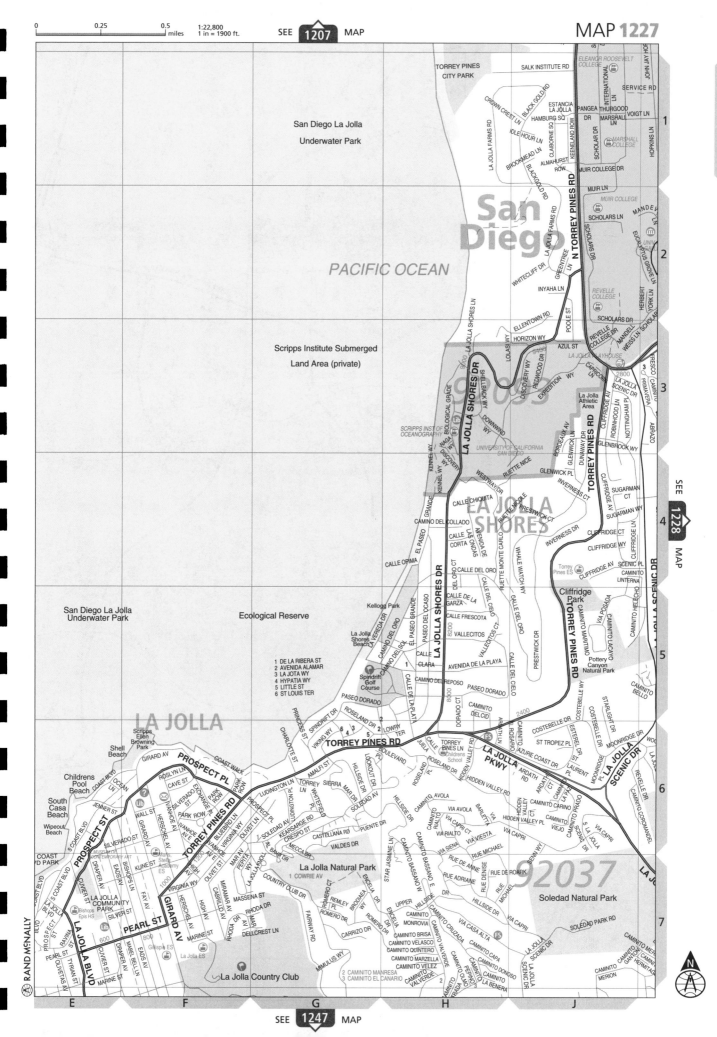

MAP **1227**

SAN DIEGO CO.

SEE **1207** MAP

0   0.25   0.5
miles
1:22,800
1 in = 1900 ft.

SAN DIEGO

ELEANOR ROOSEVELT COLLEGE

TORREY PINES CITY PARK

SALK INSTITUTE RD

San Diego La Jolla
Underwater Park

CROWN CREST LN
BLACK GOLD RD
ESTANCIA LA JOLLA
HAMBURG SQ
INTERNATIONAL
SERVICE RD
JOHN JAY HOPKINS DR
PANGEA DR
THURGOOD
VOIGT LN
IDLE HOUR LN
CLAIBORNE RD
KEENELAND ROW
MARSHALL LN
SCHOLAR DR
ALMAHURST ROW
BROOKMEAD LN
MUIR COLLEGE DR
MUIR LN
HOPKINS DR
MUIR COLLEGE
BLACKGOLD LN
LA JOLLA FARMS RD
SCHOLARS LN
MANDEVILLE LN
MARSHALL COLLEGE
SCHOLARS DR
MANDEVILLE LN
EUCALYPTUS GROVE LN

San Diego

PACIFIC OCEAN

GREENTREE LN
WHITECLIFF DR
N TORREY PINES RD
INYAHA LN
REVELLE COLLEGE
SCHOLARS DR
MANDELL WEISS LN
SCHOLARS DR
HERBERT YORK LN

ELLENTOWN RD
HORIZON WY
LA JOLLA SHORES LN
POOLE ST
REVELLE COLLEGE DR
PRIMAVERA
CAMINITO
FRESCO
ABRAZO

Scripps Institute Submerged
Land Area (private)

LOLA WY
LA JOLLA SHORES DR
DISCOVERY WY
SHELBORN WY
REDWOOD DR
AZUL ST
EXPEDITION WY
CAPRICORN WY
LA JOLLA PLAYHOUSE
2800
LA JOLLA SCENIC DR
3

92093

Scripps Inst of
Oceanography
DOWNWIND WY
La Jolla
Athletic
Area

KENNEL WY
NAGA WY
DISCOVERY
DUNAWAY DR
BORDEAUX AV
ROBINHOOD LN
NOTTINGHAM PL
TORREY PINES RD
GLENWICK LN
GLENBROOK WY
SUGARMAN DR

KENNEL WY
UNIVERSITY OF CALIFORNIA
SAN DIEGO
WESTWAY DR
RUETTE NICE
GLENWICK PL
INVERNESS CT
SUGARMAN CT
SUGARMAN WY

LA JOLLA SHORES

CALLE CHIQUITA
RUETTE MONTE CARLO
RUETTE MORE
PRESTWICK CT
INVERNESS DR
CLIFFRIDGE CT
CLIFFRIDGE LN
4

CAMINO DEL COLLADO
CALLE LAS ONDAS
AVENIDA DE
CALLE CORTA
WHALE WATCH WY
CLIFFRIDGE WY
CLIFFRIDGE AV

EL PASEO GRANDE
CALLE DEL ORO CT
CALLE DE LA GARZA
CALLE DEL CIELO
VIA POSADA
CAMINITO HELECHO

CALLE OPINA
Torrey
Pines ES
CLIFFRIDGE AV
CAMINITO LINTERNA

Kellogg Park

CAMINO DEL SOL
VEREDA DR
EL PASEO GRANDE
LA JOLLA SHORES DR
CALLE FRESCOTA
Cliffridge
Park
CAMINITO MARTIN
CAMINITO UYACOYO

San Diego La Jolla
Underwater Park

Ecological Reserve

La Jolla
Shores
Beach
CALLE CLARA
VALLECITOS
PRESTWICK DR
TORREY PINES RD
CAMINITO BELLO

1 DE LA RIBERA ST
2 AVENIDA ALAMAR
3 LA JOTA WY
4 HYPATIA WY
5 LITTLE ST
6 ST LOUIS TER

Spindrift
Golf
Course
1
CALLE DE LA PLATA
AVENIDA DE LA PLAYA
CAMINO DEL REPOSO
CALLE DEL CIELO
8000
Pottery
Canyon
Natural Park
CAMINITO
BELLO

PASEO DORADO
DORADO CT
CAMINITO
DEL CID
2400
COSTEBELLE DR
COSTEBELLE TER
STARLIGHT DR
MOONRIDGE DR

PASEO DORADO
LOWRY TER
COSTEBELLE DR
ST TROPEZ PL
LA JOLLA SCENIC DR
MOONRIDGE DR

LA JOLLA

Scripps
Ellen
Browning
Park
PRINCESS ST
SPINDRIFT DR
ROSELAND DR
6 5 4 3
VIKING WY
AZURE COAST DR
LAURENT DR
REVELLE DR
6

Shell Beach

PROSPECT PL
COAST WALK
2
TORREY PINES RD
CALLE
JUELA
Torrey
Pines LN
Childrens
School
LA JOLLA PKWY
MOONRIDGE
CAMINITO CORONADEL

Childrens
Pool Beach
JENNER ST
GIRARD AV
ROSLYN LN
CAVE ST
PARK ROW
PROSPECT
LUDINGTON PL
AMALFI ST
TORREY PINES
SIERRA MAR DR
BOULEVARD
ROSELAND
HIDDEN VALLEY RD
ARDATH RD
VIA CAPRI
S LA JOLLA DR

South
Casa
Beach
Wipeout
Beach
OCEAN LN
SILVERADO ST
EXCHANGE PL
IVANHOE AV
VIRGINIA WY
WHITEFIELD
HILLSIDE DR
SOLEDAD AV
ROSELAND PL
HIDDEN VALLEY RD
HIDDEN VALLEY PL
CAMINITO AVOLA
VIA CAPRI CT
VIA VIESTA
VIA CAPRI

COAST BLVD
S COAST BLVD
WALL ST
GIRARD AV
BLUEBIRD LN
OLIVET LN
KEARSARGE RD
SOLEDAD AV
CASTELLANA RD
PUENTE DR
CAMINITO CARINO
CAMINITO VIEJO
VIA SIENA
RUE MICHAEL

COAST RD PARK
PROSPECT ST
HERSCHEL AV
SILVERADO ST
Museum of
Contemporary Art
MARY STAR
Academy
HIGH
PEPITA ST
CRESPO DR
MECCA DR
VALDES DR
La Jolla Natural Park
1 COWRIE AV
CAMINITO BASSANO W
RUE DE ANNE
RUE ADRIANE

LA JOLLA BLVD
S COAST BLVD
DRAPER AV
EADS AV
KLINE ST
Bishops
Eps HS
La Jolla
COMMUNITY PARK
1000
VIRGINIA WY
MIRAMAR AV
CARRILLO AV
MASSENA ST
COUNTRY CLUB DR
ROMERO CT
REMLEY PL
ROMERO DR
ENCELIA DR
STAR JASMINE LN
CAMINITO VELASCO
RUE DE ROARK
RUE MICHAEL
VIA CAPRI

92037

Soledad Natural Park

PEARL ST
GIRARD AV
HERSCHEL AV
HIGH AV
RHODA DR
DELLCREST LN
FAIRWAY RD
BRODIAEA LN
ENCELIA DR
UPPER ENCELIA
HILLSIDE
MONROVIA
VIA CASA ALTA
CAMINITO CRUZADA
VIA CAPRI

PEARL ST
600
MARINE ST
RHODA DR
EADS AV
MABEL BELL LN
Gillispie ES
MIMULLUS WY
CAMINITO BRISA
CAMINITO MARZELLA
CAMINITO QUINTERO
CAMINITO VERDE
SOLEDAD PARK RD

PROSPECT
S LA JOLLA BLVD
TYRIAN ST
OLIVETAS AV
600
DRAPER AV
La Jolla ES
La Jolla
Country Club
2 CAMINITO MANRESA
3 CAMINITO EL CANARIO
CAMINITO VELEZ
CAMINITO VALVERDE
CAMINITO MERION

LA JOLLA BLVD
MARINE AV
COAST BLVD

RAND McNALLY

E   F   G   H   J

SEE 1208 MAP

1:22,800
1 in = 1900 ft.
miles 0 0.25 0.5

SEE 1227 MAP

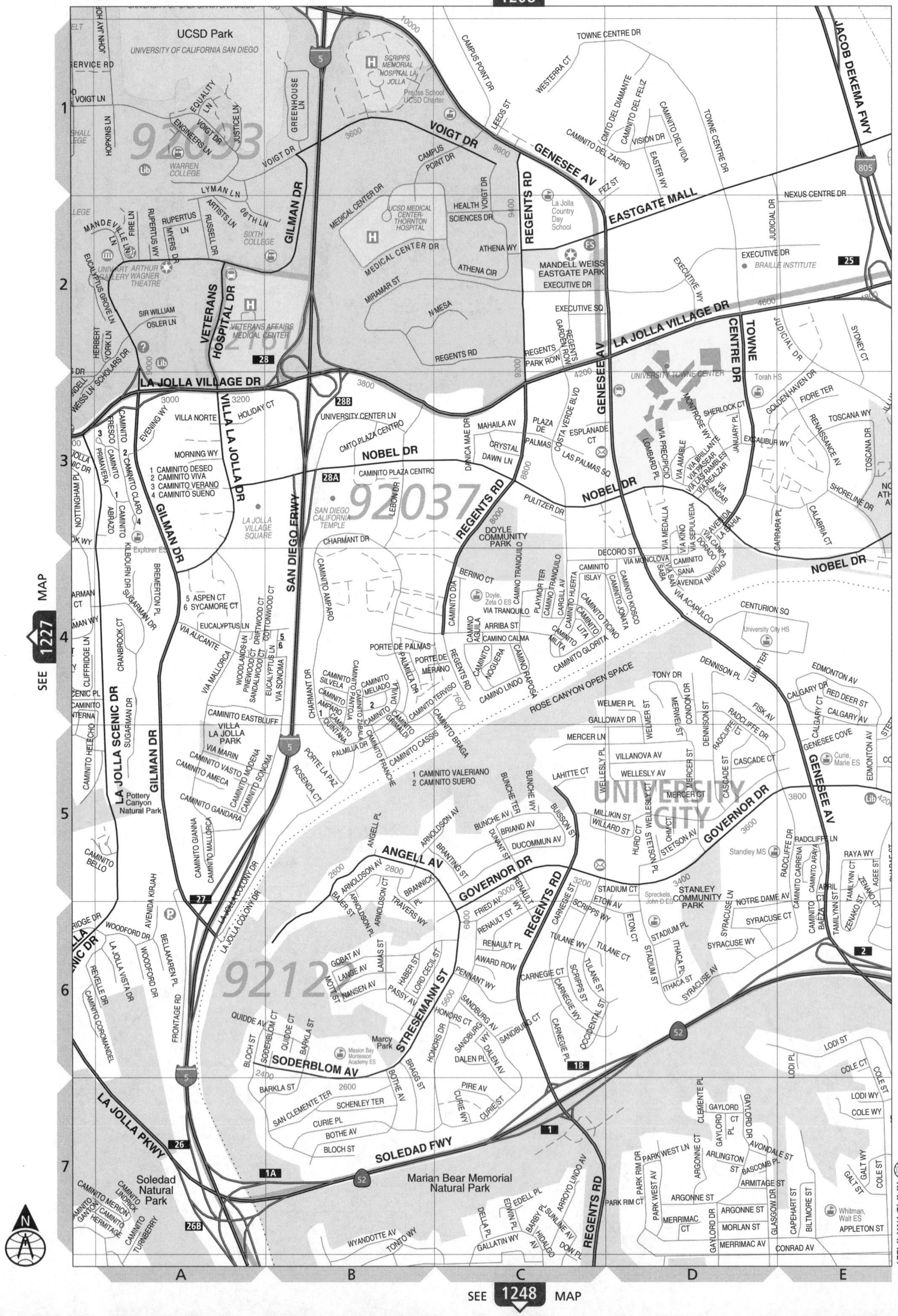

SEE 1248 MAP

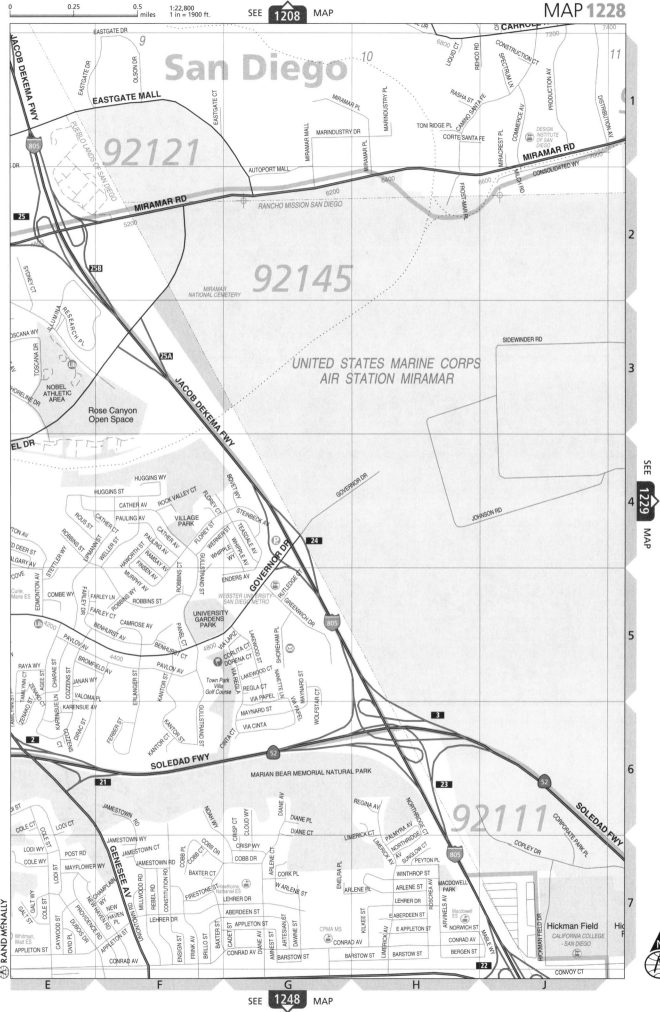

MAP **1228**

SEE **1208** MAP

SAN DIEGO CO.

San Diego

92121

92145

UNITED STATES MARINE CORPS
AIR STATION MIRAMAR

SEE **1229** MAP

92111

EASTGATE MALL

EASTGATE DR
EASTGATE DR
OLSON DR
EASTGATE CT

JACOB DEKEMA FWY

PUEBLO LANDS OF SAN DIEGO

MIRAMAR RD

MIRAMAR MALL
MARINDUSTRY DR
MIRAMAR PL
MARINDUSTRY PL

CARROLL
6800 CT
LIQUID CT
REHCO RD
CONSTRUCTION CT
SPECTRUM LN
COMMERCE AV
PRODUCTION AV
7200
7400
DISTRIBUTION AV

RASHA SANTA FE
CAMINO SANTA FE
TONI RIDGE PL
CORTE SANTA FE
MIRACREST PL

DESIGN INSTITUTE OF SAN DIEGO

MIRAMAR RD
7000
CONSOLIDATED WY

AUTOPORT MALL
6200
6400
6600
FROST-MAR PL
MILCH RD

RANCHO MISSION SAN DIEGO
5200

SYDNEY CT

TOSCANA WY
TOSCANA DR
ILLUMINA
RESEARCH PL
Lib
SHORELINE DR

NOBEL
ATHLETIC
AREA

Rose Canyon
Open Space

MIRAMAR
NATIONAL CEMETERY

SIDEWINDER RD

GOVERNOR DR

JOHNSON RD

EL DR

HUGGINS WY
HUGGINS ST
CATHER AV
ROCK VALLEY CT
FLOREY CT

BOVET WY
STEINBECK AV

VILLAGE
PARK

CATHER AV
CATHER CT
PAULING AV
PAULING AV
CATHER AV
FLOREY ST
WERNER ST
TEASDALE AV
WHIPPLE AV
WHIPPLE WY

ROUS ST
ROBBINS ST
LIPMANN ST
WELLER ST
HAWORTH ST
FINSEN AV
RAMSAY AV
MURPHY AV
ROBBINS WY
GULLSTRAND ST

STETTLER WY
EDMONTON AV
COMBE WY
FARLEY LN
ROBBINS ST
FARLEY CT
CAMROSE AV
ROBBINS CT
ENDERS AV

GOVERNOR DR

24

WEBSTER UNIVERSITY-
SAN DIEGO METRO

RUTLEDGE ST
GREENWICH DR

805

Curie,
Marie ES
RED DEER ST
CALGARY AV
COVE

FARLEY DR
BENHURST AV
Lib 4200

UNIVERSITY
GARDENS PARK

PANEL CT
BENHURST CT
4400

PAVLOV AV

RAYA WY
TAMILYNN CT
ZENAKO ST
CHARAE ST
AGEE ST

BROMFIELD AV
PAVLOV AV
KANTOR ST
ERLANGER ST

4800
VIA LAPIZ
CORLITA CT
DORENA CT
VIA REGLA
LAKEWOOD CT
LAKEWOOD ST
REGLA CT

SHOREHAM PL

LINNETTE LN
MAYNARD ST
MAYNARD CT

JANAN WY
KARENSUE LN
VALOMA PL
KARENSUE AV
COZZENS ST
DIRAC ST
SNEZZO

Town Park
Villa
Golf Course

VIA PAPEL
VIA PAPEL
VIA CINTA
VIA CINTA
WOLFSTAR ST

2

FERBER ST
FAMILY WY
KANTOR CT
KANTOR ST
GULLSTRAND ST

SOLEDAD FWY
52

21

MARIAN BEAR MEMORIAL NATURAL PARK

3

23

52

SOLEDAD FWY

LODI ST
COLE CT
COLE ST
LODI CT

JAMESTOWN RD
JAMESTOWN WY
JAMESTOWN CT
JAMESTOWN RD

NOAH WY
CRISP CT
CLOUD WY
CRISP WY

COBB PL
COBB CT
COBB DR
COBB DR
COBB DR

DIANE AV
DIANE PL
DIANE CT

REGINA AV

NORTHRIDGE CT
PALMYRA AV
NORTHRIDGE AV
SUNGLOW CT
PEYTON PL

CORPORATE PARK PL

COPLEY DR

LODI WY
COLE WY

POST RD
MAYFLOWER WY

BAXTER CT

LIMERICK CT
LIMERICK AV
ENELRA PL
ARLENE CT
CORK PL
W ARLENE ST
ARLENE PL

WINTHROP ST
ARLENE ST

MACDOWELL
PARK

GALT WY
COLE ST
LODI ST

CHAMPLAIN WY
NEW HAVEN RD
NEW HAVEN PL

GENESEE AV

MILLWOOD RD
REBEL RD
CONSTITUTION RD

FIRESTONE ST
Hawthorne,
Nathaniel ES
LEHRER DR

ARVINELS AV
Macdowell ES
NORWICH ST

Hickman Field

CALIFORNIA COLLEGE
- SAN DIEGO

GALT ST
CAYWOOD ST
DUBOIS DR
OVID PL
Whitman,
Walt ES
APPLETON ST

PROVIDENCE DR
UNIONTON RD

LEHRER DR
ABERDEEN ST
APPLETON ST
BAXTER ST
CADET ST

ENSIGN ST
FRINK AV
BRILLO ST

CONRAD AV
DIANE AV
AMNEST ST
ARTESIAN ST
DAWNE ST

CPMA MS
CONRAD AV
BARSTOW ST

BARSTOW ST

BARSTOW ST

LIMERICK AV
KILKEE ST
E ABERDEEN ST
E APPLETON ST
CONRAD AV

ROSCREA AV

BERGEN ST

MABLE WY
22
HICKMAN FIELD DR
CONVOY CT

RAND McNALLY

N

0   0.25   0.5
miles
1:22,800
1 in = 1900 ft.

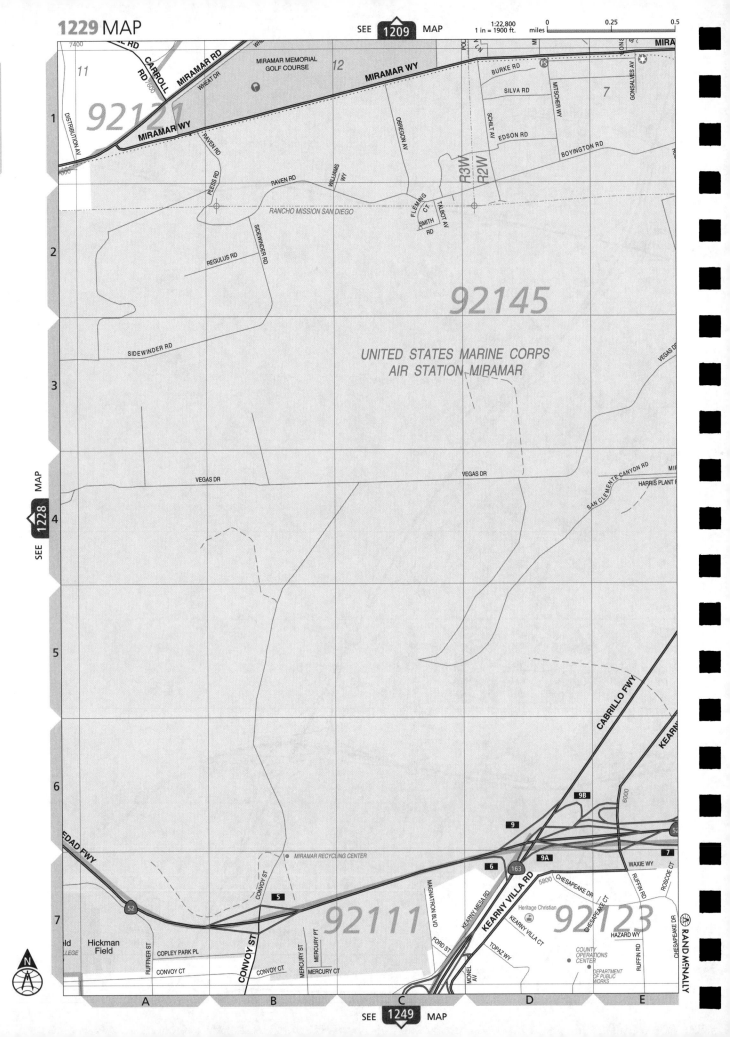

SAN DIEGO CO.

1:22,800
1 in = 1900 ft.
miles
0   0.25   0.5

92121

92145

UNITED STATES MARINE CORPS
AIR STATION MIRAMAR

RANCHO MISSION SAN DIEGO

MIRAMAR RD
CARROLL RD
MIRAMAR WY
WHEAT DR
MIRAMAR MEMORIAL GOLF COURSE
MIRAMAR WY
BURKE RD
SILVA RD
MITSCHER WY
7
GONSALVES AV
DISTRIBUTION AV
MIRAMAR WY
RAVEN RD
PLESS RD
OBREGON AV
SCHILT AV
EDSON RD
BOYINGTON RD
RAVEN RD
WILLIAMS WY
FLEMING CT
TALBOT AV
SMITH RD
R3W
R2W
REGULUS RD
SIDEWINDER RD
SIDEWINDER RD

VEGAS DR
VEGAS DR
VEGAS DR
SAN CLEMENTE CANYON RD
HARRIS PLANT R
MIR

CABRILLO FWY
KEARN
9B
6000
9
52
EDAD FWY
MIRAMAR RECYCLING CENTER
9A
WAXIE WY
7
CONVOY ST
6
163
ROSCOE CT
RUFFIN RD
CHESAPEAKE DR
5800
CHESAPEAKE CT
52
5
KEARNY MESA RD
KEARNY VILLA RD
92111
HAZARD WY
CHESAPEAKE DR
92123
Hickman Field
ld LLEGE
RUFFNER ST
COPLEY PARK PL
CONVOY CT
CONVOY ST
CONVOY CT
MERCURY ST
MERCURY PT
MERCURY ST
MAGNATRON BLVD
FORD ST
MONEL AV
TOPAZ WY
KEARNY VILLA CT
Heritage Christian
COUNTY OPERATIONS CENTER
DEPARTMENT OF PUBLIC WORKS
RUFFIN RD
RAND McNALLY

1
2
3
4
5
6
7

A   B   C   D   E

N

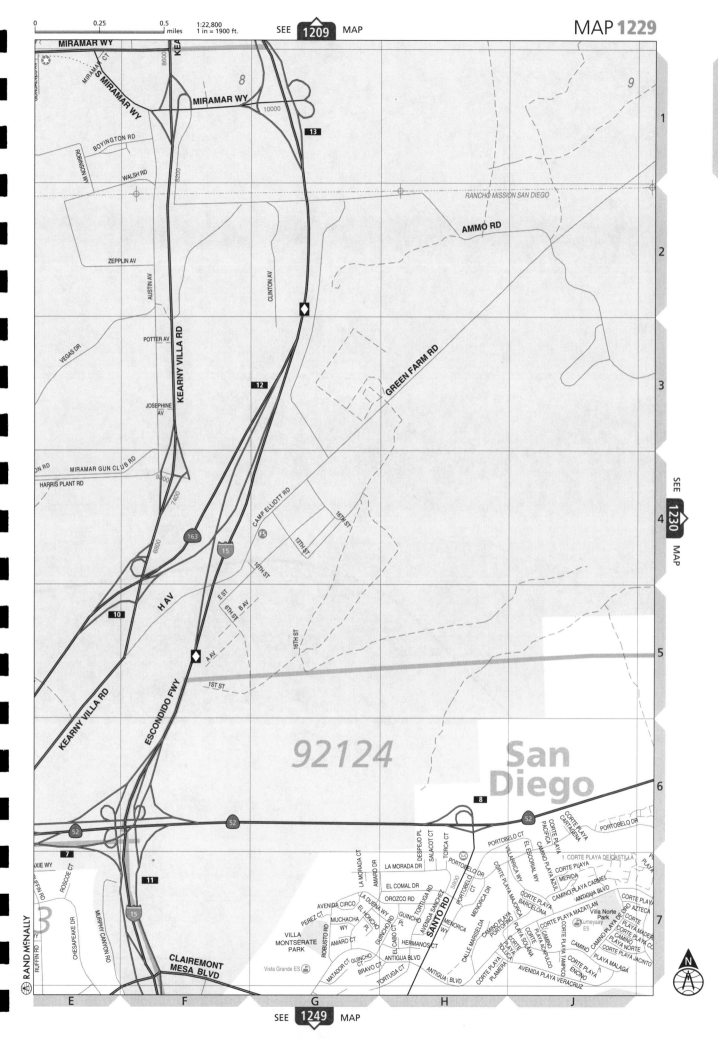

MAP **1229**

SAN DIEGO CO.

SEE **1209** MAP

0   0.25   0.5 miles
1:22,800
1 in = 1900 ft.

MIRAMAR WY

8

9

MIRAMAR CT

S MIRAMAR WY

MIRAMAR WY

10000

13

BOYINGTON RD

ROBINSON WY

WALSH RD

RANCHO MISSION SAN DIEGO

ZEPPLIN AV

AMMO RD

AUSTIN AV

CLINTON AV

VEGAS DR

POTTER AV

KEARNY VILLA RD

GREEN FARM RD

12

JOSEPHINE AV

ON RD

MIRAMAR GUN CLUB RD

HARRIS PLANT RD

CAMP ELLIOTT RD

16TH ST

163

15

FS

13TH ST

10

H AV

E ST

10TH ST

6TH ST B AV

16TH ST

SEE 1230 MAP

4

A AV

1ST ST

5

ESCONDIDO FWY

KEARNY VILLA RD

92124

**San
Diego**

6

8

52

52

52

CORTE PLAYA
CARTAGENA

PORTOBELO DR

7

DESPEJO PL

PORTOBELO CT

CORTE PLAYA
PACIFICA

CORTE PLAYA
CARTAGENA

AXIE WY

SALACOT CT

TORCA CT

PORTOBELO DR

CAMINO PLAYA AZUL

1 CORTE PLAYA DE CASTILLA

PLAYA

11

LA MORADA CT

AMARO DR

LA MORADA DR

PORTOBELO
CT

VILLARRICA WY

EL ESCORIAL WY

MERIDA

CAMINO PLAYA
BARCELONA

ANTIGUA BLVD

CORTE PLAYA
AZTECA

RUFFIN RD

ROSCOE CT

CHESAPEAKE DR

MURPHY CANYON RD

15

EL COMAL DR

AVENIDA CIRCO

PEREZ CT

LA DUENA WY

EL HONCHO

OROZCO RD

GUINCHO RD

AVENIDA SANCHEZ

SANTO RD

MENORCA

MENORCA DR

CALLE MARISELDA

CAMINO PLAYA
PORTOFINO

CORTE PLAYA MALORCA

CORTE PLAYA
MAZATLAN

CORTE
PLAYA SOLANA

CORTE PLAYA CARMEL

CAMINO PLAYA CARMEL

CORTE PLAYA MADERA

CORTE PLAYA CO

Villa Norte
Park

Kumeyaay
ES

CAMINO NORTE

CORTE PLAYA JACINTO

VILLA
MONTSERATE
PARK

ROBUSTO RD

MUCHACHA
WY

EL CABO CT

GUINCHO
RD

HERMANOS CT

ANTIGUA BLVD

CORTE
PLAYA
TOLUCA

CAMINO
PLAYA ACAPULCO

AMARO CT

MATADOR CT

GUINCHO
CT

BRAVO CT

TORTUGA CT

ANTIGUA
BLVD

CORTE PLAYA
PLAMERA

CORTE PLAYA TAMPICO

CAMINO
PLAYA MALAGA

CORTE PLAYA
ENCINO

**CLAIREMONT
MESA BLVD**

Vista Grande ES

AVENIDA PLAYA VERACRUZ

RAND M?NALLY

3

N

E   F   G   H   J

1   2   3   4   5   6   7

SEE **1249** MAP

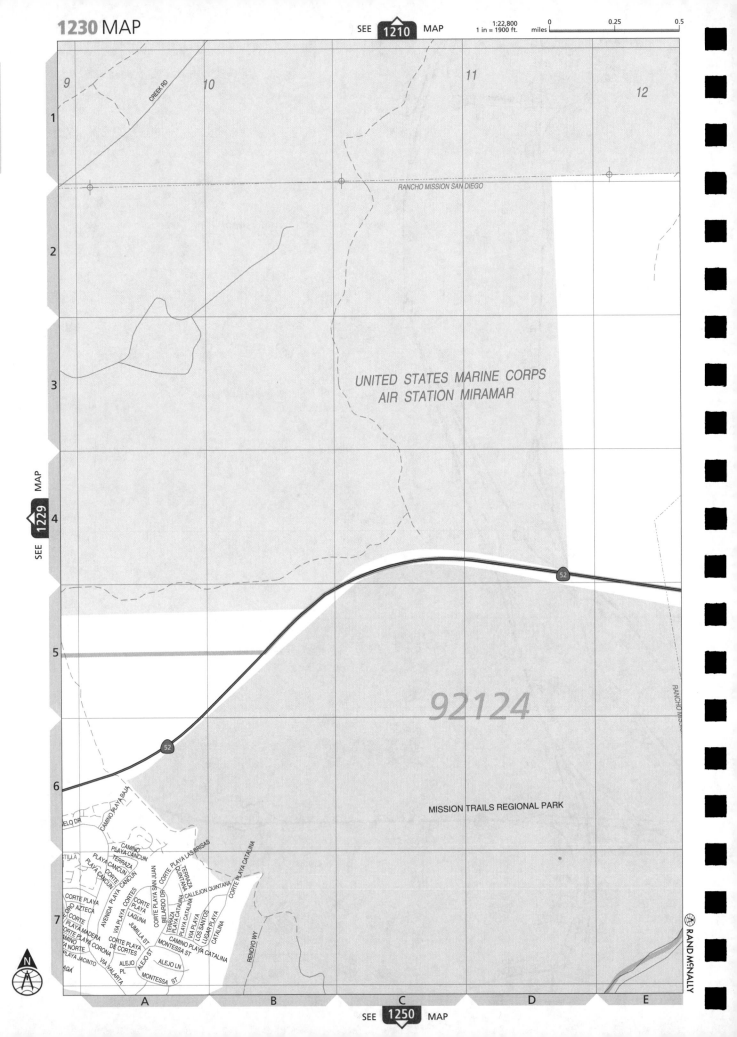

SAN DIEGO CO.

SEE 1210 MAP

1:22,800
1 in = 1900 ft.

miles   0   0.25   0.5

9   10   11   12

1

2

RANCHO MISSION SAN DIEGO

3

UNITED STATES MARINE CORPS
AIR STATION MIRAMAR

SEE 1229 MAP

4

52

5

92124

52

6

MISSION TRAILS REGIONAL PARK

CAMINO PLAYA BAJA

ELO DR

CAMINO PLAYA CANCUN

CORTE PLAYA LAS BRISAS

TILLA

TERRAZA
PLAYA CANCUN

CORTE PLAYA CANCUN

PLAYA CANCUN

CORTE PLAYA CANCUN

CORTE PLAYA SAN JUAN

BELARDO DR

CORTE PLAYA CATALINA

TERRAZA PLAYA CATALINA

CALLEJON QUINTANA

CORTE PLAYA AZTECA

SO AZTECA

CORTE PLAYA MADERA

AVENIDA PLAYA CATALINA

VIA PLAYA CORTES

CORTE PLAYA LAGUNA

JUMILLA ST

TERRAZA PLAYA CATALINA

VIA PLAYA

LOS SANTOS

LUGAR PLAYA CATALINA

RENOVO WY

7

CORTE PLAYA CORONA

CAMINO

PLAYA NORTE

CORTE PLAYA DE CORTES

CAMINO PLAYA CATALINA

MONTESSA ST

AGA

PLAYA JACINTO

VIA VALARTA

ALEJO PL

ALEJO ST

ALEJO LN

MONTESSA ST

N

RAND McNALLY

A   B   C   D   E

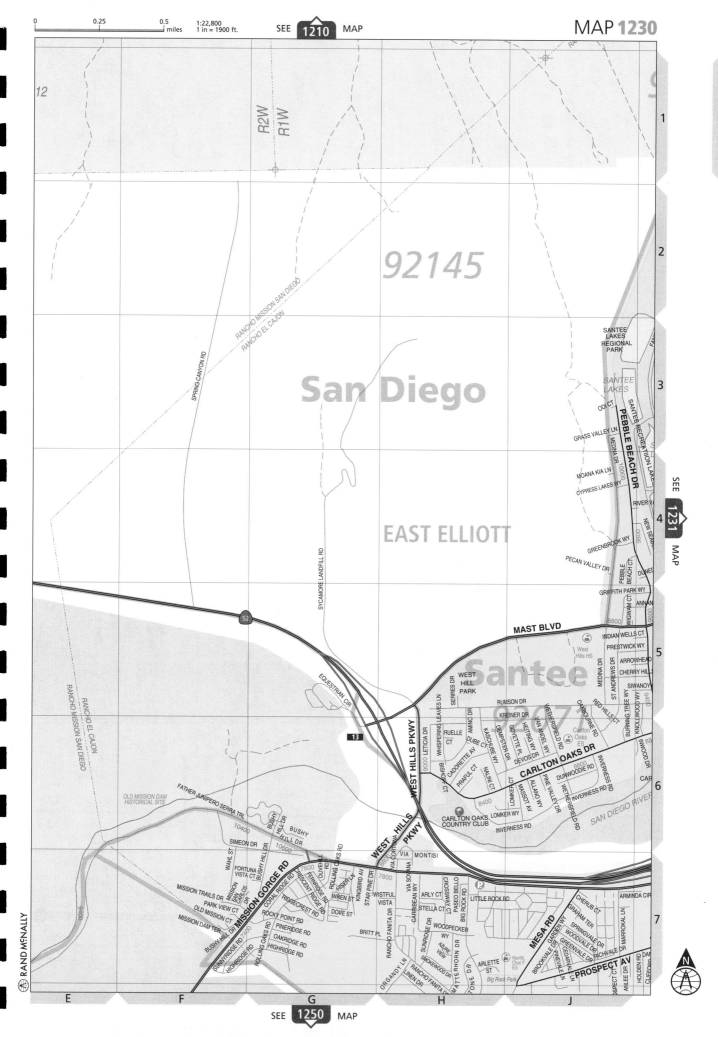

MAP **1230**

0   0.25   0.5
| miles
1:22,800
1 in = 1900 ft.

SEE 1210 MAP

12

R2W
R1W

1

92145

2

RANCHO MISSION SAN DIEGO
RANCHO EL CAJON

SPRING CANYON RD

SANTEE
LAKES
REGIONAL
PARK

SANTEE
LAKES

SANTEE RECREATION LAKES

3

San Diego

ODI CT

GRASS VALLEY LN

MOANA KIA LN

CYPRESS LAKES WY

RIVER V

PEBBLE BEACH DR

MEDINA DR 10000

EAST ELLIOTT

SEE 1231 MAP

4

GREENBROOK WY

NEW SEAB

PECAN VALLEY DR

PEBBLE
BEACH CT

DUNED

GRIFFITH PARK WY

ANNAN

SYCAMORE LANDFILL RD

52

MAST BLVD

8800

WIGWAM CT

INDIAN WELLS CT
PRESTWICK WY

West
Hills HS

5

ARROWHEAD

CHERRY HILL

SIWANOY

9400

MEDINA DR

ST ANDREWS DR

EQUESTRIAN CIR

Santee

RED HILLS CT

Carlton
Oaks
ES

92071

OAKBOURNE RD

BURNING TREE WY

KNOLLWOOD WY

WEST HILL
PARK

SERRES DR

WHISPERING LEAVES LN

RUMSON DR

KREINER DR

WETHERSFIELD DR

AMINO DR

VAN ANDEL WY

HEITING WY

GO-ETTE PL

DEMPSTER DR

DEVOS DR

PINE VALLEY DR

DUNWOODIE RD

INVERNESS RD RD

WETHERSFIELD RD

INWOOD DR

CAR

6

13

9000 LETICIA DR

RUELLE
CT

CADORETTE AV

DUBE CT

KASCHUBE WY

NALINI CT

PRAFUL CT

LOMKER CT

ALLANO WY

MASSOT AV

8400

LOMKER WY

INVERNESS RD

8600

CARLTON OAKS DR

SAN DIEGO RIVER

CARLTON OAKS
COUNTRY CLUB

FATHER JUNIPERO SERRA TRL

OLD MISSION DAM
HISTORICAL SITE

RANCHO EL CAJON
RANCHO MISSION SAN DIEGO

10400

BUSHY
HILL DR

BUSHY
HILL DR

WEST HILLS PKWY

WEST HILLS PKWY

VIA
MONTISI

SIMEON DR

10600

WAHL ST

VIA CORTE

VIA SORANA

7800

7600

ROLLING OAKS RD

OLIVENT

FERNRIDGE RD

CRESCENT RIDGE RD

KISSFLM

KINGBIRD AV

STAR PINE DR

WREN CT

DOVE ST

WISTFUL
VISTA

VIA CORTE

PASEO BELLO

ARLY CT

STELLA CT

CROSSTON

BIG ROCK RD

LITTLE ROCK RD

CHERUB CT

BRAHAM TER

SPRINGVALE DR

ARMINDA CIR

MARROKAL LN

MISSION TRAILS DR

MISSION
SAN
CARLOS
DR

FORTUNA
VISTA CT

MISSION GORGE RD

CORAL RIDGE RD

RIDGECREST RD

PARK VIEW CT

OLD MISSION CT

MISSION DAM TER

9100

ROCKY POINT RD

PINERIDGE RD

OAKRIDGE RD

HIGHRIDGE RD

BRITT PL

RANCHO FANITA DR

CARRIBEAN WY

SUNRIDGE DR

WOODPECKER
WY

AZURE
NEW

MESA RD

WOODVALE DR

GREENVALE DR

PINEVALE LN

CEDARVALE LN

WOODVALE DR

RICHVALE DR

ANLEE DR

PROSPECT AV

HOLDEN DAN

BUSHY HILL DR

SUNNYRIDGE RD

HIGHRIDGE RD

ROLLING OAKS RD

7400

ORGANDY LN

LINEN DR

RANCHO FANITA D

SMOKEWOOD
WY

MATTERHORN DR

TONE DR

ARLETTE
ST

Harritt,
Chet F
ES

Big Rock Park

BROOKVALE DR

GARDEN WY

BRAHAM TER

PROSPECT CT

ANLEE DR

CLIFFOR

RAND MᶜNALLY

E   F   G   H   J

7

SEE 1250 MAP

N

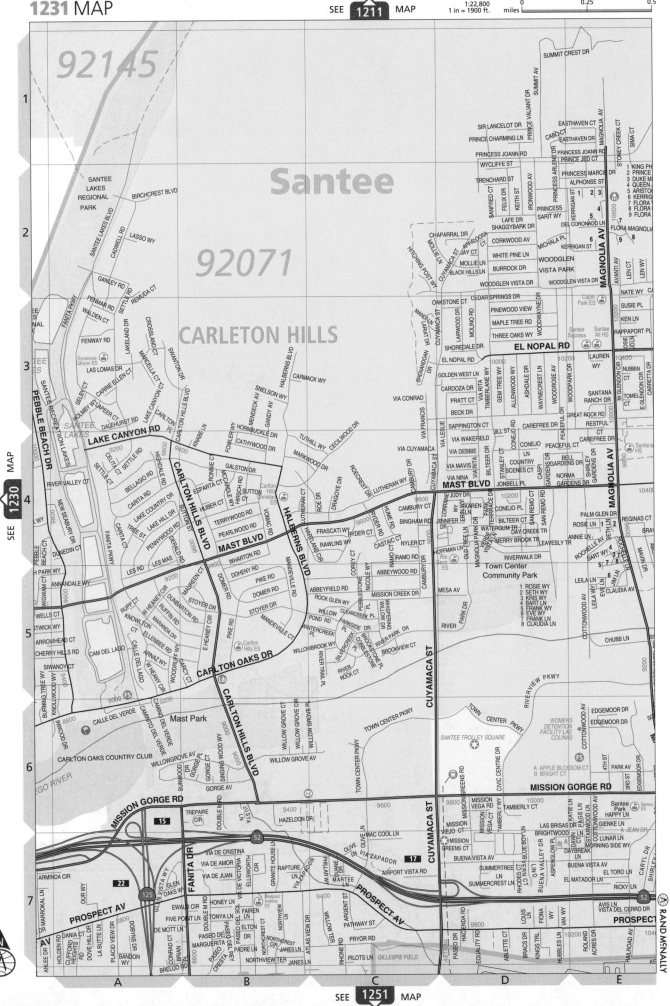

SEE 1211 MAP

1:22,800
1 in = 1900 ft.

0   0.25   0.5
miles

SAN DIEGO CO.

92145

Santee

92071

CARLETON HILLS

SANTEE LAKES REGIONAL PARK

SEE 1230 MAP

RAND McNALLY

A   B   C   D   E

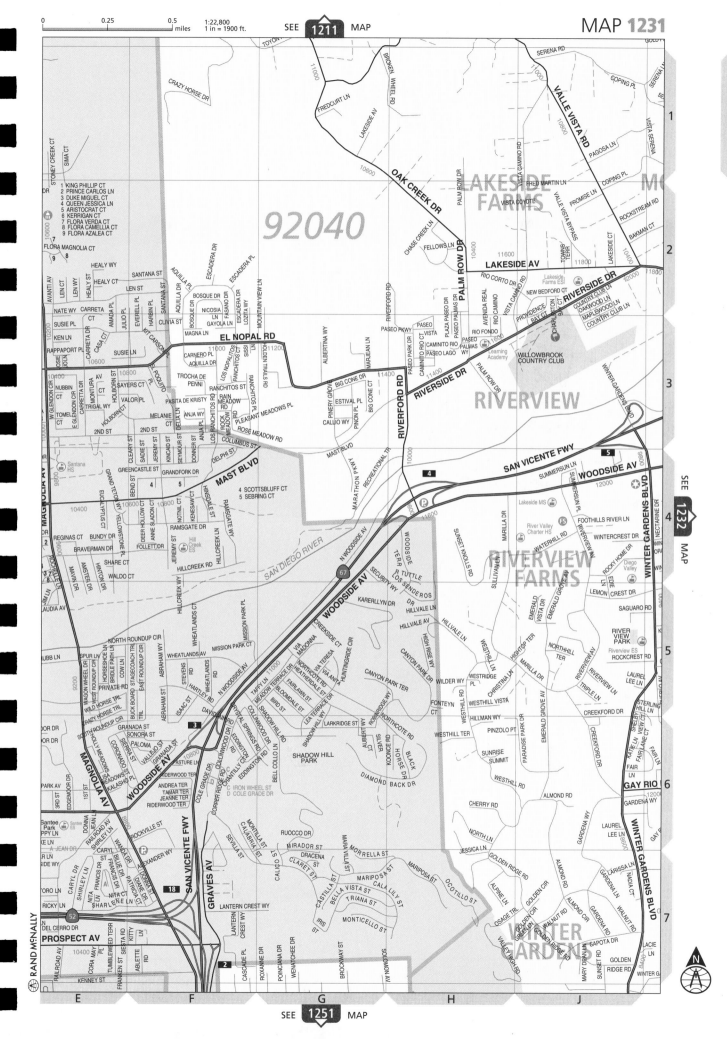

0   0.25   0.5
miles
1 in = 1900 ft.
1:22,800

92040

1 KING PHILLIP CT
2 PRINCE CARLOS LN
3 DUKE MIGUEL CT
4 QUEEN JESSICA LN
5 ARISTOCRAT CT
6 KERRIGAN CT
7 FLORA VERDA CT
8 FLORA CAMELLIA CT
9 FLORA AZALEA CT

FLORA MAGNOLIA CT

LAKESIDE FARMS

LAKESIDE AV

RIVERSIDE DR

RIVERVIEW

WILLOWBROOK COUNTRY CLUB

EL NOPAL RD

RIVERFORD RD

RIVERSIDE DR

MAST BLVD

4 SCOTTSBLUFF CT
5 SEBRING CT

SAN VICENTE FWY

WOODSIDE AV

WOODSIDE AV

San Diego River

WOODSIDE AV

RIVERVIEW FARMS

RIVER VIEW PARK

SHADOW HILL PARK

MAGNOLIA AV

WOODSIDE AV

SAN VICENTE FWY

GRAVES AV

GAY RIO

WINTER GARDENS BLVD

PROSPECT AV

WINTER GARDENS

RAND MCNALLY

N

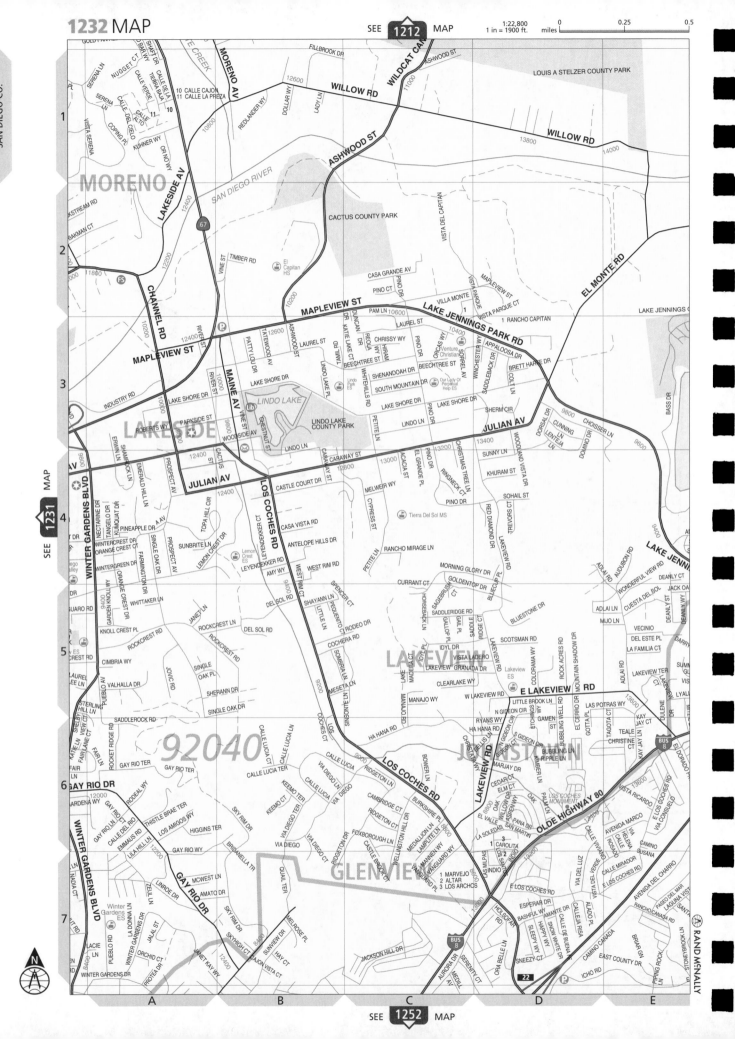

SEE **1212** MAP

1:22,800
1 in = 1900 ft.

miles 0   0.25   0.5

MORENO

SAN DIEGO RIVER

LAKESIDE

92040

LAKEVIEW

GLENVIEW

JOHNSTOWN

SEE **1231** MAP

SEE **1252** MAP

A   B   C   D   E

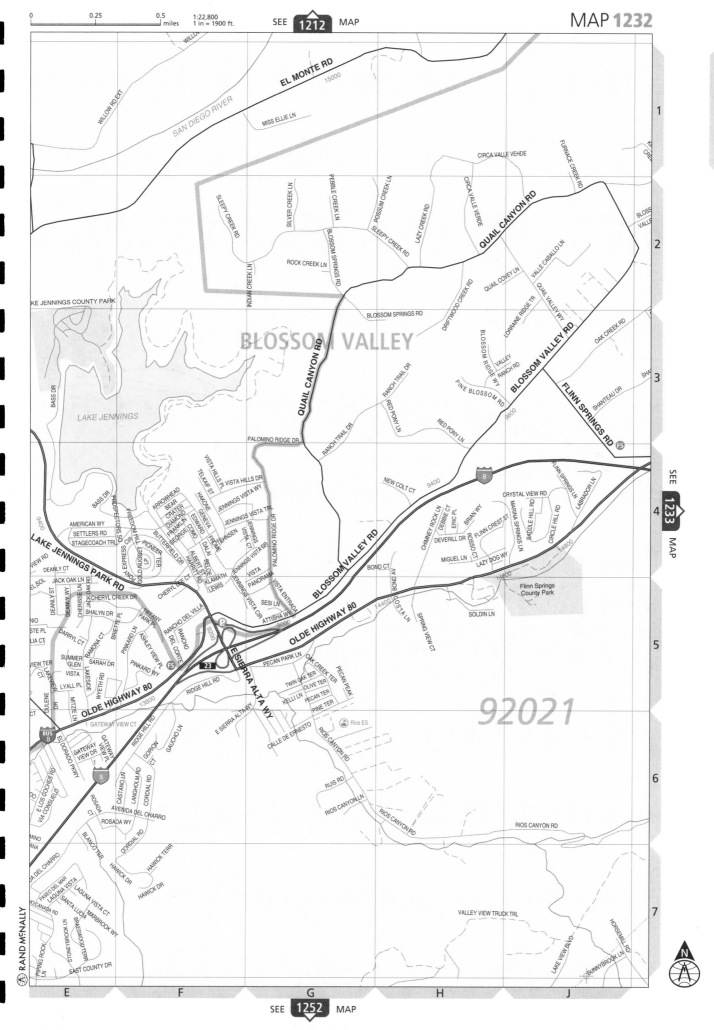

MAP **1232**

SAN DIEGO CO.

0   0.25   0.5
miles
1:22,800
1 in = 1900 ft.

EL MONTE RD   15000

SAN DIEGO RIVER

WILLOW RD EXT

WILLOW

MISS ELLIE LN

CIRCA VALLE VEHDE

FURNACE CREEK RD

KN CREEK

SLEEPY CREEK RD

SILVER CREEK LN

PEBBLE CREEK LN

POSSUM CREEK LN

LAZY CREEK RD

CIRCA VALLE VERDE

QUAIL CANYON RD

BLOSSOM VALLEY

SLEEPY CREEK RD

ROCK CREEK LN

BLOSSOM SPRINGS RD

VALLE CABALLO LN

QUAIL COVEY LN

QUAIL VALLEY WY

OAK CREEK RD

LAKE JENNINGS COUNTY PARK

INDIAN CREEK LN

DRIFTWOOD CREEK RD

LORRAINE RIDGE TR

BLOSSOM SPRINGS RD

BLOSSOM RIDGE WY

BLOSSOM SPRINGS RD

VALLEY RANCH RD

BLOSSOM VALLEY RD

SHANTEAU DR

SHA

BASS DR

LAKE JENNINGS

RANCH TRAIL DR

PINE BLOSSOM RD

RED PONY LN

RED PONY LN

9600

FLINN SPRINGS RD

FS

RANCH TRAIL DR

PALOMINO RIDGE DR

VISTA HILLS PL

VISTA HILLS DR

NEW COLT CT   9400

8

CRYSTAL VIEW RD

FLINN SPRINGS LN

LABRADOR LN

TELKAIF ST

HAKONE

JENNINGS VISTA WY

CHIMNEY ROCK LN

DEBBIE CT

ERIC PL

BRIAN WY

MARINA SPRINGS LN

SADDLE HILL RD

CIRCLE HILL RD

ARROWHEAD

BEAR

CRATER

DIAMOND

FRANKLIN

GEORGE

EDWARD

GENEVA

COMO

DALAI

JENNINGS VISTA TRL

THOMSEN

JENNINGS VISTA CT

DEVERILL DR

ROSSO CT

FLINN CREST ST

14800

AMERICAN WY

SETTLERS RD

STAGECOACH TRL

PROSPECTORS CIR

FREEDOM HILL

EXPRESS CIR

PIONEER TER

GOLD NUGGET LP

LP

BUTTERFIELD DR

ALBERT ST

HARRITT RD

KLAMATH

JENNINGS VISTA DR

PALOMINO RIDGE DR

MIGUEL LN

LAZY DOG WY

14600

Flinn Springs
County Park

VIEW RD

DEANLY CT

EL SOL

JACK OAK LN

DEANLY ST

JACK OAK RD

CHERISSE LN

JACK OAK KD

CHERYL CREEK DR

SHALYN DR

CHERYL LEE CT

LEWIS

VISTA

VISTA PANORAMA

SESI LN

BOND CT

BOND AV

ACOSTA LN

SPRING VIEW CT

SOLDIN LN

SANIO

STE PL

LIA CT

DARRYL CT

RAMONA CT

BRIETTE PL

PINKARD LN

TIFFANY
PARK PL

RANCHO DEL VILLA

RANCHO
DEL CORTE

ASHLEY VIEW PL

ATTISHA WY

VISTA ENTRADA

JENNINGS VISTA CIR

9000

OLDE HIGHWAY 80

14400

BLOSSOM VALLEY RD

VIEW TER

SUMMER
GLEN

VISTA

LAKESIDE

SARAH DR

WYETH RD

LYALL PL

PINKARD WY

FS

23

P

9200

E SIERRA ALTA WY

PECAN PARK LN

OAK CREEK TER

PECAN PEAK

92021

LAKE JENNINGS PARK RD

LAKEVIEW
CT

MITZIE LN

OLDE HIGHWAY 80   13800

1 GATEWAY VIEW CT

RIDGE HILL RD

TWIN OAK TER

KELLI LN

OLIVE TER

PECAN TER

PINE TER

Rios ES

PECAN PARK LN

DULENE
DR

BUS
8

ELDORADO PKWY

GATEWAY
VIEW DR

GATEWAY
VIEW PL

RIDGE HILL RD

GORION
CT

GAUCHO LN

E SIERRA ALTA WY

CALLE DE ERNESTO

RIOS CANYON RD

VIA LOS COCHES RD

E LOS
CONSUELO

8

CASTANO LN

LANGHOLM RD

CORDIAL RD

ROSADA

AVENIDA DEL CHARRO

ROSADA WY

BLANCO TER

CORDIAL RD

HAWICK TERR

RUIS RD

RIOS CANYON LN

RIOS CANYON RD

RIOS CANYON RD

DA DEL CHARRO

MINO
ANA

PASEO DEL MAR

LAGUNA VISTA

LAGUNA VISTA CT

SANTA LUCIA

MARBROOK WY

HAWICK DR

HAWICK DR

O CANADA RD

PIPING ROCK
LN

STONEYBROOK LN

BRAESWOOD TERR

EAST COUNTY DR

VALLEY VIEW TRUCK TRL

LAKE VIEW BLVD

HORSEMILL RD

SUNNYBROOK LN

RAND M⁹NALLY

E   F   G   H   J

1   2   3   4   5   6   7

N

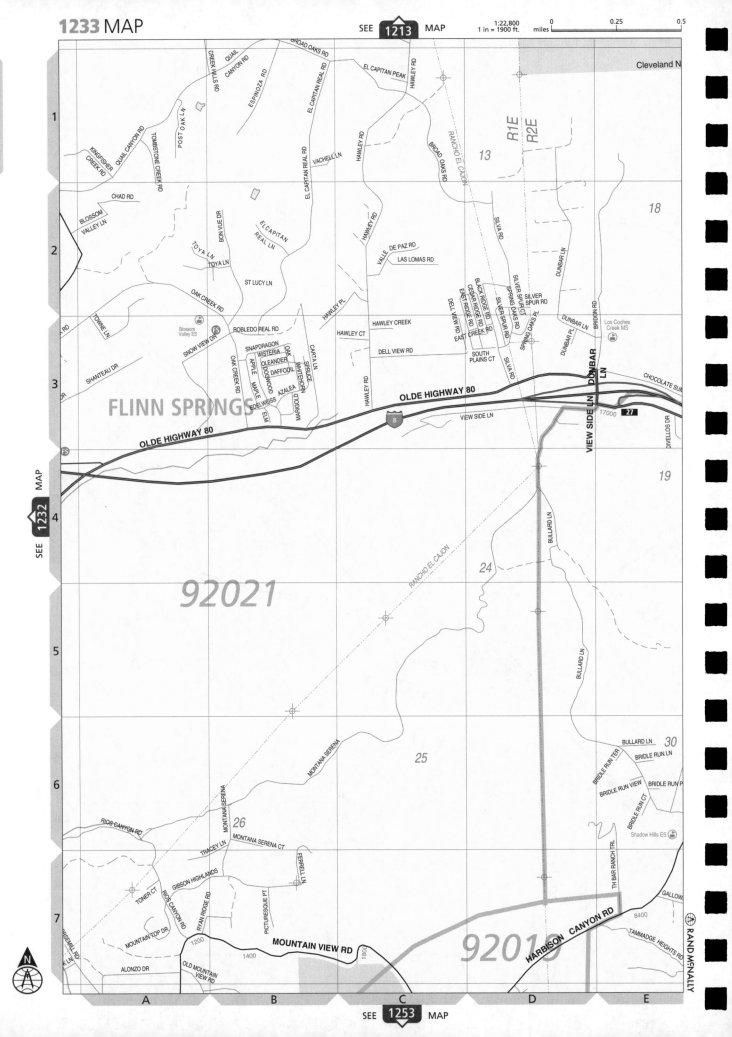

1:22,800
1 in = 1900 ft.

0   0.25   0.5
miles

SAN DIEGO CO.

Cleveland N

QUAIL CANYON RD
CREEK HILLS RD
ESPINOZA RD
BROAD OAKS RD
EL CAPITAN PEAK
HAWLEY RD

R1E
R2E

1

13

18

KINGFISHER CREEK RD
QUAIL CANYON RD
TOMBSTONE CREEK RD
POST OAK LN
EL CAPITAN REAL RD
VACHELL LN
HAWLEY RD
BROAD OAKS RD
RANCHO EL CAJON
SILVA RD

CHAD RD
BON VUE DR
EL CAPITAN REAL LN
HAWLEY RD

BLOSSOM VALLEY LN

2

TOYA LN
TOYA LN
ST LUCY LN
VALLE DE PAZ RD
LAS LOMAS RD
SILVER SPUR CT
SPRING OAKS RD
DUNBAR LN

TOWNE LN
OAK CREEK RD
SHANTEAU DR
SNOW VIEW DR
Blossom Valley ES FS
ROBLEDO REAL RD
HAWLEY PL
HAWLEY CREEK
BLACK RIDGE RD
CEDAR RIDGE RD
EAST RIDGE RD
DELL VIEW RD
SILVER SPUR RD
SILVER SPUR RD
SPRING OAKS PL
SILVER SPUR RD
SILVER SPUR RD
SPRING OAKS RD
DUNBAR LN
Los Coches Creek MS
BRIDON RD
DUNBAR PL

SNAPDRAGON
WISTERIA
OAK
OLEANDER
DOGWOOD
DAFFODIL
OAK CREEK RD
APPLE
MAPLE
MARIGOLD
SPRUCE
WHITEHORN
AZALEA
EDELWEISS
ELM
CARTA LN
HAWLEY CT
HAWLEY RD
DELL VIEW RD
SOUTH PLAINS CT
SILVA RD
DUNBAR LN
CHOCOLATE SUM

3

FLINN SPRINGS

OLDE HIGHWAY 80
OLDE HIGHWAY 80
[8]
VIEW SIDE LN
17000
[27]
VIEW SIDE LN
DUNBAR LN
DIVELLOS DR

FS

19

4

92021

RANCHO EL CAJON
BULLARD LN

24

5

BULLARD LN

MONTANA SERENA

25

BULLARD LN
30

RIOS CANYON RD
MONTANA SERENA
MONTANA SERENA CT
26
BRIDLE RUN TER
BRIDLE RUN LN
BRIDLE RUN VIEW
BRIDLE RUN CT
BRIDLE RUN P

6

TRACEY LN
FERRELL LN
Shadow Hills ES

TONER CT
GIBSON HIGHLANDS
PICTURESQUE PT
RIOS CANYON RD
RYAN RIDGE RD
TH BAR RANCH TRL
GALLOW

7

ARSENILL RD
MOUNTAIN TOP DR
1200
OLD MOUNTAIN VIEW RD
ALONZO DR
1400
MOUNTAIN VIEW RD
1800
92019
HARBISON CANYON RD
8400
TAMMADGE HEIGHTS RD

RAND McNALLY

N

A   B   C   D   E

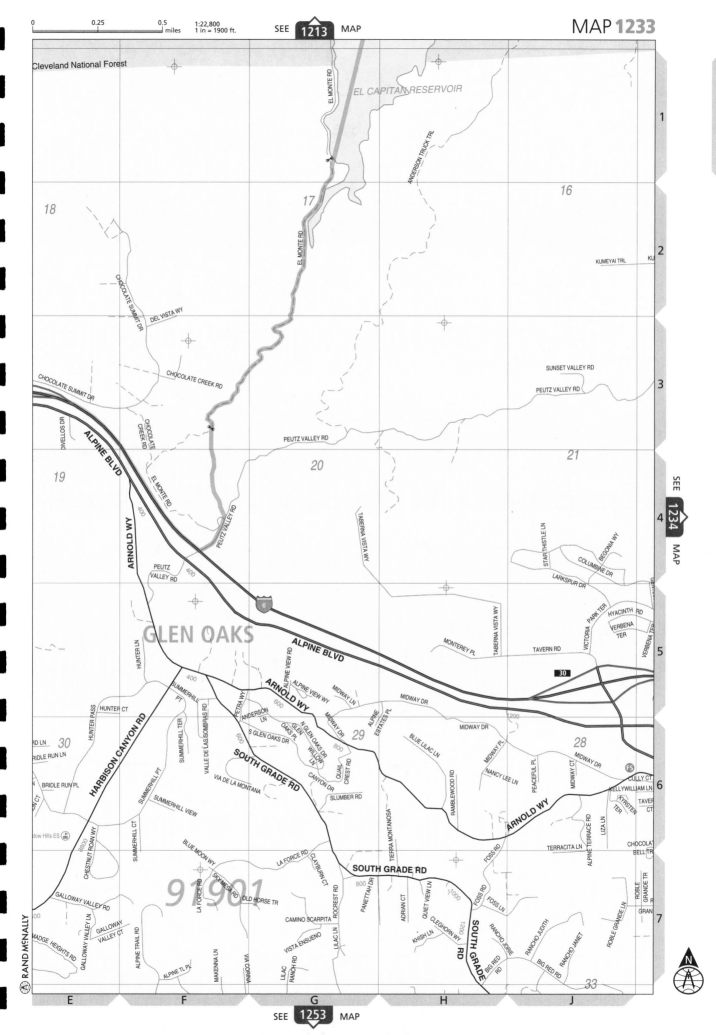

MAP **1233**

SAN DIEGO CO.

0   0.25   0.5
miles
1:22,800
1 in = 1900 ft.

SEE 1213 MAP

SEE 1234 MAP

SEE 1253 MAP

Cleveland National Forest

EL CAPITAN RESERVOIR

EL MONTE RD

ANDERSON TRUCK TRL

18

17

16

KUMEYAI TRL   KU

DEL VISTA WY

CHOCOLATE SUMMIT DR

CHOCOLATE CREEK RD

SUNSET VALLEY RD

PEUTZ VALLEY RD

CHOCOLATE SUMMIT DR

ALPINE BLVD

DIVELLOS DR

19

CHOCOLATE CREEK RD

EL MONTE RD

PEUTZ VALLEY RD

20

21

PEUTZ VALLEY RD

TABERNA VISTA WY

STAR THISTLE LN

BEGONIA WY

COLUMBINE DR

LARKSPUR DR

ARNOLD WY

400

PEUTZ VALLEY RD

400

8

TABERNA VISTA WY

VICTORIA PARK TER

HYACINTH RD

VERBENA TER

GLEN OAKS

ALPINE BLVD

MONTEREY PL

TAVERN RD

30

5

HUNTER LN

400

SUMMERHILL PT

ALPINE VIEW RD

ALPINE VIEW WY

MIDWAY LN

MIDWAY DR

1200

HUNTER PASS

HUNTER CT

SUMMERHILL TER

ARNOLD WY

600

ANDERSON LN

N GLEN OAKS DR

MIDWAY DR

ALPINE ESTATES PL

MIDWAY DR

MIDWAY PL

MIDWAY CT

MIDWAY DR

FS

CULLY CT

HARBISON CANYON RD

RD LN

BRIDLE RUN LN

30

SUMMERHILL PT

VALLE DE LAS SOMBRAS RD

PETRA WY

GLEN OAKS PL

S GLEN OAKS DR

WILLOW LN

800

QUAIL CREST RD

CANYON DR

BLUE LILAC LN

29

RAMBLEWOOD RD

NANCY LEE LN

PEACEFUL PL

28

KELLYWILLIAM LN

TAVER

N CT

BRIDLE RUN PL

SUMMERHILL CT

SUMMERHILL VIEW

SOUTH GRADE RD

VIA DE LA MONTANA

SLUMBER RD

ARNOLD WY

LIZA LN

KYRSTEN TER

CHOCOLAT

BELL TR

dow Hills ES

CHESTNUT ROAM WY

8800

BLUE MOON WY

TIERRA MONTANOSA

ALPINE TERRACE RD

TERRACITA LN

ROBLE GRANDE TR

GRAN

91901

LA FORCE RD

SKY MESA RD

OLD HORSE TR

LA FORCE RD

CLAYBURN CT

SOUTH GRADE RD

800

PANETTAH DR

ADRIAN CT

QUIET VIEW LN

FOSS RD

FOSS LN

1000

ROBLE GRANDE LN

GALLOWAY VALLEY RD

MADGE HEIGHTS RD

GALLOWAY VALLEY LN

GALLOWAY VALLEY CT

ALPINE TRAIL RD

ALPINE TL PL

MAKENNA LN

VIA CORINA

LILAC RANCH RD

VISTA ENSUENO

CAMINO SCARPITA

LILAC LN

ROCREST RD

KHISH LN

CLEGHORN WY

SOUTH GRADE RD

1200

RANCHO JOBIE

RANCHO JUDITH

BIG RED RD

BIG RED RD

RANCHO JANET

33

RAND McNALLY

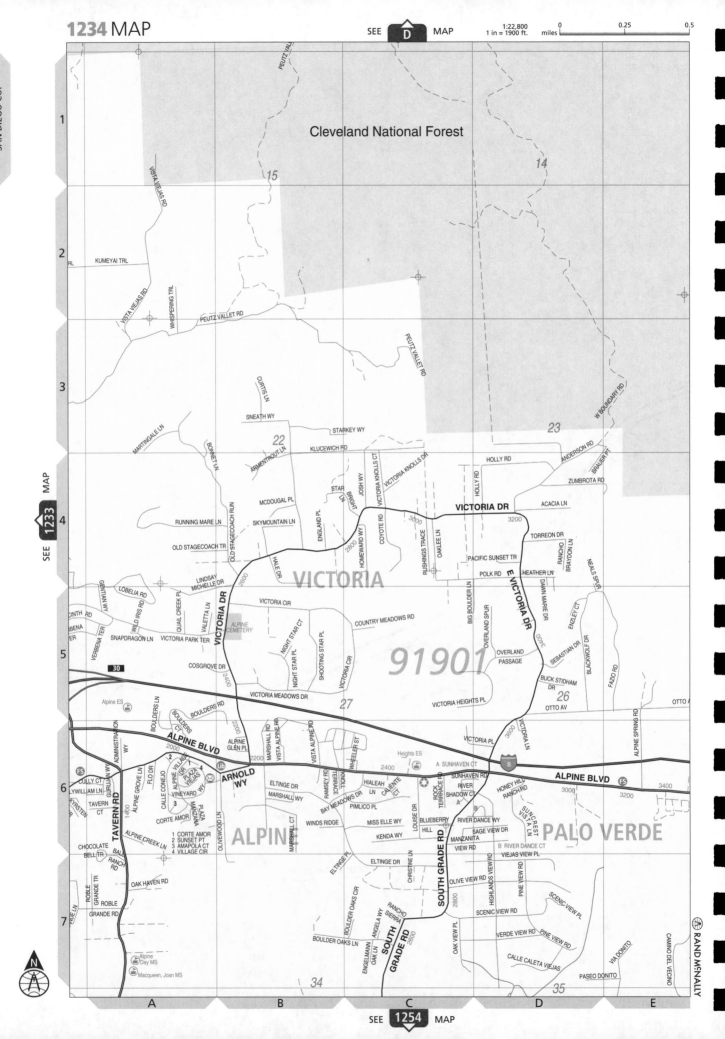

SEE **D** MAP

1:22,800
1 in = 1900 ft.

miles   0   0.25   0.5

SAN DIEGO CO.

Cleveland National Forest

15   14

SEE **1233** MAP

KUMEYAI TRL

VISTA VIEJAS RD

WHISPERING TRL

PEUTZ VALLET RD

CURTIS LN

SNEATH WY

MARTINGALE LN

BONNET LN

ARMENTROUT LN

MCDOUGAL PL

STARKEY WY

KLUCEWICH RD

22

STAR LN

BRIGHT LN

JOSH WY

VICTORIA KNOLLS CT

VICTORIA KNOLLS DR

HOLLY RD

HOLLY RD

ANDERSON RD

BRAUER PT

ZUMBROTA RD

W BOUNDARY RD

23

RUNNING MARE LN

SKYMOUNTAIN LN

ENGLAND PL

HOMEWARD WY

COYOTE RD

3000

RUSHINGS TRACE

OAKLEE LN

VICTORIA DR

ACACIA LN

3200

TORREON DR

RANCHO BRAYDON LN

OLD STAGECOACH TR

OLD STAGECOACH RUIN

HALER DR

2800

2600

PACIFIC SUNSET TR

POLK RD

HEATHER LN

DAWN MARIE DR

NEALS SPUR

LINDSAY MICHELLE DR

VICTORIA

GENTIAN WY

LOBELIA RD

QUAIL CREEK PL

VALETTA LN

VICTORIA DR

VICTORIA CIR

ALPINE CEMETERY

NIGHT STAR CT

COUNTRY MEADOWS RD

BIG BOULDER LN

OVERLAND SPUR

E VICTORIA DR

3400

ENZLEY CT

BLACKWOLF DR

FAZIO RD

CINTH RD

BENA ER

VERBENA TER

WILD IRIS RD

SNAPDRAGON LN

VICTORIA PARK TER

NIGHT STAR PL

SHOOTING STAR PL

VICTORIA CIR

91901

OVERLAND PASSAGE

SEBASTIAN DR

30

COSGROVE DR

2400

VICTORIA MEADOWS DR

27

BUCK STIDHAM DR

26

VICTORIA HEIGHTS PL

OTTO AV

OTTO A

Alpine ES

BOULDERS LN

BOULDERS RD

BOULDERS CT

2200

ALPINE GLEN PL

MARSHALL RD

VISTA ALPINE RD

VISTA ALPINE RD

WHEELER ST

2400

Heights ES

A SUNHAVEN CT

VICTORIA PL

3600

VICTORIA LN

I-8

ALPINE SPRING RD

ALPINE BLVD

2000

ALPINE VILLAGE DR

PLAZA VIEJAS

Lib

ARNOLD WY

ELTINGE DR

RAMSEY RD

TERRACE VIEW RD

TIONAI

HIALEAH

CALIENTE CT

ROCK TERRACE A

RIVER SHADOW CT

SUNHAVEN RD

HONEY HILL RANCH RD

ALPINE BLVD

FS

3000

3200

3400

FS

CULLY CT

YWILLIAM LN

GURUAN WY

ADMINISTRATION WY

ALPINE GROVE LN

FLO DR

CALLE CONEJO

VINEYARD

MARSHALL WY

MANZANA

PIMLICO PL

BAY MEADOWS DR

MISS ELLE WY

LOUISE DR

RIVER DANCE WY

BLUEBERRY HILL

SAGE VIEW DR

SUNCREST VISTA LN

B RIVER DANCE CT

PALO VERDE

KYRSTEN

TAVERN LN

1400

TAVERN RD

CORTE AMOR

ALPINE CREEK LN

OLIVEWOOD LN

WINDS RIDGE

KENDA WY

MANZANITA VIEW RD

ALPINE

CHOCOLATE BELL TR

BALL RANCH RD

OAK HAVEN RD

MARSHALL CT

ELTINGE PL

ELTINGE DR

CHRISTINE LN

VIEJAS VIEW PL

OLIVE VIEW RD

HIGHLANDS VIEW RD

PINE VIEW RD

SCENIC VIEW PL

1 CORTE AMOR
2 SUNSET PT
3 AMAPOLA CT
4 VILLAGE CIR

PINE LN

ROBLE GRANDE TR

ROBLE

GRANDE RD

BOULDER OAKS CIR

RANCHO SIERRA

SOUTH GRADE RD

2800

SCENIC VIEW RD

SCENIC VIEW PL

Alpine Day MS

Macqueen, Joan MS

BOULDER OAKS LN

ENGELMANN OAK LN

ANGELA WY

SOUTH GRADE RD

2600

OAK VIEW PL

VERDE VIEW RD

PINE VIEW RD

CALLE CALETA VIEJAS

VIA DONITO

CAMINO DEL VECINO

PASEO DONITO

34   35

N

RAND McNALLY

SEE **1254** MAP

A   B   C   D   E

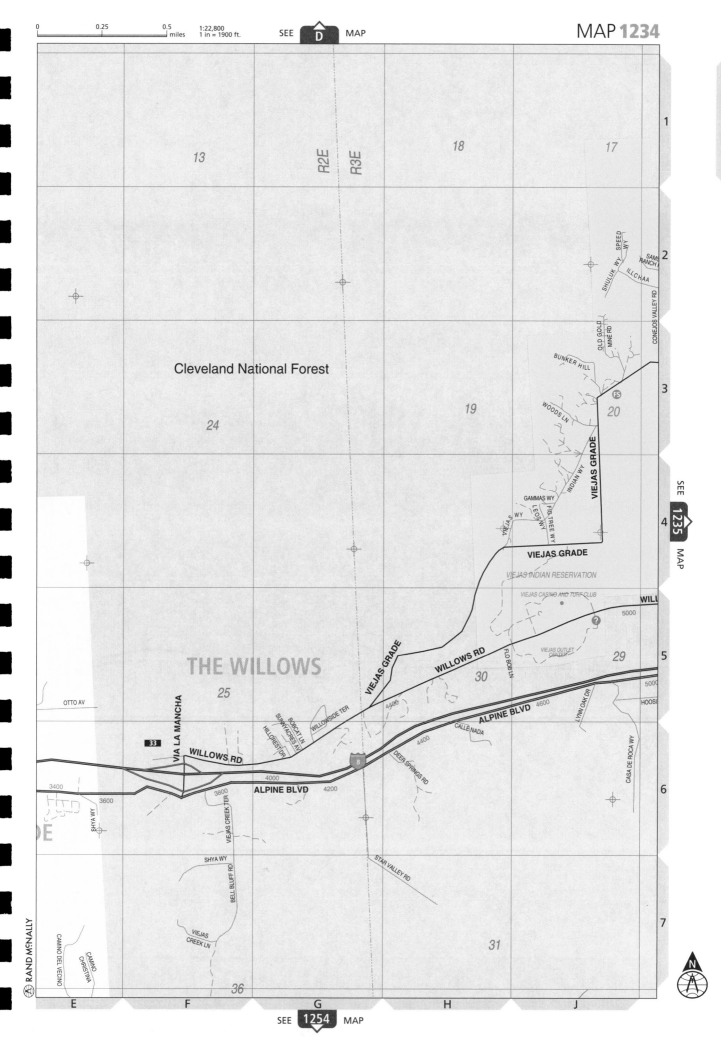

MAP **1234**

0   0.25   0.5
miles
1:22,800
1 in = 1900 ft.

SEE D MAP

SAN DIEGO CO.

13

R2E   R3E

18

17

1

SHULLUK WY   SPEED WY

ILLCHAA

SAMS RANCH

2

Cleveland National Forest

OLD GOLD MINE RD

CONEJOS VALLEY RD

BUNKER HILL

19

WOODS LN

FS

20

3

24

VIEJAS GRADE

INDIAN WY

SEE 1235 MAP

GAMMAS WY

FIG TREE WY

LEOS WY

VIEJAS WY

4

VIEJAS GRADE

VIEJAS INDIAN RESERVATION

VIEJAS CASINO AND TURF CLUB

WILL

WILLOWS RD

5000

THE WILLOWS

VIEJAS GRADE

FLO BOB LN

VIEJAS OUTLET CENTER

?

29

5

25

WILLOWS RD

30

5000

OTTO AV

4496

WILLOWSIDE TER

HOOSI

BOBCAT LN

ALPINE BLVD

4600

SUNNY ACRES AV

HILLCREST DR

CALLE NADA

LYNN OAK DR

33

VIA LA MANCHA

WILLOWS RD

8

4400

WILLOWSIDE TER

DEER SPRINGS RD

CASA DE ROCA WY

3400

3600

VIEJAS CREEK TER

3800

ALPINE BLVD   4200

4000

6

SHYA WY

DE

SHYA WY

BELL BLUFF RD

STAR VALLEY RD

VIEJAS CREEK LN

CAMINO DEL VECINO

CAMINO CHRISTINA

31

7

RAND McNALLY

36

E   F   G   H   J

N

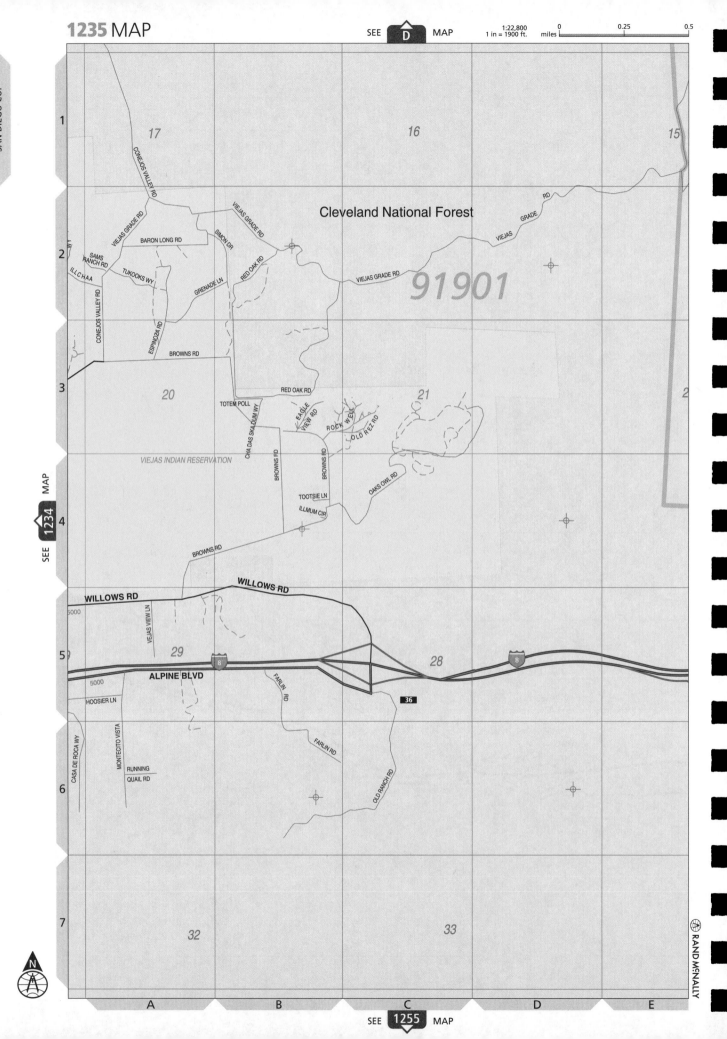

SEE **D** MAP

1:22,800
1 in = 1900 ft.   miles

0   0.25   0.5

1

17   16   15

Cleveland National Forest

CONEJOS VALLEY RD

VIEJAS GRADE RD

VIEJAS GRADE RD

VIEJAS GRADE RD

VIEJAS GRADE

RD

2

SAMS RANCH RD

BARON LONG RD

SIMON DR

ILLCHAA

TUKOOKS WY

GRENADE LN

RED OAK RD

VIEJAS GRADE RD

91901

CONEJOS VALLEY RD

ESPINOZA RD

BROWNS RD

3

20

RED OAK RD

21

2

TOTEM POLL

CHA DAS SKADUM WY

EAGLE VIEW RD

ROCK WELL

OLD REZ RD

BROWNS RD

BROWNS RD

VIEJAS INDIAN RESERVATION

OAKS OWL RD

4

TOOTSIE LN

ILLMUM CIR

SEE **1234** MAP

BROWNS RD

WILLOWS RD

WILLOWS RD

WILLOWS RD

5000

VIEJAS VIEW LN

5

9

29

8

28

8

ALPINE BLVD

5000

FARLIN RD

36

HOOSIER LN

CASA DE ROCA WY

MONTECITO VISTA

RUNNING QUAIL RD

FARLIN RD

6

OLD RANCH RD

7

32   33

A   B   C   D   E

N

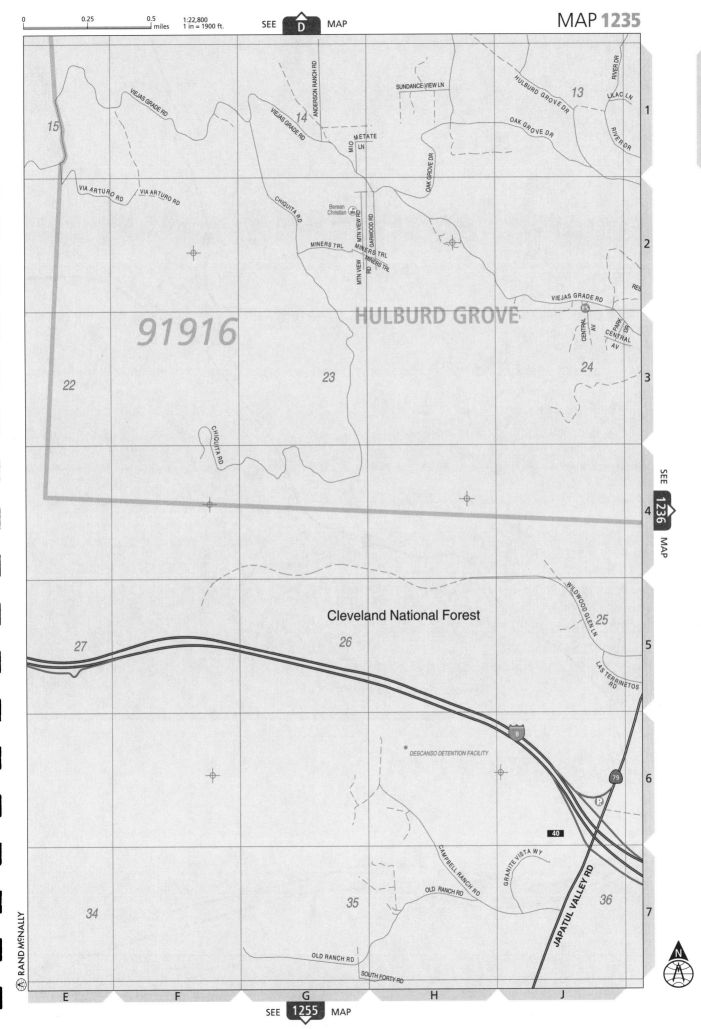

MAP **1235**

0   0.25   0.5   1:22,800
miles   1 in = 1900 ft.

SEE D MAP

SAN DIEGO CO.

RIVER DR

LILAC LN

HULBURD GROVE DR

13

SUNDANCE VIEW LN

OAK GROVE DR

RIVER DR

1

VIEJAS GRADE RD

ANDERSON RANCH RD

VIEJAS GRADE RD

14

MIO

METATE LN

OAK GROVE DR

15

VIA ARTURO RD

VIA ARTURO RD

CHIQUITA RD

Berean Christian

GARWOOD RD

MTN VIEW RD

RES

2

MINERS TRL

MTN VIEW RD

MINERS TRL

MINERS TRL

VIEJAS GRADE RD

HULBURD GROVE

FS

CENTRAL AV

PARK DR

CENTRAL AV

91916

22

23

24

3

CHIQUITA RD

SEE 1236 MAP

4

WILDWOOD GLEN LN

Cleveland National Forest

25

27

26

LAS TERRINETOS RD

5

8

DESCANSO DETENTION FACILITY

79

P

6

40

CAMPBELL RANCH RD

GRANITE VISTA WY

JAPATUL VALLEY RD

OLD RANCH RD

34

35

36

7

RAND MC NALLY

OLD RANCH RD

SOUTH FORTY RD

E   F   G   H   J

N

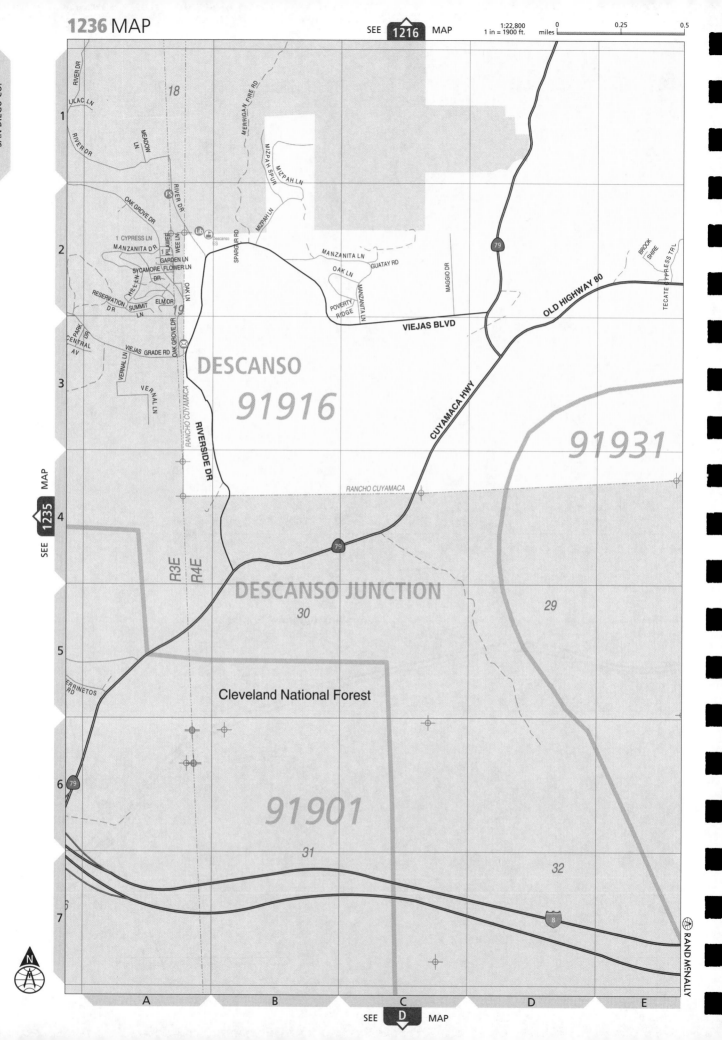

SEE 1216 MAP

SAN DIEGO CO.

1:22,800
1 in = 1900 ft.

0   0.25   0.5
miles

1

18

LILAC LN

RIVER DR

RIVER DR

MEADOW LN

MERRIGAN FIRE RD

MIZPAH SPUR

MIZPAH LN

MIZPAH LN

OAK GROVE DR

RIVER DR

FS

2

1 CYPRESS LN

MANZANITA DR

PILIWEE WEE LN

GARDEN LN

FLOWER LN

SYCAMORE DR

HILL LN

ELM DR

SUMMIT LN

RESERVATION DR

OAK LN

SPARGUR RD

Descanso ES

MANZANITA LN

GUATAY RD

OAK LN

MANZANITA LN

POVERTY RIDGE

MAGGIO DR

79

BROOK SHIRE

TECATE CYPRESS TRL

VIEJAS BLVD

OLD HIGHWAY 80

19

DESCANSO
91916

91931

PARK DR

CENTRAL AV

VIEJAS GRADE RD

VERNAL LN

OAK GROVE DR

RANCHO CUYAMACA

3

VERNAL LN

RIVERSIDE DR

CUYAMACA HWY

RANCHO CUYAMACA

SEE 1235 MAP

R3E

R4E

4

79

DESCANSO JUNCTION

30

29

5

ERRINETOS RD

Cleveland National Forest

6

79

91901

31

32

7

8

A   B   C   D   E

N

RAND MCNALLY

SEE D MAP

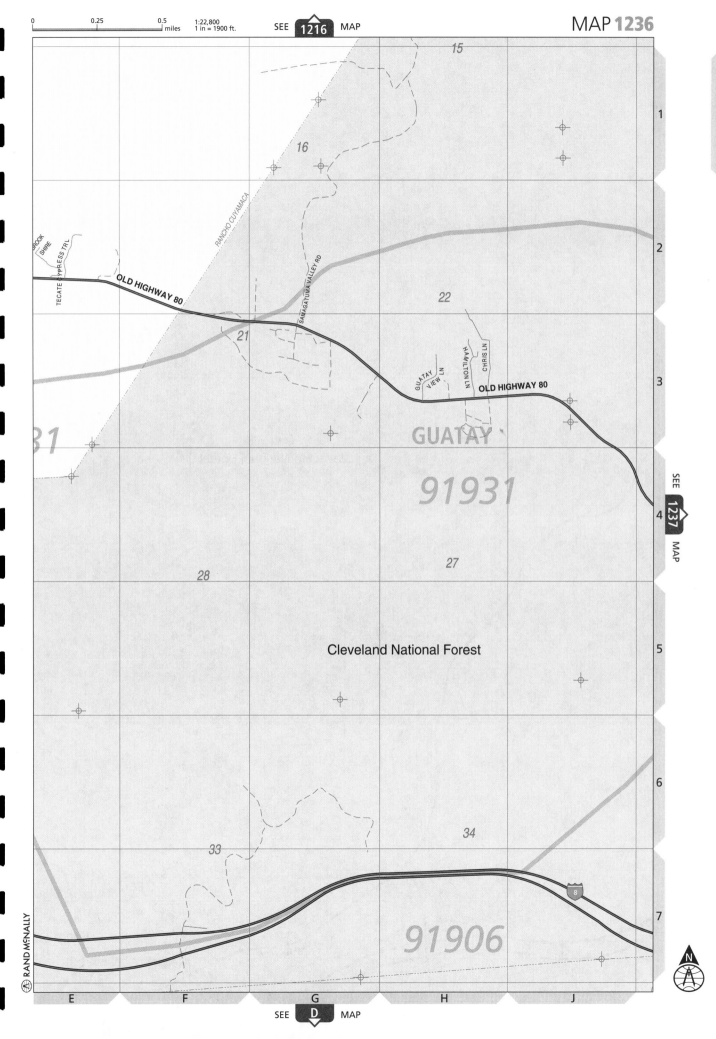

MAP **1236**

SAN DIEGO CO.

0   0.25   0.5
miles
1:22,800
1 in = 1900 ft.

15

16

RANCHO CUYAMACA

BROOK
SHIRE
TECATE CYPRESS TRL

OLD HIGHWAY 80

SANAGATUMA VALLEY RD

21

22

GUATAY VIEW LN
HAMILTON LN
CHRIS LN
OLD HIGHWAY 80

GUATAY

91931

31

28

27

SEE **1237** MAP

Cleveland National Forest

33

34

91906

8

E   F   G   H   J

1   2   3   4   5   6   7

RAND McNALLY

N

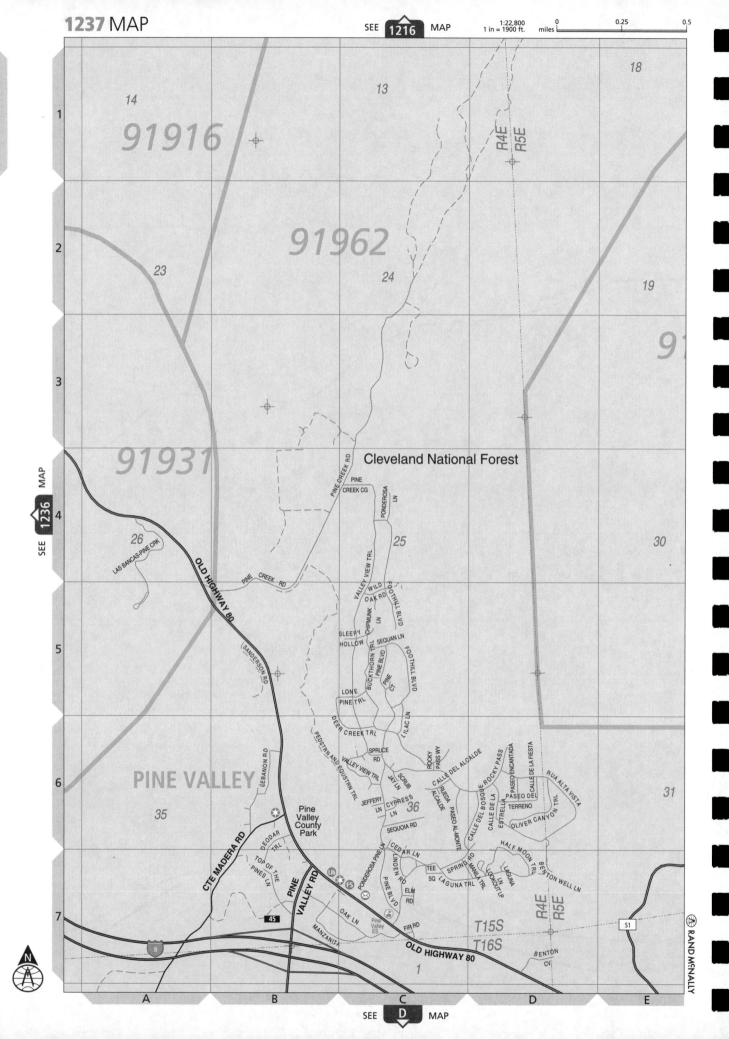

SEE 1216 MAP

1:22,800
1 in = 1900 ft.
0   0.25   0.5
miles

SAN DIEGO CO.

14
91916

13

18

R4E R5E

1

23

91962

24

19

2

3

91931

PINE CREEK RD

Cleveland National Forest

PINE CREEK CG

PONDEROSA LN

91

SEE 1236 MAP

26

LAS BANCAS-PINE CRK

OLD HIGHWAY 80

PINE CREEK RD

25

30

PINE CREEK RD

4

SANDERSON RD

VALLEY VIEW TRL

WILD OAK RD

FOOTHILL BLVD

CHIPMUNK LN

SLEEPY HOLLOW

SEQUAN LN

BUCKTHORN TRL

PINE BLVD

FOOTHILL BLVD

5

PINE CT

LONE PINE TRL

LILAC LN

DEER CREEK TRL

PEDSTRN AND EQUSTRN TRL

SPRUCE RD

ROCKY PASS WY

CALLE DEL ALCALDE

ROCKY PASS

PASEO ENCANTADA

CALLE DE LA FIESTA

RUA ALTA VISTA

PINE VALLEY

VALLEY VIEW TRL

JAY LN

SCRUB

RUEDA ALCALDE

CALLE DE LA

CALLE DEL BOSQUE

PASEO DEL TERRENO

OLIVER CANYON TRL

35

LEBANON RD

JEFFERY LN

CYPRESS LN

36

PASEO AL MONTE

ESTRELLA

31

6

Pine Valley County Park

SEQUOIA RD

HALF MOON TRL

BENTON WELL LN

CTE MADERA RD

DEODAR TRL

TOP OF THE PINES LN

PINE VALLEY RD

Lib

PONDEROSA PINE LN

CEDAR LN

LINDEN RD

SPRING RD

MANLA TRL

LAGUNA LN

LOOKOUT LP

R4E R5E

TEE SQ

LAGUNA TRL

ELM RD

51

7

45

OAK LN

Pine Valley ES

FIR RD

T15S

MANZANITA

OLD HIGHWAY 80

T16S

8

1

BENTON CV

N

A   B   C   D   E

SEE D MAP

RAND McNALLY

MAP **1237**

SEE 1216 MAP

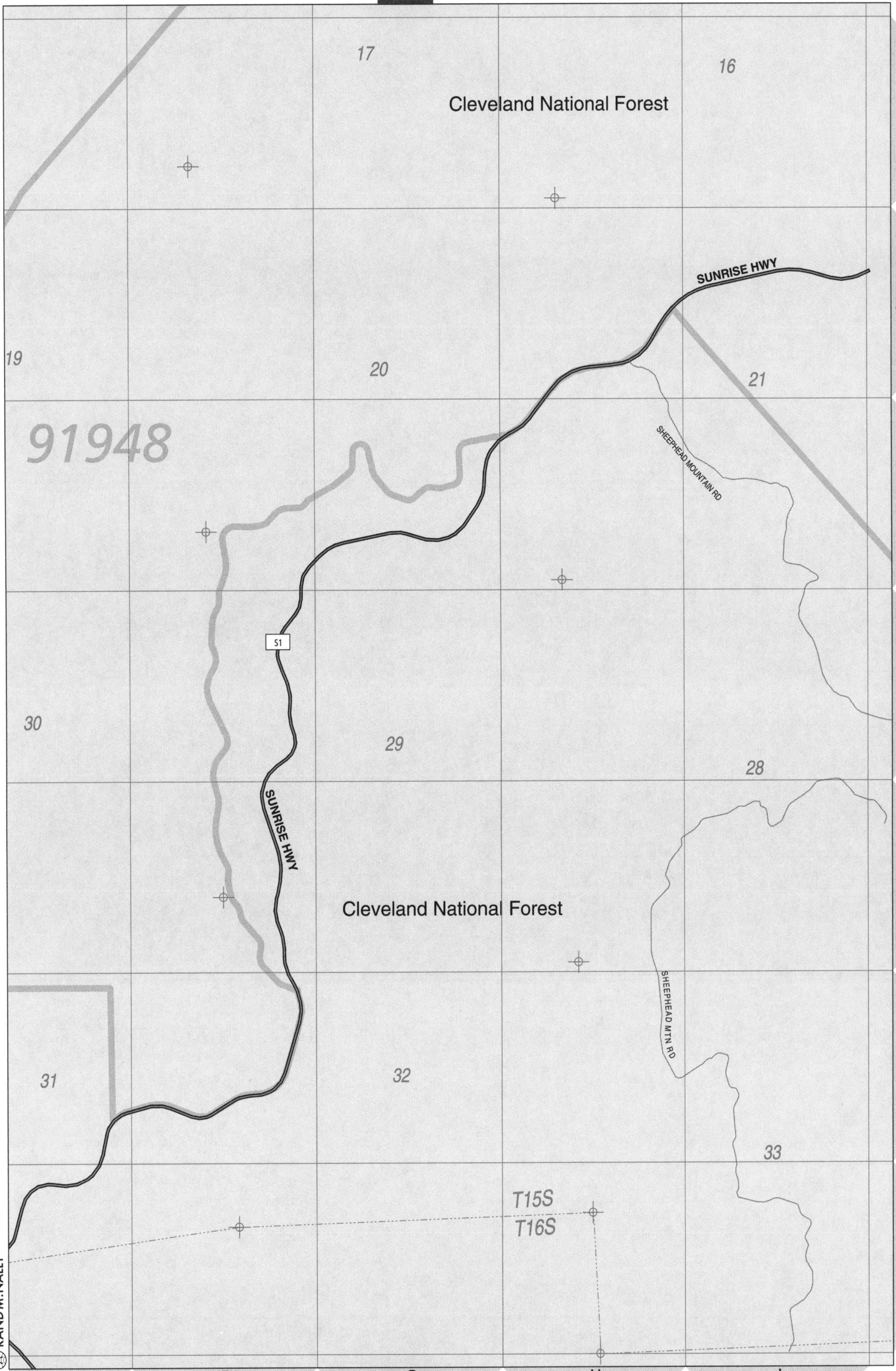

SAN DIEGO CO.

17

16

Cleveland National Forest

1

SUNRISE HWY

2

19

20

21

91948

SHEEPHEAD MOUNTAIN RD

3

S1

SEE D MAP

4

30

29

28

SUNRISE HWY

Cleveland National Forest

5

SHEEPHEAD MTN RD

31

32

6

33

T15S
T16S

7

RAND McNALLY

E   F   G   H   J

SEE D MAP

N

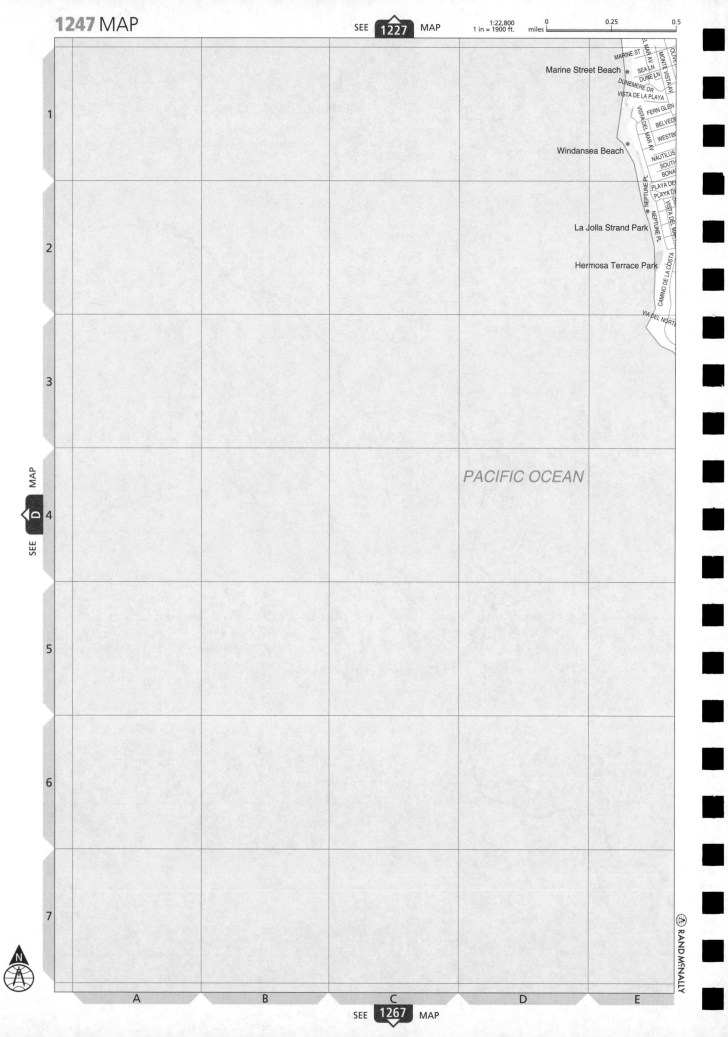

1:22,800
1 in = 1900 ft.

0   0.25   0.5
miles

SAN DIEGO CO.

Marine Street Beach

Windansea Beach

La Jolla Strand Park

Hermosa Terrace Park

MARINE ST
EL MAR AV
MONTE VISTA AV
OLIVE
SEA LN
DUNE LN
DUNEMERE DR
VISTA DE LA PLAYA
VISTA DEL MAR AV
FERN GLEN
BELVEDE
WESTBO
NAUTILUS
SOUTH
BONA
PLAYA DEL
PLAYA DE
NEPTUNE PL
VISTA DEL MAR
NEPTUNE PL
CAMINO DE LA COSTA
VIA DEL NORTE

PACIFIC OCEAN

SEE D 4 MAP

A   B   C   D   E

1

2

3

4

5

6

7

N

RAND McNALLY

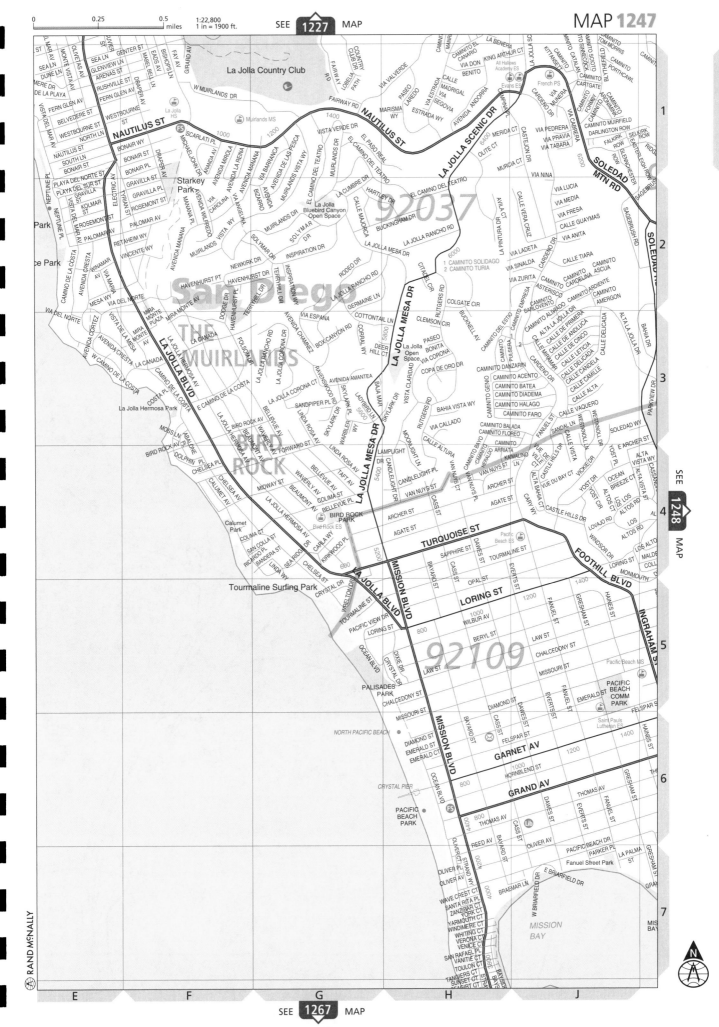

MAP **1247**

0   0.25   0.5
miles
1:22,800
1 in = 1900 ft.

SEE **1227** MAP

La Jolla Country Club

92037

San Diego
THE
MUIRLANDS

BIRD
ROCK

La Jolla Hermosa Park

La Jolla
Bluebird Canyon
Open Space

La Jolla
Open Space

Starkey
Park

NAUTILUS ST

NAUTILUS ST

LA JOLLA SCENIC DR

SOLEDAD MTN RD

SOLEDAD DR

LA JOLLA BLVD

LA JOLLA MESA DR

LA JOLLA BLVD

MISSION BLVD

MISSION BLVD

TURQUOISE ST

LORING ST

FOOTHILL BLVD

INGRAHAM ST

GARNET AV

GRAND AV

92109

Tourmaline Surfing Park

Calumet
Park

Bird Rock
PARK

La Jolla Hermosa Park

PALISADES
PARK

NORTH PACIFIC BEACH

CRYSTAL PIER

PACIFIC
BEACH
PARK

PACIFIC
BEACH
COMM
PARK

Fanuel Street Park

MISSION
BAY

SEE **1248** MAP

RAND M^cNALLY

E   F   G   H   J

1   2   3   4   5   6   7

N

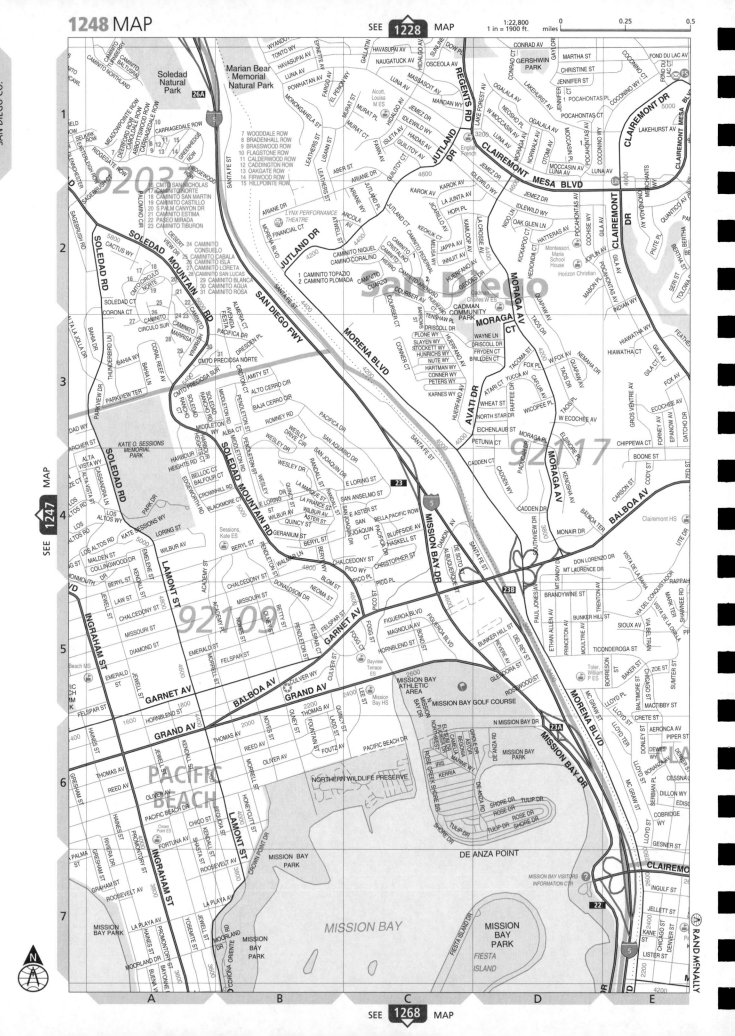

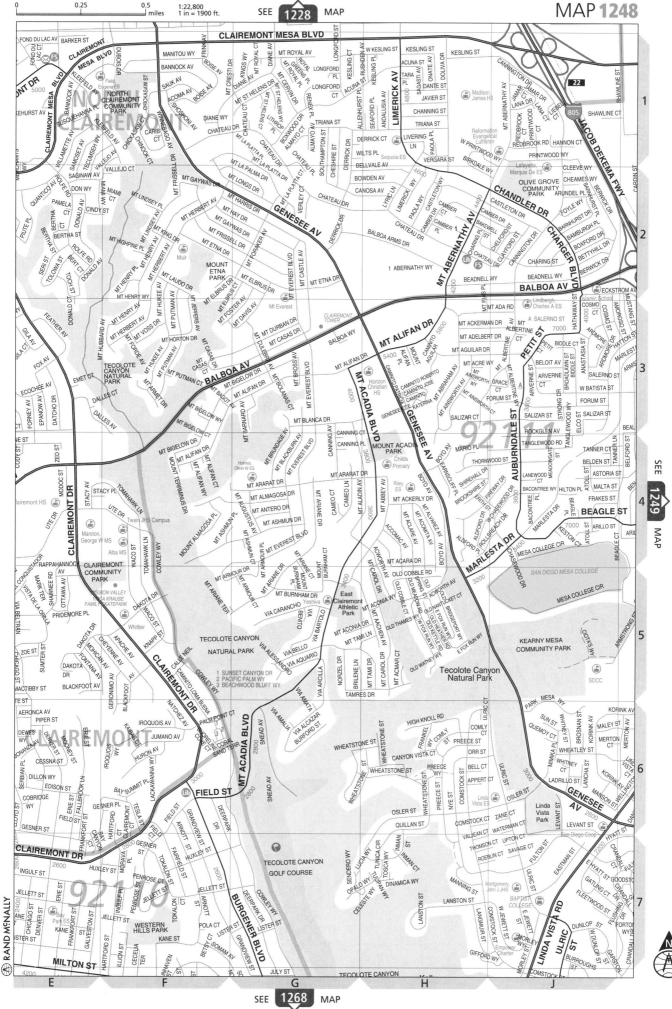

SAN DIEGO CO.

RAND McNALLY

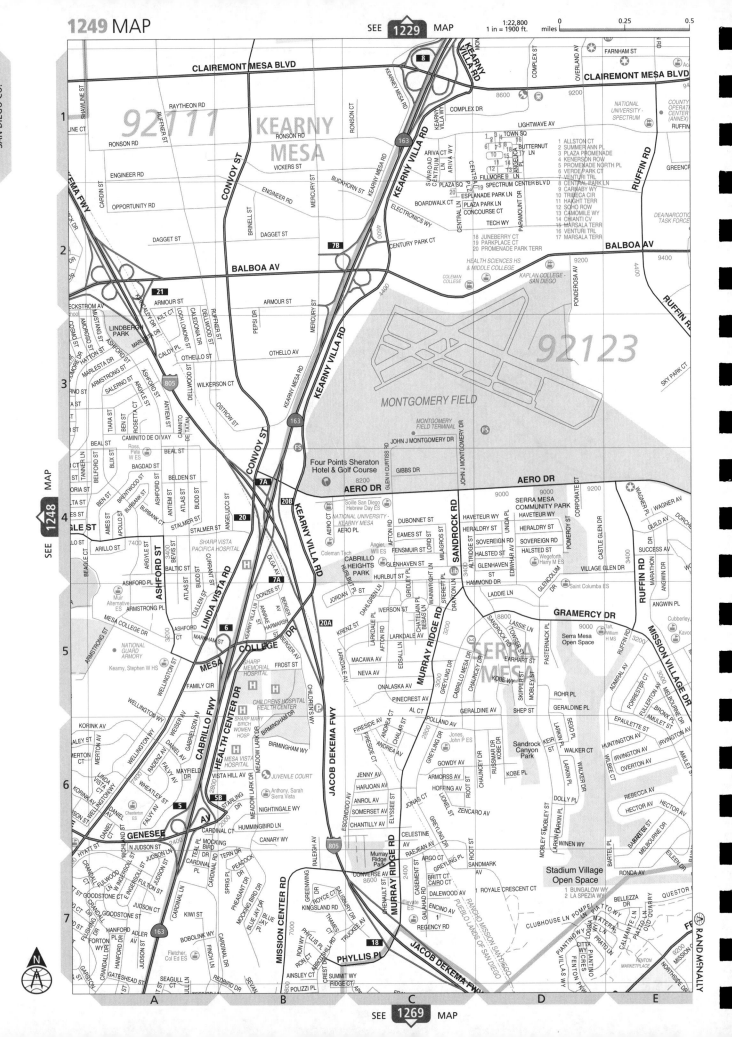

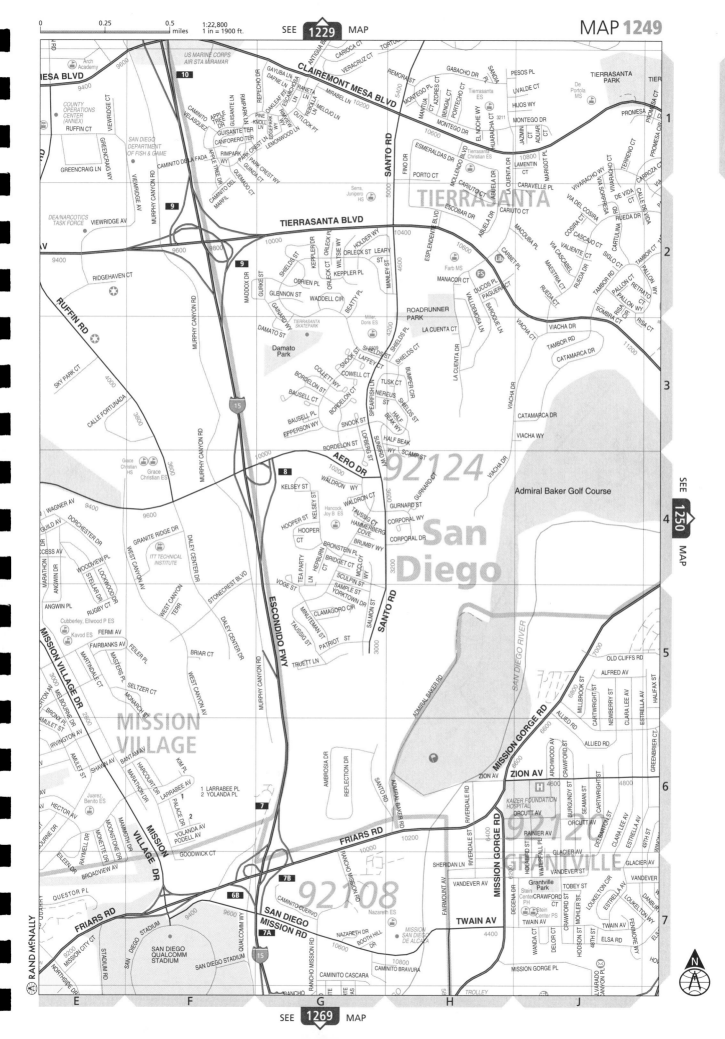

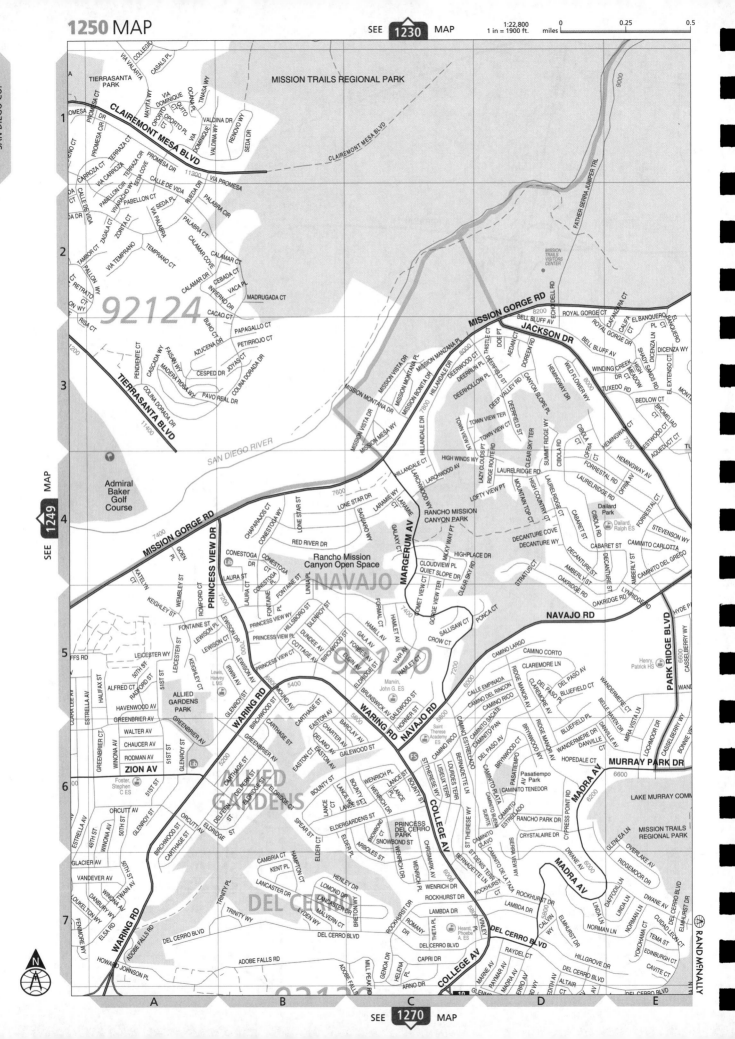

SEE 1230 MAP

1:22,800
1 in = 1900 ft.

miles 0   0.25   0.5

SAN DIEGO CO.

MISSION TRAILS REGIONAL PARK

TIERRASANTA PARK

CLAIREMONT MESA BLVD

MISSION TRAILS VISITORS CENTER

92124

TIERRASANTA BLVD

SAN DIEGO RIVER

MISSION GORGE RD

JACKSON DR

Admiral Baker Golf Course

SEE 1249 MAP

MISSION GORGE RD

PRINCESS VIEW DR

Rancho Mission Canyon Open Space

NAVAJO

Rancho Mission Canyon Park

MARGERUM AV

NAVAJO RD

PARK RIDGE BLVD

92120

WARING RD

GLENROY ST

ALLIED GARDENS PARK

WARING RD

NAVAJO RD

ZION AV

ALLIED GARDENS

COLLEGE AV

MURRAY PARK DR

MADRA AV

Princess Del Cerro Park

Lake Murray Comm

MISSION TRAILS REGIONAL PARK

DEL CERRO

MADRA AV

WARING RD

DEL CERRO BLVD

COLLEGE AV

92120

SEE 1270 MAP

RAND McNALLY

A   B   C   D   E

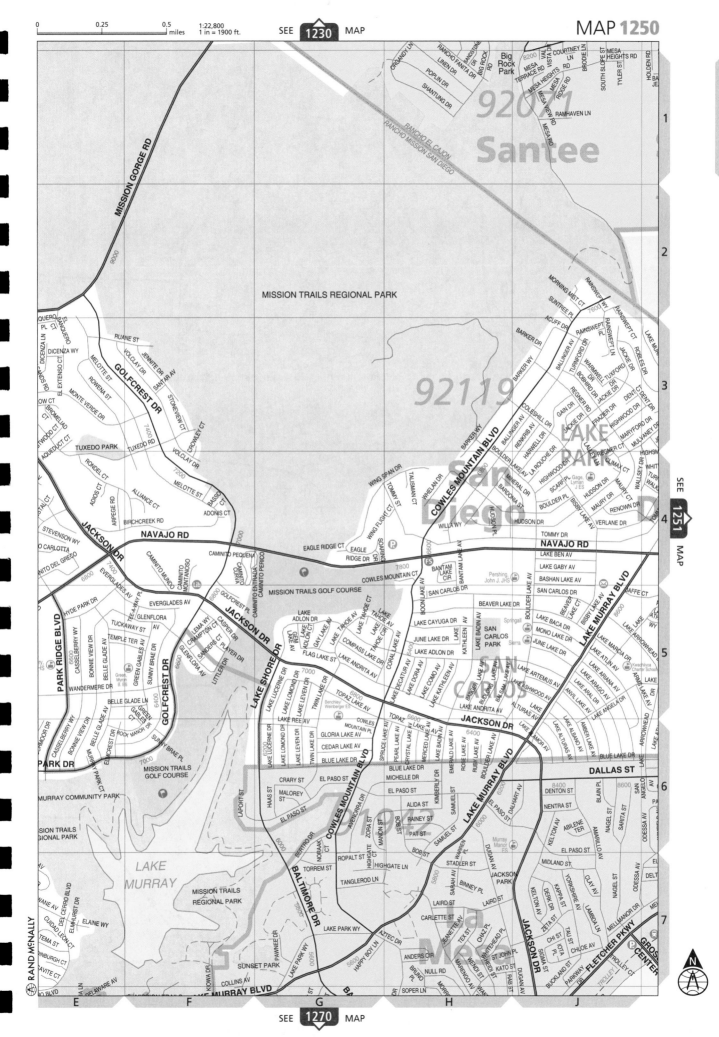

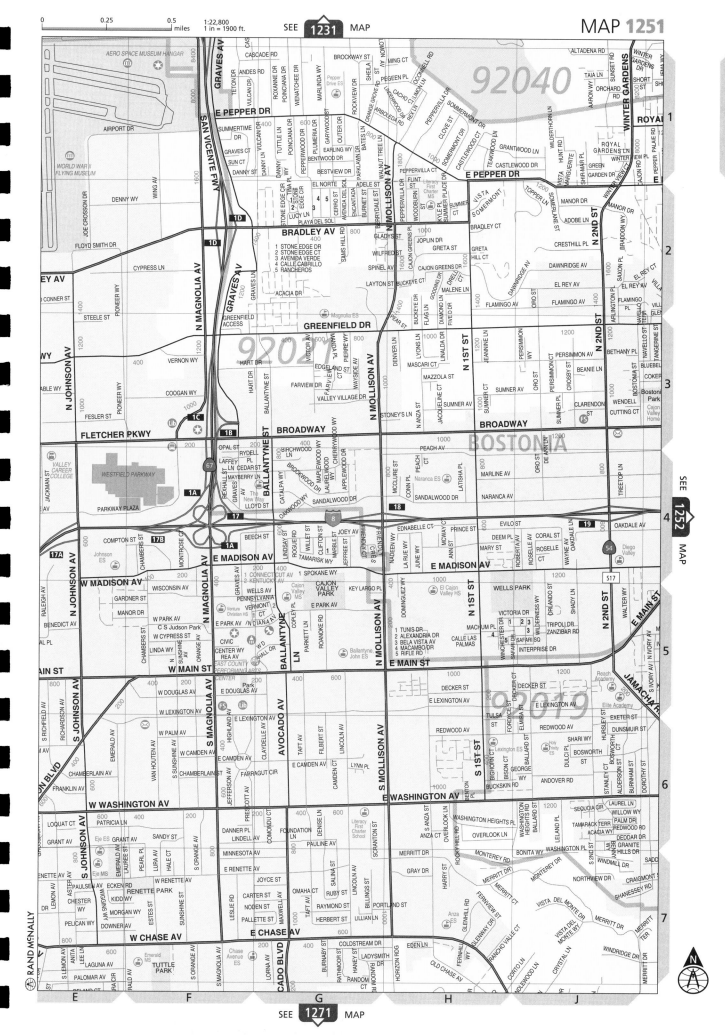

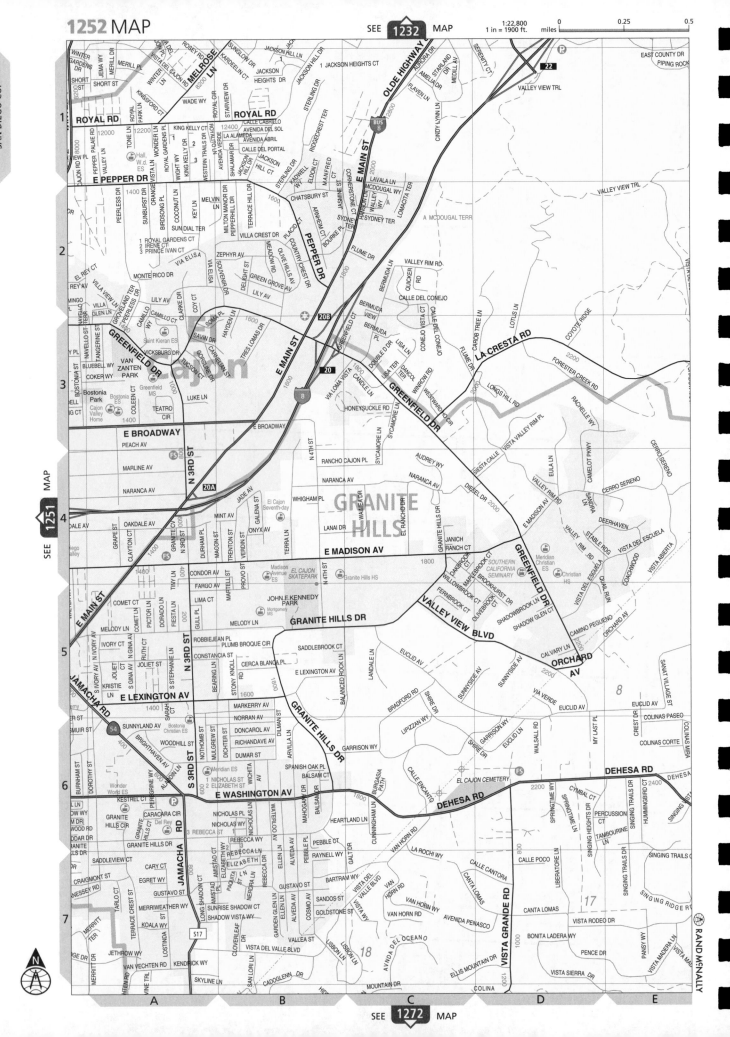

1:22,800
1 in = 1900 ft.
miles   0   0.25   0.5

SAN DIEGO CO.

SEE **1251** MAP

GRANITE HILLS

El Cajon

RAND McNALLY

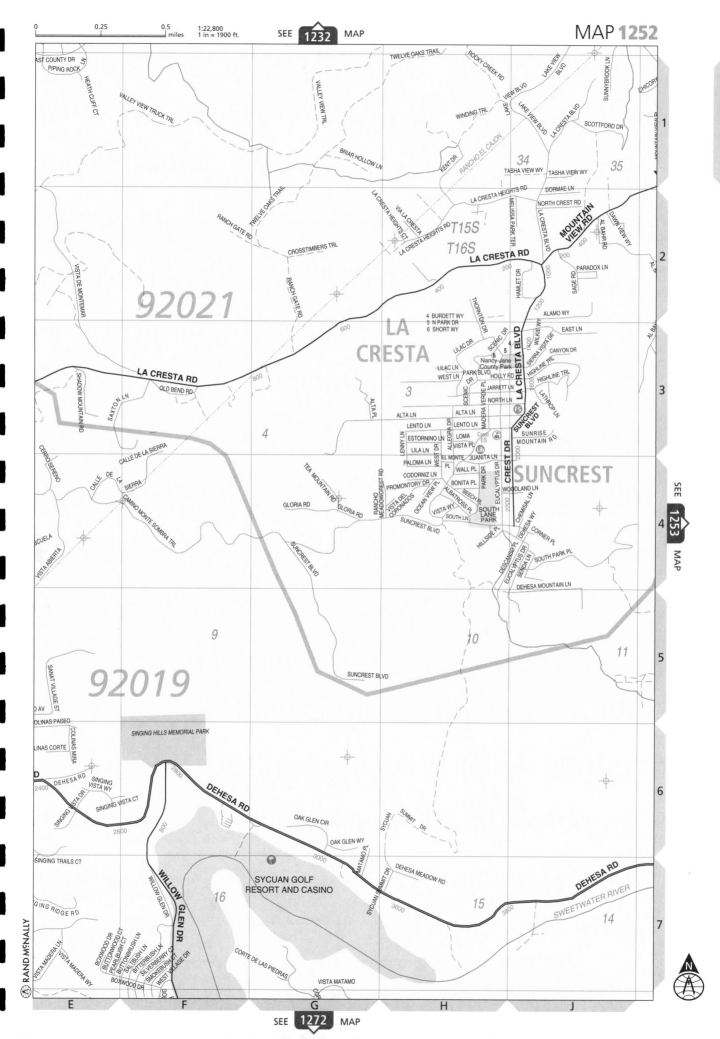

MAP 1252

SAN DIEGO CO.

SEE 1253 MAP

0   0.25   0.5
miles
1:22,800
1 in = 1900 ft.

LA CRESTA

SUNCREST

92021

92019

SYCUAN GOLF RESORT AND CASINO

SINGING HILLS MEMORIAL PARK

Nancy Jane County Park

SWEETWATER RIVER

RAND MCNALLY

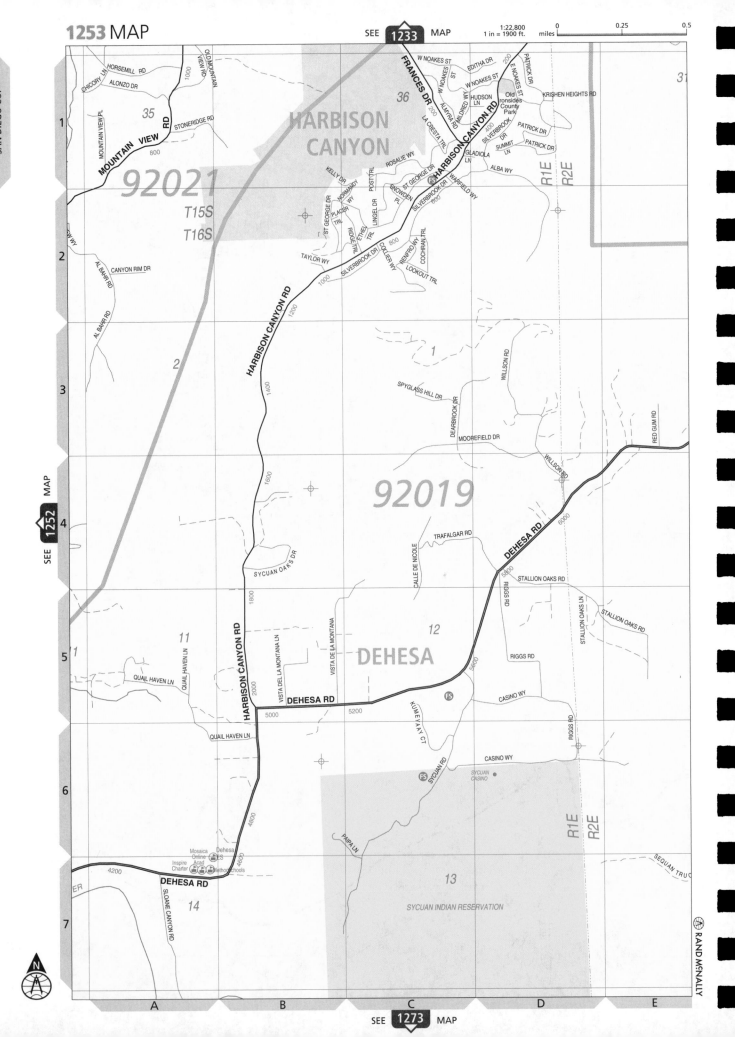

SAN DIEGO CO.

SEE 1233 MAP

1:22,800
1 in = 1900 ft.

miles 0 0.25 0.5

HARBISON CANYON

92021

T15S
T16S

36

W NOAKES ST
W NOAKES ST
W NOAKES ST

EDITHA DR

PATRICK DR

Old Ironsides County Park

KRISHEN HEIGHTS RD

FRANCES DR

MILDRED WY
HUDSON LN
ALMYRA RD

E NOAKES ST

PATRICK DR

LA CRESTA TRL

HARBISON CANYON RD

SILVERBROOK DR

SUMMIT LN

PATRICK DR

ROSALIE WY

GLADIOLA LN

ALBA WY

KELLY DR

ST GEORGE DR

POST TRL

SNOWDEN PL

WARFIELD WY

NORMANDY

PLACER WY

LINGEL DR

SILVERBROOK DR

ST GEORGE TRL

ETHEL TRL

RIDGE TRL

COLLIER WY

RENFRO WY

COCHRAN TRL

TAYLOR WY

SILVERBROOK DR

LOOKOUT TRL

CANYON RIM DR

AL BAHR RD

AL BAHR RD

HARBISON CANYON RD

1000

1200

1400

1600

1800

2000

5000

4800

4600

4200

MOUNTAIN VIEW RD

800

35

CHICORY LN

HORSEMILL RD

ALONZO DR

OLD MOUNTAIN VIEW RD

1000

STONERIDGE RD

MOUNTAIN VIEW PL

2

1

SPYGLASS HILL DR

DEARBROOK DR

MOOREFIELD DR

WILLSON RD

WILLSON RD

RED GUM RD

92019

DEHESA RD

6000

5800

5600

TRAFALGAR RD

CALLE DE NICOLE

DEHESA

12

STALLION OAKS RD

RIGGS RD

STALLION OAKS LN

STALLION OAKS RD

SYCUAN OAKS DR

VISTA DEL LA MONTANA LN

VISTA DE LA MONTANA

11

1

QUAIL HAVEN LN

QUAIL HAVEN LN

DEHESA RD

5200

QUAIL HAVEN LN

KUMEYAAY CT

RIGGS RD

CASINO WY

RIGGS RD

CASINO WY

SYCUAN CASINO

SYCUAN RD

13

PAIPA LN

Mosaica Online Acad

Dehesa ES

Inspire Charter

Methodist Schools

DEHESA RD

14

SLOANE CANYON RD

SYCUAN INDIAN RESERVATION

SEQUAN TRUC

R1E R2E

R1E R2E

31

2

SEE 1252 MAP

SEE 1273 MAP

A B C D E

1 2 3 4 5 6 7

N

RAND McNALLY

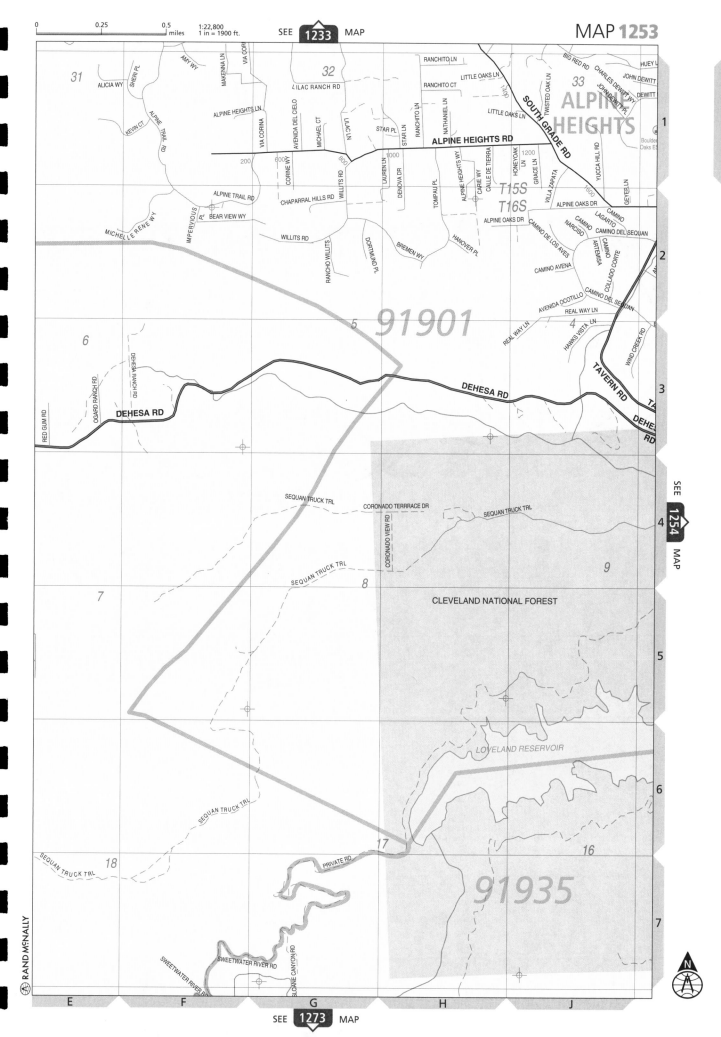

MAP **1253**

SEE ⌃ 1233 MAP

0   0.25   0.5
miles
1:22,800
1 in = 1900 ft.

SAN DIEGO CO.

31

ALICIA WY
SHERI PL
KEVIN CT
ALPINE TRAIL RD
MICHELLE RENE WY
AMY WY
MAKENNA LN
VIA COR
VIA CORINA
ALPINE HEIGHTS LN
AVENIDA DEL CIELO
CORINE WY
MICHAEL CT
LILAC CT
LILAC RANCH RD
LILAC LN
WILLITS RD
ALPINE TRAIL RD
IMPERVIOUS PL
BEAR VIEW WY
CHAPARRAL HILLS RD
WILLITS RD
RANCHO WILLITS
DORTMUND PL
BREMEN WY

32

RANCHITO LN
RANCHITO CT
RANCHITO CT
STAR PL
STAR LN
LAUREN LN
DENOVA DR
TOMPAU PL
HANOVER PL

RANCHITO LN
LITTLE OAKS LN
NATHANIEL LN
ALPINE HEIGHTS WY
CARIE WY
CALLE DE TIERRA
ALPINE OAKS DR

ALPINE HEIGHTS RD

BIG RED RD
CHARLES DEWITT WY
JOHN DEWITT
HUEY L
DEWITT
JOHN DEWITT PL
TWISTED OAK LN
LITTLE OAKS LN

33

ALPINE
HEIGHTS

SOUTH GRADE RD

YUCCA HILL RD
GEYER LN
Boulder
Oaks ES

HONEYOAK LN
GRACE LN
VILLA ZAPATA
CAMINO LAGARTO
CAMINO NARCISO
CAMINO ARTEMISA
CAMINO DEL SEQUAN
CAMINO DE LOS AVES
CAMINO AVENA
COLLADO CORTE
CAMINO DEL SEQUAN
AVENIDA OCOTILLO
REAL WAY LN
HAWKS VISTA LN

T15S
T16S

ALPINE OAKS DR

1

2

91901

5

6

OGARD RANCH RD
RED GUM RD
DEHESA RANCH RD

DEHESA RD

DEHESA RD

REAL WAY LN
4
HAWKS VISTA LN

WIND CREEK RD

TAVERN RD
TA
DEHES
RD

3

SEE ⌃ 1254 MAP

SEQUAN TRUCK TRL
CORONADO TERRRACE DR
CORONADO VIEW RD
SEQUAN TRUCK TRL

SEQUAN TRUCK TRL

7

8

CLEVELAND NATIONAL FOREST

9

4

5

LOVELAND RESERVOIR

6

SEQUAN TRUCK TRL

SEQUAN TRUCK TRL

18

17
PRIVATE RD

16

91935

7

SWEETWATER RIVER RD
SWEETWATER RIVER RD
SLOANE CANYON RD

E   F   G   H   J

SEE ⌄ 1273 MAP

N

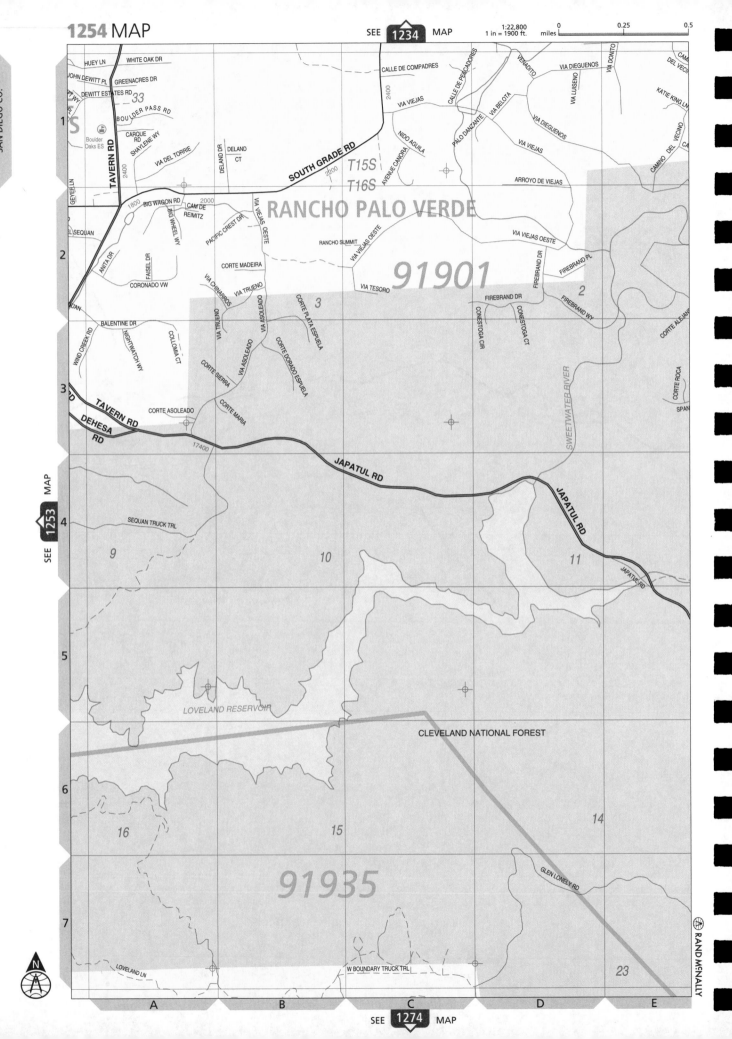

1:22,800
1 in = 1900 ft.

miles 0 — 0.25 — 0.5

SAN DIEGO CO.

HUEY LN
WHITE OAK DR
JOHN DEWITT PL
GREENACRES DR
DEWITT ESTATES RD
33
BOULDER PASS RD
CARQUE RD
SHAYLENE WY
Boulder Oaks ES
VIA DEL TORRIE
DELAND DR
DELAND CT
SOUTH GRADE RD

CALLE DE COMPADRES
CALLE DE PESCADORES
VENADITO
VIA DIEGUENOS
VIA DONITO
CAMINO DEL VECINO
VIA LUISENO
VIA BELOTA
KATIE KING LN
VIA VIEJAS
NIDO AGUILA
PALO DANZANTE
VIA DIEGUENOS
AVENUE CANORA
VIA VIEJAS
CAMINO DEL VECINO

TAVERN RD
GEYEELIN
1800
BIG WAGON RD
CAM DE REIMITZ
BIG WHEEL WY
PACIFIC CREST DR
2000
EL SEQUAN
ANITA DR
FAISEL DR
CORONADO VW
CORTE MADEIRA
VIA VIEJAS OESTE
VIA CHINARROS
VIA TRUENO
VIA ASOLEADO

RANCHO PALO VERDE

RANCHO SUMMIT
VIA VIEJAS OESTE
VIA TESORO
ARROYO DE VIEJAS
VIA VIEJAS OESTE
FIREBRAND DR
FIREBRAND PL
FIREBRAND DR
FIREBRAND WY
CONESTOGA CT
CONESTOGA CIR

T15S
T16S

91901

2

CORTE ALEJAN

CORTE ROCA
SPAN

BALENTINE DR
WIND CREEK RD
NIGHTWATCH WY
COLLOMIA CT
CORTE SIERRA
VIA ASOLEADO
CORTE PLATA ESPUELA
CORTE DORADO ESPUELA
CORTE MARIA
CORTE ASOLEADO

3

SWEETWATER RIVER

TAVERN RD
DEHESA RD
17400
JAPATUL RD

JAPATUL RD

SEQUAN TRUCK TRL

9

10

11

JAPATUL RD

LOVELAND RESERVOIR

CLEVELAND NATIONAL FOREST

16

15

14

GLEN LONELY RD

91935

23

LOVELAND LN

W BOUNDARY TRUCK TRL

N

RAND McNALLY

A   B   C   D   E

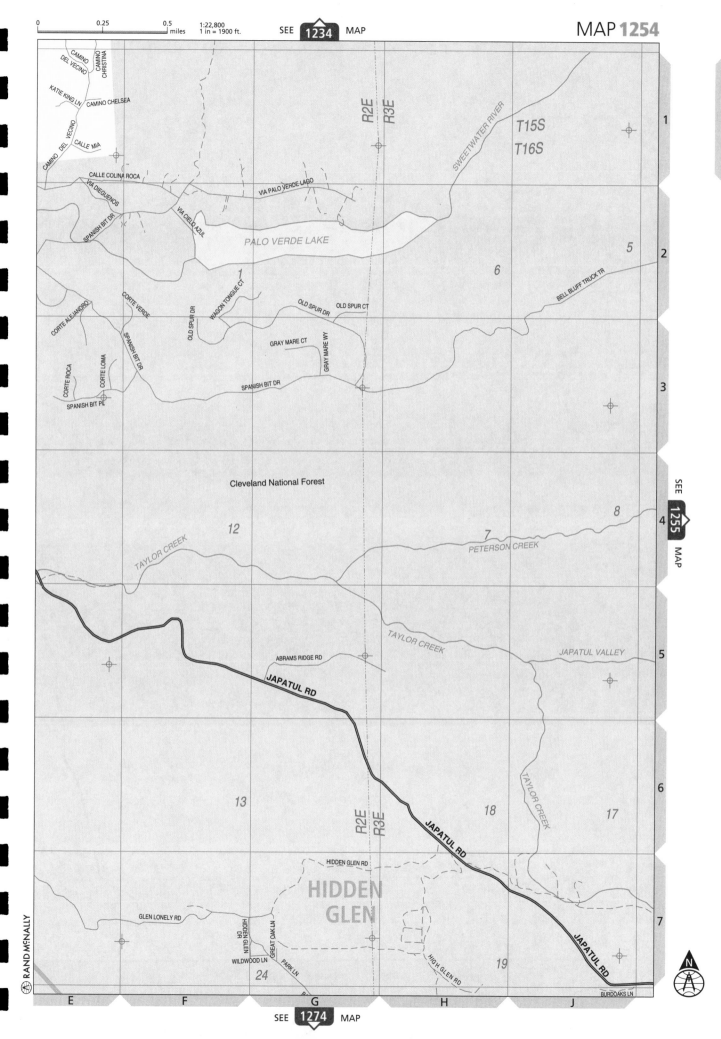

MAP **1254**

SAN DIEGO CO.

SEE 1234 MAP

SEE 1255 MAP

0   0.25   0.5 miles
1:22,800
1 in = 1900 ft.

CAMINO DEL VECINO
CAMINO CHRISTINA
KATIE KING LN   CAMINO CHELSEA
CAMINO DEL VECINO
CALLE MIA
CAMINO

CALLE COLINA ROCA
VIA DIEGUENOS
SPANISH BIT DR
VIA CIELO AZUL
VIA PALO VERDE LAGO

PALO VERDE LAKE

R2E
R3E

T15S
T16S

SWEETWATER RIVER

1

5

2

BELL BLUFF TRUCK TR

CORTE ALEJANDRO
CORTE VERDE
OLD SPUR DR
WAGON TONGUE CT
OLD SPUR DR   OLD SPUR CT
GRAY MARE CT
GRAY MARE WY
SPANISH BIT DR
SPANISH BIT DR
CORTE ROCA
CORTE LOMA
SPANISH BIT PIL

1

6

3

Cleveland National Forest

12

TAYLOR CREEK

7

8

PETERSON CREEK

4

ABRAMS RIDGE RD

JAPATUL RD

TAYLOR CREEK

JAPATUL VALLEY

5

13

JAPATUL RD

R2E
R3E

18

JAPATUL RD

TAYLOR CREEK

17

6

HIDDEN GLEN RD

HIDDEN
GLEN

GLEN LONELY RD
HIDDEN GLEN DR
GREAT OAK LN
WILDWOOD LN
PARK LN

24

19

HIGH GLEN RD

JAPATUL RD

BURDOAKS LN

7

E   F   G   H   J

RAND MCNALLY

N

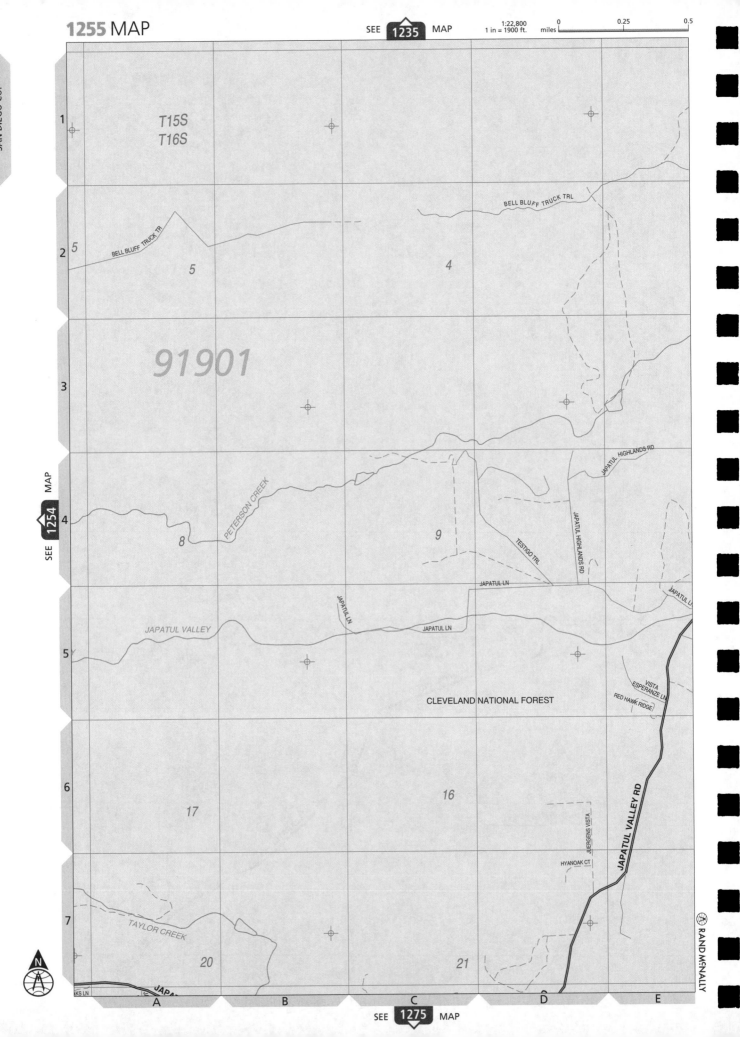

1:22,800
1 in = 1900 ft.

miles

0   0.25   0.5

SAN DIEGO CO.

T15S
T16S

91901

SEE ⬠1254 MAP

BELL BLUFF TRUCK TR.

BELL BLUFF TRUCK TRL

5

5

4

PETERSON CREEK

8

9

JAPATUL HIGHLANDS RD

JAPATUL HIGHLANDS RD

TESTIGO TRL

JAPATUL LN

JAPATUL LN

JAPATUL VALLEY

JAPATUL LN

JAPATUL LN

Y

CLEVELAND NATIONAL FOREST

VISTA
ESPERANZE LN

RED HAWK RIDGE

JAPATUL LA

17

16

JUERGENS VISTA

JAPATUL VALLEY RD

HYANOAK CT

TAYLOR CREEK

20

21

KS LN

JAPA

N

A   B   C   D   E

RAND McNALLY

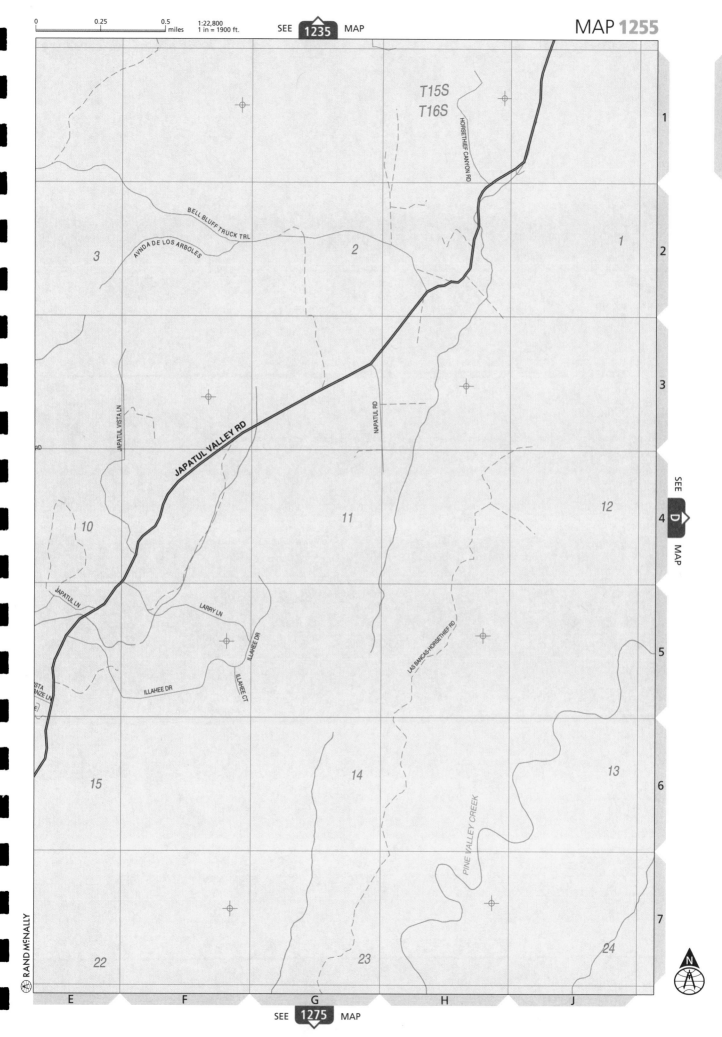

MAP **1255**

SAN DIEGO CO.

SEE **1235** MAP

0   0.25   0.5
miles
1:22,800
1 in = 1900 ft.

T15S
T16S

HORSETHIEF CANYON RD

BELL BLUFF TRUCK TRL

AVNDA DE LOS ARBOLES

3

2

1

JAPATUL VISTA LN

JAPATUL VALLEY RD

NAPATUL RD

10

11

12

SEE D MAP

JAPATUL LN

LARRY LN

ILLAHEE DR

ILLAHEE CT

ILLAHEE DR

LAS BANCAS-HORSETHIEF RD

VISTA
NZE LN
E)

15

14

13

PINE VALLEY CREEK

22

23

24

RAND MCNALLY

1
2
3
4
5
6
7

E   F   G   H   J

SEE **1275** MAP

N

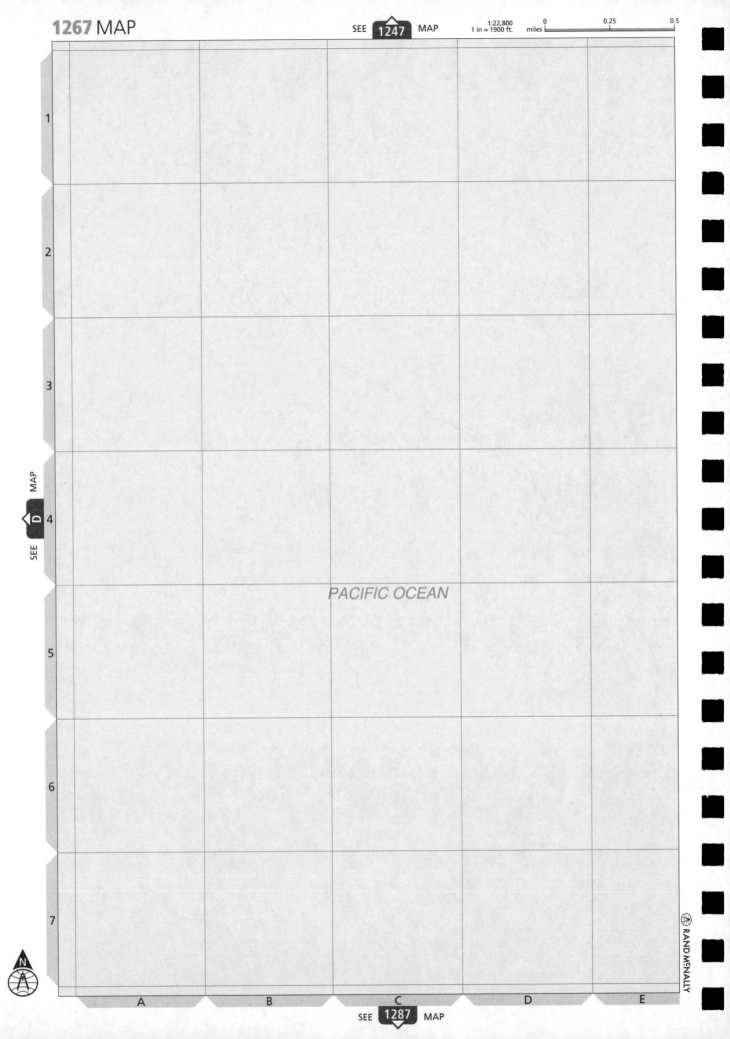

SEE 1247 MAP

1:22,800
1 in = 1900 ft.

0   0.25   0.5
miles

SAN DIEGO CO.

SEE D MAP

PACIFIC OCEAN

1   2   3   4   5   6   7

A   B   C   D   E

RAND McNALLY

SEE 1287 MAP

MAP **1267**

0   0.25   0.5
miles
1:22,800
1 in = 1900 ft.

SEE 1247 MAP

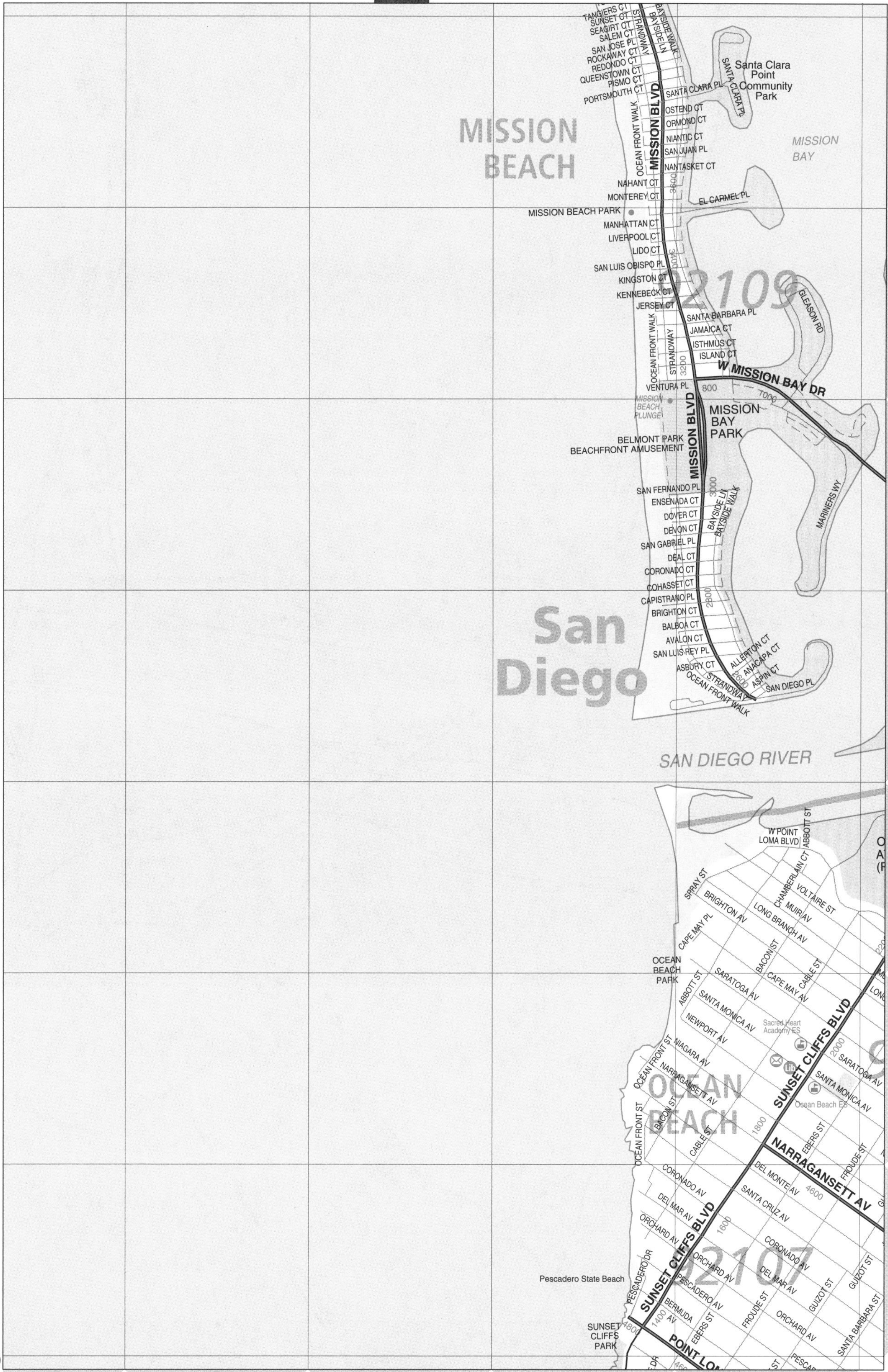

MISSION
BEACH

2109

TANGIERS CT
SUNSET CT
SEAGIRT CT
SALEM CT
SAN JOSE PL
ROCKAWAY CT
REDONDO CT
QUEENSTOWN CT
PISMO CT
PORTSMOUTH CT

SANTA CLARA PL
OSTEND CT
ORMOND CT
NIANTIC CT
SAN JUAN PL
NANTASKET CT

NAHANT CT
MONTEREY CT

MISSION BEACH PARK

MANHATTAN CT
LIVERPOOL CT
LIDO CT
SAN LUIS OBISPO PL
KINGSTON CT
KENNEBECK CT
JERSEY CT

SANTA BARBARA PL
JAMAICA CT
ISTHMUS CT
ISLAND CT

VENTURA PL

MISSION
BEACH
PLUNGE

BELMONT PARK
BEACHFRONT AMUSEMENT

SAN FERNANDO PL
ENSENADA CT
DOVER CT
DEVON CT
SAN GABRIEL PL
DEAL CT
CORONADO CT
COHASSET CT
CAPISTRANO PL
BRIGHTON CT
BALBOA CT
AVALON CT
SAN LUIS REY PL
ASBURY CT

OCEAN FRONT WALK
STRANDWAY
OCEAN FRONT WALK
STRANDWAY

MISSION BLVD

BAYSIDE WALK

SANTA CLARA
POINT
COMMUNITY
PARK

Santa Clara
Point
Community
Park

MISSION
BAY

EL CARMEL PL

GLEASON RD

W MISSION BAY DR

MISSION
BAY
PARK

MARINERS WY

BAYSIDE LN
BAYSIDE WALK

ALLERTON CT
ANACAPA CT
ASPIN CT
SAN DIEGO PL

San
Diego

SAN DIEGO RIVER

SEE 1268 MAP

W POINT
LOMA BLVD

ABBOTT ST

SPRAY ST
BRIGHTON AV
LONG BRANCH AV

CHAMBERLAIN CT
VOLTAIRE ST
MUIR AV

OCEAN
BEACH
PARK

CAPE MAY PL

SARATOGA AV
CAPE MAY AV

BACON ST
CABLE ST

SUNSET CLIFFS BLVD

LONG

SANTA MONICA AV

Sacred Heart
Academy ES

ABBOTT ST
SANTA MONICA AV
NEWPORT AV

SARATOGA AV
SANTA MONICA AV

2000

OCEAN FRONT ST
NIAGARA AV

Ocean Beach ES

OCEAN

BEACH

NARRAGANSETT AV

CABLE ST

EBERS ST

FROUDE ST

NARRAGANSETT AV

OCEAN FRONT ST

1800

DEL MONTE AV

4600

CORONADO AV

DEL MAR AV
SANTA CRUZ AV

DEL MONTE AV

SUNSET CLIFFS BLVD

GUIZOT ST

CORONADO AV

DEL MAR AV

GUIZOT ST

SANTA BARBARA ST

2107

ORCHARD AV

1600

Pescadero State Beach

PESCADERO DR

ORCHARD AV
PESCADERO AV

BERMUDA
AV

SUNSET
CLIFFS
BLVD

1400

EBERS ST
FROUDE ST

ORCHARD AV

FROUDE ST

GUIZOT ST

SUNSET
CLIFFS
PARK

DR

POINT LOMA

PESCADERO

SEE 1287 MAP

RAND MCNALLY

E   F   G   H   J

N

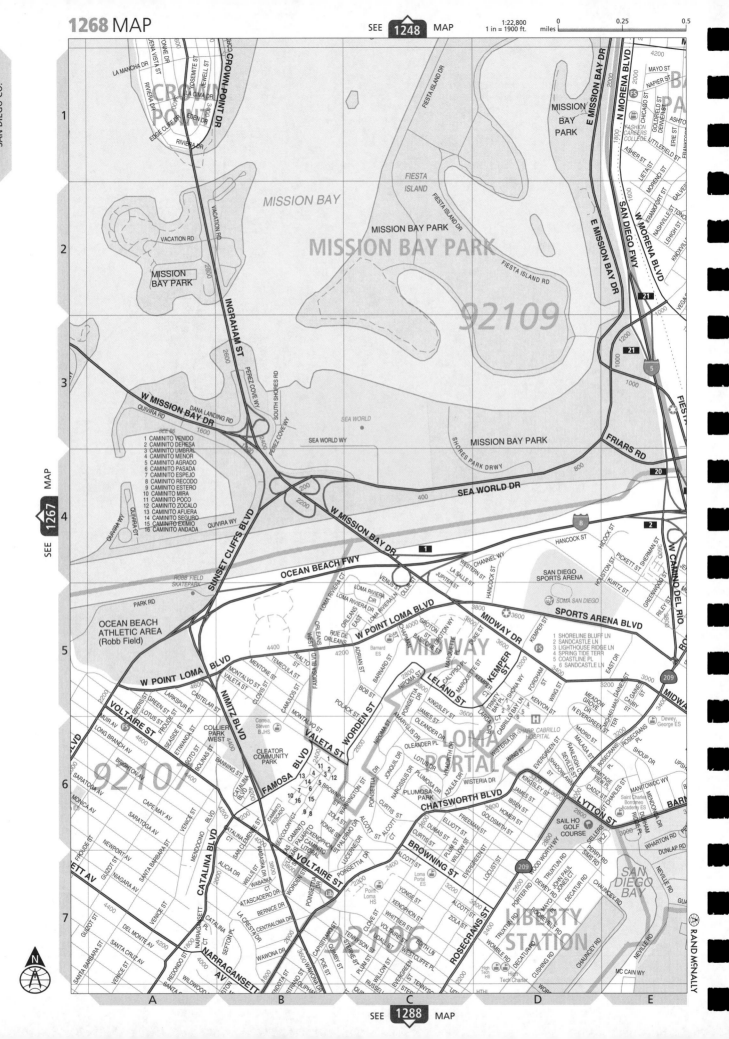

SAN DIEGO CO.

1:22,800
1 in = 1900 ft.
0   0.25   0.5
miles

CROWN POINT

CROWN POINT DR

LA MANCHA DR

MISSION BAY

FIESTA ISLAND DR

MISSION BAY PARK

N MORENA BLVD

W MORENA BLVD

MISSION BAY PARK

FIESTA ISLAND

92109

MISSION BAY PARK

INGRAHAM ST

VACATION RD

MISSION BAY PARK

E MISSION BAY DR

21

W MISSION BAY DR

DANA LANDING RD

QUIVIRA RD

SEA WORLD

I-5

21

FIESTA

SEE 1267 MAP

1 CAMINITO VENIDO
2 CAMINITO DEHESA
3 CAMINITO UMBRAL
4 CAMINITO MENOR
5 CAMINITO AGRADO
6 CAMINITO PASADA
7 CAMINITO ESPEJO
8 CAMINITO RECODO
9 CAMINITO ESTERO
10 CAMINITO MIRA
11 CAMINITO POCO
12 CAMINITO ZOCALO
13 CAMINITO AFUERA
14 CAMINITO SEGURO
15 CAMINITO EXIMIO
16 CAMINITO ANDADA

SEA WORLD WY

MISSION BAY PARK

SHORES PARK DRWY

SEA WORLD DR

FRIARS RD

QUIVIRA WY

QUIVIRA RD

SUNSET CLIFFS BLVD

W MISSION BAY DR

OCEAN BEACH FWY

8

2

HANCOCK ST

SAN DIEGO SPORTS ARENA

W CAMINO DEL RIO

ROBB FIELD SKATEPARK

PARK RD

LOMA RIVIERA CIR

W POINT LOMA BLVD

MIDWAY DR

SPORTS ARENA BLVD

SOMA SAN DIEGO

OCEAN BEACH ATHLETIC AREA
(Robb Field)

ORLEANS

MIDWAY

1 SHORELINE BLUFF LN
2 SANDCASTLE LN
3 LIGHTHOUSE RIDGE LN
4 SPRING TIDE TERR
5 COASTLINE PL
6 SANDCASTLE LN

W POINT LOMA BLVD

NIMITZ BLVD

KEMPER ST

LELAND ST

MIDWAY

209

92107

VOLTAIRE ST

COLLIER PARK WEST

WORDEN ST

VALETA ST

LOMA PORTAL

SHARP CABRILLO HOSPITAL

FAMOSA BLVD

CLEATOR COMMUNITY PARK

CATALINA BLVD

CHATSWORTH BLVD

LYTTON ST

BARN

SAIL HO GOLF COURSE

BROWNING ST

209

SAN DIEGO BAY

92106

ROSECRANS ST

LIBERTY STATION

NARRAGANSETT AV

SEE 1288 MAP

A   B   C   D   E

N

RAND MCNALLY

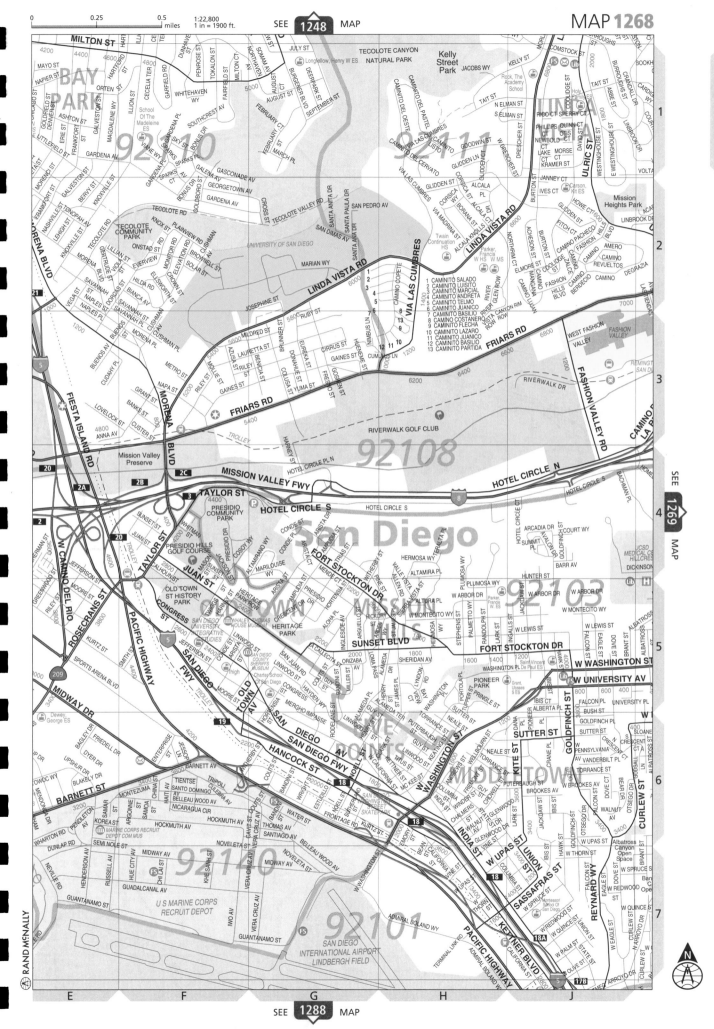

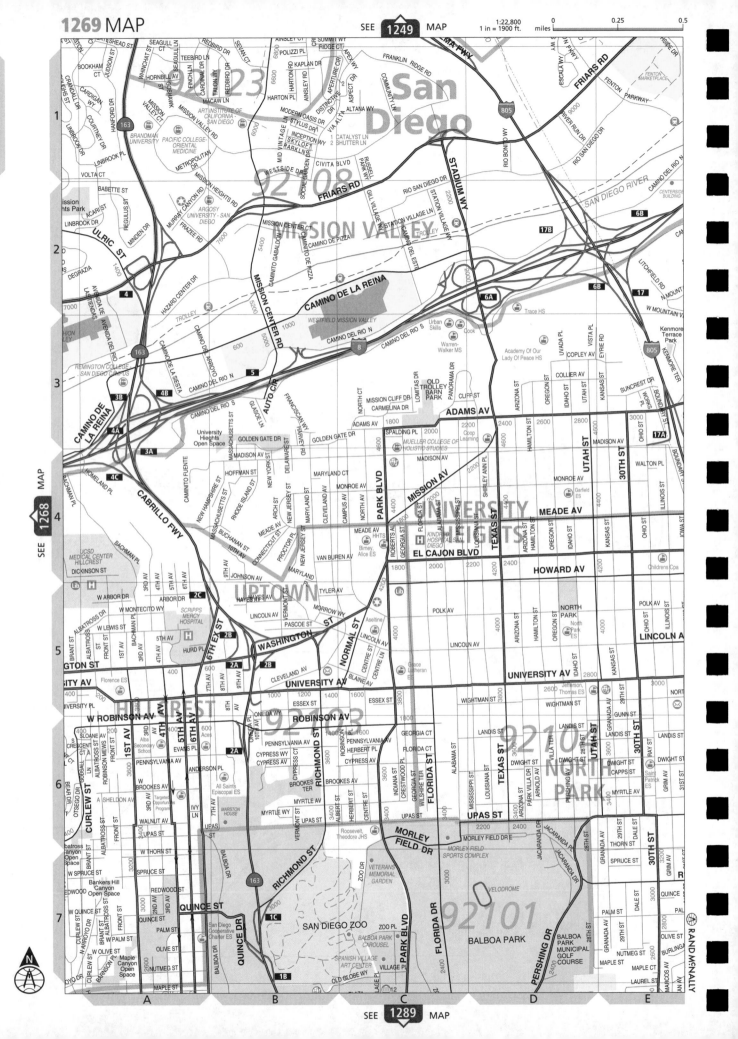

1:22,800
1 in = 1900 ft.

SAN DIEGO CO.

San Diego

MISSION VALLEY

MISSION VALLEY

CAMINO DE LA REINA

Westfield Mission Valley

UNIVERSITY HIGHTS

UPTOWN

HILLCREST

NORTH PARK

ROBINSON AV

San Diego Zoo

BALBOA PARK

RAND McNALLY

A   B   C   D   E

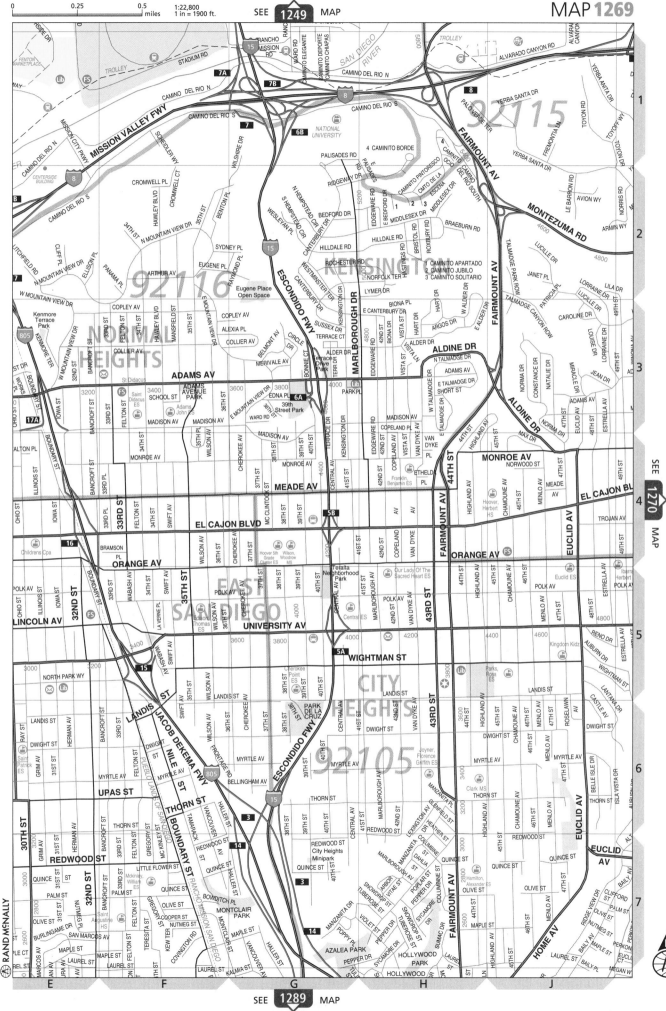

MAP 1269

SEE 1249 MAP

SAN DIEGO CO.

0   0.25   0.5
miles
1 in = 1900 ft.
1:22,800

92115

92116

NORMAL HEIGHTS

KENSINGTON

EAST SAN DIEGO

CITY HEIGHTS

92105

MISSION VALLEY FWY

ESCONDIDO FWY

FAIRMOUNT AV

MONTEZUMA RD

ADAMS AV

MEADE AV

EL CAJON BLVD

ORANGE AV

UNIVERSITY AV

WIGHTMAN ST

EL CAJON BL

MONROE AV

ORANGE AV

EUCLID AV

EUCLID AV

REDWOOD ST

UPAS ST

THORN ST

HOME AV

SAN DIEGO RIVER

NATIONAL UNIVERSITY

RAND MCNALLY

N

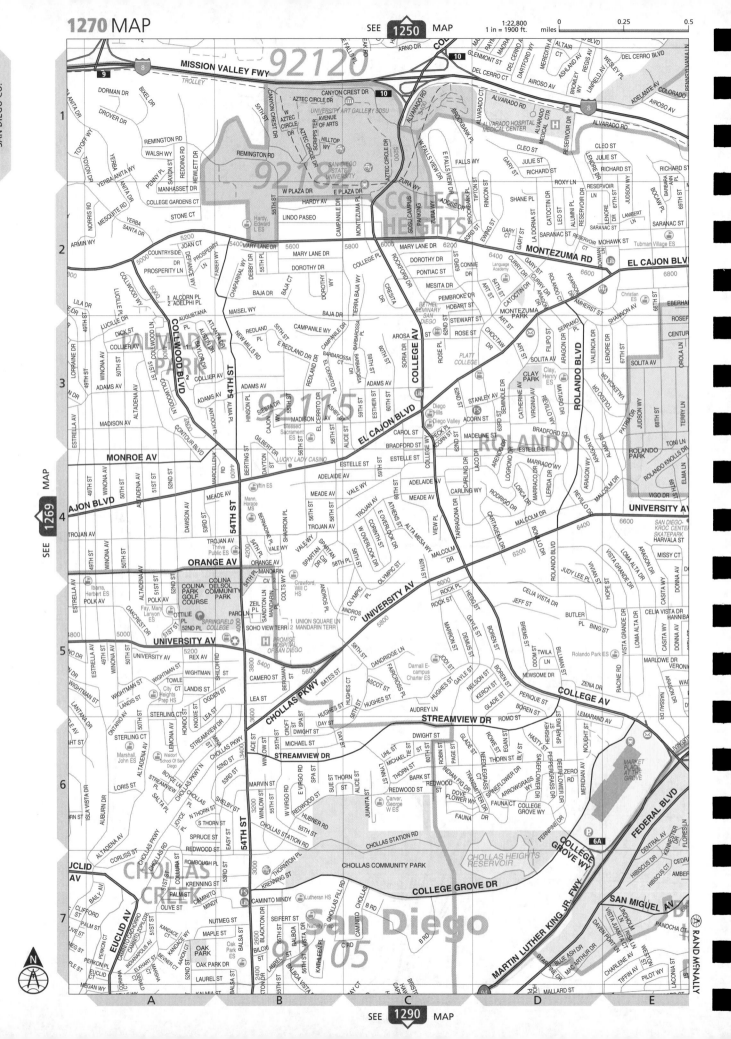

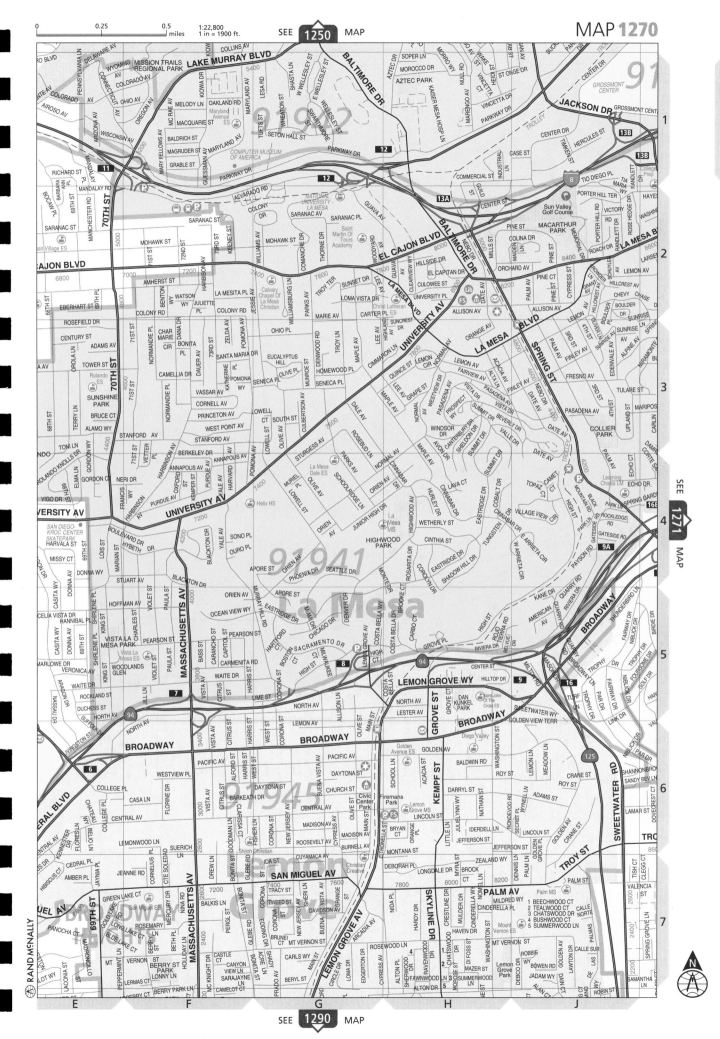

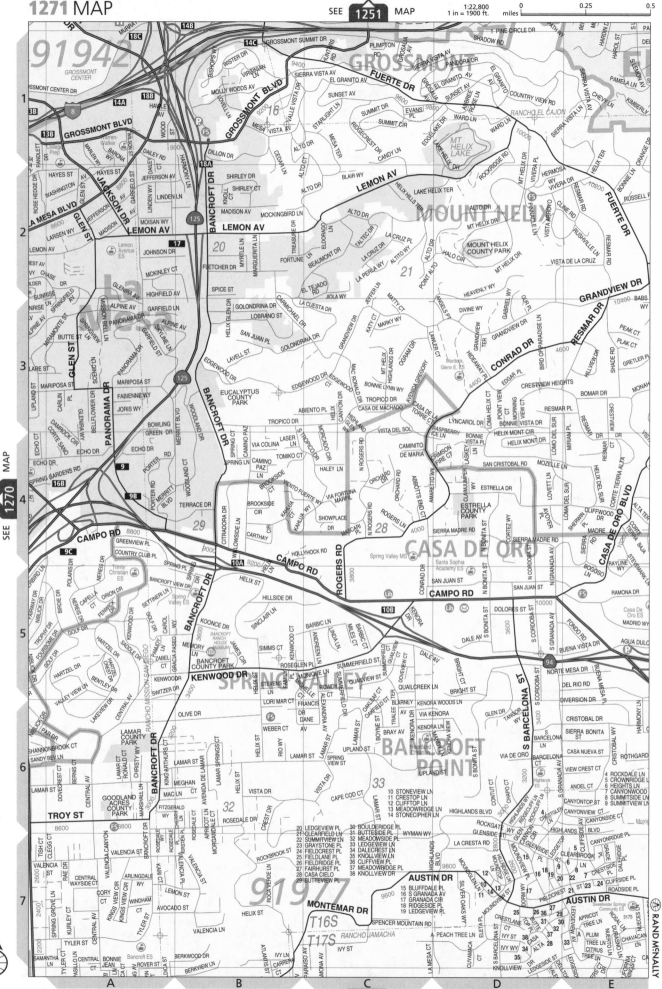

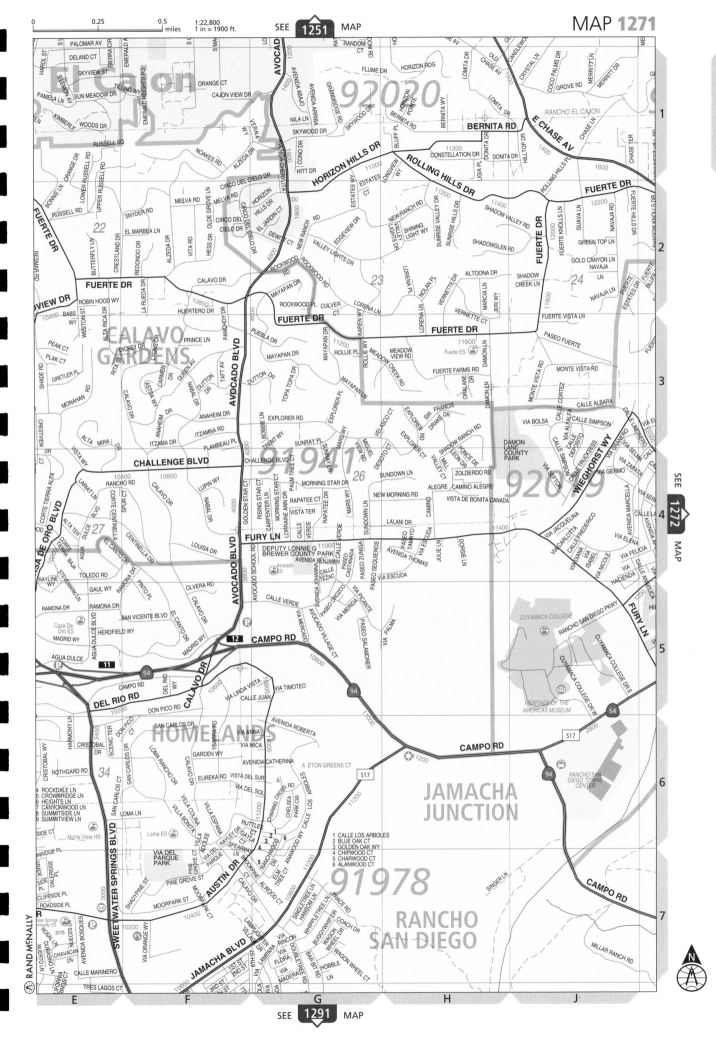

MAP 1271

SAN DIEGO CO.

El Cajon

92020

22

CALAVO
GARDENS

23

24

91941

26

92019

WIEGHORST WY

27

CASA DE ORO BLVD

HOMELANDS

34

JAMACHA
JUNCTION

91978

RANCHO
SAN DIEGO

CUYAMACA COLLEGE

HERITAGE OF THE
AMERICAS MUSEUM

RANCHO SAN DIEGO TOWNE CENTER

1 Calle Los Arboles
2 Blue Oak Ct
3 Golden Oak Wy
4 Chipwood Ct
5 Charwood Ct
6 Alanwood Ct

4 Rockdale Ln
5 Crownridge Ln
6 Heights Ln
7 Canyonwood Ln
8 Summitside Ln
9 Summitview Ln

RAND MCNALLY

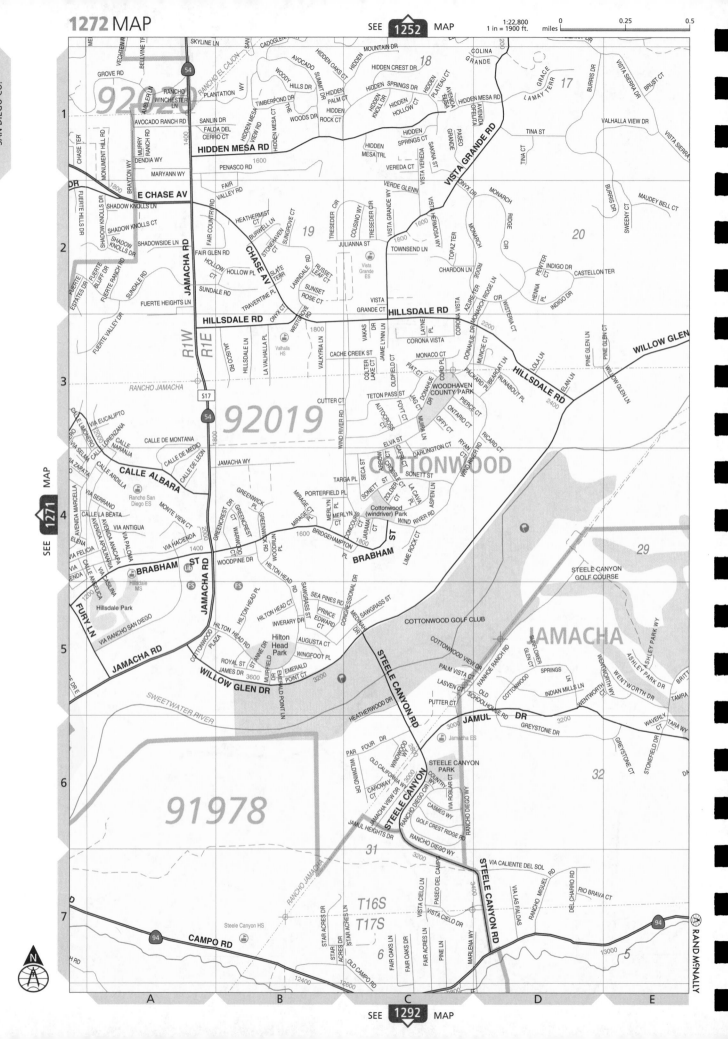

MAP **1272**

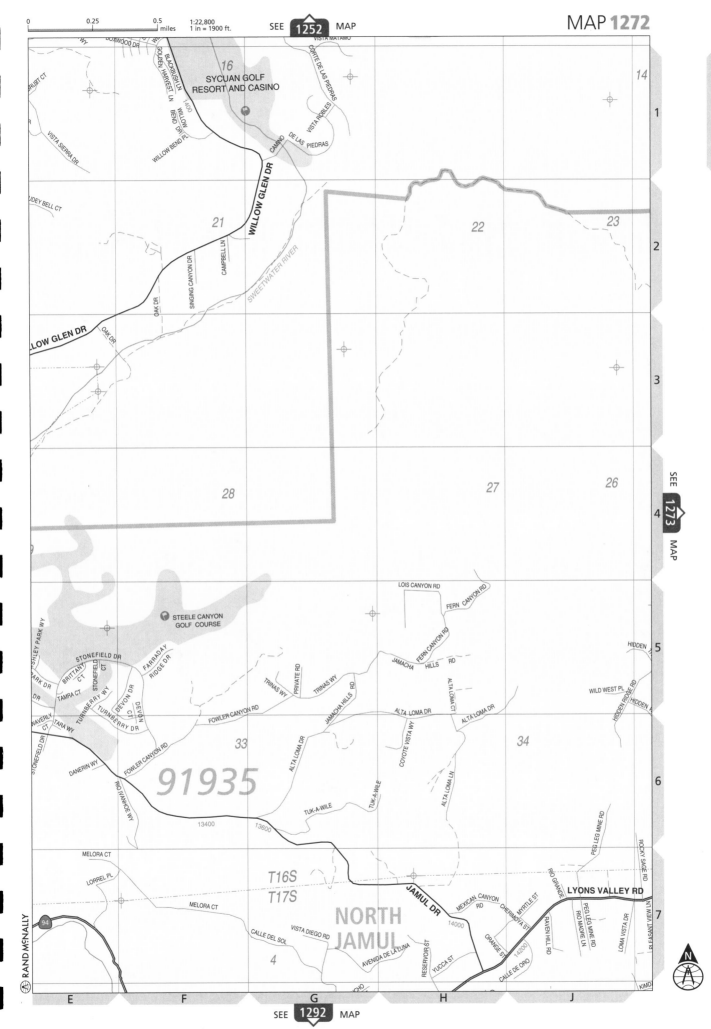

SAN DIEGO CO.

0   0.25   0.5
miles
1:22,800
1 in = 1900 ft.

16

SYCUAN GOLF
RESORT AND CASINO

14

1

VISTA MATAMO

CORTE DE LAS PIEDRAS

VISTA ROBLES

CAMINO DE LAS PIEDRAS

BOXWOOD DR

BLACKBUSH LN

GOLDEN HARVEST LN

WILLOW BEND DR

WILLOW BEND PL

CRUST CT

VISTA SIERRA DR

UDEY BELL CT

WILLOW GLEN DR

21

SINGING CANYON DR

CAMPBELL LN

OAK DR

SWEETWATER RIVER

22

23

2

LOW GLEN DR

OAK DR

3

28

27

26

SEE 1273 MAP

4

LOIS CANYON RD

FERN CANYON RD

STEELE CANYON
GOLF COURSE

FERN CANYON RD

JAMACHA   HILLS   RD

HIDDEN

5

ASHLEY PARK WY

STONEFIELD DR

BRITTANY CT

STONEFIELD CT

FARRADAY RIDGE DR

TAMRA CT

TURNBERRY WY

DEVON DR

DEVON CT

TURNBERRY DR

TRINAS WY

PRIVATE RD

TRINAS WY

JAMACHA HILLS RD

ALTA LOMA CT

ALTA LOMA DR

ALTA LOMA DR

WILD WEST PL

HIDDEN RIDGE RD

HIDDEN

PARK DR

DR

WAVERLY CT

TARA WY

FOWLER CANYON RD

ALTA LOMA DR

COYOTE VISTA WY

33

34

STONEFIELD DR

DANERIN WY

FOWLER CANYON RD

RIO IVANHOE WY

91935

ALTA LOMA LN

TUK-A-WILE

PEG LEG MINE RD

ROCKY SAGE RD

6

13400

13600

TUK-A-WILE

TUK-A-WILE

MELORA CT

LORREL PL

MELORA CT

T16S
T17S

JAMUL DR

RIO GRANDE

LYONS VALLEY RD

MEXICAN CANYON RD

CHERIMOYA ST

MYRTLE ST

PEG LEG MINE RD

RIO MADRE LN

7

94

VISTA DIEGO RD

CALLE DEL SOL

**NORTH
JAMUL**

4

AVENIDA DE LA LUNA

14000

RESERVOIR ST

YUCCA ST

ORANGE ST

CALLE DE ORO

14200

RAVEN HILL RD

LOMA VISTA DR

PLEASANT VIEW LN

RANCHO

KIMD

RAND M*NALLY

N

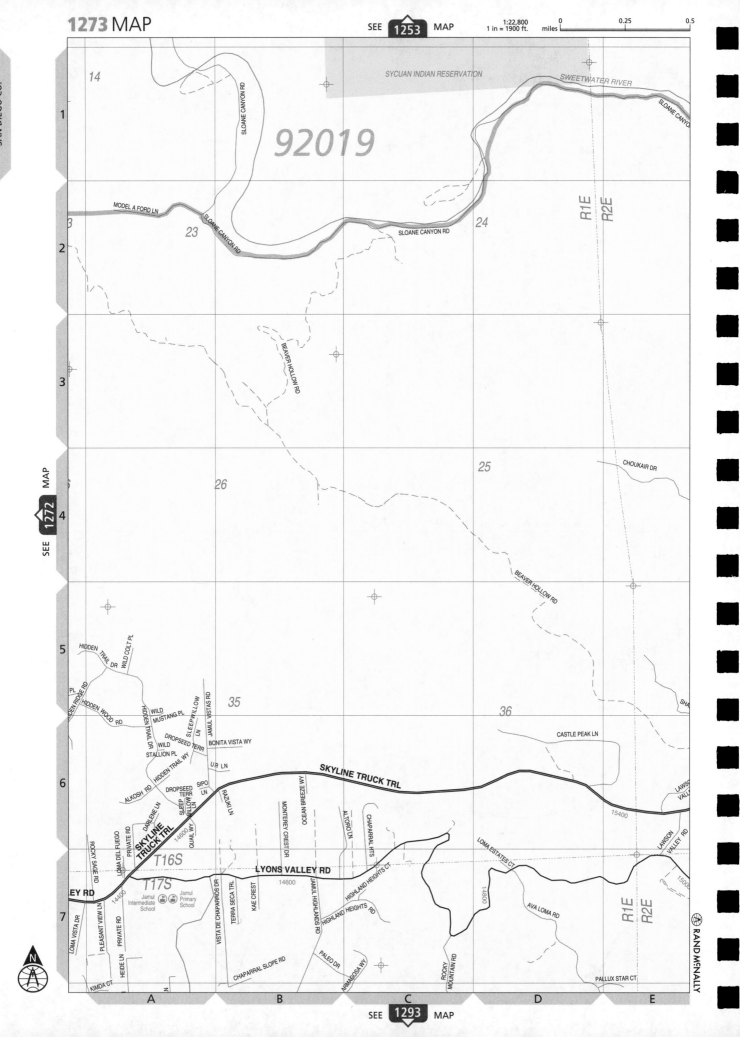

SAN DIEGO CO.

SEE **1253** MAP

1:22,800
1 in = 1900 ft.

0   0.25   0.5
miles

14

1

SYCUAN INDIAN RESERVATION

SWEETWATER RIVER

92019

SLOANE CANYON RD

SLOANE CANYON

R1E
R2E

MODEL A FORD LN

23

SLOANE CANYON RD

SLOANE CANYON RD

24

2

SEE **1272** MAP

BEAVER HOLLOW RD

3

26

25

CHOUKAIR DR

4

BEAVER HOLLOW RD

5

HIDDEN TRAIL DR   WILD COLT PL

PL

OLDEN RIDGE RD

HIDDEN WOOD RD

HIDDEN TRAIL DR

WILD MUSTANG PL

SLEEPWILLOW LN

JAMUL VISTAS RD

35

36

CASTLE PEAK LN

DROPSEED TERR

WILD STALLION PL

BONITA VISTA WY

HIDDEN TRAIL WY

U R LN

SKYLINE TRUCK TRL

6

ALKOSH RD

DROPSEED TERR

SIPO LN

RAZUKI LN

SLEEP WILLOW LN

MONTEREY CREST DR

OCEAN BREEZE WY

SKYLINE TRUCK TRL

15400

LAWSO VALLE

DARLENE LN

SKYLINE TRUCK TRL

QUAIL WY

14600 WY

ALTORO LN

CHAPARRAL HTS

LOMA ESTATES CT

LAWSON VALLEY RD

PRIVATE RD

LOMA DEL FUEGO

T16S

LYONS VALLEY RD

1500

ROCKY SAGE RD

T17S

14600

HIGHLAND HEIGHTS CT

 R1E
R2E

LEY RD

14400

Jamul Intermediate School

Jamul Primary School

VISTA DE CHAPARROS DR

TERRA SECA TRL

KAE CREST

JAMUL HIGHLANDS RD

HIGHLAND HEIGHTS RD

14800

AVA LOMA RD

7

LOMA VISTA DR

PLEASANT VIEW LN

PRIVATE RD

HEIDE LN

KIMDA CT

N

CHAPARRAL SLOPE RD

PALEO DR

ARMAGOSA WY

ROCKY MOUNTAIN RD

PALLUX STAR CT

N

A   B   C   D   E

RAND McNALLY

SEE **1293** MAP

MAP **1273**

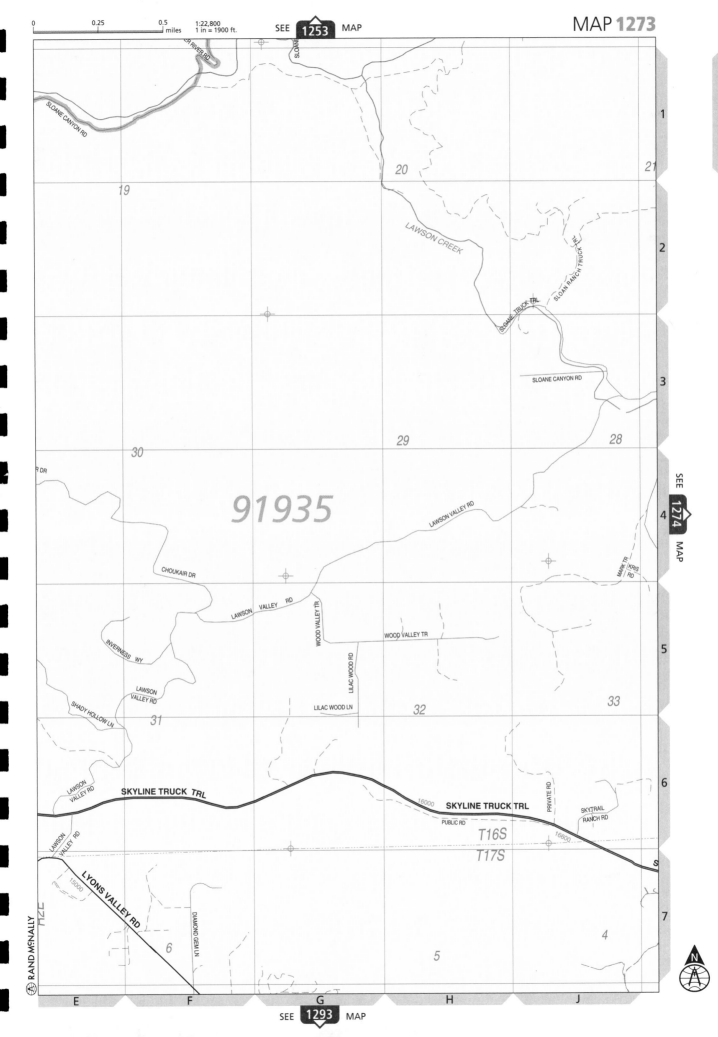

SEE 1253 MAP

SEE 1274 MAP

SEE 1293 MAP

0   0.25   0.5
miles
1:22,800
1 in = 1900 ft.

SLOANE CANYON RD

SLOANE CANYON RD

CR RIVER RD

19

20

21

1

LAWSON CREEK

SLOAN RANCH TRUCK TRL

SLOANE TRUCK TRL

2

3

30

29

28

91935

R DR

LAWSON VALLEY RD

CHOUKAIR DR

MARK TR   KRIS RD

4

LAWSON   VALLEY   RD

WOOD VALLEY TR

WOOD VALLEY TR

INVERNESS   WY

LILAC WOOD RD

5

LAWSON VALLEY RD

SHADY HOLLOW LN

LILAC WOOD LN

31

32

33

LAWSON VALLEY RD

SKYLINE TRUCK TRL

SKYLINE TRUCK TRL

16000

PUBLIC RD

PRIVATE RD

SKYTRAIL RANCH RD

6

LAWSON VALLEY RD

T16S

16600

T17S

S

LYONS VALLEY RD

15000

HZL

DIAMOND GEM LN

6

5

4

7

RAND MCNALLY

E   F   G   H   J

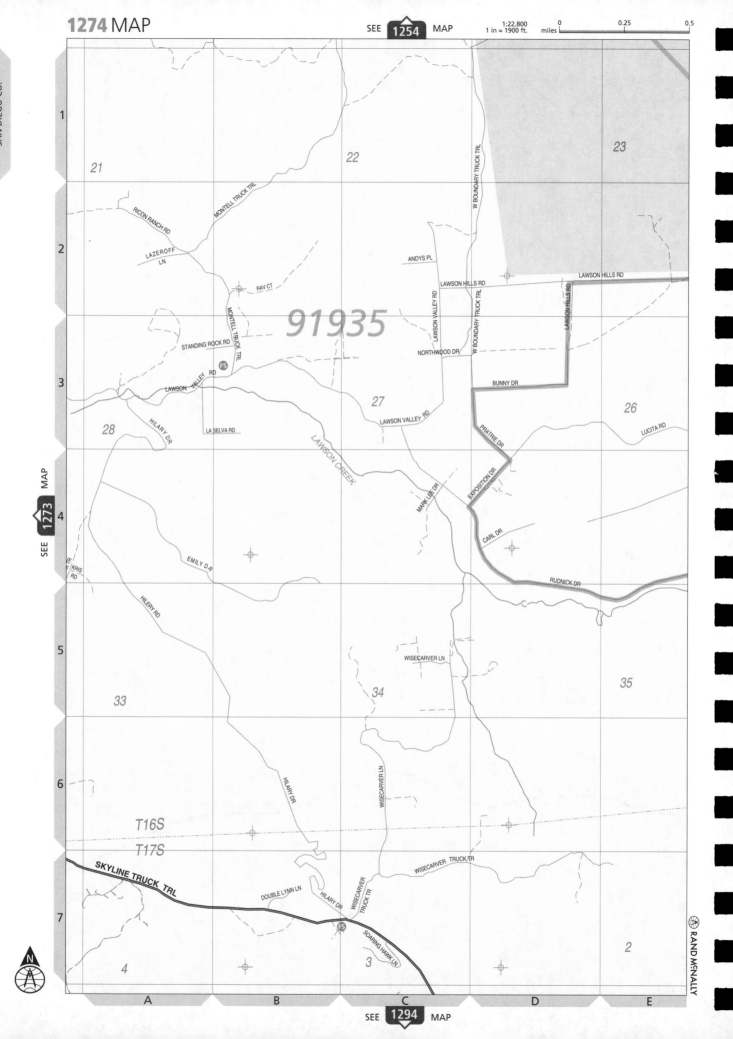

1:22,800
1 in = 1900 ft.

SAN DIEGO CO.

SEE 1273 MAP

91935

RICON RANCH RD
LAZEROFF LN
MONTELL TRUCK TRL
RAV CT
STANDING ROCK RD
MONTELL TRUCK TRL
LAWSON VALLEY RD
LAWSON VALLEY RD
LA SELVA RD
HILARY DR
HILERY RD
KRIS RD
EMILY DR
HILARY DR
LAWSON CREEK
ANDYS PL
LAWSON HILLS RD
LAWSON VALLEY RD
NORTHWOOD DR
W BOUNDARY TRUCK TRL
LAWSON HILLS RD
LAWSON HILLS RD
BUNNY DR
LUCITA RD
PRATRIE DR
EXPOSITION DR
MARK LEE DR
CARL DR
RUDNICK DR
WISECARVER LN
WISECARVER LN
SKYLINE TRUCK TRL
DOUBLE LYNN LN
HILARY DR
WISECARVER TRUCK TR
WISECARVER TRUCK TR
SOARING HAWK LN

T16S
T17S

21 22 23
28 27 26
33 34 35
4   3   2

A B C D E

RAND MCNALLY

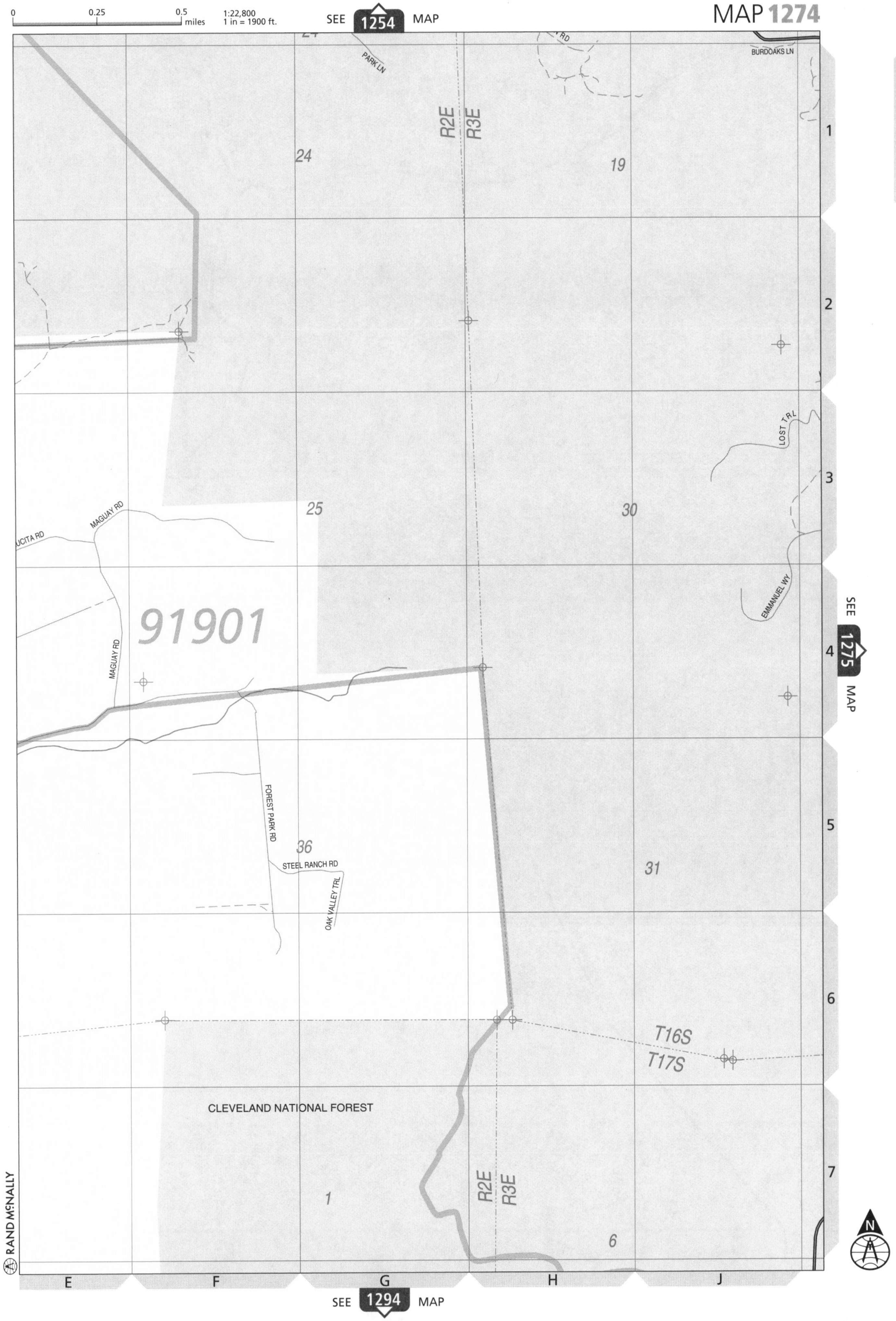

MAP **1274**

0 | 0.25 | 0.5
miles
1:22,800
1 in = 1900 ft.

SEE 1254 MAP

BURDOAKS LN

R2E
R3E

24

24

19

1

2

LOST TRL

MAGUAY RD

UCITA RD

25

30

3

91901

EMMANUEL WY

MAGUAY RD

SEE 1275 MAP

4

FOREST PARK RD

36

STEEL RANCH RD

31

5

OAK VALLEY TRL

6

T16S
T17S

CLEVELAND NATIONAL FOREST

7

1

R2E
R3E

6

RAND M℠NALLY

E | F | G | H | J

SEE 1294 MAP

N

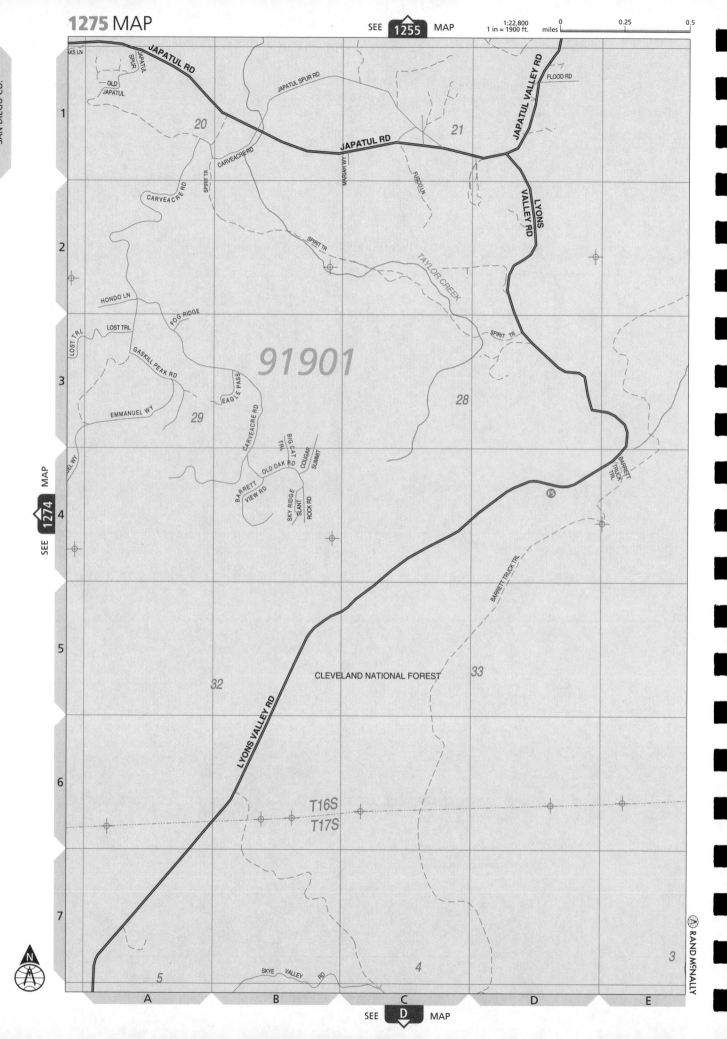

SAN DIEGO CO.

SEE 1255 MAP

1:22,800
1 in = 1900 ft.

0   0.25   0.5
miles

KS LN

JAPATUL RD

JAPATUL SPUR

OLD JAPATUL

JAPATUL SPUR RD

FLOOD RD

JAPATUL VALLEY RD

1

20

JAPATUL RD

21

CARVEACRE RD

MARIAH WY

FUSCO LN

SPIRIT TR

LYONS VALLEY RD

CARVEACRE RD

2

SPIRIT TR

TAYLOR CREEK

HONDO LN

FOG RIDGE

LOST TRL

LOST TRL

SPIRIT TR

91901

GASKILL PEAK RD

EAGLE PASS

3

EMMANUEL WY

29

CARVEACRE RD

28

BIG CAT TRL

COUGAR SUMMIT

BARRETT TRUCK TRL

OLD OAK RD

EL WY

BARRETT VIEW RD

SKY RIDGE

SLANT ROCK RD

SEE 1274 MAP

4

FS

BARRETT TRUCK TRL

5

BARRETT TRUCK TRL

32

CLEVELAND NATIONAL FOREST

33

LYONS VALLEY RD

6

T16S

T17S

7

N

LYONS VALLEY RD

5

SKYE VALLEY RD

4

3

A   B   C   D   E

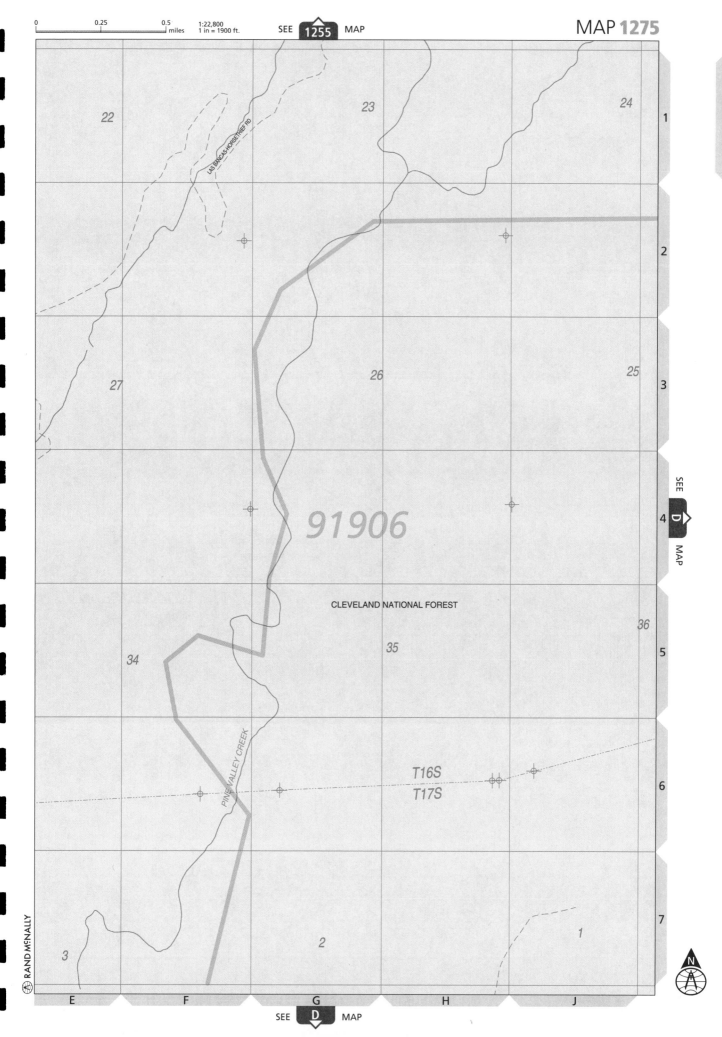

MAP **1275**

SAN DIEGO CO.

0   0.25   0.5
⌐—————————⌐ miles
1:22,800
1 in = 1900 ft.

22

23

24

1

LAS BANCAS-HORSE THIEF RD

27

26

25

3

91906

SEE ▸ D ▸ MAP

4

CLEVELAND NATIONAL FOREST

36

34

35

5

PINE VALLEY CREEK

T16S
T17S

6

3

2

1

7

RAND MCNALLY

E   F   G   H   J

N

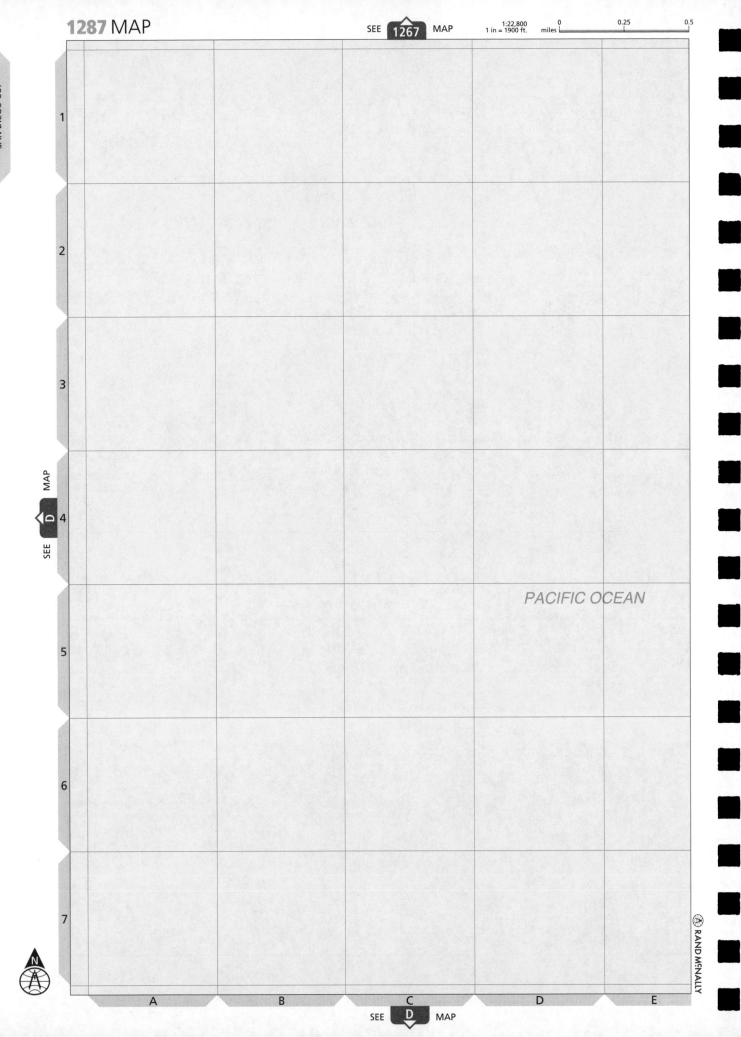

SAN DIEGO CO.

1:22,800
1 in = 1900 ft.

0   0.25   0.5
miles

SEE D MAP

PACIFIC OCEAN

RAND McNALLY

N

A   B   C   D   E

MAP **1287**

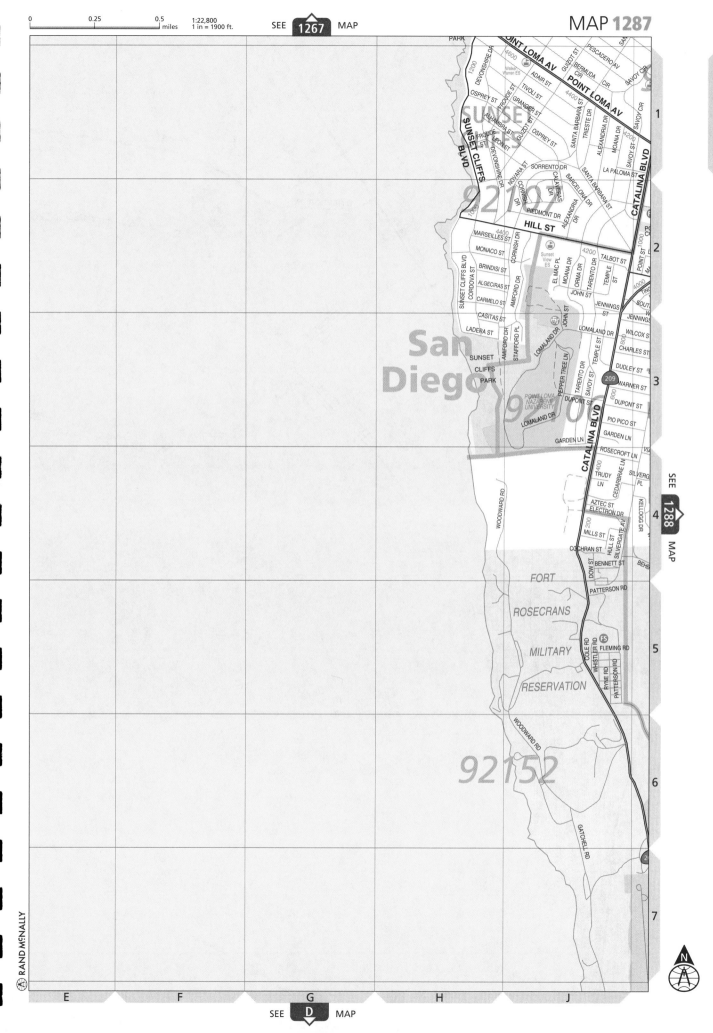

0   0.25   0.5 miles
1:22,800
1 in = 1900 ft.

SEE **1267** MAP

SUNSET
CLIFFS
BLVD

SUNSET ES

92107

POINT LOMA AV
POINT LOMA AV

CATALINA BLVD

HILL ST

San
Diego

92106

SUNSET
CLIFFS
PARK

POINT LOMA
NAZARENE
UNIVERSITY

LOMALAND DR

CATALINA BLVD

SEE **1288** MAP

WOODWARD RD

FORT

ROSECRANS

MILITARY

RESERVATION

WOODWARD RD

92152

RAND MCNALLY

E   F   G   H   J

SEE **D** MAP

92107

92147

92106

92135

SAN DIEGO BAY

U S NAVAL AIR STATION NORTH ISLAND

LA PLAYA

PENINSULA

ROSEVILLE

FLEETRIDGE

SHORELINE PARK

Shoreline Park Beach

NIMITZ MARINE FACILITY

US NAVAL RESERVATION

FORT ROSECRANS NATIONAL CEMETERY

SEE 1287 MAP

RAND MCNALLY

A   B   C   D   E

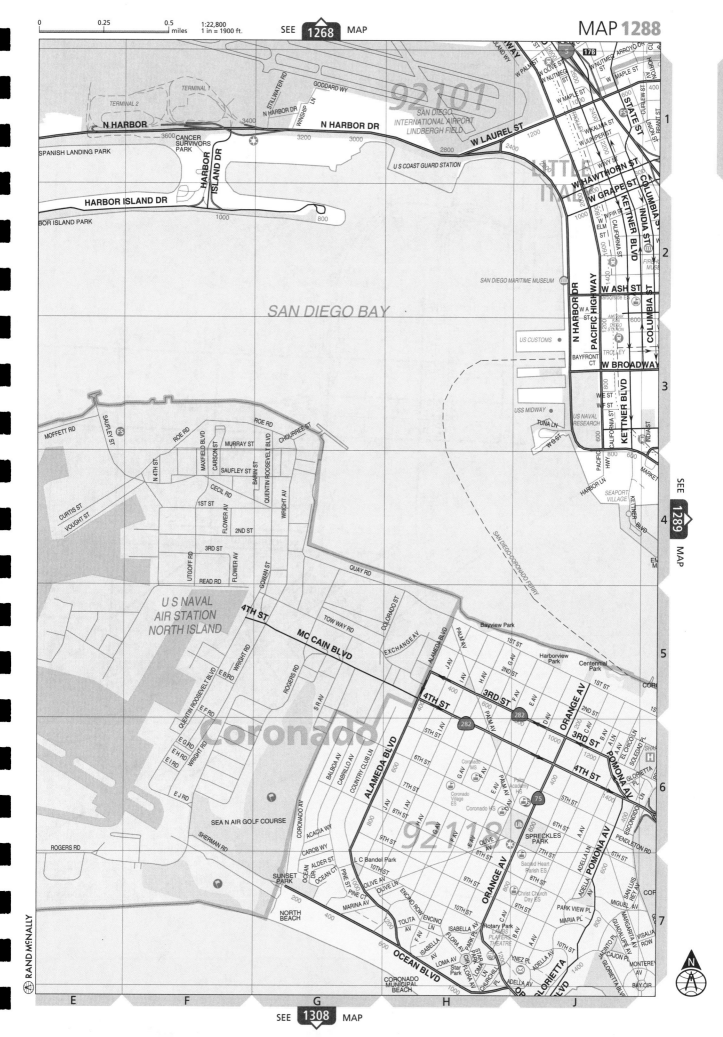

MAP **1288**

SEE ◆1268◆ MAP

0 0.25 0.5
miles
1:22,800
1 in = 1900 ft.

92101

TERMINAL 2

TERMINAL 1

STILLWATER RD

GODDARD WY

N HARBOR DR

SAN DIEGO
INTERNATIONAL AIRPORT
LINDBERGH FIELD

N HARBOR

WINSHIP LN

3400

N HARBOR DR

3200   3000

W LAUREL ST

2800

W PALMS
W OLIVE ST
W NUTMEG ST
W MAPLE
W KALMIA ST
W JUNIPER ST

2600
2400

17B

STATE ST

W NUTMEG AV
MAPLE ST

HORTON AV

500   400

1

CANCER
SURVIVORS
PARK

3600

SPANISH LANDING PARK

HARBOR ISLAND DR

HARBOR ISLAND DR

1000   800

BOR ISLAND PARK

U S COAST GUARD STATION

W HAWTHORN ST

W GRAPE ST

W FIR ST
W ELM ST

1000

W BROADWAY

LITTLE
ITALY

KETTNER BLVD

INDIA ST

CALIFORNIA ST

COLUMBIA ST

FIRE
MUSE

1200

2

SAN DIEGO MARITIME MUSEUM

SAN DIEGO BAY

W ASH ST

Harborside ES

AMTRAK
SAN
DIEGO
STATION

N HARBOR DR

PACIFIC HIGHWAY

KETTNER BLVD

COLUMBIA ST

600

W A
600

US CUSTOMS

BAYFRONT CT

W BROADWAY

TROLLEY

3

MOFFETT RD

SAUFLEY ST

FS

ROE RD

ROE RD

CHOURREE ST

USS MIDWAY

TUNA LN

W G ST

U S NAVAL
RESEARCH

W E ST
W F ST

800

PACIFIC HWY

600

600

MARKET

INDIA ST

SEE ◆1289◆ MAP

N 4TH ST

MAXFIELD BLVD

CARSON ST

MURRAY ST

SAUFLEY ST

BARIN ST

QUENTIN ROOSEVELT BLVD

WRIGHT AV

HARBOR LN

SEAPORT
VILLAGE

KETTNER
BLVD

EM
M

4

CURTIS ST

VOUGHT ST

CECIL RD

1ST ST

FLOWER AV

2ND ST

QUAY RD

COLORADO ST

SAN DIEGO-CORONADO FERRY

UTGOFF RD

3RD ST

READ RD

FLOWER AV

OGWAN ST

U S NAVAL
AIR STATION
NORTH ISLAND

4TH ST

MC CAIN BLVD

TOW WAY RD

EXCHANGE AV

ALAMEDA BLVD

PALM AV

Bayview Park

1ST ST

J AV
I AV
H AV
G AV
F AV

2ND ST

Harborview
Park

Centennial
Park

ORANGE AV

1ST ST

COR

1ST

5

WRIGHT RD

QUENTIN ROOSEVELT BLVD

E B RD
E F RD
E G RD
E H RD
E I RD

WRIGHT RD

ROGERS RD

S AV

Coronado

4TH ST

5TH ST

PALM AV

400
600

3RD ST

E AV
F AV

D AV

282

E AV

C AV
1000

2ND ST

D AV

ORANGE AV

200

3RD ST

B AV

EL CHICO LN

1200

POMONA AV

SOLEDAD PL

GLORIETTA
PL

H

6

E J RD

BALBOA AV

CABRILLO AV

COUNTRY CLUB LN

ALAMEDA BLVD

6TH ST

600

7TH ST

J AV
I AV

8TH ST

Coronado
MS

Coronado
Village
ES

Palm
Academy
HS

G AV
F AV

E AV

Coronado HS

PALM AV

D AV

4TH ST

400

5TH ST

75

6TH ST

A AV

600

Lib

PENDLETON RD

6TH ST

ESCONDIDO

POMONA AV

SAN LUIS REY AV

COR

SEA N AIR GOLF COURSE

CORONADO AV

ACACIA WY

CAROB WY

9TH ST

H AV

G AV

F AV

E AV

92118

SPRECKLES
PARK

D AV

OLIVE
AV

C AV

7TH ST

Sacred Heart
Parish ES

8TH ST

A AV

9TH ST

ADELLA LN

PARK VIEW PL

MARIA PL

600

MARGARITA AV

GUADALUPE AV

ROGERS RD

SUNSET
PARK

ALDER ST

OCEAN
DR

OCEAN CT

PINE ST

PINE CT

L C Bandel Park

10TH ST

OLIVE AV

OLIVE LN

ENCINO ROW
ENCINO

F AV

E AV

D AV

Christ Church
Day ES

C AV

B AV

9TH ST

Rotary Park

Star
Park

DAMES
PLAYERS
THEATRE

10TH ST

MIGUEL AV

COR

7

NORTH BEACH

MARINA AV

400

TOLITA
AV

200

F AV

ISABELLA AV

FLORA AV

LOMA AV

CIR FLORA AV

STAR
PARK

CHURCHILL
AV

PARK PL

YNEZ PL

C AV

B AV

A AV

JACINTO PL

GUADALUPE AV

CAJON AV

1400

VISALIA
ROW

MONTEREY
AV

600

OCEAN BLVD

1000

CORONADO
MUNICIPAL BEACH

ISABELLA
AV

FLORA AV

LOMA AV

ADELLA AV

2200

GLORIETTA

GLORIETTA BLVD

BAY CIR

E   F   G   H   J

SEE ◆1308◆ MAP

RAND MᶜNALLY

N

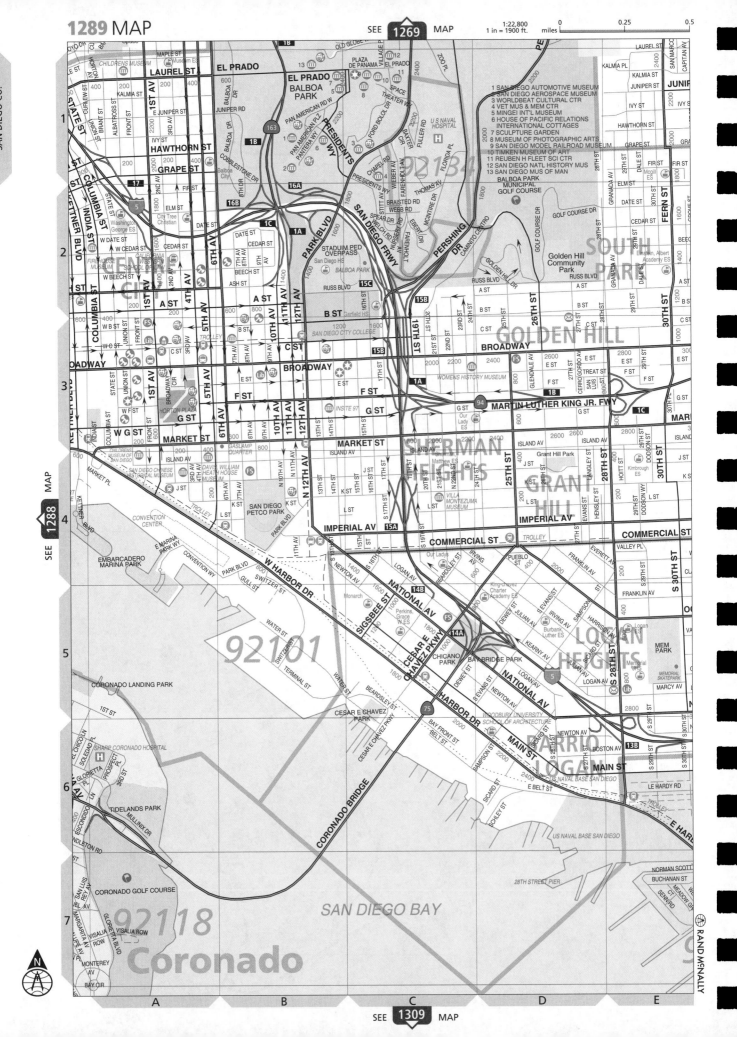

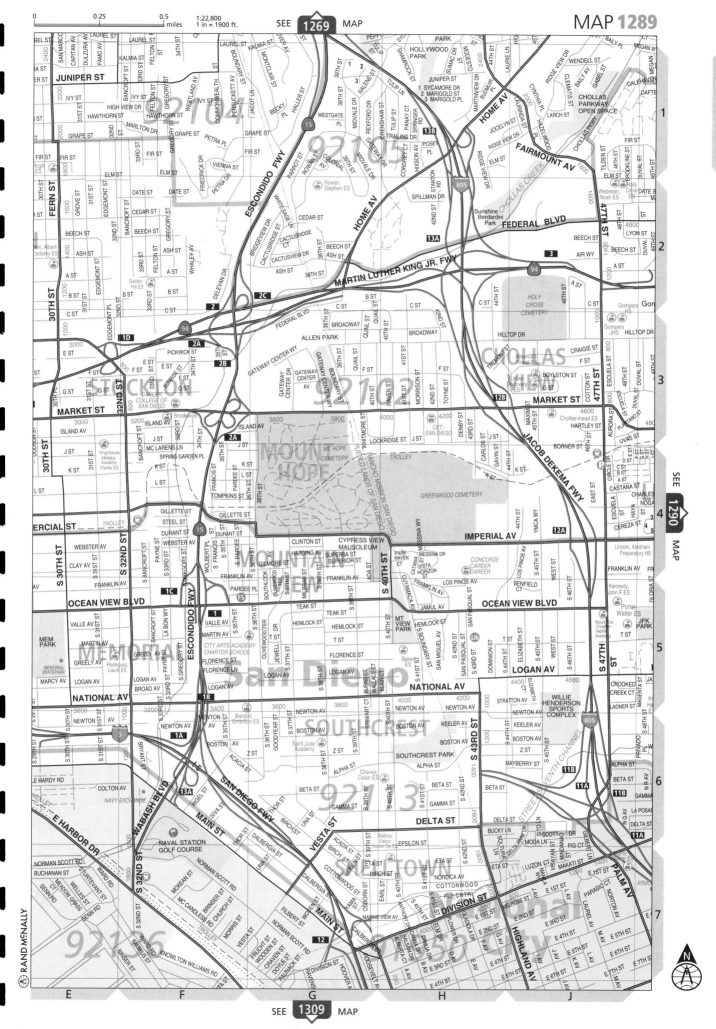

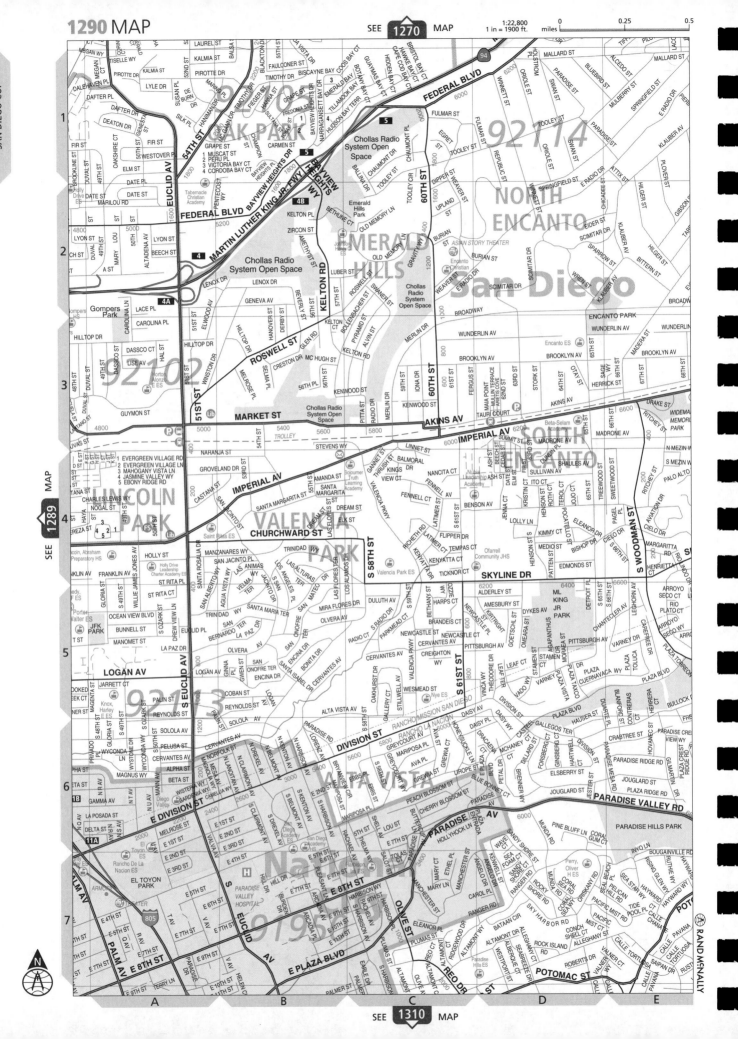

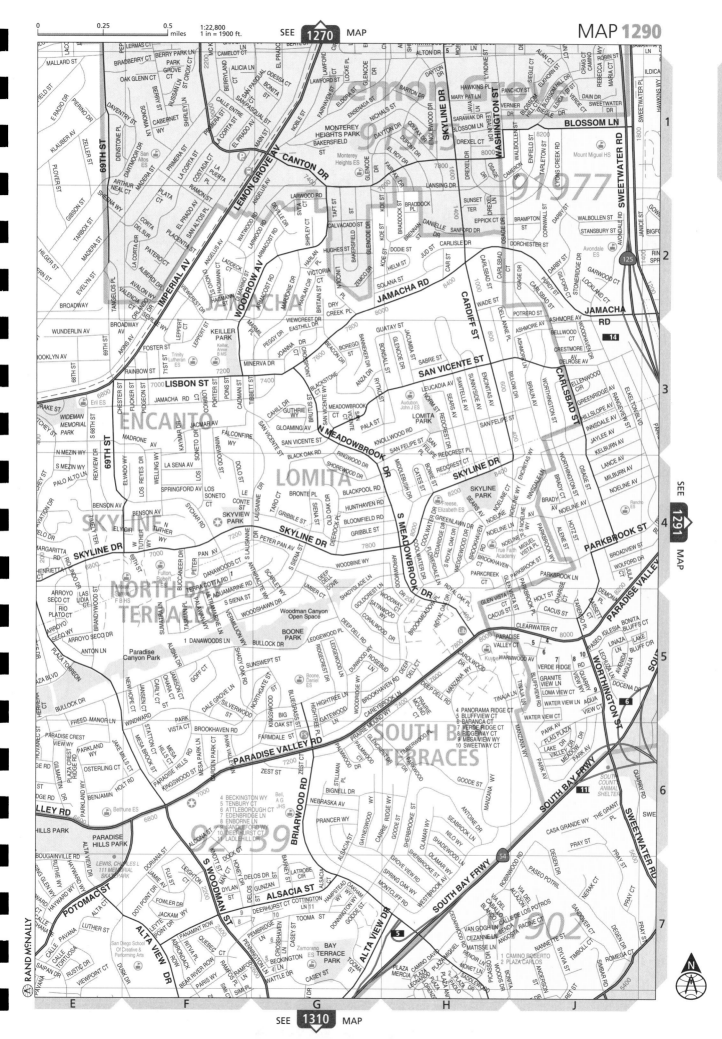

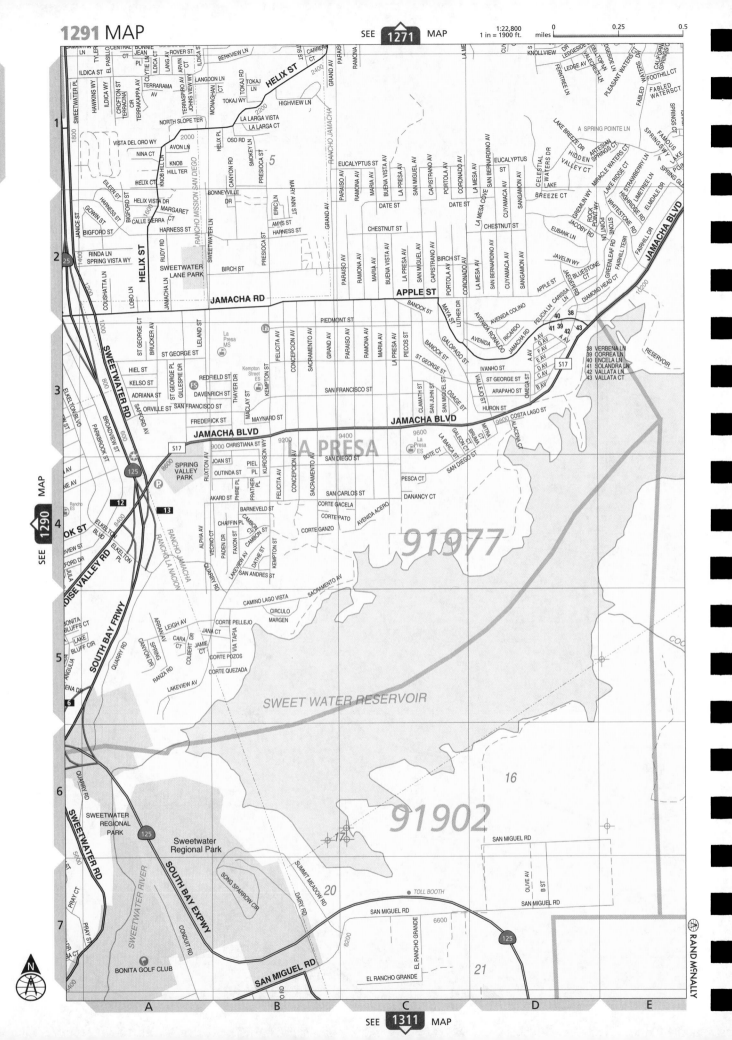

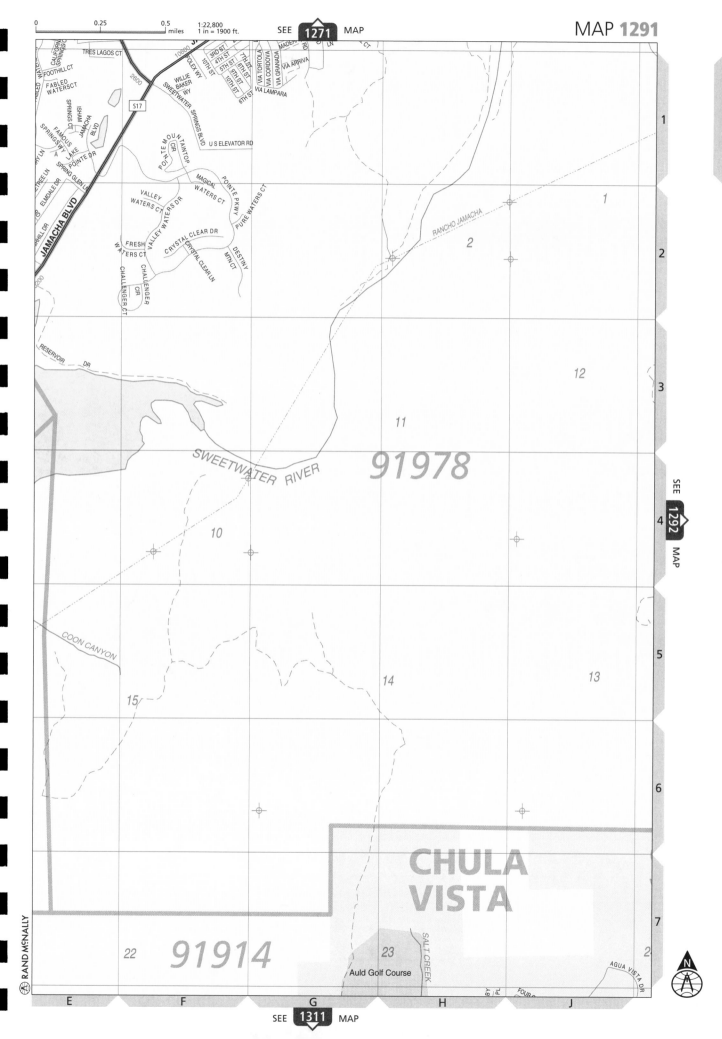

MAP **1291**

SEE **1271** MAP

0   0.25   0.5 miles
1:22,800
1 in = 1900 ft.

CALIFORNIA SPRINGS
TRES LAGOS CT
FOOTHILL CT
FABLED WATERS CT
FAMOUS SPRINGS CT
ISHAM
SPRINGSWY
SPRING GLEN LN
ELMDALE DR
JAMACHA BLVD
JAMACHA BLVD
S17
2600
10600

3RD ST
4TH ST
5TH ST
7TH ST
8TH ST
9TH ST
10TH ST
6TH ST
WILLIE BAKER WY
FOLEX WY
SWEETWATER SPRINGS BLVD
VIA TORTOLA
VIA CORDOVA
VIA GRANADA
VIA ARRIVA
VIA LAMPARA
MADEN RD
LN
CT

POINTE MOUNTAINTOP CIR
U S ELEVATOR RD
MAGICAL WATERS CT
VALLEY WATERS CT
VALLEY WATERS DR
POINTE PKWY
PURE WATERS CT
CRYSTAL CLEAR DR
CRYSTAL CLEAR LN
CRYSTAL CLEAR CT
DESTINY MTN CT
FRESH WATERS CT
CHALLENGER
CHALLENGER CIR
CHALLENGER CT
POINTE DR

RANCHO JAMACHA

1

2

12

11

RESERVOIR DR

SWEETWATER RIVER

91978

10

COON CANYON

14

13

15

SEE **1292** MAP

5

6

7

CHULA VISTA

22 **91914**

23
Auld Golf Course

SALT CREEK

AGUA VISTA DR

E   F   G   H   J

RAND M‹NALLY

SEE **1311** MAP

SAN DIEGO CO.

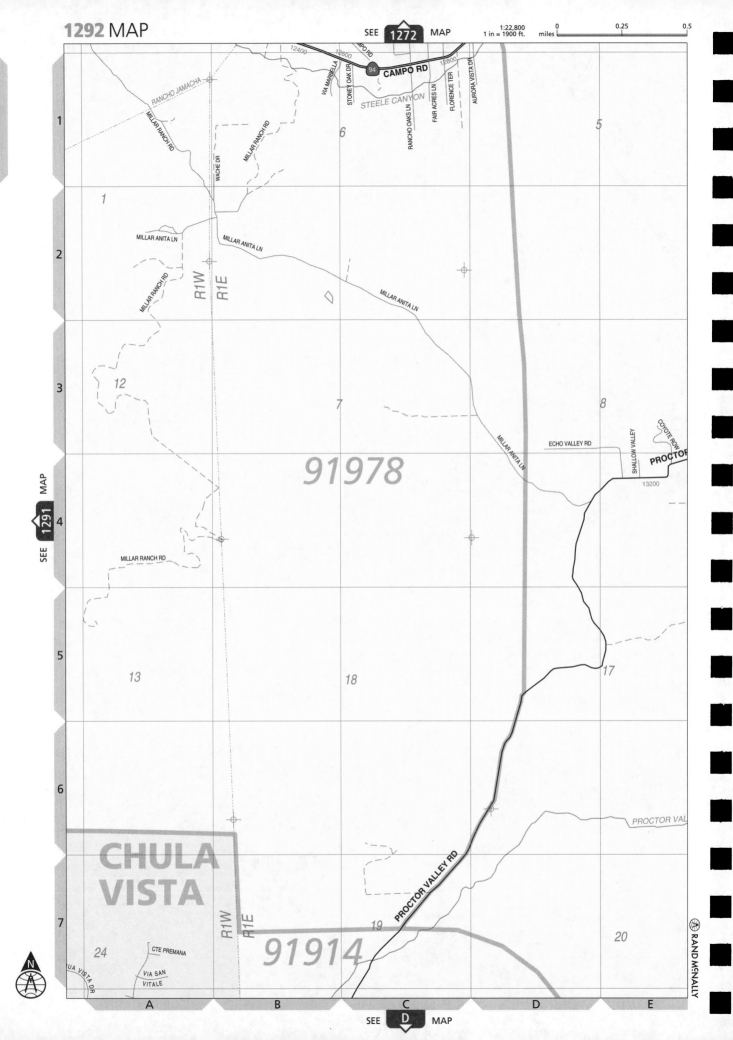

SEE ⌂ 1272 MAP

1:22,800
1 in = 1900 ft.

miles   0   0.25   0.5

CAMPO RD

12400   12600   94   12800

RANCHO JAMACHA

STEELE CANYON

VIA MARBELLA
STONEY OAK DR
RANCHO OAKS LN
FAIR ACRES LN
FLORENCE TER
AURORA VISTA DR

MILLAR RANCH RD

6

5

WACHE DR

MILLAR RANCH RD

1

MILLAR ANITA LN

MILLAR ANITA LN

MILLAR ANITA LN

MILLAR RANCH RD

R1W   R1E

2

MILLAR ANITA LN

12

3

7

8

91978

MILLAR ANITA LN

ECHO VALLEY RD

SHALLOW VALLEY
COYOTE ROW
PROCTOR

13200

SEE ⌂ 1291 MAP

MILLAR RANCH RD

4

13

18

17

5

6

PROCTOR VAL

**CHULA
VISTA**

R1W   R1E

PROCTOR VALLEY RD

7

19

20

24   CTE PREMANA

91914

UA VISTA DR

VIA SAN
VITALE

N

A   B   C   D   E

SEE ⌂ D MAP

RAND McNALLY

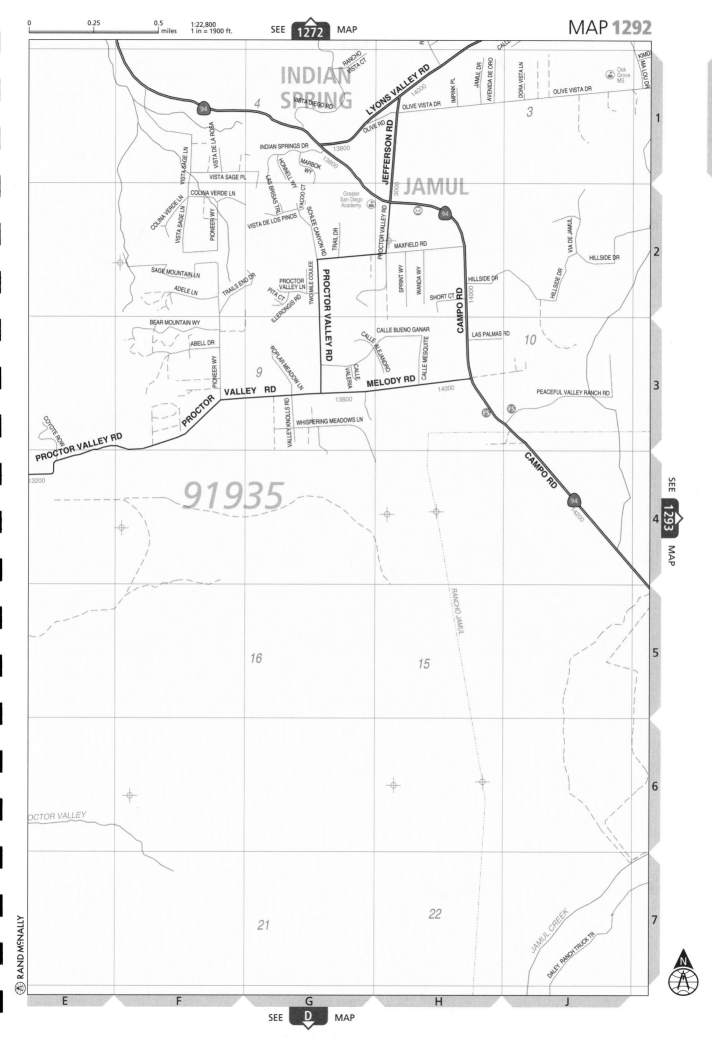

SAN DIEGO CO.

INDIAN
SPRING

JAMUL

1272

1293

SEE

1293

MAP

91935

RAND MᶜNALLY

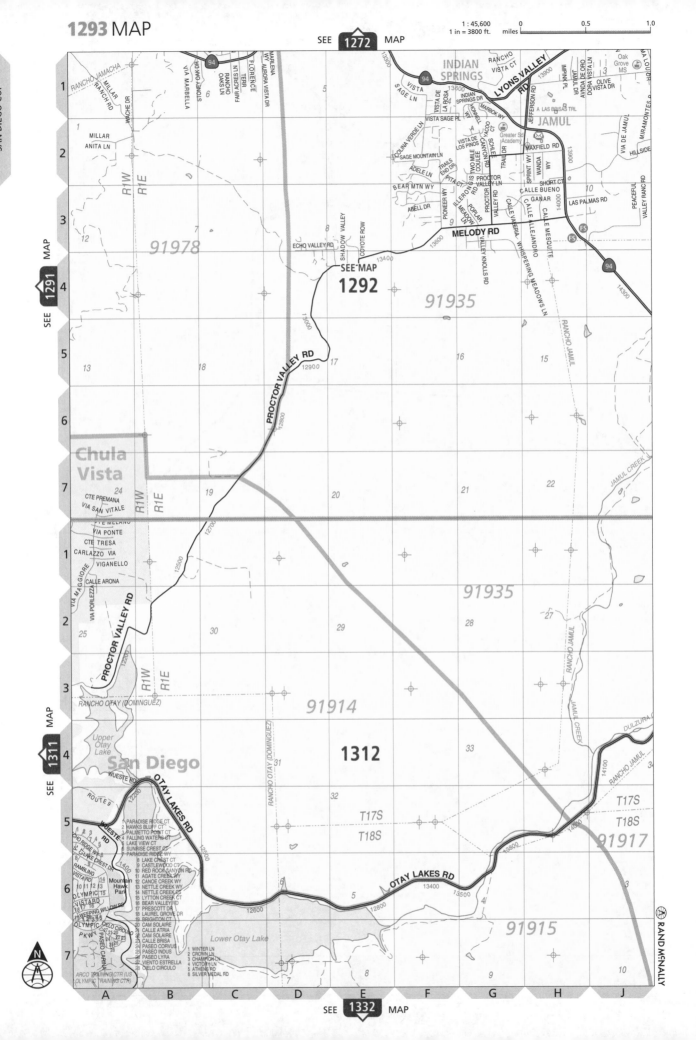

SAN DIEGO CO.

1 : 45,600
1 in = 3800 ft.   miles

0   0.5   1.0

SEE 1272 MAP

INDIAN SPRINGS

LYONS VALLEY RD

RANCHO VISTA CT

JAMUL

Greater SD Academy

WAXFIELD RD

MELODY RD

SEE MAP 1292

91978

91935

PROCTOR VALLEY RD

SEE 1291 MAP

Chula Vista

91935

PROCTOR VALLEY RD

RANCHO OTAY (DOMINGUEZ)

91914

1312

SEE 1311 MAP

Upper Otay Lake

San Diego

WUESTE RD

OTAY LAKES RD

ROUTE 9

1 PARADISE RIDGE CT
2 HAWKS BLUFF CT
3 PALMETTO POINT CT
4 FALLING WATERS CT
5 LAKE VIEW CT
6 SUNRISE CREST CT
7 PARADISE RIDGE WY
8 LAKE CREST CT
9 CASTLEWOOD CT
10 RED ROCK CANYON RD
11 AGATE CREEK WY
12 CANOE CREEK WY
13 NETTLE CREEK WY
14 NETTLE CREEK CT
15 LYTTON CREEK CT
16 BEAR VALLEY RD
17 PRESCOTT DR
18 LAUREL GROVE DR
19 BRIGHTON CT
20 CAM SOLAIRE
21 CALLE ATRIA
22 CAM SOLAIRE
23 CALLE BRISA
24 PASEO CORVUS
25 PASEO INDUS
26 PASEO LYRA
27 VIENTO ESTRELLA
28 CIELO CIRCULO

OTAY LAKES RD

T17S
T18S

T17S
T18S

91917

Lower Otay Lake

OLYMPIC PKWY

PASEO CARINA

91915

1 WINTER LN
2 CROWN LN
3 CHAMPION LN
4 VICTORY LN
5 ATHENS RD
6 SILVER MEDAL RD

ARCO TRAINING CTR (US OLYMPIC TRAINING CTR)

SEE 1332 MAP

RAND M^cNALLY

A B C D E F G H J

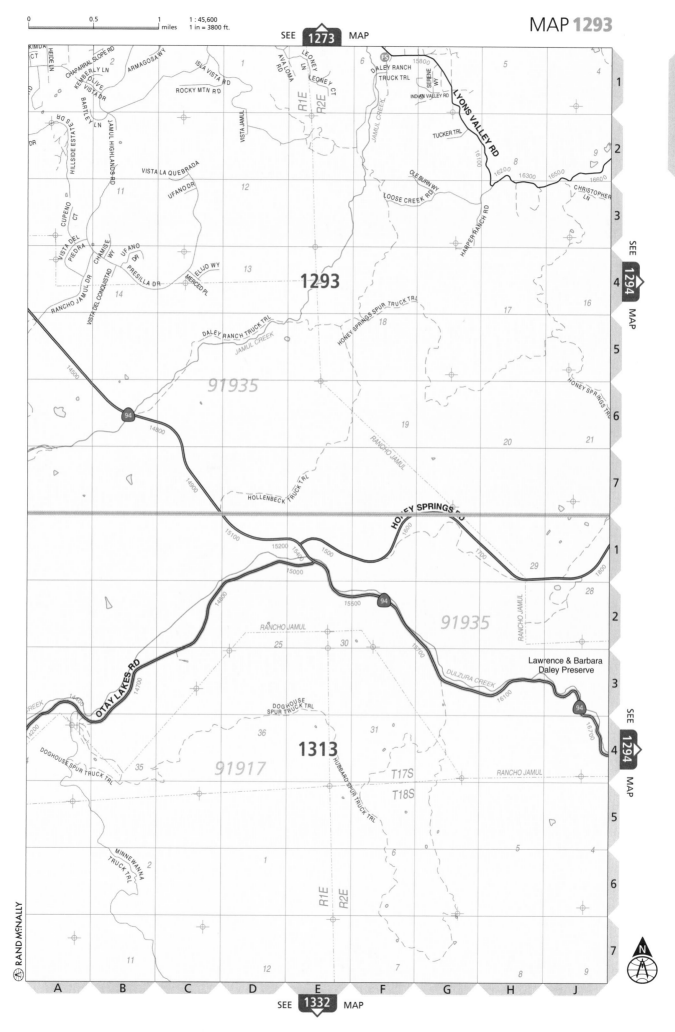

MAP **1293**

SAN DIEGO CO.

0   0.5   1
miles
1 : 45,600
1 in = 3800 ft.

SEE 1273 MAP

KIMDA CT
HEIDEN LN
CHAPARRAL SLOPE RD
KEMBERLY LN
OLIVE
VISTA DR
BARTLEY LN
ARMAGOSA WY
ISLA VISTA RD
ROCKY MTN RD
VISTA JAMUL
R1E
R2E
AVALOMA RD
LEONEY LN
LEONEY CT
DALEY RANCH TRUCK TRL
FS
15800
SERENE WY
INDIAN VALLEY RD
LYONS VALLEY RD
TUCKER TRL
16100
16200
16300
18500
16600
8
9
4
5
6
1
2

JAMUL HIGHLANDS RD
JAMUL CREEK
OLE BURN WY
LOOSE CREEK RD
HARPER RANCH RD
CHRISTOPHER LN
11
12
VISTA LA QUEBRADA
UFANO DR
3

HILLSIDE ESTATES DR
DR
CUPENO CT
VISTA DEL PIEDRA
RANCHO JAMUL DR
VISTA DEL CONQUISTAD
CHAMISE WY
UFANO DR
PRESILLA DR
ELIJO WY
MERCED PL
13
14
1293
HONEY SPRINGS SPUR TRUCK TRL
18
17
16
4
5

DALEY RANCH TRUCK TRL
JAMUL CREEK
91935
94
14500
14800
14900
HONEY SPRINGS TRL
6
7

19
20
21
RANCHO JAMUL

HOLLENBECK TRUCK TRL
15100
HONEY SPRINGS RD
1600
1700
1800
1

15200
1540
1500
15000
29
28
1

14800
15400
94
15500
91935
RANCHO JAMUL
2

OTAY LAKES RD
14900
14700
RANCHO JAMUL
25
30
15700
Lawrence & Barbara Daley Preserve
DULZURA CREEK
16100
94
16700
3

CREEK
14400
4200
DOGHOUSE SPUR TRUCK TRL
DOGHOUSE SPUR TRUCK TRL
36
31
1313
HUBBARD SPUR TRUCK TRL
T17S
T18S
RANCHO JAMUL
4

35
91917
5

MINNEWANNA TRUCK TRL
2
1
R1E
R2E
6
6
5
4
6

11
12
7
8
9
7

A B C D E F G H J

RAND MCNALLY

SEE 1294 MAP

SEE 1294 MAP

SEE 1332 MAP

N

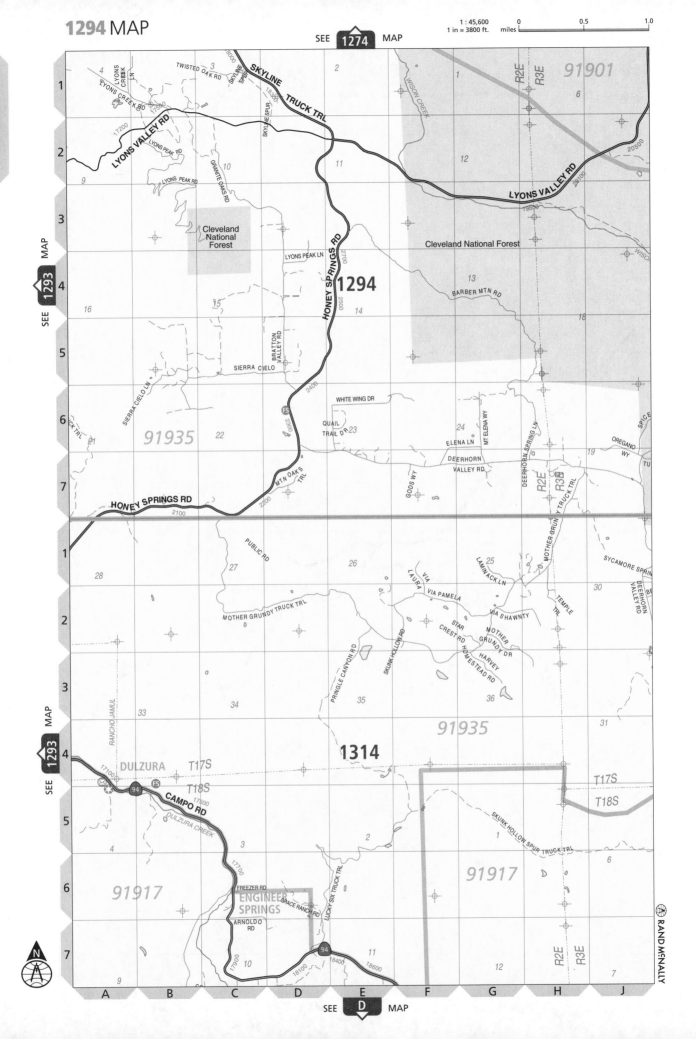

SAN DIEGO CO.

SEE **1274** MAP

SEE **1293** MAP

SEE **1293** MAP

LYONS CREEK
LYONS CREEK RD
TWISTED OAK RD
SKYLINE SPUR
SKYLINE TRUCK TRL
SKYLINE SPUR
LYONS VALLEY RD
LYONS PEAK RD
LYONS PEAK RD
GRANITE OAKS RD
91901
WISON CREEK
R2E R3E
LYONS VALLEY RD

Cleveland
National
Forest

LYONS PEAK LN
HONEY SPRINGS RD
1294
Cleveland National Forest
BARBER MTN RD
WISON

4
3
2
1
9
10
11
12
6
13
14
18
15
16

BRATTON VALLEY RD
SIERRA CIELO
SIERRA CIELO LN
FS
WHITE WING DR
QUAIL TRAIL DR
ELENA LN
MT ELENA WY
DEERHORN VALLEY RD
DEERHORN SPRING LN
GODS WY
MTN OAKS TRL
OREGANO WY
SPICE
TU
MOTHER GRUNDY TRUCK TRL
R2E R3E

21
22
23
24
19
91935

HONEY SPRINGS RD

PUBLIC RD
MOTHER GRUNDY TRUCK TRL
PRINGLE CANYON RD
SKUNK HOLLOW RD
VIA LAURA
VIA PAMELA
VIA SHAWNTY
STAR CREST RD
LAMINACK LN
MOTHER GRUNDY DR
HARVEY HOMESTEAD RD
TEMPLE TRL
SYCAMORE SPRING
DEERHORN VALLEY RD

28
27
26
25
30
33
34
35
36
31
91935

RANCHO JAMUL
DULZURA
T17S
T18S
FS
94
CAMPO RD
1314
T17S
T18S
SKUNK HOLLOW SPUR TRUCK TRL

DULZURA CREEK
FREEZER RD
GRACE RANCH RD
ENGINEER SPRINGS
ARNOLDO RD
LUCKY SIX TRUCK TRL
94

4
3
2
1
6
91917
91917

9
10
11
12
7

R2E R3E

RAND MCNALLY

A B C D E F G H J

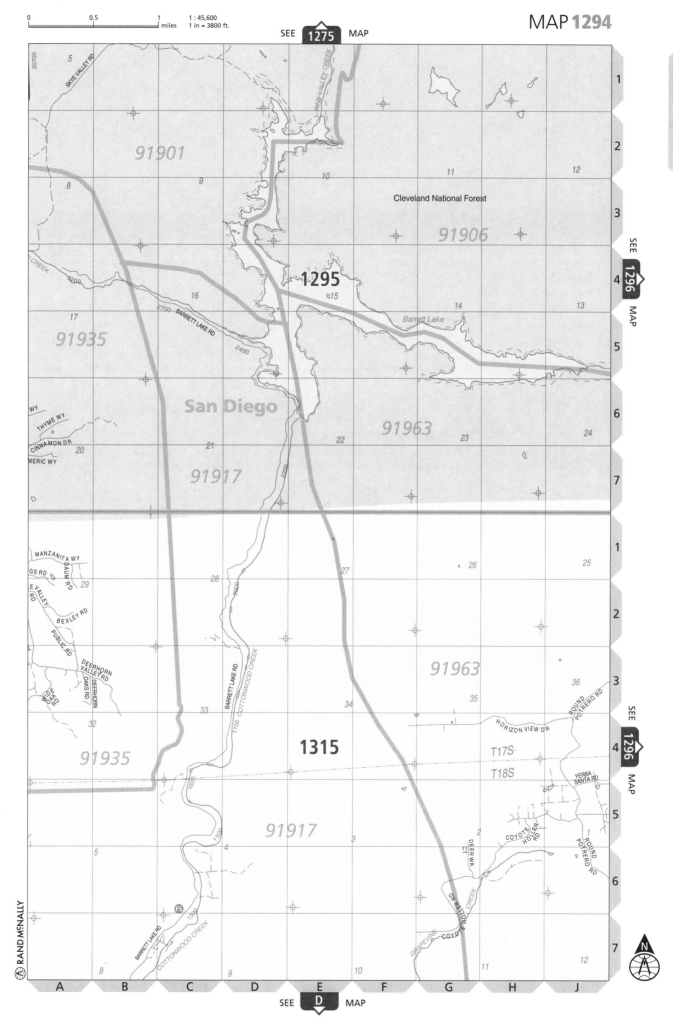

MAP **1294**

SAN DIEGO CO.

SEE **1275** MAP

0   0.5   1   1 : 45,600
miles   1 in = 3800 ft.

20700   5   SKYE VALLEY RD

91901

8   9   10   11   12

Cleveland National Forest

91906

SEE **1296** MAP

1295

I CREEK   3200   16   2700   BARRETT LAKE RD   15   14   13

17   Barrett Lake

91935   2400

WY   THYME WY   San Diego   91963

CINNAMON DR   20   21   22   23   24

MERIC WY

91917   2200

MANZANITA WY   DAUM RD   26   25

GS RD   29   28   27

LE VALLEY RD   BEXLEY RD   2400

PUBLIC RD   91963

DEERHORN VALLEY RD   OAKS RD   DEERHORN

DE   LK   BARRETT LAKE RD   COTTONWOOD CREEK   36   ROUND POTRERO RD

WOLK RD   33   1700   34   35   HORIZON VIEW DR

32   **1315**   T17S   SEE **1296** MAP

91935   T18S   YERBA SANTA RD

1600   91917   COYOTE HOLLE... RD   ROUND POTRERO RD

5   1500   4   3   DEER WK   CT

FS   1300

BARRETT LAKE RD   COTTONWOOD CREEK   GRAPEVINE   COYOTE HOLLER RD

8   9   10   11   12

RAND M?NALLY

A   B   C   D   E   F   G   H   J

SEE **D** MAP

N

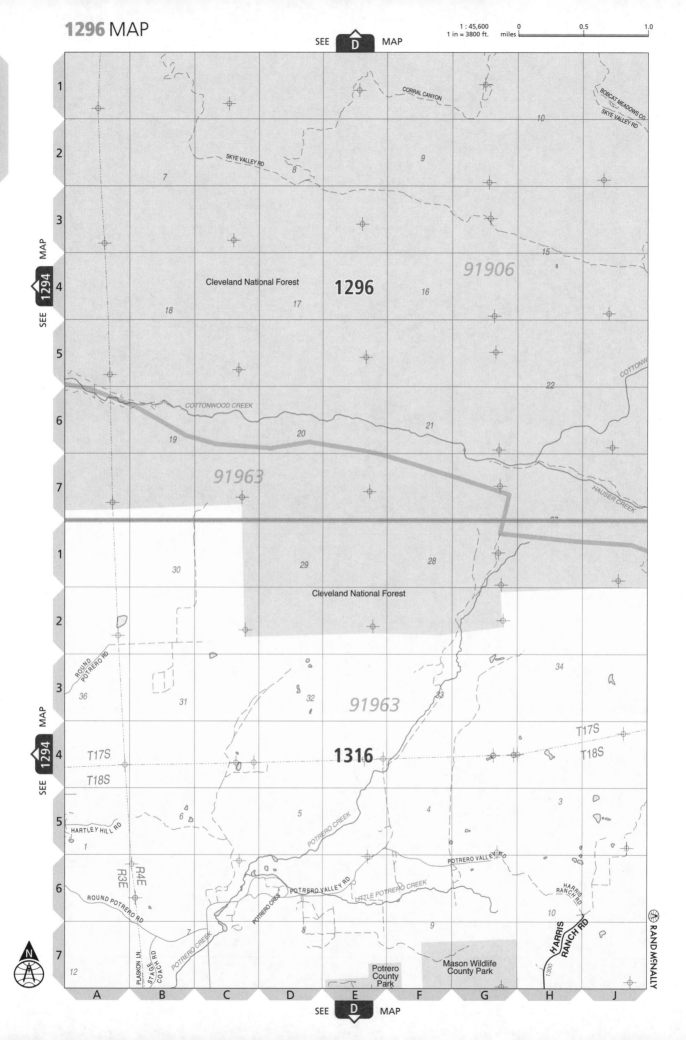

SAN DIEGO CO.

1 : 45,600
1 in = 3800 ft.   miles
0   0.5   1.0

SEE ◇1294◇ MAP

Cleveland National Forest

1296

91906

CORRAL CANYON

BOBCAT MEADOWS CG
SKYE VALLEY RD

SKYE VALLEY RD

7

8

9

10

18

17

16

15

COTTONWOOD CREEK

19

20

21

22

COTTONW

91963

HAUSER CREEK

27

SEE ◇1294◇ MAP

30

29

28

Cleveland National Forest

ROUND POTRERO RD

36

31

32

91963

33

34

T17S
T18S

T17S
T18S

1316

T17S
T18S

HARTLEY HILL RD

1

6

5

4

3

R4E
R3E

ROUND POTRERO RD

POTRERO CREEK

POTRERO CREEK

POTRERO CRES

POTRERO VALLEY RD

POTRERO VALLEY RD

LITTLE POTRERO CREEK

8

9

10

HARRIS RANCH RD

12

PLASKON LN

STAGE COACH RD

Potrero County Park

Mason Wildlife County Park

1300

HARRIS RANCH RD

RAND M^cNALLY

N

MAP **1296**

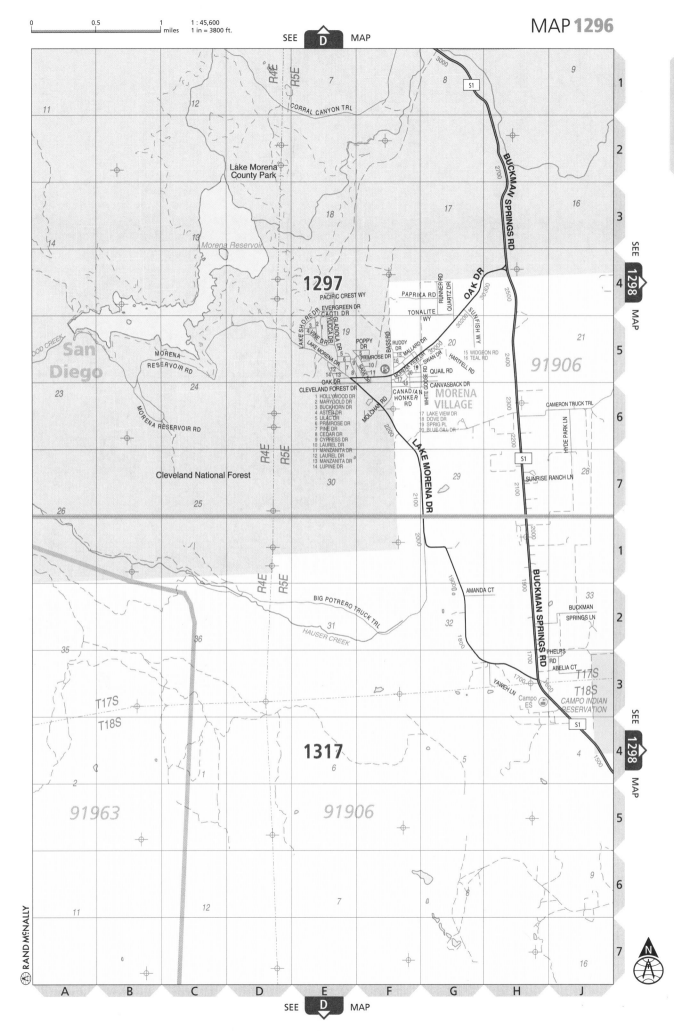

0   0.5   1   1 : 45,600
miles   1 in = 3800 ft.

R4E R5E   7   8   S1   9

CORRAL CANYON TRL   3000   1

11   12   2

Lake Morena
County Park   17   16   3

18   2700   BUCKMAN SPRINGS RD

14   13   Morena Reservoir   OAK DR   SEE 1298 MAP   4

WOOD CREEK   1297   PACIFIC CREST WY   RUNNER RD QUARTZ DR   3000   2500
San   PAPRIKA RD
Diego   EVERGREEN DR   TONALITE WY   3030
CACTI DR   302000   SUNFISH WY   21
GLADIOLA DR   19   20   WIDGEON RD   91906   5
LAKE SHORE DR   YUCCA DR   POPPY   15 TEAL RD
MORENA   VINE DR   DR   BASS RD   16   2400
RESERVOIR RD   LAKE MORENA DR   PRIMROSE DR   RUDDY   15 MALLARD DR   HARTFELL RD
24   OAK DR   DR   SWAN DR   QUAIL RD
23   CLEVELAND FOREST DR   SIGER RD   CANVASBACK DR   2300   CAMERON TRUCK TRL
1 HOLLYWOOD DR   MOLCHAN RD   CANADIAN   MORENA   6
2 MARYGOLD DR   HONKER   VILLAGE   HYDE PARK LN
3 BUCKHORN DR   2200   RD   17 LAKE VIEW DR
4 ASTER DR   18 DOVE DR   S1
5 LILAC DR   LAKE MORENA DR   19 SPRIG PL   28
6 PRIMROSE DR   20 BLUE GILL DR   SUNRISE RANCH LN   2100
7 PINE DR   2200
8 CEDAR DR   Cleveland National Forest   29
9 CYPRESS DR   30
10 LAUREL DR   25
11 MANZANITA DR   2100
12 LAUREL DR
13 MANZANITA DR   26
14 LUPINE DR

R4E R5E

2000   1

BIG POTRERO TRUCK TRL   1900   AMANDA CT   2000   BUCKMAN SPRINGS RD
R4E R5E   33   2
31   32   BUCKMAN SPRINGS LN
35   36   HAUSER CREEK   1800
PHELPS
1800   RD
1700   ABELIA CT   T17S   3
T17S   1700   T18S
T18S   YAWEH LN   1600   CAMPO INDIAN
Campo   RESERVATION   SEE 1298 MAP
L ES   S1
1317   6   1500   4
2   1   5   4
91963   91906   5
11   12   7   9   6

RAND McNALLY   16   7

A   B   C   D   E   F   G   H   J

N

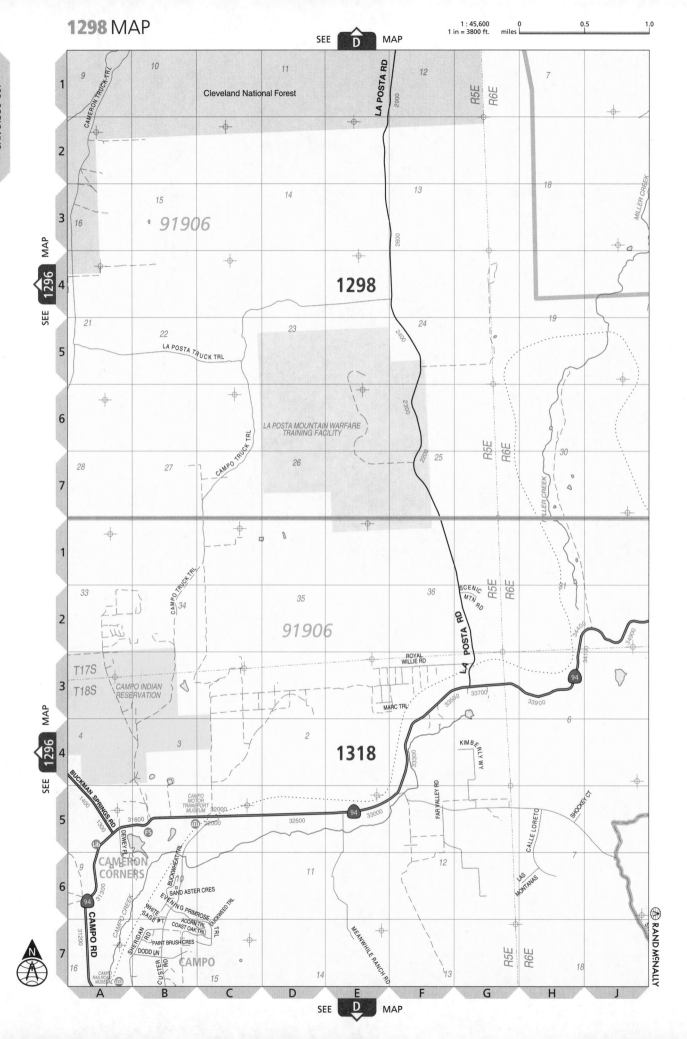

SAN DIEGO CO.

1 : 45,600
1 in = 3800 ft.
miles
0   0.5   1.0

SEE **D** MAP

Cleveland National Forest

9   10   11   LA POSTA RD   12   R5E R6E   7

2900

SEE **1296** MAP

15   14   13   18   MILLER CREEK

91906

16   2600

1298

21   22   23   24   19

LA POSTA TRUCK TRL   2400

6   LA POSTA MOUNTAIN WARFARE
TRAINING FACILITY   2300   R5E R6E   30

CAMPO TRUCK TRL   2200

28   27   26   25

33   34   35   36   SCENIC
MTN RD   R5E R6E   31   3440 0

91906   LA POSTA RD   3410 0   3480 0

CAMPO TRUCK TRL   ROYAL
WILLIE RD

T17S
T18S   CAMPO INDIAN
RESERVATION   94

MARC TRL   3350 0   33700   33900   6

4   3   2   **1318**   33300   KIMBERLY WY

BUCKMAN SPRINGS RD   1400

1300   CAMPO MOTOR
TRANSPORT
MUSEUM   32000   FAR VALLEY RD   CALLE LORETO   SHOCKEY CT

31600   32000   32500   94   33000   7

DEWEY PL   FS   Lib   LAS
MONTANAS

CAMERON
CORNERS   9   BUCKWHEAT TRL   10   SAND ASTER CRES   11   12

31300   94   EVENING PRIMROSE   BUCKWEED TRL

CAMPO CREEK   31300   WHITE
SAGE PT   ACORN TRL
COAST OAK TRL

CAMPO RD   31200   SHERIDAN
RD   CUSTER
RD   DODD LN   PAINT BRUSH CRES   MEANWHILE RANCH RD

16   CAMPO
RAILROAD
MUSEUM   **CAMPO**   15   14   13   R5E R6E   18

N

RAND M?NALLY

SEE **D** MAP

A   B   C   D   E   F   G   H   J

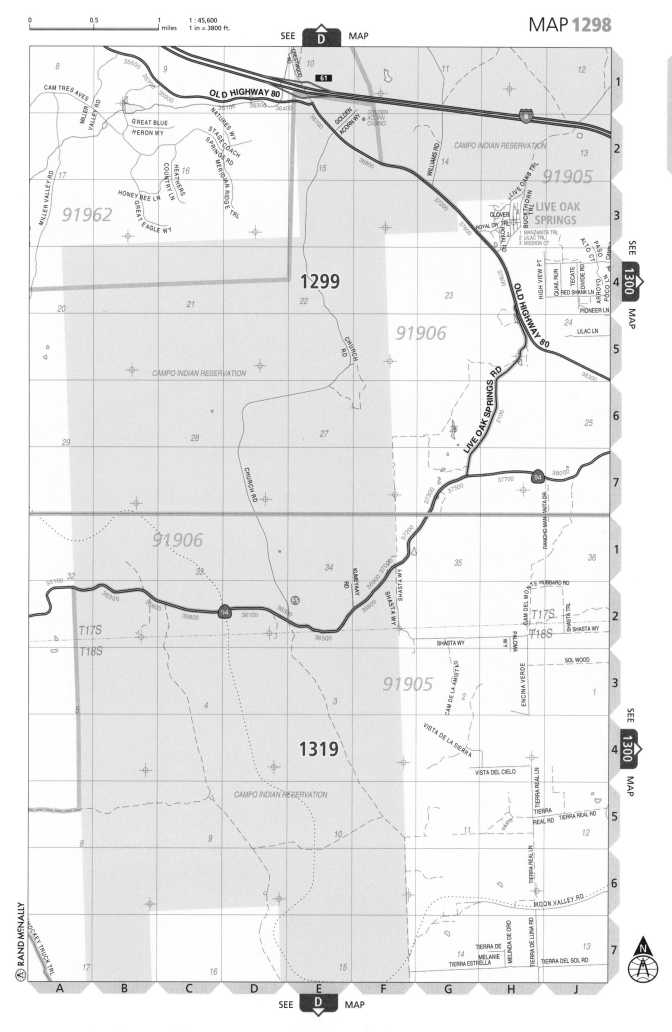

MAP **1298**

SAN DIEGO CO.

1 : 45,600
1 in = 3800 ft.

0   0.5   1
miles

SEE **D** MAP

SEE **1300** MAP

SEE **1300** MAP

SEE **D** MAP

8

9

10

11

12

CAM TRES AVES

MILLER VALLEY RD

GREAT BLUE HERON WY

NATURES WY

STAGECOACH SPRINGS RD

MERIDIAN RIDGE TRL

OLD HIGHWAY 80

35600
35700
35900
36100
36300
36400
36600
36700

61

8

GOLDEN ACORN WY

GOLDEN ACORN CASINO

WILLIAMS RD

CAMPO INDIAN RESERVATION

13

17

16

HEATHERS COUNTRY LN

HONEY BEE LN

GREAT EAGLE WY

91962

36800

15

14

37200

37600

LIVE OAKS TRL

BUCKTHORN TRL

CLOVER

ROYAL DR TRL

OLD ROYAL DR

91905

LIVE OAK SPRINGS

1 MANZANITA TRL
2 LILAC TRL
3 MISSION CT

PASO ALTO CT

HIGH VIEW PT

QUAIL RUN

TECATE

RED SHANK LN

DIVIDE RD

ARROYO

POCO LN

PIONEER LN

LILAC LN

1299

20

21

22

23

24

CHURCH RD

37800

OLD HIGHWAY 80

38300

91906

CAMPO INDIAN RESERVATION

29

28

27

26

25

CHURCH RD

LIVE OAK SPRINGS RD

2100

94

37300
37500
37700
38000

T17S
T18S

35100
35300
35600
35800
36100
36300

94

FS

KUMEYAAY RD

91906

32

33

34

35

36

SHASTA WY

36800 37000

36900

36500

SHASTA WY

CAM DEL MONTE

HUBBARD RD

SHASTA TRL

T17S
T18S

SHASTA WY

RANCHO MANZANITA DR

37200

SHASTA WY

PALOMA WY

SOL WOOD

ENCINA VERDE

5

4

3

2

1

CAM DE LA AMISTAD

VISTA DE LA SIERRA

91905

10

11

12

VISTA DEL CIELO

TIERRA REAL LN

TIERRA REAL RD

TIERRA REAL RD

1319

CAMPO INDIAN RESERVATION

TIERRA REAL LN

MOON VALLEY RD

MELINDA DE ORO

TIERRA DE LUNA RD

8

9

10

11

12

13

HOCKEY TRUCK TRL

17

16

15

14

TIERRA DE MELANIE

TIERRA ESTRELLA

TIERRA DEL SOL RD

RAND M^cNALLY

A   B   C   D   E   F   G   H   J

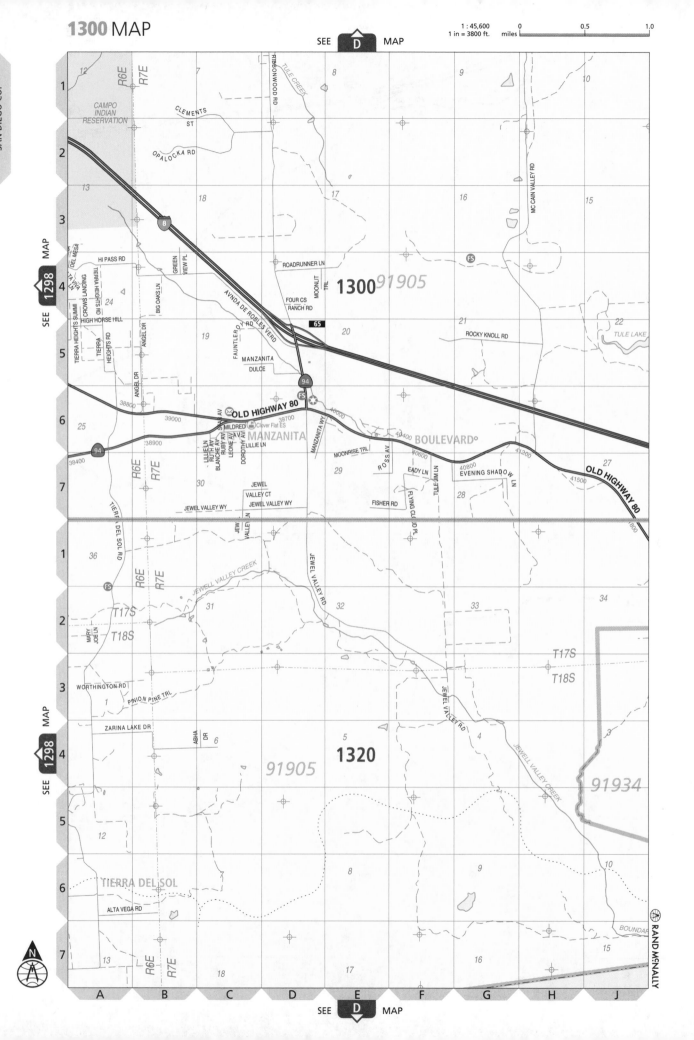

SEE **D** MAP

1 : 45,600
1 in = 3800 ft.

SAN DIEGO CO.

CAMPO INDIAN RESERVATION

R6E | R7E

CLEMENTS ST

OPALOCKA RD

8

RIBBONWOOD RD

TULE CREEK

SEE 1298 MAP

HI PASS RD

DEL MESA

TIERRA HEIGHTS RD

CROWS LANDING

TIERRA HEIGHTS SUMMI

HIGH HORSE HILL

GREEN VIEW PL

BIG OAKS LN

ANGEL DR

TIERRA HEIGHTS RD

TIERRA HEIGHTS RD

ANGEL DR

ROADRUNNER LN

MOONLIT TRL

1300 *91905*

FS

FOUR CS RANCH RD

AVNDA DE ROBLES VERD

FAUNTLEROY RD

65

MANZANITA DULCE

94

MC CAIN VALLEY RD

ROCKY KNOLL RD

TULE LAKE

FS

OLD HIGHWAY 80

38800

39000

MILDRED

Clover Flat ES

39700

MANZANITA

LILLIE LN

RUTH AV

BLANCHE AV

LEONE AV

RUBY AV

DOROTHY AV

LILLIE LN

MANZANITA WY

MOONRISE TRL

ROSS AV

40000

40400

BOULEVARD

38900

94

38400

R6E | R7E

JEWEL VALLEY CT

JEWEL VALLEY WY

JEWEL VALLEY WY

JEW VALLEY

EADY LN

FLYING CLOUD PL

FISHER RD

TULE JIM LN

40600

40800

EVENING SHADOW LN

41200

41500

OLD HIGHWAY 80

9800

TIERRA DEL SOL RD

FS

JEWELL VALLEY CREEK

T17S
T18S

MARY JOE LN

JEWEL VALLEY RD

T17S
T18S

WORTHINGTON RD

PINION PINE TRL

ZARINA LAKE DR

ABHA DR

JEWEL VALLEY RD

1320

91905

JEWELL VALLEY CREEK

91934

TIERRA DEL SOL

ALTA VEGA RD

BOUNDARY

N

SEE **D** MAP

A | B | C | D | E | F | G | H | J

RAND McNALLY

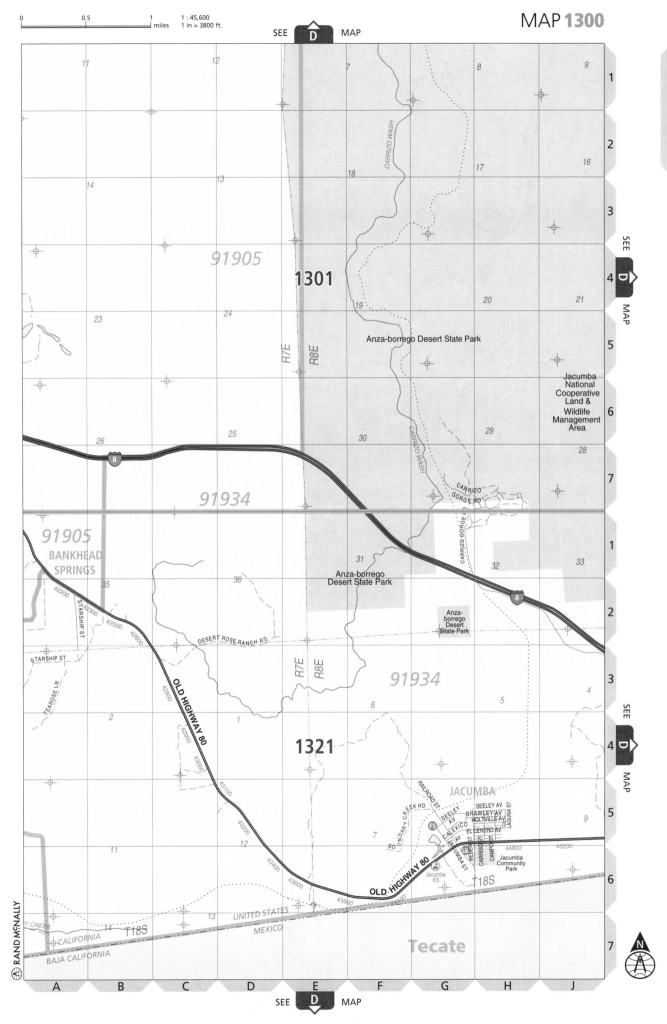

MAP **1300**

SAN DIEGO CO.

0   0.5   1
miles
1 : 45,600
1 in = 3800 ft.

SEE D MAP

11   12   7   8   9   1

18   17   16   2

14   13   3

91905   23   24   19   20   21   4

1301

Anza-borrego Desert State Park   5

R7E   R8E

Jacumba National Cooperative Land & Wildlife Management Area   6

26   25   30   29   28   7

CARRIZO WASH

91934   CARRIZO GORGE RD   1

91905
BANKHEAD SPRINGS   31   32   33

35   36   8   2

42200   42300   42500   42600
STARSHIP ST   Anza-borrego Desert State Park   Anza-borrego Desert State Park

STARSHIP ST   DESERT ROSE RANCH RD   R7E   R8E

TEAROSE LN   42800   91934   3

OLD HIGHWAY 80   42900   1   6   5   4

43000   2

43100   **1321**   4

RAILROAD ST   JACUMBA

43200   7   SEELEY AV   9

BOUNDARY CREEK RD   BRAWLEY AV   LAGUNA ST
43400   12   SEELEY AV   HOLTVILLE AV
CALEXICO AV   EL CENTRO AV   5

11   OLD HIGHWAY 80   HEBER ST   CARRISO ST   CAMPO ST   44800   45200
JACUMBA ST   Jacumba Community Park
43600   Jacumba ES   T18S   6

44100
43900   44100

13   UNITED STATES
14   T18S   MEXICO   7
Y CREEK   CALIFORNIA
BAJA CALIFORNIA   Tecate

A   B   C   D   E   F   G   H   J

SEE D MAP

SEE D MAP

N

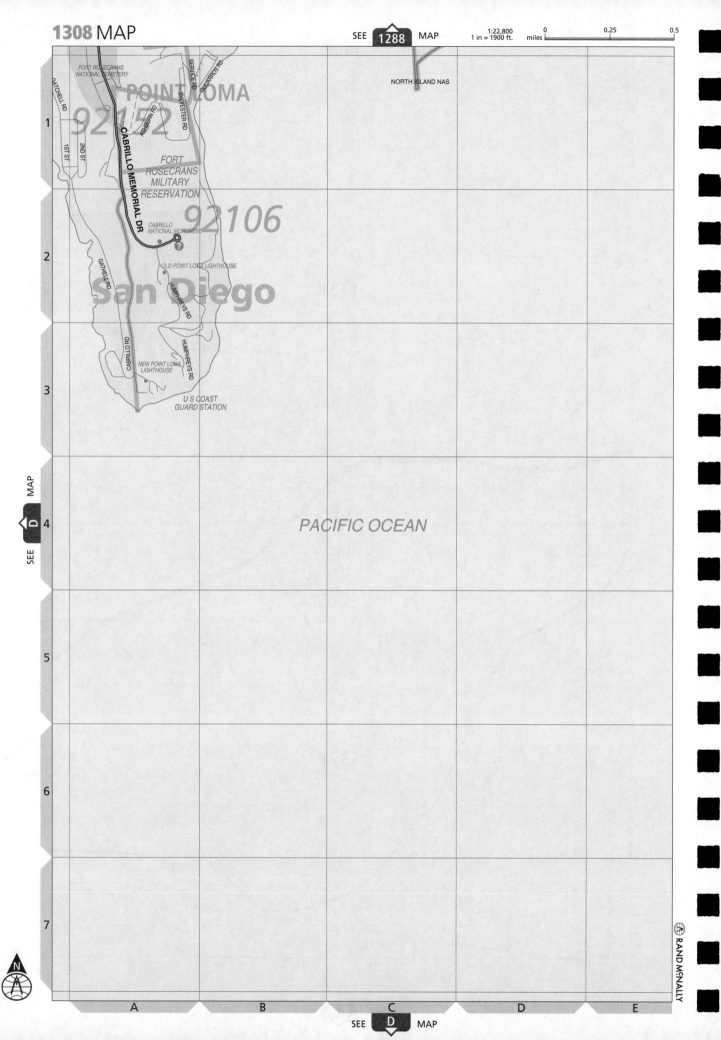

SAN DIEGO CO.

1:22,800
1 in = 1900 ft.

0   0.25   0.5
miles

POINT LOMA

92152

FORT ROSECRANS
NATIONAL CEMETERY

SERVICE RD

RICHARDS RD

NORTH ISLAND NAS

GATCHELL RD

1ST ST

2ND ST

ASHBURN RD

SYLVESTER RD

CABRILLO MEMORIAL DR

FORT
ROSECRANS
MILITARY
RESERVATION

92106

CABRILLO
NATIONAL MONUMENT

San Diego

OLD POINT LOMA LIGHTHOUSE

GATHELL RD

HUMPHREYS RD

CABRILLO RD

HUMPHREYS RD

NEW POINT LOMA
LIGHTHOUSE

U S COAST
GUARD STATION

SEE D MAP

PACIFIC OCEAN

SEE D MAP

RAND McNALLY

A   B   C   D   E

1 2 3 4 5 6 7

MAP **1308**

0   0.25   0.5   1:22,800
└─────┴─────┘ miles 1 in = 1900 ft.

SEE 1288 MAP

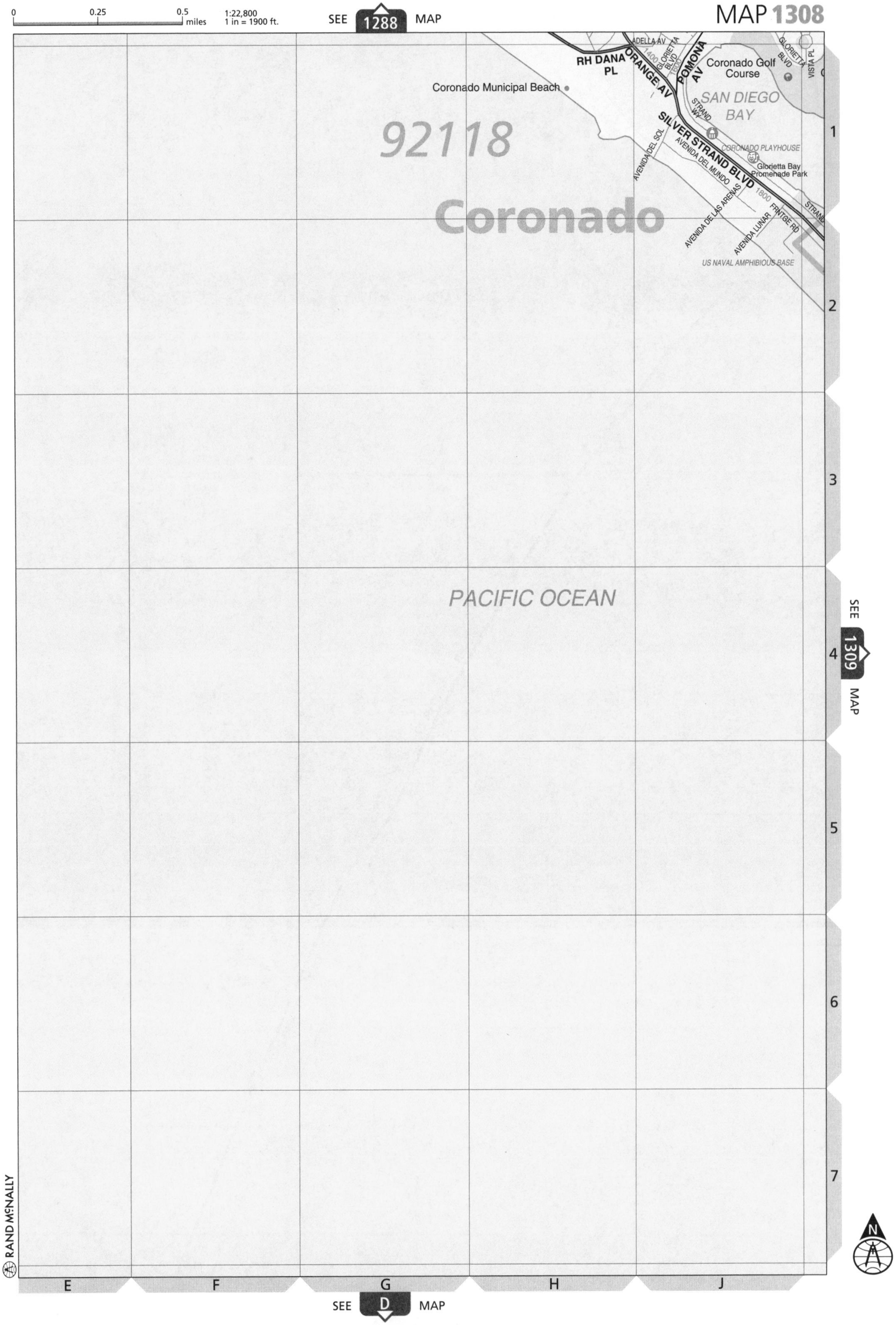

RH DANA PL

ORANGE AV

POMONA AV

ADELLA AV

Coronado Golf Course

GLORIETTA BLVD

VISTA PL

Coronado Municipal Beach

SAN DIEGO BAY

92118

SILVER STRAND BLVD

AVENIDA DEL SOL

AVENIDA DEL MUNDO

STRAND WY

CORONADO PLAYHOUSE

Glorietta Bay Promenade Park

1800

STRAND

Coronado

AVENIDA DE LAS ARENAS

AVENIDA LUNAR

FRNTGE RD

US NAVAL AMPHIBIOUS BASE

PACIFIC OCEAN

SEE 1309 MAP

1

2

3

4

5

6

7

RAND M?NALLY

E   F   G   H   J

SEE D MAP

SEE 1289 MAP

1:22,800
1 in = 1900 ft.
miles
0   0.25   0.5

SAN DIEGO CO.

GLORIETTA BLVD

VISTA PL

Coronado Golf
Course

HOUSE

ta Bay
ade Park

Glorietta Bay
Promenade Park

INCHON RD

ENIWETOK RD

KWAJALEIN RD

BOUGAINVILLE RD

ENIWETOK RD

TULAGI RD

Coronado

92135

ATTU RD

MAKIN RD

GUADALCANAL RD

RIO RD

BOUGAINVILLE RD

TULAGI RD

MUNDA RD

FRNTGE RD

STRAND WY

RENDOVA RD

TARAWA RD

GUADALCANAL RD

VELLA LA VELLA RD

TULAGI RD

RENDOVA CRES

RENDOVA RD

BASE

FRNTGE RD

2000

SAN DIEGO BAY

75

2200

SILVER STRAND BLVD

U S NAVAL
AMPHIBIOUS
BASE

92118

2200

SEE 1308 MAP

NAVY
YACHT
CLUB

PALAU RD

PALAU RD

OKINAWA RD

LEYTE RD

PALAU
CIR

SAIPAN RD

LEYTE RD

WAKE RD

3000

3400

PACIFIC OCEAN

Silver
Strand
ES

DA NANG DR

LEYTE RD

ATTU AV

INCHON CT

SILVER STRAND BAY

75

4000

N

BAY RD

CORONADO BAY RD

SS

RAND McNALLY

	A	B	C	D	E
1					
2					
3					
4					
5					
6					
7					

SEE 1329 MAP

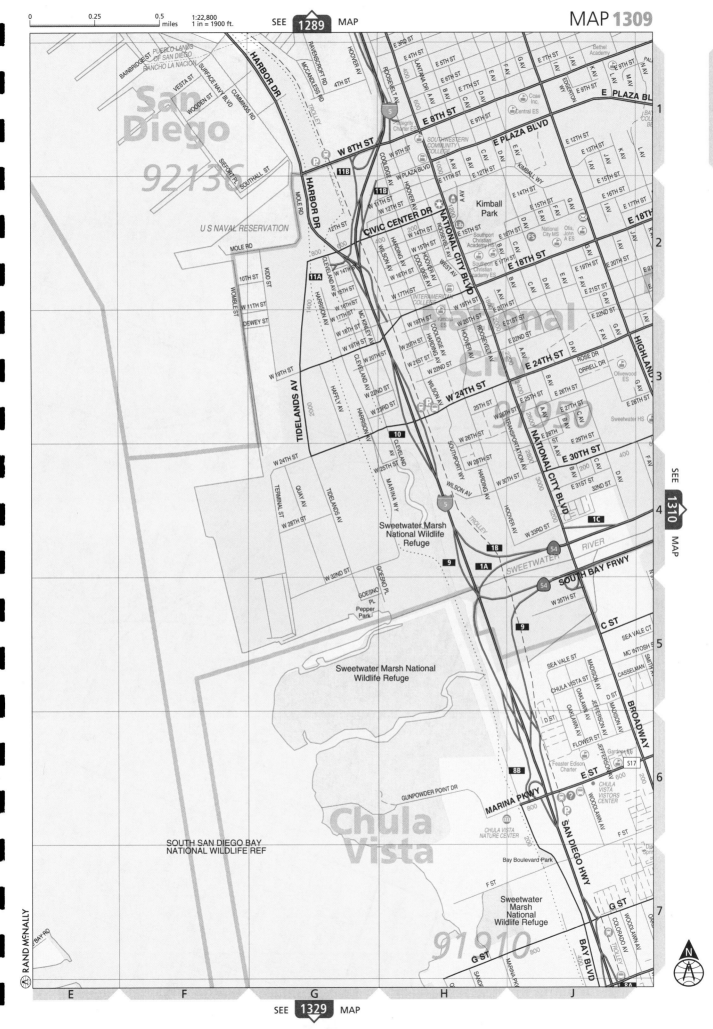

0   0.25   0.5
miles
1:22,800
1 in = 1900 ft.

San Diego
92136

PUEBLO LANDS
OF SAN DIEGO
BAINBRIDGE ST
RANCHO LA NACION

HARBOR DR

VESTA ST
WOODEN ST
CUMMINGS RD
SURFACE NAVY BLVD

SIEFORT PL
SOUTHALL ST

RAVENSCROFT RD
MCCANDLESS RD
4TH ST
HOOVER AV
ROOSEVELT AV

E 3RD ST
E 4TH ST
E 5TH ST
E 6TH ST
E 7TH ST

E 9TH ST
Bethel
Academy

E PLAZA BL

Ccae
Inc.
Central ES

E PLAZA BLVD

W 8TH ST
E 8TH ST
E 9TH ST
Integrity
Charter ES

SOUTHWESTERN
COMMUNITY
COLLEGE

E 12TH ST
KIMBALL WY
E 13TH ST
E 15TH ST
E 16TH ST

W PLAZA BLVD
W 11TH ST
W 12TH ST

CIVIC CENTER DR

NATIONAL CITY BLVD

Kimball
Park

Southport
Christian
Academy-HS
Southport
Christian
Academy ES

E 18TH ST

E 17TH ST

National
City MS
Otis,
John
A ES

W 14TH ST
W 15TH ST
WILSON AV
HARDING AV
COOLIDGE AV
HOOVER AV
W 16TH ST

W 17TH ST

INTER-AMERICAN
COLLEGE

National
City

91950

E 19TH ST
E 20TH ST
E 21ST ST
E 22ND ST

E 24TH ST

Kimball
ES

W 19TH ST
W 18TH ST
W 19TH ST
MC KINLEY AV
CLEVELAND AV
W 20TH ST
W 21ST ST
W 22ND ST

HARRISON AV
HAFFLY AV

W 24TH ST

ROSE DR
ORRELL DR

Olivewood
ES

E 27TH ST
E 28TH ST

HIGHLAND

TIDELANDS AV

W 19TH ST
W 22ND ST
W 23RD ST

25TH ST
E 25TH ST
E 26TH ST

Sweetwater HS

SOUTHPORT WY
WILSON AV
HARDING AV
HOOVER AV

TRANSPORTATION AV

E 29TH ST

E 30TH ST
E 31ST ST
32ND ST

W 24TH ST
W 25TH ST
CLEVELAND
MARINA WY

W 26TH ST
W 28TH ST
W 30TH ST

NATIONAL CITY BLVD

1C

W 28TH ST

TERMINAL ST
QUAY AV
TIDELANDS AV

GOESNO PL

W 32ND ST

Pepper
Park

Sweetwater Marsh
National Wildlife
Refuge

WILSON AV

TROLLEY

W 33RD ST

SOUTH BAY FRWY
54

SWEETWATER RIVER

SEE 1310 MAP

Sweetwater Marsh National
Wildlife Refuge

W 35TH ST

9

C ST

SEA VALE CT

MC INTOSH

SEA VALE ST
CHULA VISTA AV
MADISON AV
OAKLAWN AV
D ST
CASSELMAN

SMITH

BROADWAY

JEFFERSON AV
MADISON AV
OAKLAWN AV
FLOWER ST
JEFFERSON AV

Gardner ES
S17

D ST

Feaster Edison
Charter

E ST

600
200

GUNPOWDER POINT DR

MARINA PKWY

CHULA
VISTA
VISTORS
CENTER

WOODLAWN AV

Chula
Vista

CHULA VISTA
NATURE CENTER

SAN DIEGO HWY

F ST

Bay Boulevard Park

Sweetwater
Marsh
National
Wildlife Refuge

SOUTH SAN DIEGO BAY
NATIONAL WILDLIFE REF

BAY RD

RAND MCNALLY

91910

G ST

BAY BLVD

WOODLAWN AV
COLORADO AV
TROLLEY

G ST

8A

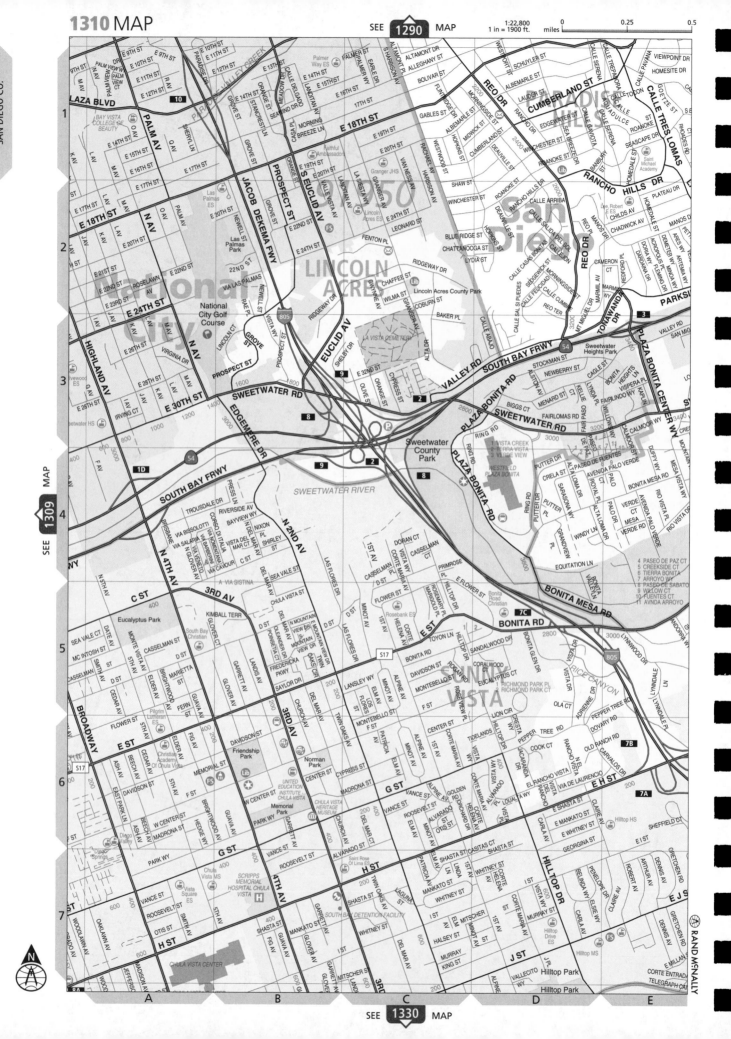

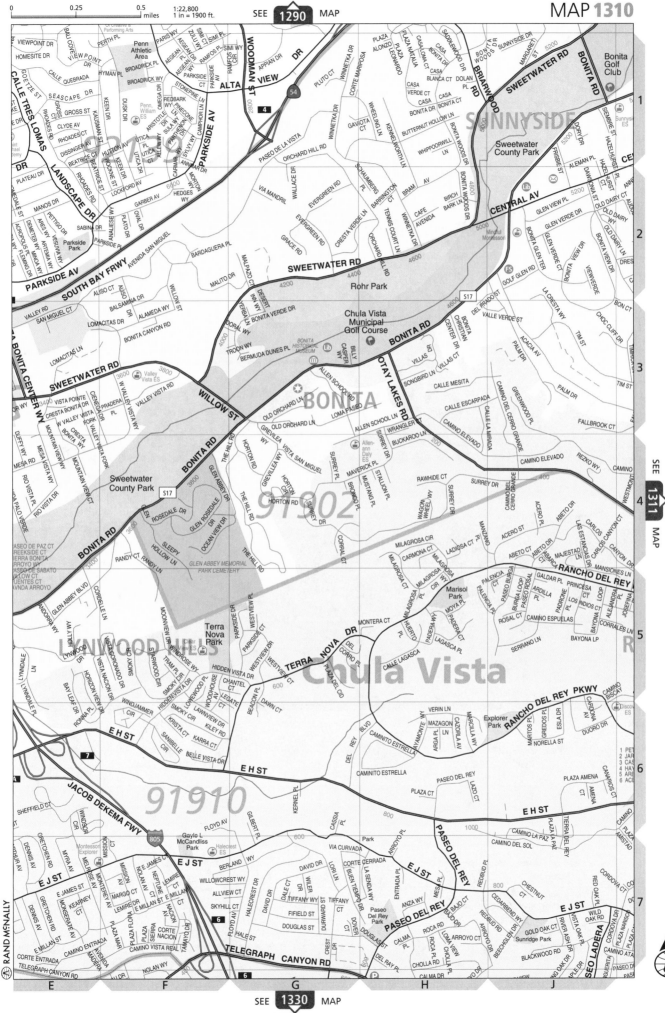

MAP 1310

SAN DIEGO CO.

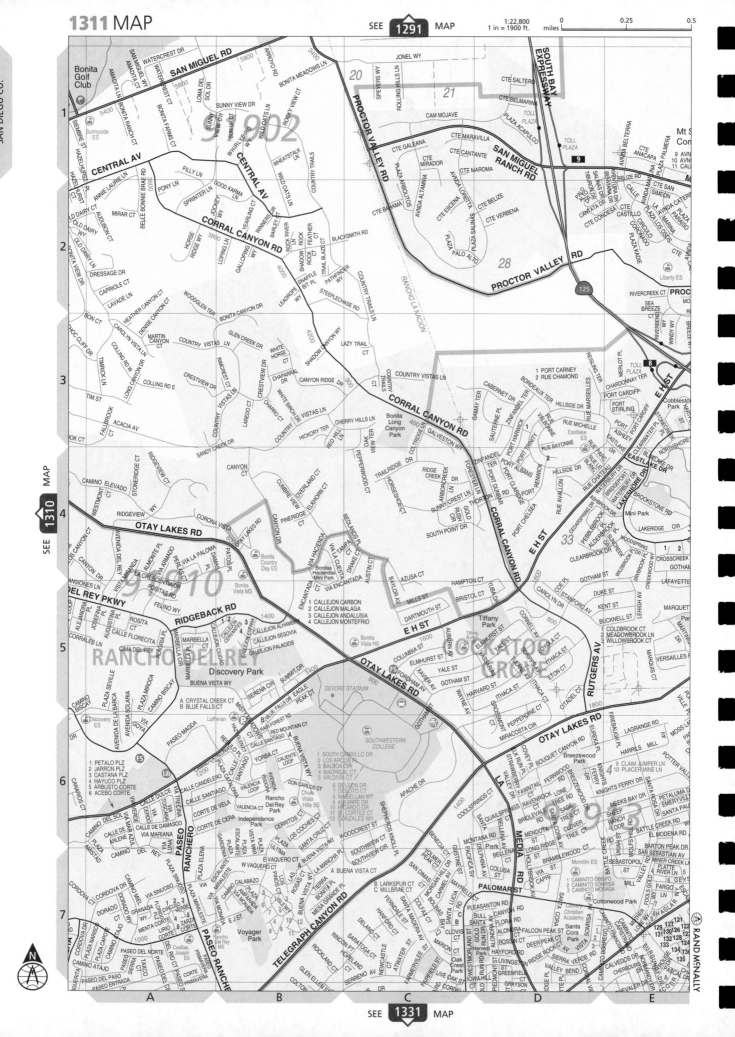

SEE 1291 MAP

1:22,800
1 in = 1900 ft.

SAN DIEGO CO.

SEE 1310 MAP

RAND McNALLY

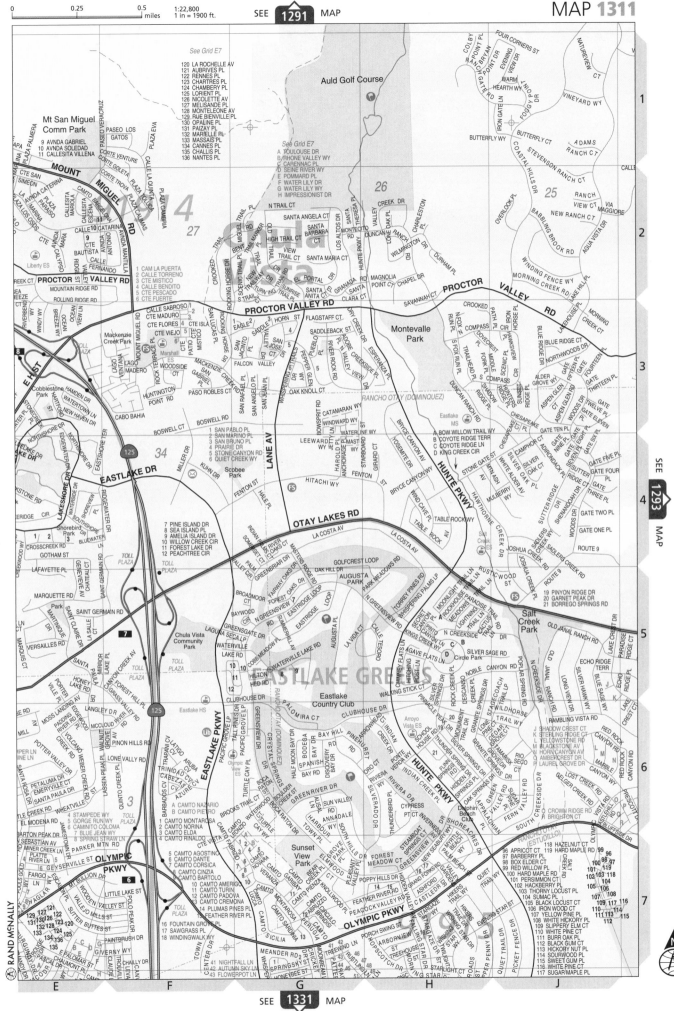

SEE 1309 MAP

1:22,800
1 in = 1900 ft.

miles   0   0.25   0.5

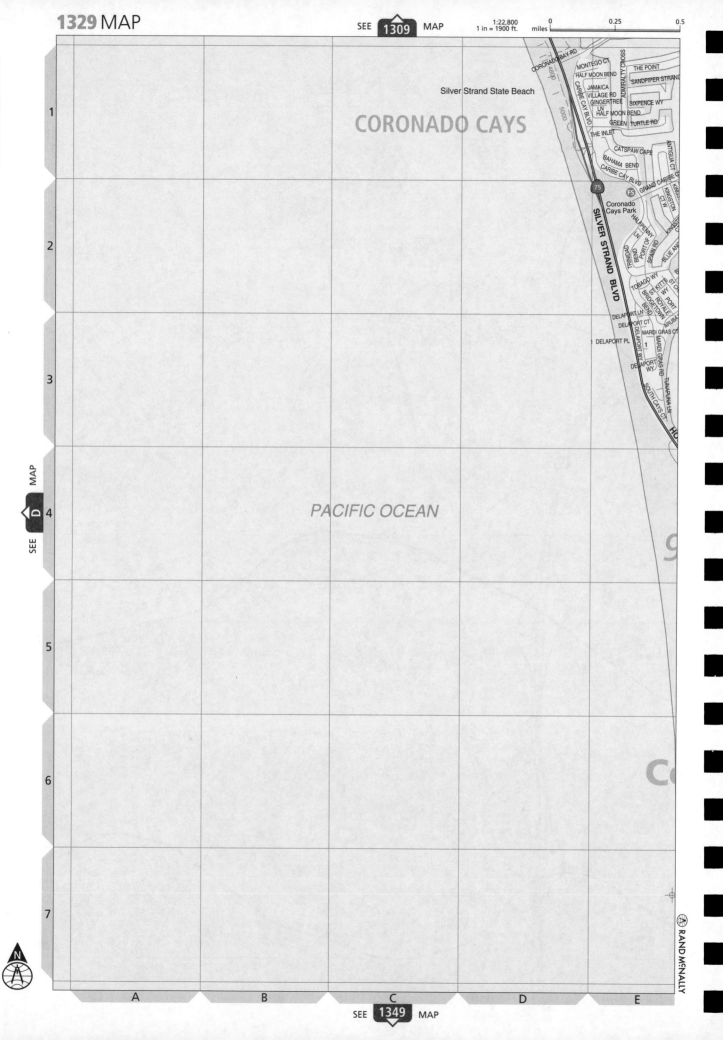

SAN DIEGO CO.

Silver Strand State Beach

CORONADO CAYS

CORONADOBAY RD

MONTEGO CT
HALF MOON BEND
JAMAICA
VILLAGE RD
GINGERTREE
LN
HALF MOON BEND
GREEN
THE INLET

THE POINT
SANDPIPER STRAND
SIXPENCE WY
TURTLE RD

CATSPAW CAPE
BAHAMA BEND
CARIBE CAY BLVD

ADMIRALTY CROSS

ANTIGUA CT

GRAND CARIBE C

75

Coronado
Cays Park

F5

KINGSTON
CT W

KINGSTO

SILVER STRAND BLVD

HALFPENNY
LN

PORT OF
SPAIN RD

BLUE AN

THRINL

BEND

TOBAGO WY
BRIDGETOWN
BRIDGE
BEND
PORT

ST KITTS
WY
ROYALE
PORT

ST CA

ARUBA

DELAPORT LN
DELAPORT CT
DELAPORT WY
1 DELAPORT PL
DELAPORT
WY

MARDI GRAS CT
MARDI GRAS RD
TUNAPUNA LN
SOUTH CAYS CT

1

9

SEE D MAP

PACIFIC OCEAN

Co

N

RAND MCNALLY

A   B   C   D   E

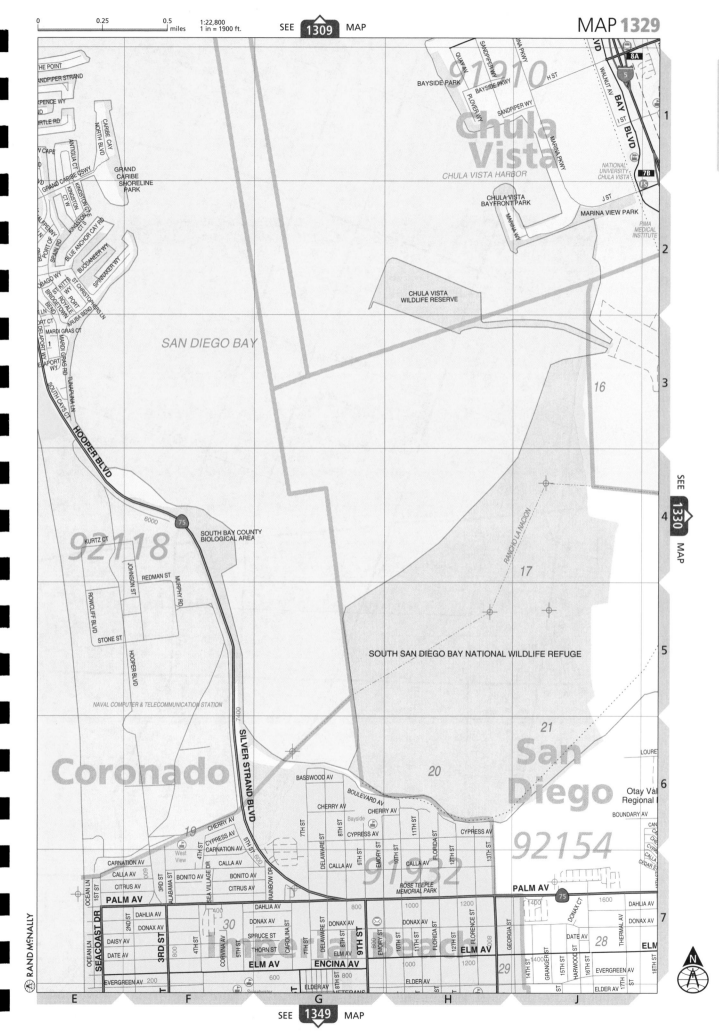

MAP **1329**

SEE 1309 MAP

SEE 1330 MAP

0   0.25   0.5   miles
1:22,800
1 in = 1900 ft.

Chula Vista
91910
BAYSIDE PARK
Chula Vista Harbor
CHULA VISTA BAYFRONT PARK
MARINA VIEW PARK
NATIONAL UNIVERSITY CHULA VISTA
PIMA MEDICAL INSTITUTE

GRAND CARIBE SHORELINE PARK

CHULA VISTA WILDLIFE RESERVE

SAN DIEGO BAY

HOOPER BLVD

92118

SOUTH BAY COUNTY BIOLOGICAL AREA

KURTZ CT
REDMAN ST
JOHNSON ST
ROWCLIFF BLVD
STONE ST
MURPHY RD
HOOPER BLVD

RANCHO LA NACION

SOUTH SAN DIEGO BAY NATIONAL WILDLIFE REFUGE

NAVAL COMPUTER & TELECOMMUNICATION STATION

SILVER STRAND BLVD

Coronado

San Diego

92154

Otay Valley Regional

BOUNDARY AV

92932

BASSWOOD AV
BOULEVARD AV
CHERRY AV   CHERRY AV
CYPRESS AV   CYPRESS AV
CARNATION AV
CALLA AV
BONITO AV   BONITO AV
CITRUS AV   CITRUS AV
CARNATION AV
CALLA AV
CITRUS AV
DELAWARE ST
EMORY ST
CALLA AV   CALLA AV
FLORIDA ST

ROSE TEEPLE MEMORIAL PARK

PALM AV

PALM AV 75

Bayside

West View

DAHLIA AV   DAHLIA AV   DAHLIA AV
DONAX AV   DONAX AV   DONAX AV   DONAX AV   DONAX AV
DAISY AV   SPRUCE ST
DATE AV   THORN ST   DATE AV
                                                ELDER AV
ELM AV   **ELM AV**   **ENCINA AV**   **ELM AV**   **ELM**
EVERGREEN AV   ELDER AV   EVERGREEN AV
                                                                            ELDER AV

Imperial Beach

SEACOAST DR
OCEAN LN
1ST ST
2ND ST
3RD ST
4TH ST
5TH ST
CORVINA AV
SEA VILLAGE DR
RAINBOW DR
7TH ST
8TH ST
9TH ST
DELAWARE ST
CAROLINA ST
10TH ST
11TH ST
FLORIDA ST
13TH ST
GEORGIA ST
14TH ST
15TH ST
16TH ST
17TH ST
18TH ST
HARWOOD ST
GRANGER ST
THERMAL AV

30
28
29

RAND McNALLY

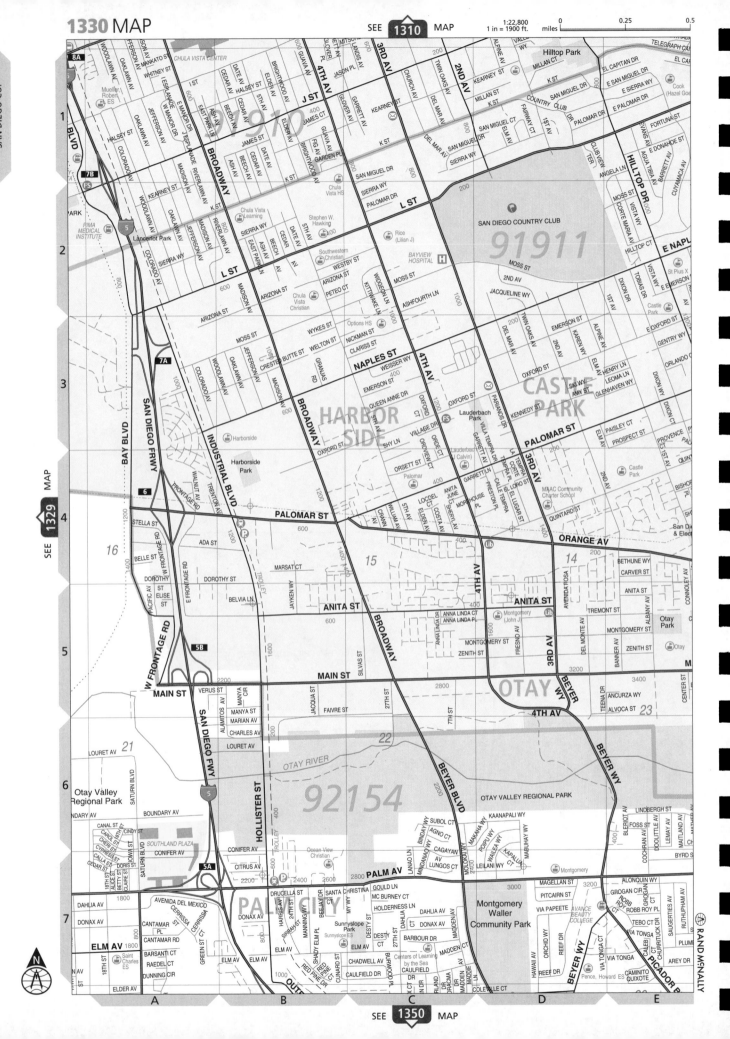

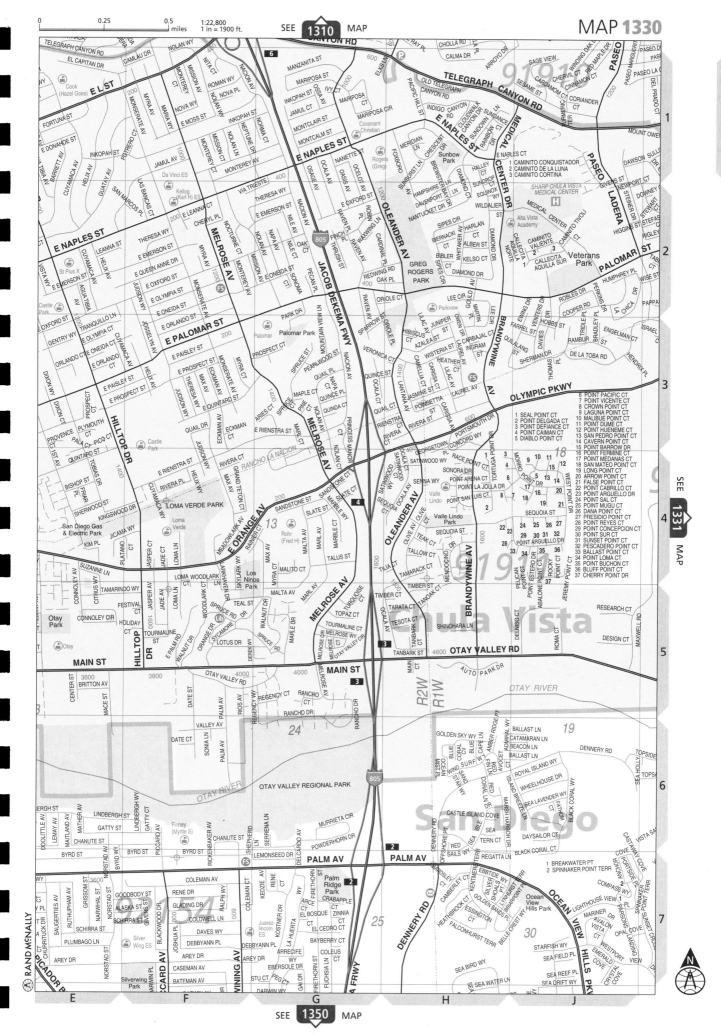

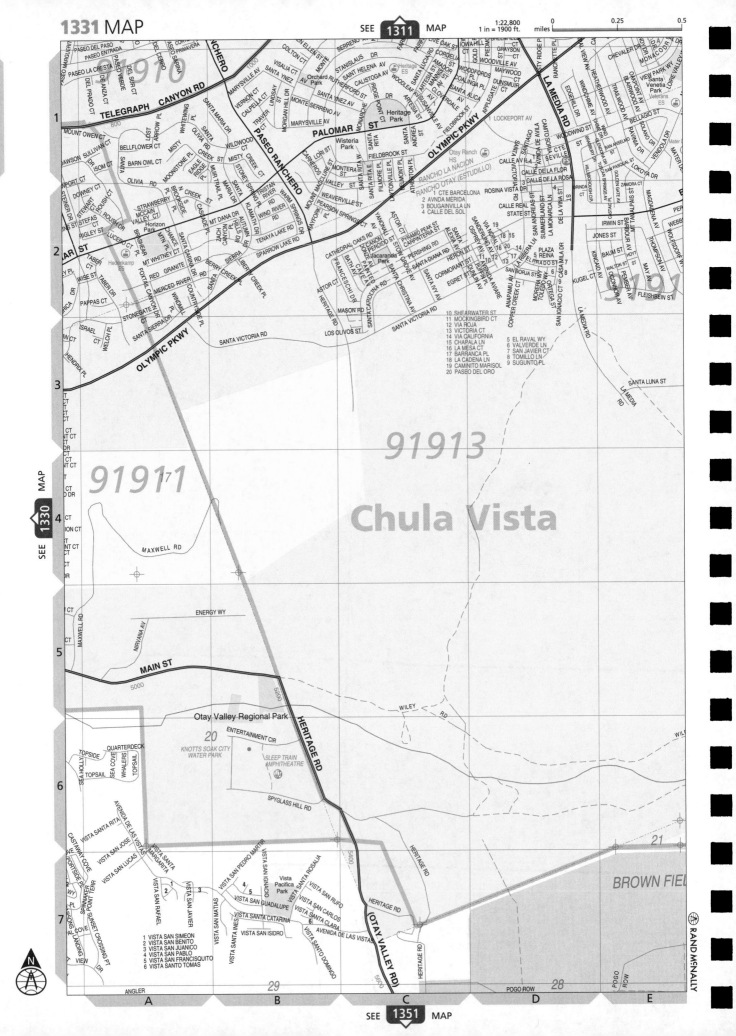

SAN DIEGO CO.

91910

TELEGRAPH CANYON RD

PASEO RANCHERO

PALOMAR ST

Heritage Park

OLYMPIC PKWY

Rancho La Nacion
Rancho Otay (Estudillo)

1 CTE BARCELONA
2 AVNDA MERIDA
3 BOUGAINVILLA LN
4 CALLE DEL SOL

10 SHEARWATER ST
11 MOCKINGBIRD CT
12 VIA ROJA
13 VICTORIA CT
14 VIA CALIFORNIA
15 CHAPALA LN
16 LA MESA CT
17 BARRANCA PL
18 LA CADENA LN
19 CAMINITO MARISOL
20 PASEO DEL ORO

5 EL RAVAL WY
6 VALVERDE LN
7 SAN JAVIER CT
8 TOMILLO LN
9 SUGUNTO PL

LA MEDIA RD

91191

OLYMPIC PKWY

SANTA VICTORIA RD

91913

Chula Vista

91911

MAXWELL RD

SEE 1330 MAP

ENERGY WY

MAIN ST

WILEY RD

Otay Valley Regional Park

HERITAGE RD

20 ENTERTAINMENT CIR
Knotts Soak City Water Park
Sleep Train Amphitheatre

SPYGLASS HILL RD

21

BROWN FIEL

HERITAGE RD

(OTAY VALLEY RD)

1 VISTA SAN SIMEON
2 VISTA SAN BENITO
3 VISTA SAN JUANICO
4 VISTA SAN PABLO
5 VISTA SAN FRANCISQUITO
6 VISTA SANTO TOMAS

Vista Pacifica Park

AVENIDA DE LAS VISTAS

ANGLER

N

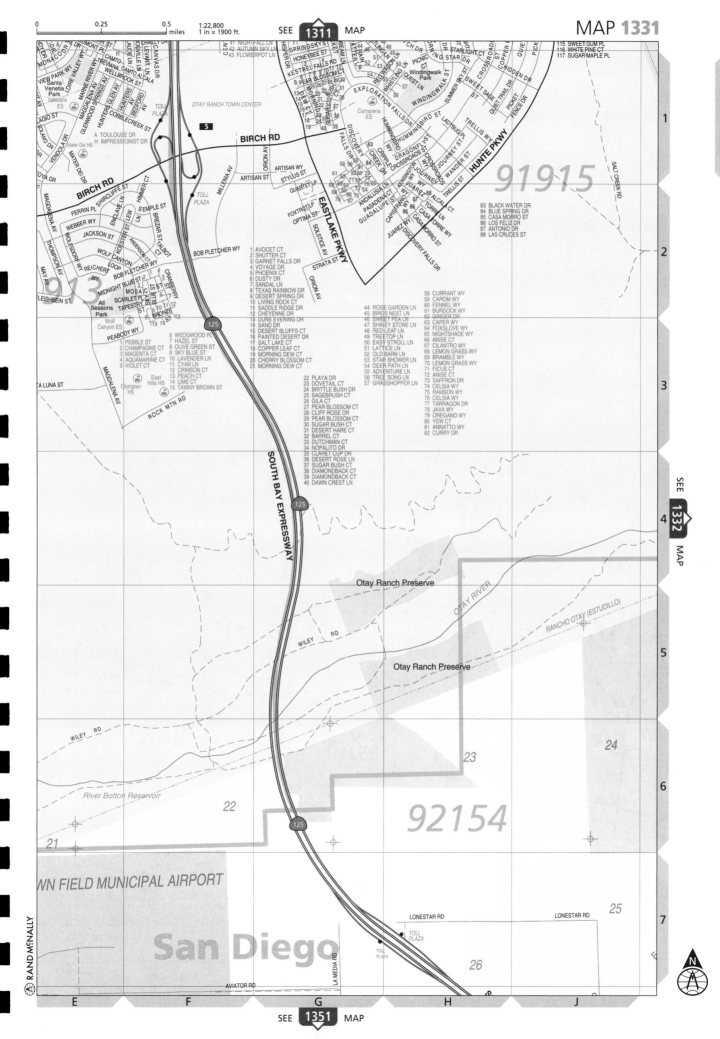

SEE 1311 MAP

SEE 1332 MAP

SEE 1351 MAP

0   0.25   0.5
miles   1:22,800
1 in = 1900 ft.

91915

91913

92154

BIRCH RD

EASTLAKE PKWY

HUNTE PKWY

SOUTH BAY EXPRESSWAY

Otay Ranch Town Center

Otay Ranch Preserve

Otay Ranch Preserve

OTAY RIVER

RANCHO OTAY (ESTUDILLO)

River Botton Reservoir

WN FIELD MUNICIPAL AIRPORT

San Diego

ROCK MTN RD

WILEY RD

WILEY RD

LONESTAR RD   LONESTAR RD

TOLL PLAZA

TOLL PLAZA

AVIATOR RD

LA MEDIA RD

1 AVOCET CT
2 SHUTTER CT
3 GARNET FALLS DR
4 VOYAGE DR
5 PHOENIX CT
6 DUSTY DR
7 SANDAL LN
8 TEXAS RAINBOW DR
9 DESERT SPRING DR
10 LIVING ROCK CT
11 SADDLE RIDGE DR
12 CHEYENNE DR
13 DUNE EVENING DR
14 SAND DR
15 DESERT BLUFFS CT
16 PAINTED DESERT DR
17 SALT LAKE CT
18 COPPER LEAF CT
19 MORNING DEW CT
20 CHERRY BLOSSOM CT
21 MORNING DEW CT

1 PEBBLE ST
2 CHAMPAGNE CT
3 MAGENTA CT
4 AQUAMARINE CT
5 VIOLET CT

6 WEDGWOOD PL
7 HAZEL ST
8 OLIVE GREEN ST
9 SKY BLUE ST
10 LAVENDER LN
11 CYAN LN
12 CRIMSON CT
13 PEACH CT
14 LIME CT
15 TAWNY BROWN ST

22 PLAYA DR
23 DOVETAIL CT
24 BRITTLE BUSH DR
25 SAGEBRUSH CT
26 GILA CT
27 PEAR BLOSSOM CT
28 CLIFF ROSE DR
29 PEAR BLOSSOM CT
30 SUGAR BUSH CT
31 DESERT HARE CT
32 BARREL CT
33 DUTCHMAN CT
34 NOPALITO DR
35 CLARET CUP DR
36 DESERT ROSE LN
37 SUGAR BUSH CT
38 DIAMONDBACK CT
39 DIAMONDBACK CT
40 DAWN CREST LN

41 NIGHTFALL LN
42 AUTUMN SKY LN
43 FLOWERPOT LN

44 ROSE GARDEN LN
45 BIRDS NEST LN
46 SWEET PEA LN
47 SHINEY STONE LN
48 RED LEAF LN
49 TREETOP LN
50 EASY STROLL LN
51 LATTICE LN
52 OLD BARN LN
53 STAR SHOWER LN
54 DEER PATH LN
55 ADVENTURE LN
56 TREE SONG LN
57 GRASSHOPPER LN

58 CURRANT WY
59 CAROM WY
60 FENNEL WY
61 BURDOCK WY
62 GINGER DR
63 CAPER WY
64 FOXGLOVE WY
65 NIGHTSHADE WY
66 ANISE CT
67 CILANTRO WY
68 LEMON GRASS WY
69 BRAMBLE WY
70 LEMON GRASS WY
71 FICUS CT
72 ANISE CT
73 SAFFRON DR
74 CELSIA WY
75 RAMSON WY
76 CELSIA WY
77 TARRAGON DR
78 JAVA WY
79 OREGANO WY
80 YEW CT
81 ANNATTO WY
82 CURRY DR

83 BLACK WATER DR
84 BLUE SPRING DR
85 CASA MORRO ST
86 LOS FELIZ DR
87 ANTONIO DR
88 LAS CRUCES ST

115 SWEET GUM PL
116 WHITE PINE CT
117 SUGAR MAPLE PL

RAND McNALLY

SAN DIEGO CO.

1 : 45,600
1 in = 3800 ft.

0   0.5   1.0
miles

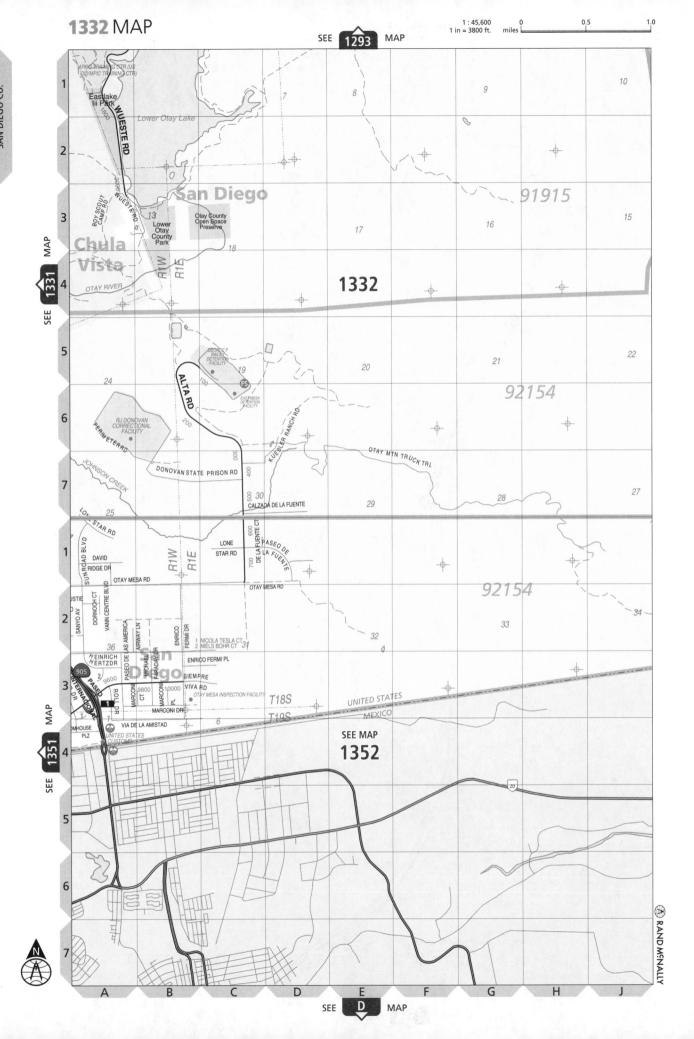

SEE 1293 MAP

ARCO TRAINING CTR (US OLYMPIC TRAINING CTR)

Eastlake Iii Park

WUESTE RD

Lower Otay Lake

BOY SCOUT CAMP RD

WUESTE RD

San Diego

13

Lower Otay County Park

Otay County Open Space Preserve

Chula Vista

R1W R1E

OTAY RIVER

91915

10

7   8   9

17   16   15

18

1332

ALTA RD

GEORGE F BAILEY DETENTION FACILITY

19

EAST MESA DETENTION FACILITY

RJ DONOVAN CORRECTIONAL FACILITY

PERIMETER RD

20   21   22

92154

JOHNSON CREEK

KUEBLER RANCH RD

DONOVAN STATE PRISON RD

OTAY MTN TRUCK TRL

LONE STAR RD

24

25

CALZADA DE LA FUENTE

30

29   28   27

SEE 1331 MAP

LONE STAR RD

SUN ROAD BLVD

DAVID RIDGE DR

R1W R1E

LONE STAR RD

PASEO DE LA FUENTE

DE LA FUENTE CT

OTAY MESA RD

OTAY MESA RD

92154

JUSTIE

SANYO AV

DORNOCH CT

VANN CENTRE BLVD

AIRWAY LN

FERMI DR

ENRICO

PASEO DE LAS AMERICAS

ENRICO FERMI PL

1 NICOLA TESLA CT
2 NIELS BOHR CT

31

San Diego

HEINRICH HERTZ DR

MICHAEL FARADAY DR

SIEMPRE

905

INTERNATIONAL

PASEO

ROLL DR

9600

MARCONI CT

9800

MARCONI PL

10000

VIVA RD

OTAY MESA INSPECTION FACILITY

T18S

UNITED STATES

36

1

MARCONI DR

6

MEXICO

T19S

VIA DE LA AMISTAD

OMHOUSE PLZ

UNITED STATES CUSTOMS

32   33   34

SEE 1351 MAP

SEE MAP
1352

70

N

SEE D MAP

A   B   C   D   E   F   G   H   J

RAND MCNALLY

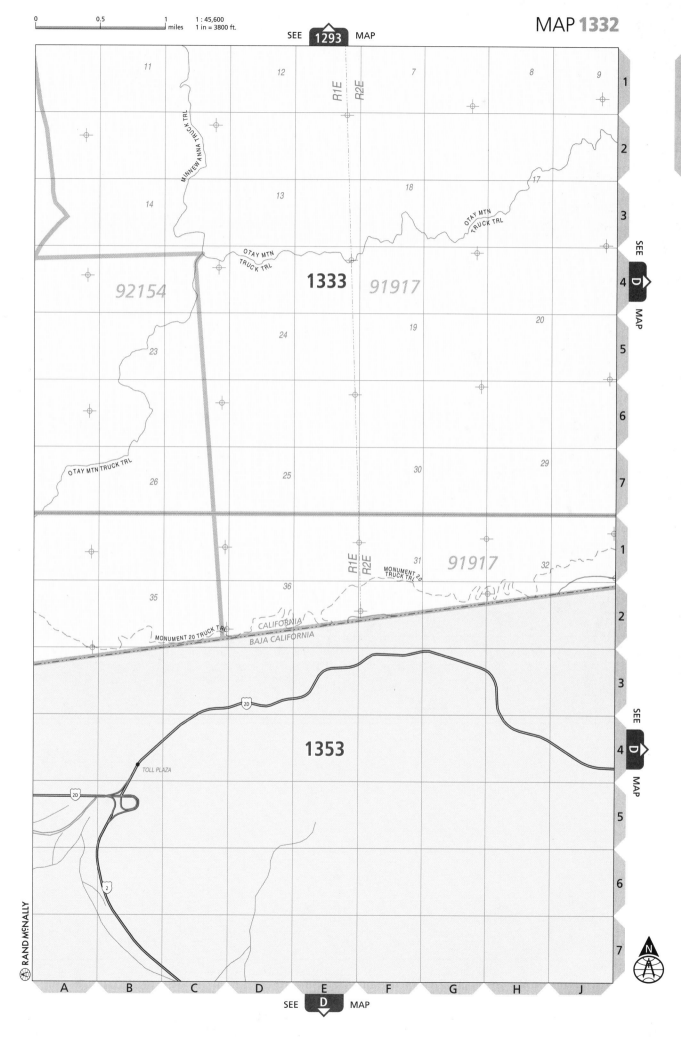

MAP **1332**

SAN DIEGO CO.

SEE **1293** MAP

0   0.5   1   1 : 45,600
miles   1 in = 3800 ft.

11

12

R1E R2E

7

8

9

1

2

MINNEWANNA TRUCK TRL

14

13

18

17

OTAY MTN TRUCK TRL

3

OTAY MTN TRUCK TRL

SEE D MAP

92154

1333

91917

4

23

24

19

20

5

6

OTAY MTN TRUCK TRL

26

25

30

29

7

35

36

R1E R2E

31

MONUMENT 20 TRUCK TRL

91917

32

1

MONUMENT 20 TRUCK TRL

CALIFORNIA

BAJA CALIFORNIA

2

3

2D

SEE D MAP

1353

4

TOLL PLAZA

2D

5

6

2

RAND MᶜNALLY

7

A   B   C   D   E   F   G   H   J

N

SEE D MAP

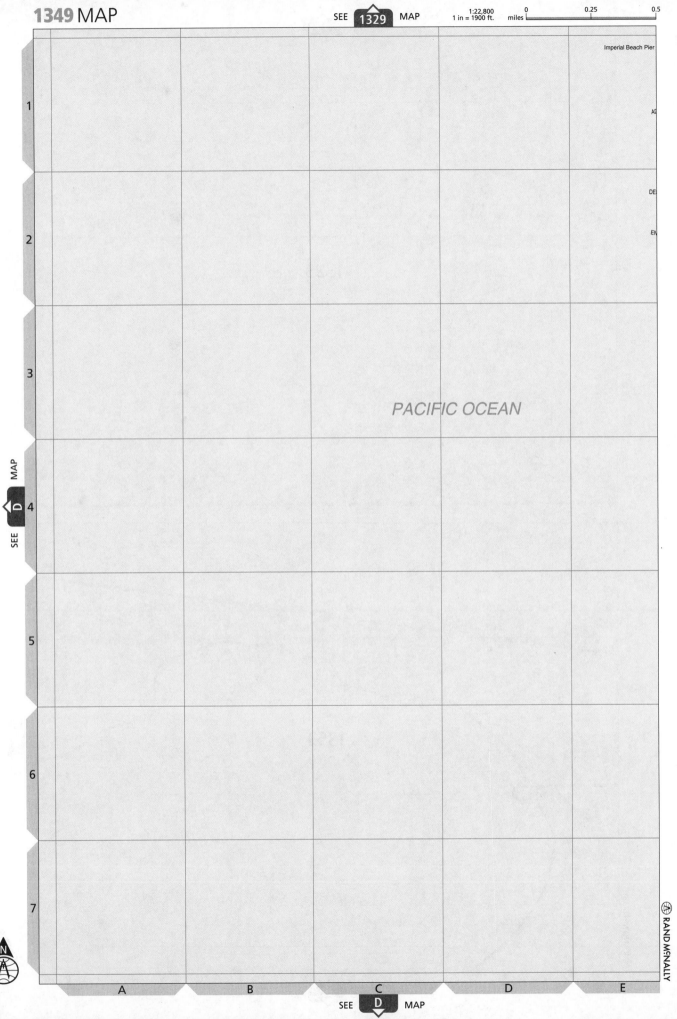

SAN DIEGO CO.

1:22,800
1 in = 1900 ft.   miles   0   0.25   0.5

Imperial Beach Pier

PACIFIC OCEAN

SEE **D** MAP

1

2

3

4

5

6

7

A   B   C   D   E

SEE **D** MAP

RAND MCNALLY

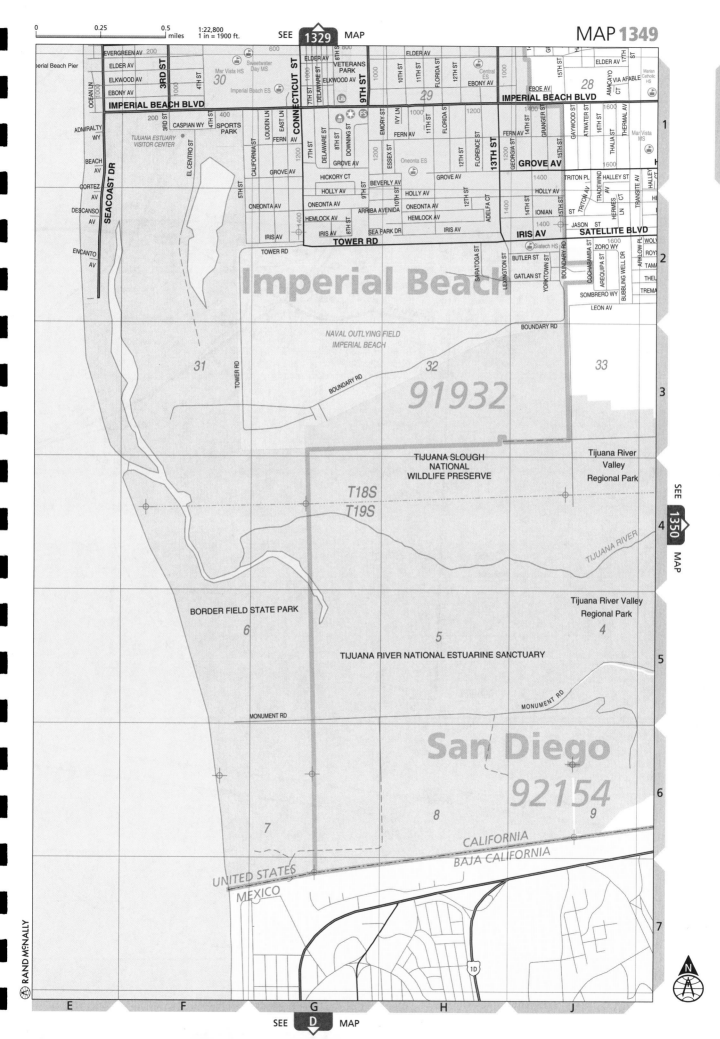

MAP **1349**

SAN DIEGO CO.

SEE **1329** MAP

0   0.25   0.5
miles
1:22,800
1 in = 1900 ft.

Imperial Beach Pier

EVERGREEN AV 200
ELDER AV
ELKWOOD AV
EBONY AV

3RD ST

4TH ST

Mar Vista HS
30
Sweetwater Day MS
Imperial Beach ES
VETERANS PARK

ELDER AV
ELKWOOD AV
EBONY AV

9TH ST

CONNECTICUT ST

IMPERIAL BEACH BLVD

ELDER AV

10TH ST
11TH ST
FLORIDA ST
12TH ST

29

EBOE AV

28

ELDER AV 17TH
AMACAYO CT
VIA AFABLE

Marian Catholic HS

IMPERIAL BEACH BLVD

1

ADMIRALTY WY

200
3RD ST
CASPIAN WY
EL CENTRO ST

400
4TH ST
SPORTS PARK

Tijuana Estuary Visitor Center

BEACH AV

CORTEZ AV

DESCANSO AV

SEACOAST DR

5TH ST

LOUDEN LN
EAST LN
FERN
CALIFORNIA ST

GROVE AV

7TH ST
8TH ST
DELAWARE ST
DOWNING ST

GROVE AV

EMORY ST
ESSEX ST
IVY LN
11TH ST
FERN AV

Oneonta ES

FLORIDA ST

FERN AV
14TH ST
GRANGER ST
GEORGIA ST
15TH ST

13TH ST

GAYWOOD ST
ATWATER ST
16TH ST
THALIA ST
THERMAL AV

Mar Vista MS

GROVE AV

HICKORY CT

HOLLY AV

ONEONTA AV
HEMLOCK AV

9TH ST

BEVERLY AV
HOLLY AV

ONEONTA AV
ARRIBA AVENIDA
HEMLOCK AV

10TH ST

12TH ST

GROVE AV

HOLLY AV

ONEONTA AV

ADELFA CT

HOLLY AV

14TH ST
IONIAN ST
15TH ST

1400

TRITON PL
TRADEWIND AV
TRITON AV
HERMES LN CT
JASON ST

HALLEY ST
TRANSITE AV
HALLEY
HE

1400

IRIS AV

TOWER RD

IRIS AV
8TH ST

SEA PARK DR

IRIS AV

IRIS AV

SATELLITE BLVD

Siatech HS

JASON ST

COCHABAMBA ST
ZORO WY
AREQUIPA ST
BUBBLING WELL DR

ARKLOW PL
ROYS

WOL
WOLY

2

TOWER RD

TOWER RD

SARATOGA ST
BUTLER ST
GATLAN ST

LEXINGTON ST
YORKTOWN ST

BOUNDARY RD

SOMBRERO WY

LEON AV

TAMA
THEL
TREMA

Imperial Beach

NAVAL OUTLYING FIELD
IMPERIAL BEACH

BOUNDARY RD

31

TOWER RD

BOUNDARY RD

32

33

91932

3

Tijuana River Valley Regional Park

TIJUANA SLOUGH NATIONAL WILDLIFE PRESERVE

T18S
T19S

SEE **1350** MAP

Tijuana River

4

BORDER FIELD STATE PARK

6

5

Tijuana River Valley Regional Park

4

TIJUANA RIVER NATIONAL ESTUARINE SANCTUARY

5

MONUMENT RD

MONUMENT RD

San Diego

92154

6

7

8

9

CALIFORNIA
BAJA CALIFORNIA

UNITED STATES
MEXICO

7

1D

E   F   G   H   J

SEE **D** MAP

N

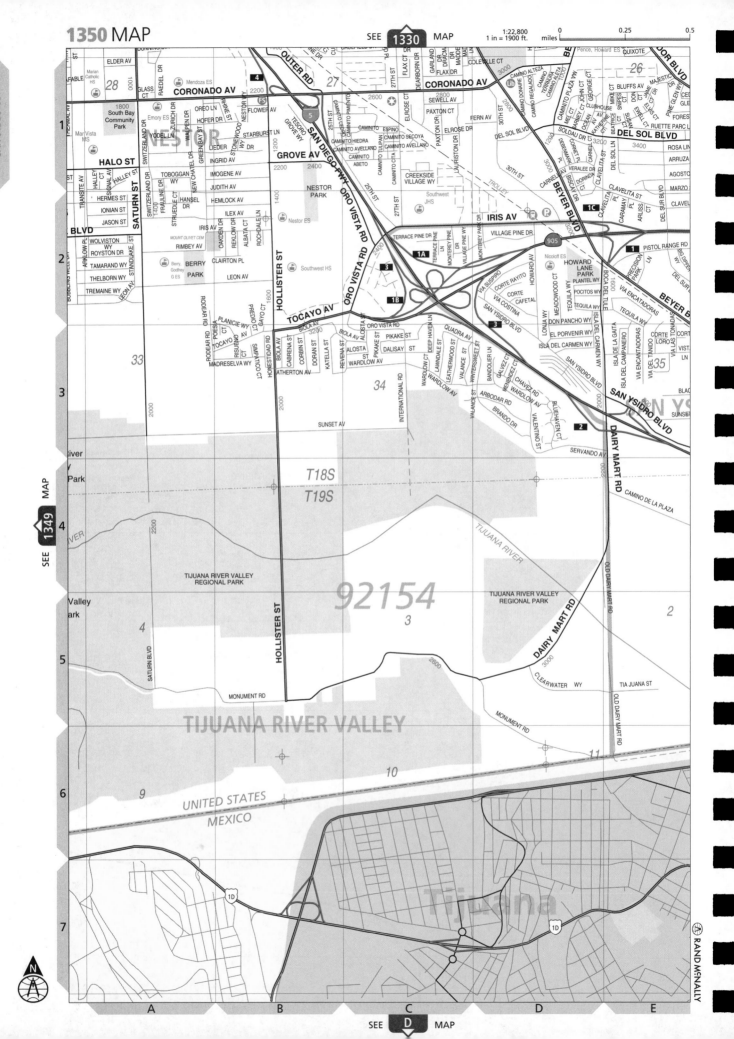

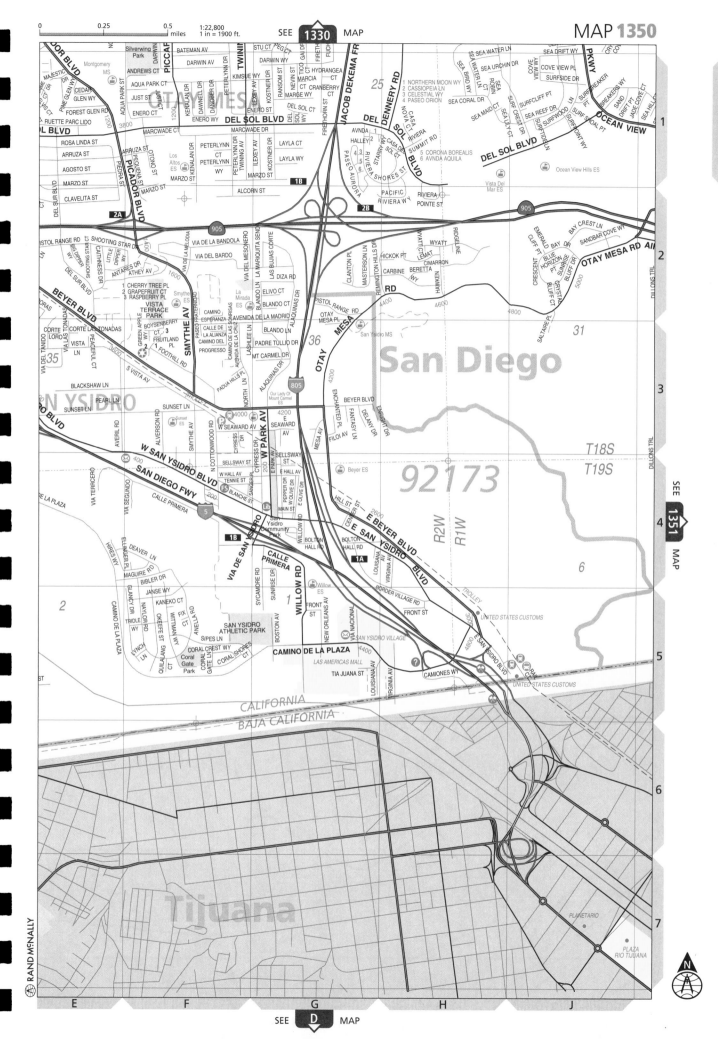

MAP 1350

SEE 1330 MAP

0   0.25   0.5 miles   1:22,800
1 in = 1900 ft.

OTAY MESA

SAN YSIDRO

San Diego

92173

T18S
T19S

R2W   R1W

SEE 1351 MAP

CALIFORNIA
BAJA CALIFORNIA

Tijuana

PLANETARIO

PLAZA
RIO TIJUANA

RAND M\NALLY

SEE D MAP

N

E   F   G   H   J

SAN DIEGO CO.

1:22,800
1 in = 1900 ft.
miles
0   0.25   0.5

29   28

POGO ROW   POGO ROW

ANGLER
SEA STRAND
HIDDEN TRAILS
SEAGREEN

EXECUTIVE CENTER CT
EXPOSITION WY
INNOVATIVE DR

VALLEY RD
OTAY

San Diego Jet Engine Museum

DRIFT PT
JADE COVE CT
SEA HILL CT
SEA FIRE PT
SANDY CAPE
SEAGLEN WY
SEAGREEN
VIEW HILLS PKWY
BERYL KNOLL
ISLAND KNOLL
OCEAN GATE LN
LEEWARD ISLE PT
MAR REEF CV
ROCK BLUFF WY
EMERALD CREST
GULL CV
AQUA COVE
SURFRIDER WY

1

CORPORATE CENTER WY
CORPORATE CENTER DR
PROGRESSIVE AV
BUSINESS CENTER CT

DATSUN ST
5800
INNOVATIVE DR

HERITAGE RD
5600

CURRAN ST
SIKORSKY ST   ST   SIKORSKY ST   LYCOMING ST
FAIRCHILD ST   GRUMMAN ST   BALCHEN WY
A STEARMAN ST ST BOEING ST

CONTINENTAL ST

OTAY MESA RD

SA RD AIRWAY RD
CALIENTE AV

San Ysidro HS

A SANTA REGINA
B SANTA SOFIA
SANTA ALICIA
SAN EUGENIO ST
SAN VICTORIO
SAN ROBERTO
SANTA GLORIA
SAN FRANCISCO
SAN JOVANI
DILLONS TRL
AIRWAY RD
SANTA ROSA

OTAY MESA FRWY   905

HERITAGE RD

1600   6600
PACIFIC RIM CT   CAMINO MAQUILADORA   OTAY HEIGHTS CT

905

2

32

1800
GATEWAY PARK DR

33

AIRWAY RD

BRITANNIA BLVD

3

DILLONS TRL

CACTUS RD

T18S
T19S

SIEMPRE VIVA RD

92154

CACTUS CT   2400

5

4

MARTINEZ RANCH RD

CALLE DE LINEA

4

CALIFORNIA
BAJA CALIFORNIA

5

Tijuana

6

7

PLAZA RIO TIJUANA

RAND McNALLY

A   B   C   D   E

0   0.25   0.5
miles
1 in = 1900 ft.
1:22,800

AVIATOR RD

27
BROWN FIELD MUNICIPAL AIRPORT

SOUTH BAY EXPRESSWAY

DEAD STICK RD

HARVEST RD

WINDSOCK ST

26

AIR WING RD

PIPER RANCH RD

125

RADAR RD

FLIGHTPATH WY

APPROACH RD

1

OTAY MESA RD

FS

OTAY MESA RD

OTAY MESA RD

8800

OTAY MESA RD

LA MEDIA RD

ST ANDREWS COVE 7600

8200

GAILES BLVD

ST ANDREWS TERR

AILSA CT

OTAY MESA CENTER RD

ST ANDREWS AV

7

LA MEDIA RD

HARVEST RD

ST ANDREWS AV

6

SAINT ANDREWS AV

OTAY MESA FRWY

SR 905

905

PASE

PANASONIC WY   WATERVILLE RD

EXCELLANTE ST

GIGANTIC ST

PIPER RANCH RD

AIRWAY RD

DUBLIN DR

34

CENTURION ST

Southwestern
College-
Otay Mesa

35

AIRWAY RD

AVENIDA COSTA AZUL

AVENIDA DE LA FUENTE NORTE

AIRWAY RD

OTAY CENTER CT

BRITANNIA BLVD

AIRWAY RD

AVENIDA COSTA NORTE

HARVEST RD

AVENIDA COSTA DEL SOL

AVENIDA COSTA BLANCA

AVENIDA COSTA ESTE

PASEO DE LA FUENTE

AVENIDA DE LA FUENTE SUR

OTAY CENTER DR

San Diego

LA MEDIA RD

AVENIDA DE LA FUENTE

BRITANNIA CT

3

SIEMPRE VIVA CT

BRITANNIA PARK PL

AVENIDA COSTA SUR

PASEO DE LA FUENTE

T18S
T19S

AVENIDA COSTA BRAVA

SIEMPRE VIVA RD

NICO

CUSTOMHOUSE PLZ

BRISTOW CT

OTAY PACIFIC DR

SIEMPRE VIVA RD

8400

LAS CALIFORNIAS DR

3

MELKSEE ST

SARNEN ST

2

DRUCKER LN

CUSTOMHOUSE CT

BRITANNIA BLVD

KERNS ST

KERNS ST

SEE [1352] MAP

BRITANNIA CT

R1W T19S

UNITED STATES

4

MEXICO

• Terminal

GENERAL ABELARDO L RODRIGUEZ INTERNATIONAL AIRPORT

5

H

6

7

RAND McNALLY

E   F   G   H   J

N

SEE ⌂ 1332 MAP

1:22,800
1 in = 1900 ft.

0   0.25   0.5
miles

LONE STAR RD

SUNROAD BLVD

DAVID RIDGE DR

VANN CENTRE BLVD

R1W
R1E

LONE STAR RD

DE LA FUENTE CT

ALTA RD

PASEO DE LA FUENTE

ACCESS RD

OTAY MESA RD

OTAY MESA RD

CARNOUSTIE RD

DORNOCH CT

ALTA RD

OTAY CROSSINGS PL

CALLE VENTNER

ENRICO FERMI DR

2

36

SANYO AV

AIRWAY LN

AIRWAY RD

AIRWAY RD

31

HEINRICH HERTZ DR

PASEO INTERNACIONAL

NIELS BOHR CT

MICHAEL FARADAY DR

ENRICO FERMI PL

San Diego

SIEMPRE VIVA RD

SIEMPRE VIVA RD

3

MARCONI CT

MARCONI PL

ROLL RD

PASEO DE LAS AMERICA

MARCONI DR

OTAY MESA INSPECTION FACILITY

9

9400

905

T18S
T19S

UNITED STATES

6

VIA DE LA AMISTAD

1

MEXICO

NICOLA TESLA CT

PASEO DE LA FRONTERA

US CUSTOMS

MHOUSE PLZ

MEXICO CUSTOMS

SEE ⌂ 1351 MAP

4

5

6

7

A   B   C   D   E

N

SEE D MAP

RAND McNALLY

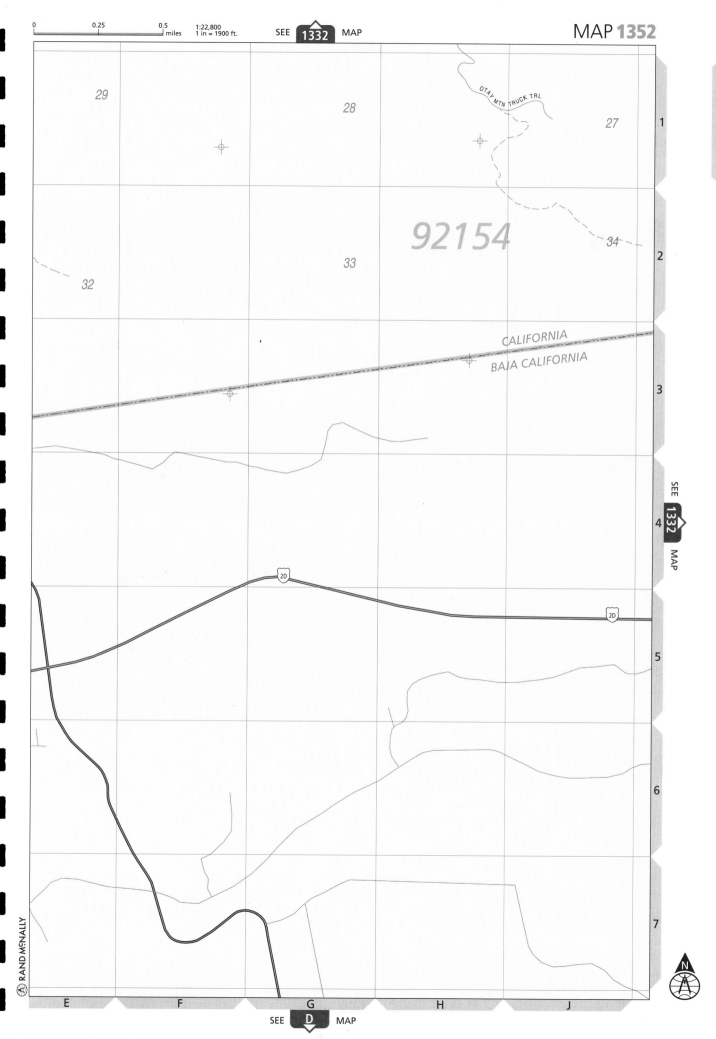

MAP **1352**

1:22,800
1 in = 1900 ft.

SAN DIEGO CO.

OTAY MTN TRUCK TRL

29   28   27

92154

33   34

32

CALIFORNIA
BAJA CALIFORNIA

2D

2D

RAND MCNALLY

E   F   G   H   J

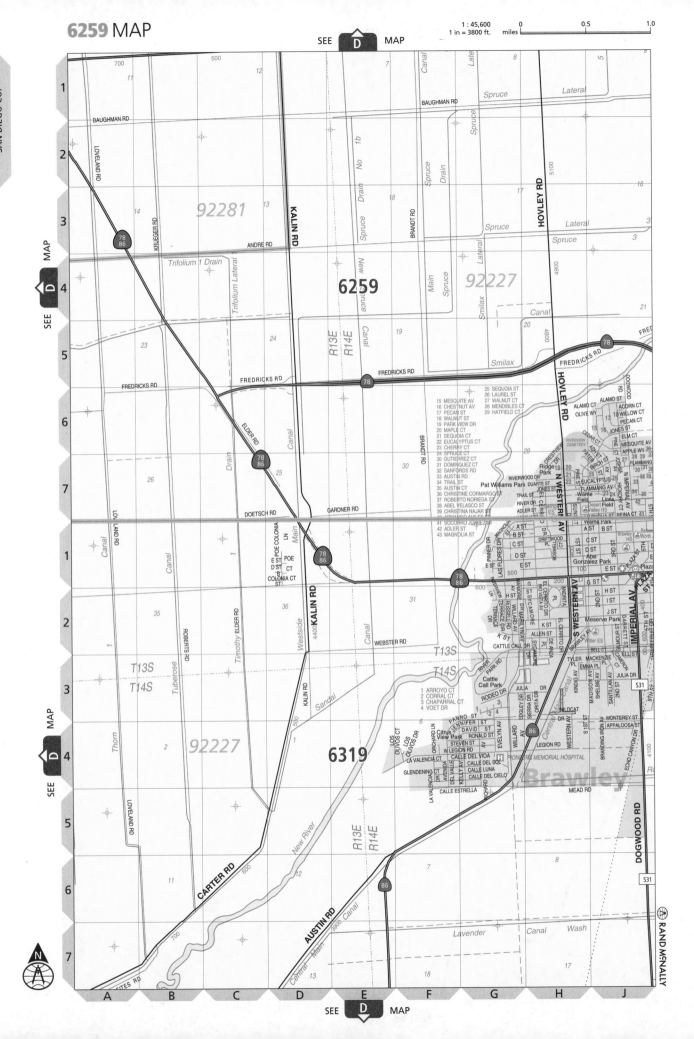

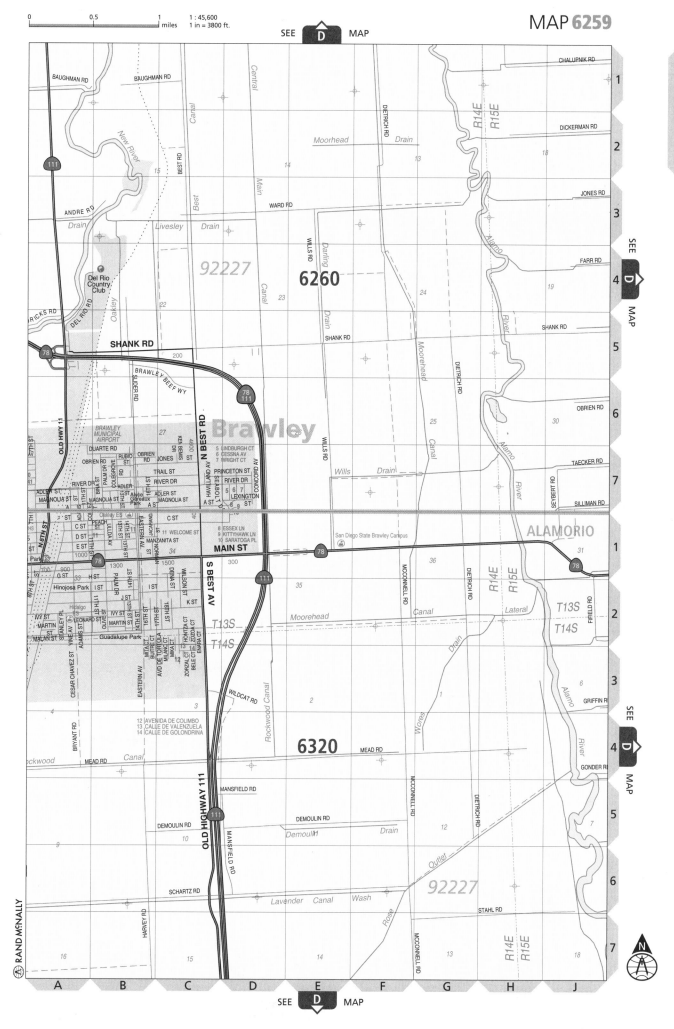

MAP **6259**

SAN DIEGO CO.

1 : 45,600
1 in = 3800 ft.

0   0.5   1
miles

CHALUPNIK RD

BAUGHMAN RD
BAUGHMAN RD

DICKERMAN RD

Moorhead   Drain

DIETRICH RD

R14E R15E

New River

JONES RD

WARD RD

Best

Canal

Main

Central

Canal

WILLS RD

DARLING RD

92227

6260

Del Rio
Country
Club

SHANK RD

78

BRAWLEY BEEF WY

SLIDER RD

OLD HWY 11

N BEST RD

Brawley

WILLS RD

Wills   Drain

BRAWLEY
MUNICIPAL
AIRPORT

DIETRICH RD

Moorhead   Canal

Alamo   River

SHANK RD

OBRIEN RD

TAECKER RD

SEYBERT RD

SILLIMAN RD

ALAMORIO

MAIN ST

San Diego State Brawley Campus

78

111

S BEST AV

McCONNELL RD

DIETRICH RD

R14E R15E

78

T13S

T14S

FIFIELD RD

Moorehead   Canal   Lateral

Drain

Alamo   River

GRIFFIN RD

Rockwood Canal

6320

MEAD RD

GONDER RD

BRYANT RD

MANSFIELD RD

OLD HIGHWAY 111

DEMOULIN RD

McCONNELL RD

DIETRICH RD

Demoulin   Drain

SCHARTZ RD

Outlet

92227

Lavender   Canal   Wash

Rockwood   Canal   MEAD RD

HARVEY RD

MANSFIELD RD

STAHL RD

RAND MCNALLY

A   B   C   D   E   F   G   H   J

SEE  D MAP

1:22,800
1 in = 1900 ft.

0   0.25   0.5
miles

SAN DIEGO CO.

34
T14S
T15S
35
HARRIS RD
36

1

NEW RIVER

COY RD

AUSTIN RD

LARSEN RD

LARSEN RD

LARSEN RD

WIENERT RD
3

LA RSEN RD

Eucalyptus

Canal

2

Canal

2

1

Dahlia

LA BRUCHERIE RD

Canal

3

AUSTIN RD

Main

12

NECKEL RD

PRECIADO RD

APOLONIA RD

FLORA LN

SEE D MAP

10

Central

11

BELFORD RD

LA BRUCHERIE RD

C ST

Irvir

92251

WINONA CT

POWELL CT

NANCE RD

MURPHY RD

MURPHY RD

IRONWOOD RD

COYNE RD

LEE RD

LA BRUCHERIE RD

5

HAMBLETT RD

HAMBLET CT

NANCE RD

13

F5

15

WORTHINGTON RD

WORTHINGTON RD

500

DAHLIA LN

700

WORTHINGTON RD

S28

700

14

DANDELION LN

600

2600 RD

LA BRUCHERIE RD

B ST

Hula
ES
5T

900

OLIVERITE ST

MENVIEILE ST

SAGUARO ST

PALO BREA ST

TOPAZ ST

SAVANNA WY

RUBY ST

CINNABAR ST

NANCE RD

BANTA RD

500

BANTA RD

6

PYRITE ST

OASIS ST

QUARTZ ST

JADE TREE ST

EMERALD

PEARL RD

C ST

GRANITE ST

JEWEL ST

CACTUS ST

GARNET ST

RUSSELL DR

B ST

AUSTIN RD

OPAL CT

SAND STONE ST

ZIRCON ST

DESERT ROSE ST

VILLA SERENA

2600

DIAMOND ST

BREWER RD

BREWER RD

Eucalyptus
Lateral

10

COSTA AZUL ST

MIRADOR ST

VALLE VERDE LN

BAHIA ST

HORIZONTE ST

VISTA DEL MAR ST

24

7

NICHOLS RD

MONTERREY PARK LN

LAS DUNAS ST

LAS LOMAS ST

Imperial

LA BRUCHERIE RD

Dahlia

22

23

Central

LAS CUSPIDES ST

F5

N

RAND McNALLY

A   B   C   D   E

SEE 6499 MAP

MAP **6439**

SAN DIEGO CO.

0   0.25   0.5
miles
1:22,800
1 in = 1900 ft.

HARRIS RD

T14S
T15S

31

Newside

32

HARRIS RD

Dolson   Drain

86

1

LARSEN RD

6

5

R13E
R14E

CLARK RD

Dolson
Drain

2

RALPH RD

RALPH RD

Date

RALPH RD

Dahlia

N IMPERIAL AV

SUNSET DR
HORSESHOE CT
SILVER SPUR CT
TAIL CREEK DR
TRAIL DR
DUSTY
CANON DR
BRANDING IRON DR
BUCKSKIN RANCH DR
CAHUILLA DR
SHOSHONEAN DR
RODEO DR

Lateral

Date

3

Canal

SANTA ROSA DR
LOS COYOTES CT
CABAZON CT
CANON DR
SABOBA CT
RAMONA CT
NECKEL RD

7

9

NECKEL RD

NECKEL RD

Date

8

FLORA LN
MALLARD LN
TEAL LN

BUTTERFIELD TR
CHAPARRAL CT
RODEO DR
SILVERADO TR
VAQUERO TR
ARROYO SECO
CHISOLM TR
ROADRUNNER LN
MUSTANG CT
MUSTANG
WINCHESTER LN
LARIAT LN

MORNINGSIDE CT
SUNRISE CT
DAWN CT
MORNINGSIDE DR
SYCAMORE CT
HUMMING
BIRD CT
SUNSHINE WY
SUMMER CT

SEE D MAP

4

BELFORD RD

Frank Wright MS

IMPERIAL AV

SAGE CT

CONESTOGA LN

CLARK RD

SHORT RD

LATHROP RD

ELLEN RD
BRISTOW LN
FRANKLIN RD

15TH ST

15TH ST

LA BRUCHERIE RD

Irving Park

14TH ST
13TH ST
12TH ST
11TH ST
10TH ST

C ST
D ST
E ST

14TH ST

IMPERIAL AV

14TH ST
13TH ST
12TH ST
11TH ST
10TH ST

14TH ST
13TH ST
12TH ST
11TH ST
10TH ST

Date

5

PALMER PERFORMING ARTS CENTER

City Park

H ST
J ST
K ST
L ST
M ST
N ST
O ST

9TH ST

9TH ST

9TH ST

FS

Imperial HS

200

BARIONI ST

WORTHINGTON RD

S28

17

7TH ST

18

7TH ST
6TH ST

700   500   400   300   200   100

7TH ST
6TH ST
5TH ST

LN

Hulse ES

B ST
C ST

5TH ST

4TH ST

D ST
E ST
F ST
G ST
H ST

IMPERIAL AV

5TH ST
4TH ST

K ST
L ST
M ST

Canal

6TH ST
5TH ST

4TH ST

6

TA RD

Emerson Park

3RD ST

2ND ST

B ST
C ST
G ST

3RD

2ND ST

3RD ST

2ND ST

2ND ST

86

1ST ST

1ST ST

1ST ST

E FIELDBROOK ST

HUSTON RD

R13E
R14E

SAN DIEGO BLVD

FRONT ST

19

CLARK RD

20

7

Dahlia

LA BRUCHERIE RD

IMPERIAL COUNTY AIRPORT

AIRPORT

IMPERIAL COUNTY EXPO

FS

BOOL DR

ROSARITO DR

E   F   G   H   J

RAND MCNALLY

N

6499 MAP

SEE 6439 MAP

SAN DIEGO CO.

1:22,800
1 in = 1900 ft.

miles 0   0.25   0.5

92251

Imperial

LAS CUSPIDES ST

IMPERIAL COUNTY AIRPORT

BOLEY FIELD CT
MCCARRAN CT
STAPLETON AV
O HARE
LAGUARDIA AV
FLYING CLOUD AV
BOLEYFIELD DR
EARHART AV
MCCARRAN DR
FLYING CLOUD DR
LA BRUCHERIE RD

AUSTIN RD

DULLES CT
SHEFFIELD AV
KITTY HAWK CT
SKY VIEW CT
ATEN RD
STAPLETON CT
O HARE CT
LAGUARDIA CT
EARHART
KITTY HAWK DR
SKY VIEW DR
SKY HARBOR WY
DULLES DR
SHEFFIELD DR
ATEN RD
INDUSTRY RD

22   23   24

ATEN RD

DESERT WILLOW ST
BAYWOOD ST
SEQUOIA ST
JUNIPER ST
JOSHUA TREE ST
MESQUITE ST
SAGEBRUSH ST
SILVERWOOD ST

BRUSHWOOD AV
SMOKEWOOD AV
SANDALWOOD GLEN AV
MORNING GLORY TR
POPPY
LANTANA LN
TIGER LILY LN
LILAC LN
WISTERIA CT
LARKSPUR LN
SUNFLOWER LN
SNAPDRAGON WY
JOSHUA TREE ST
TAMARISK ST
SILVERWOOD ST
YUCCA ST
WILD ROSE LN
BLUE SAGE CT
BUFFALO GRASS CT
VERBENA WY
BLAZING STAR TR
BOUGAINVILLEA TR
MESQUITE ST
SAGEBRUSH ST
SILVERWOOD ST
PALOVERDE AV
CALLE HELENA
DESERT ROSE CT
SHAMROCK CT
PASEO
CAMINO
TUMBLEWEED AV

T L Waggoner ES

27   26   25

Central   Drain

NICHOLS RD

2300

El Centro

SEE D MAP

2100 AUSTIN RD

Eucalyptus

92243

34   35   36

NICHOLS RD

2000

FORRESTER RD

Lotus

EVAN HEWES HWY   ADAMS

S80

EVAN HEWES HWY   600   Sunflower Park

900   800   700

Canal

W MAIN ST   W MAIN ST

AUSTIN RD

Sunflower ES   22ND ST
23RD ST

Lotus AV
STATE ST

Leeper Park   OLIVE AV   OLIVE
AV

SMITH LN

GLENWOOD RD
SANTA ROSA
SUNSET DR
HASKELL DR
MOIOLA AV
BRIGHTON AV
ORANGE

JOHNSON LN

3   2

NICHOLS RD

1800

Canal

HOLT CIR
HEIL CIR
ELM CIR
HAMILTON AV

HASKELL DR

Lotus Park
23RD ST
HOL
HEIL
ELM
HAMILTON

Drain   Wildflower Park

LOTUS AV
VINE ST
23RD ST

WENSLEY AV   WENSLEY AV
DR   LENREY AV   LENR

RAND McNALLY

A   B   C   D   E

SEE 6559 MAP

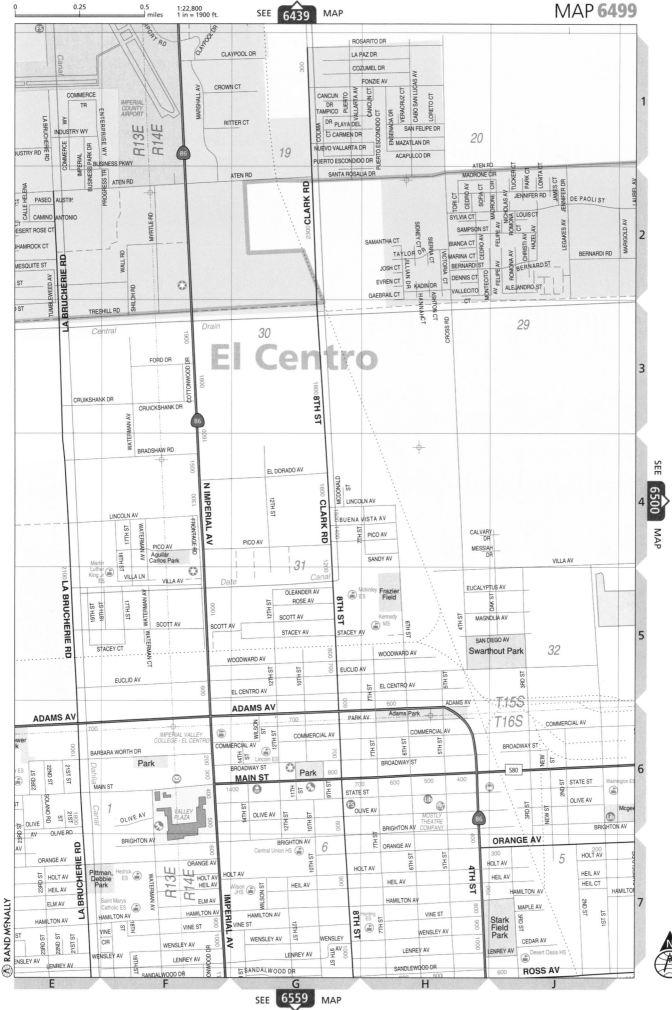

MAP **6499**

SAN DIEGO CO.

SEE **6439** MAP

SEE **6500** MAP

SEE **6559** MAP

El Centro

0   0.25   0.5
miles
1:22,800
1 in = 1900 ft.

RAND M°NALLY

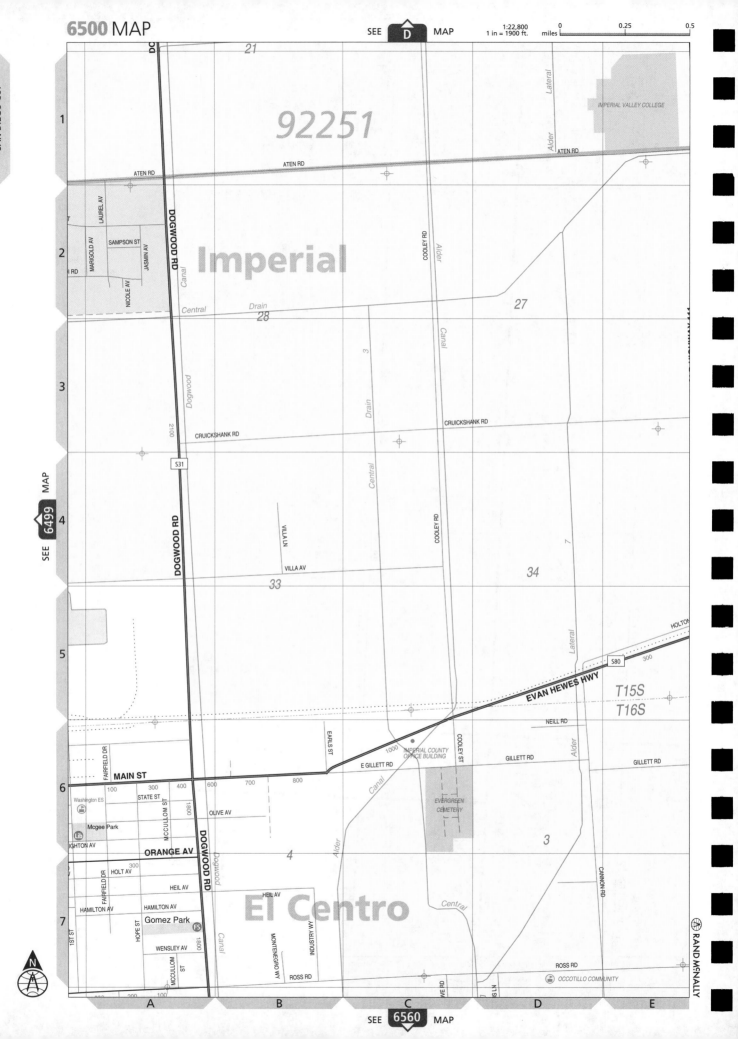

6500 MAP

1:22,800
1 in = 1900 ft.

0   0.25   0.5
miles

SAN DIEGO CO.

92251

Imperial

IMPERIAL VALLEY COLLEGE

ATEN RD
ATEN RD
ATEN RD

LAUREL AV

MARIGOLD AV

SAMPSON ST

JASMIN AV

NICOLE AV

DOGWOOD RD

Canal

COOLEY RD

Alder

27

Central

Drain
28

Drain

3

Canal

Dogwood

2100

S31

CRUICKSHANK RD

CRUICKSHANK RD

Drain

Central

Canal

CRUICKSHANK RD

DOGWOOD RD

VILLA LN

VILLA AV

Cooley RD

34

33

7

Lateral

HOLTON

S80

300

EVAN HEWES HWY

T15S
T16S

NEILL RD

EARLS ST

1000

IMPERIAL COUNTY
OFFICE BUILDING

COOLEY ST

GILLETT RD

GILLETT RD

FAIRFIELD DR

MAIN ST

E GILLETT RD

Canal

Alder

Washington ES

STATE ST

100   300   400   600   700   800

McCULLOM ST

1800

OLIVE AV

EVERGREEN
CEMETERY

Mcgee Park

Lib

RIGHTON AV

ORANGE AV

DOGWOOD RD

Dogwood

4

Alder

3

CANNON RD

FAIRFIELD DR

HOLT AV

300

HEIL AV

HAMILTON AV

HAMILTON AV

HEIL AV

Central

El Centro

HOPE ST

Gomez Park

FS

1ST ST

McCULLOM ST

WENSLEY AV

1800

MONTENEGRO WY

INDUSTRY WY

ROSS RD

Canal

VE RD

1ST ST

ROSS RD

OCOTILLO COMMUNITY

200   100

RAND McNALLY

N

A   B   C   D   E

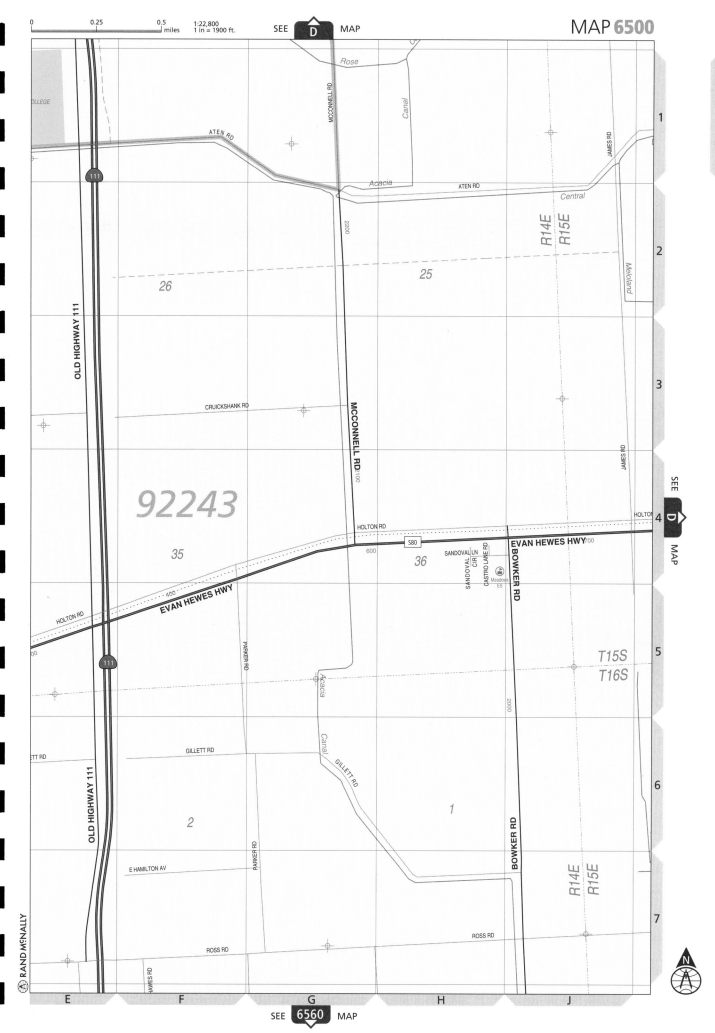

MAP **6500**

SAN DIEGO CO.

0   0.25   0.5
miles
1:22,800
1 in = 1900 ft.

SEE **D** MAP

Rose

Canal

McCONNELL RD

ATEN RD

1

Acacia

ATEN RD

Central

JAMES RD

R14E
R15E

2200

2

25

26

Meloland

3

CRUICKSHANK RD

McCONNELL RD 100

JAMES RD

OLD HIGHWAY 111

92243

SEE **D** MAP

HOLTON RD

HOLTON

4

35

S80

SANDOVAL LN
CIR

CASTRO LANE RD

EVAN HEWES HWY 700

BOWKER RD

600

36

SANDOVAL

Meadows
ES

400

EVAN HEWES HWY

HOLTON RD

PARKER RD

Acacia

T15S
T16S

5

GILLETT RD

Canal

GILLETT RD

2000

6

2

1

BOWKER RD

R14E
R15E

E HAMILTON AV

PARKER RD

7

RAND McNALLY

ROSS RD

ROSS RD

HAWES RD

E   F   G   H   J

N

111

111

OLD HIGHWAY 111

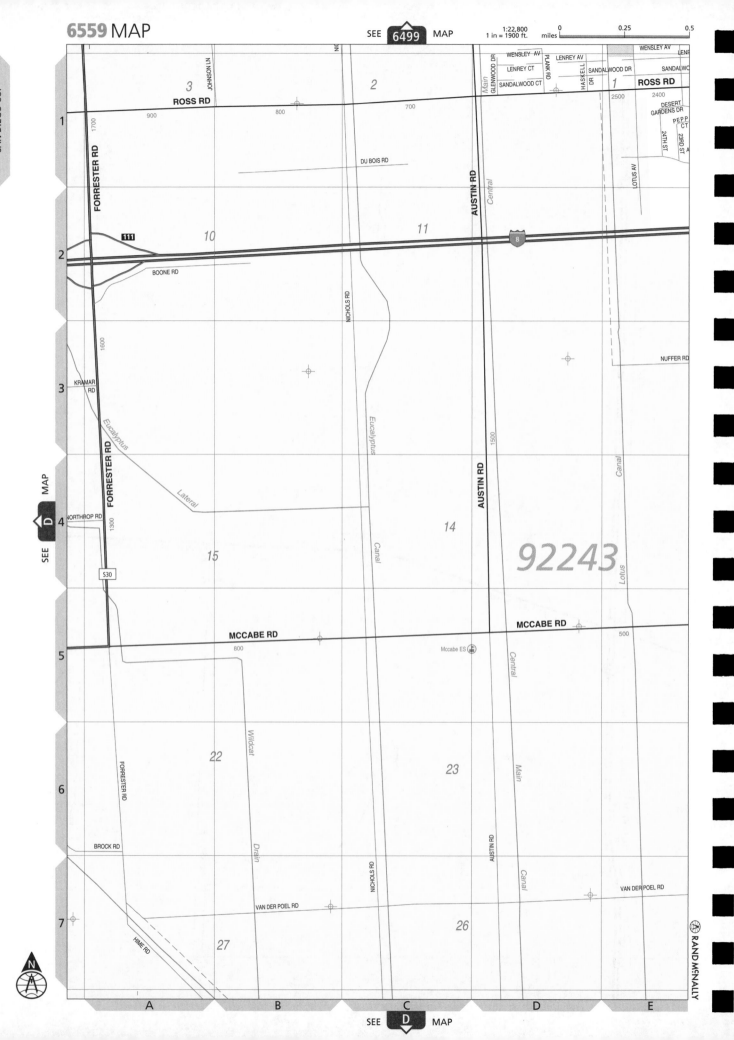

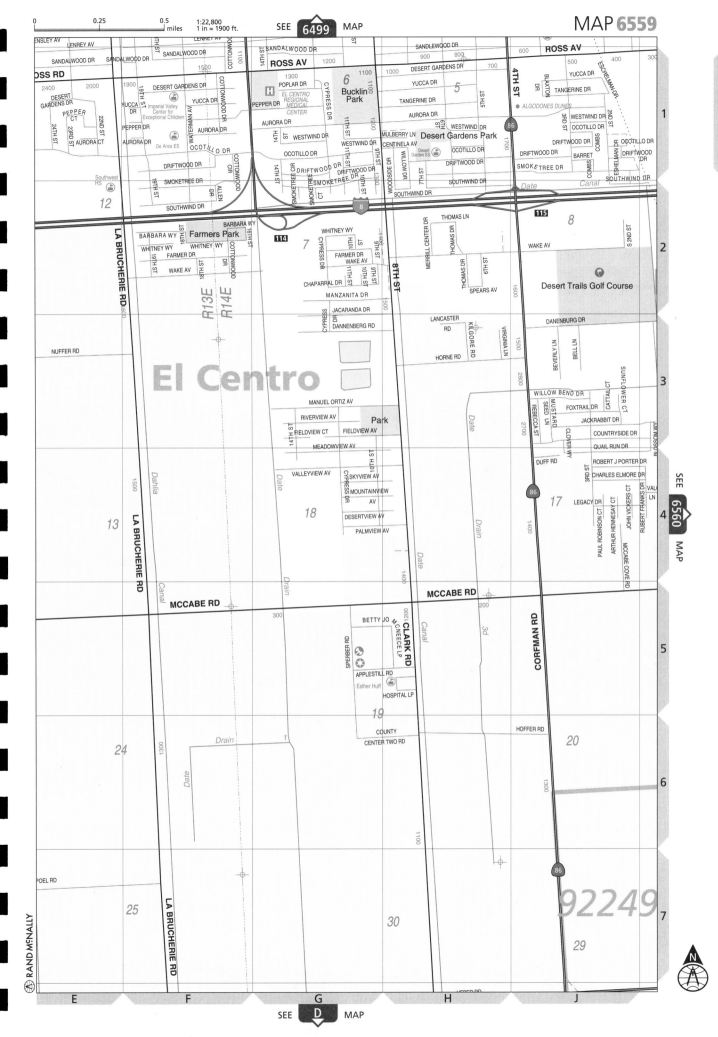

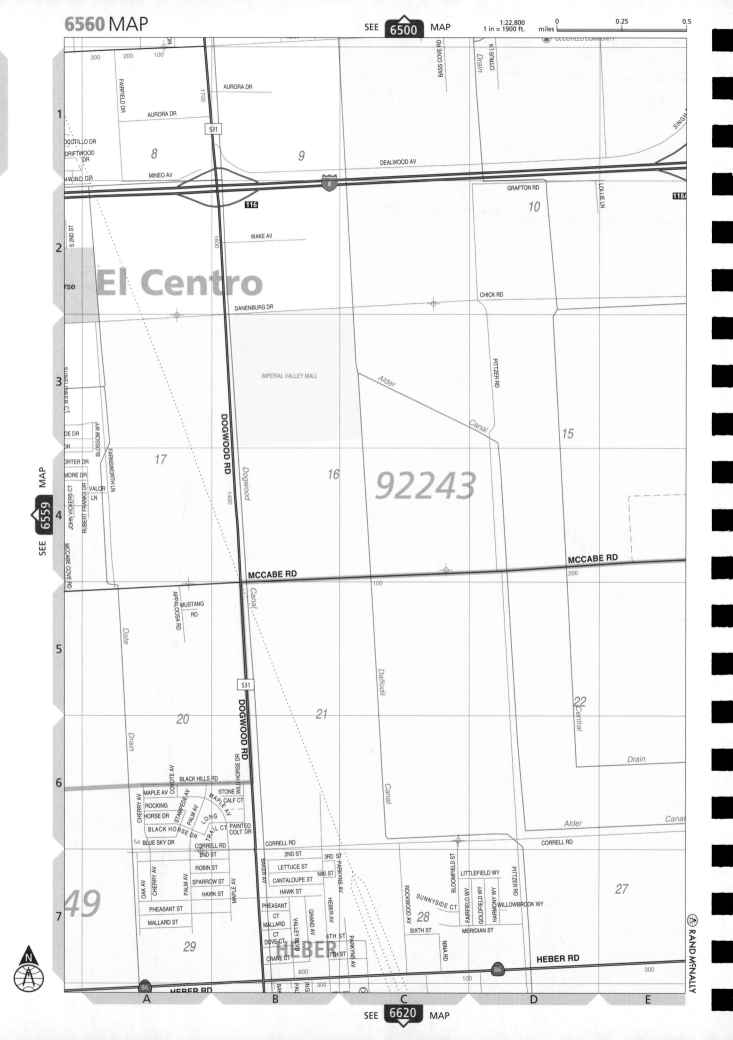

1:22,800
1 in = 1900 ft.

miles 0 0.25 0.5

SAN DIEGO CO.

OCOTILLO COMMUNITY

BASS COVE RD

CITRUS LN

Drain

SINGH

FAIRFIELD DR

300 200 100

MC

1700

AURORA DR

AURORA DR

S31

8

9

OCOTILLO DR

DRIFTWOOD DR

HWIND DR

MINEO AV

DEALWOOD AV

I-8

116

118A

GRAFTON RD

LOLLIE LN

10

S 2ND ST

1600

WAKE AV

2

El Centro

rse

CHICK RD

DANENBURG DR

PITZER RD

IMPERIAL VALLEY MALL

Alder

Canal

15

SUNFLOWER CT

DOGWOOD RD

Dogwood

3

DE DR

DR

ORTER DR

MORE DR

BLOSSOM WY

FARNSWORTH LN

17

VALOR LN

16

92243

JOHN VICKERS CT

RUBERT FRANKS DR

1400

SEE 6559 MAP

MCCABE COVE RD

MCCABE RD

4

MCCABE RD

MCCABE RD

200

100

Canal

APPALOOSA RD

MUSTANG RD

Date

Daffodil

5

DOGWOOD RD

S31

20

21

22

Central

Drain

Drain

Canal

6

COYOTE AV

BLACK HILLS RD

STONE

CALF CT

CHERRY AV

MAPLE AV

ROCKING HORSE DR

STAMPEDE AV

PALM AV

LONG

MAPLE AV

WILD HORSE RD

MAPLE AV

Alder

Canal

BLACK HORSE DR

TRAIL CT

PAINTED COLT DR

BLUE SKY DR

CORRELL RD

CORRELL RD

CORRELL RD

CORRELL RD

49

2ND ST

2ND ST

3RD ST

BAKER AV

LETTUCE ST

NIKI ST

PARKYNS AV

BLOOMFIELD ST

LITTLEFIELD WY

PITZER RD

27

OAK AV

CHERRY AV

PALM AV

ROBIN ST

SPARROW ST

MAPLE AV

CANTALOUPE ST

HEBER AV

ROCKWOOD AV

SUNNYSIDE CT

FAIRFIELD WY

GOLDFIELD WY

HARMONY WY

WILLOWBROOK WY

HAWK ST

HAWK ST

7

PHEASANT ST

MALLARD ST

PHEASANT CT

MALLARD CT

DOVE CT

GRAND AV

VALLEY BLVD

6TH ST

7TH ST

PARKYNS AV

SIXTH ST

28

MERIDIAN ST

29

CRANE CT

HEBER

800

INN RD

100

86

HEBER RD

300

N

86

HEBER RD

86

BAK

PAL

ING

300

A B C D E

RAND MCNALLY

MAP **6560**

SAN DIEGO CO.

0   0.25   0.5 miles
1:22,800
1 in = 1900 ft.

SINGH RD

HAWES

PARKER RD

GRESHAM RD

DEALWOOD RD

DEALWOOD RD

118B

8

120

Acacia

1

R14E
R15E

7

11

118A

12

GRESHAM RD

1600

Canal

BOWKER RD

2

YOURMAN RD

CHICK RD

CHICK RD

111

3

13

18

Acacia   5   Drain   14

YOURMAN RD

SEE D MAP

MCCABE RD

MCCABE RD

Acacia

4

300

800

92249

19

23

24

5

CHIEF FS PETE PEDROSA MEMORIAL HWY

3

YOURMAN RD

6

Canal

ABATTI RD

ABATTI RD

111

25

26

Central

7

HEBER RD

86

HEBER RD

RAND M?NALLY

300

SCARONI RD

E   F   G   H   J

N

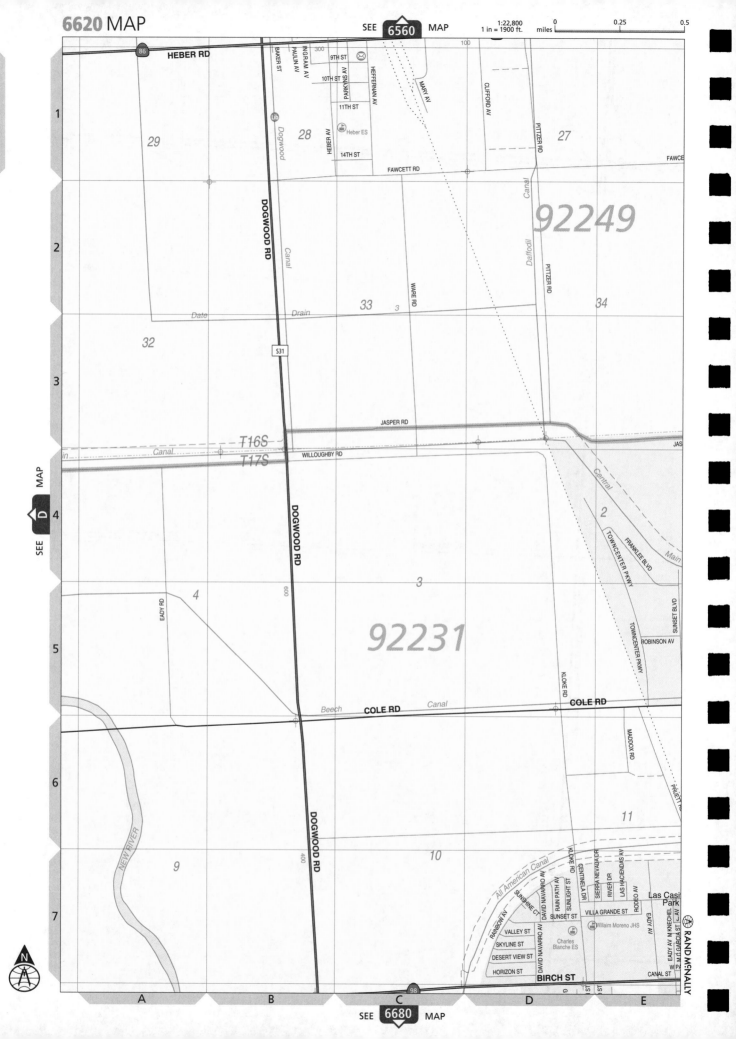

SAN DIEGO CO.

1:22,800
1 in = 1900 ft.

0   0.25   0.5
miles

HEBER RD

86

300

9TH ST
10TH ST
11TH ST

BAKER ST
INGRAM AV
PAULIN AV
PARKYNS AV

HEFFERNAN AV

MARY AV

CLIFFORD AV

PITZER RD

100

FAWCE

29

28

Lib

Dogwood

HEBER AV
Heber ES

14TH ST

FAWCETT RD

27

Canal

Daffodil

1

92249

DOGWOOD RD

Canal

Date

Drain

33

3

WARE RD

PITZER RD

34

2

32

S31

3

JASPER RD

T16S

Canal

JAS

DOGWOOD RD

T17S

WILLOUGHBY RD

Central

4

Main

2

FRANKLEE BLVD

TOWNCENTER PKWY

SUNSET BLVD

EADY RD

4

600

3

92231

TOWNCENTER PKWY

ROBINSON AV

5

KLOKE RD

Beech

COLE RD

Canal

COLE RD

MADDOX RD

6

New River

11

9

400

10

All American Canal

RAINBOW AV

SUNSHINE CT

DAVID NAVARRO AV

RAIN PATH AV

SUNLIGHT ST

SUNSET ST

KLOKE RD

CENTINELA DR

SIERRA NEVADA DR

RIVER DR

LAS HACIENDAS AV

RODEO AV

EADY AV

Las Casi
Park

7

VALLEY ST

SKYLINE ST

DESERT VIEW ST

HORIZON ST

DAVID NAVARRO AV

VILLA GRANDE ST

Willaim Moreno JHS

Charles
Blanche ES

BIRCH ST

CANAL ST

RAND MCNALLY

N

A   B   C   D   E

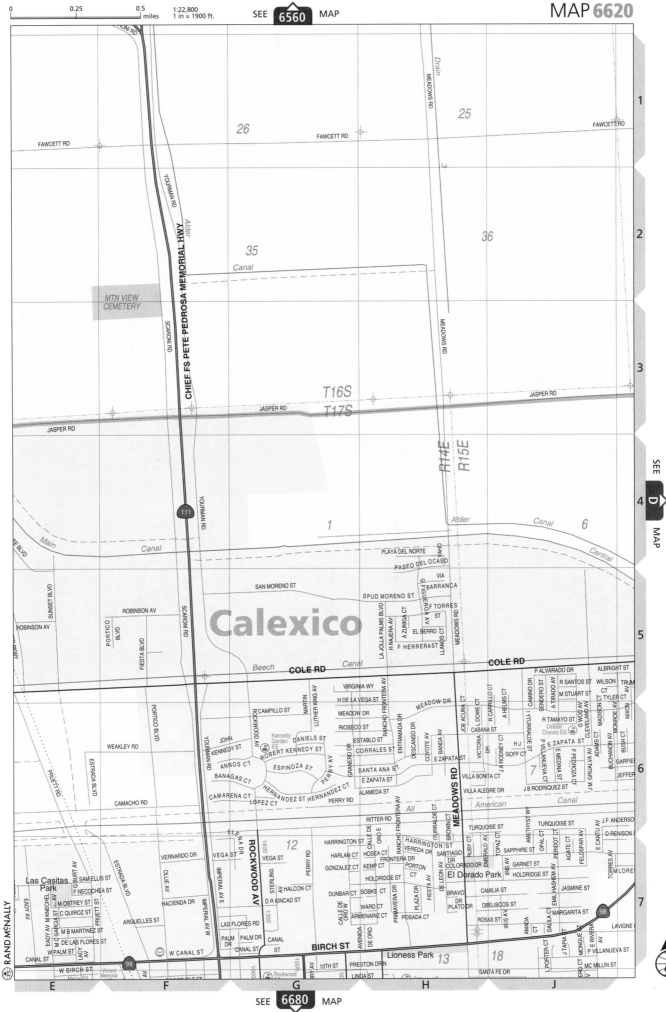

MAP **6620**

SAN DIEGO CO.

SEE **6560** MAP

0 0.25 0.5 miles
1:22,800
1 in = 1900 ft.

1

26

25

FAWCETT RD

FAWCETT RD

FAWCETT RD

2

36

35

Canal

MTN VIEW
CEMETERY

CHIEF FS PETE PEDROSA MEMORIAL HWY

YOURMAN RD

Alder

SCARONI RD

Drain

MEADOWS RD

MEADOWS RD

3

T16S
T17S

JASPER RD

JASPER RD

JASPER RD

R14E
R15E

111

YOURMAN RD

SEE
D
MAP

4

1

Alder

Canal

6

Central

Main

Canal

PLAYA DEL NORTE

PASEO DEL OCASO

SUNSET BLVD

PORTICO BLVD

SCARONI RD

FIESTA BLVD

ROBINSON AV

ROBINSON AV

ROBINSON AV

Calexico

SAN MORENO ST

SPUD MORENO ST

VIA
BARRANCA

G FIGUEROA AV

LA JOLLA PALMS BLVD

H NAJERA AV

A ZUNIGA CT

EL BERRO

F HERRERA ST

F TORRES
ST

MEADOWS RD

OHV

5

Beech

COLE RD

Canal

COLE RD

P ALVARADO DR

ALBRIGHT ST

WEAKLEY RD

PORTICO BLVD

ESTRADA BLVD

CAMACHO RD

YOURMAN RD

JOHN KENNEDY ST

ANNOS CT

BANAGAS CT

CAMARENA CT

ROCKWOOD AV

Kennedy Garden ES

ROBERT KENNEDY ST

ESPINOZA ST

HERNANDEZ ST HERNANDEZ CT

LOPEZ CT

MARTIN
LUTHER KING AV

DANIELS ST

PERRY AV

DESCANSO DR
ENTRAMADA DR
RANCHO FRONTERA AV

VIRGINIA WY

H DE LA VEGA ST

MEADOW DR

RIOSECO ST

GRANERO DR

ESTABLO ST

CORRALES ST

SANTA ANA ST

E ZAPATA ST

ALAMEDA ST

PERRY RD

MEADOW DR

BANDA AV

COYOTE AV

E ZAPATA ST

CAMPILLO ST

JOE ACUNA CT

L DOWE CT

CABANA ST

VICTORIA DR

J A RODNEY CT

VILLA BONITA CT

VILLA ALEGRE DR

R CAPRILLO CT

A HELMS CT

CAMINO DR

SENDERO ST

R TAMAYO ST

P VILLANUEVA CT

HJ
GOFF CT

Céssar
Chavez ES

G WOO AV

CLEVELAND ST

E ZAPATA ST

E MEDINA ST

J B RODRIQUEZ ST

R SANTOS ST

M STUART ST

A TIRADO CT

MADISON CT

ADAMS CT

P VILLANUEVA CT

F PEDROZA CT

J M GRUALVA AV

WILSON
CT

TYLER
CT

MONROE AV

BUCHANON AV

TRUM

NIXON
CT

BUSH CT

GARFIE

JEFFER

7

MEADOWS RD

All

American

Canal

PRUETT RD

ESTRADA BLVD

Las Casitas
Park

EADY AV

M KNECHEL
AV

M G GARCIA ST

C QUIROZ ST

W PALM ST

CANAL ST

SAM ELLIS ST

F NECOCHEA ST

DE LAS FLORES ST

J M OSTREY ST

M B MARTINEZ ST

LACY AV

W BIRCH ST

MaiselES

VERNARDO DR

OLLIE AV

HACIENDA DR

ARGUELLES ST

VEGA ST

IMPERIAL AV E

IMPERIAL AV W

LAS FLORES RD

PALM
DR

PALM DR

CANAL ST

W BIRCH ST

Vincent
Memorial

98

ROCKWOOD AV

EL ENA DR

VEGA ST

STERLIG

PERRY RD

1800

1300

12

RITTER RD

CALLE DE
ORO E

HARRINGTON ST

HARLAN CT

GONZALEZ ST

HOLDRIDGE ST

DUNBAR CT

AV HALCON CT

D R KINCAD ST

CALLE DE
ORO W

LINDA ST

RANCHO FRONTERA AV

HOSEA CT

KEMP CT

SOBKE CT

WARD CT

ARMENARIZ ST

AVENIDA
DE ORO

HARRINGTON ST
VEREDA DR

FRONTERA ST

PORTON
CT

DE LEON AV

PRIMAVERA AV

PLAZA CT

POSADA CT

10TH ST

PRESTON DR IN

ITURRALDE CT

BROWN CT

RUBY CT

SANTIAGO
ST

DE COLORADO DR

FIESTA AV

BRAVO
DR

PLATO DR

El Dorado Park

Rockwood

TURQUOISE ST

EMERALD AV

AMETHYST WY

OPAL ST

IRIS AV

ROSAS ST

SANTA FE DR

TURQUOISE ST

SAPPHIRE ST

PERIDOT CT

GARNET ST

CAMILIA ST

OBELISCOS ST

J F ANDERSO

E RENISON
ST

E CANTU AV

AGATE CT

FELDSPAR CT

HOLDRIDGE ST

JASMINE ST

E HASHEM AV

DALILA ST

MARGARITA ST

AMADA

TORRES AV

M LORE

98

LAVIGNE

L PORTER CT

J TAPIA

J RIVERA
AV

P VILLANUEVA ST

MC MILLIN ST

EMIL HASHEM AV

ERO CT

MONGUE

BIRCH ST

Lioness Park

13

18

1000

E F G H J

1:22,800
1 in = 1900 ft.

miles
0   0.25   0.5

SAN DIEGO CO.

BIRCH ST

98

G LUNA ST
DAVID NAVARRO AV
PADILLA
H FRITSCH ST
D MERCADO ST
W L MORENO
SALVADOR GUILIN ST
BRANDENBURG
CONTRERAS CT
SHERIDAN ST
NOSOTROS ST
KEMP RD
9
MENDOZA ST
MATILDE GOMEZ
CHAVEZ AV
GRANT ST
KLOKE AV
ALDER AV
MCK
LINCOLN S
GRANT ST

1

M ACUNA AV
THIELEMANN AV
R D PLATERO AV
MATALLANA CT
LINHOLM AV
CALEXICO ST

Nosotros Little
League Field

Wistaria
Canal
NEW RIVER
W SHERMAN ST
WOZENCRAFT ST
AMINAL SHELTER DR

16
Lateral
15

CALEXICO
INTERNATIONAL
AIRPORT

2

92231

P2

Wistaria
ANZA RD

ANZA RD
22
23

21
UNITED STATES
MEXICO

ANZA RD

3

SEE D MAP
4

5

6

7

N

A   B   C   D   E

RAND MCNALLY

SEE D MAP

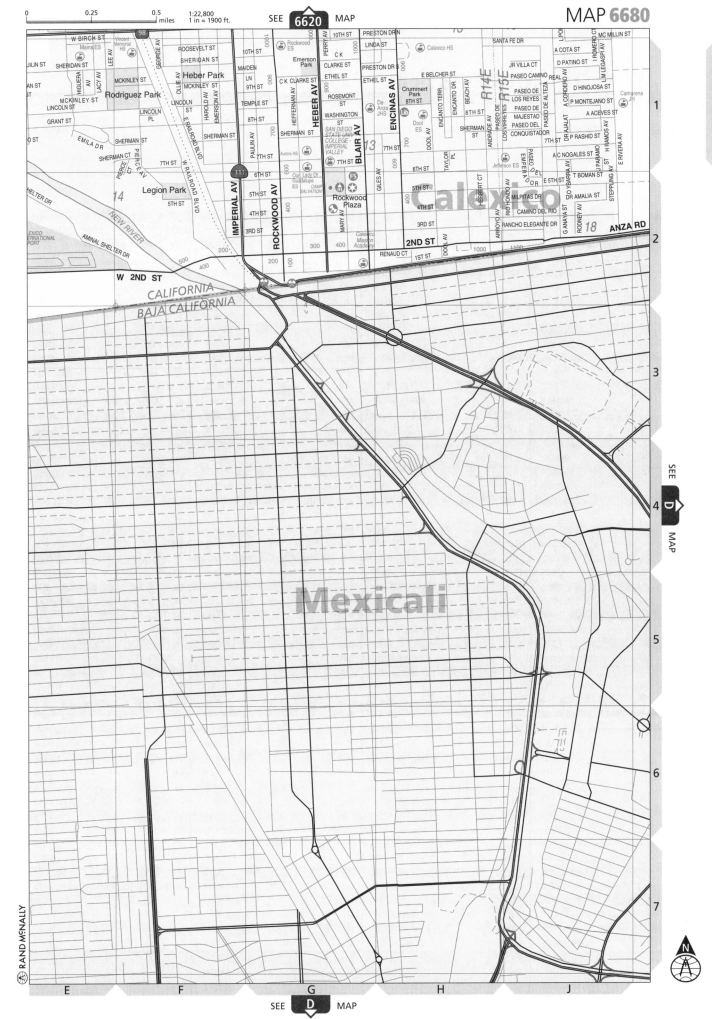

MAP **6680**

SAN DIEGO CO.

SEE 6620 MAP

0   0.25   0.5
miles
1:22,800
1 in = 1900 ft.

W BIRCH ST
Mains ES
Vincent Memorial HS
SHERIDAN ST
HIGUERA AV
LACY AV
LEE AV
GEORGE AV
W RAILROAD BLVD
E RAILROAD BLVD
ROOSEVELT ST
SHERIDAN ST
Heber Park
MAIDEN LN
10TH ST
Rockwood ES
PERRY AV
10TH ST
PRESTON DR N
LINDA ST
PRESTON DR
Calexico HS
SANTA FE DR
MC MILLIN ST
A COTA ST
D PATINO ST
I ROMERO CT
L M LEGASPI AV
McKINLEY ST
MCKINLEY AV
McKINLEY ST
Rodriguez Park
LINCOLN ST
LINCOLN PL
LINCOLN
HAROLD AV
EMERSON ST
McKINLEY
LINCOLN
9TH ST
C K CLARKE ST
CLARKE ST
ETHEL ST
E BELCHER ST
Emerson Park
JR VILLA CT
PASEO CAMINO
REAL AV
D HINOJOSA DR
A CORDERO AV
P MONTEJANO ST
A ACEVES ST
Camarena
GRANT ST
TEMPLE ST
8TH ST
ROSEMONT
WASHINGTON
Calexico HS
8TH ST
ENCANTO DR
PASEO DE LOS REYES
PASEO DE MAJESTAD
ST
EMILA DR
SHERMAN ST
PAULIN AV
7TH ST
SHERMAN ST
De Anza JHS
Dool ES
SHERMAN AV
ANDRADE AV
8TH ST
7TH ST
LOS VIRREYES
R14E
R15E
PASEO DEL CONQUISTADOR
DR AJALAT
DR P RASHID ST
SHERMAN ST
SHERMAN CT
PIERCE AV
SHERMAN ST
San Diego State Univ College - Imperial Valley
A C NOGALES ST
PASEO DEL EMPERADOR
7TH ST
Jefferson ES
E 5TH ST
ST
PIERCE AV
Aurora HS
7TH ST
6TH ST
TAYLOR PL
T BOMAN ST
DR AMALIA ST
STEPPLING AV
E RIVERA AV
Legion Park
6TH ST
Our Lady Of Guadalupe ES
CAMP SALVATION
ES
7TH ST
FS
6TH ST
5TH ST
HERBERT CT
RIO HONDO AV
MILPITAS ST
DR AMALIA ST
IMPERIAL AV
5TH ST
5TH ST
GILES AV
Calexico
5TH ST
4TH ST
CAMINO DEL RIO
G ANAYA ST
RODNEY AV
18
ANZA RD
4TH ST
MARY AV
Rockwood Plaza
4TH ST
4TH ST
ARROYO AV
RANCHO ELEGANTE DR
3RD ST
3RD ST
3RD ST
2ND ST
Calexico Mission Academy
2ND ST
RENAUD CT
1ST ST
DOOL AV
1000
1100
W 2ND ST
NEW RIVER
500
400
200
100
200
300
400
ANZA RD
AMINAL SHELTER DR
MEXICO INTERNATIONAL PORT
SHELTER DR
CALIFORNIA
BAJA CALIFORNIA
W 2ND ST

Calexico

Mexicali

SEE D MAP

SEE D MAP

RAND McNALLY

14

13

1

2

3

4

5

6

7

E   F   G   H   J

N

List of Abbreviations

ADMIN	ADMINISTRATION	CO	COUNTY	JCT	JUNCTION	REG	REGIONAL
AGRI	AGRICULTURAL	CT	COURT	KNL	KNOLL	RES	RESERVOIR
AG	AGRICULTURE	CT HSE	COURT HOUSE	LK	LAKE	RST	REST
AFB	AIR FORCE BASE	CV	COVE	LNDG	LANDING	RDG	RIDGE
ARPT	AIRPORT	CR	CREEK	LN	LANE	RIV	RIVER
AL	ALLEY	CRES	CRESCENT	LIB	LIBRARY	RD	ROAD
AMER	AMERICAN	CROSS	CROSSING	LDG	LODGE	ST.	SAINT
ANX	ANNEX	CURV	CURVE	LP	LOOP	STE.	SAINTE
ARC	ARCADE	CTO	CUT OFF	MNR	MANOR	SCI	SCIENCE/SCIENTIFIC
ARCH	ARCHAEOLOGICAL	DEPT	DEPARTMENT	MKT	MARKET	SHOP CTR	SHOPPING CENTER
AUD	AUDITORIUM	DEV	DEVELOPMENT	MDW	MEADOW	SHR	SHORE
AVD	AVENIDA	DIAG	DIAGONAL	MED	MEDICAL	SKWY	SKYWAY
AV	AVENUE	DIV	DIVISION	MEM	MEMORIAL	S	SOUTH
BFLD	BATTLEFIELD	DR	DRIVE	METRO	METROPOLITAN	SPR	SPRING
BCH	BEACH	DRWY	DRIVEWAY	MW	MEWS	SQ	SQUARE
BLTWY	BELTWAY	E	EAST	MIL	MILITARY	STAD	STADIUM
BND	BEND	EL	ELEVATION	ML	MILL	ST FOR, SF	STATE FOREST
BIO	BIOLOGICAL	ENV	ENVIRONMENTAL	MON	MONUMENT	ST HIST SITE, SHS	STATE HISTORIC SITE
BLF	BLUFF	EST	ESTATE	MTWY	MOTORWAY	ST NAT AREA, SNA	STATE NATURAL AREA
BLVD	BOULEVARD	EXH	EXHIBITION	MND	MOUND	ST PK, SP	STATE PARK
BRCH	BRANCH	EXPM	EXPERIMENTAL	MT	MOUNT	ST REC AREA, SRA	STATE RECREATION AREA
BR	BRIDGE	EXPO	EXPOSITION	MTN	MOUNTAIN	STA	STATION
BRK	BROOK	EXPWY	EXPRESSWAY	MUN	MUNICIPAL	ST	STREET
BLDG	BUILDING	EXT	EXTENSION	MUS	MUSEUM	SMT	SUMMIT
BUR	BUREAU	FCLT	FACILITY	NAT'L	NATIONAL	SYMPH	SYMPHONY
BUS	BUSINESS	FRGDS	FAIRGROUNDS	NAT'L FOR, NF	NATIONAL FOREST	SYS	SYSTEMS
BSWY	BUSWAY	FT	FEET	NAT'L HIST PK, NHP	NATIONAL HISTORIC PARK	TECH	TECHNICAL/TECHNOLOGY
BYP	BYPASS	FY	FERRY	NAT'L HIST SITE, NHS	NATIONAL HISTORIC SITE	TER	TERRACE
BYWY	BYWAY	FLD	FIELD	NAT'L MON, NM	NATIONAL MONUMENT	TERR	TERRITORY
CL	CALLE	FLT	FLAT	NAT'L PK, NP	NATIONAL PARK	THTR	THEATER
CLJN	CALLEJON	FOR	FOREST	NAT'L REC AREA, NRA	NATIONAL RECREATION AREA	THEOL	THEOLOGICAL
CMTO	CAMINITO	FK	FORK	NAT'L WLD REF, NWR	NATIONAL WILDLIFE REFUGE	THWY	THROUGHWAY
CM	CAMINO	FT	FORT	NAT	NATURAL	TOLL FY	TOLL FERRY
CYN	CANYON	FOUND	FOUNDATION	NAS	NAVAL AIR STATION	TIC	TOURIST INFORMATION CENTER
CAP	CAPITOL	FRWY	FREEWAY	NK	NOOK	TWP	TOWNSHIP
CATH	CATHEDRAL/CATHOLIC	GDN	GARDEN	N	NORTH	TRC	TRACE
CSWY	CAUSEWAY	GEN HOSP	GENERAL HOSPITAL	ORCH	ORCHARD	TRFWY	TRAFFICWAY
CEM	CEMETERY	GLN	GLEN	OHWY	OUTER HIGHWAY	TR	TRAIL
CTR	CENTER/CENTRE	GC	GOLF COURSE	OVL	OVAL	TRAN	TRANSIT
CENT	CENTRAL	GOV'T	GOVERNMENT	OVLK	OVERLOOK	TRANSP	TRANSPORTATION
CIR	CIRCLE	GRN	GREEN	OVPS	OVERPASS	TUN	TUNNEL
CRLO	CIRCULO	GRDS	GROUNDS	PK	PARK	TPK	TURNPIKE
CH	CITY HALL	GRV	GROVE	PKWY	PARKWAY	UNPS	UNDERPASS
CIV	CIVIC	HBR	HARBOR/HARBOUR	PAS	PASEO	UNIV	UNIVERSITY
CLF	CLIFF	HVN	HAVEN	PSG	PASSAGE	VLY	VALLEY
CLB	CLUB	HQS	HEADQUARTERS	PASS	PASSENGER	VET	VETERANS
CLTR	CLUSTER	HT	HEIGHT	PTH	PATH	VW	VIEW
COL	COLISEUM	HTS	HEIGHTS	PN	PINE	VIL	VILLAGE
COLL	COLLEGE	HS	HIGH SCHOOL	PL	PLACE	VIS BUR	VISITORS BUREAU
COM	COMMON	HWY	HIGHWAY	PLN	PLAIN	VIS	VISTA
COMS	COMMONS	HL	HILL	PLGND	PLAYGROUND	WK	WALK
COMM	COMMUNITY	HIST	HISTORIC/HISTORICAL	PLZ	PLAZA	WY	WAY
CO.	COMPANY	HLLW	HOLLOW	PT	POINT	W	WEST
CONS	CONSERVATION	HOSP	HOSPITAL	PND	POND	WLD	WILDLIFE
CONT HS	CONTINUATION HIGH SCHOOL	HSE	HOUSE	PRES	PRESERVE	WMA	WILDLIFE MANAGEMENT AREA
CONV & VIS BUR	CONVENTION AND VISITORS BUREAU	IND RES	INDIAN RESERVATION	PROV	PROVINCIAL		
CONV CTR	CONVENTION CENTER	INFO	INFORMATION	RR	RAILROAD		
COR	CORNER	INST	INSTITUTE	RWY	RAILWAY		
CORP	CORPORATION	INT'L	INTERNATIONAL	RCH	RANCH		
CORR	CORRIDOR	I	ISLAND	RCHO	RANCHO		
CTE	CORTE	IS	ISLANDS	REC	RECREATION		
CC	COUNTRY CLUB	ISL	ISLE	REF	REFUGE		

SAN DIEGO CO.

Cities and Communities Index

Community Name	Abbr.	County	Map Page
Alamorio		Imperial	6259
Alpine		San Diego	1234
Alpine Heights		San Diego	1253
Alta Vista		San Diego	1290
-- Baja California	MX		
Ballena		San Diego	1154
Bancroft Point		San Diego	1271
Bankhead Springs		San Diego	1300
Banner		San Diego	1156
Barona		San Diego	1192
Barrio Logan		San Diego	1289
Bear Valley		San Diego	1111
Birch Hill		San Diego	1052
Blossom Valley		San Diego	1232
Bonita		San Diego	1310
Bonsall		San Diego	1067
Borrego Springs		San Diego	1058
Bostonia		San Diego	1251
Boulevard		San Diego	1300
* Brawley	BRAW	Imperial	6259
Broadway Heights		San Diego	1270
Buena		San Diego	1108
Calavo Gardens		San Diego	1271
* Calexico	CALX	Imperial	6680
Cameron Corners		San Diego	1298
Campo		San Diego	1298
Camp Pendleton		San Diego	1085
* Carlsbad	CRLB	San Diego	1106
Carmel Mountain Ranch		San Diego	1190
Carmel Valley		San Diego	1188
Casa de Oro		San Diego	1271
Centre City		San Diego	1289
Chappo		San Diego	1066
Chollas Creek		San Diego	1270
Chollas View		San Diego	1289
* Chula Vista	CHLV	San Diego	1310
* Coronado	CORD	San Diego	1308
Coronado Cays		San Diego	1329
Cottonwood		San Diego	1272
Crown Point		San Diego	1268
Cuyamaca		San Diego	1176
Dehesa		San Diego	1253
Del Dios		San Diego	1149
* Del Mar	DLMR	San Diego	1187
De Luz		San Diego	996
Descanso		San Diego	1236
Descanso Junction		San Diego	1216
Desert Lodge		San Diego	1098
Dulzura		San Diego	1294
East Elliott		San Diego	1230
Eastlake Greens		San Diego	1311
Eden Gardens		San Diego	1187
* El Cajon	ELCJ	San Diego	1251
* El Centro	ELCN	Imperial	6499
El Monte Park		San Diego	1213
Emerald Hills		San Diego	1290
* Encinitas	ENCT	San Diego	1147
Engineer Springs		San Diego	1294
* Escondido	ESCN	San Diego	1129
Eucalyptus Hills		San Diego	1211
Fairbanks Country Club		San Diego	1188
Fairbanks Ranch		San Diego	1168
Fallbrook		San Diego	1027
Fernbrook		San Diego	1192
Fleetridge		San Diego	1288
Flinn Springs		San Diego	1233
Foster		San Diego	1211
Glen Oaks		San Diego	1233
Glenview		San Diego	1232
Granite Hills		San Diego	1252
Grant Hill		San Diego	1289
Green Valley Falls		San Diego	1216
Guatay		San Diego	1216
Harbison Canyon		San Diego	1253
Harmony Grove		San Diego	1129
Harrison Park		San Diego	1156
Heber		Imperial	6560
Hidden Glen		San Diego	1254
Hidden Meadows		San Diego	1089
Homelands		San Diego	1271
Hulburd Grove		San Diego	1235
* Imperial	IMPE	Imperial	6439
* Imperial Beach	IMPB	San Diego	1349
-- Imperial County	ImCo		
Indian Springs		San Diego	1292
Irvings Crest		San Diego	1192
Jacumba		San Diego	1300
Jamacha (SDCo)		San Diego	1272
Jamacha (SDCO)		San Diego	1290
Jamacha Junction		San Diego	1271

Community Name	Abbr.	County	Map Page
Jamul		San Diego	1292
Jesmond Dene		San Diego	1109
Johnstown		San Diego	1232
Julian		San Diego	1136
Kearny Mesa		San Diego	1249
Kentwood-In-The-Pines		San Diego	1156
La Cresta		San Diego	1252
La Jolla Amago		San Diego	1052
La Jolla Shores		San Diego	1227
Lake San Marcos		San Diego	1128
Lakeside		San Diego	1232
Lakeside Farms		San Diego	1231
Lakeview		San Diego	1232
* La Mesa	LMSA	San Diego	1270
La Presa		San Diego	1291
* Lemon Grove	LMGR	San Diego	1270
Liberty Station		San Diego	1268
Lilac		San Diego	1069
Lincoln Acres		San Diego	1310
Lincoln Park		San Diego	1290
Little Italy		San Diego	1288
Live Oak Park		San Diego	1028
Live Oak Springs		San Diego	1298
Lomas Santa Fe		San Diego	1167
Lomita		San Diego	1290
Lynwood Hills		San Diego	1310
Manzanita		San Diego	1300
Memorial		San Diego	1289
* Mexicali	MXCL	Baja California	6680
Middletown		San Diego	1268
Midway		San Diego	1268
Miramar		San Diego	1209
Miramar Ranch North		San Diego	1209
Mission Bay Park		San Diego	1268
Mission Valley		San Diego	1269
Mission Village		San Diego	1249
Morena Village		San Diego	1296
Moreno		San Diego	1232
Mountain View		San Diego	1289
Mount Helix		San Diego	1271
Mount Hope		San Diego	1289
Mount Laguna		San Diego	1218
* National City	NATC	San Diego	1309
Navajo		San Diego	1250
North Bay Terraces		San Diego	1290
North Encanto		San Diego	1290
North Jamul		San Diego	1272
Oak Park		San Diego	1290
Ocean Beach		San Diego	1267
Ocean Hills		San Diego	1107
* Oceanside	OCSD	San Diego	1086
-- Orange County	OrCo		
Pacific Highlands Ranch		San Diego	1188
Pala		San Diego	1029
Pala Mesa		San Diego	1048
Palomar Mountain		San Diego	1052
Palo Verde		San Diego	1234
Paso Picacho		San Diego	1176
Pauma Valley		San Diego	1051
Peninsula		San Diego	1288
Pine Hills		San Diego	1155
Pine Valley		San Diego	1237
* Poway	POWY	San Diego	1190
Rainbow		San Diego	998
Ramona		San Diego	1152
Rancho Palo Verde		San Diego	1254
Rancho San Diego		San Diego	1271
Rancho Santa Fe		San Diego	1168
Rincon		San Diego	1051
-- Riverside County	RivC		
Riverview		San Diego	1231
Riverview Farms		San Diego	1231
Rock Haven		San Diego	1171
Rolando		San Diego	1270
Rosemont		San Diego	1192
Roseville		San Diego	1288
Sabre Springs		San Diego	1189
* San Clemente	SCLE	Orange	1023
* San Diego	SDGO	San Diego	1289
San Diego Country Estates		San Diego	1173
-- San Diego County	SDCo		
San Luis Rey Heights		San Diego	1048
* San Marcos	SNMS	San Diego	1108
San Onofre		San Diego	1023
San Pasqual		San Diego	1131
Santa Ysabel		San Diego	1135
* Santee	SNTE	San Diego	1231
San Ysidro		San Diego	1350
Shelltown		San Diego	1289
Shelter Valley Ranchos		San Diego	1138
Sherman Heights		San Diego	1289

Community Name	Abbr.	County	Map Page
Skyline		San Diego	1290
* Solana Beach	SOLB	San Diego	1187
Sorrento Mesa		San Diego	1208
South Bay Terraces		San Diego	1290
Southcrest		San Diego	1289
South Encanto		San Diego	1290
South Oceanside		San Diego	1106
Spring Valley		San Diego	1271
Stockton		San Diego	1289
Suncrest		San Diego	1252
Sunnyside		San Diego	1310
* Tecate	TECT	Baja California	1300
The Narrows		San Diego	1100
The Willows		San Diego	1234
Tierra del Sol		San Diego	1300
Tierrasanta		San Diego	1249
* Tijuana	TJNA	Baja California	1351
Tijuana River Valley		San Diego	1350
Torrey Highlands		San Diego	1189
Torrey Hills		San Diego	1208
Torrey Pines		San Diego	1187
Uptown		San Diego	1269
Valencia Park		San Diego	1290
Valley Center		San Diego	1090
Via de la Valle		San Diego	1187
Victoria		San Diego	1234
* Vista	VSTA	San Diego	1087
Whispering Pines		San Diego	1136
Winter Gardens		San Diego	1231
Winterwarm		San Diego	1048
Wynola		San Diego	1135

* Indicates incorporated city

San Diego County Street Index

STREET Block City Map# Grid

HIGHWAYS

ALT - Alternate Route
BIA - Bureau of Indian Affairs
BUS - Business Route
CO - County Highway/ Road
FM - Farm to Market Road
HIST - Historic Highway
I - Interstate Highway
LP - State Loop
PK - Park & Recreation Road
PROV - Provincial Highway
RTE - Other Route
SPR - State Spur
SR - State Route/ Highway
TCH - Trans-Canada Highway
US - United States Highway

CO-S1
700 SDCo 1218 F6
1300 SDCo 1317 J4
(See Page 1296)
1300 SDCo 1318 A5
(See Page 1298)
6800 SDCo 1237 H2
12200 SDCo 1176 H3
12200 SDCo 1217 J1
(See Page 1216)
CO-S1 Buckman Springs Rd
1300 SDCo 1317 J4
(See Page 1296)
1300 SDCo 1318 A5
(See Page 1298)
CO-S1 Sunrise Hwy
700 SDCo 1218 F6
6800 SDCo 1237 E6
(See Page 1216)
12200 SDCo 1197 J7
(See Page 1176)
CO-S2
6600 SDCo 1138 C7
CO-S2 Great Sthn Ovld Rte-1849
6600 SDCo 1138 A4
CO-S3
2500 SDCo 1078 J2
(See Page 1058)
3500 SDCo 1099 A1
(See Page 1098)
CO-S3 Borrego Springs Rd
2500 SDCo 1078 J2
(See Page 1058)
3500 SDCo 1099 A1
(See Page 1098)
CO-S3 Yaqui Pass Rd
3800 SDCo 1099 F1
(See Page 1098)
CO-S4
11000 SDGO 1189 H6
11600 POWY 1190 E4
11600 SDGO 1190 B5
14900 POWY 1191 C1
CO-S4 Poway Rd
11000 SDGO 1189 H6
11600 POWY 1190 J2
11600 SDGO 1190 B5
14900 POWY 1191 C1
CO-S4 Rancho Penasquitos Blvd
- SDGO 1189 G6
CO-S5
12700 POWY 1170 G7
14500 POWY 1190 G2
16900 SDGO 1170 C1
17600 SDGO 1150 C7
CO-S5 Espola Rd
- SDGO 1170 D3
14500 POWY 1190 G2
14800 POWY 1170 G7
CO-S5 Pomerado Rd
16900 SDGO 1170 C1
17600 SDGO 1150 B7
CO-S5 Rancho Bernardo Rd
12500 SDGO 1170 C3
12700 POWY 1170 D3
CO-S6
100 DLMR 1187 F2
100 ESCN 1129 F5
100 SOLB 1187 F2
500 ESCN 1130 A2
1700 ESCN 1110 E7
2700 SDGO 1187 H2
3600 SDCo 1188 C1
3600 SDGO 1188 A1
6200 SDCo 1168 C7
8000 SDCo 1148 J7
8100 SDCo 1149 E1
9500 ESCN 1149 E1
9900 SDCo 1129 E7
24800 SDCo 1110 F1
26900 SDCo 1090 E7
30400 SDCo 1091 B2

CO-S6
31400 SDCo 1071 D6
31700 SDCo 1052 E1
33900 SDCo 1032 E5
34800 SDCo 1051 E7
CO-S6 E 2nd Av
100 ESCN 1129 J3
CO-S6 W 2nd Av
100 ESCN 1129 J3
CO-S6 Canfield Rd
33100 SDCo 1052 E1
33900 SDCo 1032 E5
CO-S6 Del Dios Hwy
1700 ESCN 1129 F5
7000 SDCo 1168 H1
8000 SDCo 1148 J7
8100 SDCo 1149 B7
9500 ESCN 1149 E1
9900 SDCo 1129 E7
CO-S6 S Grade Rd
31700 SDCo 1052 C6
CO-S6 W Grand Av
600 ESCN 1129 H3
CO-S6 Paseo Delicias
6200 SDCo 1168 E2
CO-S6 Valley Blvd
100 ESCN 1129 J2
CO-S6 E Valley Pkwy
100 ESCN 1129 J2
500 ESCN 1130 C1
1700 ESCN 1110 E7
CO-S6 W Valley Pkwy
1700 ESCN 1129 F5
10300 SDCo 1129 E6
CO-S6 Valley Center Rd
24700 ESCN 1110 F1
24800 SDCo 1110 F1
26900 SDCo 1090 E4
30400 SDCo 1091 A2
31400 SDCo 1071 D6
34800 SDCo 1051 E7
CO-S6 Via de la Valle
100 DLMR 1187 F2
100 SOLB 1187 F2
2700 SDGO 1187 H2
3600 SDCo 1188 A1
3600 SDGO 1188 A1
15100 SDCo 1168 E3
CO-S7
21300 SDCo 1052 H5
CO-S7 Canfield Rd
33100 SDCo 1052 F3
CO-S7 E Grade Rd
21500 SDCo 1052 F3
CO-S7 State Park Rd
21300 SDCo 1052 F3
CO-S8
100 SOLB 1167 F7
1500 SDCo 1167 J6
4000 SDCo 1168 D3
CO-S8 Linea del Cielo
4000 SDCo 1168 A6
CO-S8 Lomas Santa Fe Dr
- SDCo 1168 A6
100 SOLB 1167 G7
1500 SDCo 1167 J6
CO-S8 Paseo Delicias
6100 SDCo 1168 D3
CO-S9
10 ENCT 1147 C6
100 ENCT 1167 J1
200 SDCo 1167 J1
4800 SDCo 1168 A2
CO-S9 Encinitas Blvd
10 ENCT 1147 E7
2000 ENCT 1167 J1
CO-S9 La Bajada
17400 SDCo 1168 A2
17600 SDCo 1167 J1
CO-S9 La Granada
4800 SDCo 1168 C3
CO-S9 Los Morros
17200 SDCo 1168 A3
CO-S9 Rancho Santa Fe Rd S
100 ENCT 1167 J1
200 SDCo 1167 J1
CO-S10
- CRLB 1148 A1
100 SNMS 1108 D6
400 SNMS 1128 C1
800 SDCo 1128 C1
1600 CRLB 1128 B6
7700 CRLB 1147 H3
CO-S10 Rancho Santa Fe Rd
- CRLB 1148 A1
1600 CRLB 1128 B6
1600 SNMS 1128 A5
7700 CRLB 1147 H3
CO-S10 N Rancho Santa Fe Rd
100 SNMS 1108 D6
CO-S10 S Rancho Santa Fe Rd
100 SNMS 1108 D6
400 SNMS 1128 C1
800 SDCo 1128 C1
2000 CRLB 1128 A5
CO-S11
- OCSD 1106 G2
200 ENCT 1147 F7
400 ENCT 1167 G1

CO-S11
2500 CRLB 1106 G2
5000 CRLB 1107 C7
5600 CRLB 1127 E3
7300 CRLB 1147 E1
CO-S11 El Camino Real
- ENCT 1147 F4
- OCSD 1106 G2
2500 CRLB 1106 H5
4900 CRLB 1107 C7
5600 CRLB 1127 D1
7300 CRLB 1147 E1
CO-S11 N El Camino Real
100 ENCT 1147 F7
CO-S11 S El Camino Real
200 ENCT 1147 F7
400 ENCT 1167 G1
CO-S11 Manchester Av
3000 ENCT 1167 G4
CO-S12
- CRLB 1128 A2
100 SDCo 1108 J1
100 SNMS 1108 H7
200 SDCo 1088 J7
200 SDCo 1109 A1
500 SDCo 1089 B7
500 SNMS 1128 F1
600 CRLB 1126 H3
1000 CRLB 1127 J2
1600 SDCo 1128 C2
2100 VSTA 1128 A2
CO-S12 Deer Springs Rd
100 SDCo 1108 J1
100 SNMS 1108 J1
200 SDCo 1088 J7
200 SDCo 1109 A1
500 SDCo 1089 B7
CO-S12 Palomar Airport Rd
- CRLB 1128 A2
- SNMS 1128 A2
- VSTA 1128 A2
100 CRLB 1126 G3
1000 CRLB 1127 A3
CO-S12 W San Marcos Blvd
100 SNMS 1108 H7
400 SNMS 1128 A2
1600 SDCo 1128 C2
2100 VSTA 1128 A2
CO-S12 N Twin Oaks Valley Rd
- SNMS 1108 H7
CO-S13
100 SDCo 1027 G2
100 VSTA 1087 J5
1000 VSTA 1088 A4
2200 SDCo 1088 A1
2400 SDCo 998 B7
2400 SDCo 1068 A7
2600 SDCo 1047 J6
2800 SDCo 1067 J6
3000 SDCo 1028 F1
4500 SDCo 1048 A7
CO-S13 N Main Av
100 SDCo 1027 F2
CO-S13 S Main Av
100 SDCo 1027 F3
CO-S13 E Mission Rd
100 SDCo 1027 J1
2400 SDCo 998 B7
3000 SDCo 1028 F1
CO-S13 N Mission Rd
100 SDCo 1027 F2
CO-S13 S Mission Rd
100 SDCo 1027 F4
2600 SDCo 1047 H3
4500 SDCo 1048 A7
CO-S13 W Mission Rd
100 SDCo 1027 F2
CO-S13 Old Highway 395
- SDCo 1028 F1
CO-S13 E Vista Wy
400 VSTA 1087 J5
1000 VSTA 1088 A4
2200 SDCo 1088 A1
2400 SDCo 1068 A7
2800 SDCo 1067 J6
CO-S13 W Vista Wy
100 VSTA 1087 G7
CO-S13 Vista Village Dr
200 VSTA 1087 G7
CO-S14
- OCSD 1067 C7
100 SNMS 1108 D5
100 VSTA 1087 G4
400 SNMS 1109 A7
500 ESCN 1129 G2
800 OCSD 1087 F2
1000 VSTA 1108 A1
1100 SNMS 1129 C1
1400 SDCo 1108 B2
2100 SDCo 1087 F2
CO-S14 W Mission Av
500 ESCN 1129 G2
CO-S14 Mission Rd
1200 ESCN 1129 F2
CO-S14 E Mission Rd
100 SNMS 1108 H7
400 SNMS 1109 A7
1100 SNMS 1129 C1
1500 ESCN 1129 D2

CO-S14 W Mission Rd
100 SNMS 1108 F7
CO-S14 N Santa Fe Av
- OCSD 1067 C7
200 VSTA 1087 F2
800 OCSD 1087 D1
2100 SDCo 1087 F2
CO-S14 S Santa Fe Av
100 VSTA 1087 H7
1000 VSTA 1108 A1
1400 SDCo 1108 B2
2300 SNMS 1108 D5
CO-S15
100 SDCo 1027 H3
1700 SDCo 1028 A4
CO-S15 E Fallbrook St
100 SDCo 1027 H3
CO-S15 W Fallbrook St
100 SDCo 1027 F3
CO-S15 Reche Rd
1500 SDCo 1027 J4
1700 SDCo 1028 F3
CO-S15 S Stage Coach Ln
400 SDCo 1027 J3
CO-S16
35000 SDCo 1029 H2
39100 RivC 999 G1
CO-S16 Pala Rd
47200 RivC 999 G1
CO-S16 Pala Temecula Rd
35000 SDCo 1029 H2
37100 SDCo 999 G7
CO-S17
100 ELCJ 1251 J5
200 ELCJ 1252 A7
1000 SDCo 1252 A7
1100 ELCJ 1272 A1
1400 SDCo 1272 A1
2800 SDCo 1271 G7
8600 SDCo 1291 E2
CO-S17 N 2nd St
100 ELCJ 1251 J5
CO-S17 Campo Rd
11400 SDCo 1271 H6
CO-S17 Jamacha Blvd
8600 SDCo 1291 F1
10600 SDCo 1271 G7
CO-S17 Jamacha Rd
100 ELCJ 1251 J5
200 ELCJ 1252 A7
1000 SDCo 1252 A7
1100 ELCJ 1272 A1
1400 SDCo 1272 A1
2800 SDCo 1271 H6
CO-S21
- CRLB 1147 A2
- DLMR 1187 G7
- SDGO 1187 G7
- SDGO 1208 A7
- SOLB 1167 E7
100 OCSD 1086 A7
100 OCSD 1106 C3
600 ENCT 1147 A2
800 OCSD 1085 J7
900 ENCT 1167 C1
1400 SDCo 1085 J6
3200 SOLB 1187 F1
3900 CRLB 1106 E7
4600 CRLB 1126 F1
7400 CRLB 1146 J1
10300 SDGO 1207 J6
CO-S21 Camino del Mar
400 DLMR 1187 F1
400 SDGO 1187 G6
3200 SOLB 1187 F1
CO-S21 Carlsbad Blvd
- CRLB 1147 A2
- ENCT 1147 A2
- OCSD 1106 D4
3900 CRLB 1106 E7
4600 CRLB 1126 F1
7400 CRLB 1146 J1
CO-S21 N Coast Hwy
100 OCSD 1086 A7
800 OCSD 1085 J7
1400 SDCo 1085 J6
CO-S21 S Coast Hwy
100 OCSD 1086 A7
100 OCSD 1106 C3
2200 CRLB 1106 D4
CO-S21 N Coast Highway 101
10 ENCT 1147 C7
CO-S21 S Coast Highway 101
10 ENCT 1147 B6
900 ENCT 1167 C1
CO-S21 Genesee Av
- SDGO 1207 J7
- SDGO 1208 A7
CO-S21 N Hill St
100 OCSD 1086 A7
CO-S21 S Hill St
100 OCSD 1086 A7
100 OCSD 1106 C3
CO-S21 Old Highway 101
- DLMR 1187 F2
- ENCT 1167 E6
- SOLB 1167 E7
- SOLB 1187 E1

CO-S21 N Torrey Pines Rd
- DLMR 1187 G7
- SDGO 1187 G7
10300 SDGO 1207 J6
CO-S22
- SDCo 1098 A2
200 SDCo 1078 F2
(See Page 1058)
CO-S22 Borrego Salton Seaway
2500 SDCo 1059 J4
(See Page 1058)
CO-S22 Montezuma Valley Rd
- SDCo 1078 D7
(See Page 1058)
- SDCo 1098 D1
CO-S22 Palm Canyon Dr
700 SDCo 1078 J2
(See Page 1058)
CO-S22 Peg Leg Rd
1300 SDCo 1059 J6
(See Page 1058)
CO-S26
600 ImCo 6259 A1
CO-S26 Boarts Rd
600 ImCo 6259 A1
CO-S28
10 ImCo 6439 E6
10 IMPE 6439 E6
CO-S28 E Barioni Blvd
100 IMPE 6439 F6
700 ImCo 6439 G6
CO-S28 W Barioni Blvd
10 IMPE 6439 E6
500 ImCo 6439 E6
CO-S28 E Worthington Rd
- ImCo 6439 J5
- IMPE 6439 J5
CO-S28 W Worthington Rd
10 ImCo 6439 B6
10 IMPE 6439 E6
CO-S30
1000 ImCo 6559 A3
1800 ImCo 6499 A7
CO-S30 Forrester Rd
1400 ImCo 6559 A3
1800 ImCo 6499 A7
CO-S30 W McCabe Rd
1000 ImCo 6559 A5
CO-S31
100 BRAW 6319 J1
(See Page 6259)
100 ELCN 6500 A6
800 ImCo 6620 B7
1100 ImCo 6560 B7
1300 ImCo 6500 A1
1400 ELCN 6560 A1
2100 IMPE 6500 A1
3700 ImCo 6319 J7
(See Page 6259)
CO-S31 Dogwood Rd
2100 ELCN 6500 A4
2100 ImCo 6500 A1
2100 IMPE 6500 A1
3700 ImCo 6319 J7
(See Page 6259)
4000 BRAW 6319 J5
(See Page 6259)
CO-S31 N Dogwood Rd
1300 ELCN 6500 A6
1300 ImCo 6500 A5
CO-S31 S Dogwood Rd
100 ELCN 6500 A6
800 ImCo 6620 B7
1100 ImCo 6560 B7
1400 ELCN 6560 A1
CO-S31 S Imperial Av
200 BRAW 6319 J2
(See Page 6259)
CO-S31 S Imperial Pl
700 BRAW 6319 J2
(See Page 6259)
CO-S31 S Plaza St
100 BRAW 6319 J1
(See Page 6259)
CO-S80
100 ELCN 6499 F6
100 ELCN 6500 A6
100 ImCo 6500 E5
600 ImCo 6499 B6
CO-S80 N 4th St
100 ELCN 6499 H6
CO-S80 Adams Av
- ImCo 6499 E6
400 ELCN 6499 F6
CO-S80 W Adams Av
2000 ELCN 6499 E6
2000 ImCo 6499 E6
CO-S80 E Evan Hewes Hwy
- ELCN 6500 C5
100 ImCo 6500 H4
CO-S80 W Evan Hewes Hwy
600 ImCo 6499 B6
CO-S80 E Main St
100 ELCN 6499 J6
100 ELCN 6500 A6
900 ImCo 6500 C5

CO-S80 W Main St
100 ELCN 6499 J6
I-5
- CHLV 1309 J7
- CHLV 1329 J1
- CHLV 1330 A2
- CRLB 1106 E4
- CRLB 1126 H4
- CRLB 1127 A7
- CRLB 1147 B1
- ENCT 1147 D7
- ENCT 1167 D1
- NATC 1289 G7
- NATC 1309 H1
- OCSD 1085 J6
- OCSD 1086 A7
- OCSD 1106 C1
- SCLE 1023 C2
- SDCo 1023 H6
- SDCo 1085 F1
- SDGO 1187 J5
- SDGO 1207 J2
- SDGO 1208 A3
- SDGO 1228 A6
- SDGO 1248 A1
- SDGO 1268 F5
- SDGO 1288 J1
- SDGO 1289 D5
- SDGO 1330 B7
- SDGO 1350 F4
- SOLB 1167 G7
- SOLB 1187 G1
- TJNA 1350 H5
I-5 San Diego Frwy
- CHLV 1309 J7
- CHLV 1329 J1
- CHLV 1330 A2
- CRLB 1106 G7
- CRLB 1126 G1
- CRLB 1127 A7
- CRLB 1147 A1
- ENCT 1147 B4
- ENCT 1167 E3
- NATC 1289 G7
- NATC 1309 G1
- OCSD 1085 J6
- OCSD 1086 A7
- OCSD 1106 C1
- SCLE 1023 C2
- SDCo 1023 E3
- SDCo 1085 F1
- SDGO 1187 J7
- SDGO 1207 J2
- SDGO 1208 B6
- SDGO 1228 A6
- SDGO 1248 C3
- SDGO 1268 F5
- SDGO 1288 J1
- SDGO 1289 D5
- SDGO 1330 B7
- SDGO 1350 C2
- SOLB 1167 G7
- SOLB 1187 G1
- TJNA 1350 H5
I-8
- ELCJ 1251 H4
- ELCJ 1252 C1
- ELCJ 1271 C1
- ELCN 6559 J2
- ELCN 6560 A2
- ImCo 6559 B2
- ImCo 6560 E1
- LMSA 1251 B7
- LMSA 1270 E1
- LMSA 1271 B1
- SDCo 1237 A7
(See Page 1216)
- SDCo 1232 E7
- SDCo 1233 E3
- SDCo 1234 J5
- SDCo 1235 G5
- SDCo 1236 C7
- SDCo 1237 A7
- SDCo 1252 C1
- SDCo 1299 E1
(See Page 1298)
- SDCo 1300 D5
- SDGO 1268 H4
- SDGO 1269 E2
- SDGO 1270 B1
I-8 BUS
100 ELCN 6499 H6
12800 ELCJ 1252 C1
12800 SDCo 1252 C1
13000 SDCo 1232 C7
I-8 BUS N 4th St
100 ELCN 6499 H6
I-8 BUS Adams Av
400 ELCN 6499 G6
I-8 Mission Valley Frwy
- SDGO 1268 H4
- SDGO 1269 A3
I-8 Ocean Beach Frwy
- SDGO 1268 C4
I-15
- ESCN 1109 E2
- ESCN 1129 J7
- ESCN 1150 A1
- RivC 999 A1
- SDCo 998 H4
- SDCo 1028 H6
- SDCo 1048 H1
- SDCo 1068 J7
- SDCo 1088 J1
- SDCo 1089 A2
- SDCo 1109 E3
- SDCo 1129 F1
- SDCo 1130 A7
- SDCo 1150 A1

I-15
- SDCo 1209 F7
- SDGO 1150 A4
- SDGO 1169 G6
- SDGO 1170 A1
- SDGO 1189 F7
- SDGO 1209 F7
- SDGO 1229 G2
- SDGO 1249 F1
- SDGO 1269 G1
I-15 Avocado Hwy
- ESCN 1109 F6
- ESCN 1129 F1
- RivC 999 A1
- SDCo 998 F7
- SDCo 1028 F1
- SDCo 1048 H1
- SDCo 1068 J1
- SDCo 1088 J1
- SDCo 1089 A2
- SDCo 1109 E3
- SDCo 1129 F1
I-15 Escondido Frwy
- ESCN 1109 F6
- ESCN 1129 J7
- ESCN 1150 A4
- SDCo 998 F7
- SDCo 1028 F1
- SDCo 1048 H1
- SDCo 1068 J1
- SDCo 1088 J1
- SDCo 1089 A2
- SDCo 1109 E3
- SDCo 1129 F1
- SDCo 1130 A7
- SDCo 1150 A1
- SDCo 1209 F7
- SDGO 1150 A4
- SDGO 1169 J5
- SDGO 1170 A3
- SDGO 1189 J1
- SDGO 1209 F7
- SDGO 1229 F7
- SDGO 1249 F7
- SDGO 1269 G1
I-15 Temecula Valley Frwy
- RivC 998 J2
- RivC 999 A1
I-805
- CHLV 1310 F7
- CHLV 1330 G4
- NATC 1289 J6
- NATC 1290 A7
- NATC 1310 A1
- SDCo 1310 B3
- SDGO 1208 B5
- SDGO 1228 H7
- SDGO 1248 J1
- SDGO 1249 C7
- SDGO 1269 D1
- SDGO 1289 J6
- SDGO 1330 G7
- SDGO 1350 G1
I-805 Jacob Dekema Frwy
- CHLV 1310 F7
- CHLV 1330 G4
- NATC 1289 J6
- NATC 1290 A7
- NATC 1310 B3
- SDCo 1310 B3
- SDGO 1208 B5
- SDGO 1228 E1
- SDGO 1248 J1
- SDGO 1249 C7
- SDGO 1269 E3
- SDGO 1289 H2
- SDGO 1330 G7
- SDGO 1350 G3
MX-1D
- MX 1349 H7
- MX 1350 B7
- TJNA 1350 D7
MX-1D Crtra Ensenada-Tijuana
- MX 1349 H7
- MX 1350 B7
- TJNA 1350 D7
MX-2
- MX 1353 B6
(See Page 1332)
MX-2D
- MX 1353 E3
(See Page 1332)
- MX 1352 J5
SR-15
- SDGO 1269 G2
- SDGO 1289 G1
SR-15 Escondido Frwy
- SDGO 1269 G6
- SDGO 1289 F6
SR-52
- SDGO 1228 J6
- SDGO 1229 C7
- SDGO 1230 A6
- SNTE 1230 J7
SR-52 Soledad Frwy
- SDGO 1228 C7
SR-54
- CHLV 1309 J4
- CHLV 1310 A3
- NATC 1309 J4
- NATC 1310 A3
- SDCo 1290 H6
- SDCo 1291 A5
- SDCo 1310 G1

SR-54
- SDGO 1290 H6
- SDGO 1310 D3
100 ELCJ 1251 J4
200 ELCJ 1252 A5
1000 SDCo 1252 A7
1100 ELCJ 1272 A1
1100 SDCo 1272 A1
2800 SDCo 1271 J5
SR-54 N 2nd St
100 ELCJ 1251 J4
SR-54 S Bay Frwy
- CHLV 1309 J4
- CHLV 1310 A3
- NATC 1309 J5
- NATC 1310 A3
- SDCo 1290 H6
- SDCo 1291 A5
- SDCo 1310 E2
- SDGO 1290 H6
- SDGO 1310 D3
SR-54 Jamacha Rd
100 ELCJ 1251 J5
200 ELCJ 1252 A5
1000 SDCo 1252 A7
1100 ELCJ 1272 A1
1100 SDCo 1272 A1
2800 SDCo 1271 J5
SR-56
- SDGO 1188 C7
- SDGO 1189 A4
- SDGO 1208 A1
SR-56 Ted Williams Pkwy
- SDGO 1188 F5
- SDGO 1189 A4
- SDGO 1208 A1
SR-67
- ELCJ 1251 F3
- SDCo 1231 J4
- SDCo 1251 F3
- SNTE 1231 G5
- SNTE 1251 F1
1000 SDCo 1152 E7
2200 SDCo 1172 B4
10800 SDCo 1232 A3
10900 SDCo 1212 A7
12500 SDCo 1211 G2
13200 SDCo 1191 G7
14500 POWY 1191 D1
14900 POWY 1171 D7
15800 SDCo 1171 E5
SR-67 Julian Rd
3400 SDCo 1172 C3
SR-67 Main St
1000 SDCo 1152 E7
2200 SDCo 1172 E1
SR-67 San Vicente Frwy
- ELCJ 1251 F3
- SDCo 1231 J4
- SDCo 1232 A3
- SDCo 1251 F3
- SNTE 1231 G5
- SNTE 1251 F1
SR-75
- CORD 1329 E2
- SDGO 1289 B7
300 CORD 1288 J6
500 IMPB 1329 G7
1300 CORD 1308 H1
1300 SDGO 1329 J7
1500 CORD 1289 A6
1700 SDGO 1330 A7
5000 CORD 1309 C6
SR-75 Fourth St
1100 CORD 1288 J6
1500 CORD 1289 A6
SR-75 Orange Av
300 CORD 1288 J6
1300 CORD 1308 H1
SR-75 Palm Av
800 IMPB 1329 G7
1300 SDGO 1329 J7
1700 SDGO 1330 A7
SR-75 Pomona Av
300 CORD 1288 J6
SR-75 San Diego-Corondo Bay Br
- CORD 1289 B7
- SDGO 1289 B7
SR-75 Silver Strand Blvd
- CORD 1308 J1
- CORD 1329 E2
- IMPB 1329 F6
5000 CORD 1309 A3
SR-75 Third St
1100 CORD 1288 J6
SR-76
- OCSD 1085 J7
- OCSD 1086 H3
- OCSD 1087 A1
2300 SDCo 1048 B6
5200 SDCo 1049 A1
5200 SDCo 1068 A1
5500 OCSD 1067 G6
5800 SDCo 1067 J2
8400 SDCo 1029 E5
12100 SDCo 1030 G7
15000 SDCo 1050 J2
15600 SDCo 1051 E7
19200 SDCo 1052 A6
SR-76 Mission Av
- OCSD 1086 J2
- OCSD 1087 A1
5500 OCSD 1067 D7
5800 SDCo 1067 G6

SR-76 Mission Rd
5200 SDCo 1048 A7
5200 SDCo 1068 A1
29700 OCSD 1067 G6
29700 SDCo 1067 J2
SR-76 Pala Rd
2300 SDCo 1048 E4
5200 SDCo 1049 A1
8400 SDCo 1029 C7
12100 SDCo 1030 G7
15000 SDCo 1050 H2
15600 SDCo 1051 A4
SR-76 Pala Mission Rd
9700 SDCo 1029 D7
SR-76 San Luis Rey Msn Expwy
- OCSD 1085 J6
- OCSD 1086 A5
SR-78
- BRAW 6260 A5
(See Page 6259)
- CRLB 1106 H2
- OCSD 1106 E3
- OCSD 1107 B2
- SDCo 1118 C6
(See Page 1098)
- SDCo 1108 B4
- SDCo 1129 F2
- SDCo 1138 B1
- SNMS 1108 F7
- SNMS 1109 A7
- SNMS 1128 H1
- SNMS 1129 C1
- VSTA 1087 F7
- VSTA 1107 E1
- VSTA 1108 A3
100 ESCN 1129 J2
100 ESCN 1130 A1
100 SDCo 1152 D2
200 SDCo 1136 G7
300 ImCo 6259 A3
500 SDCo 1130 F5
600 SDCo 1153 B5
2400 SDGO 1130 F5
2600 SDCo 1135 A3
4500 SDCo 1120 G1
(See Page 1100)
15500 SDGO 1131 J7
15900 SDCo 1131 E6
25200 SDCo 1154 F2
35900 SDCo 1156 H1
SR-78 10th St
100 SDCo 1152 G6
SR-78 N Ash St
100 ESCN 1130 A1
SR-78 S Ash St
100 ESCN 1130 B2
SR-78 Banner Rd
200 SDCo 1136 C7
35900 SDCo 1156 H1
SR-78 N Broadway
600 ESCN 1129 H1
SR-78 W Haverford Rd
900 SDCo 1152 F3
SR-78 Julian Rd
100 SDCo 1152 J4
600 SDCo 1153 B5
2200 SDCo 1136 A7
2600 SDCo 1135 F7
25200 SDCo 1154 B2
SR-78 Main St
100 SDCo 1152 J5
1800 SDCo 1136 B7
SR-78 E Main St
100 BRAW 6319 J1
(See Page 6259)
1500 ImCo 6320 C1
(See Page 6259)
SR-78 W Main St
100 BRAW 6319 H1
(See Page 6259)
600 ImCo 6319 G1
(See Page 6259)
SR-78 Pine St
100 SDCo 1152 G5
SR-78 Ronald Packard Pkwy
- CRLB 1106 H2
- ESCN 1129 H1
- OCSD 1106 E3
- OCSD 1107 B2
- SDCo 1129 F2
- SNMS 1108 F7
- SNMS 1109 A7
- SNMS 1128 H1
- SNMS 1129 C1
- VSTA 1087 F7
- VSTA 1107 D1
SR-78 Ronald Packard Pl
- SNMS 1109 B7
SR-78 Ronald Packard Pkwy Pkwy
- SDCo 1108 B4
- SNMS 1108 E7
- VSTA 1107 J1
- VSTA 1108 A3
SR-78 San Pasqual Valley Rd
400 ESCN 1130 B2
500 ESCN 1130 F5
1200 SDCo 1152 C2
2400 SDGO 1130 F5
15500 SDGO 1131 A7
15900 SDCo 1131 E6
SR-78 E Washington Av
100 ESCN 1129 J2

4 INDEX

SR-78 E Washington Av

San Diego County Street Index

Albatross Wy

INDEX 4

SAN DIEGO CO.

STREET
Block City Map# Grid

SR-78 E Washington Av
600 ESCN 1130 A1
SR-78 Washington St
2700 SDCo 1136 B7
SR-79
1800 SDCo 1136 B7
2600 SDCo 1135 B1
3400 SDCo 1156 D2
5100 SDCo 1176 D5
6600 SDCo 1235 J6
7800 SDCo 1236 A6
(See Page 1216)
36600 SDCo 1033 J1
SR-79 Cuyamaca Hwy
- SDCo 1136 B7
3400 SDCo 1156 F6
5100 SDCo 1176 E7
8400 SDCo 1216 F2
8400 SDCo 1236 D1
SR-79 Japatul Valley Rd
6600 SDCo 1235 J6
7800 SDCo 1236 A6
(See Page 1216)
SR-79 Julian Rd
2200 SDCo 1136 A7
2600 SDCo 1135 E4
SR-79 Main St
1800 SDCo 1136 B7
SR-79 Washington St
2700 SDCo 1136 B7
SR-86
- ImCo 6259 D7
- ImCo 6620 A1
- IMPE 6439 F6
10 ImCo 6560 E7
100 ELCN 6499 H7
1100 ImCo 6559 J5
1200 ELCN 6559 H1
2200 ImCo 6499 F3
2200 IMPE 6499 F3
3100 ImCo 6439 F2
4100 BRAW 6319 G4
(See Page 6259)
SR-86 S 1st St
100 BRAW 6319 H1
(See Page 6259)
SR-86 N 4th St
100 ELCN 6499 H6
SR-86 S 4th St
100 ELCN 6499 H7
1200 ELCN 6559 H1
2500 ImCo 6559 J3
SR-86 Adams Av
400 ELCN 6499 H6
SR-86 S Brawley Av
600 BRAW 6319 H2
(See Page 6259)
SR-86 Corfman Rd
1100 ImCo 6559 J5
1500 ELCN 6559 J3
SR-86 E Heber Rd
- ImCo 6560 E7
SR-86 W Heber Rd
- ImCo 6560 B7
- ImCo 6620 A1
SR-86 N Imperial Av
- ImCo 6319 E6
(See Page 6259)
- IMPE 6439 F6
800 ELCN 6499 F3
2200 ImCo 6499 F3
2200 IMPE 6499 F3
3100 ImCo 6439 F2
SR-86 E Main St
10 ImCo 6560 C7
SR-86 W Main St
10 ImCo 6560 B7
100 BRAW 6319 H1
(See Page 6259)
SR-86 W Main St
600 ImCo 6319 G1
(See Page 6259)
SR-94
- LMGR 1270 D7
- LMSA 1270 G5
- LMSA 1271 B5
- SDCo 1270 J4
- SDCo 1271 F5
- SDGO 1270 E6
- SDGO 1289 E3
- SDGO 1290 C1
12300 SDCo 1272 A7
13100 SDCo 1292 J4
16900 SDCo 1314 A4
(See Page 1294)
31100 SDCo 1318 A7
(See Page 1298)
38000 SDCo 1300 D6
SR-94 Campo Rd
10800 SDCo 1271 J7
12500 SDCo 1292 B1
(See Page 1293)
12800 SDCo 1272 E7
13100 SDCo 1292 J4
16900 SDCo 1314 A4
(See Page 1294)
31100 SDCo 1318 A7
(See Page 1298)
38000 SDCo 1300 A6
SR-94 NW Innis Arden Wy
37100 SDCo 1319 F1
(See Page 1298)
38000 SDCo 1300 A6

SR-94 Martin L King Jr Frwy
- LMGR 1270 G5
- LMSA 1270 F5
- LMSA 1271 B5
- SDCo 1270 J4
- SDCo 1271 F5
- SDGO 1270 E6
- SDGO 1289 J2
- SDGO 1290 C1
SR-94 Old Highway 80
39300 SDCo 1300 C6
SR-94 Ribbonwood Rd
39900 SDCo 1300 D6
SR-98
10 CALX 6620 J7
10 CALX 6680 B1
10 ImCo 6680 A1
1600 ImCo 6620 J7
SR-98 E Birch St
10 CALX 6620 F7
SR-98 W Birch St
- ImCo 6620 E7
10 CALX 6620 F7
100 CALX 6680 D1
SR-111
- ImCo 6260 D6
(See Page 6259)
- ImCo 6500 E2
- ImCo 6560 F4
- ImCo 6620 F2
- MXCL 6680 G2
100 BRAW 6320 A1
(See Page 6259)
100 CALX 6680 F1
1000 CALX 6620 F2
SR-111 1st St
100 CALX 6680 G2
SR-111 N 8th St
100 BRAW 6320 A1
(See Page 6259)
SR-111 Chief FS Pedrosa Mem Hy
- CALX 6620 F2
- ImCo 6560 F7
- ImCo 6620 F2
SR-111 Imperial Av
300 CALX 6680 F1
1000 CALX 6620 F6
SR-111 Imperial Av S
100 CALX 6680 F2
SR-125
- CHLV 1311 D2
- CHLV 1331 F1
- ELCJ 1251 A3
- LMGR 1270 J7
- LMGR 1290 J1
- LMSA 1251 A7
- LMSA 1270 J6
- LMSA 1271 A1
- SDCo 1270 J6
- SDCo 1271 A3
- SDCo 1290 J2
- SDCo 1291 A4
- SDCo 1311 D2
- SDCo 1331 G6
- SDCo 1351 J1
- SDGO 1251 A4
- SDGO 1331 G7
- SDGO 1351 H1
- SNTE 1231 A7
- SNTE 1251 A1
SR-125 S Bay Expwy
- CHLV 1311 F7
- CHLV 1331 F1
- SDCo 1291 C7
- SDCo 1311 D2
- SDCo 1331 G6
- SDCo 1351 J1
- SDGO 1331 G7
- SDGO 1351 H1
SR-163
- SDGO 1229 D7
- SDGO 1249 A7
- SDGO 1269 A4
- SDGO 1289 B2
SR-163 Cabrillo Frwy
- SDGO 1229 D7
- SDGO 1249 A7
- SDGO 1269 A1
- SDGO 1289 B2
SR-282
300 CORD 1288 H5
SR-282 Alameda Blvd
300 CORD 1288 H5
SR-282 Fourth St
300 CORD 1288 H5
SR-282 Pomona Av
300 CORD 1288 J6
SR-282 Third St
300 CORD 1288 H5
SR-905
- MX 1352 A4
(See Page 1332)
- SDCo 1351 G2
- SDGO 1350 C2
2500 SDGO 1352 A4
(See Page 1332)
6100 SDGO 1351 E2
SR-905 Otay Frwy
- SDGO 1350 F2
SR-905 Otay Mesa Rd
- SDCo 1351 G2
6100 SDGO 1351 G2

SR-905 Paseo Internacional
- MX 1352 A4
(See Page 1332)
- SDCo 1351 J2
- SDGO 1351 J3
2500 SDGO 1352 A4
(See Page 1332)

A

A Aceves St
1200 CALX 6680 J1
A Av
500 CORD 1288 J6
200 NATC 1289 H7
1800 NATC 1309 H2
- SDCo 1066 B1
12200 SDCo 1232 A4
- SDCo 1291 D3
- SDGO 1229 F5
A C Nogales St
1200 CALX 6680 J1
A Cordero Av
800 CALX 6680 J1
A Cota St
1200 CALX 6680 J1
A Helms Ct
- CALX 6620 J6
A Ln
200 CORD 1288 J6
A St
1000 BRAW 6260 A7
(See Page 6260)
- BRAW 6319 G1
(See Page 6319)
7300 CRLB 1126 J7
300 ENCT 1147 B6
- OCSD 1106 J1
- SDCo 1066 G1
- SDCo 1085 G3
2700 SDCo 1136 B7
700 SDCo 1152 G5
1100 SDGO 1289 B2
4900 SDGO 1290 A2
W A St
900 SDGO 1288 J2
A Tirado Av
- CALX 6620 J6
A Zuniga Ct
- CALX 6620 H5
Aaron Ct
2500 SDGO 1270 A7
Aaron Wy
8200 SDCo 1251 J1
Abajo Dr
15900 SDCo 1173 F4
Abalar Wy
24800 SDCo 1173 G3
Abalone Landing Terr
- SDGO 1208 B4
Abalone Pl
5600 SDGO 1247 F3
Abalone Point Ct
1600 CHLV 1330 J5
Abalone Point Wy
700 OCSD 1066 F7
Abana Ct
16000 SDCo 1173 F3
Abanto St
6700 CRLB 1127 G6
Abarca Ct
1000 CHLV 1310 J4
Abatti Rd
- ImCo 6560 G6
Abbe St
1900 SDGO 1268 J1
Abbey Glen
2700 ESCN 1110 E7
Abbey Ln
1300 SNMS 1128 D7
Abbey Rd
800 SDCo 1152 F1
Abbeyfield Rd
9700 SNTE 1231 C5
Abbeywood Rd
9700 SNTE 1231 C5
Abbotshill Rd
8200 SDGO 1249 B7
Abbott St
2200 SDGO 1267 J5
Abbotts End Ct
4000 SDCo 1271 C4
Abbottswood Row
6000 SDGO 1248 A1
Abby Wood Ct
14000 SDGO 1210 F2
Abbywood Dr
700 OCSD 1087 C2
Abedul Pl
6700 CRLB 1127 G5
Abedul St
2700 CRLB 1127 H5
Abejorro St
2700 CRLB 1127 H6
Abel Velasco St
- BRAW 6259 F7
(See Page 6259)
Abelia Av
- CRLB 1127 A5

Abelia Ct
2100 SDCo 1317 H3
(See Page 1317)
Abelia Ln
2000 SDCo 1108 C3
Abell Dr
13800 SDCo 1292 F3
(See Page 1292)
Aber St
2800 SDGO 1248 B1
Aberdeen Av
- SNMS 1108 G7
Aberdeen Ct
4700 CRLB 1107 A5
Aberdeen Dr
100 ENCT 1167 D3
Aberdeen St
4700 SDGO 1228 G7
E Aberdeen St
5200 SDGO 1228 H7
Aberdeen Wy
3100 ESCN 1150 C1
Abernathy Wy
5700 SDGO 1248 H2
Abeto Ct
1000 CHLV 1310 J4
Abeto Dr
400 CHLV 1310 J4
Abha Dr
1400 SDCo 1320 B4
(See Page 1320)
Abiento Pl
9400 SDCo 1271 B3
Abilene Ter
8400 LMSA 1250 J6
Abing Av
13000 SDGO 1189 B5
Abington Ln
1600 ENCT 1147 H7
Abington Rd
300 ENCT 1147 G7
Ablette Ct
8500 SNTE 1231 D7
Ablette Rd
8500 SNTE 1231 F7
Abra Dr
12600 SDGO 1170 C2
Abra Pl
12800 SDGO 1170 C2
Abra Wy
17000 SDGO 1170 C2
Abraham St
9200 SNTE 1231 F6
Abraham Wy
9400 SNTE 1231 F5
Abrams Ridge Rd
- SDCo 1254 G5
Abrell Rd
300 SDCo 1086 A2
Abrigo Wy
17300 SDCo 1173 E1
Abuela Dr
5000 SDGO 1249 H2
Abundante Ct
10600 SDCo 1169 G4
Abundante St
16800 SDCo 1169 F4
Acacia Av
200 CRLB 1106 E6
4400 LMSA 1270 H3
800 OCSD 1086 C5
3700 SDCo 1310 J3
4300 SDCo 1311 A3
500 SOLB 1167 E6
S Acacia Av
100 SOLB 1167 E7
Acacia Cir
1500 VSTA 1107 E1
Acacia Dr
3300 SDCo 1156 D1
300 SDCo 1251 G2
- SNMS 1128 B2
Acacia Glen Ct
- SDGO 1190 A7
Acacia Ln
1600 SDCo 1048 A1
3100 SDCo 1234 D4
Acacia Pl
300 ESCN 1109 H7
Acacia St
3200 LMGR 1270 H6
9600 SDCo 1232 C4
3500 SDGO 1289 F6
Acacia Ter
12600 POWY 1190 C2
Acacia Wy
100 CORD 1288 G6
- ELCJ 1251 J6
Academy Dr
700 SOLB 1167 G7
Academy Ln
- VSTA 1107 G2
Academy Pl
4700 SDGO 1248 A5
Academy Rd
300 OCSD 1086 H2
- SDCo 1131 F7
Academy St
4800 SDGO 1248 A5
Acadia Ln
- ESCN 1130 A6

Acadia Wy
- SDCo 1212 B7
Acama Ct
11300 SDGO 1209 A2
Acama Pl
7700 SDGO 1209 A2
Acama St
7800 SDGO 1209 A2
Acanto Dr
17200 SDCo 1173 E1
Acapulco Dr
- IMPE 6499 H1
Acari St
7200 SDGO 1269 A2
Acaso Ct
7600 SDGO 1209 A2
Acaso Wy
11100 SDGO 1209 A2
Acateno Av
300 VSTA 1087 H4
Accent Wy
3700 OCSD 1086 H4
Access Rd
600 SDCo 1352 D1
- SNMS 1128 B5
Accomac Av
3500 SDGO 1248 H4
Accra Ln
11100 SDGO 1210 A2
Ace St
3400 SDGO 1270 B6
Ace Wy
1100 SDCo 1079 C5
(See Page 1079)
Acebo Corte
1100 CHLV 1311 A6
Acebo Dr
16700 SDGO 1170 B3
Acebo Pl
12100 SDGO 1170 B3
Aceituno St
18600 SDGO 1150 D6
Acena Dr
17000 SDGO 1170 B2
Acero Pl
400 CHLV 1310 J4
Acero St
1000 CHLV 1310 J4
Acheson St
1400 SDGO 1268 J2
Acietuno St
18200 SDGO 1150 D7
Acker Wy
2100 ESCN 1129 H7
Acoma Av
4500 SDGO 1248 F1
Acorn Cres
13600 SDCo 1070 D2
Acorn Ct
- BRAW 6259 J6
(See Page 6259)
Acorn Glen
1900 ESCN 1110 B5
Acorn Patch Ln
13600 POWY 1170 E4
Acorn Patch Rd
13700 POWY 1170 F4
5000 SDCo 1156 A7
5600 SDCo 1176 A1
(See Page 1176)
Acorn Rd
1900 SNMS 1128 B2
Acorn St
1700 ESCN 1130 C1
6200 SDGO 1270 C3
Acorn Trl
32200 SDCo 1318 B6
(See Page 1318)
Acropolis Pl
2900 SDGO 1310 E2
Acropolis Wy
200 VSTA 1088 D5
Acrux Dr
11200 SDGO 1209 C1
Activity Dr
- VSTA 1108 B7
Activity Rd
8900 SDGO 1209 D6
Activity Wy
400 OCSD 1086 B6
Acton Av
13500 POWY 1190 H3
Acton Ct
14600 POWY 1190 H3
Acuff Dr
8400 SDGO 1250 J3
Acuna Ct
2600 CRLB 1127 G6
Acuna St
5000 SDGO 1248 G1
Acworth Av
3400 SDGO 1248 H4
Ada St
700 CHLV 1330 A4
200 SDGO 1289 G5
Adagio Wy
11200 SDCo 1089 H7
Adah Ln
13100 POWY 1190 G4
Adair St
4500 SDGO 1287 J1

Adair Wy
3800 CRLB 1106 G6
Adalane Pl
1700 SDCo 1028 A4
Adam Ct
9700 SDCo 1069 C3
Adams Av
700 ELCN 6499 E6
400 ESCN 1129 J1
6800 LMSA 1270 E3
1600 SDGO 1269 C3
5600 SDGO 1270 C3
Adams Ct
- CALX 6620 J6
Adams Dr
15100 SDCo 1030 H6
- SDCo 1031 A7
- SDCo 1051 A1
Adams Ranch Ct
3000 CHLV 1311 J1
Adams Run
3300 ENCT 1148 D4
Adams St
500 BRAW 6320 A1
(See Page 6320)
3200 CRLB 1106 F5
8300 LMGR 1270 J6
4800 OCSD 1067 A7
Adcock Ln
10600 SDGO 1209 A4
Addax Ct
12400 SDGO 1189 C6
Addington Wy
- SOLB 1187 F2
Addison St
3500 SDGO 1288 A2
Adelaide Av
6000 SDGO 1270 C4
Adelaide Glen
400 ESCN 1109 H3
Adelante Av
5400 SDGO 1270 E1
Adele Ln
13600 SDCo 1292 F2
(See Page 1292)
- SNMS 1129 B2
Adele St
800 ELCJ 1251 G2
Adelfa Ct
1400 IMPB 1349 H2
Adelia Wy
- OCSD 1086 H3
Adeline Ct
3100 SNMS 1108 C5
Adella Av
1100 CORD 1288 H7
Adella Ln
400 CORD 1288 J7
Adelphi Pl
4700 SDGO 1270 A2
Adena Wy
1100 SNMS 1109 A4
Aderman Av
10700 SDGO 1208 J4
Aderman Dr
10500 SDGO 1209 A4
Adios Ct
7300 SDGO 1250 E4
Adirondack Pl
900 CHLV 1311 J4
Adirondack Row
2300 SDGO 1290 F7
Adkins Wy
7600 SDGO 1209 A4
Adlai Ln
13500 SDCo 1232 D5
Adlai Rd
9400 SDCo 1232 D4
Adler Av
7400 SDGO 1249 A7
Adler Creek Ln
2300 SDCo 1048 B1
Adler St
300 BRAW 6259 G7
(See Page 6259)
700 BRAW 6260 A7
(See Page 6260)
- BRAW 6319 F1
(See Page 6319)
Adler Wy
4700 OCSD 1087 A1
Administration Wy
1300 SDCo 1234 A6
Admiral Av
2900 SDGO 1249 E5
Admiral Baker Rd
2400 SDGO 1249 H5
Admiral Boland Wy
3300 SDGO 1268 H7
Admiral Wy
- SDGO 1330 H6
Admiralty Cross
- CORD 1329 E1
Admiralty Wy
- IMPB 1349 E1
Adobe Bluffs Dr
8800 SDGO 1189 C2
Adobe Cir
600 OCSD 1067 A5
Adobe Creek Ln
- SDCo 1130 D4

Adobe Dr
6200 SDGO 1270 C2
Adobe Estates Dr
400 VSTA 1087 F3
Adobe Falls Pl
5600 SDGO 1250 B7
Adobe Falls Rd
5100 SDGO 1250 A7
Adobe Ln
1200 SDCo 1251 J2
Adobe Norte Av
1100 SDCo 1027 H4
Adobe Pl
- CHLV 1311 G3
Adobe Ridge Rd
12200 POWY 1190 C1
Adobe Ter
1200 VSTA 1107 E1
Adobe Villa Dr
- ESCN 1110 E7
- SDCo 1168 F7
Adolphia Ct
12700 SDGO 1189 D5
Adolphia St
9400 SDGO 1189 E6
Adonis Ct
7300 SDGO 1250 F4
Adorno Pl
11900 SDGO 1170 A2
Adra Wy
4600 OCSD 1107 F4
Adrian Ct
1700 SDCo 1233 H7
Adrian St
13600 POWY 1190 F2
2900 SDGO 1268 C5
Adriana Ct
1800 VSTA 1107 G5
Adriana St
8700 SDCo 1291 A3
Adrianne Ln
- VSTA 1088 A2
Adriatic Pl
11200 SDGO 1209 A2
Adrienne Dr
4300 SDCo 1310 D6
Adrienne Wy
- SDCo 1172 A2
Aduar Ct
5300 SDGO 1249 J1
Adventure Ln
2200 CHLV 1331 G3
1200 SNMS 1109 C6
Adventurine Pl
2200 CRLB 1127 F6
Aedan Ct
14300 POWY 1190 E2
8100 SDGO 1250 D3
Aegean Ct
7500 SDGO 1209 A2
Aegean Dr
2600 SDGO 1310 F1
Aegean Pl
6700 SDGO 1310 F1
Aegean Wy
6700 SDGO 1310 F1
Aegina Wy
5000 OCSD 1107 F5
Aeola Wy
4000 OCSD 1107 E5
Aerie Heights Rd
1300 SDCo 1068 B4
Aerie Rd
- SDCo 1069 J7
28500 SDCo 1070 A7
28300 SDCo 1090 A1
Aero Ct
3600 SDGO 1249 B4
Aero Dr
9000 SDGO 1249 D4
Aero Pl
8200 SDGO 1249 B4
Aero Wy
600 ESCN 1129 D2
Aeronca Av
4100 SDGO 1248 E6
Affinity Ct
- SDGO 1209 F2
African Holly Tr
6000 SDGO 1188 F4
Afton Farmes Ln
- SDCo 1068 F2
Afton Rd
3400 SDGO 1249 C4
Afton Wy
2200 CRLB 1106 G4
Agapanthus Dr
1200 SDGO 1290 D5
Agar Ct
10300 SDGO 1209 B5
Agate Creek Wy
1400 CHLV 1312 A6
(See Page 1312)
Agate Ct
- CALX 6620 J7
Agate Gn
- ESCN 1110 C7
Agate Ln
4400 OCSD 1107 D3
Agate St
1100 SDGO 1247 H4

Agate Wy
- CRLB 1127 C4
Agave Flats Ln
- CHLV 1311 H5
Agee St
6000 SDGO 1228 E5
Agno Ct
2700 SDGO 1330 C6
Agora Wy
4700 OCSD 1107 E5
Agosto St
3600 SDGO 1350 E1
Agrarian Rd
- SDCo 1153 G2
Agreste Pl
11600 SDGO 1150 A7
Agsten Ln
13600 POWY 1190 F3
Agua Dulce
3600 SDCo 1271 E5
Agua Dulce Blvd
3900 SDCo 1271 E4
Agua Dulce Ct
7500 CRLB 1147 J1
Agua Hill Rd
- SDCo 1047 H2
Agua Tibia Av
1100 CHLV 1330 E2
Agua Vista Dr
400 CHLV 1291 J7
600 CHLV 1311 J2
Agua Vista Wy
300 SDGO 1290 B5
Aguacate Ln
15200 SDCo 1070 J6
Aguacate Wy
17800 SDGO 1149 J6
Aguamarina Pt
13000 SDGO 1150 D6
Aguamiel Rd
17700 SDGO 1149 J7
Aguila St
4000 CRLB 1106 F7
Aguilera Ln
- SDCo 1028 F1
20300 SDCo 1148 G2
Aguirre Dr
1200 CHLV 1311 B6
Ahern Ct
10300 SDGO 1209 B5
Ahern Ranch Rd
- SDCo 1091 C2
Ahlrich Av
1300 ENCT 1147 F7
Ahmu Ter
200 VSTA 1087 H2
Ahwahnee Wy
13600 POWY 1190 D3
Aida St
- SDGO 1188 C6
Aidan Cres
4000 CRLB 1106 G7
Ailsa Ct
- SDGO 1351 F2
Ainsley Ct
8200 SDGO 1249 B7
Ainsley Rd
1900 SDGO 1269 B1
Air Mail Ln
- SDCo 1171 J3
Air Park Rd
- SDCo 1027 G6
Air Strip
- SDCo 1100 C4
(See Page 1100)
Air Wing Rd
1300 SDGO 1351 H1
Air Wy
4500 SDGO 1289 J2
Airborne Dr
1400 VSTA 1088 B2
Aircraft Rd
- CRLB 1127 D3
Airflight Dr
- SDCo 1069 G4
Airoso Av
6500 SDGO 1270 D1
Airport Dr
10500 ELCJ 1251 E1
Airport Rd
- IMPE 6439 F7
200 OCSD 1086 D5
Airport Vista Rd
9700 SNTE 1231 C7
Airway Ln
- SDCo 1352 A2
Airway Rd
10200 SDCo 1352 C2
7200 SDGO 1351 E3
0 SDGO 1352 B2
Ajanta Ct
11300 SDGO 1169 J6
Ajay St
1500 ELCJ 1251 B3
Akard St
9100 SDCo 1291 A4
Akins Av
6900 LMGR 1290 E3
5900 SDGO 1290 C3
Akita Ln
1400 ENCT 1148 D4

Akron St
1000 SDGO 1288 A2
Akuunyaa Wy
2000 SDCo 1192 J4
(See Page 1192)
Al Bahr Dr
1400 SDGO 1227 G6
Al Bahr Rd
300 SDCo 1252 J2
300 SDCo 1253 A2
Al Ct
8600 SDGO 1249 C5
Alabama St
600 IMPB 1329 F7
4300 SDGO 1269 C4
Alabar Wy
4100 OCSD 1087 C6
Alacena Ct
500 SDCo 1291 D3
Alacran Ct
17700 SDGO 1149 J7
Aladdin Ln
600 ELCJ 1252 A6
Alado Pl
8400 SDCo 1232 D7
Alagria Pl
600 CHLV 1311 A5
Alamar Rd
- SDCo 1090 B2
Alameda Blvd
700 CORD 1288 G6
Alameda Cres
2600 CRLB 1127 G2
Alameda Dr
4900 OCSD 1107 F3
4000 SDGO 1268 H5
Alameda Gn
1500 ESCN 1110 A4
Alameda Pl
3800 SDGO 1268 G6
Alameda St
- CALX 6620 G6
Alameda Ter
1900 SDGO 1268 G5
Alameda Wy
3800 SDCo 1310 F3
Alamitos Av
7000 SDGO 1330 B6
Alamitos Pl
2900 ESCN 1110 F7
Alamitos Wy
500 SNMS 1108 C6
Alamo
- OCSD 1086 H2
Alamo Ct
- BRAW 6259 H6
(See Page 6259)
Alamo Dr
4400 SDGO 1270 E4
Alamo Gn
- ESCN 1150 C1
Alamo Ln
700 ESCN 1150 C1
Alamo St
- BRAW 6259 J6
(See Page 6259)
Alamo Wy
6900 LMSA 1270 E3
100 SDCo 1252 J2
Alamosa Park Dr
5100 OCSD 1087 C1
Alan Ct
2100 LMGR 1270 J7
Alana Cir
4100 OCSD 1087 C7
Alana Wy
1500 ESCN 1110 A5
Alander Ct
3500 CRLB 1107 B6
Alando Pl
14700 POWY 1190 G1
Alanwood Ct
2900 SDCo 1271 G7
Alapat Dr
1600 ESCN 1130 C2
Alaquinas Dr
2000 SDGO 1350 G3
Alaska St
3700 SDGO 1330 E7
Alaya Cir
8000 SDGO 1209 B4
Alba Ct
2200 SDGO 1248 B3
Alba Rosa Dr
11400 SDCo 1211 G7
Alba Wy
200 SDCo 1253 D1
Albany Av
1600 CHLV 1330 E5
Albata Ct
1500 SDGO 1350 B2
Albatross Dr
- SDCo 1023 F3
1000 SDGO 1268 J5
Albatross Pl
100 SDCo 1252 H4
Albatross St
4000 SDGO 1269 A5
2300 SDGO 1289 A1
Albatross Wy
4400 OCSD 1087 A3

5 INDEX

INDEX 5

Albemarle St

Anawood Wy

San Diego County Street Index

SAN DIEGO CO.

STREET
Block City Map# Grid

Albemarle St
5600 SDGO 1310 C1
Alber St
- CHLV 1330 H2
Alberdi Dr
7300 LMGR 1290 F2
Alberni Ct
11300 SDGO 1209 D1
Alberque Ct
2000 SDGO 1290 D7
Alberson Ct
4800 SDGO 1188 D4
Albert Av
17000 SDCo 1169 E2
Albert Ct
- ESCN 1110 E6
Albert Pl
10500 SDCo 1169 F1
Albert St
- SDCo 1232 F4
3400 SDGO 1269 C6
Alberta Av
1000 OCSD 1106 B1
Alberta Ct
- NATC 1289 H7
Alberta Pl
1000 SDGO 1268 J5
Albertina Wy
11400 SDCo 1231 G3
Albertus Ln
- SDCo 1071 A4
Albion St
1000 SDGO 1288 A2
Alborada Dr
11400 SDGO 1149 J6
Albright Pl
2600 ESCN 1110 D6
Albright St
- CALX 6620 J5
5400 OCSD 1067 E7
Albuquerque St
4600 SDGO 1248 C4
Albury Ct
11600 SDGO 1209 H1
Alcacer Del Sol
12600 SDGO 1170 C6
Alcala Ct
1800 CHLV 1331 H2
1500 SDGO 1268 H2
Alcala Dr
- OCSD 1086 F2
Alcala Knolls Dr
6500 SDGO 1268 H2
Alcala Pl
1500 SDGO 1268 H2
Alcalde Ct
11400 SDGO 1149 J7
Alcamo Rd
7800 SDGO 1209 A4
Alcaras Ct
400 OCSD 1086 J4
Alcedo St
2100 SDGO 1290 E1
Alcona St
6900 SDGO 1290 F6
Alcorn Pl
5200 SDGO 1270 A2
Alcorn St
4100 SDGO 1350 F2
Alcott Ct
2400 SDGO 1268 C6
Alcott St
3600 SDGO 1268 C6
Alcyon Ct
- SDCo 1127 B7
N Alda Dr
700 SNMS 1108 J5
Aldabra Ct
9400 SDGO 1189 D3
Aldama Ct
16500 SDCo 1169 G4
Aldea Dr
700 OCSD 1067 A5
Aldea Pl
7600 CRLB 1147 H1
Alden Wy
- OCSD 1087 C2
Alder Av
1000 CALX 6680 E1
3900 CRLB 1106 H5
Alder Dr
4000 SDGO 1269 G3
- SNMS 1109 A3
E Alder Dr
4800 SDGO 1269 H3
W Alder Dr
4800 SDGO 1269 H3
Alder Grove Wy
- CHLV 1311 J3
Alder Pl
300 ESCN 1109 H7
13200 POWY 1190 E2
Alder St
100 CORD 1288 G7
Alderbranch Pt
10400 SDGO 1209 J4
Alderbrook Dr
10400 SDGO 1209 H4
Alderbrook Pl
1900 CHLV 1311 D4

Aldercrest Pt
- SDGO 1210 A1
Aldergrove Av
2000 ESCN 1129 E3
Alderhill Terr
- SDGO 1210 A1
Alderidge Ct
- SDGO 1209 H1
Alderidge Ln
- SDGO 1209 J1
Alderley St
6100 SDGO 1290 D5
Alderney Ct
1200 OCSD 1106 D2
Aldersgate Rd
1700 ENCT 1147 A2
Alderson St
600 ELCJ 1251 J6
Alderwood Cir
1900 VSTA 1107 G6
Alderwood Ln
17000 POWY 1170 E2
Alderwood Rd
6800 CRLB 1127 A5
Alderwood St
100 SDCo 1086 B2
Aldford Dr
3400 SDGO 1248 H4
Aldford Pl
6200 SDGO 1248 H4
Aldine Dr
4300 SDGO 1269 H3
Aldolphia Dr
- CRLB 1127 D6
Aldorado Dr
1300 SDCo 1068 A5
Aldrin Av
13300 POWY 1190 H4
Aldrin St
14600 POWY 1190 H4
Aldwych Rd
500 ELCJ 1251 C4
Alegre Vista Ct
600 SDCo 1028 E3
Alegria Pl
2000 ESCN 1109 C5
Alejandra Pl
600 CHLV 1310 J5
Alejandro St
- IMPE 6499 H2
Alejo Ln
11200 SDGO 1230 A7
Alejo Pl
11100 SDGO 1230 A7
Alejo St
5000 SDGO 1230 A7
Aleman Pl
5200 SDCo 1310 J2
Alemania Rd
- SDGO 1189 E7
- SDGO 1209 E1
Alene St
500 SDCo 1290 J4
Alessandro Ln
1200 VSTA 1088 C4
Alessandro Trl
1900 SDCo 1088 C4
1800 VSTA 1088 C4
Alestar St
200 VSTA 1087 J6
Alex Rd
- OCSD 1086 D4
10300 SDCo 1029 D2
Alex Wy
600 ENCT 1147 E5
Alexander Dr
2100 ESCN 1129 J7
1900 ESCN 1130 A6
2400 SDCo 1149 J1
Alexander Wy
- SNTE 1231 F7
Alexandra Av
- SDCo 1271 C5
Alexandra Ln
1000 ENCT 1147 D4
Alexandri Ct
- CRLB 1127 D5
Alexandria Dr
- ELCJ 1251 H5
1100 SDGO 1287 J1
Alexandrine Ct
5400 OCSD 1067 B2
Alexia Pl
3600 SDGO 1269 F3
Alford St
3200 LMGR 1270 F6
Alfred Av
4600 SDGO 1249 J5
Alfred Ct
4900 SDGO 1250 A5
Alga Ct
1400 VSTA 1107 H4
Alga Rd
1400 CRLB 1127 B5
Algeciras St
4400 SDGO 1287 H2
Algiers Av
2500 ESCN 1110 E7
Algonquin Ct
- SDGO 1188 C6

Alhambra St
4600 SDGO 1287 H1
Alhudson Dr
1700 ESCN 1129 G5
Ali Wy
400 SDCo 1027 E5
Alicante Rd
6500 CRLB 1127 F3
Alicante Wy
4900 OCSD 1107 F5
Alice St
600 SDCo 1152 E5
4600 SDGO 1270 C3
600 SDGO 1330 A7
Alicia Dr
4000 SDGO 1268 B7
Alicia Ln
7300 LMGR 1290 F1
Alicia Wy
100 OCSD 1086 H3
200 SDCo 1253 E1
200 SNMS 1128 H3
Alida Row
6100 SDGO 1188 F4
Alida St
7900 LMSA 1250 H6
Alidade Glen
0 ESCN 1129 H2
Aliento Ct
11400 SDGO 1149 J7
- VSTA 1107 D1
Alipaz Ct
3900 OCSD 1086 G2
16300 SDCo 1169 F4
Alisa Pl
- SDCo 1070 F1
Alisal Ln
1300 CHLV 1311 G6
Alisha Dr
- SDGO 1290 F5
Aliso Canyon Rd
18400 SDCo 1148 F6
Aliso Ct
3700 SDCo 1310 E2
Aliso Dr
3400 SDCo 1310 F2
Aliso Pl
1400 ESCN 1110 A6
Aliso Valley Wy
6600 SDGO 1188 H4
Aliso Wy
4700 OCSD 1087 A2
Alita Ln
1300 ESCN 1110 B5
Alkaid Dr
11500 SDGO 1209 C1
Alkali Heath Ln
1800 CRLB 1127 E5
Alkosh Rd
14500 SDCo 1273 A6
Allano Wy
9200 SNTE 1230 J6
Allbill Wy
8900 SDGO 1251 A3
Allbrook Dr
11900 POWY 1190 B5
Allea Ln
1200 VSTA 1108 A1
Alleghany Ct
2000 SDGO 1290 D7
Alleghany St
6100 SDGO 1290 D7
5500 SDGO 1310 C1
Allegra Dr
1800 SDCo 1252 H3
Allegretto Ln
14600 SDGO 1168 J7
Allegro Ln
7600 SDGO 1168 J6
Allen Dr
2100 ELCN 6559 F2
Allen Rd
4200 SDGO 1268 H4
Allen School Ln
4300 SDCo 1310 G3
Allen School Rd
4000 SDCo 1310 G3
Allen St
400 BRAW 6319 G2
(See Page 6319)
Allenbrook Wy
8900 SDGO 1189 C3
Allende Av
4500 OCSD 1086 J1
Allende Ct
100 SOLB 1167 H4
Allenhurst Pl
4700 SDGO 1248 G1
Allenwood Ln
500 ESCN 1129 D3
Allenwood Wy
10000 SNTE 1231 D3
Allerton Ct
800 SDGO 1267 J4
Allew Wy
2800 SDGO 1310 F1
Alliance Ct
7200 SDGO 1250 F4
Allied Rd
4700 SDGO 1249 J5

Allison Av
8000 LMSA 1270 H2
Allison Ln
3600 LMGR 1270 G6
600 SNMS 1108 G6
Allspice Wy
500 OCSD 1086 H4
Allston Ct
- SDGO 1249 D1
Allston St
- CRLB 1127 F3
Allview Ct
400 CHLV 1310 F7
Allysum Rd
900 CRLB 1127 A6
Alma Pl
4600 SDGO 1270 B3
Alma St
- SDGO 1288 A4
Alma Wy
- SDGO 1288 A4
Almaden Ln
7000 CRLB 1127 F7
Almagro Ln
1800 SDCo 1109 E6
Almahurst Row
- SDGO 1227 J1
Almanor Wy
16200 SDCo 1169 B2
Almayo Av
4600 SDGO 1248 G1
Almayo Ct
4900 SDGO 1248 G1
Almazon St
11100 SDGO 1169 H6
Almeda Ln
- ENCT 1147 F5
Almendra Ct
2700 SDCo 1028 H7
Almendro Ln
18000 SDGO 1150 A7
Almeria Ct
2300 SDGO 1248 B2
1000 VSTA 1107 H4
Almona Wy
28400 SDCo 1090 H1
Almond Cir
8500 SDCo 1231 J7
Almond Ln
- OCSD 1086 G3
Almond Orchard Ln
15100 SDGO 1210 H2
Almond Rd
8800 SDCo 1231 J6
600 SNMS 1128 H3
Almond St
100 SDCo 1027 F4
Almondwood Wy
- SDGO 1188 C6
Almonte Pl
500 CHLV 1311 A4
Almyra Rd
200 SDCo 1253 C1
Aloe Ct
1100 SNMS 1129 B1
Aloha Dr
1000 ENCT 1167 E1
Aloha Ln
2000 SDCo 1088 B2
Aloha Pl
4200 SDGO 1268 G5
Alonda Ct
11000 SDGO 1209 A2
Alonda Wy
7500 SDGO 1209 A2
Alondra Av
- CHLV 1311 D7
Alondra Ct
- CHLV 1311 D7
12700 SDGO 1170 C3
Alondra Dr
16700 SDGO 1170 C3
Alondra Wy
4800 CRLB 1106 J7
Alonquin Wy
3400 SDGO 1330 E7
Alonzo Ct
- SDCo 1086 A2
Alonzo Dr
1000 SDCo 1233 A7
- SDCo 1253 A1
Alora Pt
13000 SDGO 1188 G4
Alora St
14400 POWY 1190 H3
Alosta St
2400 SDGO 1350 C3
Alpha Av
300 SDCo 1291 A4
Alpha St
1600 NATC 1289 J6
2200 NATC 1290 A6
3800 SDGO 1289 G6
Alphecca Wy
8800 SDGO 1209 D2
Alphonse St
10300 SNTE 1231 E2
Alpine Av
200 CHLV 1310 C5
1100 CHLV 1330 D3
8500 LMSA 1270 J3

Alpine Av
8900 LMSA 1271 A3
Alpine Blvd
400 SDCo 1233 E3
3000 SDCo 1234 D6
- SDCo 1235 A5
Alpine Creek Ln
1900 SDCo 1234 A6
Alpine Dr
13000 POWY 1190 D5
Alpine Estates Pl
1200 SDCo 1233 G6
Alpine Glen Pl
- SDCo 1234 B6
Alpine Grove Ln
1400 SDCo 1234 A6
Alpine Heights Ln
500 SDCo 1253 F1
Alpine Heights Rd
1000 SDCo 1253 H1
Alpine Heights Wy
2200 SDCo 1253 H2
Alpine Ln
300 OCSD 1106 C2
11600 SDCo 1231 H7
Alpine Oaks Dr
1000 SDCo 1253 H2
Alpine Pl
1400 ESCN 1110 A6
1400 SNMS 1128 D1
Alpine Ridge Rd
8400 SDGO 1189 B4
Alpine Spring Rd
- SDCo 1234 E6
Alpine Terr
- SDGO 1190 A7
Alpine Terrace Rd
1600 SDCo 1233 J7
Alpine Tl Pl
- SDCo 1233 F7
Alpine Trail Rd
- SDCo 1233 F7
400 SDCo 1253 F2
Alpine View Rd
1000 SDCo 1233 G5
Alpine View Wy
600 SDCo 1233 G5
Alpine Village Dr
100 SDCo 1234 A6
Alpine Wy
600 ESCN 1129 E2
Alps Ln
- SDCo 1089 H4
Alps Terr
11400 SDCo 1089 H4
Alps Wy
- SDCo 1089 J4
Alsacia Ct
2200 SDGO 1290 G7
Alsacia St
7300 SDGO 1290 G7
Alston Av
3600 NATC 1310 D3
Alta Bahia Ct
5300 SDGO 1247 J4
Alta Calle Dr
1000 VSTA 1087 J7
Alta Camino Ct
- ESCN 1110 D5
Alta Carmel Ct
12100 SDGO 1170 A6
Alta Ct
6600 SDGO 1290 E7
600 SNMS 1108 E5
Alta Dr
3000 SDCo 1310 C3
Alta La Jolla Dr
1800 SDGO 1247 J3
Alta Laguna Wy
9400 SDGO 1209 E2
Alta Ln
4500 LMSA 1270 H3
200 SDCo 1252 H3
Alta Loma Ct
3800 SDCo 1272 H5
Alta Loma Dr
3300 SDCo 1272 G6
3800 SDCo 1310 D4
Alta Loma Gn
800 ESCN 1109 F5
Alta Loma Ln
13600 SDCo 1272 H6
Alta Meadow Ln
- ESCN 1110 D6
Alta Mesa Dr
100 VSTA 1088 B5
Alta Mesa Wy
5900 SDGO 1270 C4
Alta Mira Dr
4200 SDCo 1271 E3
Alta Mira Ln
- SDCo 1069 H5
Alta Panorama Wy
- OCSD 1086 E5
Alta Pl
1800 SDCo 1252 G3
Alta Rd
100 SDCo 1332 B5
(See Page 1332)
900 SDCo 1352 C2

Alta Rica Dr
4600 SDCo 1271 E3
Alta Ter
10200 SDCo 1271 E4
Alta Vega Rd
38500 SDCo 1320 A6
(See Page 1320)
Alta Verde Dr
3100 SDCo 1048 A2
Alta View Dr
1800 SDGO 1290 E6
2300 SDGO 1310 F1
Alta Vista
- CRLB 1127 J7
- SNMS 1128 C1
- SNMS 1129 C2
Alta Vista Av
1100 ESCN 1109 J6
1800 ESCN 1110 A6
5800 SDGO 1290 B5
Alta Vista Ct
4200 OCSD 1086 J3
Alta Vista Dr
2500 SDCo 1028 A7
2900 SDCo 1048 A1
3300 SDCo 1156 E1
600 VSTA 1087 J6
1400 VSTA 1088 A5
Alta Vista St
5100 SDGO 1247 J4
Alta Vista Ter
900 VSTA 1088 A7
Alta Vista Wy
1700 SDGO 1247 J4
Alta Viva Ln
2500 SDCo 1299 J4
(See Page 1299)
Altadena Av
4600 SDGO 1270 A3
1500 SDGO 1290 A2
Altadena Rd
11800 SDCo 1251 J1
Altair Ct
6500 SDGO 1250 D7
Altamar Ct
14400 SDCo 1188 E1
Altamira Ct
- VSTA 1107 E2
Altamira Pl
1800 SDGO 1268 H4
Altamirano Wy
4200 SDGO 1268 F4
Altamont Cir
1900 SDGO 1290 C7
Altamont Ct
1900 SDGO 1290 C7
Altamont Dr
5900 SDGO 1290 D7
5700 SDGO 1310 C1
Altamont Pl
1900 SDGO 1290 C7
Altamont Rd
9100 LMSA 1251 B5
Altamont Wy
1900 SDGO 1290 C7
Altana Wy
7800 SDGO 1269 C1
Altar
- SDCo 1232 C7
Althea Ln
3800 CRLB 1106 G5
Altisma Wy
2300 CRLB 1127 G7
Altito Wy
4800 SDCo 1271 C2
Altiva Pl
7300 CRLB 1127 G7
Alto Cerro Cir
2400 SDGO 1248 B3
Alto Ct
9400 SDCo 1271 B2
Alto Dr
9500 LMSA 1271 C2
9400 SDCo 1271 B2
Alto St
4000 OCSD 1107 C3
Alton Dr
7900 LMGR 1290 H1
Alton Pl
2200 LMGR 1270 H7
Alton Wy
4000 ESCN 1150 D4
Altoona Dr
11600 SDCo 1271 H2
Altoro Ln
3200 SDCo 1273 B6
Altozano Dr
1900 ELCJ 1251 B2
Altozano Wy
- ELCJ 1251 C2
Altridge St
3500 SDGO 1249 C4
Altura Cir
- SNMS 1108 B7
Altura Dr
2900 OCSD 1107 B1
- SNMS 1108 C7
Altura Pl
1800 SDGO 1268 H5
Alturas Ln
700 SDCo 1027 E3

Alturas St
500 SDCo 1027 E3
Alumni Pl
5100 SDGO 1270 D2
Alva Ln
100 SDCo 1027 J2
Alva Rd
17900 SDCo 1149 E7
17100 SDCo 1169 G2
Alvarado Av
- LMSA 1251 A7
Alvarado Canyon Pl
4700 SDGO 1269 J1
Alvarado Canyon Rd
4500 SDGO 1269 J1
Alvarado Ct
100 SDCo 1027 H2
6300 SDGO 1270 D1
Alvarado Medical Ctr
- SDGO 1270 D1
Alvarado Pl
- CHLV 1310 D6
Alvarado Rd
7400 LMSA 1270 F2
6100 SDGO 1270 C1
Alvarado St
100 CHLV 1310 C6
1400 OCSD 1106 C3
200 SDCo 1027 F2
1800 SDCo 1028 A3
E Alvarado St
1700 SDCo 1027 J2
Alvarado Ter
400 VSTA 1087 H5
Alvarez Meadow Ct
11300 SDGO 1208 J2
Alveda Av
1000 ELCJ 1252 B7
Alveo Wy
11600 SDGO 1149 J7
Alverson Rd
100 SDGO 1350 F3
Alverton Dr
6200 CRLB 1127 F3
Alvin St
600 SDGO 1290 C3
Alviso Wy
400 ENCT 1147 C5
Alvoca St
3300 CHLV 1330 E5
Alwood Ct
2900 SDCo 1271 G7
Alwyne Sq
16100 SDGO 1170 B4
Alydar Ct
15500 SDCo 1168 E7
Alyssum Wy
- OCSD 1086 J4
Alzeda Dr
5200 ELCJ 1271 F1
4800 SDCo 1271 F2
Amacayo Ct
1000 SDGO 1349 J1
Amada Ct
- CALX 6620 J7
Amada Pl
10300 SNTE 1231 E3
Amadita Ct
3300 SDCo 1311 A1
Amadita Ln
5500 SDCo 1311 A1
Amador Av
1100 VSTA 1087 E7
Amador Dr
4900 OCSD 1107 F3
Amador St
- CHLV 1331 C1
Amalfi Dr
1800 ENCT 1147 C1
Amalfi Pl
1200 ESCN 1110 A6
Amalfi St
1700 SDGO 1227 G6
Amalia Ct
11100 SDGO 1169 H7
Amalia St
15100 SDGO 1169 J7
Amanda Ct
29500 SDCo 1317 G2
(See Page 1317)
Amanda Ln
2100 SDCo 1129 G6
Amanda St
5500 SDGO 1290 B4
Amanecer Pl
3000 ESCN 1110 E6
Amante Ct
- CRLB 1127 D5
Amante Dr
13400 SDCo 1232 D7
Amantha Av
10600 SDGO 1209 B4
Amapola Ct
- SDCo 1234 A6
Amaranth St
12700 SDGO 1189 D5
Amaretto Wy
4100 SDCo 1271 D4
Amargosa Dr
7900 CRLB 1147 G3
- ENCT 1147 G4

Amarillo Av
5900 LMSA 1250 J6
Amarillo Pl
1900 ESCN 1129 J6
Amarillo Rd
- SDCo 1171 G1
Amaro Ct
10300 SDGO 1229 G7
Amaro Dr
5800 SDGO 1229 G7
Amaryllis Dr
3700 SDGO 1268 C5
Amaryllis St
500 SDCo 1086 B3
Amatista Wy
200 OCSD 1106 J2
Amato Dr
8500 SDCo 1232 A7
Amaya Ct
9100 LMSA 1251 A7
Amaya Dr
5600 LMSA 1251 B6
Ambassador Av
10100 SDGO 1209 B5
Ambassador Ct
8100 SDGO 1209 B5
Amber Creek Ct
1500 VSTA 1088 A3
Amber Crest Pl
13600 SDGO 1189 J3
Amber Ct
- SDCo 1086 A2
Amber Dr
900 SNMS 1109 C5
Amber Hill Ln
12800 POWY 1190 D4
Amber Lake Av
6300 SDGO 1250 J6
Amber Ln
6800 CRLB 1127 G5
2200 ESCN 1109 F4
3500 OCSD 1107 D2
300 VSTA 1087 J6
Amber Lynn Ln
2500 SDCo 1172 D4
Amber Oak Ln
- SDGO 1130 H3
Amber Pl
6800 LMGR 1270 E7
- SDGO 1188 J3
Amber Ridge Pt
300 SDGO 1330 H6
Amber Sky Ln
13900 SDGO 1189 D3
Amber View Pt
5200 SDGO 1208 D2
Amber Vista
2900 SDCo 1048 A1
Ambercrest Dr
1500 CHLV 1311 J6
Amberglades Ln
- SDGO 1208 E2
Amberglen Dr
- SDCo 1089 A1
Amberhill Terr
- SNMS 1128 B6
Amberly Cir
9000 SDGO 1209 D3
Amberly St
6300 SDGO 1250 D4
Amberstone Ct
11200 SDGO 1210 H2
Ambersweet Wy
- ESCN 1110 F5
Ambervale Ter
3900 SDGO 1188 A5
Amberwood Ct
4700 CRLB 1106 J6
Amberwood Dr
2700 OCSD 1087 E5
Amberwood Ln
- SDCo 1130 H2
Amble Dr
21700 SDCo 1129 C5
Ambler Ln
1200 SDCo 1272 A1
Ambrose Ln
16400 SDCo 1169 F4
Ambrosia Dr
6400 SDGO 1249 G6
Ambrosia Ln
6400 CRLB 1127 D4
Ambrosia Rd
- CRLB 1127 D5
Amby Ct
14400 SDGO 1189 C1
Amelia Ct
200 VSTA 1087 G2
Amelia Dr
8100 SDCo 1252 C1
Amelia Island Dr
2300 CHLV 1311 F4
Amelia Pl
1100 ESCN 1109 J4
Amena Ct
800 CHLV 1310 J6
America Wy
- SOLB 1187 G1
American Av
3800 LMSA 1270 J5

American Rd
39100 SDCo 996 G4
American Wy
- SDCo 1232 E4
Americe Ct
3900 OCSD 1107 E4
Ames Pl
3500 CRLB 1106 J4
Ames St
3500 SDGO 1249 A4
Amesbury St
6200 SDGO 1290 D5
Amethyst Ct
800 OCSD 1087 B2
Amethyst St
1300 SDGO 1290 B2
Amethyst Wy
- CALX 6620 J7
- CRLB 1127 C4
900 ESCN 1129 D3
Amherst St
6600 SDGO 1270 D2
Amick St
2300 OCSD 1086 C6
Amie Ct
1800 SNMS 1109 D7
Amiford Dr
700 SDGO 1287 J2
Amigos Ct
3600 OCSD 1107 D3
Amigos Rd
200 SDCo 1152 J5
400 SDCo 1153 A6
Amigos Wy
100 SDCo 1027 H2
Aminal Shelter Dr
- CALX 6680 E2
Amino Dr
8400 SNTE 1230 H6
Amistad Ct
- ELCJ 1252 B7
Amistad Pl
900 ELCJ 1252 A7
Amity St
2400 SDGO 1248 B3
Ammo Rd
- SDGO 1229 H2
Ammonite Pl
6900 CRLB 1127 G6
Ammons Wy
40700 SDCo 997 H3
Ammunition Rd
- SDCo 1027 D5
Amnest St
5000 SDGO 1228 G7
Amor Pl
1400 ESCN 1110 A6
Amorosa Glen
2100 ESCN 1109 F4
Amoroso St
4100 SDGO 1248 J3
Amparo Ct
2000 ESCN 1130 B5
Amparo Dr
300 SDCo 1130 B6
Amphitheater Dr
- ESCN 1150 B1
Amphitheatre Dr
600 DLMR 1187 G5
Ampudia St
4400 SDGO 1268 G4
Amso St
15000 POWY 1170 C7
Amstel Ln
2300 SDCo 1087 J1
Amster Dr
9500 SNTE 1231 E4
Amulet St
2800 SDGO 1249 E6
Amy St
100 CHLV 1330 D3
Amy Wy
- SDCo 1232 B4
- SDCo 1253 F1
Amys Pl
600 ESCN 1110 C6
Amys St
9200 SDCo 1291 B2
Anabella Dr
14200 POWY 1190 C2
Anacapa Ct
800 SDGO 1267 J4
Anaconda Ln
2000 ENCT 1147 H7
Anaheim Dr
10700 SDCo 1271 F3
Anaheim St
2600 SDCo 1130 D7
2900 SDCo 1150 E1
Anaheim Ter
- SDCo 1150 D1
Analiese Wy
3000 SDGO 1310 F2
Anapamu Av
- CHLV 1331 D2
Anastasia St
3900 SDGO 1248 J3
Anatra Ct
- CRLB 1127 A7
Anawood Wy
2900 SDCo 1271 G7

SAN DIEGO CO.

San Diego County Street Index

STREET
Block City Map# Grid

Anchor Cir
3200 OCSD 1107 A2
Anchor Cove
500 SDGO 1330 J7
Anchor Pl
1400 SNMS 1128 F6
Anchor Wy
400 CRLB 1106 F6
Anchorage Av
500 CRLB 1126 J7
Anchorage Ln
1100 SDGO 1288 B3
Anchorage Pl
800 CHLV 1311 G4
Ancona Ln
10700 SDGO 1210 A2
Ancurza Wy
3300 CHLV 1330 E5
Anda Lucia Wy
2100 OCSD 1106 J1
Andalusia Av
4700 SDGO 1248 H1
Andalusia Ln
2200 CHLV 1331 G2
Andalusian Wy
200 SDCo 1028 H6
Andante Ln
14600 SDGO 1168 J7
Andanza Wy
11600 SDGO 1150 A7
Andasol St
7500 SDGO 1209 A2
Anders Cir
7900 LMSA 1250 H7
Anderson Av
- SDGO 1209 C7
Anderson Ct
1800 CHLV 1331 F2
Anderson Ln
1700 SDCo 1233 F6
Anderson Pl
500 SDGO 1269 A6
Anderson Ranch Rd
9800 SDCo 1235 G1
Anderson Rd
- SDCo 999 B3
500 SDCo 1234 D4
Anderson Ridge Pl
12400 SDGO 1188 F6
Anderson St
- SDCo 1023 E2
3000 SDCo 1290 J7
Anderson Truck Trl
- SDCo 1213 J7
- SDCo 1233 H2
Andes Rd
300 SDCo 1251 F1
Andorra Ct
1300 VSTA 1107 H4
Andorra Wy
3000 OCSD 1106 J1
3100 SDCo 1310 E5
15000 SDGO 1169 J7
Andorre Glen
1400 ESCN 1149 F1
Andover Av
2800 CRLB 1107 A4
Andover Rd
1100 ELCJ 1251 J6
Andrade Av
900 CALX 6680 H1
Andre Pl
- VSTA 1107 F1
Andre Rd
500 ImCo 6259 C3
(See Page 6259)
- ImCo 6260 A3
(See Page 6260)
Andrea Av
1700 CRLB 1106 G5
2800 SDGO 1249 C6
Andrea Ct
8500 SDGO 1249 C6
Andrea Lee Pl
13400 SDGO 1189 A3
Andrea Ter
10700 SNTE 1231 F6
Andrea Vista Wy
3500 SDCo 1028 E2
S Andreasen Dr
- ESCN 1129 D4
N Andreason Dr
100 ESCN 1129 F3
S Andreason Dr
100 ESCN 1129 E4
Andreen Ln
3700 SDCo 1271 C5
Andreen Rd
30600 SDCo 1069 E4
Andrew Av
100 ENCT 1147 A2
Andrew Jackson St
5000 OCSD 1067 A6
Andrews Ct
- OCSD 1106 F2
3700 SDGO 1350 F1
Andrews St
3500 SDGO 1268 H6
Andrita Pl
200 BRAW 6319 H2
(See Page 6319)

Andromeda Rd
8500 SDGO 1209 C2
Andros Ct
5800 SDGO 1270 B5
Andros Pl
5600 SDGO 1270 B5
Andros Wy
4100 OCSD 1107 E5
Andy Ln
1800 OCSD 1106 D2
Andys Pl
18000 SDCo 1274 C2
Aneas Ct
16200 SDCo 1173 F3
Anella Rd
3100 SDGO 1350 F5
Anemore Wy
- CRLB 1127 B4
Angel Dr
2500 SDCo 1300 B5
(See Page 1300)
Angel Pl
1500 SDCo 1152 F7
Angel St
200 SDCo 1085 G1
Angela Ct
- SDCo 1071 B3
Angela Ln
- CHLV 1330 D1
Angela Wy
2600 SDCo 1234 C7
Angeleno Rd
7600 SDGO 1209 A2
Angeles Glen
1900 ESCN 1129 E6
Angeles Vista Dr
100 VSTA 1087 G3
Angelica Pl
4800 SDGO 1249 D1
Angelina Rd
5200 OCSD 1087 C3
Angeline Pl
15800 SDGO 1169 D4
Angelique St
11600 SDGO 1210 B1
Angell Av
2800 SDGO 1228 B5
Angell Pl
6200 SDGO 1228 B5
Angelo Dr
800 NATC 1290 C7
Angels Pt
4700 SDCo 1271 D2
Angelucci St
3500 SDGO 1249 B4
Angelus Av
- ESCN 1130 C1
1100 LMGR 1290 G2
900 SDGO 1290 F2
Angeton Ct
10500 SDGO 1208 J5
Angeton Dr
7500 SDGO 1208 J4
Angila Dr
8400 SNTE 1251 C1
Angler
- SDGO 1351 A1
Anglim Ct
- SDCo 1023 E3
Angola Cir
7500 SDGO 1209 A3
Angola Rd
10800 SDGO 1209 A3
Angosto Wy
12900 SDGO 1150 D5
Angouleme
- SDGO 1188 E6
Anguila Pl
- CRLB 1127 J5
Angus Ct
1000 SNMS 1109 B6
Angwin Dr
3400 SDGO 1249 E5
Angwin Pl
9300 SDGO 1249 E5
Anillo Wy
7900 CRLB 1147 F2
Anise Ct
2100 CHLV 1331 H3
Anita Dr
- SDCo 1254 A2
Anita June Ct
400 CHLV 1330 C4
Anita Lee Ln
1100 ELCJ 1251 E7
Anita St
300 CHLV 1330 D5
Anja Pl
10000 SDCo 1231 F3
Anja Wy
10900 SDCo 1231 F3
Anjuli Ct
2700 ELCJ 1251 A3
Anka Ln
1600 SDCo 1109 E7
Anlee Dr
8500 SNTE 1250 J1
Ann Arbor Ln
11400 SDGO 1209 H2
Ann Dr
3400 CRLB 1106 G5

Ann St
500 ELCJ 1251 H4
600 OCSD 1067 A5
Ann-O-Reno Ln
13300 POWY 1190 G4
Anna Av
5200 SDGO 1268 E3
Anna Linda Ct
400 CHLV 1330 C5
Anna Linda Dr
1600 CHLV 1330 C5
Anna Linda Pl
400 CHLV 1330 C5
Anna Ln
1800 SDCo 1108 B3
- SNMS 1109 C5
Anna Marie Ln
- SDCo 1048 D7
Anna Rose Ln
1200 SDCo 1172 F1
Anna Wy
- SDCo 996 H3
Annadale Wy
2200 CHLV 1311 G6
Annandale Wy
8800 SNTE 1231 A5
Annapolis Av
7200 LMSA 1270 F4
Annatto Wy
2100 CHLV 1331 H3
Anne Sladon Ct
9700 SNTE 1231 F4
Anne Sladon St
4600 OCSD 1066 H7
Annette St
2800 OCSD 1087 C7
Annette Wy
1500 ELCJ 1251 D7
Annie Laurie Ln
5300 SDCo 1311 A2
Annie Ln
10300 SNTE 1231 E4
Annmar Dr
6700 SDGO 1310 F1
Annos Ct
100 CALX 6620 F6
Annrae St
3100 SDGO 1249 B5
Anns Wy
800 VSTA 1087 F6
Anoche Glen
1400 ESCN 1109 E4
Anoel Ct
10000 SDCo 1271 E6
Anrol Av
8600 SDGO 1249 C6
Anta Ct
2700 CRLB 1127 H5
Antares Dr
400 SDGO 1350 E2
Antelope Hills Dr
12600 SDCo 1232 B4
Antelope Station
- POWY 1170 F1
Anthony Dr
2100 SDGO 1289 H7
Anthony Heights Dr
1400 SDCo 1109 E7
Anthony Hollow
- SDCo 1070 C4
Anthony Ln
- SDCo 1070 B5
Anthony Rd
- SDCo 1070 C4
Anthony Ridge Rd
- SDCo 1070 C5
Anthracite Wy
- SDGO 1290 F4
Antibody Wy
- OCSD 1087 A5
Antiem St
4000 SDGO 1249 A3
Antietam Rd
9900 SDCo 1169 G4
Antigua Blvd
5800 SDGO 1229 H7
5600 SDGO 1249 G1
Antigua Ct
- CORD 1329 E1
Antigua Dr
- VSTA 1107 G5
Antilla Pl
11200 SDGO 1209 D2
Antilla Wy
800 SNMS 1128 F6
Antilope St
6700 CRLB 1127 H5
Antioch Pl
4600 SDGO 1270 A3
Antlers
- SNMS 1128 A5
Antlers Dr
4000 SDCo 1156 E2
Antoine Dr
1300 SDGO 1290 H6
Anton Ln
6700 SDGO 1290 E5
Antonio Dr
2200 CHLV 1331 H2
16700 SDGO 1170 C3

Antonio Rd
- SDCo 1130 D4
Antrim Wy
10200 SDGO 1209 B5
Anvil Lake Av
6300 SDGO 1250 J5
Anza Av
1600 VSTA 1087 J3
Anza Ct
1000 ELCJ 1251 H6
Anza Dr
8000 SDGO 1290 G3
Anza Park Trl
500 SDCo 1058 F1
(See Page 1058)
Anza Pl
1700 ESCN 1110 C7
Anza Rd
- CALX 6680 D2
- ImCo 6680 B3
N Anza St
900 ELCJ 1251 H3
S Anza St
700 ELCJ 1251 H6
Anza Wy
700 CHLV 1310 H7
Anzio Dr
3800 SDCo 1099 D2
(See Page 1099)
Apache Av
3300 SDGO 1248 F5
Apache Dr
1500 CHLV 1311 C6
34600 SDCo 1176 D4
(See Page 1176)
Apache Glen
1800 ESCN 1110 A5
Apache Rd
13500 POWY 1190 F3
Apache Trl
4300 OCSD 1087 C5
Apapas Rd
34900 SDCo 1029 J4
Aperture Cir
2300 SDGO 1269 B1
Apex Wy
2100 SDGO 1269 C1
Apollo Dr
300 VSTA 1087 H4
Apollo St
3500 SDGO 1249 A4
Apolonia Rd
500 ImCo 6439 D4
Apore St
4000 LMSA 1270 F4
Apostal Rd
3300 SDCo 1150 E2
Appalachian Pl
1400 CHLV 1311 H6
Appalachian Wy
13400 SDGO 1189 E4
Appaloosa Ct
- SNTE 1231 D2
Appaloosa Dr
13400 SDCo 1232 D3
Appaloosa Rd
- ImCo 6560 A5
9700 SDGO 1209 G5
Appaloosa St
- BRAW 6319 J4
(See Page 6319)
Appaloosa Wy
1600 OCSD 1067 F7
Appert Ct
6600 SDGO 1248 H6
Appian Dr
7000 SDGO 1310 G1
Appian Rd
2400 CRLB 1106 H4
Apple
- SDCo 1233 B3
Apple Blossom Ct
8800 SNTE 1231 D6
Apple Blossom Ln
200 SDCo 1108 D4
Apple Blossom Wy
3500 OCSD 1086 F2
Apple Glen
200 ESCN 1130 A4
Apple Hill Pl
4600 CRLB 1107 B5
Apple Ln
2600 SDCo 1136 C7
Apple St
1900 OCSD 1086 D7
9500 SDCo 1291 C2
Apple Tree Dr
9700 SDGO 1249 F1
Apple Tree Ln
100 SDCo 1029 H5
Apple Wy
- BRAW 6259 J7
(See Page 6259)
Appleby Ct
14600 POWY 1190 F1
Appleby Ln
14600 POWY 1190 F1
Applegate St
- CHLV 1331 D1
Appleridge Dr
800 ENCT 1167 G1

Applestill Rd
- ImCo 6559 G5
Appleton Ct
800 OCSD 1087 C2
Appleton St
4000 SDGO 1228 E7
E Appleton St
5200 SDGO 1228 H7
Applewilde Dr
800 SNMS 1128 F2
Applewood Ct
15000 SDGO 1210 H1
Applewood Dr
700 ELCJ 1251 G4
Applewood Ln
2000 VSTA 1107 F5
Approach Rd
8700 SDGO 1351 H1
Apricot Ct
2700 CHLV 1311 J7
Apricot Ln
2900 SDCo 1271 B7
Apricot Tree Ln
2900 SDCo 1271 E7
Apricot Tree Wy
3400 OCSD 1086 E3
April Ct
3800 SDGO 1228 E5
April Leigh Ter
11300 SDGO 1208 J2
Aqua Azul Wy
- SDCo 1090 D7
Aqua Cove
5600 SDGO 1351 A1
Aqua Hill Rd
2300 SDCo 1047 G2
Aqua Ln
3600 OCSD 1107 A1
200 SDCo 1152 H5
Aqua Mansa Rd
7900 SDGO 1209 A2
Aqua Park Ct
3700 SDGO 1350 F1
Aqua Park St
1100 SDGO 1350 E1
Aqua View Ct
8300 SDCo 1290 J5
Aquaduct Rd
32200 SDCo 1048 H7
31000 SDCo 1068 G3
Aquamarine
- OCSD 1067 A3
Aquamarine Ct
1800 CHLV 1331 E3
Aquamarine Rd
7000 SDGO 1290 F5
Aquarius Dr
8600 SDGO 1209 C1
Aquarius Pl
11200 SDGO 1209 C1
Aqueduct Ct
6700 SDGO 1250 E4
Aqueduct Rd
32700 SDCo 1048 H6
Aquilla Dr
10100 SDCo 1231 F3
Aquilla Pl
10300 SDCo 1231 F2
Aquitaine
- SDGO 1188 E7
Ara Pl
8600 SDGO 1209 C2
Arabella Wy
- OCSD 1086 H3
Arabian Crest Rd
11400 SDGO 1208 C2
Arabian Ranch Ln
2600 SDCo 1087 H1
Arabian Ranch Rd
500 SDCo 1087 H1
Arabian Trl
2400 SDCo 1047 G2
Arabian Wy
1600 OCSD 1067 E7
12500 POWY 1190 C6
Aragon Dr
4700 SDGO 1270 D3
Aragon Wy
4300 SDGO 1270 D4
Aramon Pl
15000 SDGO 1169 F6
Aranda Av
6600 SDGO 1247 F1
Arapaho Pl
3700 CRLB 1107 C6
Arapaho St
9700 SDCo 1291 D3
Arawak Ct
17700 SDGO 1169 H1
Arbalest Dr
300 SDCo 1058 G7
(See Page 1058)
Arbodar Rd
2800 SDGO 1350 D3
Arbol Ln
- SDCo 1172 A4
Arboleda Rd
800 SDCo 1251 G1
Arboleda Vista Dr
12500 SDCo 1070 A4

Arboles Ct
4100 SDCo 1028 G7
Arboles Pl
2000 ESCN 1129 F6
Arboles St
5800 SDGO 1250 C6
Arbolita Ln
1700 SDCo 1027 H6
Arbolitos Ct
14200 POWY 1190 D2
Arbolitos Dr
14100 POWY 1190 D2
Arbolitos Rd
13900 POWY 1190 C3
Arbor Cove Cir
- OCSD 1066 G7
Arbor Ct
1400 ENCT 1147 B3
Arbor Dr
400 SDGO 1269 A5
W Arbor Dr
1600 SDGO 1268 H5
200 SDGO 1269 A5
Arbor Glen
1900 SDCo 1130 A6
Arbor Glen Ln
700 VSTA 1108 A4
Arbor Glen Wy
4500 OCSD 1087 A1
Arbor Grove Ct
- SDGO 1208 F4
Arbor Heights Ln
- SDGO 1208 F4
Arbor Ln
1100 SNMS 1109 B7
Arbor Park Pl
10500 SDGO 1209 H4
Arbor Rose Dr
6200 CRLB 1127 F3
Arbor View St
2300 CHLV 1311 H7
Arbor Vitae St
4100 SDGO 1269 H7
Arborcreek Ln
600 CHLV 1311 C4
Arboretum Pl
10600 SDGO 1209 G5
Arborlake Wy
11800 SDGO 1210 A3
Arborside Wy
11200 SDGO 1210 A2
Arborview Dr
- SNMS 1108 B7
Arborwood Pl
2000 ESCN 1129 E6
Arbuckle Pl
700 CRLB 1106 E5
Arbusto Corte
- CHLV 1311 A6
Arbusto Ct
7900 CRLB 1147 G3
Arbutus St
- SDGO 1208 C6
Arcadia Av
2400 LMGR 1270 G7
700 NATC 1290 B7
1400 VSTA 1088 A3
Arcadia Bluff Ct
600 SNMS 1108 J4
Arcadia Dr
4300 SDGO 1268 J4
Arcadia Pl
800 NATC 1290 B7
Arcadia Rd
1000 ENCT 1167 D1
Arcadia Wy
4000 OCSD 1107 E5
Arcaro Ln
300 SOLB 1187 F2
Arcata Bay Wy
4200 OCSD 1066 F6
Arce Ct
4300 SDGO 1330 G7
Arch St
4400 SDGO 1269 B4
Archer Rd
- SNMS 1128 D6
Archer St
200 OCSD 1086 B6
1200 SDGO 1247 H4
E Archer St
1700 SDGO 1247 J4
Arches Wy
6400 CRLB 1127 G3
Archie Moore Rd
- SDCo 1151 F7
16000 SDCo 1171 F3
Archie Moore Ring
- SDCo 1171 F2
Archie Moore Tr
- SDCo 1151 F7
Archstone Pl
- SDGO 1209 G1
Archwood Av
6600 SDGO 1249 J6
Archwood Pl
1400 ESCN 1109 H6
Arco Dr
11000 SDCo 1109 G1
Arcola Av
2800 SDGO 1248 B2

Arcturus Wy
8800 SDGO 1209 C2
Ardath Av
2000 ESCN 1130 D1
Ardath Ct
2500 SDGO 1227 J6
Ardath Ln
7800 SDGO 1227 H5
Ardath Rd
2400 SDGO 1227 J6
Arden Dr
700 ENCT 1147 C7
1000 ENCT 1167 C1
Arden Wy
1400 SDCo 1027 J4
4200 SDGO 1268 G5
Ardena Ln
17500 SDGO 1170 A1
Ardere Ct
14900 SDGO 1169 D5
Ardilla Pl
1000 CHLV 1310 J5
Ardilla Rd
- SDCo 1029 J5
- SDCo 1049 H1
Ardilla Wy
- SNMS 1108 F4
Ardisia Ct
17800 SDGO 1149 J7
Ardmore Ct
7000 SDGO 1248 J3
Ardmore Dr
3900 SDGO 1248 J3
Ardys Pl
200 VSTA 1087 H5
Arena Cir
1000 VSTA 1087 G5
Arena Dr
16100 SDCo 1173 D3
Arena Pl
16200 SDCo 1173 D3
Arena Wy
23700 SDCo 1173 D2
Arenal Ln
7100 CRLB 1127 F6
Arenal Rd
1800 CRLB 1127 E7
Arenas St
500 SDGO 1247 E1
Arendo Dr
4400 SDGO 1270 D4
Arequipa St
1500 SDGO 1349 J2
Ares Wy
2900 SDGO 1310 E2
Arey Dr
3500 SDGO 1330 E7
Arga Pl
600 CHLV 1310 H6
Argent St
8600 SNTE 1231 C7
Argo Ct
8700 SDGO 1249 C7
Argonauta St
2700 CRLB 1127 H6
Argonauta Wy
7100 CRLB 1127 G6
Argonne Ct
5000 SDGO 1228 D7
Argonne St
3600 SDGO 1228 D7
- SDGO 1268 F6
Argos Dr
4300 SDGO 1269 H3
Argosy Ln
4800 CRLB 1106 H7
Arguelles St
300 CALX 6620 F7
Arguello St
4200 SDGO 1268 G5
Argus Wy
200 OCSD 1087 A1
Argyle St
3900 SDGO 1249 A3
Aria Av
500 SDCo 1109 H2
Ariana Rd
1100 SNMS 1109 A4
Ariane Dr
2600 SDGO 1248 B2
Ariane Wy
4500 SDGO 1248 C2
Ariel Pl
1000 ESCN 1130 F1
Aries Ct
1400 CHLV 1330 G3
Aries Glen
3700 ESCN 1150 C3
Aries Rd
8400 SDGO 1209 C2
Arietis Cove
- SDGO 1290 D3
Arikara Dr
13300 POWY 1190 E4
Arillo St
7000 SDGO 1248 J4
7200 SDGO 1249 A4
Arirang Ln
11300 SDCo 1089 H7
Arista Ct
2400 SDGO 1268 G4

Arista Dr
4400 SDGO 1268 G4
Arista St
3900 SDGO 1268 F5
Arista Wy
3900 OCSD 1086 G2
Aristocrat Ct
10600 SNTE 1231 E2
Aristotle Dr
2700 SDGO 1310 F1
Aristotle Glen
1200 ESCN 1109 J7
Ariva Ct
8700 SDGO 1249 C1
Ariva Wy
4800 SDGO 1249 C1
Arizona Av
5400 LMSA 1270 E1
Arizona St
500 CHLV 1330 B2
4700 SDGO 1269 D3
Arjons Dr
8300 SDGO 1209 C6
Arjuna Ct
300 ENCT 1147 H6
Arklow Pl
1500 SDGO 1350 A2
Arland Rd
2700 CRLB 1106 F4
Arlene Ct
5100 SDGO 1228 G7
Arlene Pl
5100 SDGO 1228 G7
Arlene St
5200 SDGO 1228 H7
W Arlene St
4800 SDGO 1228 G7
Arlene Wy
1500 SDCo 1152 F7
Arlette St
8100 SNTE 1230 H7
Arlingdale Wy
8900 SDCo 1271 A7
Arlington Cres
32000 SDCo 1048 B7
Arlington Dr
200 OCSD 1086 J4
Arlington Pl
1300 ELCJ 1251 J3
Arlington St
3600 SDGO 1228 D7
Arliss Ct
1500 SDGO 1350 E2
Arly Ct
7900 SNTE 1230 H7
Armacost Rd
1200 SDGO 1290 G2
Armada Dr
- SDCo 1126 H2
Armada Pl
3000 SDGO 1288 A3
Armada Ter
900 SDGO 1288 B3
Armadale Rd
1700 SDCo 1027 H6
Armagosa Wy
3300 SDCo 1293 C1
Armando Aviles St
- BRAW 6319 F1
(See Page 6319)
Armenariz Ct
700 CALX 6620 G7
Armentrout Ln
2400 SDCo 1234 B4
Armero Ct
11000 SDGO 1169 H1
Armin Wy
4900 SDGO 1269 J2
Arminda Cir
8600 SNTE 1230 J7
Armitage St
3600 SDGO 1228 D7
Armorlite Dr
1300 SNMS 1108 E6
Armorss Av
8800 SDGO 1249 C6
Armory St
1100 ELCJ 1251 D5
Armour St
7900 SDGO 1249 B2
Arms Lake Av
6300 SDGO 1250 J5
Armstrong Cir
1000 ESCN 1110 A7
Armstrong Pl
7400 SDGO 1249 A5
Armstrong Ranch Rd
- SDCo 1091 C4
Armstrong St
3000 SDGO 1248 J5
3900 SDGO 1249 A3
Arnaz Wy
9200 SNTE 1231 A5
Arnel Av
300 VSTA 1087 G5
Arnele Av
700 ELCJ 1251 E4
Arnheim Ct
1600 ELCJ 1252 B2
Arnies Alley
3100 OCSD 1106 G2

Arno Dr
6100 SDGO 1270 C1
Arnold Av
3500 SDGO 1269 D6
Arnold Wy
100 SDCo 1233 F4
2100 SDCo 1234 B6
Arnoldo Rd
1400 SDCo 1314 C7
(See Page 1314)
Arnoldson Av
2900 SDGO 1228 B5
Arnoldson Ct
6100 SDGO 1228 B6
Arnoldson Pl
6100 SDGO 1228 B5
Arnott St
2700 SDGO 1248 F6
Arosa St
6100 SDGO 1270 C3
Arouba Rd
- SDCo 999 C6
Arpege Rd
7200 SDGO 1250 E4
Arran Av
200 SDCo 1291 A5
Arrecife Ct
900 SDGO 1330 G7
Arrecife Wy
4300 SDGO 1330 G7
Arredondo St
200 SDCo 1085 F1
Arriba Avenida
900 IMPB 1349 G2
Arriba Linda Av
16900 SDCo 1169 F3
Arriba St
4000 SDGO 1228 C4
E Arrieta Cir
4100 LMSA 1270 J4
W Arrieta Cir
4100 LMSA 1270 J4
Arrow Ct
2000 SDCo 1272 C4
Arrow Glen
500 ESCN 1130 B2
Arrow Point Ct
600 CHLV 1330 J4
Arrow Rock Av
10100 SDGO 1209 C5
Arrow Wood Ln
1600 VSTA 1088 B5
Arrowgrass Wy
- SDGO 1270 D6
Arrowhead
- SDCo 1232 F4
Arrowhead Ct
2400 CHLV 1311 G6
4600 OCSD 1087 C3
8800 SNTE 1230 J5
Arrowwood Dr
200 SDGO 1290 H4
Arroya Vista Rd
13300 POWY 1170 E5
Arroyo Av
- CALX 6680 H2
1900 OCSD 1087 C5
Arroyo Canyon Rd
- SDCo 1130 D7
Arroyo Ct
- BRAW 6319 F3
(See Page 6319)
700 CHLV 1310 H7
Arroyo Dale Ln
13500 SDGO 1188 G3
Arroyo De Viejas
3700 SDCo 1254 D1
Arroyo Dr
900 CHLV 1310 H7
1000 CHLV 1330 H1
300 ENCT 1147 C6
- SDCo 1028 F4
600 SDGO 1288 J1
N Arroyo Dr
2900 SDGO 1269 A7
Arroyo Gn
- ESCN 1109 D5
Arroyo Grande Rd
7200 SDGO 1188 J4
Arroyo Hondo
14500 SDGO 1168 J7
Arroyo Lindo Av
5000 SDGO 1228 C7
Arroyo Pacifica
1100 SDCo 1028 C3
Arroyo Pl
800 CHLV 1310 H7
Arroyo Poco Ln
2500 SDCo 1299 J4
(See Page 1299)
Arroyo Rd
3400 SDCo 1311 B1
Arroyo Rosita
14800 SDCo 1188 B1
Arroyo Seco
400 IMPE 6439 F4
Arroyo Seco Ct
6700 SDGO 1290 E5
Arroyo Seco Dr
700 SDGO 1290 E5

7 INDEX

Arroyo Seco Truck Trl

INDEX 7

Avenida Mira Vista

SAN DIEGO CO.

San Diego County Street Index

STREET
Block City Map# Grid

Arroyo Seco Truck Trl
- SDCo 1216 C1
(See Page 1216)
Arroyo Seco Wy
- SDGO 1290 E5
Arroyo Sorrento Pl
4100 SDGO 1208 B2
Arroyo Sorrento Rd
3300 SDGO 1208 A2
Arroyo Vista
- CRLB 1127 J7
300 SDCo 1027 H3
Arroyo Vista Wy
4200 OCSD 1086 J3
- VSTA 1087 E7
Arroyo Willow Ln
1800 CRLB 1127 D5
Arroyo Wy
4100 NATC 1310 E4
Arruza St
3800 SDGO 1350 E1
Art St
4800 SDGO 1270 D3
Artemia Wy
3000 SDGO 1310 E2
Artesia St
1300 CHLV 1331 C1
Artesian Gateway
8100 SDGO 1169 A3
Artesian Rd
- SDCo 1168 G3
9800 SDCo 1169 C2
Artesian Ridge
15400 SDGO 1169 A4
Artesian Spring Rd
15400 SDGO 1169 A3
Artesian Springs Ct
- SDCo 1291 D1
Artesian St
5000 SDGO 1228 G7
Artesian Trl
1800 SDCo 1169 A3
Arthur Av
600 CHLV 1310 E7
800 OCSD 1067 B5
3400 SDGO 1269 F2
Arthur Hennesay Ct
- ELCN 6559 J4
Arthur Neal Ct
1400 LMGR 1290 E1
Artisan St
- CHLV 1331 F1
Artisan Wy
2000 CHLV 1331 G1
Artists Ln
- SDGO 1228 A2
Aruba Bend
- CORD 1329 E3
Aruba Cv
0 CHLV 1311 F6
Arucauna Ct
7400 SDGO 1188 J7
Arucauna Wy
12200 SDGO 1188 J7
Arundel Av
2500 CRLB 1127 F3
Arundel Pl
6500 SDGO 1248 J2
Arverne Ct
6800 SDGO 1248 J3
Arverne St
3900 SDGO 1248 J3
Arvilla Ln
1700 ELCJ 1252 B6
Arvin Ct
2100 SDCo 1291 A1
Arvinels Av
5000 SDGO 1228 H7
Arviso Ln
4900 SDCo 1071 E3
Arvita Ct
- OCSD 1067 A5
Aryana Dr
1700 ENCT 1147 D2
Asbury Ct
700 SDGO 1267 H4
Ascend Rd
1700 SDCo 1108 G2
Ascot Av
2700 CRLB 1127 G4
Ascot Dr
600 VSTA 1087 F6
Ascot St
5800 SDGO 1270 C5
Ash Av
300 CHLV 1310 A6
800 CHLV 1330 B2
Ash Creek Pl
- SDGO 1209 J2
Ash Hollow Crossing Rd
- POWY 1170 E2
Ash Ln
20100 SDCo 1149 E1
700 SNMS 1108 J5
Ash Rd
- SDCo 1085 J2
- SDCo 1086 A4
Ash St
- BRAW 6259 H6
(See Page 6259)
100 OCSD 1106 A1
200 SDCo 1027 F3
1200 SDCo 1152 F4
800 SDGO 1289 B2
- SDGO 1290 D4
- SNMS 1128 C1
2400 VSTA 1108 B6
N Ash St
1500 ESCN 1109 J6
1700 SDCo 1109 H4
S Ash St
300 ESCN 1130 B2
W Ash St
800 SDGO 1288 J2
Ashberry Rd
- CRLB 1107 A7
Ashbourne Glen
400 ESCN 1110 D6
Ashbrook Dr
700 CHLV 1311 D4
Ashburn Rd
- SDGO 1308 A1
Ashburton Rd
17400 SDGO 1170 A1
Ashbury St
100 ENCT 1147 A2
Ashby Ct
3600 CRLB 1107 A3
Ashby St
4600 SDGO 1270 B3
Ashdale Dr
10000 SNTE 1231 D3
Asher St
4200 SDGO 1268 E1
Ashford Castle Dr
1400 CHLV 1311 H7
Ashford Ct
7500 SDGO 1249 A5
Ashford Glen
2400 ESCN 1110 D6
Ashford Pl
7400 SDGO 1249 A5
Ashford St
4000 SDGO 1249 A3
Ashfourth Ln
300 CHLV 1330 C2
Ashgate Pl
13000 POWY 1190 F5
Ashland Av
5700 SDGO 1270 D1
Ashlar Pl
10800 SDGO 1209 J2
Ashley Ct
- SDCo 1070 G2
Ashley Falls Ct
- SDGO 1188 D5
Ashley Falls Dr
12800 SDGO 1188 D5
Ashley Ln
900 VSTA 1088 C5
Ashley Park Dr
3300 SDCo 1272 E5
Ashley Park Wy
3100 SDCo 1272 E5
Ashley Pl
- SDGO 1190 B7
Ashley Rd
- SDCo 1172 H2
Ashley View Pl
9300 SDCo 1232 F5
Ashlock Ln
- SDGO 1209 G1
Ashlock Wy
- SDGO 1209 G1
Ashmore Av
8800 SDCo 1290 J3
8600 SDGO 1290 J3
Ashmore Ln
700 SDGO 1290 J3
Ashton Ct
- IMPE 6499 H2
900 VSTA 1108 A4
Ashton St
4500 SDGO 1268 E1
Ashwood Ct
3400 OCSD 1086 E2
Ashwood St
10100 SDCo 1232 B3
Asilado St
200 OCSD 1066 J7
Askew Wy
400 SDCo 1152 E6
Asolear Pl
18600 SDGO 1150 D6
Aspect Dr
- SDGO 1269 C1
Aspen Creek
- OCSD 1086 J2
Aspen Creek Ct
9700 SDGO 1209 B6
Aspen Ct
900 CRLB 1127 A5
12700 POWY 1190 C1
3300 SDGO 1228 A4
2000 SNMS 1128 A2
Aspen Dr
3800 SDCo 998 E3
Aspen Glen
10500 SDCo 1089 F4
Aspen Glen Ct
- CHLV 1311 J3
Aspen Glen Rd
- CHLV 1311 J3
Aspen Ln
2000 SDCo 1272 C4
Aspen Rd
3400 SDCo 998 D4
Aspen Sr
- SNMS 1129 C2
Aspen St
3400 OCSD 1086 E2
Aspen View Ct
- SDGO 1190 B6
Aspen View Dr
- SDGO 1190 A7
Aspen Wy
300 ESCN 1109 H7
- SDCo 1232 D6
- VSTA 1127 H1
Aspendell Dr
- SDGO 1209 F1
Aspendell Wy
- SDGO 1209 F1
Aspenglow Dr
1700 ENCT 1147 F4
Aspenglow Pl
8700 SNTE 1231 D7
Aspenwood Ln
200 ENCT 1147 E5
Aspero Ct
1500 ESCN 1109 H5
Aspin Ct
800 SDGO 1267 J4
Aster Av
900 ELCJ 1251 E7
Aster Dr
2500 SDCo 1297 E6
(See Page 1297)
Aster Meadows Pl
5700 SDGO 1188 E4
Aster Pl
7000 CRLB 1127 E6
Aster St
600 ESCN 1110 B7
2400 SDGO 1248 B4
E Aster St
2500 SDGO 1248 C4
Asterwood Ln
2800 SDCo 1108 B6
Asti Wy
5800 LMSA 1251 B7
Aston Av
1800 CRLB 1127 B2
Astor
- SDGO 1248 C6
Astor Ct
1200 CHLV 1331 B2
Astorga Pl
600 SNMS 1109 C6
Astoria St
- CRLB 1127 G3
7100 SDGO 1248 J4
Astra Wy
4400 SDCo 1271 F3
Astro Ct
200 VSTA 1087 H7
Asturian Wy
35600 SDCo 1028 H6
Atadero Ct
2800 CRLB 1147 G3
Atari Ct
3200 SDGO 1248 D3
Atascadero Dr
3800 SDGO 1268 B7
Atchison Wy
11200 SDCo 1069 H6
Aten Rd
500 IMPE 6499 C2
- IMPE 6500 A1
800 ImCo 6499 A2
- ImCo 6500 H2
Atex Ct
23600 SDCo 1173 D5
Athena Cir
9300 SDGO 1228 C2
Athena St
100 ENCT 1147 A5
Athena Wy
- SDGO 1228 C2
Athens Av
2700 CRLB 1106 J4
Athens Pl
1300 ESCN 1109 E4
Athens Rd
2800 CHLV 1312 B7
(See Page 1312)
Athens St
4300 SDGO 1270 C4
Atherton Av
2100 SDGO 1350 B3
Atherton Pl
- CHLV 1331 C2
Atherton St
600 SNMS 1128 F5
Athey Av
300 SDGO 1350 F2
Athos Wy
4700 OCSD 1107 E5
Atkins Pl
15800 SDGO 1169 C3
Atlanta Dr
4700 SDGO 1270 A3
Atlantic St
1400 SNMS 1108 E6
Atlantis St
9200 SDCo 1271 B7
Atlas St
3500 SDGO 1249 A4
Atlas View Ct
- SNTE 1251 B1
Atlas View Dr
8600 SNTE 1231 C7
8500 SNTE 1251 C1
Atoka Pl
13600 POWY 1190 E3
Atoll St
3400 SDGO 1248 J4
Atosana Dr
32100 SDCo 1051 B6
Atrium Dr
10500 SDGO 1209 G5
Attebury Rd
- SDCo 1128 G6
- SNMS 1128 H5
Atteridge Rd
20100 SDCo 1153 G1
Attisha Wy
- SDCo 1232 G5
Attix St
1700 SDGO 1290 E1
Attleborough Ct
7000 SDGO 1290 F6
Attu Av
1500 CORD 1309 D6
Attu Rd
- CORD 1309 A1
Atwater St
- CHLV 1311 C7
1100 SDGO 1349 J1
Atwell St
4400 SDGO 1248 B2
Atwood Ct
10600 SDGO 1209 G1
Au Bon Climat Ct
30200 SDCo 1067 J5
Auberge Cir
8000 SDGO 1169 C5
Aubergine Ct
- OCSD 1087 D2
Aubert Wy
9000 SNTE 1231 G6
Aubree Rose Ln
10000 SDCo 1271 D1
Aubrey St
13600 POWY 1190 E2
Aubrives Pl
1800 CHLV 1311 F1
Auburn Av
700 CHLV 1311 C5
2700 CRLB 1106 J4
4100 OCSD 1087 C5
400 SNMS 1108 J6
Auburn Dr
4700 SDGO 1269 J5
5200 SDGO 1270 A6
Auburn Gn
- ESCN 1110 D7
Auburn Ridge Wy
- SDGO 1189 B4
Auburn Woods Dr
1000 SDCo 1107 J3
Auburndale St
3900 SDGO 1248 J4
Auden Pl
- CRLB 1107 A7
Audrey Ct
2200 SDCo 1028 A3
Audrey Ln
3400 SDGO 1270 C5
Audrey Pl
900 VSTA 1088 C5
Audrey Wy
800 SDCo 1252 C4
Audubon Ct
3600 SDCo 1311 A2
Audubon Glen
2000 ESCN 1110 B5
Audubon Rd
9400 SDCo 1232 E4
August Ct
2200 SDGO 1268 G1
August St
5000 SDGO 1268 G1
Augusta Cir
1000 OCSD 1067 A4
Augusta Ct
14100 POWY 1150 G5
1700 SDCo 1272 B5
Augusta Dr
4400 OCSD 1066 G7
14300 SDCo 1090 G4
700 SNMS 1109 D7
Augusta Pl
1000 CHLV 1311 G5
Augustana Pl
5200 SDGO 1270 A3
Augustina Pl
600 CHLV 1311 A5
Augustus Ct
12700 SDGO 1150 C6
Auklet Wy
4300 OCSD 1086 J3
Aura Cir
2000 CRLB 1106 J6
Auralie Dr
2600 SDCo 1130 B7
Aurora Av
200 SNMS 1128 H3
Aurora Ct
- ELCN 6559 E1
Aurora Dr
1900 ELCN 6559 E1
200 ELCN 6560 A1
13100 SDCo 1232 C7
13000 SDCo 1252 C1
Aurora St
400 SDGO 1289 J3
Aurora Vista Dr
3100 SDCo 1292 C1
(See Page 1292)
Austerlitz Pl
11900 SDGO 1170 A1
Austin Av
- SDGO 1229 F2
Austin Ct
- BRAW 6259 F7
(See Page 6259)
1500 CHLV 1311 C5
1300 VSTA 1087 E7
Austin Dr
9700 SDCo 1271 C7
4700 SDGO 1270 A3
Austin Hill Ct
8200 SDGO 1169 B3
Austin Rd
800 BRAW 6259 F7
(See Page 6259)
1900 ELCN 6499 C6
1300 ELCN 6559 C2
- IMPE 6439 C6
2100 IMPE 6499 C3
3900 ImCo 6319 D7
(See Page 6319)
- ImCo 6439 C3
1300 ImCo 6559 C4
Austin Terr
2900 CRLB 1106 G3
Austin Wy
1400 ESCN 1130 D2
2300 SDCo 1136 C6
Australia St
1300 ELCJ 1251 C3
Autillo Wy
10900 SDGO 1169 H1
Auto Center Ct
1000 CRLB 1126 G2
Auto Cir
4900 SDGO 1269 B3
Auto Park Dr
500 CHLV 1330 H5
Autocross Ct
1900 SDCo 1272 C3
Autopark Wy
1400 ESCN 1129 F4
N Autopark Wy
1900 ESCN 1129 F3
S Autopark Wy
1500 ESCN 1129 F4
Autoport Mall
5700 SDGO 1228 G2
Autumn Breeze Ln
- SDCo 1068 D5
Autumn Dr
2200 OCSD 1087 D6
200 SNMS 1108 G7
Autumn Gold Wy
- SDGO 1188 G4
Autumn Hill Ln
- SDCo 1089 A1
Autumn Hills Dr
1400 CHLV 1331 B2
Autumn Leaf Dr
900 SDCo 1027 G4
Autumn Ln
1800 VSTA 1088 A2
Autumn Pl
1800 ENCT 1147 H5
Autumn Rose Ln
200 SDCo 1028 A2
Autumn Sky Ln
1500 CHLV 1331 F1
Autumn Woods Pl
1500 ESCN 1129 F6
Autumnview Ln
10100 SDGO 1209 D5
Ava Ln
14200 SDCo 1070 F4
Ava Loma Rd
3200 SDCo 1273 D7
Ava Pl
5800 SDGO 1290 C6
Ava St
1300 SDGO 1290 C6
Avalon Av
2700 CRLB 1106 J4
Avalon Bay
300 OCSD 1066 J6
Avalon Ct
800 SDGO 1267 H4
Avalon Dr
4300 SDGO 1268 J4
400 VSTA 1087 J6
Avalon Vista Ct
5100 SDGO 1330 J7
Avalon Wy
6900 LMGR 1290 F2
900 SNMS 1128 F6
Avanti Av
10400 SNTE 1231 E2
Avati Dr
4100 SDGO 1248 C3
Avd Arroyo Pasajero R
16700 SDCo 1168 F5
Avd Cuatro Vientos
15900 SDCo 1188 C1
6000 SDCo 1168 H5
Avd Cuesta Del Sol
16400 SDCo 1168 F6
Avd De Los Olivos
16300 SDCo 1168 F6
Avd Del Norte
- SNMS 1109 B5
Avd Del Parque
- SDCo 1168 D7
Avd Del Sol
- SNMS 1109 B5
Avd Grande
- ENCT 1147 F5
Ave Companero
2100 SDCo 1108 E3
Ave De Benito Juarez
500 VSTA 1087 G5
Ave De La Luna
- VSTA 1087 G6
Ave De La Plaza
300 VSTA 1087 G5
Ave De Los Claveles
200 ENCT 1147 G7
Ave De San Clemente
900 ENCT 1147 E7
Avena Ct E
- CRLB 1127 C5
Avena Ct W
- CRLB 1127 C6
Avena Pl
11600 SDGO 1170 A3
Avenel Ln
15900 SDCo 1173 H4
Avenger Ct
9800 SDGO 1209 F2
Avenger Rd
11300 SDGO 1209 E2
Avenida Abajo
400 ELCJ 1271 G1
Avenida Abeja
- SDGO 1169 H5
700 SNMS 1108 E4
Avenida Abril
- ESCN 1109 G7
- SDCo 1252 B1
Avenida Acero
9400 SDCo 1291 C4
Avenida Adobe
400 ESCN 1149 J3
Avenida Aguila
500 SNMS 1108 E5
Avenida Alamar
7900 SDGO 1227 G5
Avenida Alcachofa
15600 SDGO 1170 B5
Avenida Alcor
- CRLB 1127 H7
Avenida Almada
1600 OCSD 1087 C3
Avenida Alondra
17900 SDCo 1168 B1
Avenida Alozdra Av
17900 SDGO 1150 D6
Avenida Alta Mira
1700 OCSD 1087 C4
Avenida Alteras
6000 SDCo 1168 H4
Avenida Amantea
1000 SDGO 1247 G3
Avenida Amigo
700 SNMS 1108 E5
Avenida Amorosa
3500 ESCN 1150 A3
Avenida Anacapa
3200 CRLB 1147 J3
11600 SDCo 1272 A4
Avenida Andante
1600 OCSD 1087 C4
Avenida Andorra
1500 OCSD 1087 C4
6800 SDGO 1247 H1
Avenida Angulia
8400 SDCo 1290 J5
Avenida Apolinaria
- SDCo 1272 A4
Avenida Aragon
- CRLB 1147 H4
Avenida Arana
1300 SNMS 1108 E4
Avenida Arriba
1500 ELCJ 1271 G1
Avenida Aveiro
16000 SDGO 1170 C5
Avenida Aviare
1600 CHLV 1331 D2
Avenida Avocado
500 SDCo 1027 E2
Avenida Azul
1300 SNMS 1108 E5
Avenida Benjamin
10900 SDCo 1271 G4
Avenida Bizarro
6600 SDGO 1247 G2
Avenida Blanco
500 SNMS 1108 E5
Avenida Bosques
2300 SDCo 1271 E7
Avenida Brisa
4000 SDCo 1188 C1
Avenida Calma
15900 SDCo 1188 C1
Avenida Canora
400 OCSD 1087 A4
Avenida Cantante
- SDCo 1188 H1
Avenida Cantaria
5200 SDGO 1188 D3
Avenida Carmelo
100 SCLE 1023 B1
Avenida Castana
- CRLB 1147 G2
Avenida Catherina
10700 SDCo 1271 F6
Avenida Cereza
- CRLB 1147 G2
Avenida Chamnez
5900 SDGO 1247 G3
Avenida Chapala
100 SNMS 1109 C7
Avenida Chelsea
1200 VSTA 1107 J7
Avenida Cherylita
1600 ELCJ 1271 G1
Avenida Christina
3000 CRLB 1127 J4
Avenida Cielo
- SNMS 1128 B2
Avenida Circo
5700 SDGO 1229 G7
Avenida Ciruela
- CRLB 1147 H3
Avenida Codorniz
- SNMS 1108 F4
Avenida Colino
9700 SDCo 1291 D3
Avenida Consentido
12000 SDGO 1170 B4
Avenida Cordillera
18700 SDGO 1150 D6
Avenida Cordoba
600 SNMS 1108 E5
Avenida Cortez
200 SDGO 1247 E3
Avenida Costa Azul
2000 SDGO 1351 H3
Avenida Costa Blanca
8500 SDGO 1351 H3
Avenida Costa Brava
- SDGO 1351 H4
Avenida Costa Del Sol
2300 SDGO 1351 G3
Avenida Costa Este
2300 SDGO 1351 H3
Avenida Costa Norte
8500 SDGO 1351 H3
Avenida Costa Sur
8500 SDGO 1351 H3
Avenida Cresta
6000 SDGO 1247 E3
Avenida De Acacias
17400 SDCo 1168 D2
Avenida De Aguacate St
2100 ESCN 1109 E4
Avenida De Colimbo
- BRAW 6320 B4
(See Page 6320)
Avenida De Contenta
- SDCo 1168 J1
Avenida De Espuela
12600 POWY 1170 C6
Avenida De La Barca
700 CHLV 1311 A6
Avenida De La Cantin
10200 SDGO 1189 G4
Avenida De La Cruz
1800 SDGO 1350 F3
Avenida De La Fuente
8400 SDGO 1351 H3
Avenida De La Fuente Norte
- SDGO 1351 J3
Avenida De La Fuente Sur
- SDGO 1351 J3
Avenida De La Luna
- SDCo 1272 G7
Avenida De La Madrid
100 SDGO 1350 F3
Avenida De La Plata
5100 OCSD 1087 C3
Avenida De La Playa
- ESCN 1109 F7
2300 SDGO 1227 H5
Avenida De La Ronda
6800 SDCo 1168 F7
Avenida De Lamar
3000 SDCo 1271 B6
Avenida De Las Adelsas
1500 ENCT 1167 G1
Avenida De Las Arenas
- CORD 1308 J2
Avenida De Las Flore
- SNMS 1128 A2
Avenida De Las Lilas
1500 ENCT 1147 G7
Avenida De Las Ondas
8500 SDGO 1227 H4
Avenida De Las Palmeras
- SCLE 1023 B2
Avenida De Las Pesca
6600 SDGO 1247 G2
Avenida De Las Rosas
400 ENCT 1167 G1
- SNMS 1128 B1
Avenida De Las Tiendas
- SDGO 1269 A2
Avenida De Las Vida
5100 SDCo 1068 A1
Avenida De Las Vistas
- SDGO 1331 A6
Avenida De Los Lirios
1500 ENCT 1147 G7
Avenida De Los Lobos
11200 SDGO 1169 H5
Avenida De Los Pinos
5300 SDCo 1068 A1
Avenida De Loyola
3400 OCSD 1086 H7
Avenida De Monaco
100 ENCT 1167 C2
Avenida De Nog
1600 SDCo 1027 J6
Avenida De Oro
1100 CALX 6620 G7
Avenida De Palais
- CRLB 1127 F7
Avenida De Portugal
3100 SDGO 1288 B2
Avenida De Sueno
- CRLB 1147 J4
Avenida De Suenos
1700 OCSD 1087 C4
Avenida De Suerte
200 SNMS 1108 C5
Avenida De Tortola
- BRAW 6320 B3
(See Page 6320)
Avenida Del Alba
- CRLB 1147 H4
Avenida Del Charro
13800 SDCo 1232 E6
Avenida Del Cielo
2100 SDCo 1253 G1
Avenida Del Diablo
2300 ESCN 1129 D5
Avenida Del Duque
6300 SDCo 1148 E6
Avenida Del Gado
100 OCSD 1087 A2
Avenida Del Gato
11000 SDGO 1209 B3
Avenida Del General
13000 SDGO 1189 G4
Avenida Del Mar
- SNMS 1128 B2
Avenida Del Mexico
2000 SDGO 1330 A7
Avenida Del Mundo
1700 CORD 1308 J1
Avenida Del Oro
1900 OCSD 1087 B5
Avenida Del Paisano
0 RivC 999 E1
Avenida Del Paraiso
6500 CRLB 1127 G5
Avenida Del Rey
- CHLV 1311 A4
Avenida Del Rio
- SDGO 1269 A3
Avenida Del Sol
1700 CORD 1308 J1
- ESCN 1109 G7
- SDCo 1251 G2
- SDCo 1252 B1
Avenida Del Valle
- BRAW 6319 F4
(See Page 6319)
Avenida Descanso
100 OCSD 1066 H7
- OCSD 1086 H1
Avenida Diestro
7900 CRLB 1148 A2
Avenida Dolores
100 SCLE 1023 B1
Avenida Elena
100 SNMS 1109 C7
Avenida Elisa
- SDCo 1272 C1
Avenida Empresa
4800 OCSD 1087 B3
Avenida Encinas
5400 CRLB 1126 G2
7300 CRLB 1127 A6
- SDCo 1126 J7
Avenida Esperanza
100 ENCT 1147 J7
Avenida Esteban
1100 ENCT 1147 H4
Avenida Feliz
3800 SDCo 1188 C1
Avenida Fiesta
5500 SDGO 1248 B2
Avenida Florencia
16400 POWY 1170 D4
Avenida Flores
- ENCT 1147 H4
Avenida Floresta
6200 SDCo 1168 F5
Avenida Fragata
- SNMS 1108 F4
Avenida Frontera
1100 OCSD 1087 A3
Avenida Granada
13100 POWY 1170 D3
Avenida Grande
13000 SDGO 1189 G4
Avenida Gregory
4300 SDCo 1271 C3
Avenida Guillermo
1500 OCSD 1087 C3
Avenida Hacienda
3300 ESCN 1149 J3
Avenida Helecho
- CRLB 1147 G2
Avenida Insurgentes
14700 SDCo 1188 H1
Avenida Joaquin
1900 ENCT 1147 H4
Avenida Johanna
3700 SDCo 1271 G5
Avenida Josefa
1800 ENCT 1147 H4
Avenida Kirjah
7800 SDGO 1228 A6
Avenida La Bahia
7100 SDGO 1228 D3
Avenida La Cima
- CRLB 1147 J4
2300 SDCo 1130 E4
Avenida La Cuesta
- SNMS 1128 G2
Avenida La Posta
1400 ENCT 1147 G4
Avenida La Reina
6600 SDGO 1247 F2
Avenida La Valencia
12800 POWY 1170 C4
Avenida Ladera
1500 ELCJ 1251 C2
Avenida Lamego
15800 SDGO 1170 C5
Avenida Las Brisas
200 OCSD 1086 J2
Avenida Las Perlas
16400 SDCo 1168 F7
Avenida Leon
1400 SNMS 1108 E4
Avenida Limon
500 SDCo 1027 E2
Avenida Linda
- POWY 1190 G4
Avenida Loma De Oro
6200 SDCo 1168 F5
Avenida Lorenzo
4300 OCSD 1086 J3
Avenida Lucia
100 SCLE 1023 B1
Avenida Luis
16900 SDCo 1168 E3
Avenida Lunar
- CORD 1308 J2
Avenida Madera
800 CHLV 1310 E7
Avenida Magnifica
2200 CRLB 1106 G3
10100 SDGO 1209 J4
10300 SDGO 1210 B3
Avenida Magoria
3000 ESCN 1149 J2
3200 ESCN 1150 A2
Avenida Manana
6600 SDGO 1247 F2
Avenida Manessa
4500 OCSD 1087 A4
Avenida Mantilla
1500 OCSD 1087 C3
Avenida Maravillas
5200 SDCo 1168 A3
Avenida Marbella
13000 SDGO 1150 D7
Avenida Marcella
11700 SDCo 1271 J4
Avenida Marco
8600 SDCo 1232 E6
Avenida Margarita
200 OCSD 1087 A2
Avenida Maria
10900 SDGO 1169 H7
Avenida Mariposa
- SNMS 1128 B1
Avenida Melodia
1600 ENCT 1147 H4
Avenida Michelle
- SNMS 1128 B1
Avenida Miguel
1200 ENCT 1147 H5
Avenida Mimosa
1800 ENCT 1147 H5
Avenida Mira Vista
1700 OCSD 1087 C4

8 INDEX
Avenida Mirola

San Diego County Street Index

Barker Valley Spur
INDEX 8
SAN DIEGO CO.

STREET — Block City Map# Grid

Avenida Mirola — 6500 SDGO 1247 F2
Avenida Molino Viejo — 16600 SDCo 1168 F6
Avenida Montuosa — 15000 SDGO 1169 H7
Avenida Navidad — 7900 SDGO 1228 D4
Avenida Nieve — - CRLB 1147 J3
Avenida Nobleza — 16200 SDGO 1170 A4
Avenida Obertura — - CRLB 1147 J3
Avenida Oceano — 1600 OCSD 1087 C4
Avenida Ocotillo — 2500 SDCo 1253 J2
Avenida Ofelita — - SDCo 1272 D1
Avenida Olmeda — 3100 CRLB 1127 J4
Avenida Ortega — - SNMS 1128 H2
Avenida Pacifica Wy — 5500 OCSD 1067 E7
Avenida Pala — 100 SCLE 1023 B1
Avenida Palizada — - SDGO 1188 D2
Avenida Palo Verde — 3700 SDCo 1310 D4
Avenida Pantera — - SDCo 1148 A4
Avenida Penasco — 2000 SDCo 1252 C7
Avenida Peregrina — 17300 SDCo 1168 G1
Avenida Picacho — 6100 SDCo 1168 G4
Avenida Pimentera — - CRLB 1147 G3
Avenida Playa Cancun — 5000 SDGO 1230 A7
Avenida Playa Veracruz — 10800 SDGO 1229 J7
Avenida Primavera — 400 DLMR 1187 F4
Avenida Privado — 4500 OCSD 1087 A3
Avenida Real — 10200 SDCo 1231 H3
Avenida Regina — 3000 SNMS 1108 D5
Avenida Reposo — 3200 ESCN 1149 J3
Avenida Ricardo — 9700 SDCo 1291 D3
Avenida Roberta — 10800 SDCo 1271 G6
Avenida Ronaldo — - SDCo 1291 D2
Avenida Rorras — 15400 SDGO 1170 A6
Avenida Rosa — 1500 CHLV 1330 D5
Avenida San Diego — 100 SCLE 1023 B1
Avenida San Miguel — 3900 SDCo 1310 F2
Avenida Sanchez — 5700 SDGO 1229 H7
Avenida Secreto — - CRLB 1147 H4
Avenida Segovia — 1700 OCSD 1087 C5
Avenida Sereno — 1300 ENCT 1147 H4
Avenida Sevilla — 1700 OCSD 1087 C4
Avenida Sierra — 3300 ESCN 1150 A3
Avenida Sivrita — 11800 SDGO 1169 J6; 11900 SDGO 1170 A6
Avenida Sobrina — 1100 OCSD 1087 A3
Avenida Solaria — 700 CHLV 1311 A6
Avenida Soledad — 4300 OCSD 1086 J2
Avenida Soria — 3300 CRLB 1147 J1
Avenida Suavidad — 16300 SDGO 1170 A4
Avenida Taxco — 800 VSTA 1088 C5
Avenida Theresa — 2900 CRLB 1147 H4
Avenida Thomas — 11200 SDCo 1271 H4
Avenida Tineo — 12500 SDGO 1170 C4
Avenida Topanga — 3100 CRLB 1127 J4
Avenida Toronja — - CRLB 1147 F2
Avenida Valera — - CRLB 1127 G7
Avenida Venusto — 14900 SDGO 1170 B6
Avenida Verde — - SDCo 1251 G2; - SDCo 1252 B1; 500 SNMS 1108 E5
Avenida Verde N — - ESCN 1109 G7
Avenida Verde S — - ESCN 1109 G7
Avenida Villaha — 15900 SDGO 1170 C5
Avenida Vista Del Oceano — 200 SCLE 1023 B1
Avenida Vista Labera — 1700 OCSD 1087 C4
Avenida Wilfredo — 6500 SDGO 1247 F2
Avenida Ysidora — 800 CHLV 1311 B6
Avenido Limero — - CRLB 1127 J4
Avenorra Dr — 5900 LMSA 1250 G6
Aventura Dr — 200 CHLV 1311 E1
Avenue Buena Ventura — 100 SCLE 1023 B1
Avenue Canora — 2400 SDCo 1254 C1
Avenue Of Arts — - SDGO 1270 B1
Avenue Of Industry — 11800 SDGO 1170 A7
Avenue Of Nations — - SDGO 1209 H6
Avenue Of Science — 15200 SDGO 1170 A6
Avenue Of The Trees — - CRLB 1106 F4
Avenue Santa Margarita — 100 SCLE 1023 B1
Averil Rd — 100 SDGO 1350 E3
Avery Rd — 1600 SNMS 1128 D7
Avery St — 4500 OCSD 1066 H7
Aves Ln — 1200 SDCo 1027 H3
Aviara Dr — - CRLB 1127 C6
Aviara Pkwy — - CRLB 1127 B4
Aviary Ct — 10800 SDGO 1209 H4
Aviary Dr — 9700 SDGO 1209 G5
Aviation Dr — 6600 SDGO 1290 E4
Aviation Rd — 400 SDCo 1027 F3
E Aviation Rd — 300 SDCo 1027 F3
Aviator Rd — - SDGO 1351 F1
Avila Av — 4900 CRLB 1106 J6
Avila Ct — 2000 SDGO 1247 H2
Avila Ln — 1500 VSTA 1087 F3
Avilar Ct — - SNMS 1108 C6
Avion Wy — 4800 SDGO 1269 J2
Avis Ln — 10300 SNTE 1231 E7
Avnda Altamira — 100 CHLV 1311 C2
Avnda Amapola — 7300 CRLB 1148 B2
Avnda Amistad — 1200 SNMS 1108 F4
Avnda Antonio — 400 CHLV 1311 F2
Avnda Apice — 18200 SDCo 1149 B5
Avnda Aquila — 4400 SDGO 1350 H1
Avnda Arroyo — 4100 NATC 1310 E5
Avnda Barranca — - SDCo 1149 C5
Avnda Belterra — - CHLV 1311 E1
Avnda Campana — 800 SDCo 1027 G3
Avnda Caterina — - CHLV 1311 E2
Avnda Cenit — 18100 SDCo 1149 B5
Avnda De Anita — 2800 CRLB 1106 H3
Avnda De Avila — 1500 CHLV 1331 D1
Avnda De La Madre — 2800 SDCo 1028 C4
Avnda De Las Estrell — 32600 SDCo 1051 D5
Avnda De Los Arboles — - SDCo 1255 F2; - SNMS 1128 B1
Avnda De Louisa — 2800 CRLB 1106 H3
Avnda De Nog — 3800 SDCo 1271 G5
Avnda De Oro — 3000 SDCo 1292 H1 (See Page 1292)
Avnda De Pompeii — - SDCo 1168 H3
Avnda De Robles Verd — 39100 SDCo 1300 C4 (See Page 1300)
Avnda Del Oceano — 1000 SDCo 1252 C7
Avnda Encinas — 6700 CRLB 1126 J5
Avnda Gabriel — 400 CHLV 1311 E1
Avnda Halley — 4500 SDGO 1350 G1
Avnda Jinete — 5800 SDCo 1048 B7
Avnda Loretta — 100 CHLV 1311 C1
Avnda Manantial — - SDCo 1149 B5
Avnda Mantilla — 400 CHLV 1311 F2
Avnda Mara — 2200 CHLV 1311 E2
Avnda Maravilla — 3500 CRLB 1148 A1
Avnda Marlina — 300 CHLV 1311 E2
Avnda Merida — 1500 CHLV 1331 C2
Avnda Mil Flores — 7900 SDCo 1068 H4
Avnda Milagro — - SDCo 1089 J2
Avnda Mirador — - SDCo 1149 C5
Avnda Naranja — 1200 SDCo 1152 F3
Avnda Nordeste — - SDCo 1078 J2 (See Page 1078)
Avnda Olinda — 10500 SDCo 1169 G2
Avnda Orilla — - SDCo 1149 C5
Avnda Pantera — 1300 SNMS 1108 F4
Avnda Parada — - CRLB 1128 A6
Avnda Platino — 3300 CRLB 1128 B6
Avnda Ricardo — 800 SNMS 1129 D1
Avnda Serena — 3300 CRLB 1128 B7
Avnda Soledad — - CHLV 1311 E1; - CRLB 1128 A6
Avnda Sureste — 700 SDCo 1078 J2 (See Page 1078)
Avnda Visalia — 17000 SDCo 1169 F2
Avo Dr — 100 SDCo 998 E7; 100 SDCo 1028 E1
Avocado Av — 300 ELCJ 1251 G6; 1000 ESCN 1129 G1; - SDCo 1028 F4
Avocado Blvd — 1600 ELCJ 1271 G1; 4300 SDCo 1271 F3
Avocado Crest — 100 SDCo 1130 A6
E Avocado Ct — 700 SOLB 1187 H1
Avocado Dr — 1600 SDCo 1108 A2
Avocado Frwy — - SDCo 999 A1
Avocado Hwy — 0 SDCo 1028 G3; 0 SDCo 1048 H3; 0 SDCo 1068 J3; 0 SDCo 1089 B4; 1300 SDCo 1109 F6; - SDCo 1129 F1
Avocado Knoll Ln — 2000 SDCo 1027 G6
Avocado Ln — 700 CRLB 1106 F6
Avocado Park Ln — 5000 SDCo 1048 J2
Avocado Park Wy — 5000 SDCo 1048 J2
E Avocado Pl — 200 SDGO 1187 H1; 700 SOLB 1187 H1
W Avocado Pl — 600 SOLB 1187 H1
Avocado Pt — - SDGO 1187 H1
Avocado Ranch Rd — 1900 SDCo 1272 A1
Avocado Rd — 1800 OCSD 1106 E2
Avocado School Rd — 3800 SDCo 1271 G5
Avocado St — 100 ENCT 1147 A3; 9000 SDCo 1271 A7
Avocado Summit Dr — 1400 SDCo 1272 B1
Avocado Village Ct — 3600 SDCo 1271 G5
Avocado Vista — 5000 SDCo 1048 J3
Avocado Vista Ln — 3300 SDCo 1048 J2
Avocado Wy — 1500 SDCo 1109 E7
Avocet Ct — 1500 CHLV 1331 F2; - CRLB 1127 C6; 1200 ENCT 1167 F3; 400 SDGO 1330 H6
Avocet Wy — 4400 OCSD 1087 A3
Avohill Dr — - SDCo 1068 G6
Avon Dr — 4200 LMSA 1270 H3
Avon Ln — 1900 SDCo 1291 A1
Avondale Cir — 3500 CRLB 1106 G4
Avondale Rd — 1300 SDCo 1290 J2
Avondale St — 3600 SDGO 1228 D7
Avonette Ct — - SDGO 1210 B1
Avorg Ln — 15500 SDCo 1070 J1
Avowick Ct — 30200 SDCo 1069 D5
Avowood Ct — 1900 SDCo 1028 A6
Avoyer Pl — 4100 SDCo 1271 D4
Awana Glen — 1000 ESCN 1110 A7
Award Row — 3000 SDGO 1228 C6
Ayamonte Wy — 600 CHLV 1310 H6
Ayers Ln — - SDCo 1070 H2
Azado Ct — 11600 SDGO 1150 A7
Azahar Ct — 3000 CRLB 1147 H1
Azahar Pl — 3200 CRLB 1147 J1
Azahar St — 3000 CRLB 1147 H1
Azalea — - SDCo 1233 B3
Azalea Av — - POWY 1190 F3; 2700 SDCo 1155 H3; 800 SNMS 1128 J3
Azalea Ct — - SNMS 1108 H6
Azalea Dr — 100 SDCo 1108 C4; 2700 SDGO 1268 C6
Azalea Glen — 3800 ESCN 1150 C3
Azalea Pl — 7300 CRLB 1127 A6
Azalea Spring Fire Rd — - SDCo 1196 C2 (See Page 1196)
Azalea St — 500 CHLV 1330 H3
Azalea Wy — 200 OCSD 1086 J2
Azimuth Pl — 3700 CRLB 1107 A3
Azofar Ct — 18400 SDGO 1150 D7
Azores Ct — 5400 SDGO 1249 H1
Aztec Circle Dr — - SDGO 1270 B1
W Aztec Circle Dr — - SDGO 1270 B1
Aztec Dr — 5600 LMSA 1250 G7; 5500 LMSA 1270 H1
Aztec St — - OCSD 1087 C5; 3700 SDGO 1287 J4
Azuaga St — 10200 SDGO 1189 G4
Azucar Wy — 17600 SDGO 1149 J7
Azucena Dr — 11400 SDGO 1250 A3
Azul Ct — 1000 OCSD 1067 A3
Azul Luna Wy — 6700 SDGO 1188 H3
Azul St — 2700 SDGO 1227 J3
Azul Vista — 1700 SDCo 1128 B4
Azul Wy — 200 OCSD 1087 A2
Azure Cir — 3600 CRLB 1106 H5
Azure Coast Dr — 2500 SDGO 1227 J6
Azure Cv — 2000 CHLV 1311 F6
Azure Lado Dr — 3600 OCSD 1107 C3
Azure Ln — 2300 VSTA 1108 A5
Azure Ter — 1900 SDCo 1272 C2
Azure View — 8000 SNTE 1230 H7
Azure Wy — 1900 ENCT 1147 H5
Azurite Pl — 2200 CRLB 1127 F6
Azusa Ct — 1600 CHLV 1311 C5
Azusa St — 1200 SDGO 1268 F3
Azzuro Ct — 12700 SDGO 1188 C6

B

B Av — 100 CORD 1288 J6; 200 NATC 1289 H7; 1600 NATC 1309 H2; - SDCo 1066 B2; - SDCo 1291 D3; - SDGO 1229 F5
B Rd — - SDGO 1270 C7
E B Rd — - CORD 1288 F5
B St — 400 BRAW 6319 G1 (See Page 6319); 7200 CRLB 1126 J7; - ENCT 1147 B6; 2700 IMPE 6439 E6; - ImCo 6319 D1 (See Page 6319); - SDCo 1085 H3; - SDCo 1108 G2; 2500 SDCo 1136 B7; 1100 SDCo 1152 G6; - SDCo 1291 D7; 1200 SDGO 1289 B2
W B St — 400 SDGO 1289 A3
Baba Dr — 16900 SDCo 1173 E1
Babauta Rd — 9500 SDGO 1189 E7
Babbling Brook Rd — 2900 CHLV 1311 J2
Babcock St — 16000 SDGO 1169 C3
Babette St — 7300 SDGO 1269 A2
Babilonia St — 7200 CRLB 1127 H6
Babs Wy — - SDCo 1271 E3
Baby Turtle Dr — 500 SDCo 1078 H5 (See Page 1078)
Bacadi Dr — 7800 SDGO 1209 A5
Bacara Ct — 15700 SDGO 1210 J2
Baccharis Av — - CRLB 1127 D6
Baccus Ct — 10300 SDGO 1209 B5
Bach St — 300 ENCT 1167 D2; 600 VSTA 1087 F5
Bachelor Ln — 11000 SDCo 1089 G6
Bachimba Ct — - SDGO 1170 B6
Bachman Pl — 4200 SDGO 1268 J4; 4200 SDGO 1269 A4
Back Nine Dr — 2700 SDCo 1079 B4 (See Page 1079)
Back Nine St — 2300 OCSD 1106 J1
Backer Ct — 9900 SDGO 1209 B6
Backer Rd — 7600 SDGO 1209 A6
Bacon St — 1600 SDGO 1267 H6
Bacontree Pl — 3500 SDGO 1248 J4
Bacontree Wy — 6900 SDGO 1248 J4
Badajoz Pl — 2400 CRLB 1147 G1
Badami Cir — 7900 SDGO 1209 A1
Badger Ct — 12800 SDCo 1212 D5
Badger Glen — 2000 ESCN 1129 E6
Badger Lake Av — 6300 SDGO 1250 H5
Badger Ln — - CRLB 1107 D7
Badger Wy — 1000 VSTA 1108 A5
Badillo Rd — 3500 SNMS 1108 D6
Baffin Dr — 10000 SDGO 1209 A5
Bafle St — 900 SDCo 1027 G5
Bagdad St — 7400 SDGO 1249 A4
Bagley Dr — 3400 SDGO 1268 E6
Bagwell Cove — 7600 SDGO 1209 A5
Bahama Bend — - CORD 1329 E1
Bahama Cove — 14100 SDGO 1187 H5
Bahama Dr — - ESCN 1129 J5
Bahia Dr — 2200 SDGO 1248 A3
Bahia Ln — 100 ESCN 1109 H6; 100 OCSD 1086 G3; 5400 SDGO 1248 A3
Bahia St — - IMPE 6439 C7
Bahia Vista Wy — 1600 SDGO 1247 H3
Bahia Wy — 1900 SDGO 1248 A3
Bailey Ct — 300 SDCo 1086 A2; 900 SNMS 1108 F7
Bailey Dr — 1800 OCSD 1106 F1
Bailey Meadow Rd — 33300 SDCo 1052 D3 (See Page 1052)
Bailey Rd — - SDCo 1028 C4
Baileyana Ln — 13900 SDGO 1188 H3
Baily Av — 2500 SDGO 1269 J7; 2700 SDGO 1270 A7; 2300 SDGO 1289 J1
Baily Pl — 4700 SDGO 1269 J7
E Bainbridge Rd — 2700 SDGO 1288 C1
Bainbridge St — - SDGO 1309 F1
Baja Cerro Cir — 2400 SDGO 1248 B3
Baja Ct — 4900 SDGO 1270 B2
Baja Dr — 5700 SDGO 1270 B2
Baja Mar — 5700 SDGO 1247 G3
Baja Mission Rd — 4500 SDCo 1047 J5
Baja Vista Dr — 3900 OCSD 1086 G1; 1500 SDCo 1048 A3
Baja Wy — 1100 SNMS 1128 E3
Bajada Rd — 12100 SDGO 1170 A1
Bajer St — 6200 SDGO 1228 B5
Bajo Ct — 700 CHLV 1310 H7; 3300 CRLB 1128 A7
Bajo Dr — 900 CHLV 1310 H7
Baker Av — - ImCo 6560 B7
Baker Pl — 2900 SDCo 1310 C3
Baker St — - ImCo 6620 B1; 3600 SDGO 1248 E5
Baker Wy — - OCSD 1086 G1
Bakersfield St — 1600 LMGR 1290 G2
Bakewell St — 5800 SDGO 1248 H2
Bakman Ct — 12100 SDCo 1231 J2
Bakten Wy — - SDCo 1069 E4
Balanced Rock Ln — - SDCo 1252 C5
Balboa Arms Dr — 5100 SDGO 1248 H2
Balboa Av — 600 CORD 1288 G6; 2000 DLMR 1187 F3; 3700 SDGO 1248 E4; 7800 SDGO 1249 B2
Balboa Cir — 1200 CHLV 1311 B6; 2000 VSTA 1107 J4
Balboa Ct — 800 SDGO 1267 H4
Balboa Dr — 3700 OCSD 1107 A1; 3000 SDGO 1269 B6; 2300 SDGO 1289 B1
Balboa Pl — - SDCo 1149 D4
Balboa St — 100 SNMS 1108 E6
Balboa Ter — 3700 SDGO 1248 D4
Balboa Vista Dr — 2300 SDGO 1270 B7
Balboa Wy — 4100 SDGO 1248 G3
Balchen Wy — - SDGO 1351 D2
Baldrich St — 7100 LMSA 1270 F1
Baldwin Ln — 4000 CRLB 1106 F7; 100 SNMS 1108 H7
Baldwin Rd — 8100 LMGR 1270 H6
Balentine Dr — 1900 SDCo 1254 A3
Balfour Ct — 5900 CRLB 1127 D2; 2100 SDGO 1248 A4
Bali Cove — 2400 SDGO 1290 E7
Bali Hai Rd — - ESCN 1129 J5
Bali Ln — 10900 SDGO 1209 A3
Bali Wy — 100 OCSD 1087 A1
Balkis Ln — 7200 LMGR 1270 F7
Ball Av — 700 ESCN 1109 J7
Ball Ranch Rd — - SDCo 1234 A6
Ballantyne Ln — 100 ELCJ 1251 G5
Ballantyne St — 900 ELCJ 1251 G3
Ballard St — 700 ELCJ 1251 J6
Ballast Ln — 4800 SDGO 1330 H6
Ballast Point Ct — 1600 CHLV 1330 J4
Ballata Ct — 1100 VSTA 1107 H4
Ballena Wy — 6900 CRLB 1127 J5
Ballerina Ln — - SDCo 1090 E2
Ballina Dr — 1800 SDGO 1290 C1
Ballinger Av — 6900 SDGO 1250 H3
Ballista Dr — 300 SDCo 1058 F6 (See Page 1058)
Ballow Wy — 800 SNMS 1128 J3
Ballybunion Pl — 2000 ESCN 1129 F7
Ballybunion Sq — 11400 SDGO 1189 J2
Ballystock Ct — - SDGO 1209 H1
Balmoral Ct — 1400 SNMS 1109 D7
Balmoral Dr — 5800 SDGO 1290 C4
Balour Dr — 1000 ENCT 1167 F1
Balsa St — 2600 SDGO 1270 B7; 2300 SDGO 1290 B1
Balsam Ct — 600 ELCJ 1252 B6
Balsam Dr — 700 ELCJ 1252 B6; - NATC 1289 H7
Balsam Lake Av — 6300 SDGO 1250 H5
Balsamina Dr — 3800 SDCo 1310 F3
Baltic St — 7400 SDGO 1249 A4
Baltimore Dr — 5700 LMSA 1250 G7; 5000 LMSA 1270 H2
Baltimore Pl — 1500 ESCN 1130 B4
Baltimore St — 3300 SDGO 1248 E5
Baltusrol Glen — 2200 ESCN 1109 D3
Bamboo Ln — 100 SDCo 1027 H2
Bamburgh Pl — 6700 SDGO 1248 J2
Banagas Ct — 100 CALX 6620 F6
Banbury Ct — 2600 CRLB 1106 J5
Banbury Dr — - SDCo 1090 E5
Banbury St — 6000 SDGO 1310 D1
Bancroft Dr — 5000 LMSA 1271 B2; 3700 SDCo 1271 B5
Bancroft Glen — 400 ESCN 1110 D6
Bancroft St — 4800 SDGO 1269 E3; 400 SDGO 1289 F4
S Bancroft St — 500 SDGO 1289 F5
Bancroft View Dr — 8900 SDCo 1271 A5
Banda Av — - CALX 6620 H6
Bandak Ct — - SNMS 1108 J4
Bandell Ct — 10500 SDGO 1209 A4
Bandera St — 300 SDGO 1247 G4
Bandini Pl — 300 VSTA 1087 H7
Bandini St — 4100 SDGO 1268 G5
Bandolier Ln — 1900 SDGO 1350 D3
Bandon Wy — 8800 SNTE 1231 A7
Bandy Canyon Rd — 15200 SDCo 1150 H3; 18000 SDGO 1131 D7; 15500 SDGO 1151 A2
Banff Ct — 2700 CRLB 1107 A5
Banfield Ln — - SDGO 1188 A5
Bangalore Ln — 10700 SDGO 1209 A4
Bangerter Ct — 3600 ESCN 1110 F4
Bangor Pl — 3300 SDGO 1288 A2
Bangor St — 1200 SDGO 1288 A1
Banjo Ct — 600 SNMS 1109 A6
Banjo Ln — 1400 SDCo 1152 J7
Banks St — 5300 SDGO 1268 F3
Banneker Dr — 800 SDGO 1290 G3
Banner Av — 1300 CHLV 1330 E5
Banner Dr — 2300 SDCo 1136 C6
Banner Rd — 1200 SDCo 1136 C5; 36100 SDCo 1156 H1
Banner View Dr — 1200 SDCo 1136 C6
Banning St — 4300 SDGO 1268 A6
Bannister Ln — 7500 SDGO 1208 J4
Bannister Wy — 10500 SDGO 1208 J4
Bannock Av — 4100 SDGO 1248 E1
Banock St — 800 SDCo 1291 C3
Banta Rd — - IMPE 6439 E6; 500 ImCo 6439 D6
Bantam Av — 9400 SDGO 1249 E6
Bantam Lake Av — 6500 SDGO 1250 H4
Bantam Lake Cir — 6500 SDGO 1250 H4
Banty Ct — 12200 SDGO 1188 J7
Banuelo Cove — 12300 SDGO 1188 B7
Banyan Ct — 700 SNMS 1109 A5
Banyan Dr — 1300 SDCo 998 B7
Banyan Wy — 300 ESCN 1109 H7; 13400 SDGO 1188 G3
Banyonwood Dr — 700 OCSD 1087 C1
Bar Bit Rd — 2300 SDCo 1271 G7
Bar O Dr — 3300 SDCo 1078 H6 (See Page 1078)
Baranca Ct — 8300 SDCo 1290 H6
Barbados Av — 1800 VSTA 1107 G5
Barbados Cir — 300 SDCo 1027 F5
Barbados Cv — 2000 CHLV 1311 F6
Barbados Wy — 13300 SDGO 1187 J7; 10800 SDGO 1209 A3
Barbara Ann Ln — 1100 SDCo 1152 J6
Barbara Ann Pl — 5100 SDGO 1270 E2
Barbara Av — 400 SOLB 1167 E6
Barbara Dr — - ESCN 1109 C4; 1200 SDCo 1108 B1
Barbara Jean St — 8700 SNTE 1251 A1
Barbara Ln — 1700 ENCT 1147 B2; 2700 OCSD 1087 B6
Barbara Worth Dr — 1800 ELCN 6499 E6
Barbara Wy — - ELCN 6559 F2
Barbarossa Ct — 5800 SDGO 1270 B3
Barbarossa Dr — 4700 SDGO 1270 C3
Barbarossa Pl — 4800 SDGO 1270 C3
Barbary Pl — 5700 SDCo 1048 B7
Barber Mtn Rd — 2300 SDCo 1294 F4 (See Page 1294)
Barberry Pl — 1500 CHLV 1311 J7; - CRLB 1127 A5
Barbic Ct — 3700 SDCo 1271 C5
Barbic Ln — 9400 SDCo 1271 C5
Barbour Av — 1600 CHLV 1331 E2
Barbour Dr — 2800 SDGO 1330 C7
Barby Pl — 3000 SDGO 1228 C7
Barcelona Ct — 9900 SDCo 1271 D6; 1900 VSTA 1107 H3
Barcelona Dr — 1100 SDGO 1287 J1
S Barcelona Ln — 3200 SDCo 1271 D6
S Barcelona St — 3300 SDCo 1271 D6
Barcelona Wy — 4500 OCSD 1107 E4
Barclay Av — 5600 SDGO 1250 B6
Bardaguera Pl — 3900 SDCo 1310 F2
Bardonia St — 6700 SDGO 1250 H4
Bardsley Ct — - SDGO 1330 H7
Bareback Sq — 5100 SDGO 1188 C2
Barelia Rd — 1600 SDCo 1131 C3
Bareta Star Ranch Rd — - SDCo 1173 G6
Barger Pl — 1100 SDCo 1152 G7
Barham Dr — 1400 ESCN 1129 C1; 400 SNMS 1128 J1; 500 SNMS 1129 A1
E Barham Dr — 100 SNMS 1128 H1
W Barham Dr — - SNMS 1128 G2
Barham Ln — 400 SNMS 1129 A1
Barhaven Ln — 100 SDCo 1027 H3
Bari Ct — 5800 LMSA 1251 B7
Barin St — - CORD 1288 G4
Barioni St — 200 IMPE 6439 F6
Bark St — 5900 SDGO 1270 C6
Barkeath Dr — 7300 LMGR 1270 F6
Barker Dr — 8400 SDGO 1250 J3
Barker St — 4200 SDGO 1248 E1
Barker Valley Spur — - SDCo 1033 D6

9 INDEX

Barker Wy

INDEX 9

Berkview Ln

SAN DIEGO CO.

San Diego County Street Index

STREET
Block City Map# Grid

Barker Wy
6900 SDGO 1250 H3
Barkla St
5500 SDGO 1228 B6
Barles Ct
38800 SDCo 997 A3
Barley Ct
5700 SDCo 1311 B2
Barley Dr
2300 VSTA 1108 A5
Barlows Landing Cove
4800 SDGO 1208 C2
Barn Owl Ct
- CHLV 1331 A1
Barnard Dr
3600 OCSD 1107 A1
Barnard St
2800 SDGO 1268 C5
Barnaville Ln
500 SNMS 1108 G6
Barnes Canyon Rd
9800 SDGO 1208 E6
Barnes St
100 OCSD 1086 B6
Barnett Av
3600 SDGO 1268 F6
Barnett Cir
- SDCo 1067 A2
Barnett Dr
500 SNMS 1108 J6
Barnett Rd
1500 SDCo 1172 H1
Barnett St
3000 SDGO 1268 E6
Barneveld St
9100 SDCo 1291 B4
Barney Ct
- SDGO 1350 D1
Barney St
2200 SDGO 1290 G7
Barnhurst Dr
6600 SDGO 1248 J2
Barnhurst Pl
4500 SDGO 1248 J2
Barnson Pl
2700 SDGO 1269 A7
Barnwell Pl
500 OCSD 1086 E7
E Barnwell St
2900 OCSD 1086 D6
N Barnwell St
100 OCSD 1086 D6
S Barnwell St
100 OCSD 1086 E6
Barolo Ct
15100 SDGO 1169 F6
Baron Dr
10300 SDGO 1209 C4
Baron Ln
10500 SDGO 1209 C4
Baron Long Rd
- SDCo 1235 A2
Baron Pl
900 ESCN 1129 F1
Barona Mesa Rd
23600 SDCo 1173 D5
Barona Mesa Wy
- SDCo 1173 D5
Barona Rd
15200 SDCo 1173 C6
- SDCo 1192 F6
(See Page 1192)
Barona Wy
5100 LMSA 1271 A1
Baroness Av
10100 SDGO 1209 B5
Baroque Ln
10900 SDGO 1249 H2
Baroque Pl
500 ESCN 1109 J7
Baroque Ter
4800 OCSD 1087 B2
Barr Av
900 SDGO 1268 J4
Barranca Ct
- CRLB 1107 B3
Barranca Pl
1600 CHLV 1331 C3
Barranca Rd
3500 SNMS 1108 D5
Barrego Wy
23600 SDCo 1173 D3
Barrel Blossom Ln
2700 SDCo 1108 D1
Barrel Ct
2100 CHLV 1331 G3
Barrel Dr
700 SDCo 1078 J4
(See Page 1078)
Barret
- ELCN 6559 J1
Barrett Av
1000 CHLV 1330 E2
Barrett Lake Rd
2500 SDCo 1295 C5
(See Page 1295)
1600 SDCo 1315 D3
(See Page 1315)
Barrett Truck Trl
- SDCo 1275 D5

Barrett View Rd
3400 ELCJ 1275 B4
Barrington Ct
4600 SDCo 1310 H2
Barrows St
4300 SDGO 1248 C2
Barry St
5100 OCSD 1067 B5
Barrymore St
14200 SDGO 1189 C2
Barrywood Wy
10300 SDGO 1210 B4
Barsanti Ct
1900 SDGO 1330 A7
Barsby St
600 SDCo 1087 H2
Barsky Ln
1000 SDCo 1027 H4
Barstow St
5200 SDGO 1228 G7
Bart Ln
9500 SNTE 1231 D5
Bart Wy
10300 SNTE 1231 E4
Bartel Pl
2400 SDGO 1249 E7
Bartel St
2400 SDGO 1249 E6
Bartels Ct
1000 SDCo 1152 G7
Bartizon Dr
300 SDCo 1058 F6
(See Page 1058)
Bartlett Av
3500 OCSD 1086 F5
Bartlett Dr
1000 VSTA 1087 H4
Bartley Ln
14700 SDCo 1293 A1
Bartley Pl
1200 ESCN 1109 J5
Bartola Rd
- SDCo 998 G7
Barton Dr
7800 LMGR 1290 H1
Barton Peak Dr
- CHLV 1311 E6
Bartram Wy
1500 SDCo 1252 B7
Basalto St
6500 CRLB 1127 H5
Bascomb Pl
3600 SDGO 1228 D7
Basel St
2900 OCSD 1106 G1
Bashan Lake Av
8300 SDGO 1250 J4
Bashful Wy
8500 SDCo 1232 D7
Basil St
100 ENCT 1147 B5
Basilica St
200 OCSD 1086 H3
Basilone Rd
- SDCo 1023 D3
Basilone St
3800 SDGO 1268 C5
Basin Rd
4700 CRLB 1107 B5
Bass Cove Rd
1700 ImCo 6560 C1
Bass Dr
10100 SDCo 1232 E3
Bass Ln
- OCSD 1086 G2
15800 SDGO 1169 D4
Bass Rd
2400 SDCo 1297 F5
(See Page 1297)
Bass St
3800 LMSA 1270 F5
Bassett Ct
16300 SDCo 1173 D2
100 SDCo 1290 J5
Bassett Wy
23500 SDCo 1173 D3
Bassmore Dr
13700 SDGO 1189 F3
Basso Ct
7300 SDGO 1250 F4
Basswood Av
1200 CRLB 1106 F5
700 IMPB 1329 G6
Bataan Cir
5900 SDGO 1290 D7
Batavia Cir
11100 SDGO 1209 A2
Batavia Rd
7700 SDGO 1209 A2
Batchelder Ct
1900 ELCJ 1251 C5
Bateman Av
3900 SDGO 1350 F1
Bates Ln
1200 SDCo 1251 G1
Bates St
5700 SDGO 1270 B5
Bates View Ct
100 SNMS 1108 H5
Bath Av
1500 CHLV 1331 C2

Bathurst Pl
1400 ELCJ 1251 D5
Batiquitos Dr
6900 CRLB 1127 A5
- SDCo 1127 A7
Batiquitos Rd
- CRLB 1127 C7
N Batiquitos Wy
- CRLB 1127 A7
W Batista St
7000 SDGO 1248 J3
Battle Creek Rd
- CHLV 1311 E6
Bauer Pl
600 VSTA 1107 F1
Bauer Rd
- SDGO 1209 C7
Baughman Rd
- ImCo 6259 A2
(See Page 6259)
- ImCo 6260 A1
(See Page 6260)
Baum St
1600 CHLV 1331 E2
Bausell Ct
10100 SDGO 1249 G3
Bausell Pl
10100 SDGO 1249 G3
Bautista Av
2100 SDCo 1087 G1
Bautista Ct
100 OCSD 1086 H3
Bavaria Dr
200 SDCo 1108 A2
Bavarian Dr
13100 SDGO 1189 C4
Bavarian Wy
8400 SDGO 1189 C4
Baxter Canyon Rd
2200 VSTA 1107 H7
Baxter Cir
- SDGO 1289 C1
Baxter Ct
4600 SDGO 1228 F7
Baxter St
5000 SDGO 1228 F7
Bay Berry Pl
- ENCT 1147 C5
Bay Blvd
400 CHLV 1309 J7
500 CHLV 1329 J1
1100 CHLV 1330 A4
Bay Canyon Ct
2700 SDGO 1248 E6
Bay Cir
900 CORD 1308 J1
Bay Crest Ln
5100 SDGO 1350 J2
Bay Front St
2000 SDGO 1289 C6
Bay Hill Dr
- SNMS 1108 J3
Bay Hill Rd
2300 CHLV 1311 G6
Bay Leaf Dr
300 CHLV 1310 E5
Bay Ln
6900 CRLB 1126 J5
Bay Meadows Dr
1500 SDCo 1234 B6
Bay Meadows Ln
- SOLB 1187 G1
Bay Morgan Ln
35700 SDCo 1028 J5
Bay Pony Ln
- SDGO 1190 A7
Bay Sable Ln
35800 SDCo 1028 H5
Bay Summit Pl
4600 SDGO 1248 F6
Bay View Ct
4000 SDGO 1268 H5
Bayamon Rd
9500 SDGO 1189 E4
Bayard St
5100 SDGO 1247 H4
Bayberry Ct
4300 SDGO 1330 G7
800 SNMS 1109 A6
Bayberry Dr
1800 OCSD 1106 E2
Baycane Wy
- SDGO 1190 A7
Baycliff Wy
4100 OCSD 1107 C3
Bayfront Ct
- SDGO 1288 J3
Bayleaf Wy
3800 OCSD 1086 H5
Baylee Ln
10000 SDCo 1169 E4
Bayliss Ct
4900 SDGO 1188 C4
Baylor Av
700 CHLV 1311 C4
Baylor Dr
4700 SDGO 1270 A3
900 SNMS 1128 F6
Bayona Loop
500 CHLV 1310 J5

Bayona Lp
1000 CHLV 1310 J5
Bayonet Ter
13400 SDGO 1189 J4
Bayonne Dr
3600 SDGO 1248 A7
Bayshore Dr
4700 CRLB 1106 H7
4700 CRLB 1126 H1
Bayshore Ln
- SNMS 1128 F2
Bayside Ln
3600 SDGO 1247 H7
2900 SDGO 1267 J3
Bayside Pkwy
900 CHLV 1329 H1
Bayside Walk
3600 SDGO 1247 H7
2900 SDGO 1267 J3
Bayview Heights Dr
1700 SDGO 1290 B2
Bayview Heights Pl
5400 SDGO 1290 B1
Bayview Heights Wy
1800 SDGO 1290 B1
Bayview Pl
- CRLB 1107 B4
Bayview Wy
200 CHLV 1310 B4
Baywind Pt
- SDGO 1188 D6
Baywood Av
10400 SDGO 1209 D4
Baywood Cir
1000 CHLV 1311 F5
5100 OCSD 1087 D2
Baywood Ln
10300 SDGO 1209 D5
Baywood St
- IMPE 6499 C2
Beach Av
800 CALX 6680 H1
- IMPB 1349 E1
Beach Bluff Rd
4100 CRLB 1106 H6
Beach Club Dr
100 SOLB 1187 E2
Beach Club Rd
- SDCo 1023 E3
Beach Crest Ct
900 CRLB 1126 J4
Beach Front Dr
700 SOLB 1187 E2
Beach St
600 ENCT 1147 D7
Beachcomber Ct
- SDGO 1188 D5
Beachwood Bluff Wy
2900 SDGO 1248 F5
Beachwood Ct
4700 CRLB 1106 H7
Beachwood Ln
100 OCSD 1106 C2
Beacon Bay Dr
- CRLB 1127 A5
Beacon Ct
600 VSTA 1087 F5
Beacon Dr
700 SDGO 1290 G3
Beacon Hill Ct
1100 SNMS 1128 A2
Beacon Ln
4800 SDGO 1330 H6
Beacon Pl
500 CHLV 1310 G6
700 ESCN 1130 A3
Beacons Ct
8200 SDGO 1189 B5
Beadnell Wy
6200 SDGO 1248 H2
Beagle Ct
3400 SDGO 1249 A4
Beagle Pl
3400 SDGO 1248 J4
Beagle St
7100 SDGO 1248 J4
Beak Pt
9300 SDGO 1189 E6
Beal St
7300 SDGO 1249 A3
Beaman Ln
- SDCo 1027 G4
Bean St
3200 SDGO 1268 H7
Beanie Ln
1200 SDCo 1251 J3
Bear
- SDCo 1232 F4
Bear Creek Pl
2300 CHLV 1311 G7
Bear Dance Wy
11100 SDGO 1149 H7
Bear Dr
3500 SDGO 1268 J6
Bear Mtn Wy
13600 SDCo 1292 F3
(See Page 1292)
Bear River Row
6800 SDGO 1310 F1
Bear Rock Glen
2200 ESCN 1109 C3

Bear Valley Heights Rd
- SDCo 1111 E1
Bear Valley Ln
- SDCo 1111 E1
Bear Valley Oaks
1900 SDCo 1130 C4
Bear Valley Pkwy
2700 ESCN 1110 E7
1900 ESCN 1130 D2
3400 ESCN 1150 B3
1200 SDCo 1130 D3
Bear Valley Rd
2700 CHLV 1312 A6
(See Page 1312)
Bear View Wy
- SDCo 1253 F2
Bearcat Ln
1800 SDCo 1272 D3
Beardsley St
700 SDGO 1289 C5
Bearing Ln
100 ELCJ 1252 A5
Bears Pl
400 ENCT 1147 B2
Beartrap Pl
2100 ESCN 1130 D1
Beatitude Dr
- SDCo 1090 B1
Beaton Ct
11100 SDGO 1209 D2
Beatrice Ct
6300 SDGO 1310 E1
- SDGO 1350 E1
Beatrice St
2800 SDGO 1310 E1
Beatty Pl
4600 SDGO 1249 G2
Beauchamp Ct
4900 SDGO 1188 C5
Beaumont Av
5600 SDGO 1247 F3
Beaumont Cir
1000 VSTA 1088 A6
Beaumont Ct
300 VSTA 1088 A6
Beaumont Dr
4800 LMSA 1271 C2
100 VSTA 1088 A6
Beaumont Glen
300 ESCN 1109 G6
N Beaumont Ln
100 VSTA 1088 A6
S Beaumont Ln
- VSTA 1088 A6
Beaver Hollow Rd
3100 SDCo 1273 D4
Beaver Lake Ct
6400 SDGO 1250 J5
Beaver Lake Dr
7900 SDGO 1250 H5
Beavercreek Ln
200 SDCo 1028 A3
Bebas Ln
3100 SDGO 1249 C5
Beck Dr
9900 SNTE 1231 D3
Beckington Ln
7000 SDGO 1290 G7
Beckington Wy
2600 SDGO 1290 F6
Becky Ln
600 SDCo 1108 G1
Becky Pl
2100 SDGO 1289 G1
Bedel Ct
9100 SDGO 1189 D1
Bedfont Cir
10400 SDGO 1209 D4
Bedford Av
1500 CHLV 1331 F1
3900 OCSD 1087 B7
Bedford Cir
3500 CRLB 1106 H4
Bedford Dr
4100 SDGO 1269 G2
E Bedford Dr
5100 SDGO 1269 H2
Bedford Hill
16000 SDGO 1169 C3
Bedford Pl
1900 ESCN 1129 F7
Bedfordshire Ct
12600 SDGO 1150 C6
Bedlow Ct
6700 SDGO 1250 E3
Bee Valley Rd
20500 SDCo 1314 J2
(See Page 1314)
Beech Av
300 CHLV 1310 A6
800 CHLV 1330 B2
400 CRLB 1106 D5
Beech Fern Ct
- SDGO 1209 J2
Beech Ln
20300 SDCo 1149 E1
Beech Pl
1400 ESCN 1109 J6
100 SDCo 1252 H4
Beech St
200 ELCJ 1251 F4

Beech St
500 SDCo 1027 E3
700 SDGO 1289 B2
- SDGO 1290 D4
N Beech St
800 ESCN 1110 A7
500 ESCN 1130 A1
S Beech St
300 ESCN 1130 B2
W Beech St
800 SDGO 1289 A2
Beechglen Dr
1000 CHLV 1310 J7
Beechtree Dr
100 ENCT 1147 F7
Beechtree Rd
- SNMS 1128 D6
Beechtree St
13100 SDCo 1232 C3
Beechwood Ct
8000 LMGR 1270 J7
Beechwood St
600 ESCN 1130 A1
- POWY 1190 D3
Beejay Dr
700 SDGO 1330 B7
Beeler Canyon Rd
10900 POWY 1210 D1
Beeler Canyon Terr
- SDGO 1210 D2
Beeler Creek Trl
12700 POWY 1190 B5
Beethoven Dr
700 ESCN 1150 C3
Beflora Wy
- OCSD 1087 A4
Begonia
- SDGO 1248 C6
Begonia Ct
900 CRLB 1127 A6
Begonia St
800 ESCN 1110 B6
3800 SDGO 1208 C6
Begonia Wy
2500 SDCo 1233 J4
Behberg Rd
- SDGO 1288 A4
Beinn Bhreagh
17200 SDCo 1156 D7
17200 SDCo 1176 C1
(See Page 1176)
Bel Air Ct
3100 ESCN 1130 F1
Bel Air Dr
600 VSTA 1087 J5
Bel Air Ter
1800 ENCT 1167 H3
Bel Esprit Cir
- SNMS 1108 H5
Bel Ln
- SDCo 1129 C5
Bela Vista Av
- ELCJ 1251 H5
Belair Dr
1100 SDCo 1027 H2
Belardo Dr
5200 SDGO 1230 A7
E Belcher St
- CALX 6680 H1
Belcourt Pl
- SDGO 1208 B1
Belden Pl
2100 ESCN 1129 H7
Belden St
7100 SDGO 1248 J4
7500 SDGO 1249 A4
Bele Ct
- BRAW 6320 C3
(See Page 6320)
Belfast Cir
8700 SDGO 1209 C4
Belfast Glen
100 ESCN 1110 E7
Belford Rd
400 IMPE 6439 F4
500 ImCo 6439 D4
Belford St
3700 SDGO 1249 A4
Belgian St
10900 SDGO 1209 D3
Belinda Wy
600 CHLV 1310 D7
Belio Ln
- LMGR 1270 E6
Belize Rd
- CHLV 1311 E2
Belize Wy
200 OCSD 1087 A2
Belknap Wy
2000 ESCN 1110 B6
2800 SDGO 1288 C1
Bell Bluff Av
6400 SDGO 1250 D3
Bell Bluff Rd
- SDCo 1234 F7
Bell Bluff Truck Tr
- SDCo 1254 J2
- SDCo 1255 A2
Bell Bluff Truck Trl
- SDCo 1255 D2

Bell Collo Ln
9100 SNTE 1231 G6
Bell Ct
- BRAW 6319 H2
(See Page 6319)
6600 SDGO 1248 H6
Bell Dr
- SNMS 1128 H3
Bell Gardens Dr
10200 SNTE 1231 D4
Bell Ln
- ELCN 6559 J3
Bell Rd
900 VSTA 1107 J1
Bella Azul Ct
1400 ENCT 1147 D2
Bella Colina St
- OCSD 1087 C3
Bella Collina
3200 ENCT 1148 C5
Bella Collina St
5100 OCSD 1087 C3
Bella Laguna Ct
1600 ENCT 1147 D1
Bella Linda Dr
30100 SDCo 1069 H5
Bella Pacific Row
4800 SDGO 1248 C4
Bella Rosa Dr
- SDCo 1088 B2
Bella Siena
15800 SDCo 1168 E6
Bella Vista Dr
1500 ENCT 1147 D2
2100 SDCo 1108 D3
Bella Vista St
5200 SNTE 1231 G7
Bella Vita Ln
2500 SDCo 1108 D1
Belladonna Wy
- SDGO 1209 G2
Bellagio Rd
900 ESCN 1130 F1
9200 SNTE 1231 A4
Bellagio St
1700 CHLV 1331 E1
Bellaire Ct
800 ELCJ 1251 A4
Bellaire St
300 DLMR 1187 F4
Bellakaren Pl
7800 SDGO 1228 A6
Bellatrix Ct
11400 SDGO 1209 C1
Bellatrix Dr
- SDGO 1209 E7
Bellbottom Wy
- SDCo 1174 B4
Belle Bonnie Brae Rd
3600 SDCo 1311 A2
Belle Crest Wy
800 SDGO 1330 H7
Belle Fleur Wy
12600 SDGO 1189 G5
Belle Glade Av
6600 SDGO 1250 E5
Belle Glade Ln
6900 SDGO 1250 E5
Belle Haven Dr
6600 SDGO 1250 D5
Belle Helene Ct
17600 SDCo 1150 A7
Belle Isle Dr
3300 SDGO 1269 J6
Belle Ln
3300 CRLB 1106 G4
Belle St
800 CHLV 1330 A4
Belle Vista Dr
400 CHLV 1310 F6
Belleaire St
1400 OCSD 1106 D1
Belleau Wood Av
- SDGO 1268 F6
Bellechase Cir
17700 SDGO 1150 A7
Belleflower Rd
- CRLB 1127 A4
Bellegrove Rd
1800 ENCT 1147 J7
Bellemeade Rd
1700 ENCT 1147 H7
Bellemore Dr
25400 SDCo 1173 J4
26000 SDCo 1174 A4
Bellena Av
- CHLV 1311 D6
Bellena Ct
- CHLV 1311 D7
Bellerive Ct
100 VSTA 1088 A6
Bellerive Dr
200 VSTA 1088 A6
Belleview Av
1300 ENCT 1167 C1
Bellevue Av
5700 SDGO 1247 G3
Bellevue Pl
700 SDGO 1247 G4
Belleza Ranch Rd
- SDGO 1188 H4

Bellezza Dr
2700 SDGO 1249 E7
Bellflower Ct
- CHLV 1331 A1
Bellflower Dr
4300 LMSA 1271 A4
Bellflower Gln
2000 ESCN 1109 G5
Bellinda St
2000 ESCN 1109 F5
Bellingham Av
3600 SDGO 1269 F6
Bellingham Dr
900 OCSD 1067 B4
Bellington Ln
1700 SDCo 1027 J3
Bellis Ln
- SDCo 1232 D6
Bello Hills Ln
1800 ESCN 1109 H5
Bello Mar Dr
- ENCT 1147 D2
Belloc Ct
2100 SDGO 1248 A4
Bellota Dr
16800 SDGO 1170 B3
Bellota Pl
12100 SDGO 1170 B3
Bells Dr
1100 OCSD 1067 A3
Bellvale Av
5100 SDGO 1248 G2
Bellver Cir
1200 SDCo 1027 H3
Bellvine Trl
1100 SDCo 1272 A1
Bellvista Dr
14400 SDCo 1188 E1
Bellwood Ct
8800 SDCo 1290 J3
Bellwood Ln
900 VSTA 1108 B6
Belmont Av
3800 SDGO 1269 G3
N Belmont Av
- NATC 1290 B6
S Belmont Av
100 NATC 1290 B6
Belmont Ct
300 SNMS 1108 G6
Belmont Park Rd
1500 OCSD 1067 G7
- OCSD 1087 G1
Belmont Pl
- CHLV 1331 C2
Belmont Terr
1100 SDCo 1108 C1
Belmont Trail Ct
6200 SDGO 1188 G7
6200 SDGO 1208 G1
Belmore Ct
1900 ELCJ 1251 B2
Beloe
- SDCo 1232 F4
Beloit Av
6800 SDGO 1248 J3
Belshire Ln
11400 SDGO 1209 D2
Belt St
2000 SDGO 1289 C6
E Belt St
2500 SDGO 1289 D6
Beltaire Ln
15600 SDCo 1169 B4
Belton Dr
7500 SDGO 1208 J5
Belvedere Dr
13800 POWY 1190 G3
4600 SDCo 1156 C5
Belvedere St
400 SDGO 1247 E1
Belvia Ln
700 CHLV 1330 B5
Belvista Ct
4600 SDGO 1188 C6
Belvue Dr
3700 LMSA 1270 H5
Ben St
3800 SDGO 1249 A3
Benavente Pl
9700 SDGO 1189 F5
Benavente St
9500 SDGO 1189 F6
Benavente Wy
12600 SDGO 1189 F6
Benbow Ct
13400 SDGO 1189 C4
Benchley Rd
13200 SDGO 1188 A4
Benchmark Ct
29700 SDCo 1069 A5
Bend St
9800 SNTE 1231 F4
Bendigo Cove
10700 SDGO 1209 A4
Bendigo Rd
7700 SDGO 1209 A5
Bending Elbow Dr
2900 SDCo 1078 H4
(See Page 1078)

Bendito Dr
12600 SDGO 1170 C4
Benecia Ct
1100 CHLV 1311 C6
Benedict Av
700 ELCJ 1251 E5
Benet Hill Rd
600 OCSD 1086 C4
Benet Rd
400 OCSD 1086 C4
Benevente Dr
300 OCSD 1086 J4
Benfield Ct
4400 SDGO 1289 J5
Benfold Dr
- SDGO 1209 D7
Bengal Ct
5400 SDGO 1249 H1
Benhurst Av
4300 SDGO 1228 E5
Benhurst Ct
6300 SDGO 1228 F5
Benicia St
1000 SDGO 1268 G3
Benicia Wy
- OCSD 1086 H3
Benjamin Holt Rd
6800 SDGO 1290 E6
Benjamin Pl
1000 ELCJ 1251 E7
Bennett Av
800 SNMS 1109 D6
1300 SNMS 1129 C1
Bennett Ct
1300 SNMS 1129 C1
Bennett St
- SDGO 1287 J4
Bennington Ct
3700 CRLB 1107 A4
Bennington St
8600 SDGO 1209 C4
Benny Wy
- ELCJ 1251 J6
Bennye Lee Dr
16100 POWY 1170 D4
Benson Av
6100 SDGO 1290 C4
Benson Pl
100 OCSD 1086 D6
Bent Av
100 SNMS 1128 F1
Bent Trail Dr
- CHLV 1311 G2
Bent Tree Ct
14300 POWY 1170 G5
Bent Tree Pl
2200 ESCN 1109 J4
Bent Tree Rd
15800 POWY 1170 H5
Bentley Dr
3500 SDCo 1271 A5
Bento Wy
23900 SDCo 1173 E2
Benton Cv
6800 SDCo 1237 D7
Benton Pl
600 ELCJ 1251 H6
5100 SDGO 1269 F2
Benton Well Ln
29600 SDCo 1237 D7
Benton Wy
4800 LMSA 1270 F2
Bentwood Dr
700 SDCo 1251 G1
Benviana Dr
200 CHLV 1311 E1
Benway Ln
1600 SDCo 1108 D2
Berea Ct
12200 POWY 1210 C1
Berenda Pl
1400 ELCJ 1251 D5
Beretta
- SDGO 1350 H2
Berg Rd
39600 SDCo 996 J2
Bergen Peak Pl
3700 CRLB 1107 B6
Bergen St
5400 SDGO 1228 H7
Berger Av
3100 SDGO 1249 B5
Bergman St
- SDGO 1270 B5
Beringer Ln
1300 VSTA 1107 H3
Berino Ct
3900 SDGO 1228 C4
Berkeley Av
2700 CRLB 1106 J5
Berkeley Dr
7200 LMSA 1270 F4
Berkeley Wy
800 VSTA 1088 B7
Berkshire Ct
900 ESCN 1129 J6
- SNMS 1108 J3
Berkshire Pl
600 ESCN 1110 E5
Berkview Ln
9000 SDCo 1291 B1

San Diego County Street Index

STREET
Block City Map# Grid

Berkwood Dr
- SDCo 1271 A7
Berland Wy
400 CHLV 1310 F7
Berlin St
12900 POWY 1190 D5
Bermuda Av
4700 SDGO 1267 H7
Bermuda Cir
4300 SDGO 1287 J1
Bermuda Dunes Pl
4000 CHLV 1310 G3
4400 OCSD 1066 G7
Bermuda Ln
1400 ELCJ 1252 C2
- ESCN 1129 J4
Bermuda Pl
1200 ELCJ 1252 C3
Bermuda View
1200 ELCJ 1252 C2
Bernabe Ct
14200 SDGO 1189 H2
Bernabe Dr
10600 SDGO 1189 G2
Bernabeo Ct
- SDCo 1070 F6
Bernadette Ln
6200 SDGO 1250 C6
Bernadine Pl
4200 SDGO 1270 B4
Bernadotte Ln
13900 POWY 1190 F3
Bernard St
- IMPE 6499 J2
Bernardi Rd
- IMPE 6499 J2
Bernardi St
- IMPE 6499 H2
Bernardino Ln
3400 SDCo 1088 F7
Bernardo Av
- ESCN 1129 H5
2100 SDCo 1129 H6
3000 SDCo 1149 H2
Bernardo Center Ct
11900 SDGO 1170 A2
Bernardo Center Dr
15600 SDGO 1169 G5
17500 SDGO 1170 A3
W Bernardo Ct
11500 SDGO 1169 J2
W Bernardo Dr
18100 SDGO 1149 J7
19500 SDGO 1150 A5
17100 SDGO 1169 J2
Bernardo Heights Pkwy
15900 SDGO 1170 A5
Bernardo Lakes Dr
- SDCo 1169 C2
Bernardo Ln
5700 SDCo 1149 D4
Bernardo Mountain Dr
- SDCo 1149 H3
Bernardo Oaks Ct
12100 SDGO 1170 B1
Bernardo Oaks Dr
17200 SDGO 1170 B3
Bernardo Plaza Ct
11600 SDGO 1170 A3
Bernardo Plaza Dr
11900 SDGO 1170 A2
Bernardo Ridge Rd
- ESCN 1149 G1
Bernardo Ter
11800 SDGO 1170 A2
Bernardo Trails Ct
18300 SDGO 1150 C6
Bernardo Trails Dr
18500 SDGO 1150 C6
Bernardo Trails Pl
17800 SDGO 1150 C7
Bernardo Vista Dr
17200 SDGO 1170 A1
Berney Pl
1700 ESCN 1109 D5
Bernice Dr
3800 SDGO 1268 B7
Bernie Dr
3100 OCSD 1107 B1
Bernis Ct
3100 SDCo 1271 A6
Bernita Rd
1300 SDCo 1271 H1
Bernita Wy
1400 SDCo 1271 H1
Bernwood Pl
3600 SDGO 1188 A5
Berry Creek Pl
1300 CHLV 1331 A2
Berry Park Ln
7000 LMGR 1290 F1
Berry Rd
31700 SDCo 1069 G1
N Berry Rd
11100 SDCo 1069 G2
Berry Run
27700 SDCo 1090 D3
Berry St
- LMGR 1270 F7
1900 LMGR 1290 F1

Berrydale St
1700 ELCJ 1251 G2
Berryessa Ct
23900 SDCo 1173 E2
Berryessa Ln
10600 SDCo 1169 F2
Berryessa St
5100 SDCo 1107 F4
Berryhill Dr
500 SNMS 1109 B6
Berryknoll St
11200 SDGO 1209 A2
Berryland Ct
2000 LMGR 1290 F1
Berryman Canyon
1200 ENCT 1167 G2
Bert Acosta St
10000 ELCJ 1251 D2
Bert Ct
4200 SDGO 1248 E2
Bert Ln
100 OCSD 1086 G3
Bertha Ct
4400 SDGO 1248 E2
Bertha St
4400 SDGO 1248 E2
Berting St
4400 SDGO 1270 B4
Bertro Dr
5900 LMSA 1250 G7
Bervy St
1500 SDGO 1268 E2
Berwick Dr
4500 SDGO 1248 J2
Berwick Woods
2100 SDCo 1027 G6
Berwyn Rd
8000 SDGO 1209 B4
Beryl Cove
- SDGO 1351 A1
Beryl St
7400 LMGR 1270 G7
1000 SDGO 1247 H5
2200 SDGO 1248 B4
Beryl Wy
- CRLB 1127 F6
4700 SDGO 1248 B4
Bessemer St
2900 SDGO 1288 B3
S Best Av
- BRAW 6320 C1
(See Page 6320)
Best Rd
5000 ImCo 6260 C2
(See Page 6260)
N Best Rd
4600 BRAW 6260 C7
(See Page 6260)
Bestview Dr
700 SDCo 1251 G1
Bestwood Ct
6700 SDGO 1250 E4
Beta Ct
- SDGO 1209 E6
Beta Dr
- SDGO 1209 E6
Beta St
1600 NATC 1289 J6
2200 NATC 1290 A6
3600 SDGO 1289 G6
Betelgeuse Wy
8800 SDGO 1209 C1
Beth Pl
2500 LMGR 1270 F7
Bethany Pl
- ELCJ 1251 J3
Bethany St
400 SDGO 1290 C5
Bethune Ct
5600 SDGO 1290 B2
Bethune Wy
100 CHLV 1330 E4
Betsworth Ln
- SDCo 1090 B2
Betsworth Rd
- SDCo 1089 J2
- SDCo 1090 C2
Betsy Ct
2500 SDGO 1248 F7
Betts St
1200 ELCJ 1251 C3
Betty Jo McNeece Lp
- ImCo 6559 G5
Betty Lee Wy
13200 POWY 1190 E2
Betty St
4600 SDGO 1248 B5
600 SDGO 1330 A7
Bettyhill Dr
6900 SDGO 1248 J2
Beven Dr
3100 ESCN 1110 E5
Beverley Wy
1100 ESCN 1110 A7
Beverly Av
900 IMPB 1349 G1
Beverly Dr
4300 LMSA 1270 H3
1000 VSTA 1088 B4
Beverly Glen Dr
4500 OCSD 1087 D5

Beverly Ln
1500 ELCN 6559 J3
Beverly Pl
500 SNMS 1128 D1
Beverly St
2300 SDCo 1152 D7
1000 SDGO 1290 B2
Bevis St
3400 SDGO 1249 A4
Bevner Ct
5100 SDGO 1270 A7
Bewicks Ct
- SDCo 1127 B7
Bexley Rd
20500 SDCo 1315 A2
(See Page 1315)
Beyer Blvd
2200 SDGO 1330 C6
4400 SDGO 1350 G3
E Beyer Blvd
2700 SDGO 1350 G4
Beyer Wy
100 CHLV 1330 D5
300 SDGO 1330 D6
800 SDGO 1350 D1
Biada St
1300 VSTA 1107 H4
Bianca Av
5000 SDGO 1268 F2
Bianca Ct
- IMPE 6499 H2
Bibler Ct
- CHLV 1330 H2
Bibler Dr
3500 SDGO 1350 F4
Biddeford St
14500 POWY 1190 H4
Biddle Ct
7000 SDGO 1248 J3
Biddle St
- SDCo 1067 A2
3900 SDGO 1248 J3
Bidwell Ct
13400 SDGO 1189 C4
Bienaventura Dr
3300 SDCo 998 D7
Bienvenida Cir
1800 CRLB 1106 J7
Bienvenido Ln
1900 ESCN 1109 H5
Biernacki Ct
- CHLV 1330 H2
Big Bend Wy
- OCSD 1086 G1
12600 SDCo 1090 C2
Big Boulder Ln
- SDCo 1234 C5
Big Bucks Trl
- POWY 1150 J6
Big Canyon Ln
11500 SDGO 1210 H1
Big Canyon Ter
1400 ENCT 1167 F2
Big Cat Trl
3500 SDCo 1275 B3
Big Cone Ct
10200 SDCo 1231 G3
Big Cone Dr
11200 SDCo 1231 G3
Big Dipper Wy
1600 SDGO 1350 E2
Big Horn Rd
300 SDCo 1058 H5
(See Page 1058)
1300 SDCo 1059 D5
(See Page 1059)
Big Oak Ranch Rd
1100 SDCo 1047 H1
Big Oak St
7200 SDGO 1290 G5
Big Oaks Ln
2500 SDCo 1300 B4
(See Page 1300)
Big Pine Ln
35000 SDCo 1156 E7
Big Pine Rd
2300 SDCo 1130 E2
Big Potrero Truck Trl
2000 SDCo 1317 E2
(See Page 1317)
Big Red Rd
1200 SDCo 1233 H7
1400 SDCo 1253 J1
Big Rock Rd
8600 SNTE 1230 H7
8500 SNTE 1250 H1
Big Sky Dr
500 OCSD 1086 D3
Big Sky Rd
1800 SDCo 1173 A2
Big Springs Wy
15800 SDGO 1169 J4
Big Sur St
4500 OCSD 1066 H6
Big View Rd
6200 OCSD 1067 G4
Big Wagon Rd
2500 SDCo 1254 A2
Big Wheel Wy
2600 SDCo 1254 A2
Bigford St
8700 SDCo 1291 A2

Biggs Ct
3000 NATC 1310 D3
Bighorn Ct
600 ELCJ 1251 H6
Bignell Dr
7300 SDGO 1290 G6
Bijou Lime Ln
700 ESCN 1110 E5
Billings St
1000 ELCJ 1251 G7
Billman St
3800 SDGO 1270 D5
Billow Dr
500 SDGO 1290 H3
Billy Casper Wy
- CHLV 1310 G3
Billy Glen
2000 ESCN 1109 D4
Billy Ln
14600 POWY 1190 E1
Billy Mitchell Dr
1100 ELCJ 1251 D2
Biloxi St
5400 SDGO 1270 B7
Bilteer Ct
10000 SNTE 1231 D4
Bilteer Dr
9800 SNTE 1231 D4
Biltmore Av
- ESCN 1130 C1
Biltmore St
5000 SDGO 1228 E7
Bilue Dr
100 SNTE 1231 E7
Bimini Wy
1800 VSTA 1107 G6
Bina St
600 BRAW 6260 A7
(See Page 6260)
Binday Wy
2200 SDGO 1330 C6
Bing Crosby Blvd
17300 SDCo 1148 J7
17000 SDCo 1168 J2
17200 SDCo 1169 A1
Bing St
6500 SDGO 1270 D5
Bingham Dr
100 SNMS 1108 F7
Bingham Rd
9700 SNTE 1231 C4
Binnacle Dr
- CRLB 1127 A7
Binnacle Wy
3500 OCSD 1086 E6
Binney Pl
8100 LMSA 1250 H7
Binser St
- SDGO 1289 E7
Biola Av
2300 SDGO 1350 B3
Biological Grade
8500 SDGO 1227 H3
Biona Dr
4600 SDGO 1269 H3
Biona Pl
4200 SDGO 1269 H3
Biosite Wy
- SDGO 1208 H6
Birch Av
800 ESCN 1130 B2
1100 ESCN 1130 C3
Birch Bark Ln
4800 SDCo 1310 H2
Birch Bluff Av
10600 SDGO 1210 C4
Birch Bluff Ct
12500 SDGO 1210 C3
Birch Bluff Pl
12500 SDGO 1210 C3
Birch Briar Ln
- SDCo 1130 D3
Birch Canyon Pl
9700 SDGO 1209 B6
Birch Dr
- SDCo 1086 A4
Birch Glen Ct
11700 SDGO 1209 J3
Birch Hill Pt
5200 SDGO 1208 D1
Birch Hill Rd
32700 SDCo 1052 H4
(See Page 1052)
Birch Ln
13000 POWY 1191 A4
Birch Rd
1800 CHLV 1331 E2
Birch St
- BRAW 6259 H7
(See Page 6259)
- CALX 6620 G7
- ImCo 6620 D7
9000 SDCo 1291 B2
3500 SDGO 1289 G6
- SNMS 1128 C1
- SNMS 1129 C2
2400 VSTA 1108 A6
W Birch St
- CALX 6680 E1
Birch Tree Ln
13300 POWY 1190 E3

Birch Wy
- SDCo 1130 C3
Birchbrook Ct
12600 POWY 1170 D3
Birchcreek Rd
7000 SDGO 1250 E4
Birchcrest Blvd
9100 SNTE 1231 A2
Birchley Pl
700 OCSD 1106 C1
Birchview Dr
900 ENCT 1167 G1
Birchwood Cir
4600 CRLB 1106 J6
Birchwood Dr
1700 SNMS 1109 B3
Birchwood Ln
400 ELCJ 1251 G4
Birchwood Pl
- SNMS 1108 J5
Birchwood St
6900 SDGO 1250 B5
Birchwood Wy
2400 OCSD 1106 F1
Bird Ct
- SNMS 1108 F5
Bird Haven Ln
1300 SDCo 1027 H4
Bird Of Paradise Ln
4500 SDCo 1271 D3
Bird Rock Av
400 SDGO 1247 F3
Bird St
9100 SNTE 1231 G5
Birdie Dr
3600 SDCo 1271 A5
Birdie St
2300 OCSD 1106 J1
Birds Nest Ln
2200 CHLV 1331 G2
Birds View Ct
11100 SDGO 1208 J2
Birdsell Ln
17000 SDCo 1156 D7
Birdsell Rd
34800 SDCo 1176 D1
(See Page 1176)
Birdsong Dr
32400 SDCo 1049 B6
Birdsong Pl
1600 SDCo 1252 A2
Birkdale Wy
5500 SDGO 1248 H1
1800 VSTA 1108 A4
Birmingham Dr
100 ENCT 1167 D3
7900 SDGO 1249 B6
Birmingham Wy
7900 SDGO 1249 B6
Bisby Lake Av
6700 SDGO 1250 J4
Biscay Dr
3200 SDCo 1350 D1
Biscayne Bay
- SDGO 1290 B1
Biscayne Cove
12900 SDGO 1207 J1
Biscayne Pl
14100 POWY 1150 G6
Bishoff Ct
8300 SNTE 1230 H6
Bishop Dr
6400 SDGO 1290 D4
Bishop St
- CHLV 1330 E4
Bishops Ln
7700 SDGO 1227 F7
7100 SDGO 1247 F1
Bishops Wy
5400 SDCo 1271 B1
Bishopsgate Rd
100 ENCT 1147 A2
Bison Ct
600 ELCJ 1251 H6
Bitterbush Ln
1100 SDCo 1252 F7
Bittercreek Ln
9100 SDGO 1189 B3
Bittern Ct
1800 CRLB 1127 D7
Bittern St
1100 SDGO 1290 E2
Bitterroot Ct
1500 SNMS 1109 D6
Bittersweet Hill
1700 SDCo 1108 C2
Bittersweet St
1000 ESCN 1109 F5
Bixbite Pl
6900 CRLB 1127 G6
Bixby St
16900 SDCo 1169 E2
Bixel Dr
5100 SDGO 1270 A1
Bjoin Wy
24700 SDCo 1173 F3
Bkuebird Canyon Ct
3800 SDCo 1108 G1
Black Canyon
- OCSD 1086 H2

Black Canyon Rd
1700 SDCo 1153 A1
Black Coral Ct
- SDGO 1330 J7
Black Coral Wy
- SDGO 1330 J6
Black Eagle Dr
1500 SDGO 1209 D6
Black Gold Rd
9700 SDGO 1227 J1
Black Granite Dr
17500 SDCo 1169 F1
Black Gum Ct
2700 CHLV 1311 J7
Black Hills Ct
9400 SDGO 1189 E4
Black Hills Ln
- SNTE 1231 D2
Black Hills Rd
- ImCo 6560 A6
13400 SDGO 1189 E4
Black Hills Wy
9400 SDGO 1189 D4
Black Horse Dr
- ImCo 6560 A6
8900 SNTE 1231 H6
Black Lion Ct
1500 SDGO 1209 D6
Black Locust Ct
2700 CHLV 1311 J7
Black Mountain Rd
4100 LMSA 1270 J4
- SDGO 1169 E4
3000 SDGO 1188 A5
13200 SDGO 1189 D5
10300 SDGO 1209 E4
Black Mtn Rd
5100 SDGO 1188 D4
14700 SDGO 1189 D1
Black Mustard Ln
1800 CRLB 1127 E5
Black Oak Ln
3200 SDCo 1155 G4
Black Oak Rd
7400 SDGO 1290 G4
Black Opal Rd
10500 SDCo 1169 F1
Black Pine Pl
4600 SDGO 1188 B4
Black Rail Ct
- CRLB 1127 C6
Black Rail Rd
- CRLB 1127 C4
Black Ridge Rd
9700 SDCo 1233 D2
Black Skimmer Dr
- CRLB 1127 E5
Black Swan Pl
- CRLB 1127 C7
Black Walnut Dr
- SNMS 1128 C6
Black Water Dr
- CHLV 1331 H2
Blackberry Ct
800 SNMS 1109 A6
Blackberry Wy
5400 OCSD 1067 D6
Blackbird Cir
2000 CRLB 1127 D6
Blackbird Dr
500 VSTA 1087 F4
Blackbird St
1000 ELCJ 1251 D3
Blackbird Wy
200 OCSD 1086 J1
Blackburn Ln
8400 SDGO 1169 B4
Blackbush Ln
2700 SDCo 1272 F1
Blackduck Wy
4200 OCSD 1086 J3
Blackfoot Av
4300 SDGO 1248 E5
Blackgold Rd
9600 SDGO 1227 J1
Blackhawk Av
1800 OCSD 1087 C5
Blackhawk Cir
- VSTA 1107 G1
Blackhawk Glen
1300 ESCN 1129 G6
Blackhorse Row
- SDGO 1188 D2
Blackmore Ct
2100 SDGO 1248 A4
Blackpool Rd
7700 SDGO 1290 G4
Blacks Beach St
1200 OCSD 1087 B5
Blackshaw Ln
500 SDGO 1350 E3
Blacksmith Rd
6000 SDCo 1311 B2
Blackstilt Ct
- SDCo 1127 B7
Blackstone Av
- CHLV 1311 J6
Blackstone Ct
7600 SDGO 1290 G3
Blackthorne Av
500 ELCJ 1251 D6

Blackthorne Ct
1600 ELCJ 1251 C7
Blackton Dr
4100 LMSA 1270 F4
2500 SDGO 1270 B7
2300 SDGO 1290 B1
Blacktooth Rd
11900 SDCo 1029 H4
Blackwell Dr
3100 SDCo 1067 J6
Blackwell Rd
4500 OCSD 1107 D2
Blackwolf Dr
3400 SDCo 1234 D5
Blackwood Dr
700 SDGO 1330 F7
Blackwood Rd
900 CHLV 1310 J7
Blain Pl
6100 LMSA 1250 J6
Blaine Av
1500 SDGO 1269 C5
Blair Av
500 CALX 6680 G1
Blair Ct
900 SDGO 1289 H5
Blair Wy
9500 SDCo 1271 C2
Blairwood Av
1400 CHLV 1331 E1
Blaisdell Pl
13700 POWY 1190 F6
Blake Glen
1100 ESCN 1109 J4
Blake Pl
5700 LMSA 1251 A7
Blakely Dr
3100 SDGO 1268 E6
Blakstad Ct
7100 SDGO 1208 J4
Blanchard Rd
100 ELCJ 1251 B5
Blanche Av
2100 SDCo 1300 C7
(See Page 1300)
Blanche St
100 SDGO 1350 F4
Blanco Ct
12800 POWY 1190 D5
Blanco Ter
8500 SDCo 1232 E6
Blando Ct
100 SDGO 1350 G2
Blando Ln
1800 SDGO 1350 G3
Blanford St
1500 SDGO 1290 E5
Blann St
300 SDCo 1086 A5
Blanton Ct
11700 SDGO 1190 A6
Blanton Ln
12400 SDGO 1190 A6
Blarney Av
9600 SDCo 1271 C6
Blaxton Dr
1500 ELCN 6559 J1
Blazewood Pl
11200 SDGO 1169 J4
Blazewood Wy
16000 SDGO 1169 J4
Blazing Star Ln
5700 SDGO 1188 E4
Blazing Star Tr
- IMPE 6499 E2
Blenkarne Dr
3000 CRLB 1106 G4
Bleriot Av
500 SDGO 1330 E6
Blessed Mother Dr
3400 SDCo 1047 J2
Bliss Cir
2200 OCSD 1087 D6
Blix St
7400 SDGO 1249 A4
Bloch St
5600 SDGO 1228 A6
Blockton Dr
200 SDCo 1108 A2
Blom St
2300 SDGO 1248 B4
Bloomdale St
9100 SNTE 1231 G5
Bloomfield Av
900 SNMS 1128 J3
Bloomfield Rd
7700 SDGO 1290 G4
Bloomfield St
- ImCo 6560 C7
Blossom Field Wy
1600 ENCT 1147 F4
Blossom Hill Ct
8200 LMGR 1290 J1
Blossom Hill Dr
8300 LMGR 1290 J1
Blossom Hill Ln
2200 ESCN 1129 G7
Blossom Ln
8000 LMGR 1290 H1
Blossom Ridge Wy
9600 SDCo 1232 H3

Blossom Springs Rd
9800 SDCo 1232 G3
Blossom Valley Ln
15000 SDCo 1233 A2
Blossom Valley Rd
9200 SDCo 1232 G5
Blossom Wy
- ELCN 6560 A4
3500 OCSD 1086 F3
Blue Anchor Cay Rd
- CORD 1329 E2
Blue Ash Ct
100 ENCT 1147 H7
Blue Ash Dr
6400 LMGR 1270 D7
Blue Bell Ln
- SDCo 1086 A4
Blue Bird Canyon Rd
3800 SDCo 1108 F2
Blue Bird Park Rd
100 SDCo 1027 F1
Blue Bonnet Ct
500 NATC 1290 C6
Blue Bonnet Dr
- CRLB 1127 A4
Blue Bonnet Pl
1800 ENCT 1147 F4
Blue Boy Ln
8700 SNTE 1231 D7
Blue Breton Dr
35600 SDCo 1028 J5
Blue Cape Ln
300 SDGO 1330 H6
Blue Coral Cv
300 SDGO 1330 H6
Blue Crane Wy
16800 SDCo 1169 G4
Blue Crystal Trl
- POWY 1191 B2
Blue Cypress Dr
- SDGO 1210 A1
Blue Dawn Tr
6000 SDGO 1188 F4
Blue Diamond Ct
- SDGO 1210 B1
Blue Dolphin Wy
700 CRLB 1127 A7
Blue Falls Ct
- CHLV 1311 A5
Blue Falls Dr
1300 CHLV 1311 B6
Blue Gill Dr
2400 SDCo 1297 F6
(See Page 1297)
Blue Granite Dr
10500 SDCo 1169 F1
Blue Haven Dr
- POWY 1170 G7
14700 POWY 1190 G1
Blue Heron Av
1400 ENCT 1147 D2
Blue Heron Dr
- SDCo 1128 G3
Blue Horizon Pt
5000 SDGO 1350 J2
Blue Jay Ct
500 OCSD 1086 D3
Blue Jay Dr
3100 SDCo 1155 H3
2400 SDGO 1249 B7
Blue Jay Pl
7900 SDGO 1249 B7
Blue Jean Wy
1200 CHLV 1311 E6
Blue Lace Tr
13500 SDGO 1188 F3
Blue Lake Ct
- LMGR 1270 E7
Blue Lake Dr
7700 SDGO 1250 G6
8700 SDGO 1251 A6
Blue Lilac Ln
1300 SDCo 1233 H6
Blue Moon Wy
- SDCo 1070 G1
- SDCo 1233 F6
Blue Morning Ln
- SDCo 1169 B2
Blue Oak Ct
3000 SDCo 1271 G6
Blue Oak Pl
2500 SNMS 1128 B6
Blue Of The Night Ln
17100 SDCo 1149 A7
Blue Orchid Ln
6900 CRLB 1127 E6
Blue Point Dr
- SDCo 1127 A5
Blue Ridge Ct
- CHLV 1311 J3
Blue Ridge Dr
- CHLV 1311 J3
Blue Ridge St
5500 SDGO 1310 C2
Blue Ridge Trl
14000 POWY 1170 G4
Blue Sage Ct
- IMPE 6499 D2
Blue Sage Ln
13800 SDCo 1070 E7

Blue Sage Rd
14300 POWY 1170 G4
Blue Sage Wy
- CHLV 1311 J5
- OCSD 1086 J4
Blue Shadows Ln
16800 SDCo 1168 J1
Blue Skies Ridge
17100 SDCo 1149 A7
Blue Sky Dr
1200 ENCT 1167 E1
- ImCo 6560 A6
Blue Sky Ln
100 OCSD 1107 D2
Blue Sky Ranch Rd
- SDCo 1212 F3
Blue Spring Dr
2200 CHLV 1331 H2
Blue Summit Ct
- SDGO 1209 G2
Blue Water Ln
1700 SNMS 1128 F6
Blue Water Wy
1900 OCSD 1106 F1
Blue Wing Ct
12300 POWY 1190 B6
Bluebell Ct
6600 CRLB 1127 A5
Bluebell Ln
1900 SDCo 1028 C6
Bluebell Wy
1300 ELCJ 1251 J3
Blueberry Cir
400 OCSD 1086 G2
Blueberry Hill
2700 SDCo 1234 C6
Blueberry Hill Ln
- SDCo 1090 D2
Blueberry Hill Rd
- SDCo 998 G5
Blueberry Run
13500 SDCo 1090 D4
Bluebird Canyon Rd
3700 SDCo 1108 F1
Bluebird Canyon Trl
1300 SDCo 1088 G7
1500 SDCo 1108 F1
Bluebird Ln
200 OCSD 1086 H2
- SDCo 1127 D4
1400 SDGO 1227 F6
Bluebird St
1300 ELCJ 1251 D3
2100 SDGO 1290 D1
Bluebonnet Ct
- SDCo 1128 G3
Bluecup Pl
- SDCo 1232 D5
Bluefield Ct
6600 SDGO 1250 D5
Bluefield Pl
6400 SDGO 1250 D6
Bluegill Ln
- OCSD 1086 G2
Bluegrass
- OCSD 1067 A3
Bluegrass Ln
- SDCo 1127 D4
Bluegrass Rd
- SDCo 1171 H1
1100 VSTA 1087 E6
Bluegrass St
400 SDGO 1290 G5
Bluehaven Ct
1800 SDGO 1350 D3
Bluejack Rd
900 ENCT 1167 F1
Bluejay Ln
1000 SNMS 1128 E2
Bluelake Dr
- CHLV 1311 E4
Blueridge Pl
400 ESCN 1109 G4
Blueridge St
1900 OCSD 1087 C5
Bluesage Dr
1000 SDCo 1128 B2
Bluesprings Ln
200 OCSD 1106 C2
Bluestar Wy
16200 SDCo 1169 B2
Bluestone Ct
10100 SDCo 1291 D2
Bluestone Dr
13300 SDCo 1232 D5
Bluestone St
10600 SDCo 1169 F2
Bluet Pt
- SDGO 1210 A1
Bluewater Ln
2100 CHLV 1311 E4
Bluewater Rd
800 CRLB 1126 J5
Bluff Ct
- CRLB 1107 B3
Bluff Dr
100 OCSD 1085 J6
Bluff Pl
3900 ESCN 1150 C3
5000 SDCo 1271 H1

11 INDEX
Bluff Point Ct
INDEX 11
Bridle Creek Ln
SAN DIEGO CO.

San Diego County Street Index

STREET Block City Map# Grid

Bluff Point Ct 1600 CHLV 1330 J4
Bluff Point Rd 100 SDCo 1027 F1
Bluff View Wy 4000 CRLB 1106 G6
Bluff Wy 200 OCSD 1086 F6
Bluffcrest Ln 800 ENCT 1147 F4
Bluffdale Pl 2700 SDCo 1271 C7
Bluffs Av - SDGO 1350 E1
Bluffside Av 2600 SDGO 1248 C4
Bluffside Dr 1500 CHLV 1311 J6
Bluffview Ct 8200 SDCo 1290 H5
Bluffview Rd 500 SDCo 1290 J5
Bly St 3400 SDGO 1270 D6
Blythe Ct 8100 SDGO 1209 B2
Blythe Rd 11000 SDGO 1209 B2
Boardacres - SNMS 1128 A5
Boardwalk 900 SNMS 1128 F1
Boardwalk Ct 8700 SDGO 1249 C2
Boat Basin Rd - SDCo 1085 H4
Bob Fletcher Wy 1800 CHLV 1331 E2
Bob Ln - OCSD 1086 G3
Bob Pletcher Wy 1900 CHLV 1331 F2
Bob St 6000 LMSA 1250 H6; 3900 SDGO 1268 C5
Bobbie Ln 4200 SDCo 1271 G3
Bobcat Ct - CRLB 1107 F7
Bobcat Glen 2400 ESCN 1129 E6
Bobcat Ln 1300 SDCo 1234 G5
Bobcat Meadows Cg - SDCo 1296 J1 (See Page 1296)
Bobhird Dr 7100 SDGO 1250 J3
E Bobier Dr 400 VSTA 1087 H3
W Bobier Dr 100 VSTA 1087 G3
Bobolink Dr 1300 VSTA 1087 G4
Bobolink Wy 7700 SDGO 1249 A7
Bobritt Ln - SDCo 1068 E2
Bobritt Rd 31800 SDCo 1068 E1
Bobwhite Ln 1500 ELCJ 1251 D2
Boca Del Tule 1700 SDGO 1350 E2
Boca Raton Dr 1200 CHLV 1311 G6
Boca Raton Ln 17200 POWY 1170 F2
Boca Raton St 2200 CHLV 1311 G6; 2700 SDGO 1187 H7
Boca St 2200 CRLB 1147 F2
Bocage Pt 17500 SDGO 1170 A1
Bocaw Pl 5100 SDGO 1270 E2
Bodega Bay Dr 1200 CHLV 1311 G6
Bodega Bay Wy 4200 OCSD 1066 F6
Bodega Ct 12400 SDGO 1150 B7
Bodega Pl 12400 SDGO 1150 B7
Bodega Rd 12400 SDGO 1150 C7
Bodega Wy 12400 SDGO 1170 B1; 1300 VSTA 1107 H4
Bodie Ct 13600 SDGO 1189 B3
Boeing St - SDGO 1351 D2
Bogata Cir 8900 SDGO 1209 D3
Bogey Dr - OCSD 1067 B5
Bogoso Ln 3900 SDCo 1271 E5
Bogota Av 5500 SDCo 1067 H1
Boiling Springs Rd - SDCo 1218 E6
Boise Av 4800 SDGO 1248 F1
Bolero Dr 12000 SDGO 1170 B3
Bolero Ln 2100 SDCo 1108 D3
Bolero St 7300 CRLB 1127 H7
Boleroridge Pl 200 ESCN 1109 G4
Bolex Wy 900 SNMS 1128 H3
Boley Field Ct - IMPE 6499 C1
Boleyfield Dr - IMPE 6499 D1
Bolin St 10100 SDGO 1208 J5
Bolinas Bay Ct - CHLV 1311 C7
Bolinas St 2200 SDGO 1268 A6
Bolivar Dr 1900 SDCo 1058 H7 (See Page 1058)
Bolivar St 3600 OCSD 1107 C3; 5500 SDGO 1310 C1
Bolivia Ln 3700 OCSD 1107 B2
Bollenbacher St 800 SDGO 1290 B3
Bolo Pl 7700 CRLB 1147 G2
Bolotin Ln - SNMS 1128 H1
Bolsa Chica Glen 2000 ESCN 1109 E5
Bolseria Ln - SDGO 1189 F7; - SDGO 1209 F1
Bolton Hall Rd 400 SDGO 1350 G4
Bomar Dr 4400 SDCo 1271 E3
Bon Ct 3800 SDCo 1310 J3
Bon Vue Dr 9900 SDCo 1233 B2
Bonair Dr 1700 VSTA 1088 A3
Bonair Pl 500 SDGO 1247 F1
Bonair St 200 SDGO 1247 E1
Bonair Wy 500 SDGO 1247 F1
Bonanza Av 4100 SDGO 1248 E6
Bond Av 9300 SDCo 1232 H5
Bond Ct 14400 SDCo 1232 G4
Bond St 4400 SDGO 1248 C5
Bonillo Dr 4200 SDGO 1270 D4
Bonita Bluffs Ct 8500 SDCo 1290 J5
Bonita Canyon Dr 200 CHLV 1311 B3
Bonita Canyon Rd - SDCo 1310 F3
Bonita Christian Center Dr - SDCo 1310 H3
Bonita Dr 700 ENCT 1147 E7; 1100 ENCT 1167 E1; 4200 OCSD 1107 C2; 5400 SDGO 1290 B5; 700 VSTA 1087 E6
Bonita Farms Ct 3600 SDCo 1311 A1
Bonita Glen Dr 200 CHLV 1310 D5
Bonita Glen Ter 3600 SDCo 1310 J2
Bonita Heights Ln - NATC 1310 E3
Bonita Ladera Wy 2100 SDCo 1252 D7
Bonita Ln 1700 CRLB 1106 F5
Bonita Meadows Ln - SDCo 1311 B1
Bonita Mesa Rd 3800 SDCo 1310 D5
Bonita Pl 7200 LMSA 1270 F3; 100 SDCo 1252 H4
Bonita Ranch Ct 3600 SDCo 1311 A1
Bonita Rd - CHLV 1310 C5; 3100 SDCo 1310 E4
Bonita St 2400 LMGR 1270 F7; 2000 LMGR 1290 G1
N Bonita St 3900 SDCo 1271 D4
S Bonita St 3600 SDCo 1271 D5
Bonita Valle 400 SDCo 1047 F4
Bonita Valley Ln 2700 SDCo 1310 D4
Bonita Verde Dr 3600 CHLV 1310 G3
Bonita View Dr 3600 SDCo 1310 J2
Bonita Vista - POWY 1190 D5
Bonita Vista Dr 2600 SDCo 1136 D7
Bonita Vista Wy 14700 SDCo 1273 A6
Bonita Woods Dr 3000 SDCo 1290 H7; 3400 SDCo 1310 H2
Bonita Wy 1100 SDCo 1251 J7
Bonito Av 400 IMPB 1329 F7
Bonjon Ln 10800 SDGO 1210 A2
Bonnet Ln 2300 SDCo 1234 A3
Bonneyville Dr 1700 SDCo 1291 A2
Bonnie Bluff Cir 1300 ENCT 1147 D2
Bonnie Bluff Ct 1500 ENCT 1147 D2
Bonnie Brae Pl 1000 VSTA 1087 J6
Bonnie Ct 4700 SDGO 1269 G3
Bonnie Jean Pl 8800 SDCo 1271 A7
Bonnie Ln 10300 SDCo 1271 E2
Bonnie Lynn Wy 9500 SDCo 1271 C3
Bonnie View Dr 6600 SDGO 1250 E5
Bonnie Vista Dr 9900 SDCo 1271 D3
Bonnie Vista Pl 9800 SDCo 1271 D4
Bonsall St 800 SDGO 1290 G3
Bonus Dr 1800 SDGO 1268 F2
Bookham Ct 7400 SDGO 1268 J1
Boomer Ct 13200 SDGO 1189 C4
Boomvang Ct 300 OCSD 1086 E5
Boon Lake Av 6500 SDGO 1250 H5
Boone Rd - ImCo 6559 A1
Boone St 4000 SDGO 1248 E4
Boortz Ln 16200 SDCo 1172 A3
Boot Wy 5600 OCSD 1067 E6
Bootes St 11100 SDGO 1209 D2
Booth Bay Pl 8500 SDGO 1189 C5
Booth Hill Dr - SDGO 1249 G7
Boquita Dr 14100 SDGO 1187 H5
Borana St 1500 SDGO 1268 H2
Bordeaux Av 2700 SDGO 1227 J4
Bordeaux Ter 1900 CHLV 1311 D3
Bordelon Ct 3700 SDGO 1249 G3
Bordelon St 10200 SDGO 1249 G3
Borden Cir 400 SNMS 1108 J6
Borden Ct 4700 CRLB 1107 A5
Borden Rd 1600 ESCN 1109 F6; - ESCN 1129 G1; - SDCo 1108 F5; 1400 SNMS 1108 E5; 900 SNMS 1109 B5
W Borden Rd - SNMS 1108 G6
Border Av 100 SOLB 1187 F2
Border Village Rd 4500 SDGO 1350 G5
Borealis Rd 8400 SDGO 1209 C2
Borego St 7700 SDGO 1290 G3
Boren St 3600 SDGO 1270 D5
Borica Ct 1500 SDCo 1099 D2 (See Page 1099)
Borla Pl 7300 CRLB 1128 A7
Borne Ct - SDGO 1209 E1
Borner St 4500 SDGO 1289 J4
Borra Ct 4100 OCSD 1087 C6
Borra Pl - ESCN 1129 E4
Borrego Air Ranch Rd 2400 SDCo 1100 B3 (See Page 1100)
Borrego Ct 200 OCSD 1086 J4
Borrego Hills Rd 2100 SDCo 1099 F5 (See Page 1099)
Borrego Springs Rd 1300 CHLV 1311 J5; 1000 SDCo 1058 G2 (See Page 1058); 3000 SDCo 1078 J6 (See Page 1078); 5200 SDCo 1099 H3 (See Page 1099); 6100 SDCo 1100 C6 (See Page 1100)
Borrego Valley Rd 1300 SDCo 1059 C3 (See Page 1059); 2500 SDCo 1079 C2 (See Page 1079)
Borreson St 3400 SDGO 1248 E5
Borzoi Wy 8100 SDGO 1189 B7
Bosal Ct 18200 SDCo 1091 E4
Bosna Pl - SDCo 1108 C3
Bosque Dr 10300 SDCo 1231 F3
Bosstick Blvd 200 SNMS 1108 D5
Boston Av 2800 SDGO 1289 D6; - SDGO 1350 G5
Boston Ct 7400 LMSA 1270 G5
Bostonia St 900 ELCJ 1251 J3
Boswell Ct 300 BRAW 6319 H1 (See Page 6319); 2300 CHLV 1311 F4
Boswell Rd 2300 CHLV 1311 F3
Bosworth Ct 500 ELCJ 1251 J6
Bosworth St 1200 ELCJ 1251 J6
Botany Bay Ct - SDGO 1290 C1
Bote Ct 9600 SDCo 1291 C4
Botella Pl 2300 CRLB 1147 G1
Botero Dr 17100 SDGO 1169 J2
Bothe Av 5400 SDGO 1228 B6
Bottle Tree Ln 1400 ENCT 1147 A3
Bottlebrush Ct 700 OCSD 1086 F1
Bottlebrush Pl 2100 ENCT 1147 J7
Bottlebrush Wy 900 CRLB 1127 A5; 200 SDCo 1028 A2
Boucher Heights Rd 16700 SDCo 1071 D5
Boudinot Ct 400 ESCN 1110 F5
Bougainvilla Ln 1500 CHLV 1331 C2
Bougainville Rd - CORD 1309 A2; 6300 SDGO 1290 E7
Bougainvillea Tr - IMPE 6499 D3
Bougher Rd 1100 SDCo 1109 C4; 400 SNMS 1109 C7
Boulder Creek Rd 1600 OCSD 1087 D4; 4700 SDCo 1155 G6; - SDCo 1175 E4 (See Page 1175); 13300 SDCo 1195 G3 (See Page 1195)
Boulder Creek St 2200 CHLV 1311 G6
Boulder Dr 8500 LMSA 1270 J2
Boulder Knolls Dr - SDCo 1089 E2
Boulder Lake Av 6900 SDGO 1250 H3
Boulder Legend Ln 2400 SDCo 1110 A3
Boulder Mountain Rd 15400 POWY 1170 E6
Boulder Oaks Cir 2500 SDCo 1234 C7
Boulder Oaks Dr 16900 SDCo 1171 D2
Boulder Oaks Ln 2400 SDCo 1234 B7
Boulder Pass 11100 SDCo 1089 G4
Boulder Pass Rd 1800 SDCo 1254 A1
Boulder Pl 4700 LMSA 1270 J3; 1000 OCSD 1067 A4; 8400 SDGO 1250 J4
Boulder Point Rd 12200 POWY 1190 B6
Boulder Ridge Ct 14500 SDGO 1210 G1
Boulder Ridge Ln 15600 POWY 1170 E6
Boulder View Dr 12200 POWY 1190 B6
Boulderidge Dr - SNMS 1128 A5
Boulderidge Pl 2300 SDCo 1271 C6
Boulders Ct - SDCo 1234 A5
Boulders Ln - SDCo 1234 A6
Boulders Rd - SDCo 1234 A5
Boulderview Dr 1000 OCSD 1067 B3
Boulevard Av 700 IMPB 1329 G6
Boulevard Dr 7000 LMSA 1270 E4
Boulevard Pl 1100 ELCJ 1251 E7; 7800 SDGO 1227 G6
Boulton Av 11600 SDGO 1190 A2
Boundary Av 2300 SDCo 1172 D2; 1800 SDGO 1329 J6; 1900 SDGO 1330 A6
Boundary Creek Rd 43300 SDCo 1321 F5 (See Page 1321)
Boundary Rd - IMPB 1349 G3
W Boundary Rd - SDCo 1234 D3
Boundary St 4600 SDGO 1269 E3; 600 SDGO 1289 G3
S Boundary St 600 SDGO 1289 H5
Boundary Truck Trl - SDCo 1216 C3 (See Page 1216)
W Boundary Truck Trl 17800 SDCo 1254 C7; - SDCo 1274 D3
Bounty Ct 6400 SDGO 1250 C6
Bounty St 5600 SDGO 1250 B6
Bounty Wy 14200 POWY 1170 G5
Bouquet Canyon Rd - CHLV 1311 D6
Bouquet Dr 100 SNMS 1108 H6
Bourbon Ct 9900 SDGO 1209 H5
Bourbon Rd 1000 ESCN 1109 F6
Bourgeois Wy 14200 SDGO 1189 D2
Bourke Pl 1700 ELCJ 1252 B2
Boussock Ln 3500 OCSD 1086 F5
Bovet Wy 7400 SDGO 1228 G4
Bow Willow Trail Wy - CHLV 1311 H4
Bowden Av 5100 SDGO 1248 G2
Bowditch Pl 2800 SDGO 1269 F7
Bowdoin Rd 14500 POWY 1190 H4
Bowen Rd 8300 LMGR 1270 J7
Bower Ln 8900 SDCo 1232 C6
Bowie St 300 SDGO 1290 H4
Bowker Rd 2000 ImCo 6500 H4; 1600 ImCo 6560 J2
Bowl Creek Rd - POWY 1170 E5
Bowling Green Dr 8800 LMSA 1271 A3
Bowman Ln 4900 SDGO 1270 E2
Bowron Rd 13100 POWY 1190 E5
Bowspirit Wy - CRLB 1127 A4
Bowsprit Dr 3500 OCSD 1086 F6
Bowsprit Rd 800 CHLV 1311 G4
Box Canyon Rd 1000 SDCo 1027 G1; 5800 SDGO 1247 G3
Box Elder Ct 2700 CHLV 1311 J7
Box Elder Pl 11400 SDGO 1169 J5
Box Elder Wy 11500 SDGO 1169 J5
Box S Dr 3300 SDCo 1078 J6 (See Page 1078)
Boxford Dr 6800 SDGO 1248 J2
Boxthorn Wy 1000 CRLB 1127 A6
Boxwood Ct 900 CRLB 1127 A5; 12700 POWY 1170 C7; - SNMS 1128 C6
Boxwood Dr 2500 SDCo 1252 E7; 4600 SDGO 1248 G1
Boxwood Glen 500 ESCN 1110 C7
Boxwood Rd - SDCo 1086 B2
Boy Scout Camp Rd - CHLV 1332 A3 (See Page 1332)
Boyce Ln 3300 SDGO 1270 A6
Boyd Av 3100 SDGO 1248 H4
Boyington Pl 2400 ELCJ 1251 B3
Boyington Rd - SDGO 1229 D1
Boyle Av 1500 ESCN 1130 C2
Boyle Pl 1700 ESCN 1130 D2
Boylston St 4500 SDGO 1289 J3
Boyne St 3400 SDCo 1271 C6
Boysen Ln - OCSD 1086 G3
Boysenberry Ct 13400 SDCo 1090 D3; - SDGO 1350 F3
Boysenberry Wy 600 SDCo 1067 C7
Bozanich Cir 600 VSTA 1087 J7
Brabham St 1800 SDCo 1272 C4
Bracero Pl 800 ESCN 1129 J6
Bracero Rd 700 ENCT 1147 E7
Bracken Fern Cove - SDGO 1209 J1
Bracs Dr 8500 SNTE 1231 D7
Bradberry Ct - LMGR 1290 E1
Bradbury Dr 1500 CHLV 1331 D1
Braddock Pl 8100 SDGO 1290 H2
Braddock St 1300 SDGO 1290 H2
Braddon Wy 1600 SDCo 1251 J2
Bradenhall Row 6000 SDGO 1248 B1
Bradford Rd 600 SDCo 1252 C5
Bradford St 6000 SDGO 1270 C3
Bradley Av 800 ELCJ 1251 G2
W Bradley Av 700 ELCJ 1251 E2
Bradley Ct 1100 SDCo 1251 H2
Bradley Pl - CHLV 1330 J3
Bradley St 2400 OCSD 1087 C6
Bradshaw Ct 4900 SDGO 1188 D6
Bradshaw Rd - ELCN 6499 F4
Brady Av 8700 SDCo 1290 J4
Brady Cres 1600 CRLB 1106 G5
Brady Ct 600 SDCo 1290 J4
Brae Mar Ct 600 ENCT 1147 E5
Braeburn Rd 4400 SDGO 1269 H2
Braemar Ln 900 SDGO 1247 H7
Braemar Terr 600 SDCo 1027 G6
Braeswood Terr - SDCo 1232 E7
Bragg St 5300 SDGO 1228 B6
Brahms Rd 1600 ENCT 1167 D2
Braidwood St 2000 ELCJ 1251 B1
Braisted Rd - SDGO 1289 C2
Bralorne Ct 11200 SDGO 1209 C1
Bralorne Wy 8700 SDGO 1209 D1
Bram Av 4700 SDCo 1310 H2
Brambi View Ln 16800 SDCo 1191 E5
Bramble Rd 9100 LMSA 1251 B7
Bramble Wy 2100 CHLV 1331 H3; - SDGO 1209 E3
Bramblewood Ct - CHLV 1311 D7
Bramblewood St - CHLV 1311 D7
Brampton St 8100 SDCo 1290 J2
Bramson Pl 3200 SDGO 1269 F4
Branch Ct 3600 OCSD 1086 F2
Branco Wy 11200 SDGO 1209 B2
Brand Crest 3700 ENCT 1167 H2
Brand Iron St - SDCo 1172 A4
Brandee Wy 200 SDCo 1027 G2
Brandeis Ct 6000 SDGO 1290 C5
Brandeis Dr 2800 OCSD 1087 A7
Brandenburg 900 CALX 6680 D1
Branding Iron Av - BRAW 6319 J4 (See Page 6319)
Branding Iron Cir 1200 VSTA 1107 F2
Branding Iron Ct - SDCo 1085 J4
Branding Iron Dr - IMPE 6439 F3
Brando Dr 2900 SDGO 1350 D3
Brandon Cir 2900 CRLB 1107 B4
Brandon Rd 100 SDCo 1027 G2
Brandonburg Ln 100 SDCo 1027 G2
Brandt Rd 5000 ImCo 6259 F3 (See Page 6259)
Brandywine Av 1400 CHLV 1330 H2
Brandywine St 3600 OCSD 1086 G5; 3100 SDGO 1248 D5
Brandywood St 200 SDGO 1290 E5
Branford Rd 10000 SDGO 1189 F3
Branicole Ln 12100 SDGO 1189 F6
Brannick Pl 2800 SDGO 1228 B5
Brant Canyon Ln 0 SDCo 1027 J3
Brant Ln 1800 CRLB 1127 E5
Brant St 4000 SDGO 1268 J5; 3200 SDGO 1269 A7; 2400 SDGO 1289 A1
Branta Av - CRLB 1127 C7
Branting St 6100 SDGO 1228 C5
Brantner Ln 15900 SDCo 1172 A4
Brashear Pl 1400 CHLV 1331 A2
Brasilia Pl 31600 SDCo 1067 J1
Brass Buttons St 6900 CRLB 1127 E5
Brass Lantern Rd 700 SNMS 1109 A5
Brass Ln 100 VSTA 1087 F7
Brass Pl 6900 CRLB 1127 F5
Brass Wy 900 ENCT 1167 E1
Brassica St 12200 SDGO 1189 B7
Brasswood Row 6000 SDGO 1248 B1
Bratton Valley Rd 2600 SDCo 1294 D5 (See Page 1294)
Brauer Pt 500 SDCo 1234 D4
Braun Av 300 SDGO 1290 J3
Brava Pl - ESCN 1109 H5
Brava St 7400 CRLB 1147 J1
Bravata Ct 18800 SDGO 1150 C5
Braverman Dr 10500 SNTE 1231 E4
Bravo Ct 5500 SDGO 1229 G7
Bravo Dr - CALX 6620 H7
Brawley Av 600 BRAW 6319 H2 (See Page 6319); 44600 SDCo 1321 G5 (See Page 1321)
Brawley Beef Wy - ImCo 6260 B5 (See Page 6260)
Braxton Sq 12100 SDGO 1190 B1
Bray Av 9500 SDCo 1271 C6
Brayton Wy 1400 SDCo 1272 A2
Brazo Wy 10500 SDCo 1169 F4
Brazos St 600 SDCo 1152 F6
Breakaway Dr 1000 OCSD 1067 B4
Breakers Wy - SDGO 1350 J1
Breakwater Pt - SDGO 1330 J7
Breakwater Rd 100 CRLB 1126 H6
Breakwater Wy 100 OCSD 1085 J7
Breckenridge Dr - SDGO 1209 G2
Breckenridge Wy - SDGO 1209 G2
Breeze Hill Rd 800 VSTA 1087 F7; 700 VSTA 1107 F1
Breeze St 1300 OCSD 1086 B5
Breeze Villa Ln 900 VSTA 1107 F1
Breeze Villa Pl 1000 VSTA 1107 F1
Breezeway Pl 14200 SDGO 1190 A2
Breezewood Dr - CHLV 1311 D6
Breezy Wy 200 SNMS 1129 A1
Brelco Rd 8900 SNTE 1251 A1
Bremen Wy 900 SDCo 1253 H2
Bremerton Pl 3100 SDGO 1228 A4
Brems St 3700 SDGO 1270 D5
Brenda Wy 15700 SDCo 1071 A5
Brengle Wy 1500 VSTA 1088 B6
Brenna Ct 400 ENCT 1147 G6
Brennan St 8100 SDGO 1290 H2
Brenner Springs Wy 11300 SDGO 1208 J2
Brenner Wy 1600 SDGO 1290 D6
Brent Ln - VSTA 1087 H5
Brentford Av 8800 SDGO 1209 D3
Brentwood Ct 2800 CRLB 1106 F3
Brentwood St 7400 SDGO 1249 A4
Bresa De Loma Dr 21300 SDCo 1129 B5
Bressi Ranch Wy 2600 CRLB 1127 G3
Breton Wy 5700 SDGO 1250 C7
Brett Harte Dr 13500 SDCo 1232 D3
Brett Pl 100 ESCN 1110 F6
Bretton Wood Ct - SDGO 1208 E1
Brewer Rd 500 IMPE 6439 D7
Brewley Ln 1200 VSTA 1107 J4
Brewster Bay Dr - CHLV 1330 H1
Brewster Ct 11900 SDGO 1190 A2
Brezar St 1600 CHLV 1331 F2
Brian Park Ln 13300 POWY 1190 E1
Brian Pl 1500 ESCN 1129 J5; 8500 SNTE 1231 A7
Brian Wy - SDCo 1232 H4
Briana Ct 4700 SDCo 1047 F6
Briand Av 3100 SDGO 1228 C5
Briant St 900 SNMS 1109 C5
Briar Ct 9600 SDGO 1249 F5
Briar Gn - SDCo 1232 E7
Briar Hollow Ln - SDCo 1252 G1
Briar Knoll Wy - SDGO 1189 J7
Briarcliff Dr 11100 SDGO 1209 H4
Briarcliff Wy 10400 SDGO 1209 H4
Briarcrest Pl - SDGO 1188 E6
Briardale Wy 12300 SDGO 1190 A6
E Briarfield Dr 1000 SDGO 1247 J7
W Briarfield Dr 1000 SDGO 1247 J7
Briargate Ct 3700 SDGO 1188 A5
Briargate Pl 1900 ESCN 1129 F7
Briaridge Rd 4600 OCSD 1087 D3
Briarlake Woods Dr - SDGO 1208 E2
Briarleaf Wy - SDGO 1190 B7
Briarpoint Pl 700 SDGO 1330 H7
Briarway Ct 1000 VSTA 1087 G5
Briarwood Ct 2400 SDCo 1130 D6
Briarwood Pl 2300 ESCN 1109 J3; 900 OCSD 1087 C2; 12700 POWY 1170 C7
Briarwood Rd 6800 CRLB 1127 A5; 500 SDGO 1290 G6; 1200 SDGO 1310 H1
Brickellia St 12100 SDGO 1189 C6
Brickfield Ln 5100 SDGO 1208 D2
Bricklane Rd 900 SDCo 1172 F1
Bridanella Tr 8700 SDCo 1232 B6
Bridge Ln 2200 ESCN 1110 B5
Bridgecrest Ln 12400 SDGO 1190 A6
Bridgehampton Pl 1700 SDCo 1272 B4
Bridgehampton St 1200 SNMS 1128 B3
Bridgeport 2000 CHLV 1311 E4
Bridgeport Ct - SNMS 1128 F3
Bridgeport St 1000 ESCN 1110 A6
Bridget Ct 10200 SDGO 1249 G4
Bridgetown Bend - CORD 1329 E2
Bridgeview Dr 1400 SDGO 1289 G2
Bridgewood Wy 11700 SDGO 1190 A6
Bridle Creek Ln 3300 SDCo 1088 G5

12 INDEX
Bridle Path Ln
San Diego County Street Index
Cabazon Ct
INDEX 12
SAN DIEGO CO.

STREET
Block City Map# Grid

Bridle Path Ln
200 SNTE 1231 E5
Bridle Path Wy
1000 OCSD 1067 E7
Bridle Run Ct
200 SDCo 1233 E6
Bridle Run Ln
300 SDCo 1233 E6
Bridle Run Pl
300 SDCo 1233 E6
Bridle Run Ter
200 SDCo 1233 D6
Bridle Run View
200 SDCo 1233 E6
Bridlepath Ln
11400 SDCo 1211 J6
Bridlespur Dr
14900 POWY 1190 J4
Bridlevale Rd
- CHLV 1311 D6
Bridlewood Ln
13000 SDCo 1090 D6
Bridlewood Rd
16400 POWY 1170 F3
4100 SDCo 1048 A4
Bridon Rd
9900 SDCo 1233 E3
Bridoon Terr
- ENCT 1148 D3
- SDCo 1148 D2
Brienwood Dr
- SDCo 1089 A1
Brier Rd
9200 LMSA 1251 B7
Briercrest Dr
9200 LMSA 1251 B7
Briette Pl
9200 SDCo 1232 E5
Brigantine Rd
- CRLB 1127 B5
Brigatine Ct
2100 ENCT 1147 H7
Briggs Av
- ENCT 1167 C1
Bright Creek Ln
300 OCSD 1107 D3
Bright Ct
3400 SDCo 1271 D5
8700 SNTE 1231 D6
Bright St
9800 SDCo 1271 D5
Brighthaven Av
500 ELCJ 1252 A6
Brighton Av
600 ELCN 6499 H6
400 ENCT 1167 D2
14000 POWY 1190 F3
5100 SDGO 1267 J5
4600 SDGO 1268 A6
Brighton Ct
2700 CHLV 1311 J6
2700 CHLV 1312 A7
(See Page 1312)
800 SDGO 1267 H4
900 VSTA 1108 A4
Brighton Dr
1100 OCSD 1087 D1
Brighton Glen Rd
1500 SNMS 1128 A3
Brighton Hill Ct
1700 SNMS 1128 A3
Brighton Rd
2600 CRLB 1106 J5
Brighton Ridge Ct
10700 SDGO 1210 A2
Brightside Wy
- SDCo 1153 A2
Brightwood Av
100 CHLV 1310 A5
700 CHLV 1330 B1
Brightwood Ct
- OCSD 1086 D2
Brightwood Dr
1000 SNMS 1128 F6
Brightwood Ln
10200 SNTE 1231 D7
Brilene Ln
3100 SDGO 1248 G5
Brillden Ct
3100 SDGO 1248 C3
Brillo St
4900 SDGO 1228 F7
Brillwood Hill Rd
15000 SDCo 1130 J4
Brindisi St
4400 SDGO 1287 H2
Brinell St
4600 SDGO 1249 B2
Brinser St
- SDGO 1289 F7
Brioso Ct
1100 VSTA 1107 H4
Brisas Ct
200 OCSD 1086 G1
600 VSTA 1087 H5
Brisas St
- OCSD 1086 G1
Brisbane
- CHLV 1310 A4
Brisbane Wy
- OCSD 1086 G1

Bristlecone Ct
4600 OCSD 1087 D4
Bristlewood Ct
2600 SDCo 1172 D5
Bristlewood Dr
2600 SDCo 1172 D5
Bristol Bay Ct
- SDGO 1270 C7
Bristol Ct
1700 CHLV 1311 C5
Bristol Rd
400 ENCT 1167 D2
5000 SDGO 1269 H2
Bristol Ridge Ln
8300 SDGO 1169 B3
Bristol Ridge Terr
15400 SDGO 1169 B4
Bristow Ct
7500 SDGO 1351 E4
Bristow Ln
- ImCo 6439 E4
Britain St
900 SDGO 1290 G2
Britannia Blvd
1900 SDGO 1351 E3
Britannia Ct
7500 SDGO 1351 E4
Britannia Park Pl
- SDGO 1351 E3
Britt Ct
8700 SDGO 1249 C7
Britt Pl
7700 SNTE 1230 G7
Brittain Rd
34900 SDCo 1029 J4
Brittany Ct
3500 SDCo 1272 E5
Brittany Forest Ln
- SDGO 1208 F1
Brittany Park Ln
- POWY 1170 D4
Brittany Rd
800 ENCT 1147 C4
Brittany Wy
3500 CRLB 1107 A3
Brittle Bush Dr
1600 CHLV 1331 G3
Britton Av
3600 CHLV 1330 E5
Brixton Pl
13000 SDGO 1188 C5
Briza Placida
- SDGO 1188 J2
Broad Av
3300 SDGO 1289 F5
Broad Oaks Rd
15300 SDCo 1213 B7
15600 SDCo 1233 C1
Broadlawn St
3900 SDGO 1248 J3
Broadmoor Ct
1000 CHLV 1311 G5
Broadmoor Dr
6000 LMSA 1251 C6
Broadmoor Pl
9400 LMSA 1251 B6
Broadrick Pl
6500 SDGO 1310 F1
Broadrick Wy
2600 SDGO 1310 F1
Broadview Av
9300 SDGO 1249 E7
Broadview St
400 SDCo 1290 J4
600 SDCo 1291 A3
Broadway
- CHLV 1309 J5
1500 CHLV 1330 C5
400 ELCJ 1251 G3
6900 LMGR 1270 F6
1700 OCSD 1106 C3
2400 SDGO 1289 D3
6000 SDGO 1290 C3
E Broadway
1600 ELCJ 1252 B3
300 VSTA 1087 H6
N Broadway
2300 ESCN 1109 G4
700 ESCN 1129 H1
27000 SDCo 1089 H5
26100 SDCo 1109 G1
S Broadway
100 ESCN 1129 J3
1100 ESCN 1130 A4
W Broadway
800 SDGO 1288 J3
Broadway Av
6900 LMGR 1290 E3
Broadway Cir
700 SDGO 1289 A3
Broadway Ln
8300 LMGR 1270 J5
Broadway Pl
1300 ESCN 1130 A4
Broadway St
- ELCN 6499 F6
Brock Ct
8100 LMGR 1270 H7
Brockbank Pl
5100 SDGO 1270 D2
Brockton St
1000 ELCJ 1251 B3

Brockway St
11200 SDCo 1231 G7
11300 SDCo 1251 G1
Brockwood Dr
500 ELCJ 1251 G4
Brodea Ln
4300 SDCo 1048 F2
Brodiaea Wy
7300 SDGO 1227 G7
Brodie Ln
8500 SNTE 1250 J1
Brogue Ct
1500 VSTA 1107 J5
Broken Arrow Ln
1400 SDCo 1027 J4
Broken Arrow Rd
3200 SDCo 1078 H6
(See Page 1078)
Broken Bow Ct
17000 SDGO 1169 H2
Broken Cinch Trl
7500 SDCo 1138 C7
(See Page 1138)
Broken Hitch Rd
1300 OCSD 1087 D3
Broken Oak Ln
34300 SDCo 1176 D4
(See Page 1176)
Broken Rock Rd
1700 SNMS 1128 B2
Broken Wheel Rd
10800 SDCo 1231 G1
Bromac Pl
1100 SDCo 1108 C1
Brome Ct
- CRLB 1127 D6
Brome Wy
12900 SDGO 1189 D5
Bromegrass Ct
15800 POWY 1170 F5
Bromeliad Ct
6700 SDGO 1250 E3
Bromfield Av
4300 SDGO 1228 E5
Bromley Wy
5600 SDGO 1270 D1
Bronco Ln
16400 POWY 1170 E4
Bronco Pl
300 CHLV 1310 G4
Bronco Wy
1600 OCSD 1067 E7
13300 POWY 1170 E4
Bronstein Pl
10200 SDGO 1249 G4
Bronte Pl
7500 SDGO 1290 G4
Bronx Pl
2800 SDGO 1249 E5
Bronze St
1800 CHLV 1331 F3
Bronze Wy
100 VSTA 1087 F7
Brook Canyon Rd
- SDCo 1130 C7
Brook Rd
1400 SNMS 1109 C7
Brook Shire
- SDCo 1236 E2
Brookburn Dr
- SDGO 1188 C6
Brookdale Pl
100 SOLB 1167 F7
Brookdel Av
1000 SNMS 1109 B7
Brooke Crest Ln
1300 SDCo 1027 H6
Brooke Ct
3900 LMSA 1270 H5
Brooke Dr
- SDGO 1209 F2
Brooke Glen
1300 SDCo 1027 H6
Brooke Hollow Rd
- SDCo 1028 C4
Brooke Rd
2100 SDCo 1027 J6
Brooke Vista Ln
7900 SDGO 1189 A3
Brookes Av
1200 SDGO 1268 J6
1600 SDGO 1269 B6
W Brookes Av
800 SDGO 1268 J6
200 SDGO 1269 A6
Brookes Ter
1200 SDGO 1269 B6
Brookfield Wy
- CRLB 1107 A4
Brookhaven Ct
8100 SDGO 1290 H4
Brookhaven Pass
2200 VSTA 1107 H7
2200 VSTA 1127 H1
Brookhaven Rd
7500 SDGO 1290 G5
Brookhills Rd
3700 SDCo 1048 B4
Brookhollow Ct
10700 SDGO 1208 J4

Brookhurst Av
10400 SDGO 1209 D4
Brookhurst Dr
1900 ELCJ 1252 D4
Brookhurst Ln
2600 SDCo 1130 B7
10300 SDGO 1209 D5
Brookins Ln
700 VSTA 1087 E6
Brookite Ct
6600 CRLB 1127 F4
Brookline St
1700 SDGO 1289 J2
Brooklyn Av
5900 SDGO 1290 C3
Brookmead Ln
2600 SDGO 1227 H1
Brookmeadow Pl
7900 SDGO 1290 H5
Brookpine Ct
3000 SDCo 1271 F7
Brookprinter Pl
12700 POWY 1190 D6
Brooks Glen
1900 ESCN 1129 F5
Brooks St
200 OCSD 1086 B7
400 OCSD 1106 B1
Brooks Trail Ct
2200 CHLV 1311 F6
Brooks Wy
4300 CRLB 1106 G7
Brookshire St
3500 SDGO 1248 H4
Brookside Cir
9200 SDCo 1271 B4
Brookside Ct
600 CRLB 1126 H6
9200 SDCo 1271 B4
- SNMS 1128 C6
Brookside Ln
3200 ENCT 1148 B5
100 OCSD 1107 D2
- SDGO 1210 D2
N Brookside Pl
- CHLV 1331 A2
S Brookside Pl
- CHLV 1331 A2
Brookstone Ct
12600 POWY 1190 C1
Brookstone Dr
14900 POWY 1170 C7
14700 POWY 1190 C1
Brookstone Pl
- SNTE 1231 C5
Brookstone Rd
700 CHLV 1311 E4
Brooktree Ln
800 VSTA 1108 A4
Brooktree Ter
10400 SDGO 1209 H4
Brookvale Dr
100 SNTE 1230 J7
Brookview Ct
- SNTE 1231 C5
Brookview Ln
10600 SDGO 1209 H4
N Brookville Dr
11800 SDGO 1189 G7
S Brookville Dr
10700 SDGO 1209 H1
Brookwood Ct
4700 CRLB 1107 A5
2200 ESCN 1109 H4
Brookwood Pl
900 OCSD 1087 D1
Brosnan St
2800 SDGO 1248 J6
Brotherton Rd
700 ESCN 1129 J6
100 ESCN 1130 A6
Brougham Ct
3100 OCSD 1106 H1
Brown Ct
- CALX 6620 H7
Brown Deer Rd
9200 SDGO 1208 G7
Brown Dr
2600 ELCJ 1251 B3
Brown Galloway Ln
35400 SDCo 1028 H6
Brown St
3900 OCSD 1107 A1
Brownell St
5100 SDGO 1268 F2
Browning Ct
1200 VSTA 1087 E6
Browning Rd
5300 CRLB 1107 C7
Browning St
3800 SDGO 1268 B6
Browns Rd
- SDCo 1235 B4
Brubaker Ct
- SDGO 1188 D6
Bruce Ct
6900 LMSA 1270 E3
Bruce Rd
1700 CRLB 1106 H7
Bruceala Ct
2000 ENCT 1167 F3

Bruckart Sq
9900 SDGO 1209 H5
Brucker Av
900 SDCo 1291 A3
Brule Pl
13000 POWY 1190 D3
Bruma Ct
500 SDCo 1291 D3
Brumby Wy
10200 SDGO 1249 G4
Brunei Ct
7400 LMGR 1270 G7
Brunner St
1200 SDGO 1268 G3
Bruno Pl
5600 LMSA 1250 H7
Bruns Rd
1700 SDCo 1068 H5
Brunswick Av
5600 SDGO 1250 C5
Brushwood Av
- IMPE 6499 C3
Brushwood Ln
3200 SDCo 1048 C5
Brust Ct
- SDCo 1272 E1
Brutus St
500 SDGO 1290 G3
Bruyere Ct
13800 SDGO 1189 D3
Bryan Ct
7800 LMGR 1270 H6
Bryan Glen Ct
- SDGO 1189 B3
Bryan Glen Wy
- SDGO 1189 B3
Bryan Point Dr
300 CHLV 1311 H1
Bryan St
4100 OCSD 1087 C6
Bryant Dr
2200 CRLB 1127 C1
Bryant Rd
- ImCo 6320 A4
(See Page 6320)
Bryant St
1300 SDGO 1289 F6
Bryanview Cir
1300 SDGO 1290 B6
Bryce Canyon Av
- CHLV 1311 H3
Bryce Canyon Wy
- CHLV 1311 H4
Bryce Cir
4700 CRLB 1106 H7
4700 CRLB 1126 H1
Bryce Ln
100 SDCo 1027 H2
Bryce Pt
14100 POWY 1150 G6
Brynwood Ct
6200 SDGO 1250 D6
Brynwood Wy
6600 SDGO 1250 D6
Bryson Ter
4600 SDGO 1188 C5
Bubbling Ln
13400 SDCo 1232 D6
Bubbling Well Dr
1500 SDGO 1349 J2
Bubbling Well Rd
9000 SDCo 1232 D6
Buccaneer Dr
100 SDGO 1290 F5
Buccaneer Wy
- CORD 1329 E2
Buchanan St
800 ESCN 1110 A7
- SDGO 1269 B4
- SDGO 1289 E7
Buchanon Av
- CALX 6620 J6
Buck Board Trl
- SNTE 1231 F6
Buck Ridge Av
3500 CRLB 1107 B6
Buck Stidham Dr
3000 SDCo 1234 D5
Buckaroo Ln
900 CHLV 1310 H4
Buckboard Dr
1500 OCSD 1067 F7
Buckboard Ln
1400 SDCo 1027 J4
Buckboard Trl
7000 SDCo 1138 C5
(See Page 1138)
Buckeye Ct
- ELCJ 1251 H2
Buckeye Dr
1300 SDCo 1251 H3
Buckhorn Av
600 SNMS 1128 F3
Buckhorn Dr
29300 SDCo 1297 E6
(See Page 1297)
Buckhorn St
8200 SDGO 1249 B1
Buckhurst Av
10800 SDGO 1209 D3

Buckingham Dr
1500 SDGO 1247 G2
Buckingham Ln
4600 CRLB 1107 A5
Buckland St
8400 LMSA 1270 J1
Buckley St
12900 POWY 1190 D5
Buckman Springs Ln
2200 SDCo 1317 J2
(See Page 1317)
Buckman Springs Rd
2600 SDCo 1297 H2
(See Page 1297)
1800 SDCo 1317 H1
(See Page 1317)
Bucknell Av
5800 SDGO 1247 H3
Bucknell St
1900 CHLV 1311 D5
Buckshot Canyon Rd
- SDCo 1088 H1
Buckskin Dr
1400 ESCN 1129 G7
Buckskin Glen
1900 ESCN 1110 A4
Buckskin Ranch Dr
- IMPE 6439 F3
Buckskin Rd
1100 ELCJ 1251 H6
400 SDCo 1058 G6
(See Page 1058)
Buckskin Trl
12500 POWY 1190 C6
Buckthorn Ct
1900 CRLB 1147 E3
Buckthorn Trl
8100 SDCo 1237 C5
2400 SDCo 1299 H3
(See Page 1299)
Buckwheat Ct
12600 SDGO 1189 D6
Buckwheat St
9000 SDGO 1189 D6
Buckwheat Trl
1300 SDCo 1318 B6
(See Page 1318)
Buckwood St
14600 POWY 1190 D1
Bucky Ln
800 NATC 1289 H6
Budd St
3500 SDGO 1249 A4
Budlong Lake Av
6300 SDGO 1250 H5
Budmuir Pl
4300 SDGO 1289 H1
Budwin Ln
14800 POWY 1170 F7
14500 POWY 1190 F1
Buechner Dr
19200 SDCo 1192 B2
(See Page 1192)
Buen Tiempo Dr
800 CHLV 1310 G7
Buena Capri
900 SDCo 1027 H7
Buena Creek Rd
2100 SDCo 1108 C3
Buena Crest Ln
- SDCo 1108 G1
Buena Flores
2500 SDCo 1027 H7
Buena Hills Dr
3100 OCSD 1107 A1
Buena Mesa Pl
10100 SDCo 1271 E5
Buena Pl
900 CRLB 1106 E4
Buena Rosa
2500 SDCo 1027 G7
Buena Rosa Ct
900 SDCo 1027 H7
Buena St
1300 OCSD 1086 B7
Buena Suerte
900 SDCo 1047 H1
Buena Ter
800 ELCJ 1251 D4
Buena Tierra Wy
700 OCSD 1086 J3
Buena Valley Dr
8700 SNTE 1231 D7
Buena Vida Rd
- SDCo 1212 C4
Buena Village Dr
1900 SDCo 1108 C2
Buena Vista
- ESCN 1109 G7
- POWY 1190 E5
Buena Vista Av
700 ELCN 6499 G4
1100 ESCN 1109 J6
3400 LMGR 1270 G6
1000 SDCo 1291 C2
9800 SNTE 1231 D7
Buena Vista Cir
2400 CRLB 1106 D4
S Buena Vista Cir
2300 CRLB 1106 D4
Buena Vista Ct
- CHLV 1311 B7

Buena Vista Dr
1200 SDCo 1107 G3
10000 SDCo 1271 D5
1000 VSTA 1107 G2
Buena Vista Ln
100 OCSD 1085 J6
Buena Vista St
3600 SDGO 1248 A7
Buena Vista Wy
800 CHLV 1311 B6
1200 CRLB 1106 E4
Buenaventura Ct
100 SOLB 1167 H5
Buenos Aires Wy
31200 SDCo 1067 H2
Buenos Av
900 SDGO 1268 E3
Buenos St
1100 SDGO 1268 E3
Buenos Tiempos
0 SDCo 1027 H7
Buffalo Grass Ct
- IMPE 6499 D2
Buffum Dr
3500 OCSD 1086 F5
Buford Wy
13700 POWY 1190 F3
Buggywhip Dr
10800 SDCo 1271 G7
Buho Ct
4000 SDGO 1250 A3
Buisson St
6200 SDGO 1228 C5
Buitre Ct
- BRAW 6320 B3
(See Page 6320)
Buka Pl
31400 SDCo 1067 H1
Bull Canyon Rd
- CHLV 1311 D7
Bullard Ln
- SDCo 1233 D4
Bullock Dr
6700 SDGO 1290 E5
Bullrush Glen
2000 ESCN 1110 B4
Bullrush Ln
2100 ENCT 1167 E3
Bulrush Ct
- CRLB 1127 B6
Bumann Rd
- ENCT 1148 D5
Bumper Cir
4000 SDGO 1249 H3
Buna Pl
100 VSTA 1087 H5
Bunche Av
3100 SDGO 1228 C5
Bunche Ter
6300 SDGO 1228 C5
Bunche Wy
6300 SDGO 1228 C5
Bund Ln
- SDCo 997 J7
Bundy Dr
9600 SNTE 1231 E4
Bungalow Wy
9200 SDGO 1249 D7
Bunker Hill
- SDCo 1234 J3
Bunker Hill St
3400 SDGO 1248 D5
Bunker View Wy
3400 OCSD 1106 J1
Bunkhouse Ct
- SDCo 1085 J3
Bunnell St
4800 SDGO 1290 A5
Bunnie King Ln
1300 SDCo 1172 G3
Bunny Bell Ln
1400 VSTA 1108 A2
Bunny Dr
- SDCo 1274 D3
Buoy Av
- CRLB 1127 A7
Burbank Ct
3500 SDGO 1249 A4
Burbank St
7400 SDGO 1249 A4
Burbury Wy
1700 SNMS 1128 C7
Burden Dr
700 NATC 1290 B7
Burdett Wy
100 SDCo 1252 H2
Burdoaks Ln
20600 SDCo 1274 J1
Burdock Wy
2100 CHLV 1331 H2
Burford St
5300 SDGO 1248 G6
Burga Loop
1000 CHLV 1310 J5
Burgasia Path
500 SDCo 1252 C6
Burgener Blvd
2300 SDGO 1248 G7
2200 SDGO 1268 G1
Burgos Ct
2400 CRLB 1147 F1

Burgundy Dr
1300 CHLV 1311 E7
Burgundy Rd
1500 ENCT 1147 C2
Burgundy St
6500 SDGO 1249 J6
Burian St
6000 SDGO 1290 C2
Burke Rd
7100 SDGO 1229 D1
800 VSTA 1087 E6
Burkshire Av
600 ENCT 1167 D2
Burkshire Pl
8800 SDCo 1232 C6
Burlingame Dr
3000 SDGO 1269 E7
Burlington Pl
1800 ESCN 1109 D5
Burlington Wy
7800 SDGO 1209 A4
Burma Ct
3900 SDCo 1047 E4
Burma Rd
500 SDCo 1047 E4
Burma Spur
3900 SDCo 1047 F4
Burnaby St
1100 ELCJ 1251 G7
Burned Oak Ln
10300 SDCo 1089 E3
Burned Oak Ter
28200 SDCo 1089 F3
Burnell Av
7600 LMGR 1270 G6
Burnet Dr
- ESCN 1110 E4
Burnet St
1700 ELCJ 1251 G2
Burnham St
500 ELCJ 1251 J6
Burning Bush St
800 ENCT 1147 E6
Burning Hills Dr
13300 POWY 1170 E1
Burning Tree Wy
9300 SNTE 1230 J6
Burns Ct
900 SDGO 1289 G5
Burnt Maple Wy
1800 VSTA 1107 G5
Burnt Mountain Rd
- SDCo 1090 A3
Burnt Mtn Rd
- SDCo 1090 A4
Burnt Pine Fire Rd
- SDCo 1196 C5
(See Page 1196)
Burnt Rancheria Cres
800 SDCo 1218 F7
Burr Ct
12400 SDGO 1189 C6
Burr Ln
8400 SDGO 1189 C6
Burr Oak Pl
1600 CHLV 1311 J7
Burris Dr
1600 SDCo 1272 E2
Burrock Dr
10000 SNTE 1231 D2
Burroughs St
1600 OCSD 1106 D2
2200 SDGO 1248 J7
2000 SDGO 1268 J1
N Burroughs St
1400 OCSD 1106 C2
S Burroughs St
1800 OCSD 1106 D3
Burrows Ct
- SDCo 1066 J2
Burton Ct
500 CRLB 1126 J7
Burton St
1900 SDGO 1268 J2
Burwell Ln
1500 SDCo 1272 B2
Burwood Pl
900 SDGO 1330 C7
Busch Dr
800 SDCo 1107 D2
700 VSTA 1107 D2
Bush Ct
- CALX 6620 J6
Bush Ln
600 SNMS 1108 G6
Bush St
1700 OCSD 1086 C6
600 SDGO 1268 J6
Bushard Dr
1000 SDCo 1129 H7
Bushwood Ct
7800 LMGR 1270 J7
Bushy Hill Dr
- SDGO 1230 G6
8500 SNTE 1230 F7
Business Center Ct
- SDGO 1351 B1
Business Park Dr
2300 VSTA 1107 J6
2500 VSTA 1128 A1

Business Pkwy
- IMPE 6499 E2
Businesspark Av
9600 SDGO 1209 F5
Butano Ct
8700 SDGO 1189 C3
Butano Wy
13700 SDGO 1189 C3
Butler Pl
6400 SDGO 1270 D5
Butler St
- IMPB 1349 J2
2800 OCSD 1086 D6
Butte St
8600 LMSA 1271 A3
Butte Top Pl
- SDCo 1271 D7
Buttercup Ln
600 NATC 1290 C6
Buttercup Rd
900 CRLB 1127 A6
1600 ENCT 1147 F5
Butterfield Dr
- SDCo 1232 F4
Butterfield Ln
700 SNMS 1109 D6
Butterfield Rd
700 OCSD 1067 B5
Butterfield Tr
- IMPE 6439 F4
- POWY 1170 F2
Butterfield Trl
- SNMS 1109 D6
Butterfly Ct
2900 CHLV 1311 J1
Butterfly Ln
4800 SDCo 1271 E2
Butterfly Wy
2900 CHLV 1311 H1
Butternut Hollow Ln
4800 SDCo 1310 H1
Butternut Ln
8900 SDGO 1249 D1
Butters Rd
1700 CRLB 1106 F3
Butterwood Av
500 SNMS 1109 D7
Butterwood Ct
12600 POWY 1190 D3
Butteside Pl
2400 SDCo 1271 C7
Butteview Pl
2400 SDCo 1271 B7
Button St
9700 SNTE 1231 A4
Buttonbrush Ln
1200 SDCo 1252 E7
Buttonwood Ct
1200 SDCo 1252 E7
Buxton Av
13400 POWY 1190 H4
Byrd St
3500 SDGO 1330 E7
Byrd Wy
600 SDGO 1330 E7
Byron Pl
- CRLB 1107 B7
Byron St
3300 SDGO 1288 B2

C

C Av
900 CORD 1288 H7
600 NATC 1309 H1
- SDCo 1066 B1
- SDCo 1291 D3
C K Clarke St
300 CALX 6680 G1
C Quiroz St
500 CALX 6620 E7
C Rd
- SDGO 1270 B7
C St
400 BRAW 6319 G1
(See Page 6319)
1000 BRAW 6320 A1
(See Page 6320)
500 CHLV 1309 J5
200 CHLV 1310 B4
100 ENCT 1147 B7
1000 ENCT 1148 A5
600 IMPE 6439 E5
- SDCo 1085 H4
2400 SDCo 1136 B7
2700 SDGO 1289 D3
W C St
400 SDGO 1289 A3
Caballero Canyon Rd
- SDCo 1089 G7
Caballo Ln
3400 SDCo 1048 D2
Caballos Pl
- SDGO 1188 D5
Cabana St
- CALX 6620 H6
Cabano Ct
300 SDCo 1086 A2
Cabaret St
6600 SDGO 1250 D4
Cabazon Ct
- IMPE 6439 F3

13 INDEX
INDEX 13
Cabela Dr
Calle Mejor
SAN DIEGO CO.

San Diego County Street Index

STREET
Block City Map# Grid

Cabela Dr
17800 SDGO 1150 A7
17500 SDGO 1169 J1
Cabela Pl
- CRLB 1127 C5
11400 SDGO 1169 J1
Cabernet Dr
1800 CHLV 1311 D3
Cabernet Wy
7100 LMGR 1290 F1
Cabezas Cv
1200 CHLV 1311 F6
Cabezon Pl
12500 SDGO 1189 F6
- VSTA 1107 E1
Cable Ct
600 OCSD 1086 F2
Cable St
2000 SDGO 1267 J6
Cabo Bahia
- CHLV 1311 F3
Cabo Ct
3300 CRLB 1147 J1
400 OCSD 1086 G2
10900 SNTE 1231 D1
Cabo San Lucas Av
- IMPE 6499 H1
Cabo Wy
3300 CRLB 1147 J1
Cabot Ct
1100 VSTA 1107 J4
Cabot Dr
9300 SDGO 1209 C6
Cabrena St
1800 SDGO 1350 B3
Cabrillo Av
600 CORD 1288 G6
7500 SDGO 1227 F7
Cabrillo Bay Ln
3100 SDGO 1268 D6
Cabrillo Cir
1100 VSTA 1087 J4
Cabrillo Fwy
- SDGO 1229 E6
- SDGO 1249 A6
- SDGO 1269 A4
Cabrillo Ln
1100 VSTA 1087 J4
Cabrillo Memorial Dr
- SDGO 1288 A7
- SDGO 1308 A1
Cabrillo Mesa Dr
2900 SDGO 1249 C5
Cabrillo Pl
2600 CRLB 1106 E5
- SDCo 1149 D4
Cabrillo Rd
- SDGO 1308 A3
Cabrillo St
21800 SDCo 1135 B3
Cacao Ct
11600 SDGO 1250 A2
Cacatua Pl
2900 CRLB 1127 H4
Cacatua St
2800 CRLB 1127 H5
Cache Creek St
1700 SDCo 1272 B3
Cacho Ct
- SDCo 1251 H1
Cacti Dr
29400 SDCo 1297 E4
(See Page 1297)
Cactus Av
8900 SDCo 1030 A4
Cactus Ct
6800 SDGO 1351 D4
Cactus Pl
2000 ESCN 1110 C7
Cactus Rd
1900 SDGO 1351 D4
Cactus St
- IMPE 6439 C6
9700 SDCo 1232 B3
Cactus Trail Ln
- CHLV 1311 H5
Cactus Wy
5700 SDGO 1248 A2
Cactusridge Ct
3600 SDGO 1289 G2
Cactusridge St
1400 SDGO 1289 G2
Cactusview Dr
3600 SDGO 1289 G2
Cacus St
8100 SDCo 1290 H5
Cadden Ct
3200 SDGO 1248 C4
Cadden Dr
3300 SDGO 1248 D4
Cadden Wy
3900 SDGO 1248 D4
Caddie Ct
2300 OCSD 1106 J1
Caddington Row
6000 SDGO 1248 B1
Caddy Row
12100 SDGO 1170 A4
Cade Ter
9000 SDGO 1209 D1
Cadena Dr
3900 OCSD 1086 G2
Cadence Ct
11000 SDCo 1109 G1
Cadence Grove Wy
11300 SDGO 1208 B2
Cadence Isle Ct
10800 SDGO 1188 G7
Cadencia Glen
800 ESCN 1109 F5
Cadencia Pl
13000 SDGO 1188 G4
Cadencia St
3100 CRLB 1127 J7
3300 CRLB 1128 A7
3000 CRLB 1147 H1
Cadencia Wy
1600 ESCN 1129 J5
Cades Wy
2400 VSTA 1108 A6
Cadet St
5000 SDGO 1228 G7
Cadillac Cir
300 OCSD 1086 C7
Cadiz St
2800 SDGO 1268 D6
Cadley Ct
9100 SDGO 1189 D1
Cadman St
600 SDGO 1290 F3
Cadmus St
100 ENCT 1147 A5
Cado View Ct
26700 SDCo 1090 D7
Cadoglenn Dr
- SDCo 1272 B1
Cadorette Av
9300 SNTE 1230 H6
Cadwell Rd
10400 SNTE 1231 A2
Caesar Rd
18900 SDCo 1153 E3
Caesena Wy
5000 OCSD 1107 F5
Cafanzara Ct
8200 SDGO 1250 E3
Cafe Avenida
4700 SDCo 1310 H2
Caffey Ln
7600 SDGO 1209 A5
Caflur Av
4100 SDGO 1248 D3
Cagayan Av
2800 SDGO 1330 C7
Cagle St
3700 NATC 1310 D3
Cahill Dr
7400 SDGO 1290 G3
Cahuilla Dr
- IMPE 6439 F3
Cahuilla Rd
500 SDCo 1078 H1
(See Page 1078)
Cahuka Ct
- SDCo 1050 J6
Cain Ln
1200 SDCo 1130 C3
Cairo Ct
8700 SDGO 1249 C7
Caithness Dr
1600 SDGO 1350 E2
Cajon Cir
600 OCSD 1066 J5
1100 VSTA 1087 G4
Cajon Greens Dr
1000 ELCJ 1251 H2
Cajon Greens Pl
1500 ELCJ 1251 H2
Cajon Pl
1600 CORD 1288 J7
Cajon Rd
7900 SDCo 1251 J2
Cajon View Dr
100 ELCJ 1271 F1
Cajon Vista Ct
12500 SDCo 1232 B7
Cajon Wy
4600 SDGO 1270 B3
Cala Lily St
6000 SNTE 1231 G7
Calabrese St
300 SDCo 1028 J6
Calabria Ct
7100 SDGO 1228 E3
Calabria St
1100 SNTE 1231 F6
Calac Ln
- SDCo 1071 F3
Calais Dr
13400 SDGO 1187 H7
Calamar Cove
11600 SDGO 1250 A2
Calamar Ct
11600 SDGO 1250 A2
Calamar Dr
11700 SDGO 1250 A2
Calaveras Dr
1000 SDGO 1287 J1
Calavo Ct
1700 CRLB 1106 G7
Calavo Dr
1500 SDCo 1109 E7
1300 SDCo 1129 E1
4300 SDCo 1271 F3
Calavo Rd
1500 SDCo 1027 H5
Calcatterra Sq
9900 SDGO 1209 H5
Caldas De Reyes
15600 SDGO 1170 C5
Calderon Ct
8400 SDGO 1189 B3
Calderon Rd
13500 SDGO 1189 B3
Calderwood Row
2800 SDGO 1248 B1
Caldy Pl
7600 SDGO 1249 A3
Caleb Ct
900 SDGO 1330 E7
Caledonia Dr
4100 SDGO 1249 A2
Calenda Rd
11100 SDGO 1169 H2
Calera St
1300 VSTA 1087 H4
Caleta Ct
2000 CRLB 1127 F6
Caleta Wy
12400 SDGO 1170 B2
Calevero
3500 OCSD 1107 D2
Calexico Av
44400 SDCo 1321 G5
(See Page 1321)
Calexico St
900 CALX 6680 E1
Calgary Av
4000 SDGO 1228 E4
Calgary Ct
6500 SDGO 1228 E5
200 VSTA 1087 D7
Calgary Dr
6500 SDGO 1228 E4
Calgary Wy
11100 SDCo 1069 G2
Calhoun Ct
- SDCo 1108 C5
Calhoun St
2600 SDGO 1268 F4
Caliban Ct
200 ENCT 1147 G6
Caliban Dr
1700 ENCT 1147 H6
Calico Cir
10400 SDGO 1209 B4
Calico Ln
1400 SDCo 1129 C4
Calico Ranch Gate
3600 SDCo 1135 G5
Calico Ranch Rd
3700 SDCo 1135 F5
Calico Rd
- SDCo 1086 A3
Calico St
8000 SDGO 1209 B4
3000 SNTE 1231 G7
Calidris Ln
- SDCo 1127 B7
Caliente Av
- SDGO 1351 A2
Caliente Ct
1400 SDCo 1234 C6
Caliente Glen
2000 ESCN 1129 E6
Caliente Loop
1300 CHLV 1311 B6
Caliente Lp
- CRLB 1107 A4
Califa Ct
8100 SDGO 1250 E3
E California Av
200 VSTA 1087 H5
W California Av
300 VSTA 1087 G5
California Oak Dr
600 SDCo 1107 H3
California Poppy St
2800 SDCo 1129 C6
California Springs Ct
2000 SDCo 1291 E1
California St
2000 ENCT 1147 J5
1100 IMPB 1349 G1
700 OCSD 1106 C2
- SDCo 1085 J4
2900 SDGO 1268 H7
1600 SDGO 1288 J2
W California St
3800 SDGO 1268 G6
Calina Wy
7700 CRLB 1147 G2
Calinda Dr
2600 SDCo 1108 C5
Calistoga Av
- CHLV 1331 C1
Calistoga Dr
15500 SDCo 1173 D4
Calistoga Pl
23400 SDCo 1173 C5
Calistoga Wy
- SNMS 1128 E6
Calla Av
100 IMPB 1329 E7
Calla St
- SDGO 1208 B6
1800 SDGO 1330 A7
Callado Ct
16700 SDGO 1170 A3
Callado Rd
12100 SDGO 1170 B3
Callan Rd
2900 SDGO 1207 J5
Callcott Wy
13000 SDGO 1188 C5
Calle Abajo
3000 SDGO 1310 D3
Calle Abuelito
- SDGO 1189 G5
Calle Acervo
3400 CRLB 1147 J3
- SDCo 1147 J4
Calle Adela
300 SNMS 1109 C7
Calle Aguadulce
2400 SDGO 1310 E1
Calle Albara
11700 SDCo 1271 J3
12100 SDCo 1272 A4
Calle Alhena
- CRLB 1147 H3
Calle Alicia
400 SCLE 1023 B2
Calle Allejandro
3000 SDCo 1292 H3
(See Page 1292)
Calle Alma
- CRLB 1127 J7
Calle Alta
1500 SDGO 1247 J3
Calle Alto
- SDCo 1232 A1
Calle Altura
1400 SDGO 1247 H3
Calle Ambiente
18300 SDCo 1148 H6
Calle Amistad Dr
300 SDCo 1152 J6
Calle Amistad Ln
1200 SDCo 1152 J6
Calle Ana
16500 POWY 1170 D4
Calle Anacapa
1000 ENCT 1148 A5
Calle Andalucia
14300 SDGO 1188 D2
Calle Andar
7700 CRLB 1147 J2
Calle Andrea
- SDCo 1173 D1
Calle Angelica
- SDCo 1271 J4
Calle Antonio
1800 VSTA 1088 B5
Calle Ardilla
- SDCo 1272 A4
Calle Ariana
4000 SCLE 1023 B2
Calle Arona
3100 CHLV 1312 A1
(See Page 1312)
Calle Arquero
4900 OCSD 1067 A4
Calle Arriba
5800 SDGO 1310 D2
Calle Arroyo
2700 CRLB 1106 G3
Calle Asturtas
15500 SDGO 1170 C5
Calle Atria
1600 CHLV 1312 A7
(See Page 1312)
Calle Avila
1500 CHLV 1331 D1
Calle Barcelona
1900 CRLB 1147 E3
Calle Bendito
- CHLV 1311 F2
Calle Bienvenido
1600 VSTA 1087 J3
Calle Bolero
200 OCSD 1087 A1
Calle Bonita
300 ESCN 1150 A3
Calle Brisa
1600 CHLV 1312 A7
(See Page 1312)
Calle Buena Ventura
2000 OCSD 1086 H7
2100 OCSD 1106 H1
Calle Bueno Ganar
13900 SDCo 1292 G3
(See Page 1292)
Calle Caballero
2700 CRLB 1106 G3
Calle Caballeros
13000 SDGO 1189 G4
Calle Cabrillo
- ESCN 1109 F6
- SDCo 1251 G2
- SDCo 1252 B1
Calle Cabrillo
- SNMS 1109 B5
Calle Cajon
- SDCo 1232 A1
Calle Caleta Viejas
- SDCo 1234 D7
Calle Calzada
8200 SDGO 1209 B2
Calle Camille
1500 SDGO 1247 J3
Calle Campesino
200 SCLE 1023 B1
Calle Camposeco
6100 SDCo 1168 F4
Calle Cancuna
- CRLB 1147 F4
Calle Candela
1500 SDGO 1247 J3
Calle Candelero
1200 CHLV 1311 A6
Calle Canonero
3900 SDCo 1028 F6
Calle Cantora
2000 SDCo 1252 C7
Calle Capistrano
500 SNMS 1108 F5
Calle Caracas
- CRLB 1147 F3
Calle Cardenas
13900 SDGO 1188 D3
Calle Carla
14500 SDCo 1188 F2
Calle Casas Bonitas
5700 SDGO 1310 D2
Calle Catalina
- ESCN 1129 G6
Calle Catalonia
- SDCo 1147 J5
Calle Catarina
2200 CHLV 1311 E2
Calle Cerro
- SNMS 1109 B5
Calle Chanate
2200 SDGO 1290 E7
Calle Chaparro
5400 SDCo 1168 B4
Calle Chapultepec
500 VSTA 1087 G6
Calle Charmona
12600 SDGO 1170 C5
Calle Chiquita
2300 SDGO 1227 H4
Calle Christopher
1400 ENCT 1167 G2
Calle Clara
2200 SDGO 1227 H5
Calle Cobre
- CRLB 1128 B7
Calle Codorniz
32300 SDCo 1049 G6
Calle Colina
13200 POWY 1170 E3
Calle Colina Roca
3500 SDCo 1254 E1
Calle Colnett
1200 SNMS 1109 C7
Calle Colorado
1600 VSTA 1087 J3
Calle Conejo
100 SDCo 1234 A6
Calle Conifera
7300 CRLB 1148 A1
Calle Corazon
400 OCSD 1087 A4
Calle Cordoba
- SDCo 1147 J4
Calle Corredor
- SDCo 998 B6
Calle Corta
16700 POWY 1170 D3
2300 SDGO 1227 H4
Calle Corte
17100 SDCo 1168 D3
Calle Cortejo
3700 SDCo 1168 D7
Calle Cortez
- SDCo 1271 J3
Calle Cortita
12500 SDGO 1170 C1
Calle Cozumel
7900 CRLB 1147 J4
Calle Cressa
10500 SDCo 1169 F2
Calle Cristobal
7300 SDGO 1208 H3
8100 SDGO 1209 A2
Calle Crucero
1300 SNMS 1109 C7
Calle Cumbre
2900 SDGO 1310 D2
Calle Dario
11200 SDGO 1209 B2
Calle De Adele
- ENCT 1147 B6
Calle De Alcala
900 ESCN 1150 D3
Calle De Alicia
- ENCT 1147 F5
Calle De Andluca
1500 SDGO 1247 J3
Calle De Arlene
- CHLV 1311 A6
- ENCT 1147 F5
Calle De Arroyo
1700 SDCo 1128 B3
Calle De Barbara
- ENCT 1147 F5
Calle De Baston
1100 SDCo 1128 B3
Calle De Buena Fe
8500 SDCo 1232 D7
Calle De Casitas
4600 OCSD 1066 H7
Calle De Cherie
- ENCT 1147 F5
Calle De Cinco
1500 SDGO 1247 J3
Calle De Compadres
2600 SDCo 1254 C1
Calle De Connector
4600 OCSD 1066 J7
Calle De Cristo
- SDCo 1088 G4
Calle De Damasco
- CHLV 1311 A6
Calle De Encinas
- SDCo 1091 F5
Calle De Encinas Ct
27000 SDCo 1091 F6
Calle De Ensueno
- SDCo 1070 A5
Calle De Ernesto
14100 SDCo 1232 G6
Calle De Flores
- ENCT 1147 F5
Calle De Fuentes
- CRLB 1127 J7
Calle De Golondrina
- BRAW 6320 B4
(See Page 6320)
Calle De Halcones
12300 SDCo 1049 H4
Calle De Katrina
- ENCT 1147 F5
Calle De La Alianza
200 SDGO 1350 F3
Calle De La Estrella
7700 SDCo 1237 D6
Calle De La Fiesta
7700 SDCo 1237 D6
Calle De La Flor
1600 CHLV 1331 D1
Calle De La Garza
2300 SDGO 1227 H5
Calle De La Paloma
200 SDCo 1027 H3
Calle De La Paz
500 ESCN 1149 J3
Calle De La Plata
8000 SDGO 1227 H5
Calle De La Reina
- SDCo 1069 D7
Calle De La Rosa
1500 CHLV 1331 D2
Calle De La Siena
12700 SDGO 1188 B6
Calle De La Sierra
600 SDCo 1252 E4
Calle De La Tierra Baja
- SDCo 1232 A1
Calle De La Vuelta
4700 SDCo 1048 B5
Calle De Lagrima
- SDGO 1168 H7
Calle De Las Brisas
31600 SDCo 1068 A1
Calle De Las Estrellas
31600 SDCo 1068 A2
Calle De Las Focas
3800 SCLE 1023 B1
Calle De Las Lomas
7200 SDCo 1148 G6
Calle De Las Piedras
- SDCo 1068 F5
Calle De Las Rosas
12700 SDGO 1189 E5
Calle De Leon
12000 SDCo 1272 A4
Calle De Lepanto
900 ESCN 1150 D3
Calle De Limar
1000 SDCo 1027 H6
Calle De Linea
6700 SDGO 1351 D4
Calle De Los Ninos
13000 SDGO 1189 F4
Calle De Los Potros
5100 SDCo 1290 H7
Calle De Los Serrano
1100 SDCo 1128 A3
Calle De Luz
39500 SDCo 996 H2
Calle De Madera
200 ENCT 1147 B4
Calle De Malibu
2800 SDCo 1149 J2
Calle De Maria
- ENCT 1147 E5
Calle De Medio
12000 SDCo 1272 A4
Calle De Montana
12000 SDCo 1272 A3
Calle De Newman
- SDGO 1189 D1
Calle De Nicole
1800 SDCo 1253 C5
Calle De Oro E
1200 CALX 6620 G7
Calle De Oro W
1200 CALX 6620 G7
Calle De Pescadores
2400 SDCo 1254 C1
Calle De Portal
- ESCN 1109 G7
Calle De Portola
300 SNMS 1128 J1
Calle De Primera
1500 SDGO 1247 J3
Calle De Retiro
4600 OCSD 1066 H7
Calle De Rob
13100 SDCo 1191 D5
Calle De Salud
8400 SDCo 1149 B3
Calle De Sereno
200 ENCT 1147 B5
Calle De Soto
700 SNMS 1129 A2
Calle De Sueno
4200 SDCo 1047 F4
Calle De Talar
- SDCo 1068 G2
Calle De Tierra
2200 SDCo 1253 H2
Calle De Valenzuela
- BRAW 6320 B4
(See Page 6320)
Calle De Vida
4300 SDGO 1249 J2
4500 SDGO 1250 A1
Calle De Vista
13800 SDCo 1090 E3
Calle De Vista Oeste
9200 SDGO 1189 D1
Calle Del Alcalde
7700 SDCo 1237 C6
Calle Del Alcazar
- SDCo 1168 F5
Calle Del Arco
1400 SDCo 998 H7
Calle Del Baston
1100 SDCo 1128 A2
Calle Del Bosque
7600 SDCo 1237 D6
Calle Del Campanario
- SDCo 1168 E6
Calle Del Campo
13300 SDGO 1189 A4
Calle Del Cielo
- BRAW 6319 G4
(See Page 6319)
- SDCo 1232 A1
8300 SDGO 1227 H4
Calle Del Conejo
1800 ELCJ 1252 C2
Calle Del Cruce
- SDCo 1168 H5
Calle Del Establo
3800 SCLE 1023 B1
Calle Del Greco
- OCSD 1087 B4
Calle Del Humo
8100 SDGO 1209 B1
Calle Del Lago
9400 SNTE 1231 A5
Calle Del Nido
- SDCo 1168 E6
Calle Del Oro
2300 SDGO 1227 H4
Calle Del Palo
4500 OCSD 1066 H6
Calle Del Portal
- ESCN 1109 G7
- SDCo 1252 B1
Calle Del Rancho
100 SDCo 1130 B6
Calle Del Rio
11800 SDCo 1232 A6
Calle Del Sol
- BRAW 6319 F4
(See Page 6319)
1500 CHLV 1331 C2
13700 SDCo 1272 G7
200 VSTA 1087 G6
Calle Del Sur
- CRLB 1147 J2
Calle Del Verano
- SNMS 1129 A2
Calle Del Verde
9000 SNTE 1231 A6
Calle Del Vida
- BRAW 6319 F4
(See Page 6319)
Calle Delgado
1400 NATC 1310 B1
Calle Delicada
1700 SDGO 1247 J3
Calle Deposito
11800 SDCo 1271 J4
Calle Descanso
1000 SDCo 1152 G6
Calle Devanar
1500 SDCo 1128 C3
Calle Diegueno
14600 SDCo 1188 F2
Calle Dos Lagos
7800 SDCo 1168 H2
Calle Dos Lomas
2200 SDCo 1048 B2
Calle Dos Palmas
4200 SDCo 1028 G1
Calle Dulce
- CHLV 1311 A6
1600 VSTA 1087 J3
Calle El Potrero
31900 SDCo 1052 A6
(See Page 1052)
Calle Elegante
- VSTA 1087 G5
Calle Emparrado
1100 SNMS 1108 F5
Calle Empinada
6100 SDGO 1250 C5
Calle Encanto
500 SDCo 1252 C6
Calle Entre
1900 LMGR 1290 F1
Calle Escarpada
1000 CHLV 1310 H3
Calle Estepona
18100 SDGO 1150 D6
Calle Estrella
- BRAW 6319 F5
(See Page 6319)
4700 OCSD 1066 J7
Calle Familia
- SDCo 1167 J4
Calle Fanita
8000 SNTE 1251 A1
Calle Fantasia
1300 SNMS 1108 E4
Calle Felicidad
5700 SDGO 1310 D2
Calle Feliz
16400 SDCo 1168 E4
Calle Fernando
2200 CHLV 1311 E2
Calle Florecita
1100 CHLV 1311 A5
200 ESCN 1150 A3
Calle Flores
18500 SDCo 1148 G5
Calle Fortunada
3800 SDGO 1249 E3
Calle Francesca
300 SCLE 1023 B1
Calle Frederico
- SDCo 1271 J4
Calle Frescota
2300 SDGO 1227 H5
Calle Fuego
- CRLB 1127 J7
Calle Gavanzo
3500 CRLB 1148 A2
Calle Gaviota
2500 SDGO 1310 D1
Calle Goya
- OCSD 1087 B3
Calle Guaymas
2200 SDGO 1247 J2
Calle Guernica
100 SNMS 1109 C7
Calle Helena
- IMPE 6499 E2
Calle Hermosa
- SDCo 1169 A3
Calle Hidalgo
3500 CRLB 1128 A5
Calle Hierro
- CRLB 1128 A7
Calle Huerto
100 VSTA 1088 D5
Calle Independencia
500 VSTA 1087 G5
Calle Isabel
100 SNMS 1109 C7
Calle Isabelino
- SDGO 1208 B3
Calle Isabella
4000 SCLE 1023 B2
Calle Jalapa
11200 SDGO 1209 B2
Calle Jalisco
7900 CRLB 1147 J3
Calle Jon Norte
- SDCo 1168 D3
Calle Jon Sur
- SDCo 1168 D3
Calle Joven
- OCSD 1086 J1
Calle Joya
- SDCo 1068 H3
Calle Juan
10700 SDCo 1271 F5
Calle Juanita
300 SNMS 1109 C7
Calle Juanito
15100 SDGO 1169 H7
Calle Juego
3600 SDCo 1168 D7
Calle Juela
7800 SDGO 1227 H6
Calle Jules
1200 VSTA 1087 J4
Calle Jules Av
1300 VSTA 1087 J4
Calle La Beata
- SDCo 1271 J4
Calle La Marina
- CHLV 1311 E2
Calle La Mirada
200 CHLV 1310 H3
Calle La Preza
- SDCo 1232 A1
Calle La Quinta
- CHLV 1311 F1
Calle La Reina
- SDCo 1068 D4
Calle La Serra
18400 SDCo 1148 F5
Calle Ladera
600 ESCN 1130 B4
30100 SDCo 1071 A4
Calle Lagasca
800 CHLV 1310 H5
Calle Las Casas
1600 OCSD 1087 C4
Calle Las Moras
- VSTA 1088 B4
Calle Las Palmas
- ELCJ 1251 H5
1800 OCSD 1087 C4
Calle Las Positas
4700 OCSD 1066 J7
Calle Lechuza
1200 SDCo 1027 H5
Calle Leticia
1500 SDGO 1247 J3
Calle Limonero
11900 SDCo 1271 J3
Calle Linda
200 SDCo 1047 G4
Calle Lisa
4000 SCLE 1023 B2
Calle Loma Ln
- SDCo 1068 B4
Calle Lomas
- CRLB 1147 F3
Calle Lomeda
1400 SDCo 997 H7
Calle Lorenzana
11900 SDCo 1272 A4
Calle Loreto
1200 SDCo 1318 H5
(See Page 1318)
Calle Los Arboles
3000 SDCo 1271 G6
Calle Los Santos
4700 OCSD 1066 J7
Calle Louisa
4000 SCLE 1023 B2
Calle Lucia
9200 SDCo 1232 B6
Calle Lucia Ct
9000 SDCo 1232 B6
Calle Lucia Ln
9000 SDCo 1232 B6
Calle Lucia Ter
12400 SDCo 1232 B6
Calle Luna
- BRAW 6319 F4
(See Page 6319)
- CRLB 1127 J7
Calle Madero
7600 CRLB 1147 H1
Calle Madrid
7900 CRLB 1147 H3
Calle Madrigal
1900 SDGO 1247 H1
Calle Magdalena
100 ENCT 1147 D7
Calle Majorca
6200 SDGO 1247 G2
Calle Mar De Armonia
- SDGO 1208 C3
Calle Mar De Ballenas
- SDGO 1208 B3
Calle Mar De Mariposa
- SDGO 1208 B4
Calle Marbella
1400 OCSD 1087 C3
Calle Margarita
- ENCT 1148 B3
Calle Maria
1100 SDCo 1109 C5
Calle Maribel
100 SNMS 1109 C7
Calle Marietta
15500 SDCo 1051 A7
Calle Marinero
10100 SDCo 1271 E7
Calle Mariposa
300 OCSD 1066 J7
Calle Mariselda
6100 SDGO 1229 H7
Calle Marlena
4000 SCLE 1023 B2
Calle Mayor
17600 SDCo 1168 G5
Calle Mejillones
- SDGO 1208 B3
Calle Mejor
- CRLB 1147 F3

San Diego County Street Index

STREET
Block City Map# Grid

Calle Mesita
1000 CHLV 1310 H3
Calle Mesquite
3000 SDCo 1292 H3
(See Page 1292)
Calle Messina
4500 SDCo 1148 G5
Calle Mia
3400 SDCo 1254 E1
Calle Minas
8200 SDGO 1209 B2
Calle Mirador
8600 SDCo 1232 D7
Calle Miramar
5700 SDGO 1247 J3
Calle Montecito
500 OCSD 1066 J7
Calle Montelibano
14800 SDCo 1188 G1
Calle Montera
600 ESCN 1150 C3
Calle Morelos
8400 SDGO 1209 C2
Calle Nada
- SDCo 1234 H6
Calle Naranja
12000 SDCo 1272 A3
11900 SDGO 1170 B3
Calle Narcisos
1500 ENCT 1167 G1
Calle Neil
4800 SDGO 1248 F5
Calle Nerja
7400 CRLB 1147 J1
Calle Niguel
4100 OCSD 1087 B5
Calle Nobleza
11700 SDGO 1170 A4
Calle Norte
8500 LMGR 1270 J7
Calle Nublado
14400 SDGO 1189 D2
Calle Nueva
8100 SDGO 1209 B1
Calle Odessa
- CRLB 1147 J2
Calle Olivia
- CRLB 1147 G2
Calle Opima
8400 SDGO 1227 H4
Calle Oro Verde
10900 SDCo 1049 E6
Calle Orquideas
1500 ENCT 1147 G7
Calle Osuna
3200 OCSD 1106 J2
Calle Ovieda
23600 SDCo 1173 D1
Calle Palmito
3500 CRLB 1148 B2
Calle Paracho
11600 SDGO 1170 A5
Calle Parral
11800 SDGO 1170 A6
Calle Paula
600 SOLB 1167 J6
Calle Pavana
6300 SDGO 1290 E7
6200 SDGO 1310 E1
Calle Pensamientos
1500 ENCT 1167 G1
Calle Pequena
6600 SDCo 1168 H5
Calle Pera
7300 CRLB 1148 A1
Calle Perico
8800 SDGO 1189 C3
Calle Pinabete
- CRLB 1147 G2
Calle Pino
8200 SDGO 1209 B1
Calle Pinon
- CRLB 1147 H3
Calle Pl
1400 ESCN 1109 J6
Calle Plata
7200 CRLB 1128 B7
Calle Platico
1700 OCSD 1087 C4
Calle Platino
4000 OCSD 1087 B6
Calle Plumerias
1600 ENCT 1167 G1
Calle Poco
- SDCo 1252 D7
Calle Ponte Bella
6100 SDCo 1148 E4
Calle Portone
6800 SDCo 1148 F5
Calle Posada
7900 CRLB 1147 J3
Calle Potranca
200 SCLE 1023 B1
Calle Potro
200 SCLE 1023 B1
Calle Primera
300 SDGO 1350 F4
Calle Privada
- SDCo 1188 F1
Calle Prospero
1300 SNMS 1108 E4

Calle Pueblito
15300 SDGO 1170 B5
Calle Pulido
16400 SDGO 1170 A3
Calle Quebrada
2400 SDGO 1310 E1
Calle Querido
100 SNMS 1129 C1
Calle Quinn
100 SDCo 1108 B3
Calle R Tuttle
1000 SNTE 1231 H4
Calle Rancho Vista
- ENCT 1148 A5
Calle Rayo
300 SNMS 1109 B7
Calle Real
1500 CHLV 1331 D2
Calle Redonda Ln
1400 ESCN 1109 E5
Calle Regal
700 ENCT 1147 D7
Calle Reina
6500 SDCo 1148 E6
Calle Ricardo
700 SDCo 1109 G1
Calle Rociada
1900 SDCo 996 E2
Calle Rosado
8700 SDCo 1232 E6
Calle Rosas
31800 SDCo 1051 E5
Calle Roxanne
40100 SDCo 996 E1
Calle Ryan
- ENCT 1167 G2
Calle Sabroso
2300 CHLV 1311 F3
Calle Sal Si Puedes
5700 SDGO 1310 D3
Calle Salida Del Sol
2800 SDGO 1310 D2
Calle San Blas
3300 CRLB 1147 J4
Calle San Clemente
2400 ENCT 1148 A5
Calle San Felipe
7900 CRLB 1147 H3
Calle San Miguel
2400 ENCT 1147 J5
Calle Santa Catalina
- ENCT 1148 A5
Calle Santa Cruz
900 ENCT 1148 A5
Calle Santa Fe
1500 SOLB 1167 J6
Calle Santander
- OCSD 1087 B4
Calle Santiago
1200 CHLV 1311 B6
- CRLB 1147 F4
Calle Saucillo
12200 SDGO 1170 B6
Calle Scott
- ENCT 1167 G2
Calle Seco
13400 POWY 1190 F5
Calle Serena
- SDCo 1168 H6
2200 SDGO 1290 D7
2300 SDGO 1310 D1
Calle Sierra
8700 SDCo 1291 A2
Calle Simeon
- SDCo 1169 F2
Calle Simpson
11300 SDCo 1271 J3
Calle Sinaloa
1900 VSTA 1088 C5
Calle Sobrado
4900 OCSD 1087 C3
Calle Solimar
4700 OCSD 1066 J7
Calle Sonia
1200 SDCo 1027 H4
Calle Stellina
18300 SDCo 1148 E5
Calle Suntuoso
11900 SDGO 1170 A4
Calle Sur
8500 LMGR 1270 J7
Calle Talentia
800 ESCN 1150 D3
Calle Tamarindo
10500 SDCo 1169 G2
Calle Tamega
12500 SDGO 1170 B5
Calle Tarifa
7200 CRLB 1148 A1
Calle Tecolotlan
1300 SDCo 1028 E4
Calle Tempra
- CHLV 1330 D4
Calle Tesoro
- CHLV 1311 H5
Calle Tezac
10900 SDCo 1271 G4
Calle Tiara
3800 SCLE 1023 B1
2200 SDGO 1247 J2

Calle Tiburon
- SCLE 1023 B1
Calle Tierra Blanca
- SDCo 1188 G1
Calle Tijera
1800 VSTA 1088 B5
Calle Timiteo
3400 CRLB 1147 J2
Calle Tocon
6100 SDGO 1310 E1
Calle Torreno
2300 CHLV 1311 F2
Calle Tortuosa
2400 SDGO 1290 E7
Calle Tragar
8800 SDGO 1189 C3
Calle Tramonto
18400 SDCo 1148 E5
Calle Trepadora
2200 SDGO 1290 D7
Calle Tres Lomas
2600 SDGO 1310 E1
Calle Tres Vistas
3300 ENCT 1148 B4
Calle Trevino
17000 SDCo 1169 F2
Calle Trucksess
11700 SDCo 1271 J4
Calle Tulipanes
1500 ENCT 1167 G1
Calle Ultimo
1300 OCSD 1087 B4
Calle Valeria
3000 SDCo 1292 G3
(See Page 1292)
Calle Vallarta
3200 CRLB 1147 H4
Calle Vallecito
400 OCSD 1066 J7
Calle Valperizo
6500 CRLB 1127 J4
Calle Vaquero
1400 SDGO 1247 J3
Calle Vela
300 SNMS 1109 B7
Calle Velasco
30400 SDCo 1071 A4
Calle Venado
1600 SDCo 1128 A3
Calle Venecia
14000 SDGO 1188 D3
Calle Ventner
7300 SDCo 1352 C2
Calle Vera Cruz
6100 SDGO 1247 J2
Calle Verano
- CRLB 1127 J7
Calle Verde
- SDCo 1232 A1
- SDCo 1271 G4
Calle Vida Buena
17900 SDCo 1168 A1
Calle Viento
- CRLB 1127 J6
Calle Violetas
1500 ENCT 1147 G7
Calle Vista
5300 SDGO 1247 J3
Calle Vista Av
1100 ESCN 1109 J6
Calle Viviano
8600 SDCo 1232 D6
Calle Vivienda
11700 SDGO 1170 A5
Callecita Aquilla Norte
- CHLV 1330 H2
Callecita Aquilla Sur
- CHLV 1330 J2
Callecita Wy
2300 OCSD 1087 C5
Calleja Risa
8400 SDCo 1232 D7
Callejo Feliz Dr
- SDCo 1071 A4
Callejo Feliz Ter
- SDCo 1071 A3
Callejo Felize Rd
30100 SDCo 1071 B4
Callejon
2800 SDGO 1310 D2
Callejon Alhambra
1300 CHLV 1311 B5
Callejon Andalusia
1300 CHLV 1311 B5
Callejon Carbon
1300 CHLV 1311 B5
Callejon Cervantes
1300 CHLV 1311 B5
Callejon Ciudad
700 CHLV 1311 A5
Callejon Espana
- CHLV 1311 B5
Callejon Malaga
- CHLV 1311 B5
Callejon Montefrio
1300 CHLV 1311 B5
Callejon Musica
14400 SDGO 1189 D1
Callejon Palacios
1300 CHLV 1311 B5

Callejon Quintana
11500 SDGO 1230 A7
Callejon Segovia
1300 CHLV 1311 B5
Callesita Escena
300 CHLV 1311 E2
Callesita Mariola
300 CHLV 1311 E2
Callesita Villena
- CHLV 1311 E1
Calliandra Rd
- CRLB 1127 D5
8700 SDGO 1209 C3
Calligraphy Ct
4700 OCSD 1087 B2
Callio Wy
11200 SDCo 1231 G3
Callisia Ct
- CRLB 1127 D4
Calloway Dr
16300 SDCo 1169 E4
Calma Ct
12700 SDGO 1170 C3
1200 VSTA 1107 H4
Calma Dr
1000 CHLV 1330 H1
Calma Pl
600 CHLV 1310 H7
Calmante Ln
9200 SDGO 1249 E7
Calmar Dr
2800 SDCo 1149 J2
Calmeria Pl
- CRLB 1127 A4
Calmin Dr
1600 SDCo 1027 J4
1900 SDCo 1028 A5
Calmin Wy
1600 SDCo 1027 J4
Calmoor St
4100 NATC 1310 E3
Calmoor Wy
3700 NATC 1310 E3
Calpella Ct
- CHLV 1331 B1
Calston Pl
7100 SDGO 1208 J4
Calston Wy
10600 SDGO 1208 J4
Calumet Av
5400 SDGO 1247 F4
Calvacado St
7500 LMGR 1290 G2
Calvados Pl
13500 SDGO 1190 A3
Calvary Dr
300 ELCN 6499 H4
Calvary Ln
- ELCJ 1252 D5
Calvary Rd
13900 POWY 1190 G3
Calvedos Dr
1800 CHLV 1311 E7
Calvin Ln
2600 ELCJ 1251 B5
1200 ESCN 1129 H5
Calvin Wy
5700 SDGO 1250 D7
Calypso Dr
- VSTA 1107 G5
Calypso Pl
3000 SDGO 1268 C5
Calzada De La Fuente
7300 SDCo 1332 C7
(See Page 1332)
Calzada Del Bosque
5600 SDCo 1168 C5
Cam Arriba
16300 SDCo 1173 E3
Cam Baja Cerro
1200 OCSD 1047 D7
Cam Bello
- CRLB 1148 B2
Cam Bello Mar
10500 SDCo 1169 G2
Cam Caldera
- SDCo 1169 F2
Cam Cereza
3400 CRLB 1148 A1
Cam Cielo
3000 SDCo 1047 H2
Cam Cielo Azul
20700 SDCo 1148 E1
20700 SNMS 1148 E1
Cam Corto
200 VSTA 1087 G6
Cam Culebra
2000 SDCo 1088 C3
Cam De Amigos
6700 CRLB 1128 A4
Cam De Arriba
7600 SDCo 1148 H5
Cam De La Amistad
1600 SDCo 1319 G3
(See Page 1319)
Cam De La Luna
- SDGO 1168 J7
Cam De La Paz
500 SNMS 1128 J2
Cam De La Rosa
7500 SDGO 1168 J7

Cam De Nog
- SDCo 1027 J6
1700 SDCo 1028 A6
Cam De Nog Ct
- SDCo 1027 J6
Cam De Nog Wy
0 SDCo 1027 J6
Cam De Palmas
1300 SDCo 1027 H7
Cam De Pricilla
2500 SDCo 1108 D4
Cam De Reimitz
2000 SDCo 1254 A2
Cam De Tierra
25100 SDCo 1216 D7
(See Page 1216)
Cam Del Arroyo Dr
900 SDCo 1128 C4
Cam Del Cielo
5500 SDCo 1048 C7
5500 SDCo 1068 B1
Cam Del Lago
- SNTE 1231 A5
Cam Del Monte
1600 SDCo 1319 H2
(See Page 1319)
Cam Del Sur
- SDGO 1169 C3
14300 SDGO 1189 A1
Cam Del Venado
10300 SDCo 1049 D4
Cam Hermoso
400 SNMS 1129 A2
Cam Junipero
- CRLB 1148 B2
Cam La Puerta
- CHLV 1311 F2
Cam Lago De Cristal
16800 SDCo 1168 G6
Cam Marcilla
17000 SDCo 1169 G2
Cam Minero
- CRLB 1148 B2
Cam Mojave
1800 CHLV 1311 C1
Cam Portofino
3100 SDCo 1048 A2
Cam Rainbow
1800 SDCo 998 J6
Cam San Thomas
10300 SDCo 1169 E2
Cam Sin Puente
7700 SDCo 1148 H4
Cam Solaire
2800 CHLV 1312 A7
(See Page 1312)
Cam Tres Aves
35200 SDCo 1299 A1
(See Page 1299)
Cam Verde
400 SNMS 1129 A1
Cam Vida Roble
- CRLB 1127 E3
Cam Zara
1200 SDCo 1028 D4
Camacho Rd
300 ImCo 6620 E6
Camara Ct
1400 VSTA 1107 H4
Camarena Ct
100 CALX 6620 F6
Camarena Rd
12700 SDGO 1188 B5
Camarero Ct
12500 SDGO 1188 B6
Camarillo Av
3200 OCSD 1107 B1
Camarosa Cir
11200 SDGO 1209 C2
Camassia Ln
- SDCo 1127 D4
Camber Ct
5600 SDGO 1248 H2
Camber Dr
5800 SDGO 1248 H2
Camber Pl
5600 SDGO 1248 H2
Camberley Ct
- SDGO 1330 H7
Camberwell Ct
12500 SDGO 1150 B6
Camberwell Ln
18300 SDGO 1150 C6
Cambon Ct
9100 SDCo 1291 B4
Cambon St
9100 SDCo 1291 B4
Cambria Ct
5500 SDGO 1250 B7
Cambria Pl
1600 ESCN 1129 G7
- SDCo 1147 F5
Cambria Wy
- SDCo 1147 F5
Cambridge Av
2200 ENCT 1167 E3
Cambridge Ct
3800 OCSD 1087 A7
8800 SDCo 1232 C6
1300 SNMS 1128 B3

Cambridge Ln
1900 VSTA 1108 A4
Cambridge Wy
4500 CRLB 1107 B4
Cambury Ct
9700 SNTE 1231 C4
Cambury Dr
9600 SNTE 1231 C4
E Camden Av
100 ELCJ 1251 F6
W Camden Av
100 ELCJ 1251 F6
Camden Cir
3400 CRLB 1106 G4
Camden Ct
500 ELCJ 1251 G6
Camden Dr
2800 VSTA 1108 B5
Camden Glen
- ESCN 1110 D7
Camden Pl
15500 SDGO 1210 H1
1700 SNMS 1108 J3
Camelas Walk
16400 SDCo 1169 F4
Camelia
1100 OCSD 1106 C2
- SDGO 1248 C6
Camelia Wy
13300 SDGO 1188 F4
Camellia
- SDCo 1028 F4
Camellia Ct
1400 CHLV 1330 H3
Camellia Dr
7100 LMSA 1270 F3
Camellia Pl
700 CRLB 1106 F6
Camellia St
1000 ESCN 1110 B6
Camellia Wy
2300 NATC 1290 A6
Camelot Ct
7200 LMGR 1290 F1
Camelot Dr
300 OCSD 1086 E6
Camelot Pkwy
- SDCo 1252 D4
Cameo Ct
3700 SDGO 1248 G4
Cameo Dr
500 ESCN 1109 H6
3700 OCSD 1087 A7
3400 OCSD 1106 J1
1700 VSTA 1087 D6
Cameo Ln
3700 SDGO 1248 G4
Cameo Rd
2200 CRLB 1106 H5
Camero St
- SDGO 1270 B5
Cameron Ct
- BRAW 6319 J3
(See Page 6319)
6000 SDGO 1310 D2
Cameron Dr
8100 SDCo 1290 H1
Cameron Pl
2700 ESCN 1110 D6
Cameron Truck Trl
2200 SDCo 1297 H6
(See Page 1297)
- SDCo 1298 A2
(See Page 1298)
Camet Ct
- LMSA 1270 J4
Camilia St
- CALX 6620 H7
Camille Wa
- SDCo 1089 A1
Camillo Ct
1400 ELCJ 1252 A2
Camillo Wy
1300 ELCJ 1252 A3
Camina Del Mesa
2600 SDCo 1299 J4
(See Page 1299)
Caminata Amador
14000 SDGO 1189 H3
Caminata Breve
13900 SDGO 1189 G3
Caminata Deluz
10700 SDGO 1189 H3
Caminata Duoro
11000 SDGO 1189 H2
Caminata Ebro
10800 SDGO 1189 G2
Caminata Soleado
14200 SDGO 1189 H2
Caminata Taugus
14300 SDGO 1189 H2
CaminitO Cuesta
10800 SDGO 1210 C3
Caminita Amador
14100 SDGO 1189 H2
Caminito Abeto
2600 SDGO 1350 C1
Caminito Abrazo
8700 SDGO 1228 A3
Caminito Acento
1300 SDGO 1247 H3

Caminito Aclara
11200 SDGO 1208 H2
Caminito Afuera
2300 SDGO 1268 A4
Caminito Agadir
10300 SDGO 1209 G5
Caminito Agrado
2300 SDGO 1268 A4
Caminito Agua
5400 SDGO 1248 A2
Caminito Aguar
1500 SDCo 1128 C3
Caminito Aguilar
3800 SDGO 1248 H3
Caminito Aire Puro
16000 SDGO 1170 B5
Caminito Alegria
11000 SDGO 1210 C2
Caminito Aliviado
1600 SDGO 1247 J3
Caminito Almonte
14000 SDGO 1189 G3
Caminito Alto
- SDGO 1210 C3
Caminito Alvarez
10300 SDGO 1208 J5
Caminito Amapola
100 SNMS 1109 B7
100 SNMS 1129 C1
Caminito Amarillo
1100 SNMS 1108 F5
Caminito Ameca
3200 SDGO 1228 A5
Caminito Amergon
- SDGO 1247 J2
Caminito Amparo
- SDGO 1228 B4
Caminito Andada
2300 SDGO 1268 A4
Caminito Andreta
6200 SDGO 1268 H2
Caminito Angelico
- SDGO 1188 C5
Caminito Anzio
13700 SDGO 1189 H3
Caminito Apartado
5200 SDGO 1269 H2
Caminito Aralia
10300 SDGO 1209 G6
Caminito Araya
6200 SDGO 1228 E5
Caminito Arboles
10900 SDGO 1210 B2
Caminito Arcada
- SDGO 1209 H1
Caminito Ardiente
1700 SDGO 1247 J2
Caminito Arenoso
3100 SDGO 1248 C2
Caminito Armida
11400 SDGO 1210 A5
Caminito Aronimink
2500 SDGO 1247 J1
Caminito Arriata
1300 SDGO 1247 H3
Caminito Ascua
1700 SDGO 1247 J2
Caminito Asterisco
1600 SDGO 1247 J2
Caminito Atico
15700 SDGO 1170 A5
Caminito Atildado
4800 SDGO 1188 C7
Caminito Avellano
2500 SDGO 1350 B1
Caminito Avola
7500 SDGO 1227 H6
Caminito Azul
800 CRLB 1126 J5
Caminito Badalona
3000 SDGO 1187 H2
Caminito Baeza
6100 SDGO 1228 E6
Caminito Balada
1300 SDGO 1247 H3
Caminito Balata
- SDGO 1170 D1
Caminito Baltusral
6400 SDGO 1248 A1
Caminito Banyon
10300 SDGO 1209 G5
Caminito Barbuda
14700 SDGO 1188 B2
Caminito Barlovento
1600 SDGO 1247 J2
Caminito Basilio
6300 SDGO 1268 H3
Caminito Bassano E
7300 SDGO 1227 H6
Caminito Bassano W
7300 SDGO 1227 H6
Caminito Basswood
10500 SDGO 1209 H5
Caminito Batea
1300 SDGO 1247 H3
Caminito Bautizo
- SDGO 1188 C5
Caminito Baya
17400 SDGO 1169 J1

Caminito Bayo
5300 SDGO 1247 H4
Caminito Baywood
10500 SDGO 1209 D4
Caminito Bello
2900 SDGO 1227 J5
Caminito Beso
- SDGO 1188 C5
Caminito Blanca
5400 SDGO 1248 A2
Caminito Blythefield
6400 SDGO 1247 J1
Caminito Bodega
12900 SDGO 1207 H2
Caminito Bolsa
9700 SDGO 1189 E4
Caminito Bonanza
7700 CRLB 1148 A2
Caminito Borde
5400 SDGO 1269 H1
Caminito Borrego
- CHLV 1311 D7
- SDGO 1188 E6
Caminito Bracho
13000 SDGO 1170 D1
Caminito Braga
7000 SDGO 1228 B4
Caminito Bravura
10700 SDGO 1249 G7
Caminito Brioso
12400 SDGO 1210 C3
Caminito Brisa
1800 SDGO 1227 H7
Caminito Buena Suerte
6200 SDGO 1250 D6
Caminito Cabala
2200 SDGO 1248 A2
Caminito Cabana
9400 SDGO 1209 E5
Caminito Cabo Viejo
3300 SDGO 1187 J1
Caminito Cachorro
4900 SDGO 1270 A7
Caminito Cadena
12000 SDGO 1170 B2
Caminito Cala
2300 SDGO 1207 H1
Caminito Caldo
17400 SDGO 1169 J2
Caminito Calmoso
- SDGO 1188 B4
Caminito Calor
9700 SDGO 1210 A5
Caminito Camelia
- SDGO 1188 J1
Caminito Campana
11900 SDGO 1170 B2
Caminito Campaneo
4700 SDGO 1188 B5
Caminito Canada
10900 SDGO 1210 C3
Caminito Canasto
17200 SDGO 1169 J1
17600 SDGO 1170 A1
Caminito Cancion
12700 SDGO 1170 C3
Caminito Canelo
12400 SDGO 1210 C3
Caminito Canon
12400 SDGO 1210 C3
Caminito Canor
- SDGO 1188 B4
Caminito Cantaras
- SOLB 1187 H1
Caminito Cantilena
18600 SDGO 1150 A5
Caminito Capa
2000 SDGO 1227 H7
Caminito Cape
Sebastian
- ENCT 1167 E4
Caminito Capistrano
- CHLV 1311 E7
Caminito Carboneras
3000 SDGO 1187 H2
Caminito Cardelina
5900 SDGO 1247 J2
Caminito Carino
2600 SDGO 1227 J6
Caminito Carlotta
7200 SDGO 1250 E4
Caminito Carmel
12700 SDGO 1207 J1
Caminito Carolina
1200 ENCT 1148 B5
Caminito Carrena
6200 SDGO 1228 E6
Caminito Cartgate
2500 SDGO 1247 J1
Caminito Cascara
10500 SDGO 1249 G7
Caminito Cassis
3900 SDGO 1228 B5
Caminito Castillo
2200 SDGO 1248 A2
Caminito Catalan
6400 SDGO 1227 J7
Caminito Cedro
1200 SDGO 1350 B1

Caminito Cedros
2700 SDGO 1207 H2
Caminito Centro
1300 SDGO 1289 C2
Caminito Cercado
15700 SDGO 1170 A5
Caminito Cerezo
10900 SDGO 1210 C2
Caminito Chiapas
5900 SDGO 1269 G1
Caminito Chiclayo
- SDGO 1170 C1
Caminito Chirimolla
9900 SDGO 1209 G5
Caminito Chollas
2700 SDGO 1270 C7
Caminito Chueco
10600 SDGO 1209 D4
Caminito Cielo Del Mar
3700 SDGO 1188 A7
Caminito Ciera
13300 SDGO 1189 G4
Caminito Circulo Sur
2000 SDGO 1248 A3
Caminito Cita
1200 SDGO 1350 C1
Caminito Claro
8800 SDGO 1228 A3
Caminito Clasica
- SDGO 1188 C7
Caminito Clavo
6100 SDGO 1250 C6
Caminito Coloma
1200 CHLV 1311 E6
Caminito Colorado
10800 SDGO 1210 C2
Caminito Conquistador
- CHLV 1330 H1
Caminito Consuelo
5500 SDGO 1248 A2
Caminito Coromandel
7500 SDGO 1227 J6
Caminito Corriente
11500 SDGO 1170 A5
Caminito Cortina
- CHLV 1330 H1
Caminito Covewood
10200 SDGO 1209 G6
Caminito Cristalino
4500 SDGO 1248 C2
Caminito Cristo
- SDGO 1188 E6
Caminito Cristobal
13000 SDGO 1187 H7
Caminito Cruzada
7100 SDGO 1227 H7
Caminito Cuadro
9800 SDGO 1189 F4
Caminito Cuarzo
4400 SDGO 1248 C2
Caminito Cuervo
10200 SDGO 1249 G7
Caminito Curva
6900 SDGO 1250 F4
Caminito Daniella
3300 SDGO 1187 J1
Caminito Danzarin
5600 SDGO 1247 H3
Caminito Davila
4000 SDGO 1228 B5
Caminito De Hoy
11700 SDGO 1170 A5
Caminito De La Fada
9700 SDGO 1249 F1
Caminito De La Gallarda
12500 SDGO 1170 C2
Caminito De La Luna
- CHLV 1330 H1
Caminito De La Taza
5900 SDGO 1250 D6
Caminito De Las
Missiones
11800 SDGO 1170 A5
Caminito De Las Noches
16000 SDGO 1170 A5
Caminito De Las Olas
12900 SDGO 1207 H1
Caminito De Las Palmas
16700 SDCo 1168 H3
Caminito De Linda
16000 SDGO 1170 A5
Caminito De Los
Cepillos
- SDCo 1067 H3
Caminito De Maria
- SDCo 1271 C4
Caminito De Oi Vay
- SDGO 1249 A3
Caminito De Pizza
8000 SDGO 1269 B2
Caminito De Tatan
3800 SDGO 1249 A3
Caminito Dehesa
3900 SDGO 1268 A3
Caminito Del Barco
2100 SDGO 1207 G1
Caminito Del Canto
2200 SDGO 1207 G1
Caminito Del Cervato
- SDGO 1268 H1

15 INDEX

Caminito Del Cid

INDEX 15

Camino Mayor

San Diego County Street Index

SAN DIEGO CO.

SAN DIEGO CO.

STREET	Block	City	Map#	Grid
Caminito Del Cid	7900	SDGO	1227	H5
Caminito Del Estio	5800	SDGO	1247	H3
Caminito Del Feliz	9600	SDGO	1228	D1
Caminito Del Greco	6700	SDGO	1250	E4
Caminito Del Mar	800	CRLB	1126	J4
Caminito Del Marfil	9700	SDGO	1249	F2
Caminito Del Oeste	6000	SDGO	1268	H1
Caminito Del Pasaje	12900	SDGO	1207	H1
Caminito Del Pastel	6300	SDGO	1268	H1
Caminito Del Reposo	800	CRLB	1126	J4
Caminito Del Rocio	13000	SDGO	1207	G1
Caminito Del Sol	800	CRLB	1126	J4
Caminito Del Verde	9200	SNTE	1231	A6
Caminito Del Vida	9600	SDGO	1228	D1
Caminito Del Vientecito	-	SDCo	1168	J3
Caminito Del Zafiro	4300	SDGO	1228	C1
Caminito Delicia	-	SDGO	1188	D6
Caminito Deporte	5900	SDGO	1269	G1
Caminito Derecho	10600	SDGO	1209	D4
Caminito Deseo	2900	SDGO	1228	A3
Caminito Destello	12600	SDGO	1188	E6
Caminito Dia	7900	SDGO	1228	C4
Caminito Diablo	-	SDGO	1188	E6
Caminito Diadema	1300	SDGO	1247	H3
Caminito Diego	-	SDGO	1188	E6
Caminito Doha	9700	SDGO	1209	G5
Caminito Donoso	7000	SDGO	1227	H7
Caminito Dosamantes	-	SDGO	1170	C1
Caminito Dulce	11000	SDGO	1210	B2
Caminito Duro	10600	SDGO	1209	D4
Caminito Eastbluff	3200	SDGO	1228	A4
Caminito El Canario	2000	SDGO	1227	G7
	2000	SDGO	1247	H1
Caminito El Rincon	3500	SDGO	1187	J7
Caminito El Rosario	7800	SDGO	1227	J5
Caminito Elado	11400	SDGO	1210	A5
Caminito Eldorado	2700	SDGO	1187	H7
	2700	SDGO	1207	H1
Caminito Elegante	5900	SDGO	1269	G1
Caminito Empresa	5800	SDGO	1247	J3
Caminito En Flor	12800	SDGO	1207	H1
Caminito Encantar	-	SDGO	1188	D6
Caminito Encanto	7700	CRLB	1147	J2
	11000	SDGO	1210	C2
Caminito Entrada	6900	SDGO	1250	G5
Caminito Esmero	12300	SDGO	1188	D6
Caminito Espejo	4000	SDGO	1268	A4
Caminito Espino	2500	SDGO	1350	C1
Caminito Estero	2300	SDGO	1268	A4
Caminito Estima	5600	SDGO	1248	A2
Caminito Estrada	900	CRLB	1126	J4
	-	SDGO	1247	H1
Caminito Estrella	-	CHLV	1310	G6
Caminito Estrellado	6100	SDGO	1250	D6
Caminito Eva	-	SDGO	1188	C6
Caminito Evangelico	-	SDGO	1188	B4
Caminito Eximio	2300	SDGO	1268	A4
Caminito Exquisito	12600	SDGO	1188	D6
Caminito Faceto	-	SDGO	1188	B4
Caminito Faro	1300	SDGO	1247	H3
Caminito Festivo	12300	SDGO	1210	B2
Caminito Flecha	6300	SDGO	1268	H3
Caminito Floreo	1300	SDGO	1247	H3
Caminito Flores	10500	SDGO	1209	D4
Caminito Florindo	11400	SDGO	1169	J2
Caminito Formby	6400	SDGO	1247	J1
Caminito Fortaleza	3000	SDGO	1187	H2
Caminito Franche	7000	SDGO	1228	B5
Caminito Francisco	-	CHLV	1311	D7
Caminito Fresco	8900	SDGO	1228	A3
Caminito Fuente	4400	SDGO	1269	A4
Caminito Gabaldon	1300	SDGO	1269	B2
Caminito Gandara	3200	SDGO	1228	A5
Caminito Ganton	2800	SDGO	1227	J7
Caminito Garcia	11400	SDGO	1210	A5
Caminito Genio	5600	SDGO	1247	H3
Caminito Gianna	8100	SDGO	1228	A5
Caminito Gijon	3000	SDGO	1187	H2
Caminito Gilbar	15700	SDGO	1170	A5
Caminito Girasol	-	SDGO	1188	C5
Caminito Glenellen	10500	SDGO	1209	D4
Caminito Glorita	7800	SDGO	1228	C4
Caminito Goma	10300	SDGO	1209	G5
Caminito Graciela	1200	ENCT	1148	B5
Caminito Granate	12300	SDGO	1188	D6
Caminito Grimaldi	7000	SDGO	1228	B4
Caminito Gusto	11500	SDGO	1210	A5
Caminito Halago	1300	SDGO	1247	H3
Caminito Helecho	8300	SDGO	1227	J5
Caminito Heno	17400	SDGO	1169	J1
Caminito Heraldo	5400	SDGO	1247	H4
Caminito Hercuba	-	SDGO	1170	C1
Caminito Herminia	5400	SDGO	1248	A2
Caminito Hermitage	6600	SDGO	1228	A7
Caminito Hiedra	2500	SDGO	1350	B1
Caminito Hierro	4400	SDGO	1248	C2
Caminito Huerta	7900	SDGO	1228	C4
Caminito Impersado	-	SDGO	1188	B4
Caminito Inocenta	11200	SDGO	1208	H3
Caminito Isla	5600	SDGO	1248	A2
Caminito Islay	4100	SDGO	1228	C4
Caminito Jonata	7800	SDGO	1228	D4
Caminito Jose	5500	SDGO	1248	H3
Caminito Joven	9700	SDGO	1210	A5
Caminito Jovial	10100	SDGO	1209	E5
Caminito Juanico	6200	SDGO	1268	H2
Caminito Jubilo	5200	SDGO	1269	H2
Caminito Katerina	5500	SDGO	1248	H3
Caminito Kiosco	8000	SDGO	1228	D4
Caminito Kittansett	6500	SDGO	1247	J1
Caminito La Bar	11400	SDGO	1208	J2
Caminito La Benera	7000	SDGO	1227	H7
Caminito La Paz	2500	SDGO	1227	J6
Caminito La Torre	15600	SDGO	1170	B5
Caminito Lacayo	8200	SDGO	1227	J5
Caminito Ladera	15000	SOLB	1167	H7
Caminito Lapiz	-	SDGO	1188	C5
Caminito Laswane	9800	SDGO	1210	A4
Caminito Laura	1300	ENCT	1148	B5
Caminito Lazanja	-	SDGO	1188	J1
	-	SDGO	1189	A2
Caminito Lazaro	6300	SDGO	1268	H3
Caminito Leon	7700	CRLB	1148	A2
Caminito Lindrick	6600	SDGO	1228	A7
Caminito Linterna	8300	SDGO	1227	J4
Caminito Listo	6400	SDGO	1268	H1
Caminito Lita	4100	SDGO	1228	C4
Caminito Litoral	3800	SDGO	1268	B6
Caminito Lobes	-	SDGO	1170	C1
Caminito Loma Buena	-	SDGO	1248	F5
Caminito Loreta	2000	SDGO	1248	A2
Caminito Luisito	6200	SDGO	1268	H2
Caminito Luna Nueva	3300	SDGO	1187	J1
Caminito Madrigal	900	CRLB	1126	J4
Caminito Magnifica	11500	SDGO	1210	A5
Caminito Maguey	10200	SDGO	1209	F6
Caminito Malaga	7700	CRLB	1147	J2
Caminito Mallorca	8000	SDGO	1228	A5
Caminito Manresa	7000	SDGO	1227	G7
	7000	SDGO	1247	H1
Caminito Manso	10600	SDGO	1209	D4
Caminito Mar Villa	13300	SDGO	1187	G7
Caminito Maracaibo	14700	SDGO	1188	C2
Caminito Marcial	6200	SDGO	1268	H2
Caminito Maria	15200	SDCo	1188	F1
Caminito Marisol	1600	CHLV	1331	C3
Caminito Maritimo	8200	SDGO	1227	J5
Caminito Marlock	9800	SDGO	1209	G5
Caminito Marrisa	2100	SDGO	1248	A3
Caminito Marzella	1800	SDGO	1227	H7
Caminito Masada	17300	SDGO	1169	J1
Caminito Mayten	10400	SDGO	1209	G5
Caminito Meliado	4000	SDGO	1228	B4
Caminito Membrillo	9900	SDGO	1209	G6
Caminito Memosac	10500	SDGO	1209	G5
Caminito Mendiola	13100	SDGO	1188	G4
Caminito Menor	4000	SDGO	1268	A4
Caminito Merion	2800	SDGO	1227	J7
Caminito Milita	7800	SDGO	1228	C4
Caminito Mindy	5200	SDGO	1270	A7
Caminito Mira	2300	SDGO	1268	A4
Caminito Mira Del Mar	12600	SDGO	1188	A7
Caminito Mirada	12300	SDGO	1210	C2
Caminito Miranda	11400	SDGO	1208	J2
Caminito Modena	8200	SDGO	1228	A5
Caminito Mojado	9700	SDGO	1210	B5
Caminito Monarca	7700	CRLB	1147	F2
Caminito Monrovia	1800	SDGO	1227	H7
Caminito Montanoso	6800	SDGO	1250	F5
Caminito Moraga	-	CHLV	1311	D7
Caminito Muirfield	2500	SDGO	1247	J1
Caminito Mulege	10100	SDGO	1209	E5
Caminito Mundano	5500	SDGO	1188	E6
Caminito Mundo	6800	SDGO	1250	F4
Caminito Munoz	9700	SDGO	1210	A5
Caminito Niquel	3000	SDGO	1248	B2
Caminito Noguera	7700	SDGO	1228	C4
Caminito Norte	5700	SDGO	1248	A2
Caminito Northland	6400	SDGO	1248	A1
Caminito Nuez	10200	SDGO	1209	G5
Caminito Obispo	-	CHLV	1311	D7
Caminito Obra	10500	SDGO	1209	D4
Caminito Ocean Cove	2400	ENCT	1167	E4
Caminito Ocio	4400	SDGO	1269	H1
Caminito Olmo	7100	SDGO	1227	H7
Caminito Orense Este	14700	SDGO	1189	J1
Caminito Pacifica	-	SDGO	1188	B2
Caminito Pajarito	2300	SDGO	1268	B6
Caminito Pan	6100	SDGO	1250	C6
Caminito Pantoja	-	SDGO	1228	B4
Caminito Partida	6300	SDGO	1268	H3
Caminito Pasada	2300	SDGO	1268	A4
Caminito Pasadero	18500	SDGO	1150	B6
Caminito Patricia	3900	SDGO	1248	H3
Caminito Pedernal	4400	SDGO	1248	C2
Caminito Pelon	9800	SDGO	1210	A4
Caminito Pepino	7100	SDGO	1227	H7
Caminito Pequena	7300	SDGO	1250	F4
Caminito Peral	12300	SDGO	1210	C2
Caminito Perico	6900	SDGO	1250	G5
Caminito Pescado	2200	SDGO	1268	B6
Caminito Pimiento	1200	SDGO	1350	C1
Caminito Pinero	17800	SDGO	1150	A7
Caminito Pintoresco	4200	SDGO	1269	H2
Caminito Pitaya	10200	SDGO	1209	G6
Caminito Plata	6100	SDGO	1250	D6
Caminito Plaza Centro	-	SDGO	1228	B3
Caminito Plaza Vw	-	SDGO	1350	D1
Caminito Plomada	4400	SDGO	1248	B2
Caminito Poco	4000	SDGO	1268	A4
Caminito Pollo	10500	SDGO	1209	D4
Caminito Porthcawl	2500	SDGO	1247	J1
Caminito Prado	2700	SDGO	1227	J6
Caminito Prenticia	11700	SDGO	1210	A5
Caminito Primavera	8800	SDGO	1228	A3
Caminito Propico	-	SDGO	1208	H3
Caminito Prospero	-	SDGO	1188	C7
Caminito Providencia	-	SDGO	1188	D1
Caminito Pudregal	9700	SDGO	1210	B4
Caminito Puerto	7700	CRLB	1147	J2
Caminito Pulsera	5700	SDGO	1247	H3
Caminito Quevedo	14100	SDGO	1189	H3
Caminito Quintana	-	SDGO	1228	B4
Caminito Quintero	1800	SDGO	1227	H7
Caminito Quixote	3100	SDGO	1330	E7
Caminito Radiante	-	SDGO	1188	D6
Caminito Recodo	2300	SDGO	1268	A4
Caminito Redondo	300	SNMS	1109	C7
Caminito Rialto	7400	SDGO	1227	H6
Caminito Ricardo	3100	ENCT	1148	B5
Caminito Rimini	10400	SDGO	1189	G3
Caminito Rio	-	SDCo	1231	H3
Caminito Rio Alta	-	SOLB	1187	H1
Caminito Rio Branco	10200	SDGO	1209	G5
Caminito Rio Ct	-	SDCo	1231	H3
Caminito Roberto	5500	SDGO	1248	H3
Caminito Rodar	11200	SDGO	1208	H2
Caminito Rogelio	9800	SDGO	1210	A5
Caminito Ronaldo	-	SDGO	1170	A1
Caminito Rosa	800	CRLB	1126	J5
	5400	SDGO	1248	A2
Caminito Rosita	12500	SDGO	1170	C5
Caminito Ryone	11900	SDGO	1170	A5
Caminito Sacate	6100	SDGO	1250	C6
Caminito Sagunto	3000	SDGO	1187	H2
Caminito Salado	6200	SDGO	1268	H2
Caminito San Lucas	5400	SDGO	1248	A2
Caminito San Marino	-	SDGO	1207	H2
Caminito San Martin	2100	SDGO	1248	A2
Caminito San Pablo	2700	SDGO	1207	H2
Caminito Sana	-	SDGO	1228	D4
Caminito Santico	16900	SDGO	1170	C3
Caminito Sanudo	11800	SDGO	1210	B5
Caminito Saragossa	-	SDGO	1188	D1
Caminito Scioto	6500	SDGO	1227	J7
Caminito Secoya	2600	SDGO	1350	C1
Caminito Seguro	2300	SDGO	1268	A4
Caminito Septimo	1200	ENCT	1167	F1
Caminito Sereno	12300	SDGO	1210	C2
Caminito Siega	17300	SDGO	1169	J2
Caminito Sierra	3500	CRLB	1148	A2
Caminito Silvela	-	SDGO	1228	B4
Caminito Sinnecock	6500	SDGO	1227	J7
Caminito Solidago	1400	SDGO	1247	H2
Caminito Solitario	5200	SDGO	1269	H2
Caminito Sonoma	8200	SDGO	1228	A5
Caminito Sonrisa	-	CHLV	1311	D7
Caminito Sopadilla	10500	SDGO	1209	G6
Caminito Suelto	9700	SDGO	1210	A5
Caminito Sueno	6800	CRLB	1128	A5
	-	SDGO	1228	A3
Caminito Suero	4000	SDGO	1228	B5
Caminito Sulmona	10400	SDGO	1189	G3
Caminito Surabaya	10200	SDGO	1209	G5
Caminito Tamborrel	11700	SDGO	1210	A5
Caminito Tamega	12400	SDGO	1170	A5
Caminito Tecera	4400	SDGO	1188	B1
Caminito Telmo	6200	SDGO	1268	H2
Caminito Tenedor	-	SDGO	1250	D6
Caminito Terviso	4200	SDGO	1228	B4
Caminito Tiburon	2100	SDGO	1248	A2
Caminito Ticino	4100	SDGO	1228	C4
Caminito Tierra	10900	SDGO	1210	C3
Caminito Tierra Del Sol	-	SDGO	1170	A5
Caminito Tingo	7700	CRLB	1148	A2
Caminito Tirada	9500	SDGO	1209	E5
Caminito Tivoli	-	CHLV	1330	J2
Caminito Tizona	9600	SDGO	1209	E5
Caminito Toga	9500	SDGO	1209	E5
Caminito Tom Morris	2600	SDGO	1227	J7
Caminito Tomas	16000	SDGO	1170	A5
Caminito Tomatillo	9900	SDGO	1209	G6
Caminito Topazio	3000	SDGO	1248	B2
Caminito Toronjo	10200	SDGO	1209	G6
Caminito Torreblanca	3000	SDGO	1187	H2
Caminito Tulipan	1200	SDGO	1350	C1
Caminito Turia	1600	SDGO	1247	H2
Caminito Turnberry	2800	SDGO	1228	A7
	2800	SDGO	1248	A1
Caminito Umbral	4000	SDGO	1268	A4
Caminito Valeriano	-	SDGO	1228	B5
Caminito Valiente	-	CHLV	1330	J2
Caminito Valioso	12400	SDGO	1188	D7
Caminito Valverde	7200	SDGO	1227	H7
Caminito Vantana	11700	SDGO	1210	A4
Caminito Vasto	3300	SDGO	1228	A5
Caminito Vecinos	16500	SDGO	1170	C3
Caminito Velasco	1800	SDGO	1227	H7
Caminito Velasquez	5300	SDGO	1249	F1
Caminito Velez	1800	SDGO	1227	H7
Caminito Venido	2400	SDGO	1268	A3
Caminito Vera	8900	SDGO	1209	D4
Caminito Verano	-	SDGO	1228	A3
Caminito Verde	800	CRLB	1126	J5
Caminito Verdugo	2700	SDGO	1207	H2
Caminito Vibrante	12300	SDGO	1210	C2
Caminito Viejo	2500	SDGO	1227	J6
Caminito Vilos	13000	SDGO	1170	D1
Caminito Violeta	-	SNMS	1109	B7
Caminito Vista Estrellado	14700	SDGO	1187	J1
Caminito Vista Lujo	5200	SDGO	1188	D7
Caminito Vista Pacifica	11000	SDGO	1209	H3
Caminito Vista Serena	11100	SDGO	1209	H3
Caminito Viva	8800	SDGO	1228	A3
Caminito Vizzini	13700	SDGO	1189	G3
Caminito Volar	10100	SDGO	1209	F5
Caminito Vuelo	12500	SDGO	1150	C7
Caminito Westchester	10500	SDGO	1209	E4
Caminito Zabala	7100	SDGO	1228	B4
Caminito Zar	10100	SDGO	1209	E5
Caminito Zocalo	2400	SDGO	1268	A4
Caminito Zopilote	2600	SDGO	1270	A7
Camino Abrojo	11000	SDGO	1169	H5
Camino Acampo	17100	SDCo	1168	G5
Camino Aguila	7800	SDGO	1228	C4
Camino Alegre	-	CRLB	1147	H4
	-	ENCT	1147	J4
	4200	SDCo	1271	H4
Camino Aleta	3000	SDGO	1350	D1
Camino Alisos	1000	SDCo	1028	C3
Camino Alteza	3000	SDGO	1350	D1
Camino Alvaro	7900	CRLB	1147	H3
Camino Amero	6900	SDGO	1268	J2
Camino Ancho	17700	SDGO	1150	D7
Camino Antonio	-	IMPE	6499	E2
Camino Arena	-	CRLB	1148	A3
Camino Armilla	-	SDGO	1169	H5
Camino Arroyo	-	CRLB	1127	J7
Camino Artemisa	2600	SDCo	1253	J2
Camino Atajo	-	CHLV	1310	J7
	-	CHLV	1311	A7
Camino Avena	2500	SDCo	1253	J2
Camino Bailen	400	ESCN	1149	J2
	100	ESCN	1150	A2
Camino Bajada	3600	ESCN	1150	C2
Camino Berdecio	6800	SDGO	1268	J2
Camino Biscay	1100	CHLV	1310	J5
	1100	CHLV	1311	A5
Camino Brisa Del Mar	17300	SDCo	1169	C1
Camino Cabrillo	3200	CRLB	1147	F3
Camino Calabazo	-	SDCo	1311	B7
Camino Calafia	100	SDCo	1088	G5
Camino Calma	4000	SDGO	1228	C4
Camino Canada	13800	SDCo	1232	D7
Camino Cantera	2000	SDCo	1088	C1
Camino Capistrano	6500	CRLB	1127	H4
Camino Carta	-	SNMS	1128	H2
Camino Catalina	600	SOLB	1167	J5
Camino Catalonia	1200	CHLV	1311	A6
Camino Chelsea	-	SDCo	1254	E1
Camino Christina	-	SDCo	1234	E7
	-	SDCo	1254	E1
Camino Ciego	1000	VSTA	1088	A4
Camino Ciego Ct	1100	VSTA	1088	A4
Camino Cielo Azul	-	SDCo	1128	F7
Camino Codorniz	15900	SDGO	1169	H5
Camino Conejo	-	SDCo	1071	A7
Camino Copete	1400	SDGO	1268	H2
Camino Coralino	2900	SDGO	1248	B2
Camino Coronado	3200	CRLB	1147	J3
Camino Corte	-	SDCo	1147	J4
Camino Corto	1500	OCSD	1047	E7
	6200	SDGO	1250	D5
	100	VSTA	1087	G6
Camino Costanero	6300	SDGO	1268	H3
Camino Crest Dr	3100	OCSD	1106	G2
Camino Crisalida	15700	SDGO	1169	G5
Camino Culebra	1900	VSTA	1088	C3
Camino David	4800	SDCo	1290	H7
Camino De Aguas	-	CRLB	1127	J7
Camino De Amor	500	SDCo	1152	H7
Camino De Arriba	-	SDCo	1148	H6
Camino De Astilla	-	SDCo	1171	G2
Camino De Cima Ln	300	SNMS	1129	B2
Camino De Clara	600	SOLB	1167	H6
Camino De Estrellas	-	SDCo	1149	A7
Camino De Indio	-	SDCo	1171	F2
Camino De La Breccia	-	SDGO	1150	C7
Camino De La Cima	400	SNMS	1129	A2
Camino De La Costa	5800	SDGO	1247	F3
E Camino De La Costa	700	SDGO	1247	F3
W Camino De La Costa	-	SDGO	1247	E3
Camino De La Dora	7900	SDCo	1148	J7
Camino De La Mitra	7700	SDCo	1148	H7
Camino De La Plaza	4100	SDGO	1350	E4
Camino De La Reina	100	SDGO	1268	J3
	1300	SDGO	1269	B2
Camino De La Siesta	5000	SDGO	1269	A3
Camino De Las Flores	200	ENCT	1147	G7
Camino De Las Lomas	30600	SDCo	1068	J5
	30400	SDCo	1069	A4
	3600	SDCo	1088	F6
Camino De Las Ondas	900	CRLB	1126	J5
	1000	CRLB	1127	A5
Camino De Las Palmas	2100	LMGR	1290	J1
Camino De Las Piedras	2900	SDCo	1272	G1
Camino De Las Sonrisas	1800	SDGO	1350	F3
Camino De Las Villas	1100	SOLB	1167	H4
Camino De Los Aves	2500	SDCo	1253	J2
Camino De Los Caballos	-	SDCo	1068	D3
Camino De Los Coches	3600	CRLB	1147	J2
	3700	CRLB	1148	A2
Camino De Montecillo	17100	SDCo	1168	H6
Camino De Orchidia	500	ENCT	1147	E7
Camino De Oro	15800	SDCo	1071	B5
Camino De Pilar	3600	ESCN	1150	C3
Camino De Pizza	-	SDGO	1269	B2
Camino De Sablo	-	SDCo	1171	G2
Camino De Vela	1400	SDCo	1128	C3
Camino Degrazia	6900	SDGO	1268	J2
Camino Del Aguila	19300	SDCo	1150	J3
	19900	SDCo	1151	A5
Camino Del Arco	-	CRLB	1127	J7
Camino Del Arroyo	5000	SDGO	1269	A3
Camino Del Arroyo Dr	1500	SDCo	1128	B3
Camino Del Cerro Grande	200	CHLV	1310	J3
Camino Del Collado	2100	SDGO	1227	H4
Camino Del Este	5000	SDGO	1269	C2
Camino Del Lago	1300	SDCo	1128	C3
Camino Del Lemine	-	SDCo	1171	F2
Camino Del Mar	800	DLMR	1187	F5
Camino Del Norte	-	SDCo	1169	G4
	-	SDGO	1169	E3
	14400	SDGO	1170	B7
Camino Del Oro	8300	SDGO	1227	G5
Camino Del Pajaro	6200	SDCo	1168	F5
Camino Del Parque	6400	CRLB	1126	J4
Camino Del Postigo	-	ESCN	1150	A2
Camino Del Prado	6700	CRLB	1126	J5
Camino Del Progresso	200	SDGO	1350	F3
Camino Del Rancho	3000	ENCT	1148	B5
Camino Del Reposo	2200	SDGO	1227	H5
Camino Del Rey	-	CHLV	1311	A7
	6900	SDCo	1068	E3
Camino Del Rincon	6000	SDGO	1250	C5
Camino Del Rio	-	CALX	6680	H2
W Camino Del Rio	3600	SDGO	1268	E4
Camino Del Rio N	1700	SDGO	1269	B3
Camino Del Rio S	1800	SDGO	1269	C3
Camino Del Rio South	-	SDGO	1269	H2
Camino Del Roca	-	SDCo	1171	G2
Camino Del Sequan	1500	SDCo	1253	J2
Camino Del Sol	-	CHLV	1310	J7
	-	CHLV	1311	A6
	8100	SDGO	1227	H5
	1200	SNMS	1108	E5
Camino Del Sol Cir	1100	CRLB	1106	F6
Camino Del Suelo	13700	SDGO	1189	C3
Camino Del Sur	-	SDGO	1169	B3
Camino Del Tierra	11600	SDCo	1211	H7
Camino Del Valle	12800	POWY	1170	C4
Camino Del Vecino	-	SDCo	1234	E7
	2500	SDCo	1254	E1
Camino Del Venado	-	SDCo	1049	D4
Camino Del Verde	9200	SNTE	1231	A6
Camino Deliciada	16000	SDCo	1168	D7
Camino Donaire	1100	SDGO	1350	D1
Camino Dr	-	CALX	6620	J6
	2100	ESCN	1109	D4
Camino Eldorado	500	ENCT	1147	E7
Camino Elena	-	SDCo	1089	D5
Camino Elevado	200	CHLV	1310	H3
Camino Emparrado	12600	SDGO	1150	C7
Camino Encanto	-	CRLB	1147	F3
Camino Entrada	100	CHLV	1310	E7
Camino Esmerado	5600	SDCo	1168	C7
Camino Esperanza	1800	SDGO	1350	F2
Camino Espuelas	1000	CHLV	1310	J5
Camino Estrellado	6700	SDGO	1250	C5
Camino Gato	7900	CRLB	1147	H3
Camino Hills Dr	2300	CRLB	1107	C7
	2300	CRLB	1127	B1
Camino Jasmine Rd	5300	SDCo	1067	G1
Camino La Paz	-	CHLV	1310	J6
Camino Lagarto	2500	SDCo	1253	J2
Camino Lago Vista	9100	SDCo	1291	B5
Camino Largo	100	SDCo	1087	G2
	-	SDCo	1147	J4
	6000	SDGO	1250	D5
Camino Linda	1300	SDCo	1128	B3
Camino Lindo	4000	SDGO	1228	C4
Camino Linoo	-	SDCo	1148	A3
Camino Loma Verde	1900	VSTA	1088	C4
Camino Lorado	1600	SDCo	1128	B4
Camino Lujan	1300	SDGO	1268	J2
Camino Magnifica	-	SNMS	1108	F5
Camino Mangana	1400	SDGO	1268	J2
Camino Maquiladora	6800	SDGO	1351	D2
Camino Marglesa	3600	ESCN	1150	C3
Camino Marzagan	3200	ESCN	1150	A2
Camino Mateo	300	SNMS	1109	C7
Camino Mayor	3700	SDCo	1088	G4

16 INDEX

Camino Michelle

San Diego County Street Index

INDEX 16

Carmel Brooks Wy

STREET Block City Map# Grid

Camino Michelle
3400 CRLB 1127 J5
Camino Miel
- CHLV 1311 A7
Camino Monte Sombra Trl
2400 SDCo 1252 F4
Camino Murrillo
17700 SDGO 1150 C7
Camino Narciso
2500 SDCo 1253 J2
Camino Pacheco
6900 SDGO 1268 J2
Camino Parque
300 OCSD 1086 H4
Camino Patricia
100 VSTA 1087 G6
Camino Paz
4200 SDCo 1271 B4
Camino Paz Ln
9200 SDCo 1271 B4
Camino Pegueno
100 ELCJ 1252 D5
Camino Playa Acapulco
5000 SDGO 1229 J7
Camino Playa Azul
5200 SDGO 1229 J6
Camino Playa Baja
- SDGO 1230 A6
Camino Playa Cancun
- SDGO 1230 A6
Camino Playa Carmel
10900 SDGO 1229 J7
Camino Playa Catalina
11500 SDGO 1230 A7
Camino Playa De Oro
5100 SDGO 1229 J7
Camino Playa Malaga
5300 SDGO 1229 J7
Camino Playa Norte
5300 SDGO 1229 J7
Camino Playa Portofino
5000 SDGO 1229 H7
Camino Privado
4300 SDCo 1167 J3
Camino Puente
6600 CRLB 1128 A4
Camino Rainbow
- SDCo 998 J4
Camino Ramillette
13000 SDGO 1150 D7
Camino Raposa
7700 SDGO 1228 C4
Camino Regalado
1100 SDGO 1350 D1
Camino Revueltos
6900 SDGO 1268 J2
Camino Rico
6100 SDGO 1250 D5
Camino Rio
12100 SDCo 1212 A7
Camino Roberto
4800 SDCo 1290 H7
Camino Robledo
- CRLB 1147 F2
Camino Rociar
1600 SDCo 1128 C3
Camino Ruis
- SDGO 1189 B7
Camino Ruiz
- SDGO 1168 J7
- SDGO 1169 A7
- SDGO 1188 J1
9700 SDGO 1209 C5
Camino San Bernardo
16200 SDCo 1169 E4
15800 SDGO 1169 D4
Camino Sandoval
4200 SDGO 1188 B6
Camino Santa Barbara
700 SOLB 1167 J5
Camino Santa Fe
5200 SDGO 1188 D2
10700 SDGO 1208 H3
8100 SDGO 1208 H1
Camino Sante Fe
- SDCo 1169 D1
Camino Saucito
6600 SDCo 1168 G6
Camino Scarpita
700 SDCo 1233 G7
Camino Selva
6100 SDCo 1168 D3
Camino Serbal
- CRLB 1147 H2
Camino Sereno
- SDCo 1148 H2
Camino Siego
3100 CRLB 1127 J4
Camino Sierra Del Sur
16700 SDCo 1168 G6
Camino Sin Nobre
12600 SDCo 1070 B3
Camino Sin Puente
7900 SDCo 1148 J4
Camino Sueno
1100 SDCo 1088 D7
Camino Susana
13700 SDCo 1232 E6
Camino Tablero
300 ESCN 1150 A2
Camino Teresa
1300 SOLB 1167 H6
Camino Terrnura
1100 SDGO 1350 D1
Camino Tranquilo
7900 SDGO 1228 C4
Camino Valencia
3400 CRLB 1127 J5
Camino Vallareal
3200 ESCN 1150 A2
Camino Verde
2300 SDCo 1028 B5
Camino Vida Roble
1900 CRLB 1127 C3
Camino Vista
19200 SDCo 1153 E3
Camino Vista Real
200 CHLV 1310 F7
Camino Vuelo
12500 SDGO 1150 C7
Camino Ynez
600 SOLB 1167 H6
Camino Zalce
1400 SDGO 1268 J2
Caminto A Casa
500 SNMS 1129 B2
Camiones Wy
4700 SDGO 1350 H5
Camlau Dr
100 CHLV 1330 E1
Camomile Wy
8900 SDGO 1249 D2
Camp De Luz Rd
- SDCo 996 G5
Camp Elliott Rd
- SDGO 1229 G4
Camp Kettle Dr
200 SDCo 1058 F7
(See Page 1058)
Campanera Ct
- SDCo 1085 J3
Campania Av
- SDCo 1169 E2
Campanile Dr
5100 SDGO 1270 B2
Campanile Wy
5600 SDGO 1270 B3
Campbell Ln
- SDCo 1272 F2
Campbell Pl
2500 CRLB 1127 E2
- ESCN 1110 D6
Campbell Ranch Rd
7500 SDCo 1235 H7
Campbell Rd
- VSTA 1107 J1
Campbell Wy
1100 SDCo 1172 G1
Campesino Pl
1800 OCSD 1106 F1
Camphor Ct
2700 CHLV 1311 J4
Camphor Ln
- SDCo 1089 B2
6800 SDGO 1310 F1
Camphor Pl
- CRLB 1127 B5
Campillo Ct
12300 SDGO 1170 B1
Campillo Dr
17300 SDGO 1170 B1
Campillo St
- CALX 6620 G6
Campina Dr
9100 LMSA 1251 A7
Campina Pl
6400 SDGO 1247 H1
Campo Pl
2100 ESCN 1110 B5
Campo Rd
8800 LMSA 1271 A4
9600 SDCo 1271 C5
12100 SDCo 1272 A7
14500 SDCo 1293 A5
17400 SDCo 1314 B5
(See Page 1314)
31200 SDCo 1318 A6
(See Page 1318)
Campo St
1200 SDCo 1321 H6
(See Page 1321)
Campo Truck Trl
2100 SDCo 1298 C7
(See Page 1298)
1800 SDCo 1318 B2
(See Page 1318)
Campo Verde Ct
- ESCN 1109 H4
Campobello St
4500 SDGO 1188 C6
Campolina Ct
300 SDCo 1028 H5
Campus Av
4600 SDGO 1269 C4
Campus Dr
3600 OCSD 1107 A1
Campus Point Ct
4100 SDGO 1208 B7
Campus Point Dr
10300 SDGO 1208 B7
9800 SDGO 1228 B1
Campus View
300 SNMS 1128 H2
Campus View Ct
- SDGO 1187 J7
Campus View Dr
- SNMS 1128 J1
Campus Wy
- SNMS 1128 J1
Camrose Av
4400 SDGO 1228 F5
Camta Cortina
3100 SDCo 1048 B2
Camto Abruzzo
2200 CHLV 1311 G7
Camto Agostino
1300 CHLV 1311 F7
Camto Alcala
1900 CHLV 1331 E1
Camto Amerigo
1300 CHLV 1311 F7
Camto Azul
400 VSTA 1087 G6
Camto Barcelona
300 CHLV 1311 E2
Camto Bartolo
2100 CHLV 1311 F7
Camto Caroline
13900 SDGO 1189 A3
Camto Cinzia
2100 CHLV 1311 F7
Camto Connie
1100 SDCo 1172 H1
Camto Corsica
1300 CHLV 1311 F7
Camto Cremona
1500 CHLV 1311 F7
Camto Dante
1300 CHLV 1311 F7
Camto De Conejos
7000 SDCo 1168 E1
Camto Elda
2100 CHLV 1311 F6
Camto Fabrizio
1300 CHLV 1311 F6
Camto Garibay
1400 CHLV 1311 G7
Camto Leonzio
2100 CHLV 1311 F6
Camto Lorren
14700 SDGO 1187 J1
Camto Lucca
1400 CHLV 1311 G7
Camto Montarosa
1300 CHLV 1311 F6
Camto Nazario
1300 CHLV 1311 F6
Camto Norina
2100 CHLV 1311 F6
Camto Novara
2100 CHLV 1311 G7
Camto Orense Oeste
14700 SDGO 1189 J1
Camto Padova
1400 CHLV 1311 F7
Camto Perugia
1500 CHLV 1311 G7
Camto Pienza
2200 CHLV 1311 G7
Camto Pietro
1300 CHLV 1311 F6
Camto Quieto
32100 SDCo 1048 H7
Camto Rinaldo
2100 CHLV 1311 F7
Camto Santaluz East
7900 SDGO 1169 A6
Camto Santaluz Norte
7900 SDGO 1169 A6
Camto Santaluz Sur
7800 SDGO 1189 A1
Camto Santaluz West
8100 SDGO 1169 A7
Camto Santiago
1500 CHLV 1331 D1
Camto Santo Tomas
14500 SDCo 1188 H2
Camto Sardinia
1400 CHLV 1311 G7
Camto Sicilia
1400 CHLV 1311 G7
Camto Soria
1500 CHLV 1331 D1
Camto Stella
6500 SDGO 1188 F6
Camto Treviana
1800 CHLV 1331 E1
Camto Turin
2200 CHLV 1311 F7
Camto Veranza
1300 CHLV 1311 G7
Camto Via Campestre
14700 SDGO 1187 J1
Camto Vistana
14000 SDGO 1188 J2
14000 SDGO 1189 A2
Camulos St
2700 SDGO 1268 B5
Cana Ln
1300 SDCo 1027 J5
Canadian Honker Rd
29800 SDCo 1297 F6
(See Page 1297)
Canal Rd
16600 SDCo 1091 C3
Canal St
600 CALX 6620 E7
1800 SDGO 1330 A6
W Canal St
- CALX 6620 F7
Canaleja Wy
- SDGO 1189 F7
Cananea St
200 VSTA 1087 H4
Canario St
4000 CRLB 1106 F7
Canarios Ct
800 CHLV 1310 J6
Canary Ct
1100 SNMS 1128 E3
Canary Wy
7900 SDGO 1249 B6
Canarywood Ct
10800 SDGO 1209 J2
Canberra Ct
10500 SDCo 1169 F2
Cancha De Golf
100 SDCo 1168 C7
Canciones Del Cielo
1900 VSTA 1088 C3
Cancun Ct
- IMPE 6499 G1
400 SDCo 1027 E5
Cancun Dr
- IMPE 6499 G1
Candela Pl
13000 SDGO 1187 J5
Candera Ln
200 SNMS 1109 B7
Candia Ct
4200 OCSD 1087 C6
Candice Ct
- SDCo 1048 A4
Candice Pl
100 VSTA 1087 G3
Candida St
9400 SDGO 1209 E6
Candil Pl
2900 CRLB 1127 H7
Candle Ln
1800 SDCo 1252 C3
Candle Wy
- SDCo 1090 D1
Candleberry Ct
11200 SDGO 1189 J2
Candlelight Dr
5300 SDGO 1247 H4
Candlelight Glen
1600 ESCN 1129 G5
Candlelight Pl
900 SDGO 1247 H4
Candlelight St
5200 OCSD 1107 F4
Candlelite Dr
900 SNMS 1109 A5
Candlewood Ln
1100 SDCo 1271 J1
Candlewood Pl
2700 OCSD 1087 E5
Candy Ln
100 ENCT 1167 J1
9600 SDCo 1271 C1
Candy Rose Ct
12200 SDGO 1210 B1
Candy Rose Wy
- SDGO 1190 B7
- SDGO 1210 B1
Candy Tuft Path
13500 SDGO 1188 F4
Cane Rd
14200 SDCo 1070 F4
Caneel Bay Ct
4600 OCSD 1066 J6
Caneridge Pl
- SDGO 1190 A7
Caneridge Rd
- SDGO 1190 A7
Canfield Pl
18200 SDGO 1150 C6
Canfield Rd
35600 SDCo 1032 E4
Canforero Ter
9700 SDGO 1249 F1
Canis Ln
8800 SDGO 1209 D2
Canna Dr
- NATC 1289 H7
Cannas Ct
1700 CRLB 1127 E6
Canneli Dr
13800 POWY 1190 F4
Cannes Pl
1800 CHLV 1311 F1
Canning Av
3800 SDGO 1248 G4
Canning Ct
5200 SDGO 1248 G4
Canning Pl
5200 SDGO 1248 G4
Cannington Dr
4800 SDGO 1248 J1
Cannon Gate
2200 SDCo 1027 G6
Cannon Rd
2200 CRLB 1107 D5
700 CRLB 1126 G2
- CRLB 1127 A1
1800 ImCo 6500 D7
3400 OCSD 1107 E4
- SDCo 1126 H2
Cannondale Ct
800 SNMS 1128 F4
Canoe Creek Wy
1400 CHLV 1312 A6
(See Page 1312)
Canon Dr
- IMPE 6439 F3
Canon Perdido St
1300 CHLV 1331 C2
Canon St
2800 SDGO 1288 B2
Canonita Dr
3500 SDCo 1028 E5
Canopus Dr
1600 SDGO 1209 E6
Canopy Dr
600 SNMS 1108 G6
Canopy Ridge Ln
6600 SDGO 1208 G4
Canosa Av
5100 SDGO 1248 G2
Canright Wy
9900 SDGO 1209 A5
Canta Lomas
2000 SDCo 1252 C7
Cantaberra Ct
7000 SDGO 1188 H4
Cantaloupe St
- ImCo 6560 B7
Cantamar Pl
1900 SDGO 1330 A7
Cantamar Rd
1900 SDGO 1330 A7
Cantara Ln
- VSTA 1107 E2
Cantara Wy
24800 SDCo 1173 G3
Cantaranas
16900 SDCo 1168 B3
Cantare Trl
13600 SDGO 1188 H3
Cantata Dr
2100 CHLV 1311 D2
Cantata Ln
7600 SDGO 1168 J7
Cantegra Glen
- ESCN 1150 B1
Canter Heights Dr
- SDGO 1208 C2
Canter Rd
1200 SDCo 1130 C3
Canterbury Ct
4700 OCSD 1087 D4
Canterbury Dr
4300 LMSA 1270 H3
4900 SDGO 1269 G2
E Canterbury Dr
4100 SDGO 1269 H3
Canterbury Pl
- ESCN 1129 H4
Canterbury St
- CRLB 1107 A4
Cantero Wy
3000 CRLB 1147 H1
Cantil St
6700 CRLB 1127 H5
Cantle Ln
- ENCT 1148 C3
Canton Ct
1200 ENCT 1167 F1
Canton Dr
7300 LMGR 1290 G1
Canton Ridge Terr
15500 SDGO 1169 B3
E Cantu Av
- CALX 6620 J7
Canvas Dr
1400 CHLV 1311 F7
Canvas St
- OCSD 1087 B1
Canvasback Ct
1000 CRLB 1127 B6
Canvasback Dr
30000 SDCo 1297 G6
(See Page 1297)
Canyon Back Ln
13300 POWY 1190 E1
Canyon Bluff Ct
6200 SDGO 1208 G3
Canyon Breeze Dr
7300 SDGO 1208 J3
Canyon Country Ln
- SDCo 1089 D1
Canyon Creek Av
- CHLV 1311 F5
Canyon Creek Rd
2400 ESCN 1130 D6
Canyon Creek Wy
1000 ESCN 1130 D6
Canyon Crest Dr
2500 ESCN 1130 F2
- SDGO 1270 B1
Canyon Crest Pt
- SDGO 1188 F4
Canyon Ct
1400 CHLV 1311 B4
Canyon De Oro
3800 SDCo 1148 E3
Canyon Dr
500 CHLV 1311 B4
100 OCSD 1086 C6
1100 SDCo 1108 D1
10300 SDCo 1109 F1
1300 SDCo 1136 C6
3100 SDCo 1156 D1
- SDCo 1233 G6
- SDCo 1252 J3
500 SOLB 1167 F6
N Canyon Dr
- SDCo 1086 B5
Canyon Estates Rd
30400 SDCo 1068 A4
Canyon Glen Ct
7200 SDGO 1188 J4
Canyon Heights Rd
900 SDCo 998 H6
Canyon Hill Ct
7200 SDGO 1208 J3
Canyon Hill Ln
10900 SDGO 1208 J4
Canyon Hill Pl
7100 SDGO 1208 J3
Canyon Hill Wy
7200 SDGO 1208 J3
Canyon Lake Dr
10400 SDGO 1209 G4
Canyon Ln
- ESCN 1130 A6
Canyon Lodge Pl
- OCSD 1086 D7
Canyon Mesa Ln
10900 SDGO 1209 A3
Canyon Oak Pl
2700 ESCN 1129 D4
Canyon Park Dr
11500 SNTE 1231 H5
Canyon Park Ter
9100 SNTE 1231 G5
Canyon Pass
15100 POWY 1171 A6
Canyon Peak Ln
7300 SDGO 1208 J3
Canyon Pl
1800 CRLB 1106 G4
600 SOLB 1167 F5
Canyon Point Ct
11000 SDGO 1209 A3
Canyon Point Ln
7600 SDGO 1209 A3
Canyon Rd
2200 ESCN 1130 D6
2600 ESCN 1150 C1
- SDCo 1090 D1
2600 SDCo 1130 C7
1700 SDCo 1291 B1
Canyon Ridge Dr
300 CHLV 1311 B3
Canyon Ridge Ln
1200 SDCo 1130 D6
Canyon Rim Dr
400 SDCo 1253 A2
Canyon Rim Row
6600 SDGO 1268 H3
Canyon Slope Pl
7900 SDGO 1250 D3
Canyon St
3100 CRLB 1106 G4
Canyon Ter
2400 ESCN 1130 D6
Canyon Verde Ln
2400 SDCo 1028 A7
Canyon View Dr
3200 OCSD 1086 D3
Canyon View Glen
2200 ESCN 1109 C3
Canyon View Ln
7300 LMGR 1270 F7
Canyon View Rd
2200 SDCo 996 H3
Canyon View Wy
15500 POWY 1171 A6
Canyon Vista Ct
6500 SDGO 1248 H6
Canyon Vista Dr
2300 SDCo 1028 A1
Canyon Vista Wy
4400 OCSD 1086 J3
Canyon Wash Ct
29700 SDCo 1069 A5
Canyon Way Ct
29700 SDCo 1069 A5
Canyonridge Pl
10300 SDCo 1271 E7
Canyonside Ct
10000 SDCo 1271 E6
Canyonside Park Drwy
- SDGO 1189 C7
Canyonside Wy
300 OCSD 1086 B6
Canyontop St
10000 SDCo 1271 E6
Canyonview Ct
10000 SDCo 1271 E6
Canyonwood Ln
10000 SDCo 1271 E6
Capalina Rd
3500 SNMS 1108 D6
Capazo Ct
2900 CRLB 1127 H4
Capcano Rd
8800 SDGO 1189 D7
Cape Aire Ln
1100 CRLB 1106 G7
Cape Breton Rd
700 SDCo 1088 D7
Cape Cod Bay Ct
- SDGO 1270 C7
Cape Cod Cir
2900 CRLB 1107 A4
Cape Cod Ct
9400 SDCo 1271 C6
Cape Horn
1700 SDCo 1136 B7
Cape Jewels Tr
5700 SDGO 1188 E4
Cape May
1700 CRLB 1106 H6
Cape May Av
5000 SDGO 1267 J6
4500 SDGO 1268 A6
Cape May Pl
2000 SDGO 1267 J5
Capehart St
5000 SDGO 1228 E7
Capella Ct
3700 SDCo 1271 A5
Capella Dr
- SDGO 1209 E7
Capello Ct
- SDCo 1169 E2
Caper Wy
2100 CHLV 1331 H3
Capewood Ln
13900 SDGO 1189 J2
Capilla Ct
17000 SDGO 1169 J2
Capilla Pl
17000 SDGO 1169 H2
Capilla Rd
11100 SDGO 1169 H2
Capistrano Av
1600 SDCo 1291 C2
Capistrano Dr
600 OCSD 1085 J6
900 OCSD 1086 A4
Capistrano Gn
- ESCN 1109 D5
Capistrano Ln
1200 VSTA 1107 E1
Capistrano Pl
800 SDGO 1267 H4
Capistrano St
2000 SDGO 1268 B7
1800 SDGO 1288 B1
Capistrano Wy
2200 CHLV 1331 H2
- SNMS 1129 C1
Capitan Av
2400 SDGO 1289 E1
Capitol St
3800 LMSA 1270 F5
Capps St
2800 SDGO 1269 E6
Capra Wy
- SDCo 1028 C1
Capri Ct
2000 SDCo 1272 C3
Capri Dr
6100 SDGO 1250 C7
700 VSTA 1087 J5
Capri Rd
900 ENCT 1147 C3
Capri Wy
3400 OCSD 1106 J2
Caprice Pl
11300 SDCo 1089 H7
Capricho Wy
300 OCSD 1086 G2
Capricorn Ln
4100 SDGO 1227 J3
Capricorn Wy
8500 SDGO 1209 C2
Capriole Ct
5300 SDCo 1311 A2
Caprise Dr
1100 SNMS 1128 E6
Caps Wy
2500 SDCo 998 B6
Capstan Dr
- CRLB 1127 A7
Capstone Dr
13100 SDGO 1188 B4
Captain's Ct
8600 SDCo 1068 J4
Car Country Dr
5200 CRLB 1126 H2
Car St
1100 SDGO 1290 H2
Cara Ct
8800 SDCo 1291 A5
Cara Ln
16000 SDCo 1071 B6
Cara St
400 ESCN 1130 A6
Caracara Cir
1400 ELCJ 1252 A6
Caracas Pl
5600 SDCo 1067 J1
Caracol Ct
2000 CRLB 1127 F6
Caramay Pl
1500 SDGO 1350 E2
Carancho St
3800 LMSA 1270 F5
Caras Cir
15900 SDCo 1174 B4
Caravallo Ct
3200 CRLB 1147 J1
Caravelle Pl
10800 SDGO 1249 J2
Caraway St
2000 ESCN 1109 F5
9700 SDCo 1232 B3
Carbajal Ct
- CHLV 1330 H3
Carbet Pl
10800 SDGO 1249 H2
Carbine Wy
- SDGO 1350 H2
Carbo Ct
3800 LMSA 1270 H5
Cardamom Ct
800 CHLV 1330 J1
Cardeno Dr
6200 SDGO 1247 J1
Cardiff Bay Dr
4800 OCSD 1066 J6
Cardiff Dr
1100 ENCT 1167 F2
Cardiff St
700 SDGO 1290 H2
Cardigan Wy
1900 SDGO 1269 A1
Cardin St
4600 SDGO 1249 A2
Cardinal Ct
7700 SDGO 1249 A6
1000 SNMS 1128 E3
Cardinal Dr
2100 SDGO 1249 A7
2000 SDGO 1269 A1
Cardinal Ln
2500 SDGO 1249 A7
Cardinal Pl
1200 CHLV 1330 G2
7600 SDGO 1249 A7
Cardinal Rd
2600 SDGO 1249 A7
Cardinal Wy
200 OCSD 1086 J1
- SDCo 1023 F3
Cardona Av
700 CHLV 1310 J5
Cardoza Dr
9900 SNTE 1231 D3
Carefree Dr
700 SDGO 1290 E5
10100 SNTE 1231 D3
Caren Rd
1100 VSTA 1087 E6
Carennac Pl
1900 CHLV 1311 G1
Caretta Wy
500 ENCT 1167 D2
Carey Rd
100 OCSD 1086 C6
N Carey Rd
700 OCSD 1086 C6
Careybrook Ln
7500 SDGO 1290 G5
Cargill Av
8100 SDGO 1228 C4
Cari Ann Ct
500 SDCo 1028 F3
Carib Ct
4400 SDGO 1248 F1
Carib Dr
- SDCo 1128 F7
- SDCo 1148 F1
Caribe Cay Blvd
- CORD 1329 D1
Caribe Cay North Blvd
- CORD 1329 E1
Caribou Ct
- CRLB 1127 G1
7100 SDGO 1188 J4
Carie Wy
2200 SDCo 1253 H2
Carillo Cir
600 OCSD 1066 J5
Carillo Rd
3300 SDCo 1078 J6
(See Page 1078)
Carillon Ct
10700 SDGO 1209 J2
Caringa Wy
2300 CRLB 1127 G7
Carino Wy
3900 OCSD 1086 G2
Carioca Ct
10200 SDGO 1249 G1
Carissa Av
1400 CHLV 1330 H3
Carissa Ct
1400 CHLV 1330 H3
Carissa Dr
200 OCSD 1087 A1
Carissa Ln
10000 SDCo 1291 D2
Carissa Wy
- SDCo 1127 D4
Carita Cove
13000 SDGO 1188 F4
Carita Ct
9700 SNTE 1231 A4
Carita Rd
9200 SNTE 1231 A4
Cariuto Ct
10800 SDGO 1249 H2
Carl Dr
18000 SDCo 1274 D4
Carla Av
500 CHLV 1310 D6
Carla Ct
10600 SDCo 1089 G3
Carla Wy
500 SDGO 1247 G4
Carlann Dr
100 SNMS 1108 H6
Carlann Ln
600 ESCN 1110 C6
Carlata Ln
27400 SDCo 1091 G4
Carleton Sq
1400 SDGO 1288 A1
Carleton St
3300 SDGO 1288 B2
Carlette St
8000 LMSA 1250 H7
Carley Cir
8900 SDGO 1209 D1
Carlin Heights
- SDCo 1130 D7
Carlin Pl
4400 LMSA 1271 A3
Carlin St
100 SDCo 1152 D7
Carlina St
7400 CRLB 1147 J1
Carling Dr
4400 SDGO 1270 C4
Carling Wy
6100 SDGO 1270 C4
Carlisle Dr
8400 LMGR 1290 H2
Carlo St
400 SNMS 1108 C6
Carlos Canyon Ct
500 CHLV 1310 J4
Carlos Canyon Dr
1100 CHLV 1310 J4
Carlos Dr
- OCSD 1086 F2
Carlos St
300 SDGO 1289 H4
Carlota St
11000 SDGO 1169 J6
Carlotta Wy
- OCSD 1086 H3
Carlow Ct
600 ELCJ 1251 B4
Carlow Ln
- ELCJ 1251 B4
Carlow St
2600 ELCJ 1251 B4
Carlow Wy
600 ELCJ 1251 B4
Carls Wy
7400 LMGR 1270 G7
Carlsbad Blvd
2200 CRLB 1106 D4
- CRLB 1126 G4
7400 CRLB 1146 J1
Carlsbad Ct
1000 SDGO 1290 H2
Carlsbad St
1100 SDCo 1290 J2
1300 SDGO 1290 H2
Carlsbad Village Dr
300 CRLB 1106 E5
2900 CRLB 1107 A4
Carlson Ct
14400 POWY 1190 H1
300 VSTA 1107 C1
Carlson St
14600 POWY 1190 H1
Carlton Hills Blvd
10000 SNTE 1231 B4
Carlton Oaks Dr
8500 SNTE 1230 J6
9400 SNTE 1231 B5
Carlton Pl
9900 SNTE 1231 A3
Carlton Wy
- SDCo 1048 E1
Carly Ct
1400 SDGO 1290 F5
Carmack Wy
9500 SNTE 1231 B3
Carmar Wy
2800 SDGO 1310 F2
Carmel Av
- CHLV 1311 C7
Carmel Brooks Wy
4000 SDGO 1188 A7

17 INDEX
Carmel Canyon Rd
INDEX 17
Centerstage Glen

San Diego County Street Index

SAN DIEGO CO.

STREET
Block City Map# Grid

Carmel Canyon Rd
- SDGO 1188 C6
Carmel Cape
12400 SDGO 1188 A7
Carmel Center Rd
4500 SDGO 1188 B6
Carmel Cir
700 VSTA 1087 J3
Carmel Country Rd
11700 SDGO 1188 C6
- SDGO 1208 D1
Carmel Creek Rd
- SDGO 1188 B5
- SDGO 1208 B3
Carmel Creeper Pl
- ENCT 1147 C5
Carmel Dr
4300 CRLB 1106 J5
Carmel Grove Rd
- SDGO 1188 A7
Carmel Knolls Dr
- SDGO 1188 D5
Carmel Knolls Rd
4500 SDGO 1188 C6
Carmel Mission Rd
- SDGO 1188 B6
Carmel Mountain Rd
8900 SDGO 1189 C4
12000 SDGO 1190 A1
- SDGO 1208 C3
Carmel Mtn Rd
11600 SDGO 1190 A1
- SDGO 1208 G1
Carmel Park Dr
12000 SDGO 1188 B7
Carmel Pointe
12400 SDGO 1188 A7
Carmel Ridge Rd
13900 SDGO 1190 A2
Carmel Springs Wy
3900 SDGO 1188 A7
Carmel St
400 SNMS 1108 J7
E Carmel St
100 SNMS 1128 J1
S Carmel St
200 SNMS 1129 A1
Carmel Ter
- SNMS 1128 J1
Carmel Valley Rd
100 DLMR 1187 G7
- SDGO 1169 D7
5300 SDGO 1188 E5
- SDGO 1189 A2
2500 SDGO 1207 H1
Carmel View Rd
3700 SDGO 1188 A7
Carmel Vista Rd
12100 SDGO 1187 J7
Carmelina Dr
1800 SDGO 1269 C3
Carmelita Pl
200 SOLB 1167 F7
Carmelo Dr
1500 OCSD 1085 J6
Carmelo St
4400 SDGO 1287 H2
Carmen Ct
900 SDCo 1109 B5
Carmen Dr
4400 SDCo 1271 F3
Carmen St
5500 SDGO 1290 B1
Carmena Rd
23500 SDCo 1173 D3
Carmenita Rd
7200 LMSA 1270 F5
Carmichael Dr
9300 SDCo 1271 B2
Carmir Dr
8800 SNTE 1251 A1
Carmona Ct
400 CHLV 1310 H4
Carnaby Ct
4500 CRLB 1106 J5
Carnaby Wy
4800 SDGO 1249 D2
Carnation Av
100 IMPB 1329 E7
3300 SDCo 1172 C3
Carnation Ct
600 SNMS 1128 H3
Carnation Dr
6700 CRLB 1127 A6
Carnation Glen
3700 ESCN 1150 C3
Carnation Ln
600 SDCo 1027 G4
Carnation St
- SDCo 1086 A4
Carnegie Ct
3200 SDGO 1228 C6
Carnegie Dr
3700 OCSD 1087 A7
Carnegie Pl
3100 SDGO 1228 C6
Carnegie St
5800 SDGO 1228 C6
Carnegie Wy
3200 SDGO 1228 C6
Carnelian Ct
2200 CRLB 1127 F6
Carnelian Ln
3400 OCSD 1107 D2
Carnelian St
1100 ELCJ 1252 A3
Carnell Av
3200 SDGO 1350 D1
Carnell Ct
1300 SDGO 1350 D1
Carnero Pl
10200 SDCo 1231 F3
Carneros Valley St
- CHLV 1331 B1
Carnes Rd
- SDCo 1086 A2
Carney Ln
13000 SDCo 1050 C4
Carney Rd
36300 SDCo 1050 C5
Carnitas St
14300 POWY 1190 G1
Carnoustie Rd
9500 SDGO 1352 A2
Carnton Wy
17400 SDGO 1170 A1
Carny St
- SDGO 1288 A5
Carob Ln
1700 SDCo 1099 F2
(See Page 1099)
Carob Tree Ln
1800 SDCo 1252 D3
Carob Wy
100 CORD 1288 G7
200 OCSD 1086 J2
Carol Ann Ln
0 RivC 999 G1
Carol Ct
700 SNMS 1109 B6
Carol Glen Ct
7700 SDGO 1189 A3
Carol Pl
800 CRLB 1106 F6
1300 NATC 1290 C7
Carol Rd
- SDCo 1172 B3
Carol St
6000 SDGO 1270 C3
1800 SDGO 1330 A6
Carol View Dr
2300 ENCT 1167 E3
Carol Wy
3700 SDCo 1271 A5
Caroldale Row
6000 SDGO 1248 A1
Carolee Av
13100 SDGO 1189 D4
Carolina Ln
900 SDGO 1290 A3
Carolina Pl
4900 SDGO 1290 A3
Carolina Rd
400 DLMR 1187 F5
Carolina St
700 IMPB 1329 G7
Caroline Dr
4700 SDGO 1269 J3
Caroline Ln
4900 SDCo 1047 E6
Caroline Wy
100 ESCN 1129 G4
Carolita
- SDCo 1232 D6
Carolton Ln
1900 SDCo 1028 A6
Carolwood Dr
500 SDGO 1290 H5
Carolyn Cir
3200 OCSD 1086 E5
Carolyn Dr
1800 CHLV 1311 D5
Carolyn Pl
2300 ENCT 1147 J7
Carolyn Vista Ln
5300 SDCo 1311 A3
Carom Wy
1700 CHLV 1331 H2
Carousel Ln
13100 SDGO 1187 J7
Caroway Ct
- SDCo 1272 C6
Carowind Ln
11500 SDGO 1210 G1
Carpa Ct
7200 CRLB 1128 A7
Carpenter Ln
4000 SDCo 1271 G4
Carpenter Rd
2300 OCSD 1086 C5
Carpinteria St
1400 CHLV 1331 C2
Carque Rd
- SDCo 1254 A1
Carr Dr
3100 OCSD 1107 B1
Carrando Dr
2700 SDCo 1099 G4
(See Page 1099)
Carranza Dr
17000 SDGO 1169 H1
Carrara Pl
7100 SDGO 1228 E4
Carrera Ct
2400 SDCo 1271 B7
Carreta Ct
10300 SNTE 1231 E2
Carreta Dr
10200 SNTE 1231 E3
Carretta Dr
10100 SNTE 1231 E3
Carriage Cir
2400 OCSD 1106 H1
1600 VSTA 1107 D1
Carriage Ct
- SDGO 1188 D5
Carriage Heights Cir
- POWY 1190 D4
Carriage Heights Wy
- POWY 1190 D4
Carriage Hills Ct
17000 POWY 1170 D2
Carriage Ln
1700 SDCo 1028 B5
Carriage Rd
- POWY 1190 D3
900 SNMS 1109 A5
S Carriage Rd
12800 POWY 1190 D5
Carriage Run Dr
4800 SDGO 1208 C2
Carriagedale Row
2600 SDGO 1248 A1
Carribean Wy
8600 SNTE 1230 H7
Carrie Cir
500 SNMS 1108 H6
Carrie Ellen Ct
10100 SNTE 1231 A3
Carrie Ln
- SNTE 1231 E3
Carrie Ridge Wy
7400 SDGO 1290 G6
Carrillo Wy
- CRLB 1127 J4
Carrington Dr
10500 SDGO 1208 J4
Carrio Dr
1300 SDCo 1068 A6
Carriso St
1200 SDCo 1321 H6
(See Page 1321)
Carrizo Dr
7200 SDGO 1227 G7
Carrizo Gorge Rd
1900 SDCo 1301 G7
(See Page 1301)
1900 SDCo 1321 G1
(See Page 1321)
Carrizo Pl
1600 ESCN 1110 A5
Carroll Canyon Rd
4900 SDGO 1208 E7
9400 SDGO 1209 E5
Carroll Center Rd
9200 SDGO 1209 E5
Carroll Ln
2300 SDCo 1130 F3
Carroll Park Ct
9200 SDGO 1208 H7
Carroll Park Dr
9200 SDGO 1208 H7
Carroll Rd
6500 SDGO 1208 G7
7600 SDGO 1209 A7
7600 SDGO 1229 A1
Carroll Wy
8900 SDGO 1209 A7
Carrollton Sq
12100 SDGO 1190 A1
Carrot Wood Glen
1100 ESCN 1129 F1
Carroza Ct
11200 SDGO 1249 J1
Carryll Park Ct
1000 SDCo 1027 H3
Carson Pl
9700 SDCo 1149 D4
Carson St
- CORD 1288 F4
3800 SDGO 1248 E4
Carstenz
- SNMS 1128 C1
Carta Ln
9600 SDCo 1233 B3
Cartagena Dr
4200 SDGO 1270 D4
Cartegena Wy
2300 OCSD 1106 J1
Carter Pl
7800 LMSA 1270 G2
Carter Rd
600 ImCo 6319 B6
(See Page 6319)
Carter St
200 ELCJ 1251 F7
Carthage St
6900 SDGO 1250 B6
Carthay Cir
9200 SDCo 1271 B4
Cartulina Rd
4200 SDGO 1249 J2
Cartwright St
6800 SDGO 1249 J6
Carvalos Dr
500 SDCo 1310 D6
Carveacre Rd
3500 SDCo 1275 B4
Carver St
100 CHLV 1330 E4
Cary Ct
1400 ELCJ 1252 A7
Cary Wy
1300 SDGO 1247 J4
Caryl Dr
- SNTE 1231 E7
Caryl St
- SNTE 1231 E7
Caryn Ct
25700 SDCo 1174 A3
Casa Alta
2200 SDCo 1271 D7
Casa Avenida
12600 POWY 1170 C6
Casa Blanca Ct
3100 SDCo 1310 H1
Casa Blanca Pl
8100 SDGO 1209 B4
Casa Bonita Ct
4800 SDCo 1310 H1
Casa Bonita Dr
3100 SDCo 1310 H1
Casa Bonita Wy
1900 ESCN 1129 J6
1100 VSTA 1107 F1
Casa Buena Wy
4200 OCSD 1086 J3
Casa Cielo
2200 SDCo 1271 B7
Casa Ct
12800 POWY 1190 D5
- SNTE 1231 E3
Casa De Carol
2300 SDCo 1173 A6
Casa De La Torre Ct
9600 SDCo 1271 C3
Casa De Machado
4200 SDCo 1271 C3
Casa De Oro Blvd
10100 SDCo 1271 E4
Casa De Oro Pl
800 ESCN 1129 J6
Casa De Roca Wy
1300 SDCo 1234 J6
Casa De Vereda
2000 SDCo 1088 D4
Casa Del Sol
28700 SDCo 1090 A1
Casa Del Sol Ct
4500 SDGO 1350 H1
Casa Dr
4800 OCSD 1066 J7
Casa Grande Av
13100 SDCo 1232 C2
Casa Grande Wy
5700 SDCo 1290 J6
Casa Hermosa Ct
- ENCT 1148 A5
Casa Linda Wy
2700 SNMS 1108 C5
Casa Ln
7000 LMGR 1270 F6
Casa Loma Ct
3100 SDCo 1310 H1
Casa Mila Dr
1600 CHLV 1331 D2
Casa Morro St
1800 CHLV 1331 H2
Casa Nova Ct
4500 SDGO 1350 H1
Casa Nueva St
10000 SDCo 1271 E6
Casa Pl
1600 NATC 1310 B1
Casa Real Ct
700 VSTA 1087 F5
Casa Real Ln
1500 SNMS 1109 D6
Casa Torre Wy
1800 CHLV 1331 H2
Casa Verde Ct
3200 SDCo 1310 H1
Casa Vista
- POWY 1190 E5
Casa Vista Rd
12600 SDCo 1232 B4
Casaba Ln
- OCSD 1086 G3
Casablanca Ct
1900 VSTA 1107 H4
Casablanca Wy
3400 SDCo 1028 D7
Casals Pl
4800 SDGO 1250 A1
Casca Wy
3300 CRLB 1148 A1
Cascada Wy
- SDGO 1250 A3
Cascade Crossing
14200 POWY 1150 G7
Cascade Ct
3700 SDGO 1228 D5
Cascade Pl
- CHLV 1331 A2
1400 SDCo 1231 F7
Cascade Pl
1400 SDCo 1251 F1
Cascade Rd
300 SDCo 1251 F1
Cascade St
- CRLB 1107 B6
6300 SDGO 1228 D5
Cascade Wy
5000 OCSD 1067 A6
Cascadia Ln
1400 ENCT 1147 E5
Cascadita Cir
4500 OCSD 1087 A2
Cascajo Ct
10800 SDGO 1249 J2
Casco Ct
- SDGO 1189 B6
Case Springs Rd
- SDCo 996 B6
Case St
8300 LMSA 1270 H1
Caseman Av
3900 SDGO 1330 F7
Casement St
2300 SDGO 1249 C7
Caseras Dr
3400 OCSD 1086 J7
Casero Ct
12200 SDGO 1170 B3
Casero Pl
1700 ESCN 1129 F6
12200 SDGO 1170 B3
Casero Rd
16500 SDGO 1170 B3
Casey Glen
16000 SDGO 1169 B3
Casey St
2500 SDGO 1290 G7
Casino Wy
5400 SDCo 1253 D5
Casita Ln
700 SNMS 1108 E5
Casita Wy
3900 SDGO 1270 E5
Casitas Ct
- CHLV 1310 C7
Casitas Del Sol
2300 SDCo 1028 B2
Casitas Ln
- ESCN 1129 F4
Casitas St
4400 SDGO 1287 H3
Casmeg Wy
3000 SDCo 1272 C6
Casner Rd
19700 SDCo 1154 A2
Casper Dr
7200 SDGO 1250 F5
Casper Ln
200 VSTA 1087 J6
Casper St
1300 OCSD 1087 D3
Caspi Gardens Dr
9800 SNTE 1231 D4
Caspian Dr
5000 OCSD 1087 B1
Caspian Pl
11300 SDGO 1210 J2
Caspian Wy
1100 CRLB 1127 B5
300 IMPB 1349 F1
Cass St
5300 SDGO 1247 H4
Cassandra Ln
5100 SDGO 1248 A4
Cassanna Wy
4300 OCSD 1087 A4
Casselberry Wy
6600 SDGO 1250 E5
Casselman Ct
- CHLV 1310 C4
Casselman Pl
- CHLV 1310 C4
Casselman St
500 CHLV 1309 J5
400 CHLV 1310 A5
Cassia Glen Dr
10200 SDCo 1169 E2
Cassia Pl
700 CHLV 1310 G6
17600 SDGO 1149 J7
Cassia Rd
2800 CRLB 1127 E4
- SDCo 1127 D5
Cassidy St
200 OCSD 1106 C3
Cassini Ct
- SDGO 1210 B1
Cassins St
- SDCo 1127 B6
Cassio Ct
1200 VSTA 1107 H4
Cassioepia Wy
8800 SDGO 1209 D1
Cassiopeia Ln
1300 SDGO 1350 H1
Cassou Rd
800 SDCo 1108 G2
100 SNMS 1108 J2
Cassowary Ct
- SDGO 1209 H1
Castaic Ct
9700 SNTE 1231 C4
Castaic Pl
1600 CHLV 1331 E2
Castana Plz
1000 CHLV 1311 A6
Castana St
4700 SDGO 1289 J4
5100 SDGO 1290 A4
Castaneda Dr
- ESCN 1150 B1
Castano Ln
8600 SDCo 1232 F6
Castaway Cove
700 SDGO 1330 J6
Casteel Ct
1500 SDGO 1290 D6
Casteel Ln
- SDCo 1172 G2
Castejon Dr
6100 SDGO 1247 J1
Castelar St
4600 SDGO 1268 A5
Castellana Rd
1700 SDGO 1227 G6
Castellano Dr
5100 OCSD 1067 A5
Castello Cir
- SDCo 1169 E2
Castellon Ter
2500 SDCo 1272 D2
Castile Wy
11600 SDGO 1190 A3
Castilian Ct
35500 SDCo 1028 J6
Castilla Pl
2800 CRLB 1147 G2
Castilla St
6100 SNTE 1231 G7
Castilla Wy
2100 OCSD 1106 J1
Castillo Glen
5400 SDGO 1188 D4
Castle Av
4700 SDGO 1269 J5
Castle Brook Ct
8800 SDCo 1232 C6
Castle Court Dr
12600 SDCo 1232 B4
Castle Creek Ln
- SDCo 1068 J6
Castle Creek Wy
- SDCo 1069 A6
Castle Ct
7200 LMGR 1270 F7
Castle Glen
1800 ESCN 1129 F5
Castle Glen Dr
3400 SDGO 1249 D4
Castle Heights Rd
10700 SDCo 1069 F5
Castle Hills Dr
5100 SDGO 1247 J4
Castle Island Cove
- SDGO 1330 H6
Castle Peak Ln
- SDCo 1273 D6
Castle View Dr
- SDCo 1069 D7
Castlebay
2100 SDCo 1027 G6
Castlecrest Dr
- SDCo 1069 F5
Castlegarden Ct
3400 SDCo 1068 F6
Castlegate Ln
2300 VSTA 1088 C6
Castlehill Rd
2700 CHLV 1311 J6
Castleridge Rd
- SDCo 1069 D6
Castleton Dr
5900 SDGO 1248 H2
Castleton Wy
4500 SDGO 1248 H2
Castlewood Ct
2800 CHLV 1312 B6
(See Page 1312)
- SDCo 1251 H1
Castlewood Dr
- SDCo 1251 H1
Castro Lane Rd
2000 ImCo 6500 H5
Castro St
700 SOLB 1187 G1
Catalina Av
2100 SDCo 1088 C5
2400 VSTA 1088 D5
Catalina Blvd
2200 SDGO 1268 B6
400 SDGO 1287 J4
1100 SDGO 1288 A2
Catalina Cir
2400 OCSD 1087 E4
Catalina Ct
4200 SDGO 1268 B6
Catalina Dr
3400 CRLB 1106 H4
4500 OCSD 1066 H6
Catalina Heights Wy
2800 SDCo 1088 D5
Catalina Pl
4100 SDGO 1268 A7
Catalpa Ln
400 SDCo 1027 G2
Catalpa Rd
1700 CRLB 1127 E6
Catalpa Wy
700 ELCJ 1251 G4
Catalyst Ln
- SDGO 1269 B1
Catamaran Dr
6800 CRLB 1126 H6
Catamaran Ln
4800 SDGO 1330 H6
Catamaran Wy
2500 CHLV 1311 G3
1900 OCSD 1106 F1
Catamarca Dr
3900 SDGO 1249 J3
Catania St
200 SDGO 1289 H4
Cataract Pl
2800 ELCJ 1251 A5
Catarina Dr
200 SDCo 1058 G4
(See Page 1058)
Catarina Ln
11000 SDGO 1189 H6
Catawba Dr
13600 POWY 1190 E3
Cates St
700 SDCo 1067 A1
300 SDGO 1290 H4
Catfish Ln
- OCSD 1086 G2
Cathan Ln
1800 SDCo 1108 C2
Cathedra Wy
- SDCo 1174 B4
Cathedral Glen
1800 ESCN 1129 F5
Cathedral North Pl
- SDGO 1188 E4
Cathedral Oaks Rd
1200 CHLV 1331 B2
Cather Av
4800 SDGO 1228 F4
Cather Ct
7100 SDGO 1228 E4
Catherine Av
4500 SDGO 1270 D3
800 SNMS 1109 B6
Catherine Rd
4200 SDCo 1067 E1
Cathy Ct
600 ESCN 1109 J7
Cathy Dr
39800 SDCo 997 B2
Cathy Ln
700 ENCT 1167 E1
Cathywood Dr
9400 SNTE 1231 B4
Catoctin Dr
5100 SDGO 1270 D2
Catspaw Cape
- CORD 1329 E1
Catspaw Pl
1100 ESCN 1129 F5
Cattail Ct
- ELCN 6559 J3
1300 SNMS 1128 D7
Cattail Pl
- CRLB 1127 B6
Cattail Rd
15700 SDGO 1169 J5
Cattle Call Dr
300 BRAW 6319 G2
(See Page 6319)
Cauby St
3000 SDGO 1268 E5
Caudor St
1400 ENCT 1147 C3
Caulfield Dr
2500 SDGO 1330 B7
Caurina Ct
- CRLB 1127 C5
Causey Wy
5400 SDCo 998 J4
Cavalier Ct
- SDCo 1089 E3
Cavallo St
12400 SDGO 1188 C6
Cavalry Ct
13000 SDGO 1189 C4
Cave St
1200 SDGO 1227 F6
Cavern
- CRLB 1107 B4
Cavern Point Ct
1500 CHLV 1330 J3
Cavit St
- SDGO 1268 G6
Cavite Ct
6700 SDGO 1250 E7
Cay Dr
- CRLB 1107 B3
Cayenne Creek Ct
15300 SDCo 1169 F5
Cayenne Creek Pl
16100 SDCo 1169 F5
Cayenne Creek Rd
16200 SDCo 1169 F4
Cayenne Creek Wy
15200 SDCo 1169 F5
Cayenne Ln
6400 CRLB 1127 G4
Cayenne Ridge Rd
16300 SDCo 1169 F4
Cayman Wy
1800 VSTA 1107 G5
Cayote Av
13000 SDGO 1189 C4
Cayote Ct
- CRLB 1107 D7
Cayucos Ct
13900 SDGO 1189 C3
Cayucos Wy
8700 SDGO 1189 C3
Cayuga Dr
13400 POWY 1190 D4
Caywood St
5000 SDGO 1228 E7
Cazadero Dr
2600 CRLB 1127 H5
Cazadero St
2800 CRLB 1127 H5
Cazador Ln
3600 SDCo 1047 F3
Cazorla Av
600 CHLV 1310 H6
Ceanothus Ct
- CRLB 1127 D6
Ceanothus Pl
4800 OCSD 1067 A7
Cebada Ct
11600 SDGO 1250 A2
Cebu Ct
2800 CRLB 1127 H5
Cebu Pl
2800 CRLB 1127 H5
Cecelia Jo Rd
- SDCo 1172 B3
Cecelia Ter
2200 SDGO 1248 F7
2000 SDGO 1268 F1
Cecil Rd
- CORD 1288 F4
Cecilia Wy
- OCSD 1086 H3
Cecilwood Dr
9600 SNTE 1231 C4
Cedar Av
100 CHLV 1310 A5
800 CHLV 1330 B2
200 ELCN 6499 J7
Cedar Bridge Wy
- CRLB 1107 A5
Cedar Ct
- BRAW 6259 H6
(See Page 6259)
- SDCo 1232 D6
Cedar Dr
4000 SDCo 1156 E2
2400 SDCo 1297 E6
(See Page 1297)
Cedar Glen
200 ESCN 1130 A4
Cedar Glen Wy
3600 SDGO 1350 E1
Cedar Grove Av
- OCSD 1087 E5
Cedar Grove Ct
2500 CHLV 1311 H6
Cedar Hill Ct
9500 SDGO 1189 F3
Cedar Lake Av
7700 SDGO 1250 G6
Cedar Ln
20200 SDCo 1149 E2
28900 SDCo 1237 C6
5000 SDCo 1271 B1
Cedar Peak Rd
- SDCo 1174 H4
Cedar Rd
2800 OCSD 1087 C7
100 VSTA 1107 C1
Cedar Ridge Ct
14500 POWY 1190 H3
Cedar Ridge Pl
4600 OCSD 1087 D3
Cedar Ridge Rd
9700 SDCo 1233 D2
Cedar Springs Dr
10000 SNTE 1231 D3
Cedar St
200 ELCJ 1251 F4
1900 SDCo 1152 D4
800 SDGO 1289 B2
- SDGO 1290 D4
1800 SDGO 1329 J7
600 SNMS 1108 J6
- SNMS 1128 C1
- SNMS 1129 C2
N Cedar St
800 ESCN 1130 A1
S Cedar St
400 ESCN 1130 A2
W Cedar St
800 SDGO 1289 A2
Cedar Summit Dr
1100 SDCo 1152 D4
Cedar Trails Ln
9200 SDCo 1069 B6
Cedar Trails Rd
29500 SDCo 1069 B6
Cedar Tree Wy
12600 POWY 1170 D3
Cedar Vale Wy
3700 SDCo 1048 C3
Cedar Wy
900 ESCN 1110 A7
Cedarbend Wy
800 CHLV 1310 J7
Cedarbrae Ln
3600 SDGO 1287 J4
Cedarbrook St
1000 ESCN 1130 A1
Cedarcrest Wy
- SDGO 1208 G3
Cedarhurst Ln
11700 SDGO 1190 A1
Cedaridge Dr
100 SDGO 1290 H4
Cedarspring Dr
1900 CHLV 1311 D4
Cedarvale Ln
100 SNTE 1230 J7
Cedarwood Rd
3000 SDCo 1290 H7
Cedarwood Wy
2800 CRLB 1106 F3
Cedilla Pl
13000 SDGO 1150 D7
Cedral Pl
6800 LMGR 1270 E7
Cedro Av
- IMPE 6499 H2
N Cedros Av
100 SOLB 1167 E7
S Cedros Av
100 SOLB 1167 E7
800 SOLB 1187 F1
Celadon Ct
- OCSD 1087 D2
Celata Ct
7500 SDGO 1189 A7
Celata Ln
7300 SDGO 1188 J7
Celaya Ct
100 SOLB 1167 H4
Celeste Dr
3900 OCSD 1107 B1
Celeste Wy
6200 SDGO 1248 G7
Celestial Ct
12600 POWY 1190 C4
Celestial Rd
13600 POWY 1190 C4
Celestial Waters Dr
10400 SDCo 1291 D2
Celestial Wy
4400 SDGO 1350 H1
Celestine Av
8700 SDGO 1249 C6
Celia Vista Dr
6300 SDGO 1270 D5
Celinda Dr
3300 CRLB 1106 H4
Celita Ct
9800 SNTE 1231 A4
Celle De Las Rosas
31500 SDCo 1068 A1
Celome Ct
- SDGO 1188 J7
Celome Ln
- SDGO 1188 J7
Celome Wy
- SDGO 1188 J7
Celsia Wy
1700 CHLV 1331 H3
Celtic Ct
24800 SDCo 1173 G3
- SDGO 1189 B2
Centaurus Wy
8800 SDGO 1209 D2
Centella St
7800 CRLB 1147 J2
Centella Wy
13900 SDGO 1188 H3
Centennial Dr
800 VSTA 1107 F2
Centennial Wy
- ESCN 1109 J5
1800 ESCN 1110 A5
Center Av
1100 OCSD 1086 B7
Center Dr
8700 LMSA 1251 A7
8400 LMSA 1270 J1
600 SNMS 1129 D1
Center Pl
2300 ELCJ 1251 B5
Center St
200 CHLV 1310 B6
100 CHLV 1330 E5
8100 LMGR 1270 H5
8100 LMSA 1270 H2
100 SDGO 1350 G4
W Center St
300 CHLV 1310 B6
Centerstage Glen
600 ESCN 1130 B4

SAN DIEGO CO.

18 INDEX
INDEX 18
Centinela Av
Cielo Pl
SAN DIEGO CO.
SAN DIEGO CO.

San Diego County Street Index

STREET
Block City Map# Grid

Centinela Av
700 ELCN 6559 G1
Centinela Dr
1300 CALX 6620 D7
Centinella Dr
10200 SDCo 1271 F4
Central Av
7000 LMGR 1270 E6
24300 SDCo 1235 J3
3300 SDCo 1271 A6
5000 SDCo 1310 J2
5300 SDCo 1311 A1
4400 SDGO 1269 G4
Central Ct
8700 SDCo 1271 A7
Central Ln
4600 SDGO 1249 C2
Central Park Ln
- SDGO 1249 D2
Central Plz
4600 SDGO 1249 C1
Central Wayside Ct
2400 SDCo 1271 A7
Centraloma Dr
3800 SDGO 1268 B7
Centre City Pkwy
- ESCN 1130 A7
N Centre City Pkwy
2000 ESCN 1109 F5
400 ESCN 1129 H2
26500 SDCo 1089 D7
25200 SDCo 1109 E2
S Centre City Pkwy
500 ESCN 1129 H3
1700 ESCN 1130 A5
- ESCN 1150 A1
3000 SDCo 1150 A2
Centre Ln
3900 SDGO 1269 C5
Centre St
3900 SDGO 1269 C5
Centurion Pl
900 ESCN 1129 F1
Centurion Sq
- SDGO 1228 D4
Centurion St
2000 SDGO 1351 G3
Century Park Ct
- SDGO 1249 C2
Century St
6800 LMSA 1270 E3
Century Wy
1800 ESCN 1110 A5
Cepin Dr
- SDCo 1089 J2
28400 SDCo 1090 A2
Ceramic Ln
700 SDCo 1027 F1
Cerca Blanca Pl
1600 SDCo 1252 B5
Cerca Del Arroyo
8200 SDCo 1149 A4
Cerco Rosado
100 SNMS 1109 C7
Cereus Ct
1700 CRLB 1127 E6
Cereus St
200 ENCT 1147 B5
Cereza St
4700 SDGO 1289 J4
Cerezo Dr
200 CRLB 1126 G2
Cerrissa Ct
2000 SDGO 1330 A7
Cerrissa St
700 SDGO 1330 A7
Cerritos Ct
1300 CHLV 1311 B6
Cerro Av
3600 OCSD 1107 C3
Cerro Bonita Dr
700 SNMS 1129 E1
Cerro De Oro
- VSTA 1088 C3
Cerro De Pauma Rd
15300 SDCo 1050 J7
Cerro De Paz
11500 SDCo 1211 H5
Cerro Del Sol
17900 SDCo 1149 B5
Cerro Del Sur
7800 SDGO 1169 B5
Cerro Gordo Av
700 SDGO 1289 D3
Cerro Largo Dr
1000 SOLB 1167 H6
Cerro Lindo
1600 VSTA 1088 B5
Cerro Pedregoso
19900 SDCo 1148 F3
Cerro Sereno
2100 SDCo 1252 D4
Cerro St
100 ENCT 1147 G7
- SDCo 1251 G2
Cerro Verde Dr
1000 SOLB 1167 H6
Cerro Vista Wy
24100 SDCo 1173 E1
Cerros Redondos
3300 SDCo 1148 B7

Cerulean
- OCSD 1067 A3
Cervantes Av
6000 SDGO 1290 C5
Cerveza Baja
10200 SDCo 1089 E3
Cerveza Ct
- SDCo 1089 F2
Cerveza Dr
10200 SDCo 1089 E2
Cesar Chavez St
- BRAW 6320 A3
(See Page 6320)
Cesar E Chavez Pkwy
1100 SDGO 1289 C5
Cesped Dr
11500 SDGO 1250 A3
Cessna Av
- BRAW 6260 C7
(See Page 6260)
Cessna Ln
4200 SDCo 1100 B4
(See Page 1100)
Cessna St
4200 SDGO 1248 E6
Cetus Rd
8600 SDGO 1209 C1
Cezanne Ln
5200 SDCo 1290 H7
Cha Das Ska Dum Wy
200 SDCo 1235 B4
Chabad Wy
16900 POWY 1170 D2
Chablis Ct
- ESCN 1129 E4
Chablis Ln
800 VSTA 1087 D6
Chablis Rd
- SDCo 1171 H2
Chabola Rd
9300 SDGO 1189 E7
Chaco Ct
13500 SDGO 1189 C4
Chad Ct
400 VSTA 1087 G4
Chad Rd
15100 SDCo 1233 A2
Chadamy Pl
7700 SDGO 1189 A3
Chadwell Av
2500 SDGO 1330 C7
Chadwick Av
6100 SDGO 1310 E2
Chaffee St
2700 SDCo 1310 C2
Chaffin Pl
9000 SDCo 1291 B4
Chaffinch Ct
- SDGO 1209 G2
Chagall Ct
1700 SDCo 1027 F5
Chailly Dr
1900 CHLV 1311 F7
Chaisson Dr
- SDCo 1023 D2
Chalar St
2800 SDGO 1249 C6
Chalcedony St
600 SDGO 1247 G5
2500 SDGO 1248 B4
Chalet Dr
5000 OCSD 1087 C2
Chalet Pl
8000 SDGO 1209 B4
Chalice Dr
- SDCo 1089 A1
Chalk Ct
4800 OCSD 1087 B2
Challenge Blvd
10800 SDCo 1271 F4
Challenger Cir
10000 SDCo 1291 F2
Challenger Ct
10100 SDCo 1291 E2
Challis Pl
1300 CHLV 1311 F1
Chalmers St
1600 SDGO 1268 H6
Chalon Ln
11900 SDGO 1190 A3
Chalupnik Rd
- ImCo 6260 J1
(See Page 6260)
Chamberlain Av
600 ELCJ 1251 E6
Chamberlain Ct
2200 SDGO 1267 J5
Chamberlain Pl
800 ESCN 1150 C1
Chamberlain St
100 ELCJ 1251 F6
Chambers St
500 ELCJ 1251 F4
1600 ESCN 1129 F5
Chambery Pl
1800 CHLV 1311 F1
Chambord Ct
1200 OCSD 1106 D3
Chambord Wy
- SDGO 1188 E5

Chamisal Ct
- CRLB 1127 D6
Chamisal Pl
- SDGO 1208 E4
Chamise Ct
800 SNMS 1108 H6
Chamise Vista Ln
13500 SDGO 1188 G3
Chamise Wy
- SDCo 1293 B4
Chamoune Av
4300 SDGO 1269 J4
Champa St
100 VSTA 1087 G3
Champagne Blvd
29000 SDCo 1068 J7
27000 SDCo 1089 C5
Champagne Ct
1800 CHLV 1331 E3
Champagne Village Dr
- SDCo 1089 A3
Champion Ln
1500 CHLV 1312 B7
(See Page 1312)
Champion St
1900 SDGO 1290 B1
Champions Valley Ct
- SDGO 1187 J7
Championship Rd
1100 OCSD 1067 B3
Champlain St
5200 OCSD 1087 D1
Champlain Wy
4400 SDGO 1228 E7
Chance Mtn Pl
1400 CHLV 1331 A2
Chancellor Wy
13900 POWY 1190 G4
Chancery Ct
4500 CRLB 1106 J5
Chandelier Ct
800 SNMS 1128 E5
Chandelle Ln
1200 SDCo 997 H7
Chandler Ct
- ESCN 1110 E5
Chandler Dr
5900 SDGO 1248 J2
Chandler Hill Ct
8200 SDGO 1169 B3
Chandon Ct
- SDGO 1188 D6
Chaney St
1300 ELCJ 1251 D4
Channel Island Dr
800 ENCT 1147 D5
Channel Ln
300 OCSD 1106 C2
Channel Rd
100 CRLB 1126 H6
10200 SDCo 1232 A2
Channel Wy
3500 SDGO 1268 D4
Channing St
5200 SDGO 1248 H1
Chantecler Av
- SDGO 1290 D5
Chantel Ct
500 CHLV 1310 F5
Chantilly Av
8600 SDGO 1249 C6
Chantilly Ct
10900 SNTE 1231 F6
Chanute St
3600 SDGO 1330 E6
Chapala Canyon Ct
7000 SDGO 1188 H4
Chapala Ct
100 SOLB 1167 H4
Chapala Ln
1600 CHLV 1331 C3
Chapala Wy
- SOLB 1167 H5
Chapalita Dr
200 ENCT 1147 H7
300 ENCT 1167 G1
Chaparajos Ct
5400 SDGO 1250 B4
Chaparal Valley Ct
10200 SDGO 1210 C3
Chaparral Ct
- BRAW 6319 F3
(See Page 6319)
- IMPE 6439 F4
Chaparral Dr
1500 CHLV 1311 B3
- ELCN 6559 G2
1500 SNMS 1109 D7
- SNTE 1231 C2
1800 VSTA 1108 A4
Chaparral Hills Rd
700 SDCo 1253 G2
Chaparral Hts
- SDCo 1273 C6
Chaparral Ln
700 SDCo 1130 C5
Chaparral Rd
13900 SDCo 1090 E2
Chaparral Ridge Rd
12900 SDGO 1188 C5

Chaparral Slope Rd
- SDCo 1273 B7
Chaparral Wy
1400 OCSD 1067 E6
16300 POWY 1171 D6
4900 SDGO 1270 B2
Chaparro Hills Pl
12700 SDGO 1188 D4
Chaparro Wy
- SDGO 1208 F3
Chapel Dr
- CHLV 1311 H2
Chapel Ln
- SDCo 1172 B3
Chapel Rd
- SDGO 1289 C1
Chapin Dr
900 SDCo 1136 D7
Chapman St
3900 SDGO 1268 C5
Chapo Ct
3000 SDCo 1271 D6
Chapuli Rd
4100 SDCo 1029 H3
Chapulin Ln
1700 SDCo 1028 A4
Char Marie Cir
7100 LMSA 1270 F3
Charae St
6000 SDGO 1228 E5
Charbono Pt
10800 SDGO 1210 B2
Charbono St
12000 SDGO 1210 B3
Charbono Ter
10700 SDGO 1210 B3
Chardon Ln
2100 SDCo 1272 C2
Chardonnay Pl
10900 SDGO 1210 B2
Chardonnay St
12100 SDGO 1210 B2
Chardonnay Ter
2000 CHLV 1311 E3
Chardonney Wy
800 ESCN 1129 D3
Charger Blvd
4400 SDGO 1248 J2
Charing Cross Rd
10800 SDCo 1271 G6
Charing Pl
4300 SDGO 1248 H2
Charing St
5900 SDGO 1248 J2
Chariot Ct
- SDCo 1068 A4
Charise Ct
200 SDCo 1290 J5
Charise St
2200 ESCN 1130 A6
Charity Wy
15000 SDCo 1130 J5
Charlan Rd
13800 SDCo 1090 E4
Charleen Cir
2000 CRLB 1106 G5
Charlene Av
6600 SDGO 1270 E7
Charles Av
2200 SDGO 1330 B6
Charles Dewitt Wy
2100 SDCo 1253 J1
Charles Dr
700 OCSD 1067 A5
Charles Elmore Dr
- ELCN 6559 J4
Charles Lewis Wy
4800 SDGO 1289 J4
Charles Ln
- SDCo 1172 G2
Charles St
- LMSA 1270 F5
3600 SDGO 1287 J3
Charles Swisher Ct
300 SDCo 1027 J2
Charles Wy
2100 ELCJ 1251 B5
Charleston Bay Ct
10200 SDCo 1231 J3
Charleston Ln
1700 ENCT 1147 J7
Charleston Pl
- CHLV 1311 H2
Charlie Horse Wy
1600 OCSD 1067 E7
Charlotta Wy
1300 ESCN 1110 A5
Charlotte Dr
500 SNMS 1108 H6
Charlotte St
- SDGO 1227 G6
Charlyn Ln
1000 SDCo 1027 H6
Charmaine Wy
- SDGO 1209 G1
Charmant Dr
7500 SDGO 1228 B3
Charro Ct
1500 CHLV 1311 B3
Charro St
1600 ENCT 1147 G7

Chart House St
9000 SDGO 1209 D3
Charter Av
5600 SDGO 1250 B6
Charter Oak Dr
3400 CRLB 1106 G4
Chartres Pl
1300 CHLV 1311 F1
Charwood Ct
3000 SDCo 1271 G7
Chase Av
- SDCo 1272 B2
E Chase Av
100 ELCJ 1251 F7
1600 SDCo 1271 J1
1900 SDCo 1272 A2
W Chase Av
1100 ELCJ 1251 E7
Chase Creek Ln
10400 SDCo 1231 H2
Chase Ct
4700 CRLB 1107 A6
3200 OCSD 1107 B1
Chase Ln
1200 SDCo 1271 J1
Chase Ter
1400 SDCo 1271 J1
Chase Wy
6600 SDGO 1188 G3
Chasewood Dr
- SDGO 1248 J4
W Chasewood Dr
3500 SDGO 1248 H4
Chasin St
4100 OCSD 1087 C7
Chateau Ct
- CHLV 1311 E5
4600 SDGO 1248 G1
Chateau Dr
3800 SDCo 1156 E2
5000 SDGO 1248 G2
Chateau Haute Brion
30800 SDCo 1068 B3
Chateau Lafite
1500 SDCo 1068 B3
Chateau Montelena
1200 SDCo 1068 B3
Chateau Pl
600 ESCN 1129 D3
4600 SDGO 1248 G1
Chateau St Jean
1400 SDCo 1068 A3
Chateau Wy
3100 LMGR 1270 E6
Chatelain Pl
3100 SDGO 1249 C5
Chatham Dr
3500 CRLB 1107 A4
Chatham Rd
3700 CRLB 1107 A4
Chatham St
2300 ELCJ 1251 B5
Chatsbury St
1600 ELCJ 1252 B2
Chatswood Dr
2300 LMGR 1270 H7
Chatsworth Blvd
2700 SDGO 1268 C6
1500 SDGO 1288 A1
Chatsworth Wy
- CRLB 1107 A4
Chattanooga St
5500 SDGO 1310 C2
Chaucer Av
4900 SDGO 1250 A6
Chaumont Dr
5800 SDGO 1290 C1
Chaumont Pl
1900 CHLV 1311 E7
1900 SDGO 1290 C1
Chauncey Dr
2900 SDGO 1249 C5
Chauncey Rd
3500 OCSD 1107 F3
- SDGO 1268 D7
- SDGO 1288 D1
Chavacan Ln
10000 SDCo 1271 E7
Chavez Av
800 CALX 6680 D1
Chavez Cir
- SDCo 1029 J3
Chavez Rd
2900 SDGO 1350 D3
Chaz Pl
8100 LMSA 1250 H7
Cheames Wy
6500 SDGO 1248 J2
Chelan Ct
13400 SDGO 1189 C3
Chelauren
17000 SDCo 1171 E2
Chelford St
4300 SDGO 1248 J2
Chelly Ct
13500 SDGO 1189 C4
Chelsea Av
5300 SDGO 1247 F4
Chelsea Ct
4500 CRLB 1107 A5
1000 VSTA 1088 A7

Chelsea Ln
800 ENCT 1148 A5
Chelsea Park Cir
3100 SDCo 1271 G6
Chelsea Pl
300 SDGO 1247 F4
Chelsea St
5200 SDGO 1247 G4
Chelterham Ter
5100 SDGO 1188 D4
Chemisal Ln
2200 SDCo 1252 J4
Chemise Creek Rd
- SDCo 1173 G7
14900 SDCo 1193 G1
(See Page 1193)
Chenault St
2300 SDGO 1249 C7
Cherbourg Dr
1800 CHLV 1311 E7
Cheri Ln
14300 POWY 1150 G7
Cheri St
1800 SDGO 1330 A6
Cherimoya Dr
2200 SDCo 1108 C4
Cherimoya Glen
3200 ESCN 1150 C1
Cherimoya St
- SDCo 1272 H7
Cherisse Ln
9400 SDCo 1232 E5
Cherokee Av
4300 SDGO 1269 G4
Cherokee Ln
2000 ESCN 1109 F5
4200 SDCo 1100 C4
(See Page 1100)
Cherokee St
1500 SNMS 1108 D7
Cherrish Wy
- SDCo 1174 B4
Cherry Av
100 CRLB 1106 E6
400 IMPB 1329 F6
- ImCo 6560 A6
Cherry Blossom Ct
2100 CHLV 1331 F3
Cherry Blossom Ln
10400 SDCo 1169 F2
Cherry Blossom St
3700 NATC 1290 C6
Cherry Ct
- BRAW 6259 F6
(See Page 6259)
800 SNMS 1109 D6
Cherry Dr
- SDCo 1086 A4
Cherry Hill Dr
10700 SDGO 1208 D1
Cherry Hills Ln
400 CHLV 1311 B3
Cherry Hills Rd
8800 SNTE 1230 J5
Cherry Ln
2900 SDCo 1271 B6
Cherry Pl
1600 ESCN 1130 C1
Cherry Point Dr
1600 CHLV 1330 J4
Cherry Rd
8800 SDCo 1231 H6
Cherry Tree Ct
1300 ENCT 1147 F7
Cherry Tree Ln
- ESCN 1129 E5
Cherry Tree Pl
- SDGO 1350 E2
Cherrybrook Ct
3500 SDCo 1048 E2
Cherrypoint Ct
3100 SDCo 1048 E1
Cherrystone St
3700 OCSD 1086 F2
Cherrywood Dr
5000 OCSD 1087 C2
Cherrywood St
12600 POWY 1190 C1
1900 VSTA 1107 G5
Cherrywood Wy
800 ELCJ 1251 G4
Chert Dr
- SNMS 1128 F5
Cherub Ct
8500 SNTE 1230 J7
Chervil Ct
800 CHLV 1330 J1
Cheryl Creek Dr
13800 SDCo 1232 E5
Cheryl Lee Ct
14000 SDCo 1232 F5
Cheryl Ln
1000 SNMS 1109 B6
2000 VSTA 1087 C7
Cheryl Pl
200 CHLV 1330 F2
Cheryl Ridge Ct
11600 SDGO 1208 J1
Chesapeake Ct
2700 CHLV 1311 J4
5700 SDGO 1229 D7

Chesapeake Ct
100 SNMS 1108 H5
Chesapeake Dr
9100 SDGO 1229 D7
Chesapeake Pl
800 CHLV 1311 J3
Chesfield Ct
14800 SDGO 1169 D6
Cheshire Av
3600 CRLB 1107 A3
Cheshire St
4500 SDGO 1248 G2
Cheshire Wy
1700 ESCN 1109 D5
Chester St
500 SDGO 1290 E3
Chester Wy
700 ELCJ 1251 E7
Chesterfield Cir
500 SNMS 1108 J5
Chesterfield Dr
200 ENCT 1167 D3
Chesterwood Pl
- SDGO 1208 B1
Chestnut Av
- BRAW 6259 F6
(See Page 6259)
1400 CRLB 1106 F5
400 SNMS 1108 J6
Chestnut Ct
900 CHLV 1310 J7
Chestnut Dr
900 ESCN 1130 A3
Chestnut Hill Ln
- SDGO 1190 B2
Chestnut Ln
300 ESCN 1130 A4
1400 VSTA 1088 A7
Chestnut Roan Wy
8800 SDCo 1233 E7
Chestnut St
700 ESCN 1130 A3
9700 SDCo 1232 B3
9400 SDCo 1291 C2
Chestnut Wy
200 OCSD 1086 J2
Chetenham Ct
18300 SDGO 1150 C6
Chetenham Ln
12500 SDGO 1150 B6
Chevalier Dr
1800 CHLV 1331 E1
Cheviot Ct
10400 SDGO 1208 J5
Chevy Chase Dr
8500 LMSA 1270 J2
Chevy Ln
10400 SDCo 1271 E1
Cheyenne
- SNMS 1128 A5
Cheyenne Av
3300 SDGO 1248 E5
Cheyenne Cir
1900 OCSD 1087 C5
Cheyenne Dr
1600 CHLV 1331 F2
Cheyenne Ln
300 ESCN 1109 G5
Cheyenne Tr
14300 POWY 1150 G6
Cheyenne Wy
1700 SDCo 1058 G6
(See Page 1058)
Cheyne Rd
25600 SDCo 1109 F3
Chi Lai St
- SDGO 1268 F7
Chi St
8400 LMSA 1250 J7
Chianti Cv
4800 SDGO 1249 D2
Chica Rd
2700 SDCo 998 J3
Chicadee St
1500 SDGO 1290 E2
Chicago Dr
7500 LMSA 1270 G5
Chicago St
3400 SDGO 1248 E5
1800 SDGO 1268 E1
Chicarita Creek Rd
14100 SDGO 1189 J2
Chick Rd
- ImCo 6560 C2
Chickadee Wy
4400 OCSD 1087 A3
Chickasaw Ct
4600 SDGO 1248 F1
Chickasaw St
4700 SDGO 1248 F1
Chico Ln
- OCSD 1086 G3
Chico St
1800 SDGO 1248 A6
Chicory Ln
- SDCo 1252 J1
Chief Fs Pete Pedrosa
Memorial Hwy
- CALX 6620 F3
- ImCo 6560 F6

Chieftain Ct
18000 SDGO 1149 J7
Children's Wy
2900 SDGO 1249 B5
Childs Av
6100 SDGO 1310 E2
Chiltern Ct
- OCSD 1067 A3
Chimney Flats Ln
- CHLV 1311 H5
Chimney Rock Dr
700 OCSD 1086 D3
Chimney Rock Ln
9300 SDCo 1232 H4
China St
- SDGO 1268 F6
Chinaberry Ln
200 SNMS 1108 G7
Chincoteague Ct
5500 OCSD 1067 D6
Chinon Cir
10800 SDGO 1208 J4
Chinook Ct
4500 SDGO 1248 F1
Chinquapin Av
1100 CRLB 1106 F6
Chipmunk Ln
8300 SDCo 1237 C5
Chippenham Wy
11600 SDGO 1190 A2
Chippewa Ct
3800 SDGO 1248 E3
Chipwood Ct
3000 SDCo 1271 G7
Chiquita Rd
- SDCo 1235 F3
Chiriqui Ln
6400 CRLB 1127 H4
Chisholm Trl
1300 SNMS 1109 C6
Chisolm Tr
300 IMPE 6439 F4
Chiswick Ct
1500 ELCJ 1251 C5
Chloe Av
8500 LMSA 1250 J7
Choc Cliff Dr
5100 SDCo 1310 J3
Chocolate Bell Tr
- SDCo 1233 J6
Chocolate Creek Rd
10000 SDCo 1233 F3
Chocolate Summit Dr
9700 SDCo 1233 E3
Choctaw Dr
4700 SDGO 1270 D3
Choctaw Ridge Rd
12400 SDCo 1090 B1
Choctaw Wy
- POWY 1190 D5
Choisser Ln
13600 SDCo 1232 D3
Cholla Pl
1000 CHLV 1310 H7
Cholla Rd
700 CHLV 1310 H7
Chollas Fill Rd
2600 SDGO 1270 B7
Chollas Pkwy
5400 SDGO 1270 B6
4600 SDGO 1289 J1
Chollas Pkwy N
5200 SDGO 1270 A6
Chollas Pl
3200 SDGO 1270 A6
Chollas Rd
3000 SDGO 1270 A7
Chollas Station Rd
5400 SDGO 1270 B6
Chopin Wy
300 ENCT 1167 D2
1900 OCSD 1106 F2
Chorlito St
6300 CRLB 1127 H4
Choufa Ct
15500 SDCo 1051 A7
Choukair Dr
- SDCo 1273 E4
Chourree St
- CORD 1288 G3
Choward Ln
- SDCo 1023 E1
Choya Canyon Rd
2200 SDCo 1130 C6
Chretian Ct
- SDGO 1150 A7
Chris Dee Dr
14200 SDCo 1050 F6
Chris Ln
9000 SDCo 1236 H3
Chrismark Av
6100 SDGO 1250 C6
Chrissy Wy
13100 SDCo 1232 C3
Christa Ct
5800 LMSA 1251 B7
Christata Wy
- SDCo 1232 C6
Christen Wy
100 SNMS 1108 H6

Christi Av
- IMPE 6499 J2
Christi Dr
1800 VSTA 1087 H3
Christi Wy
1000 SDCo 1027 J4
Christiana St
9000 SDCo 1291 B3
Christiansen Wy
- CRLB 1106 D5
Christianson Ct
- SDCo 1086 A3
Christina Ct
400 OCSD 1086 G1
Christina Ln
9300 SDCo 1231 H5
Christina Najar St
- BRAW 6259 F7
(See Page 6259)
Christina Wy
- SDCo 1172 F1
Christine Cormargo St
- BRAW 6259 F7
(See Page 6259)
Christine Ln
- SDCo 1234 C7
Christine Pl
- ENCT 1147 B3
Christine St
3600 SDGO 1248 D1
Christmas Tree Ln
9600 SDCo 1232 C3
Christopher Ridge Terr
8400 SDGO 1169 B4
Christopher St
2600 SDGO 1248 C4
Christy Ln
2100 DLMR 1187 F4
Christy Wy
3100 SDCo 1271 A6
Chroma Dr
- OCSD 1087 B3
Chubb Ln
10300 SNTE 1231 E5
Chuckwagon Rd
- SDCo 1172 G7
Chula Vista St
600 CHLV 1309 J5
200 CHLV 1310 B5
Chumash Trl
900 SDCo 1067 J6
Chuparosa Ln
1800 SDCo 1099 F4
(See Page 1099)
Chuparosa Wy
1300 CRLB 1106 E4
Church Av
200 CHLV 1310 B5
700 CHLV 1330 C1
Church Rd
36600 SDCo 1299 E5
(See Page 1299)
Church Sq
12100 SDGO 1190 B1
Church St
7600 LMGR 1270 G6
- SDGO 1289 F7
Church Wy
400 ELCJ 1251 B5
Churchill Downs
15400 SDCo 1168 E7
Churchill Downs Rd
5800 OCSD 1067 G7
Churchill Ln
200 SNMS 1128 J2
Churchill Pl
1200 CORD 1308 H1
Churchward St
5600 SDGO 1290 B4
Churrituck Dr
800 SDGO 1330 E7
Chutnicutt Rd
11700 SDCo 1029 H4
Ciardi Ct
- CRLB 1107 B7
Cibola Ct
8000 SDGO 1250 D3
Cibola Rd
6400 SDGO 1250 D4
Cicada Ct
7900 SDGO 1189 A6
Cicero Ct
13200 POWY 1190 F4
Cicero Wy
13200 POWY 1190 F4
Cichlid Wy
8100 SDGO 1189 B6
Cielita Linda Dr
1100 VSTA 1087 E5
Cielo Av
4200 OCSD 1107 C3
Cielo Circulo
2800 CHLV 1312 A7
(See Page 1312)
Cielo Ct
17900 POWY 1150 E7
Cielo Dr
6500 SDGO 1290 D4
Cielo Pl
3000 CRLB 1147 H1

19 INDEX
INDEX 19
Cielo Ranch Rd
College Grove Dr
SAN DIEGO CO.

San Diego County Street Index

STREET — Block City Map# Grid

- Cielo Ranch Rd: 13400 SDGO 1188 H4
- Cielo Vista: - SDCo 1089 D2
- Cienega Dr: 3700 SDCo 1310 E3
- Ciera Ct: 14300 POWY 1150 G7
- Cigno Ct: - SDCo 1127 A7
- Cijon St: 12600 SDGO 1189 F6
- Cilantro Glen: 2400 ESCN 1149 G1
- Cilantro Wy: 2100 CHLV 1331 H3
- Cima Ct: 2000 CRLB 1147 F2
- Cima Del Rey: 1200 CHLV 1311 A5
- Cima Dr: 1100 SNMS 1128 E3
- Cimarron: - SDGO 1350 H2
- Cimarron Canyon Dr: 10000 SDCo 1169 E4
- Cimarron Crest Dr: 16600 SDCo 1169 E3
- Cimarron Crest Wy: 10000 SDCo 1169 E4
- Cimarron Ter: 900 SDCo 1129 J7
- S Cimarron Ter: 2500 SDCo 1149 J1
- Cimbria Wy: 12200 SDCo 1232 A5
- Cimmaron Ln: 7800 LMSA 1270 G3
- Cinchona St: 1200 VSTA 1087 E7
- Cinchring Dr: 14900 POWY 1190 J4
- Cinco Arroyos: 43200 SDCo 998 A5
- Cinderella Pl: 8100 LMGR 1270 H7
- Cinderella Wy: 2600 LMGR 1270 H7
- Cindy Av: 4900 CRLB 1107 A6
- Cindy Jo Ln: 1100 SDCo 1109 J2
- Cindy Ln: 400 VSTA 1087 G5
- Cindy Lynn Ln: 8000 SDCo 1252 C1
- Cindy St: 4200 SDGO 1248 E2; 1800 SDGO 1330 A6
- Cinnabar Dr: 8100 LMSA 1270 H4
- Cinnabar St: - IMPE 6439 D6
- Cinnabar Wy: 6400 CRLB 1127 E4
- Cinnamon Ct: 800 CHLV 1330 J1
- Cinnamon Dr: 20600 SDCo 1295 A7 (See Page 1295)
- Cinnamon Rock Rd: - SDCo 1153 G5
- Cinnamon Teal St: 7000 CRLB 1127 B6
- Cinnamon Wy: 3800 OCSD 1086 H5
- Cinque Terre Dr: 21000 SDCo 1152 B2
- Cinta Ct: 4800 SDGO 1228 F6
- Cinthia St: 7900 LMSA 1270 H4
- Ciota's Wy: - SDGO 1248 J5
- Cipriano Ln: 2300 CRLB 1106 E4
- Circa De Cerro: 14600 SDCo 1070 G2
- Circa De Lindo: 16000 SDCo 1168 D7
- Circa De Loma: 5200 SDCo 1047 G7
- Circa De Media: 7100 SDCo 1148 F2
- Circa De Tierra: 3100 ENCT 1148 B6
- Circa Del Cielo: - SDCo 1047 G7
- Circa Del Lago: 1600 SDCo 1128 C3
- Circa Del Norte: 16900 SDCo 1168 F5
- Circa Del Sur: 6800 SDCo 1168 F7
- Circa Oriente: 17000 SDCo 1168 G6
- Circa Valle Vehde: 10100 SDCo 1232 H1
- Circa Valle Verde: 9800 SDCo 1232 H2
- Circle Dr: 1000 ESCN 1130 B3; 7600 LMGR 1270 G7; 100 OCSD 1085 J7; 2800 SDCo 1149 H2; 3600 SDCo 1156 E2; - SDGO 1248 C6; 4800 SDGO 1269 G3; - SDGO 1289 J4
- E Circle Dr: 600 SOLB 1167 E6
- W Circle Dr: 600 SOLB 1167 E6
- Circle Hill Rd: 14600 SDCo 1232 J4
- Circle J Dr: 500 SDCo 1078 H2 (See Page 1078)
- Circle P Ln: - SDCo 1089 E5
- Circle Park Ln: 1900 ENCT 1147 H5
- Circle R Course Ln: - SDCo 1068 J6
- Circle R Creek Ln: - SDCo 1068 J5
- Circle R Ct: 29700 SDCo 1069 A5
- Circle R Dr: 8700 SDCo 1068 J5; 9700 SDCo 1069 C3
- Circle R Greens Dr: 29600 SDCo 1069 A6
- Circle R Ln: 30000 SDCo 1069 C4
- Circle R Oaks Ln: - SDCo 1069 A6
- Circle R Valley Ln: - SDCo 1068 J6
- Circle R View Ln: - SDCo 1069 A6
- Circle R Wy: 29800 SDCo 1069 A5
- Circle Ranch Wy: 1500 OCSD 1067 E7
- Circle View Dr: - SDCo 1068 B1
- Circo De Verde: - ENCT 1147 C3
- Circo Del Cielo Dr: 1700 ELCJ 1271 F2
- Circo Del Parque: - ENCT 1147 D3
- Circo Diegueno Ct: 6100 SDCo 1188 F1
- Circo Diegueno Rd: 15700 SDCo 1168 F7; 14800 SDCo 1188 F1
- Circo Digueno Ct: 14800 SDCo 1188 F1
- Circulo Adorno: 3400 CRLB 1147 J3
- Circulo Brindisi: 0 CHLV 1311 G7
- Circulo Coronado: 300 CHLV 1311 E2
- Circulo Dardo: 12800 SDGO 1150 C7
- Circulo Margen: 9100 SDCo 1291 B5
- Circulo Papayo: 7300 CRLB 1148 A1
- Circulo Ronda: 7300 CRLB 1147 J1
- Circulo Santiago: 2700 CRLB 1106 G3
- Circulo Sequoia: 7400 CRLB 1148 A1
- Circulo Verde: 1000 CHLV 1311 A7
- Cirque Ct: 1600 ENCT 1147 G5
- Cirro Vista Wy: 3900 SDCo 1047 J4
- Cirrus St: 5900 SDGO 1268 G3
- Cita Av: 2600 SDCo 1149 J1
- Citadel Cir: 5900 SDGO 1247 H2
- Citadel Ct: 1800 CHLV 1311 D5
- Citadel Ln: 100 OCSD 1086 E5
- Citracado: - CRLB 1127 H2
- Citracado Dr: 34300 SDCo 1030 J7; 34500 SDCo 1050 J1
- Citracado Pkwy: - ESCN 1129 D3; 300 ESCN 1130 A7; 400 SDCo 1129 C2
- N Citracado Pkwy: 700 ESCN 1129 D2
- Citradora Dr: 4000 SDCo 1271 B4
- Citrine Dr: 6800 CRLB 1127 G5; - ESCN 1110 F4
- Citrine Wy: 900 SNMS 1128 F6
- Citron Pl: 2300 ESCN 1130 E1
- Citronella St: 2800 LMGR 1270 G7
- Citrus Av: 100 IMPB 1329 E7; 2200 SDGO 1330 B7
- N Citrus Av: 200 ESCN 1110 D7; 1100 VSTA 1087 H4
- S Citrus Av: 1100 ESCN 1130 E2; 1500 SDCo 1130 D3; 200 VSTA 1087 H6
- Citrus Crest Dr: - SDCo 1070 J3
- Citrus Dr: 4000 SDCo 1028 F6
- Citrus Glen Ct: 1800 SDCo 1130 E3
- Citrus Glen Dr: 1700 SDCo 1130 E3
- Citrus Hills Ln: 1600 SDCo 1130 D3
- Citrus Ln: 1700 ImCo 6560 D1; 4300 SDCo 1028 F5
- Citrus Park Ln: 1400 SDCo 1130 D3
- Citrus Pl: 800 CRLB 1106 F6
- Citrus Ridge: 1400 SDCo 1130 D4
- Citrus St: 3400 LMGR 1270 F6; 3600 LMSA 1270 F5
- N Citrus St: 600 ESCN 1110 C6
- Citrus Tree Ln: 2200 SDCo 1271 E7
- Citrus View Ct: 9200 SDGO 1209 D2
- Citrus Wy: 1500 CHLV 1330 E5; 500 OCSD 1086 F3
- Citta Wy: 9100 SDGO 1249 D7
- City Lights Wy: 8100 SDCo 1169 A1
- City View Ln: - ESCN 1109 G4
- Civic Center Dr: 200 NATC 1309 G2; 900 OCSD 1086 A7; 13200 POWY 1190 E4; - SNMS 1108 J7
- Civic Center Wy: 100 ELCJ 1251 F5
- Civic Centre Dr: - SNTE 1231 D6
- Civita Blvd: - SDGO 1269 B1
- Cl Del Sol: - SNMS 1129 C1
- Cl Pacifica: - SNMS 1129 C1
- Cl Serena: - SNMS 1129 C2
- Cl Vista: - SNMS 1129 C1
- Claiborne Sq: 9800 SDGO 1227 J1
- Claim Jumper Ln: 1300 CHLV 1311 E6
- Claimjumper Wy: 4100 SDCo 1271 D4
- Clair Dr: 13000 POWY 1190 G5
- Claire Av: 500 CHLV 1310 D6
- Claire Dr: 4700 OCSD 1066 J6; 4900 OCSD 1067 A5
- Claire St: 600 SDGO 1330 A7
- Clairemont Ct: 2800 SDGO 1248 F7
- Clairemont Dr: 3400 SDGO 1248 E4
- Clairemont Mesa Blvd: 9700 SDGO 1229 F7; 3200 SDGO 1248 D1; 7100 SDGO 1249 A1; 11100 SDGO 1250 A1
- N Clairmont Av: - NATC 1290 B6
- S Clairmont Av: - NATC 1290 B6
- Clairton Pl: 2100 SDGO 1350 A2
- Clamagoro Cir: 10200 SDGO 1249 G5
- Clamath St: 600 SDCo 1291 C3
- Clambake Dr: 7900 SDCo 1168 J1
- Clanton Pl: - SDGO 1350 G2
- Clara Lee Av: 6800 SDGO 1249 J6
- Claremore Av: 6800 SDGO 1250 D5
- Claremore Ln: 6300 SDGO 1250 D5
- Clarence Dr: 1300 SDCo 1108 B1
- Clarence Ln: 300 ESCN 1150 A1; 600 SDCo 1149 J1
- Clarendon St: 1200 ELCJ 1251 J3
- Claret Ct: 11900 SDGO 1210 B4
- Claret Cup Dr: 1600 CHLV 1331 G4
- Claret St: 5500 SNTE 1231 G7
- Claridge Ct: - SDGO 1209 H2
- Clariss St: 400 CHLV 1330 C3
- Clarissa Ct: - LMGR 1270 F6
- Clark Av: 700 ENCT 1147 C4
- Clark Ct: 1400 VSTA 1107 J5
- Clark Rd: 1500 ELCN 6499 G4; - IMPE 6439 G4; 2300 IMPE 6439 G2; 3000 ImCo 6439 G2; 1200 ImCo 6559 H5
- Clark St: 100 ESCN 1129 J2; 3700 SDGO 1268 G6; 300 SOLB 1167 E7
- Clarke Dr: 1200 ELCJ 1252 A3
- Clarkview Ln: 14300 SDCo 1188 H2
- Clasico Ct: 10500 SDCo 1169 F3
- Classique Wy: 14100 SDGO 1189 D2
- Clatsop Ln: 8500 SDGO 1189 B3
- Clatsop Wy: 13800 SDGO 1189 B3
- Claudan Rd: 2000 SDCo 1129 E6
- Claude Ln: 1400 CHLV 1311 F7
- Claudia Av: 10300 SNTE 1231 E5
- Claudia Ln: 10300 SNTE 1231 D5
- Claudia Wy: 100 OCSD 1086 H3
- Claudina Ln: - SDCo 1071 E2
- Clauser St: 10100 SDGO 1208 J5
- Clavelita Pl: 1500 SDGO 1350 D2
- Clavelita St: 3600 SDGO 1350 E2
- Clay Av: 5800 LMSA 1250 J7; 3000 SDGO 1289 E4
- Clayburn Ct: - SDCo 1233 G7
- Claydelle Av: 300 ELCJ 1251 G6
- Clayford St: 4300 SDGO 1248 J2
- Claymont Ct: 12900 SDGO 1188 B5
- Claymore Ct: - SDGO 1189 B2
- Claypool Dr: 100 IMPE 6499 F1
- Clayton Ct: 500 ELCJ 1252 A4
- Clayton Dr: 9400 SDGO 1209 D6
- Clayton Parkinson Ct: 200 SDCo 1027 J2
- Clayton Pl: - SDCo 1089 A6; 1900 VSTA 1088 B2
- Clear Crest Cir: 1300 VSTA 1087 H4
- Clear Sky Rd: 7500 SDGO 1250 C5
- Clear Sky Ter: 6700 SDGO 1250 D4
- Clear Valley Rd: 1900 ENCT 1147 H5
- Clear View Glen: - ESCN 1109 C3
- Clearbrook Dr: 1900 CHLV 1311 D4
- Clearbrook Ln: 10000 SDCo 1271 D7; 1000 VSTA 1087 J5
- Clearcreek Pl: - SNTE 1231 C5
- Clearcrest Ln: 2400 SDCo 1027 H7
- Clearfield Ln: 2500 SDCo 1271 B7
- Clearlake Wy: 9100 SDCo 1232 C5
- Clearspring Rd: 11300 SDGO 1209 C2
- Clearview Dr: 4200 CRLB 1106 H6
- Clearview Ln: 18700 SDCo 1091 F3
- Clearview Rd: - POWY 1171 B7
- Clearview Wy: 4800 LMSA 1270 H2; 1400 SNMS 1128 D6
- Clearwater Ct: 8300 SDCo 1290 J5
- Clearwater Pl: 2000 CHLV 1311 E4; 1600 ENCT 1147 F4
- Clearwater Rd: 8400 SDCo 1028 J1
- Clearwater Ridge: 1500 VSTA 1107 H7
- Clearwater St: 6900 CRLB 1126 J5
- Clearwater Wy: 2800 SDGO 1350 D5
- Clearwood Ct: 11700 SDGO 1210 A2
- Cleary St: 9800 SNTE 1231 F4
- Cleburn Dr: 8700 LMSA 1251 A6
- Cleeco Ct: 17300 POWY 1170 D2
- Cleeve Wy: 6400 SDGO 1248 J2
- Clegg Ct: 2700 SDCo 1271 A7
- Cleghorn Wy: - SDCo 1233 H7
- Clematis St: 2100 SDGO 1289 J1
- Clemens Ct: - CRLB 1127 A1
- Clemente Pl: 5300 SDGO 1228 D7
- N Clementine St: 700 OCSD 1086 A6
- S Clementine St: 100 OCSD 1086 A7; 1700 OCSD 1106 C3
- Clements St: 39200 SDCo 1300 B1 (See Page 1300)
- E Clemmens Ln: - SDCo 1027 F4
- W Clemmens Ln: 300 SDCo 1027 F4
- Clemson Cir: 1600 SDGO 1247 H3
- Cleo Ct: 1100 ESCN 1110 B6
- Cleo St: 6600 SDGO 1270 D1
- Cleveland Av: - CALX 6620 J6; 2100 NATC 1309 G3; 800 SDCo 1109 H3; 4600 SDGO 1269 B4
- Cleveland Forest Dr: - SDCo 1297 E6 (See Page 1297)
- N Cleveland St: 700 OCSD 1085 J7
- S Cleveland St: 1100 OCSD 1106 B2
- Cleveland Trl: 1500 SDCo 1108 D1
- Clews Ranch Rd: 11500 SDGO 1188 C7
- Cliff Cir: - CRLB 1107 A4
- N Cliff Dr: - OCSD 1085 J6
- Cliff Pl: 5000 SDGO 1269 E2
- Cliff Rose Dr: 1600 CHLV 1331 G3
- Cliff St: 2200 SDGO 1269 C3
- E Cliff St: 200 SOLB 1167 E6
- W Cliff St: 200 SOLB 1167 E6
- Cliff Swallow Ln: 1800 CRLB 1127 D5
- Cliff Wy: 3600 OCSD 1107 D3
- Cliffdale Rd: 1500 ELCJ 1251 C3
- Clifford Av: 1000 ImCo 6620 D1
- Clifford Heights Rd: 8500 SNTE 1231 A7; 8500 SNTE 1251 A1
- Clifford St: 4700 SDGO 1269 J7
- Cliffridge Av: 8800 SDGO 1227 J3
- Cliffridge Ct: 2800 SDGO 1227 J4
- Cliffridge Ln: 8300 SDGO 1227 J4
- Cliffridge Wy: 2800 SDGO 1227 J4
- Cliffrose Dr: 900 SDCo 1153 A3
- Cliffside Av: 2900 SDCo 1271 E7
- Cliffside Pl: 10100 SDCo 1271 E7
- Clifftop Av: 1500 SNMS 1128 F6
- Clifftop Ln: 2600 SDCo 1271 C6
- Cliffview Pl: 9900 SDCo 1271 C7
- Cliffwood Dr: 10100 SDCo 1271 E4
- Clifton St: 500 ELCJ 1251 G4
- Climax Ct: 8600 SDGO 1250 J4
- Cline Rd: 4900 SDCo 1271 D2
- Clinton Av: - SDGO 1229 G2
- Clinton St: 3700 SDGO 1289 G4
- Clipper Ct: 1000 SOLB 1187 G1
- Cliquot Ct: 17100 POWY 1170 E2
- Clivia St: 10900 SNTE 1231 F3
- Clos Duval: 1200 SDCo 1068 A2
- Cloud Wy: 5300 SDGO 1228 G7
- Cloudbreak Av: 12600 SDGO 1189 B5
- Cloudcrest Dr: 11300 SDGO 1169 J4
- Cloudcroft Ct: 13500 POWY 1170 E2
- Cloudcroft Dr: 16900 POWY 1170 E3
- Cloudesly Dr: 12500 SDGO 1150 B6
- Cloudview Ln: 500 ENCT 1147 H5
- Cloudview Pl: 5900 SDGO 1250 C4
- Cloudwalk Canyon Dr: 1100 CHLV 1330 H1
- Cloudy Moon Dr: 600 SDCo 1078 H2 (See Page 1078); - SDCo 1171 F5
- Clove St: 1300 SDCo 1251 H1; 2100 SDGO 1268 C7; 1500 SDGO 1288 B2
- Clove Wy: 3700 OCSD 1086 H5
- Clover Cir: 9000 SDGO 1209 D3
- Clover Ct: 6700 CRLB 1126 J4
- Clover Glen Ct: 9200 SDGO 1209 D2
- Clover Hill Wy: 13600 SDGO 1188 F3
- Clover Tree Ct: - CHLV 1311 D6
- Clover Trl: 37800 SDCo 1299 H3 (See Page 1299)
- Clover Wy: - ELCN 6559 J3; 1900 ESCN 1109 C5
- Cloverdale Av: 1300 CHLV 1331 C1
- Cloverdale Rd: - ESCN 1130 G2; 1900 SDCo 1130 G4; 2200 SDGO 1130 G5
- Cloverfield Pt: 10800 SDGO 1210 B2
- Cloverhurst Wy: - SDGO 1208 D1
- Cloverleaf Ct: 1900 VSTA 1107 J3
- Cloverleaf Dr: 1100 ELCJ 1252 B7
- Clovis Ct: - CHLV 1311 C7
- Clovis St: 2600 SDGO 1268 B5
- Club Cres: 3100 SDCo 1079 B5 (See Page 1079)
- Club Dr: - SDCo 1028 F4
- Club Heights Ln: 1700 VSTA 1107 H5
- Club Ln: 200 OCSD 1106 C2
- Club View Ter: 900 CHLV 1330 D1
- Club Vista Ln: 31300 SDCo 1068 B2
- Clubhouse Av: - SDGO 1350 D1
- Clubhouse Dr: 2200 CHLV 1311 F6; - SDCo 998 G5; - SDCo 1091 F4; 14400 SDCo 1188 E2
- Clubhouse Ln: 2800 SDGO 1249 D7
- Clyde Av: 6300 SDGO 1310 E1
- Clydesdale Ct: - OCSD 1067 F7
- Clytie Ln: 2100 SDCo 1291 A1
- Cmto Carmel Harbour: 12100 SDGO 1187 J7
- Cmto Carmel Landing: 3600 SDGO 1188 A7
- Cmto Circulo Norte: 2100 SDGO 1248 A2
- Cmto De La Escena: 4300 SDGO 1269 H2
- Cmto De Los Escoses: 17500 SDCo 1168 J1
- Cmto Del Diamante: 4300 SDGO 1228 D1
- Cmto Del Mar Cove: 3900 SDGO 1188 A7
- Cmto Del Mar Sands: 12200 SDGO 1188 A7
- Cmto Del Mar Shores: 12100 SDGO 1188 A7
- Cmto Del Mar Surf: 3900 SDGO 1188 A7
- Cmto Mar De Plata: 14700 SDGO 1187 H2
- Cmto Plaza Centro: 8800 SDGO 1228 B3
- Cmto Pointe Del Mar: 12700 SDGO 1207 J1
- Cmto Porta Delgada: 14700 SDGO 1188 B2
- Cmto Porto Alegre: 14700 SDGO 1187 J2
- Cmto Preciosa Norte: 2200 SDGO 1248 A3
- Cmto Preciosa Sur: 2200 SDGO 1248 A3
- Cmto Punta Arenas: 14700 SDGO 1187 H1
- Cmto San Nicholas: 2000 SDGO 1248 A2
- Cmto San Sebastian: 4600 SDGO 1188 B1
- Cmto Vista Soledad: 12500 SDGO 1188 E6
- Coach Dr: 2400 SDCo 1271 G7
- Coach Horse Ct: - SDGO 1208 C2
- Coach Ln: - SDGO 1188 D5
- Coach Rd: - ESCN 1150 D4
- Coachman Ct: 3100 OCSD 1106 H2; 12700 POWY 1170 C5
- Coachwood: 300 ELCJ 1252 E5
- Coalinga Pl: - CHLV 1331 G4
- Coast Av: - SNMS 1128 A3
- Coast Blvd: 1800 DLMR 1187 F4; 900 SDGO 1227 E6
- S Coast Blvd: 1000 SDGO 1227 E6
- N Coast Hwy: 300 OCSD 1086 A7
- S Coast Hwy: 2100 OCSD 1106 C4
- N Coast Hwy 101: 1600 ENCT 1147 A2
- Coast Oak Trl: 1100 SDCo 1318 B7 (See Page 1318)
- Coast Walk: 1300 SDGO 1227 F6
- Coastal Hills Dr: 500 CHLV 1311 J1
- Coastline Av: 4400 CRLB 1106 H7
- Coastline Pl: 3400 SDGO 1268 D5
- Coastview Ct: - CRLB 1107 B3
- Coastwood Rd: 10700 SDCo 1169 G3
- Cobalt: - OCSD 1067 A3
- Cobalt Dr: 1900 CRLB 1127 E5; 4200 LMSA 1270 H4; 300 VSTA 1087 F6
- Coban St: 5100 SDGO 1290 B5
- Cobb Ct: 5200 SDGO 1228 F7
- Cobb Dr: 4600 SDGO 1228 F7
- Cobb Ln: 27900 SDCo 1091 A2
- Cobb Meadow Pl: 2200 CHLV 1311 G5
- Cobb Pl: 5200 SDGO 1228 F7
- Cobblecreek Ln: 15500 SDGO 1210 J1
- Cobblecreek St: 1800 CHLV 1331 E1
- Cobblestone Creek Rd: 12700 POWY 1190 B5
- Cobblestone Creek Trl: 12600 POWY 1190 B6
- Cobblestone Dr: - SDGO 1289 B1
- Cobblestone Ln: 2300 VSTA 1108 A5
- Cobblestone Pl: - SNTE 1231 C5
- Cobblestone Rd: - CRLB 1127 B4
- Cobra Wy: 6600 SDGO 1208 H4
- Cobridge Wy: 4100 SDGO 1248 E6
- Coburn St: 2800 SDCo 1310 C2
- Cocapah St: 600 VSTA 1087 F5
- Cochabamba St: 1500 SDGO 1349 J2
- Cochera Rd: 12800 SDCo 1232 B5
- Cochise Ct: - VSTA 1087 H4
- Cochise Wy: 4500 SDGO 1248 D2
- Cochran Av: 500 SDGO 1330 E7
- Cochran St: - SDGO 1287 J4
- Cochran Trl: 800 SDCo 1253 C2
- Cockatoo Cir: 500 VSTA 1087 G4
- Cockatoo Ct: 3500 OCSD 1067 B2
- Coco Palms Dr: 600 OCSD 1086 F2; 1100 SDCo 1271 J1
- Coconino Ct: 3700 SDGO 1248 E1
- Coconino Wy: 4600 SDGO 1248 D1
- Coconut Grove Ct: 7800 SDCo 1168 J2
- Coconut Ln: 1600 SDCo 1252 A2
- Coconut Wy: 3500 OCSD 1086 F2
- Cocos Dr: - SNMS 1128 J3; 800 SNMS 1129 A3
- Codorniz: 5500 SDCo 1168 C3
- Codorniz Ln: 300 SDCo 1252 H4
- Cody Ln: 700 ESCN 1150 C1
- Cody St: 3800 SDGO 1248 E4
- Coe Pl: 1900 CHLV 1311 D5
- Coeur D Alene Ct: 14200 SDCo 1090 G5
- Cofair Av: 100 SOLB 1187 F1
- Cofair Ct: 800 SOLB 1187 F2
- Coffee Bean Ln: - SDCo 1129 C5
- Coffee Pot Trl: 700 SDCo 1138 B6 (See Page 1138)
- Cohansey Rd: 11500 SDGO 1209 H1
- Cohasset Ct: 800 SDGO 1267 H4
- Cokeley Ct: 2800 ESCN 1110 E7
- Coker Wy: 1300 ELCJ 1252 A3
- Colbert Dr: 100 SDCo 1291 A5
- Colby Ln: 31800 SDCo 1051 C7
- Colby Point Pl: 300 CHLV 1311 H1
- Cold Spring Trl: 33500 SDCo 1052 D2 (See Page 1052)
- Cold Springs Ct: 10900 SDGO 1189 J4
- Coldbrook Ct: 800 CHLV 1311 D5
- Coldstream Dr: 700 ELCJ 1251 G7
- Coldwater Ct: 12100 SDGO 1190 B3
- Coldwell Ln: 3900 SDGO 1330 F7
- Cole Brook: - ESCN 1150 B1
- Cole Ct: - ESCN 1109 J7; 4100 SDGO 1228 E6
- Cole Grade Dr: 3000 SNTE 1231 F6
- Cole Grade Rd: - SDCo 1050 F5; 33400 SDCo 1051 A3; 30200 SDCo 1070 F4; 28400 SDCo 1090 F2
- Cole Ranch Rd: 300 ENCT 1147 J7; 700 ENCT 1148 A6
- Cole Rd: 100 CALX 6620 G5; 100 ImCo 6620 C5; - SDGO 1287 J5
- Cole St: 5300 SDGO 1228 E6
- Cole Wy: 300 OCSD 1106 D1; 4100 SDGO 1228 E7
- Coleen Ct: 900 ELCJ 1252 A3
- Colegrove Rd: - BRAW 6260 B7 (See Page 6260)
- Coleman Av: 3900 SDGO 1330 F7
- Coleman Cir: 2900 SDCo 1136 A7
- Coleman Ct: 300 ESCN 1110 F5; 700 SDGO 1330 F7
- Coleridge Ct: - CRLB 1107 B7; - CRLB 1127 B1
- Coleshill Dr: 6900 SDGO 1250 J3
- Coleus Ct: 4300 SDGO 1330 G7
- Coleville Ct: 2900 SDGO 1350 C1
- Colfax Ct: 1100 CHLV 1311 C7
- Colfax Dr: 1700 LMGR 1290 H1
- Colgate Cir: 1700 SDGO 1247 H2
- Colgate Dr: 2800 OCSD 1087 A7
- Colibri Ln: 2600 CRLB 1127 G5
- Colima Ct: - IMPE 6499 G1; 300 SDGO 1247 F4
- Colima St: 300 SDGO 1247 G4
- Colin Ct: 2200 SDCo 1109 J4
- Colina Creek Trl: 900 SDCo 1028 B1
- Colina Ct: 3900 OCSD 1086 G1
- Colina Dorada Dr: 3800 SDGO 1250 B3
- Colina Dr: 4900 LMSA 1270 H2
- Colina Encantada Wy: - SDCo 1148 H3
- Colina Fuerte: 18300 SDCo 1148 C6
- Colina Grande: 2000 SDCo 1272 C1
- Colina Linda: - SOLB 1187 H1
- Colina Norte: 18200 SDCo 1148 D7
- Colina Ter: 200 VSTA 1088 A5
- Colina Verde Ln: 3000 SDCo 1292 F2 (See Page 1292)
- Colina Vista: 1600 SDCo 1028 D5
- Colinas Corte: 2400 SDCo 1252 E6
- Colinas Mira: 600 SDCo 1252 E6
- Colinas Paseo: 2400 SDCo 1252 E6
- Collado Corte: 2600 SDCo 1253 J2
- College Av: 6000 SDGO 1250 C6; 4500 SDGO 1270 C3
- College Blvd: - CRLB 1107 B4; 6000 CRLB 1127 B2; 100 OCSD 1067 A7; - OCSD 1087 B3; 3200 OCSD 1107 B1
- College Gardens Ct: 5200 SDGO 1270 A2
- College Grove Dr: 6000 SDGO 1270 C7

20 INDEX
College Grove Wy

San Diego County Street Index

Corte De Vela
INDEX 20
SAN DIEGO CO.

STREET	Block	City	Map#	Grid
College Grove Wy	3100	SDGO	1270	D6
College Pl	3200	LMGR	1270	E6
	5000	SDGO	1270	C2
College St	700	SDCo	1027	E3
College Wy	4500	SDGO	1270	C4
Collegio Dr	11100	SDGO	1250	A1
Collett Wy	10100	SDGO	1249	G3
Colley Ln	3000	SDCo	1150	D1
Collier Av	2600	SDGO	1269	D3
	5300	SDGO	1270	A3
Collier Wy	700	SDCo	1253	C2
Colling Rd E	4300	SDCo	1311	A3
Colling Rd W	4200	SDCo	1311	A3
Collingwood Dr	1600	SDGO	1248	A4
Collinos Wy	4700	OCSD	1107	E5
Collins Av	5500	LMSA	1270	F1
Collins Ln	-	SDCo	1136	C7
Collins Ranch Ct	-	SDGO	1188	J3
Collins Ranch Pl	-	SDGO	1188	H3
Collins Ranch Ter	-	SDGO	1188	H3
Collins Ter	600	SDCo	1109	H5
Collinswood Ln	1100	VSTA	1107	G1
Collinwood Dr	11000	SNTE	1231	F5
Collomia Ct	2100	SDCo	1254	A3
Collura St	2900	SDGO	1270	A7
Collwood Blvd	4800	SDGO	1270	A3
Collwood Ln	4600	SDGO	1270	A3
Collwood Wy	5000	SDGO	1270	A2
Collyn St	500	VSTA	1087	D7
Colo Ct	-	SDGO	1189	E7
Coloma Cir	7500	CRLB	1147	J1
Colonel Ct	500	SDCo	1152	G4
Colonia Ct	-	ImCo	6319	C1
(See Page 6319)				
Colonial Av	1800	SDGO	1289	G1
Colonial Wy	5200	OCSD	1067	A4
Colonnades Pl	-	SDGO	1150	A7
Colony Dr	7400	LMSA	1270	F2
	12300	POWY	1190	B1
Colony Pl	2700	ESCN	1130	F1
Colony Rd	7300	LMSA	1270	F2
	7000	SDGO	1270	F2
Colony Ter	-	ENCT	1167	J1
Colony Wy	14600	POWY	1190	B1
Colorado Av	400	CHLV	1309	J7
	600	CHLV	1330	A1
	6900	LMSA	1270	E1
Colorado Dr	-	CALX	6620	H7
Colorado St	-	CORD	1288	H5
Colorama Wy	9200	SDCo	1232	D5
Colt Ln	9800	SDCo	1232	D3
Colt Pl	-	CRLB	1127	G2
Colt Ter	-	SDGO	1188	D5
Colter Lake Ct	1700	SDCo	1272	C3
Colton Av	-	SDGO	1289	E6
Colton Ct	-	CHLV	1311	B7
Coltrane Pl	1900	ESCN	1130	D2
Coltridge Ln	1700	CHLV	1311	C4
Coltridge Pl	1800	ESCN	1129	F7
Colts Wy	4000	SDGO	1270	B5
Colucci Dr	-	SDCo	1087	J2
Columbia Dr	2800	OCSD	1087	A7
Columbia Pl	11000	SDGO	1209	C3
Columbia St	1600	CHLV	1311	C5
	29800	SDCo	1135	C3
	3600	SDGO	1268	H6
	2000	SDGO	1288	J1
	1300	SDGO	1289	A3
Columbine Dr	7000	CRLB	1127	E6
	2400	SDCo	1233	J4
Columbine St	200	SDCo	1086	B2
	2900	SDGO	1269	H7
Columbus Cir	-	CRLB	1126	J2
Columbus St	8000	SDGO	1209	B4
	11000	SNTE	1231	F3
Columbus Wy	2000	VSTA	1107	J4
Colusa Dr	4900	OCSD	1107	F3
Colusa St	-	CHLV	1311	D7
	1000	SDGO	1268	G3
Colusa Wy	200	VSTA	1087	E7
Colver Wy	25800	SDCo	1109	E1
Colvin Dr	8300	SNTE	1251	B1
Comalette Ln	8500	SDGO	1209	C2
Comanche Dr	4900	LMSA	1270	G2
Comanche St	1900	OCSD	1087	C5
Combe Wy	4100	SDGO	1228	E5
Combs	1900	ELCN	6559	J1
Comet Cir	-	SNMS	1108	E6
Comet Ct	1300	ELCJ	1252	A5
Comet Ln	200	ELCJ	1252	A5
Comet View Ct	7400	SDGO	1250	C5
Comly Ct	6600	SDGO	1248	H6
Comly St	6500	SDGO	1248	H6
Commerce Av	8600	SDGO	1228	J1
Commerce St	1100	OCSD	1106	C1
	900	SNMS	1128	E1
Commerce Tr	-	IMPE	6499	E1
Commerce Wy	-	IMPE	6499	E2
	2500	VSTA	1108	A7
Commercial Av	-	ELCN	6499	F6
Commercial St	1100	ELCJ	1251	E5
	1800	ESCN	1129	E2
	8100	LMSA	1270	H1
	1700	SDGO	1289	C4
Commodore Dr	3800	SNMS	1108	D7
Commonwealth St	2100	SDGO	1289	F1
Community Church Dr	32000	SDCo	1051	B5
Community Ln	-	SDGO	1269	C1
Community Park Pt	-	SDGO	1188	F4
Community Rd	13600	POWY	1190	E3
Como	-	SDCo	1232	F4
Comoesta Ct	25100	SDCo	1173	G3
Comondu Ct	700	ELCJ	1251	G6
Compadre Wy	24200	SDCo	1173	E2
N Compass Cir	-	CHLV	1311	H3
S Compass Cir	-	CHLV	1311	H3
Compass Ct	600	CRLB	1127	A7
Compass Lake Dr	7700	SDGO	1250	G5
Compass Point Dr N	11500	SDGO	1209	E1
Compass Point Dr S	9400	SDGO	1209	E2
Compass Rd	300	OCSD	1086	F6
Compass Wy	500	SDGO	1330	J7
Complex Dr	8700	SDGO	1249	C1
Complex St	5300	SDGO	1249	D1
Composition Ct	4900	OCSD	1087	B2
Compton St	400	ELCJ	1251	E4
Comstock Av	300	SNMS	1108	J6
Comstock Ct	6600	SDGO	1248	H6
Comstock St	3000	SDGO	1248	H6
	2100	SDGO	1268	J1
Comuna Dr	13700	POWY	1190	E3
Concannon Ct	4900	SDGO	1188	C5
Concepcion Av	600	SDCo	1291	B3
Concerto Glen	600	ESCN	1150	C4
Concerto Ln	7600	SDGO	1168	J7
Conch Shell Ct	6100	SDGO	1290	D7
Concha Ln	400	SNMS	1108	E5
Conchita Rd	-	SDCo	1091	F3
Concho Ct	18200	SDCo	1091	E4
Concho Pl	4900	OCSD	1067	A5
Conchos Dr	14900	POWY	1190	C1
Concord Av	-	BRAW	6260	D7
(See Page 6260)				
Concord Ct	900	VSTA	1108	A4
Concord Hill Rd	16000	SDCo	1171	G4
Concord Pl	-	SNMS	1108	J4
Concord Ridge Terr	15800	SDGO	1169	C3
Concord St	3300	CRLB	1106	J3
	1000	SDGO	1288	A2
Concord Woods Wy	-	SDGO	1208	F2
Concord Wy	1500	CHLV	1330	H3
Concordia Ln	3900	SDCo	1047	F4
Concours Ct	2100	SDCo	1272	C4
Concourse Ct	8700	SDGO	1249	C2
Condado Wy	400	SDCo	1130	B5
Conde Pl	4400	SDGO	1268	G4
Conde St	3900	SDGO	1268	F5
Condesa Dr	14000	SDGO	1187	G5
Condessa Ct	200	OCSD	1087	A1
Condon Dr	6900	SDGO	1228	D4
Condor Av	1500	ELCJ	1252	A4
Condor Ct	1300	ENCT	1147	D2
Condor Glen	1300	ESCN	1129	G6
Condor Ln	500	SNMS	1129	A1
Conduit Rd	3100	SDCo	1291	A7
Coneflower Dr	-	CRLB	1127	B4
Coneflower St	200	ENCT	1147	E6
Conejo Ln	-	SNTE	1231	D4
Conejo Pl	10000	SNTE	1231	D4
Conejo Rd	4900	SDCo	1047	E6
	9800	SNTE	1231	D4
Conejo Vista Ct	1300	ELCJ	1252	C3
Conejos Valley Rd	-	SDCo	1194	G5
(See Page 1194)				
	-	SDCo	1235	A1
Conestoga Cir	-	SDCo	1254	D2
Conestoga Ct	-	SDCo	1254	D2
	7300	SDGO	1250	B4
Conestoga Dr	5300	SDGO	1250	B4
Conestoga Ln	400	IMPE	6439	F4
Conestoga Pl	7200	SDGO	1250	B5
Conestoga Wy	7500	SDGO	1250	B4
Conference Wy	11900	SDGO	1170	A7
Congress St	2700	SDGO	1268	F5
Congressional Dr	2300	SDCo	1272	C5
Congressional Glen	1700	ESCN	1109	D3
Conifer Av	1900	SDGO	1330	A7
Conifer Dr	200	OCSD	1087	A1
Conifer Glen	400	ESCN	1109	G6
Conifer Ln	22600	SDCo	1052	J3
(See Page 1052)				
Conifer Rd	32200	SDCo	1052	J5
(See Page 1052)				
Conley St	12900	POWY	1190	D5
Conn Pl	700	ELCJ	1251	H4
Connay Dr	1100	ESCN	1110	A6
Connecticut Av	300	ELCJ	1251	F4
	5400	LMSA	1270	E1
E Connecticut Av	200	VSTA	1087	H6
W Connecticut Av	300	VSTA	1087	G5
Connecticut St	1100	IMPB	1349	G1
	-	SDGO	1269	B4
Connell Rd	9900	SDGO	1210	A4
Connemara Dr	-	SDCo	1149	C5
Conner Ct	4100	SDGO	1248	C3
Conner Wy	3000	SDGO	1248	C3
Connie Dr	6300	SDGO	1270	C2
Connie Ln	4200	SDCo	1100	B4
(See Page 1100)				
Connoley Av	1500	CHLV	1330	E5
Connoley Cir	-	CHLV	1330	E5
Cono Dr	1700	ELCJ	1271	G1
Conosa Wy	-	CRLB	1127	D6
Conquistador	4200	OCSD	1087	B4
Conquistador Rd	3100	SDCo	997	E4
Conquistador Wy	12300	SDGO	1170	B2
Conrad Av	3700	SDGO	1228	D7
	3400	SDGO	1248	D1
Conrad Ct	4800	SDGO	1248	D1
	8500	SNTE	1231	A7
Conrad Dr	3800	SDCo	1271	C5
Conrock Rd	-	SDGO	1209	D5
Consolidated Wy	6700	SDGO	1228	J2
Constance Dr	4600	SDGO	1269	J3
Constancia St	1500	ELCJ	1252	A5
Constant Creek Rd	700	SDCo	1027	G4
Constellation Dr	11200	SDCo	1271	H1
Constitution Rd	5100	SDGO	1228	F7
Construction Ct	7100	SDGO	1228	J1
Continental Ln	1900	ESCN	1129	F7
Continental St	-	SDGO	1351	E1
Contour Blvd	4500	SDGO	1270	A3
Contour Ct	4800	OCSD	1087	B2
Contour Pl	-	CRLB	1107	B4
Contreras Ct	700	CALX	6680	D1
	1500	SDGO	1290	E6
Contut Ct	3000	SDCo	1271	D6
Conure Ct	1100	OCSD	1067	B2
Convention Wy	500	SDGO	1289	A4
Converse Av	8600	SDGO	1249	C7
Convertible Ln	700	SDCo	1027	H1
Convoy Ct	7100	SDGO	1228	J7
	7400	SDGO	1229	A7
Convoy St	-	SDGO	1229	B7
	4600	SDGO	1249	B2
Conway Dr	2400	ESCN	1109	H3
	1500	ESCN	1110	A6
	-	SDCo	1109	H2
Coogan Wy	300	ELCJ	1251	F3
Cook Cir	1500	CRLB	1126	J2
Cook Ct	-	CHLV	1310	D6
Cook Pl	2100	SDCo	1172	E2
Cook St	1100	SDCo	1172	F2
Cooke St	-	SNMS	1128	D6
Cookie Ln	800	SDCo	1027	G4
Cool Lake Ter	10900	SDGO	1189	H4
Cool Lake Wy	13400	SDGO	1189	H4
Cool Ridge Heights	1500	SDCo	1130	E5
Cool Valley Highlands Rd	-	SDCo	1070	H4
Cool Valley Ln	30100	SDCo	1071	A4
Cool Valley Ranch Ln	30700	SDCo	1070	G2
Cool Valley Ranch Rd	-	SDCo	1070	G3
Cool Valley Rd	14200	SDCo	1070	F3
Cool Water Ranch Rd	-	SDCo	1090	G3
	27100	SDCo	1091	A5
Cooley Rd	-	ImCo	6500	C4
Cooley St	1900	ELCN	6500	C6
Coolidge Av	1700	NATC	1309	H2
Coolidge St	1900	SDGO	1268	J1
Coolngreen Wy	2100	ENCT	1147	J5
Coolsprings Ct	-	CHLV	1311	C6
Coolwater Dr	100	SDGO	1290	H4
Coolwater Ranch Ln	-	SDCo	1091	A3
Coop Ct	100	ENCT	1147	A3
Coop St	1400	ENCT	1147	A3
Cooper Canyon Rd	13000	SDGO	1188	J5
Cooper Rd	-	CHLV	1330	J2
Cooper St	3400	SDGO	1269	F7
Cooperage Ct	13200	POWY	1170	E2
Coos Bay Ct	-	SDGO	1290	B1
Copa De Oro Dr	1600	SDGO	1247	H3
Copal Pl	6900	CRLB	1127	F6
Cope Rd	15800	SDCo	1173	J4
Copeland Av	4500	SDGO	1269	H4
Copeland Pl	4200	SDGO	1269	H3
Coping Pl	12300	SDCo	1231	J1
	12200	SDCo	1232	A1
Copley Av	2700	SDGO	1269	D3
Copley Dr	5700	SDGO	1228	J7
Copley Park Pl	-	SDGO	1229	A7
Copley Pl	300	ELCJ	1251	G5
Copper Av	200	VSTA	1087	F7
Copper Canyon Rd	1800	SDCo	1131	C4
Copper Creek Ct	1600	CHLV	1331	D3
Copper Crest Rd	3500	ENCT	1148	B3
Copper Ct	-	SNMS	1128	C6
Copper Dr	600	VSTA	1087	F7
Copper Leaf Ct	2100	CHLV	1331	F3
Copper Penny Dr	1600	CHLV	1331	H1
Copper Ridge Rd	2000	SNTE	1231	F6
Copper View Ct	800	SDCo	1152	C5
Copper Wy	2400	CRLB	1127	E4
Copperwind Ln	13300	SDGO	1188	J4
Copperwood Wy	100	OCSD	1086	E4
Cora May Pl	8500	SNTE	1231	E7
Coral Berry Ln	1400	ENCT	1147	A3
Coral Cove Wy	-	ENCT	1147	A2
Coral Crest Wy	3800	SDGO	1350	F5
Coral Dr	3100	OCSD	1107	A1
Coral Gate Ln	3200	SDGO	1350	F5
Coral Gum Ct	6100	SDGO	1290	D6
Coral Lake Av	6400	SDGO	1250	H5
Coral Reef Av	600	CRLB	1126	J6
	5400	SDGO	1248	A3
Coral Ridge Glen	-	ESCN	1130	C6
Coral Ridge Rd	-	SNTE	1230	G7
Coral Sand Terr	5000	SDGO	1248	F6
Coral Sea Rd	1700	SDGO	1290	D7
Coral Sea Wy	6100	SDGO	1290	D7
Coral Shores Ct	3800	SDGO	1350	F5
Coral St	1100	ELCJ	1251	J4
	2400	VSTA	1108	A6
Coral Tree Ln	3000	SDCo	1048	A1
Coral Wy	-	CRLB	1127	B4
	-	SNMS	1128	D6
Coralwood Cir	4600	CRLB	1106	J6
Coralwood Ct	200	CHLV	1310	D5
Coralwood Dr	200	SDGO	1290	G5
Corazon Pl	17600	SDGO	1149	J7
Corbel Ct	17500	SDGO	1150	D7
Corbel Wy	2500	SNMS	1128	B6
Corbett Ct	12800	SDGO	1188	C5
Corbie Cir	-	VSTA	1087	G4
Corbin St	1800	SDGO	1350	B3
Cord Ln	8900	SDGO	1209	D4
Cord Pl	1800	SDCo	1272	C3
Cordelia Ct	14800	SDGO	1210	G2
Cordelia St	-	CHLV	1331	C1
Cordell Ct	1800	ELCJ	1251	C2
Cordelle Ln	4200	SDCo	1310	E5
Cordero Rd	2100	SDGO	1187	G6
Cordgrass Ct	7000	CRLB	1127	B6
Cordial Rd	8600	SDCo	1232	F6
Cordoba Bay Ct	-	SDGO	1290	A1
Cordoba Cove	2700	SDGO	1187	H6
Cordoba Pl	2000	CRLB	1106	J7
N Cordoba St	3900	SDCo	1271	D5
S Cordoba St	3600	SDCo	1271	D5
Cordoba Wy	4600	OCSD	1107	E4
	1100	VSTA	1107	H4
Cordobes Cove	4200	SDGO	1188	B7
Cordova Ct	1000	CHLV	1310	J7
Cordova Dr	1000	CHLV	1310	J7
	1000	CHLV	1311	A7
Cordova St	1000	SDGO	1287	H2
Cordrey Ct	1800	SDGO	1289	H1
Cordrey Dr	2900	SDCo	1129	C7
Cordrey Ln	3100	SDCo	1129	C7
Corelli Ln	7500	SDGO	1168	J7
Corey Ct	9500	SNTE	1231	C5
Corfman Rd	1400	ImCo	6559	J5
Coriander Ct	800	CHLV	1330	J1
Corine Wy	2200	SDCo	1253	G1
Corinia Ct	-	ENCT	1147	J6
Corinna Ct	2400	SDGO	1290	A1
Corinth St	4200	SDGO	1270	C4
Corinthia Wy	5000	OCSD	1107	F5
Corintia St	6800	CRLB	1127	H5
	-	CRLB	1128	A5
Cork Pl	4800	SDGO	1228	G7
Cork Tree Ln	-	ESCN	1129	E5
Corkwood Av	10000	SNTE	1231	D2
Corley Ct	11400	SDGO	1209	B1
Corliss St	4900	SDGO	1270	A7
Corlita Ct	4900	SDGO	1228	G5
Cormorant Dr	-	CRLB	1127	C6
Cormorant St	1400	CHLV	1331	C2
Cornelius Pl	2700	LMGR	1270	F7
Cornell Av	800	CHLV	1311	D5
	7200	LMSA	1270	F3
Cornell Dr	3700	OCSD	1087	A7
Corner Creek Ln	2200	SDCo	1028	A3
Corner Pl	500	SDCo	1252	J4
Cornerstone Ct	1900	ELCJ	1252	C1
Cornerstone Ct E	6100	SDGO	1208	F6
Cornerstone Ct W	5900	SDGO	1208	F6
Cornet Pl	1300	SDGO	1350	D1
Cornflower Tr	5700	SDGO	1188	F4
Corniglia Dr	19200	SDCo	1152	B2
Cornish Dr	500	ENCT	1147	C7
	1200	ENCT	1167	C1
	1300	OCSD	1086	F7
	1000	SDGO	1287	J2
Cornwall Glen	400	ESCN	1110	D6
Cornwall St	2500	OCSD	1106	E1
	1400	SDCo	1290	J2
Cornwallis Sq	12100	SDGO	1190	B1
Cornwell Ct	900	SNMS	1109	C5
Corolyn Dr	3900	LMSA	1270	H4
Corona Borealis	4400	SDGO	1350	H1
Corona Ct	2400	SDGO	1248	A3
	600	VSTA	1107	H1
Corona Dr	700	OCSD	1087	C1
Corona Oriente Rd	3500	SDGO	1268	B1
Corona St	3400	LMGR	1270	G6
	3700	LMSA	1270	G5
Corona Vista	1300	CHLV	1311	A4
	1900	SDCo	1272	C3
Corona Wy	600	ENCT	1167	D1
	-	POWY	1190	D5
Coronado Av	800	CORD	1288	G6
	1600	SDCo	1291	C2
	4900	SDGO	1267	H7
	3800	SDGO	1288	A1
	1900	SDGO	1350	A1
Coronado Bay Rd	-	CORD	1309	E7
	4000	CORD	1329	D1
Coronado Bridge	-	SDGO	1289	B6
Coronado Cir	600	VSTA	1087	H4
Coronado Ct	800	SDGO	1267	H3
Coronado Dr	4500	OCSD	1066	H6
Coronado Hills Dr	800	SNMS	1129	A3
Coronado Pl	2600	VSTA	1107	J5
Coronado St	-	SNTE	1231	E6
Coronado Terrrace Dr	-	SDCo	1253	G4
Coronado View Rd	-	SDCo	1253	H4
Coronado Vw	-	SDCo	1254	A2
Coronado Wy	-	SNMS	1129	C2
Corporal Dr	3200	SDGO	1249	H4
Corporal Wy	10400	SDGO	1249	H4
Corporate Center Dr	-	SDGO	1351	B2
Corporate Centre	-	OCSD	1087	A5
Corporate Ct	-	SDGO	1209	F1
	3500	SDGO	1249	D4
Corporate Dr	400	ESCN	1129	C2
Corporate Park Pl	5400	SDGO	1228	J6
Corporate View	3200	VSTA	1128	A1
Corral Canyon	-	SDCo	1296	F1
(See Page 1296)				
Corral Canyon Rd	300	CHLV	1311	C3
	3900	SDCo	1311	A2
Corral Canyon Trl	29900	SDCo	1297	D1
(See Page 1297)				
Corral Ct	-	BRAW	6319	F3
(See Page 6319)				
	700	CHLV	1310	G4
Corral Glen	1100	ESCN	1129	F1
Corral View Av	-	CHLV	1311	D7
Corral Wy	5800	SDGO	1247	G3
Corrales Ln	1100	CHLV	1310	J5
Corrales St	-	CALX	6620	G6
Corre Camino	1800	SDCo	1088	C1
Corre Camino Wy	-	SDCo	1088	B1
Correa Ln	900	SDCo	1291	D3
Correll Rd	-	ImCo	6560	B6
Corridor St	9900	SDGO	1209	J5
Corrigan St	14200	SDGO	1189	G2
Corro Del Cerro	-	SDCo	1168	A4
Corsair Pl	9800	SDGO	1209	F2
Corsica St	1600	SDGO	1268	H1
Corsica Wy	3300	OCSD	1106	J1
	6400	SDGO	1268	H2
Corso Di Italia	-	CHLV	1310	A4
Corta Del Sur	1500	LMGR	1290	F2
Corta Madre Wy	24100	SDCo	1173	E2
Corta St	-	OCSD	1086	G1
Corte Acebo	-	CRLB	1147	F3
Corte Acuario	-	SDGO	1208	B4
Corte Al Fresco	4300	SDGO	1188	B6
Corte Alacante	5000	OCSD	1066	J5
Corte Alejandro	2800	SDCo	1254	E3
Corte Almeria	1300	OCSD	1066	J5
Corte Alveo	1300	OCSD	1066	J4
Corte Amarillo	1800	OCSD	1087	B4
Corte Amor	-	SDCo	1234	A6
Corte Ananas	-	CRLB	1147	F2
Corte Andante	1600	OCSD	1087	C3
Corte Arauco	12800	SDGO	1150	D6
Corte Arboles	-	CRLB	1147	F4
Corte Asoleado	2000	SDCo	1254	A3
Corte Aurora	-	SDCo	1148	A4
Corte Avispon	1300	SNMS	1108	E4
Corte Azul	4500	OCSD	1087	B4
Corte Baldre	-	CRLB	1147	H3
Corte Barquero	17700	SDGO	1150	C7
Corte Belieza	-	SDGO	1208	C2
Corte Bella Vista	13200	SDGO	1189	A4
Corte Bellagio	800	SDCo	1129	E1
Corte Bello	1200	SNMS	1108	E6
Corte Bocina	1300	OCSD	1066	J5
Corte Bravo	1400	SNMS	1108	E4
Corte Cadiz	1100	OCSD	1087	A3
	-	SDCo	1147	J4
Corte Cafetal	2800	SDCo	1350	D2
Corte Calandria	10900	SDGO	1169	H5
Corte Cangrejo	-	SDGO	1208	B3
Corte Capriana	1500	SDCo	1129	E1
Corte Cardo	7900	CRLB	1148	A2
Corte Carolina	-	CRLB	1147	H3
Corte Casitas	2500	CRLB	1127	G6
Corte Castillo	-	SDCo	1148	A4
Corte Celeste	2900	CRLB	1147	H4
Corte Centinella	4100	SDCo	1271	E4
Corte Cerrada	600	CHLV	1310	G7
Corte Cicuta	-	CRLB	1147	F2
Corte Cidro	-	CRLB	1147	F3
Corte Cielo	1200	SNMS	1108	E5
Corte Cierna	12700	SDGO	1170	C1
Corte Cisco	6500	CRLB	1127	J5
Corte Clasica	1400	SNMS	1108	E4
Corte Codorniz	10900	SDGO	1169	H5
Corte Cresta	1700	OCSD	1087	C4
Corte Crisalida	10700	SDGO	1169	H5
Corte Cristal	-	SNMS	1108	F4
Corte Curva	-	SDCo	1147	J4
Corte Daniel	1500	OCSD	1087	B4
Corte De Aceitunos	18100	SDGO	1150	D7
Corte De Candilejas	13100	SDGO	1150	D7
Corte De Casares	18200	SDGO	1150	D6
Corte De Cera	1200	CHLV	1311	A6
Corte De Chucena	13300	SDGO	1150	D7
Corte De Comares	13300	SDGO	1150	D7
Corte De Estepona	13300	SDGO	1150	D6
Corte De La Fonda	4300	SDGO	1188	B6
Corte De La Pina	2200	CRLB	1127	E3
Corte De La Siena	4100	SDGO	1188	B6
Corte De La Vista	2700	CRLB	1127	G7
Corte De Las Piedras	3100	SDCo	1252	F7
Corte De Marin	-	SDGO	1208	C4
Corte De Mija	1500	OCSD	1087	B3
Corte De Sausalito	-	SDGO	1208	B4
Corte De Vela	1200	CHLV	1311	A6

21 INDEX
Corte De Verdad
INDEX 21
Crespi Ct
SAN DIEGO CO.

San Diego County Street Index

STREET
Block City Map# Grid

Corte De Verdad 14400 SDGO 1189 D2
Corte Del Abeto 6200 CRLB 1127 D3
Corte Del Cedro 6100 CRLB 1127 E3
Corte Del Nogal 2000 CRLB 1127 D3
Corte Del Sol 8000 SNTE 1251 A1
Corte Delgado 10500 SDCo 1169 F4
Corte Deseo 1400 SNMS 1108 E4
Corte Diana - CRLB 1127 H5
Corte Dolor - ENCT 1147 J4
Corte Domingo - SDCo 1148 A3
Corte Dorado Espuela 2100 SDCo 1254 B3
Corte Dorotea 12800 POWY 1170 D4
Corte Dulce
4500 OCSD 1087 B4
- SDCo 1148 A4
1200 SNMS 1108 E5
Corte Emarrado 17800 SDGO 1150 C7
Corte Encanto 1200 SNMS 1108 E5
Corte Ensenada 3300 CRLB 1147 J3
Corte Entrada 800 CHLV 1310 E7
Corte Erizo 17700 SDGO 1150 C7
Corte Esperanza - SDCo 1148 A3
Corte Esplendor - CRLB 1147 J3
Corte Facil - SDGO 1188 B6
Corte Famosa 1200 SNMS 1108 E5
Corte Favor - SDGO 1188 B5
Corte Felipe - CRLB 1147 H3
Corte Fragata 8400 SDGO 1189 B4
Corte Gacela 9400 SDCo 1291 B4
Corte Galante 600 SNMS 1108 E5
Corte Ganso 13800 SDGO 1189 B3
Corte Ganzo 9300 SDCo 1291 B4
Corte Goleta - CHLV 1311 E1
Corte Goya - OCSD 1087 B4
Corte Guera 11600 SDGO 1169 J5
Corte Helena Av 100 CHLV 1310 C5
Corte Huasco - SDGO 1150 D7
Corte Isabelino - SDGO 1208 B3
Corte Jardin - CRLB 1147 H3
Corte Jardin Del Mar - SDGO 1208 C4
Corte Juana 12800 POWY 1170 D3
Corte La Bella - ENCT 1148 B3
Corte La Mantua 1400 SDCo 1129 F1
Corte La Paz - CRLB 1127 H4
Corte Ladera
1600 ESCN 1130 B4
1100 SNMS 1108 F5
Corte Lagarto 15800 SDGO 1169 H5
Corte Lampara 14400 SDGO 1189 D1
Corte Langostino - SDGO 1208 B3
Corte Largo - SDCo 1168 D3
Corte Las Lenas - SDGO 1189 B5
Corte Las Tonadas 3500 SDGO 1350 E3
Corte Limon - CRLB 1147 F3
Corte Lira 1300 SNMS 1108 E4
Corte Loma
6600 CRLB 1127 J5
2700 SDCo 1254 E3
Corte Lomas Verdes 17400 POWY 1170 E1
Corte Loren 600 SNMS 1108 E5
Corte Loro 3400 SDGO 1350 E3
Corte Luisa - SDCo 1148 A4
Corte Luz - CRLB 1127 J4
Corte Luz Del Sol - SDGO 1208 C3
Corte Macido - CRLB 1147 F3
Corte Madeira - SDCo 1254 B2
Corte Magna 1300 OCSD 1066 J5
Corte Mango - CRLB 1147 F3
Corte Manolito - SNMS 1108 F4
Corte Mar Asombrosa - SDGO 1208 C4
Corte Mar De Brisa - SDGO 1208 B3
Corte Mar De Cristal - SDGO 1208 B3
Corte Mar De Delfinas - SDGO 1208 B3
Corte Mar De Hierba - SDGO 1208 B3
Corte Mar Del Corazon - SDGO 1208 C2
Corte Maria
- CRLB 1127 J5
2100 SDCo 1254 B3
Corte Maria Av
- CHLV 1310 C4
1000 CHLV 1330 E2
Corte Marin - CRLB 1147 F3
Corte Mariposa 4700 SDCo 1310 G1
Corte Mason 10500 SDCo 1169 F3
Corte Mazatlan - CRLB 1147 J4
Corte Mejillones - SDGO 1208 C3
Corte Merano 800 SDCo 1129 F1
Corte Montanoso 15500 SDGO 1169 J6
Corte Montecito 6500 CRLB 1127 J4
Corte Moral - CRLB 1147 F2
Corte Morea 14400 SDGO 1189 D1
Corte Morera - CRLB 1147 G2
Corte Morita 11600 SDGO 1169 J5
Corte Nacion 300 CHLV 1310 F7
Corte Napoli 12100 SDGO 1190 B2
Corte Nina - CRLB 1127 H7
Corte Orchidia - CRLB 1127 C5
Corte Paguera 1300 OCSD 1066 J4
Corte Papaya - CRLB 1147 G3
Corte Pastel 4500 OCSD 1087 B4
Corte Pato 9300 SDCo 1291 B4
Corte Paulina 16500 POWY 1170 D4
Corte Pedro 2900 CRLB 1147 H3
Corte Pellejo 8900 SDCo 1291 B5
Corte Penca - SDCo 1148 A3
Corte Pescado - SNMS 1108 F4
Corte Pintura 5200 OCSD 1067 A4
Corte Plata Espuela - SDCo 1254 B2
Corte Playa Azteca 11200 SDGO 1229 J7
Corte Playa Barcelona 10900 SDGO 1229 J7
Corte Playa Cancun 11300 SDGO 1230 A7
Corte Playa Cartagena 5400 SDGO 1229 J6
Corte Playa Catalina 5100 SDGO 1230 B7
Corte Playa Corona 11200 SDGO 1229 J7
Corte Playa De Castilla 4900 SDGO 1229 J7
Corte Playa De Cortes 11300 SDGO 1230 A7
Corte Playa Encino 4900 SDGO 1229 J7
Corte Playa Jacinto 5300 SDGO 1229 J7
Corte Playa Laguna 11400 SDGO 1230 A7
Corte Playa Las Brisas 11500 SDGO 1230 A7
Corte Playa Madera 11200 SDGO 1229 J7
Corte Playa Majorca 10800 SDGO 1229 H7
Corte Playa Mazatlan 10900 SDGO 1229 J7
Corte Playa Merida 11000 SDGO 1229 J7
Corte Playa Pacifica 5300 SDGO 1229 J6
Corte Playa Plamera 4900 SDGO 1229 H7
Corte Playa San Juan 5100 SDGO 1230 A7
Corte Playa Solana 10800 SDGO 1229 J7
Corte Playa Tampico 11000 SDGO 1229 J7
Corte Playa Toluca 10800 SDGO 1229 H7
Corte Pleno Verano - SDGO 1208 B3
Corte Poco - CRLB 1147 J2
Corte Potosi 12800 SDGO 1150 D7
Corte Pozos 8900 SDCo 1291 A5
Corte Presido - CRLB 1147 F3
Corte Primavera 1100 CHLV 1311 A7
Corte Promenade - CRLB 1147 F3
Corte Pulsera 1800 OCSD 1087 C4
Corte Quezada 8900 SDCo 1291 A5
Corte Quinta Mar 2000 CRLB 1127 F7
Corte Rapallo 1400 SDCo 1129 F2
Corte Raposo 15600 SDGO 1169 J6
Corte Raquel 600 SNMS 1108 E5
Corte Rayito
12700 POWY 1170 C6
2800 SDGO 1350 D2
Corte Real 6600 CRLB 1128 A4
Corte Roberto 1500 OCSD 1087 B4
Corte Roca 2700 SDCo 1254 E3
Corte Rosado - SDCo 1148 A3
Corte Sabio 12200 SDGO 1170 B5
Corte San Rio - SNMS 1128 G2
Corte Sano 4300 LMSA 1271 A3
Corte Santa Fe 6900 SDGO 1228 H1
Corte Santico 4900 OCSD 1087 C3
Corte Sasafras - CRLB 1147 H3
Corte Segundo 1800 OCSD 1087 C5
Corte Sierra - SDCo 1254 A3
Corte Sobrado 17700 SDGO 1150 D7
Corte Sol Del Dios - SDGO 1208 C3
Corte Sonrisa - SDCo 1147 J4
Corte Sosegado 11700 SDGO 1170 A4
Corte Stellina 13200 SDGO 1188 J5
Corte Suave 4500 OCSD 1087 B3
Corte Susana 13000 POWY 1170 D4
Corte Templanza 11700 SDGO 1170 A4
Corte Tezcuco 11900 SDGO 1150 A7
Corte Tiburon 3300 CRLB 1147 J3
Corte Tierra Alta 4000 SDCo 1271 E4
Corte Tierra Baja 10200 SDCo 1271 E4
Corte Tilo - CRLB 1147 H3
Corte Torero 1800 OCSD 1087 C4
Corte Trabuco 3000 CRLB 1127 H4
Corte Trova - CHLV 1311 E2
Corte Valdez 6500 CRLB 1127 J4
Corte Ventana 1700 OCSD 1087 C4
Corte Venture - CHLV 1311 E1
Corte Vera Cruz 3200 CRLB 1147 J3
Corte Verano 1600 OCSD 1087 C4
Corte Verde 2900 SDCo 1254 E2
Corte Verso - CRLB 1147 J3
Corte Vicenza 12100 SDGO 1190 B1
Corte Viejo
3400 CRLB 1127 J5
1700 OCSD 1087 C4
Corte Villanueva 13200 SDGO 1188 J5
Corte Violeta - CRLB 1147 J3
Cortez Av
1800 ESCN 1109 E5
- IMPB 1349 E2
600 VSTA 1087 J4
Cortez Ct - BRAW 6320 A1
(See Page 6320)
Cortez Glen 1300 ESCN 1109 E5
Cortez Pl 19200 SDCo 1149 D4
Cortez Wy
3700 OCSD 1107 A2
4100 SDCo 1271 D4
Cortile Bellaza 7400 SDGO 1188 J5
Cortina Cir
2200 ESCN 1129 G7
- ESCN 1149 G1
Cortina Ct 7600 CRLB 1147 H1
Cortina Wy - SDGO 1209 F1
Corto Ln 1200 SDCo 1251 H7
Corto St
2800 OCSD 1086 E7
300 SOLB 1167 F7
Corvalla Dr 1000 SDCo 1087 J2
Corvallis St 3400 CRLB 1106 J4
Corvidae St - SDCo 1127 B7
Corvina Av 800 IMPB 1329 F7
Corvus Pl 8800 SDGO 1209 D2
Cory Ct - SDCo 1271 A7
Cosala St - VSTA 1087 H4
Cosgrove Dr 2200 SDCo 1234 A5
Cosira Ct 4200 SDGO 1249 J2
Cosmit Ln 7200 SDCo 1175 J3
(See Page 1175)
Cosmit Wy - SDCo 1175 J3
(See Page 1175)
Cosmo Av 900 ELCJ 1252 B7
Cosmo Ct 7000 SDGO 1248 J3
Cosmo St 4100 SDGO 1248 J3
Cosmo Wy - SNMS 1128 B6
Cosmos Ct 2200 CRLB 1127 E3
Cosoy Wy 4200 SDGO 1268 F4
Costa Alta Dr 3200 CRLB 1127 J5
Costa Av 1300 CHLV 1330 C4
Costa Azul St - IMPE 6439 C7
Costa Bella Dr 3800 LMSA 1270 H5
Costa Bella St 3600 LMSA 1270 H5
Costa Bella Wy 3800 LMSA 1270 G5
Costa Del Mar Rd 1600 CRLB 1147 E1
Costa Del Rey 3700 OCSD 1087 B7
Costa Del Sur 700 SNMS 1128 F5
Costa Lago St 9800 SDCo 1291 D3
Costa Ln 14400 SDCo 1232 H5
Costa Pl - SDGO 1247 F3
Costa Verde Blvd 8700 SDGO 1228 C3
Costa Verde Ln 1700 SDCo 1108 C2
Costa Vista Wy 2000 OCSD 1106 G1
Costada Ct 1700 LMGR 1290 F1
Costalot Ln 11800 SDCo 1211 J5
Costalota Rd 29300 SDCo 1069 B6
Costebelle Dr 2700 SDGO 1227 J5
Costebelle Wy 7900 SDGO 1227 J5
Cota Ln 500 VSTA 1087 F3
Cotorro Rd 18000 SDGO 1150 A7
Cotorro Wy 12100 SDGO 1150 B7
Cottage Av 5400 SDGO 1250 B5
Cottage Dr 6300 CRLB 1127 G2
Cottage Garden Rd 15700 SDCo 1071 A6
Cottage Glen Ct 1600 ENCT 1147 F4
Cottage Grove Dr 1800 ENCT 1147 H6
Cottage Grove Ln 200 ENCT 1147 E5
Cottage Wy
- ENCT 1147 F4
2200 VSTA 1108 A4
Cottingham Ct 200 OCSD 1086 E5
Cottingham St 2800 OCSD 1086 D5
Cottington Ln 7100 SDGO 1290 G7
Cotton St 600 SDGO 1289 J3
Cottonpatch Wy 100 ELCJ 1251 C6
Cottontail Ln
- SDCo 1068 D2
1400 SDGO 1247 G3
Cottontail Rd 1000 VSTA 1108 A5
Cottonwood Av
1700 CRLB 1127 E6
9300 SNTE 1231 E5
Cottonwood Cir 2000 ELCN 6559 F1
Cottonwood Ct
8500 SDGO 1228 B4
1400 SNMS 1109 C6
Cottonwood Dr
- ELCN 6499 F3
- ELCN 6559 F2
1200 OCSD 1087 C2
1700 VSTA 1107 D2
Cottonwood Fld Cntrl - SDGO 1289 H7
Cottonwood Grove Ct - SDGO 1190 A7
Cottonwood Ln 1100 VSTA 1108 A5
Cottonwood Pl 1800 ESCN 1109 D5
Cottonwood Plaza 2400 SDCo 1272 A5
N Cottonwood Rd 200 SDGO 1350 F4
Cottonwood Springs Ln 3100 SDCo 1272 D5
Cottonwood St
200 SDCo 1086 B2
3800 SDGO 1289 G7
Cottonwood View Dr - SDCo 1272 C5
Cougar Pass Rd
27000 ESCN 1089 H4
- SDCo 1089 G3
Cougar Summit 3500 SDCo 1275 B4
Coulter Creek Rd 29700 SDCo 1069 G6
Coulter Ln 2100 SDCo 1156 A5
Coulter Ridge Dr 200 SDCo 1156 F5
Couna Wy 23900 SDCo 1173 E2
Country Club Dr
100 CHLV 1330 D1
1800 SDCo 1129 C5
3100 SDCo 1156 E1
7600 SDGO 1227 G7
7200 SDGO 1247 G1
Country Club Ln
400 CORD 1288 G6
1700 ESCN 1109 D5
200 OCSD 1086 C7
- SDCo 1129 D2
- SDCo 1231 J2
Country Club Pl 8800 SDCo 1271 A4
Country Club Rd 3200 SDCo 1078 H6
(See Page 1078)
Country Creek Rd
13900 POWY 1190 F1
- SDCo 1108 J1
Country Crest Dr 1500 ELCJ 1252 B2
Country Day Dr 16300 POWY 1170 G3
Country Estates Dr 1200 VSTA 1088 A2
Country Garden Ln - SDCo 1088 J6
Country Girl Ln 17200 SDCo 1149 A7
Country Glen Rd - SDCo 1047 G5
Country Grove Ln 1900 ENCT 1147 H5
Country Heights Rd 2300 SDCo 1109 G4
Country Hill Rd 15100 POWY 1170 H7
Country Living Wy - SDCo 1129 C5
Country Ln 1700 ESCN 1130 B5
Country Meadow Ln 3600 SDCo 1150 D2
Country Meadows Rd - SDCo 1234 C5
Country Oaks Ln 26900 SDCo 1090 G5
Country Pl 2100 ESCN 1109 G5
Country Rd
3400 SDCo 1028 E6
- SDCo 1070 B4
Country Ridge Ct 25000 SDCo 1109 G4
Country Rose Cir 3400 ENCT 1148 C4
Country Scenes Ct 10100 SNTE 1231 D4
Country Squire 1700 VSTA 1107 H5
Country Squire Dr 15800 POWY 1170 C5
Country Ter 500 SDCo 1152 G4
Country Trails 3900 SDCo 1311 B2
Country Trails Ct 4300 CHLV 1311 C3
Country Trails Ln - SDCo 1311 C2
Country View Glen 2300 ESCN 1109 B4
Country View Ln 1400 VSTA 1107 H4
Country View Rd 10000 SDCo 1271 D1
Country Villa Rd - SDCo 1173 D4
Country Villas Pl 13900 SDGO 1189 A3
Country Vistas Ln 1700 CHLV 1311 C3
Country Wy 2900 SDCo 1272 C6
Countryhaven Ct 2000 ENCT 1147 H6
Countryhaven Rd 100 ENCT 1147 H7
Countryside Dr
- ELCN 6559 J3
5100 SDGO 1270 A2
1600 VSTA 1107 H5
Countryside Pl
1500 CHLV 1331 A2
1700 VSTA 1107 H5
Countrywood Ct 2000 ENCT 1147 E5
Countrywood Ln
400 ENCT 1147 E5
1100 VSTA 1107 J3
Countrywood Wy 2000 ENCT 1147 H6
County Center Two Rd - ImCo 6559 G6
Courageous Ln 4800 CRLB 1106 H7
Courier Wy 13900 POWY 1190 F4
Courser Av 3100 SDGO 1248 C2
Courser Ct 4300 SDGO 1248 C2
Court St 2100 DLMR 1187 F3
Court Wy 900 SDGO 1268 J4
Courtland Ter 13200 SDGO 1187 J5
Courtney Dr 7200 SDGO 1269 A1
Courtney Ln 8300 SNTE 1250 J1
Courtyard Dr 9900 SDGO 1209 H5
Courtyard View Dr 8800 SDCo 1069 A6
Couser Canyon Rd 33300 SDCo 1049 E3
Couser Wy - SDCo 1049 E2
Coushatta Ln 1100 SDCo 1291 A2
Cousino Wy 1700 SDCo 1272 C2
Cousteau Ct - VSTA 1107 H7
Couts St 3900 SDGO 1268 G5
Cove Ct
1400 SNMS 1129 C1
2600 VSTA 1107 H5
Cove Dr 4500 CRLB 1106 H7
Cove View Pl - SDGO 1350 J1
Cove View Wy - SDGO 1350 J1
Coventry Rd
2600 CRLB 1106 J5
1200 VSTA 1088 A6
Covey Ln
- SDCo 1049 C7
9300 SDCo 1069 C1
Covey Pl - CHLV 1311 D6
Covina Cir 8600 SDGO 1209 C5
Covina Ct 10200 SDGO 1209 C5
Covina Pl 10200 SDGO 1209 C5
Covina St 8500 SDGO 1209 C5
Covington Av 800 SNMS 1128 J3
Covington Rd 2600 SDGO 1269 F7
Cow Ln 200 SNTE 1231 E5
Cowboy Ct 100 SDCo 1152 J5
Cowell Ct 10200 SDGO 1249 G3
Cowles Mountain Blvd
6000 LMSA 1250 G6
6600 SDGO 1250 H4
Cowles Mountain Ct 7800 SDGO 1250 G4
Cowles Mountain Pl 7800 SDGO 1250 G6
Cowley Wy 3100 SDGO 1248 F5
Cowrie Av - SDGO 1227 G7
Cox Rd 300 SNMS 1109 A2
Coy Ct 1300 ELCJ 1252 A2
Coy Rd - ImCo 6439 B2
Coyne Rd 600 ImCo 6439 D5
Coyote Av
- CALX 6620 H6
- ImCo 6560 A6
Coyote Bush Dr
- SDCo 1169 D2
- SDGO 1169 D3
Coyote Canyon Rd 2500 SDCo 1150 D2
Coyote Chase Dr 2800 SDCo 1099 H4
(See Page 1099)
Coyote Creek Trl 16100 POWY 1171 C6
Coyote Crest 1700 SDCo 1028 A5
Coyote Ct
17000 POWY 1170 D2
1700 VSTA 1087 J3
Coyote Hill Gn - ESCN 1109 F3
Coyote Holler Rd 22800 SDCo 1315 H5
(See Page 1315)
Coyote Rd 700 SDCo 1234 C4
Coyote Ridge 1800 SDCo 1252 D3
Coyote Ridge Ln - CHLV 1311 H4
Coyote Ridge Terr - CHLV 1311 H4
Coyote Row 2800 SDCo 1292 E4
(See Page 1292)
Coyote Run Rd - SDCo 1070 G4
Coyote Tr - SDCo 1069 F3
Coyote Vista Wy - SDCo 1272 H6
Coyotero Dr 13100 POWY 1190 E4
Coyotes Wy 1100 SNMS 1128 E3
Cozumel Ct 100 SOLB 1167 H4
Cozumel Dr - IMPE 6499 G1
Cozy Ct 800 SDCo 1027 E3
Cozzens Ct 4300 SDGO 1228 E6
Cozzens St 6000 SDGO 1228 E5
Crabapple Ct 4300 SDGO 1330 G7
Crabtree St 6400 SDGO 1290 E6
Cradle Mountain Ln - SDCo 1212 B6
Craftsman Wy 10300 SDCo 1169 E3
Craig Ct 2100 LMGR 1290 J1
Craig Rd - SDGO 1288 B5
Craigie St 4500 SDGO 1289 J3
Craigmont St 1300 ELCJ 1251 J7
Craigmore Av 1900 ESCN 1130 D2
Crampton Ct 6600 SDGO 1250 F5
Cranberry Ct 4300 SDGO 1350 G1
Cranberry St
1800 CHLV 1331 F2
5300 OCSD 1067 D6
Cranbrook Ct 3000 SDGO 1228 A4
Crandall Ct 2500 SDGO 1248 J7
Crandall Dr
2300 SDGO 1248 J7
2200 SDGO 1249 A7
1900 SDGO 1268 J1
Crane Av 3200 ESCN 1110 F5
Crane Ct
- CRLB 1127 C6
- ImCo 6560 B7
Crane Pl 3700 SDGO 1268 J6
Crane St 3200 LMGR 1270 J6
Crann Av 1300 CHLV 1330 C4
Cranston Crest 200 ESCN 1130 A7
Cranston Dr 2300 ESCN 1130 A7
Crary St 7500 LMSA 1250 G6
Crater - SDCo 1232 F4
Crater Dr 11000 SDGO 1209 D2
Crater Lake Wy - OCSD 1086 G1
Crater Pl 11100 SDGO 1209 C2
Crater Rim Rd 4700 CRLB 1107 B5
Craven Dr - SNMS 1128 H2
Craven Rd
4100 OCSD 1086 H3
- SDCo 1128 F2
- SNMS 1129 B2
Craven Ridge Wy - SDGO 1208 E1
Craven St - SDGO 1289 G7
Crawford Ct 4600 SDGO 1249 J7
Crawford St 6500 SDGO 1249 J6
Cray Ct - SDCo 1207 J6
Crazy Colt Ln 800 VSTA 1107 H2
Crazy Horse Dr
11400 SDCo 1211 F7
11100 SDCo 1231 F1
Crazy Horse Trl 100 SNTE 1231 E6
Creciente Ct 11300 SDGO 1149 J7
Creciente Wy 17800 SDGO 1149 J6
Cree Ct 12900 POWY 1190 D4
Cree Dr 12900 POWY 1190 D4
Creek Bluff Dr - SDGO 1210 C1
Creek Hills Rd
15500 SDCo 1213 C7
14900 SDCo 1233 B1
Creek Hollow Pl 2200 ESCN 1109 J3
Creek Hollow Rd - SDCo 1153 H4
Creek Oak Dr 5100 SDCo 1047 G7
Creek Park Dr 13000 POWY 1190 E5
Creek Park Ln 13200 POWY 1190 E5
Creek Rd
400 OCSD 1086 G2
11300 POWY 1210 D1
17300 SDCo 1156 E7
- SDGO 1210 D3
- SDGO 1230 A1
Creek St 1500 SNMS 1108 D7
Creekbridge Pl 10800 SDGO 1189 H6
Creekford Dr - SDCo 1231 J5
Creeknettle Rd - SDCo 1128 G2
Creekside Av 600 OCSD 1067 D6
Creekside Ct
4100 NATC 1310 E4
12200 SDGO 1210 A2
9300 SNTE 1231 G5
Creekside Dr - SNMS 1128 F1
N Creekside Dr - CHLV 1311 H5
Creekside Ln
13200 POWY 1190 E5
1700 VSTA 1107 D1
Creekside Pl
- CHLV 1311 G3
2100 ESCN 1129 E7
Creekside Village Wy 2700 SDGO 1350 C1
Creekstone Ln 11300 SDGO 1189 J6
Creekview Dr 12300 SDGO 1189 H6
Creekview Ln 2100 SDCo 1027 H6
Creekwood Ct 12600 SDGO 1189 C5
Creekwood Ln 8700 SDGO 1189 C5
Creekwood Wy 800 CHLV 1311 E5
Creelman Ln
- SDCo 1172 F2
- SDCo 1173 A2
Creencia Pl 1400 ESCN 1110 A6
Cregar St 100 OCSD 1086 C6
Creighton Wy 6000 SDGO 1290 C5
Crela St 3000 SDCo 1310 D4
Crenshaw St 1900 SDGO 1289 H1
Crescendo Dr
26400 SDCo 1089 H7
26200 SDCo 1109 H1
Crescendo Ln 7500 SDGO 1168 J7
Crescent Bay Dr 5000 SDGO 1350 J2
Crescent Bend 900 SDCo 1027 H4
Crescent Bend Pl 1100 SDCo 1027 H4
Crescent Creek Dr 16800 SDCo 1169 A1
Crescent Ct 600 VSTA 1088 A7
N Crescent Ct 600 SDGO 1268 J6
S Crescent Ct 600 SDGO 1268 J6
Crescent Dr
600 CHLV 1330 H1
3800 SDCo 1156 E2
2300 SDGO 1268 G5
800 VSTA 1087 J7
Crescent Heights Dr 4700 OCSD 1087 D3
Crescent Hill Wy - SDCo 1089 E3
Crescent Knolls Glen 1600 ESCN 1129 F6
Crescent Ln 600 VSTA 1088 A7
Crescent Moon Dr - SDCo 1070 G1
Crescent Pl - SNMS 1128 C6
Crescent Point Rd 4000 CRLB 1106 H6
N Crescent Ridge Dr 1100 SDCo 1027 H4
Crescent Ridge Rd - SNTE 1230 G7
Cresita Dr 4900 SDGO 1270 C2
Crespi Ct 4700 CRLB 1107 A5

SAN DIEGO CO.

22 INDEX
Crespo St
INDEX 22
Dalles Ct
SAN DIEGO CO.

San Diego County Street Index

STREET
Block City Map# Grid

Crespo St
1700 SDGO 1227 G6
Cressa Ct
- CRLB 1127 C7
Cressy Ct
1500 ELCJ 1251 B3
Crest Dr
900 CHLV 1310 G7
2500 CRLB 1106 F3
700 ENCT 1147 F7
2200 ENCT 1167 F3
- ESCN 1130 A6
600 SDCo 1252 E6
9300 SDCo 1271 B6
2100 SDGO 1249 B7
400 VSTA 1087 J7
Crest Heights
4000 SDCo 1028 F4
Crest Hill Ln
2200 SDCo 1027 H7
Crest Knolls Ct
12600 SDGO 1188 A6
Crest Ln
300 VSTA 1087 G3
Crest Rd
1200 DLMR 1187 G5
12000 POWY 1190 B5
Crest St
1300 ENCT 1167 C1
100 ESCN 1129 H1
Crest View Ct
2100 ESCN 1109 B3
Crest Wy
14000 SDGO 1187 G5
Cresta Bonita Dr
- SDCo 1310 E3
Cresta Bonita Wy
3700 SDCo 1310 E3
Cresta Ct
3600 OCSD 1107 D3
12500 SDGO 1170 C2
Cresta Dr
16900 SDGO 1170 C3
Cresta Loma
2800 SDCo 1130 E7
Cresta Loma Dr
1300 SDCo 1047 J1
Cresta Loma Ln
2800 SDCo 1047 J1
Cresta Pl
12500 SDGO 1170 C2
Cresta Verde Ln
4400 SDCo 1310 G2
Cresta Wy
- CHLV 1310 D5
12500 SDGO 1170 C3
Crestbrook Pl
12400 SDCo 1190 A6
Crestcourt Ln
400 SDCo 1027 H1
Crested Butte St
500 CHLV 1330 B3
Crestglen Ln
9900 SDCo 1271 D6
Cresthaven Dr
6200 LMSA 1251 C6
1900 VSTA 1087 H2
Cresthaven Pl
1400 OCSD 1087 E3
Cresthill Pl
- SDCo 1251 J2
Crestland Dr
4800 SDCo 1271 E2
Crestlane Ct
9900 SDCo 1271 D7
Crestline Dr
2500 LMGR 1270 H7
2100 OCSD 1086 C6
14500 POWY 1191 D3
Crestline Rd
21800 SDCo 1052 G3
(See Page 1052)
Crestmar Pt
8900 SDGO 1208 J7
Crestmont Pl
4700 OCSD 1087 E3
Crestmore Av
8800 SDCo 1290 J3
Creston Dr
5300 SDGO 1290 B3
Crestop Ln
2500 SDCo 1271 C6
Crestridge Ct
9500 SDCo 1089 C1
Crestridge Dr
1300 OCSD 1086 E7
Crestside Pl
10100 SDCo 1271 E7
Creststone Pl
3800 SDGO 1188 A4
Crestview Ct
15200 POWY 1170 G7
700 SNMS 1128 E2
Crestview Dr
1000 BRAW 6259 H7
(See Page 6259)
300 CHLV 1311 B3
4900 CRLB 1107 A7
1400 OCSD 1087 E3
4300 SDCo 1271 E3
Crestview Estates Pl
2400 SDCo 1130 E2
Crestview Glen
- ESCN 1109 G5
Crestview Heights
10100 SDCo 1271 D3
Crestview Pl
300 VSTA 1107 J1
Crestview Rd
700 VSTA 1107 H1
Crestwick Ct
12200 SDGO 1190 B1
Crestwind Rd
21400 SDCo 1129 A5
Crestwood Av
14300 POWY 1190 C1
Crestwood Dr
500 OCSD 1086 D3
Crestwood Pl
600 ESCN 1109 H4
3600 SDGO 1269 C6
Crete Ct
600 ENCT 1147 C3
Crete St
3700 SDGO 1248 E6
Cribbage Ln
400 SNMS 1128 F1
Cricket Dr
1500 CHLV 1311 G7
Cricket Hill
13400 POWY 1170 E4
Cricket Hill Dr
13400 POWY 1170 E4
Crimson Cedar
8300 SDGO 1189 B3
Crimson Ct
1800 CHLV 1331 F3
Crimson Dr
1000 SNMS 1109 A4
Crimson Fire Ct
9700 SDCo 1271 C4
Cripple Creek Dr
1700 CHLV 1331 G1
Crisie Ln
- SDCo 1130 C7
Crisp Ct
5300 SDGO 1228 G7
Crisp Wy
4700 SDGO 1228 G7
Crisscross Ln
12200 SDGO 1189 B7
Cristallo Pl
12900 SDGO 1188 B5
Cristianitos Rd
- SDCo 1023 C1
Cristobal Dr
10000 SDCo 1271 E6
Cristobal Wy
3300 SDCo 1271 E6
Crocker Rd
15000 POWY 1170 H7
14800 POWY 1190 H1
Crockett St
8700 LMSA 1251 A6
Crocus Ct
- ENCT 1147 B4
Croft St
3600 SDGO 1270 B6
Crofton Ln
1700 ESCN 1110 B7
Crofton St
2000 SDCo 1291 A1
Cromwell Ct
5200 SDGO 1269 F2
Cromwell Pl
3400 SDGO 1269 F2
Cromwell Wy
700 VSTA 1088 A7
Cronan Cir
7900 SDGO 1209 B3
Crooked Creek Ct
4700 SDGO 1289 J5
Crooked Oak Ln
28300 SDCo 1089 E3
Crooked Path Pl
- CHLV 1311 H3
Crooked Trail Rd
- CHLV 1311 F2
Crosby Club Dr
7900 SDCo 1169 A1
Crosby St
1100 SDCo 1251 J3
Crosby Tennis Dr
7900 SDCo 1169 A1
Cross Creek Ln
2400 ESCN 1130 D6
Cross Creek Pl
2400 ESCN 1130 D7
Cross Creek Rd
1600 SDCo 1068 B6
Cross Fox Ct
16000 POWY 1170 G4
Cross Rd
2100 IMPE 6499 H3
Cross St
1800 SDGO 1268 G2
Cross Stone Dr
15000 SDCo 1169 F5
Cross Stone Pl
- SDCo 1169 F5
Crossbill Ct
- SDCo 1127 D4
Crosscreek Rd
2000 CHLV 1311 E4
Crosscreek Ter
10300 SDGO 1209 H4
Crosshaven Ln
2500 SDGO 1290 G7
Crossland Ct
10100 SNTE 1231 A3
Crossle Ct
2000 SDCo 1272 C4
Crosspoint Ct
800 SDGO 1290 G3
Crossroads St
1900 CHLV 1331 H1
Crossroads Wy
- CHLV 1331 H1
Crossrock Rd
14000 POWY 1190 B3
Crosstimbers Trl
3200 SDCo 1252 G2
Crossway Ct
8700 SNTE 1230 H7
Crosswinds Rd
1400 SDCo 1152 F3
Crosthwaite Cir
12300 POWY 1190 F6
Croswaithe St
- OCSD 1106 B3
Croton Ct
5300 SDGO 1248 B3
Crouch St
100 OCSD 1086 D7
700 OCSD 1106 D1
Crow Ct
5900 SDGO 1250 C5
Crowder Ln
- LMSA 1270 J2
Crowell St
3500 SDGO 1268 H6
Crowley Ct
7100 SDGO 1250 F4
Crown Crest Ln
2600 SDGO 1227 H1
Crown Ct
- IMPE 6499 F1
1600 SDCo 1027 J5
Crown Hill Ln
- SDCo 1111 D3
Crown Ln
1500 CHLV 1312 B7
(See Page 1312)
Crown Point Ct
1500 CHLV 1330 J3
Crown Point Dr
3900 SDGO 1248 B7
3500 SDGO 1268 B1
Crown Ridge Rd
2700 CHLV 1311 J6
Crown St
5100 SDGO 1268 F2
Crown Valley Rd
15900 POWY 1170 D5
Crown View Wy
2100 OCSD 1106 J1
Crownhill Rd
2100 SDGO 1248 A4
Crownpoint Av
- CRLB 1107 B4
Crownpoint Pl
2700 ESCN 1130 F1
Crownridge Ln
2700 SDCo 1271 E6
Crownview Ct
300 SNMS 1108 J4
Crows Landing
2400 SDCo 1300 A4
(See Page 1300)
Crows Nest Ct
1000 OCSD 1067 B3
Crows Nest Ln
7200 SDGO 1208 J3
Croydon Ln
100 ELCJ 1251 C5
Cruickshank Dr
- ELCN 6499 F3
Cruickshank Rd
200 ImCo 6500 C3
Cruikshank Dr
- ELCN 6499 E3
Crusader Av
- ESCN 1130 C1
Crystal Bluff Ct
1800 SDGO 1350 J2
Crystal Clear Dr
2000 SDCo 1291 F2
Crystal Clear Ln
- SDCo 1291 F2
Crystal Cove
1100 SDGO 1350 J1
Crystal Cove Wy
- SNMS 1128 A3
Crystal Creek Ct
800 CHLV 1311 A5
Crystal Ct
3100 SDCo 1150 D1
- SNMS 1128 D6
Crystal Dawn Ln
4000 SDGO 1228 C3
Crystal Downs Glen
500 ESCN 1109 H3
Crystal Dr
5100 SDGO 1247 G5
Crystal Grove Ct
- SDGO 1188 J3
Crystal Lake Av
6200 SDGO 1250 H6
Crystal Ln
1100 SDCo 1251 J7
1100 SDCo 1271 J1
Crystal Oaks Wy
- SDGO 1209 G2
Crystal Ridge Ct
29100 SDCo 1089 C2
1600 VSTA 1107 G4
Crystal Ridge Dr
9700 SDCo 1089 C2
Crystal Ridge Glen
- ESCN 1109 B3
Crystal Ridge Rd
2900 ENCT 1148 A5
Crystal Ridge Wy
1700 VSTA 1107 G4
Crystal Springs Dr
1200 CHLV 1311 G6
Crystal Springs Pl
1000 ESCN 1129 F1
Crystal Springs Rd
10900 SNTE 1231 F5
Crystal St
4100 OCSD 1087 C6
Crystal View Ln
15800 POWY 1191 B2
Crystal View Rd
14800 SDCo 1232 H4
Crystal Wood Dr
3400 OCSD 1086 E3
Crystalaire Dr
6400 SDGO 1250 D6
Crystalline Dr
7000 CRLB 1127 B6
Crystallite Ln
13600 SDCo 1070 E2
Cte Aciano
3400 CRLB 1148 A1
Cte Adalina
6700 CRLB 1128 A4
Cte Aliso
3200 CRLB 1127 J5
Cte Altura
3400 CRLB 1128 A6
Cte Anacapa
2100 CHLV 1311 E1
Cte Bagalso
1300 SNMS 1108 E4
Cte Bahama
- CHLV 1311 C2
Cte Barcelona
1500 CHLV 1331 C2
Cte Bautista
2200 CHLV 1311 E2
Cte Belize
1900 CHLV 1311 D2
Cte Belmarina
2000 CHLV 1311 D1
Cte Bosque
3200 CRLB 1127 J6
Cte Brezo
3400 CRLB 1148 A1
Cte Brisa
7300 CRLB 1148 B1
Cte Calypso
300 CHLV 1311 E2
Cte Cantante
1900 CHLV 1311 C1
Cte Carlazzo
3100 CHLV 1312 A1
(See Page 1312)
Cte Casera
3600 CRLB 1128 B7
Cte Castillo
300 CHLV 1311 E2
Cte Claro
- CRLB 1148 B2
Cte Condesa
2100 CHLV 1311 D2
Cte De La Donna
9500 SNTE 1251 C1
Cte De Luz
7800 SDGO 1169 B7
Cte De Powell
1500 SDCo 1153 B5
Cte Del Cruce
3300 CRLB 1147 J4
Cte Delfinio
3500 CRLB 1148 A2
Cte Diego
6800 CRLB 1128 A5
Cte Escena
1900 CHLV 1311 C2
Cte Fiaba
- SDCo 1148 F5
Cte Flores
2300 CHLV 1311 F3
Cte Fortuna
3400 CRLB 1128 A7
Cte Fresa
3400 CRLB 1148 A1
Cte Fresco
18500 SDCo 1148 F5
Cte Fuerte
600 CHLV 1311 F2
Cte Galeana
1800 CHLV 1311 C1
Cte Hortensia
7300 CRLB 1148 B2
Cte Isla
2300 CHLV 1311 F3
Cte Laguna
7000 SDCo 1148 F5
Cte Langosta
6900 CRLB 1127 J5
Cte Lupe
3500 CRLB 1128 A5
Cte Lusso
6900 SDCo 1148 G5
Cte Madera Rd
7400 SDCo 1237 A7
Cte Maduro
2300 CHLV 1311 F3
Cte Manzana
3400 CRLB 1148 A1
Cte Maravilla
1900 CHLV 1311 C1
Cte Maroma
1900 CHLV 1311 C1
Cte Melano
3200 CHLV 1312 A1
(See Page 1312)
Cte Mirador
1800 CHLV 1311 C1
Cte Mistico
- CHLV 1311 F3
Cte Mora
3500 CRLB 1128 A5
Cte Pacifica
3200 CRLB 1127 J6
Cte Paloma
3200 CRLB 1127 J6
Cte Panorama
- CRLB 1128 A7
Cte Patio
600 CHLV 1311 F3
Cte Pescado
2300 CHLV 1311 F2
Cte Pino
3400 CRLB 1148 A1
Cte Premana
3200 CHLV 1292 A7
(See Page 1292)
Cte Ramon
3500 CRLB 1128 A5
Cte Romero
- CRLB 1148 A1
Cte Saltero
2000 CHLV 1311 D1
Cte San Luis
700 OCSD 1086 J3
Cte San Simeon
2100 CHLV 1311 E2
Cte Segura
3600 CRLB 1128 B7
Cte Selva
3400 CRLB 1148 A1
Cte Seville
1500 CHLV 1331 D1
Cte Soledad
- LMGR 1270 F7
Cte Spagna
6900 SDCo 1148 F5
Cte Tamarindo
3100 CRLB 1127 J5
Cte Terral
3300 CRLB 1128 A5
Cte Tomillo
7300 CRLB 1148 B2
Cte Tradicion
3100 CRLB 1147 J2
Cte Verbena
1900 CHLV 1311 D2
Cte Verde
4200 OCSD 1086 J3
Cte Viejo
2300 CHLV 1311 F3
Cte Vino
3700 CRLB 1128 B7
Cte Vista
2100 CHLV 1311 F7
Cte Yolanda
3500 CRLB 1128 A4
Cte Zafiro
1200 SNMS 1108 F4
Cuadro Vista
1700 SDCo 1128 B4
Cuatro Ln
1500 SDCo 1027 J4
Cubist Ct
4700 OCSD 1087 B1
Cuca St
14200 SDGO 1189 H2
Cuchara Dr
1200 DLMR 1187 G5
Cuchillo St
700 SDCo 1067 C7
Cudahy Pl
1000 SDGO 1268 E3
Cuervo Rd
1900 SDCo 1088 C7
Cuesta De Camellia
32200 SDCo 1050 J6
Cuesta Del Sol
- SDCo 1232 E5
Cuesta Los Osos Av
- SDCo 1168 E6
Cuesta Norte
1300 SDCo 1027 H5
Cuesta Pl
3300 CRLB 1147 J1
Cuidad Leon Ct
5800 SDGO 1250 E7
Cuisse Ln
1800 SDCo 1058 G6
(See Page 1058)
Culbertson Av
4400 LMSA 1270 G3
Culebra Av
- SDGO 1268 F6
Culebra St
400 DLMR 1187 F4
Cullen Crest Tr
5600 SDGO 1188 E4
Cullen St
7600 SDGO 1249 A5
Culloden Ct
800 SDCo 1027 G5
Cully Ct
- SDCo 1233 J6
Culowee St
7900 LMSA 1270 H2
Culver Ct
- ESCN 1110 E5
11200 SDCo 1271 G2
Culver Rd
2300 SDCo 996 J3
Culver St
4400 SDGO 1248 B5
Culver Wy
2300 SDGO 1248 B5
Cumana Ter
17500 SDGO 1150 D7
Cumberland Dr
15800 POWY 1170 G4
Cumberland St
5700 SDGO 1310 C1
Cumbre Ct
2000 CRLB 1147 F2
Cumbre Del Cielo
- SDCo 1149 C5
Cumbre Pl
2100 ELCJ 1251 C1
Cumbre View
1500 CHLV 1311 B4
Cumbres Rd
12400 SDCo 1070 B5
Cumbres Terr
12400 SDCo 1070 A5
Cummings Rd
- NATC 1309 F1
Cummins Pl
9900 SDGO 1209 H4
Cumulus Ln
6000 SDGO 1268 G3
Cunard St
900 SDGO 1330 B7
Cunning Ln
13600 SDCo 1232 D3
Cunningham Ln
600 SDCo 1252 C6
Cupeno Ct
- SDCo 1293 A3
Curie Pl
2500 SDGO 1228 B7
Curie St
3000 SDGO 1228 C7
Curie Wy
5400 SDGO 1228 C7
Curlew St
2900 SDGO 1268 J7
3500 SDGO 1269 A6
2400 SDGO 1289 A1
Curlew Terr
- CRLB 1127 B5
Curran Ct
30900 SDCo 1070 J1
Curran St
- SDGO 1351 D1
Currant Ct
- SDCo 1232 C5
Currant St
3300 SDGO 1249 A4
Currant Wy
1700 CHLV 1331 H2
200 OCSD 1086 J1
Curry Comb Dr
1700 SNMS 1108 E5
Curry Dr
1700 CHLV 1331 H3
4900 SDGO 1270 D2
Curry Wy
3700 OCSD 1086 H4
Curtis Dr
- SDCo 1087 H2
Curtis Ln
1400 SDCo 1234 B3
Curtis St
- CORD 1288 E4
3500 SDGO 1268 C6
Cushing Rd
- SDGO 1268 D7
- SDGO 1288 D1
Cushman Av
1200 SDGO 1268 F3
Cushman Pl
5200 SDGO 1268 F3
Custer Av
900 SNMS 1128 J3
Custer Rd
1000 SDCo 1318 B7
(See Page 1318)
Custer St
5300 SDGO 1268 F3
Customhouse Ct
- SDGO 1351 J4
Customhouse Plz
- SDGO 1351 J4
Cutter Ct
1800 SDCo 1272 B3
Cuvaison
30900 SDCo 1068 B3
Cuvee Ct
17200 POWY 1170 E2
Cuvier St
7400 SDGO 1227 E7
Cuyamaca Av
1200 CHLV 1330 E3
7500 LMGR 1270 G7
1000 SDCo 1291 D2
400 SDGO 1289 H4
Cuyamaca College Dr E
12100 SDCo 1271 J5
Cuyamaca College Dr W
12100 SDCo 1271 J5
Cuyamaca Ct
2100 SDCo 1271 D7
Cuyamaca Forest Rd
15800 SDCo 1176 E3
(See Page 1176)
Cuyamaca Hwy
2700 SDCo 1136 B7
3500 SDCo 1156 E3
8700 SDCo 1236 C3
Cuyamaca Meadows Rd
17900 SDCo 1156 G7
Cuyamaca Peaklookout Rd
- SDCo 1196 C3
(See Page 1196)
Cuyamaca St
1400 ELCJ 1251 D3
- SDCo 1085 J4
9700 SNTE 1231 C4
Cuyamaca Wy
1400 CHLV 1330 F4
Cyan Ln
1800 CHLV 1331 F3
Cycad Dr
900 SNMS 1129 A3
Cymbal Ct
2200 SDCo 1252 D6
Cynthia Ct
600 SNMS 1109 B6
Cynthia Ln
1300 CRLB 1106 E4
13600 POWY 1190 F4
Cynthia Pl
4400 SDGO 1289 J1
Cypress Av
200 CRLB 1106 D5
400 IMPB 1329 F6
3000 LMGR 1270 G6
1000 SDGO 1269 B6
Cypress Canyon
- SDGO 1210 B1
Cypress Canyon Park Rd
11400 SDGO 1210 C1
Cypress Canyon Rd
- SDGO 1210 B2
Cypress Creek Ct
1500 VSTA 1088 A3
Cypress Crest Ter
300 ESCN 1130 B5
Cypress Ct
1200 SDGO 1269 B6
Cypress Del Mar
3900 SDGO 1188 A7
Cypress Dr
- ELCN 6559 G3
- SDCo 1297 E6
(See Page 1297)
200 SDGO 1350 F3
800 VSTA 1088 B7
1100 VSTA 1108 A1
Cypress Glen Pl
4600 SDGO 1188 B6
Cypress Hill Rd
2700 CRLB 1106 F3
Cypress Hills Dr
600 ENCT 1147 E5
Cypress Lakes Wy
8800 SNTE 1230 J4
Cypress Ln
500 ELCJ 1251 F2
24700 SDCo 1236 A2
28900 SDCo 1237 C6
Cypress Meadows Trl
6400 SDGO 1188 G3
Cypress Point Glen
1700 ESCN 1109 D4
Cypress Point Rd
6200 SDGO 1250 D6
Cypress Point Wy
800 OCSD 1066 F7
Cypress Pt
14300 POWY 1150 G6
Cypress Pt Ct
1300 CHLV 1311 H6
Cypress Pt Terr
14400 SDCo 1090 G5
Cypress Rd
3600 OCSD 1086 F1
Cypress Ridge
- SDCo 1090 D5
Cypress St
200 CHLV 1310 B6
4800 LMSA 1270 J2
9600 SDCo 1232 C4
3200 SDCo 1310 C3
1800 SDGO 1330 A6
W Cypress St
300 ELCJ 1251 F5
Cypress Terrace Pl
11900 SDGO 1210 B1
Cypress Valley Dr
11800 SDGO 1210 A1
Cypress Woods Ct
12500 SDGO 1210 C1
Cypress Woods Dr
11400 SDGO 1210 C1
Cypress Wy
900 SDGO 1269 B6
Cyprus Island Ct
4100 SDCo 1028 G5
Cyrus Wy
4600 OCSD 1107 E5

D

D Av
600 CORD 1288 H6
200 NATC 1289 H7
600 NATC 1309 H1
- SDCo 1066 B2
- SDCo 1291 D3
W D Hall Dr
100 ELCJ 1251 G5
D Hinojosa St
1200 CALX 6680 J1
D Mercado St
1000 CALX 6680 D1
D Patino St
1200 CALX 6680 J1
D R Kincad St
200 CALX 6620 G7
D Renison St
- CALX 6620 J7
D St
400 BRAW 6319 G1
(See Page 6319)
1000 BRAW 6320 A1
(See Page 6320)
600 CHLV 1309 J5
100 CHLV 1310 C5
300 ENCT 1147 B7
600 IMPE 6439 E5
- ImCo 6319 C1
(See Page 6319)
- SDCo 1108 G2
2500 SDCo 1136 B7
1200 SDCo 1152 G6
- SDCo 1289 J4
500 SNMS 1108 D7
E D St
200 ENCT 1147 C7
Da Gama Ct
1800 SDCo 1109 E6
Da Nang Dr
1500 CORD 1309 D6
Da Vinci St
4500 SDGO 1188 C7
Dabney Dr
10600 SDGO 1209 A4
Daffodil
- SDCo 1233 B3
Daffodil Ln
5700 SDGO 1250 E7
Daffodil Pl
7200 CRLB 1127 B6
Daffodil St
- SDCo 1086 A4
- SDGO 1208 B6
Dafne Ln
10100 SDGO 1249 G1
Dafter Dr
4900 SDGO 1290 A1
Dafter Pl
4900 SDGO 1290 A1
Dagget St
7900 SDGO 1249 B2
Daggett Wy
5800 LMSA 1251 C7
Dahlgren Ln
3300 SDGO 1249 C5
Dahlia Av
200 IMPB 1329 F7
1800 SDGO 1329 J7
2700 SDGO 1330 C7
Dahlia Ct
800 SDGO 1330 C7
Dahlia Dr
- NATC 1289 H7
100 SOLB 1187 E1
Dahlia Ln
100 IMPE 6439 E6
Dahlia St
- SDCo 1086 B2
2900 SDGO 1269 H7
Dahlia Wy
800 CRLB 1127 A6
Dailey Ct
5100 LMSA 1271 A2
Dailey Rd
8900 LMSA 1271 A1
Daily Dr
2800 SDCo 997 B2
Daily Rd
- SDCo 996 H2
- SDCo 997 A1
Dain Ct
2200 LMGR 1270 J7
Dain Dr
1900 LMGR 1290 J1
Dairy Mart Rd
3000 SDGO 1350 D5
Dairy Rd
3200 SDCo 1291 B7
Daisy Av
900 CRLB 1127 A6
100 IMPB 1329 E7
6000 SDGO 1290 C5
Daisy Ct
1000 CRLB 1127 B6
Daisy Ln
2500 SDCo 1028 G7
400 SNMS 1128 F1
Daisy Pl
3900 OCSD 1107 A1
6000 SDGO 1290 C6
Daisy St
800 ESCN 1110 B6
Daisy Wy
1400 SDGO 1290 D5
Dakota Dr
4200 SDGO 1248 E5
Dakota St
12800 POWY 1190 D5
Dakota Wy
500 OCSD 1087 A4
Dalai
- SDCo 1232 F4
Dalbergia Ct
3800 SDGO 1289 G7
Dalbergia St
3500 SDGO 1289 G6
Dalby Cove
8900 SDGO 1209 D2
Dalby Pl
11200 SDGO 1209 D2
Dale Av
400 ESCN 1109 H7
4300 LMSA 1270 G3
9700 SDCo 1271 C5
Dale Ct
800 CHLV 1310 G7
900 SNMS 1109 C5
Dale Grove Ln
300 SDGO 1290 F5
Dale St
3300 SDGO 1269 E6
1300 SDGO 1289 E2
Dalea Pl
4700 OCSD 1087 A1
Dalecrest Ln
2200 SDCo 1271 C7
Dalehaven Pl
4900 SDGO 1289 J1
Dalehurst Rd
9200 SNTE 1231 A3
Dalen Av
5400 SDGO 1228 C6
Dalen Pl
3000 SDGO 1228 C6
Daleridge Pl
2700 SDCo 1271 E7
Dalewood Av
8700 SDGO 1249 C7
Daley Center Dr
- SDCo 1249 F5
3400 SDGO 1249 F4
Daley Flat Rd
3800 SDCo 1135 E7
3300 SDCo 1155 D1
Daley Ranch Truck Tr
- SDCo 1293 B6
Daley St
2400 SDCo 1152 D7
Daley Truck Trail
- SDCo 1293 F1
Dalhart Av
6100 LMSA 1250 H6
Dalhousie Rd
14200 SDGO 1189 D2
Dalia Dr
14200 SDCo 1188 D2
Dalila Ct
- CALX 6620 J7
Dalisay St
2600 SDGO 1350 C3
Dallas Rd
1100 SDCo 1028 A4
Dallas St
8400 LMSA 1250 J6
900 LMSA 1251 A6
Dalles Av
3900 SDGO 1248 E3
Dalles Ct
4300 SDGO 1248 E3

San Diego County Street Index

Street	Block	City	Map#	Grid
Dalton Ct	-	CRLB	1127	C2
Damas Pl	500	CHLV	1311	A4
Damasco Ct	12400	SDGO	1150	B7
Damato St	4500	SDGO	1249	G3
Damon Av	2900	SDGO	1248	C4
Damon Ln	4400	SDCo	1271	H3
Damrock Cir	8600	LMSA	1271	A3
Dan Wy	800	ESCN	1129	G2
Dana Ct	2300	CRLB	1106	H4
Dana Dr	4600	LMSA	1270	F3
	700	VSTA	1087	F5
Dana Landing Rd	1600	SDGO	1268	A3
Dana Ln	-	ESCN	1110	E5
Dana Pl	3700	SDGO	1268	J6
Dana Point Ct	1600	CHLV	1330	J4
Dana Point Wy	800	OCSD	1066	G7
Dana Vista	-	POWY	1190	E5
Danancy Ct	-	SDCo	1291	C4
Danawoods Ct	7200	SDGO	1290	F4
Danawoods Ln	100	SDGO	1290	F5
Danbury Wy	6200	SDGO	1250	A7
Danby Ct	9100	SDGO	1189	D1
Dancer Ct	2000	ESCN	1109	C5
Dancer Pl	1700	ESCN	1109	C5
Dancol Ter	1800	SDCo	1252	C3
Dancy Ct	10500	SDGO	1209	A5
Dancy Pl	10400	SDGO	1208	J4
Dancy Rd	7600	SDGO	1208	J4
	7700	SDGO	1209	A4
Dandelion Ln	2600	IMPE	6439	C6
Dandelion Wy	6500	SDGO	1188	G3
	-	SNMS	1128	D6
Dandridge Ln	5900	SDGO	1270	C5
Dane Av	-	SDCo	1271	B6
Dane Dr	600	SNMS	1108	J5
	700	SNMS	1109	A5
Danenburg Dr	100	ELCN	6559	J3
	200	ELCN	6560	B2
Danerin Wy	-	SDCo	1272	E6
Danes Rd	12400	POWY	1190	C5
Dania Ct	8700	SNTE	1231	A7
Danica Mae Dr	8800	SDGO	1228	C3
Danica Pl	600	ESCN	1129	J6
Danica Wy	1900	ESCN	1129	J6
Daniel Av	2800	SDGO	1249	A6
Daniel Ct	7300	SDGO	1249	A6
Daniel Glen	2600	ESCN	1110	E7
Danielle Dr	-	LMGR	1290	H2
Daniels St	200	CALX	6620	G6
Danielson St	13000	POWY	1190	E6
Dannan Ct	12700	SDGO	1188	D4
Dannenberg Rd	-	ELCN	6559	G3
Danner Pl	100	ELCJ	1251	F6
Danny Boy Rd	8000	SDCo	1169	A2
Danny Ln	1600	SDCo	1251	G1
Danny St	400	SDCo	1251	F1
Danny Wy	1600	SDCo	1251	G1
Danober Dr	1100	SDGO	1350	F1
Dante St	5300	SDGO	1248	H1
Dante Ter	2200	SDCo	1108	D2
Danube Ln	9000	SDGO	1209	D1
Danvers Cir	11900	SDGO	1190	A2
Danville Av	6600	SDGO	1250	D6
Danville Ct	6500	SDGO	1250	D6
Danza Cir	11500	SDGO	1149	J7
Daphne Ct	800	CRLB	1127	A6
Daphne St	100	ENCT	1147	A5
Dapper Ct	8400	SDGO	1209	C1
Dapple Ct	-	SDGO	1190	B7
Dapple Gray Pl	16200	SDCo	1169	F4
Dapple Wy	-	SDGO	1190	B7
Darby St	2100	ESCN	1130	A6
	1300	SDCo	1290	J2
Darcy Ct	9300	SNTE	1231	A5
Darcy Ln	-	SDCo	1172	F2
Dardaina Dr	2900	SDGO	1310	E2
Dardanelle Gn	-	ESCN	1110	D7
Darden Ct	7500	SDGO	1209	A5
Darden Rd	10300	SDGO	1208	J5
	10400	SDGO	1209	A5
Daren Glen	2000	ESCN	1109	D4
Darien Dr	100	ENCT	1167	H1
Darkwood Rd	12300	SDGO	1189	B6
Darla Ln	700	SDCo	1027	F1
Darlene Ln	3300	SDCo	1273	A6
Darling Dr	1500	SDCo	1089	D7
Darlington Ct	2000	SDCo	1272	C4
Darlington Row	-	SDGO	1247	J1
Darrow Gn	-	ESCN	1130	D2
Darryl Ct	-	SDCo	1232	E5
Darryl St	8000	LMGR	1270	H6
Dartford Wy	5600	SDGO	1270	D1
Dartington Wy	6100	CRLB	1127	F2
Dartmoor Cir	-	OCSD	1067	F7
Dartmoor Dr	1700	LMGR	1290	F1
Dartmouth Dr	2800	OCSD	1087	A7
Dartmouth St	1600	CHLV	1311	C5
Dartolo Rd	16100	SDCo	1173	G3
Darview Ln	13300	SDGO	1189	B4
Darwell Ct	10500	SDGO	1208	J4
Darwin Av	3900	SDGO	1350	F1
Darwin Berry Ct	-	SDCo	1090	D4
Darwin Ct	5900	CRLB	1127	C2
Darwin Dr	1300	OCSD	1087	E3
Darwin Pl	1000	SDGO	1350	F1
Darwin Wy	4200	SDGO	1350	G1
Dash Wy	14700	POWY	1190	E1
Dashero Pl	1700	ESCN	1129	F6
Dassco Ct	4900	SDGO	1290	A3
Dassco St	800	SDGO	1290	A3
Dassia Wy	5000	OCSD	1107	F5
Datcho Dr	4000	SDGO	1248	E3
Date Av	-	CHLV	1310	A5
	800	CHLV	1330	B2
	200	CRLB	1106	F7
	100	IMPB	1329	E7
	4800	LMSA	1270	H2
	1500	SDGO	1329	J7
Date Ct	3900	CHLV	1330	F6
Date Ln	-	OCSD	1086	G3
	20200	SDCo	1149	E2
Date Palm Ct	2500	SDCo	1088	D6
Date Pl	4900	SDGO	1290	A2
Date St	100	CHLV	1330	F5
	1300	ESCN	1109	J6
	9600	SDCo	1291	C2
	900	SDGO	1289	B2
	-	SDGO	1290	D4
	1600	VSTA	1087	C7
N Date St	500	ESCN	1130	A1
W Date St	300	SDGO	1289	A2
Dathe St	200	SDCo	1291	B4
Datsun St	-	SDGO	1351	C1
Daucus Ct	8400	SDGO	1189	B6
Dauer Av	4600	LMSA	1270	F3
Daum Rd	20800	SDCo	1315	A1
(See Page 1315)				
Dauntless St	9800	SDGO	1209	E2
Daven Port Ln	-	LMGR	1270	D7
Davenport Av	14000	SDGO	1189	D2
Davenport Ln	500	CHLV	1330	H2
Davenrich St	9000	SDCo	1291	A3
Daventry St	6900	LMGR	1290	E1
Daves Wy	3900	SDGO	1330	F7
Davey Wy	900	SNMS	1109	B5
David Dr	800	CHLV	1310	G7
	1500	ESCN	1109	D5
David Glen	-	ESCN	1109	D4
David Navarro Av	1300	CALX	6620	D7
	800	CALX	6680	D1
David Pl	2200	CRLB	1106	G3
David Ridge Dr	6900	SDCo	1352	A1
David St	-	BRAW	6319	F4
(See Page 6319)				
	1800	SDGO	1268	J1
David Wy	2100	DLMR	1187	F3
Davidann Rd	10800	SNTE	1231	F5
Davidson Av	7600	LMGR	1270	G7
Davidson St	-	CHLV	1310	C5
Davies Dr	-	CHLV	1330	J3
Davis Av	2600	CRLB	1106	E4
	3300	SDGO	1209	B7
Davis Ct	300	SDCo	1086	A2
	-	VSTA	1107	H2
Davis Cup Ln	15500	SDCo	1173	H4
Davis Dr	1800	SDCo	1027	J1
Davis Pl	2600	CRLB	1106	E4
Davis St	800	SDCo	1152	E5
Dawes Ct	1900	VSTA	1107	J4
Dawes St	5100	SDGO	1247	H4
Dawn Crest Ln	-	CHLV	1331	G4
Dawn Ct	500	CHLV	1310	G5
	-	IMPE	6439	F4
	1700	SNMS	1129	C1
	8700	SNTE	1231	E7
Dawn Ln	4200	OCSD	1107	C2
Dawn Marie Dr	-	SDCo	1234	D4
Dawn Pl	1700	ESCN	1110	C7
Dawn View Glen	2900	ESCN	1109	B3
Dawn View Wy	100	SDCo	1252	J2
Dawncrest Ct	2500	SDCo	1136	D6
Dawne St	4900	SDGO	1228	G7
Dawnell Dr	1100	SDGO	1350	F1
Dawnridge Av	1200	ELCJ	1251	J2
	1100	SDCo	1251	H2
Dawson Av	4300	SDGO	1270	A4
Dawson Dr	-	CHLV	1330	J1
	1500	VSTA	1107	H6
Dawsonia St	3600	SDCo	1310	J2
Dax Ct	13200	SDGO	1189	C4
Daxi Ln	1100	SDCo	1129	H6
Day Creek Tr	10000	SNTE	1231	D4
Day Lily Ct	800	SNMS	1129	B1
Day St	200	SDCo	1152	E7
	3400	SDGO	1270	B6
Day Star Ct	1800	VSTA	1087	J2
Day Star Wy	-	SDCo	1152	D2
Daybreak Ct	5500	OCSD	1067	D6
Daybreak Ln	10200	SNTE	1231	D7
Daybreak Pl	1600	ESCN	1110	A5
	800	VSTA	1087	J3
Dayflower Wy	13400	SDGO	1188	F4
Daylight Pl	23500	SDCo	1173	D2
Daylily Dr	-	CRLB	1127	B4
	2200	SDCo	1028	E6
Daymark Ct	-	SDGO	1190	B7
Daysailor Ct	-	SDGO	1330	J6
Dayton Dr	1700	LMGR	1290	G1
Dayton St	4400	SDGO	1270	B4
Daytona St	7700	LMGR	1270	G6
Daza Dr	16200	SDCo	1173	G3
De Acacias Av	-	SDCo	1168	D2
De Ann Ln	800	ELCJ	1251	J4
De Anza Ct	1100	CHLV	1331	A1
	400	OCSD	1086	J4
De Anza Dr	1400	SDCo	1058	G5
(See Page 1058)				
De Anza Pl	600	BRAW	6319	H2
(See Page 6319)				
De Anza Rd	4100	SDGO	1248	D6
De Anza Spur	400	SDCo	1058	G5
(See Page 1058)				
De Anza Trl	800	SDCo	1058	J1
(See Page 1058)				
De Bann Dr	1600	ENCT	1167	E2
De Burn Dr	5100	SDGO	1290	A1
De Camp Dr	6200	LMSA	1251	B6
De La Fuente Ct	600	SDCo	1352	C1
De La Garza St	-	SDCo	1023	E2
De La Ribera St	2100	SDGO	1227	G5
De La Rondo	100	OCSD	1087	A2
De La Rosa Ln	6000	OCSD	1067	D3
De La Toba Rd	-	CHLV	1330	J3
De La Valle Pl	14800	SDCo	1188	A1
De La Vina St	1500	CHLV	1331	D2
De Las Flores St	500	CALX	6620	E7
De Leon Av	-	CALX	6620	H7
De Luz Heights Dr	3400	SDCo	997	E3
De Luz Heights Rd	2700	SDCo	997	C3
De Luz Murrieta Rd	40000	SDCo	996	G1
De Luz Rd	-	SDCo	996	G3
	38100	SDCo	997	B5
	-	SDCo	1027	F1
De Mayo Rd	2100	SDGO	1187	G6
De Mott Ln	9000	SNTE	1231	A7
De Paoli St	-	IMPE	6499	J2
De Quz Heights Rd	-	SDCo	997	E3
De Sola St	16300	SDCo	1169	F4
De Soto Pl	19200	SDCo	1149	D4
De Soto St	4600	SDGO	1248	C4
De Vida Ct	10900	SDGO	1249	J2
Deacon Dr	-	SDCo	1051	E4
Dead Stick Rd	8700	SDGO	1351	H1
Deadwood Dr	-	SNMS	1128	H5
Deal Ct	700	SDGO	1267	H3
Dealwood Av	500	ELCN	6560	C1
Dealwood Rd	-	ImCo	6560	G1
Dean Dr	1100	ENCT	1167	F3
Deana Pl	1000	ESCN	1130	A3
Deanly Ct	13800	SDCo	1232	E4
Deanly St	9400	SDCo	1232	E5
Deanly Wy	13800	SDCo	1232	E5
Dearborn Dr	1000	SDGO	1350	C1
Dearborn Pl	12100	POWY	1190	F7
Dearborn St	3700	OCSD	1086	G5
Dearbrook Dr	-	SDCo	1253	C3
Deaton Dr	4900	SDGO	1290	A1
Deauville St	2500	SDGO	1310	D2
Deaver Ln	3500	SDGO	1350	F4
Deavers Dr	-	SNMS	1109	D7
Debbie Ct	-	SDCo	1232	H4
Debbie Pl	600	ESCN	1109	J7
Debby Dr	5000	SDGO	1270	B2
Debby St	400	SDCo	1027	H3
Debbyann Pl	4100	SDGO	1330	F7
Debco Dr	2200	LMGR	1270	J7
Debenmark Pl	1200	SDGO	1350	D1
Debi Ln	-	SDCo	1070	E1
Deborah Pl	7800	LMGR	1270	H7
Debra Ann Dr	600	SDCo	1027	H3
Debra Cir	4100	OCSD	1087	C7
Debra Ln	1800	VSTA	1087	H3
Debra Pl	500	SNMS	1128	D1
Debreceni Wy	10500	SDCo	1169	G2
Decant Dr	13100	POWY	1170	D2
Decanture Cove	7200	SDGO	1250	D4
Decanture St	6400	SDGO	1250	D4
Decanture Wy	7200	SDGO	1250	D4
Decatur Cir	9000	SDGO	1209	D3
Decatur Rd	10900	SDGO	1209	D3
	-	SDGO	1268	D7
	-	SDGO	1288	C1
Decatur Wy	-	ESCN	1129	G1
Decena Dr	6100	SDGO	1249	J7
Decision St	-	VSTA	1128	A1
Deck	-	SDCo	1023	E2
Decker Ct	100	ELCJ	1251	J5
Decker St	1000	ELCJ	1251	H5
Decora Cir	3500	SNMS	1108	C7
Decoro St	4300	SDGO	1228	C4
Deddar Dr	-	ELCJ	1251	J6
Deddie Ter	200	SDCo	1027	F5
Dedo Pl	11400	SDGO	1209	B1
Deeb Ct	3000	SDCo	1088	E6
Deeb Dr	2900	SDCo	1088	E6
Deelan Ln	13100	POWY	1190	H4
Deem Pl	1100	ELCJ	1251	H4
Deep Canyon Ct	-	SDCo	1089	F3
Deep Canyon Dr	-	SDCo	1089	G3
Deep Dell Cove	7400	SDGO	1290	G4
Deep Dell Ct	7600	SDGO	1290	H5
Deep Dell Rd	100	SDGO	1290	G5
Deep Haven Ln	1800	SDGO	1350	C3
Deep Valley Rd	6800	SDGO	1250	D3
Deep Well Tr	3800	SDCo	1099	E1
(See Page 1099)				
Deer Canyon Ct	13000	SDGO	1210	D2
Deer Canyon Dr	-	SDCo	1154	E2
Deer Canyon Pl	-	SDGO	1189	A4
Deer Creek Trl	28700	SDCo	1237	B6
Deer Creek Wy	-	OCSD	1086	J2
Deer Grass Dr	-	SDCo	1129	C5
Deer Hill Ct	1400	SDGO	1247	G3
Deer Hollow Ct	9700	SNTE	1231	F4
Deer Lake Park Rd	3400	SDCo	1155	J2
	3500	SDCo	1156	B2
Deer Park Rd	-	SDCo	1197	C2
(See Page 1197)				
	11000	SDCo	1217	E6
(See Page 1217)				
Deer Park Wy	-	SDGO	1188	E5
Deer Path	300	ENCT	1147	A2
Deer Path Ln	-	CHLV	1331	G3
Deer Peak Ct	-	CHLV	1311	D7
Deer Ridge Ct	16100	SDCo	1169	E4
Deer Ridge Pl	9800	SDCo	1169	E4
Deer Ridge Rd	16700	SDCo	1169	E3
Deer Springs Pl	-	SDCo	1089	A6
Deer Springs Rd	200	SDCo	1088	J7
	600	SDCo	1089	B7
	-	SDCo	1234	H6
Deer Trail Ct	16200	SDCo	1169	E5
Deer Trail Dr	9800	SDCo	1169	E4
Deer Trail Pl	9600	SDCo	1169	E5
Deer Trail Wy	9600	SDCo	1169	E5
Deer Valley	-	OCSD	1086	H2
Deer Valley Estates	18000	POWY	1150	H7
Deer View Dr	10100	SDCo	1089	D5
Deer Wk Ct	1400	SDCo	1315	G5
(See Page 1315)				
Deerben Rd	20100	SDCo	1153	G1
Deerbrook Dr	-	SNMS	1108	H4
Deerfield Ct	800	OCSD	1086	E2
Deerfield Rd	1700	ENCT	1147	G6
Deerfield St	7800	SDGO	1250	D3
Deerflower Dr	-	SDGO	1270	D6
Deerfoot Dr	11900	SDGO	1210	B2
Deerford Row	6000	SDGO	1248	A1
Deergrass Ct	13800	POWY	1170	F5
Deergrass Wy	1900	CRLB	1147	F2
Deerhaven	500	ELCJ	1252	D4
Deerhaven Dr	1000	VSTA	1087	J5
Deerhollow Pl	6800	SDGO	1250	C3
Deerhorn Oaks Rd	21000	SDCo	1315	A3
(See Page 1315)				
Deerhorn Spring Ln	2300	SDCo	1294	H7
(See Page 1294)				
Deerhorn Valley Rd	19200	SDCo	1294	F7
(See Page 1294)				
	20800	SDCo	1314	J1
(See Page 1314)				
	20800	SDCo	1315	A3
(See Page 1315)				
Deerhurst Ct	0	SDGO	1290	F6
Deering St	10800	SDGO	1209	B3
Deerock Pl	100	SDGO	1290	G4
Deerpark Dr	2700	SDGO	1248	F6
Deerpark St	2100	SDGO	1268	G1
Deerrun Pl	6800	SDGO	1250	C3
Deerwood Ct	6700	SDGO	1250	C3
Deerwood St	14600	POWY	1190	C1
Defender Ct	-	SOLB	1187	G1
Defiance Wy	5000	SDGO	1270	A2
Defreitas Av	9200	SDGO	1189	D3
Degen Dr	2800	SDCo	1290	J6
Dehesa Ct	7500	CRLB	1147	J1
Dehesa Meadow Rd	3500	SDCo	1252	H7
Dehesa Mountain Ln	3600	SDCo	1252	J4
Dehesa Ranch Rd	-	SDCo	1253	F3
Dehesa Rd	1900	SDCo	1252	C6
	5900	SDCo	1253	D4
Dehesa Wy	-	SDCo	1252	J4
Dehia St	15500	POWY	1190	H3
Del Amo Ct	16200	SDCo	1173	E3
Del Amo Pl	24000	SDCo	1173	E2
Del Amo Rd	24500	SDCo	1153	F7
	24200	SDCo	1173	E2
Del Cero	3000	OCSD	1107	D3
Del Cerro Av	3600	OCSD	1107	C2
	5600	SDGO	1270	D1
Del Cerro Blvd	5400	SDGO	1250	A7
	6700	SDGO	1270	E1
Del Cerro Ct	6300	SDGO	1270	D1
Del Charro Rd	3300	SDCo	1272	D7
Del Cielo Este	31900	SDCo	1048	B7
Del Cielo Oeste	32000	SDCo	1048	B7
Del Coronado Ln	10300	SNTE	1231	D2
Del Corro Pl	500	CHLV	1310	G5
Del Diablo Ln	14800	SDGO	1189	H1
Del Diablo St	11200	SDGO	1169	J7
	11100	SDGO	1189	H1
Del Diablo Wy	11100	SDGO	1169	H7
Del Dios Hwy	7800	SDCo	1148	J7
S Del Dios Hwy	900	ESCN	1129	G5
	10200	ESCN	1149	E1
Del Este Dr	-	ESCN	1129	F4
Del Este Wy	3400	OCSD	1107	C2
Del Flora St	-	OCSD	1086	F1
Del Fresno Av	-	SNMS	1109	B5
Del Mar Av	-	CHLV	1310	B4
	1100	CHLV	1330	D3
	4800	SDGO	1267	H7
	3900	SDGO	1288	A1
N Del Mar Av	100	CHLV	1310	B4
Del Mar Corporate Ct	-	SDGO	1187	J7
Del Mar Ct	400	CHLV	1310	C6
Del Mar Downs Rd	800	SOLB	1187	F2
Del Mar Glen	3900	SDGO	1188	A7
Del Mar Heights Pl	-	SDGO	1188	A5
Del Mar Heights Rd	2000	DLMR	1187	G6
	4200	SDGO	1188	C5
Del Mar Hills Rd	13800	SDGO	1187	J6
Del Mar Meadows	3900	SDGO	1188	A7
Del Mar Mesa Rd	-	SDGO	1188	D7
Del Mar Oaks	12300	SDGO	1188	A6
Del Mar Rd	1600	OCSD	1067	G7
Del Mar Scenic Pkwy	2200	SDGO	1207	G1
Del Mar Shores Ter	100	SOLB	1187	E1
Del Mar Trails Rd	4100	SDGO	1188	B7
Del Marino Av	13500	POWY	1190	H4
Del Mesa St	-	OCSD	1086	G1
Del Monte Av	100	CHLV	1330	D5
	4700	SDGO	1267	J7
	4300	SDGO	1268	A7
Del Norte	16100	POWY	1170	D4
Del Oro Av	-	OCSD	1087	B5
Del Oro Ct	8300	SDGO	1227	H5
Del Oro Ln	1900	SDCo	1130	C4
Del Paso Av	6300	SDGO	1250	D5
Del Paso Ct	3600	OCSD	1107	D3
Del Paso Dr	17700	POWY	1150	F7
Del Paso Pl	6800	SDGO	1250	D5
Del Pena Ct	11100	SDGO	1189	J3
Del Poniente Ct	15200	POWY	1170	F7
Del Poniente Rd	-	POWY	1170	E7
Del Prado Ct	1100	CHLV	1331	A1
Del Prado St	4800	SDCo	1310	H3
Del Ray Pl	600	CHLV	1310	H7
Del Rey Av	3100	CRLB	1147	J1
Del Rey Blvd	-	CHLV	1310	G6
Del Rey Dr	-	OCSD	1086	J3
Del Rey St	3500	SDGO	1248	D5
Del Riego Av	700	ENCT	1147	C4
Del Rincon Pl	-	ESCN	1109	H4
Del Rio Av	700	ENCT	1147	C4
Del Rio Ct	1100	CHLV	1311	A7
	3300	CRLB	1147	J1
Del Rio Rd	-	ImCo	6260	A5
(See Page 6260)				
	10000	SDCo	1271	D5
Del Rio Wy	-	SDCo	1271	F5
	300	VSTA	1087	G5
Del Rosa Ln	1300	SDCo	1128	B3
Del Roy Dr	300	SNMS	1108	H4
Del Sol Blvd	3000	SDGO	1350	D1
Del Sol Ct	4200	SDGO	1350	G1
Del Sol Ln	1300	SDGO	1350	E1
Del Sol Rd	12500	SDCo	1232	B5
Del Sol Wy	1200	SDGO	1350	G1
Del Sur Blvd	1600	SDGO	1350	E2
Del Sur Ct	1100	CHLV	1331	A1
	7900	SDGO	1169	B5
Del Sur Ridge Rd	-	SDGO	1169	D3
Del Valle Dr	800	SDCo	1047	E5
Del Vino Ct	-	SDGO	1188	G7
Del Vista Wy	16300	SDCo	1233	F3
Delage Ct	400	ENCT	1167	G1
Delage Dr	300	ENCT	1167	G1
Delancy Ct	-	CRLB	1127	A1
Deland Ct	600	ELCJ	1271	E1
	2100	SDCo	1254	B1
Deland Dr	2400	SDCo	1254	B1
Delano Av	5600	SDGO	1250	B6
Delano Ct	-	CHLV	1311	C7
Delany Dr	2200	SDGO	1350	G3
Delaport Ct	-	CORD	1329	E3
Delaport Ln	-	CORD	1329	E3
Delaport Pl	-	CORD	1329	D3
Delaport Wy	-	CORD	1329	E3
Delaware Av	6800	LMSA	1270	E1
Delaware St	500	IMPB	1329	G7
	1100	IMPB	1349	G1
	4600	SDGO	1269	B4
Delbarton St	6300	SDGO	1249	J6
Delcardo Av	600	SDGO	1330	G7
Delecia Ct	100	SOLB	1167	H4
Deleon Dr	1100	CHLV	1311	B6
Deleone Rd	3400	SNMS	1108	D5
Delevan Dr	1100	SDGO	1289	F2
Delfern St	6600	SDGO	1250	B6
Delfina	7500	SDGO	1168	J7
	7500	SDGO	1188	J1
Delfina Pl	3000	CRLB	1147	H2
Delgado Ct	7500	CRLB	1147	J1
Delgado Pl	800	ESCN	1129	J5
Delia Ln	9900	SNTE	1231	F3
Delight St	1500	ELCJ	1252	B2
Delight Wy	-	ESCN	1109	J7
Dell Anne Pl	800	SDGO	1290	H2
Dell Ct	400	SOLB	1167	F6
Dell Rim Ct	7900	SDGO	1209	A1
Dell St	600	SOLB	1167	F6
Dell View Rd	15600	SDCo	1233	C3
Della Ct	1600	OCSD	1106	D1
Della Pl	4900	SDGO	1228	C7
Dellcrest Ln	1300	SDGO	1227	F7
Dellcrest Wy	700	ESCN	1130	C2
Delltop Ln	2100	SDCo	1271	D7
Dellwood St	4100	SDGO	1249	A2
Delniso Ct	1700	CHLV	1330	J5
Delor Ct	6000	SDGO	1249	J7
Delos Dr	7000	SDGO	1290	F7
Delos St	2200	SDGO	1290	F7
Delos Wy	4900	OCSD	1107	E5
Delphi St	9900	SNTE	1231	F4
Delphinium St	100	ENCT	1147	E6

STREET
Block City Map# Grid

Delphinus Wy
11000 SDGO 1209 D2
Delridge Ln
- SDCo 1091 F5
Delrose Av
8800 SDCo 1290 J3
Delta Ln
300 VSTA 1087 F7
Delta Park Ln
200 NATC 1289 J7
Delta Rd
- SDGO 1209 C7
Delta St
8700 LMSA 1251 A7
1700 NATC 1289 J6
4300 SDGO 1289 H6
Delta Wy
- CRLB 1107 B4
Deluga Dr
800 SNMS 1109 C5
Demeter Wy
4800 OCSD 1107 E6
2900 SDGO 1310 E2
Demler Dr
2800 SDCo 1129 C5
Demona Pl
100 SDCo 1290 J5
Demoulin Rd
- ImCo 6320 E5
(See Page 6320)
Dempster Dr
9300 SNTE 1230 H6
Demus St
3800 SDGO 1270 C5
Dena St
- BRAW 6320 C1
(See Page 6320)
Denara Rd
13200 SDGO 1187 J5
Denby St
400 SDGO 1289 H3
Dendia Wy
1900 SDCo 1272 A1
Deneb Av
- SDGO 1209 E7
Denia Wy
4700 OCSD 1107 F5
Denise Canyon Ct
3800 SDCo 1311 A3
Denise Cir
1400 OCSD 1106 D1
Denise Ct
1000 SNMS 1129 B3
Denise Ln
700 ELCJ 1251 G6
Denison Wy
300 SDCo 1087 G1
Denk Ln
2200 ENCT 1167 J1
Dennery Rd
- SDGO 1330 H7
- SDGO 1350 H1
Dennig Pl
11300 SDGO 1208 J2
Denning Dr
- CRLB 1128 B7
- CRLB 1148 C1
Dennis Av
600 CHLV 1310 E7
Dennis Ct
- IMPE 6499 H2
Dennis Ln
2700 LMGR 1270 J7
Dennison Pl
7100 SDGO 1228 D4
Dennison St
6500 SDGO 1228 D5
Dennstedt Ct
1000 ELCJ 1251 C7
Dennstedt Pl
900 ELCJ 1251 D7
Denny Wy
200 ELCJ 1251 E2
Denova Dr
2300 SDCo 1253 H2
Denstone Pl
1700 LMGR 1290 E1
Dent Ct
8600 SDGO 1250 J3
Dent Dr
8600 SDGO 1250 J3
Dentata Ln
13900 SDGO 1188 H3
Denton St
8400 LMSA 1250 J6
Dentro De Lomas
- SDCo 1068 E6
Dentro De Lomas Rd
1500 SDCo 1067 J3
1600 SDCo 1068 B4
Denver Dr
3900 LMSA 1270 G5
Denver Ln
1100 ELCJ 1251 H3
Denver St
3100 SDGO 1248 E6
1800 SDGO 1268 E1
Denwood Rd
4600 LMSA 1270 G3
Deodar Rd
1100 ESCN 1109 F7

Deodar Rd
1000 SDCo 1129 F1
700 SNMS 1129 E1
Deodar Trl
7600 SDCo 1237 B7
Deprise Cove
11200 SDGO 1210 G2
Derald Rd
9600 SNTE 1231 A4
Derby Ct
- OCSD 1067 G7
Derby Downs Ct
- SDGO 1188 A4
Derby Downs Ln
- SDGO 1188 A4
Derby Farms Rd
- SDGO 1188 D2
Derby Hill Pt
- SDGO 1208 D2
Derby St
900 SDGO 1290 B3
Derek Wy
1600 CHLV 1330 F5
Derk Dr
5700 LMSA 1250 J7
Dermid Rd
- SDCo 1070 C5
Deron Av
13100 SDGO 1189 D4
Derrick Ct
5100 SDGO 1248 G1
Derrick Dr
4300 SDGO 1248 G2
Derrick Wy
2200 ESCN 1129 H7
Derringer Pl
2700 ESCN 1110 D6
Derringer Rd
14800 POWY 1170 G7
Derrydown Wy
- SDGO 1208 E1
Desart Dr
3800 SDCo 1099 F1
(See Page 1099)
Descanso Av
- IMPB 1349 E2
1500 SNMS 1108 D6
Descanso Creek Pl
- CHLV 1311 H6
Descanso Dr
- CALX 6620 H6
Descanso Pl
2400 SDCo 1252 H4
Deseret Rd
10100 SDCo 1049 D2
Desert Bluffs Ct
2100 CHLV 1331 F3
Desert Gardens Dr
2200 ELCN 6559 E1
Desert Glen
1600 ESCN 1109 D6
Desert Hare Ct
2100 CHLV 1331 G3
Desert Inn Wy
3500 CHLV 1310 G2
Desert Oriole Dr
4600 SDCo 1099 G5
(See Page 1099)
Desert Rose Ct
- IMPE 6499 E2
Desert Rose Ln
- CHLV 1331 G4
Desert Rose Ranch Rd
42800 SDCo 1321 C2
(See Page 1321)
Desert Rose St
- IMPE 6439 C7
Desert Rose Wy
- ENCT 1148 A5
Desert Spring Dr
1600 CHLV 1331 F2
Desert View Dr
5700 SDGO 1248 A2
Desert View St
1000 CALX 6620 D7
Desert Vista Dr
4500 SDCo 1099 F4
(See Page 1099)
Desert Vista Terr
1900 SDCo 1099 F4
(See Page 1099)
Desert Willow St
- IMPE 6499 C2
Desertview Av
- ELCN 6559 G4
Design Ct
700 CHLV 1330 J5
Desiree Ln
8400 SNTE 1251 C1
Desmond Cir
4600 OCSD 1107 F3
Desoto Ct
1100 CHLV 1311 B6
4200 SDCo 1271 G4
Despejo Pl
5800 SDGO 1229 H7
Destiny Mtn Ct
10000 SDCo 1291 F2
Destree Rd
1100 SDCo 1130 C2

Desty Ct
2600 SDGO 1330 C7
Desty St
800 SDGO 1330 C7
Detrick Wy
3000 SDCo 1155 H3
Detroit Pl
400 SDGO 1290 D5
Detwiler Rd
- SDCo 1149 B4
Devereux Rd
17700 SDGO 1170 B1
Deverill Dr
- SDCo 1232 H4
Deville Dr
7400 LMGR 1290 G2
Devin Dr
1400 SDCo 1027 J5
Deviney Ln
- SDCo 1172 G5
Devon Ct
3300 SDCo 1272 F5
700 SDGO 1267 H3
Devon Dr
13200 SDCo 1272 E5
Devon Pl
1800 SDCo 1108 C2
Devonshire Dr
700 ENCT 1147 C7
1000 ENCT 1167 C1
1000 SDGO 1287 H1
Devonshire Glen
400 ESCN 1110 D6
Devos Dr
16600 SDGO 1170 C3
Dew Point Av
500 CRLB 1126 J7
Dewane Dr
600 ELCJ 1251 D4
Dewberry Ct
13400 SDCo 1090 D3
Dewes Wy
4100 SDGO 1248 E6
Dewey Pl
1200 SDCo 1318 A5
(See Page 1318)
Dewey Rd
- SDGO 1268 D7
Dewey St
- NATC 1309 F3
1100 SDGO 1289 C5
Dewitt Av
700 ENCT 1147 C7
1100 ENCT 1167 C1
Dewitt Ct
300 ELCJ 1271 G2
Dewitt Estates Rd
1700 SDCo 1253 J1
Dewsbury Av
9100 SDGO 1209 D3
Dexter Pl
1200 ESCN 1129 H7
Di Foss St
2300 LMGR 1270 H7
Di Giorgio Rd
1500 SDCo 1059 A5
(See Page 1059)
2500 SDCo 1079 A3
(See Page 1079)
Di Marino St
900 SDGO 1290 F2
Di Novo St
7100 SDGO 1290 F2
Di Vita Dr
6300 CRLB 1127 G3
Dia Del Sol
16200 SDCo 1071 B7
Diablo Ct
1500 ESCN 1109 H5
Diablo Glen
1300 ESCN 1130 B2
Diablo Pl
1200 VSTA 1107 E1
Diablo Point Ct
- CHLV 1330 J3
Diamante Wy
- OCSD 1106 J2
Diamond
- SDCo 1232 F4
Diamond Back Dr
8800 SNTE 1231 G6
Diamond Bar Rd
600 SDCo 1078 J3
(See Page 1078)
Diamond Cir
4100 OCSD 1087 C6
Diamond Ct
- CHLV 1330 H1
Diamond Dr
600 CHLV 1330 H2
1100 SDCo 1172 H1
Diamond Gem Ln
- SDCo 1273 F7
Diamond Gn
- ESCN 1110 C7
Diamond Head Ct
10100 SDCo 1291 D2
Diamond Head Dr
1300 ENCT 1167 F1

Diamond Hill Pvt Rd
- SDCo 1052 F7
(See Page 1052)
Diamond Ln
1300 SDCo 1251 H3
Diamond Ranch Rd
1800 SDCo 1130 F5
Diamond St
- IMPE 6439 C7
1000 SDGO 1247 H5
1700 SDGO 1248 A5
1800 SNMS 1128 B6
Diamond Wy
600 VSTA 1087 F7
Diamondback Ct
2100 CHLV 1331 G4
Diana St
100 ENCT 1147 A4
Diane Av
5500 SDGO 1228 G6
4800 SDGO 1248 G1
Diane Ct
4900 SDGO 1228 G6
Diane Dr
- SNTE 1231 F7
Diane Lyn Ct
500 SDCo 1028 E2
Diane Pl
600 ESCN 1109 J7
4900 SDGO 1228 G6
Diane Wy
4500 SDGO 1248 F1
Diaz Dr
16600 SDGO 1170 C3
Diaz Glen
2700 ESCN 1110 E7
Diaz Rd
30600 SDCo 1069 E3
Dicenza Ln
8000 SDGO 1250 E3
Dicenza Wy
6700 SDGO 1250 E3
Dichondra Pl
9900 SDGO 1209 J4
Dichoso Dr
1600 ESCN 1130 B4
Dichter St
500 ELCJ 1252 B6
Dick St
4900 SDGO 1270 A3
Dickens St
3200 SDGO 1288 B2
Dickerman Rd
- ImCo 6260 J2
(See Page 6260)
Dickerson Dr
- CRLB 1127 A1
Dickey Dr
4500 SDCo 1271 E3
Dickey St
- SDCo 1028 A4
Dickinson St
200 SDGO 1268 J4
Diego Dr
16700 SDGO 1170 A3
Diego Estates Dr
3400 SDCo 1048 D2
Diegos Ct
4300 SDCo 1028 H7
Diegueno Rd
2000 SDCo 1078 H1
(See Page 1078)
Diesel Dr
1800 SDCo 1252 C4
Diet Ln
1200 SDCo 1027 H5
Dietrich Rd
4200 ImCo 6260 G5
(See Page 6260)
- ImCo 6320 G5
(See Page 6320)
Dillard St
1600 SDGO 1290 D6
Dillon Dr
9200 LMSA 1271 B1
Dillon Wy
4100 SDGO 1248 E6
Dillons Trl
1700 SDGO 1351 A2
Dilman St
- SDCo 1252 B6
Dimaio Wy
600 ESCN 1110 D5
Dinamica Wy
6300 SDGO 1248 H7
Dinara Dr
2300 SDCo 1129 D3
Dipper St
6000 SDGO 1290 C2
Dippon Ln
2200 ESCN 1110 B5
Dirac St
5800 SDGO 1228 E6
Directors Pl
4900 SDGO 1208 D6
Discovery Bay Dr
1200 CHLV 1311 G6
Discovery Falls Dr
1900 CHLV 1331 H2
Discovery Rd
2500 CRLB 1127 F2

W Discovery St
1200 SDCo 1128 D2
1100 SNMS 1128 E2
Discovery Wy
- SDGO 1227 H3
Disney Ln
- SDCo 1068 E4
Dissinger Av
6300 SDGO 1310 E1
Distinctive Dr
8200 SDGO 1269 B1
Distribution Av
9800 SDGO 1208 J7
9500 SDGO 1228 J1
Distribution St
200 SNMS 1129 A1
1400 VSTA 1107 J6
N Ditmar St
300 OCSD 1086 A7
S Ditmar St
1700 OCSD 1106 C3
Divellos Dr
- SDCo 1233 E4
Diversey Dr
13300 POWY 1190 G4
Diversion Dr
3400 SDCo 1271 D6
Divine Wy
4700 SDCo 1271 D3
Division St
1400 OCSD 1086 B7
3700 SDGO 1289 G7
6200 SDGO 1290 D5
E Division St
2100 NATC 1290 A6
Dixie Dr
6100 LMSA 1251 B6
4900 SDGO 1247 H5
Dixie Ln
7900 SDCo 1168 J1
Dixie St
1700 OCSD 1086 C7
Dixon Ct
1300 CHLV 1330 E3
Dixon Dr
1100 CHLV 1330 E2
Dixon Ln
- ESCN 1130 A6
Dixon Pl
3700 SDGO 1288 A1
Dixon Rd
5200 OCSD 1087 E1
Dixon Wy
1200 CHLV 1330 E3
Diza Rd
100 SDGO 1350 G2
Doane Valley Rd
34700 SDCo 1032 A7
Dobyns Dr
8500 SNTE 1231 A7
8500 SNTE 1251 A1
Docena Dr
8400 SDCo 1290 J5
Docena Rd
- CRLB 1127 C5
Dock Ct
6900 SDGO 1290 F7
Dock St
- SDGO 1288 A5
Dodd Ln
1200 SDCo 1318 B7
(See Page 1318)
Dodder Ct
13800 POWY 1170 F5
Dodge Dr
700 SDGO 1247 F3
Dodie St
8100 SDGO 1290 H2
Dodson St
300 SDGO 1289 E4
Dodson Wy
- SDGO 1289 E4
Doe Pt
8100 SDGO 1250 D3
Doetsch Rd
500 ImCo 6259 C7
(See Page 6259)
Doghouse Spur Truck Trl
- SDCo 1313 D3
(See Page 1313)
Dogwood
- SDCo 1233 B3
Dogwood Ct
4500 OCSD 1087 D4
Dogwood Glen
27800 SDCo 1089 F4
Dogwood Ln
- SDCo 1089 D4
Dogwood Pl
100 ESCN 1109 G4
Dogwood Rd
- BRAW 6319 J6
(See Page 6319)
2500 CRLB 1127 F3
- ELCN 6500 A6
1300 ELCN 6560 A3
- IMPE 6500 A1
- ImCo 6259 J5
(See Page 6259)
2100 ImCo 6500 A4
- ImCo 6560 B5

Dogwood Rd
- ImCo 6620 B2
14000 POWY 1170 G4
100 SDCo 1086 B2
Dogwood Trl
33500 SDCo 1052 E2
(See Page 1052)
Dogwood Wy
13500 SDGO 1188 G3
2400 VSTA 1108 B6
Doheny Bay Ct
300 OCSD 1066 J6
Doheny Rd
9400 SNTE 1231 B5
Dolan Pl
3200 SDCo 1310 H1
Dole Wy
100 SNMS 1128 H3
Doliva Dr
4800 SDGO 1248 H1
Dollar Wy
10800 SDCo 1232 B1
Dollimore Rd
100 ENCT 1147 C6
Dolly Pl
9000 SDGO 1249 D6
Dolo St
200 SDGO 1290 F4
Dolomite Wy
- SNMS 1128 F5
Dolore Pl
1400 ESCN 1110 A6
Dolores Ct
300 SNMS 1109 B7
Dolores Dr
3000 SDCo 1156 E1
Dolores St
9900 SDCo 1271 D5
Dolphin Cir
1200 VSTA 1088 B4
Dolphin Cove Ct
200 DLMR 1187 G6
Dolphin Cres
800 ENCT 1147 C3
Dolphin Ct
- CRLB 1127 F1
Dolphin Pl
5600 SDGO 1247 F4
Dolphin Rd
- SDCo 1085 H6
Dolstra Ln
900 SDCo 1027 G1
Domer Rd
9400 SNTE 1231 B5
Domingo Glen
2100 ESCN 1109 F5
Dominguez Ct
- BRAW 6259 F7
(See Page 6259)
Dominguez Wy
300 ELCJ 1251 H5
Dominican Dr
16800 SDGO 1170 B3
Dominion St
800 SDGO 1289 H5
Domino Dr
9600 SDCo 1232 D4
Don Alberto Dr
3400 CRLB 1107 C6
Don Alvarez Dr
3400 CRLB 1107 B6
Don Arturo Dr
3400 CRLB 1107 B6
Don Carlos Ct
1300 CHLV 1311 B6
Don Carlos Dr
3400 CRLB 1107 C6
Don Cota Dr
3400 CRLB 1107 B6
Don Ct
- SDGO 1350 E1
Don Diablo Dr
3300 CRLB 1107 B7
Don Felipe Dr
5400 CRLB 1107 C6
Don Jose Dr
3400 CRLB 1107 B6
Don Juan Dr
3100 CRLB 1107 B6
Don Lee Pl
1800 ESCN 1129 D2
Don Lorenzo Dr
- CRLB 1107 C6
3500 SDGO 1248 D4
Don Luis Dr
5400 CRLB 1107 C6
Don Mata Dr
5100 CRLB 1107 B6
Don Miguel Dr
5100 CRLB 1107 B6
Don Ortega Dr
3400 CRLB 1107 C6
Don Pablo Dr
3300 CRLB 1107 B7
Don Pancho Wy
4000 SDGO 1350 D2
Don Pico Ct
10300 SDCo 1271 E6
Don Pico Rd
10300 SDCo 1271 F5

Don Porfirio Dr
3400 CRLB 1107 B6
Don Quixote Dr
3300 CRLB 1107 C7
Don Ricardo Dr
3300 CRLB 1107 B6
Don Rolando
3000 SDCo 1150 E1
Don Rudolfo Dr
5100 CRLB 1107 B6
Don Station Ct
- SDCo 1085 J4
Don Tamaso Dr
3300 CRLB 1107 B7
Don Valdez Dr
5200 CRLB 1107 B7
Don Wy
4200 SDGO 1248 E2
E Donahoe St
- CHLV 1330 E1
Donahue Dr
2100 SDCo 1272 C3
Donahue St
1000 SDGO 1268 G3
Donaker St
- SDGO 1189 B2
Donald Av
4500 SDGO 1248 E2
Donald Ct
4100 SDGO 1248 E3
Donald Wy
1200 ESCN 1110 B6
Donaldson Dr
4700 SDGO 1248 B5
Donalor Dr
1800 ESCN 1130 D2
1600 SDCo 1130 D3
Donart Dr
14000 POWY 1190 G2
Donax Av
500 IMPB 1329 F7
1600 SDGO 1329 J7
2200 SDGO 1330 B7
Donax Ct
1500 SDGO 1329 J7
Doncarol Av
1500 ELCJ 1252 B6
Dondero Trl
6700 SDGO 1188 H3
Donee Diego Dr
3000 SDCo 1150 E1
Donita Dr
1500 SDCo 1271 H1
Donley St
3200 SDGO 1248 E6
Donna Av
4000 SDGO 1270 E5
Donna Ct
3700 CRLB 1106 G5
Donna Dr
3200 CRLB 1106 G4
Donna Jean Ln
8800 SNTE 1231 E6
Donna St
- SNTE 1231 F7
Donna Wy
6800 SDGO 1270 E4
Donnan Pl
900 VSTA 1088 A5
Donner St
9900 SNTE 1231 F4
Donnil Ln
2200 SDCo 997 B4
Donnington Wy
2300 SDGO 1290 G7
Donovan State Prison Rd
- SDCo 1332 B7
(See Page 1332)
Donray Dr
- SDCo 1172 H1
Dons Wy
- SDCo 1088 D6
Donze Av
1500 CHLV 1331 C2
Donzee St
8000 SDGO 1249 B5
Dool Av
- CALX 6680 H2
Doolittle Av
500 SDGO 1330 E7
Doomey Dr
- SDCo 1152 E4
Dophin Ct
- SNMS 1128 D6
Dora Dr
1700 ENCT 1167 F2
Dora Vista Ln
3000 SDCo 1292 J1
(See Page 1292)
Dorado Ct
1000 CHLV 1311 A7
7900 SDGO 1227 H6
Dorado Ln
200 ELCJ 1252 A5
Dorado Pl
3300 CRLB 1147 J1
Dorado Wy
- CHLV 1311 A7
Doral Ct
4600 OCSD 1087 A1

Doral Glen
1700 ESCN 1109 D4
Doral Wy
4000 CHLV 1310 F3
Doran Ct
- CHLV 1310 C4
Doran St
1800 SDGO 1350 B3
Dorcas St
1400 SDGO 1268 E2
Dorchester Dr
3500 SDGO 1249 E4
Dorchester Pl
4400 CRLB 1106 J5
Dorchester St
8100 SDCo 1290 H2
Doreen Ln
2100 SDCo 1108 G1
Doreen Rd
8200 SDGO 1250 D3
Doreet Wy
2900 CRLB 1106 G3
Dorena Ct
4900 SDGO 1228 G5
Doria Wy
2900 SDGO 1310 E2
Doriana St
2100 SDGO 1290 F7
Dorinda Ct
1500 SDGO 1350 D1
Dorinda Dr
600 OCSD 1087 B1
Doris Dr
700 ENCT 1147 F7
Doris Jean Pl
1600 VSTA 1087 D7
Doris St
1800 SDGO 1330 A7
Dorm Wy
2500 SDCo 1271 D7
Dormae Ln
100 SDCo 1252 J2
Dorman Dr
5100 SDGO 1270 A1
Dormouse Ct
7900 SDGO 1189 A6
Dormouse Rd
12200 SDGO 1188 J7
12400 SDGO 1189 A6
Dornoch Ct
1800 SDGO 1352 A2
Dorothea Av
- SDCo 1028 A5
700 SNMS 1109 B5
Dorothea Ter
12900 POWY 1190 B5
Dorothy Av
2100 SDCo 1300 C7
(See Page 1300)
Dorothy Ct
200 ESCN 1130 D1
Dorothy Dr
5500 SDGO 1270 B2
Dorothy Ln
- SDCo 1071 B5
Dorothy St
700 CHLV 1330 A4
500 ELCJ 1252 A6
Dorothy Wy
5600 SDGO 1270 B2
Dorsal Dr
9600 SDCo 1232 D3
Dorset Wy
13300 POWY 1170 E2
Dorsey Wy
200 VSTA 1087 G4
Dorsie Ln
3900 SDCo 1271 H4
Dortmund Pl
2500 SDCo 1253 G2
Dory Dr
3500 SDCo 1310 J1
Dory Ln
500 CRLB 1126 J7
Dos Amigos Rd
31600 SDCo 1049 A7
Dos Amigos Tr
- POWY 1190 J3
Dos Amigos Wy
17100 POWY 1190 J3
Dos Arrons Wy
2700 VSTA 1107 J7
Dos Cabazos
300 ESCN 1149 J2
Dos Cameos Dr
38400 SDCo 997 C5
Dos Hermanos Glen
1200 ESCN 1110 B5
Dos Hermanos Rd
- POWY 1191 D2
Dos Lomas
2900 SDCo 1048 C2
Dos Lomas Pl
2800 SDCo 1048 C2
Dos Ninas
32100 SDCo 1048 G7
Dos Ninos Rd
3700 SDCo 1028 E5
Dos Picos Park Rd
17400 SDCo 1171 H5

Doti Point Dr
6700 SDGO 1290 F7
Double Bridle Terr
11300 SDGO 1208 B2
Double Canyon Rd
33000 SDCo 1049 C4
Double D Dr
1800 SDCo 1252 C3
Double Eagle Glen
100 ESCN 1109 H3
Double K Rd
28400 SDCo 1069 H7
- SDCo 1089 J1
Double Ll Ranch Rd
- ENCT 1148 B4
Double Lynn Ln
- SDCo 1274 B7
Double M Rd
- SNTE 1231 B6
Double O Rd
2600 SDCo 1079 A3
(See Page 1079)
Double Peak Dr
800 SNMS 1128 F5
Doubletree Rd
2300 SDCo 1271 G7
Doug Hill
7700 SDGO 1169 A7
- SDGO 1189 B1
Doug Hill Ct
7800 SDGO 1169 A7
7700 SDGO 1188 J1
Dougherty Grove
500 SDCo 1027 E2
Dougherty St
400 SDCo 1027 E2
Dougherty St E
300 SDCo 1027 F1
Douglas Av
600 SNMS 1109 D6
E Douglas Av
100 ELCJ 1251 F5
W Douglas Av
300 ELCJ 1251 F5
Douglas Dr
700 OCSD 1066 G7
5200 OCSD 1067 A3
200 OCSD 1086 G2
1300 VSTA 1088 A2
Douglas St
600 CHLV 1310 G7
Douglaston Glen
2500 ESCN 1109 H3
Dovary Rd
200 SDCo 1310 D6
Dove Canyon Rd
16700 SDCo 1169 F3
Dove Cir
500 VSTA 1087 F5
Dove Creek Rd
15300 SDCo 1169 F5
Dove Ct
- ImCo 6560 B7
3600 SDGO 1268 J6
Dove Dr
29900 SDCo 1297 F6
(See Page 1297)
Dove Flower Wy
- SDGO 1270 C6
Dove Hill Dr
8500 SNTE 1231 A7
Dove Hollow Rd
3300 ENCT 1148 C3
Dove Ln
- CRLB 1127 E5
Dove Run Rd
900 ENCT 1148 A4
Dove Song Wy
900 ENCT 1148 A4
Dove St
1300 ELCJ 1251 D3
3900 SDGO 1268 J5
- SNTE 1230 G7
Dove Tail Dr
2700 SNMS 1128 B7
Dove Tail Ter
11000 SDGO 1189 J5
Dovecrest Ct
3100 SDCo 1271 A6
Dovecrest Pl
- CHLV 1311 H3
Dover Ct
800 CHLV 1310 G7
700 SDGO 1267 H3
- SNMS 1128 F2
Dover St
1400 OCSD 1067 A3
Dover Wy
4500 CRLB 1107 B4
Doverfield Ln
- SDGO 1209 E3
Doverhill Rd
11000 SDGO 1209 J2
Dovetail Ct
2100 CHLV 1331 G3
Doveview Ct
3500 SDCo 1271 C5
Dovewood Ct
15700 POWY 1170 F5
Dow Pl
3000 SDGO 1228 C7

San Diego County Street Index

STREET Block City Map# Grid

Dow St
- SDGO 1287 J4
Dowdy Dr
9400 SDGO 1209 B6
Dowitcher Ct
1100 CRLB 1127 A4
Dowitcher Wy
4200 OCSD 1086 J3
Dowling Ln
32100 SDCo 1049 J7
- SDCo 1050 A6
Down Memory Ln
16500 SDCo 1169 A2
Downer Av
600 ELCJ 1251 E7
Downey Ct
- CHLV 1330 J2
Downing
- SDGO 1210 E2
Downing St
1100 IMPB 1349 G1
Downs St
1200 OCSD 1086 D7
1800 OCSD 1106 E2
Downwind Wy
- SDGO 1227 H3
Doyle St
- SDGO 1289 G7
Dr Ajalat
700 CALX 6680 J1
Dr Amalia St
- CALX 6680 J2
Dracaena Ct
6100 SDGO 1290 D6
Dracena St
5500 SNTE 1231 G7
Dracma Dr
1000 SDGO 1350 C1
Draco Rd
10900 SDGO 1209 D3
Dragonfly St
2200 CHLV 1331 H1
Dragoye Dr
9700 SNTE 1231 C4
Dragt Pl
- ESCN 1129 F4
Drake Bay
300 OCSD 1066 H6
Drake Ct
1500 CHLV 1311 C4
Drake St
6700 SDGO 1290 E3
Drake Wy
1700 CRLB 1126 J2
Drakewood Ter
4800 SDGO 1188 C4
Draper Av
7700 SDGO 1227 E7
7100 SDGO 1247 F1
Drayton Hall Wy
17600 SDGO 1150 A7
Drayton Ln
3300 SDGO 1249 C5
Drazil Rd
1100 SDCo 1027 H5
Dream St
5600 SDGO 1290 B4
Drell Ct
1500 ELCJ 1251 H2
Drescher St
1900 SDGO 1268 J1
W Drescher St
1700 SDGO 1268 H1
Dresden Pl
2400 SDGO 1248 B3
Dressage Dr
5300 SDCo 1311 A2
Dressage Ln
- SDGO 1188 E5
Drew Ln
2700 LMGR 1270 F7
Drew Rd
2100 ESCN 1110 B5
Drew View Ln
500 SDGO 1290 A5
N Drexel Av
- NATC 1290 B6
S Drexel Av
300 NATC 1290 B6
Drexel Ct
8000 LMGR 1290 H1
Drexel Dr
1600 LMGR 1290 H1
Drexel Ln
1500 LMGR 1290 H2
Drifting Circle Dr
1100 VSTA 1107 G2
Driftwood Cir
4600 CRLB 1106 J6
- SDGO 1209 E3
Driftwood Creek Rd
14900 SDCo 1232 H3
Driftwood Ct
8500 SDGO 1228 A4
500 VSTA 1087 D7
Driftwood Dr
1800 ELCN 6559 F1
Driftwood Ln
700 SDCo 1027 G3
Driftwood Pl
300 BRAW 6319 H1
(See Page 6319)
Driftwood Wy
4700 OCSD 1087 B3
Driscoll Dr
3100 SDGO 1248 C3
Driver Wy
3300 OCSD 1086 H7
Dropseed Terr
- SDCo 1273 A6
Drover Dr
5500 SDGO 1270 A1
Drucella St
2300 SDGO 1330 B7
Drucker Ln
- SDGO 1351 J4
Drumcliff Av
10100 SDGO 1209 C5
Drury Ln
1600 VSTA 1088 B4
Dry Bark Ct
11500 SDGO 1209 A1
Dry Creek Dr
- CHLV 1311 G3
Dry Creek Pl
7700 SDGO 1290 G2
Dryden Pl
6200 CRLB 1127 B3
Dryden Rd
2000 ELCJ 1251 B5
Du Bois Rd
- ImCo 6559 C1
Duane Dr
8700 SNTE 1231 C7
Duarte Pl
1500 SDGO 1290 D5
Duarte Rd
- BRAW 6260 A7
(See Page 6260)
Duarte St
200 BRAW 6259 G7
(See Page 6259)
Dube Ct
8300 SNTE 1230 H6
Dublin Dr
100 ENCT 1167 E4
1900 SDGO 1351 F3
Dublin Ln
1500 ESCN 1110 B4
Dubois Dr
5000 SDGO 1228 E7
4900 SDGO 1248 F1
Dubois Truck Trl
21900 SDCo 1195 D6
(See Page 1195)
Dubonnet St
8500 SDGO 1249 C4
Dubuque St
1400 OCSD 1086 B6
Duchess St
6800 SDGO 1270 E5
Duck Pond Ln
2900 SDCo 1172 D5
Duck Pond Pl
- SDGO 1188 G7
Duck Pond Trl
6600 SDGO 1188 G7
Duckwalk Rd
- SNMS 1108 H4
Duckweed Trl
1200 SDCo 1318 C7
(See Page 1318)
Ducommun Av
2900 SDGO 1228 C5
Ducos Pl
4900 SDGO 1249 H2
Dudley St
3600 SDGO 1287 J3
3500 SDGO 1288 A3
Duenda Rd
11200 SDGO 1149 J7
11600 SDGO 1169 J1
Duff Rd
100 ImCo 6559 J4
Duffer Ct
3100 SDCo 1079 B5
(See Page 1079)
Duffwood Ln
- SDCo 1070 H6
Duffy Wy
3700 SDCo 1310 E3
Dufresne Pl
13100 SDGO 1189 B4
Dufresne Wy
8300 SDGO 1189 B4
Dugan Av
5800 LMSA 1250 H6
Duke Miguel Ct
10600 SNTE 1231 E2
Duke St
1900 CHLV 1311 D5
3200 SDGO 1268 C5
Dukes Pl
1200 SDCo 1152 J6
Dulci Pl
500 ELCJ 1251 J6
Dulene Dr
9100 SDCo 1232 E6
Dulin Pl
4400 OCSD 1087 A3
Dulin Rd
4600 SDCo 1048 G4
Dulles Ct
- IMPE 6499 C1
Dulles Dr
- IMPE 6499 D1
Duluth Av
5800 SDGO 1290 C5
Dulzura Av
2400 SDGO 1289 E1
Dumar St
1500 ELCJ 1252 B6
Dumas St
3300 SDGO 1268 C6
Dump Rd
1100 SDCo 1192 H6
(See Page 1192)
Dun Blazer Wy
200 SDCo 1028 J6
Dunant St
6000 SDGO 1228 C5
Dunaway Dr
8600 SDGO 1227 J4
Dunbar Ct
700 CALX 6620 G7
Dunbar Ln
9700 SDCo 1233 D3
Dunbar Pl
16000 SDCo 1233 D3
Dunbarton Rd
9200 SNTE 1231 A5
Dunbrook Rd
7800 SDGO 1209 A6
Duncan Ct
11300 SDGO 1209 D1
1000 SNMS 1128 H5
Duncan Dr
10100 SDCo 1232 C2
Duncan Ranch Rd
- CHLV 1311 H2
Duncan Rd
8700 SDGO 1209 C3
Duncan Terr
32200 SDCo 1050 F6
Duncan Wy
11000 SDCo 1069 F1
Duncannon Ct
8500 SDGO 1209 C1
Dundee Av
5400 SDGO 1250 B5
Dundee Ct
2700 CRLB 1107 A5
Dundee Glen
2500 ESCN 1109 H3
Dundee Ln
500 SNMS 1108 G6
Dundee Wy
2500 VSTA 1107 J5
Dune Evening Dr
2100 CHLV 1331 F3
Dune Ln
7200 SDGO 1247 E1
Dunedin Ct
9700 SNTE 1231 A4
Dunemere Dr
300 SDGO 1247 E1
Dunes Pl
3400 OCSD 1086 F4
Dunham Ct
4700 SDGO 1188 C5
Dunham Wy
3600 SDGO 1188 C5
Dunhaven St
2200 SDGO 1268 F1
Dunhill Ct
4500 OCSD 1107 E2
Dunhill St
3400 SDGO 1208 A5
Dunholme St
9000 SDGO 1209 E4
Dunlap Rd
- SDGO 1268 E7
Dunlin Av
1600 CHLV 1331 D2
Dunlin Pl
300 SDGO 1290 D4
Dunlop St
2200 SDGO 1248 J7
W Dunlop St
2200 SDGO 1248 J7
Dunning Cir
1900 SDGO 1330 A7
Dunsmore Ct
400 ENCT 1147 G6
Dunsmuir Ct
- CHLV 1331 D1
Dunsmuir St
1200 ELCJ 1251 J6
Dunstan St
2300 OCSD 1086 E7
Dunwood Wy
7500 SDGO 1290 G5
Dunwoodie Rd
8500 SNTE 1230 J6
Duo Ct
800 VSTA 1087 H5
Duoro Dr
700 CHLV 1310 J6
Dupont Dr
1700 LMGR 1290 H1
Dupont St
3600 SDGO 1287 J3
Durango
- SNMS 1128 A5
Durango Cir
7200 CRLB 1127 E7
Durango Dr
13900 SDGO 1187 H6
Durant St
3500 SDGO 1289 F4
Durasno Ln
2200 SDCo 1271 E7
Durazanitos Pl
2500 SDCo 1172 C5
Durazanitos Rd
2400 SDCo 1172 C4
Durgin St
300 SDCo 1152 C7
100 SDCo 1172 D1
Durham Cir
3500 OCSD 1107 E3
Durham Pl
- CHLV 1311 H2
500 ELCJ 1252 A4
Durham Ridge Pl
2600 SDGO 1268 E6
Durham St
- SDGO 1288 A5
Durhullen Dr
14100 POWY 1170 G7
Durian Ct
1300 VSTA 1087 E6
Durian St
400 VSTA 1087 E6
Durlinnsy Rd
- SDCo 996 F1
Durward St
800 CHLV 1310 G7
Dusk Dr
2200 SDGO 1290 E7
2500 SDGO 1310 F1
Dusk Ln
4200 OCSD 1107 C2
Dusty Acres Ct
- ENCT 1147 J6
Dusty Dr
1600 CHLV 1331 F2
Dusty Rd
400 SNMS 1108 G7
Dusty Rose Pl
6900 CRLB 1127 E6
Dusty Trail Dr
- IMPE 6439 F3
Dusty Trl
3000 ENCT 1148 B3
Dutchberry Ct
27700 SDCo 1090 D3
Dutchman Ct
2100 CHLV 1331 G3
Dutton Dr
10700 SDCo 1271 F3
Duval St
600 SDGO 1289 J3
1700 SDGO 1290 A2
Duxbury Ln
10400 SDCo 1169 F2
Dwane Av
6400 SDGO 1250 D6
Dwight St
2400 SDGO 1269 D6
5600 SDGO 1270 B6
Dyanna Ct
- VSTA 1108 A1
Dyar Spring Fire Rd
- SDCo 1216 J1
(See Page 1216)
Dye Rd
- SDCo 1172 C3
Dyer Dr
2600 SDGO 1268 E6
Dyer Ln
15800 SDGO 1169 D4
Dykes Av
6300 SDGO 1290 D5
Dylan St
6900 SDGO 1290 F7
Dylan Wy
1700 ENCT 1147 D2

E

E Av
500 CORD 1288 H6
300 NATC 1289 H7
600 NATC 1309 H1
- SDCo 1066 D1
- SDCo 1291 D3
E St
600 BRAW 6319 G1
(See Page 6319)
1000 BRAW 6320 A1
(See Page 6320)
600 CHLV 1309 J6
- CHLV 1310 C5
400 IMPE 6439 E5
- ImCo 6319 C1
(See Page 6319)
1800 SDCo 1108 G2
1300 SDCo 1152 F6
- SDGO 1229 F5
2700 SDGO 1289 D3
E E St
- ENCT 1147 C7
W E St
300 ENCT 1147 B7
800 SDGO 1288 J3
Eads Av
7700 SDGO 1227 E7
7100 SDGO 1247 F1
Eady Av
1100 CALX 6620 E7
Eady Ln
40500 SDCo 1300 F7
(See Page 1300)
Eady Rd
- ImCo 6620 A5
Eagle Canyon Pl
17200 SDCo 1169 F1
Eagle Canyon Rd
10400 SDCo 1169 F1
Eagle Canyon Wy
17200 SDCo 1169 F1
Eagle Crest Ln
2400 VSTA 1107 J4
Eagle Crsg
400 OCSD 1086 B6
Eagle Dr
5900 CRLB 1127 H2
Eagle Glen
1400 ESCN 1129 G5
Eagle Hill Ln
- SDCo 1152 E1
Eagle Lake Dr
10300 SDCo 1129 F7
Eagle Ln
1500 ELCJ 1251 D2
Eagle Mine Dr
14200 POWY 1190 G4
Eagle Mountain Rd
- SDCo 1068 F4
Eagle Pass
3600 SDCo 1275 B3
Eagle Peak Ct
1400 CHLV 1311 B5
Eagle Peak Rd
7200 SDCo 1154 J7
4700 SDCo 1155 F5
15100 SDCo 1174 F3
- SDCo 1194 C2
(See Page 1194)
Eagle Ridge
3600 SDCo 1155 F4
Eagle Ridge Ct
7600 SDGO 1250 G4
Eagle Ridge Dr
7700 SDGO 1250 G4
Eagle Ridge Pl
- CHLV 1331 A1
Eagle Rock Av
10100 SDGO 1209 C5
Eagle Rock Dr
1800 SNMS 1109 E7
Eagle Rock Ln
1300 ESCN 1129 F1
Eagle Rock Wy
- OCSD 1086 B6
Eagle St
4000 SDGO 1268 J5
W Eagle St
2800 SDGO 1268 J7
Eagle Summit Pl
1900 ESCN 1109 F6
Eagle Valley Dr
- CHLV 1311 G3
Eagle View Dr
- SDCo 1089 D5
Eagle View Ln
15800 SDCo 1071 A6
Eagle View Rd
- SDCo 1235 B3
Eaglehill Rd
28000 SDCo 1090 J3
Eagles Creek Ct
11200 SDGO 1189 J4
Eagles Crest Rd
16400 SDCo 1151 C5
Eagles Nest
- SDCo 1091 F4
Eagles Nest Gln
800 ESCN 1110 D5
Eagles Nest Station
- POWY 1170 F1
Eagles Nest Wy
1700 OCSD 1086 B6
Eagles Noel
- SDCo 1070 G4
Eagles Perch Ln
31300 SDCo 1068 E2
Eagles View Glen
- ESCN 1109 A4
Eaglesview Ct
11500 SDGO 1169 J5
Eagleton Pl
5100 SDGO 1188 D5
Eames St
8500 SDGO 1249 C4
Earhart Av
- IMPE 6499 D1
Earhart Ct
- IMPE 6499 D2
Earhart St
8900 SDGO 1249 D5
Earie Ln
14000 POWY 1190 G4
Earl Glen
2000 ESCN 1109 C4
Earl St
9200 LMSA 1251 B6
2000 SDGO 1289 H7
Earle Dr
1300 NATC 1290 C7
1300 NATC 1310 C1
Earlgate Ct
13000 POWY 1190 F4
Earlham St
100 SDCo 1152 H4
Earling Wy
700 SDCo 1251 G1
Earls St
100 ELCN 6500 B6
Earnscliff Pl
3600 SDGO 1248 H4
Earth Dr
800 VSTA 1087 D6
Earthstar Ct
11500 SDGO 1169 J4
East Balboa Ct
1500 CRLB 1126 J2
East Bluff Cove
15700 SDGO 1210 J1
East County Dr
- SDCo 1232 D7
- SDCo 1252 E1
East Creek Rd
15800 SDCo 1233 C3
East Dr
3400 SDGO 1268 E5
200 VSTA 1087 G4
East Grade Rd
21600 SDCo 1052 G4
(See Page 1052)
23900 SDCo 1053 B6
(See Page 1053)
26000 SDCo 1073 J3
(See Page 1073)
East Incense Cedar Rd
700 SDCo 1156 E5
East Lake Dr
6500 SDGO 1251 A5
East Ln
1100 IMPB 1349 G1
200 SDCo 1252 J3
East Park Ln
200 CHLV 1310 A6
800 CHLV 1330 B2
East Pointe Av
1800 CRLB 1106 H6
East Ridge Rd
9700 SDCo 1233 C2
East Roundup Cir
300 SNTE 1231 F5
East St
2700 OCSD 1086 D7
200 SDGO 1289 J4
East Star Rd
3200 SDCo 1078 J6
(See Page 1078)
Eastbourne Rd
11900 SDGO 1190 B1
Eastbrook Rd
2200 VSTA 1107 H7
Eastbury Dr
700 ESCN 1130 C2
Eastcliff Ct
- SDGO 1188 C6
Easter Pl
1700 ESCN 1129 G6
Easter Wy
9500 SDGO 1228 D1
Easterleigh Row
- SDGO 1247 J1
Eastern Av
- BRAW 6320 B3
(See Page 6320)
Eastern St
14000 POWY 1190 F3
Eastfield Rd
11600 POWY 1210 C1
Eastgate Ct
6400 SDGO 1228 F1
Eastgate Dr
- SDGO 1228 E1
Eastgate Mall
4300 SDGO 1228 D2
Eastglen St
11900 SDGO 1210 A3
Easthaven Ct
10800 SNTE 1231 D1
Easthaven Dr
10200 SNTE 1231 D1
Easthill Dr
7500 SDGO 1290 G3
Eastlake Dr
- CHLV 1311 E3
Eastlake Pkwy
1100 CHLV 1311 F6
1700 CHLV 1331 G2
Eastman St
6900 SDGO 1248 J7
Eastmont Pl
900 SDCo 1109 H2
Eastmore Pl
1400 OCSD 1087 E3
Eastom Wy
2100 SDCo 1028 A6
Easton Av
5600 SDGO 1250 B6
Easton Ct
6800 SDGO 1250 B6
Eastridge Ct
12700 SDGO 1210 C1
Eastridge Dr
7500 LMSA 1270 G5
Eastridge Ln
2200 ESCN 1109 G4
Eastridge Loop
2300 CHLV 1311 G5
Eastridge Pl
11400 SDGO 1210 D1
Eastshore Ter
700 CHLV 1311 E4
Eastside Rd
1000 ELCJ 1251 D3
Eastvale Rd
15100 POWY 1170 J6
15100 POWY 1171 A6
Eastview Ct
1400 OCSD 1087 E3
11400 SDGO 1210 C1
Eastview Pt
11300 SDGO 1210 C2
Eastview Terr
2700 SDCo 1130 E7
Eastwind Pt
11400 SDGO 1209 J4
Eastwood Ln
1800 ENCT 1147 H6
Easy St
6000 CRLB 1126 H4
1700 SDCo 1108 G2
3100 SDGO 1270 B6
Easy Stroll Ln
2200 CHLV 1331 G3
Eaton Wy
100 OCSD 1106 C4
100 VSTA 1087 H5
Ebano Ct
100 SOLB 1167 H4
Ebb Tide St
- CRLB 1127 A4
Ebbs Pl
5600 SDGO 1290 C6
Ebbs St
1400 SDGO 1290 C6
Ebbtide Wy
- SDGO 1330 H7
Eberhart St
6800 SDGO 1270 E2
Eberly Ct
10800 SDGO 1209 D3
Ebers St
1800 SDGO 1267 J6
2200 SDGO 1268 A5
Ebersole Dr
4300 SDGO 1330 G7
Ebert Dr
- SDGO 1289 C2
Eboe Av
1400 SDGO 1349 J1
Ebony Av
100 IMPB 1349 E1
Ebony Ridge Rd
- SDGO 1290 A4
Ecclesia Ln
100 OCSD 1086 C5
Ecclesia St
- OCSD 1086 C5
Echo Av
2600 CRLB 1127 G3
Echo Canyon Dr
- BRAW 6319 J4
(See Page 6319)
Echo Canyon Wy
300 OCSD 1086 J1
Echo Ct
4300 LMSA 1270 J4
Echo Dell Rd
8200 SDGO 1250 D3
Echo Dr
8500 LMSA 1270 J4
8800 LMSA 1271 A4
4000 SDCo 1156 E2
Echo Hill Ln
4800 SDCo 1168 A7
Echo Ln
- SNMS 1128 G3
N Echo Ln
100 SNMS 1108 G7
Echo Pl
4000 OCSD 1107 B1
Echo Ridge Ct
2800 CHLV 1312 A5
(See Page 1312)
Echo Ridge Pl
2800 CHLV 1312 A5
(See Page 1312)
Echo Ridge Terr
1300 CHLV 1311 J5
Echo Valley Ln
1700 SDCo 1109 F4
Echo Valley Rd
2800 SDCo 1292 D3
(See Page 1292)
Ecke Ranch Rd
800 ENCT 1147 D5
Ecken Rd
600 ELCJ 1251 E7
Eckman Av
1400 CHLV 1330 F3
Eckman Ct
100 CHLV 1330 F3
Eckstrom Av
7000 SDGO 1248 J2
Eclipse Dr
1400 SNMS 1128 F6
Eclipse Pl
- SDGO 1189 A6
Eclipse Rd
- SDGO 1189 A6
Ecloga Ct
25100 SDCo 1173 H3
Ecochee Av
3800 SDGO 1248 E3
W Ecochee Av
3400 SDGO 1248 D3
Eddie Dr
200 VSTA 1087 H7
Eddie Jones Wy
3200 OCSD 1086 D4
Edding Dr
2400 LMGR 1270 G7
Eddington Rd
11000 SNTE 1231 F6
Edell Pl
2900 SDGO 1228 C7
Edelweiss
- SDCo 1233 B3
Edelweiss Ln
600 ENCT 1148 A6
Eden Ct
- SNMS 1128 C6
Eden Dr
1700 SDGO 1268 A1
Eden Grove
- POWY 1170 G6
Eden Ln
900 ELCJ 1251 H7
Eden Mills Pl
14800 SDGO 1210 G2
Eden Pl
800 ESCN 1129 G2
Eden Valley Ln
1400 SDCo 1129 C3
Edenbridge Ln
2400 SDGO 1290 F6
Edendale St
6300 CRLB 1127 F3
Edenoaks St
10600 SDGO 1210 C3
Edenvale Av
4600 LMSA 1270 J3
Edgar Pl
9800 SDCo 1271 D3
Edge Cliff Dr
1400 SDGO 1268 A1
Edgebrook Pl
1700 ESCN 1109 D5
Edgeburt Dr
100 ENCT 1147 A3
Edgefield Ln
1700 ENCT 1147 G6
Edgehill Dr
1400 CHLV 1331 D1
Edgehill Ln
400 OCSD 1086 E6
Edgehill Rd
2000 SDCo 1088 C5
16400 SDGO 1169 D4
Edgelake Dr
9800 SDCo 1271 C1
Edgeland St
700 SDCo 1251 G3
Edgemere Dr
3000 NATC 1310 B3
Edgemont Pl
1000 SDGO 1289 E3
Edgemont St
1200 SDGO 1289 E2
Edgemoor Dr
- SNTE 1231 E6
Edgemoor St
13800 POWY 1190 F3
Edgepark Wy
4800 SDGO 1249 G1
Edger Ct
- SDCo 1086 A2
Edgerton Dr
2300 LMGR 1270 G7
Edgerton Wy
800 NATC 1309 J1
Edgeview Dr
4800 SDCo 1271 G2
Edgeview St
- SNMS 1128 B1
Edgeware Rd
5100 SDGO 1269 H2
Edgeware Wy
- CRLB 1107 A4
Edgewater Av
500 OCSD 1067 D6
Edgewater Dr
700 CHLV 1311 E3
- SNMS 1129 A1
Edgewater St
5900 SDGO 1310 D1
Edgewood Bend Ct
6000 SDGO 1188 E5
Edgewood Ct
4300 SDCo 1271 C3
Edgewood Dr
100 OCSD 1086 D6
3600 SDCo 1156 E2
9300 SDCo 1271 B3
Edgewood Pl
- CHLV 1311 E6
2200 OCSD 1086 C6
11400 SDGO 1210 G1
Edgeworth Rd
5200 SDGO 1248 A4
Edgley Dr
800 BRAW 6319 G4
(See Page 6319)
Edie Ln
9500 SDCo 1231 J4
Edilee Dr
1600 ENCT 1167 E2
Edina Ct
17000 POWY 1170 D2
Edina Wy
13100 POWY 1170 D2
Edinburg Av
2200 ENCT 1167 E3
Edinburgh Ct
6700 SDGO 1250 E7
Edinburgh Dr
4700 CRLB 1107 A5
Edison Pl
- CRLB 1127 C3
Edison St
4200 SDGO 1248 E6
Edith Dr
1900 ESCN 1109 C4
Edith Ln
3100 SDGO 1268 C7
Editha Dr
200 SDCo 1253 C1
Ediwhar Av
3400 SDGO 1249 D4
Edmonds St
6300 SDGO 1290 D4
Edmonton Av
6700 SDGO 1228 E4
Edna Pl
3800 SDGO 1269 G3
Edna Wy
500 VSTA 1108 A3
Ednabelle Ct
900 ELCJ 1251 H4
Ednalyn Ln
8400 SDGO 1169 B3
Edsall Ln
3100 SDGO 1249 C5
Edson Rd
8100 SDGO 1229 D1
Edulis Ct
8700 SDGO 1189 C6
Edward
- SDCo 1232 F4
Edward St
500 ELCJ 1251 B5
Edwin Ln
1900 SDCo 1108 H2
Edwin Pl
4900 SDGO 1228 C7
Edwina Wy
900 ENCT 1167 E2
Edwords Access Rd
10200 SDCo 1109 G3
Egan St
3400 SDGO 1270 D6
Egret St
1400 CHLV 1331 C2
- CRLB 1127 D7
6000 SDGO 1290 C1
Egret Wy
1400 ELCJ 1252 A7
Eichenlaub St
3200 SDGO 1248 D3
Eider St
6300 SDGO 1290 D2
Eider Wy
1000 OCSD 1087 A3
Eileen Dr
2400 SDGO 1249 E7
Eileen St
8600 SDCo 1291 A1
Eisenhower Av
13200 POWY 1190 C3
Eklund Ct
1100 VSTA 1107 J1
El Acebo
- SDCo 1168 B4
El Acebo Del Norte
- SDCo 1168 A4
El Aguila St
2600 CRLB 1127 G4
El Aire Pl
1700 ESCN 1109 E6
El Amigo Rd
2200 SDGO 1187 G6
El Amo
- OCSD 1086 F3
El Apajo
6100 SDCo 1168 E6

San Diego County Street Index

Street	Block	City	Map#	Grid
El Arbol Dr	5000	CRLB	1126	G2
El Arco Iris	4800	SDCo	1168	A5
El Asado St	14200	SDGO	1189	C2
El Aspecto	4700	SDCo	1168	A3
El Astillero Pl	7900	CRLB	1147	G3
El Banquero Ct	8100	SDGO	1250	E2
El Banquero Pl	6700	SDGO	1250	E3
El Berro	-	CALX	6620	H5
	-	OCSD	1086	F2
El Bosque Av	2400	CRLB	1147	G3
El Bosque Ct	4300	SDGO	1330	G7
El Brazo	17900	SDCo	1149	A5
El Caballo Av	10600	SDCo	1169	F4
El Caballo Dr	700	OCSD	1067	A5
El Cabo Ct	5700	SDGO	1229	H7
El Cabrillo	-	ENCT	1147	F5
El Cajon Blvd	200	ELCJ	1251	E6
	8000	LMSA	1270	G2
	1800	SDGO	1269	C4
	5800	SDGO	1270	C3
El Cajon Ln	1700	SDCo	1172	F1
El Cajon Mtn Truck Trl	-	SDCo	1193	H5
(See Page 1193)				
El Calor Ln	-	ESCN	1109	E6
El Cam Real	200	OCSD	1086	G4
El Caminito	1000	VSTA	1107	G1
El Camino Ct	1300	ENCT	1167	G3
El Camino De Los Flor	-	ESCN	1109	F7
El Camino De Pinos	8700	SDCo	1069	A5
El Camino Del Norte	2200	ENCT	1147	J6
	2700	ENCT	1148	A6
	5300	SDCo	1148	D7
El Camino Del Teatro	6300	SDGO	1247	G2
El Camino Dr	6100	SDGO	1208	F6
El Camino Entrada	15900	POWY	1170	F5
El Camino Real	2500	CRLB	1106	G3
	5000	CRLB	1107	A6
	6100	CRLB	1127	E3
	7800	CRLB	1147	F2
	1500	ENCT	1167	G3
	300	OCSD	1086	F4
	2100	OCSD	1106	G1
	17100	SDCo	1167	J3
	15500	SDCo	1168	B6
	14800	SDGO	1187	J3
	15300	SDGO	1188	A2
	11900	SDGO	1207	J1
	-	SDGO	1208	A2
	-	SNMS	1129	C2
N El Camino Real	300	ENCT	1147	F5
	100	OCSD	1086	F3
S El Camino Real	700	ENCT	1167	G1
	3800	SCLE	1023	B1
El Camino Villas	-	OCSD	1106	H2
El Camto Rd	900	SDCo	1027	H4
El Canto Dr	3900	SDCo	1271	E4
El Capitan	-	SNMS	1129	C2
El Capitan Ct	4300	CRLB	1106	J5
El Capitan Dam	-	SDCo	1213	F6
El Capitan Dr	-	CHLV	1330	D1
	8000	LMSA	1270	H2
El Capitan Peak	15500	SDCo	1233	C1
El Capitan Real Ln	15400	SDCo	1233	B2
El Capitan Real Rd	10300	SDCo	1233	B2
El Capitan Truck Trl	-	SDCo	1173	J7
	-	SDCo	1193	G1
(See Page 1193)				
	-	SDCo	1194	A3
(See Page 1194)				
El Caporal	17200	SDCo	1168	H2
El Carmel Pl	900	SDGO	1267	J1
El Cedro Ct	4300	SDGO	1330	G7
El Centro Av	1000	ELCN	6499	F5
	44600	SDCo	1321	G5
(See Page 1321)				
El Centro St	1100	IMPB	1349	F1
El Centro Terr	-	SDCo	1218	F7
El Centro Tract	500	SDCo	1218	F7
El Cerise	2400	SDCo	1028	B1
El Cerrito Dr	-	BRAW	6259	H7
(See Page 6259)				
	600	BRAW	6319	H2
(See Page 6319)				
	4500	SDGO	1270	B3
El Cerrito Pl	4700	SDGO	1270	B3
El Cerro	-	OCSD	1086	G2
El Cerro Dr	9100	SDCo	1232	D6
El Chico Ln	200	CORD	1288	J6
	1400	SDCo	1128	C4
El Cielito	5400	SDCo	1168	B4
El Cielo	8000	SDCo	1148	J4
El Cielo Ln	1400	ESCN	1109	E6
El Circulo	5100	OCSD	1087	D2
	6300	SDCo	1168	E1
El Comal Dr	10400	SDGO	1229	H7
El Copa Ln	100	SDCo	1108	B3
El Corazon Dr	3300	OCSD	1086	H6
El Corral Ln	1300	SDCo	1128	B3
El Cortez Ct	1200	CHLV	1311	B6
El Corto St	2400	SDCo	1108	D4
El Coyote Run	2900	SDCo	998	C4
El Cruero Ct	1000	VSTA	1088	C7
El Dolora Wy	14100	POWY	1190	G1
El Dorado Av	800	ELCN	6499	G4
El Dorado Ct	1700	VSTA	1108	B1
El Dorado Dr	900	SDCo	1130	C5
El Dorado Pkwy	8900	SDCo	1232	E6
El Dorado Ter	1800	SDCo	1130	C5
El Escondido Del Dios Hwy	9700	SDCo	1149	D3
	-	SDCo	1168	G1
El Escorial Wy	5900	SDGO	1229	J6
El Extenso Ct	8000	SDGO	1250	E3
El Farra St	-	SDCo	1088	H2
El Fuego	16900	SDCo	1168	D3
El Fuerte St	-	CRLB	1127	G4
El Gavilan Ct	2500	CRLB	1127	G5
El Granada Rd	-	CHLV	1311	G2
El Grande Pl	9600	SDCo	1232	C4
El Granito Av	9500	SDCo	1271	C1
El Honcho Pl	10300	SDGO	1229	G7
El Jardin Ct	1800	ELCJ	1271	G2
El Ku Av	3100	ESCN	1150	B2
El Lando Ct	3100	OCSD	1106	H1
El Loro St	300	CHLV	1330	D4
El Lugar St	1300	CHLV	1330	D4
El Mac Pl	900	SDGO	1287	J2
El Mar Av	13500	POWY	1190	H4
El Marbea Ln	10700	SDCo	1271	F2
El Matador Ln	10300	SNTE	1231	D7
El Mercado Wy	-	OCSD	1087	B3
El Mio Dr	1200	ELCJ	1251	D6
El Mirador	17000	SDCo	1168	F3
El Mirador Wy	-	SNMS	1129	C1
El Mirar	4700	SDCo	1168	A3
El Miraso	500	VSTA	1087	H7
El Mirlo	5100	SDCo	1168	A1
El Mirlo Dr	4900	SDCo	1067	A5
El Modena Rd	-	CHLV	1311	E6
El Monte Dr	2200	OCSD	1086	C6
El Monte Pl	400	ESCN	1130	B1
	300	SDCo	1252	H4
El Monte Rd	600	ELCJ	1251	D4
	15400	SDCo	1212	J7
	15900	SDCo	1213	B5
	13900	SDCo	1232	D2
	-	SDCo	1233	F4
El Montevideo	6200	SDCo	1168	D1
El Morro Ln	-	OCSD	1086	G3
El Nido	4700	SDCo	1168	A5
El Nido Dr	1600	SDCo	1047	J3
El Noche Wy	5300	SDGO	1249	H1
El Nopal Rd	11100	SDCo	1231	F3
	10300	SNTE	1231	D3
El Nora Pl	24800	SDCo	1173	G3
El Norte	-	OCSD	1086	F2
	-	SDCo	1251	G2
El Norte Hills Pl	600	ESCN	1110	D5
El Norte Pkwy	1400	ESCN	1109	C5
E El Norte Pkwy	200	ESCN	1109	H7
	2100	ESCN	1110	B5
W El Norte Pkwy	1800	SDCo	1109	E6
El Norte Vista	-	SDCo	1091	F3
El Ontono Wy	-	SDGO	1208	E4
El Oriente Ln	-	ENCT	1147	F5
El Paisano Dr	-	SDCo	1028	B1
El Pajado Pl	900	VSTA	1088	A7
El Paseo	1200	SDCo	1068	H6
	-	SDCo	1088	H1
	1500	SDCo	1128	B3
El Paseo Grande	8400	SDGO	1227	H4
El Pasillo Ln	2100	SDCo	1291	A1
El Paso Alto	3800	SDCo	1088	F5
El Paso Alto Norte	3700	SDCo	1088	F6
El Paso Real	1500	SDGO	1247	G1
El Paso St	7600	LMSA	1250	G6
	1700	SDCo	1152	D5
El Pato Ct	6400	CRLB	1127	G4
El Pedregal Dr	300	SOLB	1167	H6
El Penon Wy	4600	SDGO	1248	B1
El Perico Ln	6400	CRLB	1127	H5
El Pico Ct	900	VSTA	1087	G5
El Pico Dr	1700	ELCJ	1251	C3
El Poquito Pl	-	SNTE	1231	F3
El Portal Dr	-	CHLV	1311	G2
El Portal St	200	ENCT	1147	B5
N El Portal St	300	ENCT	1147	B5
S El Portal St	200	ENCT	1147	A6
El Porvenir Wy	4000	SDGO	1350	D3
El Prado	1100	SDGO	1289	B1
El Prado Av	1500	LMGR	1290	F2
El Prado Ln	-	OCSD	1086	G3
El Prado Pl	1400	ESCN	1130	B1
El Prado St	1500	CHLV	1331	D2
El Presidio Tr	13400	SDGO	1188	D4
El Rancho Dr	600	SDCo	1252	C4
El Rancho Grande	3300	SDCo	1291	C7
El Rancho Ln	500	ESCN	1130	B1
	-	SDCo	1027	J1
El Rancho Verde	1600	SDCo	1128	C4
El Rancho Vista	-	SDCo	1310	D6
N El Rancho Vista	400	SDCo	1310	D6
El Rastro Ln	2600	CRLB	1147	G3
El Raval Wy	1600	CHLV	1331	D3
El Retiro	28900	SDCo	1069	J7
	-	SDCo	1089	J1
El Rey Av	1300	ELCJ	1251	J2
El Rey Ct	-	ELCJ	1251	J2
El Rey Vista	-	POWY	1190	E5
El Rocko Rd	2700	SDCo	1129	D4
El Romero	6100	SDCo	1168	D2
El Rosal Pl	1700	ESCN	1109	E6
El Roy Dr	1700	LMGR	1290	H1
El Sabo Wy	24700	SDCo	1173	G2
El Secreto	5300	SDCo	1168	B3
El Secrito	5100	OCSD	1087	D2
El Sendero Dr	34500	SDCo	1030	G7
	15000	SDCo	1050	H1
El Sentido	-	SDCo	1188	H1
El Sereno Wy	2500	SDCo	1108	C4
El Sicomoro	6300	SDCo	1168	E4
El Sol Rd	-	SDCo	1172	A2
El Sueno	400	SOLB	1167	F7
El Sur	-	OCSD	1086	G3
El Tae Rd	16000	SDCo	1051	A5
El Tejado Rd	9400	LMSA	1271	B2
El Tejon Rd	3300	SDCo	1079	A6
(See Page 1079)				
El Tiempo	8400	SDCo	1149	B3
El Tigre	200	SNMS	1108	C5
El Topo Dr	14200	POWY	1170	G7
El Tordo	6100	SDCo	1168	D3
El Toro Ln	800	SNMS	1109	C5
	10300	SNTE	1231	E7
El Valle	-	SDCo	1232	D6
El Valle Opulento	100	SDCo	1108	B3
El Vallecito	1000	VSTA	1087	G4
El Vecino Dr	3300	SDCo	1047	J2
El Verde Ct	1900	LMGR	1290	J1
El Vestido St	14300	SDGO	1189	C2
El Viento	300	SOLB	1167	F7
El Vuelo	17300	SDCo	1168	F2
El Vuelo Del Este	7000	SDCo	1168	F2
El Zorro Vista	16700	SDCo	1168	E3
El-Ku Av	3000	ESCN	1150	A2
Elaine Av	600	OCSD	1067	A5
Elaine Wy	6900	SDGO	1250	E7
Elan Ln	1800	SDCo	1272	D3
Elbert Ct	11500	SDGO	1209	D1
Elbert Ter	9000	SDGO	1209	D1
Elbert Wy	11400	SDGO	1209	D1
Elbrook Dr	300	SDCo	1027	G3
Elco St	3700	SDGO	1248	J3
Eldean Ln	1300	OCSD	1086	F7
Elden Av	1300	CHLV	1330	C4
Elden St	8700	LMSA	1251	A7
Eldenberry St	2900	SDCo	1129	C6
Elder Av	100	CHLV	1310	A5
	600	CHLV	1330	B1
	100	IMPB	1349	E1
	1500	SDGO	1349	J1
	1800	SDGO	1350	A1
Elder Ct	800	CRLB	1126	J5
	6300	SDGO	1250	B7
Elder Pl	-	CRLB	1127	B6
	700	ESCN	1129	J1
	6200	SDGO	1250	B6
Elder Rd	-	ImCo	6259	C6
(See Page 6259)				
	4200	ImCo	6319	C2
(See Page 6319)				
Elder St	700	SDCo	1153	A1
E Elder St	500	SDCo	1027	F3
W Elder St	600	SDCo	1027	E3
Elderberry Ct	800	SNMS	1109	A6
Elderberry Gn	3700	ESCN	1150	C3
Elderberry Wy	5400	OCSD	1067	D7
	13500	SDGO	1188	G3
Elderburry Ct	10800	SDGO	1209	D3
Elderburry Glen	3800	ESCN	1150	C3
Eldergardens St	5800	SDGO	1250	B6
Elderwood Ct	10900	SDGO	1210	B2
Elderwood Ln	11000	SDGO	1210	B2
Elderwood Rd	10800	SDGO	1210	B2
Eldon Ct	1700	ELCJ	1252	B2
Eldora St	2000	LMGR	1290	G1
Eldorado Dr	400	ESCN	1130	B5
Eldorado Ln	9400	LMSA	1271	C2
Eldred Ln	1700	VSTA	1087	D7
Eldridge Ct	5400	SDGO	1250	B6
Eldridge St	7000	SDGO	1250	C5
Eleanor Dr	6400	SDGO	1290	D4
Eleanor Pl	3400	NATC	1290	C7
Electric Av	6600	SDGO	1247	E2
Electron Dr	3600	SDGO	1287	J4
Electronics Wy	8500	SDGO	1249	C2
Elegans	-	SDCo	1127	B7
Elegant Tern Pl	6600	CRLB	1127	C5
Elegante Wy	-	SDGO	1188	H4
Elena Dr	1800	CALX	6620	F6
	1800	SNMS	1108	H3
Elena Ln	19300	SDCo	1294	F6
(See Page 1294)				
Elena Wy	100	OCSD	1086	H3
Eleonore Ct	-	SDGO	1210	A1
Eleta Pl	2200	SDCo	1271	D7
Elevada St	2000	OCSD	1106	F2
Elevado Hills Rd	2000	SDCo	1088	C2
Elevado Rd	2400	SDCo	1068	B7
	1700	SDCo	1088	B2
Elevation Rd	1400	SDCo	1268	F2
Elfin Forest Ln	19900	SDCo	1148	G2
Elfin Forest Rd	20700	SDCo	1128	E7
	20000	SDCo	1148	H2
	-	SNMS	1128	D6
Elfin Glen	19900	SDCo	1148	H3
Elfin Oaks Rd	7000	SDCo	1148	F2
Elfin Vista Ln	20200	SDCo	1148	G2
Elfinora Ln	-	SDCo	1148	J2
Elford Ct	8700	SDGO	1189	C1
Elgin Av	5500	SDGO	1250	B5
Eliason Dr	-	SDCo	1085	G1
Elijah Ct	3700	SDGO	1188	A6
Eliot Pl	-	CRLB	1127	B1
Eliot St	1000	OCSD	1067	A3
Elisa Ln	12600	SDGO	1189	H5
Elise St	800	CHLV	1330	A5
Elise Wy	-	OCSD	1086	H3
Elivo Ct	100	SDGO	1350	G2
Elizabeth Ct	900	SDGO	1289	J5
Elizabeth Dr	19300	SDCo	1091	H4
Elizabeth Ln	1500	ELCJ	1252	B7
	200	SDCo	1153	B5
Elizabeth St	800	ELCJ	1252	A6
	500	SDGO	1289	J5
	800	SNMS	1109	B6
Elizabeth Wy	-	ELCJ	1252	B7
	1300	SDCo	1027	G5
Elk Grove Ln	14300	SDGO	1210	G1
Elk Lake Dr	2000	SDCo	1129	F7
Elk Run Pl	-	CHLV	1311	D6
Elk St	5600	SDGO	1290	B4
Elkelton Blvd	600	SDCo	1290	J3
	400	SDCo	1291	A4
Elkelton Pl	300	SDCo	1291	A4
Elkhart St	5000	SDGO	1270	A7
Elkhorn Ct	500	CHLV	1311	B4
Elkhorn Ln	300	ESCN	1109	G5
Elkhorn St	8300	LMGR	1290	J1
Elkins Cove	11800	SDGO	1209	C1
Elks Ln	-	CHLV	1330	G1
Elkwood Av	100	IMPB	1349	E1
Ell St	300	BRAW	6319	J3
(See Page 6319)				
Ellen Ln	800	ELCJ	1252	B7
	-	OCSD	1086	G3
Ellen Rd	-	IMPE	6439	E5
Ellenbee Rd	9200	SNTE	1231	A5
Ellentown Rd	2500	SDGO	1227	J3
Ellenwood Cir	8800	SDCo	1290	J3
Ellery St	100	OCSD	1086	D6
Ellie Ln	16300	POWY	1171	D7
Ellinger Pl	3000	SDGO	1350	E4
Ellingham St	8900	SDGO	1189	C3
Elliott St	400	SDCo	1067	A1
	3300	SDGO	1268	C6
Ellis Ln	100	SDCo	1027	G2
Ellis Mountain Dr	2000	SDCo	1252	C7
Ellison Pl	5000	SDGO	1269	E2
Ellsworth Cir	8700	SNTE	1231	B7
Ellsworth Ln	8500	SNTE	1251	B1
Ellsworth St	5100	SDGO	1268	F2
Elm	-	SDCo	1233	B3
Elm Av	200	CHLV	1310	C5
	1200	CHLV	1330	D3
	700	CRLB	1106	E5
	2800	CRLB	1107	A4
	2200	ELCN	6499	E7
	500	IMPB	1329	F7
	1600	SDGO	1330	A7
Elm Cir	-	ELCN	6499	D7
Elm Ct	-	BRAW	6259	J6
(See Page 6259)				
	-	SDCo	1232	D6
Elm Dr	-	NATC	1289	H7
	9400	SDCo	1236	A2
	1600	VSTA	1088	B4
Elm Ln	20000	SDCo	1149	E2
Elm Rd	28900	SDCo	1237	C7
Elm Ridge Dr	1900	VSTA	1107	G5
Elm St	100	OCSD	1106	A1
	300	SDCo	1152	G5
	3100	SDGO	1289	E2
	-	SDGO	1290	D4
	-	SNMS	1128	C1
	-	SNMS	1129	C2
N Elm St	1300	ESCN	1109	J7
	500	ESCN	1130	A1
S Elm St	200	ESCN	1130	A2
W Elm St	800	SDGO	1288	J2
Elm Tree Ct	2900	SDCo	1271	G7
Elm Tree Dr	4700	OCSD	1087	E5
Elm Tree Ln	100	SDCo	1047	G1
	1100	SNMS	1109	A5
Elma Ln	4300	LMSA	1270	E4
N Elman St	6700	SDGO	1268	H1
S Elman St	6700	SDGO	1268	H1
Elmbranch Dr	1200	ENCT	1147	F7
Elmcrest Dr	6300	SDGO	1250	E6
Elmdale Dr	10300	SDCo	1291	E2
Elmfield Ln	12800	POWY	1170	D3
Elmhurst Dr	6300	SDGO	1250	D7
Elmhurst St	1600	CHLV	1311	C5
Elmira St	300	ELCJ	1251	J6
Elmond Dr	-	SDCo	1069	C3
Elmore St	6800	SDGO	1268	J2
Elmpark Ln	12700	POWY	1190	D4
Elmport Ln	14400	POWY	1190	H5
Elmstone Ct	11400	SDGO	1210	A2
Elmview Dr	900	ENCT	1167	G1
Elmwood Ct	1400	CHLV	1311	G7
Elmwood Dr	1100	ESCN	1130	A1
Elmwood Ln	-	OCSD	1106	C1
Elmwood St	2800	CRLB	1106	F4
Elmwood Wy	-	SNMS	1128	B1
Elon Ln	1500	ENCT	1147	G5
Elora Ln	100	SNMS	1128	H3
Elrod Av	-	SDGO	1209	C7
Elrose Ct	1100	SDGO	1350	C1
Elrose Dr	2800	SDGO	1350	C1
Elsa Rd	4800	SDGO	1249	J7
	4900	SDGO	1250	A7
Elsberry St	6300	SDGO	1290	D6
Elser Ln	1700	SDCo	1109	D6
Elsie Wy	600	CHLV	1310	D7
Elsinore Pl	3400	SDGO	1248	D3
Elsinore St	5300	OCSD	1087	E1
Elston Pl	8100	SDGO	1209	B3
Eltanin Wy	11400	SDGO	1209	D1
Eltinge Dr	2300	SDCo	1234	B6
Eltinge Pl	-	SDCo	1234	B7
Elton Dr	9200	SNTE	1231	B7
Elva Ct	1400	ENCT	1167	G1
Elva St	1900	SDCo	1272	C3
Elva Ter	1400	ENCT	1167	G1
Elvado Wy	200	SDGO	1290	F4
Elvis Ct	-	SDGO	1350	E1
Elwell Ct	11600	SDGO	1210	A1
Elwood Av	900	SDGO	1290	A3
Ely Cir	6900	SDGO	1290	E4
Ely St	100	OCSD	1086	F5
Elysian Dr	3800	SDCo	1156	E2
Elyssee St	2600	SDGO	1249	C6
Elysum Dr	-	SDGO	1248	C6
Embassy Wy	10100	SDGO	1209	B5
Emberwood Wy	2100	ESCN	1129	E6
Embry Ct	7700	SDGO	1209	A5
Embry Pt	7800	SDGO	1209	A5
Embry Wy	10000	SDGO	1209	A5
Emden Rd	9100	SDGO	1189	C1
Emelene St	4900	SDGO	1248	A4
Emelita St	1000	SDCo	1027	H2
Emerald Av	-	CALX	6620	H7
	300	ELCJ	1251	E6
	1300	ELCJ	1271	F1
Emerald Bay	-	SDGO	1290	B1
Emerald City Dr	-	SDCo	1071	B4
Emerald Cliff Pt	1700	SDGO	1350	J2
Emerald Cove	5100	SDGO	1330	J7
Emerald Crest	5300	SDGO	1351	B1
Emerald Ct	700	SDGO	1247	H6
Emerald Dr	600	OCSD	1087	D6
	3500	OCSD	1107	D2
	3800	SDCo	1156	E1
	100	VSTA	1107	D1
S Emerald Dr	100	VSTA	1107	D1
Emerald Grove Av	9400	SDCo	1231	J5
Emerald Heights Rd	1100	SDCo	1271	F1
Emerald Hill Ln	9700	SDCo	1232	A4
Emerald Hill Rd	30300	SDCo	1067	H4
Emerald Hollow Dr	-	VSTA	1107	D1
Emerald Lake Av	6200	SDGO	1250	H6
Emerald Ln	14400	SDCo	1188	F2
Emerald Oaks Glen	2500	ESCN	1130	F2
Emerald Pl	2500	ESCN	1130	F1
Emerald Point Ct	1600	SDCo	1272	B5
Emerald Point Ln	2400	SDCo	1272	B5
Emerald Ridge Rd	1500	SDCo	1027	G5
Emerald Sea Wy	-	SNMS	1128	A2
Emerald St	-	IMPE	6439	D6
	600	SDGO	1247	H6
	1900	SDGO	1248	A5
Emerald Vista Dr	9400	SDCo	1231	J5
Emeraude Glen	1300	ESCN	1149	G1
Emerson Av	700	CALX	6680	F1
Emerson St	400	CHLV	1330	C3
	3100	SDGO	1288	B2
E Emerson St	-	CHLV	1330	E2
Emeryville Ct	-	CHLV	1311	E6
Emet Ct	4200	SDGO	1248	E3
Emil Hashem Av	-	CALX	6620	J7
Emila Dr	600	CALX	6680	E1
Emilia Ln	100	SDCo	1028	A2
Emilia Pl	-	ESCN	1109	H7
Emily Dr	3900	SDCo	1274	A4
Emma Dr	900	ENCT	1167	E3
Emma Ln	-	SDCo	1088	F7
Emma Pl	-	BRAW	6319	H3
(See Page 6319)				
Emma Rd	3700	SDCo	1088	F7
Emmanuel Wy	3300	SDCo	1274	J4
	3500	SDCo	1275	A3
Emmaus Rd	-	SDCo	1232	A6
Emogene Pl	1700	ESCN	1109	C5
Emory St	800	IMPB	1329	G7
	1100	IMPB	1349	H1
	3200	SDGO	1268	H6
Empire St	8900	SDGO	1209	B7
Emporer Ln	-	OCSD	1086	G3
Empress Av	10100	SDGO	1209	B5
Enander Wy	200	SDCo	1027	G2
Enara Ct	-	BRAW	6320	C3
(See Page 6320)				
Enborne Ln	6900	SDGO	1290	F6
Encantada	-	SDCo	1251	G2
Encantada Ct	1400	CHLV	1311	B5
Encanto Av	-	IMPB	1349	E2
Encanto Dr	-	CALX	6680	H1
	6300	CRLB	1127	G3
	100	ESCN	1110	E7
Encanto Terr	800	CALX	6680	H1
Encela Ln	1000	SDCo	1291	D3
Encelia Dr	7300	SDGO	1227	G7
Encendido Rd	-	SDGO	1168	J6
	-	SDGO	1169	A6
Enchante Wy	4600	OCSD	1087	B4
Enchanted Pl	2200	SDGO	1350	G3
Enchantment Av	1500	VSTA	1107	G4
Encina Av	800	IMPB	1329	G7
Encina Cte	23500	SDCo	1173	D2
Encina Dr	5400	SDGO	1290	B5
Encina Verde	1500	SDCo	1319	H3
(See Page 1319)				
Encinas Av	800	CALX	6680	H1
Encinitas Av	500	SDGO	1290	H3
Encinitas Blvd	400	ENCT	1147	D7
Encinitas Wy	8500	SDGO	1290	J4
Encino Av	8700	SDGO	1249	C7
Encino Ct	400	SDCo	1130	B5
Encino Dr	1500	ESCN	1130	B4
	2000	SDCo	1130	B5
	300	VSTA	1087	G3
Encino Ln	800	CORD	1288	H7
Encino Row	1000	CORD	1288	H7
Enclave Ln	-	CHLV	1331	E2
End Of The Trl	39500	SDCo	997	A1
Endeavor Ln	4700	CRLB	1106	H7

San Diego County Street Index

STREET
Block City Map# Grid

Enders Av
6900 SDGO 1228 F5
Enelra Pl
5100 SDGO 1228 G7
Energy Wy
800 CHLV 1331 A5
Enero Ct
3700 SDGO 1350 F1
Enero St
4200 SDGO 1350 F1
Enero Wy
3900 SDGO 1350 F1
Enfield St
1600 SDCo 1290 J1
Engel St
100 ESCN 1129 F3
Engelman Ct
- CHLV 1330 J3
Engelmann Oak Ln
2500 SDCo 1234 C7
Engelmann Oak Trl
28200 SDCo 1089 F3
Engelmann Rd
26100 SDCo 1090 F7
Engineer Rd
7900 SDGO 1249 B2
Engineers Ln
- SDGO 1228 A1
Engineers Rd
6900 SDCo 1175 J3
(See Page 1175)
9100 SDCo 1176 B3
(See Page 1176)
England Pl
700 SDCo 1234 B4
Englewood Dr
1700 LMGR 1290 H1
Englewood Wy
- CRLB 1107 A4
English Holly Ln
800 SNMS 1129 B1
Enid Ct
11600 SDGO 1210 A1
Eniwetok Rd
- CORD 1309 B1
Enrico Fermi Dr
2000 SDCo 1352 B2
Enrico Fermi Pl
7100 SDCo 1352 B3
Enright Dr
2200 SDGO 1350 G3
Ensenada Ct
700 SDGO 1267 H3
Ensenada Dr
- IMPE 6499 H1
Ensenada St
2100 LMGR 1290 G1
Ensign St
4900 SDGO 1228 F7
Enterprise Ct
3000 VSTA 1108 A7
Enterprise St
- ESCN 1129 D4
- OCSD 1087 E3
3500 SDGO 1268 F6
300 SNMS 1128 J1
Enterprise Wy
- IMPE 6499 E1
Entertainment Cir
800 CHLV 1331 B6
Entrada Av
2200 SDCo 1108 D3
Entrada De Luz East
7900 SDCo 1169 B7
Entrada De Luz West
7900 SDCo 1169 A7
Entrada Del Sol
4300 SDCo 1067 F2
Entrada Glen
1200 ESCN 1110 B5
Entrada Lazanja
7900 SDCo 1188 J1
Entrada Ln
- ENCT 1147 F5
Entrada Pl
800 CHLV 1310 H7
Entramada Dr
- CALX 6620 H6
Entrance Dr
- ESCN 1150 B2
Entreken Av
13000 SDGO 1189 B5
Entreken Pl
8400 SDGO 1189 C4
Entreken Wy
8300 SDGO 1189 B4
Enzley Ct
3100 SDCo 1234 D5
Eolus Av
1600 ENCT 1147 B2
Epanow Av
4000 SDGO 1248 E3
Epaulette St
2900 SDGO 1249 E6
Epica Ct
12500 SDGO 1170 C3
Epinette Av
4700 SDGO 1228 B7
Epperson Wy
10000 SDGO 1249 G3

Eppick Ct
8000 LMGR 1290 H2
Epsilon St
4000 SDGO 1289 H6
Equality Ln
- SDGO 1228 A1
Equality Rd
8500 SNTE 1231 D7
Equestrian Cir
- SDGO 1230 G5
Equestrian Ct
100 SNMS 1108 J1
Equestrian Ridge
10800 SDGO 1188 G7
Equestrian Tr
- SDCo 1172 D3
Equinox Wy
1200 CHLV 1330 H2
Equitation Ln
2900 SDCo 1310 D4
Eric Ln
- SDCo 1291 B2
Eric Pl
- SDCo 1232 H4
Eric Rd
2400 SDCo 996 J1
Erica St
800 ESCN 1110 B6
Ericas Wy
11900 SDCo 1211 H5
Eridanus Ct
11400 SDGO 1209 C1
Erie Ct
5300 OCSD 1087 E1
Erie St
2900 SDGO 1248 E6
1800 SDGO 1268 E1
Erik Rd
3300 SDCo 1150 E1
Erin Dr
900 ELCJ 1251 B3
Erin Glen
700 SDCo 1067 E1
Erin Ln
14300 POWY 1190 H5
Erin Wy
9700 SNTE 1231 D4
Erins Pl
2000 ESCN 1110 B5
Erith St
6700 SDGO 1248 H4
Erlanger St
5700 SDGO 1228 F6
Erma Rd
9800 SDGO 1209 F3
Ernest Ct
400 OCSD 1087 E2
Erskine Dr
- SDCo 1023 E2
Erwin Ln
9700 SDCo 1232 A3
Escadera Dr
10300 SDCo 1231 F3
Escadera Pl
11000 SDCo 1231 F2
Escala Cv
3900 OCSD 1086 G1
Escala Dr
12500 SDGO 1150 B6
11900 SDGO 1170 A1
Escala Ln
12400 SDGO 1150 C7
Escala Wy
9100 SDGO 1269 D1
Escallonia Ct
- CRLB 1126 J7
Escalon Pl
1300 CHLV 1311 E7
Escarchosa Ln
5400 SDGO 1249 G1
Escenico Ter
2000 CRLB 1147 F2
Eschelman Dr
- ELCN 6559 J1
Escoba Pl
11400 SDGO 1149 J7
Escobar Dr
10700 SDGO 1249 H2
Escodido Frwy
- SDGO 1189 H2
Escondido Av
2600 SDGO 1249 B6
200 VSTA 1087 J6
1100 VSTA 1107 G2
N Escondido Blvd
1400 ESCN 1109 H7
1000 ESCN 1129 H1
S Escondido Blvd
1300 ESCN 1130 A4
- ESCN 1150 A1
Escondido Frwy
- ESCN 1129 G4
- SDCo 998 G5
- SDCo 1028 F2
- SDCo 1048 H1
- SDCo 1068 H4
- SDCo 1089 B5
- SDCo 1109 D1
- SDCo 1150 A1
Escondido Fwy
- SDCo 1109 E3
- SDGO 1150 A5

Escondido Fwy
- SDGO 1170 A3
- SDGO 1209 F1
- SDGO 1229 F6
- SDGO 1249 G5
- SDGO 1269 G2
- SDGO 1289 F5
Escondido Ln
300 CORD 1288 J6
Escondido Ravine Rd
900 SDCo 1218 E7
Escuela Glen
100 ESCN 1109 H6
Escuela St
600 SDGO 1289 J3
Esfera St
7200 CRLB 1128 A7
7500 CRLB 1147 J1
7300 CRLB 1148 A1
Eshelman Dr
- ELCN 6559 J1
Esla Dr
700 CHLV 1310 J6
Esmeraldas Dr
10500 SDGO 1249 H1
Esmond Ct
10800 SDGO 1209 B3
Espana Dr
- OCSD 1086 F3
Espanas Glen
100 ESCN 1129 H1
Esparta Ct
9700 SNTE 1231 B4
Esperanza Pl
- CHLV 1311 H3
Esperanza Wy
1400 ESCN 1110 A6
4200 OCSD 1087 C6
Esperar Dr
13400 SDCo 1232 D7
Esperia Wy
35700 SDCo 1028 H5
Espinosa Sq
9900 SDGO 1209 H5
Espinoza Rd
5100 SDCo 1233 B1
- SDCo 1235 A3
Espinoza St
200 CALX 6620 G6
Esplanade Ct
- SDGO 1228 C3
Esplanade Park Ln
8700 SDGO 1249 C2
Esplanade St
3600 OCSD 1107 B3
Esplanade Sta Monica
7300 SDGO 1168 H7
Esplendente Blvd
5100 SDGO 1249 H2
Esplendido Av
1900 SDCo 1108 E3
Espola Rd
16600 POWY 1170 E3
14400 POWY 1190 H2
Esprit Av
13600 SDGO 1190 B2
Espuela Ln
400 SDCo 1109 G3
Esquaro Dr
3800 SDCo 1099 D2
(See Page 1099)
Esquier Dr
- SDCo 1089 A2
Esquire Glen
1800 ESCN 1129 F5
Essence Av
800 OCSD 1087 B1
Essence Rd
13500 SDGO 1190 B3
Essex Ct
4500 CRLB 1106 J5
Essex Ln
- BRAW 6320 C1
(See Page 6320)
Essex St
1700 ELCJ 1251 C5
1200 IMPB 1349 H1
1700 SDGO 1269 C5
Essington Ct
- SDGO 1330 H7
Establo St
- CALX 6620 G6
Estada Cir
300 OCSD 1087 A1
Estada Dr
4400 OCSD 1087 A1
Estancia La Jolla
- SDGO 1227 J1
Estancia St
7800 CRLB 1147 J2
Estates Ct
4900 SDCo 1271 G2
Estates Dr
- SDCo 1048 B5
Estates Wy
4900 SDCo 1271 G2
Este Vista Ct
1300 ENCT 1167 F3
Estee Ct
1100 SDCo 1027 H1
Estela Dr
1900 ELCJ 1251 C1

Estelle St
6000 SDGO 1270 C4
Esterel Dr
7800 SDGO 1227 J6
Esterlina Dr
3500 SDCo 1048 B3
Estero St
2000 OCSD 1106 F2
Estero Wy
800 ESCN 1129 F1
Estes St
900 ELCJ 1251 F7
Esther St
4600 SDGO 1270 C3
Estival Pl
11200 SDCo 1231 G3
Estoril Pl
5700 SDCo 1067 J1
Estornino Ln
300 SDCo 1252 H3
Estrada Blvd
200 CALX 6620 E6
Estrada Wy
1900 SDGO 1247 H1
Estrelita Dr
500 SDCo 1108 D3
Estrella Av
6300 SDGO 1249 J6
6800 SDGO 1250 A6
4500 SDGO 1269 J3
3800 SDGO 1270 A5
Estrella De Mar Ct
1900 CRLB 1127 F6
Estrella De Mar Rd
6700 CRLB 1127 E5
Estrella Dr
9800 SDCo 1271 D4
Estrella Ln
- OCSD 1086 G3
Estrella St
100 SOLB 1167 E7
Estrella Vista
- POWY 1190 E5
Estremoz Ct
500 OCSD 1086 H4
Estuary Wy
3500 SDGO 1208 A5
Estudillo St
3500 SDGO 1268 G6
Esturion Ct
2800 CRLB 1127 H4
Esturion Pl
2800 CRLB 1127 H4
Esturion St
2800 CRLB 1127 H4
Eta St
800 NATC 1289 H7
3900 SDGO 1289 G7
Etcheverry St
800 SDCo 1172 E2
Etchings Wy
9100 SDCo 1232 D6
Ethan Allen Av
3500 SDGO 1248 D5
Ethel Pl
800 NATC 1290 C7
Ethel St
700 CALX 6680 G1
Ethel Trl
800 SDCo 1253 C2
Ethelda Pl
4200 SDGO 1269 H4
Ethelwyn Ln
2300 SDCo 1136 C6
Etiwanda St
2200 SDGO 1268 A6
Eton Av
3300 SDGO 1228 C5
Eton Ct
900 CHLV 1311 D5
5900 SDGO 1228 D6
Eton Greens Ct
- SDCo 1271 G6
Etude Rd
13600 SDGO 1190 B2
Eubank Ln
9900 SDCo 1291 D2
Eucalyptus Av
- BRAW 6259 H7
(See Page 6259)
300 ELCN 6499 H5
1700 ENCT 1147 A2
- ESCN 1129 G7
- ESCN 1149 F1
2400 SDCo 1149 F2
100 VSTA 1087 H6
1300 VSTA 1088 A7
Eucalyptus Ct
- BRAW 6259 F6
(See Page 6259)
200 CHLV 1310 D5
- SDCo 1029 J5
9700 SNTE 1231 E4
Eucalyptus Dr
1100 ELCJ 1251 E7
2100 SDCo 1252 H4
Eucalyptus Grove Ln
- SDGO 1227 J2
Eucalyptus Heights Rd
16000 POWY 1191 B1
Eucalyptus Hill
7400 LMSA 1270 G3

Eucalyptus Hills Dr
11700 SDCo 1211 H7
Eucalyptus Ln
4900 CRLB 1107 A6
- SDGO 1228 B4
Eucalyptus Rd
34400 SDCo 1071 F1
Eucalyptus St
300 OCSD 1106 B2
9400 SDCo 1291 C1
Eucalyptus Woods Rd
700 SDCo 1109 B2
Euclid Av
1700 ELCN 6499 E5
1800 SDCo 1252 C5
2500 SDCo 1310 B3
4500 SDGO 1269 J4
2600 SDGO 1270 A7
1600 SDGO 1290 A2
S Euclid Av
400 NATC 1290 B7
2000 NATC 1310 B1
500 SDGO 1290 A5
Euclid Ct
4900 SDGO 1270 A7
Euclid Ln
600 SDCo 1252 D6
Euclid Pl
5000 SDGO 1290 A5
Eugene Pl
3500 SDGO 1269 F2
Eugenie Av
700 ENCT 1147 D5
Eula Ln
2000 SDCo 1252 D4
Eureka Dr
500 ESCN 1110 E5
Eureka Pl
- CHLV 1311 D6
3200 CRLB 1106 F5
Eureka Rd
10600 SDCo 1271 F6
Eureka St
1100 SDGO 1268 G3
Europa St
100 ENCT 1147 A4
Eva De Luca Wy
- SDCo 1070 J3
Eva Dr
15900 POWY 1170 D5
Evalyn Ct
12900 POWY 1190 B5
Evalyn Pl
12900 POWY 1190 B5
Evan Hewes Hwy
200 ELCN 6500 D5
600 ImCo 6499 C6
400 ImCo 6500 F5
Evans Av
900 CHLV 1330 E1
Evans Pl
9700 SDCo 1271 C1
500 SDGO 1269 A6
E Evans Rd
2800 SDGO 1288 C1
Evans St
- SDGO 1289 D4
S Evans St
400 SDGO 1289 D5
Evans Wood Wy
- SDGO 1208 F2
Evanston Dr
13200 POWY 1190 G4
Eve Ln
9500 SNTE 1231 E5
Eve Wy
10300 SNTE 1231 D5
Evelyn Av
- BRAW 6319 G4
(See Page 6319)
Evelyn St
1000 SDGO 1290 E2
Evening Canyon Rd
3500 OCSD 1107 E2
E Evening Creek Dr
11000 SDGO 1189 J4
N Evening Creek Dr
13200 SDGO 1189 H4
Evening Primrose Trl
32100 SDCo 1318 B6
(See Page 1318)
Evening Shadow Ln
2000 SDCo 1300 G7
(See Page 1300)
Evening Sky Ct
13200 SDGO 1188 C5
Evening Star Cres
30700 SDCo 1070 H2
Evening Star Dr
14600 POWY 1190 G1
Evening Star St
2300 CHLV 1311 H7
Evening View Dr
400 CHLV 1311 J1
Evening Wy
3000 SDGO 1228 A3
Eveningside Glen
200 ESCN 1109 G4
Evenson Wy
15000 SDCo 1173 J7
Evenstar Ln
4600 SDCo 1155 H4

Everell Pl
10300 SNTE 1231 F3
Everett Av
2100 SDGO 1289 D4
Everett Pl
23400 SDCo 1173 C3
Everett St
5200 OCSD 1067 A3
Everglades Av
7000 SDGO 1250 E4
Evergold St
- SDGO 1210 B1
Evergreen Av
100 IMPB 1349 E1
1600 SDGO 1329 J7
Evergreen Cir
1700 CRLB 1106 F4
Evergreen Ct
3700 SDCo 1048 E1
Evergreen Dr
1200 ENCT 1167 E1
3400 SDCo 1067 J5
29400 SDCo 1297 E4
(See Page 1297)
Evergreen Ln
14100 POWY 1170 G7
800 SDCo 1067 H6
1400 SNMS 1109 D7
Evergreen Pkwy
100 OCSD 1106 C2
Evergreen Rd
3300 SDCo 1310 G2
Evergreen St
3000 SDGO 1268 D6
1000 SDGO 1288 B2
N Evergreen St
3000 SDGO 1268 D5
Evergreen Trl
33500 SDCo 1052 E2
(See Page 1052)
Evergreen Village Ln
- SDGO 1290 A4
Evergreen Village Rd
- SDGO 1290 A4
Everston Rd
12600 SDGO 1189 J6
Everts St
5000 SDGO 1247 H4
Everview Rd
1300 SDGO 1268 F2
Evilo St
1100 ELCJ 1251 H4
Evlouise Dr
- SDCo 1109 H2
Evren Ct
- IMPE 6499 G2
Evvia Ct
100 SDCo 1108 B2
Ewald Cir
9100 SNTE 1231 A7
Ewell Ct
- SDGO 1350 E1
Ewing Dr
- CHLV 1330 J3
Ewing St
5100 SDGO 1270 D2
Exbury Ct
4600 SDGO 1188 C5
Excalibur Wy
4500 SDGO 1228 D3
Excellante St
2000 SDGO 1351 F3
Exception Pl
3800 ESCN 1150 D3
Exchange Av
- CORD 1288 H5
Exchange Pl
7800 SDGO 1227 F6
Excitation Glen
4000 ESCN 1150 B3
Executive Center Ct
6200 SDGO 1351 B1
Executive Dr
4100 SDGO 1228 C2
Executive Pl
2800 ESCN 1129 C2
Executive Ridge
3200 VSTA 1128 A1
Executive Sq
4200 SDGO 1228 C2
Executive Wy
9200 SDGO 1228 D2
Exeter St
1200 ELCJ 1251 J6
Expedition Wy
- SDGO 1227 J3
Exploration Falls Dr
1600 CHLV 1331 G1
Explorer Ct
4200 SDCo 1271 H3
Explorer Pl
10900 SDCo 1271 G3
Explorer Rd
10800 SDCo 1271 G3
Exposition Dr
- SDCo 1274 C4
Exposition Wy
- SDGO 1351 B1
Eyrie Rd
4900 SDGO 1269 E3

Ezee St
600 ENCT 1147 C5
Ezra Ln
14100 POWY 1190 G1

F

F Av
500 CORD 1288 H6
300 NATC 1289 H7
600 NATC 1309 H1
3000 NATC 1310 A4
- SDCo 1066 E1
- SDCo 1291 D3
F Herrera St
- CALX 6620 H5
F Necochea St
500 CALX 6620 E7
F Pedroza Ct
- CALX 6620 J6
E F Rd
- CORD 1288 F5
F St
900 CHLV 1309 H7
- CHLV 1310 C5
- ENCT 1148 A7
200 IMPE 6439 E5
1200 SDCo 1152 G6
1500 SDGO 1289 C3
- SDGO 1290 A4
E F St
- ENCT 1147 C7
W F St
200 ENCT 1147 B7
800 SDGO 1288 J3
200 SDGO 1289 A3
F Torres St
- CALX 6620 H5
Faber Wy
5000 SDGO 1270 B2
Fabienne Wy
8800 LMSA 1271 A3
Fabled Waters Ct
10100 SDCo 1291 E1
Fabled Waters Dr
1700 SDCo 1291 E1
Fair Acres Ln
3100 SDCo 1272 C7
3100 SDCo 1292 C1
(See Page 1292)
Fair Country Rd
- SDCo 1272 A2
Fair Glen Rd
1500 SDCo 1272 A2
Fair Hill
16000 SDGO 1169 C3
Fair Lane Ct
- SDCo 1231 J6
Fair Ln
- ESCN 1129 F5
8900 SDCo 1231 J6
8900 SDCo 1232 A6
100 VSTA 1108 B1
Fair Oak Ct
2300 ESCN 1109 H4
Fair Oaks Dr
3000 SDCo 1272 C7
Fair Oaks Ln
3100 SDCo 1272 C7
Fair Paso
3400 NATC 1310 D3
Fair Valley Rd
1500 SDCo 1272 B2
Fairbanks Av
9500 SDGO 1249 E5
Fairbrook Rd
12500 SDGO 1210 C4
Fairburn St
14600 POWY 1190 J4
Fairchild St
- SDGO 1351 C2
Faircrest Wy
- SDCo 1089 F3
Faircross Pl
3900 SDGO 1270 C5
Fairdale Av
1700 ESCN 1130 C1
Faire Sky Wy
8100 SDCo 1169 A2
Fairen Ln
9200 SNTE 1231 B7
Fairfax Dr
1600 LMGR 1290 G1
Fairfield Av
- CRLB 1107 A4
Fairfield Dr
- ELCN 6500 A6
1500 ELCN 6560 A1
Fairfield St
- CHLV 1331 C1
2700 SDGO 1248 F7
2200 SDGO 1268 F1
Fairfield Wy
- ImCo 6560 C7
Fairford Rd
12600 SDGO 1190 A5
Fairgate Dr
13600 POWY 1190 F4
Fairgreen Wy
- SDCo 1068 B1
Fairgrove Ln
9400 SDGO 1189 E4

Fairhaven St
2000 LMGR 1290 G1
Fairhill Ct
600 OCSD 1087 C1
Fairhill Dr
10200 SDCo 1291 E2
Fairhill Terr
1000 SDCo 1291 E2
Fairhope Ct
17400 SDGO 1170 B1
Fairhope Lp
- VSTA 1107 G6
Fairhope Rd
11900 SDGO 1170 A1
Fairhurst Pl
2500 SDCo 1271 B7
Fairlane Av
900 SNMS 1109 B7
Fairlane Rd
- SDCo 1090 E6
Fairlawn St
9100 SNTE 1231 G5
Fairlee Dr
1900 ENCT 1167 H1
Fairlee Ln
200 ENCT 1167 H1
Fairlie Rd
17400 SDGO 1170 A1
Fairlindo Wy
3600 NATC 1310 D3
Fairlomas Rd
3200 NATC 1310 D3
Fairmount Av
6100 SDGO 1249 H7
4200 SDGO 1269 H4
1800 SDGO 1289 J1
Fairmount Pl
1500 ESCN 1110 A5
Fairport Wy
- SDGO 1208 C2
Fairtree Ter
14700 POWY 1190 D1
Fairview Av
8100 LMSA 1270 H3
Fairview Cir
3500 SDCo 1067 J5
Fairview Dr
3600 SDCo 1068 A5
Fairview Ln
3300 SDCo 1068 A5
Fairwater Pl
- CRLB 1127 C5
Fairway Circle Dr
1800 SDCo 1128 D3
Fairway Ct
800 CHLV 1330 D1
2200 OCSD 1106 G2
1500 SDCo 1058 G4
(See Page 1058)
Fairway Dr
3400 SDCo 1270 J5
Fairway Heights Row
- SDGO 1170 A4
Fairway Hill Cir
8800 SDCo 1089 B1
Fairway Ln
1500 SDCo 1058 H5
(See Page 1058)
- SDCo 1091 F4
Fairway Oaks Dr
2300 CHLV 1311 G5
Fairway Park
1800 ESCN 1109 D5
Fairway Pine Pl
- SDCo 1089 B1
Fairway Pl
5900 SDCo 1188 E1
Fairway Pointe Row
12200 SDGO 1170 B4
Fairway Rd
7100 SDGO 1227 G7
6800 SDGO 1247 G1
Fairway Vista
1500 ENCT 1147 D2
Fairwind Ct
- SDGO 1208 C2
Fairwind Wy
- SDGO 1208 B2
Faisan Wy
11400 SDGO 1250 A3
Faisel Dr
- SDCo 1254 A2
Faith Av
600 ENCT 1167 D1
Faith Cir
1400 OCSD 1106 E1
Faith Rd
- ESCN 1129 F4
Faivre St
2500 CHLV 1330 B5
Falabella Ln
300 SDCo 1028 H5
Falchion Dr
1900 SDCo 1058 G7
(See Page 1058)
Falcon Bluff Ct
16700 SDCo 1169 E3
Falcon Bluff St
9800 SDCo 1169 E3
Falcon Crest Ct
15300 SDCo 1169 G5

Falcon Crest Dr
16100 SDCo 1169 G5
Falcon Dr
3200 CRLB 1106 G4
Falcon Glen
1300 ESCN 1129 G6
Falcon Heights Rd
16200 SDCo 1151 B6
Falcon Hill Ct
800 ENCT 1167 E2
Falcon Ln
1400 ELCJ 1251 D3
Falcon Peak St
- CHLV 1311 D7
Falcon Pl
700 SDGO 1268 J5
400 SNMS 1108 J7
Falcon Ridge Ct
4500 SDGO 1188 C6
Falcon Rim Pt
10600 SDGO 1209 J3
Falcon St
4000 SDGO 1268 J5
Falcon Valley Dr
- CHLV 1311 G3
Falconer Ct
1800 VSTA 1107 J3
Falconer Rd
200 ESCN 1110 E6
900 ESCN 1130 F1
Falconfire Wy
300 SDGO 1290 F3
Falconhurst Terr
- SDGO 1330 H7
Falda Del Cerro Ct
1500 SDCo 1272 A1
Falda Pl
7700 CRLB 1147 F2
Falkirk Row
- SDGO 1247 J1
Fall Brook Pl
- SDGO 1130 H3
Fall Glen Ct
10200 SDGO 1209 D5
Fall Pl
2400 OCSD 1087 D6
Fall River Wy
9300 SDGO 1189 D4
1200 SNMS 1128 A3
Fallbrook Ct
1200 CHLV 1310 J3
1200 CHLV 1311 A3
Fallbrook Ln
2900 SDGO 1248 E6
Fallbrook Oaks Ct
1800 SDCo 1028 A4
Fallbrook St
200 SDCo 1027 F3
- SDCo 1028 A3
E Fallbrook St
1300 SDCo 1027 H3
Fallcrest Wy
10900 SDGO 1208 H3
Fallen Leaf Ln
2100 SDCo 1028 A1
Fallen Leaf Rd
13300 POWY 1170 E4
Fallen Oak Rd
700 SDCo 1047 E4
Fallen Tree Ln
- SDCo 1089 D3
Fallen Wood Ln
- SDGO 1208 F4
Fallhaven Rd
13500 SDGO 1189 B3
Falling Leaf Ct
1900 SNMS 1128 B2
Falling Star Cres
30600 SDCo 1070 G2
Falling Star Dr
1500 CHLV 1311 H7
Falling Waters Ct
2800 CHLV 1312 A5
(See Page 1312)
Fallingleaf Rd
2300 OCSD 1087 E6
Fallon Cir
3600 SDGO 1188 A5
E Falls View Dr
5300 SDGO 1270 C1
W Falls View Dr
5300 SDGO 1270 C1
Falls Wy
6300 SDGO 1270 C1
Fallsbrae Rd
4100 SDCo 1048 A5
Fallsview Ln
100 OCSD 1107 D2
Fallsview Pl
1400 ESCN 1109 J5
Fallsview Rd
2600 SNMS 1128 B6
Fallwood Av
8900 SDGO 1209 D5
Falmouth Dr
2000 ELCJ 1251 C5
6200 LMSA 1251 C6
False Point Ct
600 CHLV 1330 J4
Falvy Av
2800 SDGO 1249 A6

SAN DIEGO CO.

28 INDEX
Family Cir
San Diego County Street Index
INDEX 28
Foothill Dr
SAN DIEGO CO.

STREET Block City Map# Grid

Family Cir 7600 SDGO 1249 A5
Family Pl 3400 SDCo 1271 B5
Famosa Blvd 2900 SDGO 1268 B5
Famous Springs Wy 10400 SDCo 1291 E1
Fandango Ct - SDCo 1086 A3
Fanita Dr
1300 ELCJ 1251 B3
8000 SDGO 1251 A4
8700 SNTE 1231 B7
8600 SNTE 1251 B1
Fanita Pkwy - SNTE 1231 A3
Fanita Rancho Rd 9200 SNTE 1251 B1
Fantasia Ct - SDGO 1210 B1
Fantasia Pl 200 DLMR 1187 G7
Fantasia Wy - SDGO 1210 B1
Fantasy Ln 2200 SDGO 1350 G3
Fantero Av 2100 ESCN 1129 F6
Fanuel St 5500 SDGO 1247 J3
Fanwood Ct 1700 OCSD 1106 E2
Far Valley Rd 1300 SDCo 1318 F5 (See Page 1318)
Far View Pl 2200 SDCo 1108 D4
Faraday Av
- CRLB 1127 A1
- SDCo 1127 B1
Faraday Dr 2100 CRLB 1127 D1
Faraday Rd - VSTA 1127 H1
Faraway Ln 7800 SDCo 1148 J2
Faraway Pl 14200 SDCo 1070 F4
Farel St 2900 OCSD 1106 G1
Farenholt Av - SDGO 1289 C2
Fargate Ter 7200 SDGO 1208 J4
Fargo Av
1500 ELCJ 1252 A5
4600 SDGO 1248 B1
Fargo Glen 100 ESCN 1110 E7
Fargo Ln 1800 CHLV 1311 E7
Farina Pl - VSTA 1088 A7
Farland Pl 100 ESCN 1130 C1
Farley Ct 4200 SDGO 1228 E5
Farley Dr 6300 SDGO 1228 E5
Farley Ln 4200 SDGO 1228 E5
Farley Rd 2400 SDCo 1135 F6
Farlin Rd 1300 SDCo 1235 B5
Farmdale St 7200 SDGO 1290 G6
Farmer Dr - ELCN 6559 F2
Farmer Rd 1200 SDCo 1136 B3
Farmervilee St - CHLV 1331 C1
Farmingdale St - SDGO 1209 G2
Farmington Dr 9500 SDCo 1232 A4
Farmington Pl 1200 SNMS 1128 B3
Farms View Ct 6900 SDCo 1188 H2
Farnham St 9200 SDGO 1249 E1
Farnsworth Ct 5900 CRLB 1127 C2
Farnsworth Ln 1400 ELCN 6560 A4
Farol Ct 7700 CRLB 1147 H2
Farol Pl 7700 CRLB 1147 H2
Farr Av 1000 ESCN 1109 J7
Farr Rd - ImCo 6260 J4 (See Page 6260)
Farra St 37700 SDCo 999 E7
Farraday Ridge Dr 13400 SDCo 1272 F5
Farragut Cir - ELCJ 1251 F6
Farragut Rd - SDGO 1288 D1
Farrand Ct 1000 SDCo 1027 H5
Farrand Rd 1400 SDCo 1027 H5
Farrel St - CHLV 1330 H3
Farrier Ct - SDCo 1085 J4
Farrington Ct 9000 SNTE 1251 A1
Farrington Dr
2300 ELCJ 1251 B1
9100 SNTE 1251 B1
Farview Ct 1100 ELCJ 1251 G3
Farview Dr 600 ELCJ 1251 G3
Fasano Dr 10300 SDCo 1231 F3
Fashion Hills Blvd 6700 SDGO 1268 J2
Fashion Valley Rd 900 SDGO 1268 J3
Father Junipero Serra Trl 10400 SDGO 1230 F6
Father Serra Juniper Trl 8700 SDGO 1250 D2
Fathom Ct - SDGO 1330 J6
Faulconer St 5500 SDGO 1290 B1
Fauna Ct - SDGO 1270 D6
Fauna Dr - SDGO 1270 C6
Fauntleroy Rd 39000 SDCo 1300 C5 (See Page 1300)
Fawcett Rd - ImCo 6620 C1
Fawley Ln 1600 SDCo 1108 A2
Fawley Rd 200 SDCo 1108 A2
Fawn Av 3000 SDGO 1248 C1
Fawn Creek Ln 2400 SDCo 1109 J3
Fawn Ridge - SDGO 1208 B2
Fawntail Ct - CHLV 1311 D6
Fawntail St 900 SNMS 1128 J3
Fawnwood Ln 7900 LMGR 1270 H7
Faxon St 200 SDCo 1291 B4
Fay Av
7500 SDGO 1227 F7
7100 SDGO 1247 F1
Fayette St 1200 ELCJ 1251 D3
Fazio Rd 3400 SDCo 1234 E5
Feather Av 4200 SDGO 1248 E3
Feather Bluff Dr 16700 SDCo 1169 E3
Feather Dr - SNMS 1108 F5
Feather River Pl 1400 CHLV 1311 F7
Feather River Rd 2300 CHLV 1311 G7
Feather Rock Ct 3900 SDCo 1311 B2
Featherhill Ln 11200 SDGO 1209 E2
Featherstone Canyon Rd 22900 SDCo 1193 C5 (See Page 1193)
Febo Ct 3300 CRLB 1127 J7
February Ct 2100 SDGO 1268 G1
February St 4900 SDGO 1268 G1
Fecanin Wy 15800 SDCo 1174 A4
Federal Blvd
6800 LMGR 1270 E6
3500 SDGO 1289 G3
5100 SDGO 1290 A2
Federman Ln 4200 SDGO 1188 B5
Fegan Dr - SDCo 1023 E2
Fegan Ln - SDCo 1023 D2
Feghali Ln - SDCo 1153 A5
Feghali Rd 200 SDCo 1153 A5
Feiler Pl 3000 SDGO 1249 F5
Feldspar Av - CALX 6620 J7
Feldspar Ct 16600 SDCo 1171 F2
Feldspar Pl 6900 CRLB 1127 F5
Felice Dr
1900 ESCN 1109 C4
16400 SDGO 1170 C3
Felicia Ln
9900 SDCo 1291 D3
800 SNMS 1109 B6
Felicia Wy - SDCo 1068 E6
Felicidad Dr 900 SDCo 1027 G3
Felicita Av 700 SDCo 1291 B3
E Felicita Av 100 ESCN 1130 A5
Felicita Ct 1600 ESCN 1129 J5
Felicita Ln
1600 ESCN 1129 J5
1300 SDCo 1149 G1
1700 VSTA 1087 G3
Felicita Pl 600 ESCN 1129 J5
Felicita Rd
1900 ESCN 1129 J6
2400 SDCo 1129 J7
2800 SDCo 1149 J2
Felinda Wy 2500 OCSD 1087 C6
Felino Wy 600 CHLV 1311 A5
Felipe Av - IMPE 6499 H2
Felipe Rd 17300 SDCo 1173 F1
Felix Dr 10600 SNTE 1231 D2
Feller Cove 10500 SDGO 1209 A5
Fellows Ln 11500 SDCo 1231 H2
Felson Rd 9000 SDGO 1189 C1
Felspar Ct 4500 SDGO 1248 B5
Felspar St
1500 SDGO 1247 H6
2400 SDGO 1248 B5
Felton St
4800 SDGO 1269 F3
1300 SDGO 1289 F2
Fender Rd 35000 SDCo 1156 E7
Fenelon St 3600 SDGO 1288 A1
Fenimore Wy 6100 SDGO 1249 J7
Fennel Wy 1700 CHLV 1331 H2
Fennell Av 6000 SDGO 1290 C4
Fennell Ct 200 SDGO 1290 C4
Fenoval Dr 1800 SDCo 1058 G7 (See Page 1058)
Fensmuir St 8500 SDGO 1249 C4
Fenton Parkway - SDGO 1269 E1
Fenton Pkwy 2600 SDGO 1249 D7
Fenton Pl 2600 SDCo 1310 C2
Fenton Rd - SDGO 1208 G7
Fenton St 2300 CHLV 1311 G4
Fenway Cir 1400 OCSD 1066 J4
Fenway Rd 9200 SNTE 1231 A3
Fenwick Dr 3700 SDCo 1271 A5
Fenwick Rd 10700 SDGO 1209 B4
Ferber St 5700 SDGO 1228 F6
Ferdinand Rd 2500 ELCJ 1251 B5
Fergus St 500 SDGO 1290 C3
Ferguson Wy 8800 SDGO 1251 A4
Fermi Av 9400 SDGO 1249 E5
Fermi Ct - CRLB 1127 D1
Fern Av
600 ESCN 1110 C7
500 IMPB 1349 G1
2900 SDGO 1350 C1
Fern Canyon Rd 3400 SDCo 1272 H5
Fern Flat Fire Rd - SDCo 1196 D4 (See Page 1196)
Fern Forest Rd 1600 SDCo 1068 B6
Fern Glen Av 500 SDGO 1247 E1
Fern Meadow Rd 3300 SDCo 1052 D3 (See Page 1052)
Fern Pl
7000 CRLB 1127 E6
1300 SDCo 1107 G3
Fern Ridge Ct - OCSD 1086 D3
Fern St
400 CHLV 1310 A5
1000 ESCN 1110 B6
1900 SDGO 1289 E2
Fern Trl 33500 SDCo 1052 E2 (See Page 1052)
Fern Valley Rd 2500 CHLV 1311 J6
Fernando Ct 12200 SDGO 1150 B7
Fernando Dr 12300 SDGO 1150 B6
Fernando Wy 18300 SDGO 1150 B6
Fernbrook Ct 1900 ELCJ 1252 C5
Fernbrook Dr 13700 SDCo 1192 B3 (See Page 1192)
Ferncreek Ln - SDGO 1130 J3
Ferncrest Pl 12900 SDGO 1190 B2
Ferndale Ln 4100 SDCo 1047 E4
Ferndale St
- CHLV 1311 C7
8500 SDGO 1209 C5
Fernglen Rd 2700 CRLB 1106 F3
Fernhill Wy 1100 ELCJ 1251 H7
Fernpine Dr - SDGO 1270 D6
Fernridge Rd - SNTE 1230 G7
Ferntree Ln 2100 SDCo 1291 D1
Fernview St 1000 ELCJ 1251 H7
Fernwood Av 100 ESCN 1130 C1
Fernwood Dr 6200 LMSA 1251 C6
Fernwood Rd - CHLV 1311 D6
Ferrara Ct 1400 ESCN 1129 H5
Ferrara Wy - VSTA 1087 G6
Ferrell Ln 15000 SDCo 1233 B7
Ferris Sq 6200 SDGO 1208 G7
Fesler St 1200 ELCJ 1251 D3
Festival Ct 3700 CHLV 1330 E5
Festival Dr 200 OCSD 1066 H7
Festival Rd 1100 SNMS 1128 F5
Fez St 4300 SDGO 1228 C1
Fiat Ct 2000 SDCo 1272 C3
Ficus Ct 1700 CHLV 1331 H3
Ficus Ln 1000 SNMS 1109 C7
Fiddletown Rd 14000 POWY 1190 G1
Fidelio Ct - SDGO 1210 B1
Fidelio Wy - SDGO 1210 B1
Fieger St 2100 SDGO 1290 B1
Field Ct 2900 SDGO 1248 F6
Field St 4400 SDGO 1248 E6
Fieldbrook Pl 2700 ESCN 1110 D5
Fieldbrook St - CHLV 1331 C1
E Fieldbrook St 1100 IMPE 6439 G7
Fieldcrest Pl
2500 ESCN 1110 E7
2500 SDCo 1271 B7
Fieldcrest St 10000 SDCo 1271 D7
Fieldgate Rd 4500 OCSD 1107 D2
Fieldlane Pl 2400 SDCo 1271 B7
Fieldridge Pl 2500 SDCo 1271 B7
Fields Ct 1000 OCSD 1067 A4
Fieldstone Dr 12400 SDGO 1150 B5
Fieldstone Ln 700 ENCT 1147 G5
Fieldthorn St 9800 SDCo 1169 E3
Fieldview Av - ELCN 6559 G3
Fieldview Ct - ELCN 6559 G3
Fieldview Wy 14700 POWY 1190 D1
Fiesta Av - CALX 6620 H7
Fiesta Blvd - CALX 6620 F5
Fiesta Dr - POWY 1190 E5
Fiesta Glen 2000 ESCN 1110 B5
Fiesta Island Dr
- SDGO 1248 C7
- SDGO 1268 C2
Fiesta Island Rd 1100 SDGO 1268 E3
Fiesta Ln 200 ELCJ 1252 A5
Fiesta Wy 4200 OCSD 1086 J3
Fifield Rd 4300 ImCo 6320 J2 (See Page 6320)
Fifield St 500 CHLV 1310 G7
Fig Av
200 CHLV 1310 A6
700 CHLV 1330 B1
Fig Ct 1200 NATC 1289 J7
Fig St
600 SDCo 1027 E2
- SNMS 1128 C1
E Fig St 200 SDCo 1027 F2
N Fig St
1400 ESCN 1109 J7
600 ESCN 1129 J1
500 ESCN 1130 A1
S Fig St 200 ESCN 1130 A2
Fig Tree Wy - SDCo 1234 J4
Figtree Ct - SDGO 1210 C3
Figtree St 12400 SDGO 1210 C3
Figueroa Blvd 4400 SDGO 1248 C5
Filago Ct 9400 SDGO 1189 E6
Filaree Ct - CRLB 1127 D6
Filbert St
300 ELCJ 1251 G6
- SDGO 1289 G7
Filera Rd 12300 SDGO 1170 B4
Filipo St 4700 SDGO 1270 D3
Fillbrook Dr 10900 SDCo 1212 B7
Fillmore Ln 8800 SDGO 1249 D1
Fillmott Glen 2500 ESCN 1149 H1
Filly Ln 3600 SDCo 1311 A1
Filmore Pl - CHLV 1331 C2
Filoi Av 4500 SDGO 1350 G3
Filoli Cres 3400 CRLB 1128 A5
Financial Ct 2600 SDGO 1248 B2
Finch Ln
7000 CRLB 1127 C6
2200 SDGO 1249 A7
2000 SDGO 1269 A1
Finch Pl 1200 CHLV 1330 G2
Finch St 1200 ELCJ 1251 D3
Finchley Ter 4700 SDGO 1188 C4
Fine Ln - ESCN 1129 F5
Fink Rd 31300 SDCo 1053 J4 (See Page 1053)
Finley Av 8200 LMSA 1270 H3
Finley Pl - ESCN 1110 E5
Finnila Pl - CRLB 1127 G2
Fino Dr 5100 SDGO 1249 H1
Fino Gn 700 ESCN 1150 C4
Finsen Av 4600 SDGO 1228 F4
Fiona Pl - CRLB 1127 D5
Fiona Wy 8600 SNTE 1231 D7
Fiore Ter 5200 SDGO 1228 E3
Fiorenza Ln 12600 SDGO 1189 H6
Fiori Dr 2100 SDCo 1108 D3
Fir Ln 9700 SDCo 1149 E1
Fir Rd 29000 SDCo 1237 C7
Fir St
100 OCSD 1106 A1
200 SDGO 1289 A2
- SDGO 1290 D4
- SNMS 1128 C1
W Fir St 400 SDGO 1288 J2
Fir Tree Pl 900 CRLB 1127 A5
Firbrook Ln 12800 POWY 1170 D3
Fire Ln
- SDGO 1228 A2
- SNMS 1128 C2
Fire Mountain Dr 1700 OCSD 1106 D2
Fire Mountain Pl 200 ESCN 1109 H6
Fire Opal Ct 15200 SDCo 1169 F5
Fire Rd 3700 SDCo 1048 E3
Firebaugh Pl - CHLV 1311 E5
Firebird St 300 SNMS 1108 H7
Firebrand Dr 2700 SDCo 1254 D2
Firebrand Pl 2600 SDCo 1254 D2
Firebrand Wy 2700 SDCo 1254 D2
Firecrest Wy 1200 SDCo 1027 H7
Firenze Ln 14600 SDGO 1168 H7
Firenze Wy - OCSD 1106 J2
Fireside Av 8500 SDGO 1249 C6
Fireside Ct 2800 SDGO 1249 C6
Fireside Ln 900 VSTA 1088 B7
Fireside St 100 OCSD 1086 F3
Firestone Dr 1700 ESCN 1109 D5
Firestone St 4600 SDGO 1228 F7
Firethorn Glen 2100 ESCN 1110 A4
Firethorn Ln 4500 SDCo 1099 F4 (See Page 1099)
Firethorn St
700 SDGO 1330 G7
1200 SDGO 1350 G1
Firewater Trl 7500 SDCo 1138 C7 (See Page 1138)
Fireway Dr 3600 SDGO 1248 H4
First Light Rd 800 SNMS 1128 F6
First St 3800 SNMS 1128 C1
Firtree Ct 300 ENCT 1147 G6
Firwood Row 6000 SDGO 1248 B1
Fisher Cove 14800 SDCo 1188 A1
Fisher Ln 2900 LMGR 1270 G6
Fisher Rd 40300 SDCo 1300 E7 (See Page 1300)
Fishers Pl 2800 SDCo 1129 C6
Fisk Av 6600 SDGO 1228 D4
Fitch Ct 6900 SDGO 1268 J2
Fitch Loop - SDGO 1288 A5
Fitzgerald Wy 9000 SDCo 1271 A6
Fitzpatrick Rd 300 SNMS 1108 H7
Five Crowns Wy 100 ENCT 1147 H7
Five D Dr 1300 SDCo 1251 H3
Five Diamonds Rd 2300 SDCo 1078 G2 (See Page 1078)
Five Point Ln 9100 SNTE 1231 A7
Fix Ct 3700 SDGO 1350 F5
Flag Lake St 7600 SDGO 1250 G5
Flag Ln 1300 SDCo 1251 H3
Flag Plaza - SDCo 1290 J6
Flagship Ct - SNMS 1128 D5
Flagstaff Ct - CHLV 1311 G3
Flagstone Ct 700 SNMS 1109 C5
Flagstone Row 6100 SDGO 1248 B1
Flair Encinitas Dr 1400 ENCT 1147 G6
Flair Ln - SDCo 1174 A4
Flambeau Pl 10700 SDCo 1271 F4
Flame Tree Pl 200 OCSD 1087 A1
Flamenco St 6400 CRLB 1127 H5
Flametree Ln - SDCo 1068 C7
Flaming Tree Ln 1400 CRLB 1127 A4
Flamingo Av
1200 ELCJ 1251 J2
1100 SDCo 1251 H2
Flamingo Dr 100 OCSD 1086 F4
Flamingo Pl 1300 ELCJ 1251 J2
Flammang Av - BRAW 6259 H7 (See Page 6259)
Flanders Cove 10400 SDGO 1209 A4
Flanders Ct 10200 SDGO 1208 H5
Flanders Dr
6500 SDGO 1208 H4
8600 SDGO 1209 C4
Flanders Pl 10400 SDGO 1209 A4
Flat Rock St 3500 CRLB 1107 B4
Flatiron - SNMS 1128 B5
Flaven Ln 8100 SDCo 1252 C1
Flax Ct 1000 SDGO 1350 C1
Flax Dr 2800 SDGO 1350 C1
Flaxton Ter 4900 SDGO 1188 C4
Fledgling Dr 2900 SDCo 1129 C5
Fleet St - SDCo 1126 J2
Fleetridge Dr 1100 SDGO 1288 A2
Fleetwood St
1900 ESCN 1129 F5
2300 SDGO 1248 J7
Fleischmann Ct - SDCo 1086 A2
Fleishbein St 1600 CHLV 1331 E2
Fleming Ct - SDGO 1229 C2
Fleming Dr 3000 SDGO 1310 E2
Fleming Rd - SDGO 1287 J5
Flemish St 800 OCSD 1086 G5
Fletcher Dr 9100 LMSA 1271 B2
Fletcher Pkwy
500 ELCJ 1251 E3
8400 LMSA 1250 J7
Fletcher Pt 3400 SDCo 1155 G4
Fletcher Rd 4400 SDCo 1100 B4 (See Page 1100)
Fletcher Valley Dr 8900 SNTE 1251 A1
Flicker Ln 100 OCSD 1086 H2
Flicker St 500 SDGO 1290 F3
Flightpath Wy 8500 SDGO 1351 G1
Flinn Crest St 9300 SDCo 1232 H4
Flinn Springs Ln 9400 SDCo 1232 J4
Flinn Springs Rd
2500 CHLV 1311 H6
9700 SDCo 1232 J3
Flint Av 2100 ESCN 1130 D1
Flint Pl 12100 POWY 1190 E7
Flint St 900 ELCJ 1251 H2
Flintkote Av
11200 SDGO 1207 J3
11000 SDGO 1208 A5
Flintridge Dr 2200 SDGO 1310 C1
Flintridge Pl 600 ESCN 1109 F4
Flintwood Wy - SDGO 1188 E5
Flipper Dr 100 SDGO 1290 C4
Flo Bob Ln - SDCo 1234 H5
Flo Dr 1400 SDCo 1234 A6
Flood Rd - SDCo 1275 D1
Flora Av 1000 CORD 1288 H7
Flora Azalea Ct 10500 SNTE 1231 E2
Flora Camellia Ct 10500 SNTE 1231 E2
Flora Dr 700 OCSD 1067 A5
Flora Ln - ImCo 6439 E4
Flora Magnolia Ct - SNTE 1231 E2
Flora Verda Ct 10500 SNTE 1231 E2
Flora Vista
- POWY 1190 E5
1400 SDCo 1130 E5
Floral Av 13400 POWY 1190 H4
Floral Ct 800 SNMS 1109 A5
Florence Ln 3400 SDGO 1289 F5
Florence St
700 IMPB 1329 H7
1200 IMPB 1349 H1
3400 SDGO 1289 F5
Florence Terr 3100 SDCo 1292 C1 (See Page 1292)
Florencia Ln - VSTA 1087 G6
Flores De Oro 500 SDCo 1148 A7
Flores Ln
2900 LMGR 1270 E6
100 VSTA 1087 G3
Floresta Ct 12400 SDGO 1170 B1
Floresta Wy 12400 SDGO 1170 B1
Florey Ct 7300 SDGO 1228 F4
Florey St 7200 SDGO 1228 F4
Florida Ct 1900 SDGO 1269 C6
Florida Dr 2000 SDGO 1269 C7
Florida Pl 2300 SDGO 1289 C1
Florida St
500 IMPB 1329 H7
1000 IMPB 1349 H1
4300 SDGO 1269 C4
Florido Plz 1000 CHLV 1311 A7
Florindo Rd 11400 SDGO 1169 H2
Florine Dr 3100 LMGR 1270 F6
Florissant Ct 8400 SDGO 1189 B3
Florita St 200 ENCT 1147 B6
Flower Av
- CORD 1288 F4
2200 SDGO 1350 B1
Flower Dr - NATC 1289 H7
Flower Fields Wy 2600 CRLB 1106 H3
Flower Hill Dr - SDGO 1187 H2
Flower Hill Wy 300 SNMS 1129 B1
Flower Ln
24700 SDCo 1236 A2
300 VSTA 1087 D7
Flower Meadow Ct 11500 SDGO 1209 A1
Flower Meadow Dr 7500 SDGO 1209 A2
Flower St
600 CHLV 1309 J6
- CHLV 1310 C5
1700 ESCN 1130 C1
E Flower St - CHLV 1310 C4
Flowerdale Ln 200 SDGO 1290 H4
Flowerpot Ln 2200 CHLV 1331 F1
Flowerwood Ln 3700 SDCo 1048 C4
Floyd Av 600 CHLV 1310 F6
Floyd Smith Dr 500 ELCJ 1251 E2
Flume Dr
- ELCJ 1252 C2
1900 SDCo 1252 C3
1800 SDCo 1271 G1
Flume Rd - SDGO 1251 A6
Flushing Dr 2300 SDGO 1248 J7
Flying Cloud Av - IMPE 6499 C1
Flying Cloud Dr - IMPE 6499 D1
Flying Cloud Pl 1900 SDCo 1300 F7 (See Page 1300)
Flying Cloud Wy 4800 CRLB 1106 H7
Flying H Rd 3100 SDCo 1078 J6 (See Page 1078)
Flying Hills Ct 2000 ELCJ 1251 B3
Flying Hills Ln 1900 ELCJ 1251 B3
Flying Lc Ln 6200 CRLB 1127 J3
Flying U Rd 2500 SDCo 1078 J2 (See Page 1078)
Flynn Glen 1900 ESCN 1130 B5
Flynn Heights Dr 800 SDCo 1109 B2
Fog Ridge 21000 SDCo 1275 A3
Fogg Ct 4400 SDGO 1248 C5
Fogg St 2400 SDGO 1248 C5
Foggy Point Dr 400 CHLV 1311 J1
Folex Wy 2500 SDCo 1291 F1
Follett Dr - SNTE 1231 F4
Follette St - CRLB 1127 D5
Folsom Dr 5800 SDGO 1247 F3
Fond Du Lac Av 4100 SDGO 1248 E1
Fond Du Lac Ct 4800 SDGO 1248 E1
Fondale Ct 600 ESCN 1130 D1
Fondo Rd 10000 SDCo 1271 E5
Fontaine Pl 7100 SDGO 1250 B5
Fontaine St 5400 SDGO 1250 B5
Fontana Av 3200 SDGO 1248 E5
Fontanelle Ct 11600 SDGO 1190 A3
Fontanelle Pl 13700 SDGO 1190 A3
Fonteyn Ct 9100 SNTE 1231 H5
Fonticello Wy 17600 SDGO 1150 D7
Fonts Point Dr 2800 SDCo 1099 G4 (See Page 1099)
Fonzie Av - IMPE 6499 G1
Fools Gold Wy 1200 CHLV 1311 E7
Footbridge Wy 600 ESCN 1110 D6
Foote Path Wy 1200 SDCo 1251 D7
Foothill Av - CRLB 1107 C3
Foothill Blvd
8400 SDCo 1237 C4
5100 SDGO 1247 J4
Foothill Ct 10100 SDCo 1291 E1
Foothill Dr
2400 SDCo 1088 C6
2800 SDCo 1108 C1
2100 VSTA 1088 C5

STREET
Block City Map# Grid

Foothill Rd
300 SDGO 1350 F3
Foothill St
3200 ESCN 1150 C2
Foothill Transportation Corridor
0 SDCo 1023 C2
Foothill View Pl
- ESCN 1109 C5
Foothill View Wy
- ESCN 1109 C4
Foothills River Ln
- SDCo 1231 J4
Footman Ct
12700 POWY 1170 C5
Footman Ln
12600 POWY 1170 C5
Forbell Pl
3800 SDCo 1047 J4
Forbes Av
5500 SDGO 1250 C5
Ford Av
500 SOLB 1167 F6
Ford Bolol Dr
- SDGO 1289 C1
Ford Dr
- ELCN 6499 F3
Ford St
- SDGO 1229 C7
Fordham Av
800 CHLV 1311 C5
Fordham Ct
3600 OCSD 1087 B7
Fordham St
3200 SDGO 1268 D5
Fordyce St
300 ELCJ 1251 H6
Forecastle Ct
- CRLB 1107 C7
Forest Av
1200 CRLB 1106 E4
Forest Dr
25700 SDCo 1109 H1
Forest Glen
- ESCN 1109 G7
Forest Glen Rd
3500 SDGO 1350 E1
Forest Grove Dr
2500 OCSD 1087 E5
Forest Hill Dr
23500 SDCo 1173 D2
Forest Hill Pl
- CHLV 1311 F5
Forest Lake Dr
- CHLV 1311 F4
Forest Meadow Ct
2300 CHLV 1311 H7
Forest Meadow Rd
5600 SDCo 1175 J2
(See Page 1175)
Forest Meadow Wy
7000 SDCo 1175 J1
(See Page 1175)
Forest Oaks Dr
2300 CHLV 1311 G5
Forest Park Ln
2700 CRLB 1106 F3
Forest Park Rd
2600 SDCo 1274 F5
Forest Pl
300 VSTA 1087 D7
Forest Ranch
- OCSD 1086 J2
Forest Rd
3600 OCSD 1086 F2
Forest View Wy
2800 CRLB 1106 F3
Forest Wy
1600 DLMR 1187 G4
Forestdale Dr
1600 ENCT 1147 H7
Forester Creek Rd
1900 SDCo 1252 D3
Forester Ln
600 CHLV 1311 C4
Forestview Ln
11100 SDGO 1209 H4
Forge Ln
- SDCo 1027 F4
Formal Ct
7300 SDGO 1250 C5
Formula Pl
7600 SDGO 1209 A7
Forney Av
4000 SDGO 1248 E3
Forrest Bluff
500 ENCT 1147 F5
Forrestal Ct
6900 SDGO 1250 E4
Forrestal Rd
7700 SDGO 1250 D4
Forrester Ct
3000 SDGO 1249 E5
Forrester Rd
1100 ImCo 6559 A4
Forsberg Ct
1600 SDGO 1290 D6
Forster St
- OCSD 1106 B2
Forsters Tern Dr
7000 CRLB 1127 B5
Fort Stockton Dr
1800 SDGO 1268 G4
Fortino
- SDGO 1210 D2
Forton Wy
7400 SDGO 1248 J7
Fortuna Av
1900 SDGO 1248 A7
500 VSTA 1087 H2
Fortuna Del Este
19600 SDCo 1148 F3
Fortuna Del Norte
- SDCo 1128 F7
Fortuna Del Sur
20500 SDCo 1148 F1
Fortuna Ranch Rd
3500 ENCT 1148 C4
3700 SDCo 1148 D4
Fortuna Santa Fe
8200 SDCo 1169 A4
Fortuna St
- CHLV 1330 E1
Fortuna Vista Ct
7400 SNTE 1230 F7
Fortunada St
200 OCSD 1066 H7
Fortune Ln
9300 LMSA 1271 B2
Fortune Wy
2400 VSTA 1108 A6
Fortunella Ct
600 ESCN 1110 D5
Forty Rod Trl
7400 SDCo 1138 C7
(See Page 1138)
Forum St
6500 SDGO 1248 H3
Forward St
700 SDGO 1247 G4
Fosca St
3200 CRLB 1127 J7
3300 CRLB 1147 J1
Foss Ln
1300 SDCo 1233 H7
Foss Rd
1700 SDCo 1233 H7
Foss St
3400 SDGO 1330 E6
Foster Ln
2200 SDGO 1209 E7
Foster St
2100 OCSD 1086 C6
7000 SDGO 1290 F3
Foster Truck Tr
- SDCo 1191 J1
Foster Truck Trl
- SDCo 1191 G6
- SDCo 1192 A3
(See Page 1192)
Fostoria Ct
- SDCo 1169 D2
Foucaud Wy
8500 SDGO 1189 C7
Foundation Ln
400 ELCJ 1251 G6
Founders Rd
- SDCo 1192 G6
(See Page 1192)
Fountain Grove Pl
1400 CHLV 1311 F7
Fountain Pl
1000 ESCN 1109 F5
Fountain St
4200 SDGO 1248 B6
Four Clover Ct
3000 SDCo 1047 J1
Four Corners Rd
- SDCo 1173 G7
Four Corners St
2900 CHLV 1311 J1
Four Corners Trl
14900 SDCo 1193 H1
(See Page 1193)
Four Cs Ranch Rd
39800 SDCo 1300 D4
(See Page 1300)
Four Gee Rd
16700 SDCo 1169 E2
Four Peaks St
3500 CRLB 1107 B6
Four Season Pt
7100 CRLB 1127 C6
Foursome Dr
3500 SDCo 1270 J5
Foursome E Dr
2900 SDCo 1079 C5
(See Page 1079)
Foussat Rd
400 OCSD 1086 E4
N Foussat Rd
400 OCSD 1086 E4
S Foussat Rd
200 OCSD 1086 E5
Foutz Av
2200 SDGO 1248 B6
Fowler Canyon Rd
3400 SDCo 1272 F6
Fowler Dr
2100 SDGO 1290 F7
Fowler Wy
9800 SNTE 1231 B4
Fowles St
200 OCSD 1086 E6
Fox Av
4000 SDGO 1248 E3
W Fox Av
3400 SDGO 1248 D3
Fox Bridge Ct
- SDCo 1028 G5
Fox Glen
1200 ESCN 1129 F5
Fox Grove Pl
3600 SDGO 1187 J5
Fox Hunt Ln
14800 SDGO 1170 B7
Fox Ln
- SDCo 1089 D6
Fox Meadow Rd
9900 SDCo 1169 E4
Fox Pl
3300 SDGO 1248 D3
Fox Point Ln
4600 SDCo 1099 H4
(See Page 1099)
Fox Run Ln
29100 SDCo 1070 J6
N Fox Run Pl
- CHLV 1311 H3
S Fox Run Pl
- CHLV 1311 H3
Fox Run Row
14200 SDGO 1188 D2
E Fox Run Wy
3000 SDGO 1248 H5
W Fox Run Wy
3000 SDGO 1248 H5
Fox Valley Ct
9700 SDCo 1169 E4
Fox Valley Dr
16300 SDCo 1169 E4
Fox Valley Ln
9900 SDCo 1169 E4
Fox Valley Wy
9900 SDCo 1169 E4
Foxberry Ct
13400 SDCo 1090 D3
Foxboro Av
1100 CHLV 1330 H1
Foxborough Ln
8800 SDCo 1232 C6
Foxborough Pt
5200 SDGO 1208 D2
Foxcroft Ct
12500 SDGO 1189 C6
Foxcroft Pl
8500 SDGO 1189 C5
Foxdale Pl
100 ESCN 1130 C1
Foxfire Ln
200 SDCo 1027 F5
Foxfire Pl
1600 ESCN 1109 D5
Foxfire Rd
1800 SDCo 1027 F6
Foxglove Ln
3700 SDCo 1048 F1
Foxglove St
700 ENCT 1147 E6
Foxglove View
1000 CRLB 1127 B6
Foxglove Wy
2100 CHLV 1331 H3
13500 SDGO 1188 G3
Foxhall Ct
700 SNMS 1128 G2
Foxhall Dr
800 SNMS 1128 G2
Foxhall Glen
3000 ESCN 1150 A2
Foxhills Ter
1800 VSTA 1108 A4
Foxhollow Ct
4400 SDGO 1188 B5
Foxhound Wy
- SDGO 1208 E2
Foxley Dr
3800 ESCN 1110 F4
Foxtail Canyon Dr
1500 CHLV 1331 A2
Foxtail Ct
4500 OCSD 1087 D4
Foxtail Loop
- CRLB 1107 D7
Foxtail St
1900 VSTA 1107 J4
Foxtail Wy
6600 SDGO 1188 G3
Foxtrail Dr
- ELCN 6559 J3
Foxtrot Lp
- CHLV 1331 G2
Foxwood Dr
600 OCSD 1066 H7
Foxwood Rd
10700 SDGO 1209 B4
Foy Ln
500 ESCN 1130 A6
Foyle Wy
6500 SDGO 1248 J2
Foyt Ct
1900 SDCo 1272 C3
Frace Ln
- SDCo 1090 C4
Frakes St
7100 SDGO 1248 J4
Frame Ct
13200 POWY 1190 C4
Frame Rd
13300 POWY 1190 C4
Frames Port Pl
11600 SDGO 1208 J1
Frances Dr
100 SDCo 1253 C1
100 VSTA 1087 J4
Francesca Dr
100 OCSD 1087 A2
Franceschi Dr
1500 CHLV 1331 B2
Francine Ct
12800 POWY 1190 A5
Francine Pl
12800 POWY 1190 A5
Francine Ter
12800 POWY 1190 B5
Francis Dr
- SDCo 1271 B6
- SNTE 1231 E7
Francis St
5100 OCSD 1067 B5
200 SDGO 1289 F4
S Francis St
400 SDGO 1289 F4
Francis Wy
4200 LMSA 1270 F4
Franciscan Rd
- CRLB 1126 H5
Franciscan Wy
200 OCSD 1086 G2
1100 SDGO 1269 B3
Francisco Dr
17300 SDGO 1170 B1
Frank Daniels Wy
10600 SDGO 1210 A2
Frank Ln
10300 SNTE 1231 D5
Frank Wy
9500 SNTE 1231 D5
Frankel Wy
2900 SDGO 1248 H6
Franken St
10500 SNTE 1251 E1
Frankfort St
2300 SDGO 1248 E7
1300 SDGO 1268 E2
Franklee Blvd
- CALX 6620 E4
Franklin
- SDCo 1232 F4
Franklin Av
700 ELCJ 1251 E6
2000 SDGO 1289 D4
4800 SDGO 1290 A4
Franklin Ln
- SDCo 1172 G2
700 VSTA 1087 H5
Franklin Rd
- IMPE 6439 E5
Franklin Ridge Rd
- SDGO 1269 C1
Franzen Farm Rd
16500 SDCo 1168 J4
Frascati Wy
9500 SNTE 1231 C4
Fraternal Ct
10100 SDGO 1208 D5
Frauline Dr
1300 SDGO 1350 A2
Fraxinella St
200 ENCT 1147 E6
Frazee Rd
- OCSD 1086 J2
4700 OCSD 1087 B2
1400 SDGO 1269 A2
Frazier Dr
8600 SDGO 1250 J3
Fred Martin Ln
11800 SDCo 1231 J2
Fred Rd
13200 POWY 1190 C5
Freda Ln
2000 ENCT 1167 E3
Fredas Hill Rd
3300 SDCo 1108 E1
Fredcurt Ln
11300 SDCo 1231 G1
Frederick St
3600 SDCo 1291 A3
Fredericka Pkwy
200 CHLV 1310 B5
Fredonia St
5500 SDGO 1290 B1
Fredricks Av
400 OCSD 1086 F2
Fredricks Rd
- ImCo 6259 C5
(See Page 6259)
Freeborn Wy
2800 ELCJ 1251 A5
Freed Manor Ln
6800 SDGO 1290 E6
Freedom Ct
1000 SOLB 1187 G1
Freedom Hill
- SDCo 1232 F4
Freedom Wy
1800 VSTA 1107 G5
Freeman St
800 OCSD 1086 A7
3200 SDGO 1268 C6
N Freeman St
400 OCSD 1086 A7
S Freeman St
1600 OCSD 1106 C3
Freeport Ct
10100 SDGO 1189 F4
Freeport Rd
13700 SDGO 1189 F3
Freesia Gln
100 ESCN 1109 G5
Freeway Ln
- OCSD 1106 C1
Freezer Rd
- SDCo 1314 C6
(See Page 1314)
Fremont Pl
19200 SDCo 1149 E4
Fremont St
3500 SDGO 1268 H6
1400 VSTA 1087 J4
Fremontia Ln
5400 SDGO 1269 J1
Frenata Pl
- CRLB 1127 C5
French Ct
1400 OCSD 1106 E1
Frenzel Cir
3600 OCSD 1106 J1
Fresca Ct
700 SOLB 1187 F1
Fresca St
600 SOLB 1187 F1
Fresco Ln
13200 SDGO 1188 J4
Fresh Waters Ct
2500 SDCo 1291 F2
Freshwind Ct
11500 SDGO 1169 J5
Fresnillo Ct
100 SOLB 1167 H4
Fresnillo Wy
- SOLB 1167 H5
Fresno Av
1600 CHLV 1330 D5
8300 LMSA 1270 J3
Fresno St
1000 SDGO 1268 G3
Frey Ct
13400 POWY 1190 J4
Friant St
8700 SDGO 1209 C4
Friar Pl
1400 CHLV 1330 E4
Friars Rd
10000 SDGO 1249 G6
4500 SDGO 1268 E3
7700 SDGO 1269 B2
Fried Av
2900 SDGO 1228 C6
Friedell Dr
2600 SDGO 1268 E6
Friedrick Dr
1700 SDGO 1289 F2
Friendly Cres
800 ELCJ 1251 G4
Friendly Ct
500 ELCJ 1251 G4
Friendly Dr
1900 VSTA 1088 C4
Friendly Pl
6400 CRLB 1126 H4
Friends Wy
- SDCo 1027 H5
Friendship Dr
1800 ELCJ 1251 D1
Friendship Ln
1600 SDCo 1109 E6
Frink Av
4900 SDGO 1228 F7
4800 SDGO 1248 F1
Frisbie St
3500 SDCo 1310 J1
Frisius Dr
2400 SDCo 1155 J4
1900 SDCo 1156 B5
Frntge Rd
- CORD 1308 J1
- CORD 1309 A2
Frobisher Cir
10500 SDGO 1209 C4
Frobisher St
8600 SDGO 1209 C4
Froebel Dr
2300 ESCN 1130 B6
Frog Hollow
- SDCo 1069 H2
Frolic Wy
100 SDCo 1028 A2
Frome
- SDCo 1232 F4
Frondoso Dr
17700 SDGO 1150 C7
Frondoso Dr
17300 SDGO 1170 C1
Fronsac St
10800 SDGO 1210 B2
Front St
400 ELCJ 1251 E6
- IMPE 6439 F7
4000 SDGO 1269 A5
- SDGO 1288 A5
2200 SDGO 1289 A1
200 SDGO 1350 G5
Frontage Rd
1100 CHLV 1330 A4
1200 ELCN 6499 F4
- ESCN 1150 A2
47600 RivC 999 A2
- SDCo 1028 F1
- SDCo 1209 F6
- SDGO 1189 G6
- SDGO 1209 F1
- SDGO 1228 A6
- SDGO 1268 G6
- SDGO 1269 F6
E Frontage Rd
1300 CHLV 1330 A5
W Frontage Rd
- CHLV 1330 A4
Frontera Dr
- CALX 6620 H7
Frontera Rd
12300 SDGO 1170 B2
Frontier Dr
100 OCSD 1086 F5
Frontier Rd
- SDCo 1068 J3
- SDCo 1069 A2
Frost Av
- CRLB 1107 B7
Frost St
7800 SDGO 1249 B5
Frost-Mar Pl
9300 SDGO 1228 H2
Froude St
1800 SDGO 1267 J7
2200 SDGO 1268 A6
1200 SDGO 1287 H1
Frucht St
- SDGO 1289 G7
Fruit Tree Wy
500 OCSD 1086 E2
Fruitland Dr
2900 SDCo 1067 J6
Fruitland Pl
- SDGO 1350 F3
Fruitvale Hts
- SDCo 1071 A7
Fruitvale Ln
14400 SDCo 1070 H7
Fruitvale Rd
14600 SDCo 1070 G7
- SDCo 1071 A7
Fry Creek Cg
- SDCo 1032 D6
Fryden Ct
3100 SDGO 1248 D3
Frying Pan Rd
2600 SDCo 1078 J3
(See Page 1078)
Fuchsia Ct
1700 OCSD 1106 E2
Fuchsia Dr
- SDGO 1248 C6
Fuchsia Ln
900 SDGO 1350 G1
Fucshia Ln
900 CRLB 1126 J5
Fuentes Ct
3500 NATC 1310 E5
Fuerte Bluff Dr
1600 SDCo 1272 A2
Fuerte Dr
10900 SDCo 1271 G3
Fuerte Estates Dr
1700 SDCo 1271 J2
Fuerte Farms Rd
11400 SDCo 1271 H3
Fuerte Heights Ln
1400 SDCo 1272 A2
Fuerte Hills Dr
1600 SDCo 1271 J2
Fuerte Knolls Ln
- SDCo 1271 J2
Fuerte Ln
2000 ESCN 1109 D4
Fuerte Ranch Rd
1600 SDCo 1272 A2
Fuerte St
2200 OCSD 1106 E1
1700 SDCo 1028 A5
Fuerte Valley Dr
1700 SDCo 1272 A3
Fuerte Vista Ln
- SDCo 1271 J3
Fuji St
6800 SDGO 1290 F7
Fuller Rd
- SDGO 1289 C1
Fuller St
200 SDCo 1067 A2
Fullerton Av
9200 SDGO 1249 E6
Fulmar St
6000 SDGO 1290 C1
Fulton Rd
900 SNMS 1109 B6
Fulton St
6900 SDGO 1248 J7
7400 SDGO 1249 A7
E Fulvia St
400 ENCT 1147 B4
Fulwood Ln
- ESCN 1129 E5
7300 SDGO 1249 A7
Fun Ln
- ESCN 1129 F5
Funquest Dr
900 SDCo 1027 G3
Furlong Pl
- SDGO 1208 D2
Furnace Creek Rd
15200 SDCo 1232 J1
Furner St
2100 ELCJ 1251 B1
Fury Ln
10800 SDCo 1271 F4
Fusco Ln
22100 SDCo 1275 C1
Futura St
12600 SDGO 1188 B6
Futurity Ln
200 SDCo 1047 F3

G

G Anaya St
- CALX 6680 J2
G Av
100 CORD 1288 H5
200 NATC 1289 H7
600 NATC 1309 J1
- SDCo 1291 D3
G Burt Av
- CALX 6620 E7
G Figueroa Av
- CALX 6620 H5
G Luna St
- CALX 6680 D1
E G Rd
- CORD 1288 F6
G St
500 BRAW 6319 G2
(See Page 6319)
800 BRAW 6320 A2
(See Page 6320)
800 CHLV 1309 H7
100 CHLV 1310 C6
400 IMPE 6439 F5
- SDCo 1047 A5
800 SDCo 1152 H6
1700 SDGO 1289 C3
- SDGO 1290 A4
E G St
- ENCT 1147 C7
W G St
200 ENCT 1147 B7
1200 SDGO 1288 J3
700 SDGO 1289 A3
G Woo Av
- CALX 6620 J6
Gabacho Dr
10700 SDGO 1249 H1
Gabacho St
7800 CRLB 1147 H2
Gabarda Rd
16300 SDGO 1170 C4
Gabbiano Ln
7300 CRLB 1127 A6
Gabelwood Wy
- SDGO 1208 F2
Gabilan Rd
13300 SDGO 1189 J4
Gable Ridge Rd
14800 SDGO 1170 B7
Gable Wy
700 ELCJ 1251 E3
Gabler Dr
3000 SDCo 1069 H5
Gables St
5500 SDGO 1310 C1
Gabriel Wy
- SDCo 1049 G4
4700 SDCo 1271 D3
Gabrielieno Av
4900 OCSD 1067 B7
Gabrielle Glen
2000 ESCN 1129 E5
Gabrielson Av
2800 SDGO 1249 A6
Gaebrail Ct
- IMPE 6499 G2
Gaelyn Ct
14300 POWY 1190 E2
Gaetano Altieri Dr
- SDCo 1070 J3
Gaffney Ct
3900 SDGO 1188 A4
Gage Dr
4700 CRLB 1107 A5
200 SDCo 1086 A2
900 SDGO 1288 A2
Gage Pl
3400 SDGO 1288 A3
Gai Dr
900 SDGO 1350 G1
Gail Dr
3700 OCSD 1107 A2
300 VSTA 1087 H3
Gail Park Ln
14700 POWY 1190 F1
Gail Pl
13200 SDCo 1232 C5
Gailes Blvd
1600 SDGO 1351 F2
Gaillon Ct
12600 SDGO 1150 C6
Gain Dr
7000 SDGO 1250 J3
Gainard Wy
4600 SDGO 1249 G2
Gaines St
3300 SDGO 1268 E5
Gainsborough Av
8800 SDGO 1189 C2
Gait Wy
2900 SDCo 1129 C6
Gala Av
5400 SDGO 1250 C5
Galahad Rd
2400 SDGO 1249 C7
Galante Pl
6100 SDGO 1188 F4
Galante Wy
3900 OCSD 1086 G2
Galatea Ln
- SDCo 1089 D4
Galaxy Ct
7500 SDGO 1250 E6
Galaxy Dr
800 VSTA 1087 E6
Galbar Pl
4100 OCSD 1087 C7
Galbar St
4000 OCSD 1087 C7
Galdar Pl
1000 CHLV 1310 J5
Gale St
1000 ESCN 1110 B5
Galena Av
2300 CRLB 1127 G6
4900 SDGO 1268 F1
Galena Canyon Rd
10400 SDCo 1149 E7
Galena St
500 ELCJ 1252 B4
Galeon Ct
500 SDCo 1291 C3
Galeria Cres
23600 SDCo 1173 D2
Galewood St
6900 SDGO 1250 B6
Galicia Wy
2600 CRLB 1147 G1
4800 OCSD 1107 E5
Galician Ct
400 SDCo 1028 J6
Gallatin Wy
4900 SDGO 1228 C7
4700 SDGO 1248 C1
Gallegos Ter
6300 SDGO 1290 D6
Galleon Wy
7600 CRLB 1147 H1
Gallery Ct
800 SDGO 1290 C6
Gallery Dr
900 OCSD 1087 B2
Gallineta Wy
24700 SDCo 1173 G2
Gallinule Ct
8800 SDGO 1189 C6
Gallop Crest Ct
10700 SDGO 1208 F1
Gallop Heights
6100 SDGO 1208 F2
Gallop Pl
13200 SDCo 1232 C5
Gallop Wy
21800 SDCo 1129 C4
Galloping Wy
5600 SDCo 1311 B2
Galloway Dr
3200 SDGO 1228 C4
Galloway Pl
5700 SDCo 1048 B7
Galloway Valley Ct
300 SDCo 1233 E7
Galloway Valley Ln
8600 SDCo 1233 E7
Galloway Valley Rd
300 SDCo 1233 E7
Galopago St
800 SDCo 1291 C3
Galston Dr
9500 SNTE 1231 B4
Galt Dr
800 SDCo 1252 C7
Galt St
4100 SDGO 1228 E7
Galt Wy
5100 SDGO 1228 E7
Galvani Ln
2200 SDCo 1108 D2
Galveston St
2300 SDGO 1248 E7
1400 SDGO 1268 E2
Galveston Wy
500 CHLV 1311 C3
Galvez Ct
1900 SDGO 1350 D3
Galvin Av
9700 SDGO 1209 E2
Galway Ct
1600 ELCJ 1251 C4
Galway Pl
1800 ELCJ 1251 C4
- SDGO 1189 B2
Gam Ln
1600 SDCo 1152 F7
Gamay Ter
1800 CHLV 1311 D3
Gamay Wy
5500 SDGO 1188 E5
Gamble Ln
1600 ESCN 1129 G6
Gamble Pl
2100 SDCo 1129 H6
Gamble St
1300 ESCN 1109 H7
N Gamble St
1200 ESCN 1109 J7
900 ESCN 1129 J1
Gambusa Pl
9100 SDGO 1189 D5
Gambusa Wy
12800 SDGO 1189 D5
Gamen St
9100 SDCo 1232 D6
Gamma Av
1600 NATC 1289 J6
Gamma St
3900 SDGO 1289 G6
Gammas Wy
- SDCo 1234 J4
Gandy Av
9800 SNTE 1231 B3
Ganesta Rd
11100 SDGO 1209 C2
Ganley Rd
9100 SNTE 1231 A2
Gannet Dr
200 VSTA 1087 G4
Gannet St
5600 SDGO 1290 C4
Gannon Pl
500 ESCN 1129 H3
Ganther Sq
9900 SDGO 1209 H5
Gantry Wy
15900 SDCo 1174 A4
Garber Av
6500 SDGO 1310 F2
Garboso Pl
7700 CRLB 1147 J1
Garboso St
3000 CRLB 1147 H1
Garde Ct
8600 SDGO 1209 C3
Garde St
10900 SDGO 1209 C3
Garde Wy
8600 SDGO 1209 C3
Garden Ct
500 ENCT 1147 D7
7500 SDGO 1188 J1
Garden Gate Ln
- SDCo 1169 G4
Garden Glen Ln
- ELCJ 1252 B7
Garden Grove Ln
100 ELCJ 1251 A5
Garden House Rd
2500 CRLB 1127 F3
Garden Knoll Wy
- SDCo 1232 A5
Garden Ln
24700 SDCo 1236 A2
3600 SDGO 1287 J3
Garden Park Ct
1900 SDGO 1290 F6
Garden Path Dr
17000 SDCo 1169 F2
Garden Pl
400 CHLV 1330 B1
Garden Rd
14200 POWY 1190 G4
- POWY 1191 A4
Garden Terr
7500 SDGO 1188 J1
Garden Tr
14300 SDGO 1188 J1
Garden Valley Gln
2000 ESCN 1109 G5
Garden View Ct
700 ENCT 1147 F5
Garden View Rd
1600 ENCT 1147 F5
- SDCo 1147 F4
Garden Walk Ct
10400 SDCo 1169 G2
Garden Walk Wy
17000 SDCo 1169 F2
Garden Wy
10600 SDCo 1271 F6

SAN DIEGO CO.

San Diego County Street Index

STREET	Block	City	Map#	Grid
Garden Wy				
	100	SNTE	1230	J7
Gardena Av				
	5000	SDGO	1268	F2
Gardena Ln				
	11800	SDCo	1231	J7
Gardena Pl				
	1800	SDGO	1268	F2
Gardena Rd				
	900	ENCT	1167	D1
	8500	SDCo	1231	J7
Gardena Wy				
	8800	SDCo	1231	J6
Gardendale Rd				
	200	ENCT	1147	E5
Gardenia Av				
	14000	POWY	1190	F3
Gardenia Ct				
	-	CRLB	1127	A6
	-	SNMS	1128	E2
Gardenia Glen				
	600	ESCN	1150	C3
Gardenia St				
	4700	OCSD	1067	A7
Gardenia Wy				
	2300	NATC	1290	A6
Gardenside Ct				
	100	SDCo	1027	H2
Gardiner Ln				
	6100	SDCo	1168	F7
Gardner Dr				
	0	RivC	999	F1
Gardner Rd				
	-	ImCo	6259	D7
	(See Page 6259)			
Gardner St				
	400	ELCJ	1251	E5
Gardner Wy				
	-	SNMS	1108	J6
Garey Dr				
	400	VSTA	1087	H3
Garfield Av				
	700	ELCJ	1251	B4
Garfield Ln				
	4700	LMSA	1271	A3
Garfield Rd				
	2000	SDGO	1268	F1
Garfield St				
	-	CALX	6620	J6
	2600	CRLB	1106	D5
	5000	LMSA	1271	A2
	400	OCSD	1106	B1
N Garfield St				
	300	OCSD	1086	B7
Garibaldi Ct				
	-	SDCo	1085	H5
Garibaldi Pl				
	3300	CRLB	1106	H4
Garjan Ln				
	-	SDCo	1171	H2
Garland Av				
	-	SNMS	1128	J3
Garland Dr				
	1000	SDGO	1350	C1
Garner Pl				
	3600	ENCT	1167	H3
Garnet Av				
	1500	SDGO	1247	H6
	2400	SDGO	1248	B5
Garnet Falls Dr				
	1500	CHLV	1331	F2
Garnet Ln				
	4400	OCSD	1107	D2
Garnet Mine Tr				
	-	SDCo	1173	F7
Garnet Peak Dr				
	2500	CHLV	1311	J5
Garnet St				
	-	CALX	6620	J7
	-	IMPE	6439	C6
Garrano Ln				
	35700	SDCo	1028	J5
Garretson St				
	-	SDGO	1169	D3
Garrett Av				
	100	CHLV	1310	B5
	1200	CHLV	1330	C3
Garrett Ln				
	1300	CHLV	1330	C4
Garrett St				
	600	BRAW	6319	J2
	(See Page 6319)			
Garrison Pl				
	1500	SDGO	1288	A1
Garrison St				
	200	OCSD	1086	F6
	3000	SDGO	1288	B1
Garrison Wy				
	1700	SDCo	1252	B6
Garston St				
	2100	SDGO	1248	J7
Garwood Ct				
	8400	SDCo	1290	J2
Garwood Rd				
	9600	SDCo	1235	H2
Gary Cir				
	2400	CRLB	1106	H5
Gary Ct				
	6400	SDGO	1270	D2
Gary Ln				
	1900	ESCN	1109	D5
Gary St				
	4900	SDGO	1270	D2
Garywood St				
	1700	SDCo	1251	G1
Gasconade Av				
	5000	SDGO	1268	F1
Gascony Rd				
	1500	ENCT	1147	C2
Gaskill Peak Rd				
	3800	SDCo	1275	A3
Gaslight Ct				
	14400	POWY	1190	F1
Gaston Dr				
	7700	SDGO	1209	A4
Gatchell Rd				
	-	SDGO	1287	J6
Gate Dr				
	13000	POWY	1190	F4
Gate Eight Pl				
	-	CHLV	1311	J4
Gate Eleven Pl				
	-	CHLV	1311	J3
Gate Fifteen Pl				
	2800	CHLV	1311	J3
Gate Five Pl				
	-	CHLV	1311	J4
Gate Four Pl				
	-	CHLV	1311	J4
Gate Fourteen Pl				
	2800	CHLV	1311	J3
Gate Nine Pl				
	-	CHLV	1311	J4
Gate One Pl				
	-	CHLV	1311	J4
Gate Rd				
	-	SDGO	1288	A5
Gate Seven Pl				
	-	CHLV	1311	J4
Gate Six Pl				
	-	CHLV	1311	J4
Gate Ten Pl				
	-	CHLV	1311	J3
Gate Thirteen Pl				
	-	CHLV	1311	J3
Gate Three Pl				
	-	CHLV	1311	J4
Gate Twelve Pl				
	-	CHLV	1311	J3
Gate Two Pl				
	-	CHLV	1311	J4
Gatemoore Wy				
	-	SDGO	1209	J2
Gatepost Rd				
	1800	ENCT	1147	H6
Gateshead Rd				
	4700	CRLB	1107	A5
Gateshead St				
	7500	SDGO	1249	A7
Gateside Rd				
	8500	LMSA	1270	J4
Gateview Dr				
	-	SDCo	1047	H6
Gateway Center Av				
	3600	SDGO	1289	G3
Gateway Center Dr				
	600	SDGO	1289	G3
Gateway Center Wy				
	900	SDGO	1289	F3
Gateway Dr				
	1800	SDGO	1289	G1
	1900	VSTA	1107	J4
Gateway Park Dr				
	6600	SDGO	1351	C2
Gateway Park Rd				
	12600	POWY	1170	C5
Gateway Rd				
	-	CRLB	1127	F2
Gateway Ridge Ct				
	-	SDGO	1208	A3
Gateway View Ct				
	8900	SDCo	1232	E6
Gateway View Dr				
	13700	SDCo	1232	E6
Gateway View Pl				
	8900	SDCo	1232	E6
Gatewood Ln				
	7300	SDGO	1290	G6
Gathell Rd				
	-	SDGO	1308	A2
Gatito Ct				
	11600	SDGO	1150	A7
Gatlan St				
	-	IMPB	1349	J2
Gatling Ct				
	2300	SDGO	1248	J7
	1200	VSTA	1087	E6
Gatty Ct				
	500	SDGO	1330	F6
Gatty St				
	3700	SDGO	1330	E6
Gatun St				
	2000	DLMR	1187	G3
Gaucho Ln				
	9000	SDCo	1232	F6
Gaucho Pl				
	1100	ESCN	1129	F5
Gaul Wy				
	10200	SDCo	1271	E5
Gavan Vista Rd				
	14900	POWY	1170	J5
Gavilan Mountain Rd				
	-	RivC	997	J3
	-	SDCo	997	H4
Gavin St				
	300	SDGO	1289	H4
Gaviota Cir				
	3000	CRLB	1147	H2
Gaviota Ct				
	4600	SDCo	1310	G1
Gaviota Pl				
	7800	CRLB	1147	H2
Gavioto Ct				
	4600	OCSD	1066	J7
Gay Lake Av				
	6400	SDGO	1250	G5
Gay Ln				
	-	ESCN	1129	F5
Gay Rio Ct				
	12100	SDCo	1232	A6
Gay Rio Dr				
	12000	SDCo	1231	J6
	12200	SDCo	1232	A7
Gay Rio Ln				
	11900	SDCo	1232	A6
Gay Rio Ter				
	12200	SDCo	1232	A6
Gay Rio Wy				
	-	SDCo	1232	A7
Gayla Ct				
	3000	SDCo	1271	F6
Gayland St				
	100	ESCN	1130	C1
Gayle St				
	3900	SDGO	1270	C5
Gayle Wy				
	2000	SDCo	1106	G4
Gaylemont Ln				
	-	SDGO	1208	D2
Gaylen Rd				
	7900	SDGO	1209	B3
Gaylord Ct				
	3500	SDGO	1228	D7
Gaylord Dr				
	5300	SDGO	1228	D7
	4900	SDGO	1248	D1
Gaylord Pl				
	5200	SDGO	1228	D7
Gayneswood Wy				
	7400	SDGO	1290	G6
Gayo Ct				
	1600	SDGO	1350	B3
Gayola Ln				
	10900	SDCo	1231	F3
Gayuba Ln				
	10100	SDGO	1249	G1
Gaywood St				
	1200	SDGO	1349	J1
Gazania Ct				
	1100	SNMS	1129	B2
Gazelle Ct				
	2800	CRLB	1107	G7
Gecko Rd				
	1600	SDCo	1108	A2
Geddes Dr				
	3200	SDGO	1248	C2
Gehring Ct				
	11800	SDGO	1209	A1
Geiger Ct				
	5900	CRLB	1127	D2
Geise Ct				
	2800	ESCN	1110	E6
Gelbourne Pl				
	13300	SDGO	1188	A4
Gelger Creek Rd				
	-	CHLV	1311	J6
Gem Ct				
	13300	POWY	1190	H4
Gem Hill Ln				
	11200	SDCo	1211	F6
Gem Lake Av				
	6400	SDGO	1250	G5
Gem Ln				
	2000	SDCo	1109	E4
	1300	SDCo	1172	G3
	100	SDCo	1173	A3
Gem Tree Wy				
	10000	SNTE	1231	D3
Gem View Dr				
	2300	OCSD	1087	C6
Gemini Av				
	9000	SDGO	1209	D3
Genai Rd				
	2900	SDCo	998	C3
General Atomics Ct				
	3500	SDGO	1208	A7
Genesee Av				
	10500	SDGO	1208	A7
	8700	SDGO	1228	C3
	4600	SDGO	1248	G2
	2400	SDGO	1249	A6
Genesee Cove				
	5200	SDGO	1228	E5
Genesee Ct E				
	5500	SDGO	1248	H3
Genesis St				
	-	SDCo	1212	D4
Genesta St				
	1900	SDGO	1290	A1
Genetic Center Dr				
	10300	SDGO	1208	G5
Geneva				
	-	SDCo	1232	F4
Geneva Av				
	5100	SDGO	1290	B2
Geneva Cir				
	1800	SNMS	1128	B2
Geneva Pl				
	2100	ESCN	1130	E2
Geneva St				
	2100	OCSD	1106	G1
Genevieve Av				
	-	CHLV	1311	E4
Genevieve St				
	1000	SOLB	1167	G7
Genie Ln				
	1000	ENCT	1167	E3
Genine Dr				
	3900	OCSD	1107	B1
Genista Pl				
	3100	SDCo	1048	C3
Genoa Dr				
	5600	SDGO	1250	C7
	1400	VSTA	1107	H3
Genoa Wy				
	-	OCSD	1106	J1
	800	SNMS	1128	E6
Genter St				
	700	SDGO	1247	E1
Gentian Wy				
	2000	SDCo	1234	A4
Gentle Breeze Ln				
	1700	ENCT	1147	F4
Gentle Knoll St				
	3400	CRLB	1107	B5
Gentry Wy				
	-	CHLV	1330	E3
Geode Ln				
	2300	CRLB	1127	F4
George				
	-	SDCo	1232	F4
George Av				
	900	CALX	6680	F1
George Ct				
	-	SDGO	1350	D1
George Wy				
	1100	ELCJ	1251	H6
Georgetown Av				
	5000	SDGO	1268	F2
Georgetown Pl				
	500	CHLV	1330	H4
Georgia Ct				
	1900	SDGO	1269	C6
Georgia Ln				
	1000	VSTA	1087	G5
Georgia St				
	900	IMPB	1329	H7
	1200	IMPB	1349	J1
	4300	SDGO	1269	C4
Georgina St				
	-	CHLV	1310	D7
Georgine Rd				
	600	SDCo	1047	E5
Georgios Wy				
	16700	SDCo	1173	G2
Gerald Ct				
	2600	SDGO	1270	A7
Gerald Wy				
	1100	SDCo	1027	H3
Geraldine Av				
	8900	SDGO	1249	C5
Geraldine Pl				
	9000	SDGO	1249	D5
Gerana St				
	10800	SDGO	1189	H2
Geranium St				
	1700	CRLB	1127	E7
	2300	SDGO	1248	B4
Gerlar Ln				
	1400	SDCo	1152	G7
Germaine Ln				
	5900	SDGO	1247	G2
Geronimo Av				
	3100	SDGO	1248	F6
Geronimo Pl				
	-	VSTA	1087	H4
Gershwin St				
	1500	ENCT	1167	D2
Gertrude St				
	1300	SDGO	1268	E2
Gesner Pl				
	4600	SDGO	1248	E6
Gesner St				
	4000	SDGO	1248	E6
Gettysburg Dr				
	16500	SDCo	1169	E4
Geyer Ln				
	2400	SDCo	1253	J2
Geyserville St				
	2000	CHLV	1311	E7
Gi Gi Ct				
	3300	SDCo	1048	D2
Gianelli Ln				
	2600	ESCN	1130	C7
Gibbons St				
	2400	ELCJ	1251	B2
Gibbs Dr				
	8500	SDGO	1249	C4
Gibraltar Ct				
	17400	SDGO	1170	C2
Gibraltar Dr				
	12600	SDGO	1170	C2
Gibraltar Glen				
	2100	ESCN	1129	E6
Gibraltar St				
	7500	CRLB	1147	H1
Gibson Highlands				
	1200	SDCo	1233	A7
Gibson Pt				
	200	SOLB	1167	E6
Gibson St				
	1500	SDGO	1290	E2
Giddings Ranch Rd				
	-	SDCo	1088	C7
N Gideon Cir				
	9100	SDCo	1232	D5
S Gideon Cir				
	9000	SDCo	1232	D6
Gideon Ct				
	13300	SDCo	1232	D6
Gienke Ln				
	10300	SNTE	1231	E6
Giffin Wy				
	10500	SDGO	1209	A4
Gifford Wy				
	6700	SDGO	1248	H7
Gigantic St				
	8000	SDGO	1351	F2
Gil Wy				
	1600	SDCo	1088	B7
Gila Av				
	4200	SDGO	1248	E3
Gila Ct				
	1600	CHLV	1331	G3
	3800	SDGO	1248	E3
Gilbert Dr				
	5400	SDGO	1270	B3
Gilbert Ln				
	100	NATC	1289	J6
Gilbert Pl				
	600	CHLV	1310	G6
Gilead Wy				
	100	SDCo	1027	H2
Giles Av				
	500	CALX	6680	G2
Giles Wy				
	11700	SDGO	1209	C1
Gilford Ct				
	1200	SDCo	1290	J2
Gill Lp				
	16600	SDGO	1169	D3
Gill Village Wy				
	-	SDGO	1269	C2
Gillespie Ct				
	-	ELCJ	1251	C1
Gillespie Dr				
	900	SDCo	1291	A3
Gillespie Wy				
	1300	ELCJ	1251	D2
Gillett Rd				
	200	ELCN	6500	D6
	-	ImCo	6500	E6
E Gillett Rd				
	900	ELCN	6500	C6
Gillette St				
	3500	SDGO	1289	F4
Gillingham Ct				
	-	SDCo	1085	J4
Gilman Dr				
	-	SDGO	1228	B2
Gilmartin Dr				
	1700	SDGO	1290	E6
Gilmore Pl				
	1300	ESCN	1110	A5
Gilmore St				
	3600	SDGO	1289	G4
Gilmour St				
	600	BRAW	6319	J2
	(See Page 6319)			
N Gina Av				
	100	ELCJ	1252	A5
S Gina Av				
	100	ELCJ	1252	A5
Gina Ln				
	800	SNMS	1109	B5
Gina Wy				
	200	VSTA	1087	G5
Ginger Av				
	800	CRLB	1127	A5
Ginger Dr				
	2100	CHLV	1331	H3
Ginger Glen				
	-	SNMS	1128	E2
Ginger Glen Rd				
	13400	SDGO	1188	E4
Ginger Glen Tr				
	5700	SDGO	1188	F4
Ginger Snap Ct				
	12500	SDGO	1189	B6
Ginger Snap Ln				
	8700	SDGO	1189	C6
Ginger Wy				
	3700	OCSD	1086	H5
	2600	SDCo	1129	D2
Gingertree Ln				
	-	CORD	1329	D1
Gingerwood Cove				
	-	SDGO	1208	E2
Ginna Pl				
	800	SDGO	1290	B5
Ginny Ln				
	2000	SDCo	1130	B5
Ginsberg Ct				
	1600	SDGO	1290	D6
Ginstar Ct				
	-	SDGO	1190	B7
Ginty Wy				
	-	SDCo	1091	F4
Girard Av				
	8000	SDGO	1227	F6
	7200	SDGO	1247	F1
Girard Ct				
	-	CHLV	1311	H4
	1200	VSTA	1088	A6
Girard Wy				
	300	VSTA	1088	A6
Gird Rd				
	-	SDCo	1028	C5
	3800	SDCo	1048	D3
Gitano St				
	1600	ENCT	1147	G7
Givens St				
	-	CHLV	1330	J2
	800	SDGO	1330	F7
Giverny Wy				
	1900	CHLV	1311	E7
Glacier Av				
	4900	SDGO	1249	J7
Glacier Rd				
	1500	OCSD	1087	E1
Glade Pl				
	1600	ESCN	1129	G7
Glade St				
	3500	SDGO	1270	D5
Gladeholow Ct				
	-	SDGO	1190	B7
Glading Dr				
	3900	SDGO	1330	F7
Gladiola Dr				
	-	NATC	1289	H7
	2500	SDCo	1297	E4
	(See Page 1297)			
Gladiola Ln				
	100	SDCo	1253	C1
Gladstone Ct				
	4400	CRLB	1106	J5
	-	SDCo	1089	D3
Gladys St				
	900	ELCJ	1251	G2
Glae Jean Ct				
	1100	SDCo	1172	F1
Glancy Dr				
	3100	SDGO	1350	F4
Glaser Dr				
	3400	OCSD	1106	J1
Glasgow Av				
	2100	ENCT	1167	E3
Glasgow Ct				
	600	SNMS	1108	G6
Glasgow Dr				
	2900	CRLB	1107	A4
	4900	SDGO	1228	D7
Glasgow Ln				
	1500	ESCN	1110	C4
Glasoe Ln				
	4800	SDGO	1269	B3
Glass Ct				
	1900	SDGO	1350	A1
E Glaucus St				
	300	ENCT	1147	B3
W Glaucus St				
	100	ENCT	1147	A4
Gleason Rd				
	-	SDGO	1267	J2
Glebe Rd				
	2400	LMGR	1270	F7
Glen Abbey Blvd				
	3200	SDCo	1310	E5
Glen Abbey Dr				
	-	SDCo	1310	F4
Glen Arbor Dr				
	700	ENCT	1147	H5
Glen Arven Ln				
	17000	POWY	1170	F1
Glen Aspen Ct				
	10400	SDCo	1169	F2
Glen Aspen Dr				
	17100	SDCo	1169	F2
Glen Av				
	3700	CRLB	1107	B6
Glen Avon Dr				
	1400	SNMS	1109	C7
Glen Canyon Cir				
	2800	SDCo	1271	D7
Glen Circle Rd				
	12900	POWY	1170	D5
Glen Creek Dr				
	300	CHLV	1311	B3
Glen Dr				
	3400	SDCo	1271	D6
Glen Drew Rd				
	-	ESCN	1110	B5
Glen Ellen Pike				
	-	SNMS	1128	E7
Glen Ellen St				
	-	CHLV	1311	B7
Glen H Curtiss Rd				
	3700	SDGO	1249	C4
Glen Heather Dr				
	500	SNMS	1109	B6
Glen Hollow Ct				
	1600	ENCT	1147	G5
Glen Ln				
	13600	SDCo	1050	D7
Glen Lonely Rd				
	-	SDCo	1254	D7
Glen Meadow Ln				
	-	ESCN	1110	D6
N Glen Oaks Dr				
	700	SDCo	1233	G6
S Glen Oaks Dr				
	600	SDCo	1233	F6
Glen Oaks Pl				
	600	SDCo	1233	G6
Glen Oaks Wy				
	8700	SNTE	1231	A7
Glen Rd				
	900	SDGO	1290	B3
Glen Ridge Rd				
	1900	ESCN	1130	D2
Glen Rosedale Dr				
	-	SDCo	1310	F4
Glen St				
	5000	LMSA	1271	A2
	2300	SDCo	996	J2
Glen Tree Rd				
	15400	SDCo	1090	J2
Glen Verde Ct				
	3700	SDCo	1310	J2
Glen Verde Dr				
	5000	SDCo	1310	J2
Glen View Pl				
	5000	SDCo	1310	J2
Glen Vista Ct				
	8300	SDGO	1290	H5
Glen Vista St				
	200	SDGO	1290	H4
Glen Vista Wy				
	8700	SNTE	1231	A7
Glenair Wy				
	-	SDCo	1071	C1
Glenbrook St				
	2900	CRLB	1107	A3
Glenbrook Wy				
	2800	SDGO	1227	J3
Glencliff Wy				
	13500	SDGO	1188	C4
Glencoe Dr				
	1400	LMGR	1290	G2
	700	SDGO	1290	H3
Glencolum Dr				
	3300	SDGO	1249	D5
Glencreek Cir				
	10900	SDGO	1210	A3
Glencrest Dr				
	500	SDGO	1290	G6
	-	SNMS	1128	D5
	300	SOLB	1167	F6
Glencrest Pl				
	600	SOLB	1167	F6
Glenda Ct				
	10900	SDGO	1209	B3
Glenda Wy				
	8000	SDGO	1209	B3
Glendale Av				
	800	SDGO	1289	D3
	300	SNMS	1108	G6
Glendening Ct				
	-	BRAW	6319	F4
	(See Page 6319)			
E Glendon Cir				
	10000	SNTE	1231	E3
W Glendon Cir				
	10100	SNTE	1231	E3
Glendora Dr				
	1500	CHLV	1331	D1
	-	OCSD	1067	A4
Glendora St				
	3000	SDGO	1248	D5
Glendover Ln				
	10700	SDGO	1208	H4
Gleneagles Pl				
	1000	VSTA	1108	A4
Gleneco Ln				
	1500	SDCo	1156	C5
Glenellen Av				
	10400	SDGO	1209	D4
Glenellen Ln				
	10300	SDGO	1209	D5
Glenfield St				
	3000	SDGO	1269	H6
Glenflora Av				
	7200	SDGO	1250	F5
Glengarry Ln				
	-	SDCo	1089	D4
Glengate Pl				
	13600	POWY	1190	F5
Glenhart Pl				
	700	SDCo	1027	G6
Glenhaven Dr				
	4800	OCSD	1087	E3
Glenhaven St				
	8500	SDGO	1249	C4
Glenhaven Wy				
	100	CHLV	1330	D3
Glenhill Rd				
	1000	ELCJ	1251	H7
Glenhollow Cir				
	4800	OCSD	1087	B3
Glenhope Rd				
	11800	SDGO	1190	A5
Glenhurst Wy				
	-	SDGO	1189	J2
Glenira Av				
	8700	LMSA	1271	A2
Glenira Wy				
	-	LMSA	1271	A3
Glenlea Ln				
	5900	SDGO	1250	E6
Glenmeade Wy				
	-	SDCo	1089	E3
Glenmere Rd				
	1000	VSTA	1087	J5
Glenmont Dr				
	600	SOLB	1167	F6
Glenmont St				
	6300	SDGO	1270	C1
Glenn Crawford St				
	1700	SDCo	1027	J2
Glenn Ellen Ct				
	23800	SDCo	1173	D2
Glenn Ellen Wy				
	23300	SDCo	1173	C4
Glenn Rd				
	3100	OCSD	1107	B1
	2300	SDCo	996	J2
Glenna Dr				
	1500	SDCo	1130	B4
Glennaire Dr				
	1900	ESCN	1130	C5
Glennchester Row				
	6100	SDGO	1247	J1
Glennon St				
	10000	SDGO	1249	G2
Glenoak Rd				
	12400	POWY	1190	C2
Glenridge Apartments Drwy				
	-	CRLB	1107	B6
Glenroy St				
	7100	SDGO	1250	B5
Glenside Pl				
	10000	SDCo	1271	D7
Glenside Rd				
	4700	SDCo	1135	D4
Glenside St				
	9900	SDCo	1271	D6
Glenstone Wy				
	-	SDGO	1208	E4
Glenview Dr				
	4500	OCSD	1066	H7
Glenview Ln				
	2200	SDCo	1087	F1
	500	SDGO	1247	E1
Glenview Wy				
	2800	SDCo	1130	D7
Glenville St				
	14500	POWY	1190	H5
Glenway Dr				
	1000	ELCJ	1251	H7
Glenwick Ln				
	8600	SDGO	1227	J4
Glenwick Pl				
	2700	SDGO	1227	J4
Glenwood Dr				
	-	ELCN	6559	D1
	800	OCSD	1087	C1
	1500	SDGO	1268	H6
Glenwood Rd				
	1800	ELCN	6499	D6
Glenwood Springs Av				
	1500	CHLV	1331	E1
Glenwood Wy				
	800	ESCN	1109	H3
Glidden Ct				
	1700	SDGO	1268	H2
Glidden Ln				
	6500	SDGO	1268	H1
Glidden St				
	6300	SDGO	1268	H2
Gloaming Av				
	7400	SDGO	1290	G3
Gloria Lake Av				
	7700	SDGO	1250	G6
Gloria Ln				
	3900	CRLB	1106	G6
Gloria Rd				
	-	SDCo	1252	G4
Gloria St				
	300	SDGO	1290	A5
Glorietta Blvd				
	1000	CORD	1288	J7
	700	CORD	1289	A7
	1600	CORD	1308	J1
Glorietta Pl				
	300	CORD	1288	J6
Glover Av				
	100	CHLV	1310	B5
	700	CHLV	1330	B1
N Glover Av				
	-	CHLV	1310	A4
Glover Ct				
	-	CHLV	1310	A5
Glover Pl				
	600	CHLV	1310	B7
Gloxina St				
	200	ENCT	1147	E6
Goat Hill Dr				
	2300	OCSD	1086	C7
Gobat Av				
	2500	SDGO	1228	B6
Goddard St				
	1100	SNMS	1128	D6
Goddard Wy				
	3100	SDGO	1288	G1
Godfrey St				
	700	OCSD	1106	B2
Gods Wy				
	-	SDCo	1294	F7
	(See Page 1294)			
Godsall Ln				
	3600	SDGO	1269	A6
Godwit Dr				
	4400	OCSD	1087	A3
Goen Pl				
	7400	SDGO	1250	A4
Goesno Pl				
	3200	NATC	1309	G4
Goetschl St				
	600	SDGO	1290	D5
Goetting Wy				
	200	VSTA	1087	G6
Goetze St				
	2500	SDGO	1310	E1
Goff Ct				
	1400	SDGO	1290	F5
Going My Wy				
	16800	SDCo	1169	A2
Gold Bar Wy				
	11200	SDCo	1211	J7
	11000	SDCo	1212	A7
Gold Canyon Ln				
	12200	SDCo	1271	J2
Gold Coast Ct				
	10300	SDGO	1209	D5
Gold Coast Dr				
	9400	SDGO	1209	E5
Gold Dr				
	5000	OCSD	1067	B5
	-	VSTA	1087	F7
Gold Dust				
	6000	SDCo	1175	J2
	(See Page 1175)			
Gold Dust Ln				
	1400	SDCo	1136	D7
Gold Flower Rd				
	-	SDCo	1127	A5
Gold Lake Rd				
	-	LMGR	1270	E7
Gold Nugget Lp				
	-	SDCo	1232	F5
Gold Oak Ct				
	800	CHLV	1310	J7
Gold Palomino Wy				
	200	SDCo	1028	H6
Gold Pan Allley				
	11100	SDCo	1211	J7
Gold Run Dr				
	-	CHLV	1311	D7
Gold Run Rd				
	-	CHLV	1331	D1
Gold Rush Cir				
	600	CHLV	1311	C4
Golda Odessa Ln				
	15000	SDCo	1212	H6
Goldboro St				
	1800	SDGO	1268	F2
Goldcoast Pl				
	10300	SDGO	1209	D5
Goldcoast Wy				
	10300	SDGO	1209	D5
Goldcrest Ln				
	7600	SDGO	1290	G5
Golden Acorn Wy				
	1800	SDCo	1299	E2
	(See Page 1299)			
Golden Av				
	8000	LMGR	1270	H6
Golden Birch Wy				
	-	SDGO	1209	G2
Golden Brush Dr				
	-	CRLB	1127	B4
Golden Cir				
	11700	SDCo	1231	J7
Golden Circle Dr				
	1900	ESCN	1109	C5
Golden Crest Dr				
	1400	SDCo	1129	G6
Golden Cypress Pl				
	13500	SDGO	1188	G3
Golden Dr				
	600	SDCo	1027	G3
Golden Eagle Rd				
	12200	SDCo	1212	C4
Golden Eagle Trl				
	2000	SNMS	1128	G6
Golden Elm Ln				
	13500	SDGO	1189	B3
Golden Eye Ln				
	12500	POWY	1190	B6
Golden Gate Av				
	1500	CHLV	1331	E1
Golden Gate Dr				
	1500	SDGO	1269	B3
Golden Glen Ln				
	6700	SDGO	1208	H3
Golden Grove Pl				
	2800	LMGR	1270	J7
Golden Harvest Ln				
	1300	SDCo	1252	F7
Golden Haven Dr				
	-	SDGO	1228	D3
Golden Hill Dr				
	2500	SDGO	1289	D2

31 INDEX
Golden Hill Dr

San Diego County Street Index

Groton Wy
INDEX 31
SAN DIEGO CO.

STREET
Block City Map# Grid

Golden Hill Dr
1900 VSTA 1087 H2
Golden Larch Pl
- SDGO 1188 G3
Golden Lily Wy
- SDGO 1188 F3
Golden Ln
700 SDCo 1027 G3
Golden Meadow Ln
- SDCo 1047 H5
Golden Oak Pl
2200 ESCN 1130 H2
Golden Oak Wy
3000 SDCo 1271 G6
Golden Park Av
700 SDGO 1288 A3
Golden Park Pl
900 SDGO 1288 A3
Golden Rd
- CHLV 1310 C6
1000 ENCT 1167 D1
400 SDCo 1027 G3
Golden Ridge Dr
4500 OCSD 1087 D4
Golden Ridge Rd
8700 SDCo 1231 H7
Golden Sands Pl
- SDGO 1330 H7
Golden Sky Wy
4600 SDGO 1330 H6
Golden Star Ct
4100 SDCo 1271 F4
Golden Star Ln
- SDCo 1127 C7
Golden Sunset Ct
14500 POWY 1170 H7
14500 POWY 1190 H1
Golden Sunset Dr
- SNMS 1128 D6
Golden Sunset Ln
14200 POWY 1170 G7
Golden Trails Wy
5600 OCSD 1067 F7
Golden Trl
1000 VSTA 1107 H2
Golden View Terr
3400 LMGR 1270 H6
Golden Wagon Ct
17200 SDCo 1169 F1
Golden West Ln
9900 SNTE 1231 D3
Golden Wy
12900 POWY 1190 G4
Goldenaire Wy
17000 SDCo 1169 B1
Goldeneye Vw
- CRLB 1126 J4
- CRLB 1127 A4
Goldenleaf Pl
27700 SDCo 1089 F4
Goldenrod Ln
1800 VSTA 1108 A3
Goldenrod St
1000 ESCN 1110 B6
Goldenrod Wy
7000 CRLB 1127 E6
Goldentop Dr
- SDCo 1232 C4
Goldentop Rd
16900 SDCo 1169 F3
Golder Ln
2700 SDCo 1135 J6
Goldfield St
1800 SDGO 1268 E1
Goldfield Wy
- ImCo 6560 C7
Goldfinch Pl
- CRLB 1127 C6
700 SDGO 1268 J6
Goldfinch St
4300 SDGO 1268 J4
Goldfinch Wy
4400 OCSD 1086 J1
- SNMS 1128 E3
Goldfish Ct
12300 SDGO 1189 A6
Goldfish Wy
7700 SDGO 1189 A6
Goldonna Ln
12900 SDGO 1188 B5
Goldrush Wy
1500 OCSD 1067 E6
Goldsmith St
3300 SDGO 1268 D6
Goldspring Ln
8100 SDCo 1169 B2
Goldstone Rd
6900 CRLB 1127 F6
Goldstone St
1600 ELCJ 1252 B7
Goleta
900 OCSD 1066 H6
Goleta Rd
7900 SDGO 1209 B3
Golf Club Dr
31400 SDCo 1068 A2
Golf Course Dr
1600 SDGO 1289 D2
Golf Course Rd
- SDCo 1066 G3

Golf Crest Dr
4700 SDCo 1099 G4
(See Page 1099)
Golf Crest Ridge Rd
3000 SDCo 1272 C6
Golf Dr
8700 SDCo 1271 A5
Golf Glen Dr
500 SNMS 1108 J5
Golf Glen Rd
4900 SDCo 1310 J2
Golf Green Dr
31800 SDCo 1051 C7
Golfcrest Ct
2100 OCSD 1106 H1
Golfcrest Dr
3300 OCSD 1106 H1
7500 SDGO 1250 E3
Golfcrest Loop
2400 CHLV 1311 G4
Golfcrest Pl
7300 SDGO 1250 F5
1500 VSTA 1107 H4
Golfers Dr
3300 OCSD 1106 J2
Golfview Dr
2800 SDCo 1048 E1
Golondrina Ct
- SDCo 1086 A4
Golondrina Dr
9300 LMSA 1271 B3
Golsh Rd
54700 SDCo 1071 D2
Gomez Creek Rd
- SDCo 1029 C1
Gomez Trl
- SDCo 1030 H6
- SDCo 1031 C5
Gonder Rd
- ImCo 6320 J4
(See Page 6320)
Gonsalves Av
- SDGO 1209 E7
- SDGO 1229 E1
Gonzales St
800 SOLB 1187 G1
Gonzales Wy
1200 CHLV 1311 B6
Gonzalez Ct
700 CALX 6620 G7
Good Karma Ln
5700 SDCo 1311 A2
Goodbody St
3700 SDGO 1330 E7
Goode St
7600 SDGO 1290 H6
Gooding Dr
1500 ELCJ 1251 H2
Goodland Dr
- OCSD 1085 J6
Goodman Ln
7300 LMGR 1270 F6
Goodstone Ct
7200 SDGO 1248 J7
Goodstone St
2400 SDGO 1249 A7
Goodwick Ct
9400 SDGO 1249 F7
Goodwin Dr
2000 VSTA 1087 H2
Goodwin St
6400 SDGO 1268 H1
Goodyear St
1100 SDGO 1289 G6
Goose Valley Ln
1300 SDCo 1153 A2
Gooseberry Wy
- OCSD 1067 D6
Gopher Canyon Ct
2600 SDCo 1068 A7
Gopher Canyon Rd
2300 SDCo 1068 C6
Gordon Ct
100 ESCN 1129 G4
6900 LMSA 1270 E4
Gordon Hill Rd
28500 SDCo 1069 D6
Gordon Wy
4300 LMSA 1270 E4
Gorge Av
9200 SNTE 1231 B6
Gorge Ct
8900 SNTE 1231 B6
Gorge Pl
- CRLB 1107 C3
8900 SNTE 1231 B6
Gorge Run Wy
1200 CHLV 1311 E6
Gorge View Ter
7400 SDGO 1250 C5
Gorion Ct
13800 SDCo 1232 F6
Gorsline Dr
1000 ELCJ 1252 A3
Goshawk St
2000 SDGO 1269 A1
Goshen St
1000 SDGO 1268 G3
Gosnell Wy
100 SNMS 1108 H7

Gotham St
1600 CHLV 1311 C5
Gotta Pl
9100 SDCo 1232 D6
Goulburn Ct
400 ELCJ 1251 C4
Gould Av
- CHLV 1330 H2
Gould Ln
- SDGO 1330 C7
Governor Dr
3600 SDGO 1228 D5
Gowan St
- CORD 1288 G5
Gowdy Av
8800 SDGO 1249 C6
Gower Tktr
- SDCo 1154 B5
Gower Truck Trl
- SDCo 1173 J6
- SDCo 1174 A5
Gowin St
1300 SDCo 1291 A2
Goya Pl
- SNMS 1128 A3
Goyette Pl
9300 SNTE 1230 J6
Gozo Pl
7300 CRLB 1147 J1
Grable St
7100 LMSA 1270 F1
Grace Ct
3800 SDCo 1047 J3
6400 SDGO 1248 J3
Grace Lamay Terr
2200 SDCo 1272 D1
Grace Ln
2200 SDCo 1253 J1
Grace Ranch Rd
1700 SDCo 1314 D6
(See Page 1314)
Grace Rd
4300 SDCo 1310 G2
Grace St
100 OCSD 1086 C7
Grace Wy
1200 SDCo 1109 E7
Graceland Wy
9600 SDGO 1189 E5
Gracewood Pl
- SDGO 1208 E2
Gracey Ln
2100 SDCo 1028 B7
Gracia Ln
- ENCT 1147 F5
Gracia Paseo
3500 SDCo 1271 B5
Gracilior Ct
- SDCo 1069 A6
Gracilior Dr
- SDCo 1069 A6
Gracilior Pl
- SDCo 1069 A6
Graciosa Ct
17200 SDGO 1170 A2
Graciosa Dr
17400 SDGO 1170 A1
Graciosa Rd
17300 SDGO 1170 A1
Grade Pl
2700 SDCo 1271 E7
Grade Rd
32500 SDCo 1052 D5
(See Page 1052)
Grado Cipreso
- CRLB 1147 G2
Grado El Tupelo
- CRLB 1147 F3
Grado Marbella
7000 CRLB 1127 G6
Grady Pl
1500 CRLB 1106 G6
Grafton Rd
200 ImCo 6560 D2
Grafton St
2400 ELCJ 1251 B3
Graham Av
4500 SDGO 1209 D7
Graham Pl
1300 ESCN 1109 J5
Graham St
1300 SDGO 1248 A7
Graham Ter
8500 SNTE 1230 J7
Grain Ln
13400 SDGO 1189 E4
Grain Mill Rd
1800 SNMS 1128 F6
Grainwood Wy
12400 SDGO 1210 B4
Gramercy Dr
9000 SDGO 1249 D6
Grammer Rd
3800 SDCo 1068 G6
Granada Av
3800 SDGO 1269 E6
1400 SDGO 1289 E2
N Granada Av
3900 SDCo 1271 D5
S Granada Av
3600 SDCo 1271 D5

Granada Cir
2500 SDCo 1271 C7
Granada Dr
900 OCSD 1087 E5
- POWY 1190 E5
400 SDCo 1058 G7
(See Page 1058)
700 VSTA 1087 E6
Granada Ln
- SDCo 997 H3
Granada St
- SNTE 1231 E6
Granada Wy
- CHLV 1311 A7
2400 CRLB 1106 H4
1200 SNMS 1128 E2
Granados Av N
400 SOLB 1167 F6
Granados Av S
100 SOLB 1167 F7
400 SOLB 1187 F1
Granby Wy
10600 SDGO 1208 H4
2200 SNMS 1128 B5
Grand Av
100 CRLB 1106 D5
1700 DLMR 1187 F4
1100 ImCo 6560 B7
1200 SDCo 1291 B2
1500 SDGO 1247 H6
2200 SDGO 1248 B5
3300 SNMS 1108 C6
600 SNMS 1128 G1
3000 VSTA 1108 B6
E Grand Av
200 ESCN 1129 J2
1400 ESCN 1130 B2
W Grand Av
900 ESCN 1129 G3
Grand Caribe Cswy
- CORD 1329 E2
Grand Ct
900 ESCN 1129 H4
Grand Del Mar Ct
5100 SDGO 1188 E7
Grand Del Mar Pl
5200 SDGO 1188 E7
Grand Del Mar Wy
5000 SDGO 1188 D7
Grand Forks Rd
2300 CHLV 1311 H7
Grand Pacific Dr
5400 CRLB 1126 J2
Grand Teton Ct
1500 CHLV 1330 F4
Grand Teton Wy
10600 SNTE 1231 E4
Grand Tradition Wy
200 SDCo 1027 F5
Grand View Glen
2000 ESCN 1109 C3
Grand Vista Ln
- SDCo 1028 D2
Grande Vista
- SNMS 1129 C2
Grandee Ct
12300 SDGO 1170 B2
Grandee Pl
17300 SDGO 1170 C1
Grandee Rd
12300 SDGO 1170 B2
Grandee Wy
17000 SDGO 1170 B2
Grandfathers Ln
- SDCo 1071 A7
Grandfork Dr
10800 SNTE 1231 F4
Grandon Av
3800 SNMS 1128 C1
Grandridge Rd
5200 SDCo 1271 G1
Grandvia Pt
13300 SDGO 1187 J5
Grandview
2900 SDCo 1129 B6
Grandview Ct
700 ESCN 1109 F5
Grandview Dr
9400 SDCo 1271 C3
Grandview Heights Rd
30100 SDCo 1069 J5
Grandview Pl
3800 SDCo 1310 D4
Grandview Rd
1700 SDCo 1088 C3
1400 VSTA 1088 C4
Grandview St
100 ENCT 1147 A3
2000 OCSD 1106 D1
2700 SDGO 1248 F6
Grandview Ter
4600 SDCo 1271 D3
Grandview Wy
5700 SDCo 1176 A1
(See Page 1176)
Granero Dr
- CALX 6620 G6
Granero Pl
1800 ESCN 1129 E7
Grange Hall Rd
900 ENCT 1167 E1

Grange Pl
12400 POWY 1210 C1
Grange St
2600 LMGR 1270 G7
Granger Av
1400 ESCN 1110 A6
2000 NATC 1310 C1
2900 SDCo 1310 C2
Granger St
4500 SDGO 1287 J1
900 SDGO 1329 J7
1000 SDGO 1349 J1
Granite Creek Rd
13300 SDGO 1189 H4
Granite Crest Ct
6200 SDGO 1188 G7
6200 SDGO 1208 G1
Granite Ct
3500 CRLB 1107 B3
Granite Cv
- ELCJ 1252 A4
Granite Dr
16600 SDCo 1171 D3
Granite Hills Cir
700 ELCJ 1252 A6
Granite Hills Ct
1400 ELCJ 1252 A6
Granite Hills Dr
1300 ELCJ 1251 J6
2000 ELCJ 1252 C4
1700 SDCo 1252 B5
Granite House Ln
- SNTE 1231 B7
Granite Mtn View Rd
900 SDCo 1138 A5
(See Page 1138)
Granite Oaks Rd
17900 SDCo 1294 C2
(See Page 1294)
Granite Pl
1000 OCSD 1067 A4
Granite Rd
1200 SNMS 1108 E6
Granite Ridge Dr
9600 SDGO 1249 F4
Granite Ridge Rd
- SDCo 1089 G4
Granite Rock Rd
1700 SDCo 998 H7
Granite Springs Dr
1200 CHLV 1311 H6
Granite St
- IMPE 6439 C6
- SNMS 1129 C2
Granite View Ln
500 SDCo 1290 J5
Granite Vista Wy
24300 SDCo 1235 J7
Granjas Rd
1000 CHLV 1330 B3
Grant Av
600 ELCJ 1251 E6
8400 LMSA 1270 J2
Grant St
900 CALX 6680 D1
400 OCSD 1106 B1
5300 SDGO 1268 F3
N Grant St
300 OCSD 1086 B7
Grantwood Ln
- SDCo 1251 H1
Granville Dr
13900 POWY 1190 F4
Grape Fern Ct
- SDGO 1209 J1
Grape Ln
9700 SDCo 1149 E2
Grape St
500 ELCJ 1252 A4
1200 ESCN 1109 J7
1100 ESCN 1129 J1
7800 LMSA 1270 H3
400 OCSD 1086 G2
200 SDGO 1289 A1
5400 SDGO 1290 A1
1000 SNMS 1109 C7
N Grape St
600 ESCN 1129 J1
S Grape St
200 ESCN 1130 A2
W Grape St
1000 SDGO 1288 J2
Grapefruit Ct
- SDGO 1350 E2
Grapefruit Dr
- BRAW 6319 J3
(See Page 6319)
400 SDCo 1153 B7
Grapeharbor Ct
17100 POWY 1170 D2
Grapeharbor Wy
13100 POWY 1170 E2
Grapevine Canyon Rd
- SDCo 1118 G5
(See Page 1118)
Grapevine Ct
500 VSTA 1087 D7
Grapevine Ln
1500 VSTA 1087 D7
Grapevine Rd
700 VSTA 1087 D6
100 VSTA 1107 D1

Grass Valley Ln
8700 SNTE 1230 J3
Grass Valley Rd
- CHLV 1311 F5
Grasshopper Ln
1600 CHLV 1331 G3
Grassy Meadow Rd
15400 SDCo 1050 H3
Grassy Trail Dr
11200 SDGO 1169 J5
Grassy Wy
- SDCo 1089 F3
Graves Av
600 ELCJ 1251 F4
1200 SDCo 1251 F2
8600 SNTE 1231 F7
8000 SNTE 1251 F1
Graves Ct
300 SDCo 1251 F1
Graves Ln
1300 SDCo 1251 F2
Gravilla Pl
500 SDGO 1247 F2
Gravilla St
200 SDGO 1247 E2
Gravity Wy
1400 SDGO 1290 C2
Gray Dr
900 ELCJ 1251 H7
Gray Mare Ct
- SDCo 1254 G3
Gray Mare Wy
- SDCo 1254 G3
Gray Rabbit Hollow Ln
1900 SDCo 1028 A6
Graybar Ct
3300 OCSD 1086 J7
Graydon Rd
4100 SDGO 1188 B5
Grayfish Ln
- OCSD 1086 G2
Grayfox Dr
10200 SDGO 1209 H4
Grayson Ct
- CHLV 1331 D1
Grayson Dr
4000 SDGO 1188 A4
Graystone Pl
2500 SDCo 1271 B7
Great Blue Heron Wy
2500 SDCo 1299 B2
(See Page 1299)
Great Eagle Wy
2200 SDCo 1299 B3
(See Page 1299)
Great Meadow Dr
5200 SDGO 1208 D2
Great Oak Ln
- SDCo 1254 G7
Great Plains Rd
14000 POWY 1170 G4
Great Rock Rd
10300 SNTE 1231 D3
Great Sandy Trl
700 SDCo 1138 B7
(See Page 1138)
Great Sthrn Ovrlnd S
6800 SDCo 1138 A4
(See Page 1138)
8700 SDCo 1158 E7
(See Page 1158)
Grebe Dr
- SDCo 1127 B7
Grecourt Wy
3700 CRLB 1106 F6
Gredos Pl
700 CHLV 1310 J6
Greely Av
3000 SDGO 1289 E5
Green Acres Rd
1500 SDCo 1027 J6
Green Apple Wy
- SDGO 1350 F3
Green Av
100 ESCN 1130 A5
Green Bay St
1200 SDGO 1350 A1
Green Briar Cir
1800 SDCo 1028 A5
Green Briar Dr
2100 SDCo 1028 A5
Green Briar Ln
1600 SDCo 1028 B5
Green Canyon Ln
1500 SDCo 1028 A5
Green Canyon Rd
1400 SDCo 1028 A4
2500 SDCo 1047 J1
Green Farm Rd
- SDGO 1229 H3
Green Gables Av
6600 SDGO 1250 F5
Green Gables Ct
6500 SDGO 1250 F5
Green Garden Dr
1200 SDCo 1251 J1
Green Glen Rd
23400 SDCo 1173 D2
Green Grove Av
1600 ELCJ 1252 B2

Green Haven Ct
15800 SDCo 1173 E4
Green Haven Ln
23800 SDCo 1173 D4
Green Heather Ln
3000 SDCo 1048 A1
Green Hill Ct
800 SNMS 1108 J5
Green Hills Dr
2800 SDCo 1048 A1
Green Hills Pl
2100 SDCo 1048 A1
Green Hills Rd
6200 OCSD 1067 E3
Green Hills Wy
2300 SDCo 1088 B1
Green Lake Ct
- LMGR 1270 E7
Green Links Dr
1200 SDCo 1079 C3
(See Page 1079)
Green Ln
11500 SDCo 1231 J7
Green Meadow Dr
2400 SDCo 1108 C4
Green Mountain Ln
- SDCo 1130 E7
Green Mountain Rd
- SDCo 1130 E7
Green Oak Rd
1400 VSTA 1107 J6
1300 VSTA 1108 A5
Green Oaks Dr
11000 SDCo 1211 F7
Green Orchard Pl
1200 ENCT 1147 G4
Green River Dr
2200 CHLV 1311 G6
Green St
4600 SDGO 1268 A5
800 SDGO 1330 A7
Green Terrace Rd
13400 POWY 1170 E4
Green Top Ln
12200 SDCo 1271 J2
Green Tree Ln
- VSTA 1108 A2
Green Tree Rd
- ESCN 1129 E5
Green Turtle Rd
- CORD 1329 E1
Green Valley Ct
14100 SDGO 1210 F1
Green Valley Fire Rd
- SDCo 1216 D3
(See Page 1216)
Green Valley Heights Rd
- SDCo 1151 B6
Green Valley Rd
2500 CHLV 1311 H6
2300 SDCo 996 J3
Green Valley Truck Trl
14200 POWY 1170 G3
15900 SDCo 1151 B7
15600 SDCo 1171 A1
Green View Ln
200 SDCo 1028 A2
Green View Pl
2600 SDCo 1300 B4
(See Page 1300)
Green Vista Ln
1900 SDCo 1028 A7
Greenacres Dr
1800 SDCo 1254 A1
Greenbelt Rd
- SDCo 1171 H1
Greenberg Ln
8800 SDGO 1189 C3
Greenberg Wy
8800 SDGO 1189 C3
Greenbriar Dr
2300 CHLV 1311 G5
Greenbrier Av
5200 SDGO 1250 B6
Greenbrier Ct
6700 SDGO 1250 A6
Greenbrier Dr
2000 OCSD 1086 C7
Greenbrook St
5100 OCSD 1067 B5
Greenbrook Wy
8800 SNTE 1230 J4
Greenbush Ln
1100 SDCo 1108 D1
Greencastle St
10700 SNTE 1231 E4
Greencraig Ln
4800 SDGO 1249 E1
Greencraig Wy
5000 SDGO 1249 E1
Greencrest Ct
1500 SDCo 1272 B4
Greencrest Dr
2100 SDCo 1272 B4
Greenery Cir
700 OCSD 1067 B5
Greenfield Access
- SDCo 1251 F3
Greenfield Ct
- CHLV 1311 D7
1700 ELCJ 1252 B3

Greenfield Dr
2100 ELCJ 1252 D4
400 SDCo 1251 G3
1800 SDCo 1252 C3
Greenfield Wy
22500 SDCo 1052 J3
(See Page 1052)
Greenford Dr
10800 SDGO 1209 D3
Greenhaven Dr
6300 CRLB 1127 G3
Greenhedge Row
6000 SDGO 1248 A1
Greenhouse Ln
- SDGO 1228 B1
Greenlake Ct
900 ENCT 1167 E1
Greenlake Dr
1200 ENCT 1167 E1
Greenlawn Dr
8200 SDGO 1290 H4
Greenleaf Rd
10200 SDCo 1291 E2
Greenock Ct
2700 CRLB 1107 A5
Greenridge Av
8800 SDCo 1290 J3
Greenridge Dr
1500 VSTA 1107 H5
Greens East Rd
12300 SDGO 1170 B1
Greensgate Dr
- CHLV 1311 F5
Greenshade Rd
- SDGO 1208 E4
Greenstone Ct
13300 SDGO 1210 E2
Greensview Ct
5900 SDCo 1188 E2
Greensview Dr
1100 CHLV 1311 G6
N Greensview Rd
- CHLV 1311 G5
Greentree Ln
2600 SDGO 1227 J2
Greentree Rd
1700 ENCT 1147 H6
12200 POWY 1170 B7
Greenvale Dr
- SNTE 1230 J7
Greenview Dr
- CRLB 1127 F7
Greenview Pl
8800 SDCo 1271 A4
Greenview Rd
1800 SDCo 1109 F6
Greenview St
100 ESCN 1130 C1
Greenview Wy
- CRLB 1127 F7
Greenway Rd
1000 OCSD 1067 A3
Greenway Rise
1300 ESCN 1110 B5
Greenwich Dr
6100 SDGO 1228 G5
Greenwich St
3000 CRLB 1107 A4
Greenwick Pl
2100 SDCo 1272 B4
Greenwick Rd
2100 SDCo 1272 B4
Greenwillow Ln
- SDGO 1208 D1
Greenwing Dr
2300 SDGO 1249 B7
Greenwood Ln
100 OCSD 1106 C1
Greenwood Pl
200 CHLV 1310 J3
1600 ESCN 1129 G6
Greenwood St
3700 SDGO 1268 E5
Greenwood Trl
33500 SDCo 1052 E2
(See Page 1052)
Gregg Ct
5800 LMSA 1251 C7
12800 POWY 1190 E7
Gregg St
13000 POWY 1190 E7
Gregory Dr
2500 CRLB 1106 E4
Gregory Ln
700 OCSD 1066 H7
Gregory St
9400 LMSA 1251 B6
2800 SDGO 1269 F7
1400 SDGO 1289 F2
S Gregory St
200 SDGO 1289 F5
Gremlin Wy
1600 SDCo 1291 D2
Grenache Rose Rd
- SDCo 1171 H2
Grenade Ln
- SDCo 1235 A2
Grenadine Glen
2500 ESCN 1149 G1
Gresham Rd
- ImCo 6560 H2

Gresham St
4700 SDGO 1247 J5
3900 SDGO 1248 A7
Greta Hill Ct
1100 SDCo 1251 H2
Greta St
1000 SDCo 1251 H2
Gretchen Rd
600 CHLV 1310 E6
Gretler Pl
10400 SDCo 1271 E3
Gretna Green Wy
800 SDCo 1130 D7
700 SDCo 1150 C1
Grevilea Wy
3700 SDCo 1310 G3
Grevillea Pl
12500 SDGO 1188 G6
Grevillea Wy
3800 SDCo 1310 G4
Grewia Ct
1500 SDGO 1290 C6
Grewia St
5800 SDGO 1290 C6
Grey Hawk Ct
3200 CRLB 1127 J2
Grey Oaks Ct
1400 OCSD 1087 E3
Grey Shire Ln
300 SDCo 1028 J5
Greycourt Av
5800 SDGO 1290 C6
Greycourt Wy
1400 SDGO 1290 C6
Greyfield Ct
700 SDCo 1027 G6
Greyhawk Ct
700 OCSD 1067 C7
Greyling Dr
2900 SDGO 1249 C5
Greyling Pl
8800 SDGO 1249 C7
Greystone Av
10300 SDCo 1109 F1
Greystone Ct
2900 SDCo 1272 E6
Greystone Dr
3100 SDCo 1272 D6
Greystone Rd
15900 POWY 1170 G4
Gribble St
7700 SDGO 1290 G4
Gridley Pl
3300 SDGO 1249 C5
Griffin Rd
1000 ImCo 6320 J3
(See Page 6320)
Griffin St
1600 OCSD 1106 D2
Griffith Park Wy
8800 SNTE 1230 J5
Griffith Rd
1500 SDCo 1153 B7
1700 SDCo 1173 B1
Grillo Ct
11400 SDGO 1149 J7
Grim Av
3600 SDGO 1269 E6
Grimsley Av
12800 POWY 1190 H5
Grissom St
700 SDGO 1330 E7
Grivetta Ct
- CRLB 1127 A7
Grogan Cir
3400 SDGO 1330 E7
Grogan Ct
700 SDGO 1330 E7
Gros Ventre Av
4000 SDGO 1248 E3
Grosalia Av
9900 SDCo 1271 C1
Gross Ct
2600 SDGO 1310 E1
Gross St
6400 SDGO 1310 E1
Grosse Pointe
13500 SDGO 1190 A3
Grossmont Av
800 ELCJ 1251 D7
Grossmont Blvd
8700 LMSA 1271 A1
9100 SDCo 1271 B1
Grossmont Center Dr
5600 LMSA 1250 J7
5400 LMSA 1270 J1
Grossmont College Dr
2500 ELCJ 1251 B3
Grossmont Ct
900 CHLV 1311 D5
Grossmont Summit Dr
9300 LMSA 1271 B1
Grossmont View Dr
1600 ELCJ 1251 C6
Groton Pl
2500 SDCo 1130 D7
Groton St
3800 SDGO 1268 C5
Groton Wy
3100 SDGO 1268 C5

San Diego County Street Index

STREET Block City Map# Grid

Ground Score Ct
- OCSD 1067 B4
Grouse St
1000 ELCJ 1251 D3
Grove Av
2700 CRLB 1106 F3
700 IMPB 1349 G1
2300 SDGO 1350 B1
Grove Canyon Rd
3500 SDCo 1150 D1
Grove Ct
- LMGR 1270 H5
Grove Hill Dr
600 SNMS 1109 D7
Grove Knoll Ln
12800 SDCo 1090 C2
Grove Park Pl
2200 CHLV 1311 G7
Grove Pl
1900 ESCN 1130 D2
7900 LMSA 1270 H5
Grove Rd
1400 SDCo 1271 J1
1800 SDCo 1272 A1
Grove St
3400 LMGR 1270 H6
1800 NATC 1310 B2
1600 SDGO 1289 E2
Grove View Rd
800 OCSD 1067 E3
2300 SDGO 1290 H7
Groveland Dr
5100 SDGO 1290 A4
Groveland Ter
1400 ELCJ 1252 A3
Grubstake Trl
7500 SDCo 1158 B1
(See Page 1158)
Grulla St
6600 CRLB 1127 G5
Grumman St
- SDGO 1351 D1
Grunion Run
- ENCT 1147 A2
Grutly St
30200 SDCo 1135 B3
Guacamayo Ct
12900 SDGO 1150 C6
Guacamole Farm Rd
40000 SDCo 996 J1
Guadalajara Dr
1000 ENCT 1147 E7
Guadalcanal Av
- SDGO 1268 F7
Guadalcanal Rd
- CORD 1309 A1
Guadalimar Wy
10900 SDGO 1189 H1
Guadalupe Av
700 CORD 1288 J7
Guadalupe Dr
- OCSD 1086 F2
Guadalupe St
- CHLV 1331 G2
Guadalupe Wy
1800 VSTA 1107 G5
Guajome Lake Rd
5400 OCSD 1067 D6
2200 VSTA 1087 F1
Guajome St
100 VSTA 1087 H7
Guana Juato Ct
100 SOLB 1167 H4
Guantanamo St
- SDGO 1268 E7
Guatay Av
1000 CHLV 1330 E2
Guatay Rd
25200 SDCo 1236 C2
Guatay St
8100 SDGO 1290 G3
Guatay View Ln
9000 SDCo 1236 H3
Guava Av
300 CHLV 1310 B6
700 CHLV 1330 B1
5000 LMSA 1270 G2
Guava Glen
1700 ESCN 1109 D6
Guava Ln
1600 SDCo 1271 J2
Guava Wy
3500 OCSD 1086 F2
6500 SDGO 1188 G3
Guaymas Bay Ct
- SDGO 1290 C1
Guejito Rd
- SDCo 1111 E3
Guerrero Ct
100 SOLB 1167 H4
Guessman Av
5200 LMSA 1270 F1
Guevara Rd
1700 CRLB 1106 F3
Guidero Wy
- ENCT 1147 C5
Guijaros Rd
- SDGO 1288 B7
Guijarros Rd
- SDGO 1308 B1

Guild Av
9300 SDGO 1249 E4
Guild St
5100 LMSA 1270 H1
Guilder Glen
1800 ESCN 1129 F5
Guildford Ct
1000 ENCT 1147 D4
Guilitoy Av
3000 SDGO 1248 C1
Guilitoy Ct
4600 SDGO 1248 C2
Guincho Ct
5600 SDGO 1229 G7
Guincho Pl
10400 SDGO 1229 H7
Guincho Rd
5700 SDGO 1229 G7
Guinda Ct
5200 SDGO 1249 F1
Guinevere St
2600 OCSD 1086 E6
Guisante Ln
5200 SDGO 1249 F1
Guisante Ter
9700 SDGO 1249 F1
Guizot St
1700 SDGO 1267 J7
1800 SDGO 1268 A7
1400 SDGO 1287 J1
Gull Ct
- CRLB 1127 B5
Gull Cv
1400 SDGO 1351 A2
Gull Pl
200 ELCJ 1252 A5
Gull St
800 SDGO 1289 B4
Gullstrand St
7000 SDGO 1228 F4
Gum Tree Ct
- SDCo 1086 A3
Gum Tree Glen
3700 ESCN 1150 B3
Gum Tree Ln
1700 SDCo 1027 J1
2500 SDCo 1028 B2
Gumbark Pl
10200 SDGO 1209 H4
Gunn St
3000 SDGO 1269 E6
Gunn Stage Pl
16900 SDCo 1173 D3
Gunn Stage Rd
- SDCo 1153 G7
- SDCo 1173 D3
Gunner Av
13200 SDGO 1189 C4
Gunnison Ct
13900 SDGO 1189 B3
Gunpowder Point Dr
- CHLV 1309 H6
Gunslinger Trl
7500 SDCo 1138 C7
(See Page 1138)
Gunston Ct
4900 SDGO 1188 C4
Gunzan St
7000 SDGO 1290 G7
Guppy Ct
8200 SDGO 1189 B7
Gurke St
4700 SDGO 1249 G2
Gurnard Ct
3400 SDGO 1249 H4
Gurnard St
10400 SDGO 1249 H4
Gurujan Wy
- SDCo 1234 A6
Gustavo St
1400 ELCJ 1252 A7
Gustine St
- CHLV 1311 C6
Guthrie Wy
7400 SDGO 1290 G3
Gutierrez Ct
- BRAW 6259 F7
(See Page 6259)
Guy St
2100 SDGO 1268 G5
Guymon St
4900 SDGO 1290 A3
Gwen St
800 SDGO 1290 B5
Gwynne Av
2600 SDCo 1310 C2
Gymkhana Rd
23600 SDCo 1173 D2
Gypsy Ln
1200 SDCo 1172 G1

H

H Av
200 CORD 1288 H5
- SDGO 1229 F5
H De La Vega St
- CALX 6620 G6
H Fritsch St
- CALX 6680 D1

H J Goff Ct
- CALX 6620 J6
H Najera Av
- CALX 6620 H5
H Ramos Av
800 CALX 6680 J1
E H Rd
- CORD 1288 F6
H St
500 BRAW 6319 G2
(See Page 6319)
1100 BRAW 6320 A2
(See Page 6320)
500 CHLV 1310 A7
800 CHLV 1329 J1
500 IMPE 6439 F5
800 SDCo 1152 H6
- SDGO 1290 A4
E H St
300 CHLV 1310 F6
1500 CHLV 1311 C5
- ENCT 1147 C7
100 SDCo 1310 D6
W H St
200 ENCT 1147 B7
400 ENCT 1167 B1
Ha Hana Rd
13100 SDCo 1232 C6
Haaland Glen
8300 SDGO 1169 B4
Haas St
2400 ESCN 1150 D1
6100 LMSA 1250 G6
Haber St
5800 SDGO 1228 B6
Habero Dr
2000 ESCN 1129 F6
Hacienda Cir
2000 ELCJ 1251 C2
Hacienda Ct
200 VSTA 1087 G7
Hacienda Dr
- CALX 6620 F7
900 ELCJ 1251 C4
3500 OCSD 1086 F4
900 SDCo 1156 D1
900 VSTA 1087 E7
1900 VSTA 1107 C2
Hacienda Glen
- ESCN 1109 B4
Hacienda Ln
14200 POWY 1170 G7
Hacienda Pl
1700 ELCJ 1251 C2
Hacienda Rd
8500 SNTE 1231 D7
Hackamore Dr
1100 VSTA 1087 E7
Hackamore Rd
1600 OCSD 1067 G7
Hackberry Pl
1500 CHLV 1311 J7
700 SDCo 1027 G3
Hackney Wy
200 SDCo 1028 J7
Hada Dr
17400 SDGO 1169 J1
Hadar Dr
11400 SDGO 1209 C1
Hadden Hall Ct
18200 SDGO 1150 B6
Hadley Pl
9000 SDGO 1209 D1
Haffly Av
1900 NATC 1309 G3
Hagans Cir
8000 SDGO 1209 A1
Hagen Oakes Ln
1200 ESCN 1129 F1
Hagerswood Ct
12700 SDGO 1189 C5
Haglar Wy
1200 CHLV 1311 E7
Hagmann Ct
900 SDGO 1290 F2
Hagmann St
7200 SDGO 1290 F2
Haidas Av
3000 SDGO 1248 C1
Haight Terr
4800 SDGO 1249 D2
Hailey Ct
- SNMS 1128 F5
Haines St
4700 SDGO 1247 J5
4100 SDGO 1248 A6
Haiti Av
- SDGO 1268 F6
Hakone
- SDCo 1232 F4
Hal St
800 SDGO 1290 A3
Halberns Blvd
10100 SNTE 1231 B3
Halcon Ct
- CALX 6620 G7
Halcyon Rd
100 ENCT 1147 B5
N Hale Av
100 ESCN 1129 F3
S Hale Av
1500 ESCN 1129 E5

Hale Ct
800 ELCJ 1251 F7
Hale Dr
700 SDCo 1234 B4
Hale Pl
900 CHLV 1311 G4
Hale St
400 CHLV 1310 G7
Halecrest Dr
800 CHLV 1310 G7
900 ESCN 1130 A3
Haley Ln
9400 SDCo 1271 C4
Haley St
300 SDCo 1152 D7
Half Beak Wy
3700 SDGO 1249 G3
Half Dome Pl
2600 CRLB 1106 J5
Half Mile Dr
3700 SDGO 1188 A4
Half Moon Bay Dr
1200 CHLV 1311 G6
14200 SDGO 1187 H5
Half Moon Bay Wy
4200 OCSD 1066 F6
Half Moon Bend
- CORD 1329 D1
Half Moon Trl
29100 SDCo 1237 D6
Halfoak Terr
- SDGO 1190 B7
Halfpenny Ln
- CORD 1329 E2
Halfway Rd
- SDCo 1033 G6
Halia Ct
1400 ENCT 1147 B2
Halifax St
6800 SDGO 1250 A5
Halite Pl
6500 CRLB 1127 F3
E Hall Av
100 SDGO 1350 G4
W Hall Av
100 SDGO 1350 F4
Hall Meadow Rd
10500 SDGO 1209 G1
Haller St
3100 SDGO 1269 F6
2000 SDGO 1289 G1
Halley Ct
1200 CHLV 1330 H1
1300 SDGO 1350 A1
Halley St
1600 SDGO 1349 J1
1800 SDGO 1350 A1
Hallmark Pl
2000 ESCN 1129 F7
Halo Cir
9900 SDCo 1271 D2
Halo St
1700 SDGO 1350 A1
Halper Rd
14000 POWY 1190 C3
Halsey Rd
- SDGO 1288 D1
Halsey St
100 CHLV 1310 C7
700 CHLV 1330 A1
Halsing Ct
500 CRLB 1146 J1
Halsted St
8800 SDGO 1249 D4
Halter Pl
1500 SNMS 1108 E6
Halyard Pl
- CRLB 1127 B4
Hambaugh Wy
400 VSTA 1107 H1
Hamblet Ct
- ImCo 6439 D5
Hamblett Rd
600 ImCo 6439 C5
Hamburg Sq
3100 SDGO 1227 J1
Hamden Dr
2100 CHLV 1311 E3
Hamden Ln
- SDCo 1089 D3
Hamden Wy
3100 CRLB 1107 A3
Hamill Av
5500 SDGO 1250 C5
Hamilton Av
- ELCN 6499 D7
200 ELCN 6500 A7
E Hamilton Av
- ImCo 6500 E7
Hamilton Ln
1900 ESCN 1129 F6
- SDCo 1028 A1
500 SDCo 1129 J7
27500 SDCo 1236 H3
Hamilton Pl
2000 ESCN 1129 H7
Hamilton St
4300 SDGO 1269 D4
Hamlet Av
7300 SDGO 1250 C5

Hamlet Ct
7200 SDGO 1250 C5
Hamlet Dr
1100 SDCo 1252 J2
Hamlin Ct
2500 ESCN 1110 D5
16600 SDCo 1171 E3
Hammerberg Cove
10300 SDGO 1249 G4
Hammond Dr
8800 SDGO 1249 C5
Hampe Ct
8900 SDGO 1189 C2
Hampshire Ln
500 CHLV 1330 H2
18300 SDGO 1150 B6
Hampson Pl
16100 SDCo 1173 D3
Hampstead Wy
2300 SDGO 1290 G7
Hampton Ct
1700 CHLV 1311 C5
1100 ENCT 1147 D4
5800 SDGO 1250 B6
800 VSTA 1107 H2
Hampton Glen
- ESCN 1109 D2
Hampton Rd
34100 SDCo 1050 H1
1200 SNMS 1128 B3
Hana Ct
300 ENCT 1147 A2
Hancock Cir
4500 OCSD 1107 D2
Hancock Cres
2600 CRLB 1127 G2
Hancock St
3600 SDGO 1268 D4
Hancock Terr
500 SNMS 1108 J5
Handel Ct
7900 SDGO 1209 A4
Handel Wy
7900 SDGO 1209 A4
Handlebar Rd
- SDCo 1171 J2
Handrich Ct
11900 SDGO 1210 A4
Handrich Dr
11800 SDGO 1210 A4
Hanes Pl
100 VSTA 1087 H6
Haney St
1100 ELCJ 1251 G7
Hanford Ct
1100 CHLV 1311 C7
Hanford Dr
2100 SDGO 1249 A7
1700 SDGO 1269 A1
Hanford Glen
400 ESCN 1110 D6
Hanford Pl
7400 SDGO 1249 A7
Haniman Dr
2100 SDGO 1290 A1
Hanna St
5400 SDGO 1290 B1
Hannah Ct
- IMPE 6499 H2
Hannalei Dr
100 SDCo 1108 B2
Hannalei Ln
300 SDCo 1108 A2
Hannalei Pl
300 SDCo 1108 A3
Hannibal Pl
3900 SDGO 1270 E5
Hannigans Wy
- SNMS 1109 C6
Hannon Ct
6200 SDGO 1248 J1
Hanover Pl
1100 SDCo 1253 H2
Hanover St
900 SDGO 1290 B3
Hansel Dr
2000 SDGO 1350 A2
Hansom Ln
10800 SDCo 1271 G7
Hanson Ln
1600 ELCJ 1252 C2
1700 SDCo 1172 F1
200 SDCo 1173 A1
Hanson Wy
- SDCo 1172 F1
Happiness Wy
800 CRLB 1126 H4
Happy Boy Ln
5600 LMSA 1250 G7
Happy Hill Dr
1100 SDCo 1108 C1
Happy Hill Ln
200 SNMS 1128 G1
Happy Hollow Ln
15400 SDCo 1050 H3
Happy Lilac Trl
- SDCo 1089 D3
Happy Ln
10300 SNTE 1231 E6
Happy Wy
8400 SDCo 1232 D7

Harbin Pl
10300 SNTE 1231 F3
Harbinson Av
4300 LMSA 1270 F4
Harbison Av
- NATC 1310 C1
4900 SDGO 1270 F2
N Harbison Av
- NATC 1290 B6
S Harbison Av
200 NATC 1290 B6
1200 NATC 1310 C1
Harbison Canyon Rd
8800 SDCo 1233 E6
1800 SDCo 1253 B3
Harbison Pl
800 NATC 1290 C7
Harbison Wy
3100 NATC 1290 C7
N Harbor
3600 SDGO 1288 E1
Harbor Crest Wy
3600 OCSD 1107 D3
Harbor Dr
4000 CRLB 1106 F7
- NATC 1309 G2
- SDCo 1085 J6
2000 SDGO 1289 C5
- SNMS 1128 F2
1500 VSTA 1107 H5
E Harbor Dr
2800 SDGO 1289 E6
N Harbor Dr
1500 OCSD 1085 H5
4900 SDGO 1288 C2
S Harbor Dr
200 OCSD 1085 J6
W Harbor Dr
800 SDGO 1289 B4
Harbor Island Dr
1500 SDGO 1288 E2
Harbor Ln
500 SDGO 1288 J4
Harbor Pointe Rd
6800 CRLB 1126 J5
Harbor Rd
- SDCo 1085 H4
Harbor View Dr
1100 CRLB 1106 G6
900 SDGO 1288 B3
Harbor View Pl
800 SDGO 1288 B3
Harbor View Wy
3600 OCSD 1107 D3
Harbor Wy
4300 OCSD 1087 A4
Harbour Heights Ct
5200 SDGO 1248 A3
Harbour Heights Rd
2100 SDGO 1248 A4
Harbour Town Pl
1300 CHLV 1311 G6
Harcourt Dr
2600 SDGO 1249 F6
Hard Maple Rd
2700 CHLV 1311 J7
Hardell Ln
- SDCo 1088 E5
Hardin Dr
1200 ELCJ 1271 E1
Harding Av
1400 NATC 1309 H2
3700 SDGO 1289 G4
Harding St
2900 CRLB 1106 E5
1000 ESCN 1110 A7
500 ESCN 1130 B1
100 OCSD 1067 B6
Hardscramble Trl
7200 SDCo 1138 B7
(See Page 1138)
Hardship Dr
- SDCo 1171 H4
Hardy Av
5500 SDGO 1270 B2
Hardy Dr
2400 LMGR 1270 H7
Harjoan Av
8600 SDGO 1249 C6
Harlan Cir
900 SDGO 1290 G2
Harlan Ct
700 CALX 6620 G7
- CHLV 1330 H2
Harlan Pl
7500 SDGO 1290 G2
Harlington Dr
8800 SDGO 1209 D4
Harlow Ter
8400 SDGO 1209 B1
Harmarsh St
7900 SDGO 1249 B5
Harmony Grove Rd
1900 ESCN 1129 E4
2400 SDCo 992 AC2
2100 SDCo 1129 D4
- SDCo 1148 G4
- SDCo 1149 A1
Harmony Grove Village Pkwy
2600 SDCo 1129 D5

Harmony Heights Rd
2600 SDCo 1129 D5
Harmony Hill
3500 SDCo 1047 G3
Harmony Ln
5000 LMSA 1271 B1
3400 SDCo 1271 E6
Harmony Pl
11300 SDCo 1089 H7
Harmony Village Dr
21400 SDCo 1129 C6
Harmony Wy
- ImCo 6560 D7
Harness Pt
- SDGO 1190 B7
Harness St
9200 SDCo 1291 B2
Harney St
4000 SDGO 1268 F5
Harol St
1300 ELCJ 1271 E1
Harold Av
- CALX 6680 F1
Harold Pl
800 CHLV 1311 G4
Harold Rd
1700 ESCN 1109 D5
Harolds Rd
62000 SDCo 1052 A5
(See Page 1052)
Harper Fire Rd
- SDCo 1196 H5
(See Page 1196)
Harper Rd
1100 SDCo 1152 G3
Harps Ct
6000 SDGO 1290 C5
Harrahs Rincon Wy
700 SDCo 1071 E3
Harrier Ct
- CRLB 1127 D6
Harriet St
2700 OCSD 1087 C7
Harris Mill Av
- CHLV 1311 E6
Harrington St
700 CALX 6620 G7
Harris Av
700 SDGO 1330 B7
Harris Dr
2900 SDCo 1067 H7
Harris Plant Rd
- SDGO 1229 E4
Harris Ranch Rd
- SDCo 1316 H6
(See Page 1316)
Harris Rd
600 ImCo 6439 D1
Harris Spur Truck Trl
- SDCo 997 D3
Harris St
3200 LMGR 1270 F6
3600 LMSA 1270 F5
600 SDCo 1067 A1
Harris Trl
38700 SDCo 997 D4
Harrisburg Dr
300 ENCT 1147 G7
Harrison Av
2400 NATC 1309 G3
2200 SDGO 1289 D5
Harrison Park Rd
17500 SDCo 1156 F6
Harrison Park Trl
16700 SDCo 1156 D7
Harrison St
4000 CRLB 1106 G7
100 OCSD 1067 B6
Harritt Rd
9300 SDCo 1232 F4
Harrow Ln
15500 POWY 1170 G5
Harrow Pl
14200 POWY 1170 G5
Harry St
900 ELCJ 1251 H7
Hart Dr
- SDCo 1251 F3
4800 SDGO 1269 H3
Hartfell Rd
30100 SDCo 1297 G5
(See Page 1297)
Hartfield Av
- SDGO 1188 A5
Hartford Ct
7400 LMSA 1270 G5
2800 SDGO 1248 F7
Hartford Pl
4500 CRLB 1107 B4
Hartford St
600 CHLV 1311 E3
2100 SDGO 1268 E1
Hartland Cir
- SNTE 1231 B4
Hartley Dr
6200 SDGO 1247 G2
Hartley Hill Rd
24000 SDCo 1316 A5
(See Page 1316)
Hartley Rd
10800 SNTE 1231 F5

Hartley St
4600 SDGO 1289 J3
Hartman Dr
1300 ELCJ 1251 D4
Hartman Wy
3000 SDGO 1248 C3
Harton Pl
8200 SDGO 1269 B1
Harton Rd
1900 SDGO 1269 B1
Hartwell Ct
1600 SDGO 1290 D6
Hartwright Rd
1800 SDCo 1108 C3
Hartzel Crest Dr
3500 SDCo 1271 A5
Hartzel Dr
3600 SDCo 1271 A5
Harvala St
6800 SDGO 1270 E4
Harvard Av
4300 LMSA 1270 F4
Harvard Dr
3600 OCSD 1107 A2
Harvard St
1600 CHLV 1311 C5
Harveson Pl
2300 ESCN 1129 E3
Harvest Crescent
14300 POWY 1170 G6
Harvest Ct
5200 OCSD 1067 A3
14400 POWY 1170 H6
- SDCo 1085 J3
Harvest Dance Wy
11000 SDGO 1149 H7
Harvest Ln
1100 VSTA 1108 A5
Harvest Moon Cres
30500 SDCo 1070 G1
Harvest Point Wy
17000 SDCo 1173 D1
Harvest Rd
600 SDCo 1351 J1
800 SDGO 1351 J2
Harvest Run Dr
- SDGO 1208 D2
Harvest View Wy
10400 SDGO 1189 G6
Harvest Vista Ln
2300 SDCo 1027 H7
Harvey Homestead Rd
- SDCo 1314 G3
(See Page 1314)
Harvey Rd
- ImCo 6320 B7
(See Page 6320)
4600 SDGO 1269 B3
Harwell Dr
8400 SDGO 1250 J4
Harwich Dr
- CRLB 1107 B3
1100 SNMS 1109 C6
Harwick Ln
12800 SDGO 1188 D5
Harwick Pl
4900 SDGO 1188 C5
Harwood St
900 SDGO 1329 J7
Hasbrook Rd
10800 SDGO 1209 H1
Haskell Dr
1800 ELCN 6499 D6
- ELCN 6559 D1
Haskell St
2600 SDGO 1248 C4
Hastings Ct
- SNMS 1109 C6
Hastings Dr
3200 CRLB 1107 A3
Hastings Rd
5100 SDGO 1269 H2
Hasty St
3400 SDGO 1270 D6
Hat Creek Rd
15000 POWY 1170 G7
Hataca Rd
3100 CRLB 1147 H1
Hatcher Ln
9000 SDGO 1209 D2
Hatcreek Ct
1200 VSTA 1107 J4
Hatfield Cir
3500 OCSD 1107 E3
Hatfield Creek Dr
600 SDCo 1153 B6
Hatfield Ct
- BRAW 6259 G6
(See Page 6259)
Hatfield Dr
600 SNMS 1128 H3
Hatfield Ln
- SDCo 1153 A5
Hathaway St
4000 SDGO 1248 J3
Hatherly St
- VSTA 1087 D7
Hatteras Av
3500 SDGO 1248 D2
Hatton St
4000 SDGO 1248 J3

Hauberk Ct
300 SDCo 1058 F7
(See Page 1058)
Hauberk Dr
1800 SDCo 1058 G7
(See Page 1058)
Hauser St
6400 SDGO 1290 D6
Havasupai Av
2600 SDGO 1248 B1
Haven Brook Pl
- SDGO 1208 E2
Haven Dr
8000 LMGR 1270 H7
Haven Heights Rd
300 OCSD 1087 A2
Haven Pl
600 ESCN 1130 E1
Havencrest Dr
2600 SDCo 1027 J7
Havenhurst Dr
1000 SDGO 1247 F2
Havenhurst Pl
6100 SDGO 1247 F3
Havenhurst Pt
800 SDGO 1247 F2
Havenridge Wy
- SDGO 1208 E2
Havens Point Pl
1700 CRLB 1106 G6
Havenview Ln
100 OCSD 1107 D2
Havenwood Av
4900 SDGO 1250 A5
Havenwood Dr
1500 OCSD 1087 D4
Haverfield Wy
11200 SDGO 1209 E2
Haverford Rd
1200 SDCo 1152 D3
Haverhill Rd
700 ELCJ 1251 B4
Haverhill St
3600 CRLB 1106 J4
Haveteur Wy
8800 SDGO 1249 C4
Havilland Av
- BRAW 6260 C7
(See Page 6260)
Hawaii Av
800 SDGO 1330 D7
Hawaii Pl
900 ESCN 1109 F4
Hawes Rd
1700 ImCo 6560 F1
Hawick Dr
13900 SDCo 1232 E7
Hawick Terr
- SDCo 1232 F7
Hawk Ln
1300 ELCJ 1251 D2
Hawk Ridge Pl
1600 ESCN 1130 C2
Hawk St
- ImCo 6560 A7
4000 SDGO 1268 J5
Hawk View Dr
1800 ENCT 1147 D2
Hawke Bay Ct
- SDGO 1290 C1
Hawken
- SDGO 1350 H2
Hawkeye Downs Wy
19500 SDCo 1151 J2
Hawkeye Wy
11500 SDGO 1209 E1
Hawkhill Rd
- SDCo 1068 F6
Hawkins Pl
8100 LMGR 1290 H1
Hawkins Wy
2000 SDCo 1291 A1
Hawks Bluff Ct
2800 CHLV 1312 A5
(See Page 1312)
Hawks Peak Wy
7500 SDGO 1209 A3
Hawks View Wy
700 SDCo 1028 D3
Hawks Vista Ln
1400 SDCo 1253 J3
Hawksbury Ln
- SDCo 1070 J6
Hawksview Pl
- CHLV 1311 J3
Hawley Av
9000 LMSA 1271 A1
Hawley Blvd
4700 SDGO 1269 F3
Hawley Creek
15600 SDCo 1233 C3
Hawley Ct
15500 SDCo 1233 C3
Hawley Dr
2100 SDCo 1087 J2
Hawley Pl
15500 SDCo 1233 B3
Hawley Rd
10300 SDCo 1213 C7
9700 SDCo 1233 C3

33 INDEX
Haworth St
INDEX 33
Hilcorte Dr
SAN DIEGO CO.

San Diego County Street Index

STREET	Block	City	Map#	Grid
Haworth St	7100	SDGO	1228	F5
Hawthorn Av	900	CRLB	1127	A5
Hawthorn Glen	2400	ESCN	1110	D7
Hawthorn St	200	SDGO	1289	A1
W Hawthorn St	1100	SDGO	1288	J2
Hawthorne Av	500	ELCJ	1251	D6
Hawthorne Cir	-	VSTA	1108	A2
Hawthorne Creek Dr	900	CHLV	1311	H4
Hawthorne Ct	900	SNMS	1128	B2
Hawthorne Dr	600	SDCo	1156	E2
Hawthorne St	500	SDCo	1027	F2
Haxton Pl	13200	SDGO	1188	B4
Hay Ct	12500	SDCo	1232	B7
Haya St	100	SDGO	1289	J4
N Hayden Dr	100	ESCN	1110	E7
S Hayden Dr	300	ESCN	1110	E7
Hayden Lake Pl	15600	SDGO	1169	A3
Hayden Ln	1200	ELCJ	1252	B3
Hayden Ranch Rd	-	VSTA	1087	H3
Hayden Wy	2100	SDGO	1268	G5
Haydn Dr	1700	ENCT	1167	D2
Hayes Av	1000	SDGO	1269	B5
Hayes St	8800	LMSA	1271	A2
	-	OCSD	1106	A2
Hayford Rd	-	CHLV	1311	D7
Hayford Wy	-	SDGO	1188	D4
Hayfork Pl	-	CHLV	1331	B2
Hayloft Pl	2900	SDCo	1129	C5
Haymar Dr	2700	CRLB	1106	H2
	3700	OCSD	1106	J2
	3700	OCSD	1107	A2
Haymarket Rd	1800	ENCT	1147	A2
Hayuco Plz	1000	CHLV	1311	A6
Hayvin Rd	31700	SDCo	1050	J7
Hayward Ct	2100	SDGO	1290	E7
Hayward Pl	500	ESCN	1110	D6
Hayward Wy	6400	SDGO	1290	E7
Hazard Center Dr	7400	SDGO	1269	A2
Hazard Wy	9300	SDGO	1229	E7
Hazel Av	-	IMPE	6499	J2
Hazel Ln	9700	SDCo	1149	E2
Hazel St	1800	CHLV	1331	F3
Hazel Wy	200	OCSD	1086	J2
Hazeldon Dr	8800	SNTE	1231	B6
Hazelhurst Ct	3600	SDCo	1310	J1
Hazelhurst Pl	3600	SDCo	1310	J1
Hazelnut Ct	2700	CHLV	1311	J7
	1900	SNMS	1128	B2
Hazeltine Rd	-	SDCo	1090	H5
Hazelwood Pl	1900	SDGO	1289	J1
Hazen Dr	900	SNMS	1109	B6
Hazy Glen Ct	800	CHLV	1311	B6
Hazy Meadow Ln	15600	SDCo	1212	J6
Headquarters Pt	-	SDGO	1208	D6
Heald Ln	300	SDCo	1027	H3
Healis Pl	7300	SDGO	1188	J4
Health Center Dr	2800	SDGO	1249	B6
Health Sciences Dr	-	SDGO	1228	C2
Healthcare Dr	-	LMSA	1251	A7
Healy Ct	10600	SNTE	1231	E2
Healy St	10400	SNTE	1231	E2
Healy Wy	10600	SNTE	1231	E2
E Heaney Cir	9300	SNTE	1231	B5
W Heaney Cir	9400	SNTE	1231	A5
W Heany Cir	9300	SNTE	1231	A5
Heard Ln	700	SDCo	1152	H6
Heartland Ln	1700	SDCo	1252	B6
Heartwood Ct	-	SDGO	1209	H2
Heartwood Wy	-	SDGO	1209	G2
Heater Ct	10500	SDGO	1208	H4
Heath Cliff Ct	-	SDCo	1252	E1
Heath Ct	6700	CRLB	1126	J5
Heath Dr	14900	POWY	1170	C7
Heathbrook Ct	-	SDGO	1330	H7
Heather Canyon Ct	3800	SDCo	1311	A3
Heather Ct	500	CHLV	1330	H3
Heather Dr	1000	VSTA	1087	J5
Heather Glen Wy	14800	SDGO	1170	B7
Heather Ln	2200	DLMR	1187	F3
	3300	OCSD	1107	B1
	-	SDCo	1234	D4
Heather Pl	2500	ESCN	1110	E7
Heather Ridge Dr	10700	SDGO	1208	D1
Heather Ridge Rd	500	SNMS	1108	C6
Heather St	3000	SDGO	1269	H6
Heather Stone Ct	15200	SDCo	1169	G5
Heather Wy	800	CRLB	1127	A6
	-	SDGO	1209	E3
Heatherdale St	9100	SNTE	1231	G5
Heatherfield Ln	12500	SDGO	1150	B5
Heatheridge Ct	3300	SNMS	1108	C6
Heatherly Dr	-	SDGO	1188	J3
Heathermist Ct	1600	SDCo	1272	B2
Heathers Country Ln	2400	SDCo	1299	C2
	(See Page 1299)			
Heatherton Ct	12400	SDGO	1189	J6
Heatherwood Av	1400	CHLV	1331	D1
Heatherwood Ct	2400	ESCN	1109	H3
Heatherwood Dr	5200	OCSD	1087	D2
	3400	SDCo	1272	C6
Heatherwood Hollow Ct	-	SDGO	1190	B6
Heatherwood Ln	800	VSTA	1108	A4
Heavenly Pl	-	SDCo	1067	H1
Heavenly Wy	10000	SDCo	1271	D2
Heber Av	600	CALX	6680	G1
	1100	ImCo	6560	B7
	1000	ImCo	6620	B1
Heber Rd	100	ImCo	6560	D7
	-	ImCo	6620	A1
Heber St	1200	SDCo	1321	G6
	(See Page 1321)			
Hebrides Cir	10400	SDGO	1209	C4
Hebrides Dr	8700	SDGO	1209	C4
Hector Av	9200	SDGO	1249	E6
Hedera Hills Rd	10500	SDCo	1149	F7
Hedge Wy	300	CHLV	1310	A6
Hedgerow Wy	-	SDGO	1209	E3
Hedges Wy	6600	SDGO	1310	F2
Hedgetree Ct	12600	POWY	1190	C1
Hedgewood Row	5900	SDGO	1248	A1
Hedionda Av	1400	SDCo	1107	F3
Hedionda Ct	4400	SDGO	1248	D2
Hedy Rd	-	SDCo	1171	F4
Heffernan Av	500	CALX	6680	G1
	-	ImCo	6620	C1
Heffner Ln	9900	SDGO	1209	A6
Hegg St	4000	SDGO	1270	C5
Heide Ln	3200	SDCo	1273	A7
	3200	SDCo	1293	A1
Heiden Ct	-	SNMS	1109	A3
Heidi Cir	1400	VSTA	1087	H4
Heidi St	5600	LMSA	1250	H7
	5400	LMSA	1270	H1
Heights Ct	2000	SDCo	1130	D4
Heights Ln	2600	SDCo	1271	E6
Heil Av	2000	ELCN	6499	E7
	300	ELCN	6500	A7
Heil Cir	-	ELCN	6499	D7
Heil Ct	100	ELCN	6499	J7
Heinrich Hertz Dr	9500	SDGO	1352	A3
Heirloom Pl	3000	SDCo	1129	B5
Heise Park Rd	4900	SDCo	1156	C5
Heiting Wy	9300	SNTE	1230	J6
Helen Cir	1000	NATC	1290	B7
Helen Dr	600	OCSD	1067	B5
	39700	SDCo	997	A2
Helen James Av	8900	SDGO	1209	D5
Helen Park Ln	14700	POWY	1190	E1
Helen Rd	-	SDCo	997	A1
Helen Wy	100	SDCo	1130	B5
Helena Pl	5600	SDGO	1250	C7
Helena St	4000	SDCo	1028	F4
Helenite Pl	6800	CRLB	1127	F5
Heliotrope Dr	2800	SDCo	1136	E7
Helix Av	1300	CHLV	1330	F3
	300	SOLB	1167	E7
S Helix Av	200	SOLB	1187	E1
Helix Canyon Dr	9400	SDCo	1271	C3
Helix Ct	8700	SDCo	1291	A1
Helix Del Sur	4200	SDCo	1271	E4
Helix Glen Dr	4700	LMSA	1271	B3
Helix Hills Ter	4900	LMSA	1271	C2
Helix Ln	3900	SDCo	1271	B5
Helix Mont Cir	9900	SDCo	1271	D4
Helix Mont Dr	9900	SDCo	1271	D4
Helix Pl	1800	SDCo	1291	B1
Helix St	4000	SDCo	1271	B5
	1100	SDCo	1291	A2
Helix Ter	5000	SDCo	1271	E2
Helix View Dr	1300	ELCJ	1251	D7
Helix Village Ct	1200	ELCJ	1251	D7
Helix Village Dr	1000	ELCJ	1251	E7
Helix Vista Dr	8700	SDCo	1291	A2
Helix Wy	1400	CHLV	1330	F4
	-	OCSD	1086	J4
Hell Creek Rd	-	SDCo	1091	H3
Hellers Bend	4000	SDCo	1047	H4
Helm St	8100	SDGO	1290	H2
Helmer Ln	18000	SDGO	1210	A3
Helmsdale Rd	700	SNMS	1108	G6
Helvetia Dr	2600	SDCo	1136	D7
Helvetia St	30200	SDCo	1135	B3
Hemingway Av	7800	SDGO	1250	E4
Hemingway Ct	1900	ESCN	1130	D2
	6900	SDGO	1250	D3
Hemingway Dr	6600	SDGO	1250	D3
Hemlock Av	100	CRLB	1106	E7
	300	ESCN	1129	H1
	700	IMPB	1349	G2
	2100	SDGO	1350	A2
Hemlock St	3800	SDGO	1289	G5
Hemlock Wy	200	OCSD	1086	J1
Hemmingway Dr	-	CRLB	1107	A7
	-	CRLB	1127	A1
Hempden Ct	1300	ELCJ	1251	D5
Hemphill Ct	10300	SDGO	1209	B5
Hemphill Dr	8000	SDGO	1209	B4
	500	SNMS	1108	J6
Hemphill Pl	10300	SDGO	1209	B5
Hemphill Wy	10300	SDGO	1209	B5
N Hempstead Cir	4000	SDGO	1269	G2
S Hempstead Cir	4000	SDGO	1269	G2
Henderson Av	-	SDGO	1268	E7
Henderson Canyon Rd	500	SDCo	1058	H3
	(See Page 1058)			
	1300	SDCo	1059	C3
	(See Page 1059)			
Henderson Ct	1700	VSTA	1087	G3
Henderson Dr	6300	ELCJ	1251	C6
	6000	LMSA	1251	C6
Henderson Rd	35200	SDCo	1029	J3
	8900	SDCo	1030	A3
Henderson St	-	SDCo	1067	A1
Hendricks Ct	10100	SDGO	1209	A5
Hendricks Dr	7800	SDGO	1209	A5
Hendrix Pl	-	CHLV	1330	J3
Henie Hills Dr	1900	OCSD	1086	G7
Henley Dr	5800	SDGO	1250	B7
Henna Pl	1800	SDCo	1272	D2
Henrietta Ct	200	SDGO	1290	E4
Henry Ln	100	CHLV	1330	D3
Henry Silvers Ln	-	SDCo	1136	B6
Henry St	3800	SDGO	1268	G6
Henshaw Ct	-	SDCo	1086	A2
Henshaw Rd	1400	OCSD	1087	D1
Hensley St	-	SDGO	1289	D4
Henson Heights Dr	500	SNMS	1108	G6
Henson Ln	400	SNMS	1108	G6
Henson St	200	SDGO	1290	D4
Henson St S	100	SDGO	1290	D4
Hepburn Ct	3200	SDGO	1249	G4
Heraldry St	8800	SDGO	1249	C4
Heralds Wy	-	SDCo	1172	J1
Herbert Ct	-	CALX	6680	H2
Herbert Pl	1600	SDGO	1269	C6
Herbert St	500	ELCJ	1251	G7
	700	OCSD	1067	B5
	3400	SDGO	1269	C6
Herbert York Ln	-	SDGO	1228	A2
Herby Wy	1200	OCSD	1106	C2
Hercules Rd	2300	SDGO	1209	D7
Hercules St	8300	LMSA	1270	J1
Herder Ln	700	ENCT	1147	E7
Herdfield Wy	10200	SDCo	1271	E5
Hereford Dr	25100	SDCo	1173	H4
Herencia Dr	-	POWY	1190	D5
Heritage Ct	1300	ESCN	1130	C2
Heritage Dr	6300	CRLB	1127	G3
	18700	POWY	1150	G5
Heritage Glen Ct	12700	SDGO	1188	C6
Heritage Glen Ln	4400	SDGO	1188	B6
Heritage Hills Rd	5900	SDCo	1188	E2
Heritage Ln	1400	ENCT	1147	E6
	900	VSTA	1108	A4
Heritage Park Row	2400	SDGO	1268	F5
Heritage Ranch Rd	-	SDCo	1152	F2
Heritage Rd	-	CHLV	1331	B2
	-	SDCo	1331	B6
	1000	SDGO	1331	C7
	1900	SDGO	1351	C2
Heritage St	100	OCSD	1086	F3
Heritage Wy	14600	POWY	1190	B1
Herman Av	3600	SDGO	1269	E6
Hermana Ct	1300	VSTA	1088	A3
Hermanos Ct	10500	SDGO	1229	H7
Hermes Av	1100	ENCT	1147	B4
Hermes Ct	1300	SDGO	1349	J2
Hermes Ln	1400	SDGO	1349	J2
Hermes St	1700	SDGO	1350	A2
Hermitage View Pl	2800	SDGO	1268	D6
Hermosa Wy	10100	SDCo	1271	D2
	4400	SDGO	1268	H4
Hermosillo Glen	1100	ESCN	1109	E5
Hermosillo Wy	14100	POWY	1190	E3
Hermosita Dr	1400	SDCo	1128	B3
Hernandez Ct	400	CALX	6620	G6
Hernandez St	200	CALX	6620	G6
	800	SOLB	1187	G1
Heron Av	1700	ELCJ	1251	D3
Heron Cir	7000	CRLB	1127	B5
Heron Dr	1000	VSTA	1108	A5
Heron St	1400	CHLV	1331	C2
Herrera Ct	1500	SDGO	1290	E5
Herrick St	6500	SDGO	1290	D3
Herring Cove	11300	SDGO	1209	B1
Herrington Wy	8600	SDCo	1169	B2
Herschel Av	7700	SDGO	1227	F6
Hershey St	3400	SDGO	1270	D6
Hesby Ct	8700	SDGO	1189	C1
Hess Dr	10800	SDCo	1271	F2
Hessmay Dr	100	SDCo	1108	B3
Hesta St	15000	POWY	1170	C7
Hestia Wy	300	ENCT	1147	B4
Heston Pl	13300	SDGO	1188	A4
Hewes Sq	12100	SDGO	1190	A1
Hewlett Dr	5300	SDGO	1270	A2
Heyneman Hollow	2400	SDCo	1028	B3
Heywood Ct	-	SDCo	1067	A1
Hi Hopes Dr	-	SDCo	1211	H4
Hi Pass Rd	38500	SDCo	1300	A4
	(See Page 1300)			
Hi Ridge Rd	11500	SDCo	1211	H6
Hialeah Cir	-	SOLB	1187	F2
Hialeah Ln	2400	SDCo	1234	C6
Hiawatha Ct	3800	SDGO	1248	E3
Hiawatha Gn	1300	ESCN	1130	B2
Hiawatha Wy	3800	SDGO	1248	E3
Hibert St	9800	SDGO	1209	F3
Hibiscus Av	-	POWY	1190	F3
	2400	VSTA	1108	B5
Hibiscus Cir	3900	CRLB	1106	F7
Hibiscus Ct	500	CHLV	1330	H3
	-	LMGR	1270	E7
Hibiscus Dr	6700	LMGR	1270	E7
Hibiscus Glen	600	ESCN	1150	B3
Hickman Field Dr	5100	SDGO	1228	J7
Hickman Pl	3200	SDCo	1156	D1
Hickok Pt	-	SDGO	1350	G2
Hickory Ct	-	BRAW	6259	J7
	(See Page 6259)			
	900	CRLB	1127	A5
	700	IMPB	1349	G1
	12600	POWY	1190	D3
Hickory Nut Pl	1600	CHLV	1311	J7
Hickory Rd	-	SNMS	1108	J5
Hickory St	13900	POWY	1190	D3
	2000	SDGO	1268	G5
N Hickory St	600	ESCN	1129	J1
S Hickory St	100	ESCN	1130	A2
Hickory Ter	400	CHLV	1311	B3
Hickory Wy	3700	OCSD	1086	H4
Hickoryhill Dr	300	ENCT	1147	F7
Hicks St	1500	OCSD	1106	D2
Hicock St	3900	SDGO	1268	E4
Hidalgo Av	4900	SDGO	1228	C7
	4800	SDGO	1248	C1
Hidden Bay Ct	-	SDGO	1290	C1
Hidden Canyon Rd	19900	SNMS	1148	D1
Hidden Canyon Wy	500	OCSD	1086	D7
Hidden Cove Wy	8400	SDCo	1169	B2
Hidden Creek Ln	3000	SDCo	1109	J2
Hidden Crest Dr	1900	SDCo	1272	C1
Hidden Dr	2400	CHLV	1331	H1
Hidden Dune Ct	4900	SDGO	1188	C5
Hidden Estates Ln	3200	ESCN	1110	F7
Hidden Glen Dr	-	SDCo	1254	F7
Hidden Glen Rd	19500	SDCo	1254	G7
Hidden Haven	-	SDCo	1068	A6
Hidden Hills Ln	400	SDCo	1149	J1
Hidden Hollow Ct	-	SDCo	1272	C1
Hidden Knoll	14600	POWY	1190	H3
Hidden Knoll Dr	1300	SDCo	1272	C1
Hidden Lake Ln	-	SDCo	1067	H7
	300	SDCo	1087	H1
Hidden Ln	900	SDCo	1138	A7
	(See Page 1138)			
Hidden Mac Wy	1100	SDCo	1028	F3
Hidden Meadows Ln	10200	SDCo	1089	E4
Hidden Meadows Rd	10100	SDCo	1089	F4
Hidden Mesa Ct	1400	SDCo	1272	B1
Hidden Mesa Rd	1500	SDCo	1272	A1
Hidden Mesa Trl	1400	SDCo	1272	C1
Hidden Mesa View Rd	1400	SDCo	1272	B1
Hidden Mountain Dr	1300	SDCo	1272	C1
Hidden Oak Trl	1200	SDCo	1108	D1
Hidden Oaks Ct	1800	SDCo	1272	B1
Hidden Oaks Ln	-	SDGO	1130	H3
Hidden Oaks Rd	38400	SDCo	999	J5
Hidden Palm Ct	1800	SDCo	1272	B1
Hidden Pines Ln	400	DLMR	1187	G7
Hidden Pines Rd	300	DLMR	1187	G7
Hidden Plateau Ct	1300	SDCo	1272	C1
Hidden Ridge Ct	500	ENCT	1147	E6
Hidden Ridge Rd	3600	SDCo	1272	J6
Hidden Rock Ct	1800	SDCo	1272	B1
Hidden Springs Ct	2000	SDCo	1272	C1
Hidden Springs Dr	2000	SDCo	1272	C1
Hidden Springs Pl	1300	CHLV	1311	H6
Hidden Springs Trl	1100	SDCo	1109	J2
Hidden Trail Dr	3800	SDCo	1272	J5
	3700	SDCo	1273	A5
Hidden Trail Wy	-	SDCo	1273	A6
Hidden Trails	-	SDGO	1351	A1
Hidden Trails Rd	-	ESCN	1110	E6
Hidden Vale Dr	1000	VSTA	1107	H1
Hidden Valley Av	1400	CHLV	1311	H7
Hidden Valley Ct	2800	SDCo	1291	D1
	7700	SDGO	1227	J6
Hidden Valley Dr	15100	POWY	1190	J4
Hidden Valley Pl	2500	SDGO	1227	H6
Hidden Valley Ranch Rd	-	POWY	1170	G1
Hidden Valley Rd	6100	OCSD	1067	D1
	-	SDCo	1127	A4
	2500	SDGO	1227	H6
Hidden View Ln	800	ESCN	1110	F7
	800	SDCo	1152	G6
Hidden Vista Dr	400	CHLV	1310	F5
Hidden Walk Ln	1400	SDCo	1027	J5
Hidden Wood Rd	14500	SDCo	1272	J5
Hideaway	-	SDGO	1210	C2
Hideaway Lake Rd	-	SDCo	1090	B1
Hideaway Ln	-	SDCo	1090	C1
Hideaway Pl	4400	SDCo	1271	D3
Hideaway Rd	700	SDCo	1156	E4
Hideaway Terr	-	VSTA	1107	H1
Hiel St	8700	SDCo	1291	A3
Hierba Dr	16900	SDGO	1170	B2
Hierba Pl	12000	SDGO	1170	B2
Higa Pl	12600	SDGO	1170	C4
Higgins St	-	CHLV	1330	J2
E Higgins St	1500	OCSD	1086	B6
W Higgins St	1300	OCSD	1086	B6
Higgins Ter	12200	SDCo	1232	A6
High Av	7500	SDGO	1227	F7
High Bluff Dr	13300	SDGO	1187	J4
High Country Ct	6700	SDGO	1250	D4
High Country Rd	24600	SDCo	1173	G5
High Crest Pl	1600	ESCN	1130	B4
High Ct	-	LMSA	1270	G5
High Glen Rd	18900	SDCo	1254	H7
High Hill Rd	7900	SDCo	1176	A2
	(See Page 1176)			
High Horse Hill	38500	SDCo	1300	A5
	(See Page 1300)			
High Knoll Rd	6500	SDGO	1248	H6
High Mead Cir	2700	SDCo	1067	J7
High Meadow Ct	8000	SDGO	1250	E3
High Meadow Ranch Ln	5800	SDCo	1155	G7
	5900	SDCo	1175	G1
	(See Page 1175)			
High Meadow Ranch Sp	6000	SDCo	1175	G1
	(See Page 1175)			
High Meadow Rd	12400	SDCo	1212	D4
High Mesa Ct	18200	SDGO	1149	H7
High Mountain Dr	-	SDCo	1089	D5
High Mountain Ln	27800	SDCo	1089	E5
High Park Ln	9400	SDGO	1189	E4
High Pine St	14500	POWY	1190	H5
High Point Truck Trl	-	SDCo	1033	A1
High Ranch Rd	11300	SDCo	1211	G6
High Ridge Av	1800	CRLB	1106	H6
High Rise Wy	9200	SNTE	1231	H5
High Rose Terr	8400	SDGO	1169	B4
High Sierra Rd	14000	POWY	1170	G3
High Society Wy	8000	SDCo	1149	A7
	8000	SDCo	1169	A1
High St	7500	LMSA	1270	G5
	1100	SDCo	1129	F2
High Time Ridge	8000	SDCo	1168	J2
High Trail Ct	-	CHLV	1311	G2
High Valley Rd	14400	POWY	1170	H6
High View Dr	3200	SDGO	1289	E1
High View Pt	2500	SDCo	1299	H4
	(See Page 1299)			
High Vista Dr	-	SDCo	1089	D5
High Winds Wy	8300	SDGO	1250	C4
Highbluff Av	1200	SNMS	1128	E6
Highbridge Rd	-	SDCo	1169	E3
Highdale Rd	9700	SNTE	1231	A4
Highfield Av	8900	LMSA	1271	A2
Highgate Ct	5900	LMSA	1250	G7
Highgate Ln	7700	LMSA	1250	G7
Highgrove Dr	1500	SDCo	1130	E5
Highland Av	900	DLMR	1187	G5
	300	ELCJ	1251	F6
	4700	LMSA	1270	H3
	-	NATC	1289	J7
	2400	NATC	1309	J3
	4500	SDGO	1269	H4
Highland Cove	-	SDCo	1167	J7
Highland Ct	15800	SOLB	1187	G1
Highland Cv	-	SOLB	1187	G2
Highland Dr	2200	CRLB	1106	F3
	3500	SDCo	1156	D1
	1900	SDCo	1167	J6
	1600	SOLB	1167	J7
	1000	SOLB	1187	G1
	800	VSTA	1087	F5
Highland Glen Wy	4200	SDCo	1271	C3
Highland Heights Ct	-	SDCo	1273	C7
Highland Heights Ln	1100	SDCo	1109	E7
Highland Heights Rd	-	SDCo	1273	B7
Highland Hills Dr	19200	SDCo	1151	J2
Highland Meadow Ct	-	SDCo	1171	F1
Highland Mesa Dr	18300	SDCo	1151	B4
Highland Oaks Ct	300	SDCo	1047	F5
Highland Oaks Ln	300	SDCo	1047	F6
Highland Oaks St	4400	SDCo	1047	F5
Highland Park	700	SDCo	1027	G6
Highland Pl	300	ESCN	1130	C1
Highland Ranch Rd	14500	SDGO	1190	A1
Highland St	600	ESCN	1130	C2
Highland Trails Dr	-	SDCo	1151	D4
Highland Valley Ct	-	SDCo	1172	B3
Highland Valley Rd	15200	SDCo	1150	H3
	16400	SDCo	1151	C3
	16700	SDCo	1171	D1
	18800	SDCo	1172	A2
	12800	SDGO	1150	C5
Highland View Glen	2000	ESCN	1109	C3
Highlander Dr	-	SDCo	1171	F1
Highlands Blvd	3100	SDCo	1271	D6
Highlands Crest Wy	15400	SDCo	1151	A3
Highlands Pl	13400	SDGO	1188	F4
Highlands Ranch Cir	17800	POWY	1150	D7
Highlands Ranch Pl	17900	POWY	1150	E7
Highlands Ranch Rd	13400	POWY	1150	E7
Highlands Ranch Ter	17900	POWY	1150	E7
Highlands Ter	13700	POWY	1170	F5
Highlands View Rd	1800	SDCo	1234	D7
Highlands Village Pl	7800	SDGO	1189	A4
Highlands West Dr	2000	SDCo	1129	F7
Highlands Wy	3000	SDCo	1271	D6
Highline Trl	100	SDCo	1252	J3
Highplace Dr	5900	SDGO	1250	C4
Highridge Dr	1500	OCSD	1087	D4
Highridge Rd	1600	SDCo	1291	E2
	-	SNTE	1230	F7
Highsmith Ln	8800	SDGO	1250	J4
Hightop Ter	9200	SDCo	1231	H5
Hightree Ln	7300	SDGO	1290	G5
Hightree Pl	400	SDGO	1290	G5
Highview Ln	2300	SDCo	1291	B1
Highview Trl	2200	SDCo	1108	D2
N Highway 101	100	ENCT	1147	B5
Highwood Av	7800	LMSA	1270	H4
Highwood Dr	-	ELCJ	1251	A3
	8600	SDGO	1250	J3
Higley Wy	600	OCSD	1066	G7
Higuera Av	800	CALX	6680	E1
Hihill Wy	200	ELCJ	1251	C6
Hijos Wy	10800	SDGO	1249	H1
Hike Ln	13500	SDGO	1189	E4
Hiker Hill Rd	9500	SDGO	1189	E4
Hikers Trail Dr	1500	CHLV	1311	H7
Hikers Trail Wy	2400	CHLV	1311	H7
Hilary Dr	-	SDCo	1274	B6
Hilbert Dr	600	SDCo	997	G7
Hilcorte Dr	1600	SDCo	1109	D6
	1500	SNMS	1109	D6

34 INDEX
Hilda Rd

San Diego County Street Index

INDEX 34
Hyacinth Rd
SAN DIEGO CO.

STREET
Block City Map# Grid

Hilda Rd
5000 SDGO 1268 F2
Hildale Cir
- VSTA 1087 H7
Hile Ln
1900 SDCo 1028 A3
Hilery Rd
- SDCo 1274 A5
Hilger St
1300 SDGO 1290 E2
Hill Av
- SDCo 1027 F5
N Hill Av
400 SDCo 1027 F2
S Hill Av
1400 SDCo 1027 F4
Hill Country Dr
12300 POWY 1190 C6
Hill Ct
300 SDCo 1027 F5
Hill Dr
2600 NATC 1290 B7
400 VSTA 1087 D7
Hill Ln
9500 SDCo 1236 A2
Hill Ranch Dr
5000 SDCo 1047 F7
Hill St
1300 ELCJ 1251 D7
4400 SDGO 1287 J2
3400 SDGO 1288 A2
300 SDGO 1350 G4
200 SNMS 1129 A1
200 SOLB 1167 E7
S Hill St
0 OCSD 1106 A1
Hill Ter
100 SDCo 1149 D3
Hill Valley Dr
3000 SDCo 1129 C2
Hill Valley Rd
- SDCo 1129 C2
Hillandale Ct
6000 SDGO 1250 C4
Hillandale Dr
7900 SDGO 1250 C3
Hillbrae Ct
- SDGO 1208 F3
Hillcreek Ln
9600 SNTE 1231 F4
Hillcreek Rd
10800 SNTE 1231 F4
Hillcreek Wy
9500 SNTE 1231 F5
Hillcrest Av
8400 LMSA 1270 J2
25700 SDCo 1109 F2
Hillcrest Cir
3400 CRLB 1106 G4
Hillcrest Dr
- ENCT 1147 B2
- SDCo 1070 D2
600 SDCo 1107 H3
- SDCo 1234 G6
Hillcrest Ln
700 SDCo 1027 G1
200 SDCo 1152 J6
Hillcrest Pl
900 OCSD 1086 C5
800 SDCo 1027 J1
Hillcrest Scenic Ln
1700 ENCT 1147 A2
Hillcrest Terr
800 SDCo 1027 H1
Hillcrest View Ln
1000 SDCo 1027 H1
Hilldale Rd
2200 OCSD 1086 C6
- SDCo 1070 D3
4000 SDGO 1269 G2
Hilleary Park Pl
13500 POWY 1190 E4
Hilleary Pl
13600 POWY 1190 F4
Hillero Ct
17300 SDGO 1170 B1
Hillery Dr
8600 SDGO 1209 C4
Hillfield Ct
900 OCSD 1086 E2
Hillgreen Wy
1000 SNMS 1109 B6
Hillgrove Dr
6400 SDGO 1250 D7
Hillhaven Dr
- SNMS 1128 B1
Hillhaven Rd
900 SDCo 1130 C4
Hillman Wy
9100 SDCo 1231 H6
Hillmar Trl
13600 SDGO 1188 H3
Hillndale Wy
14400 POWY 1190 E2
Hillock Pl
500 ENCT 1147 H5
Hillpark Ln
900 SDCo 1027 H1
Hillpoint Ct
12400 SDCo 1090 B1
Hillpointe Row
6000 SDGO 1248 B2

Hillridge Ln
2600 SDCo 1271 D7
Hillrise Rd
1900 SDCo 1048 A5
Hills Lane Cir
400 ELCJ 1251 D5
Hills Lane Dr
400 ELCJ 1251 D5
Hillsboro Ct
2800 CRLB 1107 A4
Hillsboro St
7000 SDGO 1250 B5
Hillsborough Cir
1500 CHLV 1331 D1
Hillsdale Ln
1700 SDCo 1272 B3
Hillsdale Rd
1900 SDCo 1272 C3
Hillside Ct
300 VSTA 1087 H5
Hillside Dr
- CHLV 1311 D3
4500 CRLB 1106 H6
7900 LMSA 1270 H2
1500 SDCo 1047 J2
9400 SDCo 1129 C6
800 SDCo 1156 D1
9200 SDCo 1271 B5
14100 SDCo 1292 J2
(See Page 1292)
7800 SDGO 1227 G6
Hillside Ln
- OCSD 1106 C2
3400 SDCo 1047 J2
Hillside Pl
200 SDCo 1252 H4
Hillside Ter
500 VSTA 1087 H5
Hillside View Ct
29800 SDCo 1069 A5
Hillside Wy
1300 ELCJ 1251 D6
600 SNMS 1129 B1
Hillslake Dr
2200 ELCJ 1251 B2
Hillslope Av
8800 SDCo 1290 J3
Hillsmont Dr
1500 ELCJ 1251 C5
Hillsmont Pl
400 ELCJ 1251 D5
Hillstar Ln
- SDCo 1070 D2
Hillstone Av
1500 ESCN 1129 G7
Hillsview Rd
600 ELCJ 1251 D4
Hilltop Cir
15200 POWY 1170 B6
Hilltop Ct
- CHLV 1330 E2
Hilltop Dr
100 CHLV 1310 C4
1400 CHLV 1330 E3
3600 LMGR 1270 H5
- SDCo 1070 D3
1500 SDCo 1271 J1
4400 SDGO 1289 H3
5200 SDGO 1290 B3
Hilltop Ln
1800 ENCT 1147 G5
Hilltop Pl
13400 SDCo 1070 D2
Hilltop St
- CRLB 1107 B6
Hilltop Terr
13400 SDCo 1070 D2
Hilltop View Ct
30800 SDCo 1091 A2
Hilltop Wy
- SDGO 1270 B1
Hillvale Av
- SDCo 1231 H5
Hillvale Ln
9300 SDCo 1231 H5
Hillview Ct
1300 CRLB 1106 F6
Hillview Dr
- SDCo 1070 D3
4500 SDCo 1271 E3
Hillview Ln
100 OCSD 1107 D2
Hillview Wy
3700 OCSD 1107 E3
Hillward St
600 ESCN 1110 C6
Hillway Dr
400 VSTA 1088 A6
Hillyer St
- CRLB 1107 B7
Hilmen Dr
300 SOLB 1167 F6
Hilmen Pl
400 SOLB 1167 F7
Hilmer Dr
9400 LMSA 1251 B7
Hilo Dr
1700 VSTA 1107 J3
Hilo Glen
1100 ESCN 1109 E6
Hilo Wy
400 SDCo 1108 A2

Hilo Wy
500 VSTA 1107 J2
Hilton Head Ct
1600 SDCo 1272 B5
Hilton Head Glen
2200 ESCN 1109 D4
Hilton Head Pl
2300 SDCo 1272 B5
Hilton Head Rd
2000 SDCo 1272 B4
Hilton Hed Rd
2200 CHLV 1311 G5
Hilton Pl
7000 SDGO 1248 J4
Himalaya Dr
- SNMS 1128 B1
Hime Rd
1100 ImCo 6559 A7
Himmer Ct
1600 CHLV 1331 F2
Hines St
- SDGO 1288 A4
Hinrichs Wy
1300 ESCN 1130 D2
Hinsdale St
9700 SNTE 1231 F4
Hinson Pl
4600 SDGO 1270 B3
Hinterland Dr
- SDCo 1169 B2
Hinton Dr
9500 SNTE 1231 E4
Hiram Wy
10000 SDCo 1232 C3
Hires Wy
2900 SDGO 1350 E4
Hirsch Rd
9700 SNTE 1231 B4
Hiser Ln
8700 SNTE 1230 G7
Hispano Dr
16400 SDGO 1170 B4
Hitachi Wy
900 CHLV 1311 G4
Hitching Post Dr
1100 OCSD 1067 D7
Hitching Post Ln
- CHLV 1311 H5
Hitching Post Rd
800 VSTA 1107 H2
Hitching Post Wy
- SNTE 1231 C2
Hito Ct
9500 SDGO 1189 E7
Hitt Dr
1700 ELCJ 1271 G1
Hixson Av
1800 SDGO 1289 H1
Hobart St
6200 SDGO 1270 C2
Hobbit Ln
2400 SDCo 1028 B2
Hobble Ln
10800 SDCo 1271 G7
Hobbs St
- CHLV 1330 J3
Hoberg Rd
2300 SDCo 1078 F2
(See Page 1078)
Hockmuth Av
- SDGO 1268 F6
Hodges Rd
1300 OCSD 1087 E2
Hodson St
6000 SDGO 1249 J7
Hofer Dr
2100 SDGO 1350 A1
Hoffer Rd
1200 ImCo 6559 H6
Hoffing Av
8800 SDGO 1249 C6
Hoffman Av
7100 LMSA 1270 E5
Hoffman Ln
9800 SNTE 1231 C4
Hoffman St
900 SDGO 1269 B4
Hogan Ridge Ln
14400 SDCo 1070 G7
Hogan Wy
2300 OCSD 1106 H2
Hohokum Wy
11300 SDGO 1149 J7
Hoitt St
300 SDGO 1289 E4
Holabird St
6200 SDGO 1249 J7
Holborn Ct
10600 SNTE 1231 E3
Holborn St
10100 SNTE 1231 E3
Holcomb Ct
- SDCo 1067 A1
Holcombe Rd
- SDGO 1288 A5
Holden Rd
8500 SNTE 1231 A7
8500 SNTE 1251 A1
Holden Trails Rd
- SDCo 1231 G3

Holder Wy
10300 SDGO 1249 G2
Holderness Ln
- SDGO 1330 C7
Holdridge St
700 CALX 6620 G7
Holiday Ct
3700 CHLV 1330 E5
3200 SDGO 1228 A3
Holiday Wy
200 OCSD 1066 H7
Holland Gln
- ESCN 1109 G5
Holland Pl
12400 POWY 1190 C2
Holland Rd
12300 POWY 1190 B2
Hollenbeck Rd
200 SNMS 1108 D6
Hollencrest Rd
3400 SNMS 1108 D5
Holleyberry Dr
3300 SDCo 1108 E1
Holliday Ln
2400 LMGR 1270 F7
Hollingsworth Wy
10400 SDCo 1169 F3
Hollins Rd
1300 OCSD 1087 D1
Hollister St
400 SDGO 1330 B6
1800 SDGO 1350 B2
Hollow Ct
1500 SDCo 1272 A2
Hollow Glen Rd
1400 SDCo 1136 C7
Hollow Mesa Ct
7900 SDGO 1209 A2
Hollow Pl
1600 SDCo 1272 B2
Hollowbrook Ct
800 SNMS 1128 F6
Hollowglen Rd
700 OCSD 1067 B5
Hollowtree Dr
3300 OCSD 1086 D3
Holly Av
2100 ESCN 1110 C6
700 IMPB 1349 G2
25800 SDCo 1109 F1
Holly Brae Ln
3900 CRLB 1106 H5
Holly Fern Ct
- SDGO 1209 J2
Holly Fern Wy
- SDGO 1210 A2
Holly Leaf Ct
- SDCo 1169 D2
Holly Ln
4200 SDCo 1067 H5
500 SDCo 1108 D3
Holly Meadows
10700 SNTE 1231 E6
Holly Oak Ln
3300 ESCN 1130 H2
Holly Oak Wy
13600 POWY 1190 F2
Holly Rd
3000 SDCo 1234 D4
100 SDCo 1252 H3
Holly St
900 OCSD 1086 B6
4900 SDGO 1290 A4
Holly Tree Ln
13200 POWY 1190 E4
Holly Valley Dr
- SDCo 1068 E7
Holly Wy
- ESCN 1129 G1
3200 SDCo 1310 E5
Hollyberry Dr
- SDCo 1108 F1
Hollyberry Tr
3400 SDCo 1088 F7
Hollybrook Av
- CHLV 1311 D7
Hollycrest Ct
- SDGO 1208 G3
Hollyfield Ct
- SDGO 1188 B5
Hollyhill Rd
4300 SDCo 1068 H6
Hollyhock Av
1400 ESCN 1110 A6
Hollyhock Ct
800 CRLB 1127 A5
Hollyhock Ln
3800 NATC 1290 C6
Hollyhock Rd
9300 SDCo 1271 B4
Hollyridge Dr
600 ENCT 1167 G1
Hollywood Dr
2500 SDCo 1297 E6
(See Page 1297)
Holmby Wy
9200 SNTE 1231 A3
Holmgrove Dr
1200 SNMS 1128 F5
Holmwood Ln
300 SOLB 1167 F6

Holsofar Rd
8400 SDCo 1232 D7
Holstrom Pl
2300 SDGO 1270 D7
Holt Av
2000 ELCN 6499 E7
200 ELCN 6500 A7
Holt Cir
- ELCN 6499 D7
Holt St
8300 SDCo 1290 J5
Holton Rd
300 ImCo 6500 E5
Holtville Av
44600 SDCo 1321 G5
(See Page 1321)
Holzapple
700 SNMS 1108 J6
Home Av
800 CRLB 1106 E5
4400 SDGO 1269 J7
3900 SDGO 1289 G2
Homedale St
2700 SDGO 1310 E2
Homeland Pl
- SDGO 1269 A4
Homer St
3000 SDGO 1268 D6
Homesite Dr
2400 SDGO 1310 E1
Homestead Dr
- SDCo 1088 J6
Homestead Ln
0 RivC 999 F1
Homestead Pl
900 ESCN 1109 F7
Homeward Wy
700 SDCo 1234 C4
Homewood Pl
7600 LMSA 1270 G3
Hondo Ln
20700 SDCo 1275 A2
Hondo St
3600 SDGO 1270 A6
Honestidad Rd
1700 SDGO 1350 B3
Honey Bee Ln
35900 SDCo 1299 B3
(See Page 1299)
- VSTA 1107 F2
Honey Dr
2200 SDGO 1290 F7
Honey Hill Ranch Rd
3000 SDCo 1234 D6
Honey Hill Rd
1400 ELCJ 1251 D2
Honey Hill Ter
1500 ELCJ 1251 C2
Honey Lake Rd
- CHLV 1311 E5
Honey Ln
9100 SNTE 1231 B7
Honey Ridge
- SDGO 1208 B2
Honey Springs Rd
2400 SDCo 1294 E5
(See Page 1294)
1600 SDCo 1313 F1
(See Page 1313)
Honeybee St
2100 CHLV 1331 G1
Honeybell Ln
2400 ESCN 1110 C5
Honeybrook Av
16700 SDCo 1169 E3
Honeycomb Ct
100 ENCT 1147 H7
Honeycutt St
4000 SDGO 1248 B6
Honeydew Cir
700 VSTA 1087 J3
Honeyglen Dr
900 SNMS 1128 F2
Honeyoak Ln
2200 SDCo 1253 J1
Honeysuckle Ct
1600 ENCT 1147 G5
Honeysuckle Dr
900 SNMS 1128 E2
Honeysuckle Ln
900 CRLB 1127 A7
1400 SDGO 1290 C6
Honeysuckle Rd
1800 SDCo 1252 C3
Honeysuckle Wy
1100 ESCN 1109 J4
Honnell Wy
13800 SDCo 1292 G1
(See Page 1292)
Honor Ct
3100 SDCo 1079 C5
(See Page 1079)
Honors Ct
2900 SDGO 1228 B6
Honors Dr
5600 SDGO 1228 B6
Hontza Ct
- BRAW 6320 C2
(See Page 6320)
Hook Ct
3100 SDCo 1079 C5
(See Page 1079)

Hoop St
- SDGO 1288 A5
Hooper Blvd
- CORD 1329 E3
Hooper Ct
10100 SDGO 1249 G4
Hooper St
10100 SDGO 1249 G4
Hoosier Ln
- SDCo 1235 A5
Hoover Av
- NATC 1289 G7
1600 NATC 1309 H2
Hoover St
1100 CRLB 1106 G7
1200 ESCN 1110 A6
400 OCSD 1086 D6
Hope Av
2800 CRLB 1106 E5
Hope Ln
- ESCN 1129 F5
Hope St
800 ELCN 6500 A7
2600 OCSD 1087 C6
- SDCo 1172 D1
4000 SDGO 1270 E5
1600 SNMS 1128 E6
Hopedale Ct
6500 SDGO 1250 D6
Hopeland Ct
- CHLV 1311 B7
Hopi Path
3800 SDCo 1099 E2
(See Page 1099)
Hopi Pl
3300 SDGO 1248 C2
Hopkins Ln
9600 SDGO 1228 A1
Hopkins St
2500 SDGO 1310 D2
Hopper Av
1000 SDCo 1109 B5
Hopper Ln
15800 SDGO 1169 D4
Hopscotch Dr
1500 CHLV 1311 H7
Hopseed Ln
8500 SDGO 1189 C7
Horado Ct
16400 SDGO 1170 C3
Horado Rd
12200 SDGO 1170 B4
Horizon Ct
14300 POWY 1170 G4
1400 SNMS 1128 F6
Horizon Dr
4300 CRLB 1106 H7
200 ENCT 1147 G7
Horizon Hills Dr
200 ELCJ 1271 G2
11200 SDCo 1271 G2
Horizon Ln
200 OCSD 1107 D2
Horizon Pointe
- SDCo 1271 H1
Horizon Rdg
- SDCo 1251 H7
- SDCo 1271 H1
Horizon St
1000 CALX 6620 D7
Horizon View Dr
400 CHLV 1310 E5
22900 SDCo 1152 C2
23300 SDCo 1315 H4
(See Page 1315)
Horizon View Glen
- ESCN 1109 C3
Horizon Wy
2400 SDGO 1227 J3
Horizonte St
- IMPE 6439 D7
Horn Canyon Av
- CHLV 1311 J6
Hornbeam Glen
1500 ESCN 1130 A4
Hornbill Av
7600 SDGO 1269 A1
Hornblend St
1400 SDGO 1247 H6
2600 SDGO 1248 C5
Hornbuckle Dr
9400 SNTE 1231 B3
Horne Pl
900 OCSD 1106 C2
Horne Rd
200 ELCN 6559 H3
N Horne St
500 OCSD 1086 A6
S Horne St
100 OCSD 1086 B7
1900 OCSD 1106 D3
Horned Owl Rd
11500 SDCo 1212 C5
Horner St
7100 SDGO 1250 C6
Hornet Wy
2700 SDGO 1288 C1
Horning Hollow Ct
- SDCo 1089 B1
Horse Ranch Creek Rd
- SDCo 1028 H6

Horse Ridge Wy
5400 SDCo 1311 A2
Horseback Ln
- SDCo 1232 C5
Horsemans Ln
1800 SDCo 1167 J5
Horsemill Rd
1100 SDCo 1232 J7
- SDCo 1253 A1
Horseshoe Cir
700 VSTA 1107 G2
Horseshoe Ct
1700 CHLV 1311 C4
- IMPE 6439 F3
Horseshoe Ln
200 SNTE 1231 E5
Horseshoe Rd
700 SDCo 1058 G1
(See Page 1058)
Horseshoe Ridge Ct
10900 SDGO 1188 G7
Horseshoe Wy
1700 OCSD 1067 E7
Horsethief Canyon Rd
- SDCo 1255 H1
Hortensia St
4300 SDGO 1268 G5
Horton Av
3000 SDGO 1289 A1
Horton Cir
3900 SDCo 1310 G4
Horton Dr
6000 LMSA 1251 B6
Horton Rd
700 CHLV 1310 G4
3700 SDCo 1310 G4
Hosea Ct
- CALX 6620 G7
Hoska Dr
600 DLMR 1187 G5
Hoska Ln
- DLMR 1187 G5
Hoskings Ranch Rd
2800 SDCo 1135 E6
Hosmer St
400 ELCJ 1251 B5
Hosp Wy
1800 CRLB 1106 F4
Hospital Lp
- ImCo 6559 G5
Hotel Circle Ct
4400 SDGO 1268 J4
Hotel Circle N
- SDGO 1268 H4
Hotel Circle Pl N
2500 SDGO 1268 G4
Hotel Circle S
1800 SDGO 1268 G4
Hotspring Wy
- VSTA 1107 J7
Hottepaa Wy
- SDCo 1091 D3
Hotz St
500 SDCo 1290 J4
Houston St
3800 SDGO 1268 D5
Hovanec St
1600 SDGO 1290 E6
Hovenweep Ct
8400 SDGO 1189 B3
Hovland Sq
9900 SDGO 1209 H5
Hovley Rd
5000 ImCo 6259 H3
(See Page 6259)
Howard Av
300 ESCN 1129 F4
2300 SDGO 1269 D4
1600 SDGO 1350 D2
Howard Johnson Pl
5200 SDGO 1250 A7
Howard Rd
3900 SDCo 1100 C4
(See Page 1100)
Howard Ridge
18300 SDCo 1153 B7
Howe Ct
6900 SDGO 1268 J2
Howe Pl
600 ESCN 1129 J6
400 ESCN 1130 A6
Howe Rd
45400 SDGO 1209 D7
Howell Dr
5900 LMSA 1251 B6
Howell Heights Dr
400 ESCN 1129 G4
Howell St
2600 SDCo 1152 C7
Hoxie Ranch Pl
2500 SDCo 1068 D6
Hoxie Ranch Rd
29400 SDCo 1068 D6
Hoydale Row
11300 SDGO 1189 J3
Hoyt Park Dr
10000 SDGO 1209 G4
Hoyt St
1600 CHLV 1331 E2
Huaracha Ct
5300 SDGO 1249 H1

Hub Ct
1100 ELCJ 1251 D7
Hubbard Av
500 SDCo 1109 H6
Hubbard Pl
1600 ESCN 1109 J5
Hubbard Rd
600 SDCo 1319 H1
(See Page 1319)
Hubbard Spur Truck Trl
- SDCo 1313 E4
(See Page 1313)
Hubbert St
5200 OCSD 1087 E1
Hubbles Ln
8500 SNTE 1231 D7
Huber Ct
9700 SNTE 1231 B4
Hubner Rd
5500 SDGO 1270 B6
Huckleberry Ln
800 ESCN 1150 C3
- SDCo 1088 F2
Hudson Bay Terr
- SDGO 1290 B1
Hudson Dr
8500 SDGO 1250 J4
Hudson Ln
100 SDCo 1253 D1
Hudson Pl
6600 SDGO 1250 H4
Hue City Av
- SDGO 1268 F7
Huelva Ct
300 OCSD 1086 J4
Hueneme St
1200 SDGO 1268 G3
Huennekens St
9900 SDGO 1208 G5
Huerfano Av
4000 SDGO 1248 C3
Huerfano Ct
3200 SDGO 1248 C2
Huertero Dr
4600 SDCo 1271 F2
Huerto Pl
500 CHLV 1310 H5
Huey Ln
1700 SDCo 1254 A1
Huff Pl
- VSTA 1087 D7
Huff St
500 VSTA 1087 D7
100 VSTA 1107 D1
Huffstatler St
2500 SDCo 998 H4
Huggins St
4300 SDGO 1228 E4
Huggins Wy
4600 SDGO 1228 F4
Hughes Ct
3900 SDGO 1270 C5
Hughes Ln
900 SDCo 1047 H1
Hughes St
7500 LMGR 1290 G2
500 SDCo 1152 C6
6000 SDGO 1270 C5
Hugo St
3000 SDGO 1288 B2
Hulburd Grove Dr
9900 SDCo 1235 J1
Hull St
- SDGO 1287 J4
Hume Rd
9600 SNTE 1231 C4
Humiston Wy
23800 SDCo 1173 D2
Humming Bird Ct
- IMPE 6439 G4
Hummingbird Ct
700 SDCo 1252 E6
Hummingbird Hill
100 ENCT 1167 J1
Hummingbird Hill Ln
2400 SDCo 1027 H7
Hummingbird Ln
- OCSD 1086 H2
7900 SDGO 1249 B6
1400 VSTA 1088 B3
Hummingbird Rd
7100 CRLB 1127 D7
Hummingbird St
2300 CHLV 1331 H1
Hummingbird Wy
- CHLV 1331 G1
Hummock Dr
- CRLB 1107 C3
Hummock Ln
1800 ENCT 1147 H5
Humo Dr
13900 POWY 1190 G3
Humphrey Pl
- CHLV 1330 J2
1600 ESCN 1130 B4
Humphreys Rd
- SDGO 1308 A2
Huneck Dr
5700 LMSA 1251 B7
Hungry Hawk Ln
1400 SDCo 1130 F6

Hunrichs Wy
3000 SDGO 1248 C3
Hunsaker St
1700 OCSD 1106 D2
Hunt Rd
1100 SDCo 1251 J1
Huntalas Ln
2500 SDCo 1088 D6
2400 VSTA 1088 D6
Hunte Pkwy
- CHLV 1311 H2
1700 CHLV 1331 H1
Hunter Ct
300 SDCo 1233 E5
Hunter Dr
1800 SDCo 1099 F4
(See Page 1099)
Hunter Green Ct
11200 SDGO 1209 E2
Hunter Ln
300 SDCo 1233 F5
Hunter Pass
9000 SDCo 1233 E6
Hunter St
600 OCSD 1086 F2
200 SDCo 1152 E7
1100 SDCo 1172 E2
1100 SDGO 1268 J4
N Hunter St
400 SDCo 1152 D6
Hunters Av
1500 CHLV 1331 E1
Hunters Glen Av
1500 CHLV 1331 E1
Hunters Glen Dr
- SDGO 1208 E2
Hunters Rd
9400 SDCo 1271 C1
Hunters Ridge Pl
800 CHLV 1311 J3
10400 SDCo 1149 E7
Hunters Ridge Rd
17700 SDCo 1149 F7
Hunthaven Rd
7700 SDGO 1290 G4
Huntingride Cir
11200 SNTE 1231 G5
Huntington Av
9100 SDGO 1249 D6
Huntington Ct
15100 POWY 1170 G7
Huntington Dr
6300 CRLB 1127 G3
Huntington Gate Dr
15000 POWY 1170 F7
Huntington Point Rd
- CHLV 1311 F3
Huntington Rd
1100 SNMS 1128 B3
Huntley Rd
- SDCo 1029 C3
Hunza Hill Ct
13100 SDCo 1090 D2
Hunza Hill Ter
13200 SDCo 1090 D2
Hunza Hill Terr
13200 SDCo 1090 D2
Hurd Ct
6200 SDGO 1228 D5
Hurd Pl
- SDGO 1269 A5
Hurlbut Pl
3300 SDGO 1249 B4
Hurlbut St
8500 SDGO 1249 C4
Hurley Dr
4100 LMSA 1270 H4
Huron Av
4700 SDGO 1248 F6
Huron Ct
5300 OCSD 1087 E1
Huron St
9700 SDCo 1291 D3
Hursley St
400 ELCJ 1251 J6
Hurstdale Av
1000 ENCT 1167 E3
Husted Pl
- SDCo 1070 H7
Huston Rd
100 IMPE 6439 H7
Hutchins Landing
16900 SDCo 1169 E2
Hutchinson St
300 SDCo 1067 H7
2200 SDCo 1087 H2
Hutton Av
6400 SDGO 1310 F1
Huula Dr
3100 OCSD 1086 D3
Huxley St
4600 SDGO 1248 E7
Hyacinth Cir
6700 CRLB 1126 J4
Hyacinth Dr
3600 SDGO 1268 C6
Hyacinth Hills Wy
13500 SDGO 1188 F3
Hyacinth Rd
2300 SDCo 1233 J5

STREET
Block City Map# Grid

Hyacinth Wy
200 OCSD 1086 J2
Hyades Wy
10900 SDGO 1209 D3
Hyanoak Ct
22400 SDCo 1255 D7
Hyatt Av
3500 OCSD 1086 F4
Hyatt St
7200 SDGO 1248 J7
E Hyatt St
7100 SDGO 1248 J7
Hybeth Dr
7000 LMSA 1270 E4
Hyde Park Dr
6900 SDGO 1250 E5
Hyde Park Ln
2200 SDCo 1297 J6
(See Page 1297)
Hydra Ct
- SNMS 1108 D5
Hydra Ln
8200 SDGO 1209 B3
- SNMS 1108 D5
Hydrangea Ct
4300 SDGO 1350 G1
Hye Wy
- SDCo 1069 C4
Hygeia Av
1400 ENCT 1147 B3
Hygeia Ct
200 ENCT 1147 B4
Hyman Pl
6500 SDGO 1310 E1
Hymettus Av
1400 ENCT 1147 B3
Hypatia Wy
1900 SDGO 1227 G5
Hypoint Av
2800 ESCN 1110 E6
Hypoint Pl
200 ESCN 1110 F6

I

I Av
200 CORD 1288 H5
500 NATC 1289 J7
700 NATC 1309 J1
2300 NATC 1310 A3
I Esplanade
600 CHLV 1330 A1
E I Rd
- CORD 1288 F6
I Romero Ct
- CALX 6680 J1
I St
200 BRAW 6319 J2
(See Page 6319)
1500 BRAW 6320 B2
(See Page 6320)
300 CHLV 1310 B7
700 CHLV 1329 J1
600 CHLV 1330 A1
600 SDCo 1152 H6
- SDGO 1290 A4
E I St
100 CHLV 1310 E6
- ENCT 1167 C1
W I St
400 ENCT 1167 B1
I Yturralde St
- CALX 6620 J6
Ia Roca Grande
10100 SDCo 1069 D1
Ian Wy
8600 SNTE 1231 D7
Iavelli Wy
12200 POWY 1190 D6
Iberia Pl
11600 SDGO 1170 A3
Ibex Ct
14600 SDGO 1189 C1
Ibis Ct
3900 SDGO 1268 J5
Ibis Pl
7000 CRLB 1127 E6
Ibis St
3900 SDGO 1268 J5
Ibis Wy
4400 OCSD 1087 A3
Ibiza Pl
5600 SDCo 1067 H1
Ibsen St
3000 SDGO 1268 D6
Icaria Wy
4900 OCSD 1107 F5
Icarus Ln
12300 POWY 1190 C1
Ice Skate Pl
10900 SDGO 1209 E3
Ida Av
500 SOLB 1167 G7
600 SOLB 1187 G1
Ida St
7400 LMGR 1270 G7
Idaho Av
400 ESCN 1130 B4
1000 SDCo 1130 C3
Idaho Ln
1500 SDCo 1130 C3
Idaho St
4600 SDGO 1269 D3
Iden Glen
300 ESCN 1129 H2
Iderdell Ln
8200 LMGR 1270 H6
Idle Hour Ln
2600 SDGO 1227 H1
Idlewild Ln
300 OCSD 1106 C2
Idlewild Wy
3400 SDGO 1248 D2
Idyl Dr
13200 SDCo 1232 C5
Idyl Pl
9200 SDCo 1232 C5
Idyllwild Ln
8900 SDGO 1251 A3
Idyllwild Wy
900 SNMS 1128 E5
Iguala Ct
100 SOLB 1167 H4
Ildica Ct
2100 SDCo 1291 A1
Ildica St
8300 LMGR 1290 J1
9100 SDCo 1291 A1
Ildica Wy
2000 SDCo 1291 A1
Ilene St
12900 POWY 1190 D4
Ilex Av
2100 SDGO 1350 B2
Ilexey Av
1300 SDGO 1350 G1
Illahee Ct
23000 SDCo 1255 F5
Illahee Dr
23300 SDCo 1255 F5
Illchaa
- SDCo 1234 J2
Illerongis Rd
13900 SDCo 1292 F3
(See Page 1292)
Illinois St
4400 SDGO 1269 E4
Illion St
1800 SDGO 1268 F1
Illmum Cir
- SDCo 1235 B4
Illumina Wy
- SDGO 1228 E3
Illuminado
- SDGO 1168 J6
Imhoff Rd
- SDCo 1085 G4
Imogene Av
2100 SDGO 1350 A1
Imogene Wy
- SDCo 1152 J4
Impala Dr
2400 CRLB 1127 E1
Imperial Av
600 BRAW 6319 J2
(See Page 6319)
- CALX 6680 F2
800 ELCN 6499 F7
- IMPE 6439 F4
7100 LMGR 1290 F2
4300 SDCo 1289 H4
1900 SDGO 1289 D4
6300 SDGO 1290 C3
N Imperial Av
700 BRAW 6259 J7
(See Page 6259)
1300 ELCN 6499 F4
- IMPE 6439 F3
Imperial Av E
1600 CALX 6620 F7
Imperial Av W
- CALX 6620 F7
Imperial Beach Blvd
100 IMPB 1349 E1
Imperial Business Park Dr
- IMPE 6499 E2
Imperial Dr
300 ESCN 1109 F5
4000 SDCo 1156 E2
Impervious Pl
2300 SDCo 1253 F2
Impink Pl
3100 SDCo 1292 H1
(See Page 1292)
Impressionist Dr
1900 CHLV 1311 G2
1900 CHLV 1331 E1
Inca Rd
3800 SDCo 1099 E1
(See Page 1099)
Incapa Rd
15400 SDCo 1176 D4
(See Page 1176)
Inception Wy
- SDGO 1269 B1
Inchon Ct
1500 CORD 1309 D6
Inchon Rd
- CORD 1309 B1
Inclinado Dr
- ELCJ 1251 C1
Incredible Ln
- SDCo 1070 A7
Independence Wy
1500 VSTA 1088 B3
India Ln
200 SDCo 1028 G3
India St
3700 SDGO 1268 H6
1700 SDGO 1288 J2
600 SDGO 1289 A3
Indian Bend Dr
- SDCo 1050 H6
Indian Canyon Ln
13900 POWY 1170 F1
Indian Creek Dr
900 ELCJ 1251 E5
Indian Creek Ct
1200 CHLV 1311 H6
Indian Creek Ln
9900 SDCo 1232 G2
Indian Creek Pl
1300 CHLV 1311 H6
Indian Creek Rd
- SDCo 1090 F2
Indian Creek Wy
- SDCo 1089 D4
Indian Ct
5100 OCSD 1066 J4
Indian Fig Dr
- SDGO 1270 C6
Indian Head Ct
- SDCo 1173 E5
Indian Head Ranch Rd
900 SDCo 1058 G2
(See Page 1058)
Indian Hill Pl
8700 SDCo 1069 A6
Indian Hill Rd
8600 SDCo 1068 J6
Indian Hill Wy
6500 OCSD 1047 E7
Indian Lore Ct
11100 SDGO 1149 H7
Indian Mills Ln
3200 SDCo 1272 D5
Indian Oak Trl
18500 SDCo 1051 G3
Indian Oaks Rd
19800 SDCo 1152 C2
Indian Palms Ct
900 CHLV 1311 G4
Indian Peak Trl
13600 POWY 1190 F1
Indian Pl
2000 ESCN 1110 C7
Indian Potrero 2
- SDCo 1197 F7
(See Page 1197)
Indian Ridge Rd
8400 SDCo 1129 A4
E Indian Rock Rd
300 VSTA 1087 H4
W Indian Rock Rd
100 VSTA 1087 G4
Indian Springs Dr
13700 SDCo 1292 G1
(See Page 1292)
Indian Springs Rd
14500 POWY 1190 H1
Indian Summer Ct
1500 SNMS 1109 C5
Indian Summer Pl
700 SNMS 1109 C5
Indian Summer Rd
1500 SNMS 1109 D6
Indian Trail Wy
6500 OCSD 1047 E7
Indian Trl
12800 POWY 1170 D4
Indian Valley Rd
- SDCo 1293 G1
Indian View Dr
6100 OCSD 1047 D7
Indian Wells Ct
8800 SNTE 1230 J5
Indian Wy
- SDCo 1234 J4
3700 SDGO 1248 E2
Indiana Av
200 ELCJ 1251 F5
N Indiana Av
200 VSTA 1087 H6
S Indiana Av
100 VSTA 1087 H6
Indiana St
3700 SDGO 1269 C6
Indianapolis Av
2500 SDGO 1270 A7
Indigo Blossom Ln
- SDGO 1208 E4
Indigo Canyon Rd
600 CHLV 1330 H1
Indigo Dr
2500 SDCo 1272 D2
Indigo Ln
1700 SDCo 1099 F3
(See Page 1099)
Indigo St
- OCSD 1107 F4
Indigo Wy
10600 SDCo 1169 F2
Indio
- SDCo 1232 D7
Indio Wy
6700 SDGO 1208 H3
Indus Wy
2200 SNMS 1128 B6
Industrial Av
1500 ESCN 1129 F3
Industrial Blvd
1100 CHLV 1330 A3
Industrial Ct
3300 SDGO 1208 A4
2100 VSTA 1108 A4
Industrial Ln
- LMSA 1270 H1
Industrial Pl
900 ELCJ 1251 E5
Industrial St
200 SNMS 1128 J1
Industrial Wy
300 SDCo 1027 G2
Industry Rd
500 IMPE 6499 E1
12100 SDCo 1232 A3
Industry St
2300 OCSD 1086 E7
2300 VSTA 1107 J6
Industry Wy
- ELCN 6500 B7
- IMPE 6499 E1
Inez St
3500 SDGO 1288 A2
Inez Wy
- OCSD 1086 H3
Ingalls St
4000 SDGO 1268 J5
Ingelow St
3100 SDGO 1288 B1
E Ingersoll St
2400 SDGO 1249 A7
W Ingersoll St
2400 SDGO 1249 A7
Ingleside Av
4200 SDGO 1268 G5
Ingleside Pl
600 ESCN 1109 H6
Ingleton Av
2500 CRLB 1127 F3
Inglewood Ct
800 VSTA 1087 H5
Ingraham St
4800 SDGO 1247 J5
4100 SDGO 1248 A7
- SDGO 1268 B2
Ingram Av
- ImCo 6560 B7
Ingram St
- CHLV 1330 H3
Ingrid Av
2100 SDGO 1350 A1
Ingulf Pl
2500 SDGO 1248 F7
Ingulf St
4100 SDGO 1248 E7
Inkopah St
100 CHLV 1330 E1
Inman Ct
2500 SDGO 1248 H7
Inman St
6300 SDGO 1248 H7
Innis Pt
11800 SDGO 1209 C1
Innovation Dr
15100 SDGO 1170 A6
Innovation Wy
- CRLB 1127 F2
Innovative Dr
- SDGO 1351 C1
Innsdale Av
8800 SDCo 1290 J3
Innsdale Ln
8500 SDGO 1290 J4
Inuit Av
3200 SDGO 1248 C2
Inspiration Dr
1200 SDGO 1247 G2
Inspiration Ln
600 ESCN 1150 C3
Inspiration Point Rd
400 SDCo 1156 F3
Inspiration Wy
6100 SDGO 1247 G2
Integrity Ct
29400 SDCo 1068 E7
Integrity Wy
3200 SDCo 1048 A2
Interlachen Terr
14700 SDCo 1090 H4
Intermezzo St
12600 SDGO 1188 C6
International Ln
- SDGO 1227 J1
International Rd
1800 SDGO 1350 C3
Interprise Dr
- ELCJ 1251 J5
Intrepid Ct
900 SOLB 1187 H1
Intrepid Wy
- VSTA 1107 G5
Inverary Dr
1700 SDCo 1272 B5
Inverlochy Dr
- SDCo 1027 G6
Inverness Av
- CHLV 1311 H6
- SDCo 1090 H5
Inverness Ct
4700 CRLB 1107 A5
2700 SDGO 1227 J4
Inverness Dr
2700 CRLB 1107 A5
4400 OCSD 1066 H7
2700 SDGO 1227 J4
Inverness Rd
9000 SNTE 1230 H6
Inverness Wy
3100 SDCo 1273 E5
Invierno Dr
11600 SDGO 1250 A2
Inwood Dr
9200 SNTE 1231 A6
Inyaha Ln
2600 SDGO 1227 J2
Inyo Ln
6400 SDGO 1290 E7
Iola Wy
12800 POWY 1190 A5
Iona Ct
500 ESCN 1110 D6
Iona Dr
800 SDGO 1290 C3
Ionian St
1500 SDGO 1349 J2
1700 SDGO 1350 A2
Iota Pl
5600 LMSA 1250 J7
Iowa Hill Ct
- CHLV 1311 C7
Iowa St
700 SDCo 1027 F1
4600 SDGO 1269 E3
600 SDGO 1330 A7
Ipai Ct
11000 SDGO 1169 H1
Ipai Waaypuk Trl
13100 POWY 1190 D5
Ipanema Ln
2100 VSTA 1088 D5
Ipava Dr
14400 POWY 1190 H2
Ira Wy
- VSTA 1107 E1
Ireland Ln
13100 SDGO 1189 B4
Irene Ct
8000 SDCo 1252 A2
Irene Rd
600 OCSD 1067 B5
Iris
- SDGO 1248 C6
Iris Av
- CALX 6620 J7
500 IMPB 1349 G2
2900 SDGO 1350 D2
Iris Ct
1000 CRLB 1127 B6
Iris Gln
- ESCN 1109 G5
Iris Ln
14000 POWY 1190 G2
N Iris Ln
2300 ESCN 1109 G4
2000 SDCo 1109 G5
S Iris Ln
1700 SDCo 1109 G6
Iris St
- SDCo 1086 A4
5100 SNTE 1231 G7
Iris Wy
1900 ESCN 1110 B6
Irisdale Ct
1900 ENCT 1147 H7
Irish Eyes Ln
16400 SDCo 1169 A2
Irish Oaks Rd
- SDCo 1090 H2
Iron Dr
200 VSTA 1087 F7
Iron Gate Ln
400 CHLV 1311 J1
Iron Horse Ct
- SDCo 1128 G3
Iron Horse Dr
900 SNMS 1128 G3
Iron Horse Pl
- CHLV 1311 J3
Iron Mountain Dr
17000 POWY 1191 D3
Iron Mountain Tktl
- SDCo 1191 D3
Iron Springs Pl
17100 SDCo 1156 E7
Iron Springs Rd
16100 SDCo 1156 C7
Iron Springs Wy
35100 SDCo 1156 E7
Iron View Row
12100 SDGO 1170 A4
Iron Wheel St
1000 SNTE 1231 F6
Iron Wood Ct
2700 CHLV 1311 J7
Iron Wood View
- SDCo 1089 B3
Ironbark Wy
13200 POWY 1190 E2
Irongate Ln
9200 SDGO 1209 D2
Ironstone Ct
16600 SDCo 1171 E3
Ironwood Av
10600 SNTE 1231 D2
Ironwood Ct
9900 SDGO 1209 J4
Ironwood Ln
4500 SDCo 1099 F3
(See Page 1099)
Ironwood Pl
3300 OCSD 1086 H7
9900 SDGO 1209 J4
Ironwood Rd
2700 ImCo 6439 C5
10900 SDGO 1209 H5
Iroquois Av
4800 SDGO 1248 F6
Iroquois Wy
3000 SDGO 1248 F6
Irving Av
1800 SDGO 1289 C4
Irving Ct
900 NATC 1310 A3
Irving Ln
- SDGO 1169 D3
Irvington Av
9300 SDGO 1249 E6
Irwin Av
5200 SDGO 1250 B5
Irwin St
1600 CHLV 1331 E2
Isaac St
9200 SNTE 1231 F6
Isabel St
2200 SDGO 1289 J1
Isabella Av
1100 CORD 1288 H7
Isabella Dr
3200 OCSD 1106 J1
Isabella Wy
1300 VSTA 1088 A4
Isham Springs Ct
- SDCo 1291 E1
Ishihara Rd
1600 VSTA 1087 J3
Isidore St
700 OCSD 1067 B5
Isla Buena Vista
- SDCo 1293 D1
Isla De La Gaita
1700 SDGO 1350 E3
Isla Del Campanero
1800 SDGO 1350 E3
Isla Del Carmen Wy
8900 SDGO 1350 D3
Isla Del Rey
23600 SDCo 1173 D2
Isla Vista Dr
3300 SDGO 1270 A6
Island Av
2000 SDGO 1289 C4
Island Breeze Ln
- SDGO 1330 H6
Island Ct
800 SDGO 1267 J2
Island Ketch
- SDGO 1351 A1
Island Pine Wy
- SDCo 1169 D2
Island Shore Wy
- SNMS 1128 A2
Island View Ln
- ENCT 1147 F7
Island View Wy
- VSTA 1128 A1
Islander St
300 OCSD 1086 E6
Isle Dr
4000 CRLB 1106 G6
Isle Royal Ct
5000 OCSD 1087 C1
Isle Wy
1100 CHLV 1311 B7
Isleta Av
4600 SDGO 1248 C1
Isleworth Av
10400 SDGO 1209 D4
Isocoma St
12700 SDGO 1189 D5
Isom Ct
- CHLV 1331 A1
Israel Ct
- CHLV 1330 J3
Isthmus Ct
800 SDGO 1267 J2
Isthmus Dr
- CRLB 1126 J6
Isthmus Wy
300 OCSD 1086 B6
Italia Wy
3400 OCSD 1106 J2
Ithaca Ct
900 CHLV 1311 D5
Ithaca Dr
1800 VSTA 1107 F5
Ithaca Pl
5800 SDGO 1228 D6
Ithaca St
1800 CHLV 1311 D5
3400 SDGO 1228 D6
Ito Ct
6300 SDGO 1290 D4
Iturralde Ct
- CALX 6620 H7
Itzama Dr
10600 SDCo 1271 F3
Itzamna Rd
10600 SDCo 1271 F3
Ivanho St
9700 SDCo 1291 D3
Ivanhoe Av
7700 SDGO 1227 F6
Ivanhoe Av E
7700 SDGO 1227 F6
Ivanhoe Ranch Rd
- SDCo 1272 D5
Iversen Point Wy
700 OCSD 1066 F7
Iverson St
8500 SDGO 1249 C5
Ives Ct
6800 SDGO 1268 J2
Ivey Ranch Rd
1200 OCSD 1086 J4
Ivey Vista Wy
- OCSD 1086 J4
N Ivory Av
100 ELCJ 1252 A5
S Ivory Av
100 ELCJ 1252 A5
Ivory Coast Dr
8500 SDGO 1209 C4
Ivory Ct
1300 ELCJ 1252 A5
Ivory Gull Wy
200 SNMS 1129 A1
Ivory Pl
2200 CRLB 1127 F5
Ivy Ct
500 CHLV 1330 G1
Ivy Dell Ln
10300 SDCo 1109 F3
Ivy Glen Dr
1400 ENCT 1167 G1
Ivy Hill Dr
- SDGO 1189 H7
Ivy Hill Rd
- SNMS 1128 B6
Ivy Ln
2300 ESCN 1110 D6
1100 IMPB 1349 H1
300 SDCo 1027 F2
9700 SDCo 1149 E2
9200 SDCo 1271 B7
500 SDGO 1269 A6
100 VSTA 1087 H6
Ivy Pass Cres
16900 SDCo 1173 D2
Ivy Rd
1900 OCSD 1106 E2
Ivy St
900 BRAW 6319 J2
(See Page 6319)
1200 BRAW 6320 B2
(See Page 6320)
7000 CRLB 1127 A6
1400 ESCN 1109 H7
400 SDCo 1027 F2
- SDCo 1271 C7
200 SDGO 1289 A1
N Ivy St
1200 ESCN 1109 H7
1000 ESCN 1129 J1
S Ivy St
200 ESCN 1129 J2
W Ivy St
1000 SDGO 1288 J1
Ivy Terr
300 SDCo 1027 F2
Ivy Trl
33000 SDCo 1052 D2
(See Page 1052)
Ivy Wy
2200 SDCo 1271 D7
Ivywood Ct
- SNMS 1108 J5
Iwo Av
- SDGO 1268 F7

J

J A Rodney Ct
- CALX 6620 H6
J Av
100 CORD 1288 H5
- NATC 1289 J7
1300 NATC 1309 J1
2300 NATC 1310 A2
J B Rodriquez St
- CALX 6620 J6
J Esplanade
600 CHLV 1330 A1
J F Anderson St
- CALX 6620 J6
J M Grijalva Av
- CALX 6620 J6
J M Ostrey St
600 CALX 6620 E7
J Paramo St
- CALX 6680 J1
J Pl
700 CHLV 1310 D7
E J Rd
- CORD 1288 F6
J St
100 BRAW 6319 J2
(See Page 6319)
1000 BRAW 6320 B2
(See Page 6320)
- CHLV 1310 D7
800 CHLV 1329 J2
400 CHLV 1330 B1
100 ENCT 1167 C1
200 IMPE 6439 F5
- SDCo 1108 F2
1700 SDGO 1289 C4
- SDGO 1290 A4
E J St
100 CHLV 1310 E7
- ENCT 1167 C1
- SDCo 1311 B7
J Tapia Ct
900 CALX 6620 J7
Jacala Dr
12400 POWY 1170 C7
Jacaranda Av
2400 CRLB 1147 G4
Jacaranda Blossom Dr
13200 SDCo 1090 D5
Jacaranda Ct
2700 OCSD 1087 E5
Jacaranda Dr
- ELCN 6559 G2
400 SDCo 1310 D6
3200 SDGO 1269 D7
Jacaranda Pl
800 ESCN 1109 J6
2600 SDGO 1269 D6
Jacaranda St
- BRAW 6320 B1
(See Page 6320)
Jacarte Ct
13200 SDGO 1187 J5
Jacinto Pl
700 CORD 1288 J7
Jacinto Rd
- SDCo 1085 J3
Jack Creek Pl
- ESCN 1110 E5
Jack N Jill Ln
2000 SDCo 1152 F1
Jack Oak Ln
13800 SDCo 1232 E5
Jack Oak Rd
- SDCo 1232 E5
Jack Pine Ct
5200 OCSD 1087 E2
Jack Rabbit Acres
25000 ESCN 1109 G4
Jack Rabbit Rd
13600 POWY 1170 E3
Jackal Trl
7400 SDCo 1138 B7
(See Page 1138)
Jackam Wy
2100 SDGO 1290 F7
Jackass Trl
800 SDCo 1138 A7
(See Page 1138)
Jackdaw St
4000 SDGO 1268 J5
Jackie Dr
6800 SDGO 1250 J3
Jackie Ln
- ENCT 1148 A5
Jackie St
- SDCo 1171 F4
Jackman St
700 ELCJ 1251 E4
Jackrabbit Dr
- ELCN 6559 J3
Jacks Creek Rd
- ESCN 1110 E5
Jackson Cir
35200 SDCo 1029 H3
Jackson Dr
5400 LMSA 1250 J7
5200 LMSA 1270 J1
5000 LMSA 1271 A2
8100 SDGO 1250 D3
Jackson Heights Ct
8300 SDCo 1252 B1
Jackson Heights Dr
12500 SDCo 1252 B1
Jackson Hill Ct
1600 SDCo 1252 B1
Jackson Hill Dr
12600 SDCo 1232 C7
12500 SDCo 1252 B1
Jackson Hill Ln
- SDCo 1252 B1
Jackson Hill Wy
12700 SDCo 1252 B1
Jackson Pl
1100 SDCo 1109 E7
Jackson Rd
- SDCo 1047 J1
Jackson St
1700 CHLV 1331 E2
2600 SDGO 1268 F4
Jackspar Dr
- CRLB 1107 C7
Jacmar Av
7200 SDGO 1290 F3
Jacob Dekema Frwy
- SDGO 1350 G1
Jacob Dekema Fwy
- CHLV 1310 E6
- CHLV 1330 G2
- NATC 1310 B1
- SDGO 1208 C6
- SDGO 1228 F3
- SDGO 1248 J1
- SDGO 1249 B6
- SDGO 1269 F6
- SDGO 1289 J3
Jacob Ln
- ENCT 1147 B4
Jacob St
300 SNMS 1128 H3
Jacobs Wy
- SDGO 1268 H1
Jacoby Rd
10100 SDCo 1291 D2
Jacot Ln
2100 SDGO 1289 G1
Jacqua St
100 CHLV 1330 B5
Jacquelene Ct
700 ENCT 1147 J6
Jacqueline Ct
- ELCJ 1251 H3
Jacqueline Ln
3100 OCSD 1107 C1
Jacqueline Wy
1000 CHLV 1330 D2
Jacuma Dr
- SDCo 1086 A3
Jacumba St
1100 SDCo 1321 G5
(See Page 1321)
700 SDGO 1290 H3
Jadam Wy
8300 LMGR 1270 J7
Jade Av
1500 CHLV 1330 F5
1500 ELCJ 1252 B4
Jade Coast Dr
8500 SDGO 1209 C5
Jade Coast Ln
8900 SDGO 1209 D5
Jade Coast Rd
7700 SDGO 1209 B5
Jade Cove Ct
- SDGO 1350 J1
Jade Ct
1400 CHLV 1330 F4
Jade Ln
6800 CRLB 1127 G5
4400 OCSD 1107 D2
Jade Pl
1200 SNMS 1109 C5
Jade Tree St
- IMPE 6439 D6
Jadero Pl
1900 ESCN 1129 F6
Jadestone Wy
13500 SDGO 1188 A4
Jaeger Rd
1100 SDCo 1291 D2
Jaffa Ct
2600 ESCN 1110 C5
Jaffe Ct
6500 SDGO 1250 J5
6500 SDGO 1251 A5
Jag Ct
1900 SDCo 1272 C3
Jagross Ct
8300 SDGO 1209 B2
Jaguar Ct
- SDGO 1210 B1
Jaime Ct
- SDGO 1350 E1
Jaime Dr
- SDGO 1350 E1
Jaime Lynn Ln
1700 SDCo 1272 C3
Jake Ln
- SDGO 1209 E2
Jake Mills Ct
1800 SDGO 1290 E6
Jake Rd
- SDCo 1090 E1
Jake View Ln
7800 SDGO 1189 A3
Jakirk Ln
- SDCo 1152 H7
Jalal St
- SDCo 1232 A7
Jalapa Ct
100 SOLB 1167 H4
Jalisco Rd
1800 SDCo 1272 B3
Jalna Ln
2600 SDCo 998 B7
Jamacha Blvd
10600 SDCo 1271 F7
9500 SDCo 1291 C3

36 INDEX

INDEX 36

Jamacha Hills Rd

Kaitz St

San Diego County Street Index

SAN DIEGO CO.

STREET
Block City Map# Grid

Jamacha Hills Rd
13800 SDCo 1272 G6
Jamacha Ln
1100 SDCo 1291 A2
Jamacha Rd
200 ELCJ 1251 J5
800 ELCJ 1252 A7
1600 SDCo 1272 A2
8400 SDCo 1290 J2
9700 SDCo 1291 D3
7000 SDGO 1290 F3
Jamacha View Dr
3000 SDCo 1272 C6
Jamacha Wy
1600 SDCo 1272 B4
Jamaica Ct
800 SDGO 1267 J2
Jamaica Dr
1800 VSTA 1107 H5
Jamaica Ln
- ESCN 1129 J5
Jamaica Village Rd
- CORD 1329 D1
Jamar Ct
4700 SDGO 1248 J1
Jamar Dr
5900 SDGO 1248 J1
Jamboree St
4500 OCSD 1066 H7
James Cir
3500 SDCo 1271 B5
James Ct
400 CHLV 1330 B1
3500 ENCT 1148 D2
- IMPE 6499 J2
E James Ct
300 CHLV 1310 F7
James Dr
1600 CRLB 1106 F4
James Gaynor St
2000 SDCo 1028 A2
James Hill Dr
10900 SDCo 1211 F7
James Rd
2400 ImCo 6500 J1
James St
500 CHLV 1330 B1
200 ESCN 1110 E6
800 SDCo 1152 D6
3700 SDGO 1268 C5
E James St
200 CHLV 1310 E7
Jamestown Ct
4500 SDGO 1228 F7
Jamestown Dr
1200 CHLV 1311 E6
Jamestown Rd
5300 SDGO 1228 F6
Jamestown Wy
4500 SDGO 1228 F7
Jamie Av
6800 SDGO 1290 F7
Jamie Ct
8900 SDCo 1291 A5
Jamies Ln
- SDCo 1029 C7
Jamison Ct
1400 SDGO 1290 F5
Jamul Av
200 CHLV 1330 F1
4100 SDGO 1289 H5
Jamul Ct
400 CHLV 1330 G1
Jamul Dr
- SDCo 1085 J3
3000 SDCo 1272 C6
14100 SDCo 1292 H1
(See Page 1292)
Jamul Heights Dr
2800 SDCo 1272 C6
Jamul Highlands Rd
3400 SDCo 1273 B7
3000 SDCo 1293 B1
Jamul Vistas Rd
3500 SDCo 1273 A6
Jan Dr
5800 LMSA 1251 C7
Jana Ct
8900 SDCo 1291 A5
Jana Ln
28800 SDCo 1090 G1
Jana Pl
900 ESCN 1109 F5
Janal Wy
14500 SDGO 1189 H1
Janan Wy
4300 SDGO 1228 E5
Jane Ct
13100 SDGO 1189 B4
Jane St
8400 SDGO 1189 B4
Janeen
13600 POWY 1190 F4
Janemar Rd
400 SDCo 1028 E2
Janes Ln
9300 SNTE 1231 B7
Janet Cir
2000 OCSD 1106 E1
Janet Kay Wy
12400 SDCo 1232 A7
Janet Ln
9400 SDCo 1232 A5
Janet Pl
4600 SDGO 1269 J2
1000 SNMS 1109 C6
Janetta Pl
13100 SDGO 1187 J5
Janette Ln
13600 POWY 1190 F3
Janfred Wy
9500 LMSA 1251 C7
Janice Ct
10900 SDGO 1209 E2
Janice St
1300 SDCo 1291 A2
Janich Ranch Ct
1900 ELCJ 1252 C4
Janis Lynn Ln
- VSTA 1087 D7
Janis Wy
2200 CRLB 1106 H4
Janney Ct
6800 SDGO 1268 J2
Janos Hill
5600 SDCo 1067 H2
Jans Oaks View
- SDCo 1173 A6
Janse Wy
3500 SDGO 1350 F5
Jansen Ct
1400 SDGO 1290 F5
January Pl
8900 SDGO 1228 D3
Japacha Pipe Ln
- SDCo 1196 E7
(See Page 1196)
Japatul Highlands Rd
- SDCo 1255 D4
Japatul Ln
- SDCo 1255 C5
Japatul Rd
18500 SDCo 1254 D4
- SDCo 1275 A1
Japatul Spur
- SDCo 1275 A1
Japatul Spur Rd
- SDCo 1275 B1
Japatul Valley Rd
24000 SDCo 1235 J7
- SDCo 1255 F4
- SDCo 1275 D1
Japatul Vista Ln
- SDCo 1255 E4
Jappa Av
3200 SDGO 1248 C2
Jarama Ct
2100 SDCo 1272 C4
Jardin Ct
1800 VSTA 1107 J3
Jardin Del Sol
23400 SDCo 1173 C2
Jardin Rd
12700 SDGO 1170 C3
Jared Pl
1000 ESCN 1130 A3
Jarman Pl
13300 SDGO 1188 A4
Jarrett Ct
- SDGO 1290 A5
Jarrett Ln
200 SDCo 1252 H3
Jarrito Ct
11600 SDGO 1150 A7
Jarron Plz
1000 CHLV 1311 A6
Jarvis St
3000 SDGO 1288 B1
Jasmin Av
- IMPE 6500 A2
- POWY 1190 F3
Jasmine Crest
- ENCT 1148 D5
Jasmine Crest Ln
- SDGO 1208 F3
Jasmine Ct
900 CRLB 1127 B6
1000 VSTA 1108 A3
Jasmine Pl
3300 ESCN 1150 C2
Jasmine St
- CALX 6620 J7
500 CHLV 1330 H3
1800 ELCJ 1252 B2
4700 OCSD 1087 D3
Jasmine Valley Wy
- SDGO 1290 A4
Jason Ct
2500 OCSD 1087 E4
9800 SDCo 1069 D4
Jason Glen
2000 ESCN 1109 D4
Jason Ln
400 SNMS 1129 A3
Jason Pl
300 CHLV 1330 B1
Jason Rd
3000 SDCo 1047 J1
Jason St
2500 OCSD 1087 E4
1500 SDGO 1349 J2
1700 SDGO 1350 A2
E Jason St
100 ENCT 1147 A3
W Jason St
100 ENCT 1147 A3
Jasper Av
1500 CHLV 1330 F5
Jasper Ct
1400 CHLV 1330 F4
Jasper Glen
2400 ESCN 1129 E6
Jasper Ln
4400 OCSD 1107 D2
Jasper Rd
200 CALX 6620 E3
- ImCo 6620 C3
Jasper Springs Wy
3100 SDGO 1288 A4
Jasper St
100 ENCT 1147 A4
Jasper Wy
- CRLB 1127 E4
Jauregui Mountain View
16700 SDCo 1111 D6
Java Hills Dr
1400 SDCo 998 B7
Java Ln
1800 LMGR 1290 H1
Java Wy
1700 CHLV 1331 H3
Javelin Wy
9900 SDCo 1291 D2
Javier St
5200 SDGO 1248 H1
Jay Ct
- SNMS 1108 F5
- SNTE 1231 D2
Jay Jay Wy
9900 SDCo 1069 D2
Jay Tee Ct
14900 SDGO 1169 E6
Jaybird Ln
- SDCo 1172 G2
Jayken Wy
1500 CHLV 1330 B5
Jaylee Av
8800 SDCo 1290 J3
Jaynia Pl
2700 LMGR 1270 E7
S Jayton Ln
1900 ENCT 1147 H7
Jazmin Ct
5300 SDGO 1249 J1
Jean Ann Ln
- SDCo 1172 H2
Jean Av
100 ESCN 1130 D1
Jean Dr
4700 SDGO 1269 J3
- SNTE 1231 E7
Jean-O-Reno Rd
14000 POWY 1190 G4
Jeanette Av
5700 LMSA 1250 H7
Jeanne Pl
1500 CRLB 1106 G6
Jeanne Rd
7000 LMGR 1270 E7
Jeanne Ter
10700 SNTE 1231 F6
Jeannine Ln
- SDCo 1251 H3
Jed Rd
2700 ESCN 1110 E7
Jeff Park Ln
14700 POWY 1190 E1
Jeff St
6200 SDGO 1270 D5
Jeffer Ln
4700 SDCo 1271 C3
Jeffers Pl
- CRLB 1107 B7
Jefferson Av
100 CHLV 1309 J5
500 CHLV 1310 A7
1000 CHLV 1330 B3
500 ELCJ 1251 F6
2100 ESCN 1110 C6
1200 ESCN 1130 A1
8900 LMSA 1271 A2
Jefferson Rd
3000 SDCo 1292 H2
(See Page 1292)
Jefferson St
- CALX 6620 J6
2200 CRLB 1106 E3
8200 LMGR 1270 H6
3000 SDGO 1268 E4
200 VSTA 1087 H6
Jeffery Ln
28800 SDCo 1237 C6
Jeffree St
500 ELCJ 1251 G4
Jeffrey Av
1500 ESCN 1130 C2
Jeffrey Ct
10900 SDGO 1209 E3
- VSTA 1127 J1
Jeffrey Heights Rd
31800 SDCo 1050 D7
Jeffrey Pl
1400 ESCN 1130 C2
Jeffrey Rd
900 SOLB 1187 H1
Jeffries Ranch Rd
5800 OCSD 1067 F6
Jellett St
4100 SDGO 1248 E7
Jema Wy
8200 SDCo 1252 A1
Jemez Dr
3400 SDGO 1248 D2
Jenday Ct
2000 OCSD 1067 C2
Jenell St
15000 POWY 1170 C7
Jenkins St
3100 SDGO 1288 A4
Jenna Ct
200 SDGO 1290 D4
Jenna Pl
2000 ESCN 1129 F7
Jenner St
8000 SDGO 1227 E6
Jennifer Cir
1000 VSTA 1087 G4
Jennifer Ct
1100 ESCN 1109 J7
- SDCo 1048 B4
4800 SDGO 1248 D1
Jennifer Dr
- IMPE 6499 J2
9900 SNTE 1231 C4
Jennifer Ln
2300 ENCT 1147 J7
Jennifer Rd
- IMPE 6499 J2
Jennifer St
- BRAW 6319 F4
(See Page 6319)
3600 SDGO 1248 D1
Jennileah Ln
- SNMS 1109 A2
Jennings Pl
- SDGO 1288 A3
Jennings St
3800 SDGO 1287 J2
3400 SDGO 1288 A3
Jennings Vista Cir
9100 SDCo 1232 F4
Jennings Vista Ct
14200 SDCo 1232 G4
Jennings Vista Dr
14200 SDCo 1232 F4
Jennings Vista Trl
14300 SDCo 1232 F4
Jennings Vista Wy
14200 SDCo 1232 F4
Jennite Dr
7500 SDGO 1250 F3
Jenny Av
8600 SDGO 1249 C6
Jenny Jay Ct
- SDCo 1090 E1
Jenny Ln
29700 SDCo 1068 E6
Jenny Terr
- SDCo 1088 D6
Jensen Ct
700 ENCT 1147 E4
Jepson Ln
- SDGO 1189 G7
Jeraback Dr
10200 SDGO 1209 H4
Jeremy Ln
2000 ESCN 1110 B5
Jeremy Point Ct
1600 CHLV 1330 J5
Jeremy St
9900 SNTE 1231 F4
Jeremy Wy
37100 SDCo 1029 E1
Jerez Ct
7500 CRLB 1147 H1
Jergens Ct
9000 SDGO 1209 D2
Jeri Wy
4600 SDCo 1271 H2
Jericho Circle Gn
- ESCN 1110 E7
Jericho Dr
700 SDCo 1028 A1
Jericho Rd
9400 LMSA 1251 B6
Jerome Dr
14200 POWY 1170 G7
Jerrilynn Pl
1600 ENCT 1167 G1
Jersey Ct
700 SDGO 1267 H2
Jesmond Dene
Heights Pl
25200 SDCo 1109 F2
Jesmond Dene
Heights Rd
2900 SDCo 1109 F3
Jesmond Dene Rd
26300 SDCo 1089 D7
25200 SDCo 1109 F3
Jesmond Dr
10100 SDCo 1109 E2
Jessica Ln
1000 ESCN 1130 E1
Jessica Ln
11500 SDCo 1231 H7
Jessie Av
4700 LMSA 1270 G2
Jessie Ln
- VSTA 1107 J1
Jessop Ln
2300 SDGO 1268 F6
Jester St
1700 SDGO 1290 D6
Jethrow Wy
1300 ELCJ 1252 A7
Jets Pl
700 ESCN 1109 J7
Jetty Ln
800 CHLV 1311 G4
Jewel St
- IMPE 6439 C6
Jewel Valley Ct
39400 SDCo 1300 C7
(See Page 1300)
Jewel Valley Ln
1900 SDCo 1320 C1
(See Page 1320)
Jewel Valley Rd
1400 SDCo 1320 F3
(See Page 1320)
Jewel Valley Wy
39000 SDCo 1300 B7
(See Page 1300)
Jewell Dr
700 SDGO 1289 G5
Jewell Ridge
2000 VSTA 1107 H6
Jewell St
4500 SDGO 1248 A5
3500 SDGO 1268 A1
E Jewett St
2300 SDGO 1248 J7
W Jewett St
2200 SDGO 1248 J7
Jibsail St
3300 OCSD 1086 F5
Jicama Terr
13000 SDGO 1188 G4
Jicama Wy
- CHLV 1330 E4
Jicarilla Dr
3100 SDCo 1048 H1
Jicarillo Av
4500 SDGO 1248 C2
Jill Ln
3700 LMSA 1270 F5
Jill St
4400 OCSD 1066 H7
9900 SNTE 1231 D4
Jillian Dr
- IMPE 6499 H2
Jillians Wy
1800 VSTA 1088 A2
Jim Ln
9500 SNTE 1231 E5
Jimdora Wy
31900 SDCo 1048 D7
Jimenez Ct
2200 SDGO 1209 D7
Jimlojan Rd
1000 SDCo 1149 H1
Jimmy Durante Blvd
- DLMR 1187 F4
Jimzel Rd
9600 LMSA 1251 C5
Jiola Wy
9500 LMSA 1271 C3
Joan Ct
5200 SDGO 1270 A2
Joan Ln
2400 SDCo 997 B2
Joan St
9000 SDCo 1291 B4
Joann Cir
400 VSTA 1087 H4
Joann Dr
2600 OCSD 1087 C6
Joanna Dr
700 SDGO 1290 G3
Joanne Wy
800 ELCJ 1251 D7
Joannie Wy
200 SDCo 1108 A3
Jobe Hill Dr
500 VSTA 1107 E1
Jocatal Ct
11600 SDGO 1150 A7
Jocelyn St
4400 SDGO 1289 H1
Jocelyn Wy
600 ENCT 1147 C5
Jockey Club
- SDCo 1048 B7
Jockey Wy
5600 SDCo 1311 A2
Jodi Ann Ct
29800 SDCo 1069 A5
Jodi St
3800 SDGO 1270 C5
Jody Ln
2900 OCSD 1087 B7
Jody Pl
2700 ESCN 1110 E7
Joe Acuna Ct
- CALX 6620 H6
Joe Crosson Dr
1700 ELCJ 1251 E2
Joe Pl
200 ESCN 1130 D1
Joel Ln
5900 LMSA 1251 C6
Joeve Ct
8700 SDGO 1251 A3
Joey Av
400 ELCJ 1251 G4
Joey Pl
- ESCN 1109 H7
Johannesberg Dr
13800 POWY 1190 F4
Johannesberg Wy
13200 POWY 1190 F4
John Ct
- SDGO 1350 D1
John Dewitt Pl
- SDCo 1253 J1
John Henry Ln
16400 SDCo 1171 G3
John Hopkins Ct
3500 SDGO 1208 A7
John J Montgomery Dr
3700 SDGO 1249 C3
John Jay Hopkins Dr
- SDGO 1207 J6
9700 SDGO 1228 A1
John Kennedy St
100 CALX 6620 F6
John Paul Jones Ct
2600 SDGO 1268 D7
John St
3800 SDGO 1287 J2
3500 SDGO 1288 A2
John Towers Av
1800 ELCJ 1251 D1
John Vickers Ct
- ELCN 6559 J4
John Wayne Ln
28700 SDCo 1071 B7
Johns View Wy
2200 SDCo 1291 A1
Johnson Av
800 SDGO 1269 B4
N Johnson Av
1100 ELCJ 1251 E3
S Johnson Av
100 ELCJ 1251 E6
Johnson Ct
200 SDCo 1086 A3
Johnson Dr
8900 LMSA 1271 A2
3900 OCSD 1107 A1
Johnson Lake Rd
11800 SDCo 1211 H5
Johnson Ln
1900 ImCo 6499 A7
1900 ImCo 6559 A1
900 SDCo 1152 G4
Johnson Rd
- SDGO 1228 H4
Johnson St
- CORD 1329 F4
Johnston Gn
- ESCN 1129 D6
Johnston Ln
100 SNMS 1108 H7
Johnston Rd
2100 ESCN 1129 E6
Jojo Ct
200 SDGO 1290 D4
Joliet Ct
100 ELCJ 1252 A5
Joliet St
1400 ELCJ 1252 A5
Jolina Wy
400 ENCT 1147 G6
Jolley Ln
14200 POWY 1190 H5
Jon Ln
- OCSD 1086 G3
Jonah Dr
3400 OCSD 1086 D3
Jonah Rd
300 ESCN 1110 F7
Jonas Ct
8800 SDGO 1249 C6
Jonathan Park Ln
13300 POWY 1190 E1
Jonathon Pl
600 ESCN 1110 C6
4200 OCSD 1087 C7
Jonathon St
4100 OCSD 1087 C7
1600 VSTA 1087 D7
Jonbell Pl
10000 SNTE 1231 D4
Jonel Wy
6500 SDCo 1311 C1
Jonell Ct
9100 LMSA 1251 B6
Jones Ct
- SDCo 1086 A2
Jones Rd
- ImCo 6260 J3
(See Page 6260)
100 OCSD 1086 D5
Jones Rd
39500 SDCo 996 H2
Jones St
300 BRAW 6259 H7
(See Page 6259)
- BRAW 6260 B7
(See Page 6260)
1600 CHLV 1331 D2
Jones Wy
32600 SDCo 1049 A6
Joni Ln
- SDCo 1088 J6
Jonny Ln
11700 SDGO 1209 B1
Jonquil Dr
2600 SDGO 1268 C6
Joplin Av
3600 SDGO 1248 D2
Joplin Dr
900 ELCJ 1251 H2
Jordan Ridge Ct
12700 SDGO 1188 D4
Jordan St
600 ESCN 1130 D1
8200 SDGO 1249 B5
Joris Wy
8800 LMSA 1271 A3
Jose Ln
1600 ESCN 1109 H6
Josefina Pl
600 CHLV 1311 A5
Joseph St
1900 SDCo 1027 H6
Josephine Av
- SDGO 1229 F3
Josephine St
1300 SDGO 1268 F3
Josh Ct
- IMPE 6499 H2
Josh Ln
- SDGO 1209 E3
Josh Wy
600 SDCo 1234 C4
Joshua Av
- BRAW 6259 J7
(See Page 6259)
300 SNMS 1108 J6
Joshua Creek Pl
- CHLV 1311 J4
Joshua Creek Rd
- CHLV 1311 J4
Joshua Pl
900 SDGO 1330 F7
Joshua St
1100 ESCN 1109 H7
Joshua Tree Ct
- POWY 1190 F2
Joshua Tree Ln
1600 SDCo 1027 J5
Joshua Tree St
- IMPE 6499 C2
Joshua Wy
1000 VSTA 1107 J7
Josie Jo Ln
10200 SNTE 1231 E3
Josselyn Av
1200 CHLV 1330 F3
Josten Wy
400 SDCo 1027 E5
Jougland St
6300 SDGO 1290 D6
Journey St
2300 CHLV 1331 H1
Journey Wy
1700 CHLV 1331 H1
Journeys End Dr
200 SDCo 1108 B3
Jovic Rd
9200 SDCo 1232 A5
Joy Ln
- ESCN 1129 F5
Joy Rd
1400 SDCo 1027 J5
Joyas Ct
17800 POWY 1150 E7
11600 SDGO 1250 B3
Joyce Pl
5100 SDGO 1270 A6
Joyce St
200 ELCJ 1251 G7
Jr Villa Ct
- CALX 6680 H1
Juan St
2400 SDGO 1268 F4
Juaneno Av
200 OCSD 1067 B7
Juanita Ln
1700 SDCo 1027 J3
- SDCo 1108 G1
100 SDCo 1252 H4
Juanita St
3200 SDGO 1270 C6
800 SOLB 1187 G1
Juanita Ter
3900 SDCo 1108 G1
Juanita Wy
- SDCo 1070 J1
Juarez Dr
16600 SDGO 1170 B3
Juarez Wy
1800 CHLV 1331 H2
Juba Rd
- SDCo 1090 F1
Jube Wright Ct
15600 SDGO 1169 A3
Jubilee Dr
38700 SDCo 999 B4
Jubilee Wy
38600 SDCo 999 B4
Jud St
1100 SDGO 1290 H2
Judiann Ln
- SDCo 1088 D7
Judicial Dr
9300 SDGO 1228 D2
Judilyn Dr
900 VSTA 1087 F5
Judith Av
2100 SDGO 1350 A1
Judith Pl
1700 ESCN 1109 C5
Judson Ct
7500 SDGO 1249 A7
Judson Ln
2600 SDGO 1249 A7
Judson St
600 ESCN 1130 D1
2500 SDGO 1249 A7
2000 SDGO 1269 A1
N Judson St
7400 SDGO 1249 A6
Judson Wy
1400 CHLV 1330 F3
4500 LMSA 1270 E3
5100 SDGO 1270 E2
Judy Dr
9900 SNTE 1231 D4
Judy Lee Pl
6500 SDGO 1270 D4
Judy Ln
1100 ENCT 1167 F2
Juergens Vista
6100 SDCo 1255 D7
Jugador Ct
1100 SDCo 1128 E3
Jula Ct
300 SDCo 1290 J4
Julia Dr
200 BRAW 6319 G3
(See Page 6319)
Julian Av
13400 SDCo 1232 D3
2300 SDGO 1289 D5
Julian Estates Rd
800 SDCo 1156 E5
Julian Ln
- SDCo 1136 A7
Julian Orchards Dr
1000 SDCo 1136 A3
Julian Rd
29800 SDCo 1135 A3
100 SDCo 1152 H5
600 SDCo 1153 C5
26300 SDCo 1154 B2
N Julian St
100 SDCo 1152 E7
S Julian St
200 SDCo 1152 E7
Julianna St
- SDCo 1272 B2
Julie Ct
800 SNMS 1109 B6
Julie Ln
3900 SDCo 1271 H4
Julie Pl
2200 CRLB 1107 A6
Julie St
6600 SDGO 1270 D1
Julielynn Wy
3000 LMGR 1270 H6
Juliette Pl
7200 LMSA 1270 F2
1200 SDCo 1027 H3
Julinda Wy
2800 SDCo 1150 A2
Julio Pl
10200 SNTE 1231 E3
July St
5100 SDGO 1268 G1
Jumano Av
4800 SDGO 1248 F6
Jumilla St
5100 SDGO 1230 A7
Junco Pl
8700 SDGO 1189 C6
Juncus Ct
7300 SDGO 1188 J7
June Lake Dr
7900 SDGO 1250 H5
June St
1300 SDCo 1027 H3
June Wy
500 ELCJ 1251 H4
Juneberry Ct
- SDGO 1249 C2
Juneberry St
- OCSD 1067 D6
Jungle Oaks Dr
3600 SDCo 1047 H4
Junior High Dr
7600 LMSA 1270 G4
Juniper Av
200 CRLB 1106 E7
Juniper Creek Ln
8300 SDGO 1209 B6
Juniper Field Trl
23400 SDCo 1173 C2
Juniper Ln
9800 SDCo 1149 E2
900 VSTA 1108 B6
Juniper Park Ln
- SDGO 1208 E4
Juniper Rd
600 SDGO 1289 B1
Juniper Ridge Ln
1700 SDCo 1028 E5
Juniper St
500 CHLV 1330 H3
800 ESCN 1129 H1
1600 ESCN 1130 A4
- IMPE 6499 C2
3100 SDGO 1289 E1
E Juniper St
200 SDGO 1289 A1
N Juniper St
600 ESCN 1129 J2
S Juniper St
200 ESCN 1129 J3
2000 SDCo 1130 B5
W Juniper St
1000 SDGO 1288 J1
Juniper Wy
200 OCSD 1086 J2
12200 POWY 1190 C7
Juniperhill Dr
1500 ENCT 1167 G1
Juno Av
- ENCT 1147 A3
Jupiter St
100 ENCT 1147 A3
3900 SDGO 1268 C4
Just Ct
1100 SDGO 1350 F1
Just St
3700 SDGO 1350 F1
Justa Ln
8800 SNTE 1231 B6
Justice Ln
- SDGO 1228 A1
Justin Pl
- SDCo 1070 G1
Justin Rd
1300 ENCT 1167 E1
Justin Wy
500 ESCN 1110 D6
Justina Dr
300 OCSD 1086 J4
Justo Ct
- SDGO 1209 F1
Jutland Ct
3000 SDGO 1248 C2
Jutland Dr
4400 SDGO 1248 B2
Jutland Pl
4500 SDGO 1248 C2

K

K Av
400 NATC 1289 J7
800 NATC 1309 J1
1800 NATC 1310 A2
K Q Ranch Rd
300 SDCo 1156 G5
K St
600 BRAW 6319 G2
(See Page 6319)
- BRAW 6320 C2
(See Page 6320)
400 CHLV 1330 B2
100 ENCT 1167 C1
300 IMPE 6439 F5
2500 SDGO 1289 D4
- SDGO 1290 A4
Kaanapali Wy
3000 SDGO 1330 D6
Kachina Ct
17800 SDGO 1169 H1
Kaden Ct
100 SDCo 1027 H2
Kadin Dr
- IMPE 6499 H2
Kadwell Wy
1700 ELCJ 1252 B2
Kae Crest
- SDCo 1273 B7
Kahlua Ct
9300 SDCo 1271 B4
Kahlua Wy
9300 SDCo 1271 B4
Kaibab Ct
3000 SDGO 1248 F6
Kaile Ln
500 ESCN 1110 E6
Kaimalino Ln
1300 SDGO 1247 H4
Kaiser Mesa Hosp Ln
- LMSA 1270 H1
Kaiser Pl
10200 SDGO 1209 A5
Kaitz St
12600 POWY 1170 C7

SAN DIEGO CO.

San Diego County Street Index

STREET Block City Map# Grid

Kal Pl
- ESCN 1129 G5
Kalamath Dr
600 DLMR 1187 G5
Kalamis Wy
4900 OCSD 1107 E6
Kalapana St
14600 POWY 1190 G1
Kalasho Pl
- SNTE 1231 E6
N Kalbaugh St
400 SDCo 1152 D7
S Kalbaugh St
100 SDCo 1172 D1
Kalbfus St
- SDGO 1289 F7
Kalin Rd
- ImCo 6259 D3
(See Page 6259)
4300 ImCo 6319 D3
(See Page 6319)
Kalmia Cir
- SDCo 1127 D4
Kalmia Ln
9700 SDCo 1149 E2
Kalmia Pl
2800 SDGO 1289 D1
Kalmia St
100 SDCo 1027 F2
200 SDGO 1289 A1
5200 SDGO 1290 A1
S Kalmia St
500 ESCN 1129 J3
800 ESCN 1130 A3
W Kalmia St
900 SDGO 1288 J1
Kalpati St
800 CRLB 1106 F7
Kamloop Av
4500 SDGO 1248 C2
Kamwood Ct
10200 SDGO 1208 J5
Kamwood Pl
10200 SDGO 1208 J5
Kamwood St
7400 SDGO 1208 J5
Kandace Ct
5100 SDGO 1270 A7
Kandace Wy
2700 SDGO 1270 A7
Kane Dr
8200 LMSA 1270 J5
Kane St
4100 SDGO 1248 E7
Kaneko Ct
3600 SDGO 1350 F5
Kansas St
4500 SDGO 1269 E3
Kantor Ct
5800 SDGO 1228 F6
Kantor St
5900 SDGO 1228 F5
Kapalua Ct
3000 SDGO 1330 D7
Kaplan Dr
8200 SDGO 1269 B1
Kaplin
- SDCo 1310 E3
Kappa St
5800 LMSA 1250 J7
Kardeelin Ct
12500 SDCo 1252 B1
Karen Ct
900 SNMS 1109 C5
Karen Ln
- SNTE 1231 D4
Karen Wy
1000 CHLV 1330 D3
4600 SDCo 1271 G3
Karena Ct
- VSTA 1087 F4
Karensue Av
4200 SDGO 1228 E6
Karensue Ln
5900 SDGO 1228 E6
Karerllyn Dr
- SNTE 1231 G5
Kari Ct
- SDCo 1271 A7
Kari Ln
4200 SDCo 1067 G4
Karibu Ln
27000 SDCo 1091 A5
Karma Dr
9500 SDGO 1209 E3
Karnes Wy
3000 SDGO 1248 C3
Karok Av
3300 SDGO 1248 C2
Karra Ct
400 CHLV 1310 F6
Karren Ln
2000 CRLB 1106 G5
Karst Rd
4000 CRLB 1107 B4
Karwarren Ct
2000 SDCo 1109 H5
Kaschube Wy
9400 SNTE 1230 H6
Kashmere Ln
10200 SDCo 1129 E7
Kate Ct
- SDCo 1048 B3
Kate Sessions Wy
5000 SDGO 1248 A4
Katella Ct
1400 ESCN 1130 B2
Katella St
1800 SDGO 1350 B3
Katella Wy
1500 ESCN 1130 B2
Katelyn Ct
7400 SDGO 1250 A4
Katerri Dr
1200 SDCo 1088 C7
Katharine Dr
3100 ESCN 1110 F5
Katherine Claire Ct
8200 SDGO 1169 A3
Katherine Claire Ln
8200 SDGO 1169 B3
Katherine Ct
2500 ELCJ 1251 B4
- SDGO 1350 D1
Katherine Pl
4600 LMSA 1270 F3
Katherine St
2300 ELCJ 1251 B4
Kathleen Pl
2400 SDGO 1270 B7
Kathriner Pl
1200 SDCo 1172 G2
Kathryn Crosby Ct
7900 SDCo 1169 A3
Kathy St
9500 LMSA 1251 C6
Katie King Ln
- SDCo 1254 E1
Katie Lake Ct
10000 SDCo 1232 B3
Katie Lendre Dr
3600 SDCo 1048 D3
Katie Ln
9100 SDCo 1231 J6
1400 SNTE 1231 E6
Katkat Ct
32300 SDCo 1051 A6
Kato St
8100 LMSA 1250 H7
Katy Ct
4600 SDCo 1271 C3
Katy Pl
1700 ESCN 1109 D5
Katydid Cir
12200 SDGO 1189 A7
Kauana Loa Dr
2500 SDCo 1129 D4
Kaufman Wy
9900 SDGO 1209 A5
Kausman St
2700 SDGO 1310 E1
Kay Dee Ln
16000 SDCo 1171 G4
Kay Jay Ct
13600 SDCo 1232 E6
Kay Jay Ln
9000 SDCo 1232 E6
Kaylyn Wy
600 SNMS 1129 E1
Kaymar Dr
300 SDGO 1290 F3
Kaywood Cir
11400 SDCo 1109 H1
Kaywood Ct
25900 SDCo 1109 J1
Kaywood Dr
- OCSD 1087 F4
- SDCo 1089 H6
3200 SDCo 1109 H1
Kaywood Ln
11500 SDCo 1109 J2
Kaywood Pl
11500 SDCo 1109 J1
Kaywood Ter
26000 SDCo 1109 J1
Kaywood Wy
25900 SDCo 1109 J1
Kea St
1300 OCSD 1086 E7
Kear Ct
- POWY 1190 G6
Kear Pl
12100 POWY 1190 F7
Kearney Ct
200 CHLV 1310 E7
Kearney Mesa Rd
5300 SDGO 1249 C1
Kearney St
700 CHLV 1330 A2
Kearny Av
2200 SDGO 1289 D5
Kearny Mesa Rd
9500 SDGO 1209 F6
5600 SDGO 1229 C7
3800 SDGO 1249 B3
Kearny Villa Ct
9100 SDGO 1229 D7
Kearny Villa Ln
3200 SDGO 1249 B5
Kearny Villa Rd
9400 SDGO 1209 E5
6300 SDGO 1229 F3
4100 SDGO 1249 B3
Kearny Villa Wy
5300 SDGO 1249 C1
Kearsarge Rd
1500 SDGO 1227 G6
Keating St
3600 SDGO 1268 H6
Keats Pl
- CRLB 1107 B7
Keats St
3100 SDGO 1288 B1
Keck Ct
9400 SDGO 1189 E6
Kedzie Av
700 SDGO 1330 G7
Keegan Pl
13500 SDGO 1188 A4
Keeler Av
4200 SDGO 1289 H6
Keemo Ct
8800 SDCo 1232 B6
Keemo Ter
12400 SDCo 1232 B6
Keen Dr
2800 SDGO 1310 F1
Keenan St
- SDGO 1209 B7
Keeneland Dr
- CRLB 1127 G3
Keeneland Row
9700 SDGO 1227 J1
Keeney St
5000 SDGO 1270 F2
Keighley Ct
7000 SDGO 1250 A5
Keighley St
- SDGO 1250 A5
Keir St
9000 SDGO 1249 D6
Keisha Cove
7400 SDGO 1208 J2
Keisha Ct
7400 SDGO 1208 J2
Keith St
10600 SNTE 1231 D2
Kelburn Av
8800 SDCo 1290 J3
Keld Ct
12200 SDGO 1188 J7
Kelglen Dr
1300 SDGO 1108 A1
Kellam Ct
13100 SDGO 1188 A5
Kellbara Ct
14100 SDGO 1189 E2
Kelleen Dr
100 VSTA 1087 G4
Kelli Ln
14100 SDCo 1232 G5
Kellie Ct
3700 NATC 1310 D3
Kellington Ct
3500 OCSD 1107 E3
Kellington Pl
1700 ENCT 1147 G7
Kellogg Av
1900 CRLB 1127 C3
Kellogg Dr
3500 SDGO 1288 A4
Kellogg St
3200 SDGO 1288 A4
200 SNMS 1128 H3
Kellogg Wy
3400 SDGO 1288 A4
Kellrae Ln
400 SDCo 1109 G2
Kelly Av
- BRAW 6319 F4
(See Page 6319)
1900 SDCo 1152 E7
2400 SDCo 1172 D1
Kelly Ct
400 ESCN 1130 D1
Kelly Dr
4800 CRLB 1106 J7
16000 SDCo 1253 B1
Kelly Ln
- SDCo 1067 H3
Kelly St
400 OCSD 1106 C3
6500 SDGO 1268 J1
Kellyn Ln
- SDCo 1068 E4
Kellywilliam Ln
- SDCo 1233 J6
Kelowna Ln
- SDCo 1070 F1
Kelowna Rd
11100 SDGO 1209 C2
Kelsey St
3300 SDGO 1249 G4
Kelsford Pl
- SDGO 1188 A5
Kelso Ct
- CHLV 1330 H2
Kelso Rd
- SDGO 1209 D7
Kelso St
8700 SDCo 1291 A3
Kelson Pl
1800 ESCN 1129 F6
Kelton Av
6000 LMSA 1250 J6
Kelton Ct
5600 SDGO 1290 B3
Kelton Dr
3800 OCSD 1087 A6
Kelton Pl
5600 SDGO 1290 B2
Kelton Rd
1000 SDGO 1290 B2
Kemah Ln
10800 SDGO 1209 H4
Kemberly Ln
3100 SDCo 1293 A1
Kemerton Rd
10600 SDGO 1208 J4
Kemp Ct
- CALX 6620 G7
Kemp Rd
- ImCo 6680 C1
Kemper Ct
3600 SDGO 1268 D5
Kemper St
4300 LMSA 1270 F4
3300 SDGO 1268 D5
Kempf St
3200 LMGR 1270 H6
Kempton St
700 SDCo 1291 B3
Ken Bemis Dr
- BRAW 6260 C6
(See Page 6260)
Ken Ln
10400 SNTE 1231 E3
Kenalan Dr
1300 SDGO 1350 F1
Kenamar Ct
- SDGO 1209 A7
Kenamar Dr
9000 SDGO 1209 A7
Kenda Wy
2400 SDCo 1234 C6
Kendall St
4900 SDGO 1248 A4
Kendi Ln
1200 SDCo 1028 D4
Kendra Ct
14300 POWY 1190 E2
Kendra Wy
14100 POWY 1190 E2
Kendrick Wy
1400 ELCJ 1252 A7
Kenerson Row
- SDGO 1249 D1
Kenesaw Ct
9700 SNTE 1231 F4
Kenison Dr
900 SDCo 1136 D7
Kenmar Wy
- SDGO 1188 H4
Kenmore Ter
4700 SDGO 1269 E3
Kennard Av
14200 POWY 1190 E2
Kennebeck Ct
800 SDGO 1267 H2
Kennebunk St
14500 POWY 1190 H5
Kennedy Ct
400 ESCN 1110 F5
Kennedy Ln
300 OCSD 1086 D6
Kennedy St
200 CHLV 1330 D3
Kennel Wy
- SDGO 1227 H4
Kennelworth Ln
3100 SDCo 1310 H1
Kennester Dr
3000 LMGR 1270 E7
Kenney St
400 ELCJ 1251 E1
Kennicott Ln
15800 SDGO 1169 D4
Kennington Rd
1700 ENCT 1147 A2
Kenora Dr
1600 ESCN 1130 C2
3700 SDCo 1271 C5
Kenora Ln
9600 SDCo 1271 C6
Kenora St
1500 ESCN 1130 C2
Kenora View
9600 SDCo 1271 D6
Kenora Woods Ln
9700 SDCo 1271 C6
Kenosha Av
3900 SDGO 1248 D4
Kenova St
8000 SDGO 1209 B4
Kensal Ct
- SDCo 1070 H6
Kensett Pl
9100 SDGO 1209 D2
Kensington Dr
4900 SDGO 1269 G3
Kensington Glen
- ESCN 1109 D2
Kensington Pl
5700 SDCo 1048 B7
Kensington Wy
2200 CHLV 1331 H2
Kensley Wy
6900 SDGO 1208 H4
Kent Av
1400 ESCN 1110 A6
Kent Dr
800 SDCo 1252 H1
Kent Hill Wy
14500 POWY 1190 F1
Kent Pl
1700 SDCo 1108 C1
5800 SDGO 1250 B7
Kent St
1900 CHLV 1311 D5
Kentfield Ct
13500 POWY 1190 F2
Kentfield Dr
13500 POWY 1190 F2
300 SNMS 1108 J5
Kentfield Pl
14400 POWY 1190 E1
Kentmere Terr
- SDGO 1330 H7
Kentner Ct
4700 CRLB 1107 A6
N Kenton Av
- NATC 1290 B6
S Kenton Av
- NATC 1290 B6
Kentucky Av
300 ELCJ 1251 F5
Kentucky St
400 SDCo 1027 F1
Kentwood Dr
700 SDCo 1156 E1
Kenwell St
1500 SDGO 1290 D7
Kenwood Ct
3700 SDCo 1271 B5
Kenwood Dr
9000 SDCo 1271 B5
Kenwood Pl
- SNMS 1128 E7
Kenwood St
5800 SDGO 1290 C3
Kenwyn St
2300 OCSD 1106 E1
Kenyatta Ct
5900 SDGO 1290 C4
Kenyatta Dr
100 SDGO 1290 C4
Kenyon St
3400 SDGO 1268 D5
Keoki Ct
7200 SDGO 1208 H5
Keoki St
- SDGO 1208 J5
Keokuk Ct
3200 SDGO 1248 C2
Keos Wy
4900 OCSD 1107 F5
Kephart Rd
- SDGO 1288 A7
Kepler Ct
- CRLB 1127 C1
Keppler Dr
10200 SDGO 1249 G2
Keppler Pl
10200 SDGO 1249 G2
Kerch St
6100 SDGO 1270 D5
Keremeos Wy
8800 SDGO 1209 C1
Keri Wy
- SDCo 1048 A3
Kerisiano Wy
1800 OCSD 1106 E1
Kern Cs
8300 SDGO 1169 B3
Kern Ct
- OCSD 1086 H1
Kern Pl
1100 ESCN 1109 J7
Kernel Pl
- CHLV 1310 G6
Kerns St
8400 SDGO 1351 G4
Kerr Wy
1300 OCSD 1106 D2
Kerran St
12400 POWY 1190 D7
Kerri Ln
25300 SDCo 1173 H3
Kerria
- SDGO 1248 C6
Kerrick Rd
- SDGO 1288 B7
Kerrigan Ct
10500 SNTE 1231 E2
Kerrigan St
10300 SNTE 1231 D2
Kerry Ln
- SDGO 1188 J3
Kersey Pl
11900 SDGO 1190 B2
Kershaw Pl
3100 SDCo 1149 H2
Kerwood Ct
4200 SDGO 1188 B5
Kesling Ct
4800 SDGO 1248 G1
Kesling Pl
4800 SDGO 1248 H1
Kesling St
5400 SDGO 1248 H1
W Kesling St
5000 SDGO 1248 H1
Keston Ct
3400 SDGO 1248 J4
Kestral Dr
- SDCo 1128 G3
Kestrel Ct
1400 ELCJ 1252 A6
Kestrel Dr
- CRLB 1127 B6
- SDCo 1127 B7
Kestrel Falls Rd
2100 CHLV 1331 G1
Kestrel Pl
9300 SDGO 1189 D6
Kestrel Rd
400 SDCo 1028 E2
Kestrel St
12700 SDGO 1189 E5
Kestrel Wy
9400 SDGO 1189 E6
Keswick Ct
4700 SDGO 1188 C4
Ketch Wy
- CRLB 1127 A5
Ketron Av
13400 POWY 1190 E3
Kettering Ln
- SDCo 1089 D4
Kettner Blvd
3100 SDGO 1268 H7
1700 SDGO 1288 J2
Kettner St
- SDGO 1268 H6
Ketuull Unnyaa Wy
3000 SDCo 1193 B4
(See Page 1193)
Kevin Ct
- SDCo 1253 F1
Kevin Dr
- VSTA 1087 H3
Kew St
10200 SDCo 1109 E1
Kew Ter
2600 SDGO 1269 F7
Key Largo Pl
800 ELCJ 1251 G5
Key Largo Rd
1800 VSTA 1107 H5
Key Lime Wy
600 ESCN 1110 E5
Key Ln
1700 SDCo 1252 A2
Keyes Rd
1100 SDCo 1152 J6
1600 SDCo 1172 J1
Keyport St
300 OCSD 1066 H6
Keys Creek Rd
11600 SDCo 1049 H7
- SDCo 1050 B6
Keys Pl
1400 SDCo 1107 G3
Keys Tr
- SDCo 1050 A7
Keyser Ct
1500 SDCo 1172 G1
Keyser Rd
1300 SDCo 1172 G2
Keystone Cir
3500 OCSD 1107 E3
Keystone Ct
8500 SDGO 1209 C2
Keystone Wy
1300 VSTA 1127 J1
Khayyam Rd
100 ESCN 1129 J3
Khe Sanh St
- SDGO 1268 F7
Khish Ln
- SDCo 1233 H7
Khuram St
13400 SDCo 1232 D4
Kiavo Dr
27500 SDCo 1091 H3
Kiavo Rd
- SDCo 1091 H5
Kibbings Rd
13500 SDGO 1188 A4
Kibler Dr
9900 SDGO 1209 A5
Kica Ct
- SDCo 1050 J5
Kickapoo Ct
4500 SDGO 1248 D2
Kickin Horse Trl
7300 SDCo 1138 C7
(See Page 1138)
Kidd St
- NATC 1309 G2
Kidd Wy
600 ELCJ 1251 E7
Kieffer
3600 OCSD 1086 G5
Kiel Rd
1000 SDCo 1027 G4
S Kihridge Ln
100 ENCT 1167 H1
Kika Ct
9900 SDGO 1189 F7
Kilbirnie Ln
- SDCo 1068 C6
Kilbourn Dr
8600 SDGO 1228 A3
Kilby Ln
- VSTA 1108 A1
Kildare Wy
2600 ELCJ 1251 B3
Kildeer Ct
- ENCT 1147 D3
Kildeer Ln
300 OCSD 1086 H1
Kiley Rd
500 CHLV 1310 F6
Kilgore Rd
1600 ImCo 6559 H3
Kilkee St
5000 SDGO 1228 H7
Kilkenny Dr
100 ENCT 1167 E4
Killarney Terr
- SNMS 1108 J4
Kilt Ct
7600 SDGO 1249 A3
Kim Pl
1400 CHLV 1330 E4
2600 SDGO 1249 F6
Kimball St
600 ESCN 1130 C2
Kimball Terr
300 CHLV 1310 A5
Kimball Valley Rd
- SDCo 1173 B7
17300 SDCo 1192 B3
(See Page 1192)
- SDCo 1193 A1
(See Page 1193)
Kimball Wy
- NATC 1309 J1
Kimber Ln
9000 SDCo 1232 D6
Kimberly Ct
2300 CRLB 1106 G4
Kimberly Dr
6100 LMSA 1250 H6
Kimberly Ln
4100 OCSD 1087 C6
Kimberly Pl
2400 ESCN 1110 D6
Kimberly Woods Dr
1500 ELCJ 1271 E1
Kimberly Wy
1400 SDCo 1318 G4
(See Page 1318)
Kimble View
700 SDCo 1027 G3
Kimda Ct
14400 SDCo 1293 A1
Kimi Ln
6300 LMSA 1251 C5
Kimmy Ct
6300 SDGO 1290 D4
Kimsue Wy
4100 SDGO 1350 F1
Kincaid Av
1600 CHLV 1331 D2
Kincaid Rd
- SDGO 1288 E1
Kincaid St
9900 SNTE 1231 F4
Kindig Av
- BRAW 6319 H3
(See Page 6319)
King Arthur Ct
2300 SDGO 1247 H1
King Arthurs Ct
- SDCo 1271 A6
King Creek Cir
- CHLV 1311 H4
King Creek Truck Trl
- SDCo 1216 B2
(See Page 1216)
King Ct
- SDCo 1086 A2
King Kelly Ct
8000 SDCo 1252 A1
King Kelly Dr
7900 SDCo 1252 A1
King Phillip Ct
10600 SNTE 1231 E2
King Sanday Ln
- SDCo 1069 E3
King St
100 CHLV 1310 C7
3800 LMSA 1270 E5
Kingbird Av
- SNTE 1230 G7
Kingbird Ln
- SDCo 1127 D5
Kingfisher Creek Rd
10700 SDCo 1233 A1
Kingfisher Ln
- CRLB 1127 C7
Kinglet Rd
1700 SDCo 1128 A4
Kinglet Wy
- SDCo 1127 D4
Kingman Rd
15700 POWY 1170 J5
Kingridge Dr
2600 SDCo 1028 C7
Kings Av
3600 OCSD 1107 D3
Kings Creek Wy
- CHLV 1311 H5
Kings Cross Ct
- ENCT 1167 E2
Kings Cross Dr
- ENCT 1167 E2
Kings Rd
1000 ESCN 1110 B6
1700 VSTA 1088 B3
Kings Trl
8500 SNTE 1231 D7
Kings View Cir
2300 SDCo 1271 A7
Kings View Ct
5800 SDGO 1290 C4
Kings Villa Rd
1400 SDCo 1152 E2
Kings Wy
1500 ESCN 1110 A5
4800 SDGO 1248 G1
1600 VSTA 1088 B3
Kingsbury Ridge Ct
10800 SDGO 1208 G1
Kingsfield Ct
- SDGO 1188 B4
Kingsford Ct
12200 SDCo 1252 A1
Kingsgate Sq
- SDGO 1170 B4
Kingsland Rd
8400 SDGO 1249 B7
Kingsley St
3700 SDGO 1268 C5
Kingspine Av
12500 SDGO 1210 B4
Kingsport Wy
- SNMS 1128 D5
Kingston Ct
800 SDGO 1267 H2
Kingston Ct E
- CORD 1329 E2
Kingston Ct S
- CORD 1329 E2
Kingston Ct W
- CORD 1329 E2
Kingston Dr
1000 ESCN 1130 C2
Kingston St
3600 CRLB 1106 J4
Kingswood Ct
5200 OCSD 1087 D1
Kingswood Dr
- CHLV 1330 E4
Kingswood St
900 SDGO 1290 F6
Kinross Ct
1900 SDCo 1130 D4
Kinsella Pt
- SDGO 1188 B4
Kinsky Wy
35300 SDCo 1028 J6
Kiowa Dr
5400 LMSA 1270 F1
5500 SDGO 1270 F1
Kipling Ln
5300 CRLB 1107 C7
Kira Pl
- SDCo 1070 F1
Kirby Ct
9000 SDGO 1209 D1
Kirby Pl
11500 SDGO 1209 D1
Kirch Ct
2300 SDCo 1129 H7
Kirk Pl
1700 CRLB 1106 H6
Kirkcaldy Dr
4200 SDGO 1249 A2
Kirkcaldy Rd
2100 SDCo 1027 G6
Kirkham Ct
12500 POWY 1190 D6
Kirkham Rd
12100 POWY 1190 D7
Kirkham Wy
- POWY 1190 F7
Kirkland Av
2500 SDCo 1129 H7
Kirks Wy
500 SDCo 1152 J7
Kirkwall Av
4700 CRLB 1107 A5
Kirkwall Dr
900 SNMS 1108 G6
Kirkwood Pl
600 SDGO 1247 G4
Kirmar Pl
1200 OCSD 1106 D3
Kirsten Ln
- SDCo 1068 D6
Kirsten Pl
2800 SDCo 1271 B7
Kirtright St
600 SDGO 1290 D5
Kismet Rd
11600 SDGO 1189 J6
Kiso Glen
1300 ESCN 1129 H5
Kit Carson Pl
10200 SNTE 1231 F3
Kit Fox Ln
2900 SDCo 1099 G4
(See Page 1099)
Kit Ln
300 SNMS 1108 H7
Kite Hill Ln
11100 SDGO 1209 E2
Kite Ln
1000 VSTA 1108 A5
Kite Pl
- CRLB 1127 A4
Kite St
3500 SDGO 1268 J6
Kittery St
14500 POWY 1190 H4
Kittiwake Ln
900 CHLV 1330 C2
Kittiwake Wy
4400 OCSD 1087 A3
Kitty Hawk Ct
- IMPE 6499 C2
Kitty Hawk Dr
- IMPE 6499 D2
Kitty Ln
8600 SNTE 1231 F7
Kittyhawk Ln
- BRAW 6320 C1
(See Page 6320)
Kiva Ln
1500 VSTA 1087 H3
Kiwi Glen
1700 ESCN 1109 D6
Kiwi Meadow Ln
- SDCo 1069 D7
Kiwi Pl
- SDCo 1127 D5
Kiwi St
7600 SDGO 1249 A7
Kl Tu Ln
14900 POWY 1170 H7
Klamath
- SDCo 1232 F5
Klamath Dr
1400 CHLV 1331 B2
Klamath St
- OCSD 1086 H1
Klauber Av
1100 SDGO 1290 D2
Kleaveland Pl
400 VSTA 1087 H5
Kleefeld Av
4600 SDGO 1248 E1
Kline St
900 SDGO 1227 F7
Klish Wy
1000 DLMR 1187 G5
Kloke Av
- CALX 6680 E1
Kloke Rd
- CALX 6620 D6
600 ImCo 6620 D5
Klucewich Rd
2900 SDCo 1234 B3
Knabe Ln
9900 SNTE 1231 B4
Knapp Dr
1700 VSTA 1087 G3
W Knapp Dr
1500 VSTA 1087 G3
Knapp St
4600 SDGO 1248 F5
Knaul Ct
8900 SDGO 1189 C4
Knight Dr
10000 SDGO 1209 A5
Knights Brg Ct
- ENCT 1167 E2
Knights Ferry Dr
- CHLV 1311 D6
Knights Realm
- SNMS 1128 D2
Knob Hill Dr
900 SDCo 1156 D2
1600 SNMS 1109 D7
Knob Hill Ln
1900 SDCo 1291 A1
Knob Hill Rd
1200 SNMS 1109 C7
Knob Hill Ter
1900 SDCo 1291 A1
Knoll Crest Pl
- SDCo 1232 A5
Knoll Ct
5000 LMSA 1271 B2
Knoll Dr
1300 OCSD 1086 F7
Knoll Edge Ct
16400 SDCo 1173 D2
Knoll Park Gn
- ESCN 1129 H6

STREET
Block City Map# Grid

Knoll Park Ln
1400 SDCo 997 H7
700 SDCo 1027 H1
Knoll Rd
300 SNMS 1108 G7
200 VSTA 1087 G6
Knoll View
- ESCN 1129 E6
Knoll Vista Dr
900 SDCo 1128 D3
Knollfield Wy
1700 ENCT 1147 F4
Knollview Dr
9900 SDCo 1271 C7
9900 SDCo 1291 D1
Knollview Ln
2600 SDCo 1271 C7
Knollwood Av
2100 SDCo 1027 H6
Knollwood Ct
4700 OCSD 1087 D3
Knollwood Dr
- CRLB 1107 C3
Knollwood Pl
1400 CHLV 1311 G7
Knollwood Rd
7900 SDGO 1290 G3
Knollwood Wy
9300 SNTE 1231 A6
Knots Ln
500 CRLB 1146 J1
Knott St
2100 SDGO 1290 F6
Knottwood Wy
3000 SDCo 1048 D3
Knowles Av
1200 CRLB 1106 E4
Knowlton Ct
9900 SNTE 1231 A5
Knowlton Williams Rd
- SDGO 1289 F7
Knox St
- OCSD 1106 G1
4900 SDGO 1268 F2
Knoxie St
3600 SDGO 1270 A6
Knoxville St
1500 SDGO 1268 E2
Koala Wy
1400 ELCJ 1252 A7
Kobe Dr
2700 SDGO 1249 D6
Kobe Pl
8900 SDGO 1249 D6
Kobe Wy
8900 SDGO 1249 D5
Koe St
1500 LMGR 1290 G2
1100 SDGO 1290 G2
Koelper St
- SDCo 1085 H5
Koester St
1700 CHLV 1331 E2
Kolmar St
200 SDGO 1247 E2
Kona Kai Ln
- ESCN 1129 D4
Kona Wy
3000 SDGO 1288 A3
Koonce Dr
9000 SDCo 1271 B5
Koonce Rd
- SNTE 1231 H6
Korea St
- SDGO 1268 E6
Korink Av
2600 SDGO 1248 J6
Korite Pl
6800 CRLB 1127 G5
Kornblum Dr
25900 SDCo 1109 E1
Korrey Dr
14100 SDGO 1189 G2
Kory Ln
1400 SDCo 1152 J7
Kostner Dr
800 SDGO 1330 G7
1300 SDGO 1350 G1
Kozy Crest Ln
12300 POWY 1190 B1
Kraft St
1700 OCSD 1086 B5
Kramer St
6800 SDGO 1268 J1
Kreiner Dr
8400 SNTE 1230 H5
Kremeyer Cir
2600 CRLB 1106 E4
Krenning St
5300 SDGO 1270 A7
Krenz St
8200 SDGO 1249 B5
Krim Pl
1500 OCSD 1106 D2
Kris Rd
4100 SDCo 1273 J4
Kris Wy
9500 SNTE 1231 D5
Krishen Heights Rd
200 SDCo 1253 D1

Krista Ct
400 CHLV 1310 F6
Kristen Ct
- ENCT 1147 D6
Kristen Glen
15900 SDGO 1169 C3
Kristen View Ct
8500 SDGO 1169 C3
Kristen Villa Ct
- SDCo 1153 A6
Kristen Wy
9800 SDCo 1069 D5
Kristi Ct
2000 SDCo 1048 B4
Kristie Ln
1300 ELCJ 1252 A5
Kristin Ct
200 SDGO 1290 D4
Kristy Ln
200 OCSD 1106 C2
Krueger Rd
- ImCo 6259 B3
(See Page 6259)
Krug Ct
1300 VSTA 1107 J3
Krystal Pl
- SNMS 1109 D6
Kuebler Ranch Rd
- SDCo 1332 D7
(See Page 1332)
Kugel Ct
1600 CHLV 1331 D2
Kuhn Dr
800 CHLV 1311 F4
Kuhner Wy
- SDCo 1232 A1
Kumeyaay Ct
- SDCo 1253 C5
Kumeyaay Rd
4600 SDCo 1319 E1
(See Page 1319)
Kumeyaay Wy
55000 SDCo 1091 C4
Kumeyai Trl
17300 SDCo 1233 J2
17300 SDCo 1234 A2
Kumquat Dr
9400 SDCo 1232 A4
Kumquat Wy
600 OCSD 1086 F2
Kunde Ct
- SDGO 1188 J3
Kunyaaw Path
- SDCo 1091 C4
Kupa Dr
16200 SDCo 1051 B6
Kurdson Wy
500 SDCo 1291 B4
Kurenda Wy
1800 SDCo 1108 A3
Kurley Ct
2300 SDCo 1271 A7
Kurtz Ct
- CORD 1329 E4
Kurtz St
1700 OCSD 1106 D2
3400 SDGO 1268 E4
Kuutpat Cres
55000 SDCo 1071 D5
Kuutpat Wy
54000 SDCo 1071 D6
Kwaaymii Pt
- SDCo 1197 G6
(See Page 1197)
Kwajalein Rd
- CORD 1309 B1
Kyanite Pl
2300 CRLB 1127 F4
Kyle Ln
1100 VSTA 1087 J4
Kyle Pl
1700 ELCJ 1251 H2
Kyrsten Ter
1400 SDCo 1233 J6

L

L Av
400 NATC 1289 J7
800 NATC 1309 J1
1200 NATC 1310 A1
L Dowe Ct
- CALX 6620 H6
L M Legaspi Av
- CALX 6680 J1
W L Moreno
900 CALX 6680 D1
L Porter Ct
900 CALX 6680 J1
L St
400 CHLV 1330 B2
- IMPE 6439 F5
1900 SDGO 1289 C4
E L St
100 CHLV 1330 E1
La Alameda
- ESCN 1109 F7
- SDCo 1252 B1
La Alberca Av
10700 SDCo 1169 F4

La Amapola
17800 SDCo 1148 J7
La Amatista Rd
300 SDCo 1187 G6
La Bajada
17400 SDCo 1168 A2
La Barca St
500 SDCo 1291 C3
La Barranca Dr
200 SOLB 1167 H6
La Bella Cir
1800 OCSD 1106 D1
La Bon Wy
500 SDGO 1289 F5
La Bonita Ct
1600 SDCo 1128 C2
La Bonita Dr
900 SDCo 1128 C2
La Bonita Wy
1600 SDCo 1128 C2
La Brea St
2000 ESCN 1109 E5
1600 SDCo 1152 F6
2300 SDCo 1172 D1
La Brisa
17400 SDCo 1168 H1
La Brucherie Rd
2000 ELCN 6499 E5
1600 ELCN 6559 E2
2900 IMPE 6439 E3
- IMPE 6499 E3
1400 ImCo 6559 E4
La Brusca Wy
7900 CRLB 1147 G4
La Butte Ln
8600 SNTE 1231 A7
La Cadena Ln
1400 CHLV 1331 C3
La Callecita St
2200 SDGO 1268 G5
La Calma
500 ESCN 1149 J3
La Camesa St
8800 SDGO 1189 C2
La Campana
3800 SNMS 1108 C7
La Canada
600 SDGO 1247 F3
La Canada Rd
3800 SDCo 1048 A3
La Capela Pl
7900 CRLB 1147 G3
La Cartera St
8800 SDGO 1189 C2
La Casa Dr
1000 SDCo 1128 C3
La Casa Ln
1100 SDCo 1128 C3
La Casita Dr
1500 SDCo 1128 C2
La Casita Wy
4200 OCSD 1086 J3
La Catrina
17600 SDCo 1149 A6
La Cava Pl
2000 SDCo 1272 C4
La Cazadora
- SDCo 1148 C6
La Chapa Rd
11800 SDCo 1029 H4
La Chica Dr
- CHLV 1330 J2
La Chula
7700 SDCo 1148 H7
La Chusa Rd
13000 SDCo 1029 J4
La Cienaga
- SNMS 1109 C5
E La Cienega Rd
300 SNMS 1108 J3
W La Cienega Rd
- SNMS 1108 H2
La Cima Dr
1600 SDGO 1268 A1
La Cintura Ct
8800 SDGO 1189 C2
La Colina Dr
2700 ESCN 1130 F1
La Colina Rd
11500 SDGO 1210 A4
La Colusa Dr
3700 SNMS 1108 C7
La Corta Cir
1400 LMGR 1290 F2
La Corta St
1900 LMGR 1290 F1
La Coruna Pl
7600 CRLB 1147 G1
La Costa Av
- CHLV 1311 G4
700 CRLB 1147 C1
200 ENCT 1147 A1
La Costa Blvd
2600 CRLB 1127 C5
La Costa Meadows Dr
- SNMS 1128 B5
La Crescenta
5500 SDCo 1148 B7
La Crescentia Dr
1200 CHLV 1311 A4
400 SDGO 1288 A4

La Cresta Blvd
800 SDCo 1252 J1
La Cresta Dr
300 OCSD 1086 F6
3800 SDGO 1268 B7
La Cresta Heights Ct
800 SDCo 1252 G2
La Cresta Heights Rd
400 SDCo 1252 H2
La Cresta Rd
1900 SDCo 1252 D3
9800 SDCo 1271 D7
La Cresta Trl
100 SDCo 1253 C1
La Cresta Wy
3900 SDCo 1310 J2
La Crosse Av
4400 SDGO 1248 D2
La Cruz Dr
4800 LMSA 1271 C2
La Cruz Pl
4800 SDCo 1271 C2
La Cuenta Ct
10700 SDGO 1249 H3
La Cuenta Dr
5100 SDGO 1249 H2
La Cuesta De Pauma
- SDCo 1070 H1
La Cuesta Dr
9300 SDCo 1271 B3
La Cumbre Dr
1500 SDGO 1247 G2
La Dalia
7800 SDCo 1148 H7
La Daphna
17800 SDCo 1148 J7
La Donna Ln
12200 SDCo 1232 A7
La Dorna St
5200 SDGO 1270 D2
La Duela Ln
2700 CRLB 1147 G3
La Duena Wy
10300 SDGO 1229 G7
La Entrada
17400 SDCo 1167 J3
17400 SDCo 1168 A2
La Entradita
3200 SDCo 1109 G2
La Espada
6400 SDCo 1168 E4
La Familia Ct
- SDCo 1232 E5
La Felice Ln
900 SDCo 1027 H6
La Fiesta Ct
900 SDCo 1128 C2
La Fiesta Dr
1500 SDCo 1128 C2
La Fiesta Ln
900 SDCo 1128 C2
La Fiesta Pl
900 SDCo 1128 C2
La Fiesta Wy
900 SDCo 1128 C2
La Flecha
6100 SDCo 1168 D3
La Flora Dr
1600 SDCo 1128 C2
La Force Rd
- SDCo 1233 F7
La France St
2400 SDGO 1248 B4
La Fremontia
6100 SDCo 1168 D2
La Gacha Ln
7900 CRLB 1147 G3
La Garza Ct
6400 CRLB 1127 G5
La Glorieta
5500 SDCo 1168 C4
La Golondrina St
2500 CRLB 1127 G4
La Gracia
16100 SDCo 1168 D4
La Gran Avd
- ENCT 1147 F5
La Gran Avenida Norte
- ENCT 1147 F5
La Gran Via
2700 CRLB 1147 G1
La Granada
5700 SDCo 1168 C3
La Granada Dr
1300 SDCo 1128 E3
La Habra Dr
1400 SDCo 1128 C3
La Habra Glen
2000 ESCN 1109 E5
La Habra St
2000 ESCN 1109 E5
La Haina Pl
500 SDCo 1152 G6
La Haina St
1300 SDCo 1152 F7
La Harina Ct
- SDGO 1189 B2
La Honda Dr
1100 ESCN 1110 C5
La Huerta Wy
800 SDGO 1330 G7

La Jacaranda
4800 SDCo 1168 A2
La Jolla Blvd
7600 SDGO 1227 E7
5800 SDGO 1247 F3
La Jolla Colony Dr
6100 SDGO 1228 A6
La Jolla Corona Ct
800 SDGO 1247 G3
La Jolla Corona Dr
5800 SDGO 1247 G3
La Jolla Farms Rd
9700 SDGO 1227 H1
La Jolla Hermosa Av
5700 SDGO 1247 F3
La Jolla Knoll
1400 SDGO 1227 F7
La Jolla Mesa Dr
5400 SDGO 1247 G4
La Jolla Palms Blvd
- CALX 6620 H5
La Jolla Pkwy
2400 SDGO 1227 H6
3100 SDGO 1228 A7
La Jolla Pl
- SNMS 1129 C1
La Jolla Pvt Rd
- SDCo 1052 F7
(See Page 1052)
La Jolla Rancho Rd
800 SDGO 1247 G3
La Jolla Scenic Dr
8900 SDGO 1227 J3
8300 SDGO 1228 A5
6500 SDGO 1247 H2
S La Jolla Scenic Dr
- SDGO 1227 J6
La Jolla Shores Dr
8700 SDGO 1227 H4
La Jolla Shores Ln
9000 SDGO 1227 H3
La Jolla Truck Trl
- SDCo 1072 H3
(See Page 1072)
La Jolla Village Dr
4300 SDGO 1228 D2
La Jolla Vista Dr
7700 SDGO 1228 A6
La Jota Wy
7900 SDGO 1227 G5
La Junta Av
3300 SDGO 1248 C2
La Larga Ct
- SDCo 1291 B1
La Larga Vista
9100 SDCo 1291 B1
La Linda Dr
1400 SDCo 1128 D3
La Loma Dr
1400 SDCo 1128 C3
La Loma Serena
2100 SDCo 1088 C1
La Lomita Dr
100 ESCN 1109 H6
La Mac Ln
- SDCo 1070 F7
La Macarena Av
2400 CRLB 1147 G3
La Madera Ln
1600 SDCo 1128 C2
La Madreselva
15500 SDCo 1168 B7
La Mancha Dr
1500 SDGO 1268 A1
La Mancha Pl
1300 CHLV 1311 B7
La Manda Rd
15300 POWY 1170 C7
La Mantanza
7400 SDGO 1168 H7
La Manzana Ln
1700 ESCN 1109 E6
La Mariquita Senda
1600 SDGO 1350 G2
La Marque St
2300 SDGO 1248 B4
La Media Rd
- CHLV 1311 D6
- CHLV 1331 E3
1100 SDGO 1331 G7
1900 SDGO 1351 G3
La Mesa Av
300 ENCT 1147 B5
1000 SDCo 1291 D2
La Mesa Blvd
7800 LMSA 1270 H2
La Mesa Cove
1400 SDCo 1291 D2
La Mesa Ct
1400 CHLV 1331 C3
2100 SDCo 1291 D1
La Mesita Pl
7300 LMSA 1270 F2
La Milla
8100 SDCo 1148 J6
La Mirada Av
700 ENCT 1147 C4
1100 ESCN 1109 E5
La Mirada Ct
1000 VSTA 1108 A6

La Mirada Dr
4600 OCSD 1066 J7
3400 SNMS 1108 C7
1400 VSTA 1107 J6
2800 VSTA 1108 B6
La Mirada Wy
1300 ESCN 1109 E5
La Monarca Ln
1500 CHLV 1331 D2
La Morada Ct
5800 SDGO 1229 G7
La Morada Dr
10400 SDGO 1229 H7
La Moree Rd
800 SNMS 1129 B2
La Nevasca Ln
2800 CRLB 1147 H4
La Noche Dr
1100 SDCo 1128 D2
1000 SNMS 1128 E2
La Noria
4300 SDCo 1167 J2
La Orilla
4500 SDCo 1167 J4
4600 SDCo 1168 A4
La Orquidia
7700 SDCo 1148 H6
La Palma
7000 SDCo 1168 F1
La Palma Dr
700 SDCo 1027 H3
La Palma St
1300 SDGO 1247 J7
La Paloma
6200 OCSD 1067 E3
La Paloma Ct
6500 CRLB 1127 G5
La Paloma Glen
1200 ESCN 1109 E5
La Paloma St
6400 CRLB 1127 G5
4200 SDGO 1287 J1
La Paz Ct
4800 CRLB 1106 J6
La Paz Dr
- IMPE 6499 G1
5100 SDGO 1290 B5
La Paz St
2300 OCSD 1106 F2
La Perla Wy
4800 SDCo 1271 C2
La Pintura Dr
6100 SDGO 1247 H2
La Place Ct
5900 CRLB 1127 E2
La Plancha Ln
2400 CRLB 1147 G3
La Plata
14600 SDGO 1168 H7
La Plata Ct
15100 SDCo 1173 E5
La Playa Av
1700 SDGO 1248 A7
La Plaza Dr
1400 SDCo 1128 C3
La Pluma Ct
1000 SDCo 1128 C3
La Pluma Ln
2400 CRLB 1147 G3
La Portalada Dr
4100 CRLB 1106 J5
La Posada St
1700 NATC 1289 J6
La Posada Wy
3000 SDCo 1155 H4
La Posta Rd
2900 SDCo 1298 E1
(See Page 1298)
1700 SDCo 1318 G3
(See Page 1318)
La Posta Truck Trl
31300 SDCo 1298 B5
(See Page 1298)
La Pradera Dr
500 SDCo 1109 G2
La Presa Av
500 SDCo 1291 C3
La Primavera Dr
- SDCo 1068 A4
La Puerta Pl
1800 LMGR 1290 F1
La Puerte
- ESCN 1129 F4
La Purisma Wy
300 OCSD 1087 A2
La Quebrada
700 ENCT 1148 A6
La Quena Vida
900 SDCo 1027 H7
La Quinta Pl
4400 OCSD 1066 G7
La Ramada Ln
2400 ESCN 1130 E1
La Reina Dr
1000 SDCo 1128 D3
La Ribera Ln
1400 CHLV 1331 D2
La Rochelle Av
1300 CHLV 1311 F1
La Rochi Wy
700 SDCo 1252 C6

La Rosa Dr
3800 SNMS 1108 C7
La Rouche Dr
8400 SDGO 1250 J4
La Rue Av
800 SDCo 1027 G3
La Rue Wy
500 ELCJ 1251 H4
La Rueda Dr
900 SDCo 1088 D7
4600 SDCo 1271 F2
La Salina Pl
800 OCSD 1106 C2
La Salina St
1400 OCSD 1106 C2
La Salle Ct
- CHLV 1311 E5
1300 VSTA 1107 J4
La Salle St
3900 SDGO 1268 C4
La Selva Rd
4700 SDCo 1274 A3
La Selva Wy
7900 CRLB 1147 G3
La Sena Av
7000 SDGO 1290 F4
La Sencilla Ln
5600 SDCo 1168 C4
La Senda Wy
800 CHLV 1310 H7
La Sendita
5900 SDCo 1168 D3
La Serena
2500 SDCo 1130 D7
La Sierra Dr
600 SNMS 1128 C1
La Siesta Wy
2000 NATC 1310 C1
La Sobrina Ct
1300 SOLB 1167 H7
La Solana Dr
1000 SDCo 1027 H2
La Soldadera
7300 SDCo 1168 G2
La Soledad
- SDCo 1232 D6
La Soledad Wy
300 OCSD 1087 A2
La Sombra Ct
1200 ELCJ 1251 D6
La Sombra Dr
500 ELCJ 1251 D6
1000 SNMS 1128 E2
La Spezia Wy
9100 SDGO 1249 D7
La Strada Dr
800 SDCo 1027 H3
La Subida Wy
1900 SDCo 1128 E3
La Suvida Dr
9300 LMSA 1251 B7
La Tara Ln
1100 SDCo 1047 G2
La Tempra Corte
- CHLV 1330 D4
La Tenaja Trl
4000 SDCo 1156 B3
La Tenista
6100 SDCo 1168 F7
La Terraza Blvd
300 ESCN 1129 G4
La Tiera Dr
4200 OCSD 1107 C3
La Tierra Ct
1700 SDCo 1128 C2
La Tierra Dr
900 SDCo 1128 C2
La Tierra Ln
1600 SDCo 1128 C2
La Tinada Ct
2400 CRLB 1147 G3
La Tortola
12900 SDGO 1189 F5
La Tortola Ct
9800 SDGO 1189 F5
La Tortola Pl
9800 SDGO 1189 F6
La Tortuga Dr
1100 VSTA 1107 E1
La Tortuga Wy
600 VSTA 1107 F1
La Trieste Pl
2900 ESCN 1150 A1
La Trucha St
14300 SDGO 1189 C2
La Valencia Ct
- BRAW 6319 F4
(See Page 6319)
La Valencia Dr
- BRAW 6319 F5
(See Page 6319)
La Valhalla Pl
- SDCo 1272 B3
La Valle Plateada
6400 SDCo 1168 E3
La Vanco Ct
6400 CRLB 1127 G5
La Varona Pl
100 ESCN 1150 A1
La Venta Dr
13300 POWY 1190 D4

La Ventana Ct
1000 SDCo 1128 C2
La Verde Dr
1600 SDCo 1128 B3
La Verde Ln
1200 SDCo 1128 B3
La Vereda Dr
8200 SDGO 1227 G5
La Verne Pl
4000 SDGO 1269 F5
La Veta Av
300 ENCT 1147 B5
La Via Feliz
- SDCo 1168 E4
La Via Guadalupe
- ENCT 1147 E7
La Vida Cir
700 VSTA 1087 G5
La Vida Ct
- CHLV 1311 G5
La Vine Ln
- SDCo 1108 B1
La Violetta
7700 SDCo 1148 H7
La Vista
- ESCN 1109 F7
La Vista Av
1400 ELCJ 1251 D6
La Vista Wy
12700 POWY 1190 C5
La Vita Ct
10400 SDGO 1210 A3
La Vonne Av
900 SDCo 1027 G3
La Vuelta
100 SNMS 1108 H3
Labrador Ln
9500 SDCo 1232 J4
Lace Pl
4900 SDGO 1290 A2
Lacebark St
800 SNMS 1109 B5
Lacie Ln
12000 SDCo 1231 J7
Lackawanna Wy
3000 SDGO 1248 F6
Laco Dr
4500 SDGO 1270 D4
Laconia St
2200 SDGO 1290 E1
Lacosta
- SNMS 1129 C1
Lacrosse Pl
500 ESCN 1130 B4
Lacy Av
- CALX 6620 E7
800 CALX 6680 E1
Ladd St
4200 SDGO 1248 B6
Laddeck Ct
7200 SDGO 1290 F2
Laddie Ln
8800 SDGO 1249 D5
Ladera Av
1500 ELCJ 1251 C2
Ladera Ct
2000 CRLB 1147 F2
Ladera Linda
- SOLB 1187 H1
Ladera Linda Wy
- SOLB 1187 H1
Ladera Piedra Wy
- POWY 1170 D5
Ladera Sarina
4900 SDCo 1168 A7
Ladera St
4400 SDGO 1287 H3
Ladera Vista Rd
4000 SDCo 1047 G4
Ladera Wy
200 OCSD 1086 E6
Ladero Pl
1900 ESCN 1129 F6
Ladiosa Ct
900 CHLV 1310 H4
Ladlehill Dr
2300 SDGO 1290 F6
Ladner St
4700 SDGO 1289 J5
Lado De Loma Dr
200 VSTA 1087 G7
600 VSTA 1107 H1
Ladoga Ln
1700 SDCo 1108 A2
Ladrillo St
7000 SDGO 1248 J6
Lady Bess Pl
8000 SDGO 1209 B5
Lady Bess Wy
10100 SDGO 1209 B5
Lady Fern Ct
- SDGO 1209 J2
Lady Hill Rd
3400 SDGO 1187 J5
Lady Ln
10800 SDCo 1232 B1
Ladybird Ln
5600 SDGO 1247 G3
Ladybug Ln
- SDCo 1088 G6

Ladybug Pl
1700 CHLV 1331 H1
Ladys Secret Ct
5900 SDCo 1188 E1
Ladys Secret Dr
14700 SDCo 1188 F1
Ladysmith Dr
800 ELCJ 1251 G7
Lafayette Ct
2300 CRLB 1106 H4
Lafayette Pl
- CHLV 1311 E5
Lafe Dr
10000 SNTE 1231 D2
Laffey Ct
10200 SDGO 1249 G3
Laffey Ln
800 ELCJ 1251 F4
Lagan Av
1200 VSTA 1087 G4
Lagasca Pl
800 CHLV 1310 H5
Lagewaart Rd
- SDCo 1172 E4
Lago Corte
- SDCo 1188 G2
Lago De Grata
- SDGO 1208 B2
Lago Grande Dr
6400 OCSD 1067 G3
Lago Lindo
6700 SDCo 1148 F7
5700 SDCo 1168 C2
Lago Madero
- CHLV 1311 F3
Lago Marcos
- SNMS 1129 C2
Lago Sereno
3600 ESCN 1150 A4
Lago Ventana
- CHLV 1311 F3
Lago Vista
18200 SDCo 1148 E6
Lagoon View Ct
1100 ENCT 1167 F4
Lagoon View Dr
2300 ENCT 1167 F4
1800 OCSD 1106 E2
Lagrange Rd
- CHLV 1311 E6
Laguardia Av
- IMPE 6499 D1
Laguardia Ct
- IMPE 6499 D2
Laguna Av
600 ELCJ 1251 E7
Laguna Dr
500 CRLB 1106 D4
500 SNMS 1109 A6
Laguna Ln
- SDCo 1237 D7
1700 VSTA 1088 A3
Laguna Meadows Dr
- SDCo 1217 G3
(See Page 1217)
Laguna Pl
- SDCo 1149 D4
Laguna Point Ct
600 CHLV 1330 J3
Laguna Seca Lp
- CHLV 1311 F5
Laguna St
500 CHLV 1310 C7
1100 OCSD 1106 C2
1200 SDCo 1321 H5
(See Page 1321)
E Laguna St
1200 OCSD 1106 C2
Laguna Trl
29000 SDCo 1237 C7
Laguna Vista
13600 SDCo 1232 E7
Laguna Vista Ct
13500 SDCo 1232 E7
Lagunita Ln
30200 SDCo 1067 J6
Lagunita Wy
4700 OCSD 1087 A1
Lahitte Ct
3200 SDGO 1228 C5
Lahoud Dr
1800 ENCT 1167 F2
Laird St
8100 LMSA 1250 H7
Lairwood Dr
10300 SNTE 1231 D3
Laja Dr
12400 POWY 1170 C7
Lajos Ln
- SDCo 1071 A7
Lake Adlon Ct
6400 SDGO 1250 G5
Lake Adlon Dr
7600 SDGO 1250 G5
Lake Alamor Av
6200 SDGO 1250 J6
Lake Albano Av
6200 SDGO 1250 J5
Lake Alturas Av
6300 SDGO 1250 J5

39 INDEX
Lake Andrita Av

San Diego County Street Index

INDEX 39
Law St

SAN DIEGO CO.

STREET
Block City Map# Grid

Lake Andrita Av
7700 SDGO 1250 G5
Lake Angela Dr
8900 LMSA 1251 A5
8500 SDGO 1250 J6
8600 SDGO 1251 A5
Lake Apopka Pl
6300 SDGO 1251 A5
Lake Arago Av
6300 SDGO 1250 J5
Lake Aral Dr
6300 SDGO 1250 J5
Lake Ariana Av
6300 SDGO 1250 J5
Lake Arrowhead Dr
6400 SDGO 1250 J5
6200 SDGO 1251 A6
Lake Artemus Av
8300 SDGO 1250 J5
Lake Ashmere Ct
6500 SDGO 1251 A4
Lake Ashmere Dr
8800 SDGO 1250 J5
Lake Ashwood Av
8300 SDGO 1250 H5
Lake Athabaska Pl
6300 SDGO 1251 A5
Lake Athabaska Wy
8700 SDGO 1251 A5
Lake Atlin Av
6300 SDGO 1250 J5
Lake Baca Dr
8300 SDGO 1250 J5
Lake Badin Av
6400 SDGO 1250 H5
Lake Ben Av
8300 SDGO 1250 J4
Lake Bluff Cir
8500 SDCo 1290 J5
Lake Blvd
4300 OCSD 1107 D3
Lake Breeze Ct
2900 SDCo 1291 D2
Lake Breeze Dr
10400 SDCo 1291 D1
Lake Canyon Ct
9900 SNTE 1231 A3
Lake Canyon Rd
9200 SNTE 1231 A4
Lake Cayuga Dr
7900 SDGO 1250 H5
Lake Circle Av
4900 SDCo 1048 J3
Lake Circle Ct
3300 SDCo 1048 J3
Lake Circle Dr
3500 SDCo 1048 J3
Lake Circle Ln
4900 SDCo 1048 H3
Lake Circle Pl
3300 SDCo 1048 J3
Lake Circle Rd
5000 SDCo 1048 J3
Lake Circle St
5000 SDCo 1048 J4
Lake Como Av
6300 SDGO 1250 H5
Lake Country Dr
9000 SNTE 1231 A4
Lake Crest Ct
2800 CHLV 1312 B6
(See Page 1312)
Lake Crest Dr
- CHLV 1311 J5
1300 CHLV 1312 A6
(See Page 1312)
Lake Ct
6800 SDGO 1268 J1
Lake Decatur Av
6300 SDGO 1250 H5
Lake Dora Av
6300 SDGO 1250 H5
Lake Dr
1900 ENCT 1167 F3
- SDCo 1129 E7
19800 SDCo 1149 E3
- SDCo 1290 J6
18800 SDGO 1149 E5
Lake Forest Av
4700 SDGO 1248 D1
Lake Forest St
2400 ESCN 1109 J3
Lake Gaby Av
8300 SDGO 1250 J4
Lake Garden Dr
3700 SDCo 1048 E1
Lake Grove Ct
11700 SDGO 1210 A4
Lake Helix Dr
- LMSA 1271 C1
Lake Helix Ter
9700 LMSA 1271 C2
Lake Hill Dr
9200 SNTE 1231 A4
Lake Hill Pl
700 CHLV 1311 J3
Lake Jennings Park Rd
9400 SDCo 1232 E4
Lake Kathleen Av
6300 SDGO 1250 H5
Lake Leven Dr
6300 SDGO 1250 G5
Lake Lomond Dr
6300 SDGO 1250 G5
Lake Lucerne Dr
6300 SDGO 1250 G5
Lake Madera Ct
9200 SDCo 1232 C5
Lake Marcia Dr
- SDGO 1250 J5
Lake Meadow Dr
- SDCo 1089 E4
Lake Meadow Ln
- SDCo 1089 E4
Lake Mere Ct
6400 SDGO 1251 A5
Lake Morena Dr
2400 SDCo 1297 E5
(See Page 1297)
Lake Murray Blvd
6000 LMSA 1250 H6
5400 LMSA 1270 F1
8400 SDGO 1250 J5
9200 SDGO 1251 A3
Lake Park Av
3400 SDCo 1048 J3
Lake Park Ct
4900 SDCo 1048 J3
Lake Park Ln
4100 SDCo 1048 J3
Lake Park Pl
4800 SDCo 1048 J3
Lake Park Rd
3700 SDCo 1048 J3
Lake Park St
3900 SDCo 1048 J3
Lake Park Wy
5600 LMSA 1250 G7
Lake Pointe Dr
2700 SDCo 1291 E1
Lake Poway Rd
- POWY 1170 F5
Lake Rd
- SDCo 1211 G5
Lake Ree Av
7500 SDGO 1250 G6
Lake Ridge Cres
100 SDCo 1047 G3
Lake Ridge Ct
10300 SDCo 1291 E2
Lake Ridge Dr
1000 SNMS 1128 B2
Lake Ridge Rd
3600 SDCo 1047 F3
Lake Rim Rd
11200 SDGO 1209 J3
Lake San Marcos Dr
1500 SDCo 1128 C2
Lake Shore Av
3400 SDCo 1048 J3
Lake Shore Ct
4900 SDCo 1048 J3
Lake Shore Dr
13400 SDCo 1232 C3
2500 SDCo 1297 E5
(See Page 1297)
6300 SDGO 1250 G5
Lake Shore Ln
4000 SDCo 1048 J3
Lake Shore Pl
4800 SDCo 1048 J3
Lake Shore Rd
3700 SDCo 1048 J3
Lake Shore St
3900 SDCo 1048 J3
Lake Sycamore Dr
4500 SDCo 1048 A6
Lake Tahoe Av
7700 SDGO 1250 G5
Lake Tahoe Cir
6400 SDGO 1250 G5
Lake Tahoe Ct
6400 SDGO 1250 G5
Lake Vicente Dr
- SDCo 1212 B3
Lake View Blvd
100 SDCo 1232 J7
500 SDCo 1252 H1
Lake View Ct
2800 CHLV 1312 A5
(See Page 1312)
Lake View Dr
29800 SDCo 1297 F6
(See Page 1297)
Lake View Ter
- SDCo 998 G5
3300 SDCo 1149 G2
Lake View Wy
5000 SDCo 1048 J3
Lake Vista Cir
31300 SDCo 1068 B2
Lake Vista Dr
5900 SDCo 1068 B2
Lake Vista Ter
31300 SDCo 1068 B3
Lake Wohlford Ct
24800 ESCN 1110 F4
Lake Wohlford Ln
16700 SDCo 1091 D3
Lake Wohlford Rd
5400 ESCN 1110 F4
16300 SDCo 1110 J2
20900 SDCo 1111 B1
N Lake Wohlford Rd
26800 SDCo 1091 C5
Lakecrest Pt
10600 SDGO 1209 J3
Lakedale Rd
1200 SDCo 1135 D3
Lakefield Ct
- SDGO 1188 B5
Lakehouse Pl
700 CHLV 1311 J3
Lakehurst Av
- SDGO 1248 D1
Lakeland Dr
10100 SNTE 1231 A3
Lakemont Dr
2800 SDCo 1048 E1
Lakeport Rd
8000 SDGO 1209 B4
Lakeridge Cir
2000 CHLV 1311 E4
Lakeridge Ln
1400 ELCJ 1251 C2
Lakeshore Dr
- CHLV 1311 E4
- SNMS 1128 F2
Lakeside
- SDCo 1232 E5
Lakeside Av
11600 SDCo 1231 H2
12400 SDCo 1232 A2
Lakeside Cir
- SDCo 1091 F4
Lakeside Ct
- SDCo 1231 J2
Lakeside Dr
- SNMS 1128 F2
Lakeside Ln
- OCSD 1107 D2
Lakeside Rd
2100 SDCo 1108 D2
Laketree Dr
- SDCo 1028 E7
- SDCo 1048 E1
Lakeview Av
200 SDCo 1291 B4
Lakeview Ct
13700 SDCo 1232 E5
Lakeview Dr
9400 LMSA 1251 C7
39900 SDCo 997 B2
- SDCo 1136 D7
3700 SDCo 1156 E2
3400 SDCo 1271 A6
Lakeview Granada Dr
13000 SDCo 1232 C5
Lakeview Rd
16100 POWY 1170 F4
2100 SDCo 1108 D2
9500 SDCo 1232 D4
E Lakeview Rd
13500 SDCo 1232 D5
W Lakeview Rd
13200 SDCo 1232 C5
Lakeview St
25700 SDCo 1109 F2
Lakeview Ter
9200 SDCo 1232 E5
Lakewind St
- ELCJ 1251 B2
Lakewood Av
- ESCN 1130 C1
Lakewood Ct
4900 SDGO 1228 G5
Lakewood Ln
200 OCSD 1106 C2
Lakewood St
3400 CRLB 1106 J4
6200 SDGO 1228 G5
Laky Ln
900 SDCo 1152 C5
Lal Bagh Ln
- SDCo 1069 E3
Lalani Dr
11100 SDCo 1271 H4
Lalley Ln
6900 SDGO 1250 J3
Lamar Ct
3100 SDCo 1271 A6
Lamar Springs Ct
3100 SDCo 1271 B6
Lamar St
900 SDCo 1152 D5
8600 SDCo 1270 J6
9300 SDCo 1271 B6
Lamas St
5700 SDGO 1228 B6
Lambar St
1200 ESCN 1129 F4
Lambda Dr
6200 SDGO 1250 C7
Lambda Ln
5600 LMSA 1250 J7
Lambert Glen
300 ESCN 1129 H2
Lambert Ln
5000 SDGO 1270 E2
Lambert Wy
6700 SDGO 1270 E2
Lambeth Ct
4500 CRLB 1106 J5
Lamentin Ct
10800 SDGO 1249 H1
Lamia Pt
13000 SDGO 1188 G4
Lamia Wy
4900 OCSD 1107 F5
Laminack Ln
19100 SDCo 1314 G1
(See Page 1314)
Lamont St
3900 SDGO 1248 B6
Lamour Ln
8100 SDCo 1169 A2
Lampasas Wy
3900 SNMS 1128 C1
Lamplight Dr
800 SDCo 1247 G4
Lamplighter Rd
700 SNMS 1109 A5
Lamplighter Village Dr
- SDCo 1271 F7
Lamplite Ln
13200 SDCo 1232 C7
Lan Ln
9800 SDCo 1089 D2
Lana Ct
4700 SDGO 1248 J1
Lana Dr
5900 SDGO 1248 J1
Lanai Ct
600 VSTA 1107 J3
Lanai Dr
1700 SDCo 1252 B4
Lanai Wy
4700 OCSD 1087 A2
Lanakai Ln
- CRLB 1126 H5
Lanao Ln
2300 SDGO 1330 C7
Lancashire Pl
600 SNMS 1108 J4
Lancashire Wy
18500 SDCo 1150 B5
Lancaster Creek Rd
10000 SDCo 1049 B5
Lancaster Dr
5800 SDGO 1250 B7
Lancaster Mtn Rd
32600 SDCo 1049 C5
Lancaster Rd
2900 CRLB 1107 B5
200 ImCo 6559 H3
Lance Av
8800 SDCo 1290 J4
Lance Ct
6400 SDGO 1250 B6
Lance Pl
6200 SDGO 1250 C6
Lance St
5900 SDGO 1250 B6
Lance Wy
6400 SDGO 1250 B6
Lancea Ct
6600 SDGO 1188 G4
Lancelot Dr
2600 OCSD 1086 E6
Lancer Av
100 OCSD 1086 F3
Lancer Glen
1200 ESCN 1129 F5
Lancer Park Av
600 SNMS 1109 C6
Lancewood Ln
1900 CRLB 1147 E2
Lancewood Wy
3500 SDCo 1048 C2
Lancha St
2700 SDGO 1248 J6
Landais Pl
35300 SDCo 1028 J6
Landale Ln
100 SDCo 1252 C5
Landau Ct
5900 CRLB 1127 D2
Landavo Dr
1000 SDCo 1130 C4
Landavo Rancho Rd
900 SDCo 1130 C4
Landbreeze Wy
11800 SDGO 1209 A1
Landfair Ct
3600 SDGO 1187 J4
Landfair Rd
13300 SDGO 1187 J4
13600 SDGO 1188 A4
Landing Dr
1700 VSTA 1107 G4
Landis Av
100 CHLV 1310 B5
Landis St
3500 SDGO 1269 F5
5200 SDGO 1270 A5
Landmark Ct
400 SNMS 1108 J4
Landmark Pl
600 SNMS 1108 J5
Landon Pl
7900 SDGO 1209 B4
Landquist Dr
1600 ENCT 1167 G1
Lands End Ct
- CRLB 1127 A5
Lands End Wy
- OCSD 1086 B6
Landscape Dr
2900 SDCo 1310 E1
Landsford Wy
3200 CRLB 1107 B3
Lane Av
800 CHLV 1311 G4
Lanewood Ct
6800 SDGO 1248 J4
Lanewood Pl
800 ESCN 1109 H4
Lang Av
2100 SDCo 1291 A1
Langdon Ln
9000 SDCo 1291 A1
Lange Av
2600 SDGO 1228 B6
Langford St
1400 OCSD 1086 B5
Langholm Rd
8600 SDCo 1232 F6
Langley Ct
10100 SDCo 1109 E2
Langley St
300 SDGO 1289 D4
Langmuir St
2200 SDGO 1248 H7
Laning Rd
2400 SDGO 1288 D2
Lanoitan Av
2000 NATC 1310 B1
N Lanoitan Av
- NATC 1290 B6
Lanphier Ln
2700 SDCo 1135 E6
Lansdale Ct
13200 SDGO 1188 C4
Lansdale Dr
4100 SDGO 1188 C4
Lansdown Ln
3200 SDCo 1172 C3
Lansford Ln
10500 SDGO 1208 H4
Lansing Cir
300 ESCN 1129 J2
Lansing Dr
7800 LMGR 1290 H2
Lansley Wy
100 CHLV 1310 C5
Lanston St
6500 SDGO 1248 H7
Lantana Av
1400 CHLV 1330 H3
Lantana Ct
900 SNMS 1109 A5
Lantana Dr
500 NATC 1309 H1
4700 SDGO 1269 J5
Lantana Ln
- IMPE 6499 D2
Lantana Ter
7100 CRLB 1127 A6
Lantana Wy
800 VSTA 1108 A4
Lantern Crest Wy
10900 SNTE 1231 F7
Lanyard Pl
- CRLB 1107 C7
Lanza Ct
1000 SDCo 1128 C2
Lapeer Ct
9200 SNTE 1231 A3
Lapis Ln
1900 SDCo 1153 A1
Lapis Rd
2400 CRLB 1127 F4
Lapiz Dr
8100 SDGO 1209 B2
Laport St
6100 LMSA 1250 F6
Lapped Circle Dr
3300 SDCo 1078 J6
(See Page 1078)
Laramie Ct
7700 SDGO 1250 C4
Laramie St
300 SDCo 1058 G6
(See Page 1058)
Laramie Wy
5700 SDGO 1250 C4
- SNMS 1128 A5
Laraway St
100 SDCo 1085 J4
Larch St
4500 SDGO 1289 J1
Larchmont St
12700 POWY 1170 D7
Larchwood Av
5900 SDGO 1250 C4
Larchwood Dr
1200 OCSD 1087 D2
500 SNMS 1109 B6
Larchwood Wy
7700 SDGO 1250 C4
Laredo Ct
1400 CHLV 1311 B3
Laredo Ln
3400 SDCo 1150 E2
Laredo St
3600 CRLB 1106 J4
Larenda Ln
9600 SDCo 1069 C5
Larga Cir
3500 SDGO 1268 D5
Larga Ct
3100 SDGO 1268 D6
Larga Vista
- SDCo 1048 B7
31400 SDCo 1069 J1
Largo Ln
3100 SDCo 1109 H2
Lariat Dr
- SNTE 1231 C3
Lariat Ln
300 IMPE 6439 F5
10300 SDCo 1271 E4
Lariat Wy
5400 OCSD 1067 D7
Larimar Av
2300 CRLB 1127 G5
Lario Ln
- SDCo 1169 E2
Larissa Ln
11900 SDCo 1231 J7
Lark Glen
2100 ESCN 1109 E5
Lark Song Ln
1100 ENCT 1147 J5
Lark St
4000 SDGO 1268 H5
Lark Vista Dr
16700 SDCo 1169 G4
Lark Wy
200 OCSD 1086 J1
Larkdale Av
8700 SDGO 1249 C5
Larkdale Pl
3200 SDGO 1249 C5
Larkhaven Dr
1500 CHLV 1330 F4
Larkhaven Glen
1700 ESCN 1109 D4
Larkhill Dr
1100 VSTA 1088 A2
Larkin Pl
2700 SDGO 1249 D6
Larkridge St
11000 SNTE 1231 G6
Larkspur Ct
- CHLV 1311 C7
- SNMS 1128 F3
Larkspur Dr
2100 SDCo 1233 J4
Larkspur Ln
1100 CRLB 1106 F6
- IMPE 6499 D2
3700 SDCo 1028 E4
Larkspur St
4600 SDGO 1268 A5
Larkwood Ct
3100 SDCo 1048 D3
Larmier Cir
11400 SDGO 1209 J2
Larrabee Av
9400 SDGO 1249 F6
Larrabee Pl
2400 SDGO 1249 F6
Larry Ln
- ESCN 1130 A6
5700 SDCo 1255 F5
Larry St
15100 POWY 1170 D7
Larsen Rd
500 ImCo 6439 C2
Larsen Wy
8600 LMSA 1271 A2
Larson Ln
1500 SDCo 1027 J4
Larwood Rd
1600 LMGR 1290 G2
1400 SDGO 1290 F2
Las Alturas Ter
5500 SDGO 1290 B4
Las Animas Wy
5200 SDGO 1290 B4
Las Arboledas
6600 SDCo 1148 F6
Las Ardillas
2300 SDCo 1109 G4
Las Bancas Ct
1000 CHLV 1330 F1
Las Bancas-Horsethief Rd
- SDCo 1255 H5
- SDCo 1275 F1
Las Bancas-Pine Crk
- SDCo 1237 A4
Las Banderas Dr
100 SOLB 1167 H6
Las Brisas Dr
400 ESCN 1110 E6
1300 SNTE 1231 D6
Las Brisas Terr
800 VSTA 1087 H5
Las Brisas Trl
3000 SDCo 1292 H1
(See Page 1292)
Las Brisas Wy
900 ENCT 1167 E3
Las Bujias Corte
1600 SDGO 1350 G2
Las Californias Dr
2500 SDGO 1351 F4
Las Canas Ct
100 SOLB 1167 H7
Las Canas Wy
- SOLB 1167 H7
Las Casitas Dr
1900 SDCo 1099 F4
(See Page 1099)
Las Colinas
6300 SDCo 1168 E3
Las Colinas Dr
600 SDCo 1129 J7
Las Conicas
9900 SDGO 1189 F4
Las Cruces Av
3900 SNMS 1128 C1
Las Cruces St
2200 CHLV 1331 H2
Las Cuestas
- SDCo 1168 F4
Las Cuspides St
- IMPE 6499 D1
Las Dunas St
- IMPE 6439 D7
Las Encinas Dr
- SDCo 1172 A5
Las Estancias Dr
500 CHLV 1310 J4
Las Estrellas
- SNMS 1129 C1
Las Flores
- SNMS 1129 C1
Las Flores Dr
100 BRAW 6319 G1
(See Page 6319)
- CHLV 1310 B4
1200 CRLB 1106 E4
3800 SDCo 1047 J3
100 SNMS 1108 D6
700 SNMS 1128 C1
Las Flores Rd
- CALX 6620 F7
Las Flores St
100 SDGO 1290 B4
Las Flores Ter
300 SDGO 1290 B5
Las Haciendas
14500 SDGO 1168 J7
Las Haciendas Av
- CALX 6620 E7
Las Lidia Ct
6700 SDGO 1290 E5
Las Lomas Dr
9300 SNTE 1231 A3
Las Lomas Rd
15600 SDCo 1233 C2
1900 VSTA 1088 C3
Las Lomas St
- IMPE 6439 D7
2100 SDGO 1268 B7
Las Lunas
7400 SDGO 1168 H7
Las Mananas
- SDCo 1188 H1
Las Manzanitas Rd
15500 SDCo 1172 A5
Las Mientes Ln
7900 CRLB 1147 H4
Las Milpas
- SDCo 1232 D7
Las Montanas
18000 SDCo 1148 C6
33800 SDCo 1318 G6
(See Page 1318)
Las Nubes Ct
1200 SDCo 1128 E3
Las Nueces Pl
7900 CRLB 1147 G3
Las Nuevas
1000 SDCo 1027 H4
Las Olas Ct
- ENCT 1147 H4
Las Palmas Av
2600 ESCN 1130 A7
3100 SDCo 1130 C7
Las Palmas Cove
2700 SDGO 1187 J7
Las Palmas Dr
2000 CRLB 1127 D4
700 VSTA 1107 G1
Las Palmas Ln
1700 ESCN 1109 E6
Las Palmas Rd
14000 SDCo 1292 H3
(See Page 1292)
Las Palmas Sq
- SDGO 1228 C3
Las Palomas
5400 SDCo 1168 C7
Las Pesetas
8400 SDCo 1149 A3
Las Planideras
15600 SDCo 1168 B6
15100 SDCo 1188 B1
N Las Posas Rd
500 SNMS 1108 E4
S Las Posas Rd
300 SNMS 1108 E7
400 SNMS 1128 E1
Las Potras Wy
13500 SDCo 1232 D5
Las Quintas
14700 SDCo 1188 F2
Las Ramblas
700 SDCo 1027 H3
Las Repolas
17600 SDCo 1148 J6
Las Rosas Ct
1300 CHLV 1311 B7
Las Terrinetos Rd
24300 SDCo 1235 J5
Las Tiendas Wy
- OCSD 1106 J2
Las Tunas Dr
6000 OCSD 1067 E4
Las Vegas Dr
3300 OCSD 1086 E5
Las Ventanas
- SDCo 1188 H1
Las Veras Pl
500 SDCo 1109 G2
Las Villas Pl
1300 ESCN 1109 G7
Las Vistas Rd
1300 SDCo 998 D7
Las Vistillas Ln
1200 SDCo 1128 E3
Laser Ln
9300 SDCo 1271 B4
Lashlee Ln
1800 SDGO 1350 F3
Laskey Ln
- SDCo 1271 D4
Laslo Dr
1600 SDCo 1130 C4
Laslo Pl
1700 SDCo 1130 C4
Lassen Dr
4900 OCSD 1107 F3
Lassen Ln
4300 CRLB 1106 J5
Lassen Peak Pl
- CHLV 1311 F6
Lassie Ln
8800 SDGO 1249 D5
Lassing Rd
- SDGO 1288 A5
Lasso Wy
9200 SNTE 1231 A2
Last Chance Trl
7500 SDCo 1158 B1
(See Page 1158)
Last Dollar Trl
7400 SDCo 1138 C7
(See Page 1138)
Lasven Ct
- SDCo 1272 C5
Lathrop Ln
100 SDCo 1252 J3
Lathrop Rd
- ImCo 6439 J4
Latigo Canyon Pl
13100 SDGO 1188 J5
Latigo Cv
1100 CHLV 1311 F6
Latigo Rd
27100 SDCo 1091 F4
Latigo Row
- ENCT 1148 D3
Latimer Ct
5900 SDGO 1290 C4
Latimer St
6000 SDGO 1290 C4
Latisha Pl
700 ELCJ 1251 H4
Latrobe Cir
7100 SDGO 1290 G7
Lattice Ln
2200 CHLV 1331 G3
Lauder St
5900 SDGO 1310 D1
Laughton Wy
- VSTA 1107 F2
Lauhala Canyon Rd
- VSTA 1107 G3
Laura Ct
7300 SDGO 1250 B5
Laura Dr
2100 ESCN 1110 B5
Laura Ln
1000 ESCN 1130 D6
Laura St
5300 SDGO 1250 B4
Lauralynn Pl
1500 OCSD 1106 D2
Laurashawn Ln
2900 SDCo 1109 H2
Lauree St
800 ELCJ 1251 F7
Laurel Av
1400 CHLV 1330 H3
- IMPE 6500 A2
100 NATC 1289 J7
Laurel Chase Dr
- SDGO 1208 E2
Laurel Cir
1500 VSTA 1107 E1
Laurel Dr
29500 SDCo 1297 E6
(See Page 1297)
300 SNMS 1108 J5
Laurel Grove Dr
1500 CHLV 1311 J6
1500 CHLV 1312 A6
(See Page 1312)
Laurel Hill Ln
16900 SDCo 1169 F2
Laurel Lee Ln
11900 SDCo 1231 J5
Laurel Ln
- ELCJ 1251 J6
9700 SDCo 1149 E2
19200 SDCo 1192 B2
(See Page 1192)
Laurel Path
10500 SDCo 1089 F4
Laurel Rd
1600 OCSD 1106 E1
Laurel Ridge Dr
- SDCo 1069 J1
- SDCo 1070 A1
Laurel St
- BRAW 6259 G6
(See Page 6259)
1400 OCSD 1086 B6
13200 SDCo 1232 C3
3100 SDGO 1269 E7
5200 SDGO 1270 A7
200 SDGO 1289 A1
W Laurel St
1200 SDGO 1288 H1
Laurel Tree Ln
1300 CRLB 1127 A3
Laurel Tree Rd
- CRLB 1127 A3
Laurel Valley Dr
- SDCo 1068 E7
Laurel Wood Rd
900 CRLB 1127 A5
Laurelcrest Dr
11200 SDGO 1208 C3
Laurelhurst Ct
9200 SDGO 1209 D2
Laurelridge Ct
6700 SDGO 1250 D4
Laurelridge Rd
7900 SDGO 1250 D4
Laurelwood Ct
800 SNMS 1109 A5
Laurelwood St
14700 POWY 1190 D1
Laurelwood Wy
700 ELCJ 1251 G4
Lauren Ct
1400 ENCT 1147 D3
Lauren Ln
- SDCo 1253 H1
Lauren Pl
1100 SNMS 1128 G5
Lauren Wy
10000 SNTE 1231 E3
Laurentian Dr
9300 SDGO 1189 D2
Lauretta St
5600 SDGO 1268 F3
Laurie Cir
2000 CRLB 1106 G4
Laurie Ln
5500 SDCo 1168 D4
2400 SDGO 1289 H1
Laurinda St
2000 SDGO 1289 J1
Laurine Ln
- SDCo 1027 F5
Lauriston Dr
1100 SDGO 1350 C1
Lausanne Dr
200 SDGO 1290 G4
S Lausanne Dr
100 SDGO 1290 F4
Lava Ct
7900 LMSA 1270 H4
Lavade Ln
5300 SDCo 1311 A2
Lavala Ln
1800 ELCJ 1252 C1
Lavandula Ct
6600 SDGO 1188 G6
Lavell St
9100 SDCo 1271 B3
Lavender Ct
700 SNMS 1109 A5
Lavender Ln
1800 CHLV 1331 F3
200 SDCo 1108 C4
Lavender Point Ln
10300 SDCo 1069 E2
Lavender Star Dr
- SDCo 1169 D2
Lavender Wy
7000 CRLB 1127 A6
13500 SDGO 1188 G3
Lavigne Rd
- ImCo 6620 J7
Law St
800 SDGO 1247 H5
1800 SDGO 1248 A5
1100 SNMS 1128 E1

San Diego County Street Index

STREET Block	City	Map#	Grid
Lawana Dr			
1300	VSTA	1087	E7
Lawford Ct			
7600	LMGR	1290	G1
Lawford St			
7600	LMGR	1290	G1
Lawler Ct			
4600	SDCo	1271	C3
Lawndale Rd			
1800	SDCo	1272	B2
Lawndale St			
1900	SDGO	1350	C3
Lawnsdale Pl			
500	SNMS	1108	J4
Lawnview Dr			
400	CHLV	1310	F6
Lawrence Ln			
2800	SDCo	1130	E7
1800	SDCo	1172	F1
Lawrence St			
3400	CRLB	1106	J4
2900	SDGO	1288	A4
Lawrence Welk Ct			
28300	SDCo	1088	J2
Lawrence Welk Dr			
8700	SDCo	1088	J1
-	SDCo	1089	B2
Lawrence Welk Ln			
29100	SDCo	1088	H1
Lawson Hills Rd			
-	SDCo	1274	D3
Lawson Valley Rd			
16500	SDCo	1273	F5
18100	SDCo	1274	C3
Lawton Dr			
2200	LMGR	1270	J7
Layang Layang Cir			
4000	CRLB	1106	F7
Layla Ct			
4200	SDGO	1350	G1
Layla Wy			
4200	SDGO	1350	G1
Layne Pl			
1700	SDCo	1272	C3
Layton St			
900	ELCJ	1251	G2
Laytonville Pl			
-	CHLV	1331	C2
Lazanja Dr			
14500	SDGO	1168	J7
Lazanja Pass			
14400	SDGO	1189	A1
Lazarette Wy			
700	CRLB	1126	J6
Lazeroff Ln			
17400	SDCo	1274	A2
Lazo Ct			
800	CHLV	1310	H6
Lazy Acres Dr			
-	SDCo	1191	E5
Lazy Circle Dr			
700	VSTA	1107	G2
Lazy Clouds Pt			
6800	SDGO	1250	D4
Lazy Creek Rd			
15100	SDCo	1232	H2
Lazy Dog Wy			
14600	SDCo	1232	H4
Lazy H Dr			
16400	SDCo	1051	C7
-	SDCo	1071	B1
Lazy Jays Wy			
3800	SDCo	1155	J2
Lazy Ladder Dr			
200	SDCo	1078	F2
(See Page 1078)			
Lazy River Rd			
8100	SDCo	1169	A1
Lazy S Dr			
1900	SDCo	1058	G7
(See Page 1058)			
Lazy Trail Ct			
5900	SDCo	1311	B3
Le Barron Rd			
5300	SDGO	1269	J2
Le Clair Ln			
400	SDCo	1109	G3
Le Conte St			
700	OCSD	1086	G5
7300	SDGO	1290	F4
Le Hardy Rd			
-	SDGO	1289	E6
Lea St			
5400	SDGO	1270	B5
Lea Terrace Dr			
11100	SNTE	1231	G6
Leadrope Wy			
5800	SDCo	1311	B2
Leaf Ct			
6200	SDGO	1290	D5
Leaf Ln			
-	SDCo	1109	E7
Leaf Pine Ct			
-	SDCo	1089	B2
Leaf Ter			
1200	SDGO	1290	D5
Leafwood Pl			
2000	ENCT	1147	H5
10300	SDGO	1209	G4
Leah Ln			
800	SDCo	1149	H2
Leaila Ln			
13100	POWY	1190	H4
Leaning Tree Ln			
13300	POWY	1190	H4
E Leanna Ct			
200	CHLV	1330	F2
Leanna St			
-	CHLV	1330	E2
Leary St			
10300	SDGO	1249	G2
Least Tern Ct			
-	SDGO	1208	J1
Leathers St			
4500	SDGO	1248	B1
Leatherwood St			
1900	SDGO	1350	C3
Leavesly Tr			
10100	SNTE	1231	D4
Lebanon Rd			
28600	SDCo	1237	B6
Lebaun Dr			
1800	LMGR	1290	H1
Lebon Dr			
3300	SDGO	1228	B3
Lechuza Ln			
100	SDCo	1290	J5
Leda Wy			
24700	SDCo	1173	G3
Ledesma Ln			
-	SDCo	1172	F1
Ledge Av			
2100	SDCo	1291	D1
Ledge St			
-	SNMS	1128	G5
Ledgeside Ln			
2100	SDCo	1271	E7
Ledgeside St			
9900	SDCo	1291	D1
Ledgetop Pl			
2700	SDCo	1271	D7
Ledgeview Av			
2100	SDCo	1271	E7
Ledgeview Ln			
2200	SDCo	1271	C7
Ledgeview Pl			
2500	SDCo	1271	B6
Ledgewood Ln			
200	SDGO	1290	G5
Ledgewood Pl			
7400	SDGO	1290	G5
Lee Av			
900	CALX	6680	E1
2200	ESCN	1110	C6
4600	LMSA	1270	G3
Lee Barr Ranch Rd			
36000	SDCo	1029	H3
Lee Cir			
-	CHLV	1330	H2
Lee Ct			
2000	CRLB	1106	G5
25700	SDCo	1109	F2
-	SDGO	1288	D1
Lee Dr			
2000	ESCN	1110	C6
Lee Rd			
500	IMPE	6439	D5
Lee St			
4100	SDGO	1248	C5
Lee Wy			
-	SDGO	1209	E2
Leeann Ln			
-	ENCT	1147	B4
Leeds St			
-	SDGO	1228	C1
Leepish Dr			
-	OCSD	1086	E3
Leeward Av			
700	SNMS	1128	F6
Leeward Ct			
300	OCSD	1086	F6
Leeward Isle Pt			
-	SDGO	1351	A2
Leeward St			
7100	CRLB	1126	J6
Leeward Wy			
2500	CHLV	1311	G4
Legacy Canyon Pl			
11300	SDGO	1210	C2
Legacy Canyon Wy			
12700	SDGO	1210	C2
Legacy Dr			
-	ELCN	6559	J4
800	SNMS	1108	H5
Legacy Pl			
12700	SDGO	1210	D2
Legacy Rd			
12600	SDGO	1210	C1
Legacy Ter			
11400	SDGO	1210	C1
Legakes Av			
-	IMPE	6499	J2
Legate Ct			
500	CHLV	1310	F5
Legaye Dr			
1600	ENCT	1167	E2
Legend Rock Ln			
-	SDCo	1089	E5
Legend Wy			
-	SDCo	1109	G1
Legendale Dr			
11500	SDCo	1211	G6
Leghorn Av			
400	SDGO	1290	E5
Legion Rd			
-	BRAW	6319	H4
(See Page 6319)			
W Legion Rd			
-	BRAW	6319	F4
(See Page 6319)			
Lego Dr			
-	CRLB	1126	J3
Legoland Dr			
-	SDCo	1126	J2
Lehigh Av			
800	CHLV	1311	E5
Lehigh Ct			
2800	OCSD	1087	A7
Lehigh St			
1300	SDGO	1268	E2
Lehner Av			
500	SDCo	1109	H5
1200	SDCo	1110	A4
Lehrer Dr			
4700	SDGO	1228	F7
Leia Ln			
-	SDCo	1071	E2
Leicester St			
7000	SDGO	1250	A5
Leicester Wy			
5100	SDGO	1250	A5
Leigh Av			
8800	SDCo	1291	A5
Leighton Ct			
2100	SDGO	1290	F7
Leila Ln			
10300	SNTE	1231	E5
Leila Wy			
9500	SNTE	1231	E5
Leilani Wy			
3000	SDGO	1330	D7
Leisure Ln			
8600	SDCo	1068	J6
Leisure Village Dr			
4600	OCSD	1107	E4
Leisure Village Wy			
4600	OCSD	1107	E4
Lejeune St			
100	SDCo	1067	A2
Lejos Dr			
1900	SDCo	1130	B5
Leland Pl			
700	SDCo	1251	J6
Leland St			
1000	SDCo	1291	A3
3700	SDGO	1268	C5
Leland Wy			
1300	SDCo	1109	E6
Lema Wy			
6700	SDGO	1250	F5
Lemarand Av			
6500	SDGO	1270	D5
Lemat			
-	SDGO	1350	H2
Lemay Av			
500	SDGO	1330	E6
Lemire Ct			
300	CHLV	1310	F7
Lemire Dr			
300	CHLV	1310	F7
Lemnos Wy			
4000	OCSD	1107	E5
Lemon Av			
800	ELCJ	1251	E7
7500	LMGR	1270	G6
8000	LMSA	1270	H3
8900	LMSA	1271	A2
2000	SDCo	1129	H6
9200	SDCo	1271	B2
700	VSTA	1087	H5
S Lemon Av			
1300	ELCJ	1251	E7
1300	ELCJ	1271	E1
Lemon Blossom Ln			
2000	SDCo	1027	J6
Lemon Blossom Rd			
-	SDCo	1071	A6
Lemon Cir			
7900	LMSA	1270	H3
Lemon Crest Dr			
11900	SDCo	1231	J5
12300	SDCo	1232	A4
Lemon Drop Ln			
400	VSTA	1107	H1
Lemon Grass Wy			
1700	CHLV	1331	H3
Lemon Grove Av			
2400	LMGR	1270	G7
1500	LMGR	1290	F2
3700	LMSA	1270	G5
Lemon Grove Dr			
100	SDCo	1047	F4
Lemon Grove Rd			
-	SDCo	1085	H3
Lemon Grove Wy			
7800	LMGR	1270	H5
Lemon Heights Dr			
1700	OCSD	1087	D4
Lemon Hill Rd			
34500	SDCo	1030	J7
Lemon Leaf Dr			
-	CRLB	1127	B5
Lemon Line Rd			
37400	SDCo	999	D7
Lemon Ln			
3200	LMGR	1270	J6
Lemon Pine Ct			
13000	SDGO	1189	C5
Lemon Pl			
1300	SDCo	1130	D4
Lemon St			
-	LMSA	1251	C7
1300	OCSD	1086	B6
9000	SDCo	1271	A7
Lemon Tree Ct			
-	SDGO	1208	A3
1700	SNMS	1128	F6
Lemona Av			
3500	SDGO	1270	A6
Lemonberry Ln			
2000	CRLB	1147	E2
Lemonseed Dr			
4100	SDGO	1330	G7
Lemonwood Ct			
600	OCSD	1086	F2
Lemonwood Dr			
300	SDCo	1047	F7
Lemonwood Ln			
7000	LMGR	1270	E6
9900	SDGO	1249	G1
1900	VSTA	1107	J4
Lemora Ln			
-	SDCo	1130	F6
Len Ct			
10400	SNTE	1231	E2
Len Ln			
-	SDCo	1089	D1
Len St			
10700	SNTE	1231	E2
Len Wy			
10400	SNTE	1231	E2
Lena Ct			
100	SNMS	1128	H5
Lendee Dr			
1800	SDCo	1130	C4
Lennie Dr			
30300	SDCo	1069	J4
Lennon Ln			
29200	SDCo	1089	C1
Lenny Ln			
2000	SDCo	1252	H4
Lenore Dr			
4700	SDGO	1270	E3
Lenore St			
5100	OCSD	1067	A5
Lenox Ct			
3700	CRLB	1107	A4
Lenox Dr			
5400	SDGO	1290	B2
Lenrey Av			
1500	ELCN	6499	F7
-	ELCN	6559	D1
Lenrey Ct			
-	ELCN	6559	D1
Lenser Wy			
800	ESCN	1129	G2
Lenteja Ln			
13600	SDCo	1232	D3
Lento Ln			
300	SDCo	1252	H3
Leo Ct			
2000	ESCN	1109	F5
Leo Rd			
-	SDCo	1029	H3
Leo St			
5100	SDGO	1270	D2
Leoma Ln			
100	CHLV	1330	E3
Leon Av			
1400	SDGO	1349	J2
1900	SDGO	1350	B2
Leon Ln			
1200	SDCo	1156	D2
Leon St			
5200	OCSD	1067	B5
4500	SDGO	1287	H1
Leon Wy			
-	SDCo	1028	D1
Leona Ln			
12300	POWY	1190	B4
Leonard Av			
300	OCSD	1106	B2
Leonard St			
1000	BRAW	6320	A2
(See Page 6320)			
2800	NATC	1310	C2
Leone Av			
2100	SDCo	1300	C7
(See Page 1300)			
Leoney Ct			
3100	SDCo	1293	E1
Leoney Ln			
15400	SDCo	1293	E1
Leonis Pl			
1500	VSTA	1087	F3
Leora Ln			
1600	ENCT	1147	B2
600	SNMS	1129	E1
Leos Wy			
-	SDCo	1234	J4
Leppert Ct			
800	SDGO	1290	F3
Leppert St			
800	SDGO	1290	F3
Leprechaun Ln			
32200	SDCo	1048	G6
Lepus Rd			
8500	SDGO	1209	C1
Lerida Dr			
4300	SDGO	1270	D4
Lerkas Wy			
4900	OCSD	1107	E5
Lermas Ct			
7000	LMGR	1270	F7
Leroy St			
1000	SDGO	1288	B2
Les Arbres Pl			
10400	SDGO	1210	A3
Les Fleurs Ter			
10400	SDGO	1210	A3
Les Mas			
-	SNTE	1231	A5
Les Rd			
9200	SNTE	1231	A5
Lesa Rd			
5500	LMSA	1270	G1
Lesar Pl			
15800	SDGO	1169	D3
Leslie Ct			
1400	SNMS	1109	D7
Leslie Dr			
100	ESCN	1109	H6
Leslie Rd			
900	ELCJ	1251	F7
Lester Av			
7800	LMGR	1270	H5
Lethbridge Wy			
9200	SDGO	1189	D2
Leticia Dr			
9300	SNTE	1230	H6
Letton St			
200	SDCo	1152	E7
N Letton St			
100	SDCo	1152	E7
Lettuce St			
-	ImCo	6560	B7
Leucadia Av			
8200	SDGO	1290	H3
Leucadia Blvd			
600	ENCT	1147	C4
1100	SDCo	1147	E4
W Leucadia Blvd			
100	ENCT	1147	A4
Leucadia Scenic Ct			
1900	ENCT	1147	B2
Leucadia Village Ct			
-	ENCT	1147	B2
Leucite Pl			
6800	CRLB	1127	G5
Levant Ln			
1400	CHLV	1311	F7
Levant St			
6900	SDGO	1248	J6
Levant Wy			
200	OCSD	1087	A1
Levante St			
1800	CRLB	1147	E2
Levanto Ct			
19800	SDCo	1152	C2
Levee Dr			
-	CRLB	1107	C3
Levita Ct			
15000	POWY	1170	C7
Lew Ln			
-	CHLV	1331	F2
Lewis			
-	SDCo	1232	F5
Lewis Ct			
1400	VSTA	1107	J5
Lewis Ln			
2600	CRLB	1106	E4
13900	ESCN	1110	F5
Lewis St			
4200	OCSD	1087	C7
W Lewis St			
700	SDGO	1268	J5
200	SDGO	1269	A5
Lewison Av			
5200	SDGO	1250	B5
Lewison Ct			
5200	SDGO	1250	A5
Lewison Dr			
7000	SDGO	1250	B5
Lewison Pl			
5200	SDGO	1250	A5
Lewiston St			
13900	SDGO	1190	A2
Lexi Ct			
1200	SNMS	1128	G5
Lexine Ln			
-	SDCo	1130	C5
Lexington Av			
-	SDGO	1269	H7
E Lexington Av			
200	ELCJ	1251	F6
1300	ELCJ	1252	A5
1700	SDCo	1252	B5
W Lexington Av			
300	ELCJ	1251	F5
Lexington Cir			
2900	CRLB	1107	B5
-	OCSD	1086	J3
Lexington Ct			
400	OCSD	1086	J4
Lexington Dr			
1200	VSTA	1088	A6
Lexington St			
-	BRAW	6260	D7
(See Page 6260)			
-	IMPB	1349	H2
Leyendekker Ct			
-	SDCo	1232	B4
Leyendekker Rd			
9200	SDCo	1232	B4
Leyte Point Dr			
6700	SDGO	1290	F7
Leyte Rd			
1300	CORD	1309	C5
Libby St			
100	OCSD	1086	C6
Libelle Ct			
12100	SDGO	1210	B1
Liberatore Ln			
800	SDCo	1252	D7
Libertad Dr			
17200	SDGO	1169	H2
Liberty Creek Pl			
1300	CHLV	1331	B2
Liberty Dr			
300	SNMS	1108	G7
Liberty Pl			
6200	CRLB	1127	G2
1500	ESCN	1129	J5
Liberty Wy			
1200	VSTA	1127	J1
Libra Dr			
9000	SDGO	1209	D2
Libre Glen			
-	ESCN	1130	A5
Licia Wy			
12100	SDGO	1189	A7
Liddiard St			
-	ELCJ	1251	B2
Lido Ct			
800	SDGO	1267	H2
Liebel Ct			
4800	SDGO	1248	J1
Lieder Dr			
2200	SDGO	1350	A1
Lieta St			
1300	SDGO	1268	E2
Liews Wy			
13600	SDGO	1188	A4
Liggett Dr			
3600	SDGO	1288	A1
Liggett Wy			
1400	SDGO	1288	A1
Lighthouse Rd			
-	CRLB	1127	A5
-	SNMS	1128	D5
Lighthouse Ridge Ln			
3100	SDGO	1268	D5
Lighthouse View Pl			
5100	SDGO	1330	J7
Lighthouse Wy			
-	SDGO	1188	D4
Lightning Rd			
3300	SDCo	1078	H7
(See Page 1078)			
Lightning Trail Ln			
-	CHLV	1311	H5
Lightwave Av			
9000	SDGO	1249	D1
Ligia Pl			
5000	SDCo	1271	H2
Lila Dr			
4800	SDGO	1269	J2
Lila Hill Ln			
11900	SDCo	1232	A7
Lila Ln			
300	SDCo	1252	H3
Lilac Av			
1300	CHLV	1330	H2
Lilac Crest			
12000	SDCo	1069	J4
Lilac Ct			
1800	CRLB	1127	E6
-	SNMS	1128	E2
Lilac Dr			
2700	SDCo	1136	D7
200	SDCo	1252	H3
29400	SDCo	1297	E6
(See Page 1297)			
Lilac Extension Rd			
900	SDCo	1029	H5
Lilac Hill Rd			
-	SDCo	1069	J3
Lilac Hills Ln			
-	SDCo	1069	E3
Lilac Knolls Rd			
12000	SDCo	1070	A4
Lilac Ln			
-	IMPE	6499	D2
-	SDCo	1086	A4
35100	SDCo	1156	E7
1800	SDCo	1233	G7
24400	SDCo	1235	J1
8000	SDCo	1237	C6
200	SDCo	1252	H3
2100	SDCo	1253	G1
38300	SDCo	1299	J5
(See Page 1299)			
Lilac Pl			
-	SDCo	1069	C1
Lilac Ranch Rd			
500	SDCo	1233	G7
Lilac Ranch Rd			
500	SDCo	1253	G1
Lilac Rd			
34300	SDCo	1029	H6
10100	SDCo	1030	A5
-	SDCo	1049	G2
31400	SDCo	1069	H2
-	SDCo	1070	B6
-	SDCo	1090	D2
2100	SDCo	1152	G1
W Lilac Rd			
7700	SDCo	1048	G6
-	SDCo	1068	A1
-	SDCo	1069	D3
Lilac Ridge Rd			
10100	SDCo	1069	D2
Lilac St			
1800	SDCo	1152	G1
Lilac Summit			
-	ENCT	1148	D5
Lilac Trl			
2500	SDCo	1299	H3
(See Page 1299)			
Lilac Vista Dr			
-	SDCo	1069	G3
Lilac Walk			
9500	SDCo	1049	B7
Lilac Wood Ln			
-	SDCo	1273	G5
Lilac Wood Rd			
-	SDCo	1273	G5
Lilac Wy			
-	SDGO	1188	G3
Lile St			
3300	OCSD	1107	A2
Lilium Ln			
-	CRLB	1127	D4
Lillian Ln			
700	ELCJ	1251	G7
Lillian St			
4900	SDGO	1268	E2
Lillian Wy			
100	SDCo	1027	G2
Lillie Ln			
39300	SDCo	1300	C6
(See Page 1300)			
Lily Av			
1600	ELCJ	1252	B2
Lily Bird Ln			
2200	SDCo	1028	A1
Lily Pl			
7300	CRLB	1127	B6
Lima Ct			
1500	ELCJ	1252	A5
Limar Wy			
9600	SDGO	1189	E5
Limber Pine Rd			
3900	SDCo	1048	C4
Lime Ct			
1800	CHLV	1331	F3
Lime Grove Rd			
-	POWY	1170	E5
Lime Pl			
-	VSTA	1107	H2
Lime Rock Ct			
2100	SDCo	1272	C4
Lime St			
7300	LMSA	1270	F5
1100	VSTA	1107	G2
Lime Tree Wy			
500	OCSD	1086	E2
Limerick Av			
5000	SDGO	1228	H7
4800	SDGO	1248	H1
Limerick Ct			
5400	SDGO	1228	G7
Limerick Wy			
4400	SDGO	1248	H2
Limestone Ln			
-	SDCo	1169	E2
Limetree Ln			
10300	SDCo	1291	E2
Limon Ln			
8200	SDCo	1251	H1
Limonite Ct			
6700	CRLB	1127	E5
Linalda Dr			
1200	SDCo	1251	H3
Linare Ct			
100	SOLB	1167	H5
Linares Ct			
-	SOLB	1167	H5
Linares St			
11200	SDGO	1169	H6
Linaza Ln			
100	SDCo	1290	J5
Linbrook Dr			
1800	SDGO	1268	J1
Linbrook Pl			
7300	SDGO	1269	A1
Lincoln Av			
300	ELCJ	1251	G6
1700	ELCN	6499	E4
1600	SDGO	1269	C5
E Lincoln Av			
2300	ESCN	1110	C5
W Lincoln Av			
900	ESCN	1129	F2
Lincoln Ct			
2800	NATC	1310	B3
Lincoln Downs Wy			
-	SOLB	1187	F2
Lincoln Pkwy			
700	ESCN	1109	J7
-	ESCN	1129	H1
Lincoln Pl			
-	CALX	6680	F1
900	SDGO	1290	G2
Lincoln St			
700	CALX	6680	E1
3100	CRLB	1106	E6
7900	LMGR	1270	H6
1900	OCSD	1106	D3
Lincolnshire St			
18300	SDGO	1150	B6
Lind Vern Ct			
8700	SNTE	1231	D7
Linda Ct			
2400	ESCN	1110	D6
Linda Dr			
3000	OCSD	1107	B1
Linda Ln			
500	CHLV	1310	C7
2000	CRLB	1106	G4
3700	SDCo	1271	C5
6500	SDGO	1250	D7
Linda Rosa Av			
5600	SDGO	1247	G3
Linda St			
700	CALX	6680	G1
1500	SDCo	1028	A5
Linda Sue Ln			
1400	ENCT	1147	G6
Linda Vista			
-	SNMS	1129	C1
Linda Vista Ct			
2700	SDGO	1249	A6
Linda Vista Dr			
3800	SDCo	1048	B3
3800	SNMS	1108	D7
900	SNMS	1128	E1
-	VSTA	1128	B1
Linda Vista Rd			
6700	SDGO	1248	J7
7600	SDGO	1249	A5
5900	SDGO	1268	G2
Linda Vista Terr			
3500	SDCo	1048	A3
Linda Wy			
300	ELCJ	1251	F5
5300	SDGO	1247	G4
Lindamere Ln			
13500	SDGO	1190	B3
Lindbergh St			
3600	SDGO	1330	E6
Lindbergh Wy			
500	SDGO	1330	F6
Lindburgh Ct			
-	BRAW	6260	C7
(See Page 6260)			
Lindell Av			
200	ELCJ	1251	F6
Linden Dr			
900	VSTA	1087	F6
Linden Ln			
8900	LMSA	1271	A2
Linden Rd			
7500	SDCo	1237	C7
Linden Ter			
7100	CRLB	1127	A6
Linden Wy			
4900	LMSA	1271	A2
Lindenwood Dr			
1300	SDCo	1251	G1
Lindero Pl			
1200	SDCo	1027	H4
Lindholm Ln			
-	LMGR	1270	E7
Lindly Ct			
11600	SDGO	1209	H1
Lindo Lake Pl			
9900	SDCo	1232	B3
Lindo Ln			
13000	SDCo	1232	C3
Lindo Paseo			
5500	SDGO	1270	B2
Lindos Wy			
4200	OCSD	1107	F6
Lindsay Dr			
2200	CRLB	1107	C7
2200	CRLB	1127	C1
Lindsay Michelle Dr			
2100	SDCo	1234	A4
Lindsay St			
-	CHLV	1331	B1
500	ELCJ	1251	G4
Lindsey Ct			
2200	SDCo	1028	B4
Lindsley Park Dr			
1700	SNMS	1109	D7
Lindy Ln			
800	SNMS	1109	B6
Lindy Wy			
2000	SDCo	1108	G2
Linea Del Cielo			
5500	SDCo	1168	D3
Linea Del Sol			
4800	SDCo	1168	B7
Linen Dr			
7900	SNTE	1230	H7
7900	SNTE	1250	H1
Linfield Av			
5600	SDGO	1270	D1
Lingel Dr			
700	SDCo	1253	C2
Lingre Av			
13200	POWY	1190	E2
Linholm Av			
-	CALX	6680	D1
Link Dr			
3500	SDCo	1270	J6
Links Wy			
2400	VSTA	1107	J4
Linmar Ln			
3900	CRLB	1106	F6
Linna Pl			
7300	SDGO	1250	B5
Linnet St			
5900	SDGO	1290	C3
Linnie Ln			
-	POWY	1190	F5
Lino Ct			
8300	SDGO	1189	B6
Linroe Dr			
12200	SDCo	1232	A7
Linsay Pl			
1400	ESCN	1109	J5
Linview Av			
900	ESCN	1109	J6
Linwood Pl			
1100	ESCN	1130	D2
Linwood St			
600	ESCN	1130	C2
2400	SDGO	1268	F5
Lion Cir			
-	CHLV	1310	D6
Lion Valley Rd			
200	ESCN	1110	D7
Lionel St			
2600	SDGO	1249	C6
Lions Gate			
2200	VSTA	1088	C5
Lionshead Av			
3100	CRLB	1127	H2
Lipizzan Wy			
600	SDCo	1252	C6
Lipizzaner Cir			
5500	OCSD	1067	E6
Lipmann St			
6800	SDGO	1228	E4
Lipscomb Dr			
10300	SDGO	1209	D4
Liquid Amber Wy			
600	SNMS	1128	F6
Liquid Ct			
8800	SDGO	1228	H1
Liquidamber Ln			
13200	SDCo	1090	C5
Lirac Pl			
15000	SDGO	1169	F6
Lirio Corte			
1100	CHLV	1311	A7
Lirio St			
400	SOLB	1187	F1
Lirope St			
6000	SDGO	1290	C6
Lisa Av			
1600	VSTA	1087	H3
Lisa Ln			
1800	SDCo	1252	C3
Lisa Meadows			
-	SNTE	1231	E6
Lisa St			
2200	CRLB	1107	A6
Lisa Ter			
1800	SDCo	1252	C3
Lisa Wy			
1400	ESCN	1110	B5
Lisann St			
4600	SDGO	1248	B1
Lisbon Ln			
1600	SDCo	1252	B7
Lisbon Pl			
1600	ESCN	1129	F5
Lisbon St			
7000	SDGO	1290	F3
Lise Av			
4900	SDGO	1290	A3
Lisieux Terr			
6200	SDGO	1250	C6
Lismore Pl			
6200	CRLB	1127	F3
Lister St			
4100	SDGO	1248	E7
Liszt Av			
200	ENCT	1167	D2
Lita Ln			
-	SDCo	1108	B1
1100	VSTA	1088	B7
1100	VSTA	1108	B1
Litchfield Rd			
5000	SDGO	1269	E2
Lithia Canyon Rd			
29500	SDCo	1068	D6
Lithrop Pl			
4700	SDGO	1248	G1
Litten Wy			
15900	SDCo	1174	B4
Little Brook Ln			
13400	SDCo	1232	D5
Little Canyon Ln			
9700	SDCo	1089	C2
Little Creek Ln			
13800	SDCo	1070	E7

41 INDEX
Little Creek Rd
INDEX 41
Lucille Dr
SAN DIEGO CO.

San Diego County Street Index

STREET
Block City Map# Grid

Little Creek Rd
- SDCo 1128 H7
Little Dawn Ln
13400 POWY 1190 E3
Little Dipper Wy
1600 SDGO 1350 E2
Little Field Ln
- SDCo 1091 G5
Little Flower St
3400 SDGO 1269 F7
Little Gopher Canyon Rd
900 SDCo 1067 J4
Little Klondike Rd
2500 SDCo 1173 A6
Little Lake St
1300 CHLV 1311 F7
Little Ln
2900 LMGR 1270 H6
- SDCo 1232 B5
Little McGonigle Ran Rd
6400 SDGO 1188 F7
Little Oaks Ln
- SDCo 1253 H1
Little Oaks Rd
100 ENCT 1147 H7
Little Pond Rd
13600 SDCo 1070 D6
Little Quail Run
31000 SDCo 1070 J2
Little Rock Rd
3800 SDCo 997 G4
8100 SNTE 1230 H7
Little Ross Rd
40500 SDCo 997 A1
Little Sierra
15500 SDCo 1071 A5
Little Silver Ct
- SDGO 1210 B1
Little St
1900 SDGO 1227 G5
Littlefield St
4200 SDGO 1268 E1
Littlefield Wy
- ImCo 6560 C7
Littlepage Ln
26100 SDCo 1154 B4
Littlepage Rd
18800 SDCo 1154 C4
Littler Dr
6600 SDGO 1250 F5
Littler Ln
2300 OCSD 1106 J2
Littleton Ct
- SDCo 1086 A3
Littleton Rd
2400 ELCJ 1251 B4
Live Oak Creek Cir
3400 SDCo 1048 D3
Live Oak Ct
4700 OCSD 1087 D4
Live Oak Dr
400 ELCJ 1251 D6
Live Oak Ln
- SDCo 1089 B3
Live Oak Park Rd
2500 SDCo 1028 B2
Live Oak Pl
100 SDCo 1129 B6
Live Oak Ranch Rd
0 RivC 999 E1
Live Oak Rd
2300 ESCN 1129 D3
1000 VSTA 1107 H4
Live Oak Springs Rd
2100 SDCo 1299 G7
(See Page 1299)
Live Oak St
- CHLV 1311 C7
Live Oaks Dr
6300 CRLB 1127 G3
Live Oaks Trl
2600 SDCo 1299 H3
(See Page 1299)
Livering Ln
5200 SDGO 1248 H1
Liverpool Ct
800 SDGO 1267 H2
Liverpool Dr
400 ENCT 1167 D3
Livery Pl
2800 SDCo 1129 C5
Livewood Wy
10400 SDGO 1210 B4
Living Rock Ct
1600 CHLV 1331 F2
Livingston St
- CHLV 1311 D7
6800 SDGO 1270 E6
Liza Ln
- SDCo 1233 J6
Lizard Rocks Rd
28400 SDCo 1090 F2
Llama Ct
2700 CRLB 1127 H6
Llama St
7000 CRLB 1127 H6
Llanos Ct
- CALX 6620 H5
Lloyd Pl
1400 SDCo 1130 C3
3600 SDGO 1248 E5

Lloyd St
200 ELCJ 1251 F4
3200 SDGO 1248 E5
Lloyd Ter
3600 SDGO 1248 E6
Lo Cascio Wy
2700 ESCN 1110 E7
Lobelia Ct
1700 CRLB 1127 D6
Lobelia Dr
200 SDCo 1108 C3
Lobelia Path
- SDGO 1247 G1
Lobelia Rd
2600 SDCo 1234 A5
Lobo Ln
8700 SDCo 1291 A2
Lobrano St
9200 LMSA 1271 B3
Lobrico Ct
600 SDGO 1290 F3
Locdel Ct
400 CHLV 1330 C4
Loch Lomond Dr
1200 ENCT 1167 D1
Loch Lomond Highland
2000 SDCo 1088 C7
Loch Lomond St
4100 SDGO 1249 A2
Loch Ness Dr
1500 SDCo 1027 G5
Lochmoor Dr
6400 SDGO 1250 E6
Lochridge Pl
2300 ESCN 1109 G4
Lochwood Pl
700 ESCN 1109 H3
Locke Pl
2100 LMGR 1290 G1
Lockeport Av
1400 CHLV 1331 D1
Lockford Av
6500 SDGO 1310 F2
Lockland Ct
8400 SDCo 1290 J2
Lockridge St
3900 SDGO 1289 G3
Locksley St
18500 SDCo 1150 B5
Lockwood Dr
3300 SDGO 1249 E4
Lockwood Pl
700 OCSD 1087 C1
Locust Dr
200 SNMS 1128 G1
Locust St
2800 SDGO 1268 D7
1400 SDGO 1288 B2
Lodgepole Rd
1800 SNMS 1128 B2
Lodi Ct
4300 SDGO 1228 E6
Lodi Glen
1800 ESCN 1109 F6
Lodi Pl
5400 SDGO 1228 E7
Lodi St
5500 SDGO 1228 E6
Lodi Wy
4100 SDGO 1228 E7
Lofberg St
3600 SDGO 1249 G3
Lofter Dr
3000 SDCo 1079 B5
(See Page 1079)
Lofty Grove Dr
4600 OCSD 1087 E5
Lofty Trail Ct
15500 SDGO 1169 J5
Lofty Trail Dr
16000 SDGO 1169 J5
Lofty View Pl
6700 SDGO 1250 C4
Logan Av
1700 SDGO 1289 C4
5300 SDGO 1290 B5
Logan Ct
1400 ESCN 1130 D2
Loganberry Ct
800 SNMS 1109 A5
Loganberry Dr
7100 CRLB 1126 J6
Loganberry Wy
5400 OCSD 1067 D6
Loggia Wy
9100 SDGO 1249 D7
Logrono Dr
4300 SDGO 1270 D4
Logwood Pl
3600 SDCo 1048 D2
Loire Av
10700 SDGO 1210 B3
Loire Cir
12100 SDGO 1210 B3
Loire Ct
12100 SDGO 1210 B3
Loire Valley Wy
- CHLV 1331 E1
Lois Canyon Rd
3500 SDCo 1272 H5

Lois Ln
16900 SDCo 1156 E7
Lois St
4200 LMSA 1270 E4
Loker Av E
2800 CRLB 1127 G2
Loker Av W
2700 CRLB 1127 F2
Lokoya Dr
1600 CHLV 1331 E1
Lola Ln
1800 SDCo 1272 D3
Lolali Ln
1100 SDCo 1108 C1
Lolasi Wy
- SDGO 1227 H3
Lolin Ln
14300 POWY 1190 H5
Lolita St
200 ENCT 1147 B6
Lollie Ln
- ImCo 6560 D2
Lolly Ln
6200 SDGO 1290 D4
Loma Alegre
- SDCo 1148 C6
Loma Alta Dr
100 OCSD 1086 D6
4000 SDGO 1270 E4
Loma Alta Ter
700 VSTA 1087 F5
Loma Av
1000 CORD 1288 H7
Loma Corta Dr
200 SOLB 1167 H6
Loma Ct
1500 CHLV 1330 F4
4900 CRLB 1106 J7
900 ELCJ 1251 A4
Loma De Naranjas
1300 SDCo 1130 D3
Loma De Oro
1200 SDCo 1129 H6
Loma De Paz
1300 SDCo 1130 B3
Loma Del Fuego
3200 SDCo 1273 A7
Loma Del Sol Dr
3200 SDCo 1311 A1
Loma Del Sur
4200 SDCo 1271 E4
Loma Dr
2300 LMGR 1270 G7
- OCSD 1087 D1
Loma Estates Ct
3200 SDCo 1273 D6
Loma Helix Ct
4300 SDCo 1271 D3
Loma La Luna
31300 SDCo 1069 E1
Loma Laguna Dr
4900 CRLB 1106 J7
Loma Largo Dr
300 SOLB 1167 J6
Loma Linda Dr
1800 SDCo 1168 C1
Loma Ln
1400 CHLV 1330 F4
1100 CORD 1288 H7
300 SDCo 1109 F6
10300 SDCo 1271 E6
Loma Paseo
4200 SDCo 1310 G3
Loma Pass
4100 SDGO 1268 G5
Loma Portal Dr
900 ELCJ 1251 C3
Loma Rancho Dr
10300 SDCo 1271 F6
Loma Riviera Cir
4000 SDGO 1268 C5
Loma Riviera Ct
4300 SDGO 1268 B5
Loma Riviera Dr
3100 SDGO 1268 B5
Loma Riviera Ln
4200 SDGO 1268 C5
Loma Valley Rd
700 SDGO 1288 A3
Loma Verde
- ENCT 1147 F5
- ESCN 1109 F6
5100 OCSD 1087 D2
Loma Verde Dr
5600 SDCo 1168 C2
Loma View
900 CHLV 1310 H7
Loma View Ct
8200 SDCo 1290 J5
Loma Vista
- SNMS 1129 C1
Loma Vista Av
2600 ESCN 1130 A7
Loma Vista Dr
7700 LMSA 1270 G2
3200 SDCo 1272 J7
3200 SDCo 1292 J1
(See Page 1292)
Loma Vista Pl
200 SDCo 1252 H3

Loma Vista Wy
1100 SDCo 1108 C1
Loma Wy
4900 CRLB 1106 J7
3600 SDGO 1288 A2
Lomacita Ter
1600 ELCJ 1252 C2
Lomacitas Dr
3600 NATC 1310 E3
Lomacitas Ln
3500 SDCo 1310 E3
Lomaland Dr
3900 SDGO 1287 J3
Lomas De Oro Ct
900 ENCT 1147 J6
Lomas Santa Fe Dr
400 SOLB 1167 F7
1200 SOLB 1168 A7
Lomas Serenas Dr
3500 ESCN 1150 A3
Lomas Verdes Dr
13100 POWY 1170 D1
Lomax St
12700 POWY 1190 D4
Lombard Pl
8900 SDGO 1228 D3
Lombard St
1400 VSTA 1087 J4
Lomica Dr
12400 SDGO 1170 B4
Lomica Pl
2200 ESCN 1129 H7
Lomita Del Sol
800 VSTA 1087 G5
Lomita Dr
1100 SDCo 1271 H1
Lomita St
2700 OCSD 1086 D6
Lomitas Dr
4700 SDGO 1269 C3
Lomker Ct
9200 SNTE 1230 J6
Lomker Wy
8400 SNTE 1230 H6
Lomo Del Sur
4300 SDCo 1271 D4
Lomond Dr
5800 SDGO 1250 B7
Londonderry Av
10400 SDGO 1209 D4
Lone Bluff Ct
16200 SDCo 1169 E5
Lone Bluff Dr
10100 SDCo 1169 E4
Lone Bluff Wy
16200 SDCo 1169 F5
Lone Cypress Pl
12600 SDGO 1188 A6
Lone Dove Ln
3600 ENCT 1148 D3
Lone Dove St
10100 SDCo 1169 E4
Lone Hawk Dr
16300 SDCo 1169 F4
Lone Hill Ln
- ENCT 1148 C3
Lone Jack Rd
3400 ENCT 1148 C4
Lone Oak Ln
- SDCo 998 G5
2200 SDCo 1108 D2
Lone Oak Pl
- CHLV 1311 H2
Lone Oak Rd
1500 SDCo 1108 D2
Lone Oak Tr
- SDCo 1173 G7
Lone Oak Trl
14900 SDCo 1193 G1
(See Page 1193)
Lone Pine Ct
2500 CHLV 1311 H6
Lone Pine Ln
- SNMS 1108 B7
Lone Pine Trl
28700 SDCo 1237 C5
Lone Quail Rd
10100 SDCo 1169 E3
16500 SDGO 1169 E3
Lone Ray Ln
1900 VSTA 1088 B2
Lone Star Dr
5700 SDGO 1250 B4
Lone Star Rd
- SDCo 1332 A7
(See Page 1332)
- SDCo 1352 A1
Lone Star St
7600 SDGO 1250 B4
Lone Tree Rd
- CHLV 1311 D6
Lone Vally Rd
- CHLV 1311 F6
Lonesome Oak Wy
12600 SDCo 1090 C1
Lonespur Ct
4600 OCSD 1087 D3
Lonestar Rd
6600 SDCo 1331 J7
6500 SDGO 1331 H7

Long Boat Cove
2600 SDGO 1207 H2
Long Boat Wy
13000 SDGO 1207 H1
Long Branch Av
4800 SDGO 1267 J5
4700 SDGO 1268 A6
Long Canyon Dr
3900 SDCo 1311 A3
Long Crest Dr
- OCSD 1086 D3
Long Fellow Rd
- CRLB 1107 B7
Long Lake Ct
- LMGR 1270 E7
Long Palm St
- OCSD 1106 C2
Long Pl
3900 CRLB 1106 F7
Long Point Ct
1500 CHLV 1330 J4
Long Ridge St
- CHLV 1311 D7
Long Run Dr
3700 SDGO 1187 J5
Long Shadow Ct
1000 ELCJ 1252 A7
Long Trail Ct
- ImCo 6560 A6
Long Trot Dr
21800 SDCo 1129 C4
Long View Dr
- CHLV 1311 J5
Longdale Dr
8000 LMGR 1270 H7
Longdale Pl
- SDGO 1209 F2
Longden Ln
300 SOLB 1187 F2
Longfellow Ct
- OCSD 1067 A4
Longfellow Ln
13500 SDGO 1189 E4
Longfellow Rd
1300 VSTA 1107 H4
Longford Ct
4900 SDGO 1248 G1
Longford Pl
4900 SDGO 1248 G1
Longford St
4800 SDGO 1248 G1
Longhorn Dr
1600 VSTA 1107 G4
Longmont Rd
2500 VSTA 1088 D6
Longridge Wy
9200 SDGO 1209 D2
Longs Hill Rd
1900 SDCo 1252 D3
Longshore Ct
- SDGO 1208 C2
Longshore Wy
- SDGO 1208 C2
Longspur Dr
- SDCo 1023 F3
Longstaff Ct
- SNMS 1128 B6
Longview Dr
3700 CRLB 1106 H4
Longview Wy
4900 SDCo 1271 H2
Longwood St
8500 SDGO 1209 C5
Loni Ln
1200 VSTA 1108 A1
Lonicera St
- CRLB 1127 A5
Lonita Ct
- IMPE 6499 J2
Lonita Wy
3900 SNMS 1128 C1
Lonja Wy
1700 SDGO 1350 D3
Lonnie St
4000 OCSD 1087 B7
Lonny Ln
7000 LMGR 1270 F7
Lonsdale Ln
1000 VSTA 1087 H4
Lookout Av
1200 OCSD 1067 B4
Lookout Ct
3500 OCSD 1107 G4
Lookout Dr
7700 SDGO 1227 G6
Lookout Ln
20200 SDCo 1149 E1
Lookout Lp
7500 SDCo 1237 D7
Lookout Mountain Rd
- SDCo 998 G3
Lookout Mtn Rd
2000 SDCo 998 F4
Lookout Pl
- SNMS 1128 B1
Lookout Point Pl
1800 ESCN 1109 F6
Lookout Rim
- SDCo 1091 G5

Lookout Trl
800 SDCo 1253 C2
Lopelia Meadows Pl
13500 SDGO 1188 F3
Lopez Canyon Wy
6700 SDGO 1208 H3
Lopez Ct
200 CALX 6620 G6
Lopez Glen Wy
6700 SDGO 1208 H3
Lopez Pte
1100 SDGO 1208 H3
Lopez Ridge Wy
- SDGO 1208 G3
Lopez St
1600 OCSD 1106 D2
Loping Ln
5600 SDCo 1311 B2
Loquat Ct
800 ELCJ 1251 E6
Loquat Pl
2100 OCSD 1106 E1
Lor-Lar Ln
400 SDCo 1152 G5
Lorca Dr
6300 SDGO 1270 D4
Lorca Wy
4700 OCSD 1107 F5
Lord Cecil St
5700 SDGO 1228 B6
Lord St
3500 SDGO 1249 C4
Lorelei Ln
- SDCo 1028 A1
Loren Dr
9300 LMSA 1251 B7
Lorena Ln
11200 SDCo 1271 G2
Lorena Pl
4700 SDCo 1271 H2
Lorene Ln
- SDCo 1028 A1
Lorenz Av
1400 SDGO 1290 B6
Lorenzo Dr
- SDCo 1027 H7
Loreto Ct
- IMPE 6499 H1
Loreto Glen
1800 ESCN 1110 A4
Loretta Ln
1000 CRLB 1106 G7
Loretta St
1500 OCSD 1086 B5
N Loretta St
1100 OCSD 1086 A4
Lori Ct
800 SNMS 1109 B6
Lori Ln
800 CHLV 1310 G7
Lori Mar Ct
9300 SDCo 1271 B6
Lori St
- CHLV 1331 B1
Lorient Pl
1800 CHLV 1311 F1
Lorikeet St
- OCSD 1067 A3
Lorimer Ln
3600 ENCT 1167 G2
Loring St
600 SDGO 1247 G5
1900 SDGO 1248 A4
E Loring St
2500 SDGO 1248 C4
Lorirae Pl
11500 SDGO 1209 B1
Loris St
4900 SDGO 1270 A6
Lorita Ln
3900 SDCo 1028 F7
Lorna Av
1100 ELCJ 1251 G7
Lorna Ln
2400 CRLB 1106 F3
Lorraine Ann Dr
4000 SDCo 1271 G4
Lorraine Ct
- SDCo 1191 F5
Lorraine Dr
1500 ENCT 1147 A3
4900 SDGO 1269 J2
Lorraine Pl
1700 ESCN 1109 D5
Lorraine Ridge Tr
9800 SDCo 1232 J3
Lorraine Wy
9700 SNTE 1231 D4
Lorrel Pl
- SDCo 1272 E7
Lorri Wy
1900 ESCN 1109 C4
Lorry Ln
1700 ESCN 1129 F5
Los Alamits Wy
- SOLB 1187 F2
Los Alamos Dr
300 SDGO 1290 C5
Los Alamos Wy
- OCSD 1087 B3

Los Alisos Dr
3100 SDCo 1028 C3
Los Alisos North
900 SDCo 1028 B4
Los Alisos North Ln
2700 SDCo 1028 B3
Los Alisos South
700 SDCo 1028 B4
Los Altos Ct
5100 SDGO 1247 J4
Los Altos Dr
- CHLV 1311 G2
Los Altos Rd
1600 SDGO 1247 J4
Los Altos Wy
1700 SDGO 1248 A4
Los Amigos
1300 SDCo 1028 A4
- SNMS 1129 C1
Los Amigos Wy
12000 SDCo 1232 A6
W Los Angeles Dr
400 VSTA 1087 G5
Los Angeles Pl
300 SDGO 1290 B4
Los Arboles
16200 SDCo 1168 D4
Los Arboles Ranch Rd
25900 SDCo 1109 G1
Los Arbolitos Blvd
500 OCSD 1086 F3
Los Archos
- SDCo 1232 C7
Los Arcos Pl
1200 CHLV 1311 B6
Los Banditos Dr
100 SDCo 1152 J5
Los Barbos
16500 SDCo 1168 F4
Los Brazos
7300 SDGO 1168 H7
Los Caballitos
1000 SOLB 1167 G7
Los Campos Dr
3000 SDCo 1048 E1
Los Cedros Ln
1400 ESCN 1109 D5
Los Cerritos Ln
2500 SDCo 1028 B3
Los Cielos
14000 SDCo 1130 F7
Los Coches Ct
1300 CHLV 1311 B6
12700 SDCo 1232 B6
Los Coches Rd
9500 SDCo 1232 B4
E Los Coches Rd
13800 SDCo 1232 E6
Los Colinas
- ENCT 1147 F5
Los Colonas Dr
- OCSD 1086 F3
Los Companeros
1100 SDCo 1128 C3
Los Conejos
1300 SDCo 1028 A4
- SDCo 1195 D6
(See Page 1195)
Los Corderos
1100 SDCo 1128 C3
Los Coyotes Ct
- IMPE 6439 F3
Los Encinos Rd
0 RivC 999 G1
Los Eucaliptos
17500 SDCo 1168 E2
Los Feliz Dr
1800 CHLV 1331 H2
Los Flores St
200 CHLV 1310 C5
Los Hermanos Ranch Rd
18500 SDCo 1091 E4
Los Hermanos Rd
3500 SDCo 1028 D2
Los Huecos Rd
- SDCo 1218 C5
Los Indios Ct
1400 CHLV 1310 J5
Los Mirlitos
5300 SDCo 1168 B1
Los Mochis Wy
3400 OCSD 1107 C2
Los Morros
16700 SDCo 1167 J4
17500 SDCo 1168 B2
Los Morros Wy
5000 OCSD 1067 A6
Los Naranjos Ct
6200 SDCo 1168 E4
Los Nidos Ln
- SDCo 1089 E2
Los Nietos Av
14100 POWY 1190 G1
Los Nopalitos
10200 SDCo 1231 F3
Los Olivos Av
13600 POWY 1190 H4
Los Olivos Ct
- BRAW 6319 E4
(See Page 6319)

Los Olivos Dr
- BRAW 6319 F4
(See Page 6319)
300 SNMS 1108 G7
Los Olivos St
1200 CHLV 1331 B6
Los Padres Dr
4100 SDCo 1028 G7
Los Pinos
4500 SDCo 1167 J3
Los Pinos Av
4200 SDGO 1289 H5
Los Pinos Cir
7800 CRLB 1147 G3
Los Pinos Ct
1000 CHLV 1311 B7
Los Plateros
- SDCo 1149 A3
Los Ranchitos Rd
10000 SDCo 1231 F3
Los Reyes Dr
200 SDGO 1290 F4
Los Robles Dr
5000 CRLB 1126 G2
Los Robles Rd
40500 SDCo 997 G3
Los Rosales St
16300 SDCo 1169 F4
Los Sabalos St
8000 SDGO 1209 B2
Los Santos
- SDCo 1232 D6
Los Senderos Dr
1000 SNTE 1231 H4
Los Sicomoros Ln
- SDCo 1028 D7
Los Soneto Ct
7100 SDGO 1290 F4
Los Soneto Dr
200 SDGO 1290 F4
Los Vallecitos Blvd
900 SNMS 1108 E7
Los Vecinos
4200 SDCo 1047 G5
Los Verdes Dr
3100 SDCo 1048 A2
Los Vientos Serreno
6800 SDCo 1148 F2
Lost Arrow Pl
- CHLV 1331 A1
Lost Creek Rd
- CHLV 1311 J6
Lost Dutchman Dr
14200 POWY 1190 G4
Lost Horizon Dr
38000 SDCo 999 J4
Lost Oak Ln
400 SDCo 1150 A1
Lost Trl
20400 SDCo 1274 J3
20400 SDCo 1275 A3
Lostinda St
1100 ELCJ 1252 A7
Lot A Rd
2600 SDCo 1135 J6
Lott Pt
11300 SDGO 1209 B1
Lotus Av
100 ELCN 6499 E6
1700 ImCo 6559 E2
Lotus Blossom St
700 ENCT 1147 F5
Lotus Ct
1800 CRLB 1127 E7
Lotus Dr
100 CHLV 1330 F5
3700 SDGO 1268 C6
Lotus Glen
1600 ESCN 1109 D6
Lotus Ln
1900 SDCo 1252 D3
Lotus Pond Ln
- SDCo 1089 E6
Lotus St
100 OCSD 1086 D6
4600 SDGO 1268 A5
Lou St
3300 NATC 1290 C6
Loualta Wy
- CHLV 1310 D6
Louden Ln
1100 IMPB 1349 G1
Louetta Ln
14300 POWY 1190 H5
Louie Pl
1000 VSTA 1087 H4
Louis Ct
- IMPE 6499 J2
Louis Dr
1900 ESCN 1109 C4
Louis Ln
8600 SNTE 1231 D7
Louisa Dr
10600 SDCo 1271 F4
Louisana Av
100 SDGO 1350 G4
Louise Ct
2300 ELCJ 1251 B5
Louise Dr
1400 SDCo 1234 C6
4800 SDGO 1269 J3

Louise Ln
1000 SDCo 1130 D6
Louise St
2800 OCSD 1087 C7
Louisiana Av
300 SDGO 1350 G5
Louisiana St
4300 SDGO 1269 D4
Loukelton Cir
6100 SDGO 1249 J7
Loukelton Wy
4800 SDGO 1249 J7
Lourdes Terr
6200 SDGO 1250 C6
Louret Av
- SDGO 1329 J6
2200 SDGO 1330 B6
Lovajo Rd
- SDGO 1247 J4
Love Ln
- ESCN 1129 G5
- SDCo 1174 B4
Loveeny Dr
2200 SDCo 1108 C3
Loveland Ln
- SDCo 1254 A7
Loveland Rd
5000 ImCo 6259 A2
(See Page 6259)
4000 ImCo 6319 A5
(See Page 6319)
Lovell Ln
9200 LMSA 1271 B1
Lovelock St
5200 SDGO 1268 E3
Lovely Ln
1500 SDCo 1108 B2
Lovett Ln
4200 SDCo 1271 D4
Low Chaparral Dr
2100 SDCo 1109 B2
Low Chaparral Pl
200 SNMS 1109 B3
Lowder Ln
7000 CRLB 1127 A6
Lowell Ct
7400 LMSA 1270 F3
Lowell St
4200 LMSA 1270 G4
3300 SDGO 1288 B1
Lowell Wy
3400 SDGO 1288 B1
Lower Lake Ct
1500 ENCT 1167 F2
Lower Ln
900 SDCo 1108 G2
Lower Ridge Rd
3200 SDGO 1187 J5
Lower Russell Rd
10500 SDCo 1271 E2
Lower Scarborough Ct
8400 SDGO 1169 B4
Lower Scarborough Ln
8400 SDGO 1169 B4
Lower Scarborough Pl
15600 SDGO 1169 B4
Lower Springs Rd
600 SDCo 1047 E6
Lowewood Pl
500 CHLV 1310 F6
Lowry Ter
7900 SDGO 1227 H6
Loyola Ct
1800 CHLV 1311 D5
Lozana Rd
2300 SDGO 1187 H5
Lozita Wy
10300 SDCo 1231 F3
Luana Dr
3000 OCSD 1107 B1
Lubbock Av
6000 LMSA 1251 A6
Luber St
5600 SDGO 1290 B2
Lucaya Ct
1800 VSTA 1107 G6
Lucera Ct
17000 SDGO 1169 J2
Lucera Pl
11400 SDGO 1169 J2
Lucerne Cir
1800 SNMS 1128 B2
Lucerne Dr
2200 SDGO 1268 C7
Lucero Ct
- CHLV 1331 A2
Lucia Ct
7700 CRLB 1147 G2
Lucia Wy
- OCSD 1086 H3
6200 SDGO 1248 G7
Lucidi Farms Wy
15000 POWY 1171 C7
Luciernaga Ct
6800 CRLB 1127 G6
Luciernaga Pl
6700 CRLB 1127 G5
Luciernaga St
2500 CRLB 1127 G6
Lucille Dr
4700 SDGO 1269 J2

San Diego County Street Index

Street	Block	City	Map#	Grid
Lucille Dr	4900	SDGO	1270	A3
Lucille Pl	4800	SDGO	1270	A2
Lucillia St	-	SNMS	1128	C1
Lucinda St	3300	SDGO	1288	A3
Lucita Rd	18400	SDCo	1274	E3
Luckett Ct	13200	SDGO	1188	D4
Lucky Devil Trl	600	SDCo	1158	C1
(See Page 1158)				
Lucky Six Truck Trl	1800	SDCo	1314	D7
(See Page 1314)				
Lucky St	1400	OCSD	1106	C2
Lucy Ln	300	SDCo	1251	G2
Lucylle Ln	-	ENCT	1148	A6
Ludington Ln	1600	SDGO	1227	G6
Ludington Pl	7700	SDGO	1227	G6
Luelf Ct	-	SDCo	1172	D5
Luelf St	-	SDCo	1172	D5
Lugano Ln	-	SOLB	1167	J7
Lugar Playa Catalina	11600	SDGO	1230	A7
Lugo Rd	7900	SDCo	1030	A4
Luigi Ter	5100	SDGO	1228	D4
Luis Rey Heights Rd	30200	SDCo	1068	G4
Luis St	15100	POWY	1170	D7
Luiseno	12800	POWY	1170	D4
Luiseno Av	300	OCSD	1067	B7
Luiseno Circle Dr	32800	SDCo	1051	A5
Luke Ln	1500	ELCJ	1252	A3
Luminara Wy	800	SNMS	1128	E5
Luna Av	2600	SDGO	1248	B1
Luna Ct	1000	VSTA	1087	G5
Luna De Miel	17500	SDCo	1168	H1
Luna De Oro	7400	SDCo	1168	H1
Luna Dr	4900	OCSD	1067	A6
N Luna Dr	500	OCSD	1067	A6
Luna Media	14500	SDGO	1168	J7
Luna Vista Dr	800	ESCN	1130	B3
Luna Vista Pl	700	ESCN	1130	A3
Lunada Pl	12800	SDGO	1150	C5
Lunada Pt	18700	SDGO	1150	C6
Lunar Ln	10300	SNTE	1231	E7
Lund St	2500	ELCJ	1251	B1
Lundy Lake Dr	2000	SDCo	1129	F7
	2100	SDCo	1149	F1
Lundy Wy	1400	SDCo	1027	J2
Luneta Dr	1100	DLMR	1187	F5
	4500	SDCo	1155	H4
Luneta Ln	3700	SDCo	1047	E3
Luneta View	4600	SDCo	1155	H4
Lungos Ct	2700	SDGO	1330	C7
Lupin Wy	10700	SDCo	1271	F4
Lupine Dr	2400	SDCo	1297	E7
(See Page 1297)				
	700	SNMS	1128	F2
Lupine Hills Dr	1400	VSTA	1107	H3
	900	VSTA	1108	A4
Lupine Ln	3600	SDCo	1028	F6
Lupine Rd	1600	CRLB	1127	E7
Lupine Wy	-	OCSD	1086	J4
Lupita Ct	12600	SDGO	1188	B6
Lupulin Ln	-	ESCN	1129	E4
Lura Av	800	ELCJ	1251	F7
Lusardi Creek Ln	7800	SDGO	1169	B5
Lusk Blvd	7200	SDGO	1208	C5
Lustrosos St	300	OCSD	1066	J6
Luther Dr	900	SDCo	1291	C3
Luther St	2400	SDGO	1290	E7
Lutheran Ct	9700	SNTE	1231	B4
Lutheran Wy	9700	SNTE	1231	C4
Lux Canyon Dr	-	ENCT	1167	G3
Lux Dr	1300	SDCo	1130	C3
Luxembourg Wy	-	SDGO	1209	G2
Luz Pl	11300	SDGO	1169	J1
Luz Rd	11400	SDGO	1169	J1
Luz Wy	2100	OCSD	1106	J1
Luzeiro Dr	100	VSTA	1088	D5
Luzon Av	300	DLMR	1187	F4
Luzon Ct	-	NATC	1289	J7
Lyall Pl	13700	SDCo	1232	E5
Lycoming St	-	SDGO	1351	D2
Lyden Wy	5700	SDGO	1250	B7
Lydia Ln	1100	SDCo	1027	H1
Lydia St	5500	SDGO	1310	C2
Lyle Dr	5000	SDGO	1290	A1
Lyman Ln	-	SDGO	1228	A1
Lymer Dr	4100	SDGO	1269	H2
Lyncarol Dr	9800	SDCo	1271	D3
Lynch Ct	-	CRLB	1107	B7
Lynch Ln	3500	SDGO	1350	F5
Lynda Ln	2600	SDCo	997	C1
Lynda Park Ln	14700	POWY	1190	E1
Lynda Pl	3700	NATC	1310	D3
Lynden Ln	400	SDCo	1027	G2
Lyndine St	2200	LMGR	1290	H1
Lyndon Rd	1800	SDGO	1268	H5
Lyndsie Ln	-	SDCo	1152	G6
Lyndy Ln	1800	SDCo	1048	A4
Lynette Cir	4100	OCSD	1087	C7
Lynhurst Terr	-	SDGO	1330	H7
Lynmar Ln	100	VSTA	1088	B6
Lynn Ct	3100	OCSD	1086	G7
Lynn Ln	100	OCSD	1086	G2
	-	SDCo	1088	J6
Lynn Oak Dr	1300	SDCo	1234	J5
Lynn Pl	700	ELCJ	1251	G6
Lynn St	5800	SDGO	1270	C6
Lynn Wy	2500	VSTA	1108	B5
Lynndale Ln	4300	SDCo	1310	E5
Lynndale Pl	3100	CHLV	1310	E5
Lynne Anne Ln	9600	SDGO	1189	E2
Lynnette Cir	500	VSTA	1087	H4
Lynnwood Dr	4200	SDCo	1310	E5
Lynridge Rd	7200	SDGO	1250	E5
Lynwood Av	300	SOLB	1167	F6
Lynwood Dr	600	ENCT	1147	E5
	3300	SDCo	1310	E5
Lynx Glen	1800	ESCN	1109	F6
Lynx Rd	8500	SDGO	1209	C2
Lynx Wy	5500	CRLB	1107	D7
	-	SNMS	1128	B6
Lyon Cir	200	VSTA	1087	H7
Lyon Rd	1300	SDCo	1029	H3
Lyon St	4800	SDGO	1289	J2
	5000	SDGO	1290	A2
Lyons Creek Ln	-	SDCo	1293	J1
	2900	SDCo	1294	A1
(See Page 1294)				
Lyons Creek Rd	1500	SDCo	1290	J1
	17200	SDCo	1294	A1
(See Page 1294)				
Lyons Ct	2700	CRLB	1106	J4
Lyons Dr	4500	SDCo	1271	F3
Lyons Gate	2200	SDCo	1088	C7
Lyons Ln	1200	SDCo	1251	H3
Lyons Peak Ln	18300	SDCo	1294	D4
(See Page 1294)				
Lyons Peak Rd	-	SDCo	1294	B2
(See Page 1294)				
Lyons Valley Rd	14300	SDCo	1272	J7
	14600	SDCo	1273	B7
	-	SDCo	1275	B6
	13900	SDCo	1292	G1
(See Page 1292)				
	15700	SDCo	1293	G1
	19200	SDCo	1294	G3
(See Page 1294)				
Lyra Ct	10900	SDGO	1209	D3
Lyra Ln	-	SNMS	1128	F5
Lyric Ln	4600	SDGO	1248	H2
Lytham Glen	300	ESCN	1109	H4
Lytton Creek Ct	2800	CHLV	1312	A6
(See Page 1312)				
Lytton St	2800	SDGO	1268	D6
M				
M & R Ranch Rd	-	SDCo	998	A7
M 1st St W	-	CORD	1288	C7
M 2nd St W	-	CORD	1288	C7
M 3rd St W	-	CORD	1288	C7
M Acuna Av	700	CALX	6680	C1
M Av	700	NATC	1289	J7
	900	NATC	1309	J1
	1600	NATC	1310	A1
M B Martinez St	500	CALX	6620	E7
M C Garcia St	-	CALX	6620	E7
M Knechel Av	1600	CALX	6620	E7
M Lorenz St	-	CALX	6620	J7
M St	100	ENCT	1167	C1
	200	IMPE	6439	F6
M Stuart St	-	CALX	6620	J5
Ma Lou Dr	3200	SDCo	1292	J1
(See Page 1292)				
	3200	SDCo	1293	A1
Mabel Bell Ln	7200	SDGO	1227	F7
	7100	SDGO	1247	F1
Mable Wy	5000	SDGO	1228	J7
Mabon Pl	3600	SDGO	1248	D2
Mabuhay Wy	2300	SDGO	1330	D7
Mac Ln	9000	SDCo	1271	A6
Macadamia Ct	4700	OCSD	1087	A1
Macadamia Dr	700	CRLB	1126	J6
	1700	SDCo	998	B7
Macambo Dr	-	ELCJ	1251	H5
Macario Dr	5000	OCSD	1067	A6
MacArthur Av	2000	CRLB	1106	H6
MacArthur Dr	6600	LMGR	1270	D7
MacAulay St	3600	SDGO	1288	B1
Macaw Ln	7700	SDGO	1269	A1
Macawa Av	8700	SDGO	1249	C5
Maccool Ln	9600	SNTE	1231	C7
MacDonald St	2900	OCSD	1086	E6
Mace St	100	CHLV	1330	E5
Macero St	1700	ESCN	1129	F6
N Machado St	1400	OCSD	1106	C2
S Machado St	1700	OCSD	1106	D2
Machado Wy	400	VSTA	1087	F3
Machum Pl	-	ELCJ	1251	H5
MacKenzie Creek Rd	-	CHLV	1311	F3
MacKenzie Dr	-	SDCo	1128	G3
MacKenzie Pl	-	BRAW	6319	H3
(See Page 6319)				
Mackey Dr	2900	SDCo	1047	G1
Mackey Ln	800	SDCo	1047	G1
Mackinac Rd	-	ESCN	1149	J3
MacKinnon Av	2000	ENCT	1167	E3
MacKinnon Ct	700	ENCT	1167	E1
MacKinnon Ranch Rd	-	ENCT	1167	E4
MacKinzie Wy	-	SDCo	1071	B7
Macklin Wy	100	SDCo	1108	B3
Maclay St	600	SDCo	1291	B3
MacLura St	4700	OCSD	1087	A1
MacMahr Rd	1000	SNMS	1128	E2
MacNaughton Ln	-	ESCN	1110	B4
Macon St	500	ELCJ	1252	B4
Macouba Pl	10800	SDGO	1249	H2
MacQuarie St	7200	LMSA	1270	F1
MacRonald Dr	4300	SDCo	1271	C3
Mac Tan Ln	-	SDCo	1071	B6
Mactan Rd	29500	SDCo	1071	A6
	28000	SDCo	1091	A2
MacTibby St	3700	SDGO	1248	E5
Madden Av	800	SDGO	1330	C7
	1000	SDGO	1350	C1
Madden Ct	2800	SDGO	1330	C7
Maddie Ln	1000	SDGO	1330	C7
Maddox Dr	10000	SDGO	1249	F2
Maddox Rd	500	ImCo	6620	E6
Madeline St	6200	SDGO	1270	C3
Madera Ct	3100	CRLB	1147	H1
Madera Ln	1100	VSTA	1088	A3
Madera Rosa Wy	11400	SDGO	1250	A3
Madera St	1400	LMGR	1290	F2
	800	SDGO	1290	E3
Madera Verde Pl	1800	SDCo	1252	H3
Madiera Dr	2100	OCSD	1086	J7
Madison Av	-	BRAW	6319	H3
(See Page 6319)				
	-	CHLV	1309	J5
	500	CHLV	1310	A7
	900	CHLV	1330	B2
	900	ESCN	1109	J6
	7600	LMGR	1270	G6
	9100	LMSA	1271	B2
	2200	SDGO	1269	C4
	4500	SDGO	1270	B3
E Madison Av	200	ELCJ	1251	F4
	1900	SDCo	1252	D4
W Madison Av	400	ELCJ	1251	E5
Madison Ct	-	CALX	6620	J6
Madison St	2900	CRLB	1106	E5
	100	OCSD	1067	A6
Madra Av	6200	SDGO	1250	D6
	5600	SDGO	1270	D1
Madra Ln	-	OCSD	1086	G3
Madreselva Wy	2100	SDGO	1350	A3
Madrid Dr	1500	VSTA	1107	H3
Madrid St	3000	SDGO	1268	D6
Madrid Wy	10100	SDCo	1271	E5
Madrigal Ct	1200	CHLV	1311	B6
Madrigal St	11000	SDGO	1169	H6
Madrilena Wy	7700	CRLB	1147	G2
Madrona St	200	CHLV	1310	B6
Madroncillo St	2400	SDGO	1270	E7
Madrone Av	6500	SDGO	1290	D3
Madrone Cir	-	IMPE	6499	H2
Madrone Glen	1600	ESCN	1110	A5
Madrugada Ct	11700	SDGO	1250	B2
Maelee Dr	2300	SDCo	1087	G1
Maemar Dr	-	SDCo	1091	C6
Maestria Ct	10800	SDGO	1249	J2
Maestro Ct	12500	SDGO	1188	B7
Maezel Ln	3200	CRLB	1106	G4
Magarian Rd	700	SDCo	1027	H3
Magdalena Av	1900	CHLV	1331	E3
Magdalena Dr	300	OCSD	1087	A2
Magdalene Wy	1800	SDGO	1268	E1
Magee Rd	4200	SDCo	1029	H3
	-	SDCo	1030	B4
Magee Truck Tr	0	RivC	999	H1
Magellan Cir	3700	OCSD	1107	A2
Magellan Ln	2500	VSTA	1107	J4
Magellan St	7400	CRLB	1127	A7
	3000	SDGO	1330	D7
Magellan Wy	1100	CHLV	1311	B6
Magens Bay	4600	OCSD	1066	H6
Magenta Ct	1800	CHLV	1331	E3
Magenta St	900	SDGO	1290	A5
Maggio Dr	9300	SDCo	1236	C2
Magical Waters Ct	10400	SDCo	1291	F1
Magna Ln	10900	SDCo	1231	F3
Magnatron Blvd	5500	SDGO	1229	C7
Magnolia Av	1400	CRLB	1106	G5
	300	ELCN	6499	H5
	1300	ESCN	1110	A7
	-	POWY	1190	F3
	1200	SDCo	1153	A2
	2600	SDGO	1248	C5
	9800	SNTE	1231	E4
N Magnolia Av	400	ELCJ	1251	F5
	1300	SDCo	1251	F3
S Magnolia Av	600	ELCJ	1251	F6
	1100	ELCJ	1271	F1
Magnolia Cir	1600	VSTA	1107	D1
Magnolia Ct	1800	OCSD	1106	E2
	400	SNMS	1108	J6
Magnolia Hts	800	SDCo	1153	A4
Magnolia Park Dr	9700	SNTE	1231	D5
Magnolia Pl	1500	ESCN	1110	A7
	6000	SDGO	1270	C4
Magnolia Point Ct	-	CHLV	1311	H2
Magnolia Rd	3800	OCSD	1086	F2
Magnolia St	700	BRAW	6260	A7
(See Page 6260)				
	-	BRAW	6319	F1
(See Page 6319)				
Magnolia Wy	2300	NATC	1290	A6
Magnus Wy	4900	SDGO	1290	A6
Magruder St	7100	LMSA	1270	F1
Maguay Rd	3500	SDCo	1274	E3
Maguire Rd	3500	SDGO	1350	E4
Mahaila Av	3900	SDGO	1228	C3
Mahogany Cv	13300	SDGO	1210	E2
Mahogany Dr	600	ELCJ	1252	B6
	4700	OCSD	1087	E5
Mahogany Glen	400	ESCN	1109	G6
Mahogany Ranch Rd	18000	SDCo	1172	A7
Mahogany St	800	SNMS	1128	J3
Mahogany Vista Ln	-	SDGO	1290	A4
Maia Point	-	SDGO	1290	D3
Maiden Ln	-	CALX	6680	F1
	1400	DLMR	1187	F5
	4900	LMSA	1270	J2
Main Av	300	SDCo	1027	F3
Main Ct	1800	CHLV	1330	H5
Main St	300	BRAW	6320	C1
(See Page 6320)				
	4000	CHLV	1330	E5
	5000	CHLV	1331	A5
	1700	ELCN	6499	E6
	100	ELCN	6500	A6
	2900	LMGR	1270	G6
	1800	LMGR	1290	G1
	2100	SDCo	1136	B7
	500	SDCo	1152	H5
	-	SDCo	1156	H1
	2800	SDCo	1172	C2
	2100	SDGO	1289	D6
	-	SDGO	1330	A5
	100	SDGO	1350	G4
E Main St	700	ELCJ	1251	H5
	1700	ELCJ	1252	B3
W Main St	1000	ELCJ	1251	E5
	-	ELCN	6499	C6
Maine Av	10000	SDCo	1232	B3
Mainsail Rd	300	OCSD	1086	F5
Maisel Wy	5400	SDGO	1270	B2
Maitland Av	500	SDGO	1330	E6
Majano Pl	2400	CRLB	1147	G3
Majella Dr	24100	SDCo	1173	E2
Majella Rd	2400	SDCo	1087	F1
Majestad Ln	1100	CHLV	1310	J4
Majestic Dr	3400	SDGO	1350	E1
Majorca Wy	4600	OCSD	1107	E4
Majordomo Ct	-	SDCo	1085	J3
Makaha Wy	2900	SDGO	1330	C6
Makati St	1200	NATC	1289	J7
Makenna Ln	500	SDCo	1233	F7
	500	SDCo	1253	F1
Makin Rd	-	CORD	1309	A1
Malabar Dr	12200	POWY	1170	B7
Malachite Pl	6700	CRLB	1127	F4
Malaga Dr	4900	OCSD	1067	A6
Malaga St	3000	SDGO	1268	D6
Malaga Wy	1500	SDCo	1027	F5
Malan St	-	BRAW	6319	J2
(See Page 6319)				
Malcolm Dr	6000	SDGO	1270	C4
Malcolm St	5300	OCSD	1087	E1
Malden St	1600	SDGO	1248	A4
Malea Wy	6000	OCSD	1107	F5
Malee St	-	CRLB	1127	D6
Malene Ln	1000	SDCo	1251	H2
Maler Rd	9400	SDGO	1189	D1
Maley St	7200	SDGO	1248	J6
Malibu Pl	2700	ESCN	1110	D6
Malibu Point Wy	800	OCSD	1066	F7
Malibu Wy	2400	SDGO	1187	H5
Malibue Point Ct	1500	CHLV	1330	J3
Malito Ct	200	CHLV	1330	G4
Malito Dr	3400	SDCo	1310	F2
Mallard Ct	-	ImCo	6560	B7
	-	SDCo	1127	B7
Mallard Dr	29800	SDCo	1297	F5
(See Page 1297)				
Mallard Ln	2800	ImCo	6439	E4
Mallard St	-	ImCo	6560	A7
	6800	LMGR	1290	E1
	6300	SDGO	1290	D1
Mallorca Dr	1500	VSTA	1107	H3
Mallorca Pl	2600	CRLB	1147	G1
Mallow Ct	1700	CRLB	1127	E6
Maloney St	1300	SNMS	1108	H4
Malorey St	7500	LMSA	1250	G6
Malpazo Ct	3400	SDCo	1310	G2
Malpertuso Ct	19800	SDCo	1152	B2
Malta Av	1500	CHLV	1330	G4
Malta St	7100	SDGO	1248	J4
Malta Wy	3300	OCSD	1106	J1
Malvern Ct	5700	SDGO	1250	B7
Mammoth Dr	2400	SDGO	1249	E6
N Mammoth Pl	2100	ESCN	1129	E6
S Mammoth Pl	1700	ESCN	1129	F6
Manacor Ct	10800	SDGO	1249	H2
Managua Pl	2900	CRLB	1127	H7
Manajo Rd	9100	SDCo	1232	C5
Manajo Wy	13000	SDCo	1232	C5
Manana Pl	6500	SDGO	1247	F2
Manarola Ce	19800	SDCo	1152	C2
Manassas St	16500	SDCo	1169	E3
Mance Buchanon Park Rd	0	OCSD	1067	A7
Manchester Av	2000	ENCT	1167	D3
	2000	ESCN	1130	D1
Manchester Dr	5200	OCSD	1087	D1
Manchester Pl	1700	ESCN	1130	C1
Manchester Rd	5100	SDGO	1270	E2
Manchester St	1200	NATC	1290	C7
Mancilla Ct	4200	SDGO	1188	B6
Manda Pl	-	SDCo	1251	G3
Mandalay Pl	5200	SDGO	1270	E1
Mandalay Rd	6900	SDGO	1270	E2
Mandan Wy	3100	SDGO	1248	C1
Mandarin Cv	5400	SDGO	1270	B4
Mandarin Dr	5200	OCSD	1087	D2
	700	SDCo	1027	G3
Mandarin Pl	4000	SDGO	1270	B5
Mandarin Terr	4100	SDGO	1270	B5
Mandarin Wy	500	SDCo	1027	G3
Mandell Weiss Ln	-	SDGO	1227	J3
Mandevilla Ct	700	SNMS	1109	A6
Mandeville Ct	9400	SNTE	1231	B5
Mandeville Dr	1400	ESCN	1129	G7
Mandeville Ln	-	SDGO	1228	A2
Mandeville Rd	9500	SNTE	1231	B4
Mandez Dr	-	SDCo	1172	E3
Mandi Ln	100	SDCo	1152	J3
	-	SNTE	1231	C3
Mandrake Ct	-	SDGO	1210	A2
Mandrake Pt	-	SDGO	1210	A2
Mandy Ln	3300	SDCo	1271	C6
Manfred Ct	1700	ELCJ	1252	B2
Mangano Cir	100	ENCT	1147	C6
Mango Cove	14300	SDGO	1187	H5
Mango Ct	700	SNMS	1109	C6
Mango Dr	13600	SDGO	1187	H6
Mango Glen	2000	SDCo	1088	D5
Mango View Dr	-	ENCT	1147	E7
Mango Wy	2400	SDGO	1187	H5
Mangonel Dr	2000	SDCo	1078	G1
(See Page 1078)				
Mangrum Pl	2300	OCSD	1106	H2
Manhasset Dr	5100	SDGO	1270	A2
Manhattan Ct	700	SDGO	1267	H2
Manifesto Pl	12500	SDGO	1188	B7
Manila Av	10400	SDGO	1209	B4
Manila Cir	7900	SDGO	1209	B4
Manila Trl	7500	SDCo	1237	D7
Manila Wy	-	NATC	1289	J7
Manion St	2300	ELCJ	1251	B1
Manitou Wy	4500	SDGO	1248	F1
Manitowoc Wy	3100	SDGO	1268	E6
Mankato St	300	CHLV	1310	B7
	600	CHLV	1330	A1
E Mankato St	-	CHLV	1310	D6
Manley St	4700	SDGO	1249	H2
Mann Av	100	NATC	1290	A6
Mannen Wy	13200	SDCo	1232	C7
Manning St	6600	SDGO	1248	H7
Manning Wy	700	SDGO	1330	B7
Mannis Av	-	CHLV	1331	C1
Mannix Ct	7300	SDGO	1188	J7
Mannix Rd	12100	SDGO	1188	J7
Manock Cove	13000	SDGO	1188	D5
Manomet St	4800	SDGO	1290	A5
Manon St	5900	LMSA	1250	G6
Manor Dr	400	ELCJ	1251	E5
	9300	LMSA	1251	B6
	1300	SDCo	1251	J2
	1700	VSTA	1087	G3
E Manor Dr	600	CHLV	1330	A1
W Manor Dr	600	CHLV	1330	A1
	6100	LMSA	1251	B6
Manor Ridge Ln	-	SDGO	1208	D1
Manor Wy	900	SDGO	1288	A2
Manorgate Dr	11200	SDGO	1208	D3
Manos Dr	2700	SDGO	1310	D2
Manresa Ct	16900	SDGO	1170	C3
Mansfield Rd	-	ImCo	6320	C5
(See Page 6320)				
Mansfield St	5000	SDGO	1269	F3
Mansiones Ln	1100	CHLV	1310	J5
Manson St	7200	SDGO	1248	J6
Manteca Dr	-	OCSD	1067	A4
Mantilla Rd	12500	SDGO	1170	C4
Manton Wy	100	VSTA	1087	G2
Mantua Ct	5400	SDGO	1249	H1
Manuel Ortiz Av	-	ELCN	6559	G3
Manya Cir	7000	SDGO	1330	B5
Manya St	2300	SDGO	1330	B5
Manzana Wy	1200	SDGO	1290	H5
Manzanares Wy	5200	SDGO	1290	A4
Manzanilla Wy	300	OCSD	1087	A2
Manzanillo Ct	100	SOLB	1167	H5
Manzanita Av	1400	ESCN	1110	A7
Manzanita Crest Rd	-	SDCo	1070	A3
Manzanita Ct	1800	VSTA	1108	B3
Manzanita Dr	-	ELCN	6559	G2
	200	OCSD	1067	A7
	900	SDCo	1136	D7
	3200	SDCo	1155	G4
	400	SDCo	1156	E1
	24400	SDCo	1236	A2
	29500	SDCo	1297	E6
(See Page 1297)				
	3900	SDGO	1269	G7
Manzanita Dulce	39500	SDCo	1300	C5
(See Page 1300)				
Manzanita Hill Rd	15900	SDCo	1091	A3
Manzanita Ln	25000	SDCo	1236	B2
	700	SNMS	1108	J5
Manzanita Pl	300	ESCN	1129	H1
	3200	SDGO	1269	H6
Manzanita Ranch Rd	15400	SDCo	1173	H6
Manzanita Rd	11400	SDCo	1211	G6
Manzanita St	-	BRAW	6320	B1
(See Page 6320)				
	500	CHLV	1330	G1
	7200	CRLB	1127	E7
Manzanita Trl	28900	SDCo	1237	B7
	2500	SDCo	1299	H3
(See Page 1299)				
Manzanita View Rd	2800	SDCo	1234	C6
Manzanita Wy	4300	OCSD	1086	J2
	2100	SDCo	1300	D6
(See Page 1300)				
	20400	SDCo	1315	A1
(See Page 1315)				
Manzano Dr	100	CRLB	1126	G3
Manzano Pl	400	CHLV	1310	H4
Manzella Dr	14200	SDGO	1189	G2
Maple	-	SDCo	1233	B3
Maple Av	100	CRLB	1106	E6
	200	ELCN	6499	J7
	-	ImCo	6560	A6
	4800	LMSA	1270	G3
	700	SNMS	1108	J6
Maple Ct	-	BRAW	6259	F6
(See Page 6259)				
	300	CHLV	1330	G3
	2900	SDGO	1269	E7
Maple Dr	1600	CHLV	1330	G5
	4400	OCSD	1087	D5
Maple Grove Ln	15200	SDGO	1210	H2
Maple Leaf Ct	11400	SDGO	1210	H1
Maple Leaf Rd	6800	CRLB	1127	A5
Maple Ln	9700	SDCo	1149	E2
Maple Ridge	-	SDGO	1208	B2

43 INDEX
INDEX 43
Maple St
McCandless Rd
SAN DIEGO CO.

San Diego County Street Index

STREET
Block City Map# Grid

Maple St
1200 SDCo 1152 F3
2800 SDGO 1269 E7
5200 SDGO 1270 A7
200 SDGO 1289 A1
- SNMS 1129 C2
N Maple St
400 ESCN 1129 H2
S Maple St
100 ESCN 1129 J3
1300 ESCN 1130 A4
W Maple St
1000 SDGO 1288 J1
Maple Tree Rd
10000 SNTE 1231 D3
Maplebrook Ct
- ELCJ 1252 C5
Mapleleaf Ct
1600 ENCT 1167 G1
Mapleleaf Dr
2300 VSTA 1108 A5
Mapleton Ct
8500 SDGO 1169 A3
Mapleview St
12700 SDCo 1232 B2
Maplewood Cir
5100 OCSD 1087 C2
Maplewood Ct
12700 POWY 1190 C2
Maplewood Ln
- SDCo 1231 J3
Maplewood Pl
- SDCo 1130 J3
Maplewood St
14400 POWY 1190 C2
Maplewood Wy
700 ELCJ 1251 G4
Mar Av
7500 SDGO 1227 F7
Mar Azul Wy
2000 CRLB 1127 F7
Mar Mary Cres
31700 SDCo 1068 G1
Mar Reef Cv
1300 SDGO 1351 A1
Mar Scenic Dr
13700 SDGO 1187 H6
Mar Vista Dr
- SDCo 1027 G1
600 SOLB 1167 F6
1100 VSTA 1107 G3
100 VSTA 1108 A2
Mara Ln
15800 SDCo 1172 A4
Mara Villa St
5700 SNTE 1231 G6
Marabou Ln
1300 VSTA 1087 G4
Maranatha Dr
- SDGO 1169 C3
Maranatha Wy
400 SNMS 1128 F1
Maranda Dr
9200 SNTE 1231 A5
Marathon Dr
3300 SDGO 1249 E5
Marathon Pkwy
10000 SDCo 1231 G4
Marathon Wy
4800 OCSD 1107 E6
Maravilla Ln
700 SDCo 1047 E3
Maravilla Wy
2300 OCSD 1087 D6
Maravillas Av
- SDCo 1168 C3
Marazon Ln
600 VSTA 1107 E2
Marbella Cir
700 CHLV 1311 A5
Marbella Ct
1200 CHLV 1311 A5
Marbella Dr
1600 VSTA 1107 G4
Marbella Pl
1200 CHLV 1311 A5
Marble Canyon Wy
- CHLV 1311 J6
Marble Ct
1500 CHLV 1330 G4
Marble Ln
- SNMS 1128 B5
Marble St
500 ELCJ 1251 G4
Marble Wy
1500 CHLV 1330 G4
Marblehead Bay Dr
4800 OCSD 1066 J6
Marbo Ter
1000 VSTA 1087 J4
Marbok Wy
13800 SDCo 1292 G1
(See Page 1292)
Marbrisa Cir
1500 CRLB 1126 J2
Marbrook Wy
- SDCo 1232 E7
Marbury Av
10600 SDGO 1209 D3
Marc Trl
1700 SDCo 1318 E3
(See Page 1318)
Marca Pl
2300 CRLB 1147 G2
Marcasel Pl
13400 SDGO 1188 B4
Marcasite Pl
1900 CRLB 1127 F5
Marcella Ct
10100 SNTE 1231 A3
Marcella St
4100 OCSD 1087 C6
Marcellena Rd
4400 SDGO 1270 B4
March Pl
2100 SDGO 1268 G1
Marcheta St
200 ENCT 1147 B6
Marci Wy
1800 SDCo 1048 A4
Marcia Ct
4300 SDGO 1350 G1
Marcia Ln
4600 SDCo 1271 H2
Marcilla Wy
600 CHLV 1310 H6
Marconi Ct
2300 SDGO 1352 B3
Marconi Dr
9800 SDGO 1352 B3
Marconi Pl
2300 SDGO 1352 B3
Marcos St
300 SNMS 1108 H7
Marcos Vista Ln
700 SNMS 1108 C6
Marcwade Ct
3800 SDGO 1350 F1
Marcwade Dr
3900 SDGO 1350 F1
Marcy Av
- SDGO 1289 E5
Marcyn Ln
1600 ESCN 1109 H6
Mardavido Ln
2100 SDCo 1028 B6
Mardavido Pl
2300 SDCo 1028 A6
Mardi Gras Ct
- CORD 1329 E3
Mardi Gras Rd
- CORD 1329 E3
Mardi Gras St
4500 OCSD 1066 H7
Mare Rd
5300 OCSD 1067 B5
Marengo Av
5500 LMSA 1250 H7
5300 LMSA 1270 H1
Margale Ln
- SDCo 1068 F6
Margaret Ct
- SDCo 1291 A2
Margaret St
5200 SDCo 1310 J1
Margaret Wy
3800 CRLB 1106 G6
Margarita Av
700 CORD 1288 J7
Margarita Dr
600 SNMS 1109 A6
Margarita Glen
1500 SDCo 998 C6
Margarita Glen Rd
2800 SDCo 998 C5
Margarita Ln
- SDCo 1070 F2
Margarita St
- CALX 6620 J7
12600 SDGO 1208 A2
Margarita Vista
- SDCo 998 C7
Margarite Rd
900 SDCo 1029 H3
Margaritta Rd
6600 SDGO 1290 E4
Margate Av
12800 POWY 1190 H5
Marge Wy
4300 SDGO 1350 G1
Margerum Av
7600 SDGO 1250 C5
Margie Pl
500 SNMS 1128 D1
Margie Wy
2400 VSTA 1088 D6
Marginata Ct
- SDGO 1210 A1
Margo Ct
300 CHLV 1310 F7
Margo Pl
1200 VSTA 1107 E1
Marguerita Ln
4800 LMSA 1271 B2
Marguerite Canyon Rd
- SDCo 1212 H5
Marguerite Creek Wy
13500 SDGO 1188 F3
Marguerite Ln
900 CRLB 1127 A6
Marguerite Wy
- OCSD 1086 H3
Margurite Canyon Rd
12000 SDCo 1212 H6
Maria Av
800 SDCo 1291 C3
Maria Ct
- LMGR 1290 J1
Maria Ln
3600 CRLB 1106 H5
Maria Pl
1500 CORD 1288 J7
Maria Wy
900 CHLV 1330 F1
Mariah Wy
22200 SDCo 1275 C2
Marian Av
2300 SDGO 1330 B6
Marian St
4000 LMSA 1270 E4
Marian Wy
5900 SDGO 1268 G2
Mariana Dr
14200 POWY 1190 B2
Marianne Ln
2500 SDCo 1028 B4
Marianopolis Wy
14200 SDGO 1189 D2
Maricotte Pl
13200 SDGO 1187 J4
Marie Av
7600 LMSA 1270 G2
Marie Ct
- ENCT 1147 G5
Marielle Pl
1800 CHLV 1311 F1
Marietta St
400 CHLV 1310 A5
Marigold
- SDCo 1233 B3
Marigold Av
- IMPE 6499 J2
Marigold Cir
300 OCSD 1066 H6
Marigold Ct
800 CRLB 1127 A5
Marigold Dr
- POWY 1190 F2
600 VSTA 1087 F4
Marigold Pl
100 CHLV 1310 C5
2200 SDGO 1289 H1
Marigold St
2300 SDGO 1289 H1
Marigold Wy
13300 SDGO 1188 G4
- SNMS 1128 F2
Marigot Pl
5200 SDGO 1249 J1
Marilla Dr
9600 SDCo 1231 H4
Marilou Rd
4900 SDGO 1290 A2
Marilouise Wy
2400 SDGO 1268 G4
Marilyn Av
500 BRAW 6319 G2
(See Page 6319)
Marilyn Ln
2300 SDCo 1109 A1
1700 SNMS 1109 A2
Marin Dr
4900 OCSD 1107 F3
- SNMS 1108 J7
Marina Av
500 CORD 1288 G7
Marina Ct
- IMPE 6499 H2
Marina Dr
4700 CRLB 1106 H7
E Marina Park Wy
- SDGO 1289 A4
Marina Pkwy
- CHLV 1309 H6
500 CHLV 1329 J1
Marina Springs Ln
- SDCo 1232 J4
Marina Wy
1000 CHLV 1329 H2
2400 NATC 1309 H4
Marindustry Dr
6200 SDGO 1228 G1
Marindustry Pl
8400 SDGO 1228 H1
Marine Pl
- CRLB 1127 A7
Marine St
600 SDGO 1227 E7
200 SDGO 1247 E1
Marine View Av
3900 SDGO 1289 G7
100 SOLB 1167 G7
600 SOLB 1187 G1
Marine View Dr
900 SDCo 1107 H3
Marine Wy
- SDGO 1248 C6
Mariner Dr
5100 SDGO 1330 J7
Mariner St
900 CRLB 1126 J4
Mariners Bay
4500 OCSD 1066 H6
Mariners Wy
- SDGO 1267 J3
Maring Pl
5200 SDGO 1290 A1
Mario Pl
3700 SDGO 1248 H4
Marion Ct
- CHLV 1311 C7
Marion Ln
2200 SDCo 1130 D6
Mariposa
5400 SDCo 1168 C3
Mariposa Cir
600 CHLV 1330 G1
Mariposa Ct
- CHLV 1330 G1
1200 VSTA 1088 A3
Mariposa Pl
900 ESCN 1109 F5
5500 SDGO 1290 B6
Mariposa Rd
- CRLB 1127 A4
1500 SDCo 1058 F5
(See Page 1058)
Mariposa Ridge
25000 SDCo 1173 G4
Mariposa St
500 CHLV 1330 G1
8600 LMSA 1270 J3
8800 LMSA 1271 A3
1400 SDGO 1290 B6
7000 SNTE 1231 G7
Marisa Ln
900 ENCT 1147 J5
Marisa Wy
2300 ENCT 1147 J6
Marisco Pt
12300 SDGO 1188 B7
Marisma Wy
1600 SDGO 1247 G1
Marita Ln
1700 SDCo 1027 J3
Maritime Dr
- CRLB 1127 C4
Maritime Pl
13000 SDGO 1187 J5
Maritime Wy
3700 OCSD 1086 J5
Marjay Dr
13300 SDCo 1232 D6
Marjean Ln
10200 SDCo 1231 G3
Marjo Ct
2500 OCSD 1087 D6
Marjorie Av
- BRAW 6319 G1
(See Page 6319)
1500 ESCN 1110 A6
Marjorie Dr
900 SDGO 1290 G2
Marjorie Ln
3600 CRLB 1106 G5
Marjorie Pl
1200 ESCN 1110 A7
Marjorie St
1500 OCSD 1087 E2
Mark Av
2000 ESCN 1110 C6
Mark Cir
2400 CRLB 1106 H4
Mark Lee Dr
17900 SDCo 1274 C4
Mark Pl
2200 ESCN 1110 C6
Mark Stevens Rd
13600 POWY 1190 G3
Mark Ter
4000 SDGO 1248 E5
Mark Tr
16700 SDCo 1273 J4
Markab Dr
11200 SDGO 1209 C1
Markar Rd
15600 POWY 1170 J6
Markell Ln
300 SDCo 1027 F4
Marker Ln
3100 SDCo 1079 B5
(See Page 1079)
Marker Rd
- SDGO 1188 J3
Markerry Av
1500 ELCJ 1252 B5
Market Pl
100 ESCN 1129 E3
- SDGO 1288 J4
Market St
3000 SDGO 1289 E3
5400 SDGO 1290 B3
1400 VSTA 1087 J4
Markham St
7600 SDGO 1249 A5
Markwood Dr
9500 SNTE 1231 B4
Marky Wy
9700 SDCo 1271 C3
Marl Av
1500 CHLV 1330 G4
Marl Ct
1400 CHLV 1330 G3
Marlborough Av
4000 SDGO 1269 H5
Marlborough Dr
4600 SDGO 1269 G3
Marlen Wy
5100 LMSA 1271 A1
Marlena Wy
3100 SDCo 1272 C7
3100 SDCo 1292 D1
(See Page 1292)
Marlesta Dr
3300 SDGO 1248 H5
4200 SDGO 1249 A3
Marlin Ct
- SDCo 1085 H5
Marlin Dr
900 VSTA 1088 A6
Marlin Ln
- CRLB 1127 A7
Marlin Rd
- SDCo 1085 H6
Marlinda Wy
1800 SDCo 1251 G1
Marline Av
1100 ELCJ 1251 H4
1400 ELCJ 1252 A4
Marlowe Dr
6700 SDGO 1270 E5
Marlton Dr
3200 SDGO 1289 F1
Marlynn Ct
400 SDCo 1130 B5
Marmac Dr
- SDCo 1172 A4
Marmil Av
3000 SDGO 1310 D2
Marmil Pl
7300 SDGO 1290 F3
Marmil Wy
5900 SDGO 1310 D2
Marmol Ct
2600 CRLB 1127 G6
Marne Av
5600 SDGO 1250 D7
Marne River Wy
- CHLV 1331 E1
Maroon Peak Ct
- SDGO 1190 A7
Marquart Ranch Rd
32400 SDCo 1049 A6
Marquette Av
200 SNMS 1128 H3
Marquette Pl
3800 SDGO 1268 C5
Marquette Rd
- CHLV 1311 E5
Marquette St
1300 OCSD 1086 A6
2900 SDGO 1268 C5
Marquez Ct
2300 SDCo 1087 H1
Marquis Ct
- CHLV 1311 E5
Marquita Pl
2600 CRLB 1147 G2
Marraco Dr
- SDGO 1270 D4
Marraco Wy
4400 SDGO 1270 D4
Marrokal Ln
- SNTE 1230 J7
Marron Rd
2000 CRLB 1106 F3
Marron St
- OCSD 1106 B2
3800 SDGO 1270 C5
Mars Wy
4200 SDCo 1271 G4
Marsala Terr
8900 SDGO 1249 D2
Marsat Ct
600 CHLV 1330 B4
Marsden Ct
100 ELCJ 1251 D5
Marseilles St
4400 SDGO 1287 H2
Marsh Harbor Dr
- SDGO 1330 H6
Marsh Wren St
7000 CRLB 1127 B6
Marsha Ct
2600 SDGO 1270 A7
Marshall Av
- IMPE 6499 F1
N Marshall Av
700 ELCJ 1251 E4
S Marshall Av
400 ELCJ 1251 E6
Marshall Ct
- SDCo 1234 B6
Marshall Ln
3000 SDCo 1271 A6
Marshall Rd
1300 SDCo 1234 B6
Marshall St
1400 OCSD 1106 C2
Marshall Wy
19200 SDCo 1091 G3
2300 SDCo 1234 B6
Marsolan Av
600 SOLB 1187 F1
Marson St
1700 OCSD 1086 B5
Marsopa Dr
700 VSTA 1107 F2
Martee Ln
9400 SNTE 1231 C7
Martell St
300 ELCJ 1252 B5
Martha St
3600 SDGO 1248 D1
Martin Av
3000 SDGO 1289 E5
Martin Canyon Ct
4000 SDCo 1311 A3
Martin Dr
900 ESCN 1109 J7
Martin Luther King Av
- CALX 6620 G6
Martin Luther King Jr. Fwy
- SDGO 1270 D7
- SDGO 1289 D3
- SDGO 1290 A2
Martin Pl
- CHLV 1330 H2
Martin Ridge Rd
16100 SDCo 1176 C2
(See Page 1176)
Martin St
1200 BRAW 6320 B2
(See Page 6320)
4900 OCSD 1067 A6
Martina Ct
1000 SDCo 1128 C3
Martincoit Rd
16600 POWY 1170 E3
Martindale Ct
3000 SDGO 1249 E5
Martinez Ranch Rd
2600 SDGO 1351 E4
Martinez St
900 SDGO 1288 A2
Martingale Ct
- CRLB 1127 C4
Martingale Ln
2000 SDCo 1234 A4
400 SNMS 1108 D5
Martinique Dr
- CHLV 1311 E5
Martinique Wy
10900 SDGO 1209 A3
Martinview Dr
2100 SDGO 1289 H1
Martos Pl
700 CHLV 1310 J6
Marvejo
- SDCo 1232 C7
Marview Dr
400 SOLB 1167 F6
Marvin St
4000 OCSD 1087 B7
5400 SDGO 1270 B6
Marvinga Ln
2600 SDCo 997 A2
Marwood Ln
100 OCSD 1106 C2
Mary Ann St
- SDCo 1291 B1
Mary Av
300 CALX 6680 G2
1000 ImCo 6620 C1
Mary Ct
800 NATC 1290 C7
Mary Dean Ln
- SDCo 1231 J7
Mary Earl Ct
13500 POWY 1190 E1
Mary Earl Ln
13400 POWY 1190 E1
Mary Fellows Av
5300 LMSA 1270 F1
Mary Joe Ln
1600 SDCo 1320 A2
(See Page 1320)
Mary Lane Ct
1100 SDCo 1130 D7
Mary Lane Dr
5500 SDGO 1270 B2
Mary Lane Pl
2600 SDCo 1130 D7
Mary Lee Ln
- SDCo 1071 E2
Mary Lewis Dr
3400 SDCo 1048 D3
Mary Ln
3600 ESCN 1150 C2
1100 NATC 1290 C7
2600 SDCo 1130 D6
3400 SDCo 1150 D1
- SDCo 1212 B7
Mary Lou St
1400 SDGO 1290 A2
Mary Pat Ln
8000 LMGR 1290 H1
Mary South Ln
- SDCo 1150 C2
Mary St
1100 ELCJ 1251 H4
Maryann Wy
1900 SDCo 1272 A1
Maryford Dr
8600 SDGO 1250 J3
Marygold Dr
2500 SDCo 1297 E6
(See Page 1297)
Maryland Av
5300 LMSA 1270 F1
Maryland Ct
4500 SDGO 1269 B4
700 VSTA 1087 F6
Maryland Dr
1300 VSTA 1087 F4
Maryland Pl
1200 SDGO 1269 B4
Maryland St
4400 SDGO 1269 B4
Marymac Pl
1800 SDCo 1028 A6
Marymount Pl
17600 SDGO 1170 A1
Marysville Av
- CHLV 1331 B1
Marzo St
3600 SDGO 1350 E2
Mascari Ct
1000 SDCo 1251 H3
Mascari Pl
3900 SDCo 1271 C4
Mason Cir
700 SDCo 1067 J7
Mason Dr
3700 LMGR 1270 J5
Mason Heights Ln
7400 SDGO 1208 J2
Mason Rd
1200 CHLV 1331 C2
600 SDCo 1067 H7
800 SDCo 1087 J1
Mason St
4100 SDGO 1268 F4
Mason Valley Truck Trl
17900 SDCo 1176 G1
(See Page 1176)
9900 SDCo 1177 B2
(See Page 1177)
Mason Wy
2700 SDCo 1067 H7
Masonry Pl
- ESCN 1129 F5
Massachusetts Av
2000 LMGR 1270 F7
3800 LMSA 1270 F5
500 VSTA 1087 H5
Massachusetts St
4600 SDGO 1269 B4
Massais Pl
1800 CHLV 1311 F1
Massasoit Av
2900 SDGO 1248 C1
Massena St
1300 SDGO 1227 F7
Massery Ln
8500 SNTE 1251 B1
Massot Av
9200 SNTE 1230 J6
Mast Blvd
- SDCo 1231 G4
- SDGO 1230 J5
9900 SNTE 1231 D4
Mast Wy
2500 CHLV 1311 G4
Masterpiece Dr
1100 OCSD 1087 B2
Masters Dr
700 OCSD 1087 B1
Masters Pl
3000 SDGO 1249 E5
Masters Rd
- CRLB 1107 B7
Masters Ridge Rd
- CHLV 1311 G4
Masterson Ln
- SDGO 1350 G2
Mastodon Ct
3700 CRLB 1107 B6
Mata Wy
100 SNMS 1109 A7
Matador Ct
10200 SDGO 1229 G7
Matagual Ct
700 VSTA 1107 G1
Matagual Dr
500 VSTA 1107 G1
Matallana Ct
700 CALX 6680 D1
Matamo Pl
- SDCo 1252 G7
Matamoros Ct
100 SOLB 1167 H5
Matanza Rd
12700 SDGO 1170 C3
Mataro Dr
4600 SDGO 1270 D3
Match Point Dr
14200 POWY 1190 G4
Mateo Pl
2700 CRLB 1147 G2
Mater Dei Dr
1600 CHLV 1331 E1
Matera Ln
2700 SDGO 1249 D7
Mather Av
500 SDGO 1330 E6
Mathew Rd
15500 SDCo 1091 A4
Mathews Av
- SDGO 1209 E6
Mathieson St
10500 SDGO 1189 G2
Mathis Pl
8500 SDGO 1169 C3
Matilde Gomez
700 CALX 6680 D1
Matin Cir
- SNMS 1109 D7
- SNMS 1129 D1
Matinal Cir
10700 SDGO 1149 J7
11300 SDGO 1169 J1
Matinal Dr
17400 SDGO 1169 J1
Matinal Rd
17000 SDGO 1169 H2
Matisse Ln
5200 SDCo 1290 H7
Matlin Rd
25900 SDCo 1174 B4
Mator Av
- SDGO 1209 D7
Mator Dr
- SDGO 1209 D6
Mator Wy
1500 SDGO 1209 D7
Matson Pl
7600 SDGO 1208 J4
Matson Wy
10500 SDGO 1209 A4
Matt Rd
10200 SDCo 1029 A2
Matte Ln
2700 SDCo 1108 B5
Matterhorn Dr
8500 SNTE 1250 H1
Matthew Ct
900 VSTA 1107 H1
Matthew Ln
600 SNMS 1109 D6
Matthew Pl
2000 ESCN 1110 C6
Mattole St
- OCSD 1086 H1
Matty Ct
4700 SDCo 1271 C2
Maturin Dr
15200 SDGO 1169 H5
Maude Rd
13800 SDCo 1070 E5
Maudey Bell Ct
2300 SDCo 1272 E2
Mauka Dr
- SDCo 1069 J5
Maureen Ct
9500 SNTE 1231 B5
Maury Ct
8600 SDGO 1250 J4
Maury Dr
6700 SDGO 1250 J4
Maverick Ct
16600 POWY 1170 E3
Maverick Glen
1900 ESCN 1110 A4
Maverick Ln
16600 POWY 1170 E3
Maverick Pl
300 CHLV 1310 G4
Maverick Wy
- CRLB 1148 A3
Mavin Dr
9500 SNTE 1231 E4
Max Av
1300 CHLV 1330 F3
Max Dr
4500 SDGO 1269 J4
Maxam Av
- SDGO 1209 F7
Maxfield Blvd
- CORD 1288 F4
Maxfield Rd
13900 SDCo 1292 H2
(See Page 1292)
Maxie Pl
1000 ESCN 1130 E1
Maxim St
500 SDGO 1289 J3
Maxine Ln
- SDCo 1149 F7
Maxson St
2100 OCSD 1086 C7
Maxwell Av
1000 ELCJ 1251 G7
Maxwell Ln
1500 VSTA 1088 B3
Maxwell Rd
1500 CHLV 1330 J5
1400 SDCo 1331 A4
May Av
1600 CHLV 1331 E2
May Ct
3900 CRLB 1106 H6
200 ENCT 1167 D2
6900 SDGO 1290 F7
Maya Ct
1800 VSTA 1107 J3
Maya Linda Rd
9800 SDGO 1209 E5
Maya St
- CRLB 1106 F7
800 SDCo 1291 C2
Mayan Ct
11200 SDGO 1149 H7
Mayapan Dr
4300 SDCo 1271 G3
Mayapan Ln
4400 SDCo 1271 G3
Mayapple Ct
- SDGO 1209 H1
Mayapple Wy
- SDGO 1209 G1
Mayberry Ln
700 ELCJ 1251 F4
1100 VSTA 1087 G4
Mayberry St
4400 SDGO 1289 H6
Maybritt Cir
600 SNMS 1108 J5
Maycrest Ln
- SDGO 1208 G3
Maye Pl
1400 SDCo 1130 C3
Mayfair Ct
4400 CRLB 1106 J5
Mayfair St
100 OCSD 1086 F3
Mayfield Ct
- CHLV 1311 C7
Mayfield Dr
200 OCSD 1086 J4
7600 SDGO 1249 A6
Mayflower Av
- ESCN 1130 C1
Mayflower Wy
4600 OCSD 1087 A1
4300 SDGO 1228 E7
Mayita Wy
4700 SDGO 1250 A1
Maynard St
9100 SDCo 1291 B3
5100 SDGO 1228 G6
Mayo Pl
2500 SDGO 1268 D7
Mayo St
4200 SDGO 1268 E1
Mayor Cir
10100 SDGO 1209 B5
Mays Hollow Ln
- ENCT 1147 D6
Maytem Ct
4700 OCSD 1087 A1
Maywind Ct
11700 SDGO 1210 A4
Maywood Ct
- CHLV 1331 D1
Maywood Ln
- OCSD 1106 C1
Maywood St
600 ESCN 1110 C6
Mazagon Ln
800 CHLV 1310 H6
Mazatlan Ct
14100 POWY 1190 E2
Mazatlan Dr
- IMPE 6499 H1
Mazatlan Wy
14000 POWY 1190 E3
Maze Glen
600 ESCN 1150 C4
Mazer St
8100 LMGR 1270 H7
Mazzetti Ln
54700 SDCo 1071 D2
Mazzola St
1100 SDCo 1251 H3
McBurney Ct
- SDGO 1330 C7
McBurney Ridge Ln
- SDGO 1209 G2
McCabe Cove Rd
- ImCo 6559 J4
McCabe Rd
300 ELCN 6559 F5
500 ImCo 6559 D5
200 ImCo 6560 D4
McCain Blvd
- CORD 1288 G5
McCain Ln
2200 ENCT 1167 J1
McCain Rd
- SDGO 1288 E1
McCain Valley Ct
- CHLV 1331 A2
McCain Valley Rd
2500 SDCo 1300 H3
(See Page 1300)
McCain Wy
4100 SDGO 1268 E7
McCall St
3100 SDGO 1288 A4
McCandless Rd
- SDGO 1289 F7
McCandless Rd
- NATC 1309 G1

San Diego County Street Index

STREET
Block City Map# Grid

McCardle Wy
9700 SNTE 1231 B4
McCarran Ct
- IMPE 6499 C1
McCarran Dr
- IMPE 6499 D1
McCauley Ln
- CRLB 1106 F4
McCawley St
600 SDCo 1067 A1
McCellan Rd
- SDGO 1288 A6
McClelland St
1200 SNMS 1109 C6
McClintock St
4300 SDGO 1269 G4
McCloud River Rd
- CHLV 1311 E6
McCloy Wy
3200 SDGO 1249 G4
McClure St
700 ELCJ 1251 H4
McConnell Rd
1800 SDGO 1288 C2
McConnell Rd
- ImCo 6320 F4
(See Page 6320)
2100 ImCo 6500 G3
McCormac Rd
1900 SDCo 1028 A7
McCormick Ln
- SDCo 1071 E3
McCullom St
300 ELCN 6500 A6
McCune Rd
- SDGO 1288 A7
McDonald Ln
600 ESCN 1129 J6
McDonald Meadows
1100 SDCo 1027 H4
McDonald Rd
1300 SDCo 1027 H5
McDonald St
2100 ELCN 6499 G4
McDonough Ln
2000 SDGO 1288 C1
McDonough Rd
- SDGO 1288 C1
McDougal Pl
2400 SDCo 1234 B4
McDougal Terr
1800 ELCJ 1252 C2
McDougal Wy
1800 ELCJ 1252 C2
McDowell Ct
- SDGO 1209 F1
McEntee St
14000 SDGO 1189 E2
McFeron Rd
12400 POWY 1190 C4
McFeron Rd
12600 POWY 1190 C4
McGann Dr
5400 SDGO 1290 B1
McGavran View
600 VSTA 1107 F1
McGill Wy
5000 SDGO 1188 D6
McGonigle Rd
- SDGO 1207 G1
McGonigle Ter
- SDGO 1188 J3
McGraw St
3100 SDGO 1248 D5
McGregory Ln
1600 VSTA 1088 B6
McGuire Dr
4000 SDGO 1188 A5
McHaney Ct
6200 SDGO 1290 D6
McHugh St
5600 SDGO 1290 B3
McInney Rd
- SDGO 1288 A5
McIntire Cir
3500 OCSD 1106 J1
McIntire Dr
2300 SDGO 1289 C2
McIntire Ln
2100 SDCo 1109 A1
McIntosh St
500 CHLV 1309 J5
McIvers Ct
12300 POWY 1190 E6
McKean St
- SDGO 1289 F7
McKee St
1900 SDGO 1268 H6
McKellar Ct
10100 SDGO 1208 E5
McKenna Heights Ct
29900 SDCo 1071 A5
McKenzie Av
13700 POWY 1190 E3
McKenzie St
- SDCo 1023 F2
McKinley Av
1400 ESCN 1110 B7
1300 ESCN 1130 B1
1500 NATC 1309 G3

McKinley Ct
8900 LMSA 1271 A2
McKinley St
3200 CRLB 1106 F5
3100 SDGO 1269 F7
McKinley St
- CALX 6680 E1
100 OCSD 1067 B6
McKinney Ct
- SDGO 1209 G1
McKittrick Wy
4200 SDGO 1188 B5
McKnight Dr
2100 LMGR 1290 F1
McLain St
600 ESCN 1130 C2
McLane Ln
1300 SDCo 1109 E6
McLarens Ln
3200 SDGO 1289 F4
McLees Ct
1900 SDCo 1109 E6
McMahr Rd
700 SNMS 1128 E3
McMillin St
1200 CALX 6680 J1
McNally Rd
- SDCo 1049 H4
- SDCo 1050 C5
McNeil St
600 OCSD 1086 B6
McNeill Av
- ENCT 1147 C7
McRae Av
5400 LMSA 1270 F1
McWay Ct
500 ELCJ 1251 H4
McWest Ln
- SDCo 1232 A7
Mead Rd
- BRAW 6319 H5
(See Page 6319)
- ImCo 6320 F4
(See Page 6320)
Mead St
5300 OCSD 1087 E1
Meade Av
1500 SDGO 1269 C4
6000 SDGO 1270 C4
Meadow Creek Ln
14000 POWY 1190 G5
Meadow Creek Rd
11400 SDCo 1271 G3
Meadow Crest Dr
100 ELCJ 1251 A5
6200 LMSA 1251 A6
Meadow Crest Pl
3200 ESCN 1110 F6
Meadow Dr
- CALX 6620 G6
4600 CRLB 1107 B5
1400 NATC 1310 B1
- SDCo 1290 J6
Meadow Flower Pl
11300 SDGO 1169 H4
Meadow Glen Ln
1600 ENCT 1147 G4
Meadow Glen Wy
12900 POWY 1190 D5
28200 SDCo 1089 D4
Meadow Glen Wy E
10000 SDCo 1089 E4
Meadow Glen Wy W
28700 SDCo 1089 D3
Meadow Grass Ct
- SDGO 1190 A7
- SDGO 1289 E7
Meadow Grass Ln
3200 ESCN 1110 F6
11400 SDGO 1189 J6
Meadow Grove Dr
3000 SDGO 1268 D5
Meadow Grove Rd
500 ESCN 1110 E7
Meadow Lark Dr
2800 SDGO 1249 B6
Meadow Ln
3200 LMGR 1270 J6
3600 OCSD 1107 A2
9800 SDCo 1236 A1
Meadow Mesa Dr
- SDCo 1089 D1
Meadow Mesa Ln
- SDCo 1089 D2
Meadow Oak Ln
28200 SDCo 1089 E3
Meadow Oaks Ln
15500 SDCo 1213 C7
Meadow Rd
1600 ELCJ 1252 B2
Meadow Spring
- OCSD 1086 H1
Meadow Terrace Dr
11100 SNTE 1231 F5
Meadow View Dr
3400 OCSD 1086 D2
Meadow View Rd
- SDCo 998 G5
11300 SDCo 1271 H3
Meadow Vista Pl
- ESCN 1109 H4

Meadow Wood Pl
1200 ENCT 1147 G4
Meadowbrook Ct
7600 SDGO 1290 G3
Meadowbrook Dr
4800 OCSD 1087 E3
N Meadowbrook Dr
400 SDGO 1290 G3
S Meadowbrook Dr
100 SDGO 1290 H4
Meadowbrook Ln
800 CHLV 1311 D5
12300 POWY 1190 B3
Meadowbrook Pl
2600 ESCN 1130 E1
Meadowdale Ln
12800 SDGO 1210 C4
Meadowgate St
3700 SDGO 1248 J4
Meadowgreen Ct
2100 ENCT 1147 H5
Meadowhaven Ct
1800 ENCT 1147 H4
Meadowlake Dr
1000 VSTA 1088 A5
Meadowlands Wy
- SOLB 1187 F1
Meadowlark Av
100 CHLV 1330 F4
Meadowlark Dr
- SDCo 1023 F3
Meadowlark Ln
3200 CRLB 1106 G4
2600 ESCN 1110 E7
Meadowlark Ranch Cir
2100 CRLB 1128 A4
Meadowlark Ranch Ln
2000 SDCo 1128 A4
Meadowlark Ranch Rd
1800 SDCo 1128 A5
Meadowlark Ridge Rd
16900 SDCo 1169 G4
Meadowlark Wy
1100 SDCo 1152 F3
Meadowmist Ct
500 ENCT 1148 A7
Meadowmist Ln
2500 ENCT 1148 A6
Meadowood Ct
- SDGO 1350 D2
Meadowood Glen
- SDGO 1188 H3
Meadowpointe Row
6000 SDGO 1248 A1
Meadowridge Ln
9800 SDCo 1271 C6
Meadowridge Pl
2300 SDCo 1271 C7
Meadowridge Rd
4700 SDCo 1135 D4
Meadowrun Ct
9000 SDGO 1189 C2
Meadowrun Dr
4500 OCSD 1066 H7
Meadowrun Pl
9000 SDGO 1189 C2
Meadowrun St
14500 SDGO 1189 D1
Meadowrun Wy
9000 SDGO 1189 C2
Meadows Del Mar
- SDGO 1188 E7
Meadows Del Mar Drwy
5400 SDGO 1188 F7
Meadows Rd
- CALX 6620 H5
- ImCo 6620 H3
Meadows Trail Ln
- CHLV 1311 H5
Meadowside Pl
3200 ESCN 1110 F6
2300 SDCo 1271 C7
Meadowview Av
- ELCN 6559 G4
Meadowview Dr
10200 SDGO 1209 H4
Meadowvista Wy
200 ENCT 1147 J7
Meajean Pl
11800 SDGO 1189 E7
Meander Glen
500 ESCN 1129 H2
Meander Rd
2100 CHLV 1311 G7
Meandro Ct
16700 SDGO 1170 B3
Meandro Dr
16700 SDGO 1170 B3
Meandro Rd
12400 SDGO 1170 C3
Meanley Dr
10000 SDGO 1209 F4
Meanwhile Ranch Rd
1000 SDCo 1318 E7
(See Page 1318)
Mecca Dr
1600 SDGO 1227 G6
Medalist Ct
5000 OCSD 1067 C3
Medallion Ln
13200 SDCo 1232 C7

Medford Av
2100 ESCN 1110 C6
Medford Ct
2600 CRLB 1106 J4
Medford Pl
2200 ESCN 1110 C6
Medford St
600 ELCJ 1251 A4
1400 OCSD 1067 A3
Mediatrice Ln
14200 SDGO 1189 D2
Medical Center Ct
700 CHLV 1330 J2
Medical Center Dr
1000 CHLV 1330 J1
- SDGO 1228 B2
Medici Wy
3400 OCSD 1106 J2
Medill Av
8200 SDCo 1232 C7
8100 SDCo 1252 C1
Medina Dr
10000 SNTE 1230 J3
Medina Glen
2200 ESCN 1109 D4
E Medina St
- CALX 6620 J6
Medinah Dr
2400 SDCo 1272 C5
Medinah Rd
- SNMS 1108 J3
Medinah Wy
- SDCo 1090 F5
Medio St
6400 SDGO 1290 D4
Medoc Ct
10500 SDGO 1210 B3
Medoc Ln
12000 SDGO 1210 B3
Meeks Bay Dr
- CHLV 1311 E6
Megan Ct
2400 SDGO 1290 A1
Megan Ln
- CRLB 1148 B2
Megan Terr
9700 SDCo 1069 C3
Megan Wy
4900 SDGO 1289 J1
Meghan Ct
9000 SDCo 1271 A6
Meknes St
15400 SDGO 1169 J6
Meknes Wy
11400 SDGO 1169 H6
Mel Ct
- SDGO 1350 D1
Melaleuca Av
900 CRLB 1127 A5
Melaleuca Ln
- SDCo 998 B6
Melanie Ct
10800 SNTE 1231 F3
Melba Rd
200 ENCT 1167 C1
Melbourne Dr
2800 SDGO 1249 E5
Melbourne Glen
400 SDCo 1109 H2
Melic Ct
12900 SDGO 1189 E5
Melinda Av
800 SNMS 1109 B6
Melinda De Oro
900 SDCo 1319 H7
(See Page 1319)
Melinda Wy
- OCSD 1086 H3
Melisa Wy
4500 SDGO 1248 C2
Melisande Pl
1800 CHLV 1311 F1
Melissa Ct
2400 VSTA 1108 B5
Melissa Ln
13600 POWY 1190 F4
Melissa Park Ter
900 SDCo 1252 H2
Melksee St
- SDGO 1351 H4
Mellmanor Dr
8500 LMSA 1250 J7
8700 LMSA 1251 A7
Melodia Terr
- SDCo 1127 B7
Melodie Ln
14100 POWY 1190 G3
Melody Ln
1500 ELCJ 1252 B5
7200 LMSA 1270 F1
- OCSD 1086 C5
34900 SDCo 1156 E6
Melody Rd
13800 SDCo 1292 F3
(See Page 1292)
Melojo Ln
10200 SDGO 1249 G1
Melora Ct
- SDCo 1272 E7
Melotte St
7500 SDGO 1250 E3

Melrose Av
600 CHLV 1310 E7
1400 CHLV 1330 G3
3400 CRLB 1128 A5
300 ENCT 1147 B5
Melrose Cir
- CHLV 1330 G5
Melrose Ct
- CHLV 1330 G5
Melrose Dr
- CRLB 1127 H3
1300 OCSD 1067 E6
1400 OCSD 1087 E3
- OCSD 1107 G3
1700 SNMS 1128 B6
- VSTA 1107 G2
2500 VSTA 1127 H1
N Melrose Dr
1000 VSTA 1087 F4
S Melrose Dr
1500 VSTA 1107 H4
Melrose Ln
8200 SDCo 1252 A1
Melrose Pl
12500 SDCo 1232 B7
700 SDGO 1290 B3
600 VSTA 1087 F5
Melrose St
800 NATC 1289 H7
2100 NATC 1290 A6
Melrose Wy
- CHLV 1330 G5
1100 VSTA 1107 F2
Melru Ln
- SDCo 1109 J3
Melton Ct
11000 SDGO 1209 J1
Melva Rd
1700 ELCJ 1271 F2
10700 SDCo 1271 F2
Melvin Ln
1500 SDCo 1252 A2
Melweir Wy
9600 SDCo 1232 C4
Memike Pl
8900 SDGO 1251 A3
Memorial Dr
4900 LMSA 1270 J2
Memorial St
- CHLV 1310 A6
Memory Ln
1000 ESCN 1109 F5
9000 SDCo 1271 B5
1200 VSTA 1088 A4
Menard St
3200 NATC 1310 D3
Mende Ct
2200 SDGO 1268 G4
Mendeck Av
9900 SNTE 1231 B3
Mendel Rivers Rd
400 SDCo 1067 A1
Mendenaro Ct
3300 SDCo 1048 C4
Mendibles Ct
- BRAW 6259 G6
(See Page 6259)
Mendiola Pt
11800 SDGO 1189 E7
Mendip St
- OCSD 1067 A3
Mendocino Blvd
1900 SDGO 1268 A7
Mendocino Dr
1500 CHLV 1330 H4
900 SNMS 1128 G3
Mendonca Dr
2600 SDGO 1268 E6
Mendota St
- CHLV 1311 D6
1800 SDGO 1288 B1
Mendoza
- SDCo 1071 E2
Mendoza St
1000 CALX 6680 C1
Menendez Ct
1900 SDGO 1350 D3
Mengibar Av
12600 SDGO 1189 F6
Menkar Pl
11400 SDGO 1209 B1
Menkar Rd
8900 SDGO 1189 D7
8300 SDGO 1209 B2
Menlo Av
4300 SDGO 1269 J4
Mennonite Pt
13900 SDGO 1189 D2
Menocino Ct
- SDCo 1128 G2
Menorca Dr
5800 SDGO 1229 H7
Menorca Wy
10500 SDGO 1229 H7
Mensha Pl
4400 SDGO 1188 B5
Menta Corte
1100 CHLV 1311 A7
Mentone St
4300 SDGO 1268 B5
Menvielle St
- IMPE 6439 C6

Mercado Dr
13900 SDGO 1187 H6
Mercado Glen
1400 ESCN 1109 E4
Mercantile St
500 VSTA 1087 H7
Merced Dr
3600 OCSD 1107 E4
Merced Lake Av
6200 SDGO 1250 H6
Merced Pl
- SDCo 1293 C4
Merced River Rd
900 CHLV 1331 A2
Mercedes Rd
100 SDCo 1027 H2
Mercer Ct
3500 SDGO 1228 D5
Mercer Ln
3000 SDGO 1228 C5
Mercer St
6200 SDGO 1228 D5
Merchants Wy
- SDGO 1248 E2
Mercurio St
4500 SDGO 1188 C7
Mercury Ct
8100 SDGO 1229 B7
Mercury Dr
2500 LMGR 1270 F7
Mercury Pl
6900 CRLB 1127 F6
Mercury Pt
5100 SDGO 1229 B7
Mercury St
5000 SDGO 1229 B7
4600 SDGO 1249 B2
Mercy Pl
2000 ESCN 1109 J4
Mercy Rd
9500 SDGO 1189 D7
Meredith Av
5600 SDGO 1270 D1
Meredith Rd
1400 SDCo 1028 B4
Merganser Ln
- SDCo 1127 B7
Mergho Impasse
2100 SDGO 1268 G5
Merida Ct
2100 SDGO 1247 H1
Merida Dr
400 SDCo 1027 E5
Meriden Ln
11800 SDGO 1190 A2
Meridian Av
3200 SDGO 1270 D6
Meridian Ct
1000 OCSD 1067 B3
Meridian Ln
1100 CHLV 1330 H1
Meridian Ridge Trl
2300 SDCo 1299 C2
(See Page 1299)
Meridian St
- ImCo 6560 C7
Meridian Wy
500 CRLB 1126 J7
Merill Dr
- SDCo 1252 A1
Merill Pl
- SDCo 1252 A1
Merion Cir
14200 SDCo 1090 F4
Merivale Av
3800 SDGO 1269 G3
Merlin Ct
900 SNMS 1109 C5
Merlin Dr
- CRLB 1127 A4
800 SDGO 1290 C3
Merlin Pl
2700 OCSD 1086 E6
Merlo Ct
- CRLB 1127 A7
Merlot Ct
1500 VSTA 1087 D6
Merlot Pl
500 CHLV 1311 E3
17200 POWY 1170 E2
Merlyn Ct
1700 SDCo 1272 B4
Merlyn Pl
2100 SDCo 1272 B4
Mermaid Ln
7400 CRLB 1127 A7
Merriam Rd
1700 SDCo 1128 B2
Merrick Ct
4600 OCSD 1107 E3
Merrigan Fire Rd
- SDCo 1216 B6
(See Page 1216)
- SDCo 1236 B1
Merrill Center Dr
- ELCN 6559 H2
Merrimac Av
3400 SDGO 1228 D7
Merrimac Ct
5000 SDGO 1228 D7

Merrington Pl
7900 SDGO 1209 A3
Merritage
- SDGO 1210 D2
Merritt Blvd
4300 LMSA 1271 B4
Merritt Ct
900 SDCo 1251 H7
Merritt Dr
900 ELCJ 1251 H7
1100 SDCo 1251 H7
1400 SDCo 1252 A7
1500 SDCo 1271 J1
Merritt Ln
1000 SDCo 1271 J1
Merritt Park Ln
14600 POWY 1190 E1
Merritt Ter
1300 SDCo 1251 J7
Merriweather Wy
- ELCJ 1252 A7
Merry Brook Tr
10000 SNTE 1231 D4
Merry Ln
- ESCN 1129 G5
Merryfield Row
- SDGO 1208 A6
Merrymount Ct
- OCSD 1067 F7
Merrywood Ln
300 SDCo 1130 B7
Mertensia St
5100 OCSD 1107 F4
Merton Av
2800 SDGO 1249 A6
Merton Ct
7100 SDGO 1248 J6
Merwel St
6600 SDGO 1228 D4
Merwin Dr
- CRLB 1107 A7
N Mesa
- SDGO 1228 B2
Mesa Av
- NATC 1290 A6
200 SDGO 1350 G3
9800 SNTE 1231 D5
Mesa Breeze Wy
500 OCSD 1086 B6
Mesa Brook St
1500 SDGO 1290 F6
Mesa College Cir
- SDGO 1248 J4
Mesa College Dr
7200 SDGO 1249 A5
Mesa Crest Pl
13100 SDGO 1188 J4
Mesa Crest Rd
12300 POWY 1190 B5
- SDCo 1070 B4
W Mesa Crest Rd
30900 SDCo 1070 B2
Mesa Dr
3500 OCSD 1086 F5
- OCSD 1087 B3
15800 SDCo 1051 C3
30300 SDCo 1069 H4
N Mesa Dr
- SDCo 1051 E3
S Mesa Dr
- SDCo 1051 E4
Mesa Estates Ct
15200 SDCo 1173 H6
Mesa Estates Rd
25000 SDCo 1173 H5
Mesa Fire Rd
- SDCo 1216 G4
(See Page 1216)
- SDCo 1217 A3
(See Page 1217)
Mesa Grande Dr
1700 ESCN 1129 F6
Mesa Grande Pl
1300 CHLV 1311 B7
Mesa Grove Rd
2800 SDCo 1048 G1
Mesa Heights Rd
8400 SNTE 1250 J1
Mesa Hills Ct
1900 SDGO 1290 F6
Mesa Lilac Rd
32400 SDCo 1049 A6
W Mesa Loop Fire Rd
- SDCo 1196 F6
(See Page 1196)
Mesa Madera Ct
11500 SDGO 1209 J4
Mesa Madera Dr
10000 SDGO 1209 J4
Mesa Norte Dr
6400 SDGO 1188 G6
Mesa Oak Ct
- SDCo 1172 D4
Mesa Oak Pl
2200 ESCN 1130 H2
Mesa Park Ln
1900 SDGO 1290 F6
Mesa Pl
800 CHLV 1310 H7
Mesa Ranch Dr
1500 SDCo 1109 D1

Mesa Rd
8500 SNTE 1230 J7
8400 SNTE 1250 J1
Mesa Ridge Ct
10000 SDGO 1208 H6
Mesa Ridge Rd
6600 SDGO 1208 H5
8400 SNTE 1250 J1
Mesa Rim Rd
9900 SDGO 1208 G6
Mesa Rock Rd
26400 SDCo 1089 D7
25700 SDCo 1109 E2
Mesa Springs Wy
- SDGO 1209 F5
Mesa Ter
5000 SDCo 1271 C1
Mesa Terrace Rd
8400 SNTE 1250 J1
Mesa Top Pl
- SDGO 1208 G3
Mesa Trail Pl
4800 CRLB 1107 B6
Mesa Verde Dr
11500 SDCo 1069 H2
12200 SDCo 1070 A2
1600 VSTA 1088 B5
Mesa Verde Rd
3200 SDCo 1310 E4
Mesa View Rd
8400 SNTE 1250 J1
Mesa View Wy
8300 SDCo 1290 H6
Mesa Vista Av
9200 LMSA 1271 B1
Mesa Vista Pl
12400 SDGO 1210 C2
Mesa Vista Wy
4200 OCSD 1086 J3
3800 SDCo 1310 E4
Mesa Woods Av
9000 SDGO 1209 D3
Mesa Wy
300 SDGO 1247 E2
Mesamint St
16900 SDCo 1169 G3
Mescalita Ct
- OCSD 1086 G1
Meseta Ln
12800 SDCo 1232 B5
Mesita Dr
6100 SDGO 1270 C2
Mesquite Av
- BRAW 6259 F6
(See Page 6259)
Mesquite Ct
2000 CRLB 1147 E2
Mesquite Ln
4600 SDCo 1099 G5
(See Page 1099)
Mesquite Rd
5100 SDGO 1270 A2
Mesquite St
- IMPE 6499 C2
Mesquite Tree Trl
15400 POWY 1170 G6
Messara St
35800 SDCo 1028 H5
Messiah Dr
300 ELCN 6499 H4
Messina Dr
4000 SDGO 1289 H4
Messina Wy
100 SDGO 1289 H4
Mesto Ct
16200 SDGO 1170 B4
Mesto Dr
16100 SDGO 1170 B4
Metate Ln
12600 POWY 1190 C5
Metcalf Gun
- ESCN 1129 F1
Metcalf Pl
1100 ESCN 1129 F2
Metcalf St
600 ESCN 1129 G2
Metro St
5300 SDGO 1268 F3
Metropolitan Dr
7500 SDGO 1269 A1
Metropolitan St
- CRLB 1127 F3
Mewall Dr
6700 SDGO 1251 A4
Mexicali Ct
100 SOLB 1167 H5
Mexican Canyon Rd
- SDCo 1272 H7
Meyers Av
2200 ESCN 1129 C2
Meyers Rd
- SDGO 1288 A5
Meyncke Wy
7900 SDGO 1209 A1
N Mezin Wy
6700 SDGO 1290 E4
S Mezin Wy
6700 SDGO 1290 E4
Miami Ct
4300 SDGO 1248 F2

Miami Dr
- LMSA 1270 G5
Miami Wy
4500 SDGO 1248 E2
Mica Rd
2300 CRLB 1127 F4
Michac Ln
- SDCo 1029 J3
Michael Ct
2100 SDCo 1253 G1
Michael Faraday Dr
2100 SDGO 1352 B3
Michael Glen
- ESCN 1109 C4
Michael Gn
- ESCN 1109 D4
Michael St
600 OCSD 1067 A5
5500 SDGO 1270 B6
Michaeljohn Dr
6600 SDCo 1247 F1
Michaelmas Ter
3200 SDGO 1268 E6
Michala Pl
10200 SNTE 1231 D2
Michele Dr
300 VSTA 1087 H3
Michelle Ct
- SDCo 1271 B5
Michelle Dr
7800 LMSA 1250 H6
Michelle Rene Wy
2400 SDCo 1253 E2
Michigan Av
600 OCSD 1106 B1
200 VSTA 1087 H6
Micro Pl
2200 ESCN 1129 C1
Mid City Ln
- SNMS 1128 H1
Mid Vintage Ln
- SDGO 1269 B1
Midbluff Av
13100 SDGO 1189 H4
Midbury Ct
9200 SDGO 1209 D2
Middle Fork Pl
800 CHLV 1311 H3
Middle Peak Fire Rd
- SDCo 1176 B5
(See Page 1176)
Middle Ridge Ter
11300 SDGO 1189 J4
Middlebrook Sq
12200 SDGO 1190 B1
Middlebush Dr
200 SDGO 1290 H4
Middlesex Dr
4300 SDGO 1269 H2
Middleton Dr
4500 CRLB 1107 B5
Middleton Rd
5100 SDGO 1248 B3
Middleton Wy
2200 SDGO 1248 A3
Midgrove Ct
13800 POWY 1190 F3
Midland Rd
15200 POWY 1170 F7
13200 POWY 1190 F4
Midland St
8400 LMSA 1250 J7
Midnight Blue St
1800 CHLV 1331 E2
Midnight Wy
1100 OCSD 1067 A3
Midori Ct
- SOLB 1167 E6
Midori Ln
- SOLB 1167 E6
Midranch Ln
- SDCo 1212 A7
Midvale Dr
1700 SDGO 1289 G1
Midway Av
- SDGO 1268 F7
Midway Ct
1300 SDCo 1233 J6
Midway Dr
1100 ELCJ 1251 D7
800 SDCo 1233 G5
3800 SDGO 1268 D5
N Midway Dr
1200 ESCN 1110 B6
S Midway Dr
600 ESCN 1130 C1
Midway Ln
800 SDCo 1233 G5
Midway Pl
1300 SDCo 1233 H6
Midway St
600 SDGO 1247 G4
Midwick St
5700 SDGO 1310 C1
Miguel Av
1700 CORD 1288 J7
Miguel Garden Wy
13300 POWY 1190 H4
Miguel Ln
14500 SDCo 1232 H4

45 INDEX
Miguel Trail Pl

San Diego County Street Index

INDEX 45
Montez Villa Rd
SAN DIEGO CO.

STREET
Block City Map# Grid

Miguel Trail Pl
- CHLV 1311 G2
Miguel View Rd
4200 SDCo 1271 G3
Miguel Vista Pl
8400 SDGO 1290 J4
Mijo Ln
13500 SDCo 1232 D5
Mika Ct
- BRAW 6320 C3
(See Page 6320)
Mike Ct
- SDGO 1350 E1
Mil Arboles
- SDCo 1188 G2
Mil Pitrero Rd
- SDGO 1190 A7
Mil Pitreto Rd
- SDGO 1190 A7
Mil Sorpresas Dr
1800 SDCo 997 J6
2000 SDCo 998 A7
Milagros St
3500 SDGO 1249 C4
Milagrosa Cir
400 CHLV 1310 H4
Milagrosa Ct
800 CHLV 1310 H4
Milagrosa Pl
800 CHLV 1310 H5
Milagrosa Wy
- CHLV 1310 H4
Milan Gn
- ESCN 1110 A4
Milan St
1200 OCSD 1087 C3
3700 SDGO 1288 B1
Milan Wy
1600 SNMS 1128 E6
Milane Ln
900 ESCN 1110 A7
Milano Ct
- BRAW 6320 C3
(See Page 6320)
Milano Dr
2400 CRLB 1106 J6
Milano Wy
- OCSD 1087 A3
Milbank Rd
1800 ENCT 1147 A2
Milbrae St
400 SDGO 1289 G5
Milburn Av
8800 SDCo 1290 J4
Milbury Rd
8600 SDGO 1189 C1
Milch Rd
9400 SDGO 1228 J2
Milden St
9500 LMSA 1251 C7
Mildred Av
39400 SDCo 1300 C6
(See Page 1300)
Mildred St
5500 SDGO 1268 F3
Mildred Wy
8200 LMGR 1270 H7
100 SDCo 1253 C1
Mile Hi Rd
17100 SDCo 1156 F7
Miles Ct
3700 SDCo 1271 C5
Miles Ranch Rd
200 SDCo 1047 G7
Miletus Wy
4700 OCSD 1107 E5
Milford Pl
3500 CRLB 1107 A3
1800 ELCJ 1251 C4
Milissi Wy
5000 OCSD 1107 E4
Milk Ranch Rd
- SDCo 1196 C1
(See Page 1196)
Milky Way Pt
7500 SDGO 1250 C4
Mill Creek Rd
33200 SDCo 1050 H3
5500 SDGO 1188 E5
Mill Peak Rd
5600 SDGO 1250 C7
Mill Valley Ct
4100 SDCo 1271 H4
Mill Valley Rd
- CHLV 1311 E7
Millagra Dr
- SDCo 1028 G5
Millan Ct
- CHLV 1330 D1
E Millan Ct
300 CHLV 1310 F7
Millan St
100 CHLV 1330 D1
E Millan St
100 CHLV 1310 E7
Millar Anita Ln
12200 SDCo 1292 A2
(See Page 1292)
Millar Av
100 ELCJ 1251 E6

Millar Ranch Rd
- SDCo 1271 J7
3300 SDCo 1292 A1
(See Page 1292)
Millards Ranch Ln
13500 POWY 1190 H3
Millards Ranch Wy
11300 POWY 1190 J2
Millards Rd
14700 POWY 1190 J2
Millay Ct
- CRLB 1107 A7
Millbrae Ct
- CHLV 1311 C7
Millbrook Pl
800 ESCN 1109 J7
Millbrook St
6800 SDGO 1249 J5
Millco Ln
14100 SDCo 1070 F6
Millco Wy
29500 SDCo 1070 F6
Millcroft Ct
13100 SDGO 1187 J5
Millegar Ln
2200 SDCo 1108 D4
Millenia Av
1700 CHLV 1331 F2
Miller Av
1900 ESCN 1129 J6
2500 SDCo 1129 J7
2500 SDCo 1149 J1
Miller Dr
800 CHLV 1311 F4
Miller Ln
29900 SDCo 1070 F5
Miller Rd
30100 SDCo 1070 F5
28700 SDCo 1090 E1
Miller St
4100 SDGO 1268 G5
Miller Valley Rd
2800 SDCo 1299 A2
(See Page 1299)
Millikin St
3400 SDGO 1228 C5
Millpond Rd
13500 SDGO 1189 G3
Mills Ct
- SNMS 1109 D7
Mills Pl
1500 ESCN 1110 B7
Mills St
1600 CHLV 1311 C5
900 ESCN 1110 A7
4900 LMSA 1270 H2
- SDGO 1287 J4
Millstone Ct
900 SDCo 1027 G5
Millwood Rd
7300 SDCo 1176 A2
(See Page 1176)
5100 SDGO 1228 F7
Milos Wy
5100 OCSD 1107 F5
Milpas Dr
2700 SDCo 1129 C3
Milpitas Dr
- CALX 6680 H2
Milton Ct
2200 SDGO 1268 F1
Milton Manor Dr
1700 SDCo 1252 B2
Milton Rd
- CRLB 1127 B1
3700 LMGR 1270 J5
Milton St
4200 SDGO 1248 E7
Milwaukee Ct
3800 LMSA 1270 G5
Mimika Pl
2800 SDGO 1248 J6
Mimlus Pl
3000 SDCo 1129 B5
Mimosa Av
100 SDCo 1108 C5
Mimosa Creek Ln
800 SDCo 1152 G7
Mimosa Ct
1300 ESCN 1110 A5
4800 OCSD 1067 A7
Mimosa Dr
- CRLB 1127 E5
Mimosa Pl
16800 SDCo 1168 C3
Mimulus
6000 SDCo 1168 D2
Mimulus Wy
1600 SDGO 1227 G7
Mina De Oro Rd
15100 POWY 1171 C7
14800 POWY 1191 B1
Mina St
3400 SDGO 1270 A6
Mindanao St
200 NATC 1289 J7
Mindanao Wy
2300 SDGO 1330 C7
Minden Dr
1300 SDGO 1269 A2
Mine Shaft Dr
11100 SDCo 1212 A7

Mineo Av
200 ELCN 6560 A1
Miner Creek Ln
1800 CHLV 1311 E7
Mineral Dr
6700 SDGO 1250 H4
Miners Ct
1400 SDCo 1136 D7
Miners Trl
23600 SDCo 1235 G2
Minerva Dr
7400 SDGO 1290 F3
Ming Ct
11400 SDCo 1251 G1
Minneola Cir
- SDCo 1069 H5
Minneola Ct
2600 ESCN 1110 D5
Minneola Dr
5100 SDCo 1047 F7
Minnesota Av
200 ELCJ 1251 F7
600 OCSD 1106 B1
E Minnesota Av
1000 OCSD 1106 B1
Minnesota St
400 SDCo 1027 G2
Minnewanna Truck Trl
- SDCo 1313 B6
(See Page 1313)
- SDCo 1333 C3
(See Page 1333)
Minoa Wy
3000 SDGO 1310 E2
Minor Dr
700 SDCo 1130 C4
Minorca Cove
14100 SDGO 1187 H5
Minorca Wy
2600 SDGO 1187 H5
Minot Av
200 CHLV 1310 C5
Mint Av
1500 ELCJ 1252 A4
Mint Pl
3500 OCSD 1086 F4
Minuteman St
3000 SDGO 1249 G5
Minya Ln
14300 POWY 1190 H5
Mio Metate Ln
9800 SDCo 1235 G1
Mira Costa College Rd
- ENCT 1167 G3
Mira Costa St
4000 OCSD 1107 B2
Mira Este Ct
9000 SDGO 1209 B7
Mira Flores Ct
3600 OCSD 1107 D3
Mira Flores Dr
5500 SDGO 1290 B5
Mira Flores Glen
1300 ESCN 1109 E5
Mira Grande Ln
12100 SDCo 1070 A3
Mira Lago Ter
10600 SDGO 1209 J3
Mira Lago Wy
17900 SDGO 1209 J3
Mira Lee Wy
- SDGO 1209 E2
Mira Loma Ct
17900 POWY 1150 E7
Mira Loma Ln
300 ESCN 1130 B4
Mira Mar Pl
900 OCSD 1085 J7
Mira Mesa Av
3100 OCSD 1107 B1
Mira Mesa Blvd
6000 SDGO 1208 F6
8300 SDGO 1209 C4
Mira Montana Dr
13900 SDGO 1187 H6
Mira Montana Pl
2600 SDGO 1187 H7
Mira Monte Av
600 SDGO 1247 F3
Mira Monte Dr
3500 OCSD 1107 C3
Mira Monte Plaza
- SDGO 1247 F3
Mira Monte Rd
4100 SDCo 997 G3
Mira Pacific Dr
3500 OCSD 1106 J2
3700 OCSD 1107 A1
Mira Sol
2200 SDCo 1108 D3
Mira Sorrento Pl
5300 SDGO 1208 D6
Mira Verde St
4000 OCSD 1107 B3
Mira Vista Ln
6400 SDGO 1250 E6
Mira Zanja
- SDGO 1188 H2
Mira Zanja Corte
- SDGO 1188 H2

Mirabel Ln
10200 SDGO 1249 G1
Miracielo Ct
1300 SDCo 1128 E3
Miracle Dr
4700 SDGO 1269 J3
Miracle Waters Ct
- SDCo 1291 D1
Miracosta Cir
- CHLV 1311 D6
Miracrest Pl
8400 SDGO 1228 J1
Mirador
2300 SDCo 1088 C1
Mirador St
- IMPE 6439 D7
3100 SNTE 1231 G6
Mirage Ct
4200 OCSD 1107 C2
1600 SDCo 1272 B4
Mirage Pl
2100 SDCo 1272 B4
Miralani Dr
8100 SDGO 1209 C6
Miramar Av
7500 SDGO 1227 F7
Miramar Ct
- SDGO 1229 E1
Miramar Dam Rd
9800 SDGO 1209 F4
Miramar Dr
800 SDCo 1107 H2
Miramar Gun Club Rd
- SDGO 1229 E4
Miramar Mall
8200 SDGO 1228 G1
Miramar Pl
8300 SDGO 1228 H2
Miramar Rd
9100 SDGO 1209 D6
5100 SDGO 1228 F2
7300 SDGO 1229 A1
Miramar St
3700 SDGO 1228 B2
Miramar Wy
- SDGO 1209 E7
- SDGO 1229 A1
S Miramar Wy
9500 SDGO 1229 E1
Miramonte Glen
1100 ESCN 1109 E5
Miramonte St
4500 LMSA 1271 A3
Miramontes Rd
2900 SDCo 1292 J2
(See Page 1292)
2900 SDCo 1293 A1
Mirando St
14500 POWY 1190 H4
Mirar Ct
5400 SDCo 1311 A2
Mirar De Valle Rd
- SDCo 1090 D4
Mirasol Ct
12200 SDGO 1150 B7
Mirasol Dr
18000 SDGO 1150 B7
Mirasol Pl
12200 SDGO 1150 B7
Mirasol Wy
12100 SDGO 1150 B7
Miratech Dr
7000 SDGO 1208 H6
Miriam Pl
4300 SDCo 1271 E4
Miro Cir
11200 SDGO 1209 G3
Mirror Lake Pl
- CHLV 1311 E5
Misaki Wy
- SDCo 1028 J6
Miss Elle Wy
1400 SDCo 1234 C6
Miss Ellie Ln
- SDCo 1232 G1
Mission Av
700 CHLV 1310 F7
1200 CHLV 1330 F2
5400 OCSD 1067 D7
3900 OCSD 1086 G3
4600 OCSD 1087 A2
6100 SDCo 1067 H6
1900 SDGO 1269 C4
E Mission Av
2400 ESCN 1110 C6
100 ESCN 1129 J1
W Mission Av
100 ESCN 1129 H2
Mission Bay Dr
4800 SDGO 1248 C4
E Mission Bay Dr
1200 SDGO 1268 D2
N Mission Bay Dr
2700 SDGO 1248 C5
W Mission Bay Dr
800 SDGO 1267 J2
2400 SDGO 1268 B4
Mission Bell Ln
4700 LMSA 1271 A2
Mission Blvd
5100 SDGO 1247 H4
3600 SDGO 1267 H1

Mission Bonita Dr
7800 SDGO 1250 C3
Mission Carmel Cove
2400 SDGO 1187 H5
Mission Center Ct
7900 SDGO 1269 B2
Mission Center Rd
7000 SDGO 1249 B7
5400 SDGO 1269 B2
Mission City Ct
9200 SDGO 1249 E7
Mission City Pkwy
5100 SDGO 1269 E1
Mission Cliff Dr
1800 SDGO 1269 C3
Mission Creek Dr
- SNTE 1231 C5
Mission Creek Rd
1000 SDCo 1047 H2
Mission Ct
600 CHLV 1310 F7
1000 CHLV 1330 F1
- SDCo 1299 H3
(See Page 1299)
Mission Dam Ter
7300 SNTE 1230 F7
Mission Gate Dr
- OCSD 1086 J3
Mission Gorge Pl
4500 SDGO 1249 H7
Mission Gorge Rd
6600 SDGO 1249 H6
8200 SDGO 1250 C3
7500 SNTE 1230 F7
10000 SNTE 1231 D6
Mission Greens Ct
9800 SNTE 1231 D7
Mission Greens Rd
8800 SNTE 1231 D6
Mission Grove Rd
- SNMS 1109 A6
Mission Heights Rd
7600 SDGO 1269 A1
Mission Hills Ct
300 SNMS 1109 A7
Mission Ln
9700 SDCo 1149 D4
Mission Manzana Pl
7900 SDGO 1250 C3
Mission Meadow Dr
- OCSD 1067 F7
Mission Meadows Dr
- OCSD 1067 F7
Mission Mesa Wy
3400 SDGO 1250 C4
Mission Montana Dr
3600 SDGO 1250 B3
Mission Montana Pl
7800 SDGO 1250 C3
Mission Oaks Rd
100 SDCo 1027 F6
Mission Park Ct
11000 SNTE 1231 F5
Mission Park Pl
9400 SNTE 1231 F5
Mission Preserve Pl
15500 SDGO 1210 H2
Mission Rd
1300 ESCN 1129 E2
- SDCo 998 B7
800 SDCo 1027 G2
3000 SDCo 1028 C1
5400 SDCo 1048 A7
- SDCo 1067 J3
- SDGO 1149 F2
- SDGO 1150 A4
E Mission Rd
- SDCo 998 B7
500 SNMS 1109 A7
1200 SNMS 1129 C1
S Mission Rd
400 SDCo 1027 F3
3300 SDCo 1047 H2
W Mission Rd
1200 ESCN 1129 F2
100 SDCo 1027 F2
1300 SNMS 1108 E6
Mission Ridge Ln
300 SDCo 1028 F1
Mission San Carlos Dr
8600 SNTE 1230 F7
Mission Trails Dr
7300 SNTE 1230 F7
Mission Valley Ct
1800 SDGO 1269 A1
Mission Valley Fwy
- SDGO 1268 F4
- SDGO 1269 E1
- SDGO 1270 A1
Mission Valley Rd
7500 SDGO 1269 A1
Mission Vega Ct
8800 SNTE 1231 D7
Mission Vega Rd
9900 SNTE 1231 D6
Mission Viejo Ct
9800 SNTE 1231 D6
Mission View
- SDCo 1048 B7
Mission Village Dr
2800 SDGO 1249 E5

Mission Vista Dr
7800 SDGO 1250 C3
Mission Wy
- SNMS 1129 C1
Mississippi St
4300 SDGO 1269 C4
Missouri Av
600 OCSD 1106 B1
Missouri St
600 SDGO 1247 H6
2100 SDGO 1248 B5
Missy Ct
6800 SDGO 1270 E4
Mister B Pl
- SDCo 1070 F6
Mistletoe Ln
800 CRLB 1127 A5
Mistletoe St
400 VSTA 1087 E6
Mistral Pl
4400 SDGO 1188 B6
Misty Blue Ct
- SDGO 1210 B1
Misty Cir
1900 ENCT 1147 H6
Misty Creek Ct
- CHLV 1331 B1
Misty Creek St
- CHLV 1331 A1
Misty Ln
4200 OCSD 1107 C2
Misty Meadow Ln
9600 SDCo 1089 C2
Misty Meadows Ct
800 CHLV 1311 B5
Misty Oak Rd
13700 SDCo 1070 E7
Misty Ridge
- SDGO 1208 B2
Misty Ridge Pl
- CHLV 1331 D1
Misty Sea Wy
- SNMS 1128 D5
Mita Ct
- BRAW 6320 B3
(See Page 6320)
Mitchell St
1200 OCSD 1106 B2
Mitra Ct
500 SDCo 1291 D3
Mitscher Ln
2000 SDGO 1288 C1
Mitscher St
300 CHLV 1310 B7
Mitscher Wy
- SDGO 1209 D7
- SDGO 1229 D1
Mitten Ln
2500 SDCo 1152 D7
Mitzie Ln
9100 SDCo 1232 E5
Mizpah Ln
9500 SDCo 1236 B2
Mizpah Spur
9700 SDCo 1236 B1
Moa Dr
500 VSTA 1087 F4
Moana Dr
1200 SDGO 1287 J1
Moana Kia Ln
8700 SNTE 1230 J4
Mobley St
3100 SDGO 1249 D5
Moccasin Av
3500 SDGO 1248 D1
W Moccasin Av
3200 SDGO 1248 D1
Moccasin Pl
4700 SDGO 1248 D1
Mocha Ct
5100 OCSD 1107 F4
Mocking Bird Dr
7700 SDGO 1249 A6
Mockingbird Cir
700 ESCN 1130 C7
Mockingbird Ct
1400 CHLV 1331 C3
Mockingbird Ln
100 OCSD 1086 H2
9400 SDCo 1271 B2
1000 SNMS 1128 E2
Moda Ln
1000 NATC 1289 J6
Mode Dr
3100 SDCo 1109 H2
Model A Ford Ln
4300 SDCo 1273 A2
Modena Pl
3700 SDGO 1188 A3
Modern Oasis Dr
- SDGO 1269 B1
Modesto St
2300 SDGO 1289 H1
Modoc St
3800 SDGO 1248 E4
Moffett Rd
- CORD 1288 C6
- SDGO 1288 C4
Mohawk St
7400 LMSA 1270 G2
6600 SDGO 1270 D2

Mohegan Ln
4700 SDCo 1048 G1
Mohican Av
3200 SDGO 1248 E5
Mohler St
6100 SDGO 1249 J7
Moiola Av
2400 ELCN 6499 D7
Moisan Wy
8900 LMSA 1271 A2
Mola Vista Wy
800 SOLB 1167 G7
Molchan Rd
2300 SDCo 1297 F6
(See Page 1297)
Mole Rd
- NATC 1309 F2
Molina Ln
- SDGO 1188 H4
Molino Rd
10200 SNTE 1231 D3
Mollendo Blvd
5200 SDGO 1249 H2
Mollie Ln
- SNTE 1231 C2
Mollie St
1200 SDGO 1268 F3
N Mollison Av
900 ELCJ 1251 G3
S Mollison Av
300 ELCJ 1251 G6
Molly Anne Ct
15200 SDCo 1091 B2
Molly Cir
1500 OCSD 1106 E1
Molly Woods Av
9000 LMSA 1271 B1
Molokai Wy
2200 SDGO 1330 C7
Moluccan St
- OCSD 1067 B2
Momar Ln
500 ESCN 1130 D1
Mona Lisa St
12400 SDGO 1188 C7
Mona Ln
- SDGO 1188 J3
Mona Pl
1100 ELCJ 1251 E7
Monaco Ct
2000 SDCo 1272 C3
Monaco Dr
1800 CHLV 1331 E1
Monaco St
4400 SDGO 1287 H2
Monaghan Ct
2200 SDCo 1291 B1
Monahan Rd
4500 SDCo 1271 E3
Monair Dr
3400 SDGO 1248 D4
Monarch Ridge Cir
1900 SDCo 1272 C2
Monarch Ridge Ln
1900 SDCo 1272 D3
Monarch St
2700 SDGO 1249 E5
Monarch Wy
200 OCSD 1087 A1
Monarche Dr
- SDCo 1331 C1
Mondavi Cir
1300 VSTA 1107 J3
Monel Av
5300 SDGO 1229 D7
5300 SDGO 1249 D1
Monet Ln
5200 SDCo 1290 H7
Monette Dr
2400 SDGO 1249 E6
Mongue Ct
900 CALX 6620 J7
Monica Cir
600 OCSD 1067 A5
Monique Ct
1200 VSTA 1088 A3
Monique Ln
- SDCo 1271 B5
Monique Wy
3000 SDCo 1109 G3
Monitor Rd
1500 SDGO 1268 F2
Monmouth Dr
1500 SDGO 1247 J4
Mono Lake Dr
8300 SDGO 1250 J5
Monona Dr
9300 LMSA 1251 B7
Monongahela St
4600 SDGO 1248 B1
Monroe Av
- CALX 6620 J6
3000 SDGO 1269 D4
5000 SDGO 1270 A4
Monroe St
2500 CRLB 1106 F3
100 OCSD 1067 A7
Monserate Av
700 CHLV 1310 E7
1400 CHLV 1330 F3

Monserate Hill Ct
3600 SDCo 1048 E3
Monserate Hill Rd
3500 SDCo 1048 E3
Monserate Pl
3600 SDCo 1048 E4
Monserate Ter
3900 SDCo 1048 A4
Monserate Wy
1700 SDCo 1047 J4
Monserrat Wy
1800 VSTA 1107 H5
Monserrate St
- SDCo 1086 A4
Montage Glen
1400 ESCN 1129 G5
Montage Rd
600 OCSD 1087 C1
Montalvo St
4200 SDGO 1268 B5
Montana Luna Ct
400 SDCo 1130 B5
Montana Rd
- CHLV 1311 C6
Montana Serena
15000 SDCo 1233 B6
Montana Serena Ct
1400 SDCo 1233 B6
Montana St
7800 LMGR 1270 H6
Montanes Ln
7000 CRLB 1127 G7
Montanya Rd
- SDCo 1070 A4
Montara Av
7900 SDGO 1209 B2
Montara Ct
11100 SDGO 1209 B2
Montaubon Cir
- SDGO 1209 J2
Montaubon Wy
- SDGO 1209 J2
Montauk St
12600 POWY 1190 C6
Montbury Pl
15700 SDGO 1210 J1
Montcalm St
400 CHLV 1330 G1
Montclair St
400 CHLV 1330 G1
2600 SDGO 1269 F7
2400 SDGO 1289 G1
Montcliff Rd
2300 SDGO 1290 G7
Monte Alto Terr
15800 SDGO 1169 C3
Monte Azul Ln
7000 SDCo 1138 A6
(See Page 1138)
Monte De Josue
- SDCo 1151 E6
Monte Dore Ln
1300 VSTA 1088 B4
Monte Dr
- LMSA 1270 G4
Monte Fuego
- SDCo 1188 G2
Monte Mar Rd
1600 VSTA 1088 B4
Monte Mira Dr
900 ENCT 1147 C1
Monte Mira Ln
- ENCT 1147 C1
Monte Rd
5900 SDCo 1048 C7
Monte Real
3600 ESCN 1150 A4
Monte Rico Dr
1400 ELCJ 1252 A2
Monte Serreno Av
- SDCo 1331 B1
Monte Verde Dr
6900 SDGO 1250 E3
Monte View Ct
11700 SDCo 1272 A4
Monte Vista
- OCSD 1086 J2
- SNMS 1129 C1
Monte Vista Av
- CHLV 1310 A5
7300 SDGO 1247 E1
Monte Vista Dr
2200 SDCo 1108 D1
1000 VSTA 1108 A1
Monte Vista Rd
12600 POWY 1170 C6
1700 SDCo 1271 J3
Montebello St
- CHLV 1310 C5
Montecito Av
- IMPE 6499 H2
Montecito Dr
6300 CRLB 1127 G3
2700 SDCo 1047 J1
Montecito Glen
300 ESCN 1150 B1
13400 SDGO 1188 E4
Montecito Ln
1300 SDCo 1047 H1
Montecito Rd
- CHLV 1311 G2

Montecito Rd
2400 SDCo 1151 J6
2400 SDCo 1152 B6
Montecito Vista
1300 SDCo 1235 A6
Montecito Wy
1100 SDCo 1152 B5
W Montecito Wy
1800 SDGO 1268 H5
100 SDGO 1269 A5
Montefrio Ct
3900 SDGO 1188 B7
Montego Av
700 ESCN 1109 F5
Montego Bay Ct
300 OCSD 1066 H6
Montego Cove
2700 SDGO 1187 H6
Montego Ct
- CORD 1329 D1
1300 VSTA 1107 H4
Montego Dr
13400 POWY 1190 H4
10900 SDGO 1249 H1
Montego Pl
5300 SDGO 1249 H1
Montelena Ct
1400 VSTA 1088 B4
Monteleone Av
1300 CHLV 1311 F1
Montell Truck Trl
- SDCo 1274 B2
Montellano Ter
12500 SDGO 1188 A6
Montello Wy
4200 SDGO 1188 A6
Montemar Av
2200 ESCN 1110 C6
Montemar Dr
9500 SDCo 1271 C7
Montenegro Wy
- ELCN 6500 B7
Montera Ct
500 CHLV 1310 G5
Montera St
- CHLV 1331 B1
Monterey Av
700 CHLV 1310 E7
1200 CHLV 1330 F2
1900 CORD 1288 J7
Monterey Cir
1000 SNMS 1109 B5
Monterey Crest Dr
- SDCo 1273 B6
Monterey Ct
1000 CHLV 1330 F1
700 SDGO 1267 H1
Monterey Cypress Wy
12700 SDGO 1188 B6
Monterey Dr
- ESCN 1149 G1
400 OCSD 1085 J6
1100 SDCo 1251 J7
Monterey Glen
2500 ESCN 1149 G1
Monterey Ln
700 VSTA 1087 J3
Monterey Park Dr
1500 SDGO 1350 D2
Monterey Pine Dr
1500 SDGO 1350 C2
Monterey Pl
- SDCo 1147 F5
1300 SDCo 1233 H5
Monterey Rd
1100 SDCo 1251 H7
Monterey Ridge Ct
17100 SDCo 1169 F2
Monterey Ridge Dr
10400 SDCo 1169 F2
Monterey Ridge Wy
17100 SDCo 1169 F2
Monterey St
- BRAW 6319 J4
(See Page 6319)
Monterey Vista Pl
1100 ENCT 1167 F1
Monterey Vista Wy
1100 ENCT 1167 F1
Montero Ct
12500 SDGO 1170 C2
Montero Pl
1900 ESCN 1129 E7
12500 SDGO 1170 C2
Montero Rd
17400 SDGO 1170 C2
Montero Wy
12500 SDGO 1170 C2
Monterra Trl
6700 SDGO 1188 H3
Monterrey Park Ln
- IMPE 6439 D7
Montesano Rd
3100 SDCo 1149 J2
Montessa St
5100 SDGO 1230 A7
Montevideo Pl
5600 SDCo 1067 J2
Montez Villa Rd
6300 SDGO 1188 G3

SAN DIEGO CO.

STREET Block City Map# Grid

Montezuma
- SDGO 1268 F6
Montezuma Ct
1600 SDCo 1058 F6
(See Page 1058)
Montezuma Pl
5100 SDGO 1270 C2
Montezuma Rd
100 SDCo 1058 F5
(See Page 1058)
4500 SDGO 1269 J2
6400 SDGO 1270 D2
Montezuma Valley Rd
200 SDCo 1078 F3
(See Page 1078)
600 SDCo 1098 C1
(See Page 1098)
Montfort Ct
14000 SDGO 1190 A2
Montgomery Av
1900 ENCT 1167 D3
Montgomery Dr
1800 SDCo 1108 C2
Montgomery St
400 CHLV 1330 C5
Montia Ct
6700 CRLB 1126 J5
Montia Pl
2200 ESCN 1129 H7
Monticello Dr
800 SDCo 1129 J7
Monticello St
6200 SNTE 1231 G7
Monticook Ct
11200 SDGO 1149 H7
Montiel Rd
1100 SDCo 1129 F1
2300 SNMS 1129 E2
Montien
- SDGO 1168 H5
Montien Pass
- SDGO 1168 J5
Montijo Rd
- SDCo 996 D5
Montilla St
1700 SNTE 1231 F6
Montmead Rd
- SDCo 1089 C6
Montongo Cir
7900 SDGO 1209 A2
Montongo St
10700 SDGO 1209 B4
Montrachet St
30200 SDCo 1067 J5
Montros Pl
1200 ESCN 1110 A7
Montrose Ct
500 ELCJ 1251 F4
Montrose Wy
4600 OCSD 1087 A1
8900 SDGO 1228 D3
Montura Av
10100 SNTE 1231 E3
Montura Ct
10600 SNTE 1231 E3
Montura Dr
17000 SDGO 1170 C2
Montura Rd
1100 SDCo 1128 B2
Montview Dr
1000 ESCN 1129 H5
500 ESCN 1130 A6
Monument 20 Truck Trl
- SDCo 1353 B2
(See Page 1353)
Monument Hill Rd
1300 SDCo 1272 A1
Monument Pl
3900 ESCN 1150 B3
Monument Rd
700 IMPB 1349 F5
1000 SDGO 1349 J5
2900 SDGO 1350 D5
Monument Trail Dr
1300 CHLV 1311 H6
Moody Dr
900 ESCN 1130 E1
Moon Field Dr
3400 CRLB 1107 B5
Moon Rd
1400 VSTA 1087 D6
Moon Ridge Rd
- SDCo 1029 B2
Moon Rock Rd
1600 SDCo 997 G7
Moon Shadow Dr
- OCSD 1086 D3
Moon Valley Rd
37900 SDCo 1319 H6
(See Page 1319)
Moon View Wy
- SDCo 1089 E3
Moonbeam Ln
1600 CHLV 1311 G7
Mooncrest Ct
3100 SNMS 1108 B6
Mooncrest Rd
- SDCo 1154 D3
Mooney St
3100 SDGO 1248 E6
Moonflower Meadows Tr
13400 SDGO 1188 E4

Moonglow Ct
23700 SDCo 1173 D5
1900 VSTA 1107 J4
Moonglow Dr
15300 SDCo 1173 D5
Moonlight Dr
500 SNMS 1109 A6
Moonlight Glen
2300 ESCN 1109 B4
Moonlight Ln
400 ENCT 1147 B7
4200 OCSD 1107 C2
5300 SDGO 1247 H3
Moonlight Pl
31000 SDCo 1070 E2
Moonlight Trail Ln
- CHLV 1311 H5
Moonlight Wy
600 SDCo 1152 E6
Moonlit Trl
2500 SDCo 1300 D4
(See Page 1300)
Moonlite Hill Rd
1700 SDCo 1027 J7
Moonridge Dr
2800 SDGO 1227 J6
Moonridge Pl
7700 SDGO 1227 J6
Moonrise Trl
2000 SDCo 1300 E7
(See Page 1300)
Moonshadow Ridge
1700 SDCo 1027 J6
Moonshell Ct
10600 SDGO 1208 B4
Moonsong Ct
18200 SDGO 1149 H7
Moonstone Bay Dr
300 OCSD 1066 J6
Moonstone Dr
2400 SDGO 1249 E6
Moonstone Pl
- CHLV 1331 A1
13000 SDGO 1189 B5
Moonview Dr
300 CHLV 1310 F5
Moonwind Cir
8800 SDCo 1089 B1
Moore Av
- SDGO 1209 E7
Moore St
3000 SDGO 1268 E5
Moorefield Dr
5500 SDCo 1253 C3
Moorgate Rd
100 ENCT 1146 J2
Moorhen Pl
- CRLB 1127 E5
Moorland Dr
1400 SDGO 1248 A7
Moorland Hts Wy
- SDGO 1208 E4
Moorpark Ct
2900 SDCo 1271 F7
Moorpark St
10300 SDCo 1271 F7
Mora Cir
13500 POWY 1190 H3
Morada St
7700 CRLB 1147 H2
Morado Trl
13500 SDGO 1188 H3
Moraea St
1200 SDGO 1290 D5
Moraga Av
4100 SDGO 1248 D4
Moraga Ct
3300 SDGO 1248 D3
Moraga Pl
3300 SDGO 1248 D3
Moraga Wy
400 OCSD 1086 G2
Morales Ln
- SDCo 1071 E3
Moran Wy
12700 SDGO 1189 D6
Moranda Ct
11200 SDGO 1189 J4
Moratalla Ter
4000 SDGO 1188 A6
Morava Pl
- SDGO 1248 F7
Morcado Cir
- SDCo 1271 C3
Mordigan Ln
9900 SDCo 1029 C3
Morehouse Dr
5400 SDGO 1208 E6
Morehouse Pl
300 CHLV 1330 C4
Morelia Ct
- SOLB 1167 G7
Morella Wy
3200 OCSD 1106 J1
Morena Blvd
2900 SDGO 1248 D5
4900 SDGO 1268 F3
N Morena Blvd
1900 SDGO 1268 E1
W Morena Blvd
1400 SDGO 1268 E2

Morena Pl
5100 SDGO 1268 F3
Morena Reservoir Rd
- SDCo 1297 B5
(See Page 1297)
Morena View Dr
29800 SDCo 1297 F5
(See Page 1297)
Morenci St
1400 SDGO 1268 E2
Morene St
12900 POWY 1190 D5
Moreno Av
- SDCo 1211 J4
- SDCo 1212 A3
11000 SDCo 1232 B1
Moreno St
1600 OCSD 1106 D2
N Moreno St
1400 OCSD 1106 C2
S Moreno St
1900 OCSD 1106 D3
Moreno Wy
1300 OCSD 1106 C2
Morera Wy
1600 CHLV 1331 D2
Moreton Glen
13400 SDGO 1188 E4
Morgan Creek Wy
- OCSD 1086 J2
Morgan Ct
1300 SDCo 1079 C6
(See Page 1079)
Morgan Hill Dr
- CHLV 1311 C7
- SDCo 1331 B1
Morgan Pl
300 SDCo 1108 C4
Morgan Rd
2200 CRLB 1107 C7
2200 CRLB 1127 C1
Morgan St
- SDCo 1023 F2
Morgan Wy
600 ELCJ 1251 E7
Morgandale Ct
2900 SDCo 1271 B7
Morgans Av
1700 SNMS 1128 D6
Morlan St
3600 SDGO 1228 D7
Morley Field Dr
1700 SDGO 1269 C6
Morley Field Dr E
2100 SDGO 1269 C6
Morley St
2200 SDGO 1268 J1
Morley Wy
6900 SDGO 1248 J7
Morning Air Rd
14200 POWY 1170 G4
Morning Breeze Ln
1600 NATC 1310 B1
Morning Breeze Wy
9300 SDGO 1209 E2
Morning Canyon Rd
4700 OCSD 1107 E2
Morning Creek Ct
2900 CHLV 1311 J3
Morning Creek Dr N
10900 SDGO 1189 H4
Morning Creek Dr S
11100 SDGO 1189 J5
Morning Creek Rd
2800 CHLV 1311 J2
Morning Dew Ct
- CHLV 1331 F3
Morning Dove Rd
11000 SDCo 1211 F7
Morning Dove Wy
- CRLB 1127 C6
4500 OCSD 1086 J1
Morning Glory Dr
- SDCo 1232 C4
Morning Glory Ln
2700 CRLB 1106 F4
1300 VSTA 1108 A1
Morning Glory Pl
1300 VSTA 1108 A1
Morning Glory Ter
1300 VSTA 1108 A1
Morning Glory Tr
- IMPE 6499 D2
Morning Glory Wy
6300 SDGO 1188 G4
Morning Mist Ct
8300 SDGO 1250 J2
800 VSTA 1087 J2
Morning Side Wy
- SNTE 1231 E7
Morning Star Cres
30700 SDCo 1070 H2
Morning Star Ct
4100 SDCo 1271 G4
Morning Star Dr
1600 CHLV 1311 H7
10900 SDCo 1271 G4
Morning Star Ln
1300 SDCo 1027 F4
Morning Sun Ct
2200 ENCT 1147 J5

Morning Sun Dr
800 ENCT 1147 J5
Morning Terrace Glen
2600 ESCN 1130 J4
Morning View Ct
4300 SDCo 1271 D3
Morning View Dr
1200 ESCN 1109 G7
1000 ESCN 1129 G1
- OCSD 1086 D2
1800 VSTA 1087 J3
Morning Walk Ct
2700 ESCN 1110 E5
Morning Wy
3100 SDGO 1228 A3
Morningmist Glen
1900 ESCN 1109 B3
Morningside Ct
- IMPE 6439 F4
12200 POWY 1170 B7
Morningside Dr
- IMPE 6439 G4
3100 OCSD 1107 C1
14800 POWY 1170 B7
14800 POWY 1190 B1
500 VSTA 1087 J6
Morningside St
2900 SDGO 1310 D2
Morningside Ter
2800 SDCo 1149 G2
200 VSTA 1087 J6
Moro Rd
11800 SDCo 1029 H3
Morocco Dr
7900 LMSA 1270 H1
Morongo Dr
- IMPE 6439 F3
Morose St
2200 LMGR 1290 H1
Morrell St
4200 SDGO 1248 B6
Morrella St
7800 SNTE 1231 G6
Morris St
- SDGO 1289 F7
Morrison Pl
14100 SDCo 1192 B2
(See Page 1192)
Morrison St
600 SDGO 1289 H3
Morro Bay
4500 OCSD 1066 H6
Morro Heights Rd
6500 OCSD 1067 D2
Morro Hills Pl
5100 SDCo 1047 G6
Morro Hills Rd
600 SDCo 1047 E6
Morro Point Dr
600 CHLV 1330 J4
Morro Rd
1200 SDCo 1027 G4
Morro Wy
5500 LMSA 1250 H7
Morrow Wy
1400 SDGO 1269 B5
Morsa Wy
3200 CRLB 1127 J5
Morse Ct
6900 SDGO 1268 J1
Morse St
300 OCSD 1106 C3
E Morse St
1500 OCSD 1106 D2
Morton Glen
1900 ESCN 1129 H5
Morton Wy
2900 SDGO 1310 F2
Mosaic Cir
700 OCSD 1087 B1
Mosaic Glen
1400 ESCN 1129 G5
Mosaic St
1800 CHLV 1331 F2
Moselle St
10300 SDGO 1210 A3
Moselle Wy
12000 SDGO 1210 A3
Moss Landing Av
- CHLV 1311 E6
Moss Ln
- SDGO 1247 F3
Moss St
600 CHLV 1330 B3
E Moss St
300 CHLV 1330 F1
Moss Tree Wy
- SDCo 1089 D4
Mossberg Ct
1200 VSTA 1087 E5
Mosswood Cove
- SDGO 1208 E2
Mossy Rock Dr
1700 SDCo 1068 B5
Mother Grundy Dr
1900 SDCo 1314 G2
(See Page 1314)
Mother Grundy Truck Trl
1600 SDCo 1314 C2
(See Page 1314)

Mother Lode Wy
1300 CHLV 1311 E7
Motif St
4800 OCSD 1087 B2
Mott St
5700 SDGO 1228 B6
Mottino Dr
2500 OCSD 1087 C6
Moultrie Av
3500 SDGO 1248 D5
Mound Av
5400 SDGO 1250 B5
Moundglen Ln
2600 SDCo 1271 D7
Moundtop Ln
2600 SDCo 1271 D7
Moundview Pl
2600 SDCo 1271 D7
Moundview St
9900 SDCo 1271 D7
Mount Alifan Pl
- SDGO 1248 H3
Mount Almagosa Pl
3700 SDGO 1248 F4
Mount Burnham Ct
3400 SDGO 1248 G5
Mount Burnham Pl
3500 SDGO 1248 G5
Mount Hills Pl
300 ELCJ 1251 C5
Mount Israel Rd
- SDCo 1149 C4
Mount Israel Tktr
- SDCo 1148 J2
Mount MacClure St
- CHLV 1331 B2
Mount Miguel Rd
- CHLV 1311 F3
Mount Owen Ct
- CHLV 1330 J1
Mount Terrminus Dr
4000 SDGO 1248 F4
Mount Wy
1700 VSTA 1107 G4
Mountain Circle Dr
35800 SDCo 1176 C3
(See Page 1176)
Mountain Glen Ter
10300 SDGO 1209 J4
Mountain Hills Pl
1700 ESCN 1129 G6
Mountain Hts Dr
- SDCo 1149 H1
Mountain Lilac Rd
- SDCo 1089 E2
Mountain Lion Rd
12100 SDCo 1212 C4
Mountain Ln
2200 SDCo 1172 E2
Mountain Meadow Dr
1400 OCSD 1087 D3
Mountain Meadow Rd
28200 SDCo 1089 E3
Mountain Park Pl
1200 ESCN 1130 E1
Mountain Pass Cir
- VSTA 1107 H7
Mountain Pass Rd
- SDGO 1190 B7
Mountain Quail Ct
11400 SDCo 1212 C5
Mountain Ranches Rd
12000 SDCo 1212 C5
Mountain Rd
14200 POWY 1190 G1
11600 SDCo 1212 C5
Mountain Ridge Rd
2200 CHLV 1311 E2
- SDCo 1069 C3
Mountain Shadow Dr
9200 SDCo 1232 D5
Mountain Shadow Ln
- SDCo 1171 F3
Mountain Top Ct
6700 SDGO 1250 D4
Mountain Top Dr
1000 SDCo 1233 A7
Mountain Valley Ln
1900 ESCN 1129 F6
Mountain Valley Pl
15600 SDCo 1212 J6
Mountain View Av
1600 OCSD 1106 C1
Mountain View Ct
14100 POWY 1190 G2
- SDCo 1310 E4
600 VSTA 1087 F4
Mountain View Dr
2500 CRLB 1106 D5
2000 ESCN 1130 D2
2700 SDCo 1310 G3
E Mountain View Dr
100 CHLV 1310 B5
4600 SDGO 1269 G3
N Mountain View Dr
200 CHLV 1310 B5
3100 SDGO 1269 E2
S Mountain View Dr
200 CHLV 1310 B5
W Mountain View Dr
4800 SDGO 1269 E3

Mountain View Ln
1300 CHLV 1330 G3
10300 SDCo 1231 G3
Mountain View Pl
- SDCo 1253 A1
Mountain View Rd
32200 SDCo 1048 H6
1500 SDCo 1233 B7
500 SDCo 1252 J2
500 SDCo 1253 A1
Mountain View Wy
3800 SDCo 1310 E3
Mountain Vista Dr
1400 ENCT 1147 G6
Mountain Vista Wy
2000 OCSD 1106 F1
Mountain Wy
31500 SDCo 1068 G1
Mountainbrook Rd
4900 SDCo 1135 D4
Mountainside Dr
13400 POWY 1190 C4
Mountainview Av
- ELCN 6559 G4
Mower Pl
- SDGO 1188 G7
Moya Pl
500 CHLV 1310 H5
Moyla Ct
500 OCSD 1086 D3
Moyla Dr
16200 SDCo 1051 B5
Mozart Av
100 ENCT 1167 D3
Mozelle Ln
10000 SDCo 1271 D4
Mt Aachen Av
3400 SDGO 1248 H5
Mt Abbey Av
3700 SDGO 1248 H4
Mt Abernathy Av
4200 SDGO 1248 H2
Mt Abraham Av
3700 SDGO 1248 H3
Mt Acadia Blvd
3600 SDGO 1248 G3
Mt Acara Dr
5700 SDGO 1248 H4
Mt Ackerly Dr
5600 SDGO 1248 H4
Mt Ackerman Dr
6200 SDGO 1248 H3
Mt Aclare Av
3500 SDGO 1248 H4
Mt Acmar Ct
3100 SDGO 1248 H5
Mt Acomita Av
3500 SDGO 1248 H4
Mt Aconia Dr
5500 SDGO 1248 G5
Mt Aconia Wy
5500 SDGO 1248 H5
Mt Acre Wy
6300 SDGO 1248 H3
Mt Ada Rd
6400 SDGO 1248 H3
Mt Adelbert Dr
6200 SDGO 1248 H3
Mt Aguilar Dr
6300 SDGO 1248 H3
Mt Ainsworth Av
3900 SDGO 1248 H3
Mt Ainsworth Ct
6300 SDGO 1248 H3
Mt Ainsworth Wy
6300 SDGO 1248 H3
Mt Aladin Av
3800 SDGO 1248 H4
Mt Albertine Av
3800 SDGO 1248 J3
Mt Albertine Ct
6500 SDGO 1248 J3
Mt Albertine Wy
3900 SDGO 1248 J3
Mt Alifan Ct
4000 SDGO 1248 F4
Mt Alifan Dr
4400 SDGO 1248 F4
Mt Alifan Wy
4000 SDGO 1248 F4
Mt Almagosa Dr
4900 SDGO 1248 G4
Mt Alvarez Av
3500 SDGO 1248 H4
Mt Antero Dr
4900 SDGO 1248 G4
Mt Ararat Dr
5200 SDGO 1248 G4
Mt Ararat Wy
7600 SDCo 1068 G1
Mt Ariane Ct
5200 SDGO 1248 G4
Mt Ariane Dr
3600 SDGO 1248 G4
Mt Ariane Ter
5200 SDGO 1248 F5
Mt Armet Dr
4600 SDGO 1248 F3
Mt Armour Ct
3400 SDGO 1248 G5

Mt Armour Dr
4800 SDGO 1248 F5
Mt Armour Pl
3400 SDGO 1248 G5
Mt Ashmun Ct
3600 SDGO 1248 G4
Mt Ashmun Dr
4900 SDGO 1248 G4
Mt Ashmun Pl
3700 SDGO 1248 F4
Mt Augustus Av
3700 SDGO 1248 G4
Mt Bagot Av
4100 SDGO 1248 F3
Mt Barnard Av
4000 SDGO 1248 G4
Mt Bigelow Ct
4100 SDGO 1248 F3
Mt Bigelow Dr
4700 SDGO 1248 F3
Mt Bigelow Wy
4100 SDGO 1248 F3
Mt Blackburn Av
3800 SDGO 1248 G4
Mt Blanca Dr
5000 SDGO 1248 G3
Mt Bolanas Ct
4000 SDGO 1248 G3
Mt Bross Av
4100 SDGO 1248 G3
Mt Brundage Av
3800 SDGO 1248 G4
Mt Bullion Dr
1900 CHLV 1311 E7
Mt Burnham Dr
5300 SDGO 1248 G5
Mt Carmel Dr
100 SDGO 1350 F3
Mt Carol Dr
3400 SDGO 1248 H4
Mt Casas Ct
4200 SDGO 1248 F3
Mt Casas Dr
4700 SDGO 1248 F3
Mt Castle Av
4400 SDGO 1248 G2
Mt Cervin Dr
4700 SDGO 1248 G1
Mt Cresti Dr
4700 SDGO 1248 F1
Mt Culebra Av
4200 SDGO 1248 G3
Mt Dana Dr
1000 CHLV 1331 B2
Mt Davis Av
4300 SDGO 1248 G3
Mt Durban Dr
4900 SDGO 1248 G3
Mt Elbrus Ct
4300 SDGO 1248 F3
Mt Elbrus Dr
4800 SDGO 1248 F3
Mt Elena Wy
2300 SDCo 1294 G6
(See Page 1294)
Mt Etna Dr
4600 SDGO 1248 F2
Mt Everest Blvd
4400 SDGO 1248 G3
Mt Foraker Av
4300 SDGO 1248 G2
Mt Forde Av
4600 SDGO 1248 F3
Mt Foster Av
4300 SDGO 1248 F3
Mt Frissell Dr
4600 SDGO 1248 F2
Mt Gaywas Dr
4700 SDGO 1248 F2
Mt Harris Dr
4700 SDGO 1248 F2
Mt Hay Dr
4700 SDGO 1248 F2
Mt Helix Dr
5100 SDCo 1271 D2
Mt Helix Highlands Dr
4300 SDCo 1271 C3
Mt Henry Av
4200 SDGO 1248 F3
Mt Henry Pl
4500 SDGO 1248 F2
Mt Henry Wy
4500 SDGO 1248 F3
Mt Herbert Av
4100 SDGO 1248 F3
Mt Highpine Pl
4500 SDGO 1248 F2
Mt Holly Ln
- SDCo 1152 J6
Mt Horton Dr
4600 SDGO 1248 F3
Mt Hubbard Av
4500 SDGO 1248 E3
Mt Hukee Av
4300 SDGO 1248 F3
Mt Israel Pl
19300 SDCo 1149 C4
Mt Israel Rd
9000 SDCo 1149 C4

Mt Jeffers Av
4300 SDGO 1248 F2
Mt King Dr
4500 SDGO 1248 F2
Mt La Palma Dr
4700 SDGO 1248 F1
Mt La Platta Ct
4500 SDGO 1248 G2
Mt La Platta Dr
4600 SDGO 1248 G1
Mt La Platta Pl
4500 SDGO 1248 G1
Mt Langley Dr
2000 CHLV 1311 E6
Mt Laudo Dr
4600 SDGO 1248 F2
Mt Laurence Dr
3300 SDGO 1248 D4
Mt Lindsey Av
4400 SDGO 1248 F2
Mt Lindsey Pl
4500 SDGO 1248 F2
Mt Longs Dr
4700 SDGO 1248 F2
Mt Miguel Dr
3000 SDGO 1310 D3
Mt Olympus Dr
6900 SDCo 999 D4
Mt Olympus Valley Rd
9900 SDCo 999 D4
Mt Putman Av
4300 SDGO 1248 F3
Mt Putman Ct
4600 SDGO 1248 F3
Mt Rias Pl
4100 SDGO 1248 H3
Mt Royal Av
4800 SDGO 1248 G1
Mt Royal Ct
4700 SDGO 1248 G1
Mt Royal Pl
4800 SDGO 1248 G1
Mt Sandy Dr
3700 SDGO 1248 D5
Mt Shasta
- SNMS 1128 B1
Mt St Helens Ct
4700 SDGO 1248 G1
Mt St Helens Dr
4700 SDGO 1248 G1
Mt St Helens Wy
4700 SDGO 1248 G1
Mt Tamalpais St
1600 CHLV 1331 E2
Mt Tami Dr
3100 SDGO 1248 H5
Mt Tami Ln
3300 SDGO 1248 G5
Mt Vernon Av
3700 OCSD 1086 G5
Mt Vernon St
7100 LMGR 1270 E7
Mt View Rd
2900 SDCo 1129 C6
Mt Voss Dr
4200 SDGO 1248 F3
Mt Whitney Ct
900 CHLV 1331 A2
Mt Whitney Rd
2800 SDCo 1129 C4
Mt Woodson Rd
- SDCo 1171 E4
Mt. Woodson Wy
- SDCo 1171 F3
Mtn Ash Av
900 CHLV 1311 H4
Mtn Crest Glen
2500 ESCN 1130 F2
Mtn Meadow
5900 SDCo 1176 A2
(See Page 1176)
Mtn Meadow Trl
4400 SDCo 1155 J4
Mtn Oaks Trl
18400 SDCo 1294 D7
(See Page 1294)
Mtn Peak Pl
23400 SDCo 1173 D2
Mtn Rim Dr
300 SDCo 1029 B2
Mtn View Dr
600 SDCo 1156 E1
Mtn View Ln
25000 SDCo 1173 G5
Mtn View Rd
9600 SDCo 1235 G2
Muchacha Wy
10300 SDGO 1229 G7
Muddy Ln
- VSTA 1088 A6
Mudge Ln
1700 ESCN 1109 F5
Muffin Ct
9900 SDGO 1189 F3
Muir Av
4800 SDGO 1267 J5
4700 SDGO 1268 A5
Muir College Dr
- SDGO 1227 J1
Muir Ln
- SDGO 1227 J2

Muir Trail Pl
- CHLV 1331 B1
Muira Ln
2000 SDCo 1272 C3
Muirfield Av
- SDCo 1090 G5
Muirfield Dr
800 OCSD 1086 D2
2500 SDCo 1272 B5
Muirfield Glen
1700 ESCN 1109 D4
Muirfield Wy
7800 SDCo 1168 G7
- SNMS 1108 J3
Muirfields Dr
2600 CRLB 1127 F3
Muirlands Dr
1000 SDGO 1247 G2
W Muirlands Dr
900 SDGO 1247 F1
Muirlands Vista Wy
700 SDGO 1247 F2
Muirwood Dr
700 OCSD 1087 C2
Mulberry Ct
6900 CRLB 1127 A5
Mulberry Dr
1500 SNMS 1109 A3
Mulberry Ln
700 ELCN 6559 G1
- SDCo 1089 B3
Mulberry St
3800 OCSD 1086 G2
6500 SDGO 1290 E1
Mulberry Tree Ct
13600 POWY 1190 E3
Mulberry Tree Ln
13100 POWY 1190 D4
Mulberry Wy
2700 CHLV 1311 H4
Mulder Dr
2500 LMGR 1270 H7
Mulgrave Rd
11000 SDGO 1209 J1
Mulgrew St
400 ELCJ 1252 A6
Mulholland Ct
12200 SDGO 1190 B3
Mullen Wy
1000 VSTA 1107 J1
Mullin Terrace
- SDGO 1290 D3
Mullinix Dr
1000 CORD 1289 A6
Mulvaney Dr
8600 SDGO 1250 J3
Muncie Ct
1800 SDCo 1272 D3
Munda Rd
- CORD 1309 A2
1500 SDGO 1290 D6
Mundial St
- SDGO 1210 B1
Mundy Ter
600 ELCJ 1251 D4
Munevar Ct
1200 ENCT 1167 E1
Munevar Dr
700 ENCT 1167 E1
Munroe St
4600 LMSA 1270 G3
Munster Platz Wy
- SDCo 1069 G3
Mural St
600 OCSD 1087 C1
Murano Ln
- SDCo 1169 E2
Murat Ct
4600 SDGO 1248 C1
Murat Pl
4700 SDGO 1248 C1
Murat St
2900 SDGO 1248 C1
Murcia Ct
2100 SDGO 1247 H1
Murcott Wy
2900 ESCN 1110 E5
Murel Trl
14100 POWY 1190 J3
14000 POWY 1191 A2
Muriel Ln
500 ESCN 1130 A6
Muriel Pl
7400 LMSA 1270 G4
Murillo Ln
7000 CRLB 1127 G7
Murphy Av
4500 SDGO 1228 F5
Murphy Canyon Rd
5400 SDGO 1229 E7
4000 SDGO 1249 F3
Murphy Rd
- CORD 1329 F4
500 IMPE 6439 D5
- ImCo 6439 A5
Murray Av
1600 LMSA 1251 D6
Murray Canyon Rd
1400 SDGO 1269 A2
Murray Ct
100 ESCN 1129 G3

SAN DIEGO CO.

STREET Block City Map# Grid

Murray Dr
200 ELCJ 1251 D5
9700 LMSA 1251 C6
8900 LMSA 1271 A1
Murray Hill Rd
3800 LMSA 1270 F4
Murray Park Ct
6300 SDGO 1250 E6
Murray Park Dr
6600 SDGO 1250 E6
Murray Ridge Rd
2700 SDGO 1249 C5
Murray St
100 CHLV 1310 C7
- CORD 1288 F3
Murrieta Cir
4300 SDGO 1330 G6
Murry Ranch Rd
- SDCo 1272 A1
Muscat St
2000 SDGO 1290 A1
Museum Ct
900 OCSD 1087 B2
Museum Wy
- VSTA 1087 G2
Music Ln
500 SDCo 1109 H2
Muslo Ln
7300 CRLB 1148 A1
Mussey Grade Rd
- SDCo 1171 J5
15900 SDCo 1172 A4
12800 SDCo 1192 B5
(See Page 1192)
Mustang Ct
- IMPE 6439 F4
Mustang Dr
12500 POWY 1190 C6
Mustang Glen
600 ESCN 1130 B2
Mustang Ln
300 IMPE 6439 F4
Mustang Pl
300 CHLV 1310 H4
Mustang Point Wy
300 SDCo 1028 H5
Mustang Rd
- ImCo 6560 A5
Mustang Ridge Dr
11400 SDGO 1208 C2
Mustang Ridge Pt
11400 SDGO 1208 B2
Mustang St
4100 SDGO 1249 A2
Mustang Wy
1600 OCSD 1067 E7
3200 SNMS 1108 C6
Mustard Seed Ln
- ELCN 6559 J3
Muth Valley Rd
- SDCo 1212 C4
Muutama Ln
- SDCo 1050 D4
Muutama Rd
- SDCo 1050 C5
My Last Pl
600 SDCo 1252 D6
My Wy
700 SDGO 1330 C7
Mycenae Wy
5000 OCSD 1107 E5
Mycorte Dr
700 SDCo 1109 D6
Myers Country Ln
28600 SDCo 1069 H7
Myers Dr
400 SDGO 1228 A2
Myers Rd
- SDCo 1029 J3
N Myers St
400 OCSD 1086 A7
S Myers St
1900 OCSD 1106 C4
Mykonos Ln
- SDGO 1188 A6
Mykrantz Truck Tr
25700 SDCo 1173 J7
Mykrantz Truck Trl
- SDCo 1173 H7
Mynah Pl
500 VSTA 1087 F4
Myra Av
600 CHLV 1310 E7
1100 CHLV 1330 F2
Myra Ct
1300 CHLV 1330 F3
Myra St
2700 LMGR 1270 H7
Myrica Ln
17900 SDGO 1149 J7
Myricks Ct
200 SDCo 1152 G6
Myrtle Av
1200 SDGO 1269 B6
Myrtle Beach Wy
2400 CHLV 1311 H7
Myrtle Ct
900 CRLB 1127 A7
Myrtle Ln
4800 LMSA 1271 B2
- SDCo 1089 B2
Myrtle Rd
2300 IMPE 6499 F2
Myrtle St
- OCSD 1066 G7
14100 SDCo 1272 J7
Myrtle Wy
1000 SDGO 1269 B6
Myrtlewood Ct
500 ESCN 1110 D6
600 OCSD 1086 F2
Mystery Mountain Rd
- SDCo 1069 G6
Mystic Hill Rd
1600 SDCo 1068 B6
Mystik Rd
4600 OCSD 1087 D3
Mystra Dr
4000 OCSD 1107 E4
Mystra Pt
6100 SDGO 1188 G4

N

N Av
800 NATC 1310 A1
N St
400 IMPE 6439 G5
Nabal Dr
4300 SDCo 1271 F3
Nabal St
2300 ESCN 1150 D1
Nacido Ct
16200 SDGO 1170 B4
Nacido Dr
12500 SDGO 1170 C4
Nacion Av
700 CHLV 1310 F7
1400 CHLV 1330 G3
Nadeen Wy
500 ELCJ 1251 H4
Nadia Ct
8600 SDCo 1231 J7
Naga Wy
- SDGO 1227 H3
Nagel St
6000 LMSA 1250 J6
Nagorski Ln
- SDCo 1070 E5
Nahama Ln
11300 SDGO 1208 C2
Nahant Ct
700 SDGO 1267 H1
Naiad St
400 ENCT 1147 B4
Nakwakwa Ln
100 SDCo 1029 H5
Nalco St
11200 SDGO 1209 B2
Nalini Ct
9300 SNTE 1230 H6
Nance Rd
2800 ImCo 6439 D5
Nancita Ct
6000 SDGO 1290 C4
Nancy Dr
6000 LMSA 1251 B6
Nancy Lee Ln
1300 SDCo 1233 H6
Nancy Ridge Dr
6100 SDGO 1208 F7
Nancy St
700 ESCN 1130 D1
Nanday Ct
5400 OCSD 1067 B2
Nandina Ct
8800 SDCo 1069 A6
Nandina Dr
- SDCo 1069 A5
Nandina Pl
- SDGO 1188 H3
Nanette Ln
6100 SDGO 1228 G5
Nanette St
400 CHLV 1330 G1
Nannette St
5200 SDCo 1290 J7
Nansen Av
2600 SDGO 1228 B6
Nantasket Ct
700 SDGO 1267 H1
Nantes Pl
1800 CHLV 1311 F1
Nantucket Ct
- ENCT 1147 B2
Nantucket Dr
500 CHLV 1330 H2
Nantucket Glen
400 ESCN 1110 D6
Nantucket Ln
2800 CRLB 1107 A4
Nantucket Park Wy
11400 SDGO 1208 C2
Naomi Dr
1000 VSTA 1087 G4
Napa Av
1200 CHLV 1330 G2
Napa Ct
1400 CHLV 1330 G3
3600 OCSD 1107 F3
Napa Dr
- SNMS 1108 J7
Napa St
5300 SDGO 1268 F3
Napatul Rd
- SDCo 1255 G3
Napier St
4200 SDGO 1268 E1
Naples Ct
2700 CRLB 1106 J4
600 OCSD 1067 C7
E Naples Ct
700 CHLV 1330 H1
Naples Pl
4900 SDGO 1268 E2
Naples St
500 CHLV 1330 C3
4900 SDGO 1268 E2
E Naples St
- CHLV 1330 E2
Napoli St
- OCSD 1087 C3
Naranca Av
1100 ELCJ 1251 H4
1400 ELCJ 1252 A4
1800 SDCo 1252 C4
Naranja St
5100 SDGO 1290 A4
Narcissa Ct
27700 SDCo 1089 E4
Narcissus Dr
2600 SDGO 1268 C6
Narcissus Summit
- ENCT 1148 C5
Nardito Ln
600 SOLB 1187 F1
S Nardo Av
400 SOLB 1167 F7
600 SOLB 1187 F1
Nardo Rd
700 ENCT 1147 D7
1000 ENCT 1167 D1
Narragansett Av
5000 SDGO 1267 H6
3700 SDGO 1268 A7
Narragansett Bay Dr
- SDGO 1290 B1
Narragansett Ct
1800 SDGO 1268 A7
Narwhal St
700 SDGO 1330 E7
Nash Ln
1100 VSTA 1087 E7
Nashville St
1300 SDGO 1268 E2
Nassau Dr
3600 SDGO 1270 E5
Natal Wy
100 VSTA 1087 J7
Natalie Dr
4600 SDGO 1269 J3
Natalie Wy
300 SDCo 1027 G4
Natchez Av
3100 SDGO 1248 F6
Natchez Trl
34700 SDCo 1176 E4
(See Page 1176)
Nate Harrison Grade
18900 SDCo 1031 G7
16400 SDCo 1051 C2
Nate Wy
10400 SNTE 1231 E2
Nathan St
3000 LMGR 1270 H6
Nathaniel Ct
7900 SDCo 1169 A3
Nathaniel Ln
- SDCo 1253 H1
National Av
1400 SDGO 1289 C4
National City Blvd
1200 NATC 1309 H2
National Glen
1700 ESCN 1109 D4
Natoma Wy
1200 OCSD 1087 B3
Natures Wy
36100 SDCo 1299 C1
(See Page 1299)
Natureview Ct
3000 CHLV 1311 J1
Naugatuck Av
2900 SDGO 1248 C1
Nautical Dr
3700 CRLB 1106 E6
Nautilus St
- SDCo 1085 H6
200 SDGO 1247 E1
Nautilus Wy
4300 OCSD 1087 A4
Nava Ct
100 SOLB 1167 H7
Navaja Ln
- SDCo 1271 J2
Navaja Rd
1600 SDCo 1271 J2
Navajo Av
4300 OCSD 1087 C5
Navajo Pl
1800 ESCN 1129 F5
Navajo Rd
2800 ELCJ 1251 A4
34500 SDCo 1176 D4
(See Page 1176)
6400 SDGO 1250 D5
Navajo St
200 SNMS 1108 D7
Navarra Dr
2500 CRLB 1147 G1
Navarro St
4400 OCSD 1086 G1
Navel Pl
1200 SDCo 1107 G3
1400 SDCo 1130 D4
Navello St
1100 ELCJ 1252 A3
Navello Terr
- ELCJ 1251 J3
Navigator Cir
7500 CRLB 1127 A7
7500 CRLB 1147 A1
3200 OCSD 1107 A2
Navigator Ct
600 CRLB 1147 A1
Nawa Ct
15400 SDGO 1169 H6
Nawa St
15500 SDGO 1169 H6
Nawa Wy
11400 SDGO 1169 H6
Naylor Rd
3100 SDGO 1350 F5
Nazareth Dr
- SDGO 1249 G7
Nazas Dr
12400 POWY 1170 C7
Neale St
1500 SDGO 1268 H6
Neals Spur
3100 SDCo 1234 D4
Neblina Dr
4600 CRLB 1106 H7
Nebo Dr
4900 LMSA 1270 H2
Nebraska Av
7300 SDGO 1290 G6
Neches Ct
3800 SDCo 1099 D2
(See Page 1099)
Neckel Rd
- IMPE 6439 F4
600 ImCo 6439 D4
Nectar Wy
23900 SDCo 1173 E5
Nectarine Cir
3700 OCSD 1086 F2
Nectarine Dr
9600 SDCo 1232 A4
Neddick Av
13300 POWY 1190 H4
Needham Rd
2300 ELCJ 1251 B4
Needlegrass Ct
3300 SDGO 1270 D6
Needlerock Pl
800 ESCN 1150 C1
Negley Av
10900 SDGO 1209 H5
Negley Dr
11600 SDGO 1210 A4
Neighborly Ln
1000 SDCo 1153 A6
Neil Ter
200 SDCo 1067 H7
Neill Rd
200 ImCo 6500 D6
Nejo Rd
36000 SDCo 1029 H3
Nella Ln
- SDCo 1068 E6
Nelms St
1200 OCSD 1086 B6
Nelson Ct
4800 CRLB 1107 A6
Nelson Ln
13100 POWY 1190 H4
Nelson St
6100 SDGO 1270 C5
Nelson Wy
8700 SDCo 1068 J3
8800 SDCo 1069 B2
Nemaha Dr
4100 SDGO 1248 D3
Nemo St
12700 POWY 1190 D4
Nentra St
8400 LMSA 1250 J6
Neoma St
2400 SDGO 1248 B5
Neosho Pl
3200 SDGO 1248 D1
Nepeta Wy
6700 CRLB 1126 J5
Neptune Av
400 ENCT 1147 B5
Neptune Ct
700 CHLV 1310 F7
Neptune Dr
1000 CHLV 1330 F1
7400 CRLB 1127 A7
Neptune Pl
100 ESCN 1109 H6
6600 SDGO 1247 E2
Nerak Ct
5500 SDCo 1290 J7
Nerdra Ln
- ELCJ 1252 B7
Nereis Dr
3900 SDCo 1271 A5
Nereus St
10400 SDGO 1249 G3
Neri Dr
7000 LMSA 1270 E4
Nerine Wy
- CRLB 1127 D5
Nesmith Dr
11000 SDCo 1089 H7
Nesmith Pl
25500 SDCo 1089 H7
Nestor Wy
1100 SDGO 1350 B1
Nethelton Rd
- VSTA 1107 C1
Nettle Creek Ct
2800 CHLV 1312 A6
(See Page 1312)
Nettle Creek Wy
1400 CHLV 1312 A6
(See Page 1312)
Nettle Pl
3500 SDCo 1048 C2
Nettleton Rd
200 VSTA 1107 C1
Neva Av
8500 SDGO 1249 C5
Nevada Av
100 VSTA 1087 H5
Nevada Glen
2200 ESCN 1129 E6
Nevada St
900 OCSD 1086 A6
N Nevada St
400 OCSD 1086 A7
S Nevada St
200 OCSD 1086 A7
1700 OCSD 1106 C3
Neville Cres
300 SDCo 1066 J1
Neville Rd
- SDGO 1268 E7
Nevin St
1100 SDGO 1350 G1
Nevoso Wy
11500 SDGO 1149 J7
New Bedford Ct
10200 SDCo 1231 J2
New Branch Ct
- OCSD 1086 D2
New Castle Wy
- CRLB 1107 A4
New Chatel Dr
1300 SDGO 1350 A2
New Colt Ct
9400 SDCo 1232 H4
New Crest Ct
1600 CRLB 1127 C5
New Hampshire St
4400 SDGO 1269 A4
New Haven Dr
2100 CHLV 1311 E3
New Haven Pl
4500 CRLB 1107 B4
4400 SDGO 1228 F7
New Haven Rd
5100 SDGO 1228 E7
New Hope Ct
1400 SDGO 1290 F5
New Jersey Av
2900 LMGR 1270 G6
New Jersey St
4400 SDGO 1269 B4
New Man Wy
- SDCo 1135 G6
New Mills Rd
5400 SDGO 1270 B3
New Moon Ln
16500 SDCo 1111 D5
New Morning Rd
11100 SDCo 1271 G4
New Orleans Av
200 SDGO 1350 G5
New Park Ln
8300 SDGO 1169 A3
New Park Terr
15500 SDGO 1169 B3
New Ranch Ct
3000 CHLV 1311 J2
New Ranch Rd
4800 SDCo 1271 G2
New Rochelle Wy
17000 SDCo 1169 F2
New Salem Cir
10900 SDGO 1209 A2
New Salem Cove
10800 SDGO 1209 A3
New Salem Ct
10900 SDGO 1209 A3
New Salem Pl
10800 SDGO 1209 A3
New Salem Pt
10800 SDGO 1209 B3
New Salem St
8300 SDGO 1209 C3
New Salem Ter
10800 SDGO 1209 B3
New Salem Wy
10800 SDGO 1208 J4
New Seabury Dr
8900 SNTE 1231 A4
New Seabury Wy
2400 CHLV 1311 H7
New St
300 ELCN 6499 J6
New Trailway
- CHLV 1311 G2
New York St
4500 SDGO 1269 B4
Newberry St
3300 NATC 1310 D3
6800 SDGO 1249 J6
Newbold Ct
6800 SDGO 1268 J1
Newcastle Av
2000 ENCT 1167 D3
Newcastle Ct
- CHLV 1311 C7
1100 OCSD 1087 D1
6000 SDGO 1290 C5
Newcastle Pl
6100 SDGO 1290 C5
Newcastle St
5900 SDGO 1290 C5
Newcomb St
16500 SDGO 1169 D4
Newcrest Pt
3600 SDGO 1187 J4
Newell St
1800 NATC 1310 B2
2500 SDCo 1310 B2
3400 SDGO 1288 B1
Newhaven Rd
- SNMS 1128 B3
Newkirk Dr
900 SDGO 1247 F2
Newland Ct
1200 CRLB 1106 F4
Newland Rd
3500 OCSD 1107 E3
Newlin Ln
2300 SDGO 1209 E7
Newmont Dr
9000 SDGO 1189 C1
Newport Av
2400 ENCT 1167 D4
4800 SDGO 1267 J6
4700 SDGO 1268 A6
Newport Ct
- CHLV 1330 J2
Newport Dr
100 SNMS 1108 E7
800 VSTA 1087 J5
Newport St
900 OCSD 1066 H6
Newport Ter
- VSTA 1087 J5
Newport Wy
3700 CRLB 1107 A5
Newporter Wy
14000 SDGO 1190 A2
Newshire St
3000 CRLB 1107 A3
Newsome Dr
6300 SDGO 1270 D5
Newton
- SDCo 1127 C1
Newton Av
2100 SDGO 1289 D5
Newton Hill
16000 SDGO 1169 C3
Nexus Centre Dr
4700 SDGO 1228 E2
Niagara Av
4800 SDGO 1267 H6
4400 SDGO 1268 A7
Niantic Ct
700 SDGO 1267 H1
Niblick Dr
3400 SDCo 1270 J5
Niblick Ter
2100 OCSD 1106 J1
Nicado Vereda Montecita
- SDCo 998 C5
Nicaragua Cir
- SDGO 1268 F6
Nichals St
7700 LMGR 1290 G1
Nicholas Av
- IMPE 6499 J2
Nicholas Ln
700 ELCJ 1252 B6
Nicholas Pl
1500 ELCJ 1252 A6
Nicholas St
700 ELCJ 1252 A6
17100 SDCo 1067 A1
Nicholas Wy
1500 ELCJ 1252 A6
Nichols Rd
- ImCo 6439 B7
- ImCo 6499 B3
- ImCo 6559 B3
Nichols St
3100 SDGO 1288 A4
Nicklaus Dr
2300 OCSD 1106 H2
Nickman St
400 CHLV 1330 C3
Nickrose Pl
4000 SDCo 1028 F3
Nicola Ranch Rd
1100 SDCo 998 A7
Nicola Tesla Ct
9400 SDGO 1352 A4
Nicole Av
- IMPE 6500 A2
Nicole Dr
300 VSTA 1087 H4
Nicole Ridge Rd
16300 SDGO 1169 C5
Nicole St
1900 SDCo 1153 A1
Nicole Wy
9500 SNTE 1231 C5
Nicoles Vista
13800 SDCo 1050 E7
Nicolette Av
1300 CHLV 1311 F1
Nicolia Dr
- CRLB 1127 D4
Nicolina Dr
- SDCo 997 H7
Nicolo Ct
500 ESCN 1130 A6
Nicosia Ln
10900 SDCo 1231 F2
Nida Pl
2600 LMGR 1270 H7
Nido Aguila
2300 SDCo 1254 C1
Nido Ln
4500 SDGO 1248 D2
Nidrah St
1000 ELCJ 1251 E7
Niego Ln
12500 SDGO 1170 C4
Niels Bohr Ct
2200 SDGO 1352 A3
Nielsen Ct
2300 ELCJ 1251 B1
Nielsen St
2200 ELCJ 1251 B1
Niemann Ranch Rd
6600 SDCo 1188 G2
Night Star Ct
2400 SDCo 1234 B5
Night Star Pl
2400 SDCo 1234 B5
Nightfall Ln
1500 CHLV 1311 F7
Nightfall Ter
13000 SDGO 1189 H5
Nighthawk Ct
1900 CRLB 1127 D6
Nighthawk Ln
16600 SDGO 1169 D4
Nighthawk Wy
4900 OCSD 1107 E3
Nightingale Pl
1000 ESCN 1110 B5
Nightingale Wy
8000 SDGO 1249 B6
Nightshade Rd
- CRLB 1127 B5
Nightshade Wy
2100 CHLV 1331 H3
Nightsky Rd
23400 SDCo 1173 C2
Nightwatch Wy
2900 SDCo 1254 A3
Niguel St
- OCSD 1067 A5
Niki Lynn Pl
1100 CRLB 1106 E4
Niki St
- ImCo 6560 B7
Nikita Ct
12100 SDGO 1210 B1
Nikki Ln
- SDCo 1070 D1
Nila Ln
400 ELCJ 1271 G1
Nile Av
1100 CHLV 1330 G2
Nile Ct
1200 CHLV 1330 G2
Nile St
3300 SDGO 1269 F6
Nilo Wy
1700 SDGO 1290 H6
Nimbus Ln
1100 SDGO 1268 G3
Nimitz Blvd
4200 SDGO 1268 B5
2600 SDGO 1288 C1
Nina Ct
1900 SDCo 1291 A1
Nina Pl
1900 ESCN 1109 H5
Nina Rd
- ImCo 6560 C7
2600 LMGR 1270 F7
Nina St
3500 OCSD 1106 J2
Nipoma St
2700 SDGO 1268 C5
Nira Ln
31700 SDCo 1068 G1
Nirvana Av
1800 CHLV 1331 A5
Nita Ct
900 CHLV 1330 F1
- SNTE 1231 E7
Nita Ln
- SNTE 1231 E7
1000 VSTA 1087 G4
Nitens St
- SDCo 1127 B7
Nivel Ct
12000 SDGO 1170 B4
Nixon Av
- CALX 6620 J6
Nixon Cir
100 OCSD 1067 B6
Nixon Pl
200 CHLV 1310 B4
Noah Wy
5300 SDGO 1228 F6
Noakes Rd
10700 SDCo 1271 F1
E Noakes St
100 SDCo 1253 D1
W Noakes St
300 SDCo 1253 C1
Nob Av
800 DLMR 1187 G6
13700 SDGO 1187 G6
Nob Cir
700 VSTA 1087 J4
Nob Hill Dr
2200 CRLB 1106 G4
1500 ESCN 1109 H6
Nobel Ct
500 ENCT 1147 D7
Nobel Dr
4100 SDGO 1228 C3
Noble Canyon Rd
- CHLV 1311 H5
Noble St
1800 LMGR 1290 G1
Noche Tapatia
7300 SDCo 1168 G2
Nocturne Ct
300 CHLV 1330 F2
Noden St
200 ELCJ 1251 F7
Noeline Av
8900 SDCo 1290 J4
8300 SDGO 1290 H4
Noeline Ct
100 SDGO 1290 H4
Noeline Ln
8300 SDGO 1290 H4
Noeline Pl
8400 SDGO 1290 H4
Noeline Wy
100 SDGO 1290 J4
S Noeline Wy
100 SDGO 1290 J4
Noell St
3500 SDGO 1268 G6
Nogal St
4800 SDGO 1290 A4
Nogales Dr
13700 SDGO 1187 G6
Nogales Rd
39000 SDCo 1029 H4
Nokomis St
5500 LMSA 1251 B7
Nokoni Dr
13300 POWY 1190 E4
Nolan Av
700 CHLV 1310 F7
1400 CHLV 1330 G3
Nolan Ct
1400 CHLV 1330 G3
Nolan Ln
1000 CHLV 1330 F1
Nolan Pl
4700 SDCo 1271 H2
Nolan Wy
900 CHLV 1330 F1
Nolasquez Wy
11200 SDCo 1029 H3
Nolbey St
800 ENCT 1167 E2
Nolina Ct
- SDCo 1127 D4
Nolina Wy
13200 SDGO 1188 G4
Noma Ln
1600 ENCT 1147 B2
Nomad Pl
4000 ESCN 1150 D4
Nomel Ln
2700 LMGR 1270 H7
Non Rd
- SDCo 1091 B1
Nonie Ter
12400 SDGO 1189 C6
Nopalito Dr
2100 CHLV 1331 G3
Noraak Ct
5900 LMSA 1250 G7
Norcanyon Wy
7600 SDGO 1209 A1
Norcroft Rd
13200 SDGO 1188 B4
Nordahl Rd
1100 SNMS 1109 E7
700 SNMS 1129 D1
Nordica Av
4100 SDGO 1289 H7
Noreen Ct
900 SNMS 1109 C5
Noreen Pl
100 OCSD 1086 E5
Noreen Wy
1100 ESCN 1109 J6
3100 OCSD 1086 E5
Norella St
900 CHLV 1310 J6
Noren Pl
2800 SDGO 1288 B3
Norfolk Dr
300 ENCT 1167 D3
Norfolk St
2400 NATC 1290 A6
Norfolk Ter
4100 SDGO 1269 H2
Noria Dr
600 OCSD 1086 F2
Noria Ln
- ENCT 1147 F5
Norlak Av
600 ESCN 1129 H3
Norm St
600 SDGO 1290 H3
Norma Ct
1000 CHLV 1330 G1
Norma Dr
4500 SDGO 1269 J3
Norma Gardens Dr
10200 SNTE 1231 D4
Norma St
2700 OCSD 1087 C7
Normal Av
7800 LMSA 1270 G4
Normal St
3900 SDGO 1269 C5
Norman Ln
6200 SDGO 1250 D7
Norman Scott Rd
- SDGO 1289 E7
Norman St
200 BRAW 6320 B1
(See Page 6320)
Norman Strasse Rd
2700 SNMS 1108 D5
Normandie Ct
2800 SDCo 1130 E7
Normandie Pl
4400 LMSA 1270 F3
Normandy Av
800 ENCT 1147 C4
Normandy Cir
3500 OCSD 1107 E3
Normandy Dr
1400 CHLV 1311 E7
Normandy Glen
1800 ESCN 1110 B4
Normandy Hill Ln
1000 ENCT 1147 C4
Normandy Ln
200 CRLB 1106 D5
Normandy Wy
900 SDCo 1253 B2
Normanton Ct
- SDGO 1209 G2
Normantown Wy
- SDGO 1209 G2
Normark Ter
800 VSTA 1087 J6
Normount Rd
3500 OCSD 1107 F3
Norran Av
1500 ELCJ 1252 B6
Norris Rd
5100 SDGO 1270 A2
Nors Ranch Rd
1400 SDCo 1068 B4
Norse Ln
800 SDCo 1130 C4
Norstad Av
600 SDGO 1330 E7
Norstad St
800 SDGO 1330 E7
Norstar Ln
1500 SDCo 1047 J2
Norte Dr
23800 SDCo 1173 D2
Norte Mesa Dr
10000 SDCo 1271 D5
Norte Villa Wy
- ESCN 1110 D5
Norte Vista
1000 SDCo 1128 B4
North Av
1300 ESCN 1109 H2
7400 LMGR 1270 G5
- LMSA 1270 E5
4500 OCSD 1087 D5
1100 SDCo 1109 J2

SAN DIEGO CO.

San Diego County Street Index

STREET Block City Map# Grid

North Av
4400 SDGO 1269 C4
700 VSTA 1087 F4
North City Dr
200 SNMS 1128 J1
North Crest Rd
100 SDCo 1252 J2
North Ct
100 ENCT 1147 B5
4700 SDGO 1269 C3
North Dr
1100 VSTA 1087 F4
North Fork Av
3500 CRLB 1107 B6
North Fork Dr
- SDCo 1068 D5
North Ln
- SDCo 1168 A7
11500 SDCo 1231 H6
100 SDCo 1252 H3
200 SDGO 1247 E1
400 SDGO 1350 F3
- SOLB 1167 J7
North Park Wy
3100 SDGO 1269 E5
North Point Dr
- SDGO 1207 J7
North River Rd
4700 OCSD 1066 H7
5900 OCSD 1067 F5
- SDCo 1067 H4
North Roundup Cir
200 SNTE 1231 E5
North Shore Dr
100 SOLB 1187 E2
North Slope Ter
1900 SDCo 1291 A1
North Star Dr
3200 SDGO 1248 D3
North Star Wy
31300 SDCo 1070 H1
North View Ct
9800 SDCo 1069 D7
North View Ln
29100 SDCo 1069 D7
North Wy
3600 OCSD 1107 A2
Northaven Av
5000 SDGO 1268 F1
Northbrook Ct
1900 SDCo 1108 B3
Northcliff Dr
3500 SDCo 1048 E1
Northcote Rd
9000 SNTE 1231 G5
Northcrest Cir
9300 SNTE 1231 B7
Northcrest Ct
8500 SNTE 1231 B7
Northcrest Ln
- POWY 1170 E6
Northerly St
4800 OCSD 1087 D3
Northern Lights
- SDGO 1168 H6
Northern Moon Wy
4500 SDGO 1350 H1
Northfork
- SNMS 1128 B5
Northgate St
300 SDGO 1290 G5
Northhill Ter
- SDCo 1231 J5
Northmore Pl
4700 OCSD 1087 E3
Northpoint Ln
- SDGO 1207 J7
Northridge Av
5200 SDGO 1228 H7
Northridge Ct
5400 SDGO 1228 H6
Northridge Pl
9300 SNTE 1251 B1
Northrim Ct
1300 SDGO 1268 H2
Northrup Dr
7500 SDGO 1208 J5
Northrup Pl
7600 SDGO 1209 A5
Northrup Pt
10000 SDGO 1209 A5
Northshore Dr
2000 CHLV 1311 E3
Northside Dr
2400 SDGO 1249 E7
Northstar Wy
- SNMS 1128 B6
Northview Dr
1300 SDCo 1251 J7
Northview Ln
8500 SNTE 1231 B7
Northview Rd
- ESCN 1149 G1
Northview Ter
9300 SNTE 1231 B7
Northwest
- SDGO 1248 C6
Northwick Wy
- SDGO 1209 G1
Northwood Cir
- SDGO 1209 E3
Northwood Dr
3400 OCSD 1086 D2
18000 SDCo 1274 C3
Northwoods Dr
- CHLV 1311 G3
Norton Av
100 NATC 1289 J7
Norwalk Av
4600 SDGO 1248 D1
Norwalk Ln
14400 POWY 1190 E2
Norwalk St
13500 POWY 1190 E2
Norway Ct
600 ESCN 1129 J1
Norwich Pl
4500 CRLB 1107 B4
Norwich St
5400 SDGO 1228 H7
Norwood St
4500 SDGO 1269 J4
Norwood Wy
500 ESCN 1129 H4
Norwynn Ln
600 SDCo 1027 J4
Norzel Dr
3100 SDGO 1248 G5
Nosotros St
800 CALX 6680 D1
Nostalgia Pl
1000 VSTA 1108 A1
Nothomb St
400 ELCJ 1252 A6
Notnil Ct
9700 SNTE 1231 F4
Notre Dame Av
3700 SDGO 1228 D6
Nottingham Gn
- ESCN 1110 D7
Nottingham Pl
8800 SDGO 1227 J3
Nottinghill Ct
800 SNMS 1108 H5
Nought St
3400 SDGO 1270 D6
Nova Glen
1800 ESCN 1109 F6
Nova Pl
300 CHLV 1330 F1
Nova Wy
300 CHLV 1330 F1
Novak Wy
- SDGO 1209 H6
Novara St
1000 SDGO 1287 J2
Novato Pl
24400 SDCo 1173 F2
Noveleta St
- SDGO 1268 F6
Noya Wy
3200 OCSD 1106 J1
Noyes St
4700 SDGO 1248 B5
Nubbin Ct
10400 SNTE 1231 E3
Nueces Ln
2300 SDCo 1271 E7
Nuerto Ln
10000 SDCo 1271 E7
Nuestra Ln
2800 SDCo 1028 D6
Nueva Castilla Wy
7600 CRLB 1147 G1
Nuevo Mundo Rd
23300 SDCo 1173 C1
Nuevo Vallarta Dr
- IMPE 6499 G1
Nuffer Rd
600 ImCo 6559 E3
Nugent Ct
1000 ELCJ 1251 A3
Nugget Ct
12300 SDCo 1232 A1
Null Rd
5500 LMSA 1250 H7
5500 LMSA 1270 H1
Numbers Av
- OCSD 1086 E3
Nursery Rd
- SDGO 1289 C2
Nutby Ln
9700 SDCo 1049 D7
Nute Wy
3000 SDGO 1248 C3
Nutmeg Cir
1800 ESCN 1109 F6
Nutmeg Ln
9700 SDCo 1149 E2
Nutmeg Pl
2700 SDGO 1269 E7
N Nutmeg Rd
1400 ESCN 1109 F6
Nutmeg St
200 SDGO 1269 A7
5200 SDGO 1270 A7
N Nutmeg St
2000 ESCN 1109 E5
W Nutmeg St
1100 SDGO 1288 J1
Nutmeg Wy
3800 OCSD 1086 H4
Nye St
2700 SDGO 1248 H6
Nyemii Pass
16100 SDCo 1091 C3
Nyler Ct
9500 SNTE 1231 C4

O

O Av
1100 NATC 1310 A1
O Brien Pl
2600 ESCN 1110 D6
O Conner St
700 ELCJ 1251 E2
O Hare Av
- IMPE 6499 D1
O Hare Ct
- IMPE 6499 D2
O St
- IMPE 6439 G5
O Ybarra Av
500 CALX 6680 J2
Oak
- SDCo 1232 D6
- SDCo 1233 B3
Oak Av
600 CRLB 1106 E5
- ImCo 6560 A7
Oak Bluff Pl
3300 ESCN 1110 G6
Oak Br Dr
- SDCo 1068 C6
Oak Br Trl
- SDCo 1068 C4
Oak Burl Ln
700 ENCT 1147 G5
Oak Canyon Rd
15200 POWY 1171 A5
Oak Cliff Dr
3500 SDCo 1048 E1
Oak Creek
14800 SDCo 1070 H3
Oak Creek Dr
11600 SDCo 1211 F6
10700 SDCo 1231 H1
Oak Creek Rd
14800 SDCo 1232 J3
15200 SDCo 1233 B3
Oak Creek Ter
- SDCo 1232 G5
Oak Creek Trl
16200 POWY 1170 F4
Oak Crest Rd
3500 SDCo 998 G5
Oak Ct
300 CHLV 1330 G2
Oak Dr
- SDCo 1272 E3
29400 SDCo 1297 E5
(See Page 1297)
1400 VSTA 1088 A3
Oak Fern Ct
- SDGO 1209 J1
Oak Forest Pl
3300 ESCN 1110 G6
Oak Glade Dr
500 SDCo 1028 A3
Oak Glade Pl
0 SDCo 1028 A4
Oak Glen Cir
- SDCo 1252 G6
Oak Glen Dr
2100 VSTA 1107 H3
Oak Glen Ln
31100 SDCo 1070 E2
3500 SDGO 1248 D2
Oak Glen Rd
31600 SDCo 1050 E7
31600 SDCo 1070 E1
W Oak Glen Rd
- SDCo 1070 D1
Oak Glen Wy
- SDCo 1252 G6
Oak Glenn Ct
7000 LMGR 1290 E1
Oak Gn
- SDCo 1130 B6
Oak Grove Dr
3000 SDCo 1155 G4
10200 SDCo 1235 H2
9600 SDCo 1236 A2
Oak Grove Rd
17000 SDCo 1151 G3
Oak Grove Truck Trl
- SDCo 1032 J2
24200 SDCo 1033 D2
Oak Haven Rd
1800 SDCo 1234 A7
Oak Heights Rd
1200 SDCo 1156 C1
Oak Hill Dr
1000 CHLV 1311 G5
2800 ESCN 1110 E7
1300 ESCN 1130 B2
Oak Hill Ln
2700 SDCo 1135 F7
Oak Hills Ln
- SDCo 999 G4
Oak Hollow Rd
- SDCo 1153 H7
Oak Island Ln
4100 SDCo 1028 G5
Oak Knoll Ct
- CHLV 1311 G3
Oak Knoll Dr
13000 POWY 1190 B5
1200 VSTA 1088 A4
Oak Knoll Ln
14600 SDCo 1070 G3
Oak Knoll Rd
12700 POWY 1190 C5
Oak Lake Ln
17800 SDCo 1156 F7
Oak Land Rd
1200 SDCo 1156 D2
Oak Leaf Ct
2000 VSTA 1107 H3
Oak Ln
900 SDCo 1129 H7
- SDCo 1149 E1
17600 SDCo 1156 F6
25100 SDCo 1236 B2
28900 SDCo 1237 C7
Oak Meadow Dr
23800 SDCo 1173 D2
Oak Mountain Rd
- SDCo 1153 G2
Oak Park Dr
5200 SDGO 1270 A7
Oak Pl
400 CHLV 1330 G2
Oak Ranch Ln
- SDCo 1089 E3
Oak Ranch Pl
- SDCo 1089 E3
Oak Ranch Rd
- SDCo 1089 E4
Oak Ranch Wy
28000 SDCo 1089 E3
Oak Ridge Ln
18500 SDCo 1153 C6
Oak Ridge Rd
- SDCo 1089 D1
Oak Shade Ln
2800 SDCo 1172 D5
Oak Shadows Dr
- SDCo 1089 A2
Oak Springs Dr
2500 CHLV 1311 H6
16100 SDCo 1173 C3
Oak Spur Wy
10100 SDCo 1089 E4
Oak St
1000 ELCN 6499 H5
100 OCSD 1106 A2
700 SDCo 1152 G3
- SNMS 1128 C1
Oak Ter
4600 OCSD 1087 D4
Oak Trail Ct
14800 POWY 1150 J6
Oak Trail Ln
18700 POWY 1150 J6
Oak Trail Rd
- SDCo 1091 G5
Oak Tree Ln
- POWY 1190 C6
Oak Tree Pl
500 ESCN 1110 E6
Oak Valley Ln
300 ESCN 1110 G6
- SDCo 1068 E7
Oak Valley Rd
- SDCo 1172 B4
Oak Valley Trl
2400 SDCo 1274 G6
Oak View Pl
1900 SDCo 1234 C7
Oak View Ter
1600 CHLV 1311 G3
Oak View Wy
1200 ESCN 1129 D4
- SDGO 1190 B7
Oak Village Dr
1300 SDCo 1152 G7
Oak Village Pl
800 SDCo 1152 G7
Oak Wood Ln
3200 ESCN 1110 G6
Oak Wy
34800 SDCo 1156 E7
Oakana Rd
25100 SDCo 1153 G2
Oakbend Dr
10700 SDGO 1210 A3
Oakbourne Rd
9300 SNTE 1230 J5
Oakbranch Dr
300 ENCT 1167 G1
Oakbrook Ct
1900 ELCJ 1252 C4
12600 POWY 1170 D3
Oakcreek Ct
2000 VSTA 1107 H6
Oakcreek Ln
1400 VSTA 1107 J5
Oakcrest Dr
4000 SDGO 1270 A5
Oakcrest Park Dr
- ENCT 1147 F7
Oakdale Av
1300 ELCJ 1251 J4
1400 ELCJ 1252 A4
Oakdale Ln
500 ELCJ 1251 J4
Oakden Dr
1500 SDGO 1350 B2
Oakfield Ct
9500 SDCo 1271 C6
Oakfield Wy
12800 POWY 1170 D3
Oakforest Rd
1500 SDCo 1135 D4
Oakfort Ct
12400 SDGO 1210 C4
Oakfort Pl
12400 SDGO 1210 C4
Oakgate Row
6000 SDGO 1248 B1
Oakham Wy
7200 SDGO 1290 G7
Oakhurst Dr
900 SDGO 1290 C5
Oakland Rd
7400 LMSA 1270 F1
Oaklawn Av
100 CHLV 1309 J5
400 CHLV 1310 A7
1000 CHLV 1330 B3
Oakleaf Ct
3500 SDCo 1271 C6
Oakleaf Dr
600 OCSD 1086 F2
Oakleaf Ln
- SDCo 1172 G2
Oakleaf Pt
- SDGO 1249 G1
Oaklee Ln
700 SDCo 1234 C4
Oakley Ct
23400 SDCo 1173 C3
Oakley Pl
23400 SDCo 1173 C3
Oakley Rd
16000 SDCo 1173 C3
Oakline Ct
13100 POWY 1190 E1
Oakline Rd
14700 POWY 1190 D1
Oakmont Rd
27200 SDCo 1090 E5
Oakpoint Av
1300 CHLV 1331 E1
Oakridge Cove
2400 SDGO 1187 H5
Oakridge Pl
2300 ESCN 1109 G4
Oakridge Rd
6300 SDGO 1250 D4
- SNTE 1230 G7
Oakridge Wy
- VSTA 1107 H7
- VSTA 1127 H1
Oaks Ct
1400 SNMS 1109 D6
Oaks North Dr
12500 SDGO 1170 C1
Oaks Owl Rd
- SDCo 1235 C4
Oaks Rd
- SDCo 1029 J3
W Oaks Wy
- CRLB 1127 B3
Oakshire Ct
1800 SDGO 1290 A1
Oakstand Ct
15400 POWY 1170 F6
Oakstand Rd
13800 POWY 1170 F5
Oakstone Creek Pl
2900 ESCN 1110 E5
Oakstone Ct
9900 SNTE 1231 C3
Oaktree Ln
700 SNMS 1108 J6
Oaktree Wy
- SDCo 1048 E1
Oakvale Rd
15100 SDCo 1110 H3
15600 SDCo 1111 A2
Oakview Ct
3700 SDCo 1048 E1
Oakview Wy
- SDGO 1190 B7
Oakwood Creek Pl
600 ESCN 1110 E5
Oakwood Creek Wy
- ESCN 1110 D5
Oakwood Dr
3200 SDCo 1156 E1
Oakwood Glen Pl
14000 SDCo 1070 E7
Oakwood Ln
- OCSD 1106 C1
- SDCo 1231 J2
Oakwood Wy
600 ELCJ 1251 G4
Oasis Av
1100 CHLV 1330 G1
Oasis Dr
1200 SDCo 1129 E1
Oasis Ln
- VSTA 1087 D6
Oasis Rd
- SDCo 1218 B2
Oasis St
- IMPE 6439 C6
Oat Hill Rd
- SDCo 1089 D1
Obelisco Cir
7100 CRLB 1127 H6
Obelisco Ct
2700 CRLB 1127 H6
Obelisco Pl
2600 CRLB 1127 H6
Obeliscos St
- CALX 6620 H7
Oberlander Wy
200 SDCo 1028 H6
Oberlin Dr
5700 SDGO 1208 F6
Obispo Ln
16700 SDGO 1170 A3
Obispo Rd
12000 SDGO 1170 B3
Obregon Av
8200 SDGO 1229 C1
Obrien Pl
10100 SDGO 1249 G2
Obrien Rd
- BRAW 6260 A7
(See Page 6260)
- ImCo 6260 J6
(See Page 6260)
Observation Pl
3800 ESCN 1150 D3
Observation Point Dr
22500 SDCo 1052 H3
(See Page 1052)
Observatory Cg
- SDCo 1032 D6
Obsidian Dr
17000 SDCo 1171 E3
Obsidian Gn
- ESCN 1110 C7
Obsidian Pl
6700 CRLB 1127 F4
Ocala Av
1600 CHLV 1330 G5
Ocala Ct
1400 CHLV 1330 G3
Ocala Wy
- CRLB 1107 C6
Ocana Pl
4700 SDGO 1250 A1
Ocaso Dr
12600 SDGO 1170 C4
Ocaso Wy
4100 OCSD 1087 C6
Occidental St
3200 SDGO 1228 C6
E Ocean Air Dr
- SDGO 1208 C4
W Ocean Air Dr
11000 SDGO 1208 B3
Ocean Av
900 DLMR 1187 F5
- SDGO 1350 D1
Ocean Beach Fwy
- SDGO 1268 B4
Ocean Bluff Av
3900 SDGO 1208 B3
Ocean Bluff Wy
- ENCT 1147 D7
Ocean Blvd
500 CORD 1288 H7
4900 SDGO 1247 G5
Ocean Breeze Ct
5200 SDGO 1247 J4
Ocean Breeze St
- SNMS 1128 B2
Ocean Breeze Wy
500 CHLV 1311 E3
3300 SDCo 1273 B6
Ocean Cove Dr
2500 ENCT 1167 F5
Ocean Crest Av
1400 CRLB 1127 C5
Ocean Ct
- CORD 1288 G7
Ocean Dr
100 CORD 1288 G7
Ocean Front
2700 DLMR 1187 F3
Ocean Front St
1800 SDGO 1267 H6
Ocean Front Walk
3200 SDGO 1267 H2
Ocean Gate Ln
5400 SDGO 1351 A1
Ocean Heights Wy
- SDGO 1208 E3
Ocean Ln
800 IMPB 1329 E7
1000 IMPB 1349 E1
8000 SDGO 1227 E6
Ocean Mist Pl
300 SDGO 1330 H6
Ocean Ranch Blvd
3700 OCSD 1086 J5
3900 OCSD 1087 A5
Ocean Ridge Ct
1100 OCSD 1087 E2
Ocean Ridge Wy
- SDGO 1208 C2
Ocean St
2600 CRLB 1106 D5
200 SOLB 1167 E6
Ocean Surf Dr
700 SOLB 1187 E2
Ocean Valley Ln
4400 SDGO 1188 B6
Ocean View Av
100 DLMR 1187 G7
900 ENCT 1147 C4
Ocean View Blvd
2900 SDGO 1289 E5
5000 SDGO 1290 A5
Ocean View Ct
- ENCT 1147 B6
100 VSTA 1087 H7
Ocean View Dr
- SDCo 1128 J4
- SDCo 1310 F4
400 VSTA 1087 H6
Ocean View Hills Pkwy
- SDGO 1330 J7
5100 SDGO 1350 J1
Ocean View Ln
500 CHLV 1311 E3
Ocean View Pl
2400 SDCo 1252 H4
Ocean View Wy
3800 LMSA 1270 F5
Ocean Village Wy
2800 OCSD 1106 F1
Ocean Vista Rd
13200 SDGO 1187 J5
Oceancenter Dr
- OCSD 1087 D5
Oceancrest Pl
3600 OCSD 1107 D3
Oceancrest Rd
700 ENCT 1167 E1
Oceanhills Dr
4800 OCSD 1107 F5
Oceanic Dr
1000 ENCT 1167 F1
3800 OCSD 1087 A6
Oceanic Wy
3700 OCSD 1086 J6
Oceanside Blvd
3100 OCSD 1086 G6
4700 OCSD 1087 D4
200 OCSD 1106 B2
S Oceanside Blvd
1600 OCSD 1106 C1
Oceanside Harbor Dr
- OCSD 1085 J6
Oceanside Pier
- SDCo 1105 J1
Oceanview Dr
6600 CRLB 1126 H4
Oceanview Rd
2000 OCSD 1086 H7
2200 OCSD 1106 H1
Oceanview Ridge Ln
- SDGO 1208 F4
Ocelot Av
1100 CHLV 1330 G1
Ochre Ct
11000 SDGO 1189 J5
Oconnell Rd
8300 SDCo 1251 H1
Oconnor Av
1600 CHLV 1331 E2
Ocotillo Cres
400 SDCo 1078 H1
(See Page 1078)
Ocotillo Dr
1600 ELCN 6559 F1
600 VSTA 1087 G5
Ocotillo Pl
200 OCSD 1067 A7
Ocotillo St
7200 SNTE 1231 H7
Octans St
8600 SDGO 1209 C1
Oculto Ct
17000 SDGO 1169 J2
Oculto Pl
17000 SDGO 1169 J2
Oculto Rd
11400 SDGO 1169 J2
Oculto Wy
17000 SDGO 1169 J2
Odell Cir
1800 VSTA 1088 C4
Odell Pl
7900 SDGO 1209 A4
Odell Rd
10500 SDGO 1209 A4
Odessa Av
5700 LMSA 1250 J7
5900 LMSA 1251 A6
Odessa Ct
2200 LMGR 1290 G1
Odi Ct
8700 SNTE 1230 J3
Odom St
3700 SDGO 1270 D5
Odyssey Dr
- VSTA 1107 J2
Offbrook Rd
2100 SDCo 1027 J6
Offshore Pt
- SDGO 1330 H7
Offy Ct
2000 SDCo 1272 C3
Ofria Av
6800 SDGO 1250 E4
Ofria Ct
6900 SDGO 1250 D4
Oftedahl Wy
13500 SDGO 1189 F3
Ogalala Av
3400 SDGO 1248 D1
Ogard Ranch Rd
1200 SDCo 1253 E3
Ogden St
5200 SDGO 1270 A5
Ogram Dr
9800 SDCo 1271 C3
Ogunquit Av
13400 POWY 1190 H4
Ohana Wy
11100 SDCo 1211 F6
Ohara Ct
1400 SDGO 1290 F5
Ohearn Rd
100 SDCo 1027 F5
Ohio Av
6900 LMSA 1270 E1
E Ohio Av
1200 ESCN 1130 B2
Ohio Pl
7400 LMSA 1270 G3
Ohio St
4600 SDGO 1269 E3
Ohlson Crest Ct
- SDCo 999 C5
Ohm Ct
6200 SDGO 1228 D5
Ojeda Rd
1600 SDCo 1088 B1
Okeefe St
3100 SDGO 1350 F5
Okinawa Rd
- CORD 1309 C5
Okra Ct
800 CRLB 1127 A6
Ola Ct
4300 SDCo 1310 D5
Olamar Wy
1600 SDGO 1290 H6
Old Barn Ln
2200 CHLV 1331 G3
Old Barn Rd
1700 SDCo 1068 C5
Old Barona Rd
12900 SDCo 1212 F2
Old Battlefield Rd
- SDGO 1130 J4
Old Bend Rd
2000 SDCo 1252 F3
Old Bridge Rd
700 SDCo 1027 H3
Old Bridgeport Wy
2900 SDGO 1248 H5
Old California 76
- SDCo 1067 J3
Old California Wy
2800 SDCo 1272 C6
Old Campo Rd
- SDCo 1272 C7
Old Carmel Valley Rd
5300 SDGO 1188 E5
Old Carousel Ranch Rd
- SDCo 1171 H3
Old Castle Pl
8700 SDCo 1069 A6
Old Castle Rd
8600 SDCo 1068 J6
9300 SDCo 1069 C6
Old Castle Wy
- SDCo 1069 H5
Old Cedar Rd
1400 SDCo 1130 B3
Old Chase Av
1000 SDCo 1251 H7
1200 SDCo 1271 H1
Old Cliffs Rd
4700 SDGO 1249 J5
Old Coach Rd
16900 POWY 1170 F2
Old Coach Wy
18500 POWY 1150 G5
Old Cobble Ct
3400 SDGO 1248 H5
Old Cobble Rd
3600 SDGO 1248 H5
Old Cole Grade Rd
14400 SDCo 1050 G4
Old Colony Rd
- OCSD 1087 F1
2400 SDCo 1087 E1
Old Community Rd
14200 POWY 1190 E2
Old Course Rd
8100 SDCo 1169 A1
Old Creek Ct
1500 ENCT 1167 F2
Old Creek Rd
14300 SDGO 1210 G2
Old Cuyamaca Rd
2900 SDCo 1156 C1
Old Dairy Ct
5300 SDCo 1310 J2
Old Dairy Ln
3700 SDCo 1310 J2
Old Dairy Mart Rd
- SDGO 1350 E4
Old Dairy Wy
5300 SDCo 1310 J2
Old Desert Club Rd
3100 SDCo 1078 H5
(See Page 1078)
Old El Cam Real
11800 SDGO 1207 J1
Old El Camino Real
14900 SDGO 1188 A3
Old Espola Rd
16900 POWY 1170 D2
Old Glen St
1700 SNMS 1128 F7
Old Globe Wy
1300 SDGO 1269 B7
Old Gold Mine Rd
100 SDCo 1234 J3
Old Grove Market Wy
- OCSD 1086 J2
Old Grove Rd
- OCSD 1086 J1
- OCSD 1087 C4
10000 SDGO 1209 F5
Old Guejito Grade Rd
- ESCN 1110 F6
- SDCo 1110 H6
- SDCo 1111 C4
Old Heather Rd
3200 SDGO 1248 H5
Old Highway 101
- SDCo 1023 E4
Old Highway 111
- ImCo 6320 C6
(See Page 6320)
- ImCo 6500 E3
Old Highway 395
1300 SDCo 998 G5
- SDCo 1028 F3
2900 SDCo 1048 H1
- SDCo 1068 J2
Old Highway 80
26400 SDCo 1236 D2
27800 SDCo 1237 A4
37700 SDCo 1299 H4
(See Page 1299)
39400 SDCo 1300 C6
(See Page 1300)
42800 SDCo 1321 C3
(See Page 1321)
Old Hill Rd
100 SDCo 1027 J2
Old Horse Tr
1700 SDCo 1233 F7
Old Hwy 11
- BRAW 6260 A7
(See Page 6260)
Old Hwy 395
47900 RivC 999 A2
Old Janal Ranch Rd
- CHLV 1311 J5
Old Japatul
- SDCo 1275 A1
Old Julian Hwy
100 SDCo 1152 J6
24600 SDCo 1153 F4
26300 SDCo 1154 A3
Old Julian Tr
18700 SDCo 1153 G4
Old Kane Springs Rd
2900 SDCo 1120 H4
(See Page 1120)
3200 SDCo 1121 D5
(See Page 1121)
Old Kettle Rd
3100 SDGO 1248 H5
Old Lantern Ln
- SDCo 1089 D3
Old Lilac Rd
32200 SDCo 1049 H7
Old Man River Rd
- SDCo 1168 J1
Old Manzanita Rd
23800 SDCo 1111 D6
Old Meadow Rd
3400 SDGO 1248 H5
Old Melrose Ranch Rd
- SDCo 1111 C4
Old Memory Ln
5700 SDGO 1290 C2
Old Milky Wy
15000 SDGO 1130 H7
15900 SDGO 1131 A7
Old Mill Ct
1700 ENCT 1147 H6
Old Mill Rd
1700 ENCT 1147 H6
2100 SDCo 1088 B1
Old Mission Ct
7300 SNTE 1230 F7
Old Mountain View Rd
1000 SDCo 1233 A7
Old Nantucket Ct
5600 SDGO 1248 H5
Old Oak Dr
100 SDGO 1290 G4

SAN DIEGO CO.

49 INDEX
Old Oak Holler
San Diego County Street Index
Oxford St
INDEX 49
SAN DIEGO CO.

STREET
Block City Map# Grid

Old Oak Holler
10800 SDCo 1049 D3
- SDCo 1069 C1
Old Oak Rd
21200 SDCo 1275 B4
Old Oak Ridge
700 SDCo 1109 B2
Old Oak Tree Ln
3100 SDCo 1109 H2
Old Orchard Ln
4000 CHLV 1310 G3
4000 SDCo 1310 G3
Old Pomerado Rd
12600 POWY 1190 B6
Old Post Rd
3100 SDCo 1048 D2
Old Quarry Rd
2500 SDGO 1249 E7
Old Ranch Dr
28300 SDCo 1090 C2
Old Ranch Rd
5600 OCSD 1067 F6
- SDCo 1130 H2
- SDCo 1235 C6
100 SDCo 1310 D6
Old Rd
13700 SDCo 1090 E3
Old Rez Rd
- SDCo 1235 C3
Old River Rd
30700 SDCo 1067 J3
31000 SDCo 1068 A2
Old River St
4400 OCSD 1086 H1
Old San Pasqual Rd
- SDCo 1091 C3
1300 SDCo 1130 E5
Old Saybrook Dr
10700 SDGO 1189 H2
Old Schoolhouse Rd
- SDCo 1272 D5
Old Spanish Trl
2400 SDCo 1130 C7
Old Spring Ct
3400 SDGO 1248 H5
Old Springs Rd
2400 SDCo 1079 J2
(See Page 1079)
Old Spur Ct
- SDCo 1254 G2
Old Spur Dr
- SDCo 1254 F3
Old Stage Ct
300 SDCo 1027 F3
Old Stage Rd
1200 SDCo 1027 F4
Old Stagecoach Run
500 SDCo 1234 B4
Old Stagecoach Tr
2200 SDCo 1234 A4
Old Station Rd
14000 POWY 1170 G7
Old Stone Rd
12200 POWY 1190 B7
Old Stonefield Chase
8500 SDGO 1169 C4
Old Stonefield Pl
15900 SDGO 1169 C3
Old Survey Rd
16600 SDCo 1151 D1
16400 SDCo 1151 D1
Old Sycamore Dr
13200 SDGO 1189 H4
Old Taylor St
1000 VSTA 1087 J2
Old Telegraph Canyon Rd
- CHLV 1330 H1
Old Thames Wy
5500 SDGO 1248 H5
Old Town Av
3800 SDGO 1268 F5
Old Trail Dr
- CHLV 1311 G2
Old Tree Ln
9800 SNTE 1231 D4
Old Via Rancho Dr
- ESCN 1149 J2
Old Wagon Rd
- SDCo 1111 C4
23000 SDCo 1131 C1
Old Watney Wy
5500 SDGO 1248 H5
Old West Av
13000 SDGO 1189 D5
Old West Wy
13000 SDGO 1189 D5
Old Winemaster Ct
13300 POWY 1150 E7
Old Winemaster Wy
17800 POWY 1150 D7
Old Winery Ct
17700 POWY 1170 D1
Old Winery Rd
13300 POWY 1170 E1
Old Winery Wy
17700 POWY 1170 E1
Old Yucca Rd
16700 SDCo 1111 D7
Old Yucca Trl
17200 SDCo 1111 D5
Old Yucca Trl
16600 SDCo 1131 D1
Olde Grove Ln
4900 SDCo 1271 F2
Olde Highway 80
14300 SDCo 1232 G5
15600 SDCo 1233 C3
12800 SDCo 1252 C1
Oldfield Ct
1800 SDCo 1272 C3
Oldham Ct
900 ENCT 1147 D4
Oldham Wy
1000 ENCT 1147 C4
Olea Ln
- CRLB 1127 E4
Oleander
- SDCo 1233 B3
Oleander Av
1200 CHLV 1330 G2
1000 ELCN 6499 G5
3300 SNMS 1108 C6
2500 VSTA 1108 B5
Oleander Dr
100 CHLV 1310 B5
200 OCSD 1087 A1
3700 SDGO 1268 C6
Oleander Ln
1700 SDCo 1099 F2
(See Page 1099)
Oleander Pl
800 ESCN 1110 B7
700 SDCo 1108 B6
3700 SDGO 1268 C6
Oleander St
3300 SDGO 1207 J3
Oleander Wy
6700 CRLB 1126 J5
6300 SDGO 1188 G4
Olga Av
3400 SDGO 1249 B4
Olinda St
600 ESCN 1110 B7
Oliphant St
3500 SDGO 1288 B1
Olite Ct
2000 SDGO 1247 H1
Oliva Rd
12300 SDGO 1170 C4
Olive Av
1500 CHLV 1330 H4
700 CORD 1288 H6
200 CRLB 1106 F7
- ELCN 6499 E6
500 ELCN 6500 A6
4400 LMSA 1270 G3
- SDCo 1027 G1
800 SDCo 1152 J3
7300 SDCo 1291 D7
1900 SDGO 1290 C7
300 VSTA 1087 G6
Olive Crest Dr
1000 ENCT 1147 J5
Olive Crest Wy
13900 POWY 1190 E3
Olive Ct
1500 CHLV 1330 H4
Olive Dr
4000 OCSD 1087 C6
400 SDCo 1108 J2
9000 SDCo 1271 B6
E Olive Dr
- SDGO 1350 G4
W Olive Dr
100 SDGO 1350 G4
Olive Green St
1800 CHLV 1331 F3
Olive Grove Dr
13200 POWY 1190 E3
Olive Grove Ln
- SNMS 1128 C6
Olive Grove Pl
13800 POWY 1190 E3
Olive Hill Ln
2400 SDCo 1047 G1
Olive Hill Rd
3700 SDCo 1047 G3
5800 SDCo 1067 J1
Olive Hill Trl
5100 SDCo 1047 H7
Olive Hill Wy
400 SDCo 1047 G2
Olive Hills Av
4700 ELCJ 1252 B2
Olive Knoll Ct
11400 SDGO 1210 G1
Olive Ln
1000 CORD 1288 G7
28900 SDCo 1070 F7
9700 SDCo 1149 E3
8700 SNTE 1231 C7
Olive Meadows Dr
13300 POWY 1190 E3
Olive Meadows Pl
14000 POWY 1190 E3
Olive Mesa Ct
13900 POWY 1190 E3
Olive Mill Wy
13800 POWY 1190 E3
Olive Park Pl
13800 POWY 1190 E3
Olive Pl
7500 LMSA 1270 G3
Olive Rd
500 ELCN 6499 E7
Olive St
600 BRAW 6320 B2
(See Page 6320)
3500 LMGR 1270 G6
1000 NATC 1290 C7
1300 OCSD 1086 B7
400 SDCo 1027 G2
500 SDCo 1109 B2
1600 SDCo 1152 D5
3200 SDCo 1310 C3
400 SDGO 1269 A7
5100 SDGO 1270 A7
W Olive St
1000 SDGO 1268 J7
300 SDGO 1269 A7
1200 SDGO 1288 J1
Olive Ter
1000 SDCo 1152 D5
- SDCo 1232 G5
Olive Tree Ln
13300 POWY 1190 G4
Olive View Rd
2800 SDCo 1234 C7
Olive Vista Dr
14200 SDCo 1292 J1
(See Page 1292)
14700 SDCo 1293 A1
Olive Wy
- BRAW 6259 H6
(See Page 6259)
Olivebrook Ct
1900 ELCJ 1252 D5
Olivehill Rd
- SNTE 1230 G7
Oliveknoll Pl
- SDGO 1130 H3
Olivenhain Farms Rd
- ENCT 1148 B5
Olivenhain Rd
1700 CRLB 1147 G4
Olivenite St
- IMPE 6439 C6
Oliver Av
700 SDGO 1247 H7
1800 SDGO 1248 B6
Oliver Canyon Trl
7700 SDCo 1237 D6
Oliver Ct
4200 SDGO 1247 H6
Oliver Ln
4600 LMSA 1270 J2
Oliver Pl
700 SDGO 1247 H7
Olivera Av
10600 SDCo 1169 F4
Olivet Ln
1400 SDGO 1227 F6
Olivet St
1200 SDGO 1227 F7
Olivetas Av
7400 SDGO 1227 E7
7400 SDGO 1247 E1
Olivewood Ln
1400 SDCo 1234 B6
Olivewood Ter
700 SDGO 1289 G5
Olivia Glen
1900 ESCN 1130 A5
Olivine Ct
1900 CRLB 1127 F5
Olivos Ct
- SDCo 1028 G7
Ollie Av
- CALX 6620 F7
- CALX 6680 F1
Ollie St
3200 SDGO 1268 C5
Olly Ct
1000 VSTA 1107 J1
Olmeda Ct
13000 SDGO 1150 C6
Olmeda Pl
18700 SDGO 1150 D6
Olmeda St
1600 ENCT 1147 H7
Olmeda Wy
17000 SDGO 1169 H2
Olney St
4400 SDGO 1248 B5
Olson Dr
9700 SDGO 1228 F1
Olson Wy
100 OCSD 1106 F2
Olvera Av
5600 SDGO 1290 B5
Olvera Rd
10600 SDCo 1271 F5
Olvida Dr
200 SNMS 1129 A1
E Olympia Ct
- CHLV 1330 E3
Olympia Dr
2700 CRLB 1106 J4
Olympia Fields Dr
11300 SDGO 1189 J3
E Olympia St
100 CHLV 1330 F2
Olympic Pkwy
- CHLV 1311 E7
Olympic Pkwy
2700 CHLV 1312 A7
(See Page 1312)
- CHLV 1330 H3
- CHLV 1331 A3
Olympic Pl
5700 SDGO 1270 C5
Olympic Pt
18800 POWY 1150 F5
Olympic St
4000 SDGO 1270 C5
Olympic Vista Rd
- CHLV 1311 J7
2700 CHLV 1312 A6
(See Page 1312)
Olympic Wy
- OCSD 1086 G1
Olympus Loop Dr
1600 VSTA 1107 G4
Olympus St
600 ENCT 1147 B3
Oma Rd
30700 SDCo 1069 F3
Omaha Ct
400 ELCJ 1251 G7
Omar Ct
5100 OCSD 1067 B5
Omar Dr
800 ESCN 1129 J3
Omeara St
700 SDGO 1290 D5
Omega Dr
6600 SDGO 1310 F1
Omega St
700 SDCo 1291 D3
Omega Wy
- SNMS 1128 H4
Onager Dr
300 SDCo 1058 F7
(See Page 1058)
Onalaska Av
8500 SDGO 1249 C5
Onate Av
4800 SDGO 1248 H1
Onda Pl
6500 CRLB 1127 G5
E Oneida Ct
- CHLV 1330 E3
Oneida Pl
3700 SDGO 1269 B6
E Oneida St
200 CHLV 1330 F3
Oneida Wy
900 SDGO 1269 B6
Oneonta Av
500 IMPB 1349 F2
Onley Dr
600 VSTA 1087 F5
Onondaga Av
4600 SDGO 1248 E2
Onstad St
5000 SDGO 1268 F2
Ontario Av
3600 SDGO 1270 A6
Ontario Ct
2000 SDCo 1272 C3
Ontario St
900 ESCN 1129 H5
5300 OCSD 1087 D1
Onyx Av
1600 ELCJ 1252 B4
Onyx Ct
1600 SDCo 1272 B3
Onyx Dr
2000 SDCo 1272 C2
Onyx Gn
- ESCN 1110 D7
Onyx Pl
6700 CRLB 1127 G4
Oos Pl
15000 SDCo 1091 E3
Oos Rd
27700 SDCo 1091 D3
Opal Cove
5200 SDGO 1330 J7
Opal Ct
- CALX 6620 J7
- IMPE 6439 C7
Opal Dr
500 SDCo 1156 E1
Opal Gn
- ESCN 1110 D7
Opal Ln
4400 OCSD 1107 D2
Opal Ridge
2100 VSTA 1107 H6
Opal St
100 ELCJ 1251 F4
1300 SDGO 1247 H5
- SNMS 1128 B5
Opal Wy
- CRLB 1127 B4
Opaline Pl
1300 CHLV 1311 F1
Opalo Wy
2300 SDGO 1248 G7
Opalocka Rd
39200 SDCo 1300 B2
(See Page 1300)
Open View Rd
16600 SDCo 1173 D2
Opimo Ct
16400 SDGO 1170 C4
Opimo Dr
12600 SDGO 1170 C4
Oporto Ct
4700 SDGO 1250 A1
Oporto Pl
4700 SDGO 1250 A1
Opossum Ct
12100 SDCo 1212 C5
Opper St
600 ESCN 1129 D2
Opportunity Rd
7100 SDGO 1249 A2
Optima St
- CHLV 1331 G2
Optimist Wy
- VSTA 1108 A4
Or No Wy
- SDCo 1232 A1
Ora Avo Dr
700 SDCo 1088 E7
Ora Avo Ln
3100 SDCo 1088 E7
Ora Avo Ter
3000 SDCo 1088 E7
Ora Belle Ln
8300 SDCo 1232 D7
Oralane Dr
11500 SDCo 1271 H3
Oranado Ln
- SOLB 1167 J7
Orange Av
300 CHLV 1330 D4
800 CORD 1288 H7
1400 CORD 1308 H1
100 ELCJ 1251 F5
2200 ELCN 6499 E7
300 ELCN 6500 A7
2200 ESCN 1129 G7
8100 LMSA 1270 H3
400 SDCo 1027 F3
2100 SDCo 1129 G6
1700 SDCo 1153 A1
3500 SDGO 1269 F5
5400 SDGO 1270 B4
E Orange Av
- CHLV 1330 F4
300 VSTA 1087 H6
N Orange Av
200 SDCo 1027 F2
S Orange Av
700 ELCJ 1251 F7
Orange Blossom Ct
31600 SDCo 1051 A7
Orange Blossom Ln
13400 POWY 1190 E1
Orange Blossom Wy
1600 ENCT 1147 G5
1100 ESCN 1109 J4
13300 SDGO 1188 F4
Orange Crest Ct
12100 SDCo 1232 A4
Orange Crest Dr
9500 SDCo 1232 A4
Orange Ct
- ELCJ 1271 F1
Orange Dr
100 CHLV 1330 F5
- SDCo 1271 E2
Orange Grove Av
400 VSTA 1087 J6
Orange Grove Pl
- SDCo 1130 H2
Orange Grove Rd
1300 SDCo 1251 G1
Orange Haven Pl
8300 SDGO 1189 B3
Orange Hill
4300 SDCo 1048 B5
Orange Ln
9800 SDCo 1149 E1
Orange Pl
1500 ESCN 1130 A5
2800 LMGR 1270 H6
Orange St
1800 NATC 1310 B1
3100 SDCo 1272 H7
3100 SDCo 1310 C3
N Orange St
100 ESCN 1129 H3
S Orange St
1300 ESCN 1129 J4
W Orange St
100 VSTA 1087 G6
Orange Ter
28100 SDCo 1090 E2
Orange Tree Ln
- SDCo 1068 D5
Orange Vista Ln
1800 SDCo 1252 A2
Orange Wy
3800 OCSD 1086 H4
Orangeburg Av
12900 SDGO 1189 E5
Orangeburg Ct
9600 SDGO 1189 E5
Orangetree Ct
1400 ENCT 1147 G6
Orangeview Dr
1500 ENCT 1167 G1
Orangewood Dr
1000 SDCo 1130 D6
Orcas Wy
10000 SDCo 1232 C3
Orchard Av
8200 LMSA 1270 H2
2200 SDCo 1252 D5
4800 SDGO 1267 H7
Orchard Bend Rd
16200 POWY 1170 F4
Orchard Dr
400 CHLV 1310 C6
4200 SDCo 1271 C4
Orchard Gate Rd
13600 POWY 1170 E5
Orchard Glen Cir
1200 ENCT 1147 G4
Orchard Hill Rd
3400 SDCo 1310 H2
Orchard Ln
- BRAW 6319 F4
(See Page 6319)
- SDCo 1135 F3
Orchard Rd
11900 SDCo 1251 J1
- SDCo 1271 C4
Orchard View Dr
15000 POWY 1170 H7
Orchard View Ln
- SDCo 1130 H2
Orchard Vista Rd
- SDCo 1090 B5
Orchard Wood Rd
1700 ENCT 1147 G4
Orchard Wy
3400 OCSD 1086 E3
Orchid Av
- POWY 1190 F2
- SDCo 1128 G3
Orchid Ct
- SDCo 1232 A7
- VSTA 1108 B5
Orchid Glen
3700 ESCN 1150 B3
Orchid Ln
500 DLMR 1187 G5
- SDCo 1086 A4
Orchid Wy
900 CRLB 1127 A6
800 SDGO 1330 D7
Orcutt Av
4500 SDGO 1249 H6
5200 SDGO 1250 A6
Orde Ct
1200 CHLV 1330 C3
Ordview Ct
1200 CHLV 1330 C3
Ordway Rd
1300 SDCo 1028 H2
Oregano Wy
2100 CHLV 1331 H3
3800 OCSD 1086 H4
20400 SDCo 1294 J6
(See Page 1294)
Oregon Av
6900 LMSA 1270 F1
Oregon St
4600 SDGO 1269 D3
Oreo Ln
2100 SDGO 1350 A1
Organdy Ln
8500 SNTE 1250 H1
Oriba Rd
1700 DLMR 1187 G4
Orien Av
7300 LMSA 1270 F5
Oriente Dr
3000 SDCo 1067 H6
Oriente Pl
700 SDCo 1067 H6
Oriente Wy
23500 SDCo 1173 D3
Orilla Dr
16600 SDGO 1170 B3
Orinda Ct
1600 CHLV 1331 D2
Orinda Dr
2100 ENCT 1167 D3
Orinda Pl
1300 ESCN 1129 G7
Orinoco Dr
2800 SDCo 1135 G7
2800 SDCo 1155 E1
Oriole Ct
400 CHLV 1330 G2
- CRLB 1127 E5
Oriole Ln
- OCSD 1086 H2
Oriole Pl
1300 CHLV 1330 G3
Oriole St
1800 SDGO 1290 D1
Oriole Wy
1000 SNMS 1128 E2
Orion Av
- CHLV 1331 G2
Orion Ct
1400 SDGO 1209 D6
Orion Dr
3700 SDCo 1271 A5
1400 SDGO 1209 D6
Orion Pl
400 ESCN 1109 J7
400 ESCN 1129 J1
Orion St
5700 CRLB 1127 E1
Orion Wy
2500 CRLB 1127 E1
11100 SDGO 1209 D2
800 SNMS 1128 F6
Oriskany Rd
1900 SDGO 1290 D7
Orita Dr
800 BRAW 6319 H3
(See Page 6319)
Orizaba Av
2000 SDGO 1268 G5
Orkney Ln
1200 ENCT 1167 D1
Orla St
800 SNMS 1108 J5
Orlando Ct
- CHLV 1330 E3
E Orlando Ct
- CHLV 1330 E3
Orlando Dr
1200 LMGR 1290 F3
Orlando St
100 ELCJ 1251 J5
1200 SNMS 1109 C6
E Orlando St
200 CHLV 1330 F3
Orleans Av
200 ESCN 1110 E7
Orleans East
3100 SDGO 1268 B5
Orleans West
3100 SDGO 1268 B5
Orleavo Dr
1000 VSTA 1087 J6
Orleck Ct
4800 SDGO 1249 G2
Orleck Pl
4900 SDGO 1249 G2
Orleck St
10100 SDGO 1249 G2
Orma Dr
900 SDGO 1287 J2
Ormond Ct
700 SDGO 1267 H1
Ormsby St
800 SDCo 1067 J7
Ormsby Wy
2700 SDCo 1068 A7
Oro Blanco Cir
2800 ESCN 1110 E5
Oro Ct
2300 CHLV 1311 H6
Oro Glen
1500 ESCN 1109 H6
Oro Grande St
800 OCSD 1087 C1
Oro St
1400 ELCJ 1251 J2
1200 SDCo 1251 J3
Oro Verde Rd
2000 SDCo 1130 F4
Oro Vista Rd
1900 SDGO 1350 C3
Orohaven Ln
12600 POWY 1190 C4
Orola Ln
6800 LMSA 1270 E3
Orozco Rd
10400 SDGO 1229 H7
Orpha Ct
12800 POWY 1190 D5
Orpheus Av
1400 ENCT 1147 B2
Orr St
3500 OCSD 1086 E2
6600 SDGO 1248 H6
Orrell Dr
400 NATC 1309 J3
Orsett St
400 CHLV 1330 C4
Ortega Rd
11900 SDCo 1029 H4
Ortega St
1600 CHLV 1331 D2
Orten St
4500 SDGO 1268 E1
Ortez Pl
14400 POWY 1190 H1
Orvil Wy
100 SDCo 1028 A2
Orville St
8800 SDCo 1291 A3
Orwell Ln
300 ENCT 1147 H7
Orwell Rd
1500 ENCT 1167 H1
Osage Av
1100 CHLV 1330 G1
Osage Dr
1300 LMGR 1290 H2
1100 SDCo 1290 J2
Osage St
400 SDCo 1290 J4
9600 SDCo 1291 C3
1500 SNMS 1108 D6
Osage Trl
11600 SDCo 1231 H7
Osborn St
2100 SDGO 1289 G7
Osborne St
200 SDCo 1087 G1
Osborne Ter
2400 SDCo 1087 J1
Osceola Av
3000 SDGO 1248 C1
Osgood Wy
9900 SDGO 1208 J5
Oshia Ln
11300 SDCo 1069 H2
Osler St
6400 SDGO 1248 H6
Oso Rd
9100 SDCo 1291 B1
Osoyoos Pl
11300 SDGO 1209 C1
Osprey Av
1600 CHLV 1331 D2
Osprey St
4600 SDGO 1287 H1
Osprey Terr
7000 CRLB 1127 C6
Osprey Wy
- OCSD 1087 A3
Ossa Av
1000 CHLV 1330 G1
Ostend Ct
700 SDGO 1267 H1
Osterling Ct
6800 SDGO 1290 E6
Ostrow St
7800 SDGO 1249 A3
Osuna Ct
3200 OCSD 1106 J2
Osuna Dr
- CRLB 1106 G2
Otay Center Ct
2200 SDGO 1351 J3
Otay Center Dr
2100 SDGO 1351 J3
Otay Crossings Pl
800 SDCo 1352 D2
Otay Heights Ct
- SDGO 1351 D2
Otay Lakes Rd
100 CHLV 1310 H3
800 CHLV 1311 C5
12400 SDCo 1312 B4
(See Page 1312)
14600 SDCo 1313 B4
(See Page 1313)
Otay Mesa Center Rd
1600 SDGO 1351 G2
Otay Mesa Frwy
0 SDCO 1351 A2
0 SDGO 1351 H2
Otay Mesa Pl
4400 SDGO 1350 G2
Otay Mesa Rd
8700 SDCo 1351 H1
6900 SDCo 1352 A1
4200 SDGO 1350 G3
5500 SDGO 1351 B2
Otay Mtn Truck Trl
- SDCo 1332 E7
(See Page 1332)
- SDCo 1333 D4
(See Page 1333)
- SDCo 1352 H1
Otay Pacific Dr
2500 SDGO 1351 F4
Otay St
700 SDGO 1290 D3
Otay Valley Cir
- CHLV 1330 G5
Otay Valley Rd
100 CHLV 1330 F5
5600 SDGO 1331 C7
5600 SDGO 1351 C1
Otero Wy
23900 SDCo 1173 E2
Othello Av
7900 SDGO 1249 B3
Othello St
7600 SDGO 1249 A3
Otis Ct
6900 SDGO 1268 J1
Otis Pl
13800 POWY 1190 G4
Otis Post Rd
13200 POWY 1190 G4
Otis St
100 CHLV 1310 C6
Otomi Av
4700 SDGO 1248 D1
Otono St
1300 SDGO 1350 F1
Otsego Dr
500 SDGO 1268 J6
Ottawa Av
3500 SDGO 1248 E5
Ottilie Pl
5100 SDGO 1270 A5
Otto Av
3000 SDCo 1234 D5
Otto Strasse
- SDCo 1028 G2
Our Country Rd
- SDCo 1129 H7
Our Pl
- SDCo 1271 D2
Our Wy
8700 SNTE 1231 A7
Ouro Pl
7300 LMSA 1270 F4
Outer Dr
1700 SDCo 1251 G1
Outer Rd
1000 SDGO 1330 B7
Outinda St
9000 SDCo 1291 B4
Outlook Ct
2300 CRLB 1106 H4
Outlook Point Dr
8100 SDCo 1169 A1
Outlook Pt
4900 SDGO 1249 G1
Outlook Rd
13600 POWY 1190 F1
Outrigger Ln
1800 CRLB 1106 H7
Outrigger Wy
1900 OCSD 1106 F1
Oval Dr
3000 SDGO 1310 F2
Overbrook Ln
1000 SDCo 1027 J5
Overhill Dr
3000 SDCo 1088 D7
Overlake Av
5800 SDGO 1250 E6
Overland Av
5300 SDGO 1249 D1
Overland Ct
500 CHLV 1311 B4
Overland Pass
- POWY 1170 F1
Overland Passage
2900 SDCo 1234 D5
Overland Rd
400 ENCT 1147 F4
Overland Spur
3400 SDCo 1234 D5
Overland Trl
2800 SDCo 1047 G1
Overlook Cir
800 SNMS 1128 G2
Overlook Dr
4800 OCSD 1087 C2
E Overlook Dr
4200 SDGO 1270 C4
W Overlook Dr
4200 SDGO 1270 C4
Overlook Ln
800 SDCo 1251 H6
Overlook Pl
600 CHLV 1311 J2
Overlook Point Dr
2700 SDCo 1129 C5
Overlook St
600 ESCN 1130 C2
Overpark Rd
3700 SDGO 1187 J5
Overton Av
9100 SDGO 1249 E6
Overview Rd
15900 POWY 1170 F5
Ovid Pl
5000 SDGO 1228 E7
Oviedo Pl
2400 CRLB 1147 G1
Oviedo St
9100 SDGO 1189 C3
Oviedo Wy
- SDGO 1189 E2
Owega Ct
3900 SDCo 1099 D2
(See Page 1099)
Owen Dr
- CHLV 1330 H2
Owen St
3100 SDGO 1288 A4
Owens Av
1900 CRLB 1127 C3
Owl Ct
9400 SDGO 1189 E6
Owl Glen
1300 ESCN 1129 G5
Owlinguish Rd
12000 SDCo 1029 J3
Oxbow Cir
100 ENCT 1147 H7
Oxbow Ln
100 ENCT 1147 H7
Oxford Av
2000 ENCT 1167 D3
Oxford Ct
1100 CHLV 1330 C3
1900 VSTA 1107 H5
Oxford Hill
16000 SDGO 1169 C3
Oxford Pl
3800 OCSD 1087 B7
Oxford St
400 CHLV 1330 C3
3600 CRLB 1106 J4
4300 LMSA 1270 F4

50 INDEX
Oxford St
INDEX 50
Parkdale Cir
SAN DIEGO CO.

San Diego County Street Index

STREET
Block City Map# Grid

E Oxford St
- CHLV 1330 E3
Ozark Rd
1400 OCSD 1087 D1
S Ozark St
500 SDGO 1290 A5
Ozland Av
- SDCo 1071 A3
Ozzie Wy
400 SDGO 1290 C4

P

P Alvarado Dr
- CALX 6620 J5
P Montenejano St
1200 CALX 6680 J1
P Rashid St
1200 CALX 6680 J1
P Villanueva Ct
- CALX 6620 J6
P Villanueva St
- CALX 6620 J7
Paauwe Dr
32200 SDCo 1051 B6
Pabellon Cir
11200 SDGO 1250 A2
Pabellon Ct
11200 SDGO 1250 A2
Pablo Dr
16200 SDGO 1170 C4
Pablo Pl
1200 ESCN 1109 J6
Pacato Cir N
12500 SDGO 1170 C2
Pacato Cir S
12600 SDGO 1170 C2
Pacato Ct
17100 SDGO 1170 C2
Pacato Pl
17200 SDGO 1170 C2
Pacato Wy
17100 SDGO 1170 C2
Pacemont Ln
11100 SDGO 1209 E2
Pacer Ln
13300 POWY 1170 E3
Pacesetter St
500 OCSD 1067 E6
Pacific Av
1500 CHLV 1330 A5
200 CRLB 1106 D5
1100 ESCN 1129 H4
7200 LMGR 1270 F6
400 SOLB 1167 E6
Pacific Beach Dr
700 SDGO 1247 J7
2600 SDGO 1248 C6
Pacific Canyon Wy
- SDGO 1208 F4
Pacific Center Blvd
5800 SDGO 1208 E5
Pacific Center Ct
10300 SDGO 1208 F5
Pacific Crest Dr
2100 SDCo 1254 A2
Pacific Crest Wy
29400 SDCo 1297 E4
(See Page 1297)
Pacific Grove Lp
1100 CHLV 1311 F6
Pacific Grove Pl
- SDGO 1188 D6
Pacific Haven Ct
- SDGO 1208 F3
Pacific Heights Blvd
10100 SDGO 1208 F5
Pacific Highlands Pkwy
- SDGO 1188 E3
Pacific Highway
4400 SDGO 1268 F5
1000 SDGO 1288 J3
Pacific Hill St
1000 CHLV 1330 H1
Pacific Hwy
500 SDGO 1288 J4
Pacific Mesa Blvd
10000 SDGO 1208 F6
Pacific Mesa Ct
5900 SDGO 1208 F5
Pacific Mist Ct
1900 SDGO 1290 D7
Pacific Mist Rd
1900 SDGO 1290 D7
Pacific Oaks Pl
1200 ESCN 1129 E5
Pacific Palm Wy
2900 SDGO 1248 F5
Pacific Pl
- SDGO 1188 F4
Pacific Ranch Dr
1500 ENCT 1167 H2
Pacific Rim Ct
800 SDGO 1351 D2
Pacific Riviera Wy
4500 SDGO 1350 G2
Pacific Shores Wy
- SDGO 1208 C2
Pacific St
- ENCT 1147 B2
1200 OCSD 1085 H6

Pacific St
1400 SNMS 1128 D1
N Pacific St
1000 OCSD 1085 J6
100 OCSD 1106 A1
100 SNMS 1108 E6
S Pacific St
1800 OCSD 1106 C3
200 SNMS 1108 D7
500 SNMS 1128 D1
Pacific Sunset Tr
- SDCo 1234 C4
Pacific Surf Dr
700 SOLB 1187 E2
Pacific Ter
1800 OCSD 1106 C4
Pacific View Dr
600 SDGO 1247 G5
Pacific View Ln
- ENCT 1147 D6
Pacific Vista Wy
- SDCo 1108 G1
Pacifica Dr
4800 SDGO 1248 C4
Pacifica Pl
- SDCo 1147 F5
Pacifica Ranch Rd
- SDCo 1148 G7
Pacifica Sv
- CHLV 1311 C6
Pacifica Wy
4300 OCSD 1087 A4
- SDCo 1147 E5
Pacifico Rd
7100 CRLB 1127 F6
Packard Pl
2100 SDCo 1272 C3
Padding River Rd
- CHLV 1311 E6
Paddock Rd
5600 OCSD 1067 F7
Paddy Pl
2000 ESCN 1110 B6
Paden Dr
200 SDCo 1291 B4
Padera Ct
800 CHLV 1310 H5
Padera Wy
500 CHLV 1310 H5
Padgett St
9400 SDGO 1209 E6
Padilla
900 CALX 6680 D1
Padre Ln
9200 SNTE 1231 B7
Padre Tullio Dr
100 SDGO 1350 G3
Padrone Pl
500 CHLV 1310 J5
Padua Hills Pl
200 SDGO 1350 F3
Paducah Dr
3900 SDGO 1248 D4
Page Ln
1200 SNTE 1231 E6
Page Rd
- SDGO 1288 A7
Page St
3400 SDGO 1270 C6
Pageant Av
13100 SDGO 1189 D4
Pagel Pl
100 SDGO 1290 E4
Pagoda Tree Ln
- SDCo 1169 D2
Pagoda Wy
8700 SDGO 1209 C4
Pagosa Ln
12100 SDCo 1231 J1
Paguera Ct
4900 SDGO 1249 H2
Pahls Wy
900 SDCo 1153 B1
Pahvant St
2500 OCSD 1086 D6
Paige Cres
2300 SDCo 1028 A1
Paine Ct
- POWY 1190 G6
Paine Pl
12100 POWY 1190 F7
Paine St
12100 POWY 1190 F7
Paint Brush Cres
32100 SDCo 1318 B7
(See Page 1318)
Paint Mountain Rd
- SDCo 1148 F4
Paintbrush Dr
1900 CHLV 1311 E7
Painted Canyon Rd
15200 SDCo 1169 F5
Painted Cave Av
1500 CHLV 1331 C2
Painted Colt Dr
- ImCo 6560 B6
Painted Desert Dr
2100 CHLV 1331 F3
Painted Desert Rd
14000 POWY 1170 G3

Painted Nettles Glen
5600 SDGO 1188 E4
Painted Pony Cir
1000 VSTA 1107 G2
Painted Rock Rd
- SDCo 1173 F7
Painted Trail Ct
8200 SDCo 1169 B2
Paipa Ln
5400 SDCo 1253 B6
Paisley Ct
100 CHLV 1330 E3
E Paisley St
- CHLV 1330 E3
Paiute Pl
13000 POWY 1190 D3
Paizay Pl
1300 CHLV 1311 F1
Pajama Dr
100 OCSD 1086 D6
Pajaro Wy
11300 SDGO 1149 J7
Pakama Ln
- SDCo 1068 E5
Pala Ct
- CHLV 1330 E3
Pala Del Norte Rd
36300 SDCo 1029 D3
Pala Lake Dr
1700 SDCo 1028 G5
Pala Lilac Rd
38900 SDCo 1029 J6
Pala Loma Dr
10800 SDCo 1049 F3
Pala Mesa Ct
2700 SDCo 1048 F1
Pala Mesa Dr
4100 SDCo 1028 G7
3800 SDCo 1048 F1
Pala Mesa Heights Dr
200 SDCo 1028 H5
1000 SDCo 1029 A5
Pala Mesa Mtn Dr
900 SDCo 1028 J4
Pala Mesa Oaks Dr
- SDCo 1028 G5
Pala Mission Cir
2000 SDCo 1029 H4
Pala Mission Rd
- SDCo 1029 G4
1700 SDCo 1030 C4
Pala Rd
3500 OCSD 1086 F2
4400 OCSD 1087 A1
- SDCo 1029 E4
- SDCo 1030 C4
3100 SDCo 1048 C5
5300 SDCo 1049 A1
- SDCo 1050 J2
Pala St
200 SDCo 1152 E7
7900 SDGO 1290 G3
Pala Temecula Rd
- SDCo 999 G4
36400 SDCo 1029 H2
Pala Vista Dr
300 VSTA 1087 J7
Palabra Cir
11400 SDGO 1250 A2
Palabra Ct
11400 SDGO 1250 A2
Palace Dr
2400 SDGO 1249 F6
Palacio Ct
17000 SDGO 1169 H2
Palacio Dr
7700 CRLB 1147 F2
Palacio Norte
100 SDCo 1027 H2
Palacio Pl
17000 SDGO 1169 H2
Palaie Rd
- SDCo 1252 A1
Palau Cir
- CORD 1309 C5
Palau Rd
1100 CORD 1309 C5
Palawan Wy
100 SDGO 1290 F5
Pale Moon Rd
8100 SDCo 1168 J1
Palencia Ct
900 CHLV 1310 H5
Palencia Pl
900 CHLV 1310 H5
Palenque St
7700 CRLB 1147 F2
Paleo Dr
14800 SDCo 1273 B7
Palermi Pl
- CRLB 1127 C5
Palermo Ct
1900 VSTA 1107 H3
Palermo Dr
5000 OCSD 1087 B1
2300 SDGO 1268 B6
Palero Dr
800 ENCT 1147 C2
Palero Rd
12400 SDGO 1170 C3

Palette Ct
500 OCSD 1087 C1
Palima St
- SDCo 1085 J4
Palin St
5100 SDGO 1290 A5
Palisades Ct
12800 POWY 1190 D2
Palisades Dr
1800 CRLB 1106 H6
14100 POWY 1190 D2
Palisades Rd
4100 SDGO 1269 G1
E Palisades Rd
5300 SDGO 1269 H1
Palito Ct
11400 SDGO 1149 J7
Pallette St
200 ELCJ 1251 F7
Pallon Ct
4100 SDGO 1249 J2
Pallon Wy
11000 SDGO 1249 J2
Pallux Star Ct
- SDCo 1273 D7
Pallux Wy
8300 SDGO 1209 C2
Palm Av
300 CHLV 1330 F6
300 CORD 1288 H5
700 CRLB 1106 F6
1000 ELCJ 1251 E6
100 IMPB 1329 E7
- ImCo 6560 A6
8000 LMGR 1270 H7
4800 LMSA 1270 J2
200 NATC 1289 J7
200 NATC 1290 A7
1100 NATC 1310 A1
1500 SDGO 1329 J7
2800 SDGO 1330 C7
W Palm Av
300 ELCJ 1251 F6
Palm Beach Ln
9600 SDGO 1189 E5
Palm Beach St
1400 CHLV 1311 H7
Palm Canyon Dr
- SDCo 1078 E2
(See Page 1078)
1700 SDCo 1079 E2
(See Page 1079)
200 VSTA 1087 E7
S Palm Canyon Dr
2600 SDGO 1248 A2
Palm Crest Ter
3100 SNMS 1108 B6
Palm Dr
600 BRAW 6260 B7
(See Page 6260)
300 BRAW 6320 B1
(See Page 6320)
- CALX 6620 F7
3800 CHLV 1310 J3
- ELCJ 1251 J6
100 OCSD 1085 J7
4100 SDCo 1310 J3
500 VSTA 1087 H5
Palm Glen Dr
10300 SNTE 1231 E4
Palm Hill Dr
3000 SDCo 1088 E6
Palm Ln
2700 LMGR 1270 J7
9700 SDCo 1149 E3
- SDCo 1232 D6
Palm Point Ct
5000 SDGO 1248 F6
Palm Rd
400 SNMS 1108 E6
E Palm Rd
1600 CHLV 1330 F5
Palm Ridge Dr
4000 SDCo 1028 F3
Palm Row Dr
10500 SDCo 1231 H2
Palm St
8500 LMGR 1270 J7
400 SDGO 1269 A7
5100 SDGO 1270 A7
W Palm St
600 CALX 6620 E7
1100 SDGO 1268 J7
100 SDGO 1269 A7
1400 SDGO 1288 J1
Palm Ter
800 ESCN 1129 J6
Palm Tree Ct
4100 SDCo 1271 G4
Palm Valley Cir
900 CHLV 1311 G4
Palm View Ct
1400 NATC 1310 A1
Palm View Dr
1400 NATC 1310 A1
Palm View Wy
1500 NATC 1310 A1
Palm Vista Ct
- SDCo 1272 C5
Palma Vista Ct
1200 SDCo 1130 E6
Palmac St
400 SNMS 1108 E6

Palmas Ct
3600 OCSD 1107 D3
Palmas Norte
100 SDCo 1028 A2
Palmbark St
400 VSTA 1087 E6
Palmer Dr
2300 OCSD 1106 H2
Palmer St
2900 NATC 1310 B1
Palmer Wy
5700 CRLB 1127 D1
1200 NATC 1290 C7
1300 NATC 1310 C1
Palmera Dr
- OCSD 1087 D3
Palmero Dr
16700 SDGO 1170 C3
Palmetto Dr
2700 CRLB 1127 G3
4800 OCSD 1067 A7
Palmetto Point Ct
2800 CHLV 1312 A5
(See Page 1312)
Palmetto Wy
4000 SDGO 1268 H5
Palmilla Dr
7500 SDGO 1228 B4
Palmitas St
400 SOLB 1187 F1
Palmview Av
- ELCN 6559 G4
Palmwood Ct
500 SDGO 1290 G6
Palmwood Dr
500 SDGO 1290 G6
Palmyra Av
100 SDCo 1108 C3
5200 SDGO 1228 H7
Palmyra Dr
100 SDCo 1108 C3
Palo Alto Ct
800 SNMS 1108 H6
Palo Alto Dr
2100 CHLV 1311 D2
Palo Alto Ln
6700 SDGO 1290 E4
Palo Brea St
- IMPE 6439 C6
Palo Ct
3700 SDCo 1310 E4
Palo Danzante
2300 SDCo 1254 C1
Palo Dr
3800 SDCo 1310 E4
Palo Glen
1800 ESCN 1109 F6
Palo Verde Av
- IMPE 6499 D3
Palo Verde Dr
- SDCo 1085 J4
Palo Verde Ln
4600 SDCo 1099 F4
(See Page 1099)
Palo Verde Ter
4400 SDGO 1269 H1
Palo Verde Wy
3700 OCSD 1107 B2
Palo Vista Rd
2300 SDCo 1028 C7
Paloma
- SNTE 1231 F6
Paloma Bay Ct
300 OCSD 1066 J6
Paloma Ct
500 ENCT 1147 E5
- SDCo 1085 J3
Paloma Ln
300 SDCo 1252 H4
Paloma Wy
1600 SDCo 1319 H2
(See Page 1319)
Palomar Airport Rd
1300 CRLB 1126 J3
1900 CRLB 1127 C4
Palomar Av
600 ELCJ 1251 E7
300 SDGO 1247 E2
Palomar Divide Truck Trl
- SDCo 1031 E1
- SDCo 1032 C4
- SDCo 1033 C4
- SDCo 1053 H1
(See Page 1053)
Palomar Dr
300 CHLV 1330 C2
3600 SDCo 1047 J3
4500 SDCo 1048 A5
300 SNMS 1109 D7
1400 SNMS 1129 C1
E Palomar Dr
- CHLV 1330 E1
Palomar Oaks Ct
6300 CRLB 1127 D4
Palomar Oaks Wy
1900 CRLB 1127 C4
Palomar Pl
1400 VSTA 1088 B3
Palomar Point Wy
1900 CRLB 1127 C2
Palomar St
- CHLV 1311 D7

Palomar St
400 CHLV 1330 D3
- CHLV 1331 B1
E Palomar St
1900 CHLV 1311 E7
100 CHLV 1330 F3
Palomar Ter
1200 ESCN 1130 B2
Palomar Vista Dr
- OCSD 1087 D2
- SDCo 1070 F1
Palomar Vista Rd
3400 SDCo 1052 C2
(See Page 1052)
Palomar Wy
- OCSD 1087 A4
Palomarcos Av
1500 SNMS 1108 E6
Palomares Ct
1200 SDCo 1027 H6
Palomares Rd
1800 SDCo 1027 H6
Palomino Cir
2600 SDGO 1248 A2
Palomino Ct
- OCSD 1067 F7
700 SNMS 1109 C5
Palomino Dr
3400 ENCT 1148 D4
800 SNMS 1109 C5
Palomino Ln
1600 SDCo 1130 C4
Palomino Mesa Ct
16200 SDCo 1169 E5
Palomino Mesa Pl
16200 SDCo 1169 F4
Palomino Mesa Rd
15000 SDCo 1169 E5
Palomino Mesa Wy
15100 SDCo 1169 F4
Palomino Rd
400 SDCo 1027 G5
Palomino Ridge Dr
9500 SDCo 1232 G3
Palomino Valley Ct
16000 SDCo 1169 F5
Palomino Valley Pl
15100 SDCo 1169 F5
Palomino Valley Rd
16200 SDCo 1169 F5
Palomira Ct
2200 CHLV 1311 G6
Palos Tierra Rd
12400 SDCo 1070 B7
Palos Verdes Dr
31700 SDCo 1049 A7
31600 SDCo 1069 A1
Palsero Av
1900 ESCN 1129 F6
Pam Ln
13100 SDCo 1232 C2
Pambara Cir
1400 OCSD 1106 E1
Pamela Ct
4100 SDGO 1248 E2
Pamela Dr
100 SDCo 1028 E1
Pamela Ln
800 ELCJ 1271 E1
1900 ESCN 1109 D4
Pamjoy Ln
3600 SDCo 1271 A5
Pamo Av
2400 SDGO 1289 E1
Pamo Rd
1500 SDCo 1152 H2
Pamo Wintercamp Rd
- SDCo 1171 J5
Pamoosa Ln
29200 SDCo 1069 D6
Pampa St
8700 LMSA 1251 A6
Pampas Ln
1700 SDCo 1099 F2
(See Page 1099)
Pamplona Ct
2100 SDCo 1130 B5
Pamplona Wy
2200 CRLB 1127 F7
Pan American Plz
2000 SDGO 1289 B1
Pan American Rd W
2100 SDGO 1289 B1
Pana Dr
- SDCo 1232 D6
Panache Dr
4700 SDCo 1048 H1
Panama Pl
4900 SDGO 1269 F2
Panamint Row
6800 SDGO 1290 F7
Panasonic Wy
7500 SDGO 1351 E2
Panay Ct
1600 SDGO 1289 H1
Panchoy Dr
4600 SDCo 1271 F3
Panchoy St
8200 LMGR 1290 H1
Pandora Dr
9900 SDCo 1271 D1

Panel Ct
6400 SDGO 1228 F5
Panella Ct
- OCSD 1067 A5
Panettah Dr
1700 SDCo 1233 G7
Pangea Dr
- SDGO 1227 J1
Panhandle Trl
7300 SDCo 1138 B7
(See Page 1138)
Pankey Rd
100 SDCo 1028 H5
- SDCo 1048 J1
Panno St
- BRAW 6319 F4
(See Page 6319)
Pannonia Rd
4600 CRLB 1106 H7
Panocha Ct
6800 SDGO 1270 E7
Panorama Av
1400 SDCo 1128 C4
Panorama Crest
2800 SDCo 1150 A2
Panorama Dr
4600 LMSA 1271 A3
3200 SDCo 1156 E1
4700 SDGO 1269 C3
Panorama Rd
1700 VSTA 1087 G3
Panorama Ridge Ct
8300 SDCo 1290 H5
Panorama Ridge Rd
1200 OCSD 1087 D3
Panorama Trl
31400 SDCo 1073 G1
(See Page 1073)
Panorama View
15000 SDCo 1051 A6
Panoramic Dr
- SDCo 1088 C1
Panoramic Ln
- SDGO 1208 E4
Panoramic Pl
- SDCo 1088 D1
Panoramic Wy
- SDCo 1068 D7
Pansy Wy
1000 SDCo 1252 E7
Pantaneiro Pl
200 SDCo 1028 H5
Pantera Wy
- SDGO 1289 B1
Panterra Rd
13200 SDGO 1187 J4
Panterra Wy
3500 SDGO 1187 J4
Panther Wy
- VSTA 1087 H3
Paola Pl
4600 SDGO 1248 H1
Paola Wy
4400 SDGO 1248 H2
Papagallo Ct
11700 SDGO 1250 B3
Papagallo Dr
5500 OCSD 1067 C2
Papagayo Ct
1800 VSTA 1107 G6
Papago Dr
13000 POWY 1190 D4
Papago Trl
15300 SDCo 1176 E4
(See Page 1176)
Papaya St
400 VSTA 1087 E6
Papaya Wy
3500 OCSD 1086 F2
Papin St
1400 OCSD 1086 B5
Papoose Ct
11100 SDGO 1149 H7
Pappas Ct
- CHLV 1331 A2
Pappas Rd
24500 SDCo 1173 F4
Paprika Rd
30000 SDCo 1297 F4
(See Page 1297)
Paprika Wy
3800 OCSD 1086 H4
Papyrus Ct
2400 OCSD 1106 F2
Paquita St
700 ELCJ 1252 B7
Par Dr
3300 OCSD 1106 J1
3300 SDCo 1270 J5
Par Four Dr
- SDCo 1272 C6
Par Valley Rd
28900 SDCo 1088 F1
Par View Ct
- SDCo 1089 F3
Para Siempre Vista Rd
20100 SDCo 1152 D1
Paradise Av
3600 NATC 1290 C6
Paradise Cove Wy
700 OCSD 1066 F7

Paradise Creek Ln
49000 SDCo 1071 E5
Paradise Crest View Wy
6600 SDGO 1290 E6
Paradise Ct
1800 VSTA 1107 G6
Paradise Dr
900 NATC 1290 A7
1100 NATC 1310 A1
14000 POWY 1190 G3
Paradise Hills Rd
2000 SDGO 1290 F6
Paradise Meadow Ln
26900 SDCo 1091 F4
Paradise Mesa Rd
1700 SDGO 1290 D6
Paradise Mountain Rd
17200 SDCo 1091 D5
Paradise Park Dr
9000 SDCo 1231 J6
Paradise Ranch Rd
30500 SDCo 1070 G5
Paradise Rd
2600 CRLB 1127 G3
1400 SDGO 1290 B6
Paradise Ridge Ct
2800 CHLV 1312 A5
(See Page 1312)
Paradise Ridge Rd
6500 SDGO 1290 E6
Paradise Ridge Wy
1300 CHLV 1312 A6
(See Page 1312)
Paradise St
1800 ESCN 1109 H5
1900 SDGO 1290 D1
Paradise Trail Rd
- CHLV 1311 H5
Paradise Valley Ct
8100 SDCo 1290 H5
Paradise Valley Rd
- SDCo 1033 J2
8100 SDCo 1290 J5
6400 SDGO 1290 D6
Paradise View Dr
400 SDCo 1108 A2
Paradisio Pl
10400 SDCo 1169 F2
Paradox Ln
200 SDCo 1252 J2
Paragon Mesa Rd
- SDCo 1191 D5
Paraiso Av
800 SDCo 1291 C3
Paraiso Rd
3600 SDCo 1047 E3
Parakeet Pl
1100 VSTA 1087 G4
Parallel Glen
300 ESCN 1129 H2
Paramount Av
- ESCN 1130 C1
Paramount Dr
4600 SDGO 1249 D2
Parasio Ct
1400 NATC 1289 J7
Parc Ln
- SDGO 1270 B5
Pardee Pl
3500 SDGO 1289 F5
Pardee St
200 SDGO 1289 F4
S Pardee St
400 SDGO 1289 F4
Parianos Dr
1200 CHLV 1330 D3
Paris Wy
6700 SDGO 1310 F1
Parish Rd
12600 SDGO 1170 C3
Pariva Dr
1800 ENCT 1167 E3
Park Av
700 ELCN 6499 G6
- SDCo 1290 J6
10400 SNTE 1231 E6
100 VSTA 1087 H6
E Park Av
100 ELCJ 1251 F5
200 ESCN 1129 J2
100 SDGO 1350 G4
W Park Av
100 ELCJ 1251 F5
300 SDGO 1350 G4
Park Blvd
100 SDCo 1252 H3
4600 SDGO 1269 C4
1400 SDGO 1289 B2
Park Center Dr
900 VSTA 1107 J7
- VSTA 1127 H1
Park Creek Ct
300 SNMS 1129 B1
Park Crest Dr
1900 ENCT 1167 F3
Park Crest Ln
9800 SDGO 1249 F1
Park Crest Wy
5200 SDGO 1249 F1
Park Ct
4900 CRLB 1106 J7
- IMPE 6499 J2

Park Dale Ln
2000 ENCT 1147 H7
Park Dr
1300 CHLV 1330 G3
3900 CRLB 1106 G6
4900 CRLB 1107 A7
- ESCN 1150 B2
900 SDCo 1129 H7
800 SDCo 1149 H1
3800 SDCo 1156 E2
9300 SDCo 1235 J3
2300 SDCo 1252 H4
- SDGO 1248 A4
N Park Dr
100 SDCo 1252 H3
Park Grove Ct
- LMGR 1290 F1
Park Haven Ct
4000 SDGO 1289 H4
Park Hill Dr
1000 ESCN 1130 B3
Park Hill Ln
1400 ESCN 1130 B4
1000 SDCo 1130 B3
Park Hill Pl
1000 SDCo 1107 H3
Park Hill Rd
2000 SDCo 1107 H3
Park Lilac Ln
11600 SDCo 1049 H7
Park Ln
500 ENCT 1147 D7
100 ESCN 1129 J2
8500 LMSA 1270 J4
- OCSD 1085 J7
- SDCo 1254 G7
- SDCo 1274 G1
Park Meadows Rd
1000 CHLV 1311 H5
Park Mesa Wy
6900 SDGO 1248 J6
Park Pl
1000 CORD 1288 H7
700 ESCN 1129 J1
0 RivC 999 F1
4100 SDGO 1269 G3
300 SNMS 1128 F1
Park Plaza Dr
9000 LMSA 1251 A6
Park Ranch Glen
300 ESCN 1150 B1
Park Rd
- ESCN 1150 B2
- SDGO 1268 A5
Park Ridge Blvd
6600 SDGO 1250 E5
Park Ridge Dr
2500 SDCo 1130 D7
Park Rim Ct
3300 SDGO 1228 C7
Park Rim Dr
5000 SDGO 1228 D7
Park Row
1500 SDGO 1227 F6
Park Run Rd
8600 SDGO 1189 C5
Park St
25800 SDCo 1109 F2
Park Terrrace Dr
9700 SNTE 1231 D4
Park Valley Ln
1900 SDGO 1290 F6
Park View
- ESCN 1129 E6
Park View Ct
7300 SNTE 1230 F7
Park View Dr
- BRAW 6259 F6
(See Page 6259)
Park View Pl
1500 CORD 1288 J7
Park Villa Dr
3500 SDGO 1269 D6
Park Villa Pl
900 ESCN 1130 A3
Park Village Rd
7100 SDGO 1188 H7
- SDGO 1189 C6
Park Vista Ct
6900 SDGO 1290 F6
Park West Av
5000 SDGO 1228 D7
Park West Ln
3400 SDGO 1228 D7
Park Wy
300 CHLV 1310 B6
Parkbrook Ln
8400 SDGO 1290 J4
Parkbrook Pl
200 SDGO 1290 J4
Parkbrook St
300 SDCo 1290 J4
600 SDCo 1291 A3
8300 SDGO 1290 H4
Parkbrook Wy
200 SDGO 1290 J4
Parkcreek Ct
100 SDGO 1290 H4
Parkdale Av
10900 SDGO 1209 A3
Parkdale Cir
7600 SDGO 1209 A4

51 INDEX
Parkdale Cove
INDEX 51
Pebblebrook Wy
SAN DIEGO CO.

San Diego County Street Index

STREET
Block City Map# Grid

Parkdale Cove
7700 SDGO 1209 A3
Parkdale Ct
7700 SDGO 1209 A3
Parkdale Pl
7700 SDGO 1209 A4
Parker Ln
1600 SDCo 1152 F7
Parker Mtn Rd
1900 CHLV 1311 E7
Parker Pl
1200 SDGO 1247 J7
1000 VSTA 1087 J6
Parker Rd
- ImCo 6500 F5
- ImCo 6560 F1
Parker St
600 OCSD 1067 A5
E Parker St
5100 OCSD 1067 B5
Parkett Ln
100 ELCJ 1251 G5
Parkhurst Sq
- SDGO 1208 B2
Parkland Wy
1900 SDGO 1290 E6
Parklawn Dr
1600 SDCo 1251 G1
Parkmead Ct
5800 SDGO 1290 C5
Parkplace Ct
8700 SDGO 1249 C2
Parks Av
4300 LMSA 1270 G4
Parkside Av
6200 SDGO 1310 E2
Parkside Cs
8200 SDGO 1169 B3
Parkside Ct
400 CHLV 1310 G5
7000 SDGO 1310 F1
Parkside Dr
500 CHLV 1310 G5
400 OCSD 1086 E3
- SDGO 1169 D3
Parkside Glen
200 ESCN 1109 G5
Parkside Pl
4200 CRLB 1106 G6
3100 SDGO 1310 E2
- SNTE 1231 C5
Parkside St
12300 SDCo 1232 A3
Parktree Ln
2200 ESCN 1109 H5
Parkview Dr
1100 OCSD 1067 A4
5400 SDGO 1248 A3
1500 VSTA 1107 J5
Parkview Lp
15900 SDGO 1169 D3
Parkview Ter
1900 SDGO 1248 A3
Parkway Centre Dr
- POWY 1190 F7
Parkway Dr
8400 LMSA 1250 J7
7300 LMSA 1270 F1
Parkway Plaza
- ELCJ 1251 E4
Parkwood Av
900 VSTA 1108 B6
Parkwood Dr
600 SDGO 1290 H6
Parkwood Ln
400 ENCT 1147 B2
- OCSD 1106 C1
Parkyns Av
1100 ImCo 6560 B7
- ImCo 6620 B1
Parlange Pl
17600 SDGO 1170 A1
Parliament Rd
1800 ENCT 1146 J2
Parma Ct
12500 SDGO 1170 C2
Parma Ln
7600 SDGO 1209 A3
Parnassus Cir
100 OCSD 1086 E6
Parnell Ct
12400 POWY 1190 D7
Parrolette Ct
5400 OCSD 1067 B3
Parrot St
1700 SDGO 1289 G2
Parsley Wy
800 OCSD 1086 H5
Parsons Landing
1000 SDGO 1330 J7
Parsons Ln
500 SNMS 1109 A2
Parthenon Dr
2700 SDGO 1310 F1
Partridge Av
1300 ELCJ 1251 D3
Partridge Cir
400 VSTA 1087 G5
Partridge Ct
- SNMS 1128 E3

Partridge Glen
1300 ESCN 1129 G6
Partridge Ln
1300 OCSD 1086 E7
Partridge Pl
7000 CRLB 1127 D6
Parus Pt
9300 SDGO 1189 D6
Parvenu Ln
1500 SDCo 1027 H5
Parvo Ct
18100 SDGO 1150 B7
Pasadena Av
7900 LMSA 1270 H3
200 SDCo 1027 F3
Pasadena Ct
2200 CHLV 1331 G2
Pasadero Dr
1100 ESCN 1129 F5
Pasall Rd
- SDCo 1051 J6
Pasatiempo Av
6200 SDGO 1250 D6
Pasatiempo Glen
2500 ESCN 1130 B7
Pascal Ct
5900 CRLB 1127 D2
Pascal Dr
1400 CHLV 1311 E7
Pascali Ct
700 SNMS 1109 A5
Pascoe St
1200 SDGO 1269 B5
Paseo Abrazo
3100 CRLB 1127 J5
Paseo Acampo
- CRLB 1127 H2
Paseo Adelante
6500 CRLB 1127 J4
Paseo Airoso
- CRLB 1127 J2
Paseo Ajanta
15500 SDGO 1169 J6
Paseo Al-Monte
7700 SDCo 1237 C6
Paseo Alameda
- CRLB 1127 J2
Paseo Albacete
11300 SDGO 1169 J6
Paseo Aldabra
13800 SDGO 1189 D3
Paseo Alegre
200 SNMS 1109 D7
Paseo Aliso
- CRLB 1147 F3
Paseo Allegria Av
10600 SDCo 1169 F4
Paseo Almendro
- CRLB 1147 H3
Paseo Almiar
- CRLB 1127 G2
Paseo Alta Rico
- CRLB 1127 H3
Paseo Ancho
- SDCo 1147 J4
Paseo Arbolado
6100 SDCo 1168 D3
Paseo Arrayan
- CRLB 1147 H3
Paseo Aspado
- CRLB 1127 J4
Paseo Aurora
1500 SDGO 1350 G1
Paseo Austin
- IMPE 6499 E2
Paseo Avellano
- CRLB 1147 G2
Paseo Bello
8700 SNTE 1230 H7
Paseo Bonita
13700 POWY 1190 F6
1600 SDGO 1247 H3
Paseo Burga
500 CHLV 1310 J5
Paseo Callado
6200 CRLB 1127 J3
Paseo Camas
- CRLB 1127 G2
Paseo Camino Real
1200 CALX 6680 H1
Paseo Canada
600 SNMS 1128 J2
Paseo Candelero
2300 CRLB 1127 G6
Paseo Capuchina
7300 CRLB 1148 A1
Paseo Cardiel
13700 SDGO 1189 F3
Paseo Carina
1600 CHLV 1312 A7
(See Page 1312)
Paseo Carreta
- CRLB 1127 J2
Paseo Castanada
11000 SDCo 1271 G4
Paseo Cazador
- CRLB 1127 J4
Paseo Cerro
- CRLB 1127 J4
Paseo Cevera
13700 SDGO 1189 E3

Paseo Cielo
3000 SDCo 1148 A7
Paseo Colina
- CRLB 1127 H3
12400 POWY 1190 B6
Paseo Corono
- CRLB 1127 J4
Paseo Corto
- CRLB 1127 J3
Paseo Corvus
1600 CHLV 1312 A7
(See Page 1312)
Paseo Cresta
9100 SNTE 1231 B7
9100 SNTE 1251 B1
2000 VSTA 1087 G2
Paseo Cristal
- CRLB 1148 B2
3100 ESCN 1150 A2
Paseo Culzada
3100 ESCN 1150 A2
Paseo De Alicia
3400 OCSD 1106 J2
Paseo De Alteza
- CALX 6680 J1
Paseo De Anza
2000 VSTA 1087 G2
Paseo De Brisas
3400 OCSD 1106 J2
Paseo De Caballo
25200 SDCo 1173 H5
Paseo De Colores
- OCSD 1106 J2
Paseo De Columbia
- OCSD 1106 J2
Paseo De Elenita
3500 OCSD 1106 J2
Paseo De Francisco
3500 OCSD 1106 J2
Paseo De Fuentes
3300 NATC 1310 D4
Paseo De La Frontera
- SDGO 1352 A4
Paseo De La Fuente
7300 SDCo 1352 C1
- SDGO 1351 H3
Paseo De La Huerta
13600 POWY 1170 E6
Paseo De La Vista
4300 SDCo 1310 G1
Paseo De Las America
2400 SDGO 1352 A3
Paseo De Las Cumbres
13700 POWY 1170 F6
Paseo De Las Flores
- ENCT 1147 D4
Paseo De Las Plantas
- ENCT 1147 D3
Paseo De Las Verdes
1400 ENCT 1147 D5
Paseo De Laura
2300 OCSD 1106 H2
Paseo De Linda
10300 SDCo 1169 E2
Paseo De Los Americanos
3500 OCSD 1106 J2
Paseo De Los Arboles
1800 SDCo 1028 A4
Paseo De Los Californianos
3500 OCSD 1107 A2
Paseo De Los Peregri
- SDCo 1089 J1
Paseo De Los Reyes
- CALX 6680 H1
Paseo De Los Suenos
19000 SDCo 1149 A3
Paseo De Los Virreyes
- CALX 6680 H1
Paseo De Majestad
- CALX 6680 H1
Paseo De Marguerita
9100 SNTE 1231 B7
Paseo De Ocho Minos
- SDCo 1191 E6
Paseo De Olivos
3500 SDCo 1047 G3
Paseo De Paz
4100 NATC 1310 D3
Paseo De Paz Ct
3400 NATC 1310 E4
Paseo De Piedras
17300 SDCo 1169 C2
Paseo De Sabato
4000 NATC 1310 E5
Paseo De Santos
- SDCo 1089 E2
Paseo Del Arquero
100 VSTA 1088 A5
Paseo Del Arroyo
15500 POWY 1170 F6
1800 SDCo 1028 A4
Paseo Del Bianco
2800 SDCo 1130 E7
Paseo Del Bosque
500 VSTA 1107 J2
Paseo Del Campo
- SDCo 1272 C7
Paseo Del Ceilo
- ENCT 1147 D3

Paseo Del Cerro
1100 CHLV 1311 A7
Paseo Del Concho
400 SNMS 1128 J2
Paseo Del Conquistador
- CALX 6680 H1
Paseo Del Emperador
- CALX 6680 J1
Paseo Del Lago
6300 CRLB 1127 C4
900 SDCo 1047 H3
Paseo Del Lago Dr
1800 VSTA 1107 G5
Paseo Del Mar
13500 SDCo 1232 E7
Paseo Del Norte
1000 CHLV 1311 A7
5400 CRLB 1126 H2
6700 CRLB 1127 A5
Paseo Del Norte Ct
5300 CRLB 1126 G2
Paseo Del Ocaso
- CALX 6620 H5
8300 SDGO 1227 H5
Paseo Del Oro
1600 CHLV 1331 C3
Paseo Del Paso
900 CHLV 1330 J1
Paseo Del Rey
700 CHLV 1310 H6
8600 SNTE 1231 B7
1900 VSTA 1087 G2
Paseo Del Sol
2800 SDCo 1130 E7
8500 SNTE 1231 B7
- VSTA 1087 G3
Paseo Del Sur
15800 SDGO 1169 C3
Paseo Del Terreno
29300 SDCo 1237 D6
Paseo Del Verano
13000 SDGO 1170 D1
Paseo Del Verano Norte
12700 SDGO 1150 D7
Paseo Del Vista
6700 CRLB 1128 A5
Paseo Delicias
- SDCo 1168 F1
Paseo Descanso
- CRLB 1127 J3
Paseo Dominguez
- CRLB 1127 H4
Paseo Donito
2100 SDCo 1234 D7
Paseo Dorado
1900 SDGO 1227 G5
600 SNMS 1129 A2
Paseo Dr
8500 SNTE 1231 D7
Paseo Elegancia
- CRLB 1127 H3
Paseo Elegante
- ENCT 1147 C3
Paseo Encantada
7700 SDCo 1237 D6
Paseo Encino
- CRLB 1148 B2
Paseo Ensillar
- CRLB 1127 G2
Paseo Entrada
1000 CHLV 1331 A1
Paseo Escuela
- CRLB 1127 H3
Paseo Esmerado
- SDCo 1148 A4
Paseo Esplanada
8200 SDCo 1149 A3
Paseo Establo
- CRLB 1127 H4
Paseo Estribo
- CRLB 1127 H3
Paseo Fraternidad
1800 SDGO 1350 F3
Paseo Frontera
6500 CRLB 1127 H4
Paseo Fuerte
11900 SDCo 1271 J3
Paseo Grande
2100 SDCo 1272 C1
Paseo Grande Rd
- SDCo 1068 C4
Paseo Granto
- CRLB 1127 G2
Paseo Hermosa
1200 OCSD 1087 D2
17100 SDCo 1168 G5
Paseo Hermoso
15700 POWY 1170 E5
Paseo Iglesia
8400 SDCo 1290 J5
Paseo Indus
1600 CHLV 1312 A7
(See Page 1312)
Paseo Internacional
2500 SDGO 1352 A3
Paseo Jaquita
- CRLB 1127 H3
Paseo Jenghiz
15500 SDGO 1169 J6
Paseo La Cresta
900 CHLV 1330 J1

Paseo La Jolla
- CRLB 1147 F3
Paseo Ladera
1200 CHLV 1330 J1
- SNTE 1251 B1
2000 VSTA 1087 G2
Paseo Lago
11500 SDCo 1231 H3
Paseo Laredo
6900 SDGO 1247 H1
Paseo Lazo
- CRLB 1127 H4
Paseo Lindo
31700 SDCo 1067 G1
Paseo Los Gatos
- CHLV 1311 F1
Paseo Lucido
12900 SDGO 1170 B6
Paseo Lunada
- CRLB 1127 H4
Paseo Lupino
- CRLB 1148 A1
Paseo Lyra
1600 CHLV 1312 A7
(See Page 1312)
Paseo Magda
1200 CHLV 1311 A6
Paseo Marguerita
1100 CHLV 1330 J1
300 VSTA 1087 G2
N Paseo Marguerita
- VSTA 1087 G2
Paseo Membrillo
- CRLB 1147 H3
Paseo Mirada
2600 SDGO 1248 A2
Paseo Monona
- CRLB 1127 J2
Paseo Montalban
9600 SDGO 1189 E4
Paseo Montanas
4100 SDGO 1188 B6
Paseo Montanoso
11100 SDGO 1169 H6
Paseo Monte
2400 SDCo 1047 H3
Paseo Montebatalla
12200 SDGO 1150 B5
Paseo Montenero
15900 SDGO 1169 C3
Paseo Montril
9800 SDGO 1189 F5
Paseo Orion
1400 SDGO 1350 H1
Paseo Orozco
3700 SDCo 1271 G5
Paseo Pacifica
300 ENCT 1147 C6
Paseo Palero
- CRLB 1127 J3
Paseo Palmas Dr
10300 SDCo 1231 H3
Paseo Palmas Wy
11500 SDCo 1231 H3
Paseo Pantera
18400 SDCo 1153 C5
Paseo Park Dr
10200 SDCo 1231 H3
Paseo Penasco
15300 SDCo 1151 A2
Paseo Picado
- CRLB 1127 G2
Paseo Piedras
- SDCo 1149 A3
Paseo Pkwy
- SDCo 1231 G3
Paseo Plomo
7200 CRLB 1128 B6
Paseo Portero
- CRLB 1127 J4
Paseo Potril
2700 SDCo 1290 J7
Paseo Pradera
- CRLB 1127 J2
Paseo Primavera
1100 CHLV 1311 A7
- ENCT 1147 D3
Paseo Primero
- SDCo 1168 A6
Paseo Privado
- CRLB 1127 J3
Paseo Ranchero
- CHLV 1311 A7
- CHLV 1331 B1
Paseo Rio
600 VSTA 1107 E1
Paseo Roble Rd
29300 SDCo 1070 J6
Paseo Rojo
10000 SDCo 1069 D2
Paseo Rosal
500 CHLV 1310 J5
Paseo Salamoner
3500 SDCo 1271 G5
Paseo Salida Glen
- ESCN 1130 A4
Paseo Salinero
- CRLB 1127 G3
Paseo Sarina
1100 CHLV 1311 A7

Paseo Saucedal
- CRLB 1147 G2
Paseo Sequieros
3900 SDCo 1271 G5
Paseo Siembra
4100 SDCo 1067 G1
Paseo Sierra
1100 CHLV 1311 A7
Paseo Sonora Glen
- ESCN 1130 A4
Paseo Tamayo
3900 SDCo 1271 H4
Paseo Tapajos
6100 CRLB 1127 H3
Paseo Taxco
- ENCT 1147 J4
Paseo Temporada
9500 SDGO 1189 E4
Paseo Tesoro
- CRLB 1127 J2
Paseo Tiempo Glen
100 ESCN 1130 A4
Paseo Tienda
- CRLB 1127 J3
Paseo Tierra
700 SNMS 1129 A2
Paseo Tobarra
10100 SDGO 1189 G5
Paseo Tulipero
- CRLB 1147 F3
Paseo Valencia
- SDCo 1168 F7
- SDCo 1188 G1
Paseo Valiente
- CRLB 1127 J2
Paseo Valino
- CRLB 1127 J2
Paseo Valle
- CRLB 1127 G2
Paseo Valle Alto
13700 POWY 1170 F6
Paseo Veracruz
- CHLV 1311 F1
Paseo Verde
1100 CHLV 1331 A1
- CRLB 1127 J7
7600 SDGO 1189 A3
Paseo Victoria
- SDCo 1148 D7
Paseo View Ct
- SDGO 1187 J7
Paseo Vista
11500 SDCo 1231 H3
Paseo Vista Famosa
3600 SDCo 1168 D7
Paseo Volante
- CRLB 1127 J2
Paseo Vuelo
- CRLB 1127 J4
Paseo Zaldivar
13700 SDGO 1189 E3
Paseo Zuniga
3900 SDCo 1271 G4
Paseos De Las Flores
300 DLMR 1187 E4
Pasita De Kristy
10900 SDCo 1231 F3
Paso Alto Ct
2600 SDCo 1299 J3
(See Page 1299)
Paso De Flora
10000 SDCo 1069 D3
Paso Del Lagos
- SDCo 1067 G2
Paso Del Norte
400 SDCo 1109 G2
Paso Del Sol
15000 SDCo 1168 A7
Paso Oro Verde
3900 SDCo 997 G4
Paso Robles Ct
- CHLV 1311 F3
29300 SDCo 1070 J6
Paso Robles Ln
- SDCo 1070 J5
Paso Robles Pl
15200 SDCo 1070 J5
Paso Robles Rd
- SDCo 1070 J5
Paso Tenis
16100 SDCo 1168 F7
Pasqual Highlands Rd
- SDCo 1152 D1
Passerine Wy
- SDGO 1208 E4
Passiflora Av
700 ENCT 1147 D5
Passiflora Pl
1000 ENCT 1147 D4
Passing Ln
200 SDCo 1153 C5
Passion Pl
900 SDCo 1152 G6
Passy Av
2800 SDGO 1228 B6
Pastel Ct
4800 OCSD 1087 C1
Pasternack Pl
3100 SDGO 1249 D5
Pasteur Ct
2000 CRLB 1127 C2

Pastoral Rd
12000 SDGO 1170 B3
Pastoral Wy
1700 SDCo 1128 B2
Pasture Ln
9100 SNTE 1231 F6
Pat St
7900 LMSA 1250 H6
Pata Ranch Rd
13500 SDCo 1212 F4
Pata View Dr
15200 SDCo 1212 H6
Pate Rd
- SDCo 1023 D2
Pater St
- BRAW 6259 H7
(See Page 6259)
Patero Ct
1400 LMGR 1290 F2
Pathfinder Wy
5900 SDCo 1311 B2
Pathos Ct
8400 SDGO 1189 C6
Pathos Ln
12300 SDGO 1189 C6
Pathway St
9500 SNTE 1231 C7
Patiences Pl
5300 OCSD 1067 D7
Patina Ct
4800 OCSD 1087 B2
10900 SDGO 1210 A2
Patina St
17100 SDCo 1169 F2
Patmos Wy
6000 OCSD 1107 F5
Patos Pl
500 CHLV 1311 B4
Patra Wy
5000 OCSD 1107 E4
Patria Dr
4500 SDGO 1270 E3
Patricia Av
300 CHLV 1310 C6
Patricia Cir
1100 VSTA 1088 A7
Patricia Ct
- SNTE 1231 E7
Patricia Ln
600 ELCJ 1251 E6
600 VSTA 1088 A7
Patricia Pl
4600 SDGO 1269 J3
Patricia Rd
- SDCo 1050 D5
Patrick Dr
200 SDCo 1253 D1
Patrick Wy
31800 SDCo 1069 F1
Patriot St
10200 SDGO 1249 G5
Patten St
300 SDGO 1290 D4
Patterson Rd
2300 ESCN 1130 D1
- SDGO 1287 J5
Patti Dr
300 VSTA 1087 H3
Patton Oak Rd
200 SDCo 997 F7
Patty Hill Dr
200 SOLB 1167 E6
Patty Ln
300 ENCT 1147 B3
Patty Lou Dr
10100 SDCo 1232 B3
Paul Barwick Ct
11200 SDGO 1208 J2
Paul Jones Av
3600 SDGO 1248 D5
Paul Robinson Ct
- ELCN 6559 J4
Paul St
600 ESCN 1130 C2
Paul Wy
1000 ESCN 1130 C2
Paula Dr
- SDCo 1109 G6
Paula St
900 ESCN 1110 C6
4000 LMSA 1270 F5
Paula Wy
1000 ESCN 1110 B5
Paulann Ct
1500 SDCo 1027 G4
Paulin Av
400 CALX 6680 F1
- ImCo 6620 B1
Paulina Ter
16500 POWY 1170 D4
Pauline Av
500 ELCJ 1251 G6
Pauline Wy
2700 OCSD 1087 B7
Pauling Av
4700 SDGO 1228 F4
Paulsen Av
700 ELCJ 1251 E7
Pauma Alta Dr
14600 SDCo 1050 G7

Pauma Heights Ln
31300 SDCo 1070 J1
Pauma Heights Rd
32200 SDCo 1050 J5
32000 SDCo 1051 A6
31200 SDCo 1070 J1
Pauma Heights Rd (Juanita Wy)
- SDCo 1070 F1
Pauma Pl
100 ESCN 1129 F3
Pauma Rancho Rd
31600 SDCo 1051 H6
Pauma Reservation Rd
- SDCo 1031 B7
- SDCo 1050 J1
- SDCo 1051 A1
Pauma Ridge Cres
- SDCo 1050 F1
Pauma Ridge Rd
34400 SDCo 1030 F7
33600 SDCo 1050 E1
Pauma Valley Dr
- SDCo 1050 H4
15800 SDCo 1051 A6
Pauma View Dr
31700 SDCo 1050 H6
Pauma Vista Dr
- SDCo 1050 E6
Paunack St
- NATC 1309 G1
Pavlov Av
4200 SDGO 1228 E5
Pavo Ct
1000 SNMS 1128 F5
Pavo Real Dr
3900 SDGO 1250 A3
Pawnee Dr
5800 LMSA 1250 G7
Pawnee Glen
500 ESCN 1130 A6
Pawnee St
100 SNMS 1108 D7
Paxton Ct
2800 SDGO 1350 C1
Paxton Dr
1200 SDGO 1350 C1
Paxton Wy
1900 ENCT 1147 A2
Paymaster Rd
10200 SDCo 1069 E4
Paymogo Ct
11300 SDGO 1169 H6
Paymogo St
15500 SDGO 1169 H6
Payne St
200 SDGO 1289 F4
Payson Dr
2600 SDCo 1135 J6
2800 SDCo 1136 A7
Payson Rd
4000 LMSA 1270 J4
Peabody Wy
- CHLV 1331 E3
Peace Valley Ln
- SDCo 1171 H3
Peaceful Ct
1800 SDGO 1350 E3
10100 SNTE 1231 D4
Peaceful Dr
9900 SNTE 1231 D4
Peaceful Ln
100 VSTA 1087 D7
Peaceful Pl
1300 SDCo 1233 J6
Peaceful Valley Ranc Rd
14000 SDCo 1292 J3
(See Page 1292)
Peach Av
1000 ELCJ 1251 H4
1400 ELCJ 1252 A3
Peach Blossom St
3700 NATC 1290 C6
Peach Ct
1800 CHLV 1331 F3
800 ELCJ 1251 H4
Peach Grove Ln
1200 VSTA 1088 A6
Peach Point Av
7900 SDGO 1209 B3
Peach St
1100 BRAW 6320 A1
(See Page 6320)
Peach Tree Ln
2200 SDCo 1271 C7
Peach Tree Wy
3400 OCSD 1086 F2
13500 SDGO 1188 G3
Peach Wy
900 ESCN 1109 H6
6300 SDGO 1188 G4
500 SNMS 1108 J5
Peachtree Cir
- CHLV 1311 F4
Peachtree Ct
400 SNMS 1128 G2
Peachtree Ln
14100 POWY 1190 F2
Peachtree Rd
6900 CRLB 1127 A6
Peachwood Ct
12600 POWY 1190 C1

Peachwood Dr
1400 ENCT 1167 G1
Peacock Blvd
1300 OCSD 1087 D3
Peacock Dr
7700 SDGO 1249 B7
Peacock Valley Rd
2300 CHLV 1311 G7
Peak Ct
4500 SDCo 1271 E3
Peak Rd
15600 SDCo 1176 D4
(See Page 1176)
Peak Wy
36100 SDCo 1176 C3
(See Page 1176)
Pear Blossom Ct
2100 CHLV 1331 G3
Pear Blossom Pl
400 ESCN 1109 H7
800 OCSD 1086 G6
Pear Ln
- SDCo 1089 B2
Pear St
900 ELCJ 1251 H3
- SNMS 1128 C1
Pearblossom Av
3500 OCSD 1086 F5
Pearblossom Cir
3500 OCSD 1086 F5
Pearblossom Dr
3500 OCSD 1086 F5
Pearce Grove Dr
300 ENCT 1147 B3
Pearl Av
1300 ESCN 1110 A7
Pearl Dr
700 SNMS 1128 E5
Pearl Heights Rd
1500 VSTA 1107 H6
Pearl Lake Av
6200 SDGO 1250 H6
Pearl Ln
3200 OCSD 1107 A2
500 SDGO 1350 E3
Pearl Pl
800 ELCJ 1251 F7
1400 ESCN 1110 A7
Pearl Rd
2600 ImCo 6439 D6
Pearl St
400 SDGO 1227 E7
Pearlbush Ct
1200 SDCo 1252 E7
Pearleaf Ct
900 SNMS 1128 H3
Pearlman Pl
- SDGO 1188 D5
Pearlman Wy
5000 SDGO 1188 D5
Pearlwood Rd
9400 SNTE 1231 B4
Pearlwood St
300 CHLV 1330 G3
Pearman Ln
- SDCo 1172 H1
Pearson Dr
4900 SDGO 1270 D2
Pearson Springs Ct
- CHLV 1331 B2
Pearson St
7300 LMSA 1270 F5
Peartree Ct
1400 ENCT 1147 G7
Peartree Dr
6800 CRLB 1127 A5
Peartree Ln
800 OCSD 1086 G5
Peartree Pl
400 ESCN 1109 H7
Peartree Ter
12700 POWY 1190 C1
Pearwood St
700 OCSD 1086 G5
Pebble Beach Ct
8900 SNTE 1230 J4
Pebble Beach Dr
4400 OCSD 1066 H7
- SNMS 1108 J3
10000 SNTE 1230 J3
Pebble Beach Wy
14200 SDCo 1090 F5
Pebble Canyon Dr
14400 POWY 1190 H1
Pebble Creek Ln
10000 SDCo 1232 G1
Pebble Ct
800 ELCJ 1252 B6
Pebble Pl
800 ELCJ 1252 B7
Pebble Springs Ln
1000 SDCo 1109 E7
Pebble St
1800 CHLV 1331 E3
- CRLB 1107 B4
Pebblebrook Ln
14100 SDGO 1189 J2
Pebblebrook Pl
1900 CHLV 1311 D4
Pebblebrook Wy
- SDGO 1189 J2

52 INDEX

INDEX 52

Pebblestone Ln

Placer Trl

San Diego County Street Index

STREET	Block	City	Map#	Grid
Pebblestone Ln	9200	SDGO	1209	D2
Pebblestone Pl	-	SNTE	1231	C5
Pecan Ct	-	BRAW	6259	J6
	(See Page 6259)			
	1800	VSTA	1108	B3
Pecan Park Ln	14100	SDCo	1232	G5
Pecan Peak	-	SDCo	1232	G5
Pecan Pl	1200	CHLV	1330	G2
	3000	ESCN	1110	E6
Pecan St	-	BRAW	6259	F6
	(See Page 6259)			
Pecan Ter	-	SDCo	1232	G5
Pecan Valley Dr	8700	SNTE	1230	J4
Peck Pl	6100	SDGO	1270	C3
Peckham Pl	1900	ENCT	1167	H1
Pecos Dr	3800	SDCo	1099	D1
	(See Page 1099)			
Pecos St	900	SDCo	1291	C3
Pedragal Dr	500	OCSD	1086	G1
Pedregal Dr	1500	SDCo	1130	B4
Pedriza Dr	12700	POWY	1170	C5
Pedstrn And Equstrn Trl	-	SDCo	1237	B6
Peerless Dr	1700	SDCo	1252	A2
Peet Ln	2400	ESCN	1130	C7
	2500	ESCN	1150	C1
Peg Ct	4200	SDGO	1330	G7
Peg Leg Mine Rd	3200	SDCo	1272	J7
Peg Leg Rd	2000	SDCo	1059	J7
	(See Page 1059)			
Pegaso St	1400	ENCT	1167	G1
Pegasus Av	11300	SDGO	1209	D1
Pegasus Wy	-	SNMS	1108	D5
Pegeen Pl	11300	SDCo	1251	G1
Peggy Dr	700	SDGO	1290	G3
Peil Rd	-	SDCo	1173	J6
Peinado Wy	-	SDGO	1208	G3
Peirce Ln	-	SDCo	1172	G4
Pelican Hill Rd	1900	SDGO	1290	E7
Pelican Ln	-	SDGO	1209	D7
Pelican Point Ct	1600	CHLV	1330	J5
Pelican Wy	700	ELCJ	1251	E7
Pelicano Dr	700	OCSD	1086	J3
Pell Pl	-	SDGO	1188	A6
Pelton Ct	8900	SDGO	1209	D2
Pelusa St	5000	SDGO	1290	A6
Pember Av	1700	CHLV	1331	E2
Pembridge Ln	6900	SDGO	1290	F7
Pembroke Dr	6100	SDGO	1270	C2
Pena Rd	11800	SDCo	1029	H4
Penanova St	11200	SDGO	1169	H6
Penara Ct	7100	SDGO	1208	J4
Penara Pl	7300	SDGO	1208	J4
Penara St	10600	SDGO	1208	J4
Penasco Rd	1600	SDCo	1272	B1
Penasquitos Ct	14800	SDGO	1169	H7
Penasquitos Dr	15000	SDGO	1169	H7
Pence Dr	2200	SDCo	1252	D7
Pendiente Ct	-	SDGO	1250	A3
Pendleton Av	-	SDGO	1268	E6
Pendleton Rd	1500	CORD	1288	J6
Pendleton St	5000	SDGO	1248	B3
Pendon Ct	7700	CRLB	1147	F2
Pendragon Rd	15300	SDCo	1191	C5
Penelope Dr	600	CHLV	1310	D7
	400	SNMS	1109	A6
Penfield Pt	13500	SDGO	1188	D4
Penford Ct	14400	SDGO	1189	C1
Penguin Cir	900	VSTA	1087	G5
Penina St	13600	POWY	1170	E1
Peninsula Dr	-	CRLB	1107	B4
Penkea Dr	2700	OCSD	1086	D6
Penmar Rd	9200	SNTE	1231	A3
Penn St	300	SDCo	1152	J3
Pennacook Ct	17700	SDGO	1169	H1
Pennant Wy	3000	SDGO	1228	C6
Pennington Ln	2500	SDGO	1290	F7
Pennsylvania Av	-	ELCJ	1251	F5
	1200	SDGO	1269	B6
E Pennsylvania Av	400	ESCN	1129	J2
	700	ESCN	1130	A2
W Pennsylvania Av	700	SDGO	1268	J6
Pennsylvania Ln	5500	LMSA	1270	E1
Penny Ln	16000	SDGO	1169	B3
Penny Pl	5300	SDGO	1270	A2
Pennyroyal Wy	300	OCSD	1086	H1
Pennywood Rd	9200	SNTE	1231	A4
Penridge St	10500	SDGO	1208	J4
Penrod Ct	200	VSTA	1087	G4
Penrod Ln	10300	SDGO	1208	J5
Penrose Ct	4800	SDGO	1248	F7
Penrose St	2600	SDGO	1248	F7
	2200	SDGO	1268	F1
Penstemon Ct	32500	SDCo	1175	G4
	(See Page 1175)			
Penstemon Ln	32400	SDCo	1175	H4
	(See Page 1175)			
Penstemon Rd	15700	SDCo	1175	H3
	(See Page 1175)			
Pentas Ct	1800	CRLB	1127	E6
Pentecost Wy	1600	SDGO	1290	B2
Penticton Wy	9000	SDGO	1209	D2
Pentuckett Av	2100	SDGO	1289	F1
Penview Dr	3100	SDCo	1067	J6
Peony Dr	4000	SDCo	1028	F5
Pepita Wy	7400	SDGO	1227	F7
Pepper Ct	-	ELCN	6559	E1
Pepper Dr	1600	ELCJ	1252	B2
	1900	ELCN	6559	E1
	4000	SDGO	1269	G7
	100	SDCo	1350	G4
E Pepper Dr	100	ELCJ	1251	F1
	1100	SDCo	1251	H1
	1400	SDCo	1252	A1
Pepper Glen Wy	-	CHLV	1311	G3
Pepper Ln	-	SDCo	1023	E2
Pepper Tree Ln	12200	POWY	1190	C6
	100	SDCo	1027	F5
	-	SDGO	1287	J3
	1200	VSTA	1108	B1
Pepper Tree Pl	2100	ESCN	1109	G5
	1600	SDCo	1027	H5
Pepper Tree Rd	-	CHLV	1310	D6
	100	SDCo	1310	D6
Pepper Valley Ln	1800	SDCo	1252	A1
Pepperbrook Ln	10500	SDGO	1209	J3
Pepperdine Av	4100	OCSD	1087	B5
Pepperdine Ct	900	CHLV	1311	D6
Peppergrass Creek	-	SDGO	1188	F4
Peppergrass Dr	-	SDGO	1270	D6
Pepperhill Dr	1600	ELCJ	1252	B2
Peppermint Ln	2200	LMGR	1290	E1
Peppermint Pl	1800	ESCN	1129	E4
Peppertree Ct	500	SNMS	1109	D7
Peppertree Dr	2700	OCSD	1087	E5
Peppertree Ln	100	ENCT	1167	J1
	-	SOLB	1187	F1
Peppertree Wy	2700	CRLB	1127	G3
Pepperview Terr	11200	SDGO	1210	A2
Peppervilla Ct	900	ELCJ	1251	H1
Peppervilla Dr	1700	ELCJ	1251	H2
	1300	SDCo	1251	H1
Pepperwood Ct	500	CHLV	1311	C4
Pepperwood Dr	1600	SDCo	1251	G1
Pepsi Dr	4200	SDGO	1249	B3
Pequena St	1300	SDGO	1350	F1
Pequenito Ct	-	SDCo	1232	B5
Pequeno Pl	1200	ESCN	1110	A6
Pequot Dr	13400	POWY	1190	D4
Pera Alta Dr	3100	SDCo	1155	G4
Peralta St	4200	CRLB	1107	B6
Perch Ln	-	OCSD	1086	G2
Percussion Ct	2300	SDCo	1252	D6
Percy Ct	12900	SDGO	1188	B5
Perdido St	3700	SNMS	1108	C7
Perdiz St	7300	CRLB	1127	J7
Peregrine Rd	16600	SDCo	1051	C6
Peregrine Wy	-	ELCJ	1252	A6
Perez Cove Wy	2200	SDGO	1268	B3
Perez Ct	10200	SDGO	1229	G7
Pergl St	2500	LMGR	1270	F7
Peridot Ct	-	CALX	6620	J7
	2000	CRLB	1127	F5
Perimeter Rd	-	ELCJ	1251	A3
	-	SDCo	1332	A6
	(See Page 1332)			
Periouito Ct	1800	VSTA	1107	H5
Perique St	-	SDGO	1270	D5
Periwinkle St	700	ENCT	1147	E6
Periwinkle Wy	-	OCSD	1086	J4
Perkins Dr	-	CHLV	1330	J2
Perkon Ct	2500	SDGO	1270	A7
Perkon Pl	4900	SDGO	1269	J7
Perla Ct	12500	SDGO	1170	C2
Perlas Ct	1300	CHLV	1311	A4
Perrin Pl	1700	CHLV	1331	E2
Perry Av	2000	CALX	6620	G6
	-	CALX	6680	G1
Perry Rd	-	CALX	6620	G6
	-	SDGO	1268	D6
Perry St	2900	SDGO	1288	A3
Persa St	6500	CRLB	1127	G5
Persano Pl	35100	SDCo	1028	J6
Perseus Rd	8600	SDGO	1209	C2
Pershing Av	3700	SDGO	1269	D6
Pershing Dr	1400	SDGO	1289	C2
Pershing Rd	1200	CHLV	1331	C2
Persimmon Av	1200	SDCo	1251	J3
Persimmon Ct	2700	CHLV	1311	J7
	1100	SDCo	1251	J3
Persimmon Ln	30600	SDCo	1070	H4
Persimmon Wy	600	OCSD	1086	F2
	1200	SDCo	1251	J3
Perth Pl	6500	SDGO	1310	E1
Pertus Dr	-	SDCo	1023	D2
Peru Pl	5500	SDGO	1290	A1
Pesca Ct	400	SDCo	1291	C4
Pescadero Av	4700	SDGO	1267	J7
	4500	SDGO	1287	J1
Pescadero Dr	1400	SDGO	1267	H7
Pescadero Point Ct	1600	CHLV	1330	J4
Pescado Pl	400	ENCT	1147	C6
Pesos Pl	10800	SDGO	1249	H1
Petal Dr	1600	SDGO	1290	D6
Petalo Plz	1000	CHLV	1311	A6
Petaluma Dr	-	CHLV	1311	E6
Petenwell Rd	11500	SDGO	1209	H1
Peteo Ct	400	CHLV	1330	B2
Peter Pan Av	7100	SDGO	1290	F4
Peterlynn Ct	4000	SDGO	1350	F1
Peterlynn Dr	1100	SDGO	1350	F1
Peterlynn Wy	4000	SDGO	1350	F1
Peters Dr	300	VSTA	1087	H7
Peters Stone Ct	15600	SDGO	1169	B4
Peters Wy	3000	SDGO	1248	C3
Petirrojo Ct	11600	SDGO	1250	B3
Petit Ct	6900	SDGO	1248	J3
Petit St	6800	SDGO	1248	J3
Petite Ln	9700	SDCo	1232	C3
Petra Dr	1700	SDGO	1289	F2
Petra Pl	3400	SDGO	1289	F1
Petra Wy	1100	SDCo	1233	F5
Petree St	1500	ELCJ	1251	D4
Petrolia Ct	-	SDCo	1171	F1
Pettigo Dr	2900	SDGO	1310	E2
Petunia Ct	3200	SDGO	1248	C3
	200	SNMS	1108	H6
Petunia Pl	-	CRLB	1127	B4
Petunia Wy	13200	SDGO	1188	G4
Peutz Vallet Rd	-	SDCo	1234	C3
Peutz Valley Rd	200	SDCo	1233	F4
	15500	SDCo	1234	B1
Pewter Ct	1700	SDCo	1272	D2
Peyri Dr	200	OCSD	1086	G2
Peyton Pl	5300	SDGO	1228	H7
Pfeifer Ln	1200	ELCJ	1251	C3
Phantom Ln	11500	SDGO	1209	E1
Pheasant Ct	-	ImCo	6560	B7
	1100	SNMS	1128	E2
Pheasant Dr	2900	SDCo	1136	E7
	2500	SDGO	1249	B7
Pheasant Hill	-	SDCo	1109	E6
Pheasant Ln	-	OCSD	1086	H2
Pheasant Pl	1900	ESCN	1109	H5
Pheasant Run	2000	SDCo	1028	A4
Pheasant St	-	ImCo	6560	A7
Pheasant Valley Ct	-	SDCo	1027	G1
Phelps Rd	2000	SDCo	1317	H3
	(See Page 1317)			
Phil Mar Ln	1400	VSTA	1108	A2
Philbrook Sq	-	SDGO	1208	B2
Phildel St	-	SDGO	1188	A4
Phillar Wy	8700	SNTE	1231	C7
Phillips Cir	1400	VSTA	1108	A2
Phillips Ct	6800	SDGO	1268	J1
Phillips St	700	VSTA	1107	H1
	1100	VSTA	1108	A1
Phillips Wy	400	VSTA	1107	H1
Philox Ct	-	CRLB	1127	B4
Philton Dr	500	SDCo	1153	B6
Phipps Av	6000	SDGO	1209	E7
Phire Pl	400	SDCo	1291	B4
Phoebe Pl	1200	CRLB	1127	B5
Phoebe St	100	ENCT	1147	A4
Phoenix Ct	1600	CHLV	1331	F2
Phoenix Dr	7500	LMSA	1270	G4
Phoenix Wy	700	SNMS	1129	A3
Phyllis Pl	8300	SDGO	1249	B7
Piantino Cres	2600	SDGO	1249	D7
Piantino Wy	9200	SDGO	1249	D7
Piatto Ln	9200	SDGO	1249	E7
Piatto Wy	9200	SDGO	1249	D7
Piazza De Oro Wy	-	OCSD	1106	J2
Picacho Ct	600	OCSD	1067	C7
Picadilly Ct	4500	CRLB	1107	A5
Picador Blvd	900	SDGO	1330	E7
	1300	SDGO	1350	F1
Picarte Pl	12600	SDGO	1190	A5
Picasso Dr	2900	SDCo	1290	H7
Picaza Pl	11000	SDGO	1169	H1
Piccadilly Rd	1800	ENCT	1147	A2
Piccard Av	500	SDGO	1330	F7
	1200	SDGO	1350	F1
Picket Fence Dr	1700	CHLV	1331	H1
Pickett Glen	500	ESCN	1110	D6
Pickett St	3400	SDGO	1268	E4
Pickford Rd	11700	SDGO	1209	G1
Pickwick St	3400	SDGO	1289	F3
Picnic Ct	2300	CHLV	1331	H1
Picnicview Ln	200	OCSD	1107	D2
Pico Av	1500	ELCN	6499	F4
	500	SDCo	1027	F3
	300	SNMS	1108	H7
Pico Ct	-	CHLV	1330	E3
Pico De La Loma	300	ESCN	1150	A3
Pico Pl	800	ESCN	1109	J6
	-	POWY	1190	H7
	2600	SDGO	1248	C5
Pico Rd	3900	SDCo	1068	F4
Pico St	4600	SDGO	1248	C5
Pico Wy	300	ESCN	1109	H7
	2500	SDGO	1248	C4
Picrus St	12200	SDGO	1189	B7
Pictor Ln	200	ELCJ	1252	A5
Picturesque Pt	15100	SDCo	1233	B7
Pidgeon St	700	SDGO	1290	F3
Piedmont Dr	4400	SDGO	1287	J2
Piedmont Rd	800	SDCo	1152	J3
Piedmont St	-	CHLV	1331	D1
	9200	SDCo	1291	B3
Piedra St	1300	SDGO	1350	E1
Piedra Tract	600	SDCo	1218	E5
Piedras Oro Calle	700	ENCT	1147	D7
Piel Pl	9100	SDCo	1291	B4
Pienza Wy	-	OCSD	1106	J2
Pier View Wy	900	OCSD	1086	A7
Pierce Av	-	CALX	6680	F1
Pierce Ct	-	CALX	6680	E2
	2000	SDCo	1272	C3
Pierce Pl	4900	OCSD	1067	A7
N Pierce St	600	ELCJ	1251	D4
S Pierce St	100	ELCJ	1251	D5
Pierino Dr	2000	SDGO	1290	E1
Pierpoint Pl	4700	CRLB	1106	H7
Pierre Wy	1100	SDCo	1251	G3
Pikake St	2700	SDGO	1350	C3
Pike Ln	-	OCSD	1086	G2
Pike Rd	9300	SNTE	1231	B5
Pilawee Wee Ln	9500	SDCo	1236	A2
Pile St	-	SDCo	1152	H2
	700	SDCo	1153	A2
Pilgrim Wy	1400	OCSD	1067	A3
Pillar Point Wy	800	OCSD	1066	F7
Pillsbury Ln	1200	ELCJ	1251	B3
Pilon Pt	4100	SDGO	1188	B7
Pilot Wy	6700	SDGO	1270	E7
Pilots Ln	9500	SNTE	1231	C7
Pima Trl	34600	SDCo	1176	D4
	(See Page 1176)			
Pimlico Ct	15400	SDCo	1168	E7
Pimlico Dr	-	SOLB	1187	G2
Pimlico Pl	2400	SDCo	1234	C6
Pimpernel Dr	9000	SDGO	1189	C5
Pimpernel Wy	12800	SDGO	1189	D5
Pina Ln	-	VSTA	1087	H7
Pinar Pl	2100	SDGO	1187	G6
Pinata Dr	16700	SDGO	1170	B3
Pindar Wy	4100	OCSD	1107	E6
Pine Av	600	CRLB	1106	E5
Pine Blossom Rd	9600	SDCo	1232	H3
Pine Bluff Ln	1600	SDGO	1290	D6
Pine Blvd	8100	SDCo	1237	C5
Pine Circle Dr	1400	ELCJ	1271	D1
Pine Cone Dr	700	SDCo	1156	E2
Pine Creek Cg	28800	SDCo	1237	C4
Pine Creek Rd	8500	SDCo	1217	C5
	(See Page 1217)			
	8600	SDCo	1237	B4
Pine Crest Dr	2600	SDCo	1136	D7
Pine Crest Ln	0	RivC	999	F1
Pine Crest Wy	2100	CRLB	1106	F3
Pine Ct	-	BRAW	6259	J6
	(See Page 6259)			
	300	CHLV	1330	G3
	-	CORD	1288	G7
	8300	LMSA	1270	J2
	8000	SDCo	1237	C5
Pine Dr	1200	ELCJ	1251	D7
	2400	SDCo	1297	E6
	(See Page 1297)			
Pine Glen Ct	2600	SDCo	1272	E3
Pine Glen Ln	2500	SDCo	1272	D3
Pine Glen Wy	1100	SDGO	1350	E1
Pine Grove Ct	2900	SDCo	1271	F7
Pine Grove St	10300	SDCo	1271	F7
Pine Heights Wy	1400	SDCo	1129	E1
	1500	SNMS	1129	E1
Pine Hgts	-	SDCo	1152	F1
Pine Hill Pt	5200	SDGO	1208	D2
Pine Hills Crest Rd	3200	SDCo	1155	H4
Pine Hills Rd	2900	SDCo	1135	J7
	4900	SDCo	1155	H5
Pine Island Dr	-	CHLV	1311	F4
Pine Knoll Ln	9900	SDGO	1249	F1
Pine Ln	9800	SDCo	1149	E1
	3100	SDCo	1272	C7
Pine Manor Ct	12900	SDGO	1189	F4
Pine Meadow Ct	12800	SDGO	1188	B5
Pine Needles Dr	300	DLMR	1187	G7
	13700	SDGO	1187	G6
Pine Patch Wy	-	SDCo	998	G5
Pine Ridge Av	4700	SDCo	1155	H5
Pine Ridge Rd	1400	OCSD	1087	C3
Pine Ridge Wy	4700	SDCo	1155	H5
Pine St	-	BRAW	6259	H7
	(See Page 6259)			
	1000	CORD	1288	G7
	4900	LMSA	1270	H2
	100	OCSD	1106	A1
	1200	SDCo	1152	F3
	2100	SDGO	1268	G4
	-	SNMS	1128	C1
	-	SNMS	1129	C2
N Pine St	100	ESCN	1129	H3
S Pine St	200	ESCN	1129	H3
	1800	ESCN	1130	A5
Pine Ter	14200	SDCo	1232	G6
Pine Tree Ln	35200	SDCo	1156	F7
	600	VSTA	1107	H1
Pine Tree Pl	400	ESCN	1130	A4
Pine Valley Dr	9200	SNTE	1230	J6
Pine Valley Glen	2300	ESCN	1109	H3
Pine Valley Rd	7400	SDCo	1237	B7
Pine View Rd	1900	SDCo	1234	D7
Pine Vista Rd	1400	SDCo	1130	E2
Pine Wy	800	SDCo	1152	F2
Pineapple Dr	9600	SDCo	1232	A4
Pineapple Wy	-	ESCN	1129	E5
Pinebranch Dr	1300	ENCT	1167	F1
Pinebrook Ct	12600	POWY	1170	D3
Pinecastle St	10200	SDGO	1210	C4
Pinecliffs Ct	10400	SDGO	1210	A3
Pinecone Ln	6600	SDGO	1310	F1
Pinecrest Av	800	ESCN	1129	H5
	8800	SDGO	1249	C5
Pinecrest St	0	RivC	999	F1
Pinefalls Ct	10500	SDGO	1209	J3
Pinefield Rd	12800	POWY	1170	D3
Pinehurst Av	1700	ESCN	1109	D5
Pinehurst Ct	4100	SDCo	1028	G5
Pinehurst Dr	1200	OCSD	1067	B4
	11300	SDCo	1211	H6
Pinehurst Pl	15400	SDGO	1210	J1
Pinehurst Rd	1200	CHLV	1311	G6
Pineoak Ridge Rd	700	SDCo	1156	E3
Pineridge Ct	500	CHLV	1311	B4
Pineridge Rd	-	SNTE	1230	G7
Pinery Grove	10200	SDCo	1231	G3
Pinestone Ct	11200	SDGO	1189	J2
Pinetree Dr	10100	SDGO	1209	G4
Pinevale Ln	100	SNTE	1230	J7
Pinewood Ct	8500	SDGO	1228	A4
Pinewood Dr	800	OCSD	1087	C1
	14200	SDGO	1187	H5
Pinewood Rd	1900	VSTA	1107	F5
Pinewood St	2400	SDGO	1187	H5
Pinewood View	10100	SNTE	1231	D3
Pinezanita Ln	2300	SDCo	1136	A7
Pinion Pine Trl	38700	SDCo	1320	A3
	(See Page 1320)			
Pinion St	1000	SNMS	1109	B5
Pinion Trl	10400	SDCo	1089	F4
Pinkard Ln	9100	SDCo	1232	F5
Pinkard Wy	-	SDCo	1232	F5
Pinnacle Ct	1700	VSTA	1107	G4
Pinnacle Ln	10100	SDCo	1271	D2
Pinnacle Peak Dr	1200	CHLV	1311	H5
Pinnacle Pl	3800	ESCN	1150	D3
Pinnacle Wy	1600	VSTA	1107	G4
Pinner Dr	-	BRAW	6319	G1
	(See Page 6319)			
Pino Ct	13100	SDCo	1232	C2
Pino Dr	10000	SDCo	1232	C3
Pinon Hills Rd	-	CHLV	1311	F6
Pinon Pl	10200	SDCo	1231	G3
Pinos Wy	-	SDGO	1190	A7
Pinot Noir Cir	10800	SDGO	1210	B2
Pinot Pl	17200	POWY	1170	D2
Pinta St	3100	OCSD	1106	J1
Pintail Ct	12400	POWY	1190	B6
Pintail Dr	-	CRLB	1127	D6
Pinto Canyon Ln	-	CHLV	1311	H5
Pinto Ct	1000	SNMS	1109	C5
Pinto Pl	3800	SDCo	1271	F4
Pinto Ridge Ct	16300	SDCo	1169	E4
Pinto Ridge Dr	16200	SDCo	1169	E4
Pintoresco Ct	2100	CRLB	1147	F1
Pinyon Dr	-	SDCo	1085	J3
Pinyon Ridge Dr	2500	CHLV	1311	J5
Pinzolo Pt	9100	SDCo	1231	H6
Pinzon Wy	10900	SDGO	1169	H1
Pio Pico Dr	2300	CRLB	1106	E3
Pio Pico St	3600	SDGO	1287	J3
Pioneer Av	2500	VSTA	1108	B6
Pioneer Cir	1400	OCSD	1066	J3
Pioneer Ln	38400	SDCo	1299	J4
	(See Page 1299)			
Pioneer Pl	3100	ESCN	1150	C1
	3700	SDGO	1268	J6
Pioneer Ter	-	SDCo	1232	F4
Pioneer Wy	1000	ELCJ	1251	E3
	2800	SDCo	1292	F3
	(See Page 1292)			
Piovana Ct	-	CRLB	1127	A7
Pipeline Dr	1300	VSTA	1107	J6
Piper Ln	4300	SDCo	1100	C4
	(See Page 1100)			
Piper Ranch Rd	1300	SDCo	1351	H1
	-	SDGO	1351	H2
Piper St	4200	SDGO	1248	E6
Pipes Ln	400	ENCT	1147	D7
Pipestone Wy	8800	SDGO	1189	C3
Pipilo Ct	12900	SDGO	1189	D5
Pipilo St	9400	SDGO	1189	D5
Piping Rock Ln	13500	SDCo	1232	E7
	-	SDCo	1252	E1
Pipit Ct	-	SDCo	1127	D4
	12200	SDGO	1189	A7
Pipit Pl	7600	SDGO	1189	A7
Pipit Wy	12200	SDGO	1189	A7
Pipo Rd	12400	SDGO	1170	C4
Pippin Ct	-	SNMS	1128	E3
Pippin Dr	300	SDCo	1027	G4
Piraeus St	1100	ENCT	1147	C4
Piragua St	3000	CRLB	1127	J7
	3200	CRLB	1147	J1
Pire Av	5400	SDGO	1228	C7
Pirgos Wy	3500	OCSD	1107	E4
Pirineos Wy	2600	CRLB	1147	G1
Piros Wy	6000	OCSD	1107	F5
Pirotte Dr	5200	SDGO	1290	A1
Pisces Wy	11100	SDGO	1209	C2
Pismo Bay Ct	300	OCSD	1066	J5
Pismo Ct	800	SDGO	1267	H1
Pistol Range Rd	-	SDGO	1350	E2
Pita Ct	13600	SDCo	1292	F2
	(See Page 1292)			
Pitcairn St	3000	SDGO	1330	D7
Pitman Pl	900	ESCN	1110	C6
Pitman St	600	ESCN	1110	C6
Pitta St	400	SDGO	1290	C3
Pittsburgh Av	6100	SDGO	1290	C5
Pittzer Rd	1500	ImCo	6560	D3
	-	ImCo	6620	D2
Piute Pl	4400	SDGO	1248	E2
Piute Trl	34800	SDCo	1176	E5
	(See Page 1176)			
Pizarro Ln	1900	SDCo	1109	E6
Pizzo Ln	700	SDCo	1027	G4
Place Monaco	2200	SDGO	1187	G5
Place St Tropez	2200	SDGO	1187	G5
Placentia St	7300	LMGR	1290	F2
Placer Av	400	SNMS	1108	J6
Placer Mine Ln	1800	CHLV	1311	E6
Placer Trl	900	SDCo	1253	B2

SAN DIEGO CO.

53 INDEX
INDEX 53
Placerita St
Poway Rd

San Diego County Street Index

SAN DIEGO CO.

STREET
Block City Map# Grid

Placerita St
1500 ENCT 1147 G7
Placid Ct
1600 ELCJ 1252 B2
Placid View Dr
8500 SNTE 1231 A7
8500 SNTE 1251 A1
Placido Ct
2100 CRLB 1147 F2
Placitos Suenos
1700 VSTA 1087 D7
Plainview Rd
5100 SDGO 1268 F2
Plak Ct
- SDCo 1271 E3
Plane Tree View
- SDCo 1089 B2
Planet Rd
1400 VSTA 1087 D6
Planicie Wy
1600 SDGO 1350 B2
Plank Rd
- ELCN 6559 D1
Plantano St
400 SDGO 1289 J3
Plantation Wy
1500 SDCo 1272 A1
Plantel Wy
3100 SDGO 1350 D2
Plaskon Ln
1100 SDCo 1316 B7
(See Page 1316)
Plata Ct
1600 LMGR 1290 F2
Platano Ct
1400 CHLV 1330 F4
Platanus Dr
29700 SDCo 1069 A5
Platanus Pl
- SDCo 1069 A5
Plateau Av
300 SNMS 1128 H3
Plateau Dr
6200 SDGO 1310 E2
Plateau Pl
- CRLB 1107 C3
3900 ESCN 1150 C3
Platinum Rd
16800 SDCo 1191 D3
Plato Dr
- CALX 6620 H7
3000 SDGO 1310 F2
Plato Pl
600 ENCT 1147 B2
Platte River Ln
1800 CHLV 1311 E7
Playa Blanca
300 ENCT 1147 C6
Playa Catalina
5000 SDGO 1230 A7
Playa De Concord
- ESCN 1129 F4
Playa Del Alicante
- ESCN 1129 E4
Playa Del Carmen Dr
- IMPE 6499 G1
Playa Del Norte
- CALX 6620 H4
Playa Del Norte St
200 SDGO 1247 E2
Playa Del Rey
100 OCSD 1066 F7
Playa Del Rey Av
- OCSD 1086 G1
Playa Del Sol
- ESCN 1109 F7
- SDCo 1251 G2
Playa Del Sur St
200 SDGO 1247 E2
Playa Del Tokay
- ESCN 1129 E4
Playa Dr
2100 CHLV 1331 G3
Playa Rd
2000 CRLB 1127 F7
Playa Rivera Dr
1800 ENCT 1167 E3
Playa Vista
1700 SDCo 1128 B4
Player Dr
7300 SDGO 1250 F5
Players Dr
1100 OCSD 1067 B4
Playmor Ter
7900 SDGO 1228 C4
Plaza Abierto
17400 SDGO 1170 C1
Plaza Acapulco
2000 CHLV 1311 D1
Plaza Acosta
17700 SDGO 1150 D7
Plaza Ahora
17800 SDGO 1150 C7
Plaza Alonzo
3000 SDCo 1310 H1
Plaza Amada
12500 SDGO 1170 C1
Plaza Amena
1000 CHLV 1310 J6
Plaza Amistad
- CHLV 1311 A6
Plaza Amparada
- SDCo 1311 B7
Plaza Animado
17400 SDGO 1170 C1
Plaza Anita
3000 SDCo 1290 H7
Plaza Arbolitos
1800 CHLV 1311 C1
Plaza Arica
17600 SDGO 1150 C7
Plaza Ascope
17600 SDGO 1150 C7
Plaza Blvd
6800 SDGO 1290 E5
E Plaza Blvd
4100 NATC 1290 D6
500 NATC 1309 H1
W Plaza Blvd
100 NATC 1309 H2
Plaza Bonita
2200 CRLB 1127 F7
Plaza Bonita Center Wy
- SDCo 1310 E3
Plaza Bonita Rd
3000 NATC 1310 C3
Plaza Calimas
- CHLV 1311 F2
Plaza Cambria
- CHLV 1311 F2
Plaza Capote
- CHLV 1311 A7
Plaza Carlos
2900 SDCo 1290 H7
Plaza Catalonia
800 CHLV 1311 B6
Plaza Centrada
12500 SDGO 1170 D2
Plaza Cerado
17400 SDGO 1170 C1
Plaza Crest Ridge Rd
1600 SDGO 1290 E6
Plaza Ct
700 CHLV 1310 H6
Plaza Cuernavaca Wy
6400 SDGO 1290 D5
Plaza De La Costa
- CRLB 1127 F7
Plaza De La Rosa
17400 SDGO 1170 D2
Plaza De La Siena
4200 SDGO 1188 A6
Plaza De Las Flores
- CRLB 1127 F7
Plaza De Palmas
- SDGO 1228 C3
Plaza De Panama
2500 SDGO 1289 C1
Plaza Del Cid
500 CHLV 1310 G5
Plaza Del Curtidor
17400 SDGO 1170 C1
Plaza Del Mar
2400 SDCo 1150 D1
Plaza Destacado
17400 SDGO 1170 D2
Plaza Dolores
17300 SDGO 1170 D2
Plaza Dr
- CALX 6620 H7
3800 OCSD 1107 B2
E Plaza Dr
- SDGO 1270 B2
W Plaza Dr
- SDGO 1270 B2
Plaza Elena
- CHLV 1311 A7
Plaza Entrada
- NATC 1290 C6
Plaza Escalante
- SDCo 1311 B6
Plaza Eva
- CHLV 1311 F1
Plaza Fiel
17400 SDGO 1170 C2
Plaza Flora
800 CHLV 1310 F7
Plaza Gardenia
- SDCo 1311 B6
Plaza Gitana
17500 SDGO 1170 D1
Plaza Guata
12500 SDGO 1170 C1
Plaza Guillermo
17400 SDGO 1170 C1
Plaza Kadie
2100 CHLV 1311 E2
Plaza Karena
17500 SDGO 1170 D1
Plaza La Paz
- CHLV 1310 J6
Plaza Leonardo
2900 SDCo 1290 H7
3000 SDCo 1310 H1
Plaza Lorenzo
3000 SDCo 1290 H7
Plaza Los Osos
300 CHLV 1311 E2
Plaza Manzana
- SDCo 1234 A6
Plaza Mar
800 CHLV 1310 F7
Plaza Maria
17300 SDGO 1170 D1
Plaza Marlena
17500 SDGO 1170 D1
Plaza Menta
12600 SDGO 1150 C7
Plaza Mercia
3000 SDCo 1290 H7
Plaza Miguel
2900 SDCo 1290 H7
Plaza Miraleste
- SDCo 1311 A7
Plaza Miroda
700 CHLV 1311 A5
Plaza Narisco
- CHLV 1311 A7
Plaza Natalia
3000 SDCo 1290 H7
Plaza Otonal
17300 SDGO 1170 D1
Plaza Palmera
- CHLV 1311 E1
Plaza Palo Alto
1800 CHLV 1311 C2
Plaza Paolo
3000 SDCo 1290 H7
Plaza Paraiso
300 CHLV 1311 E2
Plaza Park Ln
8700 SDGO 1249 C2
Plaza Paseo Dr
10300 SDCo 1231 H3
Plaza Promenade
5000 SDGO 1249 D1
Plaza Real
1900 OCSD 1087 B5
Plaza Reina
1500 CHLV 1331 D2
Plaza Ridge Rd
6400 SDGO 1290 E6
Plaza Salinas
200 CHLV 1311 D2
Plaza Seville
700 CHLV 1311 A5
Plaza Sierra
800 CHLV 1310 F7
Plaza Sinuoso
- CHLV 1311 A7
Plaza Sonada
17400 SDGO 1170 C1
Plaza Sonrisada
17400 SDGO 1170 D1
Plaza Sq
8700 SDGO 1249 C2
Plaza St
- BRAW 6319 J1
(See Page 6319)
300 SOLB 1167 E7
Plaza Taxco
800 SDGO 1290 D5
Plaza Toluca
- CHLV 1311 F2
800 SDGO 1290 E5
Plaza Torreon
800 SDGO 1290 E5
Plaza Ultima
- SDCo 1311 B6
Plaza Valdivia
17800 SDGO 1150 C7
Plaza Viejas
- SDCo 1234 A6
Plaza Vista
- SDGO 1290 D5
Plaza Vista Mar
- SDCo 1311 B6
Plazuela St
2200 CRLB 1147 F1
Pleasan Ridge
- SDGO 1208 B2
Pleasant Grove Rd
2100 ENCT 1147 H7
Pleasant Heights Dr
2000 SDCo 1088 B2
Pleasant Hill St
1400 ESCN 1109 F7
1200 ESCN 1129 F1
Pleasant Knoll Ln
28700 SDCo 1070 G7
Pleasant Ln
700 NATC 1290 B7
Pleasant Meadows Pl
11000 SDCo 1231 F3
Pleasant Pl
1600 ENCT 1147 G5
Pleasant Vale Dr
3400 CRLB 1107 B5
Pleasant Valley Pl
2200 CHLV 1311 G7
Pleasant View Dr
500 SDCo 1156 E2
Pleasant View Ln
3200 SDCo 1273 A7
Pleasant Waters Ct
2000 SDCo 1291 E1
Pleasant Wy
300 SNMS 1108 H7
Pleasantdale Dr
1800 ENCT 1147 H7
Pleasanton Rd
- CHLV 1311 C7
Pleasantwood Ln
2100 ESCN 1109 H4
Pleiades Dr
1200 SDCo 1108 D1
Plein Aire
- SDGO 1168 H6
Plein Aire Ct
- SDGO 1168 J6
Pless Rd
- SDGO 1229 B2
Plimpton Rd
9600 SDCo 1271 C1
Plone Wy
3000 SDGO 1248 C3
Plover Ct
- CRLB 1127 D6
Plover St
1500 SDGO 1290 E1
Plover Wy
900 CHLV 1329 H1
1000 OCSD 1087 A3
Plum Ct
- SDCo 1071 A6
- SDCo 1130 H2
Plum Hollow Pl
- VSTA 1107 D2
Plum St
2500 SDGO 1268 C7
1200 SDGO 1288 B2
Plum Tree Ln
- SDCo 1130 J3
1000 SDCo 1271 E7
Plum Tree Rd
- CRLB 1127 B4
- SDCo 1127 A4
Plum Tree Wy
500 OCSD 1086 F3
13400 SDGO 1188 F4
Plum Wy
6200 SDGO 1188 G4
Plumas Pines Pl
1400 CHLV 1311 F7
Plumas St
5800 SDGO 1290 C7
Plumb Broque Cir
1700 SDCo 1252 B5
Plumbago Ln
3500 SDGO 1330 E7
Plumcrest Ln
- SDGO 1208 E1
Plumeria Dr
2700 CRLB 1127 G3
1600 SDCo 1251 G1
800 SNMS 1108 H6
Plumeria Ln
10400 SDCo 1169 F2
Plummer Ct
4700 SDGO 1188 C4
Plumosa Av
200 SDCo 1108 C4
500 VSTA 1108 B4
Plumosa Ct
2400 SDCo 1108 B4
Plumosa Dr
3600 SDGO 1268 C6
Plumosa St
- OCSD 1086 F1
Plumosa Wy
1500 SDGO 1268 H5
Plumtree Dr
1500 ENCT 1167 G1
Plumwood St
14600 POWY 1190 D1
Pluto Ct
3400 SDCo 1310 G1
Pluto Rd
1400 VSTA 1087 D6
Plymouth Ct
- CHLV 1330 E3
Plymouth Dr
100 VSTA 1087 G6
Plymouth St
1400 OCSD 1067 A3
Plz De Benito Juarez
300 VSTA 1087 G5
Poblado Ct
17100 SDGO 1169 J2
Poblado Rd
10800 SDGO 1169 H1
Poblado Wy
17100 SDGO 1169 J2
Pocahontas Av
4500 SDGO 1248 D2
Pocahontas Ct
3600 SDGO 1248 D1
Pocahontas Pl
3600 SDGO 1248 D1
Pocano Wy
13300 SDGO 1189 J4
Pocatello St
100 SDGO 1290 D4
Pochard Wy
- SDGO 1209 G2
Poche Pt
11200 SDGO 1209 J2
Pocitos Wy
3100 SDGO 1350 D2
Poco Lago
6700 SDCo 1188 G2
Poco Montana Rd
5600 SDCo 1175 H1
(See Page 1175)
Poco Pz
- SNMS 1129 C2
Poco Wy
24300 SDCo 1173 E2
Pod Dr
2300 SDCo 1108 D1
Podell Av
9400 SDGO 1249 F6
Poderio Ct
16100 SDCo 1173 H3
Poderio Dr
25200 SDCo 1173 H3
Poe Colonia Ln
- ImCo 6319 D1
(See Page 6319)
Poe Ct
- ImCo 6319 D1
(See Page 6319)
Poe St
10300 SDCo 1109 F2
3400 SDGO 1268 B7
3000 SDGO 1288 C1
Poesia Ct
1600 SDGO 1350 B3
Poets Ct
1400 SDCo 1027 F4
Poets Sq
400 SDCo 1027 F4
Pogo Row
- SDGO 1351 D1
Pohl Pl
- VSTA 1087 F5
Poinciana Dr
8200 SDCo 1231 G7
1600 SDCo 1251 G1
Poinsettia Ct
100 CHLV 1310 B5
Poinsett Rd
11000 SDGO 1209 H1
Poinsettia Av
300 SDCo 1108 C4
800 SNMS 1108 B6
1500 VSTA 1128 A1
Poinsettia Dr
2900 SDGO 1268 C5
Poinsettia Ln
500 CRLB 1126 J6
- CRLB 1127 D4
Poinsettia Park
- ENCT 1147 C5
Poinsettia Park Ct
600 ENCT 1147 C5
Poinsettia Park N
600 ENCT 1147 C5
Poinsettia Park S
600 ENCT 1147 C5
Poinsettia St
500 CHLV 1330 H3
Point Alto
4800 SDCo 1271 C2
Point Arena Ct
500 CHLV 1330 H4
Point Arguello
700 OCSD 1066 G7
Point Arguello Dr
- CHLV 1330 J4
Point Barrow Dr
- CHLV 1330 J3
Point Buchon
800 OCSD 1066 G7
Point Buchon Ct
600 CHLV 1330 J4
Point Cabrillo
700 OCSD 1066 G7
Point Cabrillo Ct
1600 CHLV 1330 J4
Point Caiman Ct
600 CHLV 1330 J3
Point Concepcion Ct
1600 CHLV 1330 J4
Point Defiance Ct
600 CHLV 1330 J3
Point Degada
4400 OCSD 1066 G7
Point Delgada Ct
1500 CHLV 1330 J3
Point Dume Ct
1500 CHLV 1330 J3
Point Estero Dr
1600 CHLV 1330 J5
Point Fermine Ct
- CHLV 1330 J4
Point Hueneme Ct
1500 CHLV 1330 J3
Point La Jolla Dr
1500 CHLV 1330 H4
Point Lobas Cir
- OCSD 1066 G7
Point Loma Av
4400 SDGO 1267 H7
4400 SDGO 1287 J1
W Point Loma Blvd
5100 SDGO 1267 J5
4100 SDGO 1268 C5
Point Loma Ct
1600 CHLV 1330 J4
Point Loma Pl
4800 OCSD 1066 J6
Point Loma Wy
1400 SDGO 1288 A1
Point Malaga Pl
4700 OCSD 1066 J6
Point Medanas Ct
600 CHLV 1330 J4
Point Mugu Ct
1600 CHLV 1330 J4
Point Pacific Ct
1500 CHLV 1330 J3
Point Rd
- ESCN 1129 J1
Point Reyes
700 OCSD 1066 G7
Point Reyes Ct
1600 CHLV 1330 J4
4300 CRLB 1106 J4
Point Sal Ct
1600 CHLV 1330 J4
Point San Luis Ct
500 CHLV 1330 H4
Point St
900 SDGO 1288 A2
Point Sur
700 OCSD 1066 G7
Point Sur Ct
1600 CHLV 1330 J4
Point Vicente
4400 OCSD 1066 G7
Point Vicente Ct
600 CHLV 1330 J3
Point View Ct
4300 SDCo 1271 D3
Point Windemere Pl
300 OCSD 1066 J6
Point Wy
1000 CRLB 1106 G7
Pointe Del Mar Wy
12800 SDGO 1207 J1
Pointe Mountaintop Cir
10500 SDCo 1291 F1
Pointe Pkwy
2300 SDCo 1291 F1
Pointed Oak Ln
10700 SDGO 1210 A3
Pointer Glen
2000 ESCN 1129 E6
Pointer Ln
100 VSTA 1088 B6
Pointillist Ct
4800 OCSD 1087 B3
Pointing Rock Dr
400 SDCo 1058 G5
(See Page 1058)
Poipu Wy
2200 SDGO 1330 D7
Pola Ct
4900 SDGO 1248 F7
Polack St
3900 SDGO 1268 B5
Polanco St
8800 SDGO 1189 C2
Polaris Av
- SDGO 1229 D1
Polaris Dr
600 ENCT 1147 D5
3800 SDCo 1271 A5
10900 SDGO 1209 D3
Polizzi Pl
8200 SDGO 1269 B1
Polk Av
2000 SDGO 1269 C5
5100 SDGO 1270 A5
Polk Rd
2800 SDCo 1234 D4
Polk St
100 OCSD 1067 B6
Polland Av
8800 SDGO 1249 C6
Polley Dr
3400 SNMS 1108 D5
Polly Ln
3800 CRLB 1106 G6
Pollyanna Ter
400 VSTA 1087 G5
Polo Club Dr
- SDCo 1068 D6
Polo Ct
- OCSD 1067 F7
Polo Peak Dr
- CHLV 1311 F7
Polo Pt
14700 SDGO 1188 B1
Polvera Av
12900 SDGO 1150 C5
Polvera Ct
12900 SDGO 1150 C6
Polvera Dr
18500 SDGO 1150 C6
Polvera Wy
18000 SDGO 1150 C6
Polvo Dr
- SDCo 1071 D6
Pomani Ct
1200 OCSD 1087 C3
Pomard Ct
17100 POWY 1170 D2
Pomard Wy
12900 POWY 1170 D2
Pomegranate Ct
- SDCo 1130 H2
Pomegranate Ln
1900 SDCo 1027 H6
Pomegranate Av
- POWY 1190 F3
Pomelo Dr
700 SDCo 1107 E2
100 VSTA 1107 E1
Pomelo Wy
- VSTA 1107 E1
Pomerado Ct
12400 SDGO 1170 C2
Pomerado Pl
12400 SDGO 1170 B2
Pomerado Rd
15400 POWY 1170 C6
13900 POWY 1190 C3
9900 SDCo 1209 F6
19000 SDGO 1150 B6
17100 SDGO 1170 C2
11400 SDGO 1209 H5
11700 SDGO 1210 B4
Pomerado Wy
17100 SDGO 1170 B2
Pomeroy St
3500 SDGO 1249 D4
Pommard Pl
1900 CHLV 1311 G2
Pommel Wy
400 SNMS 1108 E6
Pomona Av
300 CORD 1288 J6
1600 CORD 1308 J1
4600 LMSA 1270 F3
Pomona Wy
7300 LMSA 1270 F3
Pompei Ln
9000 SDGO 1249 D7
Ponca Ct
6000 SDGO 1250 D5
Ponce De Leon Dr
4100 SDCo 1271 H4
Pond Pl
100 VSTA 1087 G3
Ponder Wy
10500 SDGO 1209 B4
Ponderosa Av
4200 SDGO 1249 D2
1000 SNMS 1109 B5
Ponderosa Ct
2600 ESCN 1110 C5
Ponderosa Dr
3500 OCSD 1086 F2
700 VSTA 1088 A5
Ponderosa Ln
8600 SDCo 1237 C4
Ponderosa Pine Ln
7600 SDCo 1237 C7
Pons St
600 SDGO 1290 F3
Ponsettia Ln
- CRLB 1127 C5
Ponte Av
400 SNMS 1108 C6
Ponte Verda Wy
2400 CHLV 1311 H6
Pontiac Dr
3400 CRLB 1106 J4
4500 CRLB 1107 A5
Pontiac St
6100 SDGO 1270 C2
Ponto Dr
6500 CRLB 1126 H5
Ponto Rd
- CRLB 1126 J7
Pony Ct
5600 OCSD 1067 F7
Pony Express Cir
- SDCo 1232 F5
Pony Ln
5500 SDCo 1311 A2
Poole St
9400 SDGO 1227 J3
Poomacha Rd
- SDCo 1072 F2
(See Page 1072)
Popkorn Dr
- VSTA 1088 B4
Poplar Av
400 SNMS 1108 J6
Poplar Dr
1200 ELCN 6559 G1
Poplar Meadow Ln
2800 SDCo 1292 G3
(See Page 1292)
Poplar Rd
2000 OCSD 1086 C5
Poplar Spring Rd
- CHLV 1311 J5
Poplar St
900 SDCo 1152 F4
4200 SDGO 1269 H7
Poplar Wy
300 ESCN 1129 H1
Poplin Dr
7900 SNTE 1250 H1
Poppy Cir
300 OCSD 1066 H7
Poppy Ct
- IMPE 6499 D2
Poppy Dr
29500 SDCo 1297 E5
(See Page 1297)
Poppy Hills Dr
2300 CHLV 1311 G7
Poppy Hills Ln
3200 ENCT 1148 C6
Poppy Hills Wy
11600 SDGO 1190 A3
Poppy Ln
900 CRLB 1127 A6
3700 SDCo 1028 E4
Poppy Pl
4000 SDGO 1269 G7
Poppy Rd
- SNMS 1128 F2
Poppy St
5900 LMSA 1251 C6
Poppyfield Glen
300 ESCN 1109 H5
Poppyfield Pl
2100 ENCT 1147 J7
Poquito St
- POWY 1190 C6
Poquito Wy
4200 OCSD 1086 H3
Porcelina Ct
- SDGO 1210 B1
Porch Swing St
2300 CHLV 1311 G7
Porreca Pt
11300 SDGO 1208 J2
Port Albans
1800 CHLV 1311 D4
Port Ashley
600 CHLV 1311 E3
Port Cardiff
2000 CHLV 1311 E3
Port Carney
- CHLV 1311 D3
Port Chelsea
600 CHLV 1311 D4
Port Cir
3300 OCSD 1107 A2
Port Claridge
- CHLV 1311 D4
Port Dunbar
600 CHLV 1311 D4
Port Harwick
500 CHLV 1311 D4
Port Marnock Dr
17400 POWY 1170 E1
Port Marnock Wy
13400 POWY 1170 E1
Port Of Spain Rd
- CORD 1329 E2
Port Renwick
1800 CHLV 1311 D4
Port Royale
- CORD 1329 E2
Port Royale Cove
10200 SDGO 1209 B5
Port Royale Dr
8000 SDGO 1209 B5
Port Rush Row
11400 SDGO 1189 J3
Port Stirling
600 CHLV 1311 E3
Port Trinity
600 CHLV 1311 D4
Porta Pl
2400 CRLB 1106 H5
Portada Pl
12500 SDGO 1188 B6
Portage Wy
7300 CRLB 1126 J7
Portal Terr
12100 SDGO 1190 A7
Porte De Merano
4100 SDGO 1228 B4
Porte De Palmas
4200 SDGO 1228 B4
Porte La Paz
4000 SDGO 1228 B5
Portecho Ct
5400 SDGO 1249 H1
Porteno Ct
1000 SDCo 1128 C2
Porter Creek Rd
5500 SDGO 1188 E5
Porter Hill Rd
4900 LMSA 1270 J2
Porter Hill Ter
8400 LMSA 1270 J2
Porter Ln
1800 SDCo 1136 B7
Porter Rd
4200 LMSA 1271 A4
- SDGO 1268 D7
E Porter Rd
2800 SDGO 1288 C1
Porter St
500 SDCo 1027 G1
600 SDGO 1290 F3
Porter Ville Pl
- CHLV 1311 E5
Porter Wy
800 SDCo 1027 G1
Porterfield Pl
1700 SDCo 1272 B4
Portfolio St
4800 OCSD 1087 B2
Portia Av
200 VSTA 1087 H3
Portico Blvd
- CALX 6620 E5
Portico Dr
500 OCSD 1086 G1
Portilla Pl
4100 SDGO 1188 B7
Portillo Rd
900 SDCo 1029 G4
Portland Ct
3700 CRLB 1107 A5
Portland St
800 ELCJ 1251 G7
Porto Ct
10500 SDGO 1249 H1
Portobelo Ct
5900 SDGO 1229 H6
Portobelo Dr
10500 SDGO 1229 H7
Portofino Cir
12900 SDGO 1207 H2
Portofino Dr
1800 OCSD 1106 F1
13300 SDGO 1187 J7
12700 SDGO 1207 J1
1400 VSTA 1107 J4
Portola Av
1300 ESCN 1109 E5
1000 SDCo 1291 C2
Portola Ct
4800 CRLB 1107 A6
Portola Pl
3900 SDGO 1268 H5
Portola St
1100 VSTA 1087 J4
Porton Ct
- CALX 6620 H7
Portovenere Ct
19800 SDCo 1152 C3
Portside Pl
500 SDGO 1330 J7
- SNMS 1128 C6
Portsmouth Bay Ct
4800 OCSD 1066 J6
Portsmouth Ct
700 SDGO 1267 H1
Portsmouth Dr
500 CHLV 1330 H3
Posada Ct
- CALX 6620 H7
3900 OCSD 1086 G1
Poseidon Wy
4900 OCSD 1107 E6
Posey Pl
4200 SDGO 1289 H1
Positas Rd
1200 CHLV 1311 A5
Positive Pl
- SNMS 1108 H7
Possum Creek Ln
9900 SDCo 1232 H2
Possum Pass
18800 SDCo 1091 F3
Post Hill Pl
11400 SDCo 1211 J7
Post Hill Rd
11100 SDCo 1211 J7
Post Oak Ln
15100 SDCo 1233 A1
Post Rd
4300 SDGO 1228 E7
Post Trl
700 SDCo 1253 C2
Postal Wy
900 VSTA 1087 J7
Potomac Ridge Rd
- SDGO 1169 D3
Potomac St
6000 SDGO 1290 D7
5700 SDGO 1310 C1
Potrero Cres
1600 SDCo 1316 C6
(See Page 1316)
Potrero Ct
900 CHLV 1330 E1
Potrero St
8700 SDCo 1290 J2
Potrero Valley Rd
25500 SDCo 1316 D6
(See Page 1316)
Potter Av
- SDGO 1229 F3
Potter St
500 SDCo 1027 G3
Potter Valley Dr
- CHLV 1311 E6
Poumele Wy
1800 OCSD 1106 E1
Poverty Ridge
25100 SDCo 1236 B2
Poway Creek Rd
- POWY 1190 E5
Poway Hills Dr
13200 POWY 1190 D1
Poway Mesa Ct
14500 POWY 1190 E1
Poway Mesa Dr
14700 POWY 1190 E1
Poway Rd
12800 POWY 1190 D4
15500 POWY 1191 A2
10600 SDGO 1189 G6

San Diego County Street Index

STREET
Block City Map# Grid

Poway Springs Ct
15300 POWY 1170 F6
Poway Springs Rd
13600 POWY 1170 F6
Poway Valley Rd
13900 POWY 1190 F1
Powderhorn Dr
4300 SDGO 1330 G7
Powell Ct
2800 ImCo 6439 C5
Powell Dr
1800 ELCJ 1251 C4
Powell Rd
1500 OCSD 1087 E1
Powers Ct
13200 POWY 1190 C4
Powers Rd
13500 POWY 1190 C3
Powhatan Av
2700 SDGO 1248 B1
Poyntell Cir
10800 SDGO 1210 A3
Pozo Rico Ct
100 SOLB 1167 H5
Pradera Pl
3600 SDCo 1310 F3
Prado Ct
5100 OCSD 1087 C1
12300 SDGO 1170 B2
Prado Pl
17100 SDGO 1170 B2
Prado Rd
17200 SDGO 1170 B2
Prado Verde
500 SNMS 1109 A6
Prado Wy
12200 SDGO 1170 B2
Praful Ct
9300 SNTE 1230 H6
Prairie Dog Av
12700 SDGO 1189 C5
Prairie Dr
- CHLV 1311 F4
Prairie Fawn Ct
16700 SDCo 1169 G4
Prairie Fawn Dr
10100 SDCo 1169 E3
Prairie Mile Rd
17200 SDCo 1173 D1
Prairie Mound Ct
500 SDGO 1290 H5
Prairie Mound Wy
7500 SDGO 1290 G6
Prairie Rd
- OCSD 1067 B5
Prairie Rose Wy
400 SNMS 1128 G2
Prairie Shadow Pt
11500 SDGO 1209 A1
Prairie Shadow Rd
7700 SDGO 1209 A2
Prairie Springs Rd
10000 SDCo 1169 E3
Prairie Vista Rd
15800 POWY 1170 G5
Prairiestone Wy
2700 ESCN 1110 D5
Prairiewood Dr
11400 SDGO 1209 A2
Prancer Wy
7300 SDGO 1290 G6
Prather Pl
400 SDCo 1291 B4
Prato Ln
2600 SDGO 1249 D7
Pratrie Dr
- SDCo 1274 D3
Pratt Ct
9900 SNTE 1231 D3
Pray Ct
5600 SDCo 1290 J7
Pray St
5700 SDCo 1290 J6
Preakness Ct
3400 SDCo 1047 G2
Preciado Rd
- ImCo 6439 D4
Precious Hills Rd
500 OCSD 1067 F3
Precision Park Ln
1600 SDGO 1350 E2
Predio Ct
1600 SDGO 1350 B2
Preece St
2800 SDGO 1248 H6
Preece Wy
6500 SDGO 1248 H6
Prego Ct
12600 SDGO 1188 C6
Premier St
1700 SDCo 1028 A5
Prescott Av
500 ELCJ 1251 F6
Prescott Ct
1900 VSTA 1107 J4
Prescott Dr
1500 CHLV 1312 A6
(See Page 1312)
Prescott Glen
- ESCN 1110 D7
Presidents Wy
1900 SDGO 1289 B1
Presidio Dr
2600 SDGO 1268 F4
Presidio Point Ct
1600 CHLV 1330 J4
Presilla Dr
- SDCo 1293 C4
Presioca St
1300 SDCo 1291 B2
Presley Pl
200 VSTA 1108 A2
Presley St
10100 SDGO 1208 J5
Press Ln
100 CHLV 1310 B4
Prestige
2000 SDCo 1152 E1
Preston Dr N
700 CALX 6620 G7
Preston Dr S
700 CALX 6680 G1
Preston Pl
1300 CHLV 1330 D4
Prestwick Cir
3500 OCSD 1107 E3
Prestwick Ct
2600 SDGO 1227 J4
- SNMS 1108 J3
900 VSTA 1108 A4
Prestwick Dr
8100 SDGO 1227 J5
Prestwick Wy
8800 SNTE 1230 J5
Price Wy
- SDCo 1023 D2
Pridemore Pl
4100 SDGO 1248 E5
Priestly Dr
5800 CRLB 1127 D1
Prieto Rd
900 SDCo 998 H6
Prima Vera
1500 OCSD 1087 B4
Primavera Dr
- CALX 6620 H7
Primavera Ln
1500 DLMR 1187 G4
Primavera Wy
7600 CRLB 1147 H1
Primentel Ln
7000 CRLB 1127 G7
Primera St
1900 LMGR 1290 F1
Primero Izquierdo
6500 SDCo 1148 E6
Primrose Av
2100 SDCo 1108 C3
Primrose Ct
14200 POWY 1170 G5
Primrose Dr
1600 ELCJ 1251 C6
6300 LMSA 1251 C6
29500 SDCo 1297 F5
(See Page 1297)
Primrose Glen
3800 ESCN 1150 B3
Primrose Ln
1000 ENCT 1147 G4
7100 SDGO 1188 J4
Primrose Pl
- CHLV 1310 C4
300 SDCo 1108 C4
Primrose Wy
7100 CRLB 1127 A6
400 OCSD 1086 J4
Prince Carlos Ln
10600 SNTE 1231 E2
Prince Charming Ln
10100 SNTE 1231 D1
Prince Edward Ct
2300 SDCo 1272 B5
Prince Ivan Ct
7900 SDCo 1252 A2
Prince Jed Ct
10200 SNTE 1231 D2
Prince Ln
10700 SDCo 1271 F3
Prince St
1000 ELCJ 1251 H4
1800 SDCo 1027 J5
1800 SDCo 1028 A5
3500 SDCo 1150 D2
Prince Valiant Dr
10800 SNTE 1231 D1
Prince Wy
2300 VSTA 1088 A2
Princehouse Ln
- ENCT 1147 E6
Princesa Ct
1100 CHLV 1310 J5
Princess Arlene Dr
10700 SNTE 1231 D2
Princess Joann Rd
10300 SNTE 1231 D1
Princess Manor Ct
1400 CHLV 1330 G3
Princess Marcie Dr
10200 SNTE 1231 D2
Princess Sarit Wy
10200 SNTE 1231 D2
Princess St
7900 SDGO 1227 G5
Princess View Ct
5400 SDGO 1250 B5
Princess View Dr
7300 SDGO 1250 A5
Princess View Pl
5400 SDGO 1250 B5
Princess View Wy
5400 SDGO 1250 B5
Princeton Av
7200 LMSA 1270 F3
3500 SDGO 1248 D5
Princeton Dr
3300 OCSD 1107 A2
Princeton St
- BRAW 6260 C7
(See Page 6260)
Pringle Canyon Rd
19500 SDCo 1314 E3
(See Page 1314)
Pringle St
3900 SDGO 1268 H5
Printwood Ct
4700 SDGO 1248 J1
Printwood Wy
5900 SDGO 1248 J1
W Printwood Wy
5600 SDGO 1248 H1
Priscilla St
14800 SDGO 1169 J7
14800 SDGO 1189 J1
Prism Dr
900 SNMS 1128 F6
Privado Glen
1900 ESCN 1129 E4
Privado Pl
1300 SDGO 1290 A6
Privet Pl
- SDCo 1089 B2
Privet St
- SNMS 1109 C7
Proctor Pl
4200 SDGO 1269 B4
Proctor Valley Ln
13700 SDCo 1292 G2
(See Page 1292)
Proctor Valley Rd
10700 CHLV 1311 G3
13800 SDCo 1292 G3
(See Page 1292)
3400 SDCo 1311 D2
12100 SDCo 1312 A3
(See Page 1312)
Production Av
3200 OCSD 1086 D5
8600 SDGO 1228 J1
Production St
400 SNMS 1128 J1
Progress Ln
700 SDCo 1172 H1
Progress Pl
2800 ESCN 1129 C2
Progress St
2500 VSTA 1108 B7
Progress Tr
- IMPE 6499 E2
Progressive Av
- SDGO 1351 B1
Prohoroff Ln
100 SNMS 1108 G7
Promenade Cir
1700 VSTA 1087 D7
Promenade North Pl
8700 SDGO 1249 D1
Promenade Park Terr
4700 SDGO 1249 C2
Promenade Pl
1700 VSTA 1087 D7
Promesa Cir
4400 SDGO 1250 A1
Promesa Ct
4400 SDGO 1250 A1
Promesa Dr
11000 SDGO 1249 J1
11200 SDGO 1250 A1
Promise Ln
12000 SDCo 1231 J2
Promontory Dr
100 SDCo 1252 H4
Promontory Pl
- CRLB 1107 B3
Promontory Ridge Wy
1600 VSTA 1107 G4
Promontory St
4000 SDGO 1248 A6
Prospect Av
400 SDCo 1027 G2
9500 SDCo 1232 A4
8600 SNTE 1230 J7
8300 SNTE 1231 A7
Prospect Cir
1100 VSTA 1107 H2
Prospect Ct
- CHLV 1330 E3
8500 SNTE 1250 J1
Prospect Pl
200 CORD 1289 A6
2000 SDCo 1136 C6
7700 SDGO 1227 F6
1100 VSTA 1107 H2
Prospect St
100 CHLV 1330 E3
2200 NATC 1310 B1
2800 SDCo 1310 B3
400 SDGO 1227 E7
E Prospect St
- CHLV 1330 E3
Prospect Wy
8000 LMSA 1270 H3
Prospectors Sq
- SDCo 1232 E4
Prosperity Dr
400 SNMS 1109 A6
Prosperity Ln
5200 SDGO 1270 A2
Protea Dr
8400 SDCo 1252 A1
Protea Gardens Rd
9800 SDCo 1089 D7
Protea Vista Dr
- SDCo 1068 E7
Protea Vista Terr
3000 SDCo 1068 E6
Provencal Pl
13600 SDGO 1189 J3
Provence Ct
- CHLV 1330 E3
Providence Bay Ct
11800 SDCo 1231 J3
Providence Dr
1500 VSTA 1107 E1
Providence Ln
- CRLB 1107 A4
Providence Rd
5000 SDGO 1228 E7
Province Ct
17100 SDCo 1169 A1
Provo St
300 ELCJ 1252 B5
Pruett Dr
2400 SDCo 1087 H1
Pruett Rd
- CALX 6620 E6
Pruett St
- CALX 6620 E7
Prussian Wy
1100 OCSD 1067 A3
Pryor Rd
9500 SNTE 1231 C7
Pso De Los Castillos
8500 SNTE 1251 C1
Psom Down Wy
- SOLB 1187 F2
Public Rd
- CRLB 1127 D1
- SDCo 1273 H6
- SDCo 1314 C1
(See Page 1314)
- SDCo 1315 A2
(See Page 1315)
Puebla Dr
- OCSD 1086 F2
10900 SDCo 1271 F3
Puebla St
700 ENCT 1147 C5
2600 SDCo 1150 D1
Pueblo Av
9100 SDCo 1232 A5
Pueblo Dr
34700 SDCo 1176 E4
(See Page 1176)
Pueblo Glen
2100 ESCN 1110 B5
Pueblo Pl
- CHLV 1311 G3
Pueblo Rd
8400 SDCo 1232 A7
Pueblo St
2900 CRLB 1147 H1
1900 SDGO 1289 D4
Pueblo Vista Ln
17900 SDGO 1149 H7
Puente Dr
1800 SDGO 1227 G6
Puerta De Lomas
600 OCSD 1067 E1
300 SDCo 1047 F7
Puerta Del Sol
16200 SDCo 1168 B5
Puerto De Destino
5500 SDCo 1148 C6
Puerto Del Mundo
1700 SDCo 1028 F5
Puerto Escondido Ct
- IMPE 6499 H2
Puerto Escondido Dr
- IMPE 6499 G1
Puerto Oro Ct
700 OCSD 1087 C1
Puerto Oro Ln
- SDCo 1151 G3
Puerto Vallarta Av
- IMPE 6499 G1
Puesta Del Sol
2200 ESCN 1130 E2
Puesta Del Sol Ln
- SDCo 1171 C1
Puesta Pl
2100 ELCJ 1251 C1
Puffen Pl
- CRLB 1127 C6
Puffin Dr
200 VSTA 1087 G4
Puffin Pl
1600 CHLV 1331 D2
Pulitzer Dr
4000 SDGO 1228 C3
Puller Pl
- SDCo 1023 E2
E Puls St
1500 OCSD 1086 B6
W Puls St
1300 OCSD 1086 B6
Puma Trl
- SDCo 1070 G4
Pummelo Ct
2600 ESCN 1110 D6
Punta Arroyo
19000 SDCo 1149 A3
Punta Baja Dr
300 SOLB 1167 H6
Punta Del Norte
18000 SDCo 1148 H5
Punta Del Sur
17800 SDCo 1148 J6
Punta Dulcina
11500 SDGO 1210 H1
Purdue Av
7400 LMSA 1270 F4
Purdue Ct
1800 OCSD 1087 C5
Purdum Ln
1400 ESCN 1130 B4
Purdy St
1100 SDCo 1290 J2
Pure Waters Ct
10100 SDCo 1291 F2
Purebred Ln
21900 SDCo 1129 B4
Purer Rd
3700 SDCo 1149 G3
Puritan Dr
1400 OCSD 1067 A4
Puritan Wy
1400 OCSD 1067 A3
Purple Blossom Dr
- SDCo 1128 G3
Purple Leaf Wy
- SDCo 1169 D2
Purple Sage
7900 SDGO 1188 J1
Purple Sage St
13100 SDCo 1090 E6
Puterbaugh St
1400 SDGO 1268 H6
Putney Rd
13900 POWY 1190 F3
Putter Ct
- SDCo 1272 C5
Putter Dr
3600 SDCo 1310 D4
Putter Pl
3400 OCSD 1106 H1
3400 SDCo 1310 D4
Putter Wy
1100 SDCo 1079 B4
(See Page 1079)
Putting Green Ct
3300 OCSD 1106 J2
Putting Green Row
12100 SDGO 1170 A4
Pyeatt Truck Rd
- SDCo 996 E1
Pylos Wy
4900 OCSD 1107 E6
Pyramid Peak St
1300 CHLV 1331 C2
Pyramid Point Wy
700 OCSD 1066 F7
Pyramid St
800 SDGO 1290 C3
Pyranees
- SNMS 1128 C1
Pyrite Av
- CRLB 1127 F3
Pyrite St
- IMPE 6439 C6
Pyrus Pl
- CRLB 1127 A4

Q

Q Av
500 NATC 1290 A7
1400 NATC 1310 A1
N Q Av
100 NATC 1289 J6
Quadra Av
2800 SDGO 1350 C3
Quail Canyon Rd
9800 SDCo 1232 G3
10900 SDCo 1233 A1
Quail Covey Ln
9800 SDCo 1232 H2
Quail Creek Dr
- SDCo 997 G7
Quail Creek Pl
- SDCo 1130 H3
2500 SDCo 1234 A5
Quail Crest Rd
- SDCo 1233 G6
Quail Crossing Rd
16800 SDCo 1171 D1
Quail Ct
400 CHLV 1330 G3
Quail Dr
100 CHLV 1330 F3
17900 SDCo 1051 G5
Quail Gardens Ct
1000 ENCT 1147 D6
Quail Gardens Dr
600 ENCT 1147 D4
300 SDCo 1147 D5
Quail Gardens Ln
400 ENCT 1147 D5
Quail Glen Rd
1900 SDCo 1149 F1
Quail Glen Wy
100 SDCo 1149 F1
Quail Haven Ln
14600 SDCo 1253 A5
Quail Hill Rd
900 SDCo 1027 G1
Quail Hollow Dr
- ENCT 1147 C3
Quail Hollow Ln
29700 SDCo 1070 E5
Quail Hollow Rd
3200 SDCo 1155 G3
Quail Knoll Ln
1000 SDCo 1047 H1
Quail Ln
200 OCSD 1086 H2
Quail Meadow Rd
2000 SDCo 1152 E1
Quail Mountain Rd
15600 POWY 1171 B6
Quail Pl
300 CHLV 1330 G3
1900 CRLB 1127 E5
Quail Pointe Ln
500 ENCT 1147 D6
Quail Rd
200 ENCT 1147 D6
2700 ESCN 1109 G3
3100 SDCo 1109 G2
30000 SDCo 1297 G5
(See Page 1297)
Quail Ridge Ln
4600 SDCo 1099 G5
(See Page 1099)
Quail Ridge Rd
1600 SDCo 1130 E5
Quail Rock Rd
16200 SDCo 1171 G4
Quail Run
300 ELCJ 1252 D4
2500 SDCo 1299 J4
(See Page 1299)
Quail Run Dr
- ELCN 6559 J4
500 SDCo 1058 H5
(See Page 1058)
Quail Run St
6100 SDGO 1188 F3
Quail Springs Ct
10500 SDGO 1209 J3
Quail St
900 SDGO 1289 G3
Quail Ter
12400 SDCo 1232 B7
Quail Trail Dr
18600 SDCo 1294 D6
(See Page 1294)
Quail Valley Wy
14800 SDCo 1232 J2
Quail View Dr
1900 SDCo 1088 B2
- SDCo 1089 D5
Quail Wy
3200 SDCo 1273 A6
Quailcreek Ln
9600 SDCo 1271 C5
Quailridge Dr
4500 OCSD 1087 D5
Quails Trl
500 VSTA 1107 J3
Quailsprings Ct
- CHLV 1311 D6
Quailview Ct
3600 SDCo 1271 C5
Quailview St
3500 SDCo 1271 C5
Quaker Hill Ln
- SDGO 1208 D2
Qualcomm Wy
- SDGO 1249 F7
Quality Rd
- SDCo 996 J2
Qualtrough St
3000 SDGO 1288 A3
Quanah Ct
3800 SDCo 1099 D2
(See Page 1099)
Quantico Av
4500 SDGO 1248 E2
Quapaw Av
4100 SDGO 1248 D3
Quarry Glen
- ESCN 1110 D7
Quarry Rd
3700 LMGR 1270 J5
3900 LMSA 1270 J5
- SDCo 1088 G5
5700 SDCo 1290 J6
6300 SDCo 1291 A4
Quarry St
200 SNMS 1128 J1
Quarry View Wy
500 SDCo 1290 J5
Quarter Horse Cir
5500 OCSD 1067 D6
Quarter Mile Dr
3700 SDGO 1188 A5
Quarterdeck
- SDGO 1331 A6
Quartet Lp
- CHLV 1331 G2
Quartz Ct
1000 SNMS 1128 E5
Quartz Dr
2500 SDCo 1297 G4
(See Page 1297)
Quartz Hill Ln
1300 SDCo 1130 C3
Quartz St
- IMPE 6439 C6
Quartz Wy
- CRLB 1127 G4
35200 SDCo 1156 F6
Quasar Dr
12500 POWY 1190 C3
Quashish Rd
11900 SDCo 1029 J3
Quate Ct
13100 POWY 1190 E4
Quay Av
400 CHLV 1329 H1
2400 NATC 1309 G4
Quay Rd
- CORD 1288 G4
Quebec Ct
6800 SDGO 1290 F7
Quebec Pl
1700 ESCN 1129 J5
Quebrada Cir
2900 CRLB 1147 H2
Quebrada Ct
3100 CRLB 1147 J2
Queen Anne Dr
400 CHLV 1330 C3
E Queen Anne Dr
100 CHLV 1330 F2
Queen Anne Ln
29500 SDCo 1069 C6
Queen Av
10500 SDCo 1271 F3
Queen Jessica Ln
10600 SNTE 1231 E2
Queens Wy
1700 VSTA 1088 B3
Queensbridge Rd
28100 SDCo 1090 J2
Queensferry Sq
16100 SDGO 1170 B4
Queenston Dr
1600 ESCN 1130 C2
Queenstown Ct
800 SDGO 1267 H1
Quemado Ct
5200 SDGO 1249 F1
Quemoy Ct
6900 SDGO 1248 J6
Quentin Ct
600 ENCT 1147 D7
Quentin Roosevelt Blvd
- CORD 1288 G4
Querida Sol
18100 SDCo 1148 D6
Quest Ln
1600 CHLV 1331 H1
Quest Rd
- SDCo 1152 E1
Questa Pt
9700 SDGO 1209 E1
Questhaven Rd
21200 SDCo 1128 G6
- SDCo 1148 H2
Questor Pl
9100 SDGO 1249 E7
Quicker Rd
1800 SDCo 1252 C2
Quidde Av
2500 SDGO 1228 A6
Quidde Ct
5600 SDGO 1228 B6
Quidort Ct
1900 ELCJ 1251 C5
Quiet Cove Dr
6900 CRLB 1126 J5
Quiet Creek Wy
- CHLV 1311 F4
Quiet Hills Dr
1700 OCSD 1087 D4
13500 POWY 1191 A4
3100 SDCo 1149 J2
800 SNMS 1109 C6
Quiet Hills Farm Rd
700 SDCo 1149 J2
Quiet Hills Pl
3100 ESCN 1149 J3
Quiet Hollow Ln
27700 SDCo 1089 G4
Quiet Oaks Trl
4800 SDCo 1155 J5
4600 SDCo 1156 A5
Quiet Pl
27500 SDCo 1090 J3
700 SDCo 1149 J2
Quiet Ranch Rd
1800 SDCo 1028 A6
Quiet Ridge Ln
4600 SDCo 1048 G1
Quiet Slope Dr
5900 SDGO 1250 C4
Quiet Trail Dr
1700 CHLV 1331 H1
Quiet Trail Wy
2400 CHLV 1311 H7
Quiet Valley Ln
15600 POWY 1191 A3
Quiet View Ln
1700 SDCo 1233 H7
Quietwood Ln
16700 SDCo 1169 A2
Quigg Pl
1000 VSTA 1088 A7
Quilalang Ct
3300 SDGO 1350 F5
Quilalang St
- CHLV 1330 H3
Quilcene Ct
2200 VSTA 1108 B4
Quill Glen
1200 ESCN 1129 F5
Quill St
- OCSD 1087 C1
Quillan St
6400 SDGO 1248 H6
Quilters Dr
2800 SDCo 1129 C5
Quimby St
3400 SDGO 1268 B7
3300 SDGO 1288 C1
Quinalt Pt
- SDGO 1210 A2
Quince Ct
13000 SDCo 1090 D7
Quince Dr
700 SDGO 1269 B7
Quince Ln
- SDCo 1149 E3
Quince Pl
300 CHLV 1330 G3
Quince St
400 CHLV 1330 G3
7800 LMSA 1270 H3
200 SDGO 1269 A7
N Quince St
700 ESCN 1129 H2
S Quince St
200 ESCN 1129 H3
1700 ESCN 1130 A5
W Quince St
1000 SDGO 1268 J7
Quincy Canyon Rd
- SDCo 1192 H7
(See Page 1192)
Quincy St
4900 SDGO 1248 B4
Quinda Ct
- CHLV 1330 G3
Quinn Ct
6900 SDGO 1268 J1
Quinn Pl
- ELCJ 1251 D7
Quinnel Ct
12900 SDGO 1188 B5
Quinta St
7500 CRLB 1147 H1
Quintain Dr
2000 SDCo 1058 G7
(See Page 1058)
Quintard St
300 CHLV 1330 D4
E Quintard St
100 CHLV 1330 F3
Quinto Creek Pl
- CHLV 1311 F6
Quinton Rd
13700 SDGO 1189 F3
Quitasol St
7700 CRLB 1147 F2
Quito Ct
4700 SDGO 1250 A1
Quivira Ct
2500 SDGO 1268 A4
Quivira Rd
1400 SDGO 1268 A3
Quivira Wy
1400 SDGO 1268 A4
Quorum Ct
100 SNMS 1128 H3

R

R Av
500 NATC 1290 A7
1100 NATC 1310 A1
N R Av
- NATC 1290 A6
S R Av
- CORD 1288 G5
R Carrillo Ct
- CALX 6620 H6
R D Platero Av
700 CALX 6680 D1
R Santos St
- CALX 6620 J5
R Tamayo St
- CALX 6620 J6
Rab St
5500 LMSA 1250 H7
Rabbit Hill
1700 SDCo 1028 C5
Rabbit Ridge Rd
5500 SDGO 1188 E5
Rabbit Run
- SDCo 1070 H4
Raccoon Ct
12200 SDCo 1212 C4
Race Point Ct
500 CHLV 1330 H4
Racetrack View Ct
13400 SDGO 1187 H4
Racetrack View Dr
- SDGO 1187 G4
Rachael Av
400 NATC 1290 B6
2300 SDGO 1310 C1
Rachel Av
800 NATC 1290 C7
Rachel Cir
1100 SDCo 1109 E6
Rachelle Pl
1900 ESCN 1129 J6
Rachelle Wy
- SDCo 1252 D3
Racine Ct
5200 SDCo 1290 J7
Racine Rd
- SDCo 1270 E5
Racquet Ct
13300 POWY 1190 H4
Radar Rd
1400 SDGO 1351 G1
Radcliffe Ct
6700 SDGO 1228 D5
Radcliffe Dr
6700 SDGO 1228 D4
Radcliffe Ln
3800 SDGO 1228 E5
Radenz Av
7400 SDGO 1249 A6
Radford St
1900 OCSD 1087 C5
5000 SDGO 1250 A5
Radio Ct
5800 SDGO 1290 C5
Radio Dr
500 SDGO 1290 C3
E Radio Dr
6000 SDGO 1290 C2
S Radio Dr
500 SDGO 1290 C5
Rae Dr
- SDCo 1271 A7
Rae Ln
100 OCSD 1086 G3
Rae Pl
2500 SDCo 1310 B2
Raecorte Pl
- SDCo 1109 D6
Raedel Ct
1900 SDGO 1330 A7
Raedel Dr
1000 SDGO 1350 A1
Raedene Wy
- SDGO 1209 G1
Raejean Av
8700 SDGO 1249 C7
Raffee Dr
4100 SDGO 1248 D3
Rafter Wy
- SDCo 1129 D5
Rag Doll Ln
3000 SDCo 1088 E3
Ragweed Ct
8800 SDGO 1189 D6
Ragweed St
12400 SDGO 1189 C6
Rail Ct
5900 SDGO 1350 J5
Railroad Av
- ESCN 1129 G3
8800 SNTE 1231 E6
E Railroad Blvd
- CALX 6680 F1
W Railroad Blvd
700 CALX 6680 F1
Railroad St
- SDCo 1321 G5
(See Page 1321)
Rain Forest Rd
1300 CHLV 1311 B6
Rain Meadow Rd
11000 SDCo 1231 F3
Rain Path Av
1300 CALX 6620 D7
Rain Patter Ln
- CHLV 1311 G7
Rainbird Rd
15700 SDCo 1173 G5

55 INDEX
INDEX 55
Rainbow Av
Red Willow Pl
SAN DIEGO CO.

San Diego County Street Index

STREET Block City Map# Grid

Rainbow Av
1200 CALX 6620 D7
Rainbow Creek Rd
- SDCo 998 J3
- SDCo 999 A3
Rainbow Crest Rd
1300 SDCo 999 B7
300 SDCo 1029 D3
Rainbow Ct
- VSTA 1107 C1
Rainbow Dr
600 CHLV 1330 H1
500 IMPB 1329 G7
Rainbow Glen Rd
- SDCo 998 E4
Rainbow Heights Ln
6400 SDCo 999 B6
Rainbow Heights Pl
38300 SDCo 999 B5
Rainbow Heights Rd
5400 SDCo 998 J5
- SDCo 999 C3
Rainbow Hills Rd
- SDCo 998 F6
Rainbow Ln
200 OCSD 1086 C7
Rainbow Oaks Dr
0 RivC 999 F1
Rainbow Peaks Rd
- SDCo 999 B5
Rainbow Peaks Trl
38700 SDCo 999 C4
Rainbow Pl
600 ESCN 1110 E7
Rainbow Ridge Ln
1300 ENCT 1147 C3
Rainbow St
6900 SDGO 1290 F3
Rainbow Terr
5700 SDCo 999 A6
Rainbow Valley Blvd
- RivC 999 A2
1000 SDCo 998 G6
Rainbow Valley Ct
1000 SDCo 998 G6
Rainbow Valley West Blvd
1600 SDCo 998 J2
Rainbow Vista Dr
4400 SDCo 998 G6
Rainbow Wy
5200 SDCo 998 J6
Rainbrook Dr
- SDCo 1029 C3
Raineer Wy
- OCSD 1086 G1
Rainey Ct
1500 ENCT 1147 D3
Rainey St
7900 LMSA 1250 H6
Rainier Av
4500 SDGO 1249 J6
Rainier Ct
100 CHLV 1330 F4
Rainswept Ct
8500 SDGO 1250 J2
Rainswept Ln
7400 SDGO 1250 J3
Rainswept Pl
8500 SDGO 1250 J3
Rainswept Wy
8400 SDGO 1250 J2
Raintree Dr
700 CRLB 1126 J6
200 ENCT 1147 A3
500 VSTA 1087 H5
Raintree Pl
2200 ESCN 1109 F4
800 VSTA 1087 H5
Raintree Wy
5600 OCSD 1067 F6
Rainwood Ct
600 OCSD 1086 D3
Raju St
11100 SDGO 1169 H7
Raleigh Av
300 ELCJ 1251 E5
- SDGO 1249 B7
Ralene St
2200 SDGO 1289 G1
Ralls St
2500 SDCo 1028 B2
Ralph Rd
- IMPE 6439 E3
- ImCo 6439 G3
Ralph Wy
700 SDGO 1330 F7
Ralphs Ranch Rd
17200 SDCo 1169 F1
Ralston Cir
12800 SDGO 1188 B5
Ram Ln
1300 SDCo 1047 H1
Rama De Las Palmas
- SDCo 1168 D7
Ramada Dr
2100 OCSD 1086 J7
16400 SDGO 1170 B4
Rambla Brisa
1400 SNMS 1109 D7
Rambla De Las Flores
16900 SDCo 1168 A4
Rambla Puesta
1400 SNMS 1109 D7
Rambla Serena
1400 SNMS 1109 D7
Ramblewood Rd
1300 SDCo 1233 H6
Rambling Rd
400 ENCT 1147 G5
Rambling Vista Rd
- CHLV 1311 J6
2700 CHLV 1312 A6
(See Page 1312)
Rambling Wy
500 SDCo 1152 C6
Rambur St
- CHLV 1330 J3
Ramfos Cir
6800 SDGO 1310 G1
Ramfos Ln
6900 SDGO 1290 F7
Ramfos Pl
2600 SDGO 1290 F7
2700 SDGO 1310 F1
Ramhaven Ln
8200 SNTE 1250 J1
Ramin Rd
- POWY 1190 F2
Ramo Ct
9700 SNTE 1231 C5
Ramo Rd
9700 SNTE 1231 C4
Ramon St
1800 LMGR 1290 F2
Ramona Airport Rd
200 SDCo 1152 B7
Ramona Av
800 SDCo 1291 C3
Ramona Ct
- IMPE 6439 F3
- SDCo 1232 E5
Ramona Dr
900 SDCo 1029 J5
4400 SDCo 1048 B5
2400 SDCo 1087 G1
700 SDCo 1136 E7
10100 SDCo 1271 E5
Ramona East Wy
100 OCSD 1086 H4
Ramona Highlands Dr
19700 SDCo 1152 B1
Ramona Highlands Rd
20800 SDCo 1152 B1
Ramona Ln
2100 SDCo 1108 D2
Ramona Oaks Rd
24700 SDCo 1173 F4
- SDCo 1174 B4
Ramona Pl
700 SOLB 1187 G1
Ramona Real
600 SDCo 1152 J1
Ramona St
600 SDCo 1152 F7
2000 SDCo 1172 F3
Ramona Trails Rd
19100 SDCo 1153 C2
Ramona View Ct
1400 SDCo 1153 B5
Ramona View Dr
18400 SDCo 1153 B4
Ramona Wy
100 OCSD 1086 H3
- SNMS 1129 C1
Rams Hill Dr
4000 SDCo 1099 F3
(See Page 1099)
Rams Hill Rd
1700 SDCo 1099 F4
(See Page 1099)
Ramsay Av
4600 SDGO 1228 F4
Ramsdell Ct
11600 SDGO 1209 H1
Ramsey Ln
1800 SDCo 1172 F1
Ramsey Rd
1400 SDCo 1234 B6
Ramsey Wy
- CRLB 1107 C6
Ramsgate Dr
10700 SNTE 1231 F4
Ramsgate Wy
9600 SNTE 1231 F4
Ramson Wy
1700 CHLV 1331 H3
Rana Ct
3000 CRLB 1147 H1
Ranch Creek Ln
13500 POWY 1170 E6
14900 SDCo 1070 H2
Ranch Creek Rd
30500 SDCo 1070 G3
Ranch Gate Rd
2900 CHLV 1311 H1
1100 SDCo 1252 F2
Ranch Glen
- ESCN 1109 G4
Ranch Hollow Rd
15900 POWY 1170 E5
Ranch House Rd
12200 SDGO 1150 B7
Ranch Rd
1300 ENCT 1147 D3
- SDCo 1153 G7
- SDCo 1154 A6
Ranch Trail Dr
14400 SDCo 1232 G4
Ranch View Ct
2900 CHLV 1311 J2
Ranch View Dr
10600 SDGO 1209 G4
Ranch View Rd
5800 OCSD 1067 F6
Ranch View Ter
2100 ENCT 1147 J7
Ranchbrook Rd
4000 SDCo 998 F5
Ranchero Dr
1500 OCSD 1067 F6
Rancheros
- SDCo 1251 G2
Rancheros Dr
100 SNMS 1108 H7
600 SNMS 1109 A7
200 SNMS 1128 J1
Ranchette Pl
- CHLV 1331 D1
Ranchito Ct
1000 SDCo 1253 H1
Ranchito Del Rio
17500 SDCo 1167 J2
Ranchito Dr
500 ESCN 1130 C6
Ranchito Ln
2100 SDCo 1253 H1
Ranchitos Ct
- SDCo 1231 F3
Ranchitos Pl
10000 SDCo 1231 F3
Ranchitos St
- SDCo 1231 F3
E Rancho
18400 SDCo 1148 G6
Rancho Adarme Ln
- SDCo 1067 F1
Rancho Agua Hadionda Dr
- OCSD 1106 J2
Rancho Alegre Rd
3600 SDCo 1028 E3
Rancho Allen Ln
100 SDCo 1153 A5
Rancho Amigos Rd
- SDCo 1068 F3
N Rancho Amigos Rd
- SDCo 1068 G2
Rancho Antiguo
14900 SDCo 1188 A1
Rancho Arroba
- CRLB 1127 J3
Rancho Ballena Ln
26700 SDCo 1154 B1
Rancho Ballena Rd
19300 SDCo 1154 C1
Rancho Barona Rd
- SDCo 1173 H5
Rancho Bernardo Rd
10600 SDCo 1169 F3
11100 SDGO 1169 H2
12100 SDGO 1170 B2
Rancho Bonita Pl
- ESCN 1109 H4
Rancho Bonito Rd
100 SDCo 1047 F4
Rancho Brasado
- CRLB 1127 J4
Rancho Bravado
- CRLB 1127 H2
Rancho Braydon Ln
800 SDCo 1234 D4
Rancho Brida
- CRLB 1127 G2
Rancho Bullard Ln
800 SDCo 1152 G7
Rancho Caballo
- CRLB 1127 J4
Rancho Caballo Rd
12600 POWY 1190 C6
Rancho Cabrillo Tr
7300 SDGO 1188 J1
Rancho Cajon Pl
1700 SDCo 1252 B4
Rancho Camino
400 SDCo 1047 H5
Rancho Camino Norte
4200 SDCo 1047 H5
Rancho Canada Rd
8500 SDCo 1232 E7
Rancho Capistrano Bend
- SDGO 1188 D4
Rancho Capitan
- SDCo 1232 D3
Rancho Carlsbad Dr
3300 CRLB 1107 C7
Rancho Carmel Dr
11200 SDGO 1169 J7
10400 SDGO 1189 J3
Rancho Carrizo
- CRLB 1127 J2
Rancho Catalina Tr
7300 SDGO 1188 J1
Rancho Charro
- CRLB 1127 H2
Rancho Cielo
6900 SDCo 1148 F7
Rancho Companero
- CRLB 1127 J3
Rancho Copa
14500 SDCo 1070 G7
Rancho Corte
2000 VSTA 1087 G2
Rancho Cortes
- CRLB 1127 J4
Rancho Costero
- CRLB 1127 H3
Rancho Ct
200 CHLV 1330 G5
5200 OCSD 1087 E2
Rancho De Carole Rd
- SDCo 1171 G2
Rancho De Kevin Rd
- SDCo 1171 G3
Rancho De La Angel Rd
- SDCo 1171 F3
Rancho De Loma Rd
100 SDCo 1028 E1
Rancho De Oro Dr
17500 SDCo 1171 J4
17500 SDCo 1172 A4
Rancho De Oro Rd
13900 POWY 1190 J2
500 SDCo 1109 G6
Rancho Del Azaleas Wy
13500 SDGO 1188 G4
Rancho Del Caballo
5600 SDCo 1047 J7
5600 SDCo 1067 J1
Rancho Del Canon
- CRLB 1127 H2
Rancho Del Cerro
- SDCo 1067 F1
Rancho Del Corte
9300 SDCo 1232 F5
Rancho Del Ladera Dr
200 SDCo 1153 A4
Rancho Del Madison
5000 SDCo 1188 A1
Rancho Del Mar Tr
- SDGO 1188 C3
Rancho Del Oro
- OCSD 1106 J2
Rancho Del Oro Dr
100 OCSD 1086 H3
Rancho Del Prado Tr
14400 SDGO 1188 J1
Rancho Del Rey
100 SDCo 1130 E7
Rancho Del Rey Pkwy
- CHLV 1310 J5
Rancho Del Rio
17500 SDCo 1168 H1
Rancho Del Sol
- SDCo 1130 E7
17700 SDCo 1151 D6
- SDGO 1188 G4
Rancho Del Verde
400 SDCo 1130 E7
Rancho Del Verde Pl
- SDCo 1130 F7
Rancho Del Villa
14000 SDCo 1232 F5
Rancho Diamonte
- CRLB 1127 H3
Rancho Diego Cir
3000 SDCo 1272 C6
Rancho Diego Wy
3400 SDCo 1272 C6
Rancho Diegueno Rd
6000 SDCo 1168 E7
6000 SDCo 1188 F1
Rancho Dorado Bend
- SDGO 1188 C3
Rancho Dr
200 CHLV 1330 G5
- ESCN 1129 G1
- SDCo 1148 H3
- SDCo 1149 D4
2300 SDGO 1310 D1
Rancho Dulzura
- CRLB 1127 H3
Rancho Elegante Dr
- CALX 6680 H2
Rancho Encinitas Dr
1100 ENCT 1148 B5
Rancho Famosa
- CRLB 1127 J2
Rancho Fanita Dr
8000 SNTE 1230 H7
Rancho Frontera Av
- CALX 6620 H6
Rancho Ganadero
- CRLB 1127 H4
Rancho Grande
4800 SDCo 1168 A7
Rancho Heights Rd
11800 SDCo 999 H2
Rancho Hills Dr
5700 SDGO 1310 D2
Rancho Jamul Rd
- SDCo 1293 A4
Rancho Janet
1800 SDCo 1233 J7
Rancho Jorie
1800 SDCo 1233 H7
Rancho Judith
1600 SDCo 1233 J7
Rancho La Cima Ct
18000 SDCo 1148 F6
Rancho La Cima Dr
6800 SDCo 1148 F6
Rancho La Mirada Ln
400 SDCo 1130 A7
Rancho La Noria
17500 SDCo 1167 J2
Rancho La Presa
- CRLB 1127 H2
Rancho Laguna Bend
- SDGO 1188 B3
Rancho Lakes Ct
- SDCo 1188 G3
Rancho Las Brisas
- SDGO 1188 B3
Rancho Las Palmas Dr
2000 SDCo 1048 A1
Rancho Latigo
- CRLB 1127 H2
Rancho Luiseno Rd
1300 SDCo 1109 C1
Rancho Madera Bend
- SDGO 1188 D3
Rancho Manzanita Dr
2000 SDCo 1319 H1
(See Page 1319)
Rancho Maria Av
3000 SDCo 1172 C2
Rancho Meadowcrest Rd
2100 SDCo 1252 G4
Rancho Mia
1400 SDCo 1027 J6
Rancho Miel
- CRLB 1127 J4
Rancho Miguel Rd
3200 SDCo 1272 D7
Rancho Milagro
- CRLB 1127 J3
Rancho Mirage Ln
9600 SDCo 1232 C4
Rancho Mission Rd
6300 SDGO 1249 G6
5900 SDGO 1269 G1
Rancho Nuevo
14900 SDCo 1188 A1
Rancho Oaks Ln
3100 SDCo 1292 C1
(See Page 1292)
Rancho Pacifica Pl
- VSTA 1087 J7
Rancho Pancho
- CRLB 1127 H4
Rancho Park Dr
6300 SDGO 1250 D6
Rancho Penasquitos Blvd
12600 SDGO 1189 F4
Rancho Posta
- CRLB 1127 G2
Rancho Quinta Bend
- SDGO 1188 C3
Rancho Rd
10300 SDCo 1271 E4
Rancho Real
15100 SDCo 1188 B1
Rancho Reata
- CRLB 1127 J2
Rancho Reposo
4600 SDCo 1188 A1
Rancho Rio Chico
- CRLB 1127 H3
Rancho River Rd
14400 SDCo 1030 F7
Rancho Roble Rd
10100 SDCo 1089 E5
Rancho Rose Wy
1400 OCSD 1067 E6
Rancho Ryan Rd
1100 SDCo 1027 H1
Rancho San Diego Pkwy
- SDCo 1271 J5
Rancho San Martin Dr
- SDCo 1171 G1
Rancho Santa Fe Ct
19000 SDCo 1153 E2
Rancho Santa Fe Farm Dr
6400 SDCo 1188 G1
Rancho Santa Fe Farm Rd
14500 SDCo 1188 G2
14000 SDGO 1188 G2
Rancho Santa Fe Lakes Dr
- SDCo 1188 H3
Rancho Santa Fe Rd
1400 CRLB 1147 H3
2800 CRLB 1148 A1
1200 ENCT 1147 H4
2300 SNMS 1128 A5
S Rancho Santa Fe Rd
800 SDCo 1128 C2
200 SDCo 1167 J1
100 SNMS 1108 D7
Rancho Santa Fe View Ct
7000 SDCo 1168 H1
Rancho Santa Teresa Dr
24800 SDCo 1153 G1
Rancho Serena
1400 SDCo 1167 J5
Rancho Sierra
2600 SDCo 1234 C7
Rancho Sierra Bend
- SDGO 1188 B3
Rancho Sol Ct
4800 SDCo 1188 A1
Rancho Solana Tr
- SDGO 1188 C3
Rancho Suenos Dr
- SDCo 1171 F1
Rancho Summit
2200 SDCo 1254 B2
Rancho Summit Dr
3800 ENCT 1148 E2
- SNMS 1148 E1
Rancho Taza Rd
8300 SDCo 998 H7
Rancho Ter
500 SDCo 1109 G3
Rancho Tierra Tr
- SDGO 1188 C3
Rancho Toyon Pl
- SDGO 1188 G7
Rancho Trails
- SDCo 1152 G1
Rancho Vacada
- CRLB 1127 H3
Rancho Valencia Dr
16000 SDCo 1168 F7
Rancho Valencia Rd
- SDCo 1168 E7
Rancho Valencia St
- SDCo 1071 A7
Rancho Valencia Vist
14800 SDCo 1188 F1
Rancho Valencia Wy
- SDCo 1071 A7
Rancho Valle Ct
1000 ELCJ 1251 H7
Rancho Ventana Tr
7300 SDGO 1188 H1
Rancho Verde Dr
2100 SDCo 1130 B6
Rancho Verde Tr
- SDGO 1188 C3
Rancho Vicente Dr
15100 SDCo 1173 A5
Rancho Viejo Dr
4800 SDCo 1188 A1
Rancho Villa Rd
2500 SDCo 1152 C1
Rancho Vista Bend
- SDGO 1188 C3
Rancho Vista Ct
12900 SDCo 1090 D4
13800 SDCo 1292 G1
(See Page 1292)
Rancho Vista Dr
18500 SDCo 1153 C4
Rancho Vista Pl
300 VSTA 1087 H7
Rancho Vista Rd
400 VSTA 1087 H7
600 VSTA 1107 H1
Rancho Vista Wy
1600 SDCo 1027 J1
Rancho Willits
- SDCo 1253 G2
Rancho Winchester Ln
1900 SDCo 1272 A1
Ranchos Ladera Rd
32500 SDCo 1048 H6
Ranchview Pl
2300 ESCN 1130 J2
Ranchwood Dr
10600 SDCo 1271 G7
Ranchwood Glen
300 ESCN 1109 G4
Ranchwood Ln
1500 SDCo 1027 J5
Randall St
5000 SDGO 1248 B4
Randlett Dr
4900 LMSA 1270 J2
Randolph St
4000 SDGO 1268 H5
Random Ct
1200 ELCJ 1251 G7
Random Rd
- SDCo 1251 G7
Randy Ct
3400 SDCo 1310 F4
Randy Ln
3300 SDCo 1310 F4
Raneta Ln
5400 SDGO 1249 G1
Range Park Pl
14500 POWY 1190 H1
Range Park Rd
14300 POWY 1190 H2
Range St
100 ENCT 1147 A3
Range View Rd
1100 VSTA 1108 C1
Rangeland Rd
18800 SDCo 1151 H3
Ranger Rd
5900 NATC 1290 C7
1000 SDCo 1028 F3
6000 SDGO 1290 D7
Rangeview St
900 SDCo 1290 J3
Rango Wy
700 SDCo 1079 A7
(See Page 1079)
Rangpur Ct
2900 ESCN 1110 E5
Ranleigh Ct
3100 SDGO 1268 D6
Ranrido Dr
800 SDCo 1130 B3
Ransom Hill Ln
100 SDCo 1153 A4
Ransom St
1100 SDGO 1350 G1
Ranza Rd
8700 SDCo 1291 A5
Rapatee Ct
10900 SDCo 1271 G4
Rapatee Dr
4000 SDCo 1271 G4
Raphael Ct
400 ENCT 1147 G6
Rappahannock Av
4100 SDGO 1248 E5
Rappaport Pl
10400 SNTE 1231 E3
Raptor Rd
15600 SDCo 1191 B6
Rapture Ln
1700 CRLB 1106 F3
Raquel Dr
4200 OCSD 1107 C2
Rascon Ct
- SDGO 1190 B6
Rasha St
6500 SDGO 1228 H1
Rasmussen Wy
14100 SDGO 1189 E2
Raspberry Ice Ln
9700 SDCo 1271 C3
Raspberry Pl
- SDGO 1350 E2
Raspberry Wy
5300 OCSD 1067 C6
Ratcliff Rd
1700 CRLB 1106 F3
Rathmoor St
1100 ELCJ 1251 G7
Raulston Ter
800 ESCN 1130 C2
Rav Ct
17500 SDCo 1274 B2
Ravean Ct
1300 ENCT 1147 D2
Ravello Terr
1300 SDCo 1027 H5
Raven Av
1300 CHLV 1330 G2
Raven Hill Pr
- SDGO 1208 D2
Raven Hill Rd
- SDCo 1272 J7
Raven Pl
1200 CHLV 1330 G2
Raven Rd
- SDGO 1229 B2
Raven Ridge Pt
7500 SDGO 1208 J2
Raven St
600 SDGO 1289 H3
Ravenrock Ct
- CHLV 1311 D6
Ravenscroft Rd
- NATC 1289 G7
- NATC 1309 G1
Ravensthorpe Wy
- SDGO 1209 G2
Ravenswood Rd
5800 SDGO 1247 G3
Ravenwood Dr
2200 LMGR 1270 H7
Ravina St
400 SDGO 1227 E7
Ravine Ct
1700 VSTA 1087 D6
Ravine Dr
3400 CRLB 1107 B5
Ravine Rd
1400 VSTA 1087 D6
Ravinia Dr
1500 CHLV 1331 E1
Rawhide
- OCSD 1086 J2
Rawhide Ct
900 CHLV 1310 H4
Rawhide Ln
2600 SNMS 1128 A5
Rawl Pl
700 SOLB 1167 F6
Rawlins Wy
9500 SNTE 1231 C4
Ray St
600 ESCN 1109 J7
3500 SDGO 1269 E6
Raya Wy
4100 SDGO 1228 E5
Raydel Ct
6300 SDGO 1250 D7
Rayford Dr
10000 SDCo 1089 E7
10000 SDCo 1109 E1
Rayley Dr
- SDCo 1271 F6
Rayline Wy
10100 SDCo 1271 E4
Raymar Av
5600 SDGO 1270 D1
Raymell Dr
2500 SDGO 1249 E7
Raymond Av
1900 SDCo 1152 E7
2500 SDCo 1172 D1
Raymond Ln
1900 OCSD 1086 C7
Raymond Pl
5000 SDGO 1269 G2
Raymond St
500 ELCJ 1251 G7
Raynell Wy
1600 ELCJ 1252 B7
Rays Wy
13000 SDCo 1050 C5
Raytheon Rd
7400 SDGO 1249 A1
Razuki Ln
3300 SDCo 1273 B6
Rea Av
100 ELCJ 1251 F5
Read Rd
- CORD 1288 F4
Reagan Cir
8600 SDGO 1209 C4
Reagan Ct
8600 SDGO 1209 C4
Reagan Glen
8400 SDGO 1169 B3
Reagan Pl
8600 SDGO 1209 C4
Reagan Rd
10600 SDGO 1209 C4
Real Tres Ninas
31300 SDCo 1070 J1
Real Way Ln
1200 SDCo 1253 H3
Realty Rd
1400 SDCo 1152 F7
Reaser Ln
1100 SDCo 1152 F3
Reata Ct
12300 SDGO 1150 B6
Reata Wy
18300 SDGO 1150 B6
Rebecca Av
9100 SDGO 1249 E6
200 VSTA 1087 H3
Rebecca Dr
- ELCJ 1252 B7
Rebecca Ln
1500 ELCJ 1252 B7
- SDCo 1070 E3
Rebecca St
800 ELCJ 1252 A6
- ELCN 6559 J3
Rebecca Wy
1500 ELCJ 1252 B6
- LMGR 1290 J1
Rebeccas Green Tr
1900 SDCo 1172 F1
Rebel Rd
5100 SDGO 1228 F7
Rebel Wind Rd
12200 SDCo 1216 A2
(See Page 1216)
Rebolla Ln
5400 SDGO 1249 G1
Reche Rd
1100 SDCo 1027 H4
3100 SDCo 1028 C5
Reche Wy
700 SDCo 1027 J4
Recluse Ln
400 ENCT 1147 G5
Recodo Ct
2200 CRLB 1147 F2
Recreation Dr
- SDCo 1028 F4
100 VSTA 1087 G6
Recreational Tr
- SDCo 1231 G4
Recuerdo Cove
2300 SDGO 1187 G5
Recuerdo Dr
14200 SDGO 1187 H5
Red Alder Pl
700 ESCN 1110 D5
Red Bark Rd
1400 ESCN 1129 F5
Red Barn Rd
1700 ENCT 1147 H6
Red Bluff Pl
4600 CRLB 1107 B5
Red Blush Rd
800 ESCN 1110 C5
Red Canyon Dr
29800 SDCo 1069 J6
Red Cedar Ct
10200 SDGO 1209 H4
Red Cedar Dr
11000 SDGO 1209 H4
Red Cedar Ln
11300 SDGO 1209 J4
Red Cedar Pl
10300 SDGO 1209 J4
Red Cedar Wy
11300 SDGO 1209 J4
Red Cloud Ln
13300 POWY 1190 H4
Red Coach Ln
2000 ENCT 1147 H6
Red Coral Av
600 CRLB 1126 J6
Red Coral Ln
- SDGO 1330 H6
Red Deer St
6500 SDGO 1228 E4
Red Diamond Dr
- SDCo 1232 D4
Red Fin Ln
400 SDGO 1330 H6
Red Fox Ln
- SNMS 1108 H4
Red Gate Rd
400 SDCo 1052 A6
(See Page 1052)
Red Granite Rd
900 CHLV 1331 A2
Red Gum Rd
1200 SDCo 1253 E3
Red Hawk Ln
14500 POWY 1190 H1
Red Hawk Rd
- SDCo 1069 C4
Red Hawk Ridge
6100 SDCo 1255 E5
Red Hawk Vista
- SDCo 1171 F2
Red Hawk Wy
1100 SNMS 1128 E3
Red Hill Ln
1600 CHLV 1311 B4
Red Hills Ct
9300 SNTE 1230 J5
Red Ironbark Dr
27200 SDCo 1090 D5
Red Knot St
6500 CRLB 1127 A4
Red Leaf Ln
2200 CHLV 1331 G3
Red Maple Dr
1000 CHLV 1330 J1
Red Maple Wy
4400 OCSD 1086 H1
Red Mountain Ct
1300 CHLV 1311 B6
Red Mountain Dr
29900 SDCo 1069 J5
Red Mtn Dam Dr
1400 SDCo 998 D7
Red Mtn Heights Dr
3000 SDCo 998 C6
Red Mtn Ln
100 SDCo 1028 E1
Red Oak Ct
- SNMS 1128 C6
Red Oak Pl
1000 CHLV 1310 J7
Red Oak Rd
- SDCo 1235 B2
Red Oak Wy
13400 SDGO 1188 G3
Red Pine Ct
900 SDGO 1330 B7
Red Pine Dr
2400 SDGO 1330 B7
Red Plum Ln
600 SDCo 1107 H3
Red Pony Ln
9600 SDCo 1232 H3
Red River Dr
5500 SDGO 1250 B4
Red Robin Pl
11000 SDGO 1208 J2
Red Rock Canyon Rd
- CHLV 1311 J6
2800 CHLV 1312 A6
(See Page 1312)
Red Rock Ct
9900 SDGO 1209 H4
Red Rock Dr
10900 SDGO 1209 H5
Red Rose Ln
10400 SDCo 1169 G2
Red Sails Wy
- SDGO 1330 H6
Red Shank Ln
38300 SDCo 1299 J4
(See Page 1299)
Red Stone Ln
- SDCo 1089 E3
Red Tail Rd
17800 SDCo 1149 E7
Red Wagon Ln
- CHLV 1331 G1
Red Willow Pl
1500 CHLV 1311 J7

STREET
Block City Map# Grid

Redbark Wy
600 SDGO 1310 F1
Redberry Ct
800 SNMS 1109 A5
Redbird Dr
2100 SDGO 1249 A7
2000 SDGO 1269 B1
Redbrook Ct
4700 SDGO 1248 J1
Redbrook Rd
6100 SDGO 1248 J1
Redbud Ct
11300 SDGO 1169 J5
Redbud Pl
800 CHLV 1310 H7
Redbud Rd
900 CHLV 1310 H7
Redcliff Ct
12000 SDGO 1210 B3
Redcrest Ct
8200 SDGO 1290 H4
Redcrest Dr
200 SDGO 1290 H3
Redcrest Pl
8200 SDGO 1290 H4
Redding Rd
5300 SDGO 1270 A1
Redel Rd
200 SNMS 1128 J1
Reden Ln
- SDCo 1069 D4
Redfern Cir
10800 SDGO 1210 A3
Redfern Ln
- SDCo 1070 C5
Redfield St
9000 SDCo 1291 A3
Redford Pl
3000 SDGO 1310 E2
Redgap Ct
2100 ENCT 1147 H7
Redhill Ln
800 SNMS 1109 B5
Redland Dr
4700 SDGO 1270 B3
E Redland Dr
5500 SDGO 1270 B3
Redland Pl
5400 SDGO 1270 B3
Redlander Wy
10800 SDCo 1232 B1
Redlands Pl
600 CHLV 1311 B4
Redlands St
400 VSTA 1087 G6
Redman St
- CORD 1329 F4
Redondo Ct
800 SDGO 1267 H1
Redondo Dr
5700 SDCo 1048 C7
4800 SDCo 1271 F2
N Redondo Dr
600 OCSD 1067 A6
W Redondo Dr
400 OCSD 1066 J6
Redondo St
1700 SDGO 1268 A7
Redtail Hawk Ct
11500 SDCo 1212 C5
Redwing Dr
- OCSD 1086 D2
Redwing Rd
400 CHLV 1330 G2
Redwing St
1700 SDCo 1128 A4
Redwing Wy
1700 SDCo 1128 A4
Redwood Av
100 CRLB 1106 E7
1000 ELCJ 1251 H6
Redwood Creek Ln
8400 SDGO 1209 C6
Redwood Crest
2000 VSTA 1107 F5
Redwood Dr
9300 SDGO 1227 J3
300 SNMS 1108 J5
Redwood Ln
9800 SDCo 1149 D3
Redwood Pl
700 ESCN 1129 J5
Redwood Rd
- ELCJ 1251 J6
Redwood St
600 ESCN 1129 H4
3500 OCSD 1086 E2
4100 SDGO 1269 H6
5500 SDGO 1270 B6
- SNMS 1129 C2
W Redwood St
1300 SDGO 1268 J7
Reed Av
800 SDGO 1247 H7
1900 SDGO 1248 B6
Reed Rd
2400 ESCN 1130 E1
Reed Ter
900 ESCN 1130 F1
Reedley Ter
4700 SDGO 1188 C4

Reef Cir
5400 CRLB 1107 C7
Reef Dr
700 SDGO 1330 D7
Rees Rd
1100 SDCo 1109 E6
1000 SNMS 1109 D7
Reese Ln
17000 SDCo 1171 H3
Reese St
900 OCSD 1106 B2
Reeve Rd
7500 CRLB 1146 J1
Reflection Cir
2200 VSTA 1107 H7
Reflection Dr
6400 SDGO 1249 G6
Reflection St
1500 SNMS 1128 F6
Reflections Cres
17100 SDCo 1169 A1
Refugio Av
4800 CRLB 1106 H7
Regal Rd
700 ENCT 1147 D7
1100 ENCT 1167 D1
Regal Ridge Rd
1000 ENCT 1148 A5
Regalo Ln
17200 SDGO 1170 A2
Regatta Ct
1200 SNMS 1128 F5
Regatta Ln
- SDGO 1330 H7
Regatta Rd
- CRLB 1127 B4
Regency Cir
4500 OCSD 1107 E2
Regency Ct
200 CHLV 1330 G5
Regency Rd
8700 SDGO 1249 C7
Regency Wy
1700 CHLV 1330 G6
Regent Rd
2600 CRLB 1106 J6
Regents Garden Row
- SDGO 1228 C2
Regents Park Row
4100 SDGO 1228 C2
Regents Rd
8000 SDGO 1228 C3
5300 SDGO 1248 C1
Regghetti Rd
3100 SDCo 1029 J5
- SDCo 1030 A5
Regina Av
5600 SDGO 1228 H6
Regina Glen
31300 SDCo 1070 E1
Regina Ln
1100 VSTA 1087 G4
Reginas Ct
10400 SNTE 1231 E4
Regis Av
5600 SDGO 1270 D1
Regis Ct
- VSTA 1087 J5
Regla Ct
4900 SDGO 1228 G5
Regner Ct
8600 SDGO 1250 J4
Regner Rd
7100 SDGO 1250 J3
Regulo Pl
800 CHLV 1311 B6
Regulus Rd
- SDGO 1229 B2
Regulus St
1500 SDGO 1269 A2
Rehco Rd
9000 SDGO 1208 H7
8800 SDGO 1228 H1
Reichert Wy
1700 CHLV 1331 E2
Reidy Canyon
- SDCo 1089 G5
Reidy Canyon Pl
11200 SDCo 1089 H6
Reidy Canyon Trl
10800 SDCo 1089 G7
Reill View Dr
2400 SDCo 1130 B7
Reina Ct
- BRAW 6259 J7
(See Page 6259)
Reineman Rd
2100 SDCo 1027 H6
Reisling Ter
500 CHLV 1311 D3
Reklow Dr
1500 SDGO 1350 B2
Reliance St
- SOLB 1187 G1
Relindo Ct
16300 SDGO 1170 C4
Relindo Dr
12600 SDGO 1170 C4
Rembrandt Glen
1200 ESCN 1109 J7

Remedios Ct
100 SOLB 1167 H4
Remijio St
1100 SDCo 1029 H4
Remington Ct
1200 VSTA 1087 E5
Remington Hills Dr
- SDGO 1350 G2
Remington Rd
5100 SDGO 1270 A1
Remley Pl
7300 SDGO 1227 G7
Remora St
10500 SDGO 1249 G1
Remsen Ct
- CRLB 1127 B5
Remuda Ct
- SDCo 1085 J3
9300 SNTE 1231 A3
Rena Dr
700 OCSD 1067 B5
- SDCo 1109 D1
Renaissance Av
5300 SDGO 1228 E3
Renato St
8900 SDGO 1189 C3
Renaud Ct
700 CALX 6680 G2
Renault Pl
2900 SDGO 1228 C6
Renault St
2900 SDGO 1228 C6
Renault Wy
5900 SDGO 1228 C5
Rendezvous Cres
16900 SDCo 1169 B2
Rendon Valley Rd
- SDCo 1171 E2
Rendova Cres
- CORD 1309 A2
Rendova Rd
- CORD 1309 A2
Rene Ct
3500 SDGO 1248 D5
Rene Dr
3900 SDGO 1330 F7
E Renette Av
200 ELCJ 1251 F7
W Renette Av
900 ELCJ 1251 E7
Renex Pl
4700 SDGO 1248 G1
Renfro Wy
800 SDCo 1253 C2
Renkrib Av
6900 SDGO 1250 J3
Rennes Pl
1800 CHLV 1311 F1
Reno Dr
4700 SDGO 1269 J5
Renoir Ln
5200 SDCo 1290 H7
Renovo Wy
4800 SDGO 1230 B7
4700 SDGO 1250 B1
Renown Dr
8500 SDGO 1250 J4
Renshaw Ct
2000 ELCJ 1251 B1
Renwick Ln
1400 SDCo 1108 B1
Reo Ct
2000 SDGO 1290 C7
Reo Dr
2100 SDGO 1290 C7
2700 SDGO 1310 D2
Reo Pl
6000 SDGO 1310 D2
Reo Real Dr
12800 POWY 1190 D5
Reo Ter
5800 SDGO 1310 D2
Reola Dr
10000 SDCo 1232 C3
Repecho Dr
5300 SDGO 1249 G1
Reposado Dr
7600 CRLB 1147 F1
Reposo Alto
17000 SDCo 1167 J3
Represa Cir
7900 CRLB 1147 G3
Republic St
1800 SDGO 1290 D1
Republican Wy
16700 SDCo 1173 F2
Requeza St
100 ENCT 1147 C7
Requlo Pl
13000 SDGO 1188 F4
Resava Ln
14200 SDCo 1070 F4
Research Ct
- CHLV 1330 J5
Research Pl
- SDGO 1228 E3
Reservation Dr
24500 SDCo 1236 A2
Reservation Rd
- SDCo 1050 J1

Reserve Dr
10300 SDCo 1169 E3
Reservoir Ct
6000 SDGO 1270 D2
Reservoir Dr
- SDCo 1291 E3
5100 SDGO 1270 D2
Reservoir Ln
6000 SDGO 1270 D2
Reservoir St
3100 SDCo 1272 H7
Resmar Ct
10000 SDCo 1271 E4
Resmar Dr
4600 SDCo 1271 E3
Resmar Pl
10000 SDCo 1271 D3
Resmar Rd
4800 SDCo 1271 E2
Resort Summit Dr
28700 SDCo 1089 B1
Restful Ct
10300 SNTE 1231 E3
Retaheim Wy
400 SDGO 1247 E2
Retrato Ct
11000 SDGO 1249 J2
Retreat Ct
300 SDCo 1027 F3
Reuben Fleet Dr
- ELCJ 1251 C2
Revelle College Dr
- SDGO 1227 J3
Revelle Dr
7700 SDGO 1227 J6
Revelstoke Ter
- SDGO 1209 D1
Revelstoke Wy
8800 SDGO 1209 D1
Revena St
1800 SDGO 1350 C3
Revere Av
3500 SDGO 1248 D5
Revere Ct
1900 VSTA 1107 J4
Revillo Dr
4300 SDGO 1270 D4
Revillo Wy
4500 SDGO 1270 D3
Rex Av
5300 SDGO 1270 A5
Rex Ln
1300 SDCo 1251 H1
Rexford Dr
1900 SDGO 1289 G1
Rexhall St
800 ELCJ 1251 F4
Rexview Dr
200 SDGO 1290 E4
Reynard Wy
3100 SDGO 1268 J7
Reynolds St
5200 SDGO 1290 B5
Reynosa Ct
100 SOLB 1167 H4
Reza Ct
29700 SDCo 1068 F6
Rezko Wy
400 CHLV 1310 J4
Rh Dana Pl
1000 CORD 1308 H1
Rhea Glen
1000 ESCN 1109 F6
Rhea Ln
- SNMS 1109 A4
Rhea Pl
1100 VSTA 1087 H5
Rhesa Ln
200 SDCo 1027 F5
Rhine St
1100 SDGO 1350 B1
Rhoades Ct
6300 SDGO 1310 E1
Rhoades Rd
2700 SDGO 1310 E2
Rhoades Wy
4100 OCSD 1107 E6
Rhoda Dr
1300 SDGO 1227 F7
Rhoda Ln
- VSTA 1087 H7
Rhode Island St
4500 SDGO 1269 B4
Rhodes Ct
8700 SNTE 1231 D7
Rhonda Ln
34200 SDCo 1050 H1
Rhone Rd
8500 SNTE 1231 C7
8500 SNTE 1251 C1
Rhone Valley Wy
1400 CHLV 1311 G1
Rialto Glen
200 ESCN 1150 B1
Rialto St
4300 SDGO 1268 B5
Riata Ct
- SDCo 1086 A3
Riata Dr
600 SDCo 1078 J5
(See Page 1078)

Ribbon Beach Wy
400 OCSD 1086 B6
Ricard Ct
2100 SDCo 1272 D3
Ricardo Dr
1200 CHLV 1311 B6
Ricardo Pl
300 SDGO 1247 F4
Ricardo Ranch Rd
19000 SDCo 1091 G4
Rice Canyon Rd
1400 SDCo 998 J6
1000 SDCo 1029 A1
Rice Ct
8400 SDGO 1189 B6
Ricebird Dr
500 VSTA 1087 F4
Ricewood Dr
3400 OCSD 1086 E3
Rich Field Dr
3400 CRLB 1107 B5
Richandave Av
1500 ELCJ 1252 B6
Richard Av
- BRAW 6319 G5
(See Page 6319)
Richard Ct
200 OCSD 1087 F2
Richard Rd
10400 SDCo 1169 F1
Richard St
6600 SDGO 1270 D1
Richardson Av
100 ELCJ 1251 E6
Richeth Rd
100 SDGO 1290 C4
S Richfield Av
100 ELCJ 1251 E6
Richland Rd
500 SNMS 1109 B6
Richland St
2600 SDGO 1249 A7
Richland View Ct
600 SDCo 1109 A3
Richlynn Ridge Rd
2700 SDCo 1150 E1
Richmar Av
400 SNMS 1108 G7
Richmond Park Ct
- CHLV 1310 D5
Richmond Park Pl
0 CHLV 1310 D5
Richmond St
3600 SDGO 1269 B6
Richvale Dr
- SNTE 1230 J7
Rick Rd
- SDCo 1128 J4
- SDCo 1129 A6
Rick St
12800 POWY 1190 D5
Rickenbaker Av
600 SDGO 1330 F7
Rickert Rd
10600 SDGO 1209 E3
Rickey Pl
200 ESCN 1110 E6
Ricks Ranch Ct
31600 SDCo 1070 D1
Ricks Ranch Rd
- SDCo 1070 C1
Ricky Ln
10300 SNTE 1231 E7
Ricky Ridge Rd
- SDCo 1089 D2
Rico Ct
6800 SDGO 1268 J1
Ricon Ranch Rd
17400 SDCo 1274 A2
Rideabout Ct
12500 SDGO 1189 C6
Rideabout Ln
8700 SDGO 1189 C5
Rider Pl
- SDGO 1188 D5
Riderwood Ter
10700 SNTE 1231 F6
Ridge Canyon Rd
14000 SDCo 1090 F6
Ridge Creek Dr
1700 CHLV 1311 C4
3000 SDCo 1028 C2
Ridge Creek Rd
30100 SDCo 1069 B5
Ridge Ct
- CRLB 1107 B3
8300 SDGO 1269 B1
1600 VSTA 1107 G4
Ridge Dr
200 SDCo 1028 C2
Ridge Heights Dr
1000 SDCo 1027 H4
Ridge Hill Rd
13800 SDCo 1232 F5
Ridge Manor Av
6700 SDGO 1250 D5
Ridge Oak Pl
14200 SDCo 1090 F7
Ridge Pl
2000 SDCo 1028 C2

Ridge Point Ct
- CHLV 1331 C1
Ridge Ranch Ct
14000 SDCo 1090 G5
Ridge Ranch Rd
13900 SDCo 1090 F6
Ridge Rd
3500 OCSD 1107 E3
1600 SDCo 1107 E2
1200 VSTA 1107 G2
Ridge Rock Ct
- CHLV 1311 D7
Ridge Route Rd
8300 SDGO 1250 D4
Ridge Run Wy
- SDGO 1209 G1
Ridge Terr
200 ENCT 1147 J7
Ridge Trl
1200 SDCo 1136 C6
900 SDCo 1253 C2
Ridge View
- ESCN 1129 E6
Ridge View Dr
2400 SDGO 1269 J7
1900 SDGO 1289 H1
Ridge View Wy
100 OCSD 1086 J3
Ridge Wy
3000 SDCo 1028 C3
Ridgeback Rd
1400 CHLV 1311 A5
Ridgecliff Ln
3000 SDCo 1271 D6
Ridgecrest Dr
3500 CRLB 1106 G4
9500 SDCo 1271 C1
200 SDGO 1290 G5
Ridgecrest Rd
- POWY 1171 B7
- SNTE 1230 G7
Ridgecrest Ter
1800 SDCo 1252 B1
Ridgedale Dr
13100 POWY 1190 C5
Ridgefield Av
2900 CRLB 1107 B4
Ridgefield Pl
8500 SDGO 1189 C5
Ridgegate Row
2500 SDGO 1248 A1
Ridgegrove Ln
- ESCN 1129 G5
Ridgehaven Ct
9500 SDGO 1249 E2
Ridgeland Ct
800 SNMS 1128 F5
Ridgeline
- SDGO 1350 H2
Ridgeline Av
2000 VSTA 1107 J7
Ridgeline Pl
3100 ESCN 1110 F7
600 SOLB 1167 G6
Ridgemont Ct
600 ESCN 1110 F7
Ridgemont Ct
1400 OCSD 1087 E3
Ridgemoor Dr
5800 SDGO 1250 E7
Ridgemoore Pl
- VSTA 1087 G4
Ridgeside Pl
2500 SDCo 1271 C7
Ridgeton Ct
8800 SDCo 1232 C6
Ridgeton Dr
12400 SDCo 1232 B7
Ridgeton Ln
8900 SDCo 1232 C6
Ridgetop Ct
4200 SDGO 1188 B6
Ridgeview Ct
400 CHLV 1311 A4
Ridgeview Ln
- SDCo 1171 G2
Ridgeview Pl
2100 ESCN 1109 G5
15200 POWY 1170 F6
Ridgeview Rd
- SDCo 1171 G3
Ridgeview Wy
1200 CHLV 1311 A4
Ridgewater Dr
800 CHLV 1311 E4
Ridgewater Ln
10400 SDGO 1209 H4
Ridgeway Ct
400 SDCo 1290 H6
Ridgeway Dr
2200 NATC 1310 B3
2800 SDCo 1310 C2
4100 SDGO 1269 G2
Ridgeway St
1400 OCSD 1106 D1
Ridgewood Dr
700 SDCo 1136 E7
1800 SDGO 1290 C7
Ridgewood Wy
- CRLB 1107 A4

Riding High Wy
16600 SDCo 1168 J2
Riding Ridge Rd
- SDGO 1188 C6
Riding Trail Dr
21400 SDCo 1129 C6
Ridley Rd
13400 SDGO 1189 E4
Rienstra Ct
400 CHLV 1330 G3
E Rienstra St
- CHLV 1330 F4
Rienza Pl
17600 SDGO 1170 A1
Riesling Ct
12200 SDGO 1210 B3
Riesling Dr
10800 SDGO 1210 B2
Rife Wy
12800 SDGO 1189 C4
Rifle Rd
- ELCJ 1251 H5
Rifle Wy
13000 SDGO 1189 D5
Rift Rd
4700 CRLB 1107 B5
Rigel St
1500 SDGO 1289 F6
Riggs Rd
- SDCo 1253 D4
Rigley St
- CHLV 1331 A2
Rigsby Dr
9300 SNTE 1251 B1
Rihely Pl
600 ENCT 1147 E5
Riley Pl
200 ESCN 1110 E6
Riley St
3700 SDGO 1268 E5
Rill Ct
- CRLB 1107 C3
Rim Cir
4600 CRLB 1107 B5
Rim Of The Valley
- SDCo 1070 J1
- SDCo 1071 A1
Rim Rd
10900 SDCo 1089 F3
Rim Rock Cir
3200 ENCT 1148 C5
Rim Rock Rd
4700 OCSD 1087 D4
Rimbach Rd
12200 POWY 1190 B4
Rimbey Av
2000 SDGO 1350 A2
Rimcrest Ct
1400 CHLV 1311 B3
Rimgate Ct
14400 SDGO 1189 C1
Rimhurst Ct
300 OCSD 1086 D2
Rimini Rd
600 DLMR 1187 G5
Rimpark Ln
5200 SDGO 1249 F1
Rimpark Wy
9700 SDGO 1249 F1
Rimridge Ln
8300 SDGO 1209 B1
Rimrock Dr
1300 ESCN 1110 A6
Rimrock Rd
500 ELCJ 1251 C4
Rimrock Summit Ln
9700 SDCo 1089 C1
Rimstone Ln
16100 SDGO 1169 J4
Rimview Wy
4900 SDGO 1249 G1
Rincado Rd
32400 SDCo 1051 F5
Rincon Av
400 ESCN 1109 G4
1400 ESCN 1109 J3
- SDCo 1110 A3
Rincon Ct
3600 OCSD 1107 F4
Rincon Del Mundo
1100 SDCo 1149 H2
Rincon Hilltop View Rd
49000 SDCo 1071 D5
Rincon Pt
1200 CHLV 1311 B7
Rincon Rancho Rd
- SDCo 1051 E4
Rincon Rd
1400 ESCN 1130 B4
Rincon Springs Rd
35000 SDCo 1051 D7
Rincon St
5100 SDGO 1270 D2
700 VSTA 1087 H7
Rincon Villa Dr
1400 ESCN 1109 J6
Rincon Villa Pl
1000 ESCN 1109 J6
Rinda Ln
8700 SDCo 1291 A2

Ring Rd
- NATC 1310 C3
13500 POWY 1190 C3
Ringdove Ct
- SDGO 1209 J1
Ringneck Ct
- SDCo 1232 C4
Ringwood Dr
300 SDGO 1290 G4
Rio Bonito Wy
2200 SDGO 1269 D1
Rio Brava Ct
13100 SDCo 1272 D7
Rio Camino
10200 SDCo 1231 H3
Rio Claro Ct
800 OCSD 1087 C1
Rio Corto Dr
11600 SDCo 1231 H2
Rio Ct
14000 POWY 1190 G1
Rio Fondo
11600 SDCo 1231 H3
Rio Grande
3200 SDCo 1272 J7
Rio Hondo Av
- CALX 6680 H2
Rio Ivanhoe Wy
13400 SDCo 1272 E6
Rio Lindo Dr
200 SDGO 1290 E4
Rio Madre Ln
3100 SDCo 1272 J7
Rio Maria Rd
- SDCo 1191 E4
Rio Plata Dr
5300 OCSD 1087 C1
Rio Plato Ct
6700 SDGO 1290 E5
Rio Rancho
14700 SDGO 1168 H7
Rio Rd
- CORD 1309 B1
Rio San Diego Dr
8700 SDGO 1269 C2
Rio Seco Ct
2600 CHLV 1311 J6
Rio Senda
7800 SDCo 1168 J1
Rio Valle Dr
5900 SDCo 1047 J7
5900 SDCo 1067 J1
Rio Verde Rd
24600 SDCo 1173 G4
Rio Viento Ct
800 OCSD 1087 C1
Rio Vista Av
4000 BRAW 6319 H1
(See Page 6319)
Rio Vista Dr
- ESCN 1129 F4
2000 SDCo 1048 B5
3300 SDCo 1310 E4
Rio Vista Pl
3800 SDCo 1310 E4
Rio Vista Rd
- SDCo 1168 J3
Rio Wy
3100 SDCo 1271 B6
1200 VSTA 1107 E1
Riomaggiore Dr
20500 SDCo 1152 C2
Rios Av
1700 CHLV 1330 F5
N Rios Av
600 SOLB 1167 E6
S Rios Av
100 SOLB 1167 F7
500 SOLB 1187 F1
Rios Canyon Ln
14100 SDCo 1232 G6
Rios Canyon Rd
14200 SDCo 1232 G6
- SDCo 1233 A6
Rios Ct
100 SOLB 1167 E6
Rios Rd
12700 SDGO 1170 C3
Rioseco St
- CALX 6620 G6
Riparian Rd
15700 POWY 1170 F5
Rippey Ct
2300 ELCJ 1251 B3
Rippey St
900 ELCJ 1251 B3
Ripple Ln
13400 SDCo 1232 D6
Ripple Wy
- SDCo 1171 J3
Risa Cir
4000 SDGO 1249 J2
Risa Ct
4000 SDGO 1249 J3
Risa Ln
- LMGR 1270 E7
Rising Dale Wy
17300 SDCo 1153 C7
Rising Glen Dr
4700 OCSD 1087 D4

Rising Glen Wy
2300 CRLB 1106 G3
2100 SDGO 1290 E7
Rising Hill Wy
1100 SDCo 1149 H1
Rising River Pl
15500 SDGO 1169 A3
Rising Star Ct
4100 SDCo 1271 G4
Risueno Ct
1700 SDGO 1350 B3
Rita St
4500 SDCo 1271 E3
Ritchey St
400 SDGO 1290 E3
Ritchie Rd
4000 SDCo 1135 E5
Ritidian Wy
11800 SDCo 1170 B1
Ritson Rd
31600 SDCo 1069 A1
Ritter Ct
- IMPE 6499 F1
9900 SDGO 1209 H4
Ritter Pl
2200 ESCN 1129 H7
Ritter Rd
- CALX 6620 G6
Ritva Pl
2300 SDGO 1290 F7
Riva Ln
1600 ESCN 1130 B1
Rivawill Ct
14900 SDGO 1169 E6
Rivendell Ln
500 SDCo 1152 D6
River Ash Dr
1000 CHLV 1310 J7
River Dance Ct
1500 SDCo 1234 D6
River Dance Wy
2900 SDCo 1234 C6
River Dr
300 BRAW 6259 G7
(See Page 6259)
1100 BRAW 6260 A7
(See Page 6260)
1300 CALX 6620 E7
10100 SDCo 1235 J1
9500 SDCo 1236 A2
River Glen Row
1200 SDGO 1268 H2
River Oaks Ct
900 CHLV 1311 G4
River Oaks Ln
900 SDCo 997 G7
River Park Dr
- SNTE 1231 C5
River Park Rd
- BRAW 6319 G3
(See Page 6319)
River Ranch
- OCSD 1086 J2
River Rim Rd
11600 SDGO 1209 A1
River Rock Ct
- SNTE 1231 C5
River Rock Rd
- CHLV 1311 G3
River Run Cir
- SNMS 1109 A5
River Run Dr
2100 SDGO 1269 D1
River Shadow Ct
2900 SDCo 1234 C6
River St
10100 SDCo 1232 A3
River Trail Pl
- SNTE 1231 C5
River Valley Ct
8900 SNTE 1230 J4
River View Ct
5100 SDCo 1048 J2
River Vista Row
1200 SDGO 1268 H3
E Rivera Av
- ImCo 6620 J7
- ImCo 6680 J1
Rivera Ct
100 CHLV 1330 F4
Rivera Pl
- CHLV 1330 F4
Rivera St
500 CHLV 1330 H3
Riverbend Ct
15700 POWY 1170 G4
Riverbend Rd
14000 POWY 1170 G5
Riverbend Wy
500 CHLV 1311 E3
Rivercreek Ct
400 CHLV 1311 E2
Rivercrest Rd
- SNMS 1128 C6
Riverdale Rd
6500 SDGO 1249 H6
Riverdale St
6200 SDGO 1249 H7
Riverford Rd
10000 SDCo 1231 H3

San Diego County Street Index

STREET / Block City Map# Grid

Riverhead Ct
13800 SDGO 1189 F3
Riverhead Dr
10000 SDGO 1189 F3
Riverlawn Av
700 CHLV 1330 A1
Riverside Av
200 CHLV 1310 B4
Riverside Dr
100 OCSD 1085 J6
600 OCSD 1086 A6
11400 SDCo 1231 H3
8900 SDCo 1236 A3
Riverton Pl
4000 SDGO 1188 A4
Rivertree Dr
600 OCSD 1086 E3
Riverview Av
- ELCN 6559 G3
9600 SDCo 1231 J4
Riverview Dr
1400 SDCo 998 A6
900 SDCo 1028 A1
Riverview Ln
200 BRAW 6319 G1
(See Page 6319)
11900 SDCo 1231 J5
Riverview Pkwy
200 SNTE 1231 D6
Riverview Pl
2400 SDCo 998 A7
Riverview Rd
2100 SDCo 996 H4
Riverview Wy
100 OCSD 1066 J7
Riverwalk Dr
- SDGO 1268 J3
- SNTE 1231 D4
Riverwood Dr
200 BRAW 6259 G7
(See Page 6259)
Riverwood Rd
1100 SDCo 1135 D4
Riviera Ct
600 SDCo 1087 H2
Riviera Dr
2400 CHLV 1311 H6
3700 LMSA 1270 H5
100 OCSD 1086 F4
2000 SDCo 1087 J2
4000 SDGO 1248 A6
3300 SDGO 1268 A1
Riviera Pointe St
1200 SDGO 1350 H2
Riviera Shores St
4500 SDGO 1350 G1
Riviera Summit Rd
1200 SDGO 1350 H1
Riviera Wy
1300 CHLV 1311 H6
- SDCo 1090 G5
Rivoli Rd
31200 SDCo 1070 E2
Roach Dr
8400 LMSA 1270 J2
Road Runner Glen
1300 ESCN 1129 G6
Road To Morocco
16500 SDCo 1168 J2
Road To Rio
16500 SDCo 1168 J2
Road To Singapore
7600 SDCo 1168 J2
Road To The Cure
10800 SDGO 1208 A5
Road To Utopia
- SDCo 1168 H3
Road To Zanzibar
7700 SDCo 1168 J2
Roadliner Av
- ESCN 1110 C7
Roadrunner Ln
400 IMPE 6439 F4
100 OCSD 1086 H2
39800 SDCo 1300 D4
(See Page 1300)
Roadrunner Rd
3000 SNMS 1108 C6
Roadrunner Rdg
30700 SDCo 1069 F4
Roadrunner Ridge
30400 SDCo 1069 F4
Roadrunner S Dr
3500 SDCo 1099 G5
(See Page 1099)
Roadside Pl
10100 SDCo 1271 E7
Roan Rd
7700 SDGO 1189 A6
Roan Wy
12200 SDGO 1189 A6
Roane Dr
5600 OCSD 1067 F6
Roanoke Rd
100 ELCJ 1251 G5
Roanoke St
5700 SDGO 1310 D2
Roaring Camp Rd
14100 POWY 1170 G7
Robb Roy Ct
- SDGO 1330 E7

Robb Roy Pl
3400 SDGO 1330 E7
Robbie Ln
- SDCo 1068 D6
Robbie Wy
8300 LMGR 1270 J7
Robbiejean Pl
1500 ELCJ 1252 A5
Robbins Ct
6800 SDGO 1228 F5
Robbins St
4200 SDGO 1228 E4
Robbins Wy
6700 SDGO 1228 F5
Robby Ln
100 OCSD 1086 G2
Robby Wy
600 SDCo 1027 G2
Robelini Dr
100 SDCo 1108 C3
Robert Av
600 CHLV 1310 E7
Robert J Porter Dr
- ELCN 6559 J4
Robert Kennedy St
200 CALX 6620 G6
Robert Ln
800 ENCT 1147 G4
Roberta Av
500 ELCJ 1251 J4
Roberta Ln
3200 OCSD 1086 E5
Roberto Noriega St
- BRAW 6259 F7
(See Page 6259)
Roberto Rio Rd
14400 POWY 1190 G1
Roberto Wy
12700 POWY 1170 C7
Roberts Al
- SDGO 1269 C4
Roberts Dr
6100 SDGO 1290 D7
Roberts Pl
2000 ESCN 1129 G7
Roberts Rd
- ImCo 6319 B2
(See Page 6319)
Roberts St
- SDGO 1288 A5
Roberts Wy
12200 SDCo 1232 A3
Robertson Dr
1100 ESCN 1130 A3
Robertson Rd
4600 CRLB 1106 J6
4800 CRLB 1107 A6
Robertson St
1800 SDCo 1152 E7
2700 SDCo 1172 C1
Robin Ct
- SNMS 1128 E3
Robin Hill Dr
1100 SNMS 1109 A5
Robin Hill Ln
400 SDCo 1109 G5
Robin Hood Wy
10600 SDCo 1271 E2
Robin Ln
1400 ELCJ 1251 D3
200 OCSD 1086 H2
Robin Pl
1200 CHLV 1330 G2
- CRLB 1127 D7
1100 SDCo 1108 D1
Robin St
- ImCo 6560 A7
8500 LMGR 1290 J1
3400 SDGO 1270 C6
Robinea Dr
- CRLB 1127 A4
Robinhood Ln
8800 SDGO 1227 J3
Robinhood Rd
1800 SDCo 1108 G2
1900 SNMS 1108 H3
Robinia Ct
17700 SDGO 1169 H1
Robinridge Wy
9000 SNTE 1231 G6
Robins Nest Wy
16900 SDCo 1169 F3
Robinson Av
- CALX 6620 E5
1200 SDGO 1269 B6
W Robinson Av
100 SDGO 1269 A6
Robinson Mews
3700 SDGO 1269 A6
Robinson Pl
3600 SDGO 1269 C6
Robinson Wy
- SDGO 1229 E1
Robinwood Dr
5200 OCSD 1087 D1
Robinwood Rd
5400 SDCo 1290 H7
Robison Blvd
12600 POWY 1190 C4
Roblar Truck Rd
- SDCo 996 F2

Roblar Truck Trl
- SDCo 996 F3
Roble Grande Ln
1500 SDCo 1233 J7
Roble Grande Rd
1700 SDCo 1234 A7
Roble Grande Tr
- SDCo 1234 A7
Roble Pl
7900 CRLB 1147 G3
Roble Verde
- SDCo 1070 B6
Roble Wy
17000 SDGO 1170 C2
Robleda Cove
12900 SDGO 1150 C6
Robleda Ct
18600 SDGO 1150 C6
Robledo Real Rd
15400 SDCo 1233 B3
Robles Dr
- CHLV 1330 J2
8600 SDGO 1250 J3
8500 SDGO 1251 A3
Robles Ln
29700 SDCo 1070 A6
Robles Rd
11800 SDCo 1029 H4
Robles Wy
1200 SDCo 1029 H4
8700 SDGO 1251 A3
Robley Pl
900 ENCT 1167 E2
Robley Ranch Rd
- POWY 1190 F5
Robusto Rd
5700 SDGO 1229 G7
Robyn Dr
1500 ESCN 1130 B4
Roca Ct
4700 SDCo 1099 G4
(See Page 1099)
Roca Dr
16600 SDGO 1170 C3
Roca Grande Dr
12700 POWY 1190 C5
Roca Pl
900 CHLV 1310 H7
600 SDCo 1067 H6
Roca Rd
700 CHLV 1310 H7
Roca Verde Ln
2600 SDCo 1271 B7
Rochdale Ln
1500 SDGO 1350 B2
Rochelle Av
10300 SNTE 1231 E4
Rochelle Ln
9500 SNTE 1231 E4
Rochester Rd
4100 SDGO 1269 G2
Rocio St
7700 CRLB 1147 G2
Rock Acres Rd
9200 SDCo 1232 D5
Rock Bluff Wy
1500 SDGO 1351 B2
Rock Canyon Ct
11000 SDGO 1209 A3
Rock Canyon Dr
7200 SDGO 1208 J3
7500 SDGO 1209 A3
Rock Creek Dr
10400 SDGO 1209 J4
10500 SDGO 1210 A3
Rock Creek Ln
13500 SDCo 1232 G2
Rock Creek Pl
- CHLV 1311 H6
Rock Creek Rd
13900 POWY 1170 G5
Rock Crest Glen
2300 ESCN 1109 B3
Rock Ct
1300 SNMS 1128 F6
Rock Dove St
- CRLB 1127 E7
Rock Glen
3300 ENCT 1148 C4
Rock Glen Wy
- SNTE 1231 C5
Rock Hill Pl
1300 ESCN 1109 F7
Rock Hill Ranch Rd
15000 SDCo 1090 H2
Rock House Rd
- SDCo 1171 F5
Rock Island Rd
6000 SDGO 1290 D7
Rock Manor Dr
6900 SDGO 1250 E6
Rock Meadow Rd
10000 SDCo 1231 F3
Rock Mountain Dr
39800 SDCo 997 G5
Rock Mtn Dr
40000 SDCo 997 H4
Rock Mtn Rd
1700 CHLV 1331 F3
Rock Pl
6000 SDGO 1270 C5

Rock Point Wy
10200 SDCo 1291 D2
Rock Rd
17000 POWY 1170 D2
Rock Ridge Ln
12800 SDCo 1090 C2
Rock Ridge Pl
400 ESCN 1130 C1
Rock River Ln
3900 SDCo 1311 B2
Rock Rose
14400 SDGO 1188 J1
Rock Springs Hollow
1100 SDCo 1109 D6
Rock Springs Pl
4600 OCSD 1087 D3
Rock Springs Rd
600 ESCN 1129 G2
1800 SDCo 1109 D6
1200 SDCo 1129 F1
700 SNMS 1109 C6
Rock St
6000 SDGO 1270 C5
Rock Stone Rd
- SDCo 1071 A3
Rock Terrace Pl
- CHLV 1311 F3
Rock Terrrace Rd
- SDCo 1234 C6
Rock Valley Ct
7100 SDGO 1228 F4
Rock View Ct
16100 SDGO 1168 H5
Rock View Glen
2200 ESCN 1109 C3
Rock Well
- SDCo 1235 B3
Rock Wren Rd
4700 SDCo 1099 G5
(See Page 1099)
Rockaway Ct
800 SDGO 1267 H1
Rockbrook St
9200 SDCo 1271 B7
Rockcliff Ln
3000 SDCo 1271 D6
Rockcrest Ln
- SDCo 1232 A5
Rockcrest Rd
11900 SDCo 1231 J5
12100 SDCo 1232 A5
Rockdale Ln
3000 SDCo 1271 E6
Rockdale Pl
2500 SNMS 1128 B6
Rocket Ridge Rd
8900 SDCo 1232 A6
Rockfield Ct
- CRLB 1107 C3
Rockfield Wy
9200 SDGO 1209 E2
Rockford Dr
4900 SDGO 1270 C2
Rockgate Wy
9900 SDCo 1271 D6
Rockglen Av
6700 SDGO 1248 J4
Rockhill Rd
100 VSTA 1088 B6
Rockhoff Ln
- SDCo 1109 E4
Rockhoff Rd
1800 SDCo 1109 E4
Rockhouse Rd
17700 SDCo 1171 G4
Rockhouse Trail Ln
- CHLV 1311 H5
Rockhurst Ct
5800 SDGO 1250 D7
Rockhurst Dr
6100 SDGO 1250 C7
Rockin Oaks Wy
- SDCo 1171 H3
Rocking Chair Dr
500 SDCo 1078 H4
(See Page 1078)
Rocking Horse Cir
3300 ENCT 1148 C4
Rocking Horse Dr
- CHLV 1311 F3
- ImCo 6560 A6
Rocking Horse Ln
5400 OCSD 1067 E7
Rocking Horse Rd
31700 SDCo 1049 A7
31700 SDCo 1069 A1
Rockinghorse Rd
700 VSTA 1107 G2
Rockland Ct
- CHLV 1311 B7
Rockland St
6800 SDGO 1270 E5
Rockledge Rd
8500 LMSA 1270 J4
Rockledge St
500 OCSD 1106 B1
Rockmint Dr
- SDCo 1128 G3
Rockne St
2800 SDGO 1310 F1

Rockport Bay Wy
4200 OCSD 1066 F7
Rockport Ct
- ENCT 1147 B2
Rockridge Rd
5100 SDCo 1271 D2
Rockrose Ct
12600 POWY 1190 D3
Rockrose Ln
30500 SDCo 1070 J3
Rockrose Terr
- CRLB 1127 B6
Rockside Ct
11000 SDGO 1208 J2
Rockstream Rd
- SDCo 1231 J2
Rockview Dr
8200 SDCo 1251 G1
Rockville St
10700 SNTE 1231 F6
Rockwall Ln
400 SNMS 1108 G6
Rockwell Ct
12800 POWY 1190 D3
Rockwell Springs Ct
900 ESCN 1129 H6
Rockwood Av
2300 CALX 6620 G6
300 CALX 6680 G2
- ImCo 6560 C7
Rockwood Pl
11000 SDCo 1271 G2
Rockwood Rd
15300 SDCo 1130 G3
- SDCo 1131 C4
10900 SDCo 1271 G2
- SDGO 1131 A5
Rocky Creek Rd
1600 SDCo 1232 H7
Rocky Dr
- SDCo 1023 D2
Rocky Hill Rd
700 ELCJ 1251 H7
Rocky Home Dr
11900 SDCo 1231 J4
Rocky Knoll Rd
40700 SDCo 1300 G5
(See Page 1300)
Rocky Ln
- SDCo 1212 B6
Rocky Mountain Rd
- SDCo 1273 C7
Rocky Mtn Trl
7200 SDCo 1138 B7
(See Page 1138)
7500 SDCo 1158 B1
(See Page 1158)
Rocky Pass
29200 SDCo 1237 D6
Rocky Pass Wy
7800 SDCo 1237 C6
Rocky Point Ct
1600 CHLV 1330 J4
Rocky Point Dr
1300 OCSD 1087 B5
Rocky Point Rd
- SNTE 1230 G7
Rocky Point Wy
1200 ESCN 1109 J4
Rocky Pt Wy
29000 SDCo 1089 D2
Rocky Rd
100 SDCo 1071 D1
19900 SDCo 1148 F2
Rocky Sage Rd
3200 SDCo 1273 A6
Rocky Shore Rd
1700 SDGO 1290 D7
Rocky Top Ln
12400 SDCo 1071 E1
Rocky View Ct
5900 SDCo 1311 B1
Rockycrest Rd
200 SDCo 1027 F5
Rocoso Ln
7900 CRLB 1147 G3
Rocoso Rd
11900 SDCo 1211 G5
Rocrest Rd
1800 SDCo 1233 G7
Rod St
- SDCo 1027 H5
Rodada Dr
16200 SDGO 1170 C4
Rodado Pl
2100 ELCJ 1251 C1
Rodeal Wy
12000 SDCo 1232 A6
Rodear Rd
1600 SDGO 1350 A2
Rodelane St
2000 SDGO 1268 G6
Rodeo Av
1200 CALX 6620 E7
Rodeo Dr
- BRAW 6319 G3
(See Page 6319)
- IMPE 6439 F3
12600 SDCo 1232 C5
1300 SDCo 1247 G2
Rodeo Queen Dr
900 SDCo 1027 G3

Rodeo Rd
1000 IMPE 6439 F4
Rodeo St
- SDCo 1085 J3
Rodin
- SDCo 998 J6
Rodman Av
4900 SDGO 1250 A6
Rodney Av
- CALX 6680 J2
100 ENCT 1147 G6
Rodrigo Dr
4300 SDGO 1270 D4
Rodrigues Ct
- SDCo 1085 J4
Rodriguez Rd
31200 SDCo 1069 D2
Roe Dr
9700 SNTE 1231 C4
Roe Rd
- CORD 1288 F3
Roeblin Ct
6700 SDGO 1248 H7
Roecrest Dr
9700 SNTE 1231 C4
Rogan Rd
200 CHLV 1310 C5
Rogers Ln
4100 SDCo 1271 C4
Rogers Rd
- CORD 1288 G5
3800 SDCo 1271 C5
N Rogers Rd
4100 SDCo 1271 C4
Rogers St
3100 SDGO 1288 A3
Rogue Isle Ct
1700 CRLB 1106 G6
Rogue Rd
500 ELCJ 1251 G4
Rohn Rd
1900 ESCN 1129 H6
Rohr Pl
9000 SDGO 1249 D5
Roja Dr
4900 OCSD 1067 A6
N Roja St
600 OCSD 1067 A5
Rojo Tierra Rd
3700 LMSA 1270 H5
Roland Acres Dr
- SNTE 1231 E7
Rolando Blvd
4700 SDGO 1270 D3
Rolando Ct
4800 SDGO 1270 D2
Rolando Knolls Dr
6800 LMSA 1270 E4
Rolfe Rd
4400 SDGO 1248 E2
Roll Dr
2300 SDGO 1352 A3
Rollie Pl
4600 SDCo 1271 G3
Rollie Wy
4500 SDCo 1271 G3
Rollin Glen Rd
13300 POWY 1190 H4
Rolling Hill Wy
11200 SDCo 1069 G4
Rolling Hills Dr
1500 OCSD 1087 D4
11100 SDCo 1271 H1
Rolling Hills Ln
3500 SDCo 1311 C1
300 SNMS 1108 J6
Rolling Hills Pl
5000 SDCo 1271 J2
Rolling Hills Rd
30300 SDCo 1069 H4
600 SDCo 1108 A3
500 VSTA 1107 J3
500 VSTA 1108 A3
Rolling Meadows Ct
- SDGO 1190 A7
Rolling Oaks Rd
- SNTE 1230 G7
Rolling Ridge Rd
2200 CHLV 1311 E2
Rolling Rock Rd
- SDCo 1089 E2
Rollingview Ln
- SDCo 1047 H6
Rollingwood Ln
- SDCo 1047 H6
Rollins St
100 VSTA 1087 G7
Rollsreach Dr
3300 SDGO 1248 H4
Roma Av
200 SNMS 1108 H7
Roma Ct
1700 CHLV 1330 J5
Roma Dr
1500 VSTA 1107 H3
Roman Wy
300 CHLV 1330 F1
Romance Rd
1400 SDCo 1129 C4
Romany Dr
6100 SDGO 1250 C7

Rombough Pl
5200 SDGO 1270 A7
Romega Ct
5400 SDCo 1290 J7
Romeria St
7600 CRLB 1147 H2
Romero Ct
7300 SDGO 1227 G7
Romero Dr
7100 SDGO 1227 G7
Romford Ct
7100 SDGO 1250 A5
Romine Rd
25000 SDCo 1173 G5
Romney Rd
2300 SDGO 1248 B3
Romneya Dr
200 OCSD 1067 B7
Romo St
6200 SDGO 1270 D6
Romona Av
- IMPE 6499 J2
Romona Ct
- IMPE 6499 J2
Ron Ct
8200 SDGO 1249 B7
Ron Wy
2200 SDGO 1249 B7
Ronald Ct
3100 SDCo 1271 A6
Ronald Ln
- VSTA 1108 A2
Ronald Packard Pkwy
- OCSD 1106 F2
- SNMS 1108 F7
- SNMS 1109 A7
- SNMS 1128 F1
- SNMS 1129 E2
- VSTA 1107 J1
- VSTA 1108 B4
Ronald Packard Pkywy
- VSTA 1107 B2
Ronald St
- BRAW 6319 G4
(See Page 6319)
Ronan Dr
19300 SDCo 1192 B2
(See Page 1192)
Ronda Av
1200 ESCN 1110 A7
9000 SDGO 1249 E7
Ronda Pl
1400 ESCN 1110 A7
Rondel Ct
7300 SDGO 1250 E4
Rondelet Wy
1300 OCSD 1087 B4
Rondevoo Rd
3000 LMGR 1270 H6
Ronica Wy
700 SDCo 1027 J4
Ronna Pl
300 CHLV 1310 E6
Ronnie Ct
9400 SNTE 1231 B4
Ronson Ct
4800 SDGO 1249 C1
Ronson Rd
7100 SDGO 1249 A1
Rookwood Dr
10400 SDGO 1209 G5
Roosevelt Av
7500 LMGR 1270 G6
400 NATC 1289 G7
1100 NATC 1309 H2
1700 SDGO 1248 A7
Roosevelt Ln
13100 SDCo 1193 B5
(See Page 1193)
Roosevelt Rd
- SDGO 1268 D7
Roosevelt St
200 CALX 6680 F1
100 CHLV 1310 C6
2900 CRLB 1106 D5
600 ESCN 1110 A7
Root St
2600 SDGO 1249 C6
Ropalt St
7700 LMSA 1250 G7
Roper Ct
100 ENCT 1147 G7
Rorex Dr
2000 ESCN 1130 A6
Rosa Ct
- ESCN 1110 E6
Rosa Linda St
3600 SDGO 1350 E1
Rosa Rancho Ln
300 SDCo 998 F4
Rosa St
400 SOLB 1187 F1
Rosa Wy
3500 SDCo 1028 D1
Rosada Ct
8600 SDCo 1232 E6
Rosada Glen
1400 ESCN 1110 A5
Rosada Wy
8500 SDCo 1232 E6
Rosal Ct
900 CHLV 1310 J5

Rosal Ln
2300 SDCo 1271 E7
Rosalie Wy
700 SDCo 1253 C1
Rosario Ln
1000 VSTA 1088 A5
Rosarita Dr
4000 LMSA 1270 H4
Rosarito Dr
- IMPE 6499 G1
Rosas St
- CALX 6620 H7
Roscoe Ct
5700 SDGO 1229 E7
Roscrea Av
5100 SDGO 1228 H7
Rose Arbor Dr
900 SNMS 1129 B2
Rose Av
1000 ELCN 6499 G5
Rose Creek Shore Dr
- SDGO 1248 C6
Rose Ct
13900 POWY 1190 F3
600 SNMS 1108 J5
Rose Dr
7100 CRLB 1127 B6
400 NATC 1309 J3
4600 OCSD 1087 E5
- SDGO 1248 D6
900 VSTA 1087 F5
Rose Fern Ln
- SDCo 1172 E2
Rose Garden
- SDGO 1210 D2
Rose Garden Ln
1500 CHLV 1331 G2
Rose Hedge Dr
4900 LMSA 1270 J2
Rose Lake Av
6200 SDGO 1250 H6
Rose Ln
30400 SDCo 1067 G3
- SDCo 1086 A4
Rose Meadow Rd
11000 SDCo 1231 F3
Rose Mtn Rd
800 SDCo 1088 G7
Rose Of Tralee Ln
16600 SDCo 1168 J2
Rose Pl
100 OCSD 1086 D6
4700 SDGO 1270 C3
Rose Ranch Rd
800 SNMS 1109 A5
Rose Rd
2300 SDCo 997 A1
Rose St
800 ESCN 1130 C2
6200 SDGO 1270 C3
N Rose St
1100 ESCN 1110 A6
S Rose St
100 ESCN 1130 C1
Rose View Pl
300 CHLV 1310 C5
Rose Wy
1500 ESCN 1110 B7
Roseann Av
3000 ESCN 1110 E6
Rosebay Dr
100 ENCT 1147 E6
Rosebud Ln
4300 LMSA 1270 G3
300 SDGO 1290 G5
Rosebush Ln
- SDCo 1091 B2
Rosecliff Pl
- SDGO 1208 B1
Rosecrans Blvd
- SDGO 1288 A6
Rosecrans Pl
3100 SDGO 1268 D6
Rosecrans St
3500 SDGO 1268 E5
1300 SDGO 1288 B2
Rosecrest Dr
- SDCo 1089 H4
Rosecroft Ct
3700 SDGO 1188 A3
Rosecroft Ln
3600 SDGO 1287 J4
Rosecroft Wy
13700 SDGO 1187 J3
Rosedale Ct
2900 SDCo 1271 B7
Rosedale Dr
9100 SDCo 1271 B6
Rosedale Pl
2800 SDCo 1271 A7
Rosedale Wy
2800 SDCo 1271 A7
Rosedown Pl
17700 SDGO 1150 A7
Rosedust Glen Dr
10500 SDCo 1169 F1
Rosefield Dr
6800 LMSA 1270 E3
Roseglen Ct
2700 ESCN 1110 E5

Roseglen Pl
9400 SDCo 1271 B5
Rosehill Ct
- SDCo 1130 D7
Rosehill Rd
2600 SDCo 1130 D7
Roseland Dr
7900 SDGO 1227 G5
Roseland Pl
7700 SDGO 1227 H6
Roselawn Av
1200 NATC 1310 A2
3600 SDGO 1269 J6
Roselle Av
500 ELCJ 1251 J4
3900 OCSD 1107 B1
Roselle Ct
1100 ELCJ 1251 J4
Roselle Meadows Tr
6000 SDGO 1188 F4
Roselle St
3500 OCSD 1087 A7
3600 OCSD 1107 B1
10400 SDGO 1208 C6
Rosemarie Ln
3000 SDCo 1048 B1
Rosemary Av
900 CRLB 1127 A6
Rosemary Ct
2500 ENCT 1148 A7
1700 ESCN 1109 C5
Rosemary Ln
7000 LMGR 1270 F7
800 VSTA 1107 H1
Rosemary Pl
100 CHLV 1310 C5
Rosemary Wy
3700 OCSD 1086 H4
Rosemere Ln
800 SDCo 1027 G3
Rosemont Ln
2200 ENCT 1167 J1
15700 SDCo 1172 A5
Rosemont St
400 CALX 6680 G1
200 SDGO 1247 E2
Rosenda Ct
4000 SDGO 1228 B5
Roseta St
200 ENCT 1147 B6
Rosetta Ct
3800 SDGO 1249 A3
Rosette Run
- SDCo 1070 J3
Rosewood Cir
2700 OCSD 1087 E5
Rosewood Dr
5100 OCSD 1087 D2
Rosewood Ln
3200 ESCN 1130 J2
7900 LMGR 1270 G7
4600 SDCo 1099 F3
(See Page 1099)
Rosewood Pl
3600 SDCo 1048 D2
Rosewood St
3000 SDGO 1248 D5
1900 VSTA 1107 G5
Rosey Rd
12400 SDCo 1232 A7
Rosie Ln
10300 SNTE 1231 E4
Rosie Wy
9600 SNTE 1231 D5
Rosina Vista Dr
1500 CHLV 1331 D2
Rosita Ct
600 CHLV 1311 A5
Roslyn Ln
1200 SDGO 1227 F6
Ross Av
1300 ELCN 6559 G1
2000 SDCo 1300 E7
(See Page 1300)
Ross Dr
300 ESCN 1129 D2
300 SDCo 1129 D2
Ross Ln
2800 ESCN 1150 A1
Ross Rd
500 ELCN 6500 B7
2300 ELCN 6559 E1
200 ImCo 6500 D7
900 ImCo 6559 A1
- SDCo 997 A2
Rossin Ct
- CHLV 1311 D7
Rossini Dr
- ENCT 1167 D3
Rossiter Ln
700 SDCo 1027 G2
Rosso Ct
9400 SDCo 1232 H4
Rostrata Hill Rd
16200 POWY 1170 F4
Rostrata Ln
- POWY 1170 F3
Rostrata Rd
13600 POWY 1170 F4
Rosvall Dr
400 SDCo 1027 F2

58 INDEX
Roswell St
San Diego County Street Index
Salina Ct
INDEX 58
SAN DIEGO CO.

STREET Block City Map# Grid

Roswell St
5400 SDGO 1290 B3
Rosy Av
13600 SDGO 1189 D3
Rotanzi St
100 SDCo 1152 D7
300 SDCo 1172 E1
Rotella Ct
11100 SDGO 1189 J4
Roth Ct
200 SDGO 1290 D4
Rotherham Av
8900 SDGO 1189 C3
Rothgard Rd
10000 SDCo 1271 E6
Rouge Dr
1800 CHLV 1311 E7
Rougemont Pl
12400 SDGO 1210 B4
Round Meadow Ct
2500 SDCo 1027 H7
Round Potrero Rd
1200 SDCo 1315 J4
(See Page 1315)
1200 SDCo 1316 A3
(See Page 1316)
Round Tree Dr
1700 OCSD 1087 D4
Round Tree Rd
15200 SDCo 1090 J2
Roundup Av
13000 SDGO 1189 D5
Rous St
4200 SDGO 1228 E4
Roush Ct
- CHLV 1331 A2
Roush Dr
- CHLV 1331 A2
Rousillon Ct
18300 SDGO 1150 B6
Route 9
- CHLV 1311 J5
- CHLV 1312 A5
(See Page 1312)
- SDCo 1311 J4
Rover St
8900 SDCo 1271 A7
Rowan Glen
1500 ESCN 1130 A4
Rowan St
1800 SDGO 1289 G1
Rowcliff Blvd
- CORD 1329 E5
Rowdy Ct
- SDCo 1271 C5
Rowe St
3400 SDGO 1270 D6
Rowell Ct
27300 SDCo 1091 F4
Rowena Av
1200 SNMS 1108 H4
Rowena St
7500 SDGO 1250 E3
Rowlett Av
9000 SDGO 1189 D4
Rowley Av
1900 SDCo 1172 E1
Rowley Wy
600 SDCo 1172 E1
Roxanne Dr
1400 SDCo 1231 G7
1300 SDCo 1251 G1
Roxboro Ct
11400 SDGO 1209 J1
Roxboro Rd
11000 SDGO 1209 H1
Roxbury Rd
5100 SDGO 1269 H2
Roxbury Terr
- SDCo 1188 H2
Roxton Cir
13300 SDGO 1187 J4
Roxy Ln
6500 SDGO 1270 D2
Roy Ln
- SDCo 1028 D2
Roy St
8200 LMGR 1270 H6
Royal Ann Av
10100 SDGO 1209 B5
Royal Birkdale Pl
6900 SDCo 1188 H1
Royal Birkdale Row
12100 SDGO 1170 B5
Royal Caribbean Dr
1800 VSTA 1107 G5
Royal Cir
8100 SDCo 1252 B1
Royal Crest Ct
200 SDCo 1130 B6
Royal Crest Dr
2400 SDCo 1130 B6
Royal Crown Row
15600 SDGO 1170 A5
Royal Dornoch Sq
13800 SDGO 1189 J3
Royal Dr
4000 CRLB 1106 G6
3600 SDCo 1156 E2
37700 SDCo 1299 G3
(See Page 1299)
Royal Gardens Ct
8000 SDCo 1252 A2
Royal Gardens Ln
- SDCo 1251 J1
Royal Gardens Pl
8000 SDCo 1252 A1
Royal Glen Dr
200 SDCo 1027 F1
Royal Gorge Ct
6500 SDGO 1250 D2
Royal Gorge Dr
8100 SDGO 1250 D3
Royal Greens Pl
4800 SDGO 1248 G1
Royal Island Wy
- SDGO 1330 J6
Royal Lytham Glen
2100 ESCN 1109 D4
Royal Lytham Row
12100 SDGO 1170 A5
Royal Lytham Sq
15600 SDGO 1170 A5
Royal Melbourne Sq
13900 SDGO 1189 J3
Royal Oak Dr
4500 OCSD 1087 D5
2300 SDCo 1130 F2
300 SDGO 1290 H5
S Royal Oak Dr
100 SDGO 1290 H4
Royal Oak Pl
7900 SDGO 1290 H4
Royal Oaks Ln
- SDCo 1171 G1
Royal Park Ln
8100 SDCo 1252 A1
Royal Pl
3700 SDCo 1310 D4
Royal Rd
3300 SDCo 1088 E7
12000 SDCo 1251 J1
12500 SDCo 1252 B1
- SDCo 1299 H3
(See Page 1299)
Royal Rim Dr
28900 SDCo 1089 D3
Royal St James Dr
2400 SDCo 1272 B5
Royal Terrn Wy
900 OCSD 1087 A3
Royal Troon Glen
2500 ESCN 1109 H3
Royal View Rd
2500 SDCo 1130 F5
Royal Vista Dr
- SDCo 1172 E3
Royal Willie Rd
33300 SDCo 1318 F3
(See Page 1318)
Royale Crescent Ct
2200 SDGO 1249 C7
Royalito Ln
8000 SDCo 1252 A1
Royce Ct
8400 SDGO 1249 B7
Royce Ln
- SDCo 1027 J7
Roymar Rd
3200 OCSD 1086 D5
Royston Dr
1700 SDGO 1350 A2
Rua Alta Vista
29400 SDCo 1237 D6
Rua Michelle
- SDCo 1109 F2
Ruane St
7100 SDGO 1250 E3
Ruben Ct
14900 SDGO 1169 E6
Rubenstein Av
1200 ENCT 1167 D1
Rubenstein Dr
1600 ENCT 1167 D2
Rubenstein Pl
200 ENCT 1167 C2
Rubert Franks Dr
- ELCN 6559 J4
Rubio St
1400 BRAW 6260 B7
(See Page 6260)
Ruby Av
2100 SDCo 1300 C6
(See Page 1300)
Ruby Ct
- CALX 6620 H7
1100 SNMS 1128 E5
Ruby Dr
800 VSTA 1087 D6
Ruby Lake Av
6200 SDGO 1250 H6
Ruby Ln
4400 OCSD 1107 D2
Ruby Rd
1900 ESCN 1109 C5
Ruby St
600 ELCJ 1251 G7
- IMPE 6439 D6
5800 SDGO 1268 G3
Ruby Wy
- CRLB 1127 B4
Rudd Rd
100 VSTA 1088 B6
Rudder Av
500 CRLB 1146 J1
Rudder Rd
2400 OCSD 1106 F1
Rudder Wy
2500 OCSD 1106 F1
Ruddy Dr
29800 SDCo 1297 F5
(See Page 1297)
Ruddy Duck Ct
2200 ENCT 1167 F4
Rudnick Dr
3200 SDCo 1274 D4
Rudy Rd
1400 SDCo 1291 A2
Rue Adriane
2300 SDGO 1227 H7
Rue Avalion
600 CHLV 1311 D4
Rue Bayonne
600 CHLV 1311 D4
Rue Biarritz
9900 SDGO 1210 B5
Rue Bienville Pl
1800 CHLV 1311 F1
Rue Cannes
10200 SDGO 1210 C5
Rue Cap Ferrat
1200 SDCo 1128 B3
Rue Chamberry
10200 SDGO 1210 B5
Rue Chamond
600 CHLV 1311 D3
Rue Chamonix
10200 SDGO 1210 C5
Rue Chantemar
10200 SDGO 1210 C5
Rue Chateau
1900 CHLV 1311 D4
Rue Cheaumont
12500 SDGO 1210 B5
Rue D Antibes
14000 SDGO 1187 G5
Rue D Azur
14000 SDGO 1187 G6
Rue De Anne
2300 SDGO 1227 H7
Rue De Fleur
25200 SDCo 1109 G2
Rue De La Mar
1700 OCSD 1106 D2
Rue De La Montagne
2000 OCSD 1106 D1
Rue De Lac
25400 SDCo 1109 F2
Rue De Orleans
3000 SDGO 1268 B5
Rue De Roark
7200 SDGO 1227 H7
Rue De Valle
1600 SNMS 1128 C1
Rue Denise
2400 SDGO 1227 H7
Rue Des Amis
12000 SDGO 1210 A3
Rue Des Chateaux
- CRLB 1106 C5
Rue Du Nuage
10400 SDGO 1210 A3
Rue Finisterre
10300 SDGO 1210 C4
Rue Fontenay
10300 SDGO 1210 B4
Rue Fontenay Ct
12400 SDGO 1210 B4
Rue Fountainebleau
12300 SDGO 1210 B4
Rue Lausanne
25400 SDCo 1109 F2
Rue Le Blanc
600 CHLV 1311 D4
Rue Marabelle
12600 SDGO 1210 C4
Rue Marseilles
600 CHLV 1311 D3
Rue Michael
7200 SDGO 1227 H7
Rue Michelle
1900 CHLV 1311 D3
Rue Monaco
14000 SDGO 1187 G6
Rue Mont Grenoble
10300 SDGO 1210 B4
Rue Montereau
12000 SDGO 1210 B5
Rue Montreux
3100 SDCo 1109 F2
Rue Parc
600 CHLV 1311 D3
12600 SDGO 1210 C5
Rue Riviere Verte
10300 SDGO 1210 C5
Rue San Remo
14000 SDGO 1187 G6
Rue Sienne Nord
12600 SDGO 1210 C5
Rue St Jean
1200 SDCo 1128 B4
Rue St Martin
1200 SDCo 1128 B3
Rue St Moritz
1200 SDCo 1128 B3
Rue St Raphael
14000 SDGO 1187 G5
Rue St Tropez
14000 SDGO 1187 G6
Rue St. Jacques
11200 SDGO 1210 B5
Rue St. Lazare
12100 SDGO 1210 B5
Rue Touraine
10200 SDGO 1210 C5
Rue Valbonne
600 CHLV 1311 D3
Rue Vincennes
12600 SDGO 1210 C5
Rueda Acayan
12700 SDGO 1170 C1
Rueda Alcalde
7700 SDCo 1237 C6
Rueda Ct
10800 SDGO 1249 J2
Rueda Dr
4300 SDGO 1249 J2
4600 SDGO 1250 A2
Rueda Margarita
300 SNMS 1109 C7
Rueda Melilla
12800 SDGO 1150 C7
Ruelle Ct
8300 SNTE 1230 H6
Ruette Abeto
17300 SDGO 1169 J1
Ruette Alliante
12400 SDGO 1188 A7
Ruette Campana
17100 SDGO 1170 B2
Ruette De Mer
- SDGO 1188 D6
Ruette De Ville
3600 SDGO 1187 J7
Ruette Le Parc
13600 SDGO 1187 J6
Ruette Monte Carlo
8500 SDGO 1227 H5
Ruette Nice
2500 SDGO 1227 H4
Ruette Nicole
2500 SDGO 1227 H4
Ruette Parc Lido
- SDGO 1350 E1
Ruette San Raphael
- SDGO 1208 A2
Ruffin Ct
9400 SDGO 1249 E1
Ruffin Rd
5700 SDGO 1229 E7
3300 SDGO 1249 E5
9200 SNTE 1231 A5
Ruffner St
5000 SDGO 1229 A7
4900 SDGO 1249 A1
Rufus Ct
7900 SDGO 1189 A7
Rugby Ct
9300 SDGO 1249 E5
Ruger Wy
2100 SDCo 1068 C7
Ruidos Wy
- SOLB 1187 F2
Ruis Rd
14300 SDCo 1232 G6
Rujean Ln
2300 SDCo 1027 H7
Rumex Ln
8600 SDGO 1189 C6
Rumson Dr
8300 SNTE 1230 H5
Run Of The Knolls
8000 SDGO 1169 A6
Run Of The Knolls Ct
8100 SDGO 1169 B6
Runabout Pl
2100 SDCo 1272 D3
Runner Rd
2500 SDCo 1297 G4
(See Page 1297)
Running Creek Rd
10100 SDCo 1049 D7
Running Creek Trl
9600 SDCo 1049 D7
Running Deer Trl
15300 POWY 1171 C6
Running M Rd
3300 SDCo 1079 A6
(See Page 1079)
Running Mare Ln
2000 SDCo 1234 A4
Running Quail Rd
5400 SDCo 1235 A6
Running Springs Pl
2200 ENCT 1147 J6
Running Stream Rd
1800 SDCo 1068 B5
Runnymead Ln
900 SDGO 1288 A3
Runway Dr
31900 SDCo 1051 C7
Runyun Ln
- POWY 1190 F1
Ruocco Dr
8700 SNTE 1231 G6
Rupertus Ln
- SDGO 1228 A2
Rupertus Wy
- SDGO 1228 A2
Rupp Ct
9000 SNTE 1231 A5
Rush Av
1700 VSTA 1087 H3
E Rush Av
200 VSTA 1087 H3
Rush Dr
- SNMS 1128 H2
Rush Rose Dr
7800 CRLB 1147 E2
Rushden Av
4800 SDGO 1248 H1
Rushings Trace
700 SDCo 1234 C4
Rushville Ln
4800 SDCo 1271 E2
Rushville St
500 SDGO 1247 E1
Rusk Cove
11500 SDGO 1209 B1
Ruskin Pl
700 SNMS 1109 B5
Russ Blvd
1400 SDGO 1289 B2
Russan Ln
7000 LMGR 1290 F1
Russelia Ct
6700 CRLB 1126 J5
Russell Av
- SDGO 1268 E7
Russell Dr
- IMPE 6439 D6
- SDGO 1228 A2
Russell Park Wy
- SDGO 1269 C1
Russell Pl
1500 ESCN 1129 H5
Russell Rd
300 BRAW 6319 G2
(See Page 6319)
1200 ELCJ 1251 D5
10300 SDCo 1271 E2
Russell Sq
- ELCJ 1271 E1
Russell St
- SDCo 1067 A2
3300 SDGO 1268 C7
Russet Ct
900 SNMS 1128 F2
Russet Leaf Ct
1700 SDCo 1272 B2
Russet Leaf Ln
13100 SDGO 1189 B4
Russet St
17100 SDCo 1169 F2
Russett Glen
2400 ESCN 1149 G1
Russmar Dr
2700 SDGO 1249 D6
Rustic Canyon Rd
1600 SDCo 1068 B6
Rustic Dr
6300 SDGO 1290 E7
Rustic Ranch Rd
- SDCo 1152 D1
Rustic Rd
700 ESCN 1130 A1
Rustic Villa Rd
- SDCo 1152 D1
Rustic Wood St
2600 CHLV 1311 H5
Rustico Dr
7600 CRLB 1147 F1
Rustling Ln
1500 CHLV 1311 G7
Rustys Hacienda Ln
- SDCo 1151 E7
Rutgers Av
900 CHLV 1311 D5
Rutgers Pl
2800 OCSD 1087 A7
Rutgers Rd
5900 SDGO 1247 H3
Ruth Av
2100 SDCo 1300 C7
(See Page 1300)
Ruth Ct
100 ELCJ 1252 A5
Rutherford Rd
1800 CRLB 1127 C2
24200 SDCo 1153 E7
24100 SDCo 1173 E1
Rutherford St
- CHLV 1331 B1
Ruthie Wy
1900 SDGO 1290 E7
Ruthlor Rd
1600 ENCT 1167 E2
Ruthupham Av
700 SDGO 1330 E7
Rutledge Ct
5200 SDGO 1228 G5
Rutledge Sq
14500 SDGO 1190 B1
Ruttles Ct
3000 SDCo 1271 F6
Ruxton Av
400 SDCo 1291 A4
Ryan Ct
2000 SDCo 1272 C3
Ryan Dr
3400 SDCo 1150 D2
300 SNMS 1128 E1
Ryan Rd
- SDGO 1288 A5
Ryan Ridge Rd
1300 SDCo 1233 A7
Ryan Wy
100 OCSD 1106 F2
11000 SDCo 1109 H2
Ryans Wy
13200 SDCo 1232 D6
Rycker Ridge Rd
800 SDCo 1153 A5
Rydell Pl
800 ELCJ 1251 F4
Ryder Ct
9600 SNTE 1231 C4
Ryder Rd
9600 SNTE 1231 C4
Ryder St
- SDGO 1288 A5
Ryne Rd
- SDGO 1287 J5
Rytko St
600 SDGO 1290 G3

S

N S Av
- NATC 1290 A6
Saba Ct
- VSTA 1088 A2
Sabadell Dr
400 OCSD 1086 H4
Sabina Dr
3000 SDGO 1310 E2
Sabinas Ct
100 SOLB 1167 H4
Sabinas Wy
- SOLB 1167 G7
Sable Ct
5200 OCSD 1087 D1
Saboba Ct
- IMPE 6439 F3
Sabre Hill Dr
10700 SDGO 1189 G5
Sabre Springs Pkwy
12800 SDGO 1189 H5
Sabre St
8200 SDGO 1290 H3
Sabre View Cv
12600 SDGO 1189 G5
Sabrina Ter
600 SDCo 1152 H6
Sabrina Wy
600 VSTA 1087 J7
Sacada Cir
2400 CRLB 1147 G1
Saco St
14500 POWY 1190 H4
Sacramento Av
700 SDCo 1291 B3
Sacramento Dr
3900 LMSA 1270 G5
Sactillo Ct
100 SOLB 1167 H4
Sadderly Sq
5100 SDGO 1188 D2
Saddle
- CRLB 1107 B4
Saddle Back Mountain Rd
- SDCo 1171 F2
Saddle Back Wy
600 SNMS 1129 B1
Saddle Bred Ln
21600 SDCo 1129 C5
Saddle Brook Dr
700 SDCo 1153 A3
Saddle Cove Ln
11300 SDGO 1208 C2
Saddle Creek Dr
15000 SDCo 1070 H2
Saddle Dr
3400 SDCo 1271 A5
Saddle Hill Rd
9400 SDCo 1232 J4
Saddle Horn St
- CHLV 1311 G3
Saddle Mountain Ct
4500 SDGO 1188 C5
Saddle Rd
500 SDCo 1078 H2
(See Page 1078)
Saddle Ridge Ct
- SDCo 1232 D5
Saddle Ridge Dr
1600 CHLV 1331 F2
Saddle Sore Trl
600 SDCo 1138 C7
(See Page 1138)
Saddle Summit Rd
- SDCo 1171 G4
Saddle Wy
1400 OCSD 1067 E6
Saddleback Dr
9900 SDCo 1232 D3
Saddleback Ln
30800 SDCo 1070 J3
Saddleback Rd
- SDCo 1070 H3
N Saddleback Rd
- SDCo 1070 J2
Saddleback St
- CHLV 1311 G3
Saddlebred St
- OCSD 1067 E6
Saddlebrook Ct
1700 ELCJ 1252 B5
Saddlebrook Ln
15000 POWY 1170 F7
Saddlecreek Rd
- SDCo 1047 G5
Saddlehorn
- OCSD 1086 H1
Saddlehorn Dr
1600 SNMS 1108 D5
Saddleridge Rd
- OCSD 1067 F6
13200 SDCo 1232 C5
Saddlerock Rd
9200 SDCo 1232 A6
Saddleview Ct
1300 ELCJ 1252 A7
Saddlewood Dr
14000 POWY 1190 D2
2900 SDCo 1290 H7
Sadie St
9900 SNTE 1231 F4
Sadlers Creek Rd
2700 CHLV 1311 J4
Sadlers Creek Wy
1100 CHLV 1311 J4
Safari Dr
100 ELCJ 1251 J5
Safari Sq
- ELCJ 1251 J5
Safford Av
700 SDCo 1291 A3
Saffron Dr
1700 CHLV 1331 H3
Saffron Glen
2400 ESCN 1149 G1
Saffron Rd
3000 SDCo 1048 B1
Saffron Wy
2100 SDCo 1048 B1
Sagamore Wy
- SDGO 1208 D1
Sagasti Av
4800 SDGO 1248 H1
Sage Brush Trl
27200 SDCo 1090 C5
Sage Canyon Dr
3600 ENCT 1167 G2
Sage Creek Rd
3600 SDCo 1028 E6
Sage Ct
6900 CRLB 1127 A6
800 IMPE 6439 F4
Sage Dr
2400 SDCo 1297 E5
(See Page 1297)
Sage Glen
3100 ESCN 1149 J3
Sage Glen Trl
- SDCo 1089 D3
Sage Hill Dr
25300 SDCo 1173 G4
Sage Hill Wy
12000 SDCo 1089 D3
Sage Meadow Ct
29700 SDCo 1070 D6
Sage Meadow Ln
13600 SDCo 1070 E6
Sage Mesa Rd
13500 SDGO 1188 G3
Sage Mountain Ln
13600 SDCo 1292 F2
(See Page 1292)
Sage Rd
3300 SDCo 1048 F3
200 SDCo 1252 J2
Sage Sparrow Wy
300 SNMS 1129 B1
Sage Tree Ct
- CHLV 1311 D6
Sage View
1000 CHLV 1330 J1
Sage View Dr
2800 SDCo 1234 C6
Sage View Rd
12200 POWY 1190 B5
Sage Wy
3700 OCSD 1086 G4
600 SDGO 1290 E3
Sagebrush Bend Wy
6200 SDGO 1188 F3
Sagebrush Ct
1600 CHLV 1331 G3
- SDCo 1232 C5
2400 SDGO 1247 J2
Sagebrush Rd
1000 CRLB 1127 B6
5800 SDGO 1247 J2
Sagebrush St
- IMPE 6499 C2
Sagebrush Terr
15400 SDCo 1051 A7
Sagebrush Wy
1400 OCSD 1067 E6
Sagecrest St
12600 POWY 1170 D7
12600 POWY 1190 D1
Sageflower Dr
- SDGO 1270 D6
Sageland Dr
23000 SDCo 1153 D7
Sagewood Dr
800 OCSD 1087 C2
13400 POWY 1170 E3
Sagewood Ln
16500 POWY 1170 F3
Sagewood Rd
- SDCo 1068 B4
Sagewood Wy
- SNMS 1128 C6
Sagina Ct
4800 OCSD 1067 A7
Saginaw Av
4200 SDGO 1248 E2
Sagittarius Rd
11100 SDGO 1209 C2
Saguaro Pl
200 OCSD 1067 A7
Saguaro Rd
9400 SDCo 1231 J5
Saguaro St
- IMPE 6439 C6
Saguaro Wy
7600 SDGO 1250 C4
Sahara Pl
3400 OCSD 1086 F4
Sahm Wy
- SDCo 1091 F4
Sailfish
1200 SDCo 1085 H5
Sailfish Pl
900 CRLB 1126 J4
St. Agnes Ct
3900 SDGO 1188 B7
St. Albans Dr
900 ENCT 1147 D4
St. Albans Pl
1000 ENCT 1147 C3
St. Andrews Av
7600 SDGO 1351 F2
St. Andrews Cove
1600 SDGO 1351 E2
St. Andrews Ct
16900 POWY 1170 E2
St. Andrews Dr
16900 POWY 1170 D2
9400 SNTE 1230 J5
St. Andrews Glen
2500 SDCo 1109 H3
St. Andrews Ln
26700 SDCo 1090 G4
St. Andrews Pl
4400 OCSD 1066 H7
13400 POWY 1170 E1
St. Andrews Rd
8100 SDCo 1168 G7
8300 SDCo 1188 G1
St. Andrews Terr
1600 SDGO 1351 F2
St. Anne Dr
2400 SDCo 1272 B5
St. Anne Glen
1800 ESCN 1109 C4
St. Charles St
3000 SDGO 1268 E6
St. Christophers Ln
- CORD 1329 E2
St. Claire Dr
- CHLV 1311 E5
St. Cloud Wy
- OCSD 1087 A4
St. Croix Ct
2100 LMGR 1290 F1
St. Croix Dr
2000 SDCo 1058 G7
(See Page 1058)
St. Denis Terr
5900 SDGO 1250 C6
St. Etienne Ln
18300 SDGO 1150 C6
St. George Ct
4500 CRLB 1106 J5
900 SDCo 1291 A3
St. George Dr
900 SDCo 1253 B2
St. George Pl
- SDCo 1291 A3
St. George St
9600 SDCo 1291 C3
St. Georges Ln
- SDCo 1070 F7
St. Germain Rd
- CHLV 1311 E5
St. Helena Av
- CHLV 1331 C1
St. Helena Ct
24100 SDCo 1173 E1
St. Helena Dr
17200 SDCo 1173 E1
St. Helene Ct
1200 OCSD 1106 D2
St. James Ct
- CRLB 1106 F5
St. James Dr
16800 POWY 1170 D2
St. James Pl
4200 SDGO 1268 H5
St. John Pl
8100 LMSA 1250 H7
St. Johns Cross
- OCSD 1067 E1
St. Kitts Wy
- CORD 1329 E2
St. Laurent Pl
2700 SDGO 1227 J6
St. Louis Ter
7900 SDGO 1227 G5
St. Lucia Wy
1800 VSTA 1107 G5
St. Lucy Ln
15400 SDCo 1233 B2
St. Malo Beach
- OCSD 1106 C4
St. Martins Ct
14100 POWY 1190 G1
St. Marys Ct
8000 SDCo 1169 A2
St. Moritz Ter
11800 SDGO 1210 A3
St. Nikola Ct
800 SDCo 1129 E1
St. Onge Dr
8100 LMSA 1270 H1
St. Paul Dr
700 SNMS 1129 E1
St. Peters Dr
1700 SDCo 1027 J3
St. Pierre Wy
- SDGO 1210 A2
St. Pierre Wy
11900 SDGO 1210 A3
St. Rita Ct
- SDGO 1290 A5
St. Rita Pl
- SDGO 1290 A4
St. Sava Pl
800 SDCo 1129 E1
St. Stefan Terr
1700 SDCo 1129 E1
St. Therese Wy
6000 SDGO 1250 C6
St. Thomas Dr
2000 SDCo 1058 G7
(See Page 1058)
St. Thomas Rd
1800 VSTA 1107 G5
St. Tropez Dr
1900 VSTA 1107 H4
St. Tropez Pl
2600 SDGO 1227 J6
St. Vincent Dr
1900 SDCo 1058 G7
(See Page 1058)
Saintsbury Glen
16800 SDGO 1169 E3
Saipan Dr
2300 SDGO 1290 E7
Saipan Rd
1300 CORD 1309 D5
Sakina St
1900 SDCo 1272 C1
Sal Ln
1100 VSTA 1088 C4
Sal Pl
- ESCN 1129 G5
Sal Rd
1100 SDCo 1029 H5
Salacot Ct
5800 SDGO 1229 H7
Salamanca Ct
100 SOLB 1167 H4
Salem Ct
1400 OCSD 1066 J4
800 SDGO 1267 H1
Salem Pl
4500 CRLB 1107 B4
Salem St
800 SDCo 1088 F7
Salerno Ct
1200 OCSD 1087 C2
Salerno St
7100 SDGO 1248 J3
7400 SDGO 1249 A3
Salet Pl
700 SNMS 1109 A5
Salida Del Luna
- SDCo 1171 C3
Salida Del Sol
15700 SDCo 1171 B2
- SDGO 1189 A2
Saliente Wy
2000 CRLB 1147 F1
Salina Cruz Ct
100 SOLB 1167 H4
Salina Ct
300 VSTA 1087 E7

59 INDEX
INDEX 59
Salina St
Santa Gloria
SAN DIEGO CO.

San Diego County Street Index

STREET
Block City Map# Grid

Salina St
800 ELCJ 1251 G7
Salinas Dr
200 CHLV 1311 D1
Salinas St
- OCSD 1066 H7
Salinas Wy
10900 SDGO 1209 A3
Salisbury Dr
4400 CRLB 1106 J5
2300 SDGO 1249 B7
Salix Ct
12100 SDGO 1189 A7
Salix Pl
7600 SDGO 1189 A7
Salix Wy
12100 SDGO 1189 A7
Salizar Ct
6400 SDGO 1248 H3
Salizar St
7100 SDGO 1248 J3
Salk Av
- CRLB 1127 C1
Salk Institute Rd
- SDGO 1227 J1
Sallisaw Ct
5900 SDGO 1250 C5
Sally Pl
1700 ESCN 1109 D5
Salmon Ln
- OCSD 1086 G2
Salmon Rd
200 SDCo 1153 B5
Salmon River Rd
13400 SDGO 1189 E4
Salmon St
3100 SDGO 1249 G5
Salot St
700 NATC 1290 C7
Salt Air Ln
- SDCo 1027 G1
Salt Creek Rd
- SDCo 1311 J7
- SDCo 1331 J1
Salt Lake Ct
2100 CHLV 1331 F3
Salt Mine Rd
17100 SDCo 1171 E2
Salta Pl
3300 SDGO 1270 A6
Saltaire Pl
1700 SDGO 1350 J3
Saltaire Wy
- CRLB 1127 A4
Saltbush Ln
1200 SDCo 1252 F7
Saltgrass Av
600 CRLB 1126 H6
Saltie Ct
7000 CRLB 1127 A6
Saltillo Ct
- SOLB 1167 G7
Salton View Dr
2100 SDCo 1136 C6
Salton Vista Dr
2500 SDCo 1136 D7
3200 SDCo 1156 E1
Saluda Av
10100 SDGO 1209 C5
Saluto Ct
4500 SDGO 1188 B7
Salvador Guilin St
900 CALX 6680 D1
Salvador Rd
11700 SDCo 1029 H4
Salvia Wy
12200 SDGO 1189 A7
Sam Ellis St
500 CALX 6620 E7
Sam Ln
16600 SDCo 1171 G2
Sam-O-Reno Rd
13900 POWY 1190 F4
Samagatuma Valley Rd
- SDCo 1236 G3
Samantha Av
13500 SDGO 1189 D3
Samantha Ct
- IMPE 6499 G2
9000 SDGO 1189 D4
Samantha Ln
8600 SDCo 1270 J7
Samar St
- SDGO 1268 E6
Samara Wy
800 CRLB 1127 A6
Sambrosa Pl
16500 SDGO 1170 C3
Samoa St
- SDGO 1268 F6
Samoa Wy
1800 OCSD 1106 E1
Samoset Av
4200 SDGO 1248 E2
Sample St
10200 SDGO 1249 G5
Sampson Rd
- SDGO 1288 C2
Sampson St
- IMPE 6499 H2
- IMPE 6500 A2
400 SDGO 1289 D5
Sams Hill Rd
1500 SDCo 1251 G2
Sams Mountain Rd
32500 SDCo 1051 C4
Sams Ranch Rd
- SDCo 1235 A2
Samuel Ct
500 ENCT 1147 E5
Samuel St
6000 LMSA 1250 H6
San Abella Dr
1000 ENCT 1147 E7
San Alberto Wy
300 SDGO 1290 A5
San Altos Pl
1500 LMGR 1290 F2
San Andrade Dr
1000 ENCT 1147 E7
San Andreas St
1500 CHLV 1331 D2
San Andres Dr
15600 SDGO 1187 H2
600 SOLB 1167 G7
San Andres St
9100 SDCo 1291 B4
San Angelo Av
6100 LMSA 1250 J6
San Angelo Pl
- CHLV 1311 G3
San Anselmo St
1600 CHLV 1331 E1
2500 SDGO 1248 B4
San Antonio Av
500 SDGO 1288 A4
San Antonio Pl
800 SDGO 1288 B3
San Antonio Rose Ct
17000 SDCo 1149 A7
San Antonio Wy
10800 SDCo 1049 F2
San Aquario Dr
5000 SDGO 1248 B3
San Ardo Cove
4000 SDGO 1188 B7
San Augustine Wy
3900 SDGO 1188 B7
San Benito
7200 CRLB 1126 J7
San Benito Ct
1400 SOLB 1167 H7
San Benito Rd
700 SDCo 1099 A1
(See Page 1099)
San Bernardino Av
1600 SDCo 1291 D2
San Bernardo Ter
5200 SDGO 1290 B5
San Blas Cir
10900 SDGO 1209 D3
San Borja St
1500 CHLV 1331 D2
San Bortolo
7200 CRLB 1126 J6
San Bristo Wy
2900 CRLB 1147 H2
San Bruno Cove
12400 SDGO 1188 B6
San Bruno Pl
- CHLV 1311 F4
San Carlos
7000 CRLB 1126 J6
San Carlos Ct
10300 SDCo 1271 E6
San Carlos Dr
3300 SDCo 1271 F6
7900 SDGO 1250 H5
San Carlos Pl
1400 ESCN 1109 E5
San Carlos Rd
700 SDCo 1079 A7
(See Page 1079)
San Carlos St
9300 SDCo 1291 B4
San Clemente Av
2200 VSTA 1088 C6
San Clemente Canyon Rd
- SDGO 1229 D4
San Clemente St
2200 SDGO 1268 B7
San Clemente Ter
2500 SDGO 1228 B7
San Clemente Wy
2300 VSTA 1088 D6
San Colla St
300 SDGO 1247 F4
San Cristobal Rd
9800 SDCo 1271 D4
San Diego Av
300 ELCN 6499 H5
- SDCo 1172 D2
2300 SDGO 1268 G6
San Diego Blvd
- IMPE 6439 F7
San Diego Frwy
- CHLV 1330 A3
3300 CRLB 1106 F5
4500 CRLB 1126 H3
7000 CRLB 1127 A6
- ENCT 1147 B2
- ENCT 1167 D2
- OCSD 1106 C1
- SDCo 1023 E3
- SDCo 1085 G2
- SDGO 1207 J2
- SDGO 1208 B7
- SDGO 1228 B4
- SDGO 1289 C2
San Diego Fwy
- ENCT 1147 C7
- ENCT 1167 E4
- SDGO 1187 H3
- SDGO 1248 B2
- SDGO 1268 F5
- SDGO 1289 F6
- SDGO 1330 A5
- SDGO 1350 F4
San Diego Hwy
- CHLV 1309 J6
San Diego Mission Rd
9600 SDGO 1249 G7
San Diego Pl
- SDGO 1267 J4
San Diego St
200 OCSD 1086 B6
9600 SDCo 1291 C4
San Diego Stadium
- SDGO 1249 F7
San Dieguito Dr
2000 DLMR 1187 G3
700 ENCT 1147 C7
San Dieguito Rd
- SDCo 1168 G6
- SDGO 1168 H5
4400 SDGO 1188 C2
San Dimas Av
200 OCSD 1086 H3
6000 SDGO 1268 G2
San Dimas Ct
1100 CHLV 1311 C7
San Dionicio St
600 SDGO 1288 A3
San Elijo Av
2300 ENCT 1167 D4
5100 SDCo 1168 B2
S San Elijo Av
1300 ENCT 1167 C1
San Elijo Rd
- SNMS 1128 G5
San Elijo St
500 SDGO 1288 A3
San Eugenio St
1700 SDGO 1351 A2
San Felipe Dr
- IMPE 6499 H1
San Felipe Pl
300 SDGO 1290 H3
San Felipe St
8500 SDGO 1290 H3
San Fernando Pl
700 SDGO 1267 H3
San Fernando St
300 SDGO 1288 A4
San Fernando Wy
- OCSD 1086 J3
San Francisco
1700 SDGO 1351 A3
San Francisco St
9200 SDCo 1291 B3
San Gabriel Dr
- OCSD 1086 F2
San Gabriel Pl
- CHLV 1311 F3
700 SDGO 1267 H3
San Gabriel Wy
10700 SDCo 1049 F4
San Gallo Ln
- SDCo 1169 E2
San Geronimo Dr
- SDCo 1049 J5
San Gorgonio St
500 SDGO 1288 A4
San Gregorio Wy
3900 SDGO 1188 B7
San Helena Dr
3200 OCSD 1086 J7
San Ignacio
1400 SOLB 1167 H7
San Ignacio Ct
1700 CHLV 1331 D3
San Jacinto Cir
5000 SDCo 1047 E7
San Jacinto Cir W
4800 SDCo 1047 F6
S San Jacinto Dr
600 SDGO 1290 B4
San Jacinto East Cres
4800 SDCo 1047 F6
San Jacinto Glen
1100 ESCN 1109 E5
San Jacinto Pl
- CHLV 1311 G3
5200 SDGO 1290 A4
San Jacinto St
100 SDGO 1290 A4
San Jacinto Terr
4600 SDCo 1047 F6
San Jacito Rd
- SDCo 1085 J4
San Javier Ct
1500 CHLV 1331 D3
San Joaquin Ct
2500 SDGO 1248 C4
San Joaquin Dr
5000 SDGO 1248 B4
San Joaquin St
4400 OCSD 1066 H7
4400 OCSD 1086 G1
San Jose Ct
- CHLV 1311 G3
San Jose Pl
800 SDGO 1267 H1
San Jose St
1500 OCSD 1086 A5
San Jovani
1700 SDGO 1351 A3
San Juan Pl
- CHLV 1311 G3
900 OCSD 1086 A5
9100 SDCo 1271 B3
700 SDGO 1267 H1
San Juan Rd
4000 SDGO 1268 G5
San Juan St
1000 OCSD 1086 B5
9800 SDCo 1271 C5
San Juan Wy
- SNMS 1129 C1
San Juhn St
600 SDCo 1291 C3
San Julian Dr
1000 SDCo 1128 D3
San Julian Ln
1300 SDCo 1128 D3
San Julian Pl
1200 SDCo 1128 D3
San Julio Dr
500 SOLB 1167 H7
San Leandro Wy
3900 SDGO 1188 B7
San Leon Ct
3500 SDCo 1079 A7
(See Page 1079)
1100 SOLB 1167 H5
San Leon Rd
700 SDCo 1079 A7
(See Page 1079)
San Lorenzo Ct
3900 OCSD 1086 H4
900 SOLB 1167 H5
San Lori Ln
1100 SDCo 1272 B1
San Lucas
7300 CRLB 1126 J7
San Lucas Ct
1300 SOLB 1167 H7
San Lucas Dr
300 SOLB 1167 H7
San Lucas Pl
- CHLV 1311 F3
San Luis
7100 CRLB 1126 J6
San Luis Av
- OCSD 1086 G2
San Luis Obispo Pl
800 SDGO 1267 H2
San Luis Opispo Dr
- OCSD 1086 F3
San Luis Rey Av
1700 CORD 1288 J7
1600 VSTA 1087 H3
San Luis Rey Dr
600 OCSD 1085 J6
- SDCo 1049 F3
San Luis Rey Mission Exwy
1900 OCSD 1086 C5
San Luis Rey Pl
800 SDGO 1267 H4
San Luis Rey Rd
2900 OCSD 1086 D5
San Luis St
700 SDGO 1289 D3
San Luiseno Ln
38000 SDCo 1071 D5
San Marcos Av
2600 SDGO 1269 E7
2400 SDGO 1289 E1
W San Marcos Blvd
1400 SNMS 1128 C2
San Marcos Ln
- SNMS 1108 H7
San Marcos Pl
100 CHLV 1330 E2
San Marino Dr
900 SDCo 1128 C3
San Marino Pl
- CHLV 1311 F4
San Mario Dr
500 SOLB 1167 J5
San Martin
3300 SDCo 1232 D6
San Martine Wy
3900 SDGO 1188 B7
San Mateo Dr
5400 SDGO 1290 B5
San Mateo Point Ct
1500 CHLV 1330 J4
San Mateo St
1500 OCSD 1086 A5
San Miguel
7200 CRLB 1126 J7
San Miguel Av
6600 LMGR 1270 E7
1200 SDCo 1291 C2
600 SDGO 1289 H5
San Miguel Ct
100 CHLV 1330 D1
3500 NATC 1310 E3
3900 OCSD 1086 H3
San Miguel Dr
200 CHLV 1330 C1
E San Miguel Dr
- CHLV 1330 E1
San Miguel Ranch Rd
- CHLV 1311 D1
San Miguel Rd
7200 SDCo 1291 D6
5600 SDCo 1311 A1
San Miguel St
600 SDCo 1291 C3
San Miguel Wy
3300 SDCo 1311 A1
San Moreno St
- CALX 6620 G5
San Moritz
15300 POWY 1170 D6
San Onofre Ter
5400 SDGO 1290 B5
San Pablo Av
3900 OCSD 1086 G4
San Pablo Ct
3500 SDCo 1079 A7
(See Page 1079)
1300 SDCo 1128 D2
San Pablo Dr
1200 SDCo 1128 D3
San Pablo Pl
- CHLV 1311 F3
San Pablo Rd
700 SDCo 1099 A1
(See Page 1099)
San Pablo Wy
900 SDCo 1128 D2
San Pasqual Ct
2000 LMGR 1290 F1
San Pasqual Rd
700 ESCN 1150 C2
14200 SDGO 1130 G7
14200 SDGO 1150 F1
San Pasqual St
1600 CHLV 1331 E1
7200 LMGR 1290 F1
500 SDGO 1289 H5
San Pasqual Trl
3300 SDCo 1130 F6
San Pasqual Valley Rd
2300 SDCo 1130 D5
17700 SDCo 1131 F6
19700 SDCo 1152 C2
15200 SDGO 1130 H5
15900 SDGO 1131 A6
San Pasqual Wy
14300 SDCo 1130 F6
San Patricio Dr
1000 SOLB 1167 H6
San Pedro Av
6100 SDGO 1268 G2
San Pedro Point Ct
1500 CHLV 1330 J3
San Placido Ct
400 ESCN 1149 J4
San Rafael Dr
- SDCo 1085 J5
San Rafael Pl
- CHLV 1311 G3
800 SDGO 1247 H7
San Rafael Rd
3300 SDCo 1079 A6
(See Page 1079)
San Ramon Dr
3900 OCSD 1086 G4
10200 SDGO 1209 C5
San Ramone
7200 CRLB 1126 J7
E San Raphael Dr
- SDGO 1208 A2
W San Raphael Dr
- SDGO 1208 A2
San Remo Cir
2200 SDCo 1108 D2
San Remo Ct
9700 SNTE 1231 D4
San Remo Dr
2000 OCSD 1086 J7
San Remo Rd
9700 SNTE 1231 D4
San Remo Wy
400 SDGO 1288 A4
San Rey Ct
4700 SDCo 1048 H4
San Rey Ln
3300 SDCo 1048 H3
San Rey Pl
4700 SDCo 1048 H4
San Ricardo Ct
1100 SOLB 1167 H5
San Roberto
5400 SDGO 1351 A2
San Rodolfo Dr
600 SOLB 1167 F7
San Roque Dr
300 SDCo 1130 B6
San Rufo Ct
16500 SDCo 1169 G4
San Salvador Ct
16600 SDGO 1170 B3
San Salvador Rd
16500 SDGO 1170 B3
San Sebastian Av
- CHLV 1311 E7
San Sebastian Wy
13800 POWY 1170 F7
San Simeon St
1400 OCSD 1086 B4
San Souci Dr
3100 SDCo 1149 F1
San Tomas Ct
12200 SDGO 1170 B3
San Tomas Dr
3200 OCSD 1086 J7
16600 SDGO 1170 B3
San Tomas Pl
12100 SDGO 1170 B3
San Vicente Av
12100 SDCo 1211 J6
- SDCo 1212 A6
San Vicente Blvd
10400 SDCo 1271 E5
San Vicente Ct
600 SDGO 1290 G3
San Vicente Fwy
- SDCo 1231 H4
- SDCo 1251 F1
- SNTE 1231 F7
San Vicente Oaks Rd
23400 SDCo 1173 D7
23400 SDCo 1193 D1
(See Page 1193)
San Vicente Rd
1100 SDCo 1152 G7
1800 SDCo 1172 G3
24400 SDCo 1173 F4
San Vicente St
7400 SDGO 1290 G3
San Vicente Ter
1200 SDCo 1172 G1
San Vicente View
- SDCo 1172 H4
San Vicente Wy
600 SDGO 1290 G3
San Victorio
1700 SDGO 1351 A2
San Ysidro Blvd
900 SDGO 1350 D3
E San Ysidro Blvd
300 SDGO 1350 G4
W San Ysidro Blvd
300 SDGO 1350 F3
San Ysidro Dr
600 SDCo 1058 H5
(See Page 1058)
Sanat Village St
2400 SDCo 1252 E5
Sancado Ter
500 SDCo 1027 E3
Sand Aster Cres
32000 SDCo 1318 B6
(See Page 1318)
Sand Aster Dr
- CRLB 1127 D6
Sand Castle Dr
900 ENCT 1167 E2
Sand Cove Wy
4000 CRLB 1106 G7
Sand Crab Pl
- SDGO 1208 C4
Sand Crest Wy
- SNMS 1128 A2
Sand Ct
3500 CRLB 1107 B4
Sand Dollar Wy
- SNMS 1128 A2
Sand Dr
2100 CHLV 1331 F3
Sand Drift Pt
- SDGO 1350 J1
Sand Dune Wy
- SNMS 1128 C5
Sand Hill Rd
14200 POWY 1170 G5
Sand Piper Av
- SDCo 1023 E3
Sand Shell Av
600 CRLB 1126 J6
Sand Star Wy
400 SDGO 1330 H6
Sand Stone St
- IMPE 6439 C7
Sand Trap Ct
2300 OCSD 1106 J1
Sand Trap Row
12100 SDGO 1170 A4
Sandal Ln
1600 CHLV 1331 F2
1400 SDGO 1247 J3
Sandalwood Ct
- ELCN 6559 D1
400 ENCT 1147 E6
8500 SDGO 1228 A4
Sandalwood Dr
- CHLV 1310 C5
500 ELCJ 1251 G4
- ELCN 6559 D1
Sandalwood Glen Av
- IMPE 6499 C3
Sandalwood Ln
1500 CRLB 1106 F5
Sandalwood Pl
500 ESCN 1110 D6
5200 OCSD 1087 C1
Sandalwood Wy
4700 OCSD 1087 B3
Sandbar Cove Wy
5100 SDGO 1350 J2
Sandbar Dr
- SNMS 1128 C5
Sandbar Wy
800 CRLB 1126 J6
Sandburg Av
5600 SDGO 1228 C6
Sandburg Ct
3000 SDGO 1228 C6
Sandburg Wy
3000 SDGO 1228 C6
Sandcastle Dr
6900 CRLB 1127 A6
Sandcastle Ln
3400 SDGO 1268 D5
Sandcastle Wy
1900 OCSD 1106 F1
Sanddollar Ct
- SDGO 1188 D6
Sandel Dr
300 VSTA 1087 E6
Sander Ct
1100 ESCN 1110 A7
Sanderling Av
1600 CHLV 1331 D2
Sanderling Ct
2000 CRLB 1127 E7
Sanders Ct
6600 SDGO 1250 F5
Sanderson Rd
8300 SDCo 1237 B5
Sandhill Ct
- SDGO 1188 D4
Sandhill Terr
- SDGO 1188 D5
Sandhurst Wy
- SDCo 1089 C3
Sandia Creek Dr
38600 SDCo 997 F4
Sandia Creek Terr
4000 SDCo 997 G2
Sandia Pl
5500 SDGO 1249 H1
Sandleford Wy
6900 SDGO 1290 F6
Sandlewood Dr
600 ELCN 6559 H1
Sandmark Av
8800 SDGO 1249 C7
Sandor Wy
3500 SDCo 1088 F7
Sandos St
1600 ELCJ 1252 B7
Sandoval Cir
2000 ImCo 6500 H5
Sandoval Ln
600 ImCo 6500 H4
Sandover Ct
2800 SDCo 1290 J7
Sandown Ct
14300 POWY 1190 E2
Sandown Wy
- SDGO 1188 E5
Sandpiper Pl
6900 CRLB 1127 F6
3500 OCSD 1107 C2
900 SDGO 1247 G3
Sandpiper Strand
- CORD 1329 E1
Sandpiper Wy
400 CHLV 1309 H7
400 CHLV 1329 H1
Sandpoint Ct
- CRLB 1107 B3
Sandra Ann Ln
11300 SDCo 1069 H3
Sandra Cir
1200 VSTA 1107 J1
1200 VSTA 1108 A1
Sandra Ln
600 ELCJ 1252 D4
Sandrock Rd
3400 SDGO 1249 C4
Sands Pl
100 OCSD 1086 F5
Sandshore Ct
4900 SDGO 1188 D6
Sandside Ct
600 CRLB 1126 H5
Sandstone Cres
1500 SDCo 1058 H5
(See Page 1058)
Sandstone Ct
300 CHLV 1330 G4
Sandstone Dr
8500 SNTE 1250 H1
Sandstone St
200 CHLV 1330 G4
Sandstone Vista Ln
1900 ENCT 1147 J7
Sandstone Wy
- CRLB 1107 B3
Sandton Ln
4000 SDGO 1270 B5
Sandy Av
600 ELCN 6499 G4
Sandy Bev Ln
8600 SDCo 1270 J6
Sandy Cape
- SDGO 1351 A1
Sandy Creek
7100 SDCo 1175 J2
(See Page 1175)
Sandy Creek Dr
400 CHLV 1311 A4
Sandy Crest Ct
12700 SDGO 1188 D6
Sandy Ct
800 ENCT 1147 C3
Sandy Ct Dr
- OCSD 1085 J6
Sandy Hill Dr
- SDCo 1069 A7
Sandy Hook Rd
10800 SDGO 1209 A3
Sandy Ln
2900 DLMR 1187 F3
600 SNMS 1129 A2
2300 VSTA 1108 A5
Sandy Pl
3200 CRLB 1106 G4
Sandy Pointe
2900 DLMR 1187 F3
Sandy Shore Ct
6000 SDGO 1290 D7
Sandy Shore St
1600 SDGO 1290 D6
Sandy St
300 ELCJ 1251 F6
Sanford Dr
7800 LMGR 1290 H2
Sanford Ln
2800 CRLB 1107 A4
Sanford St
300 ENCT 1147 B3
Sanfords Rd
- BRAW 6259 F7
(See Page 6259)
Sanfred Ct
10600 SNTE 1231 D2
Sangamon Av
1500 SDCo 1291 D2
Sanger Pl
- SDGO 1350 G4
Sanibelle Cir
400 CHLV 1310 F6
Sanlin Dr
1600 SDCo 1272 A1
Sanshey Ln
10500 SDCo 1169 F2
Santa Alexia Av
- CHLV 1331 C2
Santa Alica Av
- CHLV 1331 C1
Santa Alicia
5400 SDGO 1351 A2
400 SOLB 1167 G6
Santa Ana
- OCSD 1066 J7
Santa Ana Dr
1400 SDGO 1268 G2
Santa Ana St
- CALX 6620 G6
Santa Andrea St
- CHLV 1331 C1
Santa Angela Ct
- CHLV 1311 G2
Santa Anita Ct
- CHLV 1311 G2
Santa Anita Dr
1600 SDGO 1268 G2
Santa Anita Pl
100 VSTA 1087 J7
Santa Anita St
1000 OCSD 1086 A5
Santa Antonio Dr
- OCSD 1086 F2
Santa Arminita Av
8100 SDGO 1209 B2
Santa Asis Dr
- OCSD 1086 F3
Santa Barbara
7100 CRLB 1126 J6
Santa Barbara Ct
- CHLV 1311 G2
Santa Barbara Dr
- SDCo 1128 G2
Santa Barbara Pl
800 SDGO 1267 J2
Santa Barbara St
400 OCSD 1086 B6
1600 SDGO 1267 J6
1800 SDGO 1268 A7
1100 SDGO 1287 J1
Santa Barbara Wy
100 VSTA 1087 E7
Santa Bartola
400 SOLB 1167 G6
Santa Bella
- OCSD 1066 J7
Santa Brillo Dr
- OCSD 1086 F2
Santa Camelia Dr
700 SOLB 1167 J5
Santa Carina
500 SOLB 1167 H5
Santa Carina Dr
- CHLV 1331 A2
Santa Carolina Rd
- CHLV 1331 C3
Santa Catalina Dr
12300 SDCo 1049 H5
Santa Catalina Rd
- SDCo 1049 J4
Santa Caterina Trl
800 SDCo 1059 A1
(See Page 1059)
Santa Cecilia
400 SOLB 1167 G6
Santa Christina Av
- CHLV 1331 C2
Santa Christina Ct
2400 SDGO 1330 B7
Santa Clara
- OCSD 1066 J7
500 OCSD 1086 F3
Santa Clara Ct
- CHLV 1311 G2
Santa Clara Dr
200 VSTA 1087 E7
Santa Clara Pl
800 SDGO 1267 H1
Santa Clara Wy
3400 CRLB 1106 J4
Santa Cora Av
- CHLV 1311 D6
Santa Corina Ct
16700 SDCo 1169 F4
Santa Cristobal St
16300 SDCo 1169 F4
Santa Cruz
7100 CRLB 1126 J6
- OCSD 1066 J7
Santa Cruz Av
4700 SDGO 1267 J7
4400 SDGO 1268 A7
3800 SDGO 1288 A1
Santa Cruz Ct
1300 CHLV 1311 B7
Santa Delores Dr
- OCSD 1086 F3
Santa Delphina Av
- CHLV 1311 D6
Santa Diana Rd
- CHLV 1331 C2
Santa Dominga
400 SOLB 1167 G6
Santa Elena Ct
1500 SOLB 1167 J6
Santa Estella
900 SOLB 1167 G5
Santa Fe
- OCSD 1066 J7
Santa Fe Av
- ESCN 1129 G3
- SDCo 1085 H4
- SDCo 1108 C3
N Santa Fe Av
700 OCSD 1067 C7
2700 OCSD 1087 E1
1100 VSTA 1087 G4
S Santa Fe Av
1900 SDCo 1108 B3
2900 SNMS 1108 D5
100 VSTA 1087 H6
1200 VSTA 1108 A1
Santa Fe Canyon Pl
7000 SDGO 1188 H4
Santa Fe Dr
- CALX 6680 H1
100 ENCT 1167 C1
Santa Fe Highlands Dr
700 SDCo 1153 A3
Santa Fe Hills Dr
1400 SDCo 1153 A2
Santa Fe Knolls Ln
16700 SDCo 1168 H3
Santa Fe Palms Dr
2400 SDCo 1078 G3
(See Page 1078)
Santa Fe Pl
- VSTA 1087 J7
Santa Fe St
1900 DLMR 1187 F4
5000 SDGO 1248 C3
Santa Fe Trl
400 SDCo 1058 G6
(See Page 1058)
Santa Fe Vista Ct
- ENCT 1148 A6
Santa Flora Ct
3500 ESCN 1150 A4
Santa Flora Rd
- CHLV 1311 C7
Santa Florencia
900 SOLB 1167 G5
Santa Gabriella
1000 SOLB 1167 H5
Santa Gloria
1700 SDGO 1351 A3

60 INDEX
INDEX 60
Santa Helena
Seeforever Dr

San Diego County Street Index

SAN DIEGO CO.

STREET Block City Map# Grid

Santa Helena
500 SOLB 1167 G6
Santa Helena Park Ct
900 SOLB 1167 G6
Santa Hidalga
800 SOLB 1167 G5
Santa Ines Wy
300 OCSD 1087 A2
Santa Inez
- OCSD 1066 J7
800 SOLB 1167 G5
Santa Isabel Dr
800 SDGO 1290 B5
Santa Isabel St
6600 CRLB 1127 H5
Santa Ivy Av
- CHLV 1331 C2
Santa Lira Dr
600 OCSD 1086 F2
Santa Lucia
13500 SDCo 1232 E7
Santa Lucia Rd
- CHLV 1311 C7
- SDCo 1331 C1
Santa Luisa Dr
1200 SOLB 1167 H5
Santa Luna Ct
3600 SNMS 1108 C7
Santa Luna St
- CHLV 1331 E3
Santa Madera Av
- CHLV 1311 C7
Santa Madera Ct
1100 SOLB 1167 H6
Santa Margarita Dr
1400 SDCo 997 G6
1100 SDCo 1027 G1
Santa Margarita St
5300 SDGO 1290 B4
Santa Margarita Truck Trl
- SDCo 996 G3
Santa Maria
- OCSD 1066 J7
Santa Maria Av
- SDCo 1212 A7
Santa Maria Ct
- CHLV 1311 G2
100 VSTA 1087 G6
Santa Maria Dr
- CHLV 1331 A1
7300 LMSA 1270 F3
Santa Maria St
3500 OCSD 1106 J2
Santa Maria Ter
5300 SDGO 1290 B5
Santa Mariana Ct
16600 SDCo 1169 G4
Santa Marina Ct
400 ESCN 1150 A3
Santa Marta Ct
1400 SOLB 1167 J5
Santa Martha Glen
1000 ESCN 1110 A7
Santa Monica Av
4700 SDGO 1267 J6
Santa Nella Pl
4000 SDGO 1188 B7
Santa Olivia
700 SOLB 1167 G5
Santa Olivia Rd
- CHLV 1331 A1
Santa Paula
700 SOLB 1167 G5
Santa Paula Dr
- CHLV 1311 E5
1600 SDGO 1268 G2
Santa Paula St
800 OCSD 1086 A5
Santa Petra Dr
1400 SOLB 1167 J5
Santa Queta
1000 SOLB 1167 G5
Santa Regina
5400 SDGO 1351 A2
800 SOLB 1167 G6
Santa Rena
- OCSD 1066 J7
Santa Rita
- CHLV 1331 C1
Santa Rita E
- CHLV 1331 C2
Santa Rita Pl
700 SDGO 1247 H7
Santa Rita W
- CHLV 1331 C2
Santa Rosa
7100 CRLB 1126 J6
1800 ELCN 6499 D6
- SDGO 1351 A2
Santa Rosa Dr
- CHLV 1311 E6
- IMPE 6439 F3
- SDCo 1086 A4
Santa Rosa Rd
1300 SDCo 1058 G4
(See Page 1058)
Santa Rosa St
1400 OCSD 1086 B4
Santa Rosalia Dr
- IMPE 6499 G2
Santa Rosalia Dr
200 SDGO 1290 A5
Santa Rosalina Ct
400 ESCN 1149 J3
Santa Rosita
- OCSD 1066 J7
600 SOLB 1167 G5
Santa Rufina Ct
1100 SOLB 1167 H5
Santa Rufina Dr
700 SOLB 1167 H6
Santa Saba Ct
800 SDCo 1079 A7
(See Page 1079)
Santa Saba Rd
3400 SDCo 1079 A7
(See Page 1079)
Santa Sabina Ct
1500 SOLB 1167 J5
Santa Sierra Dr
1500 CHLV 1331 B2
Santa Sofia
5400 SDGO 1351 A2
Santa Teresita Ct
500 ESCN 1149 J4
Santa Theresa
600 SOLB 1167 H6
Santa Theresa Pl
- CHLV 1311 G2
Santa Tomasa Av
10700 SDCo 1169 F4
Santa Valera Ct
16300 SDCo 1169 F4
Santa Vela Dr
- OCSD 1086 F2
Santa Venetia St
- CHLV 1331 D1
Santa Victoria
700 SOLB 1167 H5
Santa Victoria Rd
- CHLV 1331 C3
Santa Virginia Dr
- SDCo 1049 J5
13000 SDCo 1050 A5
Santa Ynez Av
- SDCo 1331 B1
Santa Ynez Wy
3700 OCSD 1107 B2
Santa Ysabel Glen
2000 ESCN 1109 E5
Santaluz Inlet
7700 SDGO 1169 A7
Santaluz Pte
8300 SDGO 1169 B6
Santaluz Vill Grn E
8200 SDGO 1169 B6
Santaluz Vill Grn N
8100 SDGO 1169 B6
Santaluz Vill Grn S
8200 SDGO 1169 A6
Santana Ranch Dr
10300 SNTE 1231 E3
Santana St
10400 SNTE 1231 F2
Santanella St
16700 SDCo 1169 F4
Santar Av
7100 SDGO 1250 F3
Santar Pl
100 SNMS 1109 A7
Santee Lakes Blvd
10400 SNTE 1231 A2
Santee Ln
18800 SDCo 1091 F3
Santiago Av
- SDGO 1268 G6
Santiago Dr
- CALX 6620 H7
Santiago Rd
38900 SDCo 1029 H3
E Santiago Rd
12300 SDGO 1170 B3
W Santiago Rd
12100 SDGO 1170 B2
Santillan Av
- BRAW 6319 J3
(See Page 6319)
Santo Domingo Av
- SDGO 1268 F6
Santo Rd
5700 SDGO 1229 H7
3100 SDGO 1249 G5
Santo Tomas Dr
- SOLB 1167 J5
Santolina Ct
6600 SDGO 1188 G6
Santolina St
27100 SDCo 1090 D6
Santorini Wy
5000 OCSD 1107 F5
Santoro Wy
3500 SDGO 1187 J5
Sanyo Av
1700 SDGO 1352 A2
Sao Paulo Wy
24900 SDCo 1173 G3
Saponi Ct
17900 SDGO 1149 H7
Sapota Dr
11900 SDCo 1231 J7
Sapote Ct
- VSTA 1087 J5
Sapphire Dr
1400 CRLB 1127 B4
Sapphire Gn
- ESCN 1110 D7
Sapphire Ln
4400 OCSD 1107 D2
1500 VSTA 1107 H6
Sapphire Pt
- VSTA 1088 C5
Sapphire St
- CALX 6620 H7
1100 SDGO 1247 H4
Sappington Ct
9900 SNTE 1231 D3
Sara Marie Pl
1500 SDCo 1152 F7
Sara Wy
2200 CRLB 1106 H5
Sarah Ann Dr
3500 SDCo 1048 D3
Sarah Av
5800 LMSA 1250 H7
Sarah Ct
300 ELCJ 1252 A6
Sarah Dr
- SDCo 1232 E5
Sarahfaye Ct
1200 SDCo 1109 E6
Sarajayne Ln
7300 LMGR 1270 F7
Saranac Av
7500 LMSA 1270 G2
Saranac Pl
7600 LMSA 1270 G2
Saranac St
7200 LMSA 1270 F2
6500 SDGO 1270 D2
Sarape Dr
16300 SDGO 1170 C4
Sarasona Wy
3700 SDCo 1310 D4
Sarasoto Dr
1400 SDCo 1099 D2
(See Page 1099)
Saratoga Av
5000 SDGO 1267 J5
4500 SDGO 1268 A6
Saratoga Corte
5800 SDCo 1168 E7
Saratoga Ct
- CHLV 1311 C7
Saratoga Glen St
300 ESCN 1130 B7
Saratoga Pl
- BRAW 6320 C1
(See Page 6320)
Saratoga St
- IMPB 1349 H2
2400 OCSD 1086 D7
Sarawak Dr
8000 LMGR 1290 H1
Sarbonne Dr
2400 OCSD 1086 E7
Sarda Ct
- SDCo 1173 G2
Sardina Cove
12300 SDGO 1188 B7
Sardis Pl
11600 SDGO 1210 A1
Sardonyx St
- CRLB 1127 G4
Sargeant Rd
24000 SDCo 1173 E1
Sarita St
5900 LMSA 1250 J6
Sarnen St
- SDGO 1351 H4
Sarno Pl
400 ESCN 1109 G2
Sarsparilla St
12600 SDGO 1189 B6
Sartori Wy
300 SDCo 1108 C4
Sarver Ln
2600 SDCo 1088 J6
Sasha Dr
500 SDCo 1149 J1
Saskatchewan Av
9600 SDGO 1189 E5
Sass Wy
16000 SDCo 1173 H3
Sassafras St
1300 SDGO 1268 J7
Satanas St
14800 SDGO 1189 J1
Satellite Blvd
- SDGO 1349 J2
Satin Doll Ln
- SDCo 1088 F3
Satinwood Ct
1500 CHLV 1330 H4
Satinwood Wy
400 CHLV 1330 G4
200 SDGO 1290 G5
Saturn Blvd
100 SDGO 1330 A6
2300 SDGO 1350 A5
Saturn St
1500 SDGO 1350 A2
Satusuma Ct
24900 SDCo 1173 G3
Saufley St
- CORD 1288 F4
- SDGO 1288 E3
Saugerties Av
700 SDGO 1330 E7
Sauk Av
4500 SDGO 1248 F1
Saul St
- SDCo 1028 D2
Saunders Ct
11100 SDGO 1209 H4
Saunders Dr
10200 SDGO 1209 H4
Sausalito Av
2600 CRLB 1106 J5
Sauterne Pl
500 CHLV 1311 D3
10600 SDGO 1210 B3
Savage Ct
6800 SDGO 1248 J7
Savage Wy
13800 POWY 1190 G3
Savanna Wy
- IMPE 6439 D6
Savannah Creek Dr
12600 SDGO 1189 H5
Savannah Ct
- CHLV 1311 H3
Savannah Ln
- SDCo 1127 B7
Savannah Pl
5100 SDGO 1268 E2
Savannah St
5100 SDGO 1268 E2
Savannah Wy
1700 SNMS 1109 A3
Savin Dr
1500 ELCJ 1252 A3
Savona Ct
2100 SDCo 1108 C3
Savona Ln
- SNMS 1128 J3
Savona Pl
4600 SDGO 1188 C4
Savory Wy
3700 OCSD 1086 H4
Savoy Cir
1400 SDGO 1287 J1
1400 SDGO 1288 A1
Savoy St
1200 SDGO 1287 J1
Saw Leaf Ln
- SDCo 1169 D2
Sawday St
400 SDCo 1152 C7
- SDCo 1172 C1
Sawday Tktr
27100 SDCo 1154 D3
Sawgrass Cres
14300 SDCo 1090 G5
Sawgrass Dr
- OCSD 1067 B4
Sawgrass Glen
2200 ESCN 1109 D4
Sawgrass Pl
1400 CHLV 1311 F7
Sawgrass St
2300 SDCo 1272 C5
Sawtelle Av
500 SDGO 1290 H3
Sawtooth Ct
9300 SDGO 1189 D4
Sawtooth Rd
13400 SDGO 1189 D4
Sawtooth Wy
9300 SDGO 1189 D4
Sawyer Ln
2200 CRLB 1107 C7
2200 CRLB 1127 C1
Saxon Pl
1500 ELCJ 1251 J2
Saxon St
5300 SDGO 1270 A2
Saxony Ln
- ENCT 1147 C6
Saxony Pl
- ENCT 1147 C6
Saxony Rd
1400 ENCT 1147 C3
200 SDCo 1147 C6
Saxton Ln
1900 SDCo 1252 E3
Sayers Ct
10700 SNTE 1231 E3
Sayles Ct
1100 SNMS 1109 E7
Saylor Dr
- CHLV 1310 B5
Scabard Pl
13100 SDGO 1189 H5
Scamp St
3500 SDGO 1249 H4
Scandia Ct
900 SDCo 1130 C4
Scannell Ct
11100 SDGO 1209 B2
Scarberry Rd
16100 SDCo 1173 D3
Scarberry Wy
23600 SDCo 1173 D3
Scarboro St
14500 POWY 1190 H5
Scarf Pl
8400 SDGO 1250 J4
Scarlati Pl
1000 SDGO 1247 F1
Scarlet Oak Wy
4400 OCSD 1086 J2
Scarlet Pl
1800 CHLV 1331 E2
500 SNMS 1109 C6
Scarlet Sage Tr
13500 SDGO 1188 F3
Scarlet Wy
- SDGO 1290 G4
Scaroni Rd
- CALX 6620 F3
- ImCo 6560 E7
Scarsdale Wy
13500 SDGO 1190 A3
Scaup St
6500 CRLB 1127 A4
Sceneco Dr
- OCSD 1086 F2
Scenic Cres
- SNMS 1128 A2
Scenic Dr
1300 ESCN 1129 F5
- SDCo 998 G5
300 SDCo 1252 H3
Scenic Ln
4400 LMSA 1271 A3
Scenic Mtn Rd
33700 SDCo 1318 G2
(See Page 1318)
Scenic Pl
800 CHLV 1311 J3
2800 SDGO 1227 J4
Scenic Ter
3400 SDCo 1271 E6
Scenic Trail Pl
- CHLV 1311 G2
Scenic Trails Wy
- ESCN 1129 F6
Scenic Valley Pl
1800 ESCN 1129 F6
Scenic Valley Rd
26800 SDCo 1154 C2
Scenic View Pl
1800 SDCo 1234 D7
Scenic View Rd
2800 SDCo 1234 D7
Scenic Wy
1000 CRLB 1106 G7
3700 OCSD 1107 E3
Schafer Pl
500 ESCN 1129 H4
Schaler Dr
12400 POWY 1190 C4
Schartz Rd
- ImCo 6320 C6
(See Page 6320)
Schaumberg Pl
4600 SDGO 1310 G1
Scheidler Wy
5300 SDGO 1269 F1
Schenley Ter
2600 SDGO 1228 B7
Scheyer Ln
- SDCo 1023 D2
Schilling Av
6900 SDGO 1208 H4
Schilt Av
- SDGO 1209 C7
- SDGO 1229 D1
Schirra St
3700 SDGO 1330 E7
Schlee Canyon Rd
3000 SDCo 1292 G2
(See Page 1292)
Schley St
1200 SDGO 1289 D6
Schmidt Ct
- SDCo 1023 E2
Schmidt Dr
- SDCo 1023 E2
Schneple Dr
8500 SDGO 1209 C2
Scholar Dr
- SDGO 1227 J1
Scholar Dr N
- SDGO 1207 J7
Scholars Dr
- SDGO 1227 J2
- SDGO 1228 A3
Scholars Ln
- SDGO 1227 J2
Scholder Pl
- SDCo 1029 J3
School Bus Ln
28500 SDCo 1090 F1
School Daze Ln
1100 SDCo 1172 F1
School House Rd
2400 CHLV 1311 H6
700 SDCo 1153 A4
School Ln
3100 LMGR 1270 H6
School St
3400 SDGO 1269 F3
Schoolhouse Wy
- SNMS 1128 D5
Schoolridge Ln
4200 LMSA 1270 G4
Schooner Wy
1700 CRLB 1106 G6
Schubert Path
100 ENCT 1167 C3
Schuller Ln
1000 SDCo 1028 C4
Schuyler Av
4800 LMSA 1270 J2
Schuyler St
5900 SDGO 1310 D1
Science Center Dr
- SDGO 1208 A7
Science Park Rd
2900 SDGO 1207 J5
Scimitar Dr
6400 SDGO 1290 D2
Scooter Ln
1600 SDCo 1028 D5
Scorpius Wy
- SDGO 1209 D2
Scoter Pl
- CRLB 1127 C6
Scotia Wy
2300 SDCo 1108 D1
Scots Wy
13500 POWY 1190 F3
Scotsman Rd
13300 SDCo 1232 D5
Scott Av
1600 ELCN 6499 F5
Scott Dr
3900 CRLB 1106 G6
1100 NATC 1289 J6
3900 OCSD 1107 B1
Scott Pl
1600 ENCT 1147 F4
Scott St
1300 SDGO 1288 B2
- VSTA 1127 J1
Scott Wy
2300 ESCN 1110 C6
Scottford Dr
100 SDCo 1252 J1
Scottsbluff Ct
9800 SNTE 1231 F4
Scranton Rd
9600 SDGO 1208 E6
Scranton St
700 ELCJ 1251 G7
Scripps Av
900 CHLV 1311 D5
Scripps Cape Vista Pt
17900 SDGO 1209 J3
Scripps Creek Dr
11500 SDGO 1209 J1
Scripps Highlands Dr
- SDGO 1189 G7
Scripps Lake Dr
10300 SDGO 1209 G4
Scripps Poway Pkwy
12300 POWY 1190 C7
- SDCo 1191 C5
10100 SDGO 1189 G7
Scripps Preserve Rd
- SDGO 1210 D2
Scripps Ranch Blvd
10100 SDGO 1209 G4
Scripps Ranch Ct
10200 SDGO 1209 F5
Scripps Ranch Row
10700 SDGO 1209 H5
Scripps St
5600 SDGO 1228 C6
Scripps Summit Ct
- SDGO 1189 G7
Scripps Summit Dr
12000 SDGO 1189 G7
Scripps Ter
- SDGO 1270 B1
Scripps Trl
10600 SDGO 1210 A3
Scripps Vista Wy
9900 SDGO 1209 F2
Scripps Westview Cir
9900 SDGO 1209 F2
Scripps Westview Wy
9800 SDGO 1209 F2
Scripps Wy
3200 SDGO 1228 C6
Scrub Jay Ct
1100 CRLB 1127 A5
Scrub Jay Ln
7800 SDCo 1237 C6
Scrubs Oak Rd
- SDCo 1171 H3
Sculpin St
10200 SDGO 1249 G4
Sdsu Campus Parking
- SDGO 1270 C2
Sea Bird Wy
- SDGO 1330 H7
- SDGO 1350 H1
Sea Bluff Cir
4500 CRLB 1106 H7
Sea Bluffe
100 ENCT 1147 A2
Sea Breeze Ct
2100 CHLV 1311 E2
1900 ENCT 1147 A2
Sea Breeze Dr
200 CRLB 1126 H4
100 OCSD 1085 J7
2500 SDGO 1310 D1
Sea Bright Dr
4300 CRLB 1106 H7
Sea Bright Pl
4300 CRLB 1106 H7
Sea Cliff Dr
900 CRLB 1126 J4
Sea Cliff Ln
200 SOLB 1187 E1
Sea Cliff Wy
1000 OCSD 1086 J7
Sea Colony Ct
2200 SDGO 1268 B6
Sea Coral Dr
- SDGO 1350 H1
Sea Cottage Wy
700 OCSD 1085 J7
Sea Country Ln
3700 SDGO 1187 J3
Sea Cove
- SDGO 1331 A6
Sea Crest Wy
- ENCT 1147 C6
Sea Drift Wy
- SDGO 1350 J1
Sea Field Pl
- SDGO 1330 J7
Sea Fire Pt
- SDGO 1351 A1
Sea Foam Ct
6000 SDGO 1290 D7
Sea Gate Rd
900 CRLB 1126 J4
Sea Hill Ct
- SDGO 1351 A1
Sea Holly
- SDGO 1331 A6
Sea Island Pl
2300 CHLV 1311 F4
- SNMS 1128 A3
Sea Isle Dr
- SDGO 1330 H6
Sea Knoll Ct
- SDGO 1188 D5
Sea Larke Dr
1100 SDCo 1027 H5
Sea Lavender Wy
- SDGO 1330 J6
Sea Lily Ct
- SDGO 1350 H1
Sea Lion Pl
- CRLB 1127 G2
Sea Ln
500 SDGO 1247 E1
Sea Maid Ct
- SDGO 1350 H1
Sea Mist Ct
- SDGO 1208 E4
Sea Mist Wy
- SDGO 1170 A4
- SDGO 1208 D4
Sea Orbit Ln
100 DLMR 1187 F5
Sea Otter Pl
- CRLB 1127 G1
Sea Park Dr
900 IMPB 1349 G2
Sea Pearl Cv
10500 SDGO 1208 B4
Sea Pines Rd
1800 SDCo 1272 B5
Sea Reef Dr
- SDGO 1350 J1
Sea Reef Pl
- SDGO 1330 J7
Sea Ridge Dr
400 SDGO 1247 G4
Sea Ridge Rd
3500 OCSD 1086 F5
Sea Robin Ct
- SDGO 1350 H1
Sea Rocket Ln
1800 CRLB 1127 D5
Sea Scape Glen
2500 ESCN 1109 B3
Sea Star Wy
1800 SDGO 1290 E7
Sea Strand
- SDGO 1351 A1
Sea Tern Ct
- SDGO 1330 H6
Sea Turf Cir
800 SOLB 1187 F2
Sea Urchin Dr
- SDGO 1350 H1
Sea Vale Ct
500 CHLV 1309 J5
Sea Vale St
600 CHLV 1309 J5
200 CHLV 1310 B4
Sea View Av
1900 DLMR 1187 F4
Sea View Ct
- ENCT 1147 D6
Sea View Wy
- SDCo 1148 E3
Sea Village Cir
2000 ENCT 1167 F3
Sea Village Dr
1100 ENCT 1167 E3
700 IMPB 1329 F7
Sea Village Pl
- ENCT 1167 F3
Sea Village Wy
1100 ENCT 1167 F3
Sea Vista Pl
- SNMS 1128 B2
Sea Water Ln
- SDGO 1330 H7
- SDGO 1350 H1
Sea Wind Ct
900 CRLB 1126 J4
Sea World Dr
400 SDGO 1268 C4
Sea World Wy
2000 SDGO 1268 B3
Seabolt Dr
- BRAW 6260 C7
(See Page 6260)
Seabreeze Dr
2000 SDGO 1290 D7
Seabreeze Farms Dr
- SDGO 1188 D6
Seabreeze Walk
3400 OCSD 1107 C2
Seabridge Ln
14300 SDGO 1190 A2
Seabright Ln
400 SOLB 1167 E6
Seabrook Ln
1500 SDGO 1290 H6
Seabury St
3100 CRLB 1107 A3
Seachase St
- SDGO 1188 D4
Seachase Wy
- SDGO 1188 D5
Seacliff Ln
300 SOLB 1187 E1
Seacliff Wy
- SNMS 1128 F2
Seacoast Dr
800 IMPB 1329 E7
1300 IMPB 1349 E2
Seacrest Ct
2600 VSTA 1107 H5
Seacrest Dr
3300 CRLB 1106 G4
- SNMS 1128 F2
Seacrest View Rd
- SDGO 1208 F3
Seacrest Wy
3600 OCSD 1107 C3
Seafarer Dr
3500 OCSD 1086 E6
Seafarer Pl
7300 CRLB 1126 J7
Seaflower Ln
3600 OCSD 1107 A2
Seaford Pl
4700 SDGO 1248 H1
Seaforest Ct
200 DLMR 1187 F6
Seagate Wy
3500 OCSD 1086 J6
3500 OCSD 1087 A6
Seagaze Dr
900 OCSD 1086 A7
600 OCSD 1106 A1
Seagirt Ct
800 SDGO 1267 H1
Seaglass Ct
11800 SDGO 1190 A1
Seaglen Wy
- SDGO 1351 A1
Seagreen
- SDGO 1351 A1
Seagrove Ct
- SDGO 1188 D5
Seagrove Cv
5000 SDGO 1188 D4
Seagrove Pl
5100 SDGO 1188 D4
Seagrove Wy
- OCSD 1087 A4
- SDGO 1188 D4
Seagull Ct
7600 SDGO 1249 A7
Seagull Ln
200 OCSD 1086 H2
2000 SDGO 1269 A1
Seahorn Cir
3500 SDGO 1187 J5
Seahorse Ct
- SDCo 1127 A5
Seahorse Ln
- SDCo 1085 H6
Seal Beach Pl
6200 SDGO 1290 D7
Seal Point Ct
1500 CHLV 1330 J3
Sealane Dr
1000 ENCT 1167 B1
Seaman St
6500 SDGO 1249 J6
Sean Taylor Ln
7300 SDGO 1208 J2
Seapoint Wy
- SDGO 1208 F3
Seaport Rd
- CRLB 1127 B4
Seaquest Tr
- SDCo 1148 E3
Sears Av
500 SDGO 1290 H3
Seascape Dr
6800 CRLB 1127 A5
4800 OCSD 1087 B1
6200 SDGO 1310 E1
Seashell Ct
7400 CRLB 1127 A7
Seaside St
2200 SDGO 1268 A6
Seaside Wy
- CRLB 1107 A4
Seasons Rd
2300 OCSD 1087 D6
Seaspray Ln
6800 CRLB 1126 J5
Seattle Dr
2500 ELCJ 1251 A4
7600 LMSA 1270 G4
Seattle Slew Wy
1600 OCSD 1067 E7
Seaview Av
1300 OCSD 1106 D1
Seaview Pl
500 VSTA 1107 H1
Seaview Wy
3600 CRLB 1106 H5
Seaward Av
600 CRLB 1126 J5
E Seaward Av
100 SDGO 1350 G3
W Seaward Av
100 SDGO 1350 F3
Seaward Cir
3500 OCSD 1107 G4
Seawatch Ln
- CRLB 1126 J6
Seawind Cove
11200 SDGO 1209 A2
Seawind Dr
2400 NATC 1310 B1
Seawind Ln
7900 SDGO 1209 A2
Seawind Wy
1900 OCSD 1106 F2
Seaworthy Wy
700 CRLB 1126 J6
Sebago Av
13400 POWY 1190 H4
Sebastian Dr
3000 SDCo 1234 D5
Sebastopol St
- CHLV 1311 E7
Sebring Ct
9800 SNTE 1231 F4
Seca St
2000 SDCo 1272 C4
Seckel Pear St
700 OCSD 1086 G5
Secluded Ln
3500 SDCo 1047 J3
Seco Glen
1800 ESCN 1109 F6
Secret Canyon Pl
- CHLV 1311 H5
Secret Lake Ln
2600 SDCo 1028 E7
Secret Pl
3000 LMGR 1270 J6
Secretariat Ct
- SDCo 1168 E7
Section St
1400 OCSD 1086 B7
Securidad St
200 OCSD 1066 H7
Security Pl
1500 SNMS 1128 C1
Security Wy
9200 SNTE 1231 G4
Seda Cove
4600 SDGO 1250 A2
Seda Dr
4700 SDGO 1250 B1
Seda Pl
11300 SDGO 1250 A2
Sedero Ct
11500 SDGO 1149 J7
Sedge Ct
12900 SDGO 1189 E5
Sedgewick St
5700 SDGO 1310 D2
Sedona Dr
2300 SDCo 1172 H3
Sedona Gn
1500 ESCN 1110 A5
Sedorus St
8300 SDGO 1189 B4
Seeforever Dr
- SNMS 1129 B4

61 INDEX
INDEX 61
Seeley Av
Sierra Cir
SAN DIEGO CO.
SAN DIEGO CO.

San Diego County Street Index

STREET
Block City Map# Grid

Seeley Av
44400 SDCo 1321 G5
(See Page 1321)
Seeman Dr
100 ENCT 1147 E7
Sefton Pl
1800 SDGO 1268 B7
Sego Pl
2900 SDGO 1249 D6
Segovia Ct
3000 CRLB 1147 H2
15200 SDGO 1169 J7
Segovia Wy
3000 CRLB 1147 H2
Segundo Ct
14100 POWY 1190 G1
Seifert Rd
- SDGO 1288 A5
Seifert St
5500 SDGO 1270 B7
Seiler St
13100 POWY 1190 D5
Seine River Wy
1400 CHLV 1311 G2
Selby Ct
10100 SNTE 1231 A3
Selden Ln
- SDCo 1023 E1
Select Wy
- SDCo 999 A5
Selena Wy
7000 SDGO 1188 H3
Selina Dr
- SNMS 1109 A4
Selkirk Row
- SDGO 1247 J1
Sellers Plz
- SDGO 1268 D6
Sello Ln
3200 CRLB 1127 J5
Sellsway St
100 SDGO 1350 F4
Selma Ct
12800 POWY 1190 B5
Selma Dr
1300 OCSD 1106 C1
Selma Pl
700 SDGO 1290 B3
Selmalita Ter
300 VSTA 1087 G5
Selsey St
14600 POWY 1190 H5
Seltzer Ct
9400 SDGO 1249 F5
Selva Dr
16100 SDGO 1170 C5
Semi Nole St
- SDGO 1268 E6
Semillon Blvd
12000 SDGO 1210 B3
Seminole Dr
4600 SDGO 1270 D3
Seminole St
1500 SNMS 1108 D7
Semple St
1800 CHLV 1331 F2
Sencillo Ct
17900 SDGO 1150 B7
Sencillo Dr
17900 SDGO 1150 B7
Sencillo Ln
17900 SDGO 1150 B7
Senda Acantilada
12600 SDGO 1150 C7
Senda Acuario
- SDGO 1208 B4
Senda Angosta
5100 SDCo 1290 H7
Senda De La Luna
- SDCo 1168 D3
Senda Ln
2300 SDCo 1252 J4
Senda Luna Llena
- SDGO 1208 B2
Senda Mar De Ponderosa
- SDGO 1208 C3
Senda Panacea
- SDGO 1189 B6
Senda Pl
16400 SDGO 1170 C4
Senda Rd
12400 SDGO 1170 C4
Sendero Angelica
7800 SDGO 1169 B7
- SDGO 1189 A1
Sendero Av
1000 ESCN 1109 J7
Sendero De Alba
8300 SDGO 1169 B6
Sendero De La Prader
8100 SDGO 1169 C7
Sendero De Oro
7900 SDGO 1189 A1
Sendero St
- CALX 6620 J6
Sendero Wy
2400 SDGO 1248 G7
Seneca Pl
7400 LMSA 1270 F3
Senecio Pl
1700 SDGO 1188 G7
Senegal St
5400 SDCo 1067 B2
Sengme Oaks Rd
100 SDCo 1072 G2
(See Page 1072)
Senior Center Dr
3300 OCSD 1086 H6
Senn Rd
- SDGO 1289 E7
Senn Wy
7700 SDGO 1227 J7
Senna Wy
- CHLV 1330 H4
Sentenac Creek Rd
2900 SDCo 1135 F7
3300 SDCo 1155 F1
Sentinel
7900 SDGO 1169 B7
Sentinel Ln
- SNMS 1128 A5
Senwood Wy
1100 SDCo 1027 G4
Seph Wy
900 SDCo 1130 B3
Sepia Ct
700 OCSD 1087 B1
12000 SDGO 1189 H5
September St
5000 SDGO 1268 G1
Sequan Ln
28800 SDCo 1237 C5
Sequan Truck Trl
- SDCo 1253 G4
16700 SDCo 1254 A4
Sequence Dr
6500 SDGO 1208 G4
Sequoia Av
100 CRLB 1106 E7
Sequoia Cir
- ELCJ 1251 J6
Sequoia Crest
2000 VSTA 1107 G5
Sequoia Ct
- BRAW 6259 F6
(See Page 6259)
400 CHLV 1330 G4
Sequoia Ln
1500 SDCo 1107 E2
Sequoia Pl
4700 OCSD 1087 A1
Sequoia Rd
28900 SDCo 1237 C6
Sequoia St
- BRAW 6259 G6
(See Page 6259)
500 CHLV 1330 H4
- IMPE 6499 C2
4000 SDGO 1248 A6
2000 SNMS 1128 A2
Serafina Ln
10800 SDGO 1189 H5
Serbian Pl
3000 SDGO 1248 E6
Serena Av
4200 OCSD 1107 C3
Serena Cir
1300 CHLV 1311 B5
Serena Hills Rd
2200 SDCo 1172 D4
Serena Ln
10900 SDCo 1232 A1
Serena Rd
11800 SDCo 1231 J1
Serena Wy
1000 SNMS 1128 E3
Serenata Pl
4600 SDGO 1188 C6
Serendipity Ln
- SDCo 1089 C6
Serene Rd
- OCSD 1067 G7
Serene Wy
- SDCo 1293 G1
Serenidad Pl
4000 OCSD 1107 C2
Serenity Ct
8200 SDCo 1232 C7
Serenity Path
28300 SDCo 1090 E2
Sereno Ct
2100 CRLB 1147 F2
Sereno View Ln
2200 ENCT 1147 J6
Sereno View Rd
600 ENCT 1147 J6
Seri St
4100 SDGO 1248 E2
Serigraph Ct
4600 OCSD 1087 B2
Serpentine Dr
300 DLMR 1187 F4
Serra Wy
15900 SDCo 1173 C4
Serrano Dr
3100 CRLB 1147 H2
Serrano Ln
600 CHLV 1310 J5
Serrano Pl
6500 SDGO 1270 D3
Serrano St
1700 OCSD 1106 C3
Serranos Ct
4100 SDCo 1028 G7
Serrena Ln
600 SDGO 1330 G6
Serres Dr
9500 SNTE 1230 H5
Servando Av
2200 SDGO 1350 D3
Service Pl
1000 VSTA 1108 A1
Service Rd
- SDGO 1227 J1
- SDGO 1288 A7
- SDGO 1308 A1
Sesame St
700 CHLV 1330 J1
Sesame Wy
3700 OCSD 1086 G5
Sesi Ln
- SDCo 1232 G5
Sespe Pl
14400 POWY 1190 H2
Seth Ln
9600 SNTE 1231 E4
Seth Wy
10300 SNTE 1231 D5
Seton Hall St
7500 LMSA 1270 G1
Settineri Ln
3800 SDCo 1271 A5
Setting Sun Wy
- SDGO 1208 E4
Settle Ct
9800 SNTE 1231 A4
Settle Rd
10300 SNTE 1231 A3
Settlers Ct
700 SNMS 1109 A6
Settlers Pl
14400 POWY 1190 H1
Settlers Rd
- SDCo 1232 E4
Sevan Ct
7900 SDGO 1249 B7
Seven Bridges Rd
18300 SDCo 1148 F5
Seven Oakes Rd
1300 ESCN 1109 F6
1200 ESCN 1129 F1
Severin Dr
6200 LMSA 1251 B6
Severino Ln
- SDCo 1071 A6
Sevilla St
4000 SNTE 1231 F6
Sevilla Wy
4800 CRLB 1106 J7
Seville St
3100 SDGO 1268 D6
Seville Wy
- LMGR 1290 F2
Sewanee Dr
1400 SDCo 1099 D2
(See Page 1099)
Sewell Av
2800 SDGO 1350 C1
Seybert Rd
4400 ImCo 6260 J7
(See Page 6260)
Seymour St
9900 SNTE 1231 F4
Shackleford Ct
9300 SDGO 1209 E2
Shade Rd
4400 SDCo 1271 E3
Shade Tree Ln
800 SDCo 1027 H4
Shadetree Ct
13300 SDGO 1210 E2
Shadetree Dr
1800 SNMS 1128 B6
Shadetree Ln
2100 ESCN 1129 E6
Shadewood Ln
1700 SDGO 1290 H6
Shadow Canyon Wy
5800 SDCo 1311 B3
Shadow Creek Ln
11800 SDCo 1271 J2
Shadow Crest Ct
2700 CHLV 1311 J6
Shadow Glen
1700 ESCN 1129 E6
Shadow Glen Ct
100 ELCJ 1252 D5
Shadow Grove Wy
2000 ENCT 1147 H7
Shadow Hill Dr
7900 LMSA 1270 H4
Shadow Hill Rd
9200 SNTE 1231 G5
Shadow Hill Wy
11000 SNTE 1231 G6
Shadow Hills Ct
1300 SNMS 1109 C7
Shadow Hills Dr
1400 SNMS 1109 C6
Shadow Knolls Ct
1500 SDCo 1272 A2
Shadow Knolls Dr
1500 SDCo 1272 A2
Shadow Knolls Ln
1500 SDCo 1272 A2
Shadow Lake Rd
- SDCo 1069 A3
Shadow Ln
4200 OCSD 1107 C2
400 VSTA 1087 J6
Shadow Mountain Dr
1600 ENCT 1147 G6
Shadow Mountain Rd
1900 SDCo 1252 E3
Shadow Mountain Ter
1100 VSTA 1088 A4
Shadow Oak Ct
2800 SDCo 1172 D5
Shadow Ranch Rd
11400 SDCo 1271 H4
Shadow Rd
9800 SDCo 1271 D1
Shadow Ridge Dr
5100 OCSD 1107 F4
2100 VSTA 1107 H5
700 VSTA 1108 A4
Shadow Ridge Pl
- CHLV 1311 H3
Shadow Rock Ct
4000 SDCo 1311 B2
Shadow Tree Dr
- OCSD 1086 D3
Shadow Valley
2800 SDCo 1292 E4
(See Page 1292)
Shadow Valley Rd
11700 SDCo 1271 H2
Shadow Vista Wy
1500 ELCJ 1252 A7
Shadowbrook Ct
14700 POWY 1190 D1
Shadowbrook Ln
100 ELCJ 1252 D5
Shadowbrook Wy
2600 SNMS 1128 C7
Shadowcrest Ln
1200 SDCo 1027 H7
Shadowglen Rd
11700 SDCo 1271 H2
Shadowlawn St
3200 SDGO 1268 D6
Shadowline St
12700 POWY 1190 D1
Shadowood Cir
1800 VSTA 1107 G5
Shadowood Ln
- SDCo 1090 E6
Shadowside Ln
1300 SDCo 1272 A2
Shadowtree Dr
600 OCSD 1086 E3
Shadwell Pl
4700 SDGO 1188 C4
Shady Acre Cir
1900 ENCT 1147 J5
Shady Acre Ln
- LMGR 1270 G7
Shady Acres Ln
5700 SDCo 1175 J1
(See Page 1175)
Shady Bend
16400 SDCo 1171 H3
Shady Creek Dr
13800 SDCo 1070 E6
Shady Creek Ln
- SDCo 1070 E3
Shady Crest Ct
1700 ELCJ 1251 C2
Shady Crest Pl
1700 ELCJ 1251 C2
Shady Crest Rd
700 SNMS 1109 A5
Shady Elm Pl
900 SDGO 1330 B7
Shady Glen Dr
300 SDCo 1027 G3
Shady Hill Ln
- SDCo 1047 H6
Shady Hollow Ln
- SDCo 1273 E5
Shady Knoll Rd
- SDCo 1090 D2
Shady Ln
100 ELCJ 1251 J5
4300 OCSD 1107 C2
700 SDCo 1027 F1
Shady Oak Ct
- POWY 1190 C6
Shady Oak Rd
100 SDGO 1290 F5
Shady Oaks Dr
16500 SDCo 1171 G3
Shady Oaks Ln
0 RivC 999 F1
16300 SDCo 1171 G3
Shady Oaks Wy
- SDCo 1071 A5
Shady Sands Rd
8000 SDGO 1250 E3
Shadybrook Pl
400 ESCN 1109 G5
Shadyglade Ln
7600 SDGO 1290 G5
Shadypine St
2900 SDCo 1271 F7
Shadyridge Av
2200 ESCN 1129 E6
Shadytree Ln
2000 ENCT 1147 H6
Shadywood Dr
500 ESCN 1109 H4
Shafer St
1000 OCSD 1106 B1
Shafter St
1100 SDGO 1288 B3
Shaggybark Dr
10000 SNTE 1231 D2
Shahram Wy
9100 SDCo 1049 B7
Shalamar Dr
7900 SDCo 1252 B1
Shale Ct
- CRLB 1107 B4
Shale Rock Rd
3000 SDCo 1088 D7
Shalimar Cove
2600 SDGO 1187 H7
Shalimar Pl
1500 ESCN 1129 G7
13100 SDGO 1187 J7
Shallman St
12400 POWY 1190 C3
Shalom Rd
- SDCo 1174 B4
Shalyn Dr
13800 SDCo 1232 E5
Shamrock Ct
- IMPE 6499 E2
5600 SDCo 1047 H7
Shamrock Ln
9700 SDCo 1232 A3
Shamrock Pl
6200 CRLB 1127 G2
Shamrock Rd
32400 SDCo 1047 H7
32000 SDCo 1067 J1
Shamrock St
2300 SDGO 1289 H1
Shamrock Wy
2500 ESCN 1130 C7
Shanas Ln
600 ENCT 1147 G5
Shandy Ln
200 SDCo 1153 A6
Shane Pl
6400 SDGO 1270 D2
Shanessey Rd
1300 ELCJ 1251 J7
Shank Rd
- BRAW 6260 B5
(See Page 6260)
500 ImCo 6260 E5
(See Page 6260)
Shankara Rd
16200 SDCo 1091 B1
Shannon Av
6600 SDGO 1270 E3
Shannon Ridge Ln
- SDGO 1208 E1
Shannonbrook Ct
- SDCo 1270 J6
Shanteau Dr
14800 SDCo 1232 J3
14900 SDCo 1233 A3
Shantung Dr
7900 SNTE 1250 H1
Shapely Wy
- SDCo 1023 D2
Share Ct
10500 SNTE 1231 E4
Shari Wy
1200 ELCJ 1251 J6
400 OCSD 1086 G2
Sharlene Ln
- SNTE 1231 E7
Sharon Wy
700 ELCJ 1251 B4
Sharp Pl
200 ENCT 1147 G6
Sharron Pl
4200 SDGO 1270 B4
Shasta Ct
- OCSD 1086 H1
Shasta Daisy Tr
5600 SDGO 1188 E5
Shasta Dr
500 ENCT 1147 E5
Shasta Ln
5500 LMSA 1270 G1
Shasta Pl
4300 CRLB 1106 J5
Shasta St
400 CHLV 1310 B7
3700 SDGO 1248 A6
E Shasta St
- CHLV 1310 D6
Shasta Trl
1600 SDCo 1319 J2
(See Page 1319)
Shasta Wy
1600 SDCo 1319 F2
(See Page 1319)
Shaula Wy
8800 SDGO 1209 D2
Shaules Av
6300 SDGO 1290 D4
Shauna Wy
26300 SDCo 1091 F6
Shaw Lopez Row
- SDGO 1208 F4
Shaw Ridge Rd
- SDGO 1188 E6
3800 SDGO 1208 A1
Shaw St
5500 SDGO 1310 C2
Shaw Valley Rd
11900 SDGO 1188 C7
Shawline Ct
7100 SDGO 1248 J1
Shawline St
4800 SDGO 1249 A1
Shawn Av
9300 SDGO 1249 E6
Shawn Ct
2300 CRLB 1106 H4
Shawn Elise Wy
- ENCT 1147 F6
Shawnee Rd
3500 SDGO 1248 E5
Shay Pl
1100 ESCN 1109 J5
Shay Rd
- SDCo 1027 F4
Shayann Ln
- SDCo 1232 B5
Shaylene Wy
2300 SDCo 1254 A1
Shea Ct
- OCSD 1087 F2
Shearer Crossing
- SDCo 1048 J1
Shearwater St
1400 CHLV 1331 C3
Shearwater Wy
4400 OCSD 1087 A3
Shearwaters Dr
6800 CRLB 1126 J5
Sheba Wy
10000 SDGO 1189 F3
Sheena Wy
- LMGR 1290 E2
Sheep Ranch Loop
- CHLV 1311 E6
Sheephead Mountain Rd
- SDCo 1237 H3
Sheephead Mtn Rd
- SDCo 1237 H6
Sheffield Av
400 ENCT 1167 D2
- IMPE 6499 C2
Sheffield Ct
600 CHLV 1310 E6
Sheffield Dr
- IMPE 6499 D1
900 VSTA 1108 A4
Sheila Ln
300 SDCo 1028 D1
Sheila St
8300 SDCo 1251 G1
Shelbie Av
- BRAW 6319 J3
(See Page 6319)
Shelborne St
10400 SDCo 1169 F2
Shelby Dr
2900 SDCo 1310 B3
Shelby Ln
- ENCT 1147 B3
100 SDCo 1027 H2
Shelby St
5300 SDGO 1270 A6
Shelby View Ct
9000 SDCo 1231 J6
Sheldon Av
300 SDGO 1269 A6
Sheldon Dr
4300 LMSA 1270 H3
Shell Av
400 NATC 1290 C6
Shellback Wy
- SDGO 1227 H3
Shelley Pl
- CRLB 1107 B7
Shelly Dr
100 SNMS 1129 A1
Shelsteve Ter
800 VSTA 1087 J6
Shelter Cove Wy
800 OCSD 1066 F6
Shelter Island Dr
1900 SDGO 1288 B4
Shenandoah Av
- SNMS 1128 F2
Shenandoah Dr
2800 CHLV 1311 J4
3900 OCSD 1087 B7
13000 SDCo 1232 C3
Shenandoan Dr
- SNTE 1231 C3
Shep St
8900 SDGO 1249 D5
Shepherd Cir
- SDCo 1067 A1
Shepherd Ln
600 SDGO 1330 F7
Shepherds Knoll Pl
1400 CHLV 1311 C6
Sherann Dr
12300 SDCo 1232 A5
Sherbourne Dr
3900 OCSD 1087 B7
Sherbourne Ln
7100 SDGO 1188 J4
Sherbrooke St
1700 SDGO 1290 H6
Sheri Ln
2600 LMGR 1270 G7
Sheri Pl
2300 SDCo 1253 F1
Sheridan Av
700 ESCN 1109 J6
1600 ESCN 1110 A6
1800 SDGO 1268 H5
Sheridan Ln
4400 SDGO 1249 H7
Sheridan Pl
3900 CRLB 1106 F6
1500 ESCN 1110 A5
Sheridan Rd
2000 ENCT 1147 A1
4500 OCSD 1107 E2
1000 SDCo 1318 A7
(See Page 1318)
Sheridan St
600 CALX 6680 E1
Sheridan Wy
1800 SNMS 1128 C7
Sheriton Valley Rd
24500 SDCo 1216 A1
(See Page 1216)
Sherlock Ct
4500 SDGO 1228 D3
Sherm Cir
9700 SDCo 1232 D3
Sherman Ct
- CALX 6680 E1
Sherman Dr
- CHLV 1330 J3
Sherman Pl
200 ESCN 1129 J2
Sherman Rd
- CORD 1288 F6
Sherman St
- CALX 6680 E1
3800 SDGO 1268 E4
W Sherman St
1000 CALX 6680 C1
Sherman Wy
1500 VSTA 1088 B3
Sherrard Wy
- SDGO 1209 J2
Sherri Ln
100 OCSD 1106 C3
Sherrie Ln
100 DLMR 1187 F6
Sherwin Pl
4100 SDCo 1271 E4
15900 SDGO 1169 D5
Sherwood Dr
2200 LMGR 1270 H7
700 OCSD 1086 F2
Sherwood Forest Ct
- SDCo 1069 A6
Sherwood Glen
- ESCN 1129 F5
Sherwood St
- CHLV 1330 E4
Sherwood Wy
- SNMS 1128 B1
Sheryl Av
1300 CHLV 1330 C4
Sheryl Ln
1400 NATC 1310 A1
Shetland Ct
- OCSD 1067 F7
E Shetland Hills
200 SDCo 1028 H4
Shetland Wy
200 SDCo 1027 F4
Shields Av
1400 ENCT 1147 F6
Shields Ct
10400 SDGO 1249 H3
Shields Dr
- SDGO 1209 E7
Shields Pl
4200 SDGO 1249 H3
Shields St
4100 SDGO 1249 G3
Shiloh Ln
- SDCo 1091 G4
Shiloh Rd
- IMPE 6499 F3
3800 SDGO 1270 B5
Shiney Stone Ln
2200 CHLV 1331 G3
Shining Light Wy
11100 SDCo 1271 H2
Shinly Pl
1300 ESCN 1110 A5
Shinohara Ln
- CHLV 1330 H5
Shipley Ct
1400 SDGO 1290 G2
Shir-Mar Pl
- SDCo 1251 J2
Shircliffe St
1600 CHLV 1331 E2
Shire Av
- OCSD 1067 F7
Shire Dr
1900 SDCo 1252 C5
Shirehall Dr
6400 SDGO 1248 H4
Shirey Rd
32200 SDCo 1049 A7
31900 SDCo 1069 A1
Shirlene Pl
3800 LMSA 1270 E5
Shirley Ann Pl
4500 SDGO 1269 D4
Shirley Ct
9200 LMSA 1271 B2
Shirley Dr
9100 LMSA 1271 B2
300 SNMS 1108 J5
Shirley Gardens Dr
9800 SNTE 1231 E4
Shirley Ln
1900 LMGR 1290 F1
- OCSD 1086 G3
100 SNTE 1231 E7
Shirley St
200 CHLV 1310 B4
Shirra Av
- POWY 1190 H5
Shoal Creek Dr
- SDGO 1189 J2
Shoal Ct
7000 CRLB 1127 A6
Shoal Summit Dr
13500 SDGO 1190 A3
Shockey Ct
1400 SDCo 1318 H5
(See Page 1318)
Shockey Truck Trl
35000 SDCo 1318 J7
(See Page 1318)
Shoemaker Ct
300 SOLB 1187 F2
Shoemaker Ln
300 SOLB 1187 F2
Shoen Ln
- SDCo 1173 J7
Shogo Mtn Rd
37500 SDCo 997 D5
Shona Wy
3100 SDGO 1268 D5
Shooting Iron Trl
700 SDCo 1138 B6
(See Page 1138)
Shooting Star Ct
1600 SDGO 1350 E2
Shooting Star Dr
3700 SDGO 1350 E2
Shooting Star Pl
2400 SDCo 1234 B5
Shore Crest Rd
900 CRLB 1126 J4
Shore Dr
5000 CRLB 1126 F2
- SDGO 1248 C6
Shore View Ln
300 ENCT 1147 B3
Shoreacres Dr
1400 CHLV 1311 H6
Shorebird Ln
- SDCo 1127 B7
Shoredale Dr
9900 SNTE 1231 D3
Shoreham Pl
5000 SDGO 1228 G5
Shorehang Ln
200 ENCT 1167 H1
Shoreline Bluff Ln
3500 SDGO 1268 D5
Shoreline Cove Ct
2900 SDGO 1248 F6
Shoreline Dr
6900 CRLB 1126 J5
7400 SDGO 1228 E3
Shoreline Wy
4300 OCSD 1087 A4
Shorepointe Ct
- SDGO 1208 B2
Shorepointe Wy
- SDGO 1208 B2
Shores Park Drwy
- SDGO 1268 C3
Shoreview Pl
2100 CHLV 1311 E4
Shorewood Dr
7600 SDGO 1290 G4
Short Ct
14000 SDCo 1292 H3
(See Page 1292)
Short Nine E Dr
1100 SDCo 1079 B3
(See Page 1079)
Short Pl
- ESCN 1129 H6
Short Rd
- ImCo 6439 H4
Short St
12000 SDCo 1251 J1
Short St
12000 SDCo 1252 A1
4300 SDGO 1269 H3
Short Wy
100 SDCo 1252 H3
Shorthill Dr
2300 OCSD 1106 H2
Shoshone St
1300 OCSD 1086 B6
Shoshonean Dr
- IMPE 6439 F3
Shoshoni Av
4600 SDGO 1248 F1
Shoup Dr
2900 SDGO 1268 E6
Showplace Dr
9400 SDCo 1271 C4
Shropshire Ln
12400 SDGO 1150 B6
Shubin Ln
100 SNMS 1128 H1
Shuboro St
600 VSTA 1087 F5
Shuluk Wy
- SDCo 1234 J2
Shutter Ct
1500 CHLV 1331 F2
Shutter Ln
- SDGO 1269 B1
Shuttle Rd
- CRLB 1127 C7
Shy Bird Ln
10900 SDGO 1189 H4
Shy Ln
400 CHLV 1330 C3
Shya Wy
- SDCo 1234 E6
Sibimooat Cir
- SDCo 1029 H2
Sicard St
500 SDGO 1289 D5
Sicily Wy
3300 OCSD 1106 J1
Siddall Dr
1500 SDCo 1108 F2
Side Saddle Pl
2800 SDCo 1129 B4
Sidewinder Rd
- SDGO 1228 J3
- SDGO 1229 B2
Sidewinder Wy
13000 SDGO 1189 D5
Sidney Ct
- IMPE 6499 H2
Sidonia Ct
1100 ENCT 1147 D4
Sidonia St
1200 ENCT 1147 D3
Siefort Pl
400 NATC 1309 F1
Siegle Ct
2100 LMGR 1290 J1
Siegle Dr
2000 LMGR 1290 J1
Siembre St
3500 SDCo 1310 J1
Siempre Viva Ct
- SDCo 1351 F4
Siempre Viva Rd
- SDCo 1352 B3
- SDGO 1351 D4
0 SDGO 1352 A3
Siena St
100 SDGO 1290 G4
S Siena St
300 SDGO 1290 F5
Siena Wy
3400 OCSD 1106 J2
Sienna Canyon Ct
3800 ENCT 1167 H2
Sienna Canyon Dr
1800 ENCT 1167 H3
Sienna Ct
- SDGO 1189 B4
Sienna Hills Dr
10200 SDCo 1169 E1
Sienna Ridge Dr
17000 SDCo 1169 E2
Sienna Ridge Pl
10200 SDCo 1169 E2
Sienna St
3500 OCSD 1107 F4
E Sierra Alta Wy
- SDCo 1232 F5
N Sierra Av
300 SOLB 1167 E6
S Sierra Av
400 SOLB 1167 E7
- SOLB 1187 E1
Sierra Bonita
1100 SDCo 1028 D3
Sierra Bonita St
10000 SDCo 1271 E6
Sierra Cielo
17800 SDCo 1294 C5
(See Page 1294)
Sierra Cielo Ln
17400 SDCo 1294 A6
(See Page 1294)
Sierra Cir
1300 ELCJ 1271 E1

62 INDEX
Sierra Crest Ct
INDEX 62
Soledad Rd
SAN DIEGO CO.

San Diego County Street Index

STREET
Block City Map# Grid

Sierra Crest Ct
11600 SDGO 1209 J4
Sierra Ct
- IMPE 6499 H2
900 VSTA 1107 H2
Sierra Dr
800 BRAW 6319 G3
(See Page 6319)
- ESCN 1109 F7
Sierra Grande Rd
15500 SDCo 1070 J5
Sierra Linda Dr
3900 ESCN 1150 D3
Sierra Ln
14900 SDCo 1050 F3
Sierra Madre Ct
- SDCo 1086 A3
Sierra Madre Rd
9900 SDCo 1271 D4
Sierra Mar Dr
7700 SDGO 1227 G6
Sierra Mesa Ct
13100 SDGO 1188 J4
Sierra Morena Av
3500 CRLB 1106 H4
Sierra Nevada Dr
1300 CALX 6620 D7
Sierra Ridge Dr
300 ENCT 1147 J7
Sierra Rojo Ln
- SDCo 1069 J6
Sierra Rojo Rd
- SDCo 1069 J7
- SDCo 1070 A7
Sierra Rosa Tr
13500 SDGO 1188 F3
Sierra St
100 ESCN 1150 B2
100 SNTE 1231 E6
Sierra Verde
- VSTA 1087 J7
Sierra Verde Rd
- CHLV 1311 D7
- SDCo 1091 H5
Sierra View Wy
6000 SDGO 1250 D6
Sierra Vista
- SNMS 1129 B1
Sierra Vista Av
9400 SDCo 1271 B1
Sierra Vista Dr
100 SDCo 1252 J3
Sierra Vista Ln
10400 SDCo 1271 D1
Sierra Vista St
4200 SDGO 1268 H5
Sierra Wy
500 CHLV 1330 B2
E Sierra Wy
- CHLV 1330 E1
Siesta Calle
1900 SDCo 1252 D4
Siesta Dr
4800 OCSD 1066 J7
4900 OCSD 1067 A6
5400 SDGO 1270 B3
Siesta Ln
- SDCo 1091 H4
Siesta Pl
4800 OCSD 1066 J7
Siesta Rd
8600 SNTE 1231 E7
Siete Leguas
7300 SDCo 1168 G1
Siggson Av
1200 ESCN 1110 A6
Siggson Ct
600 ESCN 1109 J7
Siglo Ct
10900 SDGO 1249 J2
Sigma St
5600 LMSA 1250 J7
Signal Av
1300 SDGO 1350 A2
Sigsbee St
1100 SDGO 1289 C5
Sikes Pl
12100 POWY 1190 E7
Sikokis Pl
2000 ESCN 1130 A7
Sikorsky St
- SDGO 1351 C1
Silent Knoll Dr
4600 SDCo 1048 G1
Silent Tide Ct
8400 SDCo 1169 B2
Silhouette Rd
16600 SDCo 1169 A3
Silk Mill Pl
300 SNMS 1108 J7
Silk Pl
5100 SDGO 1290 A1
Silktree Ln
4600 SDCo 1099 F4
(See Page 1099)
Silkwood Dr
5200 OCSD 1087 D1
Silla Ct
14500 POWY 1190 H3

Silliman Rd
800 ImCo 6260 J7
(See Page 6260)
Silva Rd
9700 SDCo 1233 D3
7100 SDGO 1229 D1
Silvana Wy
500 VSTA 1087 H3
Silvas St
1600 CHLV 1330 C5
Silver Acacia
- SDGO 1188 G6
Silver Berry Pl
- ENCT 1147 C5
Silver Berry Wy
27100 SDCo 1090 D5
Silver Birch Ln
3200 SDCo 1047 J2
Silver Birch Wy
4400 OCSD 1086 J2
Silver Bluff Dr
5200 OCSD 1067 C7
4700 OCSD 1087 B1
Silver Bluff Wy
600 OCSD 1067 C7
Silver Buckle Wy
11200 SDGO 1169 H5
Silver Cloud Pass
3200 SDCo 1155 G3
Silver Creek Ln
10000 SDCo 1232 G2
Silver Crest Dr
16800 SDCo 1169 E2
Silver Crest Ln
16900 SDCo 1169 E2
Silver Ct
8900 SNTE 1231 G6
Silver Dr
700 VSTA 1087 F6
Silver Fox Ln
1700 VSTA 1087 D6
Silver Gum Wy
- SDCo 1169 D2
Silver Hawk Wy
- CHLV 1311 J5
Silver Heights Rd
14300 POWY 1190 G4
Silver Ivy Ln
13400 SDGO 1189 B4
Silver Lake Dr
13600 POWY 1190 D4
Silver Medal Rd
2800 CHLV 1312 B7
(See Page 1312)
Silver Oak
- SDGO 1210 E2
Silver Oak Ct
2700 CHLV 1311 J4
Silver Oak Ln
3300 SDCo 1088 E7
Silver Oak Pl
900 CHLV 1311 J4
2700 ESCN 1129 D3
Silver Oaks Wy
- SDCo 1271 D7
Silver Peak Pl
2200 ENCT 1147 J6
Silver Pine Ct
16900 SDCo 1169 E2
Silver Pine Pl
10300 SDCo 1169 E2
Silver Pine Rd
17000 SDCo 1169 E2
Silver Pine Wy
10300 SDCo 1169 E2
Silver Ridge Ct
- OCSD 1086 D3
Silver Ridge Pt
11600 SDGO 1209 J4
Silver Ridge Rd
14200 POWY 1190 H4
Silver Saddle Ct
16400 POWY 1170 E4
Silver Saddle Ln
13100 POWY 1170 E4
Silver Sage Rd
- CHLV 1311 H5
Silver Shadow Dr
400 SNMS 1129 A1
Silver Shoals Pt
- SDGO 1330 H7
Silver Spring Wy
- OCSD 1086 J2
Silver Springs Dr
1100 CHLV 1311 H5
Silver Springs Ln
1000 SDCo 1047 H1
Silver Springs Pl
1000 ESCN 1129 F1
Silver Spur Ct
- IMPE 6439 F3
15900 SDCo 1233 D2
Silver Spur Rd
9700 SDCo 1233 D2
Silver Spur Wy
400 SNMS 1108 E6
Silver St
700 SDGO 1227 E7
Silver Stallion Dr
1000 VSTA 1107 G2

Silver Strand Bay
3500 CORD 1309 C6
Silver Strand Blvd
2200 CORD 1308 J1
2200 CORD 1309 B4
5700 CORD 1329 E2
Silver Tree Ln
1500 SDCo 1089 D7
Silver Vine Path
13500 SDGO 1188 G3
Silverado Dr
1200 CHLV 1311 H6
1400 OCSD 1067 E6
Silverado Pl
2900 ESCN 1110 F7
Silverado St
900 SDGO 1227 E6
2100 SNMS 1128 B5
Silverado Tr
- IMPE 6439 F4
Silverberry Ct
1200 SDCo 12[illegible]2 F7
Silverbrook Dr
700 SDCo 1253 C2
Silverbush Creek St
6200 SDGO 1188 F3
Silvercreek Dr
- SNTE 1231 C5
Silvercreek Glen
200 ESCN 1150 A2
Silverfox Ln
1700 SDCo 1027 F5
Silvergate Av
- SDGO 1287 J4
700 SDGO 1288 A3
Silvergate Pl
3500 SDGO 1287 J4
Silverleaf Cres
1900 CRLB 1147 E3
Silverleaf Ln
- SDCo 1068 G7
- SDCo 1088 F1
Silverset St
14600 POWY 1190 D1
Silverton Av
7800 SDGO 1209 A7
Silverwind Dr
8100 SDCo 1169 B2
Silverwood St
- IMPE 6499 C3
600 OCSD 1086 F2
7000 SDGO 1290 F5
Silvery Ln
400 ELCJ 1251 C5
Silvery Moon Ln
7900 SDCo 1148 J7
Sima Ct
10800 SNTE 1231 E1
Simbar Rd
3100 SDCo 1290 J7
Simeon Dr
7400 SDGO 1230 F6
Simeon Pl
1200 ESCN 1129 H7
Simi Ct
2600 SDGO 1290 F7
Simi Pl
6800 SDGO 1310 F1
Simi Wy
6900 SDGO 1310 F1
Simms Ct
- SDCo 1271 B5
Simon Dr
- SDCo 1235 B2
Simons Ln
15800 SDGO 1169 D4
Simpatico Ct
1700 SDGO 1350 B3
Simple Melody Ln
16900 SDCo 1168 J1
Simpson Ct
- ESCN 1129 F3
Simpson Wy
1100 ESCN 1129 F3
Sims Rd
- SDGO 1268 D7
Simsbury Ct
3500 CRLB 1107 A3
Sinaloa Ct
100 SOLB 1167 H4
Sinclair Ln
3700 SDCo 1271 B5
Sinclair St
15900 SDGO 1169 D4
Singer Ln
11900 SDCo 1271 H7
Singh Rd
- ImCo 6560 E1
Singing Canyon Dr
4200 SDCo 1272 F2
Singing Heights Dr
700 SDCo 1252 D7
Singing Ridge Rd
900 SDCo 1252 E7
Singing Trails Ct
2300 SDCo 1252 E7
Singing Trails Dr
700 SDCo 1252 E6
Singing Vista Ct
600 SDCo 1252 E6

Singing Vista Dr
600 SDCo 1252 E6
Singing Vista Wy
2500 SDCo 1252 E6
Singing Wood Wy
8900 SNTE 1231 B6
Singingwood Pl
2100 ESCN 1129 E7
Single Oak Dr
9500 SDCo 1232 A4
Single Oak Pl
12300 SDCo 1232 A5
Singletree Ln
10800 SDCo 1271 G7
Singletree Pl
1400 SDCo 1047 J4
Sinjon Cir
9100 LMSA 1251 B6
Sinkler Wy
800 VSTA 1107 J1
Sinsonte Ln
9100 SDCo 1232 C6
Sinton Pl
6000 LMSA 1251 A6
Sintonte Ct
12200 SDGO 1150 B7
Sintonte Dr
17800 SDGO 1170 B1
Sioux Av
3900 SDGO 1248 E5
Sipes Cir
- CHLV 1330 H2
Sipes Ln
3700 SDGO 1350 F5
Sipo Ln
- SDCo 1273 A6
Sipple St
200 SDCo 1085 J5
- SDCo 1086 A4
Sir Francis Drake Dr
11400 SDCo 1271 H3
Sir Lancelot Dr
10000 SNTE 1231 D1
Sir William Osler Ln
- SDGO 1228 A2
Sirena Vista Wy
3100 CRLB 1127 J5
Sirginson St
500 SNMS 1108 J6
Sirias Rd
11200 SDGO 1209 C2
Siros Wy
5000 OCSD 1107 F5
Sirrah St
800 SDGO 1330 B7
Sissi Ln
10200 SDCo 1231 F3
Sisson St
9300 LMSA 1251 B6
Sistina Wy
3400 OCSD 1106 J2
Sitio Abeto
- CRLB 1147 H2
Sitio Abridor
- CRLB 1147 H3
Sitio Algodon
7600 CRLB 1148 A2
Sitio Andulcia
- CRLB 1147 J4
Sitio Arago
7200 CRLB 1128 B7
Sitio Avellana
3200 CRLB 1128 A6
Sitio Bahia
7100 CRLB 1128 A7
Sitio Baniano
- CRLB 1147 H3
Sitio Baya
3500 CRLB 1148 A2
Sitio Borde
3400 CRLB 1148 A2
Sitio Caballero
7100 CRLB 1127 J5
Sitio Caliente
7100 CRLB 1128 A7
Sitio Calmar
- CRLB 1147 J3
Sitio Castano
7300 CRLB 1128 B7
Sitio Catana
- CRLB 1147 J3
Sitio Caucho
- CRLB 1147 G3
Sitio Cedrela
- CRLB 1127 C5
Sitio Coco
- CRLB 1147 G2
Sitio Colina
7000 CRLB 1128 A6
Sitio Conejo
- CRLB 1148 B2
Sitio Corazon
- CRLB 1128 A6
Sitio Cordero
6900 CRLB 1127 J6
Sitio Damasco
3500 CRLB 1148 B2
Sitio Destino
7100 CRLB 1128 B6

Sitio Espino
3500 CRLB 1148 A1
Sitio Fresca
- SDCo 1148 A4
Sitio Fresno
- CRLB 1147 H2
Sitio Frontera
7000 CRLB 1128 A6
Sitio Granado
- CRLB 1147 H2
Sitio Isadora
- CRLB 1147 H1
Sitio Lima
7200 CRLB 1148 A1
Sitio Lirio
7200 CRLB 1148 A1
Sitio Manana
7600 CRLB 1148 A2
Sitio Mirto
- CRLB 1147 H2
Sitio Montecillo
3200 CRLB 1127 J6
Sitio Montilla
7400 CRLB 1128 B7
Sitio Musica
- CRLB 1147 J3
Sitio Nespero
- CRLB 1147 H3
Sitio Oceano
3200 CRLB 1127 J5
Sitio Olmo
- CRLB 1147 H2
Sitio Palmas
- CRLB 1127 H5
Sitio Peral
- CRLB 1147 G2
Sitio Redonda
- SDCo 1148 A3
Sitio Rosalia
3200 CRLB 1127 G7
Sitio Sabroso
- SDCo 1148 A4
Sitio Sago
- CRLB 1127 C5
Sitio Salvia
7300 CRLB 1148 B1
Sitio Sandia
3400 CRLB 1148 A2
Sitio Sendero
3100 CRLB 1127 J6
Sitio Solana
- CRLB 1148 A3
Sitio Tejo
- CRLB 1147 F2
Sitio Toledo
- CRLB 1147 J4
Sitio Tortuga
3200 CRLB 1128 A6
Sitio Vaquero
- SDCo 1148 A3
Sito Ln
300 NATC 1289 J6
Siva St
1600 SDGO 1289 F6
Siwanoy Ct
8800 SNTE 1230 J5
Sixes Ct
- SDCo 1172 J2
Sixpence Wy
- CORD 1329 E1
Sixth St
- ImCo 6560 C7
Ski Wy
100 CHLV 1330 D3
Skimmer Ct
- CRLB 1127 E5
Skimmer Wy
4400 OCSD 1087 A3
Skipjack Ln
- SDCo 1085 H5
Skipper St
3000 SDGO 1249 D5
Skunk Hollow Rd
- SDCo 1314 E3
(See Page 1314)
Skunk Hollow Spur Truck Trl
- SDCo 1314 G5
(See Page 1314)
Sky Blue St
1800 CHLV 1331 F3
Sky Corral
- SNMS 1128 A5
Sky Country Ct
200 SDCo 1027 F5
Sky Crest Gn
- ESCN 1129 H6
Sky Dr
26000 SDCo 1089 H7
25900 SDCo 1109 H1
Sky Harbor Rd
1800 SDGO 1290 D7
Sky Harbor Wy
- IMPE 6499 D2
Sky Haven Ln
3700 OCSD 1107 C3
Sky High Rd
15300 SDCo 1150 J2
Sky Loft Ln
1700 ENCT 1147 C2

Sky Loft Rd
- ENCT 1147 B2
Sky Mesa Rd
600 SDCo 1233 F7
Sky Park Ct
9200 SDGO 1249 E3
Sky Pilot Wy
- SDCo 1090 B1
Sky Pond Ln
- SNMS 1128 B5
Sky Ridge
3400 SDCo 1275 B4
Sky Ridge Ct
1300 SNMS 1128 D5
Sky Rim Dr
8600 SDCo 1232 B6
Sky St
4900 SDGO 1268 F1
Sky Valley Dr
16800 SDCo 1151 E5
Sky View Ct
- IMPE 6499 C2
Sky View Dr
- IMPE 6499 D2
- SDCo 1090 A2
Sky Vista Wy
300 SDCo 1027 H2
Skybrook Pl
1900 CHLV 1311 E5
Skycrest Dr
3000 SDCo 1048 D1
Skye Valley Rd
- SDCo 1275 B7
- SDCo 1295 A1
(See Page 1295)
- SDCo 1296 C2
(See Page 1296)
Skyhawk Rd
1500 SDCo 1149 F1
Skyhawk Wy
4900 OCSD 1107 E3
Skyhigh Ct
12400 SDCo 1232 B7
Skyhill Ct
400 CHLV 1310 F7
Skyhill Pl
1800 ESCN 1109 E6
Skyknoll Wy
1900 ENCT 1147 H5
Skylark Dr
2400 OCSD 1086 E7
900 SDGO 1247 G3
Skylark Pl
5700 SDGO 1247 G3
Skylark Wy
1500 CHLV 1330 F5
Skyline Av
- ESCN 1130 C1
Skyline Cir
300 SDCo 1028 H3
Skyline Dr
2400 LMGR 1270 H7
1700 LMGR 1290 H1
3000 OCSD 1086 G7
300 SDCo 1088 B6
2000 SDCo 1130 E4
- SDCo 1217 G1
(See Page 1217)
6100 SDGO 1290 D4
Skyline Ln
1500 ELCJ 1252 A7
4600 LMSA 1271 A3
Skyline Rd
3700 CRLB 1106 H5
Skyline Spur
2900 SDCo 1294 D2
(See Page 1294)
Skyline St
1000 CALX 6620 D7
Skyline Ter
1900 SDCo 1130 E4
Skyline Truck Trl
14900 SDCo 1273 B6
16700 SDCo 1274 A7
18100 SDCo 1294 C1
(See Page 1294)
Skyline View Glen
3100 ESCN 1130 J4
Skyloft Park Ln
- SDGO 1269 B1
Skymountain Ln
700 SDCo 1234 B4
Skyridge Ln
400 ESCN 1109 G4
Skyridge Rd
15000 POWY 1170 J5
- POWY 1171 A5
Skyros Wy
1300 ENCT 1147 B3
Skysail Av
800 CRLB 1126 J5
Skytrail Ranch Rd
3300 SDCo 1273 J6
Skyview Av
- ELCN 6559 G4
Skyview Glen
2100 ESCN 1110 B5
Skyview Ln
100 OCSD 1107 D2
Skyview St
600 ELCJ 1271 E1

Skywood Dr
400 ELCJ 1271 G1
10900 SDCo 1271 G1
Slack St
12900 POWY 1190 D5
Sladon Ct
14300 POWY 1190 E2
Sladon Rd
1400 ELCJ 1251 B3
Slant Rock Rd
3400 SDCo 1275 B4
Slash M Rd
300 SDCo 1078 G6
(See Page 1078)
Slate Ct
300 CHLV 1330 G4
Slate St
200 CHLV 1330 G4
Slate Terr
1700 SDCo 1272 B2
Slater Pl
- CRLB 1127 F2
Slaughterhouse Canyon Rd
- SDCo 1211 G4
Slaughterhouse Rd
27100 SDCo 1154 C2
Slayen Wy
3000 SDGO 1248 C3
Sleep Willow Ln
3400 SDCo 1273 A6
Sleeping Circle Dr
4800 SDCo 1099 F5
(See Page 1099)
Sleeping Indian Rd
1100 OCSD 1067 D3
4100 SDCo 1047 E4
Sleepwillow Ln
- SDCo 1273 A6
Sleepy Creek Rd
15400 SDCo 1232 F2
Sleepy Hill Ln
2300 SDCo 1109 E4
Sleepy Hill Rd
2300 SDCo 1109 D4
Sleepy Hollow
2200 SDCo 1136 C6
28700 SDCo 1237 C5
Sleepy Hollow Ln
- SDCo 1310 F4
Sleepy Hollow Rd
2000 SDCo 1109 D4
Sleepy Hollow Wy
- VSTA 1107 D2
Sleepy Wy
8400 SDCo 1232 D7
Slice Ct
3100 SDCo 1079 B6
(See Page 1079)
Slider Rd
- ImCo 6260 B5
(See Page 6260)
Slippery Elm Ct
2700 CHLV 1311 J7
Slivkoff Dr
2900 ESCN 1110 F7
Sloan Dr
1900 SDCo 1028 A6
Sloan Ranch Truck Trl
- SDCo 1273 J2
Sloane Av
400 SDGO 1268 J6
Sloane Canyon Rd
4300 SDCo 1253 A7
3200 SDCo 1273 C2
Sloane Truck Trl
- SDCo 1273 H3
Slope St
9400 SNTE 1251 C1
Slumber Rd
700 SDCo 1233 G6
Slumbering Oaks Trl
3200 SDCo 1156 C1
Smart Ct
100 ENCT 1147 G6
Smedley Av
- SDGO 1209 F7
Smilax Rd
200 SNMS 1108 C5
Smiliana Ln
- SDCo 1108 A2
Smith Av
- CHLV 1310 A5
Smith Canyon Ct
4900 SDGO 1188 C5
Smith Dr
800 VSTA 1087 J5
Smith Ln
800 ImCo 6499 A6
- SDCo 1023 D2
35200 SDCo 1029 H3
Smith Rd
8300 SDGO 1229 C2
Smith St
3700 SDGO 1268 F5
Smithers Ct
11400 SDGO 1209 D1
Smoke Tree Pl
200 OCSD 1087 A1
Smokebush Ct
1200 SDCo 1252 F7

Smokesignal Dr
18200 SDGO 1149 J7
Smoketree Cir
2100 ELCN 6559 G2
Smoketree Ct
2100 ELCN 6559 G2
800 SNMS 1128 E2
Smoketree Dr
1700 ELCN 6559 F2
Smoketree Glen
500 ESCN 1109 G4
Smokewood Av
- IMPE 6499 D2
Smokewood Dr
8000 SNTE 1230 H7
Smokewood Pl
2400 ESCN 1109 H3
Smokey Ln
1700 SDCo 1291 B1
Smoky Cir
400 CHLV 1310 F5
Smythe Av
2100 SDGO 1350 F3
Snaffle Bit Pl
5900 SDCo 1311 B2
Snapdragon
- SDCo 1233 B3
Snapdragon Dr
7000 CRLB 1127 A6
Snapdragon Ln
2200 SDCo 1234 A5
Snapdragon St
700 ENCT 1147 E6
Snapdragon Wy
- IMPE 6499 D2
Snead Av
2700 SDGO 1248 G6
Snead Dr
2300 OCSD 1106 H2
Sneath Wy
700 SDCo 1234 B3
Sneezy Ct
13300 SDCo 1232 D7
Snelson Wy
9400 SNTE 1231 B3
Snipe Ct
- CRLB 1127 A4
Snipes Ct
- SDGO 1350 E1
Snook St
9900 SDGO 1249 G3
Snow Creek
1000 SDCo 1027 H4
Snow View Dr
9700 SDCo 1233 A3
Snow White Dr
8400 SDCo 1232 D7
Snowbells Ln
16400 SDCo 1169 F4
Snowberry Ct
1900 CRLB 1147 F3
800 SNMS 1109 A5
Snowbond Ct
5800 SDGO 1250 C6
Snowbond St
6200 SDGO 1250 C6
Snowden Pl
400 SDCo 1253 C2
Snowdrop St
2500 SDGO 1269 H7
Snowdrop Wy
- CRLB 1127 B4
Snowfall Cir
4500 OCSD 1087 D5
Snows Rd
3200 SDCo 1047 J1
Snuz Mtn Rd
15600 SDCo 1171 H5
Snyder Rd
10600 SDCo 1271 F2
Soapstone Grade Fire Rd
- SDCo 1176 G7
(See Page 1176)
Soaring Bird Pt
13000 SDGO 1189 H5
Soaring Dr
6600 SDCo 1250 G4
Soaring Hawk Ln
- SDCo 1274 C7
Sobke Ct
1200 CALX 6620 G7
Sobre Ct
2800 SDCo 1099 F4
(See Page 1099)
Sobre Los Cerros
17200 SDCo 1168 C3
Social Garden Dr
- SDGO 1269 B2
Socin Ct
- ESCN 1110 E6
Socorro Ct
11100 SDGO 1169 J6
Socorro Juarez St
- BRAW 6319 F1
(See Page 6319)
Socorro Ln
2700 CRLB 1127 H5
Socorro Pl
15200 SDGO 1169 J6

Socorro St
11100 SDGO 1169 J6
Socorro Wy
15200 SDGO 1169 J7
Soderblom Av
2500 SDGO 1228 B6
Soderblom Ct
5500 SDGO 1228 B6
Sofia Ct
- IMPE 6499 H2
Soft Wind Rd
800 VSTA 1107 F1
Softwind Ln
2100 ENCT 1147 H5
Sohail St
13400 SDCo 1232 D4
Soho Row
8800 SDGO 1249 D2
Soho View Terr
5400 SDGO 1270 B5
Sol Dr
500 OCSD 1067 A6
Sol Sitio St
4800 OCSD 1067 A7
Sol Vista
3200 SDCo 1028 D1
Sol Vista Glen
- ESCN 1130 A3
Sol Wood
37900 SDCo 1319 J3
(See Page 1319)
Solace Ct
100 ENCT 1147 G6
Solamar Dr
6300 CRLB 1126 G3
Solana Cir
600 SOLB 1187 F2
E Solana Cir
600 SOLB 1187 F1
W Solana Cir
600 SOLB 1187 F1
Solana Dr
1000 SOLB 1167 G7
Solana Glen Ct
600 SOLB 1167 G6
Solana Gn
- ESCN 1109 D5
Solana Hills Ct
600 SOLB 1167 G6
Solana Hills Dr
300 SOLB 1167 G7
Solana Point Cir
100 ENCT 1167 E5
Solana Real
500 SDCo 1047 E7
Solana St
8000 SDGO 1290 G2
Solana Vista Dr
300 SOLB 1167 E6
Solandra Dr
- CRLB 1127 A5
Solandra Ln
900 SDCo 1291 D3
Solano Bay Dr
300 OCSD 1066 J6
Solano Dr
1500 CHLV 1331 E1
Solano Este Dr
- OCSD 1086 F2
Solano Rd
1800 ELCN 6499 E6
Solano St
7500 CRLB 1147 H1
Solar Circle Dr
- DLMR 1187 F3
Solar Ln
- SDCo 1088 H6
Solar St
5100 SDGO 1268 F2
Solar View Dr
- SDCo 1088 H6
Solazar Wy
2400 OCSD 1087 C6
Soldau Dr
3200 SDGO 1350 D1
Soldier Oaks Ln
12800 SDCo 1090 C2
Soldin Ln
- SDCo 1232 H5
Soledad Av
1900 SDGO 1227 G6
Soledad Ct
2400 SDGO 1248 A2
Soledad Fwy
- SDGO 1228 F6
Soledad Mountain Rd
5100 SDGO 1248 B3
Soledad Mtn Rd
6000 SDGO 1247 J1
Soledad Park Rd
7000 SDGO 1227 J7
Soledad Pl
200 CORD 1288 J6
3000 ESCN 1110 E6
Soledad Rancho Ct
5200 SDGO 1248 A3
Soledad Rancho Rd
2200 SDGO 1248 A3
Soledad Rd
5400 SDGO 1248 A2

63 INDEX
Soledad Wy

San Diego County Street Index

INDEX 63
Steamboat Springs Ct

STREET	Block	City	Map#	Grid
Soledad Wy				
	1700	SDGO	1247	J3
Solera Wy				
	12900	POWY	1170	D2
Solita Av				
	6400	SDGO	1270	D3
Solitary Ln				
	100	SDCo	1027	J6
Solo Roble				
	-	SNMS	1129	A3
Solola Av				
	5200	SDGO	1290	B6
Solomon Av				
	8300	SDCo	1231	G7
Solstice Av				
	-	CHLV	1331	G2
Solterra Vista Pkwy				
	-	SDGO	1188	H4
Soltura Ln				
	200	NATC	1289	H6
Solymar Dr				
	1000	SDGO	1247	F2
Soma Pl				
	1500	ELCJ	1252	A3
Somam Av				
	4900	SDGO	1248	F7
	-	SDGO	1268	G1
Sombra Ct				
	10900	SDGO	1249	J2
Sombra Del Monte				
	-	SDCo	1171	F3
Sombrero Rd				
	-	SDCo	999	C6
Sombrero Wy				
	1600	SDGO	1349	J2
Sombria Ln				
	9200	SDCo	1232	B5
Sombrosa Pl				
	2500	CRLB	1147	H4
Sombrosa St				
	2700	CRLB	1147	G3
Somercrest Glen				
	300	ESCN	1109	H4
Somerlane St				
	1700	SDCo	1251	J2
Somermont Dr				
	1300	SDCo	1251	H1
Somers Ln				
	2600	SDGO	1288	C1
Somerset Av				
	1400	ENCT	1167	D2
	8600	SDGO	1249	C6
Somerset Ct				
	900	CHLV	1311	G4
	1300	SDCo	1152	G7
Somerset Rd				
	13600	POWY	1190	F3
Somerset Wy				
	-	CRLB	1107	A4
Sommer Pl				
	6400	LMSA	1251	B5
Sommermont Dr				
	1300	SDCo	1251	H1
Sonata Ln				
	1600	SDCo	1128	C2
	7600	SDGO	1168	J7
Sondra Ct				
	2900	CRLB	1127	H7
Sondrio Ln				
	7500	SDGO	1168	J7
Sonett St				
	-	SDCo	1272	C4
Song Sparrow Cir				
	-	SDCo	1291	B7
Songbird Av				
	1600	CRLB	1127	C5
Songbird Ln				
	900	CHLV	1310	H3
Sonia Ln				
	-	CHLV	1330	F6
Sonia Pl				
	900	ESCN	1109	F5
Sonja Ct				
	3000	OCSD	1086	G7
Sono Pl				
	7300	LMSA	1270	F4
Sonoma Ct				
	1200	CHLV	1330	G2
Sonoma Dr				
	-	OCSD	1086	F2
Sonoma Ln				
	1900	LMGR	1290	F1
Sonoma Pl				
	-	SDGO	1188	E5
Sonoma St				
	-	SDCo	1128	G2
Sonora Ct				
	2400	CRLB	1106	H4
	2000	VSTA	1107	J4
Sonora Dr				
	1500	CHLV	1330	H4
Sonora Rd				
	12600	SDGO	1170	C3
Sonora St				
	200	SNTE	1231	E6
Sonora Wy				
	2200	SDCo	1152	C5
Sonrisa Glen				
	2200	ESCN	1129	G7
Sonrisa St				
	700	SOLB	1187	F1
Sonrisa Wy				
	2400	OCSD	1087	C6
Soper Ln				
	7900	LMSA	1270	H1
Sophia Dr				
	12300	POWY	1190	C2
Sophia Wy				
	-	OCSD	1086	H3
Soprano Ln				
	14700	SDGO	1168	J7
Sora Wy				
	1100	CRLB	1127	B5
	12500	SDGO	1189	C6
Sorbonne Ct				
	13700	SDGO	1190	A3
Soria Dr				
	4700	SDGO	1270	C3
Soria Glen				
	1200	ESCN	1109	G7
Sorrel Av				
	9900	SDCo	1232	C3
Sorrel Ct				
	1700	CRLB	1127	E6
Sorrel Tree Pl				
	200	OCSD	1087	A1
Sorrentino Dr				
	1900	SDCo	1130	D5
Sorrento Dr				
	2100	OCSD	1086	J7
	1000	SDGO	1287	J1
Sorrento Pl				
	1200	ESCN	1110	A6
Sorrento Valley Blvd				
	-	SDGO	1208	D5
Sorrento Valley Rd				
	12300	SDGO	1207	J2
	10400	SDGO	1208	C6
Soto St				
	1600	OCSD	1106	D2
	2300	SDGO	1268	A6
Soule St				
	12600	POWY	1190	C5
Sourwood Pl				
	1600	CHLV	1311	J7
South Bay Expressway				
	0	SDCo	1311	D1
	0	SDCo	1331	G4
	0	SDCo	1351	H1
South Bay Expwy				
	-	SDCo	1291	A7
South Bay Frwy				
	-	NATC	1309	J5
	-	NATC	1310	D3
	-	SDCo	1290	H7
	-	SDCo	1291	A5
South Cabrillo Dr				
	1100	CHLV	1311	B6
South Cays Ct				
	-	CORD	1329	E3
South Chevy Chase				
	15600	SDGO	1169	B4
South Coast Hwy 101				
	2600	ENCT	1167	D4
	100	SOLB	1187	E1
South Creekside Dr				
	1400	CHLV	1311	J6
South Forty Rd				
	23300	SDCo	1235	G7
South Grade Rd				
	500	SDCo	1233	F6
	2800	SDCo	1234	C7
	1400	SDCo	1253	J1
	2200	SDCo	1254	B1
South Hill Rd				
	-	OCSD	1067	B4
South Hills Dr				
	1300	CHLV	1311	G6
South Lake Ct				
	6200	SDGO	1251	A6
South Ln				
	-	SDCo	1167	J7
	4400	SDCo	1187	J1
	100	SDCo	1252	H4
	200	SDGO	1247	E1
South Mountain Dr				
	13000	SDCo	1232	C3
South Park Pl				
	500	SDCo	1252	J4
South Plains Ct				
	15800	SDCo	1233	D3
South Point Dr				
	1700	CHLV	1311	C4
South Roundup Cir				
	-	SNTE	1231	E6
South Shore Dr				
	100	SOLB	1187	E2
South Shore Rd				
	-	SDCo	997	B1
South Shores Rd				
	1700	SDGO	1268	B3
South Slope St				
	8500	SNTE	1250	J1
South St				
	7500	LMSA	1270	G3
South View Dr				
	1800	CRLB	1106	H7
Southall St				
	-	NATC	1309	F2
Southampton Rd				
	2700	CRLB	1106	J5
	2700	CRLB	1107	A5
Southampton St				
	4500	SDGO	1248	G2
	1200	SNMS	1128	A3
Southbridge Ct				
	-	ENCT	1147	B2
Southbrook Ct				
	11400	SDGO	1189	J6
Southcrest Av				
	4900	SDGO	1268	F1
Southern Hills Ln				
	14400	POWY	1190	H2
Southern Oak Rd				
	-	SDCo	1172	D4
Southern Pine Pl				
	10400	SDGO	1209	J4
Southern Rd				
	100	ELCJ	1251	B5
	9200	LMSA	1251	B6
Southernwood Wy				
	3700	SDGO	1288	A2
Southgate Dr				
	600	OCSD	1067	C7
	6900	SDGO	1251	A4
Southhampton Cv				
	-	SDGO	1188	D6
Southlook Av				
	300	SDGO	1289	G5
Southport Wy				
	2400	NATC	1309	H3
Southridge Wy				
	3700	OCSD	1107	E3
	11100	SDGO	1209	H4
Southshore Dr				
	800	CHLV	1311	E4
Southview Cir				
	1400	CHLV	1311	C7
Southview Dr				
	3700	SDGO	1248	D4
Southview Ct				
	1400	CHLV	1311	C7
Southwind Dr				
	1700	ELCN	6559	F2
Southwind Ln				
	3000	SDCo	1068	E6
Southwood Cir				
	-	SDGO	1209	D3
Southwood Dr				
	3300	OCSD	1086	D2
Souvenir Dr				
	1600	ELCJ	1252	B2
Sovereign Rd				
	8900	SDGO	1249	D4
Soyla Dr				
	3300	OCSD	1086	D3
Spa St				
	3600	SDGO	1270	B6
Space Theater Wy				
	1800	SDGO	1289	C1
Spalding Pl				
	1800	SDGO	1269	C3
Spangler Peak Rd				
	16000	SDCo	1173	C3
Spanish Bay Ct				
	1400	ENCT	1147	E4
Spanish Bay Rd				
	2300	CHLV	1311	G6
Spanish Bit Dr				
	-	SDCo	1254	F3
Spanish Bit Pl				
	3900	SDCo	1254	E3
Spanish Horse				
	5500	OCSD	1067	E6
Spanish Landing (Ntc				
	-	SDGO	1288	D1
Spanish Oak Av				
	500	SNMS	1109	D6
Spanish Oak Ct				
	3800	OCSD	1086	F2
Spanish Oak Pl				
	1600	ELCJ	1252	B6
Spanish Oak Wy				
	1900	VSTA	1107	F5
Spanish Spur				
	100	SDCo	1047	G4
Spanish Wy				
	3400	CRLB	1106	F5
Spar Ct				
	-	CRLB	1127	A4
Spargur Rd				
	-	SDCo	1236	B2
Sparkling Creek Wy				
	-	ESCN	1129	F1
Sparkling Oaks Tr				
	-	SDCo	1089	F3
Sparks Av				
	4800	SDGO	1268	F1
Sparks Ct				
	1800	SDGO	1268	F2
Sparks Pl				
	1800	SDGO	1268	F1
Sparling St				
	3400	SDGO	1270	D6
Sparren Av				
	13900	SDGO	1189	C3
Sparren Ct				
	13400	SDGO	1189	C4
Sparren Wy				
	8700	SDGO	1189	C3
Sparrow Ct				
	1000	SNMS	1128	E2
Sparrow Hawk Ct				
	11300	SDCo	1212	C6
Sparrow Lake Rd				
	1100	CHLV	1331	B2
Sparrow Ln				
	-	SNMS	1128	B5
Sparrow Rd				
	1300	CRLB	1127	C5
Sparrow St				
	400	CHLV	1330	G3
	-	ImCo	6560	A7
	1200	SDGO	1290	D2
Sparrow Wy				
	200	OCSD	1086	J1
Sparrs Rd				
	-	SDGO	1288	A5
Sparta Dr				
	700	ENCT	1147	C3
Spartan Cir				
	4200	SDGO	1270	B4
Spartan Dr				
	5600	SDGO	1270	B4
Spear Dr				
	-	SDGO	1289	C2
Spear St				
	6400	SDGO	1250	B6
Spearfish Ln				
	3900	SDGO	1249	G3
Spearhead Trl				
	30000	SDCo	1069	E4
Spearman Ln				
	3000	SDCo	1271	F6
Spears Av				
	-	ELCN	6559	H2
Specialty Dr				
	1300	VSTA	1108	A7
	1300	VSTA	1128	A1
Spectrum Center Blvd				
	8800	SDGO	1249	D2
Spectrum Ct				
	4800	OCSD	1087	B3
Spectrum Ln				
	8500	SDGO	1228	J1
Speed Wy				
	-	SDCo	1234	J2
Spencer Ct				
	-	OCSD	1067	A4
	-	SDCo	1232	B4
Spencer Ln				
	5300	CRLB	1107	C7
Spencer Mountain Rd				
	9600	SDCo	1271	C7
Spencerport Wy				
	-	SDGO	1209	H2
Sperber Rd				
	-	ImCo	6559	G5
Sperry Ct				
	6900	SDGO	1268	J1
Speyers Wy				
	3500	SDCo	1311	C1
Spica Dr				
	11300	SDGO	1209	C1
Spice St				
	9100	LMSA	1271	B2
Spice Wy				
	20600	SDCo	1294	J6
(See Page 1294)				
Spicewood Ct				
	-	SDGO	1208	E1
Spillman Dr				
	4100	SDGO	1289	H2
Spindeltop Rd				
	12600	SDGO	1189	C5
Spindlewood Ct				
	-	OCSD	1086	D2
Spindrift Ct				
	700	OCSD	1086	E3
Spindrift Dr				
	1800	SDGO	1227	G6
Spindrift Ln				
	800	CRLB	1126	J5
Spindrift St				
	800	SOLB	1187	H1
Spineflower Dr				
	-	SDGO	1270	D6
Spinel Av				
	900	ELCJ	1251	G2
Spinnaker Bay Ct				
	4600	OCSD	1066	J6
Spinnaker Ct				
	100	DLMR	1187	F7
Spinnaker Point Terr				
	700	SDGO	1330	J7
	700	SDGO	1331	A7
Spinnaker Wy				
	-	CORD	1329	E2
Spires St				
	600	VSTA	1087	F5
Spirit Tr				
	-	SDCo	1275	D3
Spitfire Rd				
	11200	SDGO	1209	F2
Splendorwood Pl				
	2100	ESCN	1109	G4
Split Rock Rd				
	19100	SDCo	1172	B4
Splitrail Dr				
	1600	ENCT	1147	G5
Spokane Wy				
	2700	CRLB	1106	J4
	600	ELCJ	1251	G4
Spoonbill Ln				
	7200	CRLB	1127	D7
Spoonbill Wy				
	4200	OCSD	1087	A3
Spooner Ct				
	-	SDGO	1209	J1
Sportfisher Wy				
	100	OCSD	1085	J7
	600	OCSD	1086	A7
Sports Arena Blvd				
	3600	SDGO	1268	D5
Sports Park Wy				
	1600	VSTA	1087	F3
Spotted Saddle Wy				
	200	SDCo	1028	H6
Spray St				
	2100	SDGO	1267	J5
Spreckels Ln				
	8400	SDGO	1169	B4
Spreckels Pl				
	15700	SDGO	1169	B4
Sprig Pl				
	2400	SDCo	1297	F6
(See Page 1297)				
	2600	SDGO	1249	B7
Spring Canyon				
	-	OCSD	1086	J2
Spring Canyon Dr				
	8700	SDCo	1291	A5
Spring Canyon Rd				
	10400	SDGO	1189	H7
	-	SDGO	1210	E3
	-	SDGO	1230	F3
Spring Creek Ln				
	1500	OCSD	1067	E7
Spring Creek Rd				
	-	SDCo	1108	H1
Spring Ct				
	4200	SDCo	1271	B4
Spring Dr				
	3800	SDCo	1271	B5
Spring Flower Dr				
	2100	SDCo	1028	A4
Spring Garden Pl				
	3300	SDGO	1289	F4
Spring Gardens Rd				
	8700	LMSA	1270	J4
Spring Glen Ln				
	1400	SDCo	1291	E1
Spring Grove Ln				
	2300	SDCo	1271	A7
Spring Lilac Ln				
	14300	SDCo	1090	G7
Spring Ln				
	9100	SDCo	1271	B4
Spring Manor Ct				
	10100	SDGO	1209	D5
Spring Meadow Ln				
	11300	SDGO	1189	J6
Spring Oak Wy				
	2300	SDGO	1290	H7
Spring Oaks Pl				
	9700	SDCo	1233	D3
Spring Oaks Rd				
	15900	SDCo	1233	D2
Spring Pl				
	8900	SDCo	1271	A4
Spring Pointe Ln				
	2700	SDCo	1291	D1
Spring Rd				
	29000	SDCo	1237	C7
Spring Sky St				
	2100	CHLV	1331	G1
Spring St				
	4400	LMSA	1270	J3
Spring Straw Ln				
	1800	CHLV	1311	E7
Spring Tide Terr				
	3400	SDGO	1268	D5
Spring Valley Rd				
	15500	SDCo	1050	H4
Spring View Ct				
	9200	SDCo	1232	H5
Spring View St				
	9400	SDCo	1271	C6
Spring Vista Wy				
	8600	SDCo	1291	A2
Spring Wagon Rd				
	18300	SDCo	1153	C7
Springbrook Ct				
	-	OCSD	1086	D3
Springbrook Dr				
	12600	SDGO	1189	J6
	-	SDGO	1190	A7
Springdale Ln				
	1900	ENCT	1147	H7
Springer Rd				
	1900	SDGO	1289	H1
Springfield Av				
	8600	LMSA	1271	A3
	500	OCSD	1067	D6
Springfield Ct				
	1200	VSTA	1087	E6
Springfield Rd				
	1100	SNMS	1128	E6
Springfield St				
	6300	SDGO	1290	D2
Springford Av				
	7000	SDGO	1290	F4
Springhurst Dr				
	12600	SDGO	1190	A5
Springlake Pl				
	700	ESCN	1110	D5
Springside Rd				
	11600	SDGO	1190	A6
Springtime Dr				
	4400	OCSD	1087	D6
Springtime Ln				
	2200	SDCo	1252	D6
Springtime Wy				
	700	SDCo	1252	D6
Springtree Pl				
	300	ESCN	1109	H4
Springvale Dr				
	-	SNTE	1230	J7
Springvale St				
	14500	POWY	1190	H4
Springview Ln				
	8700	LMSA	1271	A3
Springview Rd				
	1500	SDCo	1135	E4
Springwater Pt				
	12300	SDGO	1189	H6
Springwood Dr				
	23600	SDCo	1173	D3
Springwood Ln				
	900	ENCT	1147	J5
Sprint Wy				
	13900	SDCo	1292	H2
(See Page 1292)				
Sprinter Ln				
	5600	SDCo	1311	A2
Spruance Rd				
	-	SDGO	1288	D1
Spruce				
	-	SDCo	1233	B3
Spruce Ct				
	-	BRAW	6259	F7
(See Page 6259)				
	200	CHLV	1330	G3
	3500	OCSD	1086	E2
Spruce Dr				
	-	SNMS	1108	J5
Spruce Grove Av				
	10500	SDGO	1210	B4
Spruce Grove Pl				
	12200	SDGO	1210	B3
Spruce Lake Av				
	6200	SDGO	1250	G6
Spruce Ln				
	13500	POWY	1191	A4
	9800	SDCo	1149	D3
Spruce Rd				
	100	CHLV	1330	F5
	28800	SDCo	1237	C6
Spruce Run Dr				
	-	SDGO	1209	J1
	-	SDGO	1210	A1
Spruce St				
	300	CHLV	1330	G3
	2300	CRLB	1106	E3
	500	IMPB	1329	F7
	500	SDGO	1269	A7
	5200	SDGO	1270	A6
N Spruce St				
	400	ESCN	1129	G2
S Spruce St				
	100	ESCN	1129	H3
W Spruce St				
	500	SDGO	1268	J7
Spruce Woodland Wy				
	10200	SDCo	1089	E4
Sprucewood Dr				
	300	ENCT	1147	G7
Sprucewood Ln				
	-	SDCo	1130	J4
Spud Moreno St				
	-	CALX	6620	G5
Spur Av				
	5500	OCSD	1067	F7
	29700	SDCo	1067	G7
Spur Crossing Way				
	-	SDGO	1208	G1
Spur Ct				
	10300	SDCo	1271	F4
Spur Ln				
	-	SNTE	1231	E5
Spur Point Ct				
	-	SDGO	1208	E2
Spyglass Cir				
	1700	VSTA	1108	A4
Spyglass Ct				
	1800	CRLB	1106	H6
	1400	ENCT	1147	D5
Spyglass Hill Dr				
	5400	SDCo	1253	C3
Spyglass Hill Rd				
	800	CHLV	1331	B6
Spyglass Ln				
	6800	SDCo	1168	H7
Spyglass Trl				
	28600	SDCo	1090	B1
Spyglass Wy				
	3600	OCSD	1107	D3
Squamish Rd				
	11200	SDGO	1209	C2
Squire Pl				
	300	OCSD	1086	E6
Squires Pl				
	800	SDCo	1107	F2
Squirrel Rd				
	11300	SDCo	1212	B5
Stable Glen Pl				
	11300	SDGO	1208	C2
Stable Pl				
	2900	SDCo	1129	B4
Stable Rdg				
	-	ELCJ	1252	D4
Stable Vista Wy				
	-	SDGO	1208	G1
Stacey Av				
	800	ELCN	6499	G5
Stacey Ct				
	1700	ELCN	6499	E5
Stacy Av				
	3800	SDGO	1248	E4
Stacy Ln				
	-	SDCo	1172	J1
Stacy Pl				
	4300	SDGO	1248	E4
Stadden Wy				
	100	VSTA	1087	H6
Stadium Ct				
	3300	SDGO	1228	C5
Stadium Pl				
	3400	SDGO	1228	D6
Stadium Rd				
	-	SDGO	1249	E7
	-	SDGO	1269	F1
Stadium St				
	5800	SDGO	1228	D6
Stadium Wy				
	2200	SDGO	1269	C1
Stadler St				
	8000	LMSA	1250	H7
Stafford Av				
	300	ENCT	1167	D3
Stafford Pl				
	700	SDGO	1287	J3
Stage Coach Ln				
	1100	SDCo	997	J7
	-	SDCo	998	C3
	2200	SDCo	1027	H7
N Stage Coach Ln				
	200	SDCo	1027	J2
Stage Coach Pl				
	-	SDGO	1189	A4
Stage Coach Rd				
	100	OCSD	1086	G4
	14300	POWY	1150	G6
	24400	SDCo	1316	B7
(See Page 1316)				
Stage Stop Dr				
	12000	POWY	1190	C7
Stage Terr				
	2100	SDCo	997	J7
	1900	SDCo	1027	J1
Stagecoach Ln				
	1100	SDCo	1027	J5
Stagecoach Pass				
	16800	SDCo	1168	J1
Stagecoach Rd				
	-	SDCo	1066	B1
Stagecoach Springs Rd				
	36000	SDCo	1299	C2
(See Page 1299)				
Stagecoach Trail Lp				
	1100	CHLV	1311	H6
Stagecoach Trl				
	900	SDCo	1138	A5
(See Page 1138)				
	-	SDCo	1232	E4
	300	SNTE	1231	F5
Stagecoach Wy				
	300	SDCo	1058	F2
(See Page 1058)				
Staghorn Ct				
	3200	SDCo	1048	C3
Stahl Rd				
	-	ImCo	6320	G6
(See Page 6320)				
Stalker Ct				
	1500	ELCJ	1251	B3
Stallion Dr				
	100	OCSD	1067	B6
Stallion Oaks Ln				
	5600	SDCo	1253	D5
Stallion Oaks Rd				
	5500	SDCo	1253	D4
Stallion Pl				
	300	CHLV	1310	H4
Stallion Run Pl				
	5200	SDGO	1208	D3
Stallions Ln				
	10700	SDGO	1208	D2
Stalmer St				
	7600	SDGO	1249	A4
Stamen Ct				
	6300	SDGO	1290	D5
Stamen St				
	1300	SDGO	1290	D5
Stampede Av				
	-	ImCo	6560	A6
Stampede Wy				
	1200	CHLV	1311	E6
Stancrest Ln				
	1400	NATC	1310	B1
Standel Ln				
	32400	SDCo	1049	A6
Standing Rock Rd				
	800	SDCo	1274	A3
Standish Dr				
	13400	POWY	1190	H4
Standlake St				
	1600	SDGO	1350	A2
Stanfield Cir				
	10400	SDGO	1209	D4
Stanford Av				
	800	CHLV	1311	D5
	7000	LMSA	1270	E3
Stanford Ct				
	-	SDCo	1070	F1
Stanford Dr				
	3800	OCSD	1087	A7
Stanford St				
	4300	CRLB	1107	A5
Stanislaus Dr				
	-	CHLV	1331	C1
Stanley Av				
	200	ESCN	1109	H5
	800	ESCN	1109	J4
	6200	SDGO	1270	C3
Stanley Ct				
	600	ELCJ	1251	J6
	600	ESCN	1109	J7
	10000	SNTE	1231	D4
Stanley Dr				
	6100	LMSA	1251	B6
Stanley Pl				
	600	BRAW	6320	A2
(See Page 6320)				
Stanley St				
	500	OCSD	1106	B2
Stanley Wy				
	2000	ESCN	1110	B5
Stansbury St				
	8300	SDCo	1290	J2
Stanton Rd				
	1800	ENCT	1147	H7
	4200	SDGO	1289	H2
Stanwell Cir				
	10600	SDGO	1209	C4
Stanwell Ct				
	10600	SDGO	1209	C4
Stanwell Pl				
	10600	SDGO	1209	C4
Stanwell St				
	8600	SDGO	1209	C4
Stanwix Sq				
	12100	SDGO	1190	A1
Staples Rd				
	15900	SDCo	1174	A4
Stapleton Av				
	-	IMPE	6499	C1
Stapleton Ct				
	-	IMPE	6499	C2
Star Acres Dr				
	3200	SDCo	1272	B7
Star Acres Ln				
	12600	SDCo	1272	C7
Star Av				
	2100	SDCo	1300	C6
(See Page 1300)				
Star Bright Ln				
	600	SDCo	1234	B4
Star Crest Pl				
	1700	SNMS	1128	C6
Star Crest Rd				
	19400	SDCo	1314	F2
(See Page 1314)				
Star Haven Dr				
	30600	SDCo	1070	G1
Star Jasmine Ln				
	200	ENCT	1147	B3
	-	SDCo	1068	A1
	-	SDCo	1086	A4
	-	SDGO	1169	J3
	-	SDGO	1227	H7
Star Ln				
	2000	SDCo	1253	H1
Star Park Cir				
	1000	CORD	1288	H7
Star Path				
	4300	OCSD	1087	A4
Star Pine Dr				
	2300	LMGR	1270	D7
	8700	SNTE	1230	G7
Star Pl				
	900	SDCo	1253	G1
Star Ruby Ct				
	600	ESCN	1110	D6
Star Shower Ln				
	2200	CHLV	1331	G3
Star Thistle Ln				
	-	SDCo	1233	J4
Star Track Wy				
	4000	SDCo	1048	F3
Star Valley Rd				
	1500	SDCo	1234	G7
Star View Dr				
	1100	SDCo	1108	D1
Starbeam Ln				
	17900	SDCo	1051	F4
Starboard Cir				
	3500	OCSD	1086	F5
Starboard St				
	800	CHLV	1311	H4
	-	CRLB	1126	J7
Starburst Ln				
	2100	SDGO	1350	B1
Starcrest Dr				
	9300	SNTE	1251	B1
Stardust Ln				
	31600	SDCo	1050	D7
	-	SDCo	1070	D3
Starfish Wy				
	-	SDGO	1330	J7
Starflower Rd				
	800	ENCT	1147	G4
Stargaze Av				
	9400	SDGO	1189	D2
Stargaze Ct				
	-	SNMS	1128	C5
Stargaze Dr				
	1500	CHLV	1311	H7
Stargaze Ln				
	29100	SDCo	1070	H6
Stargaze Wy				
	2400	CHLV	1311	H7
Starhaven Ln				
	2500	SDCo	1088	C6
Starkey Wy				
	2500	SDCo	1234	B3
Starland Dr				
	8200	SDCo	1252	C1
Starlight Av				
	5500	OCSD	1067	D6
Starlight Ct				
	2400	CHLV	1331	H1
Starlight Dr				
	1400	ENCT	1167	D2
	7700	SDGO	1227	J5
Starlight Glen				
	2300	ESCN	1109	B4
Starlight Ln				
	9500	SDCo	1271	C1
	-	SNMS	1128	F3
Starlight Mountain Rd				
	24100	SDCo	1153	E5
Starlight Wy				
	7500	SDCo	1156	A7
	7200	SDCo	1175	J1
(See Page 1175)				
Starling Ct				
	1800	CRLB	1127	D7
Starling Dr				
	7700	SDGO	1249	B6
	500	VSTA	1087	G4
Starling Ln				
	200	OCSD	1086	H2
Starling Sight Rd				
	16900	SDCo	1169	G4
Starling Wy				
	500	SNMS	1109	C6
Starmount Wy				
	13300	POWY	1170	E1
Starridge St				
	13700	POWY	1190	D3
Starry Night Dr				
	2800	SDCo	1129	C5
Starry Wy				
	1300	SDGO	1350	G1
Starship St				
	1600	SDCo	1321	A2
(See Page 1321)				
Starside Ln				
	200	OCSD	1107	D2
Starstone Dr				
	600	SNMS	1108	C7
Starstone Pl				
	-	SNMS	1108	D7
Starting Gate Rd				
	-	POWY	1170	H4
Starvale Ln				
	-	SDCo	1153	H2
Starvation Mountain Rd				
	18800	SDCo	1151	B3
Starview Dr				
	8100	SDCo	1252	B1
Starwood				
	-	SDGO	1210	D2
Starwood Cir				
	400	CHLV	1310	F5
Starwood Ln				
	8800	SNTE	1231	E7
State Park Rd				
	-	SDCo	1051	J1
	21000	SDCo	1052	E3
(See Page 1052)				
State Pl				
	300	ESCN	1129	E3
State St				
	1500	CHLV	1331	D2
	2900	CRLB	1106	D5
	2300	ELCN	6499	E6
	200	ELCN	6500	A6
	3600	SDGO	1268	H6
	2400	SDGO	1288	J1
	1800	SDGO	1289	A2
State Tree				
	600	OCSD	1106	C1
Statice Ct				
	-	CRLB	1127	B4
Station Rd				
	31300	SDCo	1091	C2
Station Village Ln				
	-	SDGO	1269	C2
Station Village Wy				
	-	SDGO	1269	C2
Station Wagon Rd				
	-	SDCo	1153	C7
Statton Ct				
	1500	SDGO	1290	F6
Steadman St				
	10100	SDGO	1208	G5
Steamboat Springs Ct				
	2400	CHLV	1311	H7

SAN DIEGO CO.

SAN DIEGO CO.

Street	Block	City	Map#	Grid
Stearman St	-	SDGO	1351	C2
Stebick Ct	12800	SDGO	1188	C6
Steel Ranch Rd	19300	SDCo	1274	F5
Steel St	3200	SDGO	1289	F4
Steele Canyon	3000	SDCo	1272	C6
Steele Canyon Rd	2500	SDCo	1272	C5
Steele St	500	ELCJ	1251	E3
Steelfish Ln	-	OCSD	1086	G2
Steelhead Wy	300	VSTA	1087	F6
Steen Cir	1400	VSTA	1108	A2
Steeple Chase Row	14000	SDGO	1188	D2
Steeple Glen	-	ESCN	1129	F5
Steeplechase Ln	1600	VSTA	1087	D6
Steeplechase Rd	5900	SDCo	1311	B2
Steeplegate Sq	-	SDGO	1188	A6
Stefas Ct	-	CHLV	1331	A2
Steffy Rd	600	SDCo	1152	H7
	200	SDCo	1153	A7
Steiger Ln	2000	OCSD	1106	H1
Steinbeck Av	7200	SDGO	1228	G4
Steinbeck Ct	-	CRLB	1127	A1
Steiner Dr	-	CHLV	1330	J2
Stella Ct	7900	SNTE	1230	H7
Stella Maris Ln	3900	CRLB	1106	G6
Stella St	800	CHLV	1330	A4
Stellar Dr	3300	SDGO	1249	E4
Stephanie Ct	1000	SNMS	1128	E6
Stephanie Ln	100	VSTA	1088	B5
S Stephanie Ln	100	ELCJ	1252	A5
Stephanie Pl	4900	OCSD	1067	A5
Stephanie St	8900	SNMS	1128	E6
Stephens Port	400	SDCo	1047	E3
Stephens St	4100	SDGO	1268	H5
Steppling Av	-	CALX	6680	J2
Sterett Pl	3200	SDGO	1249	C5
Sterling Av	1300	CALX	6620	G7
Sterling Bridge	700	SDCo	1027	G6
Sterling Ct	1500	ESCN	1129	E2
	5100	SDGO	1270	A5
Sterling Dr	7900	SDCo	1252	B2
Sterling Grove Ln	-	SDGO	1208	D1
Sterling Hill Ln	12000	SDCo	1231	J5
Sterling Ridge Ct	2800	CHLV	1311	J6
Sterling View Dr	4200	SDCo	1028	F3
Stern Wy	500	CRLB	1147	A1
Sterne St	3400	SDGO	1268	B7
	3100	SDGO	1288	C1
Stetson Av	3500	SDGO	1228	D5
Stetson Pl	5600	OCSD	1067	F7
	6100	SDGO	1228	D5
Stettler Wy	4100	SDGO	1228	E5
Steuer Wy	-	SDGO	1209	J2
Stevemark Ln	3900	SDCo	1271	E4
Steven Cir	2400	CRLB	1106	H4
Steven Ln	100	OCSD	1086	G2
Steven St	-	BRAW	6319	F4
(See Page 6319)				
Stevens Av	200	SOLB	1167	F7
	600	SOLB	1187	G1
Stevens Ln	3400	SDCo	1271	B5
Stevens Pl	2400	ESCN	1110	C4
Stevens Rd	9300	SNTE	1231	F5
Stevens Vista	15000	SDCo	1172	J6
Stevens West Av	500	SOLB	1167	F7
Stevens Wy	5500	SDGO	1290	B3
Stevenson Ct	1500	SNMS	1109	A3
Stevenson Ranch Ct	2900	CHLV	1311	J1
Stevenson Wy	7600	SDGO	1250	E4
Stewart Canyon Rd	400	SDCo	1028	G3
Stewart Crest Rd	600	SDCo	1028	H3
Stewart Ct	-	CHLV	1331	A2
	1000	SDGO	1289	G6
Stewart Dr	500	VSTA	1087	D7
Stewart Pl	2300	ESCN	1110	C6
Stewart St	1900	OCSD	1106	D3
	-	SDCo	1085	J5
	6200	SDGO	1270	C3
Stewart Wy	-	ENCT	1147	A2
Stickley Ranch	27300	SDCo	1089	E5
Stiles Ct	900	VSTA	1087	F5
Still Brook Ln	15400	SDCo	1050	H3
Stillman Pl	2000	SDGO	1290	G6
Stillwater Cove Wy	800	OCSD	1066	F7
Stillwater Ct	3300	CRLB	1106	J3
Stillwater Glen	1700	ESCN	1109	D4
Stillwater Rd	2300	SDGO	1288	G1
Stillwell Av	1000	SDGO	1290	C5
Stimson Ct	8900	SDGO	1189	C4
Sting Ray Ct	-	SDCo	1085	J5
Stinson Rd	2600	SDCo	1100	B4
(See Page 1100)				
Stipa Ct	8700	SDGO	1189	C6
Stirling Av	2700	CRLB	1107	A5
Stirling Ct	2700	CRLB	1107	A5
Stirrup Rd	2400	SDCo	1079	A2
(See Page 1079)				
Stirrup Wy	5400	OCSD	1067	D7
Stitt Av	-	SDGO	1289	C2
Stockalper Ln	400	SDCo	1152	G5
Stockbridge Rd	9900	SDCo	1169	G4
Stockett Wy	3000	SDGO	1248	C3
Stockman St	3700	NATC	1310	D3
Stockton Ln	2400	SDCo	1087	J1
Stockton Pl	3500	CRLB	1107	A3
Stockwood Cove	11300	SDGO	1210	F1
Stone Calf Ct	-	ImCo	6560	A6
Stone Canyon Rd	-	CHLV	1311	F4
	12800	POWY	1170	C5
Stone Castle	2100	SDCo	1027	G6
Stone Ct	5200	SDGO	1270	A2
Stone Dr	1200	SNMS	1128	E1
Stone Edge Cir	1500	SDCo	1251	G2
Stone Edge Ct	300	SDCo	1251	G2
Stone Edge Dr	300	SDCo	1251	G2
Stone Gate St	-	CHLV	1311	H4
Stone Haven Wy	-	SDGO	1208	E1
Stone Pl	-	POWY	1190	G6
Stone Point Ln	10200	SDCo	1291	E2
Stone Post Wy	700	SDCo	997	G7
Stone St	-	CORD	1329	E5
Stone Valley Pl	2200	ESCN	1109	J4
Stonebridge Ct	3900	SDCo	1167	H4
Stonebridge Ln	3900	SDCo	1167	J3
Stonebridge Pkwy	16600	SDGO	1191	A7
	13600	SDGO	1210	F2
	16600	SDGO	1211	A1
Stonebridge Rd	15300	ESCN	1110	J7
Stonebrook Ln	1800	ENCT	1147	H6
Stonecipher Ln	2500	SDCo	1271	C6
Stonecreek Pl	2100	CHLV	1311	E3
Stonecrest Blvd	-	SDCo	1249	F5
Stonecrest Ct	1900	VSTA	1107	J4
Stonecrest Ln	900	SDCo	1130	B3
Stonecroft Terr	11400	SDGO	1210	E2
Stonedale Ct	11800	SDGO	1210	A2
Stonefield Ct	3500	SDCo	1272	E5
Stonefield Dr	3100	SDCo	1272	E5
Stonegate Ct	-	CHLV	1331	A3
Stonegate Dr	-	SDCo	1090	A1
Stonegate Pl	3500	SDCo	1028	E2
Stonehaven Ct	1600	SDCo	1272	B2
Stonehedge Pl	400	SNMS	1109	B7
Stonehurst Dr	10100	SDCo	1109	E1
Stonemill Dr	12200	POWY	1210	C1
Stonemont Pt	4500	OCSD	1107	D2
Stonepine Ct	11300	SDGO	1210	C7
Stonepine Ln	6600	SDGO	1310	F1
Stonepointe Dr	-	ESCN	1150	D3
Stoneridge	-	CRLB	1107	C3
Stoneridge Cir	1300	ESCN	1129	G7
Stoneridge Country Club Ln	16900	POWY	1170	E3
Stoneridge Ct	400	CHLV	1311	A4
	1300	OCSD	1087	D3
Stoneridge Dr	1100	SDCo	1290	J2
Stoneridge Rd	2300	SDCo	1129	D5
	1000	SDCo	1253	A1
Stoneridge Terr	-	VSTA	1108	A2
Stoneview Ct	7400	SDGO	1250	F3
Stoneview Ln	2500	SDCo	1271	C6
Stonewall Creek Rd	-	SDCo	1196	G3
(See Page 1196)				
Stonewall Ln	1900	SDCo	1088	C4
Stonewood Wy	1200	SDGO	1350	B1
Stoney Acres Rd	16000	POWY	1170	E4
Stoney Creek Ct	10800	SNTE	1231	E2
Stoney Creek Rd	13500	SDGO	1189	G3
Stoney Gate Pl	13700	SDGO	1189	J3
	14000	SDGO	1190	A2
Stoney Ln	15800	SDCo	1175	J3
(See Page 1175)				
Stoney Oak Dr	3100	SDCo	1292	C1
(See Page 1292)				
Stoney Peak Dr	11700	SDGO	1190	A1
Stoney Point Wy	400	OCSD	1086	B6
Stoney Spring Pl	-	CHLV	1331	B1
Stoney Wy	-	SDGO	1209	G1
Stoney's Ln	900	ELCJ	1251	G3
Stoneybrae Pl	600	ESCN	1110	D5
Stoneybrae Wy	-	ESCN	1110	D5
Stoneybrook Ln	-	SDCo	1232	E7
Stonington Wy	-	SDCo	1089	D3
Stony Knoll Rd	200	SDCo	1252	B5
Stony Ridge Ct	-	SDGO	1209	G1
Stony Ridge Wy	-	SDGO	1209	G1
Stonyhurst Ct	-	VSTA	1087	H5
Stork St	500	SDGO	1290	D3
Stormy Ln	1700	VSTA	1088	B3
Stotler Ct	12500	POWY	1190	D7
Stoutwood St	-	POWY	1190	C1
Stow Grove Av	1500	CHLV	1331	C2
Stowe Dr	12400	POWY	1190	C6
Stoyer Dr	9400	SNTE	1231	B5
Strada Fragante	6200	SDCo	1148	D6
Strada Ranch Rd	3900	SDCo	1135	E6
Straightaway Ct	1000	OCSD	1067	B3
Strand St	600	CRLB	1126	J5
Strand Wy	1600	CORD	1308	J1
	1800	CORD	1309	A1
	4100	SDGO	1247	H7
Strandway	3800	SDGO	1247	H7
	3300	SDGO	1267	H2
Stransburg Ct	4600	OCSD	1107	F3
Strata Dr	-	CRLB	1107	B4
Strata St	-	CHLV	1331	G2
Stratford Cir	4500	OCSD	1107	D2
Stratford Ct	1300	DLMR	1187	F5
	1200	SNMS	1128	B3
Stratford Dr	700	ENCT	1147	C7
	1000	ENCT	1167	C1
Stratford Knoll	800	ENCT	1148	A6
Stratford Ln	1100	CRLB	1106	E4
Stratford Park Ct	200	DLMR	1187	G7
Stratford Wy	1600	DLMR	1187	E4
Stratton Av	4400	SDGO	1289	H5
Stratus Ct	7200	SDGO	1250	D5
Strawberry Creek St	-	CHLV	1331	A2
Strawberry Glen	800	ESCN	1150	C1
Strawberry Hill Ln	-	SDCo	1067	J7
Strawberry Ln	10300	SDCo	1291	E2
Strawberry Pl	-	CRLB	1127	A5
	3500	OCSD	1107	A2
Strawberry Valley Dr	-	CHLV	1311	D6
Streamview Dr	5500	SDGO	1270	B6
Streamview Pl	3400	SDGO	1270	A6
Streamwood Ct	16300	SDCo	1169	B2
Street E	-	SNMS	1128	H1
Stresemann St	5600	SDGO	1228	B6
Stromberg Cir	2400	CRLB	1106	H5
Stromesa Ct	7900	SDGO	1209	B6
Strong Dr	3800	SDGO	1248	J3
Strothe Rd	-	SDGO	1288	A4
Struedle Ct	1300	SDGO	1350	A2
Stu Ct	4200	SDGO	1330	F7
Stuart Av	7000	LMSA	1270	E4
Stuart Mesa Rd	-	SDCo	1085	H2
Studio Ln	4500	OCSD	1087	B2
Sturgeon Ct	4200	SDGO	1188	B5
Sturgess Av	7500	LMSA	1270	G4
Sturnella Wy	-	SDCo	1070	G4
Sturtevant St	-	SDGO	1289	E7
Styles Pl	-	SDCo	1169	E2
Stylus Dr	-	SDGO	1269	B1
Stylus St	2000	CHLV	1331	G1
Su Siempre Pl	2900	ESCN	1150	B1
Subida Al Cielo	2100	SDCo	1088	C1
Subida Ter	2000	CRLB	1147	F1
Subol Ct	2700	SDGO	1330	C6
Suburban Hills Dr	1100	SDCo	1130	C4
Success Av	9300	SDGO	1249	E4
Success St	200	CRLB	1126	H4
Sudan Rd	13100	POWY	1190	G4
Sudy St	9100	LMSA	1251	B6
Sue St	3300	SDGO	1270	B6
Suemark Ter	1900	VSTA	1088	C4
Suerich Ln	7100	LMGR	1270	F6
Suerte Del Este	19600	SDCo	1148	F3
Suffolk Dr	3600	SDGO	1270	E5
Sugar Bush Ct	-	CHLV	1331	G3
Sugar Bush Wy	27000	SDCo	1090	E5
Sugar Maple Pl	1600	CHLV	1331	J1
Sugar Pine Ln	2500	SDCo	1028	E7
Sugar Pine Pl	1400	CHLV	1311	J6
Sugar Pine Rd	1700	CRLB	1127	E6
Sugar Pine St	700	OCSD	1086	F1
Sugar Pine Wy	27800	SDCo	1089	F4
Sugarbush Dr	1000	SDCo	1088	E7
	1000	SDCo	1108	E1
Sugarbush Ter	-	SDCo	1088	E7
Sugarloaf Dr	900	ESCN	1109	F7
Sugarman Ct	2800	SDGO	1227	J4
Sugarman Dr	8500	SDGO	1228	A4
Sugarman Wy	2800	SDGO	1227	J4
Sugarplum Wy	-	SDCo	1174	B5
Sugunto Pl	1700	CHLV	1331	D3
Sukat Ct	32300	SDCo	1051	A6
Sukat Trl	32300	SDCo	1051	A6
Sula Wy	2700	SDGO	1310	F1
Sullivan Av	6300	SDGO	1290	D4
Sullivan Ct	-	CHLV	1331	A1
Sullivan Ln	-	SDCo	1231	H5
Sully Wy	10200	SDGO	1209	D5
Sultana St	2000	SDGO	1290	B1
Sumac Ct	3200	SDCo	1048	F2
Sumac Dr	2400	SDGO	1269	H7
	2300	SDGO	1289	H1
Sumac Ln	800	CRLB	1127	A6
Sumac Pl	1500	CHLV	1311	J7
	4800	OCSD	1067	A7
Sumac Rd	2800	SDCo	1048	G1
Sumac Summit	-	SDCo	998	E3
Sumac Terr	15500	SDCo	1051	A7
Sumac View	-	SDCo	1089	B3
Sumac Wy	800	ESCN	1110	B7
Sumatra Ln	100	SDGO	1290	F5
Summer Ann Pl	-	SDGO	1249	D1
Summer Bloom Ln	2100	SDCo	1028	A3
Summer Creek Ct	1500	VSTA	1088	A4
Summer Ct	-	IMPE	6439	G4
	1000	SDCo	1251	H2
	1300	VSTA	1088	A2
Summer Dr	4400	OCSD	1087	D6
Summer Glen Rd	1000	SDCo	1152	D5
Summer Glen Vista	13600	SDCo	1232	E5
Summer Holly Ln	900	ENCT	1147	J5
Summer Land Rd	-	SDCo	1068	C5
Summer Moon Rd	800	SNMS	1128	F6
Summer Place Dr	-	ELCJ	1251	H2
Summer Sage Dr	15700	POWY	1170	G5
Summer Sage Rd	16300	POWY	1170	G3
Summer Set Wy	3300	OCSD	1106	H1
Summer Sky St	1700	CHLV	1331	H1
Summer View Cir	600	ENCT	1147	D7
Summer Wy	3900	ESCN	1150	C3
Summerbreeze Ln	12200	SDGO	1170	B7
Summerbreeze Wy	14800	SDGO	1190	B1
Summercreek Wy	2300	ESCN	1129	E6
Summercrest Ln	8700	SNTE	1231	D7
Summerdale Rd	8600	SDGO	1209	C3
Summerdale Wy	10900	SDGO	1209	C3
Summerdawn Pl	1500	ENCT	1147	G4
Summerfield Ct	3600	SDCo	1271	C5
Summerfield Dr	3600	SDCo	1271	C5
Summerfield Ln	12600	POWY	1170	D3
Summerfield Pl	800	ESCN	1130	E1
Summerfield St	9500	SDCo	1271	C5
Summerhill Av	-	CHLV	1311	G5
Summerhill Ct	800	ENCT	1147	F4
	400	SDCo	1233	F7
Summerhill Dr	2300	ENCT	1147	H5
	5100	OCSD	1087	C2
Summerhill Ln	2300	SDCo	1027	G7
Summerhill Pt	9000	SDCo	1233	F5
Summerhill Ter	400	SDCo	1233	F6
Summerhill View	400	SDCo	1233	F6
Summerholly Dr	500	SNMS	1128	G3
Summerland St	1500	CHLV	1331	D2
Summers Ridge Rd	9700	SDGO	1208	H6
Summerset Wy	3600	CRLB	1107	A3
Summershade Ln	11300	SDGO	1209	E2
Summerside Ln	200	ENCT	1147	J7
Summersong Ct	800	ENCT	1147	H5
Summersong Ln	700	ENCT	1147	H5
Summersun Ln	9800	SDCo	1231	J4
Summersun Pl	9800	SDCo	1231	J4
Summertime Dr	1600	SDCo	1251	F1
Summertree Ln	9900	SNTE	1231	D7
Summerview Ct	10100	SDGO	1209	D5
Summerview Wy	4100	OCSD	1087	C7
Summerwind Pl	2300	CRLB	1107	A7
Summerwood Ct	10400	SDGO	1210	A3
Summerwood Ln	8000	LMGR	1270	H7
Summit Av	1400	ENCT	1167	C2
	500	SDCo	1027	E3
	10800	SNTE	1231	D1
Summit Cir	13300	POWY	1170	E6
	9600	SDCo	1271	C1
Summit Circle Glen N	2400	ESCN	1109	B4
Summit Circle Glen S	2300	ESCN	1109	B4
Summit Cove Ln	1200	ENCT	1167	C1
Summit Crest	-	SDCo	1130	F6
Summit Crest Dr	10200	SNTE	1231	D1
Summit Dr	1400	CHLV	1311	B5
	4400	LMSA	1270	H3
	1900	SDCo	1130	D4
	9600	SDCo	1271	C1
Summit Glen	2500	ESCN	1109	B3
Summit Hill Dr	-	SDCo	1130	E4
Summit Ln	-	SDCo	1130	F6
	24500	SDCo	1236	A2
	100	SDCo	1253	D1
Summit Meadow Rd	-	SDCo	1291	B7
Summit Pl	1200	SDCo	1130	D5
	4300	SDGO	1268	J4
Summit Point	-	SNMS	1128	A3
Summit Ridge Dr	1900	SDCo	1130	E4
Summit Ridge Wy	6700	SDGO	1250	D4
Summit St	400	OCSD	1086	A7
	-	SDGO	1290	D3
Summit Trail Ct	3500	CRLB	1107	B6
Summit Trl	1000	SDCo	1130	D5
	1300	VSTA	1108	A1
Summit Vista Dr	16700	SDCo	1169	E3
Summit Wy	8300	SDGO	1249	B7
Summitside Ln	10000	SDCo	1271	E6
Summitview Ln	2600	SDCo	1271	E6
Sumner Av	1100	SDCo	1251	H3
Sumner Ct	-	SDCo	1251	H3
Sumner Pl	1000	SDCo	1251	J3
Sumner Wy	600	OCSD	1086	G1
Sumter St	3300	SDGO	1248	E5
Sun And Shadows Dr	400	SDCo	1078	G2
(See Page 1078)				
Sun And Shadows Ln	2500	SDCo	1078	H2
(See Page 1078)				
Sun Cir	600	VSTA	1107	J3
Sun Ct	300	SDCo	1251	F1
Sun Dial Ter	1500	SDCo	1252	A2
Sun Energy Rd	-	SDCo	1091	C3
Sun King Rd	-	SDGO	1209	D6
Sun Maiden Ct	18100	SDGO	1149	H7
Sun Meadow Dr	600	ELCJ	1271	E1
Sun St	6900	SDGO	1248	J6
Sun Summit Pt	16000	SDGO	1169	J4
Sun Up Ct	5800	SDCo	1311	B1
Sun Valley Ln	15100	SDCo	1168	A7
Sun Valley Rd	2200	CHLV	1311	G6
	-	SDCo	1167	J6
	4800	SDCo	1168	A7
	-	SNMS	1128	A2
	1400	SOLB	1167	J6
Sun Villa Ct	-	VSTA	1088	C6
Sun Walk Ct	17800	SDGO	1169	H1
Sunbeam Ln	300	SDCo	1027	F4
Sunbird Ct	300	SNMS	1108	J7
Sunbird Wy	3500	SDGO	1249	G3
Sunbright Ct	5000	OCSD	1087	E2
Sunbright Dr	-	OCSD	1087	E3
Sunbrite Ln	-	SDCo	1232	A4
Sunburst Dr	4500	OCSD	1087	D5
	1600	SDCo	1252	A2
Sunburst Ln	500	CHLV	1330	H2
Sunburst Rd	4600	CRLB	1106	H7
Sunbury Ct	1500	SDCo	1108	B2
Sunbury St	1800	ESCN	1109	D5
Suncreek Dr	700	CHLV	1311	E4
Suncrest Av	1900	OCSD	1087	E2
Suncrest Blvd	3200	SDCo	1252	G4
Suncrest Ct	5000	OCSD	1087	E2
Suncrest Dr	7800	LMSA	1270	H3
	2900	SDGO	1269	E3
Suncrest Vista Ln	1500	SDCo	1234	D6
Suncup Wy	7800	CRLB	1147	E2
Sundale Rd	1500	SDCo	1272	A2
Sundance Av	12700	SDGO	1189	C5
Sundance Cir	2300	OCSD	1087	D5
Sundance Ct	700	CHLV	1330	H1
	9000	SDGO	1189	D4
Sundance Dr	2200	SDCo	1028	A6
Sundance Rd	13400	SDCo	1070	D1
	-	SDCo	1171	G1
Sundance View Ln	23800	SDCo	1235	H1
Sundance Wy	1400	OCSD	1067	E6
Sunday Dr	13200	SDCo	1090	E3
Sunderland St	12900	POWY	1190	H5
Sundevil Wy	9800	SDGO	1189	E3
Sundial Ct	1000	OCSD	1067	A4
Sundial Ln	-	CRLB	1127	A7
Sundown Dr	16600	SDCo	1051	C7
Sundown Glen	1300	ESCN	1109	G7
	1200	ESCN	1129	G1
Sundown Ln	1100	CHLV	1330	H1
	4000	SDCo	1271	G4
N Sundown Ln	3400	OCSD	1107	C2
S Sundown Ln	3500	OCSD	1107	C2
Sundowner Ct	1400	SDGO	1209	D6
Sundrift Ct	-	OCSD	1087	F2
Sundrop Ct	1200	CHLV	1330	H2
Sunfish Ln	-	OCSD	1086	G2
Sunfish Wy	2400	SDCo	1297	G4
(See Page 1297)				
Sunflower Ct	-	ELCN	6559	J3
Sunflower Glen	300	ESCN	1109	H5
Sunflower Glen Ct	3100	SDCo	1272	D5
Sunflower Ln	-	IMPE	6499	D2
Sunflower St	700	ENCT	1147	E6
Sunflower Ter	2400	SDCo	1108	B4
Sunflower Wy	800	CRLB	1127	A5
Sunglow Ct	-	OCSD	1087	E2
	5300	SDGO	1228	H7
Sunglow Dr	-	OCSD	1087	E2
	12500	SDCo	1232	B7
Sungold Wy	800	ESCN	1110	D5
Sungrove Ct	1700	SDCo	1272	B2
Sunhaven Ct	2900	SDCo	1234	C6
Sunhaven Rd	1300	SDCo	1234	C6
Sunkist Dr	2800	SDCo	1088	D7
Sunlight Ct	1900	OCSD	1087	F2
Sunlight St	1300	CALX	6620	D7
Sunline Av	4900	SDGO	1228	C7
	4900	SDGO	1248	C1
Sunlit Wy	100	SDCo	1152	J5
Sunmeadow Rd	5000	OCSD	1087	E3
Sunningdale Dr	700	OCSD	1066	G7
Sunningdale Wy	-	SDCo	1090	G4
Sunny Acres Ln	4800	SDCo	1168	B7
Sunny Brae Dr	6600	SDGO	1250	F5
Sunny Brae Pl	7100	SDGO	1250	F6
Sunny Creek Rd	5000	CRLB	1107	F6
Sunny Crest Cir	1200	VSTA	1087	J4
Sunny Crest Ln	1700	CHLV	1311	C4
Sunny Dr	-	ENCT	1147	C6
Sunny Heights Rd	-	SDCo	998	C7
Sunny Hill Ct	-	SDCo	1027	H1
Sunny Hills Rd	4700	OCSD	1087	D4
Sunny Ln	13400	SDCo	1232	D4
Sunny Meadow Ct	10900	SDGO	1208	J3
Sunny Meadow St	10800	SDGO	1208	J3
Sunny Mesa Rd	-	SDGO	1208	G3
Sunny Pt	1300	SDCo	1135	D4
Sunny Slope Dr	1900	SDCo	1130	D4
Sunny Slope Ln	9700	SDCo	1149	D4
Sunny Slope Ter	1800	SDCo	1130	D4
Sunny Summit Dr	-	SDCo	1169	B3
Sunny View Dr	5700	SDCo	1311	A1
Sunny Vista Ln	1900	SDCo	1108	H2
Sunnyacres Av	1300	SDCo	1234	G5
Sunnybrook Ln	200	SDCo	1232	J7
	-	SDCo	1252	J1
Sunnycrest Ln	2000	SDCo	1028	A6
Sunnydale Ct	11200	SDGO	1169	H4
Sunnyfield Pl	15800	SDGO	1169	H4
Sunnyhill Dr	3900	CRLB	1106	H5
Sunnyland Av	1400	ELCJ	1252	A6
Sunnyridge Dr	-	SDCo	1089	B2
Sunnyridge Rd	-	SNTE	1230	F7
Sunnyside Av	2100	SDCo	1252	C5
	500	SDGO	1290	H3
	1600	SNMS	1128	E6
Sunnyside Ct	-	ImCo	6560	C7
Sunnyside Dr	5100	SDCo	1310	H1
Sunnyside Ln	-	SDCo	1089	H6
Sunray Ln	4200	SDCo	1271	G3
Sunray Pl	10900	SDCo	1271	G3
Sunrich Ln	800	ENCT	1147	C3
Sunridge Dr	400	OCSD	1087	E2
	8600	SNTE	1230	H7
Sunridge Pl	400	ESCN	1109	G4
Sunrise Av	8400	LMSA	1270	J3
Sunrise Bluff Dr	1700	SDGO	1350	J2
Sunrise Canyon Rd	14600	POWY	1190	H3

SAN DIEGO CO.

San Diego County Street Index

STREET / Block City Map# Grid

Sunrise Cir
1500 CRLB 1106 G6
300 SDCo 1088 C6
Sunrise Crest Ct
2800 CHLV 1312 A5
(See Page 1312)
Sunrise Ct
- IMPE 6439 F4
12200 POWY 1190 B1
Sunrise Dr
14800 POWY 1170 B7
1900 SDCo 1088 C6
1200 SDCo 1136 D6
200 SDGO 1350 G5
1400 VSTA 1088 B7
E Sunrise Dr
700 SDCo 1088 C7
Sunrise Hills Dr
4800 SDCo 1271 H2
Sunrise Hwy
16000 SDCo 1176 G3
(See Page 1176)
15200 SDCo 1177 A5
(See Page 1177)
12800 SDCo 1197 G5
(See Page 1197)
11400 SDCo 1218 C4
7600 SDCo 1237 F5
Sunrise Ln
8600 LMSA 1270 J3
Sunrise Mountain Dr
1200 SDCo 1109 J3
Sunrise Mountain Rd
400 SDCo 1252 J3
Sunrise Pl
400 SDCo 1088 B6
Sunrise Ranch Ln
2200 SDCo 1297 H7
(See Page 1297)
Sunrise Ranch Rd
- POWY 1190 G2
Sunrise Rd
600 SDCo 1078 J3
(See Page 1078)
Sunrise Ridge
4700 OCSD 1087 D4
Sunrise Shadow Ct
1500 ELCJ 1252 A7
Sunrise St
3300 SDGO 1289 F3
Sunrise Summit
- SDCo 1231 H6
Sunrise Trail Pl
- CHLV 1311 G2
Sunrise Valley Dr
4800 SDCo 1271 H2
Sunrise View Dr
2100 SDCo 1048 A1
Sunrise Vista
16800 SDCo 1151 E6
Sunrise Wy
- ESCN 1129 H7
1100 SNMS 1128 E3
Sunroad Blvd
- SDCo 1352 A1
Sunroad Centrum Ln
4900 SDGO 1249 C2
Sunrose Crest Wy
6200 SDGO 1188 F3
Sunrose Ct
5000 OCSD 1087 E3
Sunset Av
9500 SDCo 1271 C1
2300 SDGO 1350 B3
Sunset Bluffs Wy
4400 SDGO 1188 B5
Sunset Blvd
- CALX 6620 E5
2000 SDGO 1268 G5
Sunset Canyon Dr
3000 SDGO 1248 F5
Sunset Cliffs Blvd
1400 SDGO 1267 H7
- SDGO 1268 A5
800 SDGO 1287 H2
Sunset Crest Wy
- SDGO 1208 F3
Sunset Crossing Pt
1000 SDGO 1331 A7
Sunset Ct
800 SDGO 1267 H1
600 SNMS 1108 J5
Sunset Dr
600 BRAW 6259 H7
(See Page 6259)
1800 ELCN 6499 D6
200 ENCT 1147 B6
1900 ESCN 1130 A5
- IMPE 6439 F3
7700 LMSA 1270 G2
600 OCSD 1085 J5
15700 POWY 1170 H5
3300 SDCo 1047 H2
1400 SDCo 1107 F2
2200 SDCo 1130 B6
2200 SDCo 1136 C6
3400 SDCo 1156 E1
3600 SDGO 1150 B3
2100 VSTA 1107 D2
Sunset Grove Rd
1300 SDCo 1047 J2
Sunset Heights Ct
4700 SDGO 1188 C5
Sunset Heights Rd
1000 ESCN 1109 E6
Sunset Hill Dr
1800 CRLB 1106 H7
Sunset Hills
2600 SDCo 1150 D1
Sunset Knolls Rd
11600 SDCo 1231 H4
Sunset Ln
35400 SDCo 1156 F7
3400 SDGO 1350 E3
Sunset Mountain Wy
14600 POWY 1170 H5
Sunset Oaks Dr
19400 SDCo 1153 D2
Sunset Point Ct
1600 CHLV 1330 J4
Sunset Point Rd
- POWY 1170 J1
Sunset Pt
- SDCo 1234 A6
Sunset Pt Pl
13000 SDGO 1188 C5
Sunset Pt Wy
13100 SDGO 1188 C5
Sunset Rd
- SDCo 1071 B7
500 SDCo 1078 H3
(See Page 1078)
28300 SDCo 1091 B1
8300 SDCo 1231 J7
8300 SDCo 1251 J1
Sunset Ridge Ct
- POWY 1150 J7
Sunset Ridge Dr
10900 SDGO 1210 A2
Sunset Ridge Pl
800 CHLV 1311 J3
Sunset Rose Ct
1700 SDCo 1272 B2
Sunset St
900 CALX 6620 D7
2900 SDGO 1268 F4
Sunset Ter
- LMGR 1290 H2
16200 SDCo 1091 B1
Sunset Valley Rd
- SDCo 1233 J3
Sunset View Dr
2300 SDCo 1136 A7
Sunset View Rd
13600 POWY 1190 G3
Sunset Vista Ln
27400 SDCo 1091 E3
Sunset Wy
16100 SDCo 1071 B7
N Sunshine Av
100 ELCJ 1251 F5
S Sunshine Av
600 ELCJ 1251 F6
Sunshine Ct
1300 CALX 6620 D7
Sunshine Ln
100 SNMS 1108 H6
Sunshine Mountain Rd
2100 SDCo 1108 H1
Sunshine Peak Ct
- SDGO 1190 A7
- SDGO 1210 A1
Sunshine St
900 ELCJ 1251 F7
Sunshine Trl
1300 SDCo 1136 C5
Sunshine Valley Ln
- SDCo 1153 G3
Sunshine Valley Rd
- SDCo 1153 G2
Sunshine Wy
- IMPE 6439 G4
Sunstone Dr
16400 SDCo 1169 F4
Sunstone Pt
13100 SDGO 1188 E5
Sunswept St
200 SDGO 1290 F5
Suntree Pl
8400 SDGO 1250 J2
Sunview Dr
8300 SDCo 1232 B7
Sunview Pl
1100 OCSD 1067 B3
Sunwest Glen
100 ESCN 1130 A6
Sunwood Dr
8900 SNTE 1231 B6
Sunwood Trl
12200 POWY 1190 B6
Supale Ranch Rd
38400 SDCo 997 B5
Superba St
3800 SDGO 1289 G4
Superior Hollow Rd
12800 SDCo 1070 B4
Superior St
600 ESCN 1129 E3
3800 SDGO 1289 G4
Supreme Ct
300 SNMS 1129 B3
Surco Dr
11400 SDGO 1209 B1
Surf Crest Dr
- SDGO 1350 H1
Surf Crest St
6600 CRLB 1127 C5
Surf Pl
3500 OCSD 1107 C2
Surf Rd
1500 ENCT 1147 A3
Surf Shoal Pt
- SDGO 1350 J1
Surf View Ct
200 DLMR 1187 F6
Surface Navy Blvd
- NATC 1309 F1
Surfbird Cir
- CRLB 1127 C6
Surfbird Wy
900 OCSD 1087 A3
Surfbreaker Pt
- SDGO 1350 J1
Surfcliff Pt
- SDGO 1350 J1
Surfline Pl
3600 OCSD 1107 C3
Surfpoint Wy
- SDGO 1350 J1
Surfrider Wy
200 OCSD 1085 J7
600 OCSD 1086 A7
5500 SDGO 1351 A2
Surfside Dr
- SDGO 1350 J1
Surfside Ln
6500 CRLB 1126 H5
Surftide Ln
- SDGO 1350 J1
Surfwood Ln
- SDGO 1350 J1
Surrealist Ct
4800 OCSD 1087 B2
Surrey Ct
1500 OCSD 1067 F6
Surrey Dr
300 CHLV 1310 G4
- POWY 1190 F1
Surrey Heights
1400 SDCo 1027 H4
Surrey Hills Ct
17000 POWY 1170 D2
Surrey Ln
2700 SDCo 1129 C3
Surrey Pl
200 CHLV 1310 G4
Surrey Trl
800 SDCo 1138 B7
(See Page 1138)
Survey Pt
13000 SDGO 1187 J5
Susan Cir
3000 OCSD 1107 B2
Susan Ct
2000 SDCo 1109 E6
- SDGO 1350 E1
Susan Pl
2200 SDGO 1290 A1
Susana Ct
1000 SDCo 1128 C3
Susanna Ct
2300 SDCo 1028 B6
Susanville Av
1300 CHLV 1331 C1
Susie Ln
10800 SNTE 1231 E3
Susie Pl
10400 SNTE 1231 E3
Susie Wy
- SDCo 1172 C2
Susita Ct
11100 SDGO 1169 J7
Susita St
15100 SDGO 1169 J7
Susita Ter
11100 SDGO 1169 J7
Susquehanna Pl
4300 SDGO 1248 E1
Sussex Dr
4800 SDGO 1269 G3
Sutherland St
3500 SDGO 1268 G6
Sutter Buttes St
1400 CHLV 1311 E7
Sutter Ct
3600 OCSD 1107 E4
400 SNMS 1109 C7
Sutter Ln
1100 SNMS 1109 C7
Sutter Mill Rd
13400 POWY 1190 H4
Sutter Ridge Ct
1000 CHLV 1311 J4
Sutter Ridge Dr
2700 CHLV 1311 J4
Sutter St
2600 CRLB 1106 J5
1600 SDGO 1268 H5
Sutton Ct
9700 SNTE 1231 B4
Sutton Hill Pl
700 SDCo 1027 H3
Suzanne Ln
- CHLV 1330 E4
700 SDCo 1129 E2
Svea Ct
1600 LMGR 1290 G2
Swalero Rd
6200 LMSA 1251 A6
Swallow Dr
1700 ELCJ 1251 C2
900 VSTA 1087 G4
Swallow Ln
1900 CRLB 1127 E5
100 OCSD 1086 H2
Swallowtail Ct
- ENCT 1147 D2
Swallowtail Rd
1600 ENCT 1147 D2
Swamis Ln
400 ENCT 1147 D7
Swan Canyon Ct
10500 SDGO 1210 C2
Swan Canyon Pl
10500 SDGO 1210 C1
Swan Canyon Rd
11300 SDGO 1210 C1
Swan Dr
29900 SDCo 1297 F5
(See Page 1297)
Swan Lake Dr
- SDGO 1209 G1
Swan Rd
18600 SDCo 1153 E5
Swan St
1700 SDGO 1290 D1
Swaner St
1000 SDGO 1290 C2
Swansea Glen
400 ESCN 1110 D7
Swansea Pl
10900 SDGO 1209 A3
Swanson Ct
11100 SDGO 1209 J1
Swanton Dr
10100 SNTE 1231 A3
Swarthmore St
5300 LMSA 1270 G1
Swartz Canyon Rd
16200 SDCo 1173 E3
Swath Ct
9900 SDGO 1189 F5
Swath Pl
12900 SDGO 1189 F4
Sweeny Ct
1600 SDCo 1272 E2
Sweet Alice Ln
100 ENCT 1147 E7
Sweet Fennel Rd
- SDCo 1128 G3
Sweet Gum Pl
1600 CHLV 1311 J7
Sweet Leilani Ln
16600 SDCo 1168 J2
Sweet Lime Rd
- SDCo 1068 A5
Sweet Ln
- SDCo 1153 G6
Sweet Pea Ln
2200 CHLV 1331 G3
Sweet Pea Pl
- ENCT 1147 C5
Sweet Sage St
2400 CHLV 1331 H1
Sweet Tree Ln
- SDCo 1068 D5
Sweet Willow Wy
11500 SDGO 1210 H1
Sweetbriar Cir
- CRLB 1127 A4
Sweetbriar Ln
11800 SDGO 1210 A2
Sweetgrass Ct
2500 SDCo 1048 A6
Sweetgrass Ln
4800 SDCo 1048 A6
Sweetshade St
- OCSD 1086 G1
Sweetwater Dr
1800 LMGR 1290 J1
Sweetwater Glen
- ESCN 1129 G1
Sweetwater Ln
1300 SDCo 1291 B2
Sweetwater Pl
2100 SDCo 1290 J1
Sweetwater Rd
3200 LMGR 1270 J6
1800 LMGR 1290 J2
2800 NATC 1310 D3
5600 SDCo 1290 J6
700 SDCo 1291 A3
3500 SDCo 1310 E3
Sweetwater River Rd
- SDCo 1253 F7
Sweetwater Springs Blvd
3000 SDCo 1271 E7
2500 SDCo 1291 F1
Sweetwater St
6900 CRLB 1126 J6
Sweetwater Wy
3300 LMGR 1270 J5
Sweetway Ct
8300 SDCo 1290 H6
Sweetwood St
200 SDGO 1290 E4
Swenerick Dr
- SDCo 1211 G7
Swift Av
4300 SDGO 1269 F4
Swift Ln
1400 ELCJ 1251 D2
Swinging V Rd
3300 SDCo 1079 A6
(See Page 1079)
Switzer Dr
8900 SDCo 1271 A5
Switzer St
- SDGO 1289 B4
Switzerland Dr
1200 SDGO 1350 A1
Sword Wy
13600 SDGO 1188 C4
Sybil Ct
1200 SDCo 1109 E6
Sycamore
- SDCo 1089 B3
Sycamore Av
100 CRLB 1106 E6
14200 POWY 1190 F2
800 SDCo 1108 B4
2000 VSTA 1107 H7
400 VSTA 1108 B4
Sycamore Canyon Rd
15900 POWY 1190 J5
16200 SDCo 1191 C6
16300 SDCo 1211 C1
Sycamore Creek Ln
300 SNMS 1108 J2
Sycamore Creek Rd
20000 SDGO 1150 D5
Sycamore Crest Pl
3100 ESCN 1110 G7
Sycamore Ct
1000 IMPE 6439 F4
- SDGO 1228 A4
2200 VSTA 1108 B4
Sycamore Dr
300 BRAW 6319 G2
(See Page 6319)
1600 CHLV 1330 F5
2600 OCSD 1087 F5
1200 SDCo 1047 J2
24600 SDCo 1236 A2
4100 SDGO 1269 H7
3900 SDGO 1289 H1
2100 SNMS 1108 J1
1900 SNMS 1109 A2
Sycamore Heights
1300 SDCo 1047 J2
Sycamore Heights Pl
3100 ESCN 1110 G7
Sycamore Landfill Rd
- SDGO 1230 G5
Sycamore Ln
3000 ESCN 1130 C7
53000 SDCo 1029 G2
900 SDCo 1252 C3
Sycamore Park Dr
- SDCo 1191 E6
Sycamore Pl
1000 VSTA 1107 F2
Sycamore Rd
300 SDGO 1350 G5
Sycamore Ridge Ct
- SDGO 1210 C3
Sycamore Springs Rd
20500 SDCo 1314 J1
(See Page 1314)
Sycamore Test Rd
- SDGO 1210 C3
Sycamore Trail Rd
15000 SDGO 1210 H2
Sycamore Tree Ln
13000 POWY 1190 E3
Sycamore Valley Rd
- POWY 1191 A4
Sycamore Wy
1400 SDCo 1047 J2
Sycamoreview Dr
1100 ENCT 1167 F1
Sychar Rd
100 SDGO 1290 F4
Sycuan Oaks Dr
- SDCo 1253 B4
Sycuan Rd
- SDCo 1253 C6
Sycuan Summit Dr
- SDCo 1252 H6
Sydney Ct
9000 SDGO 1228 E2
Sydney Ln
- SDGO 1209 E2
Sydney Pl
3500 SDGO 1269 F2
Sydney Rae Pl
13400 SDGO 1189 A3
Sydney Ter
- ELCJ 1252 B2
Sydney View Wy
- SDCo 1028 D2
Sylvan St
3000 SDCo 1109 H2
Sylvester Rd
- SDGO 1288 A7
- SDGO 1308 A1
Sylvia Ct
- IMPE 6499 H2
Sylvia St
400 ENCT 1147 B6
3000 SDCo 1290 J7
Sylvie Ct
700 SDCo 1088 F7
Sylvis Wy
700 SNMS 1108 C7
Sylvy Wy
2700 SDGO 1310 F1
Syme Dr
3900 CRLB 1106 G6
Symphony Pl
1100 ESCN 1129 F5
Syracuse Av
3400 SDGO 1228 D6
Syracuse Ct
3600 SDGO 1228 D6
Syracuse Ln
6200 SDGO 1228 D6
Syracuse Wy
6100 SDGO 1228 D6
Syrah Ln
200 SNMS 1108 J6

T

T Anchor Dr
600 SDCo 1078 H3
(See Page 1078)
T Av
400 NATC 1290 A7
N T Av
100 NATC 1290 A6
T Boman St
1200 CALX 6680 J2
T St
3800 SDGO 1289 G5
Tabby Ln
1100 ESCN 1109 J7
Taber Ct
- CHLV 1331 A2
Taber Dr
- CHLV 1331 A2
Taberna Vista Wy
600 SDCo 1233 G4
Table Rock Av
- CHLV 1311 H4
Table Rock Wy
- CHLV 1311 H4
Tablero Ct
17300 SDGO 1169 H2
Tablero Pl
17200 SDGO 1169 H1
Tacayme Dr
4800 OCSD 1067 A7
Tacayme Pl
4900 OCSD 1067 A7
Tacoma Ln
1700 VSTA 1088 B4
Tacoma St
4200 SDGO 1248 D3
Taecker Rd
800 ImCo 6260 J7
(See Page 6260)
Taegan Ln
1600 ENCT 1167 G1
Taffy Ln
11000 SNTE 1231 F5
Taft Av
300 ELCJ 1251 G6
1300 ESCN 1109 H7
4500 SDCo 1271 F3
5400 SDGO 1247 G4
Taft Cir
100 OCSD 1067 B6
Taft St
1600 LMGR 1290 G2
Tag Ln
500 SDCo 1152 G6
Tagota Ct
9100 SDCo 1232 E6
Tahiti Dr
- ESCN 1129 J5
Tahoe St
2900 ELCJ 1251 A5
Taia Ln
11800 SDCo 1251 J1
Tail Creek Dr
- IMPE 6439 F3
Tait St
1000 OCSD 1106 B2
6500 SDGO 1268 H1
S Tait St
1300 OCSD 1106 B2
Takishla Pl
32200 SDCo 1051 A6
Talbot Av
9100 SDGO 1229 C2
Talbot Ct
1800 CHLV 1331 F2
Talbot St
3800 SDGO 1287 J2
2800 SDGO 1288 B3
Talca Av
13800 SDGO 1189 C3
Talca Ct
8900 SDGO 1189 C3
Taliesin Wy
32000 SDCo 1048 D7
Talisman Ct
6900 SDGO 1250 H4
Tall Oak Dr
10000 SDCo 1089 D4
Tall Oak Ln
27700 SDCo 1089 E4
Tall Pine Rd
18000 SDCo 1156 G5
Tall Pines Dr
2200 CHLV 1311 G6
Tallow Ct
500 CHLV 1330 H4
Tallow Tree Ln
- SDCo 1169 D2
Tallus Glen
9700 SDGO 1169 D3
Talmadge Canyon Row
4600 SDGO 1269 J2
E Talmadge Dr
4600 SDGO 1269 H3
N Talmadge Dr
4300 SDGO 1269 H3
W Talmadge Dr
4600 SDGO 1269 H3
Talmadge Park Row
4800 SDGO 1269 J2
Talon Ridge Wy
300 OCSD 1086 B6
Talon Wy
2000 SDGO 1269 B1
Taloncrest Wy
11100 SDGO 1208 H3
Taltec Dr
- LMSA 1271 C2
Talus St
200 CHLV 1330 G4
Talus Wy
- CRLB 1107 B4
Tam O Shanter Ct
13800 POWY 1170 F2
Tam O Shanter Dr
17100 POWY 1170 F2
500 SNMS 1109 D7
Tamar Ter
10700 SNTE 1231 F6
Tamara Dr
700 SDCo 1109 H2
Tamara Ln
2400 SDCo 1088 G7
2300 SDCo 1108 G1
Tamarack Av
1500 CRLB 1106 G6
- CRLB 1107 C3
Tamarack Ct
500 CHLV 1330 H4
Tamarack Ln
9900 SDCo 1149 D4
Tamarack St
- SDGO 1269 F6
Tamarack Terr
- ELCJ 1251 J6
Tamarak Av
300 ESCN 1109 H7
Tamarand Wy
1700 SDGO 1350 A2
Tamarindo Wy
- CHLV 1330 E5
Tamarisk Cir
4400 OCSD 1066 H7
Tamarisk Grove Dr
1300 CHLV 1311 J6
Tamarisk Ln
500 SNMS 1128 E1
Tamarisk St
- IMPE 6499 D2
Tamarisk Wy
400 ELCJ 1251 G4
Tamarme Ter
1700 ESCN 1130 A5
Tamayo Dr
800 CHLV 1310 F7
Tamberly Ct
8800 SNTE 1231 D6
Tamberly Wy
8800 SNTE 1231 D7
Tambor Ct
4200 SDGO 1249 J2
Tambor Rd
4000 SDGO 1249 J2
Tambourine Ln
2300 SDCo 1252 D6
Tamil Rd
10000 SDCo 1232 B3
Tamilynn Ct
4100 SDGO 1228 E6
Tamilynn St
6100 SDGO 1228 E6
Tammadge Heights Rd
- SDCo 1233 E7
Tampa Av
2300 ELCJ 1251 B4
Tampa Ct
1500 CHLV 1311 B4
Tampere Ct
11100 SDGO 1209 J1
Tampico Ct
7800 SDGO 1209 A3
100 SOLB 1167 H4
Tampico Dr
- IMPE 6499 G1
Tampico Glen
200 ESCN 1130 B7
Tamra Ct
3500 SDCo 1272 E5
Tamres Dr
5500 SDGO 1248 G5
Tan Bob Ln
- SDCo 1150 A2
Tan Tam Dr
2800 SDCo 1149 G1
Tana Wy
25000 SDCo 1173 G4
Tanager Dr
- CRLB 1127 D6
Tanager Ln
1300 ELCJ 1251 D2
Tanbark Ct
1600 CHLV 1330 H5
Tanbark St
400 CHLV 1330 H5
Tang Dr
- SDGO 1208 B1
Tangelo Dr
12100 SDCo 1232 A4
Tangelo Wy
29000 SDCo 1071 B7
Tangelos Pl
1100 LMGR 1290 E2
Tangerine Cove Dr
500 VSTA 1087 G7
Tangerine Dr
600 ELCN 6559 H1
Tangerine Ln
5100 SDCo 1047 G7
Tangerine St
1100 ELCJ 1252 A3
Tangerine Wy
- ESCN 1129 E5
Tangier Ct
600 OCSD 1087 B1
Tangiers Ct
800 SDGO 1267 H1
Tanglefoot Trl
7400 SDCo 1138 B7
(See Page 1138)
Tanglerod Ln
7700 LMSA 1250 G7
Tanglewood Dr
1800 SNMS 1128 G6
Tanglewood Ln
1500 ESCN 1129 G5
- SDGO 1209 E3
Tanglewood Rd
6700 SDGO 1248 J4
Tanglewood Wy
3700 SDGO 1248 J4
Tangor Wy
9900 SDCo 1271 D6
Tanner Ct
7100 SDGO 1248 J4
Tanner Ln
3700 SDGO 1248 J4
Tanner Ridge Ct
- SDGO 1169 C4
Tanner Ridge Rd
- SDGO 1169 C4
Tannin Dr
17100 POWY 1170 D2
Tanoak Ct
500 CHLV 1330 H5
Tansy St
3700 SDGO 1208 C6
Tanya Ln
900 SDCo 1027 H1
Tanzanite Dr
6800 CRLB 1127 F5
Taos Dr
4100 SDGO 1248 D3
Taos Pl
3400 SDGO 1248 D3
Tapestry St
1800 CHLV 1331 E2
Tara Ct
1400 CRLB 1106 G6
Tara Pl
5200 SDGO 1248 H1
Tara Wy
3500 SDCo 1272 E6
1700 SNMS 1128 F6
Tarakim Ln
1600 VSTA 1107 J2
Tarantella St
4600 SDGO 1188 C6
Tarascan Dr
13200 POWY 1190 E4
Tarata Ct
400 CHLV 1330 H5
Tarawa Rd
- CORD 1309 A2
Taray Ct
- SDGO 1209 F1
Tarbox St
1300 SDGO 1290 E2
Tarek Ter
- SDCo 1068 G7
Tarengo Pl
200 SDCo 1290 J5
Tarento Dr
900 SDGO 1287 J2
Targa Pl
1800 SDCo 1272 B4
Tarleton St
1600 SDCo 1290 J1
Tarlo Ct
1000 ELCJ 1252 A7
Taro Ct
100 SDGO 1290 G4
Tarocco Ct
- OCSD 1087 A2
Tarragon Dr
2100 CHLV 1331 H3
4800 OCSD 1067 B7
Tarragona Dr
6000 SDGO 1270 C4
Tartan Terr
- SDCo 1171 G1
Tarzana Rd
14100 POWY 1190 B2
Tasha View Wy
- SDCo 1252 H1
Tasman Pl
100 SDGO 1290 F5
Taspa Ct
- SDCo 1050 J5
Tassel Rd
12400 POWY 1190 C4
Tatas Pl
10300 SDCo 1109 F1
Tatewood Av
12500 SDCo 1232 B3
Tatia Ct
17600 SDGO 1170 A1
Tatler Rd
- CRLB 1127 C6
Tattenham Rd
1700 ENCT 1146 J2
Tattersall Sq
5200 SDGO 1188 D2
Tattnal Ln
1900 SDGO 1288 C1
Tatum St
600 VSTA 1087 F5
Tau St
5600 LMSA 1250 J7
Taulbees Ln
1300 SNMS 1108 E7
Taunt Pl
12500 POWY 1190 C2
Taunt Rd
12500 POWY 1190 C2
Taupa Wy
- SDCo 1051 B6
Tauri Court
- SDGO 1290 D3
Taurus Pl
8800 SDGO 1209 D2
Taussig Ct
10200 SDGO 1249 G4
Taussig St
3000 SDGO 1249 G5
Tavara Pl
400 SDGO 1288 A4
Tavern Ct
1800 SDCo 1234 A6
Tavern Rd
900 SDCo 1233 J5
1400 SDCo 1234 A6
2800 SDCo 1253 J3
2400 SDCo 1254 A2
Tavertine Ct
- SDGO 1210 C1
Tawanka Dr
13300 POWY 1190 D4
Tawny Brown St
1800 CHLV 1331 F3
Tawny Ct
700 OCSD 1087 C1
Tawny Pl
1800 ESCN 1109 D5
Tawny Wy
13100 POWY 1170 E2
Taxco Ct
1100 CHLV 1311 A7
Taylor Av
1400 ESCN 1110 B7
Taylor Dr
- IMPE 6499 H2
400 OCSD 1087 E3
Taylor Pl
500 CALX 6680 H2
2100 ESCN 1110 C6
1300 ESCN 1130 A1
Taylor St
500 SDCo 1087 J2
4400 SDGO 1268 F4
300 VSTA 1087 G2
E Taylor St
1400 VSTA 1088 A2
Taylor Wy
- SDCo 1253 B2
Taza Rd
1500 SDCo 1028 H1
Tea Mountain Rd
1900 SDCo 1252 G4
Tea Party Ln
3100 SDGO 1249 G4
Tea Tree Dr
- CRLB 1127 A5
Tea Tree Ln
- SDCo 1169 D2
Teaberry Gn
- ESCN 1110 D7

66 INDEX
Teaberry St
INDEX 66
Tonopah Av
SAN DIEGO CO.

San Diego County Street Index

STREET
Block City Map# Grid

Teaberry St
700 ENCT 1147 E6
Teak Ct
500 CHLV 1330 H4
Teak St
3800 SDGO 1289 G5
Teakwood Ct
700 SNMS 1109 A5
Teakwood Glen
400 ESCN 1109 G6
Teakwood Ln
- SDCo 1251 H1
Teakwood Wy
1800 VSTA 1107 G5
Teal Glen
2100 ESCN 1109 H5
Teal Ln
2800 ImCo 6439 E4
Teal Pl
2600 SDGO 1249 A7
Teal Rd
29800 SDCo 1297 G5
(See Page 1297)
Teal St
100 CHLV 1330 F5
Teal Stone Ct
17500 SDCo 1169 F1
Teal Stone St
10400 SDCo 1169 F1
Teal Wy
- OCSD 1067 A3
Teale Christine Ct
13500 SDCo 1232 E6
Tealwood Ct
8000 LMGR 1270 J7
Tearose Ln
1400 SDCo 1321 A3
(See Page 1321)
Teasdale Av
7000 SDGO 1228 G4
Teatro Cir
900 ELCJ 1252 A3
Tebo Ct
3400 SDGO 1330 E7
Tecalote Dr
1600 SDCo 1028 F4
Tecalote Ln
400 SDCo 1028 H6
Tecate Cypress Trl
9400 SDCo 1236 E2
Tecate Divide Rd
2500 SDCo 1299 J4
(See Page 1299)
Tecate Glen
1900 ESCN 1129 E6
Tech Center Ct
11900 POWY 1190 E7
Tech Center Dr
12100 POWY 1190 F7
Tech Wy
8700 SDGO 1249 D2
Technology Dr
16200 SDGO 1169 H4
Technology Pl
10900 SDGO 1169 H4
Tecolote Rd
1100 SDGO 1268 E2
Tecolote Valley Rd
1500 SDGO 1268 G2
Tecoma Pl
- CRLB 1127 E4
Tecumseh Wy
4300 SDGO 1248 E2
Ted Williams Fwy
- SDGO 1188 H3
- SDGO 1189 A5
- SDGO 1208 A1
Ted Williams Pkwy
- POWY 1190 B2
10800 SDGO 1189 J3
11800 SDGO 1190 A2
Teds Pl
500 SDCo 1152 D6
Tee Sq
29000 SDCo 1237 C7
Tee St
- OCSD 1067 B4
Tee-A-Way Pl
6800 SDGO 1250 F5
Teebird Ln
7600 SDGO 1269 A1
Teelin Av
1300 VSTA 1087 G4
Teena Dr
100 CHLV 1330 D5
Teepee Dr
1300 SDCo 1130 E5
Tehachapi
- SNMS 1128 C1
Tehama Dr
- SNMS 1108 J7
Tehnsen
- SDCo 1232 F4
Telegraph Canyon Rd
- CHLV 1310 E7
1000 CHLV 1311 B7
700 CHLV 1330 H1
800 CHLV 1331 A1
Telescope Av
4600 CRLB 1106 H7

Telford Ln
400 SDCo 1152 J6
Telkaif St
9500 SDCo 1232 F4
Tellypuu Rd
2200 SDCo 1091 D5
Tema St
6700 SDGO 1250 E7
Temapala Rd
10500 SDCo 1029 G3
Temecula St
- SDCo 1086 A4
4300 SDGO 1268 B5
Temecula Valley Frwy
- SDCo 999 A2
Temepa Rd
11400 SDCo 999 G4
Temet Dr
32800 SDCo 1050 J4
Tempas Ct
6000 SDGO 1290 C4
Tempera Ct
900 OCSD 1087 B2
Temple Heights Dr
1300 OCSD 1087 D3
Temple St
- CALX 6680 F1
13800 POWY 1190 F2
900 SDGO 1287 J2
Temple Ter
6900 SDGO 1250 E5
Temple Trl
2000 SDCo 1314 H2
(See Page 1314)
Templeton St
- SDGO 1169 D3
Tempra Pl
- CHLV 1330 D4
Temprano Ct
4500 SDGO 1250 A2
Tenaya Lake Rd
1100 CHLV 1331 B2
Tenbury Ct
7000 SDGO 1290 F6
Tenderfoot Ln
1100 OCSD 1067 E7
Tennie St
100 SDGO 1350 F4
Tennis Club Dr
1300 ENCT 1167 G2
Tennis Court Ln
3500 SDCo 1310 H2
Tennis Match Wy
1400 ENCT 1147 G6
Tennis Pl
1800 ENCT 1167 H3
Tennyson St
3400 SDGO 1268 B7
Tenshaw Pl
3200 SDGO 1248 C3
Tequila Wy
4000 SDGO 1350 D2
Teracewood Ln
2200 ESCN 1109 H4
Teralta Pl
4400 SDGO 1268 H4
Teran Dr
500 SDCo 1027 F3
Tercer Verde
- SOLB 1187 H1
Teresa Dr
8300 SDGO 1209 B2
Teresa St
4100 OCSD 1087 C7
Teresita St
2600 SDGO 1269 F7
Teri Dr
12300 POWY 1190 C2
Terman Ct
- SDGO 1208 J7
Terminal Link Rd
1700 SDGO 1268 H7
Terminal St
2400 NATC 1309 G4
1000 SDGO 1289 B5
Tern Dr
2600 SDGO 1249 B7
Tern Pl
7100 CRLB 1127 D7
Terol Ct
200 SDGO 1290 D4
Terr Dr
4600 SDGO 1269 G3
Terra Cotta Rd
7000 SDGO 1290 F5
Terra Ln
500 ELCJ 1252 B4
Terra Nova Dr
600 CHLV 1310 G5
Terra Seca Trl
3100 SDCo 1273 B7
Terra Vista
4100 NATC 1310 D4
Terrace Av
600 ESCN 1109 H7
Terrace Cir
300 BRAW 6319 G2
(See Page 6319)
Terrace Crest St
800 ELCJ 1252 A7

Terrace Ct
4000 SDGO 1269 G3
Terrace Dr
600 BRAW 6319 G2
(See Page 6319)
8900 LMSA 1271 B4
- SDCo 1089 B2
4500 SDGO 1269 G4
100 VSTA 1087 H7
Terrace Hill Dr
1700 SDCo 1252 B2
Terrace Knoll
1400 SDCo 1234 B6
Terrace Ln
3300 OCSD 1106 H1
100 SNMS 1108 J7
Terrace Pine Dr
2700 SDGO 1350 C2
Terrace Pine Ln
1500 SDGO 1350 C2
Terrace Pl
- CRLB 1107 B4
Terrace View
- ESCN 1129 E6
Terrace View Ln
- SDCo 1070 G4
Terrace View Pl
2100 ESCN 1109 G5
Terracina Cir
1900 SDCo 1291 A1
Terracina St
- OCSD 1087 B3
Terracina Wy
100 VSTA 1087 G6
Terracita Ln
1400 SDCo 1233 J6
Terrakappa Av
2000 SDCo 1291 A1
Terrarama Av
8800 SDCo 1291 A1
Terraspiro Av
2000 SDCo 1291 A1
Terraza Cir
4500 SDGO 1250 A1
Terraza Ct
4600 SDGO 1250 A1
Terraza Disoma
7900 CRLB 1148 A2
Terraza Floracion
10800 SDGO 1169 H5
Terraza Goya
2300 CRLB 1127 G6
Terraza Guitara
2300 CRLB 1127 G6
Terraza Mar Marvelosa
- SDGO 1208 C4
Terraza Panga
2300 CRLB 1127 G7
Terraza Playa Cancun
11300 SDGO 1230 A7
Terraza Playa Catalina
5000 SDGO 1230 A7
Terraza Portico
- CRLB 1127 J4
Terraza Quintana
5100 SDGO 1230 A7
Terraza Ribera
2300 CRLB 1127 G6
Terraza Salvo
2300 CRLB 1127 G6
Terraza St
1700 OCSD 1106 E1
Terrazzo Ct
- SDGO 1188 H4
Terrebonne Ct
15200 SDGO 1210 H1
Terrella Pl
2500 SDCo 1150 D2
Terreno Ct
4400 SDGO 1249 J1
Terrier Wy
100 SNMS 1128 H1
Terrilee Dr
13800 POWY 1190 G3
Terrilee Ln
14100 POWY 1190 G3
Terry Ln
4500 LMSA 1270 E3
1800 NATC 1310 A1
Terry St
4200 OCSD 1087 C6
Terryhill Dr
6100 SDGO 1247 F3
Terrywood Rd
9400 SNTE 1231 B4
Tesla Ln
1000 SDCo 998 A7
Tesla St
2900 SDGO 1248 F6
Tesoro Av
- SNMS 1108 F5
Tesoro Ct
12300 SDGO 1170 B2
Tesoro Dr
17000 SDGO 1170 B3
Tesoro Grove Wy
1100 SDGO 1350 B1
Tesoro Wy
24500 SDCo 1173 F3
Tesota Ct
400 CHLV 1330 H5

Testigo Trl
- SDCo 1255 D4
Teten Wy
2400 ENCT 1147 J7
Tetillas Ct
15300 SDGO 1170 A6
Teton Dr
1300 SNTE 1251 F1
Teton Pass St
1800 SDCo 1272 C3
Tewa St
500 DLMR 1187 G5
Tex St
5700 LMSA 1250 H7
Texana St
13000 SDGO 1189 C5
Texas Rainbow Dr
1600 CHLV 1331 F2
Texas St
4300 SDGO 1269 D4
Th Bar Ranch Trl
8000 SDCo 1233 E7
Thalia St
1100 SDGO 1349 J1
Thames Ct
2300 SDGO 1249 B7
Thanksgiving Ln
10200 SDGO 1209 D5
Thata Wy
31700 SDCo 1051 H5
Thatcher Ct
- POWY 1190 E7
Thayer Dr
700 SDCo 1291 B3
The Circle
100 VSTA 1087 H6
The Crossings Dr
5800 CRLB 1127 A3
The Depot Rd
5700 OCSD 1067 E7
The Grant Pl
8300 SDCo 1290 J6
The Hill Rd
3800 SDCo 1310 F4
The Inlet
- CORD 1329 D1
The Landing Wy
8100 SDCo 1169 A1
The Loop
900 SDCo 1051 A1
The Point
- CORD 1329 E1
The Preserve Ct
6900 SDGO 1188 H6
The Preserve Terr
6900 SDGO 1188 H6
The Preserve Wy
6900 SDGO 1188 H6
The River Rd
- SDCo 1168 D6
The River Tr
15800 SDCo 1168 D6
The Square
13400 POWY 1170 E2
The Strand N
600 OCSD 1085 J7
300 OCSD 1106 A1
The Strand S
200 OCSD 1106 A1
The Woods Dr
1700 SDCo 1272 B1
The Yellow Brick Rd
29100 SDCo 1071 B7
Thebes St
14600 SDGO 1189 H1
Thebes Wy
4800 OCSD 1107 F6
Thelborn Wy
1700 SDGO 1350 A2
Thelma Wy
400 NATC 1290 C6
Theodore Dr
1200 SDGO 1290 D5
Theresa Wy
1600 CHLV 1330 F3
Thermal Av
800 SDGO 1329 J7
1100 SDGO 1349 J1
Theta Glen
400 ESCN 1129 H2
Theta Pl
5700 SDGO 1250 C7
Thibodo Ct
2000 VSTA 1108 B4
Thibodo Rd
1500 VSTA 1107 J2
2000 VSTA 1108 B4
Thielemana Av
- CALX 6680 C2
Thimble Ct
8300 SDGO 1189 B6
Thistle Brae Ter
12000 SDCo 1232 A6
Thistle Ct
8100 SDGO 1250 D3
Thistle Hill Pl
- SDGO 1208 B2
Tho Ninh Pl
- ESCN 1110 B7
Thomas Av
800 SDGO 1247 H6

Thomas Av
2200 SDGO 1248 B6
- SDGO 1268 G6
- SDGO 1289 C2
Thomas Dr
- ELCN 6559 H2
Thomas Hayes Ln
11600 SDGO 1209 A1
Thomas Ln
- ELCN 6559 H2
Thomas Paine
- SDCo 1171 J5
Thomas Paine Ln
18500 SDCo 1171 J4
Thomas Pl
1500 CHLV 1330 J3
900 VSTA 1088 C5
Thomas St
4000 OCSD 1087 B7
Thomas Wy
1000 ESCN 1110 A6
Thompson Av
1600 CHLV 1331 E2
Thomsen Wy
100 SDCo 1152 H4
Thomson Ct
6700 SDGO 1248 H7
Thor St
1600 SDGO 1289 G6
Thoreau Pl
15800 SDGO 1169 C5
Thorley Wy
1700 SNMS 1128 F6
Thorn Dale Rd
- SDCo 1068 D5
Thorn Ln
9700 SDCo 1149 E3
Thorn St
500 IMPB 1329 F7
2800 SDGO 1269 E6
5700 SDGO 1270 B6
N Thorn St
5200 SDGO 1270 A6
S Thorn St
5200 SDGO 1270 A6
W Thorn St
1700 SDGO 1268 H7
100 SDGO 1269 A7
Thornbush Ct
12400 SDGO 1210 C4
Thornbush Rd
- SDCo 1174 B5
Thorne Dr
5000 LMSA 1270 G2
Thornmint Rd
10700 SDCo 1169 F3
Thornton Dr
200 SDCo 1252 H2
Thornton Pl
3000 SDGO 1270 B7
Thornwood St
6400 SDGO 1248 H4
Thorny Locust Pl
1500 CHLV 1311 J7
Thoroughbred Av
- OCSD 1067 F7
Thoroughbred Ln
5900 SDCo 1067 J1
Thoroughbred Pl
- SDGO 1188 D5
Thoroughbred St
5500 OCSD 1067 E6
Thorton Rd
- CHLV 1311 C4
Thrasher Pl
6600 CRLB 1127 C5
Thrasher Wy
100 ELCJ 1251 A5
Three Canyons Ct
6600 SDGO 1188 G6
Three Canyons Pt
12800 SDGO 1188 G6
Three Oaks Wy
10000 SNTE 1231 D3
Three Peaks Ln
2800 SDCo 1155 J4
Three Seasons Rd
9100 SDGO 1209 D5
Thrush Pl
- CRLB 1127 C6
Thrush St
400 CHLV 1330 G2
300 SDGO 1290 C4
Thumbkin Ln
2200 SDCo 1087 H2
Thunder Dr
2700 OCSD 1087 B7
3400 OCSD 1107 C2
100 VSTA 1107 C2
Thunder Glen
600 ESCN 1130 B2
Thunder Mtn Rd
24800 SDCo 1193 F1
(See Page 1193)
Thunder Spring Dr
1300 CHLV 1311 H6
Thunderbird Dr
600 OCSD 1066 H7
Thunderbird Ln
8500 SDCo 1270 J5
5400 SDGO 1248 A3

Thunderbird Pl
1300 CHLV 1311 H6
Thunderhead St
13200 SDGO 1189 C4
Thundernut Ln
- SDCo 1091 C1
Thurgood Marshall Ln
- SDGO 1227 J1
Thurston Pl
4700 SDGO 1188 C4
Thyme Wy
20700 SDCo 1295 A6
(See Page 1295)
Tia Juana St
400 SDGO 1350 E5
Tia Maria Wy
8400 LMSA 1270 J1
Tiara St
3800 SDCo 1249 A3
Tibbett St
600 SDGO 1290 F3
Tiber Ct
100 SDCo 1108 B3
Tiberon Dr
4200 OCSD 1107 C2
Tibidabo Dr
1500 ESCN 1110 A5
Tiburon Av
2700 CRLB 1106 J5
Tiburon Dr
200 CHLV 1311 D1
Tiburon St
500 SNMS 1128 G2
Ticanu Dr
2100 SDCo 1156 B3
Ticino St
- SDCo 1135 B3
Ticket St
9000 SDGO 1209 D3
Ticknor Ct
6000 SDGO 1290 C4
Tico Ct
1100 SDGO 1350 G1
Ticonderoga St
3500 SDGO 1248 D5
Tide Ct
900 CRLB 1126 J4
Tide Pool Pl
6200 SDGO 1290 E7
Tide Wy
- SNMS 1109 A4
Tidelands
- CHLV 1310 C6
Tidelands Av
2000 NATC 1309 G3
Tie St
3400 SDGO 1270 C6
Tientse
- SDGO 1268 F6
Tierney Glen
16600 SDGO 1169 B3
Tierra Alta
15000 SOLB 1167 H7
Tierra Baja Wy
4900 SDGO 1270 C3
Tierra Blanca Av
- SDCo 1085 J3
Tierra Blanca Wy
- SDCo 1085 J4
Tierra Bonita
4200 NATC 1310 E4
Tierra Bonita Ct
14000 POWY 1190 G1
Tierra Bonita Pl
1300 CHLV 1311 B7
Tierra Bonita Rd
13600 POWY 1190 G3
Tierra De Dios
3600 SDCo 1150 D2
Tierra De Luna Rd
900 SDCo 1319 H7
(See Page 1319)
Tierra De Melanie
37600 SDCo 1319 G7
(See Page 1319)
Tierra Del Cielo
1400 VSTA 1088 C4
Tierra Del Oro St
5000 CRLB 1126 F2
Tierra Del Rey
800 CHLV 1310 J6
Tierra Del Sol Rd
2000 SDCo 1300 A7
(See Page 1300)
700 SDCo 1319 H7
(See Page 1319)
Tierra Del Sur
11700 SDGO 1208 A2
Tierra Dura Rd
900 SNMS 1109 C5
Tierra Estrella
37100 SDCo 1319 G7
(See Page 1319)
Tierra Grande St
9600 SDGO 1209 E6
Tierra Heights Rd
2400 SDCo 1300 A4
(See Page 1300)
Tierra Heights Summi
2400 SDCo 1300 A5
(See Page 1300)

Tierra Libertia Rd
1800 SDCo 1089 D7
Tierra Linda Ln
3500 SDCo 1048 B3
Tierra Montanosa
1600 SDCo 1233 H7
Tierra Nuevo
300 SDCo 998 D3
Tierra Real Ln
1300 SDCo 1319 H5
(See Page 1319)
Tierra Real Rd
38100 SDCo 1319 H5
(See Page 1319)
Tierra Roja Dr
1300 SDCo 998 D7
Tierra Tesoro
- SDGO 1189 A1
Tierra Verde
2200 SDCo 1088 C7
Tierra Vista Cir
13400 SDGO 1188 G3
Tierra Vista Ct
6600 SDGO 1188 H3
Tierra Vista Pl
3900 ESCN 1150 D3
Tierrasanta Blvd
10100 SDGO 1249 G2
11200 SDGO 1250 A3
Tiffany
2000 OCSD 1086 J7
Tiffany Ct
600 CHLV 1310 G7
Tiffany Ln
1400 SDCo 1108 B1
Tiffany Park Pl
9300 SDCo 1232 F5
Tiffany Wy
500 CHLV 1310 G7
Tiffin Av
6600 SDGO 1270 E7
Tiger Lily Ln
- IMPE 6499 D2
Tiger Run Ct
- CRLB 1127 H2
Tiger Tail Ln
900 VSTA 1088 A6
Tiger Tail Rd
800 VSTA 1087 J6
900 VSTA 1088 A6
Tiger Wy
1100 SDCo 1152 J6
Tigereye Pl
2200 CRLB 1127 G5
Tiki Dr E
- VSTA 1087 E6
Tiki Dr N
- VSTA 1087 E5
Tiki Dr S
- VSTA 1087 E6
Tiki Dr W
- VSTA 1087 E6
Tiki Ln
- VSTA 1087 E6
Tilden St
1800 SDGO 1289 J1
Tilia Ct
400 CHLV 1330 G4
Tilia Pl
- CRLB 1127 D4
Tillage Ln
17000 SDCo 1169 B2
Tillamook Bay
- SDGO 1290 B1
Tilley Ln
600 SNMS 1108 C7
Tilling Wy
- ELCJ 1271 E1
Tilos Wy
4900 OCSD 1107 E6
Tilting T Dr
900 SDCo 1079 A6
(See Page 1079)
Tilton St
10100 SDGO 1208 J5
Tim St
3900 SDCo 1310 J3
Timaru Wy
11800 SDGO 1170 A1
Timber Branch Wy
- SDGO 1208 D1
Timber Brook Ln
- SDGO 1208 F2
Timber Cove Wy
700 OCSD 1066 F7
Timber Creek
- SNMS 1128 A5
Timber Creek Ln
- SDCo 1130 J3
Timber Ct
400 CHLV 1330 G5
Timber Feather Ln
500 SDCo 1027 G3
Timber Glen
1300 ESCN 1110 A5
Timber Passage
23400 SDCo 1153 C7
Timber Rd
12500 SDCo 1232 B2
Timber Ridge Rd
4500 SDGO 1188 C5

Timber St
500 CHLV 1330 H5
Timber Trail
1800 VSTA 1107 F5
Timbergate Cir
11200 SDGO 1189 J2
Timberlake Dr
11500 SDGO 1209 J3
Timberlane Wy
10000 SNTE 1231 D3
Timberline Ct
10000 SDGO 1210 A4
Timberline Ln
600 SNMS 1108 J4
Timberline Rd
2100 CRLB 1106 F3
Timberpond Dr
1300 SDCo 1272 B1
Timberwood Pl
800 ESCN 1109 H3
7500 SDGO 1290 H6
Timboll Ct
5400 SDCo 1290 J7
Timely Ter
100 SDGO 1290 E4
Timingo Gate Wy
1700 OCSD 1106 E2
Timken Cir
3200 ESCN 1110 F5
Timken St
5300 LMSA 1270 J1
Timneh Ct
2100 OCSD 1067 B2
Timothy Dr
5400 SDGO 1290 B1
Timothy Pl
1700 VSTA 1087 D7
Timrick Ln
3900 SDCo 1311 A3
Timsford Rd
11500 SDGO 1209 H1
Tin Cup Dr
- SDCo 1173 J7
Tina Ct
1400 SDCo 1272 D1
Tina Pl
1600 SDCo 1251 G2
Tina St
2200 SDCo 1272 D1
Tinaja Ln
4700 SDCo 1099 F5
(See Page 1099)
- SDGO 1290 H5
Tinamou Pl
1100 VSTA 1087 G4
Tinasa Wy
4800 SDGO 1250 A1
Tingley Ln
900 SDGO 1288 A2
Tining Dr
- POWY 1170 E2
Tining Wy
- POWY 1170 E2
Tiny Ln
300 ELCJ 1252 A5
Tio Diego Pl
8400 LMSA 1270 J1
Tioga Lake Dr
10300 SDCo 1129 F7
Tioga Trl
1500 SDCo 1047 J1
Tipperary Wy
- SDGO 1209 H1
Tipton St
5100 SDGO 1270 D2
Tisselle Wy
5000 SDGO 1290 A1
Tish Ct
2700 SDCo 1270 J7
Tisha Cir
10200 SDGO 1209 B5
Tisha St
8100 SDGO 1209 B5
Tishmal Ct
400 OCSD 1086 D4
Titan Ct
1200 SDCo 1109 E6
Titan Wy
16400 POWY 1170 G6
Titanite Pl
6600 CRLB 1127 G4
Titanium Pl
700 VSTA 1087 F7
Titus St
1800 SDGO 1268 H6
Tiverton Rd
13200 SDGO 1188 A5
Tivoli Park Row
11900 SDGO 1190 A2
Tivoli St
4500 SDGO 1287 J1
Tobacco Rd
1700 SDCo 1109 E6
Tobago Rd
10900 SDGO 1209 A3
Tobago Wy
- CORD 1329 E2
Tobey St
4700 SDGO 1249 J7
Tobias Dr
1400 CHLV 1330 E4

Tobiasson Rd
13700 POWY 1190 C3
Tobira Dr
8800 SDCo 1069 A6
Toboggan Wy
2000 SDGO 1350 A1
Tobria Terr
- CRLB 1127 E4
Toca Ln
2100 SDCo 1172 C3
Tocayo Av
3200 SDGO 1350 B2
Toch St
4200 SDGO 1248 E2
Todd Ct
200 OCSD 1086 E5
Todd St
2900 OCSD 1086 D6
Todos Santos Dr
9100 SNTE 1251 B1
Todos Santos Pl
1500 SDCo 1027 E4
Togan Av
9000 SDGO 1189 D4
Tokaj Ln
9100 SDCo 1291 B1
Tokaj Rd
2200 SDCo 1291 B1
Tokaj Wy
9100 SDCo 1291 B1
Tokalon Ct
2500 SDGO 1248 F7
Tokalon St
2700 SDGO 1248 F7
2100 SDGO 1268 F1
Tokay St
2000 SDCo 1290 B1
Tolas Ct
3400 NATC 1290 C7
Toledo Dr
4500 SDGO 1270 E3
Toledo Rd
10200 SDCo 1271 E4
Toledo Wy
1600 CHLV 1331 D2
Tolita Av
700 CORD 1288 H7
Tolkien Wy
- CRLB 1127 A1
Tolo Wy
5000 OCSD 1107 E4
Tolowa St
4200 SDGO 1248 E2
Toltec Ct
17800 SDGO 1169 H1
Toluca Ct
100 SOLB 1167 H4
Tom McGuinness Jr Cres
300 SDCo 1028 A2
Tomahawk Ln
3700 SDGO 1248 F4
Tombill Rd
- SDCo 1173 A5
Tombstone Creek Rd
15100 SDCo 1233 A1
Tomcat Pl
9800 SDGO 1209 E2
Tomel Ct
10400 SNTE 1231 E3
Tomiko Ct
9300 SDCo 1271 B4
Tomillo Ln
1500 CHLV 1331 D3
Tommie Ln
- SDCo 1171 F4
Tommy Dr
8300 SDGO 1250 J4
8700 SDGO 1251 A4
Tommy St
7800 SDGO 1250 H4
Tomorro Ln
900 SDCo 1027 G4
Tompau Pl
2200 SDCo 1253 H2
Tompkins St
3500 SDGO 1289 F4
Tomsyl Ln
10700 SDCo 1069 F5
Tonalite Wy
30200 SDCo 1297 F4
(See Page 1297)
Tonapah St
3400 OCSD 1086 E5
Tonawanda Dr
5900 SDGO 1310 D3
Tondino Ct
11700 SDGO 1210 A2
Tondino Rd
11000 SDGO 1210 A3
Tone Ln
8000 SDCo 1252 A1
Toner Ct
1300 SDCo 1233 A7
Toni Ln
4400 LMSA 1270 E3
Toni Ridge Pl
- SDGO 1228 H1
Tonopah Av
4400 SDGO 1268 E2

San Diego County Street Index

STREET
Block City Map# Grid

Tonto Wy
2700 SDGO 1228 B7
2600 SDGO 1248 B1
Tony Dr
3400 SDGO 1228 D4
Tonya Ln
9100 SNTE 1231 B7
Tooley Cir
1700 SDGO 1290 C2
Tooley St
5800 SDGO 1290 C2
Tooma St
7300 SDGO 1290 G7
Toopal Dr
3100 OCSD 1086 D4
Toota Ct
500 OCSD 1086 C4
Toothrock Rd
15200 POWY 1170 J7
Tootsie Ln
- SDCo 1235 B4
Top Gun St
6700 SDGO 1208 H4
Top O Crosby
16400 SDCo 1168 J3
Top O The Morning Wy
7500 SDCo 1168 J3
7900 SDCo 1169 A2
Top Of The Pines Ln
28700 SDCo 1237 B7
Top Rail Ln
1300 SDCo 1130 C3
Topa Hill Cir
12300 SDCo 1232 A4
Topa Rd
15200 SDCo 1030 H7
Topa Topa Dr
4400 SDCo 1271 G3
Topaz Ct
- CALX 6620 H7
300 CHLV 1330 G5
500 ESCN 1110 E7
- LMSA 1270 J4
Topaz Dr
500 SDCo 1156 E2
Topaz Lake Av
7700 SDGO 1250 G5
Topaz Ln
4400 OCSD 1107 D2
Topaz Pl
1200 SNMS 1109 C5
Topaz St
- IMPE 6439 C6
Topaz Ter
1700 SDCo 1272 C2
Topaz Wy
- CRLB 1127 B4
9100 SDGO 1229 D7
Topeka St
3400 CRLB 1106 J4
600 OCSD 1106 A1
W Topeka St
400 OCSD 1106 A1
Topgun Av
1500 SDGO 1209 D6
Topiary St
6200 CRLB 1127 F3
Topmast Dr
- CRLB 1127 A4
Topo Ln
12100 SDCo 1212 A6
Topper Ln
1200 SDCo 1251 J2
Topsail
- SDGO 1331 A6
Topsham St
14500 POWY 1190 H4
Topside
- SDGO 1330 J6
Torano Dr
200 VSTA 1087 H3
Torbett Ln
16900 SDCo 1169 G2
Torca Ct
5800 SDGO 1229 H7
Torenia Trl
6600 SDGO 1188 H3
Torero Pl
8200 SDGO 1209 B2
Tori Ct
- IMPE 6499 H2
Torole Cir
1000 VSTA 1087 J6
Toronga Wy
- SDCo 1070 J3
Torrance St
1700 SDGO 1268 H6
Torre Ln
1800 CHLV 1331 H2
Torrejon Pl
2400 CRLB 1147 F1
Torrell Wy
8300 SDGO 1209 B1
Torrem St
7600 LMSA 1250 G7
Torreon Dr
3100 SDCo 1234 D4
Torres Av
- CALX 6620 J7
Torrey Arbor Ln
- SDGO 1189 A4
Torrey Bella Ct
13800 SDGO 1189 B3
Torrey Bluff Dr
12600 SDGO 1188 B5
Torrey Circle
- SDGO 1208 C3
Torrey Crest Ct
- SDGO 1189 B4
Torrey Del Mar Dr
- SDGO 1188 J3
Torrey Dr
1200 ENCT 1167 F1
Torrey Gardens Pl
- SDGO 1189 A4
Torrey Glenn Rd
13600 SDGO 1189 B3
Torrey Gn
- ESCN 1109 D4
Torrey Hill Ct
13600 SDGO 1188 A4
Torrey Hill Ln
3800 SDGO 1188 A4
Torrey Ln
- SDCo 1023 E1
7800 SDGO 1227 G6
Torrey Meadows Dr
13200 SDGO 1188 J4
- SDGO 1189 A4
Torrey Mesa Ct
7100 SDGO 1188 J4
Torrey Park Terr
- SDGO 1189 B4
N Torrey Pines Ct
3300 SDGO 1207 J7
Torrey Pines Ln
2200 SDGO 1227 H6
Torrey Pines Park Rd
- SDGO 1207 H3
Torrey Pines Pl
700 OCSD 1086 F1
N Torrey Pines Pl
11100 SDGO 1207 J5
Torrey Pines Rd
- CHLV 1311 H5
2000 SDGO 1227 G6
N Torrey Pines Rd
12600 SDGO 1207 G1
9300 SDGO 1227 J2
Torrey Pines Scenic Dr
2800 SDGO 1207 H7
Torrey Pines Ter
200 DLMR 1187 G7
Torrey Point Rd
400 DLMR 1187 G7
Torrey Ranch Ct
- SDGO 1189 A4
Torrey Ridge Dr
12900 SDGO 1188 B5
Torrey Santa Fe Rd
7200 SDGO 1188 J4
7500 SDGO 1189 A4
Torrey View Ct
- SDGO 1208 A3
Torreyana Rd
10900 SDGO 1208 A5
Torreyanna Cir
- CRLB 1127 A4
Torrington St
- SDGO 1188 B4
Torry Ct
2700 CRLB 1127 G7
Tortilla Cir
4400 OCSD 1087 A1
Tortuga Cove
3900 OCSD 1086 G2
Tortuga Ct
5500 SDGO 1229 G7
5500 SDGO 1249 G1
Tortuga Point Dr
500 CHLV 1330 H4
Tortuga Rd
5700 SDGO 1229 H7
Tosca Wy
2400 SDGO 1248 H7
Toscana Dr
- SDGO 1228 E3
Toscana Wy
5300 SDGO 1228 E3
Toscano Ct
- ENCT 1148 B3
Totem Poll
200 SDCo 1235 B3
Toub St
2300 SDCo 1152 D7
Toucan Dr
500 VSTA 1087 F4
Toucanet Ct
5400 OCSD 1067 A3
Toulon Ct
800 SDGO 1247 H7
Toulon St
- OCSD 1087 B3
Toulouse Dr
1800 CHLV 1311 G1
1800 CHLV 1331 E1
Toulouse Ln
2800 SDCo 1048 C1
Tourmaline Ct
300 CHLV 1330 G5
Tourmaline Ln
2100 SDCo 1028 A6
Tourmaline Pl
6900 CRLB 1127 F5
Tourmaline St
- CHLV 1330 F5
600 SDGO 1247 G5
Tournament Dr
3300 OCSD 1106 J1
Toussachs Wy
- SDCo 1027 G6
Tow Way Rd
- CORD 1288 G5
Towell Ln
1600 ESCN 1129 G5
Tower Dr
1100 VSTA 1107 J1
1300 VSTA 1108 A2
Tower Ln
1200 ESCN 1109 J7
Tower Pl
700 ESCN 1109 J7
1100 VSTA 1107 J1
Tower Rd
- IMPB 1349 F3
- SDGO 1208 A6
Tower St
- LMSA 1270 E3
Towhee St
1800 SDCo 1128 A4
Towheg Ln
- CRLB 1127 C5
Towkish Dr
3200 OCSD 1086 D3
Towle Ct
5100 SDGO 1270 A5
Town Center
- OCSD 1087 B1
Town Center Dr
1400 CHLV 1311 F7
- SDGO 1170 A3
Town Center Pkwy
- SNTE 1231 C6
Town Center Pl
- CRLB 1147 F4
Town Garden Rd
2400 CRLB 1127 F3
Town Sq
- SDGO 1249 D1
Town Sq Pkwy
16900 SDCo 1169 F2
Town View Ct
6700 SDGO 1250 D3
Town View Ln
6800 SDGO 1250 C3
Town View Ter
6700 SDGO 1250 C3
Towncenter Pkwy
- CALX 6620 D4
Towne Centre Dr
8900 SDGO 1228 D2
Towne Ln
9700 SDCo 1233 A2
Towns Terr
10400 SDCo 1231 J2
Townsend Ln
1900 SDCo 1272 C2
Townsgate Dr
3800 SDGO 1188 A6
Townwood Ct
3400 OCSD 1086 E3
Townwood Wy
100 ENCT 1147 J7
Towser St
3200 SDGO 1249 D5
Toya Ln
15300 SDCo 1233 B2
Toyne St
2300 SDCo 1047 G2
600 SDGO 1289 H3
Toyoff Wy
4900 SDGO 1269 J1
Toyon Canyon Rd
9500 SDCo 1149 D4
Toyon Ct
- SNMS 1108 H5
Toyon Dr
- SDCo 1028 F4
5400 SDGO 1269 J1
Toyon Glen
1700 ESCN 1109 D6
Toyon Heights Ct
1400 SDCo 998 D7
Toyon Heights Dr
3000 SDCo 998 C7
Toyon Hills Dr
11000 SDCo 1211 F7
11000 SDCo 1231 G1
Toyon Ln
- CHLV 1310 C5
Toyon Mesa Pl
- SDGO 1188 G6
Toyon Mtn Ln
900 SDCo 1156 E5
Toyon Mtn Rd
4300 SDCo 1156 E5
Toyon Rd
5500 SDGO 1269 J1
Toyon Ridge Trl
27000 SDCo 1090 E6
Toyon Terr
300 SNMS 1108 G5
Trabert Ranch Rd
1300 ENCT 1167 H1
Trace Rd
2500 SDCo 1271 G7
Tracey Ln
1300 SDCo 1233 A7
Tracey Lyn Dr
31700 SDCo 1051 A7
Traci Ln
600 VSTA 1088 A7
Tracy Ct
- SDCo 1048 A3
Tracy St
7400 LMGR 1270 G7
Trade Pl
9100 SDGO 1209 A7
Trade St
7100 SDGO 1208 J7
7500 SDGO 1209 A7
200 SNMS 1128 J1
Trade Winds Dr
16700 SDCo 1168 J2
Tradewind Av
1300 SDGO 1349 J2
Tradewinds Dr
6800 CRLB 1126 H6
Tradition St
13600 SDGO 1190 B3
Trafalgar Ln
4600 CRLB 1107 A5
Trafalgar Rd
5600 SDCo 1253 C4
Trail Blaze Ct
4000 SDCo 1311 B2
Trail Blazer Ln
21600 SDCo 1129 C5
Trail Crest Ct
- SDGO 1189 G7
Trail Crest Dr
- SDGO 1209 G1
Trail Crest Pl
- SDGO 1189 G7
N Trail Ct
- CHLV 1311 G2
S Trail Ct
- CHLV 1311 G3
Trail Dr
3000 SDCo 1292 G2
(See Page 1292)
Trail Dust Av
13000 SDGO 1189 D5
Trail Marker Pl
- CHLV 1311 G2
Trail Ridge Dr
- SDCo 1129 C5
Trail Shrine Ln
2000 SDCo 1099 F5
(See Page 1099)
Trail St
- BRAW 6259 F7
(See Page 6259)
- BRAW 6260 B7
(See Page 6260)
Trailbrook Ln
11400 SDGO 1190 A6
Trailbrush Pt
11600 SDGO 1209 A1
Trailbrush Ter
7600 SDGO 1209 A1
Trailhead Pl
- CHLV 1311 H3
- SDGO 1189 B4
Trailing Dr
4100 SDGO 1289 H1
Trailridge Dr
500 CHLV 1311 C4
Trails End
2300 SDCo 1047 G2
Trails End Cir
10200 SDGO 1209 A5
Trails End Dr
13700 SDCo 1292 F2
(See Page 1292)
Trailside Ct
11200 SDGO 1169 H4
Trailside Pl
- SNMS 1128 F3
Trailside Rd
- SDCo 1169 A4
Trailside Wy
11300 SDGO 1169 J4
Trailview Rd
300 ENCT 1147 J6
Trailwind Rd
14300 POWY 1170 H4
Trailwood Av
1400 CHLV 1331 E1
Tralee Ter
3400 SDCo 1271 C6
Tram Pl
400 CHLV 1310 F5
Tranquil Ct
500 ENCT 1147 H5
Tranquil Wy
5000 OCSD 1067 A6
Tranquility Glen
600 ESCN 1130 B2
Tranquility Ln
- SDCo 1174 B4
Tranquillo Ln
- CHLV 1311 J3
Transformation Terr
2500 SDCo 1047 G2
S Transit St
200 OCSD 1106 A1
Transite Av
1300 SDGO 1349 J2
Transmitter Dr
- SDGO 1270 C6
Transportation Av
2600 NATC 1309 H3
Trapani Cv
1200 CHLV 1311 F6
Traske Rd
1500 ENCT 1147 G6
Traveld Wy
1500 ENCT 1147 G6
Travelers Wy
- SNMS 1128 G1
S Travelodge Dr
400 ELCJ 1251 D6
Traver Ct
- CHLV 1331 B1
Travers Wy
6100 SDGO 1228 B5
Travertine Pl
1600 SDCo 1272 B2
Travis Ct
8400 SDGO 1209 C1
Travis Pl
11300 SDGO 1209 C1
Traylor Rd
- SDCo 1171 H1
Treadwell Dr
- SDGO 1210 C1
Treasure Dr
4900 LMSA 1271 B2
Treasureview Ln
900 ENCT 1167 E1
Treat St
2700 SDGO 1289 D3
Trebol St
11300 SDGO 1209 B2
Trebuchet Dr
1900 SDCo 1058 G7
(See Page 1058)
Tree Haven Ct
10000 SDGO 1210 A4
Tree Hollow Ln
- SDGO 1189 J7
Tree Song Ln
1600 CHLV 1331 G3
Tree St
9700 SNTE 1231 A4
Tree View Pl
11700 SDGO 1210 A4
Treecrest St
13000 POWY 1190 D1
Treehill Pl
12600 POWY 1190 C2
Treehouse St
2300 CHLV 1311 H7
Treena St
10600 SDGO 1209 F4
Treeridge Ter
12700 POWY 1190 D1
Treeside Ln
10900 SDCo 1089 G3
Treetop Ln
2200 CHLV 1331 G3
- ELCJ 1251 J4
Treetop Rd
- OCSD 1067 B3
Treewind Ct
- SDGO 1190 A7
Treewind Ln
2200 CHLV 1311 G7
Treewood St
200 SDGO 1290 D4
Trelawney Ln
3000 SDCo 1028 C4
Trellis Ln
1500 ESCN 1109 H6
Trellis St
2200 CHLV 1331 H2
Trellis Wy
1700 CHLV 1331 H1
Tremaine Wy
1700 SDGO 1350 A2
Tremont St
200 CHLV 1330 D5
4300 SDGO 1289 H3
N Tremont St
800 OCSD 1085 J7
S Tremont St
1600 OCSD 1106 C3
Trenchard St
10000 SNTE 1231 D2
Trent Pl
15800 SDGO 1169 D4
Trent St
- SDCo 1086 A5
Trent Wy
10800 SDCo 1271 G4
Trento Pl
13700 SDGO 1188 A3
Trenton Av
1100 CHLV 1330 A4
3600 SDGO 1248 D5
Trenton St
600 ELCJ 1252 B4
Trenton Wy
1600 SNMS 1128 E6
Trepaire Cir
- SNTE 1231 B6
Tres Encinos
- SDCo 1088 J7
Tres Hermanas Wy
1400 ENCT 1147 G5
Tres Lagos Ct
10100 SDCo 1291 E1
Tres Lomas
2400 SDCo 1048 C1
Tres Lomas Ct
2700 SDCo 1048 C1
Tres Lomas Dr
1100 ELCJ 1252 B3
Tres Ninos Corte
1100 VSTA 1108 C1
Tres Ranchos Ln
500 SNMS 1109 A4
Tres Vista Ct
13700 SDGO 1189 E3
Treseder Cir
- SDCo 1272 B2
Treshill Rd
- IMPE 6499 E3
Trestles St
1200 OCSD 1087 B4
Tretagnier Cir
12000 SDGO 1150 A7
Trevino Av
2100 OCSD 1106 G1
Treviso Ct
13700 SDGO 1188 A4
Trevor Pl
2600 ELCJ 1251 A3
Trevors Ct
9500 SDCo 1232 D4
Treyburn Wy
- SDGO 1209 G2
Triana St
4900 SDGO 1248 G1
6300 SNTE 1231 G7
Trias St
4400 SDGO 1268 G4
Tribal Rd
65200 SDCo 1071 D2
Tribal Store Rd
- SDCo 1051 E7
- SDCo 1071 E5
Tribeca Cir
8700 SDGO 1249 D2
Tribul Ln
7400 CRLB 1126 J7
Tribuna Av
11500 SDGO 1209 J5
Tricia Ann Ct
29800 SDCo 1069 A5
Tricia Pl
28300 SDCo 1089 E3
Tricia St
14100 POWY 1190 E2
Tridle Pl
- CHLV 1330 J3
Tridle Wy
3500 SDGO 1350 F5
Trieste Dr
3400 CRLB 1106 H4
1200 SDGO 1287 J1
Trieste Wy
3500 OCSD 1106 J1
Trigal Wy
10600 SNTE 1231 E3
Trigger St
13000 SDGO 1189 C5
Trigo Ln
7400 CRLB 1147 J1
Trijullo Terr
- ESCN 1110 B5
Trillium Ct
7800 CRLB 1147 E2
- SDGO 1209 G2
Trillium Wy
- SDGO 1209 G1
Trilogy St
100 SNMS 1128 J3
Trinas Wy
3400 SDCo 1272 G5
Trinidad Bend
- CORD 1329 E2
Trinidad Cv
1200 CHLV 1311 F6
Trinidad Wy
5400 SDGO 1290 B4
Trinity Bay Pl
0 SDGO 1268 D5
Trinity Pl
5700 SDGO 1250 B7
Trinity St
- OCSD 1086 H1
Trinity Wy
5500 SDGO 1250 B7
Triple C Ranch Rd
2400 ENCT 1148 A7
Triple Crown Dr
5200 SDCo 1047 J7
5400 SDCo 1067 J1
Triple Crown Row
5100 SDGO 1188 D2
Triple J Trl
10000 SDCo 1069 D2
Triple Ln
11900 SDCo 1231 J5
Tripoli
- SDGO 1268 F6
Tripoli Dr
- ELCJ 1251 J5
Tripoli Rd
7700 SDGO 1209 A3
Tripoli Wy
3300 OCSD 1106 J1
Tripp Ct
3400 SDGO 1208 A4
Tristan River Rd
1100 CHLV 1331 B2
Tristiana Pl
17700 SDGO 1169 J1
Triton Av
1300 SDGO 1349 J2
Triton Cir
100 ENCT 1147 C7
Triton Pl
1500 SDGO 1349 J1
Triton St
1500 CRLB 1127 C5
Triumph Dr
12900 POWY 1190 D1
Triumph St
2000 VSTA 1107 G5
Trocha De Penni
10100 SDCo 1231 F3
Trojan Av
4800 SDGO 1269 J4
5800 SDGO 1270 C4
Trolley Ct
- LMSA 1250 J7
Trona Wy
2400 CRLB 1127 E4
Troon Wy
4000 CHLV 1310 F3
Tropea St
- OCSD 1067 A5
Trophy Dr
3500 SDCo 1270 J5
Trophy Wy
1200 SDCo 1079 C4
(See Page 1079)
Tropicana Dr
100 OCSD 1086 F4
Tropico Dr
9500 SDCo 1271 C3
S Tropico Dr
4200 SDCo 1271 B3
Trotter Dr
- SDGO 1208 E2
Trotting Horse Rd
1600 OCSD 1067 G7
Trousdale Dr
200 CHLV 1310 A4
Trousdale Pl
1900 ESCN 1129 F7
Trout Ln
- OCSD 1086 G3
Troutman Rd
- SDGO 1288 A5
Trouville Ln
1400 CHLV 1311 F7
Trovita Ct
500 ESCN 1110 D6
Troy Ln
4600 LMSA 1270 G3
1700 OCSD 1106 E2
Troy Pl
2000 VSTA 1088 C5
Troy St
8500 LMGR 1270 J7
8800 SDCo 1271 A6
Troy Ter
7600 LMSA 1270 G2
Truckee Av
2200 SDGO 1249 B7
Trudy Ln
3600 SDGO 1287 J4
Truesdell Ln
2000 CRLB 1106 G4
Truett Ln
10100 SDGO 1249 G5
Trujillo Rd
11800 SDCo 1029 J3
Truly Ter
600 VSTA 1087 J5
Truly Terr
600 VSTA 1087 H5
Truman Ct
- CALX 6620 J5
Truman St
9100 SDGO 1189 D6
Trumbull St
3100 SDGO 1288 B2
Trunks Bay
300 OCSD 1066 H6
Trust Dr
- ESCN 1129 F4
Truxtun Rd
- SDGO 1268 D7
- SDGO 1288 C1
Trza Mar
900 SNMS 1128 F6
Tubb Canyon Rd
200 SDCo 1098 H1
(See Page 1098)
600 SDCo 1099 A1
(See Page 1099)
Tuberose St
2700 SDGO 1269 G7
Tucana Dr
900 SNMS 1128 F5
Tuckaway St
6900 SDGO 1250 E5
Tucker Ct
- IMPE 6499 J2
Tucker Ln
1500 ENCT 1147 G6
Tucker Tr
2800 SDCo 1293 G2
Tucson Ct
1100 ELCJ 1252 A3
Tucuman St
- OCSD 1067 B2
Tudor Ln
2000 SDCo 1028 A3
Tudor St
9900 SDGO 1209 H5
Tufts St
5300 LMSA 1270 G1
Tuk-A-Wile
3800 SDCo 1272 G6
Tukmal Dr
600 OCSD 1086 D3
Tukooks Wy
200 SDCo 1235 A2
Tukwut Ct
- SDCo 1051 A6
Tulagi Rd
- CORD 1309 B2
Tulane Av
900 CHLV 1311 D5
Tulane Ct
1900 OCSD 1087 C5
3300 SDGO 1228 C6
Tulane St
5600 SDGO 1228 C6
Tulane Wy
3300 SDGO 1228 C6
Tulare Ct
3600 OCSD 1107 F3
Tulare St
8600 LMSA 1270 J3
Tularosa Ln
900 SNMS 1128 F6
Tule Ct
1800 CRLB 1127 E6
Tule Jim Ln
2100 SDCo 1300 F7
(See Page 1300)
Tule Springs Rd
- SDCo 1194 J3
(See Page 1194)
- SDCo 1195 C3
(See Page 1195)
Tule Springs Truck Trl
- SDCo 1194 C4
(See Page 1194)
31500 SDCo 1195 E3
(See Page 1195)
Tulip Dr
- SDGO 1248 C6
Tulip Ln
- SDCo 1086 A4
4100 SDGO 1289 H1
Tulip St
2400 SDGO 1289 G1
N Tulip St
200 ESCN 1129 G3
S Tulip St
500 ESCN 1129 H4
Tulip Wy
1000 CRLB 1127 B6
Tulipan Wy
2400 SDGO 1248 H7
Tulsa St
1100 ELCJ 1251 H6
Tumble Creek Ln
400 SDCo 1028 A3
Tumble Creek Terr
600 SDCo 1028 A3
Tumbleweed Av
- IMPE 6499 E3
Tumbleweed Ln
700 SDCo 1047 E4
Tumbleweed Terr
8500 SNTE 1231 E7
Tumbleweed Trl
27100 SDCo 1090 D6
Tumbleweed Wy
5600 OCSD 1067 E6
Tumeric Wy
20600 SDCo 1294 J7
(See Page 1294)
Tuna Ln
- SDGO 1288 J3
Tunapuna Ln
- CORD 1329 E3
Tungsten Dr
4100 LMSA 1270 H4
Tunica Cir
2400 SDGO 1248 H7
Tunis Dr
- ELCJ 1251 H5
Tunrif Ct
2500 SDCo 1068 D6
Tuolomne Pl
4300 CRLB 1107 A5
Tupelo Cove
7500 SDGO 1209 A2
Tupper St
1600 SDGO 1268 H5
Tura Ln
12300 POWY 1190 C2
Turf Club Dr
17200 SDCo 1169 A1
Turf Ln
3400 SDCo 1270 J5
Turf Rd
- SDGO 1187 G2
Turf View Dr
200 SOLB 1187 F2
Turfwood Ln
500 SOLB 1187 G1
Turlock Ct
13400 SDGO 1189 C3
Turmeric Ter
800 CHLV 1330 J1
Turnberry Ct
7400 SDCo 1168 G7
Turnberry Dr
3500 SDCo 1272 E5
- SNMS 1108 J3
1800 VSTA 1108 A4
Turnberry Glen
2600 SDCo 1109 H3
Turnberry Wy
3100 SDCo 1272 E6
Turnbridge Glen
2400 ESCN 1110 D6
Turnbridge Wy
6800 SDGO 1251 A4
Turnbull St
2800 OCSD 1086 D6
Turner Av
200 ENCT 1147 G6
Turner Heights Dr
- SDCo 1089 H3
Turner Heights Ln
- SDCo 1089 H3
Turner Ln
- SDCo 1071 D6
- SDCo 1089 H2
Turnford Dr
7300 SDGO 1250 J3
Turning Trail Rd
- CHLV 1311 G2
Turnstone Rd
- CRLB 1127 A4
Turnstone Wy
1000 OCSD 1087 A3
Turquoise Dr
- CRLB 1127 B4
Turquoise Ct
300 CHLV 1330 G5
Turquoise Ln
3500 OCSD 1107 D2
Turquoise St
- CALX 6620 H6
1100 SDGO 1247 H4
Turret Dr
11000 SDGO 1209 H4
Turtle Cay Pl
1200 CHLV 1311 G6
Turtle Cay Wy
1200 CHLV 1311 G6
Turtle Dove Ln
1000 ESCN 1109 F5
Turtle Point Wy
700 SNMS 1108 J4
Turtle Rock Rd
- SDCo 1090 F2
Turtleback Ct
11200 SDGO 1169 H4
Turtleback Ln
11300 SDGO 1169 J4
Turtleback Rd
16100 SDGO 1169 J4
Tuscan Springs Av
1500 CHLV 1331 E1
Tuscany Av
700 SNMS 1109 B4
Tuscany Ct
1100 ENCT 1147 C3
10600 SDCo 1169 F2
Tuscany Ln
7500 SDGO 1208 J4
Tuscany Wy
- OCSD 1087 A4
Tuscarora Dr
13000 POWY 1190 D4
Tushak Ranch Rd
- SDCo 1067 H6
Tusk Ct
10400 SDGO 1249 G3
Tustin St
12600 POWY 1190 C5
1800 SDGO 1288 B1
Tutela Heights
1500 ESCN 1109 H6
N Tuther Wy
7100 SDGO 1290 F4
W Tuther Wy
7000 SDGO 1290 F4
Tuthill Wy
9500 SNTE 1231 B4
Tuttle Ln
1200 SDCo 1251 G1

San Diego County Street Index

STREET
Block City Map# Grid

Tuttle St
2400 CRLB 1106 E4
Tuxedo Rd
6600 SDGO 1250 D3
Tuxford Dr
7300 SDGO 1250 J3
Twain Av
- CRLB 1107 B7
- CRLB 1127 B1
4400 SDGO 1249 H7
4900 SDGO 1250 A7
Twain Ct
1300 SNMS 1109 A3
Twain Wy
- SDCo 1070 H6
Tweed St
7400 LMGR 1270 G7
Twelve Oaks Trail
- SDCo 1252 F2
Twiggs St
4100 SDGO 1268 F5
Twila Ln
6300 SDGO 1270 D5
Twilight Glen
1900 ESCN 1109 A4
Twilight Ln
3500 OCSD 1107 C3
Twilight Point Wy
8100 SDCo 1169 A2
Twilight Ridge
- SDGO 1208 B2
Twilight St
1600 CHLV 1311 H7
Twilight View Terr
600 SDCo 1129 J7
Twin Circle Ct
13200 POWY 1190 E1
Twin Circle Wy
13200 POWY 1190 E2
Twin Gables Ct
14400 POWY 1190 F2
Twin Haven Rd
4500 OCSD 1087 A3
Twin Lake Dr
6200 SDGO 1250 G5
Twin Lakes Ct
- SDGO 1188 G2
Twin Mountain Cir
9300 SDGO 1209 E3
Twin Oak Ter
- SDCo 1232 G5
Twin Oaks Av
200 CHLV 1310 B5
1100 CHLV 1330 D2
Twin Oaks Cir
100 CHLV 1310 B5
Twin Oaks Crest Dr
- SDCo 1088 G4
Twin Oaks Ln
35100 SDCo 1156 E7
Twin Oaks Rd
35200 SDCo 1156 F7
Twin Oaks Valley Rd
29800 SDCo 1068 E6
3600 SDCo 1088 G4
2400 SDCo 1108 J1
1100 SNMS 1108 J4
- SNMS 1128 H5
S Twin Oaks Valley Rd
300 SNMS 1128 H2
W Twin Oaks Valley Rd
29500 SDCo 1068 F7
27700 SDCo 1088 G4
Twin Palm Cir
500 SDCo 1027 G3
Twin Peaks Pl
14400 POWY 1190 H1
Twin Peaks Rd
12300 POWY 1190 C1
Twin Pond Ter
11000 SDGO 1189 J5
Twin Trails Ct
9000 SDGO 1189 D4
Twin Trails Dr
9100 SDGO 1189 C4
Twinford Ct
9300 SDGO 1209 E2
Twining Av
900 SDGO 1350 F1
Twinleaf Ct
- SDGO 1209 J2
Twinleaf Wy
- SDGO 1209 H2
Twisted Branch Rd
14300 POWY 1170 G3
Twisted Oak Ln
- SDCo 1253 J1
Twisted Oak Rd
17800 SDCo 1294 B1
(See Page 1294)
Two Mile Coulee
13900 SDCo 1292 G2
(See Page 1292)
Tyaha St
9900 SDCo 999 D7
Tyhaven Dr
2200 SDCo 1087 J1
Tylee St
1100 VSTA 1087 E6
Tyler Av
1400 SDGO 1269 B5
Tyler Ct
- CALX 6620 J5
2200 SDCo 1291 A1
Tyler Ln
14400 SDCo 1050 F7
Tyler Pl
- BRAW 6319 H3
(See Page 6319)
Tyler Rd
14400 SDCo 1050 F7
14200 SDCo 1070 F1
Tyler St
2900 CRLB 1106 E5
4900 OCSD 1067 B7
8900 SDCo 1271 A7
- SNTE 1250 J1
Tynebourne Cir
3900 SDGO 1188 A4
Tyrian St
7400 SDGO 1227 E7
6600 SDGO 1247 E2
Tyrolean Rd
7700 SDGO 1209 A2
Tyrolean Wy
11100 SDGO 1209 A2
Tyrone St
600 ELCJ 1251 C4
Tyson St
100 OCSD 1106 A1
Tzena Wy
1500 ENCT 1147 G6

U

U Av
- NATC 1290 A6
N U Av
- NATC 1290 A6
U S Elevator Rd
10700 SDCo 1291 F1
Udall St
3400 SDGO 1268 C7
3000 SDGO 1288 C1
Ufano Dr
- SDCo 1293 B2
Uhl St
5800 SDGO 1270 C6
Ukiah St
- CHLV 1311 E7
Ullda Av
300 BRAW 6320 B1
(See Page 6320)
Ullman St
3400 SDGO 1288 A2
Ulric Ct
3000 SDGO 1248 H6
Ulric St
2700 SDGO 1248 J6
1700 SDGO 1268 J1
1400 SDGO 1269 A2
Ultimo Av
200 ESCN 1130 A7
Ultramarine Ln
100 SDGO 1290 F5
Umatilla Rd
- DLMR 1187 G5
Umber Ct
200 SDGO 1290 G4
Umbria Pl
13900 POWY 1170 F6
Umbria Wy
13900 POWY 1170 F6
Una St
1600 SDGO 1289 G6
Unicornio St
2700 CRLB 1127 G5
Unida Pl
3500 SDGO 1249 D4
Union Plaza Ct
1300 OCSD 1106 D1
Union Square Ln
4000 SDGO 1270 B5
Union St
400 ENCT 1147 C5
700 SDCo 1147 D5
3400 SDGO 1268 J7
2400 SDGO 1289 A1
Uniontown Rd
5100 SDGO 1228 F7
Unity Wy
100 VSTA 1087 G7
University Av
7200 LMSA 1270 F4
3200 SDGO 1269 D5
5800 SDGO 1270 C5
W University Av
300 SDGO 1268 J5
University Center Ln
8800 SDGO 1228 B3
University Dr
2100 VSTA 1108 B3
University Pl
8000 LMSA 1270 H2
400 SDGO 1268 J5
Unknown
- SDCo 1293 B1
Unknown Dr
3800 SDGO 1188 A6
Uno Ct
800 VSTA 1087 H5
Uno Verde Ct
1500 SOLB 1167 J7
Upas Ln
9700 SDCo 1149 D3
Upas St
1500 ESCN 1129 J5
1200 SDGO 1269 B6
N Upas St
11400 SDGO 1250 A1
200 ESCN 1129 G3
S Upas St
500 ESCN 1129 H4
W Upas St
1300 SDGO 1268 H7
Upland Dr
100 VSTA 1088 B6
Upland St
4400 LMSA 1270 J3
9600 SDCo 1271 C6
6000 SDGO 1290 C2
Upper Green Valley Rd
- SDCo 1196 H4
(See Page 1196)
Upper Hillside Dr
1700 SDGO 1227 H7
Upper Meadow Rd
33300 SDCo 1052 E3
(See Page 1052)
Upper Russell Rd
10400 SDCo 1271 E2
Upper Valley Ranch Rd
- POWY 1170 H1
Ups Cir
2000 OCSD 1106 E1
Upshur Dr
2600 SDGO 1268 E6
Upshur St
2900 SDGO 1288 B2
Upton Ct
6800 SDGO 1248 J7
Ur Ln
14700 SDCo 1273 A6
Urania Av
1100 ENCT 1147 C3
Urban Dr
5700 LMSA 1251 B7
Uribe Pl
- SDCo 1168 A7
Ursina Pl
1900 ENCT 1147 H7
Urubu St
6800 CRLB 1127 H5
Ushla Wy
32100 SDCo 1051 B6
Utah St
4700 SDGO 1269 D3
Utah Wy
600 ESCN 1129 J5
Ute Av
4300 OCSD 1087 D5
Ute Dr
3800 SDGO 1248 E4
Utgoff Rd
- CORD 1288 F4
Utica Ct
6500 SDGO 1310 F1
Utica Dr
3800 SDCo 1099 D1
(See Page 1099)
2700 SDGO 1310 F1
Utica Pl
6500 SDGO 1310 F1
Utopia Rd
13600 POWY 1190 D3
17400 SDGO 1170 C2
Utopia Wy
12500 SDGO 1170 C1
Uvada Pl
4900 SDGO 1269 D3
Uvalde Ct
10800 SDGO 1249 H1
Uvas St
4700 SDGO 1289 J3

V

V Av
500 NATC 1290 A7
Vaca Pl
11600 SDGO 1250 B2
Vacation Rd
- SDGO 1268 A2
Vachell Ln
15500 SDCo 1233 B1
Vado Wy
1300 SDGO 1290 D5
Vaho
- CALX 6620 H4
Vail Creek Ct
5100 SDGO 1188 D6
Vail Ct
- SDGO 1210 A1
Vakas Dr
1700 SDCo 1272 C3
Val Dale Dr
2700 SDCo 1130 E7
Val Sereno Dr
800 ENCT 1148 B6
Val Vista Dr
8500 SNTE 1250 J1
Valance St
1900 SDGO 1350 C3
Valborge Dr
- SNMS 1128 H5
Valbrook Dr
2100 SDCo 1028 B4
Valdes Dr
1600 SDGO 1227 G6
Valdina Dr
11400 SDGO 1250 A1
Valdina Wy
4700 SDGO 1250 A1
Valdivia Ct
1100 CHLV 1311 B6
Valdosta Av
8100 SDGO 1209 B3
Vale Blossom Ct
3400 CRLB 1107 B5
Vale Terrace Dr
1600 VSTA 1088 B5
Vale Terrace Pl
1400 VSTA 1088 B6
E Vale View Dr
1000 VSTA 1107 H1
W Vale View Dr
600 VSTA 1107 G1
Vale Wy
5800 SDGO 1270 C4
Valecrest Ln
2100 SDCo 1271 D7
Valemont St
3400 SDGO 1288 A2
Valencia Av
1800 CRLB 1106 J7
900 SNMS 1128 E3
Valencia Canyon
2600 SDCo 1271 A7
Valencia Cir
5900 SDCo 1168 F7
Valencia Ct
900 CHLV 1311 B6
6900 LMGR 1290 E2
1600 OCSD 1106 D2
Valencia Dr
1100 SDCo 1130 D5
4700 SDGO 1270 D3
100 VSTA 1087 G7
Valencia Glen Ct
1800 SDCo 1130 E3
Valencia Ln
9200 SDCo 1271 B7
Valencia Loop
1300 CHLV 1311 B6
Valencia Pkwy
- SDGO 1290 C4
Valencia Pl
- SDCo 1271 B7
Valencia St
1500 OCSD 1106 D2
8600 SDCo 1270 J7
8800 SDCo 1271 A7
Valencia Valley
31700 SDCo 1050 J7
Valencia View
12000 POWY 1190 C7
Valencia Wy
29000 SDCo 1070 J7
Valentine Ln
1200 SDCo 1028 C1
Valentine Rd
- SNMS 1109 A6
Valentino St
2000 SDGO 1350 D3
Valenzuela Rd
34700 SDCo 1029 J5
Valer Ct
4700 SDCo 1099 G4
(See Page 1099)
Valera Wy
100 OCSD 1086 H3
Valerian Vista Pl
6100 SDGO 1188 F3
Valerie Dr
2400 SDCo 1028 C7
400 VSTA 1087 H4
Valerio Gate
13400 SDGO 1188 E4
Valerio Tr
5400 SDGO 1188 D4
Valeta St
4300 SDGO 1268 B5
Valetta Ln
2500 SDCo 1234 A5
Valewood Av
2600 CRLB 1106 J5
Valewood Rd
13100 POWY 1190 C5
Valhalla Dr
- SDCo 1232 A5
Valhalla View Dr
2300 SDCo 1272 D1
Vali Hai Rd
15000 POWY 1171 A6
Valiente Ct
10800 SDGO 1249 J2
Valinda Pt
4600 SDGO 1188 B4
Valindo Wy
1900 SDCo 1108 C2
Valjean Ct
6600 SDGO 1248 H7
Valkyria Ln
1700 SDCo 1272 B3
Valladares Dr
18100 SDGO 1150 A7
Vallarta Ct
- SOLB 1167 G7
Vallata Ct
- SDCo 1291 D3
Vallata Ln
- SDCo 1291 D3
Valldemosa Ln
10800 SDGO 1249 H2
Valle Av
3000 SDGO 1289 E5
Valle Caballo Ln
9900 SDCo 1232 J2
Valle De Las Sombras Rd
1100 SDCo 1233 F6
Valle De Lobo Dr
17800 POWY 1170 F1
Valle De Lobo Wy
13600 POWY 1170 F1
Valle De Oro
- SDCo 1168 D5
Valle De Paz Rd
10100 SDCo 1233 C2
Valle Del Sol
- OCSD 1067 G2
3600 SDCo 1067 F1
Valle Del Sur Ct
14800 SDGO 1169 D6
Valle Dr
4300 LMSA 1270 H3
Valle Grande
1400 ESCN 1150 E3
Valle Lindo Rd
13900 ESCN 1110 F5
Valle Paso
- SDCo 1088 F5
Valle Verde Ln
- IMPE 6439 C7
Valle Verde Rd
16800 POWY 1170 E3
Valle Verde St
3800 SDCo 1310 H3
Valle Verde Ter
13200 POWY 1170 E3
Valle Vista
4300 SDGO 1268 H4
- SNMS 1129 C1
Valle Vista Av
2000 NATC 1310 B2
Valle Vista Bypass
- SDCo 1231 J2
Valle Vista Dr
5300 SDCo 1271 B1
Valle Vista Rd
11700 SDCo 1211 G6
10800 SDCo 1231 J1
Vallea St
1600 ELCJ 1252 B7
Vallecito Ct
- IMPE 6499 H2
Vallecito Ln
- SDCo 1085 J4
Vallecito Wy
- CHLV 1310 D7
Vallecitos
2300 SDGO 1227 H5
Vallecitos Ct
2400 SDGO 1227 H5
Vallecitos De Oro
100 SNMS 1108 F7
Vallecitos Dr
- SNMS 1108 C7
- SNMS 1128 C1
Valleda Ln
1400 ENCT 1147 G5
Vallejo Av
4300 SDGO 1248 E2
Vallejo Ct
4300 SDGO 1248 F2
Vallejo Mills St
1400 CHLV 1311 E7
Vallejo St
600 SDCo 1291 D3
100 SNTE 1231 F6
Vallery Ct
- SDGO 1188 D5
Valley
- ESCN 1129 E6
Valley Av
300 CHLV 1330 F6
600 SOLB 1167 G7
600 SOLB 1187 G1
Valley Bend St
- CHLV 1311 D7
Valley Blvd
1100 ImCo 6560 B7
Valley Center Rd
16600 ESCN 1110 F2
34800 SDCo 1051 E7
- SDCo 1071 D5
28100 SDCo 1090 E3
31100 SDCo 1091 B1
Valley Center School Rd
- SDCo 1090 F1
Valley Centre Rd
3600 SDGO 1208 A1
Valley Creek Dr
- CHLV 1311 H2
Valley Crest Dr
700 OCSD 1086 D3
700 SDCo 1088 E7
Valley Dr
400 SDCo 1088 B6
- SDCo 1290 J6
Valley Gardens Dr
2400 CHLV 1311 H7
Valley Glen Dr
3000 OCSD 1106 H2
Valley Grove Ln
500 ESCN 1130 C6
Valley Heights Dr
400 OCSD 1087 A2
Valley High Rd
8400 SNTE 1231 H7
Valley Knolls Rd
2800 SDCo 1292 G3
(See Page 1292)
Valley Lake Dr
2000 ELCJ 1251 B2
Valley Lights Dr
10900 SDCo 1271 G2
Valley Meadow Rd
500 ESCN 1110 E7
Valley Mill Rd
2100 ELCJ 1251 B2
Valley Oaks Blvd
- SDCo 1028 F4
Valley Of The King Rd
29600 SDCo 1068 F6
E Valley Pkwy
3000 ESCN 1110 E5
1100 ESCN 1130 A2
W Valley Pkwy
1800 ESCN 1129 F4
Valley Pl
1700 CRLB 1106 G5
2800 SDGO 1289 E4
Valley Ranch Ct
- POWY 1170 G2
Valley Ranch Dr
- POWY 1170 G1
Valley Ranch Rd
9700 SDCo 1232 H3
Valley Rd
3600 NATC 1310 E3
1900 OCSD 1086 G7
2000 OCSD 1106 G1
5700 SDGO 1310 C3
Valley Ridge St
- CHLV 1311 E2
Valley Rim Glen
2100 ESCN 1109 C4
Valley Rim Rd
- ELCJ 1252 D4
1900 SDCo 1252 D4
Valley Springs Rd
14000 POWY 1170 G4
Valley St
1000 CALX 6620 D7
2900 CRLB 1106 F4
Valley View Blvd
1900 ELCJ 1252 C5
Valley View Dr
1200 SDCo 1136 C7
N Valley View Dr
- CHLV 1311 G3
Valley View Glen
2500 ESCN 1109 B3
Valley View Ln
100 OCSD 1086 E6
3400 SDCo 1271 A6
Valley View Pl
2300 ESCN 1109 G4
200 VSTA 1107 J1
Valley View Rd
- SDCo 1090 A1
Valley View Trl
8200 SDCo 1237 C5
- SDCo 1252 D2
Valley View Truck Trl
- SDCo 1232 H7
- SDCo 1252 E1
Valley Village Dr
600 ELCJ 1251 G3
Valley Vista Dr
27000 SDCo 1090 J5
Valley Vista Fork
3700 SDCo 1310 E3
W Valley Vista Fork
3700 SDCo 1310 E3
Valley Vista Rd
3700 SDCo 1310 F3
Valley Vista Wy
2800 OCSD 1106 F1
W Valley Vista Wy
3600 SDCo 1310 F3
Valley Waters Ct
2500 SDCo 1291 F2
Valley Waters Dr
10300 SDCo 1291 F2
Valleydale Ln
1900 ENCT 1167 H1
Valleyside Ln
1000 ENCT 1148 A5
Valleytree Pl
300 ESCN 1109 G4
Valleyview Av
- ELCN 6559 G4
Valleyview Dr
- SDCo 996 J2
Valleyview Rd
14600 POWY 1150 H7
Valmonte Glen
2500 ESCN 1149 G1
Valner Ct
2200 SDGO 1290 D7
Valner Wy
6200 SDGO 1290 D7
Valoma Pl
4300 SDGO 1228 E5
Valor Ln
- ELCN 6559 J4
Valor Pl
10700 SNTE 1231 E3
Valpreda Rd
100 SNMS 1108 J7
Valva Av
- NATC 1290 A6
Valverde Ln
1500 CHLV 1331 D3
Van Allen Wy
5800 CRLB 1127 C2
Van Andel Wy
9300 SNTE 1230 J5
Van Buren Av
1500 SDGO 1269 B4
Van Der Poel Rd
- ImCo 6559 B7
Van Dyke Av
500 DLMR 1187 G5
4500 SDGO 1269 H4
Van Dyke Pl
4200 SDGO 1269 H4
Van Gogh Ln
5200 SDCo 1290 H7
Van Horn Rd
800 SDCo 1252 C7
Van Horn St
8700 LMSA 1251 A6
Van Horn Wy
800 SDCo 1252 C7
Van Houten Av
400 ELCJ 1251 F6
Van Ness Av
2000 NATC 1310 C1
Van Nuys Ct
5300 SDGO 1247 H4
Van Nuys Pl
5300 SDGO 1247 H4
Van Nuys St
1200 SDGO 1247 H4
Van Roy Wy
2400 OCSD 1086 D6
Van Vechten Rd
1300 ELCJ 1252 A7
Vance St
100 CHLV 1310 C6
Vancouver Av
3100 SDGO 1269 F6
Vancouver St
2600 CRLB 1106 J3
Vandegrift Blvd
800 OCSD 1067 A4
- SDCo 1066 B3
- SDCo 1067 A2
- SDCo 1085 H4
- SDCo 1086 A1
Vandemen Wy
- SDGO 1209 G2
Vanderbilt Pl
700 SDGO 1268 J6
Vandever Av
4300 SDGO 1249 H7
Vandever St
4700 SDGO 1249 J7
Vanessa Cir
1400 ENCT 1147 G5
Vanessa Wy
1000 SNMS 1128 G5
Vanguard Pl
8700 SDCo 1232 C7
Vanguard Wy
13200 SDCo 1232 C7
Vanilla Wy
700 OCSD 1086 H5
Vanita St
700 SDCo 1027 G1
Vanitie Ct
800 SDGO 1247 H7
Vann Centre Blvd
700 SDCo 1352 A1
Vann Ct
1600 ELCJ 1251 C4
Vantage Ct
- VSTA 1128 A1
Vantage Pl
1100 SDCo 1027 H7
Vantage Wy
2400 SDGO 1187 H5
Vaquero Ct
- SDCo 1086 A3
E Vaquero Ct
- CHLV 1311 B7
W Vaquero Ct
- CHLV 1311 B7
Vaquero Glen
1400 ESCN 1109 E4
Vaquero Tr
- IMPE 6439 F4
Varney Dr
6300 SDGO 1290 D5
Varona St
4200 SDGO 1288 A2
Vasquez Wy
16900 SDCo 1169 F3
Vassar Av
800 CHLV 1311 D5
7200 LMSA 1270 F3
Vaughan Rd
12400 POWY 1190 C3
Vechten Rd
- SDCo 1272 A1
Vecinio Del Este Pl
13600 SDCo 1232 E5
Vecino Ct
300 SDCo 1291 B4
Veemac Av
6000 LMSA 1251 B6
Vega St
- CALX 6620 F7
1200 SDGO 1268 E2
Vega Wy
1000 SNMS 1128 F5
Vegas Dr
- SDGO 1229 C4
Vejas View Ln
- SDCo 1235 A5
Vela Dr
11300 SDGO 1209 C1
Velasco Ct
4300 SDCo 1271 G3
Velite Dr
300 SDCo 1058 G7
(See Page 1058)
Vella La Vella Rd
- CORD 1309 A2
Velma Ter
5200 SDGO 1290 B5
Venadito
3000 SDCo 1254 D1
Venado St
3000 CRLB 1127 H7
3200 CRLB 1147 J1
Vendimia Ct
2500 VSTA 1088 D6
Vendola Dr
1700 CHLV 1331 E1
Vendor Pl
17200 POWY 1170 D2
Venetia Wy
- OCSD 1087 A4
Venice Av
1600 SNMS 1128 E6
Venice Ct
800 SDGO 1247 H7
Venice Glen
900 ESCN 1109 J7
Venice St
2000 SDGO 1268 A6
1700 SDGO 1288 A1
Ventana Dr
1400 ESCN 1149 G1
Ventana Wy
2000 ELCJ 1251 C1
4700 OCSD 1087 A1
Ventasso Wy
200 SDCo 1028 H5
Venters Dr
- CHLV 1330 J3
Ventura Pl
700 SDGO 1267 H2
Venture St
400 ESCN 1129 E3
100 SNMS 1129 A1
Venture Valley Rd
800 SDCo 1138 A6
(See Page 1138)
Venturi Trl
- SDGO 1249 D2
Venus St
4100 SDGO 1268 C4
Venus View Dr
700 VSTA 1107 G1
Vera Cir
100 VSTA 1087 J5
Vera Cruz
1200 OCSD 1087 B4
Vera Cruz Av
- SDGO 1268 F7
Vera Ln
2000 ESCN 1109 D5
Vera St
800 SOLB 1187 G1
Veracruz Ct
- IMPE 6499 H1
10200 SDGO 1249 G1
Veralee Dr
3200 SDGO 1350 D1
Veranda Ct
12400 SDGO 1189 J6
Verano Brisa Dr
- SDCo 1148 E3
Verano Ct
12000 SDGO 1150 B7
Verano Dr
18100 SDGO 1150 B6
Verano Pl
2500 ESCN 1130 C7
18300 SDGO 1150 B6
Verano Vista
1800 SDCo 1128 C4
Verbena Ct
- CRLB 1127 B4
500 ENCT 1147 E5
Verbena Dr
300 SDCo 1078 G1
(See Page 1078)
Verbena Ln
10000 SDCo 1291 D3
Verbena Ter
1900 SDCo 1233 J5
1900 SDCo 1234 A5
Verbena Wy
- IMPE 6499 E2
Verda Av
2700 ESCN 1130 A7
2800 ESCN 1150 B1
Verda Ln
6100 SDGO 1188 G4
Verdant Pl
600 VSTA 1087 J5
Verde Av
3100 CRLB 1127 J7
500 SDCo 1047 E5
Verde Ct
3200 SDCo 1310 E4
Verde Dr
4900 OCSD 1067 A6
Verde Glenn
1900 SDCo 1272 C2
Verde Oro
300 SDCo 1047 F3
Verde Park Ct
- SDGO 1249 D1
Verde Ridge Ct
400 SDCo 1290 H6
Verde Ridge Rd
8300 SDCo 1290 J5
Verde Via
1900 SDCo 1130 E4
Verde View
4100 NATC 1310 D4
Verde View Rd
2900 SDCo 1234 D7
Verde Vista Ln
10000 SNTE 1231 D4
Verdi Av
100 ENCT 1167 C2
Verdigris Valley Rd
- SDCo 1171 E1
Verdin Ct
- CRLB 1127 D4
Verdin St
500 ELCJ 1252 B4
Verdot Ct
15000 SDGO 1169 F6
Vereda Barranca
1200 SDCo 1088 C4
Vereda Callada Ln
900 SDCo 1149 H1
Vereda Ct
1900 SDCo 1272 C1
Vereda Dr
- CALX 6620 H7
Vereda Luna Llena
- SDGO 1208 C3
Vereda Luz Del Sol
- SDGO 1208 C3
Vereda Mar De Ponderosa
- SDGO 1208 C3
Vereda Mar Del Corazon
- SDGO 1208 C2
Vereda Mar Del Sol
- SDGO 1208 C3
Vereda Rd
700 SNMS 1109 A6
Vereda Sol Del Dios
- SDGO 1208 C4
Vergara St
5300 SDGO 1248 H1
Veridian Cir
- SDGO 1169 D4
Verin Ln
800 CHLV 1310 H6
Verla Ln
1600 SDCo 1130 C4
Verlane Dr
8500 SDGO 1250 J4
Verley Ct
4400 SDGO 1248 G2
Vermarine Ct
6700 CRLB 1127 G4
Vermel Av
1900 ESCN 1129 F5
Vermillion Wy
100 SDGO 1290 F5
E Vermont Av
200 ESCN 1130 A5
W Vermont Av
300 ESCN 1130 A5
Vermont Ct
200 ELCJ 1251 F5
Vermont Pl
1900 ESCN 1129 J6
Vermont St
1800 SDCo 1152 E7
2300 SDCo 1172 D1
4100 SDGO 1269 B5
Vern Dr
2300 SDCo 1028 F6
Verna Dr
- SDCo 1069 A6
Verna Wy
5100 SDCo 1271 F1

69 INDEX
INDEX 69
Vernal Ln
Via Hondita
SAN DIEGO CO.

San Diego County Street Index

STREET
Block City Map# Grid

Vernal Ln
9000 SDCo 1236 A3
Vernardo Dr
100 CALX 6620 F7
Vernazza Ct
13700 SDGO 1188 A4
Verner Wy
- VSTA 1087 G7
Vernette Ct
11600 SDCo 1271 H2
Vernette Dr
4600 SDCo 1271 H2
Vernie Vista Ln
32300 SDCo 1050 F6
Vernier Dr
8000 LMGR 1290 H1
Vernon Ct
- CHLV 1331 B1
Vernon Wy
900 ELCJ 1251 E3
Verona Ct
800 SDGO 1247 H7
Verona Hills Ct
2100 SDCo 1108 D3
Verona Hills Pkwy
- SDCo 1108 D2
Verona St
- OCSD 1087 C3
Veronica Av
6800 SDGO 1270 E5
Veronica Ct
400 CHLV 1330 G3
- CRLB 1127 B5
Veronica Pl
500 ESCN 1110 D6
Versailles Ct
12000 SDGO 1150 A7
Versailles Rd
- CHLV 1311 E5
Verus St
2200 SDGO 1330 A5
Vervain St
9400 SDGO 1189 E5
Vesper Ln
- SDCo 1127 D4
Vesper Rd
- SDCo 1071 C7
14400 SDCo 1090 G1
16300 SDCo 1091 A1
Vesta St
- NATC 1309 F1
- SDGO 1289 F7
- SDGO 1309 F1
Vesuvia Wy
3000 SDGO 1310 E2
Veterans Hospital Dr
- SDGO 1228 A2
Vetter Pl
4300 LMSA 1270 F4
Vezelay Ln
18300 SDGO 1150 B6
Via A La Casa
16400 SDCo 1168 E4
Via Abaca
10900 SDGO 1209 C3
Via Abajo
11100 SDGO 1169 H7
Via Abertura
14000 SDGO 1188 H2
Via Acantilada
17800 SDGO 1170 C1
Via Acapulco
- SDGO 1228 D4
Via Acosta
12800 SDGO 1150 C7
Via Acquaviva
4300 SDCo 1047 G5
Via Adelea
- CRLB 1147 F2
Via Adelia
- SCLE 1023 B1
Via Adriana
1700 OCSD 1087 C5
Via Afable
1600 SDGO 1349 J1
Via Agave
7000 SDGO 1188 H3
Via Alberto
10700 SDGO 1189 H2
Via Alcazar
6500 CRLB 1127 J4
5400 SDGO 1248 G6
Via Aldea
4000 OCSD 1086 H2
Via Alegre
800 SDCo 1027 H1
1700 SDCo 1130 D3
Via Alegre Dr
- SDCo 1152 J6
Via Alessandro
3200 SDGO 1248 G5
Via Alexandra
- ESCN 1109 F5
Via Alfalfa
11900 SDCo 1271 J3
Via Alicante
3000 SDGO 1228 A4
Via Alicia
3600 OCSD 1107 G4
2400 SDCo 1048 C2

Via Alisal
14100 SDGO 1190 B1
Via Allegra
800 VSTA 1107 H2
Via Allena
1700 OCSD 1087 C4
Via Allondra
1700 SDCo 1128 A4
Via Almansa
300 ENCT 1147 F6
Via Almonte
3200 SDCo 1048 H2
Via Alta
1400 DLMR 1187 G4
- SDGO 1269 B1
Via Alta Mirasol
17700 SDGO 1170 B1
Via Alta Vista
- SDCo 1048 C7
- SNMS 1108 C7
- SNMS 1128 C1
Via Altamira
3200 SDCo 1048 G2
Via Altiva
17800 SDGO 1150 B7
Via Altivo
11100 SDGO 1169 H7
Via Amable
4400 SDGO 1228 D3
Via Amador
3000 CRLB 1106 H3
Via Amalia
3100 SDGO 1248 G6
Via Amata
3100 SDGO 1248 G5
Via Ambiente
17700 SDCo 1148 H6
18500 SDCo 1149 B4
Via Ambrosa
13300 SDGO 1188 J4
Via Amistosa
3800 SDCo 1168 C7
Via Anacapa
- SNMS 1108 D4
Via Andalusia
300 ENCT 1147 F6
Via Andar
8800 SDGO 1228 D3
Via Angelina
1100 SDGO 1247 F2
Via Anita
2200 SDGO 1247 J2
9200 SNTE 1231 G5
Via Anna
10700 SDCo 1271 F6
Via Antigua
12100 SDCo 1272 A4
Via Antoinette
- SDCo 1070 C5
Via Aprilia
2200 SDGO 1207 H1
Via Apuesto
1200 SDCo 1128 B3
Via Aquario
5300 SDGO 1248 G5
Via Arango
10700 SDGO 1189 H2
Via Ararat Dr
31500 SDCo 1048 G7
Via Arboleda
1200 SDCo 1149 G2
Via Arboles
400 SNMS 1109 D7
Via Arce
- CRLB 1147 G3
Via Arcilla
3100 SDGO 1248 G5
Via Arequipa
4900 CRLB 1107 A7
Via Arezzo
14500 SDGO 1168 J7
Via Argentina
1100 VSTA 1107 E1
Via Armado
500 CHLV 1311 A4
Via Arriva
- SDCo 1291 G1
Via Arroyo
2900 SDCo 1048 B1
Via Artista
- SNMS 1108 E4
Via Arturo Rd
9500 SDCo 1235 E2
Via Ascenso
18100 SDCo 1148 D6
Via Asoleado
2800 SDCo 1254 B3
Via Asti
11000 SDGO 1189 H3
Via Astuto
2500 CRLB 1106 H3
Via Asuncion Wy
31500 SDCo 1067 H2
Via Avante
5100 SDGO 1188 D3
Via Avola
2400 SDGO 1227 H6
Via Azul
14700 SDGO 1168 J6
Via Bahia
700 SNMS 1108 F4

Via Baldona
3700 OCSD 1107 F4
Via Banco
10900 SDGO 1209 C3
Via Bandita
200 OCSD 1087 A2
Via Barberini
- CHLV 1310 A4
Via Barletta
2500 SDGO 1227 H6
Via Barlovento
1600 SDCo 1128 C3
Via Baroda
14200 SDGO 1188 D2
Via Barona
6500 CRLB 1127 J4
Via Barquero
700 SNMS 1108 F4
Via Barranca
- CALX 6620 H5
1200 SDGO 1247 G2
Via Barranca Del Zorro
- SDCo 1168 F4
Via Bartolo
3200 SDGO 1248 G5
Via Belfiore
7800 SDGO 1189 A4
Via Bella Donna
800 SNMS 1128 C1
Via Bella Maria
800 SNMS 1128 C1
Via Bella Monica
800 SNMS 1128 C1
Via Bellarado
13300 SDGO 1189 A4
Via Belleza
1200 SNMS 1109 C7
Via Bellini
14700 SDGO 1168 J6
Via Bello
5300 SDGO 1248 G5
Via Belmonte
4700 SDCo 1048 G1
Via Belota
2900 SDCo 1254 D1
Via Beltran
3500 SDGO 1248 E5
Via Benito
3300 SDGO 1248 G5
Via Bergamo
14600 SDGO 1168 J7
Via Bernardo
3600 OCSD 1107 G4
Via Bettona
14600 SDGO 1168 J7
Via Bissolotti
300 CHLV 1310 A4
Via Blanca
2100 OCSD 1106 F2
Via Bocas
2600 CRLB 1106 H3
Via Bogota
600 VSTA 1107 F1
Via Bolivia
600 VSTA 1107 E1
Via Bologna
10900 SDGO 1189 H2
Via Bolsa
11600 SDCo 1271 J3
Via Boltana
13800 SDGO 1189 E3
Via Borgia
12700 SDGO 1207 H1
Via Borregos
6800 CRLB 1128 A6
Via Botero
1500 OCSD 1087 C3
Via Brescia
10900 SDGO 1189 H2
Via Brillante
4500 SDGO 1228 D3
Via Brisa Del Lago
1500 SDCo 1128 C3
Via Broma
15900 SDCo 1168 C7
Via Buena Vista
1500 SDCo 1128 B4
Via Caandria
- SCLE 1023 B2
Via Caballo Rojo
13000 SDGO 1189 F5
Via Cabana
7000 CRLB 1127 G6
Via Cabernet
- ESCN 1129 E4
Via Cabezon
12300 SDGO 1189 F6
Via Cabo Verde
3300 ESCN 1150 A3
Via Cabrera
6300 SDGO 1247 J1
Via Cabrillo
3700 OCSD 1107 F4
Via Caceras
9800 SDGO 1189 F3
Via Cafetal
- SNMS 1108 E4
Via Cajita
3200 CRLB 1106 H4

Via Calabria
3600 ESCN 1150 D3
Via Calafia
7000 CRLB 1127 G6
Via Calanova
15600 SDGO 1170 B5
Via Caldron
- CRLB 1127 H4
Via Caliente
- SNMS 1108 F4
Via Caliente Del Sol
- SDCo 1272 D7
Via California
1500 CHLV 1331 C3
Via Callado
700 OCSD 1067 B5
5500 SDGO 1247 H3
Via Callendo
7900 CRLB 1148 A2
Via Calvillo
1800 SDCo 1067 G2
Via Camellia
1100 SNMS 1109 C7
Via Caminar
1600 SDCo 1128 C3
Via Camino Verde
2100 OCSD 1106 F1
Via Campanile
7600 CRLB 1147 J1
Via Campestre
29700 SDCo 1069 J6
- SDGO 1187 H1
Via Campo Verde
- SDCo 1168 F5
Via Canada Del Osito
5800 SDCo 1168 E5
Via Cancion
1600 SDCo 1128 A3
Via Candela
18400 SDCo 1148 E5
Via Candidiz
- SDGO 1188 B6
Via Candrejo
7000 CRLB 1127 G6
Via Cangrejo
- SDGO 1208 B3
Via Cantamar
30500 SDCo 1068 J4
Via Cantebria
100 ENCT 1147 F6
- SDCo 1147 F4
Via Canyon Dr
13100 SDGO 1188 J5
Via Capri
- CHLV 1311 D7
7600 SDGO 1227 H6
Via Capri Ct
2300 SDGO 1227 H6
Via Capriccia
6200 SDCo 1148 D4
Via Cara Loma
3700 ENCT 1148 B3
Via Caracas
8900 SDGO 1209 D3
Via Carancho
5300 SDGO 1248 G5
Via Cardel
2700 CRLB 1106 H3
Via Carina
1000 VSTA 1107 H2
Via Carlotta
11600 SDCo 1271 J4
Via Carolina
1100 SDGO 1247 F2
Via Carpa Dorado
- SDGO 1228 D3
Via Carrillo
1500 SDCo 1128 B4
7300 SDGO 1188 J4
Via Carrio
2800 CRLB 1106 H3
Via Carroza
11200 SDGO 1250 A2
Via Casa Alta
1900 SDGO 1227 H7
Via Cascabel
2300 SDCo 1130 F4
10800 SDGO 1249 J2
Via Cascada
2800 CRLB 1106 H3
Via Cascadita
4500 OCSD 1087 A2
Via Casilina
11800 SDCo 1272 A4
Via Casitas
- SDCo 1048 B7
- SDCo 1068 C1
Via Cassandra
200 SDCo 1027 F4
Via Castenet
1200 SDCo 1128 B4
Via Castilla
5100 OCSD 1067 A4
Via Catania
18600 SDCo 1148 F5
Via Cavour
300 CHLV 1310 A4
Via Cazadero
16200 SDCo 1168 F7
Via Cenote
2300 SDCo 1156 B3

Via Centre
1900 VSTA 1107 C2
Via Cerdo
- CHLV 1311 A6
Via Cerezas
10800 SDGO 1189 G2
Via Chaparral
1500 SDCo 1028 E5
Via Chardonnay
- ESCN 1129 E4
Via Chica
- ENCT 1147 J4
Via Chica Ct
300 SOLB 1167 H6
Via Chinarros
2700 SDCo 1254 A2
Via Chona
11700 SDGO 1170 A5
Via Christina
1400 VSTA 1088 A4
Via Cibola
1300 OCSD 1067 A5
Via Cielito
8300 SDCo 1149 A4
Via Cielo Azul
3700 SDCo 1254 F2
Via Cielo Vista
1100 SDCo 1149 H3
Via Cima
15000 SDGO 1169 H7
Via Cima Bella
13700 SDGO 1189 E3
Via Cimborio Cir
10700 SDGO 1210 A2
Via Cineria
- ESCN 1129 E4
Via Cinta
4900 SDGO 1228 G6
Via Clarez
2800 CRLB 1106 H3
Via Clemente
2300 CRLB 1106 G3
4200 OCSD 1087 A4
Via Codorniz
2500 SDCo 997 C5
Via Coello
7000 CRLB 1127 G7
Via Colima
2700 CRLB 1106 H3
Via Colina
- OCSD 1107 F4
9200 SDCo 1271 B4
Via Collado
15000 SDGO 1169 H7
Via Colmenar
- SDGO 1189 B5
Via Colonia
8600 SDGO 1209 C3
Via Colorado
4700 OCSD 1087 B4
Via Coloroso
- SCLE 1023 B2
Via Columbia
600 VSTA 1107 E1
Via Conca Doro
800 SDCo 1088 F7
Via Concepcion
- SDCo 1168 C5
Via Conejo
1200 SDCo 1149 H3
Via Conquistador
- CRLB 1127 J4
Via Conrad
- SNTE 1231 C3
Via Consuelo
8500 SDCo 1232 E6
Via Contenta
1100 SDCo 1149 H2
Via Contessa
- SNMS 1108 F4
Via Cordoba
6700 SDCo 1168 H6
Via Cordova
- SDCo 1291 G1
Via Corina
1800 SDCo 1233 F7
1800 SDCo 1253 F1
Via Corona
1600 SDGO 1247 H3
Via Coronado
- SDCo 1168 C7
Via Corsini
14100 SDGO 1190 B2
Via Corte
2100 SDCo 1129 H6
Via Cortina
12700 SDGO 1207 H1
Via Corto
2200 SDCo 1048 B4
Via Cortona
7600 SDGO 1168 J7
- SNTE 1230 H7
Via Coscoja
- CRLB 1147 G2
Via Costa Rica
600 VSTA 1107 F1
Via Costanza
13300 SDGO 1189 A3
Via Costina
1700 SDGO 1350 D2

Via Cresta Rd
7300 SDGO 1188 J4
Via Cristal
7600 SDGO 1188 J4
Via Cristobal
2700 CRLB 1106 H3
Via Cruz
400 OCSD 1086 J4
400 OCSD 1087 A4
Via Cuarto
1800 OCSD 1087 C5
Via Cuarto Caminos
17400 SDCo 1168 G1
Via Cuenca
9900 SDGO 1189 F3
Via Cuesta
19000 SDCo 1151 H2
Via Cuesta Arriba
- SDCo 1068 E4
Via Cuesta Mansa
6800 SDCo 1168 G7
Via Cuesta Verde
11900 SDCo 1168 G6
Via Cumbres
600 SDCo 1028 B3
Via Cumbres Ln
- SDCo 1028 C3
Via Cupeno
5100 OCSD 1067 B7
Via Curvada
600 CHLV 1310 G7
Via Cuyamaca
9800 SNTE 1231 C4
Via Dardo
12800 SDGO 1150 C7
Via Daroca
9900 SDGO 1189 F3
Via De Amo
200 SDCo 1028 B2
Via De Amor
9100 SNTE 1231 B7
Via De Anza
3700 SNMS 1108 C7
Via De Caballo
3100 ENCT 1148 B6
Via De Canto
3100 CRLB 1106 H3
Via De Casa
100 SDCo 1028 B2
Via De Cristina
9100 SNTE 1231 B7
Via De Encanto
1200 SDCo 1149 H3
Via De Fortuna
- CRLB 1127 G7
18200 SDCo 1148 C7
17500 SDCo 1168 B2
Via De Jamul
13900 SDCo 1292 J2
(See Page 1292)
Via De Juan
9100 SNTE 1231 B7
Via De La Amistad
9700 SDGO 1352 B3
Via De La Bandola
3900 SDGO 1350 F2
Via De La Cuesta
1700 SDCo 1130 D3
Via De La Cumbre
- SDCo 1168 C2
Via De La Flor
- SDCo 1068 D3
Via De La Melodia
1600 SDGO 1350 F2
Via De La Montana
1600 SDCo 1233 F6
Via De La Nola
17100 SDCo 1168 H2
Via De La Paz
4000 OCSD 1086 H4
Via De La Reina
- SDCo 1068 D4
Via De La Roca
40600 SDCo 997 H3
Via De La Valle
3300 OCSD 1086 E4
15700 SDCo 1168 D5
2700 SDGO 1187 H2
3300 SDGO 1188 A1
200 SOLB 1187 F2
Via De La Vista
- ENCT 1147 D3
Via De Las Flores
18300 SDCo 1148 G6
Via De Las Palmas
16100 SDCo 1168 C7
Via De Laurencio
- CHLV 1310 D6
Via De Los Cepillos
- SDCo 1067 H2
Via De Los Rosales
16700 SDCo 1168 F6
Via De Luna
13200 SDCo 1070 C7
Via De Maranatha
- SDCo 1028 A4
Via De Maya
7000 SDCo 1168 F2
Via De Oro
9900 SDCo 1271 D6

Via De Paz
2900 CRLB 1106 H3
30300 SDCo 1068 E4
Via De Plata
- SNMS 1108 F5
Via De San Ysidro
100 SDGO 1350 F4
Via De Santa Fe
16700 SDCo 1168 D3
Via De Sinnard
7000 SDCo 1168 F1
Via De Sueno
- SDCo 1148 C7
Via De Todos Santos
3200 SDCo 1048 H2
Via De Victoria
8700 SNTE 1231 B7
Via De Vista
300 SOLB 1167 F7
Via Debbie
9900 SNTE 1231 D4
Via Del Aguacate
2300 SDCo 1028 B7
Via Del Alba
16200 SDCo 1168 C4
Via Del Allazon
2800 SDCo 1290 J7
Via Del Astro
300 OCSD 1086 H4
Via Del Bardo
3700 SDGO 1350 F2
Via Del Bravo
17500 SDCo 1168 G1
Via Del Caballero
5800 SDCo 1047 J7
Via Del Caballo
500 SNMS 1129 A2
Via Del Caballo Blanco
2900 SDCo 1290 H7
Via Del Campo
17200 SDGO 1169 H2
600 SNMS 1129 A2
Via Del Campo Ct
16700 SDGO 1169 H3
Via Del Canon
14800 SDCo 1188 A1
Via Del Cerrito
200 ENCT 1147 J7
Via Del Cerro
1100 SDCo 1068 A6
Via Del Charro
6800 SDCo 1148 F6
Via Del Cielo
- SDCo 1028 D6
Via Del Conquistador
3600 SDGO 1248 E5
Via Del Corvo
1600 SDCo 1128 B4
Via Del Cosira
10800 SDGO 1249 J2
Via Del Gavilan
- SDCo 997 J4
- SDCo 998 A4
Via Del Lago
- SDCo 997 H5
Via Del Lobo
- SDCo 1068 C5
Via Del Luz
8600 SDCo 1232 D7
Via Del Mar
3800 SDGO 1208 A2
600 VSTA 1107 E1
Via Del Mesonero
1600 SDGO 1350 F2
Via Del Monte
200 OCSD 1086 D5
Via Del Monte Libano
- SDCo 1088 E6
Via Del Norte
500 OCSD 1086 D5
300 SDGO 1247 E2
Via Del Oro
5200 OCSD 1107 F4
1300 SDCo 1028 A4
Via Del Pardo
2600 OCSD 1106 G1
Via Del Parque
10500 SDCo 1271 F7
Via Del Prado
2000 SDCo 1088 C1
Via Del Rancho
3700 OCSD 1107 F4
Via Del Rey
- SNMS 1108 C7
Via Del Rio
- SDCo 998 A4
Via Del Robles
2700 SDCo 1028 B6
Via Del Santo
- SDCo 1068 E6
Via Del Sauce
- SDCo 1070 A5
Via Del Sol
10700 SDCo 1271 F6
Via Del Sud
10100 SDGO 1189 G5
Via Del Sur
5200 OCSD 1107 F4
Via Del Tanido
1800 SDGO 1350 E3

Via Del Toro
12800 POWY 1170 D3
Via Del Torrie
- SDCo 1254 A1
Via Del Valedor
13000 SDGO 1189 F5
Via Del Venado
32700 SDCo 1049 E5
Via Del Verde
2500 SDCo 1028 C7
Via Dello Russo
15500 SDCo 1070 J6
Via Dena Loma
- SDCo 1171 B2
Via Denise
3000 CRLB 1106 H3
Via Di Felicita
- ENCT 1148 A5
Via Diana
11600 SDCo 1271 J4
Via Dianza
- CRLB 1127 H4
Via Dicha
16300 SDCo 1168 C7
Via Diego
2800 CRLB 1106 H3
12400 SDCo 1232 B6
Via Diego Ct
8700 SDCo 1232 B6
Via Diego Ln
8800 SDCo 1232 B6
Via Diego Ter
8700 SDCo 1232 B6
Via Dieguenos
2300 SDCo 1254 D1
Via Dominique
11300 SDGO 1250 A1
Via Don Benito
2000 SDGO 1247 H1
Via Donada
12700 SDGO 1207 H1
Via Donito
- SDCo 1234 E7
- SDCo 1254 E1
Via Dora
8000 SDCo 1148 H6
8300 SDCo 1149 A6
Via Dorado
1200 SNMS 1109 D7
Via Dos Valles
6500 SDCo 1168 F5
Via Dulcea
2200 SDCo 1048 B4
Via Dwight
1300 SDCo 1152 H7
Via Eco
2600 CRLB 1106 H3
Via El Centro
200 OCSD 1086 D5
Via El Dorado
4200 SDCo 997 G3
Via Elena
11600 SDCo 1271 J4
Via Elisa
1500 ELCJ 1252 A2
Via Embeleso
16200 SDGO 1170 A4
Via Emerado
- CRLB 1147 H4
Via Emily
400 OCSD 1086 H1
Via Empresa
1200 OCSD 1087 B3
Via Encantada
600 CHLV 1311 B5
Via Encantado
- SDCo 1070 E6
Via Encantadoras
1800 SDGO 1350 E3
Via Encatadoras
1700 SDGO 1350 E2
Via Encinas Dr
1100 SDCo 1047 H3
Via Entrada
1700 SDCo 1027 J3
Via Entrada Del Lago
1500 SDCo 1128 C3
Via Escala
4700 OCSD 1087 B4
Via Escalada
- SDGO 1189 B5
Via Escalante
- CHLV 1311 A7
Via Escuda
3800 SDCo 1271 G4
Via Esmarca
2200 OCSD 1106 G2
Via Espana
1100 SDGO 1247 G3
Via Esparto
2500 CRLB 1106 H3
Via Esperia
12900 SDGO 1207 H1
Via Esprillo
16400 SDGO 1169 H4
Via Estrada
3000 CRLB 1127 J5
6900 SDGO 1247 H1
Via Estrellada
- SDCo 1027 J1

Via Eucalipto
12000 SDCo 1272 A3
Via Excelencia
9600 SDGO 1209 E6
Via Felicia
12000 SDCo 1271 J4
Via Felicidad
1100 SDCo 1149 H2
800 VSTA 1087 J3
Via Felicita
4400 OCSD 1086 J2
Via Felino
12700 SDGO 1207 H1
Via Feliz
1300 SDCo 1027 J3
- SDCo 1147 J4
Via Festivo
2700 CRLB 1106 H3
Via Fiesta
14700 SDGO 1168 J7
Via Firenze
1300 SDCo 1128 C4
Via Firul
11600 SDGO 1170 A6
Via Flora
- SDCo 1271 G7
700 SNMS 1108 C7
Via Flora Rd
700 SNMS 1129 D1
Via Flores
3500 SDGO 1288 A4
Via Floresta
100 SDCo 1027 F1
Via Forte
8600 SDGO 1209 C3
Via Fortuna Marfil
9400 SDCo 1271 C4
Via Francesco
7700 SDGO 1189 A4
Via Francis
9800 SNTE 1231 C4
Via Francisca
2300 CRLB 1106 G3
Via Fresa
2200 SDGO 1247 J2
Via Frontera
11000 SDGO 1169 H4
Via Galacia
12600 SDGO 1170 C5
Via Galan
16000 SDCo 1168 C7
Via Gardenias
10700 SDGO 1189 G2
Via Gato St
- SNMS 1108 E4
Via Gavilan
1800 SNMS 1128 B3
Via Gaviota
4500 SDCo 1167 J5
Via Germo
11800 SDCo 1271 J4
Via Giannelli
1000 SDCo 1048 E7
31900 SDCo 1068 E1
Via Gianni Turco
1700 SDCo 1028 B5
Via Gold Pan
10000 SDCo 1212 A7
Via Goya
1100 CHLV 1311 A6
Via Gracia
17600 SDGO 1170 B1
Via Granada
- SDCo 1291 G1
Via Grandar
14200 SDGO 1188 D2
Via Granero
11800 SDCo 1271 J4
Via Green Canyon Nor
- SDCo 1028 A4
Via Grenache
- ESCN 1129 E4
Via Grenada
31200 SDCo 1067 J2
Via Grimaldi
12700 SDGO 1207 H1
Via Guadalmina
18200 SDCo 1150 D7
Via Guadalupe
7000 SDCo 1168 G2
Via Hacienda
1500 CHLV 1311 B4
11800 SDCo 1271 J4
12200 SDCo 1272 A4
- SNMS 1108 D5
Via Hacienda Ct
- SNMS 1108 D5
Via Helena
8600 SDCo 1232 E6
Via Hermosa
3000 SDCo 1149 H2
Via Hillview
900 SDCo 1027 H1
Via Hinton
4900 CRLB 1107 A7
Via Hoja
- CRLB 1147 F4
Via Holgura
- SDGO 1188 A6
Via Hondita
- ESCN 1110 C5

70 INDEX
Via Hondonada

San Diego County Street Index

Via Zancas
INDEX 70
SAN DIEGO CO.
SAN DIEGO CO.

STREET
Block City Map# Grid

Via Hondonada
15000 SDGO 1169 H7
Via Huelva
13700 SDGO 1189 F3
Via Inca
4700 SDCo 1048 G2
Via Inez
7500 SDGO 1168 J7
Via Inspirar
1600 SDCo 1128 C3
Via Ipanema
- CRLB 1147 H3
Via Iris
3100 CRLB 1147 J2
Via Isabel
11600 SDCo 1271 J4
Via Isidro
1300 OCSD 1087 B4
Via Jacquelina
11600 SDCo 1271 J4
Via Jazmin
- SCLE 1023 B2
Via Juanita
2700 CRLB 1106 H3
800 SNMS 1128 C1
Via Judy
2700 CRLB 1106 H3
Via Julita
300 ENCT 1147 C6
Via Kenora
9600 SDCo 1271 C6
Via Kino
8100 SDGO 1228 D4
Via La Cantera
10000 SDGO 1189 F5
Via La Cresta
800 SDCo 1252 H2
Via La Cuesta
600 CHLV 1311 B4
1100 SDCo 1149 H2
Via La Gardenia
12700 POWY 1170 C6
Via La Gitano
15300 POWY 1170 C6
Via La Izquierda
15400 SDCo 1191 B5
Via La Jolla
4400 OCSD 1087 A2
Via La Mancha
- SDCo 1234 F6
Via La Mirada
12600 SDCo 1070 B4
Via La Orilla
2300 SDCo 1028 B7
Via La Paloma
500 CHLV 1311 A4
Via La Paz
100 SNMS 1109 C7
100 SNMS 1129 C1
Via La Plaza
1600 SDCo 1128 C4
Via La Ranchita
1300 SNMS 1109 C7
Via La Senda
14900 SOLB 1167 J7
14900 SOLB 1187 J1
Via La Venta
800 SNMS 1108 D5
Via La Ventana
15500 SDGO 1210 J2
Via Lactea
13800 SDGO 1189 E3
Via Ladera
1700 SDCo 999 B6
700 SDCo 1149 H1
- SNMS 1108 C7
Via Ladeta
2000 SDGO 1247 J2
Via Lago Azul
16500 SDCo 1168 F6
Via Lampara
- SDCo 1271 G7
- SDCo 1291 G1
Via Landini
7500 SDGO 1168 J7
Via Lapiz
4900 SDGO 1228 F5
Via Larga Vista
- SDCo 1048 C7
- SDCo 1068 C1
Via Largo
3600 OCSD 1107 G4
Via Las Brisas
- SNMS 1108 H3
Via Las Cumbres
1400 SDGO 1268 H3
Via Las Faldas
3100 SDCo 1272 D7
Via Las Lenas
- SDGO 1189 B5
Via Las Palmas
1700 NATC 1310 B2
Via Las Posadas
10700 SDGO 1189 H3
Via Las Rambles
4400 SDGO 1228 D3
Via Las Rosas
2900 OCSD 1106 G1
Via Las Tonadas
1700 SDGO 1350 E3
Via Las Villas
3700 OCSD 1107 F4
Via Latina
12800 SDGO 1207 H1
Via Laura
2000 SDCo 1314 F1
(See Page 1314)
Via Lechusa
4600 SDCo 1167 J5
Via Leslie
9900 SNTE 1231 D4
Via Libertad
2900 CRLB 1106 H3
Via Lido
- SNMS 1108 C7
Via Lima
1400 SDCo 1027 J3
Via Linda
900 SDCo 1129 H7
Via Linda Del Sur
- SDCo 1147 B5
Via Linda Vista
10700 SDCo 1271 F5
Via Lisa
14000 POWY 1190 G4
Via Livorno
11000 SDGO 1189 H1
Via Llano
11100 SDGO 1169 H7
Via Lobo
1700 SDCo 1128 B3
Via Loma Dr
17500 POWY 1170 D1
Via Loma Vista
1100 ELCJ 1252 B3
3100 SDCo 1149 G2
Via Lomas
3200 SDCo 1048 D2
Via Lombardia
10800 SDGO 1189 H2
Via Lomita
1000 ESCN 1110 B6
Via Lopez
24900 SDCo 1173 G2
Via Los Arcos
300 SNMS 1109 C7
Via Los Farolitos
16800 SDCo 1168 G6
Via Los Narcisos
10800 SDGO 1189 G2
Via Los Nopales
- SDCo 1168 C6
Via Los Padres
4000 OCSD 1086 H2
Via Los Santos
2300 CRLB 1106 G3
Via Lucia
2200 SDGO 1247 J2
Via Luiseno
3100 SDCo 1254 D1
Via Lujosa
3600 ESCN 1150 D3
Via Luna
- CHLV 1311 A7
17600 SDCo 1148 J6
Via Madeira
- ESCN 1129 F4
Via Madera
- SDCo 1271 G7
E Via Madera Circa
16100 SDCo 1168 C7
W Via Madera Circa
16100 SDCo 1168 C7
Via Madonna
11200 SNTE 1231 G5
Via Madrid
5100 OCSD 1067 A4
Via Madrina St
1500 SDGO 1268 H2
Via Magdalena
13300 SDGO 1188 J4
Via Maggiore
600 CHLV 1311 J2
600 CHLV 1312 A2
(See Page 1312)
Via Magia
2800 CRLB 1106 H3
Via Majella
- SDCo 1172 C4
Via Malaga
400 ENCT 1147 E6
Via Malaguena
5100 OCSD 1067 A4
Via Mallorca
8400 SDGO 1228 A4
Via Mandril
3400 SDCo 1310 G2
Via Manos
5000 OCSD 1067 C7
Via Mantova
14700 SDGO 1168 J7
Via Mar Azul
- CHLV 1311 A6
Via Mar De Ballenas
- SDGO 1208 B3
Via Mar De Delfinas
- SDGO 1208 B3
Via Mar Valle
2100 SDGO 1187 G7
Via Marbella
3100 SDCo 1292 B1
(See Page 1292)
Via Marbrisa
- ENCT 1147 E6
Via Marcala
14000 SDGO 1188 D3
Via Marchena
15600 SDGO 1170 B5
Via Marco
1000 VSTA 1087 J2
Via Margarita
- SDCo 1068 E2
Via Marguerita
1400 OCSD 1087 C3
Via Maria
400 OCSD 1086 H1
6300 SDGO 1247 E2
100 SNMS 1109 C7
Via Maria Elena
- SDCo 1068 C3
Via Mariana
- CHLV 1311 A6
Via Marin
3200 SDGO 1228 A5
Via Marinero
6800 CRLB 1128 A5
Via Mariposa
3000 CRLB 1128 A5
6800 SDCo 1068 E2
Via Mariposa Ct
31200 SDCo 1068 E2
Via Mariposa Norte
6900 SDCo 1068 E2
Via Mariposa Sur
6900 SDCo 1068 E2
Via Mark
13300 POWY 1190 G4
Via Marmol Rd
10000 SDCo 1109 E1
Via Marta
4900 CRLB 1107 A7
Via Masada
2600 CRLB 1106 H4
Via Mataro
- ESCN 1129 E4
Via Mavis
9900 SNTE 1231 D4
Via Maximo
- CRLB 1127 J4
Via Mayas
10800 SDGO 1189 H2
Via Medalla
- SDGO 1228 D4
Via Medanos
11700 SDGO 1170 A5
Via Media
2200 SDGO 1247 J2
Via Merano
2500 SDGO 1207 H1
Via Mercado
3700 SDCo 1271 G5
Via Mercato
3400 CRLB 1147 J2
Via Merde
3100 CRLB 1106 H3
Via Merida
11000 SDCo 1271 G5
Via Merritt
7900 SDCo 1048 H6
Via Metates
300 OCSD 1067 B7
Via Mica
10700 SDCo 1271 F6
Via Michelangelo
14200 SDGO 1189 C2
Via Mil Cumbres
1400 SOLB 1167 J6
Via Milano
12100 SDGO 1190 B1
Via Milazzo
13200 SDGO 1189 A4
Via Milpas
2500 SDCo 998 B6
Via Mindanao
5100 OCSD 1066 J4
Via Mirador
- CRLB 1147 J3
Via Miraleste
- SDCo 1311 A7
Via Molena
1200 ENCT 1147 F6
Via Molinero
- POWY 1170 G6
Via Monada
- SDCo 1311 A7
Via Monalex
- SDCo 1168 G2
Via Monclova
4300 SDGO 1228 D4
Via Monserate
2300 SDCo 1048 C5
Via Montalvo
400 ENCT 1147 E5
Via Montaneta
3100 ESCN 1150 A2
Via Montanosa
300 ENCT 1147 F6
Via Monte
16000 SDCo 1167 J5
Via Monte Alegre
3900 SDCo 1067 F1
Via Monte Claro
12600 POWY 1170 C6
Via Monte Verde
3400 ENCT 1148 B4
Via Montebello
3400 CRLB 1147 J2
7700 SDGO 1189 A4
Via Montecillo
- SNMS 1108 H3
Via Montecito
1100 ENCT 1147 E6
Via Montecristo
15600 SDGO 1169 B3
Via Montellano
- SDCo 1067 H2
Via Montenero
15700 SDGO 1169 B3
Via Monterey
16200 SDCo 1168 C6
Via Monteverde
14600 SDGO 1168 J7
Via Montevina
3000 SDCo 1028 D3
Via Montisi
- SNTE 1230 H7
Via Montoncillo
11100 SDGO 1169 H7
Via Montoro
1200 ENCT 1147 F6
Via Monzon
9800 SDGO 1189 E4
Via Morella
100 ENCT 1147 F6
Via Moura
12700 SDGO 1150 D7
Via Munera
2200 SDGO 1247 J1
Via Nacional
200 SDGO 1350 G5
Via Nancita
300 ENCT 1147 C6
Via Napoli
- SDCo 997 H4
Via Naranja
2500 CRLB 1106 H3
Via Naranjal
6400 SDCo 1148 D6
Via Nasca
12700 SDGO 1150 D6
Via Navajo
1200 SDCo 1128 B4
Via Nestore
12800 SDGO 1207 H1
Via Nicole
11600 SDCo 1271 J4
Via Nieve
- SDGO 1188 B6
Via Nina
2100 SDGO 1247 J1
9900 SNTE 1231 D4
Via Nomentana
- CHLV 1310 A4
Via Nopal
1600 CHLV 1331 D2
Via Norte
1100 SDCo 1149 H2
Via Ocioso
1600 SDCo 1128 C3
Via Oeste Dr
2200 SDCo 1028 E7
Via Olas
7000 CRLB 1127 G7
Via Opuntia
- CRLB 1147 G2
Via Orange Wy
2700 SDCo 1271 F7
Via Ordaz
10900 SDGO 1189 H2
Via Orillia
- SDCo 1148 A4
Via Oro Verde
200 SDCo 1027 F4
Via Ostiones
7000 CRLB 1127 G6
Via Ostra
6500 CRLB 1127 J4
Via Osuna
- SDCo 1168 C7
Via Otano
1500 OCSD 1087 B4
Via Pacifica
16200 SDCo 1168 C6
Via Padilla
7000 CRLB 1127 G6
Via Pajaro
2800 CRLB 1106 H3
Via Palabra
4500 SDGO 1250 A2
Via Palacio
200 ENCT 1147 F6
Via Palma
3400 SDCo 1271 H5
Via Palmilla
- ENCT 1147 D3
Via Palo Verde Lago
3900 SDCo 1254 G2
Via Paloma
1500 SDCo 1109 E7
11600 SDCo 1272 A4
Via Palomar
- SNMS 1108 C7
- SNMS 1128 C1
Via Pamela
19100 SDCo 1314 F2
(See Page 1314)
Via Panacea
- SDGO 1189 B5
Via Panorama
- SDCo 997 J3
Via Papeete
3100 SDGO 1330 D7
Via Papel
5100 SDGO 1228 G5
Via Paradiso
3700 SDCo 1088 F7
Via Paranza
- CRLB 1127 J4
Via Parma
11000 SDGO 1189 H3
Via Partricio
10800 SDCo 1049 F3
Via Pasar
9900 SDGO 1209 E5
Via Pasatiempo
3800 SDCo 1168 C7
Via Pasear
4400 SDGO 1228 D3
Via Pato
15900 SDCo 1168 A5
Via Patron
- CRLB 1127 J4
Via Pauma
5200 OCSD 1067 B7
Via Pedrera
2200 SDGO 1247 J1
Via Pedro
1500 VSTA 1088 B5
Via Pelicano
200 OCSD 1086 J3
Via Peligano
2300 CRLB 1127 G7
Via Penasco
16300 SDCo 1171 H4
Via Penoles
15400 SDGO 1170 A6
Via Pepita
2900 CRLB 1147 H4
Via Pequinto
10800 SDGO 1189 H2
Via Pereza
9500 SDGO 1189 E4
Via Perlita
3300 SNMS 1108 C6
Via Pescado
3200 CRLB 1106 H3
Via Picante
3500 SDCo 1271 G5
Via Piedra
- SDCo 1070 C7
- SDCo 1090 C1
Via Pisa
2500 SDGO 1207 H1
Via Platillo
2300 CRLB 1127 G7
Via Plato
2700 CRLB 1106 H3
Via Playa Cortes
11500 SDGO 1230 A7
Via Playa Los Santos
5000 SDGO 1230 A7
Via Poco
2500 ENCT 1167 F4
Via Ponte Tresa
3200 CHLV 1312 A1
(See Page 1312)
Via Porlezza
600 CHLV 1312 A2
(See Page 1312)
Via Portofino
1200 SDCo 1128 C4
Via Portola
5100 OCSD 1067 B7
- SNMS 1108 C7
- SNMS 1128 C1
Via Portovecchio
1200 SDCo 1128 B3
Via Posada
2800 SDGO 1227 J5
Via Posada Del Norte
6000 SDCo 1168 G5
Via Prado
1000 SDCo 1027 J5
Via Pravia
2200 SDGO 1247 J1
Via Precipicio
4400 SDGO 1228 D3
Via Premio
3100 CRLB 1106 H3
Via Primero
1800 OCSD 1087 C5
Via Privada
1100 SDCo 1149 H3
Via Promesa
11400 SDGO 1250 A1
Via Puerta
- CRLB 1127 J3
Via Puerta Del Sol
30600 OCSD 1067 G4
31000 SDCo 1067 G1
Via Quinceleaguas
39100 SDCo 999 D3
Via Quinto
1800 OCSD 1087 C5
Via Rafael
1200 SDCo 1128 B4
Via Ramon
1200 SDCo 1149 G2
Via Rancheros
2200 SDCo 1028 B7
2500 SDCo 1048 C1
Via Rancheros Wy
2800 SDCo 1048 C1
Via Ranchitos
- SDCo 997 J3
Via Rancho
200 SCLE 1023 B1
Via Rancho Cielo
8300 SDCo 1149 B5
Via Rancho Del Lago
- SDCo 1067 G2
Via Rancho Dos Ninos
- SDCo 1172 E3
Via Rancho Ln
1900 SDCo 1129 F7
Via Rancho Pacifica
- SDCo 1088 G7
Via Rancho Pkwy
2100 SDCo 1129 E7
20900 SDCo 1130 G7
1100 SDCo 1149 G2
20900 SDCo 1150 F1
E Via Rancho Pkwy
100 ESCN 1150 B3
Via Rancho Rd
4000 OCSD 1086 H4
4400 OCSD 1087 A4
Via Rancho San Diego
11300 SDCo 1272 A5
Via Ranchtos
- SDCo 997 G3
Via Ravello
4200 SDCo 1148 F4
Via Realzar
4400 SDGO 1228 D3
Via Reata
1000 VSTA 1107 H2
Via Recanto
17200 SDCo 1168 B2
Via Regla
6100 SDGO 1228 G5
Via Reposo
3900 SDCo 1168 C7
Via Rialto
2300 SDGO 1227 H6
Via Ribera
3200 ESCN 1150 A2
Via Ricardo
2800 CRLB 1106 H3
Via Rico
7700 CRLB 1147 J2
Via Rimini
13700 SDGO 1189 G3
Via Rincon
- SDCo 1271 G7
Via Rio
4000 OCSD 1086 H1
Via Risa
1500 SDCo 1128 C3
Via Rita
10100 SNTE 1231 D3
Via Rivera
7300 SDGO 1188 J4
Via Roberto
- CRLB 1106 H3
Via Roblar Ct
- SDCo 1272 C6
Via Robles
2100 OCSD 1106 G1
Via Robusta
- SDGO 1188 H3
Via Rogelio
4100 SDCo 1067 G1
Via Roja
1400 CHLV 1331 C3
Via Rojo
2500 CRLB 1106 H3
Via Romaza
- CRLB 1147 H3
Via Ronda
1400 SNMS 1109 D7
Via Rosa
3900 SNMS 1128 C1
Via Rosarita
2900 CRLB 1106 H3
Via Rose Marie Ln
900 SDCo 1027 G3
Via Rossi
7700 SDGO 1189 A3
Via Roswitha
18000 SDCo 1148 D7
Via Rota
18000 SDGO 1150 D7
Via Rovello Ct
7400 SDGO 1189 A5
Via Sabbia
13300 SDGO 1189 A4
Via Sabinas
3000 CRLB 1106 H3
Via Salaria
300 CHLV 1310 A4
Via Salerno
1500 SDCo 1129 E1
Via Salvador
- SDCo 1071 A7
Via San Aaron
- SDCo 1048 H4
Via San Alberto
200 SDCo 1048 H4
Via San Arturo
- SDCo 1048 G4
Via San Blas
10900 SDGO 1209 D3
Via San Clemente
7900 CRLB 1147 J3
Via San Jacinto
1200 SDCo 1128 B4
Via San Juan
- SDCo 1048 H4
Via San Loreno
12100 SDGO 1190 B2
Via San Lorenza
13200 SDGO 1189 A4
Via San Marco
10800 SDGO 1189 H3
Via San Saba
8000 SDGO 1228 D4
Via San Thomas
- SDCo 1048 H4
Via San Vitale
3100 CHLV 1292 A7
(See Page 1292)
Via Sansal
15300 POWY 1170 C6
Via Santa Beatrice
- SDCo 1048 G4
Via Santa Brisa
11400 SDGO 1210 H1
Via Santa Cruz
600 VSTA 1107 E1
Via Santa Delores
- SDCo 1048 G4
Via Santa Felice
- SDCo 1048 H4
Via Santa Paulo
700 VSTA 1107 E1
Via Santa Pradera
15600 SDGO 1190 J7
- SDGO 1211 A1
Via Santa Vienta
15200 SDGO 1210 H2
Via Santalina
- SNMS 1108 D4
Via Santiago
700 VSTA 1107 E1
Via Santillana
13200 SDGO 1188 J4
Via Sarasan
200 ENCT 1147 F6
Via Sassari
18600 SDCo 1148 F5
Via Savoy
400 ENCT 1147 E6
Via Scott
1900 ESCN 1109 F6
Via Sefton
11700 SDCo 1271 J4
Via Segovia
1900 SDGO 1247 H1
Via Segundo
2300 SDGO 1350 F4
Via Selma
11900 SDCo 1271 J3
Via Sendero
1200 SDCo 1149 G2
Via Sendero Vista
1200 SDCo 1149 G2
Via Sepulveda
4400 SDGO 1228 D4
Via Serena
13600 POWY 1170 E5
4300 SDCo 1067 H2
Via Serenidad
- SDCo 1171 F1
Via Serra
4000 OCSD 1086 H2
4700 SDCo 1048 H2
Via Serrano
12100 SDCo 1271 J4
Via Seville
5100 OCSD 1107 F4
- SNMS 1108 C7
- SNMS 1128 C1
Via Shawnty
19500 SDCo 1314 G2
(See Page 1314)
Via Siena
2300 SDGO 1227 H7
Via Silva
3600 OCSD 1107 F4
Via Simpatia
- CRLB 1127 J3
Via Simpatico
15300 SDCo 1168 C7
Via Sinalda
2000 SDGO 1247 H2
Via Sinsonte
- SDCo 1130 F4
Via Sinuoso
- CHLV 1311 A7
Via Sistina
300 CHLV 1310 B5
Via Sobrado
12800 SDGO 1150 C7
Via Sol Arriva
- SDCo 1150 E2
Via Solana
3100 SDCo 1149 G2
Via Solare
7700 SDGO 1189 A4
Via Solaro
100 ENCT 1147 F6
Via Soledad
800 VSTA 1087 J3
Via Sombra
3100 CRLB 1106 H3
Via Sombras
12700 POWY 1170 C6
Via Sonoma
8400 SDGO 1228 B4
Via Sonora
2100 OCSD 1106 G1
Via Soplador
300 SDCo 1027 J3
Via Sorbete
2500 CRLB 1106 H3
Via Sorpresa
4300 SDGO 1249 J1
Via Sovana
- SNTE 1230 H7
Via Stephen
13300 POWY 1190 G4
Via Subria
2300 SDCo 1088 D1
Via Suena
13000 SDCo 1070 C7
Via Suspiro
2800 SDGO 1350 D2
Via Tabara
2200 SDGO 1247 J1
Via Tala
4700 SDCo 1048 G2
Via Talavera
5200 SDGO 1188 D3
Via Tapia
100 SDCo 1291 B5
Via Taquita
200 SDCo 1152 J5
Via Tarifa
18000 SDGO 1150 D7
Via Tavira
200 ENCT 1147 F6
Via Tavito
11600 SDGO 1170 A6
Via Tazon
16900 SDGO 1169 J2
Via Teca
- CRLB 1147 H2
Via Temprano
11000 SDGO 1250 A2
Via Teramo
700 SDCo 1129 F2
Via Tercero
4200 OCSD 1087 C5
Via Teresa
1200 SNMS 1109 C7
11200 SNTE 1231 G5
Via Terrassa
1400 ENCT 1147 F6
Via Terrcero
500 SDGO 1350 E4
Via Terrceto
- SDGO 1188 B6
Via Tesoro
2200 SDCo 1254 C2
Via Tiempo
2100 ENCT 1167 F3
Via Tierra
200 ENCT 1147 E6
Via Timoteo
10800 SDCo 1271 G5
Via Tizon
5200 OCSD 1067 B7
Via Tomas
10700 SDGO 1189 H2
Via Tonala
3200 CRLB 1106 H4
Via Tonga
3400 SDGO 1330 E7
Via Tonga Ct
800 SDGO 1330 D7
Via Topacio
2800 CRLB 1106 H3
Via Tore
- SDCo 1108 A3
Via Torina
2500 SDGO 1207 H1
Via Tortola
- SDCo 1291 G1
Via Toscana
- CHLV 1311 A6
7700 SDGO 1189 A4
Via Tranquilo
- SDGO 1228 C4
Via Trato
6200 CRLB 1127 J3
Via Trecina
- CHLV 1311 A6
Via Tres Vista
13600 SDGO 1189 E3
Via Tresca
13300 SDGO 1189 A3
Via Trieste
1100 CHLV 1330 F2
Via Trueno
- SDCo 1254 B2
Via Tulipan
2700 CRLB 1106 H3
Via Ultimo
400 ENCT 1147 E6
Via Unidos
1000 SDCo 1027 H4
Via Urner Wy
8200 SDCo 1048 J7
8200 SDCo 1068 81
Via Valarta
- SDGO 1230 A7
- SDGO 1250 A1
Via Valencia
- SDCo 1070 G5
Via Valente
1400 SDCo 1149 F2
Via Valesco
3100 ESCN 1150 A2
Via Valle Verde
3900 SDCo 1168 D7
Via Valle Vista
1100 SDCo 1149 H3
Via Valverde
6800 SDGO 1247 G1
Via Varese
18600 SDCo 1148 F4
Via Vastago
1000 VSTA 1087 E6
Via Velasquez
7000 CRLB 1127 G7
Via Veltri
14100 SDCo 1070 F6
Via Veneto
- CHLV 1310 A4
2000 ESCN 1110 C6
Via Venezia
14400 SDGO 1189 H2
Via Ventada
3500 SDCo 1149 H3
Via Venusto
1400 OCSD 1087 C3
Via Vera
2600 CRLB 1106 H3
32100 SDCo 1048 E7
Via Vera Cruz
100 SNMS 1108 E7
600 SNMS 1128 E2
Via Verano
6800 CRLB 1128 A5
Via Verde
- CHLV 1311 A6
2200 SDCo 1252 D5
Via Verde Cruz
- SNMS 1128 F3
Via Verrazzano
7700 SDGO 1168 J7
Via Viajera
16000 SDCo 1168 D7
Via Vida Nueva
1300 SDCo 1109 E6
Via Viejas
2600 SDCo 1254 C1
Via Viejas Oeste
- SDCo 1254 B2
Via Viento
3700 SDCo 1028 F7
Via Viento Sauve
1200 SDCo 1128 C3
Via Viesta
2500 SDGO 1227 H6
Via Viganello
3100 CHLV 1312 A1
(See Page 1312)
Via Villegas
2300 CRLB 1127 F7
Via Villena
200 ENCT 1147 F6
Via Viso
28000 SDCo 1091 C2
Via Vista
- SDCo 1028 C4
Via Vista Canada
6500 SDCo 1168 F6
Via Vista Del Rio
3000 SDCo 1067 H7
Via Vista Grande
19600 SDCo 1151 G2
Via Vista Mejor
- SDCo 1070 A2
Via Vista Oriente
- SDCo 1168 D4
Via Vivaldi
7600 SDGO 1168 J7
Via Vonnie
- SDCo 1048 C2
Via Vuelta
3700 SDCo 1168 C7
Via Wakefield
9900 SNTE 1231 D4
Via Yuha
- OCSD 1067 C7
Via Zamia
1100 ENCT 1147 D5
Via Zamora
3200 ESCN 1150 A2
Via Zancas
- SDCo 998 B7

71 INDEX

Via Zapador

San Diego County Street Index

INDEX 71

Vladic Ln

SAN DIEGO CO.

STREET — Block City Map# Grid

Via Zapador — 9400 SNTE 1231 B7
Via Zapata — 11900 SDCo 1271 J4
Via Zara — 3400 SDCo 1028 D4
Via Zara Ct — 3400 SDCo 1028 D4
Via Zurita — 5900 SDGO 1247 H2
Viacha Ct — 10900 SDGO 1249 J3
Viacha Dr — 10400 SDGO 1249 H3
Viacha Wy — 10500 SDGO 1249 J3
Vian Rd — 13600 POWY 1190 F2
Vianda Ct — 6000 CRLB 1127 G6
Viane Wy — 4800 SDGO 1268 F1
Viar Av — 7200 SDGO 1250 C5
Vicente Meadow Dr — - SDCo 1173 A4
Vicente View Dr — 12700 SDCo 1212 B3
Viceroy Dr — 18100 SDGO 1150 B6
Vickers Rd — - SDCo 997 A1
Vickers St — 7800 SDGO 1249 B1
Vicki Pl — 500 ESCN 1109 J7; 500 ESCN 1129 J1
Vickie Dr — 5300 SDGO 1247 J4
Vicksburg Dr — 1400 ELCJ 1252 A3
Victor Av — 1200 SDCo 1251 G3
Victoria Av — 2700 CRLB 1106 J4
Victoria Bay Ct — - SDGO 1290 A1
Victoria Cir — 2300 SDCo 1234 B5
Victoria Ct — 1400 CHLV 1331 C3; - IMPE 6499 H2; 7500 SDGO 1290 G2
Victoria Dr — - CALX 6620 H6; - ELCJ 1251 H5; 3100 SDCo 1234 C4
E Victoria Dr — 3500 SDCo 1234 D4
Victoria Estates Ln — 14400 POWY 1190 E1
Victoria Glen — 1400 ESCN 1150 E3
Victoria Heights Pl — 3500 SDCo 1234 C5
Victoria Knolls Ct — - SDCo 1234 C4
Victoria Knolls Dr — - SDCo 1234 C4
Victoria Ln — - SDCo 998 F7; 3000 SDCo 1234 D5
Victoria Meadows Dr — 2300 SDCo 1234 B5
Victoria Park Ter — 1800 SDCo 1233 J5; 2200 SDCo 1234 A5
Victoria Pl — 2800 SDCo 1234 C6; 400 VSTA 1087 H4
Victoria Wy — 200 OCSD 1086 H3; 31400 SDCo 1069 C2; 1700 SNMS 1108 J3; 1700 SNMS 1109 A3
Victorian Ct — 14200 POWY 1190 F2
Victory Ct — 1000 OCSD 1067 B3
Victory Dr — 1900 SDCo 1108 D3
Victory Ln — 1500 CHLV 1312 B7 (See Page 1312)
Victory Rd — 8500 LMSA 1270 J2
Vidas Cir — 1100 SDCo 1109 E7
Viejas Blvd — 25200 SDCo 1236 C3
Viejas Creek Ln — 3900 SDCo 1234 F7
Viejas Creek Ter — - SDCo 1234 F6
Viejas Grade — - SDCo 1234 G5
Viejas Grade Rd — - SDCo 1235 B2; 24600 SDCo 1236 A3
Viejas View Pl — 2900 SDCo 1234 D7
Viejas Wy — - SDCo 1234 H4
Viejo Castilla Wy — 7500 CRLB 1147 G1
Vienna St — 3400 SDGO 1289 F1
Viento Estrella — 2800 CHLV 1312 A7 (See Page 1312)
Viento Fuerte Wy — 9300 SDCo 1271 B4
Viento Valle — 20800 SDCo 1130 F7
Vietta Ter — 11600 SDGO 1208 J1
View Crest Ct — 10000 SDCo 1271 E6
View Crest Glen — 2100 ESCN 1109 C3
View Park Wy — 1700 CHLV 1331 E1
View Pl — 4200 SDGO 1270 C4
View Point Rd — 1800 SDCo 1048 A3
View Pointe Av — 1400 ESCN 1110 A7
View Side Ln — 15700 SDCo 1233 C3
View St — 2200 OCSD 1106 E2; 200 SDCo 1027 F2
View Trail Ct — - CHLV 1311 G2
View Wy — - CRLB 1106 F7; 1600 ELCJ 1251 C5
Viewcrest Dr — 7600 SDGO 1290 G3
Viewmont Dr — 1100 SDCo 1130 C4
Viewpoint Ct — - SDGO 1290 E7
Viewpoint Dr — 6200 SDGO 1310 E1; 800 SNMS 1128 B2
Viewpoint Wy — 3400 OCSD 1106 H1
Viewridge Av — 4500 SDGO 1249 E2
Viewridge Ct — - SDGO 1249 E1
Viewridge Ln — 2300 ESCN 1109 F4
Viewridge Wy — 5000 OCSD 1107 E3
Viewverde — 3700 SDCo 1310 J2
Vigilant Wy — 4800 CRLB 1106 H7
Vigilante Rd — - SDCo 1211 H4
Vigo Dr — 6600 LMSA 1270 E4
Viking Grove Ln — - SDCo 1071 A6
Viking Ln — 900 SNMS 1109 A5
Viking Pl — 1100 ESCN 1130 E2
Viking Wy — - CRLB 1106 G5; 1800 SDGO 1227 G6; - SNMS 1109 A5
Viletta Dr — - SDCo 1130 C4
Villa Adolee — 3000 SDCo 1271 F6
Villa Alegre Dr — - CALX 6620 H6
Villa Av — 1600 ELCN 6499 F5; - ImCo 6500 B4
Villa Blanca Ct — - ENCT 1147 D7
Villa Bonita — 10500 SDCo 1271 F6
Villa Bonita Ct — - CALX 6620 H6
Villa Cardiff Dr — 1600 ENCT 1167 E2
Villa Colina — 3100 SDCo 1271 F6
Villa Crest Dr — 1500 ELCJ 1252 B2
Villa Del Cielo Dr — 31800 SDCo 1067 F1
Villa Del Dios Dr — 1800 ESCN 1129 F6
Villa Espana — 3100 SDCo 1271 F6
Villa Flora — 6100 SDCo 1068 C3
Villa Flores Glen — 2100 ESCN 1129 E7
Villa Glen Ln — 1300 ELCJ 1252 A2
Villa Grande St — 700 CALX 6620 D7
Villa Hermosa Ct — 100 SOLB 1167 H4
Villa La Jolla Dr — 8800 SDGO 1228 A3
Villa Ln — 1600 ELCN 6499 F5; - ImCo 6500 B4
Villa Medici — 6000 SDCo 1068 C4
Villa Monte — - SDCo 1232 C2
Villa Norte — 3100 SDGO 1228 A3
Villa Pavrone — 6100 SDCo 1068 C3
Villa Roma — 6000 SDCo 1068 D4
Villa Santini — 6000 SDCo 1068 C3
Villa Serena — - IMPE 6439 C7
Villa Sierra Ln — 15500 SDCo 1070 J4; 15600 SDCo 1071 A4
Villa Sierra Rd — 15000 SDCo 1070 J4; 15600 SDCo 1071 A5
Villa Sonoma Glen — 2100 ESCN 1129 E7
Villa Tempra Dr — - CHLV 1330 D3
Villa Ter — 3600 SDGO 1269 D6
Villa Toscana — 30800 SDCo 1068 C3
Villa Verde Rd — 2200 ESCN 1129 G7
Villa View Ln — 1300 ELCJ 1252 A2
Villa Zapata — 2300 SDCo 1253 J2
Village Center Dr — 400 ENCT 1147 H5
Village Center Loop Rd — 5900 SDGO 1188 F4
Village Cir — 3600 CRLB 1106 E6; - SDCo 1234 A6
Village Ct — 1000 OCSD 1067 B3
Village Dr — 400 CHLV 1330 C3; 500 CRLB 1106 E6; 5200 OCSD 1067 B3; 700 SNMS 1128 H3
Village Glen Dr — 9200 SDGO 1249 D4
Village Green Dr — 6200 CRLB 1127 F3
Village Green Rd — 200 ENCT 1147 H6
Village Ln — 400 VSTA 1087 G6
Village Park Wy — 2200 ENCT 1147 H5
Village Pine Dr — 2900 SDGO 1350 D2
Village Pine Wy — 1500 SDGO 1350 C2
Village Pl — 1900 SDGO 1269 C7; 1800 SDGO 1289 C1
Village Rd — 100 ESCN 1109 G4
Village Ridge Rd — - SDGO 1189 J7
Village Run East — 400 ENCT 1147 H6
Village Run North — 1700 ENCT 1147 G6
Village Run West — 200 ENCT 1147 G6
Village Square Dr — 100 ENCT 1147 G7
Village View Cir — - LMSA 1270 J4
Village View Pl — 500 SDCo 1027 G3
Village View Rd — 1200 ENCT 1147 G5
Village Wood Rd — 1900 ENCT 1147 H7
Village Wy — 2400 OCSD 1086 D7; 5900 SDGO 1188 F4
Villamoura Dr — 17700 POWY 1170 E1
Villamoura Wy — 13600 POWY 1170 F1
Villanitas Rd — 2100 ENCT 1147 J6
Villanova Av — 3200 SDGO 1228 D5
Villarrica Wy — 5700 SDGO 1229 H6
Villas — 7900 SDGO 1169 A7
Villas Ct — 4600 CHLV 1310 H3
Villas Dr — 4500 CHLV 1310 H3; 5400 SDCo 1068 B1
Villas Wy — 2600 SDGO 1249 D7
Vinaruz Pl — 16900 SDGO 1170 C3
Vinca Wy — 1300 SDGO 1290 D5
Vincente Wy — 400 SDGO 1247 E2
Vincetta Ct — 5400 LMSA 1270 H1
Vincetta Dr — 8200 LMSA 1270 H1
Vine Av — 600 BRAW 6320 A3 (See Page 6320)
Vine Cir — 1900 ELCN 6499 E7; 2000 VSTA 1088 C5
Vine Dr — 29300 SDCo 1297 E5 (See Page 1297)
Vine Ln — 9800 SDCo 1149 D3
Vine St — 2400 ELCN 6499 E7; 300 ESCN 1129 H4; 800 OCSD 1106 C1; 600 SDCo 1027 F3; - SDCo 1232 B2; 1500 SDGO 1268 H7
N Vine St — 500 OCSD 1106 C1; 100 SDCo 1027 F2
Vine Wood Dr — 3800 SDCo 1156 E2
Vinewood St — 100 ESCN 1129 E3
N Vinewood St — 100 ESCN 1129 F3
Vineyard Av — 2100 ESCN 1129 E3
Vineyard Ct — 200 SNMS 1108 J6
Vineyard Ln — 17700 POWY 1170 D1
Vineyard Rd — 700 SNMS 1108 J5
Vineyard Wy — 3000 CHLV 1311 J1; - SDCo 1234 A6
Vinley Pl — 5700 SDGO 1250 D7
Vintage Dr — 14500 SDGO 1189 C1
Vintage Pl — - ESCN 1110 B5
Vintage Point Dr — - SNMS 1129 B3
Vinter Wy — 13200 POWY 1170 E2
Vinwood Ct — 12800 SDGO 1188 E5
Vinyard Av — 1900 VSTA 1107 J3
Vinyard St — 4500 OCSD 1066 H7
Viola St — 1300 SDGO 1268 E2
Violet Av — 200 SNMS 1128 H3
Violet Ct — 1800 CHLV 1331 E3; 800 CRLB 1127 A6
Violet Dr — - POWY 1190 F3
Violet Glen — 3800 ESCN 1150 C3
Violet Ln — 13300 SDGO 1188 G4
Violet Ridge — - ENCT 1148 C5
Violet St — 4000 LMSA 1270 F5; 2600 SDGO 1269 G7
Viper Wy — 10500 SDGO 1208 H4
Vireo Ct — - CRLB 1127 B5
Vireo St — 1700 SDCo 1128 A4
Virgin Islands Rd — - SDCo 1068 E2
Virginia Av — 4500 SDGO 1270 D3; 100 SDGO 1350 H4
Virginia Ct — 2100 ELCJ 1251 B5
Virginia Dr — 2600 NATC 1310 A3
Virginia Ln — 900 ESCN 1110 C6; 1600 ImCo 6559 H3
Virginia Pl — 700 SNMS 1108 C7
Virginia Wy — - CALX 6620 G5; 1400 SDGO 1227 F6
Virginian Ln — 9200 SDCo 1271 B1
Virgo Pl — 11000 SDGO 1209 C2
E Virgo Rd — 3200 SDGO 1270 B6
W Virgo Rd — 3100 SDGO 1270 B6
Visalia Ct — - CHLV 1331 B1
Visalia Row — 1800 CORD 1288 J7; 1800 CORD 1289 A7
Visayan St — 200 NATC 1289 J7
Viscaya Wy — 3000 OCSD 1106 J1
Vision Ct — 11900 SDGO 1150 A7
Vision Dr — 4400 SDGO 1228 D1
Vispera Pl — 6500 CRLB 1127 G5; - SDCo 1310 E3
Vista Abierta — 300 SDCo 1252 E4
Vista Acedera — - CRLB 1147 G3
Vista Alegria — 300 OCSD 1086 H4
Vista Alpine Rd — - SDCo 1234 B6
Vista Arroyo — 4900 SDCo 1271 D2
Vista Av — 1200 ESCN 1109 J5; 3100 LMGR 1270 F6; 3600 LMSA 1270 F5; 600 SDCo 1109 H5
S Vista Av — 500 SDGO 1350 F3
Vista Azul — 3800 SCLE 1023 B1
Vista Bella — 3600 OCSD 1086 G4
Vista Blanca — 3800 SCLE 1023 B1
Vista Bonita — - CRLB 1127 H7; - VSTA 1107 J1
Vista Bonita Ln — 4100 ESCN 1150 E3
Vista Calaveras — 4000 OCSD 1107 C3
Vista Camino Rd — 10300 SDCo 1231 H3
Vista Campana N — 3800 OCSD 1086 G4
Vista Campana S — 3700 OCSD 1086 G5
Vista Canela — - CRLB 1147 G3
Vista Canon Ct — - SDGO 1188 J3
Vista Capitan — 1200 ELCJ 1251 C3
Vista Capri — 4100 OCSD 1086 J4
Vista Catalina — 15600 SDCo 1071 A4
Vista Chaparral — - CRLB 1147 F3
Vista Cielo Dr — 12800 SDCo 1272 C7
Vista Cielo Ln — 3200 SDCo 1272 C7
Vista Claridad — 1500 SDGO 1247 H3
Vista Colina Wy — 1200 SNMS 1128 E3
Vista Corona — 3500 SDCo 1048 B3
Vista Coronado Dr — 4400 SDCo 1310 F5
Vista Coyote — 11800 SDCo 1231 H2
Vista Creek — 4100 NATC 1310 D3
Vista De Bonita Canada — 11400 SDCo 1271 H4
Vista De Chaparros Dr — 3000 SDCo 1273 B7
Vista De Fortuna — 5300 SDCo 1168 C1
Vista De Golf — - SDCo 1168 D7
Vista De La Bahia — 3700 SDGO 1248 E4
Vista De La Canada — 3600 ESCN 1150 A3
Vista De La Cresta — 3300 SDCo 1149 G2
Vista De La Cruz — 10100 SDCo 1271 D2
Vista De La Mesa — 6100 SDGO 1247 E3
Vista De La Montana — 1900 SDCo 1253 B5
Vista De La Orilla — 3500 SDGO 1248 E5
Vista De La Patria — 4500 SDCo 1187 J1; 4500 SDCo 1188 A1
Vista De La Playa — 300 SDGO 1247 E1
Vista De La Rosa — 2900 SDCo 1292 F1 (See Page 1292)
Vista De La Sierra — 1400 SDCo 1319 G4 (See Page 1319)
Vista De La Tierra — 4800 SDCo 1188 A1; 4300 SOLB 1187 J1
Vista De Lomas — - SDCo 1068 B4
Vista De Los Pinos — 13700 SDCo 1292 G2 (See Page 1292)
Vista De Montemar — 1800 SDCo 1252 E2
Vista De Oro — - SDCo 1149 G3
Vista De Palomar Rd — 2500 SDCo 1048 C1
Vista De Pauma — 14900 SDCo 1050 G5
Vista De Sembrado — 2700 SDCo 1150 F1
Vista Del Agua Wy — - SDGO 1208 E4
Vista Del Cajon Pl — 8400 SDCo 1232 A7
Vista Del Cajon Rd — 12100 SDCo 1252 A1
Vista Del Canon — - SOLB 1187 H1
Vista Del Capitan — 10200 SDCo 1232 C2
Vista Del Cerro Dr — 10300 SNTE 1231 E7
Vista Del Cielo — 37600 SDCo 1319 G4 (See Page 1319)
Vista Del Conquistador — - SDCo 1293 B4
Vista Del Coronados — - SDCo 1252 H4
Vista Del Dios — 5200 SDGO 1188 D2
Vista Del Escuela — 200 ELCJ 1252 D5
Vista Del Indio — 300 SDCo 1027 J2
Vista Del La Montana Ln — 1900 SDCo 1253 B5
Vista Del Lago Dr — 1800 SDCo 997 H6
Vista Del Mar — 1800 SDCo 1068 B5
Vista Del Mar Av — 7300 SDGO 1227 E7; 6500 SDGO 1247 E2
Vista Del Mar Ct — 200 CHLV 1310 B4
Vista Del Mar St — - IMPE 6439 D7
Vista Del Monte Dr — 1200 SDCo 1251 J7
Vista Del Monte Wy — 900 SDCo 1251 J7
Vista Del Norte — 1800 SDCo 1048 A2
Vista Del Oceano — 14900 SDCo 1187 J1
Vista Del Oro — 2700 CRLB 1127 H5
Vista Del Oro Dr — 2100 OCSD 1086 J7
Vista Del Oro Wy — 8700 SDCo 1291 A1
Vista Del Otero — - SDCo 1151 H2
Vista Del Pacifico — 4300 SDCo 1028 F5
Vista Del Piedra — - SDCo 1293 A4
Vista Del Rancho — 400 CHLV 1310 D6
Vista Del Rey Dr — 300 ENCT 1147 C6
Vista Del Rio — 2900 SDCo 998 C4
Vista Del Rio Wy — 4200 OCSD 1086 J3
Vista Del Sage — 13000 SDCo 1050 C5
Vista Del Sol — 9600 SDCo 1271 C4
Vista Del Sur — 10800 SDCo 1271 F6
Vista Del Valle Blvd — 1600 SDCo 1252 B7
Vista Del Verde — 8600 SDCo 1232 D7
Vista Diego Rd — 3200 SDCo 1272 G7
Vista Dr — 8100 LMSA 1270 H3; 9200 SDCo 1271 B6; - SDCo 1310 D5
Vista Elevada — 11300 SDGO 1210 C2
Vista Ensueno — - SDCo 1233 G7
Vista Entrada — - OCSD 1086 H4; 9100 SDCo 1232 G5
Vista Esperanze Ln — - SDCo 1255 E5
Vista Flume — - ESCN 1109 F3; - SDCo 1109 G3
Vista Flume Rd — 13900 ESCN 1110 F4
Vista Glen Ln — 200 VSTA 1087 J6
Vista Grande — - CRLB 1127 H7
Vista Grande Ct — 1800 SDCo 1272 C2
Vista Grande Dr — 2100 SDCo 1088 A2; 4000 SDGO 1270 E4; 2000 VSTA 1088 B2
Vista Grande Glen — 200 ESCN 1130 A6
Vista Grande Pl — 2100 VSTA 1088 A2
Vista Grande Rd — 1000 SDCo 1252 D7; 1500 SDCo 1272 C2
Vista Grande Terr — 2100 SDCo 1088 B1
Vista Grande Wy — 700 OCSD 1086 H3; 1900 SDCo 1272 C2
Vista Gubaya — - CRLB 1147 H3
Vista Hermosa Wy — 2000 SDCo 1272 C2
Vista Higuera — - CRLB 1147 H3
Vista Hill Av — 7700 SDGO 1249 A6
Vista Hills Dr — 14200 SDCo 1232 F4
Vista Hills Pl — 9500 SDCo 1232 F4
Vista Horizon St — 200 SDGO 1289 H4
Vista Juanita Ct — - LMGR 1270 E7
Vista La Cuesta Ct — 10000 SDGO 1209 J4
Vista La Cuesta Dr — 11200 SDGO 1209 J4
Vista La Nisa — - CRLB 1147 F2
Vista La Quebrada — - SDCo 1293 B2
Vista Ladero — 13200 SDCo 1232 C5
Vista Lago Pl — 10500 SDGO 1209 G4
Vista Lago Ter — 2300 SDCo 1129 F7
Vista Laguna Rd — 2500 SDCo 1048 B3
Vista Lazanja — - SDGO 1188 J2
Vista Ln — - ENCT 1147 F5; 4700 SDGO 1269 H3; 3200 SDGO 1350 E3
Vista Loma Cir — 3300 OCSD 1107 B1
Vista Lomas Dr — 17900 POWY 1150 E7
Vista Madera Ln — 1000 SDCo 1252 E7
Vista Madera Wy — 2400 SDCo 1252 E7
Vista Mar — - CRLB 1127 H7
Vista Marazul — 300 OCSD 1086 H4
Vista Marguerite — 7900 SDCo 1251 J2
Vista Mariana — - CRLB 1127 G7
Vista Matamo — 3200 SDCo 1252 G7
Vista Merriam — - SDCo 1088 J7
Vista Miranda — 500 CHLV 1311 A5
Vista Montana — 200 OCSD 1086 E5
Vista Montanoso — - SDCo 1089 E2
Vista Mountain Dr — - VSTA 1088 D6
Vista Nacion Dr — 4400 SDCo 1310 E5
Vista Norte — - SDCo 1130 G6
Vista Nuez — - CRLB 1147 H2
Vista Oak Pl — 1000 CHLV 1310 J7
Vista Oceana — 3600 OCSD 1086 F4
Vista Pacific Dr — 2600 OCSD 1087 E5
Vista Pacifica — 3200 SDCo 1088 F6
Vista Palma — - CRLB 1147 G2
Vista Panorama — 14300 SDCo 1232 G5
Vista Panorama Wy — - OCSD 1086 H3
Vista Parque — - SDCo 1232 C2
Vista Parque Ct — - SDCo 1232 D3
Vista Pl — 400 CHLV 1310 D6; 900 CORD 1309 A1; 4900 SDGO 1269 D3
Vista Pointe — 3500 SDCo 1310 E3
Vista Pointe Blvd — 1100 OCSD 1067 B4
Vista Poniente Dr — 13700 POWY 1170 F6
Vista Pt Cir — 700 SDCo 1088 G7
Vista Ramona Rd — 13500 SDCo 1153 B6; 23400 SDCo 1173 D1
Vista Rancho — 17600 SDCo 1168 G1
Vista Rancho Ct — 7400 SDCo 1148 H7
Vista Real Dr — 14100 SDCo 1050 F6
Vista Rey — 3600 OCSD 1086 F4
Vista Rica — - CRLB 1127 H7
Vista Ricardo — 13800 SDCo 1232 E6
Vista Ridge — - SDGO 1208 B2
Vista Rim Pl — 3700 SDCo 1088 F7
Vista Robles — 3100 SDCo 1272 G1
Vista Rocosa — 3300 ESCN 1149 J3
Vista Rodeo Dr — 2500 SDCo 1252 D7
Vista Royal — 2300 SDCo 1108 D1
Vista Sage Ln — 13400 SDCo 1292 F1 (See Page 1292)
Vista Sage Pl — 13900 SDCo 1292 F2 (See Page 1292)
Vista San Benito — - SDGO 1331 A7
Vista San Carlos — - SDGO 1331 B7
Vista San Francisquito — - SDGO 1331 A7
Vista San Guadalupe — - SDGO 1331 B7
Vista San Ignacio — - SDGO 1331 B6
Vista San Isidro — - SDGO 1331 B7
Vista San Javier — - SDGO 1331 A7
Vista San Jose — - SDGO 1331 A7
Vista San Juanico — - SDGO 1331 A7
Vista San Lucas — - SDGO 1331 A7
Vista San Matias — - SDGO 1331 B7
Vista San Miguel — 3900 SDCo 1310 G4
Vista San Pablo — - SDGO 1331 A7
Vista San Pedro Martir — - SDGO 1331 B7
Vista San Rafael — - SDGO 1331 A7
Vista San Rufo — - SDGO 1331 B7
Vista San Simeon — - SDGO 1331 A7
Vista Santa Catarina — - SDGO 1331 B7
Vista Santa Clara — - SDGO 1331 B7
Vista Santa Fe Ln — 10900 SDGO 1208 H3
Vista Santa Ines — - SDGO 1331 B7
Vista Santa Margarita — - SDGO 1331 A6
Vista Santa Rita — - SDGO 1330 J6
Vista Santa Rosalia — - SDGO 1331 B7
Vista Santo Domingo — - SDGO 1331 B7
Vista Santo Tomas — - SDGO 1331 A7
Vista Secunda — 9500 SDGO 1189 E3
Vista Serena — 10600 SDCo 1231 J1
Vista Sierra Dr — 1000 SDCo 1252 D7; 1500 SDCo 1272 E1
Vista Somermont — 1100 SDCo 1251 H2
Vista Sonrisa Av — - CHLV 1311 D7
Vista Sorrento Pkwy — 10700 SDGO 1208 C5
Vista St — 4800 SDGO 1269 H3
Vista Summit Dr — 16700 SDCo 1171 E2
Vista Ter — 10900 SDCo 1271 G4
Vista Tercera — 9500 SDGO 1189 E4
Vista Terrraza Ct — - SDCo 1070 A6
Vista Valle Cam — 1000 SDCo 1028 F4
Vista Valle Ct — 10200 SDGO 1209 G4
Vista Valle Dr — 10600 SDGO 1209 G4
Vista Valle Verde — 2200 SDCo 1048 B2
Vista Valley Dr — 29500 SDCo 1068 D6
Vista Valley Ln — 2200 SDCo 1088 E1
Vista Valley Rd — - SDCo 1068 D7; - SDCo 1088 E1
Vista Valley Rim Pl — 2000 SDCo 1252 D4
Vista Verde — - OCSD 1086 J1; - SNMS 1109 B5
Vista Verde Dr — - ESCN 1110 A5; 1500 SDGO 1247 G1
Vista Verde Wy — - ESCN 1110 A4
Vista Vereda — 1500 SDCo 1272 C2
Vista Vicente Ct — 24000 SDCo 1173 E4
Vista Vicente Dr — 15600 SDCo 1173 D4
Vista Vicente Wy — 22800 SDCo 1173 D4
Vista Viejas Rd — 9800 SDCo 1234 A1
Vista View Ct — 13200 POWY 1190 F4
Vista View Dr — 13000 POWY 1190 F5
Vista Village Dr — - SDCo 1087 G7
Vista Way Village Dr — 3500 OCSD 1106 J2
Vista Wy — - CHLV 1310 C4; 1100 CHLV 1330 E2; - ESCN 1109 G7; 100 OCSD 1106 C4; 4000 OCSD 1107 B2; 3100 SDCo 1067 J6; 100 SDCo 1252 H4; 4200 SDCo 1271 E3; 2700 SDCo 1310 B3
E Vista Wy — 2500 SDCo 1088 A1; 100 VSTA 1087 H6; 1300 VSTA 1088 A4
W Vista Wy — 200 VSTA 1087 G6; 1900 VSTA 1107 C2
Vistamonte Av — - ESCN 1130 J4
Vistamonte Glen — - ESCN 1130 J4
Vistosa Pl — 2600 CRLB 1147 G1
Vita Rd — 4800 SDCo 1271 F2
Viva Ct — 800 SOLB 1187 G1
Vivaldi St — 1500 ENCT 1167 D2
Vivaracho Ct — 4300 SDGO 1249 J2
Vivaracho Wy — 10900 SDGO 1249 J2; 11100 SDGO 1250 A2
Vivera Dr — 10100 SDCo 1271 D2
Vivera Pl — 5100 SDCo 1271 D2
Vivian St — 4000 SDGO 1270 D4
Vivienda Cir — 3300 CRLB 1147 J1
Vixen Dr — - SDCo 1172 G2
Vizcaino Ct — 1900 SDCo 1109 E5
Vladic Ln — 1600 SDCo 1130 C4

72 INDEX
Voet Dr

San Diego County Street Index

INDEX 72
Westview Dr
SAN DIEGO CO.

STREET Block City Map# Grid

Voet Dr
- BRAW 6319 F3
(See Page 6319)
Voge St
10100 SDGO 1249 G4
Voigt Dr
3900 SDGO 1228 C2
Voigt Ln
- SDGO 1227 J1
Volans St
11300 SDGO 1209 C1
Volcan Preserve Rd
- SDCo 1136 D1
Volcan Rd
- SDCo 1085 J3
Volcan View Dr
1200 SDCo 1136 C6
Volcano Creek Rd
- CHLV 1311 E6
Volclay Dr
7500 SDGO 1250 E3
Volmer Peak Ct
1100 CHLV 1311 C7
Volney Ln
300 ENCT 1147 H7
Volney Rd
300 ENCT 1167 H1
Volta Ct
7200 SDGO 1269 A1
Voltaire St
5000 SDGO 1267 J5
4700 SDGO 1268 A5
Voluntary Rd
- VSTA 1087 J3
Vomac Rd
9500 SNTE 1231 B4
Voorhes Rd
- SDCo 1171 J2
- SDCo 1172 A1
Vortex Pl
4000 ESCN 1150 D4
Vought St
- CORD 1288 E4
Voyage Dr
1500 CHLV 1331 F2
Voyager Cir
3400 SDGO 1187 J6
Voyager Ct
3500 OCSD 1086 F6
Vue De Ville Ct
1300 SDGO 1247 J4
Vue Du Bay Ct
1400 SDGO 1247 J4
Vuelta Ct
2100 CRLB 1147 F2
N Vulcan Av
700 ENCT 1147 B4
S Vulcan Av
300 ENCT 1147 C7
Vulcan Dr
1300 SDCo 1251 F1
Vulcan Pl
1100 ESCN 1130 E1

W

Waash Rd
54000 SDCo 1071 D5
Wabash Av
3700 SDGO 1269 F5
Wabash Blvd
1300 SDGO 1289 F6
Wabash St
600 ESCN 1110 B7
Wabaska Ct
2100 SDGO 1268 B7
Wabaska Dr
3900 SDGO 1268 B6
Wache Dr
3000 SDCo 1292 A2
(See Page 1292)
Waco St
3400 SDGO 1248 F5
Waddell Cir
10200 SDGO 1249 G2
Wade Dr
- SNMS 1128 C1
Wade St
8500 SDGO 1290 H2
Wade Wy
12300 SDCo 1252 A1
Wadsworth Pl
15800 SDGO 1169 D4
Wadsworth St
2600 CRLB 1107 A6
Wagner Av
9300 SDGO 1249 E4
Wagner Pl
3600 SDGO 1249 E4
Wagner Rd
1100 ELCJ 1251 D4
Wagon Gn
1300 ESCN 1130 B2
Wagon Rd
3100 SDCo 1078 H6
(See Page 1078)
Wagon Tongue Ct
- SDCo 1254 F3
Wagon Trl
100 SDCo 1027 J2

Wagon Wheel Ct
- ESCN 1109 J4
2400 SDCo 1271 G7
Wagon Wheel Dr
1600 OCSD 1067 F7
10800 SDCo 1271 G7
100 SNTE 1231 E5
Wagon Wheel Wy
300 CHLV 1310 H4
Wahl St
8600 SNTE 1230 F7
Wahupa Ranch Rd
2800 SDCo 1149 J2
Waier Ford Dr
- SOLB 1187 F2
Wailea Wy
2300 SDGO 1330 D7
Waimea Dr
700 SDCo 1252 C4
Wainwright Ln
3200 SDGO 1249 C5
Waite Dr
7200 LMSA 1270 F5
6800 SDGO 1270 E5
Wakarusa St
9100 LMSA 1251 B7
Wake Av
- ELCN 6559 F2
500 ELCN 6560 B2
Wake Rd
- CORD 1309 C5
Wake St
5500 LMSA 1270 H1
Wakefield Ct
700 ELCJ 1251 B4
Wakefield Ln
15800 SDGO 1169 D4
Wala Dr
600 OCSD 1086 D3
Walbollen St
1600 SDCo 1290 J1
Walden Ct
10300 SNTE 1231 A3
Walden Glen
3100 ESCN 1130 J4
Waldgrove Pl
9900 SDGO 1209 H5
Waldo Ct
10500 SNTE 1231 E4
Waldorf Wy
- SDGO 1209 J2
Waldron Ct
10200 SDGO 1249 G4
Waldron Wy
10200 SDGO 1249 G4
Wales Dr
- ENCT 1167 F4
Wales Pl
- ENCT 1167 F4
Walinca Wy
2500 SDCo 1088 D5
Walkden Ln
8700 SDGO 1251 A4
Walker Ct
9000 SDGO 1249 D6
Walker Dr
2700 SDGO 1249 D6
Walker Farm Rd
4200 SDCo 1048 F3
Walker Ln
- SDCo 1023 E2
Walker Wy
100 VSTA 1087 G6
Walking Fern Cove
- SDGO 1209 J1
Walking H Dr
700 SDCo 1078 J5
(See Page 1078)
Walking Path Pl
13000 SDGO 1187 J5
Walking Stick Ct
- CHLV 1311 H5
Wall Pl
100 SDCo 1252 H4
Wall Rd
- IMPE 6499 F2
Wall St
1000 SDGO 1227 F6
Wallaby Ct
11200 SDGO 1189 J4
Wallace Ct
900 SDGO 1289 G5
Wallace Dr
3400 SDCo 1310 G2
Wallace Ln
100 VSTA 1108 A1
Walley Wy
1600 ELCJ 1252 C2
Wallingford Ct
7500 SDGO 1208 J4
Wallingford Rd
10800 SDGO 1208 J4
Wallsey Dr
6800 SDGO 1250 J4
Walmar Ln
2300 SDGO 1248 B4
Walnut Av
500 CHLV 1329 J1
1100 CHLV 1330 A4
500 CRLB 1106 E6
1700 SDGO 1268 H6

Walnut Av
100 SDGO 1269 A6
Walnut Ct
- BRAW 6259 G6
(See Page 6259)
2600 OCSD 1087 E5
Walnut Dr
- CHLV 1330 F5
2100 SDCo 1108 D2
Walnut Glen
200 ESCN 1110 E7
Walnut Grove Av
- CHLV 1311 E6
Walnut Hills Dr
100 SNMS 1129 A1
Walnut Rd
11800 SDCo 1231 J7
Walnut Ridge
- SDGO 1208 B2
Walnut St
- BRAW 6259 F6
(See Page 6259)
1900 SDCo 1152 D6
Walnut Tree Ln
1200 SDCo 1251 G1
Walnutcreek Dr
1400 ENCT 1167 F1
Walnutdale St
10200 SDGO 1210 C4
Walnutview Dr
1300 ENCT 1147 F7
Walpen Dr
1200 SDGO 1350 A1
Walsall Rd
600 SDCo 1252 D6
Walsh Rd
- SDGO 1229 F1
Walsh St
100 OCSD 1086 D6
Walsh Wy
5100 SDGO 1270 A1
Walsing Dr
700 SNMS 1129 E1
Walter Av
4900 SDGO 1250 A6
Walter Wy
100 ELCJ 1251 J5
Waltham St
13200 POWY 1190 H4
Walton Heath Row
15500 SDGO 1170 B5
Walton Pl
3000 SDGO 1269 E4
Walton St
1600 CHLV 1331 E2
1500 OCSD 1086 B5
Walton Wy
2300 ESCN 1110 C6
700 SDCo 1107 D2
Walz Ct
11500 SDGO 1209 B1
Wanda Ct
600 ESCN 1129 J1
6000 SDGO 1249 J7
Wanda Dr
- SNTE 1231 E6
Wanda Wy
13900 SDCo 1292 H2
(See Page 1292)
Wander St
2200 CHLV 1331 H1
Wandering Rd
- ENCT 1147 G4
800 VSTA 1087 F7
Wandering Wy
100 SNMS 1128 J3
Wandermere Ct
6600 SDGO 1250 D5
Wandermere Dr
6700 SDGO 1250 E5
Wanek Rd
2400 ESCN 1110 D6
Wanesta Dr
13000 POWY 1190 D4
Wannacut Pl
- SDGO 1209 J1
Waples Ct
10000 SDGO 1208 G5
Waples St
9300 SDGO 1208 G5
War Bonnet St
13000 SDGO 1189 C5
War Horse St
12800 SDGO 1189 C5
Warbler Ct
- CRLB 1127 D6
Warbler Wy
5500 SDGO 1247 G4
Ward Ct
800 CALX 6620 G7
Ward Ln
10000 SDCo 1271 D1
Ward Pl
1300 ESCN 1109 J5
Ward Rd
- ImCo 6260 D3
(See Page 6260)
3600 SDGO 1269 G3
- SDGO 1289 E7
Warden Ln
8400 SDGO 1169 B4

Wardlow Av
2700 SDGO 1350 C3
Wardlow Ct
1900 SDGO 1350 C3
Ware Ct
8900 SDGO 1208 J7
Ware Rd
- ImCo 6620 C2
Warfield Wy
600 SDCo 1253 C1
Warhead Rd
- SDGO 1288 A5
Waring Ct
3200 OCSD 1107 B1
Waring Rd
3900 OCSD 1107 B1
5600 SDGO 1250 C5
Warm Hearth Wy
2900 CHLV 1311 J1
Warm Springs Dr
1400 CHLV 1331 B2
Warmlands Av
- VSTA 1088 C5
Warmwell Dr
8600 SDGO 1250 J3
Warmwood Av
8200 SDCo 1290 H5
Warner Dr
900 SDCo 1079 A6
(See Page 1079)
Warner St
100 OCSD 1086 F3
3600 SDGO 1287 J3
Warnock Dr
1600 SDCo 1172 F2
Warpaint Dr
700 SDCo 1152 F7
Warpaint Pl
1700 ESCN 1129 G5
Warren Pl
5900 LMSA 1250 H7
Warrington St
2400 SDGO 1268 B6
1700 SDGO 1288 A1
Warwick Av
400 ENCT 1167 D2
Warwick Cir
4500 OCSD 1107 E2
Warwood Ct
2100 SDCo 1272 B4
Wasa Ct
16100 SDCo 1051 A5
Washenio Cir
11500 SDCo 1029 H2
Washington Av
2700 CRLB 1106 D5
8600 LMSA 1271 A2
400 OCSD 1106 B1
E Washington Av
700 ELCJ 1251 G6
1500 ELCJ 1252 A6
2800 ESCN 1110 D5
300 ESCN 1129 J2
W Washington Av
400 ELCJ 1251 E6
900 ESCN 1129 G3
Washington Cir
2900 SDCo 1129 B6
Washington Heights Pl
1000 SDCo 1251 H6
Washington Heights Rd
700 ELCJ 1251 J6
Washington Pl
1200 SDCo 1251 J7
1200 SDGO 1268 H5
Washington St
400 CALX 6680 G1
3500 LMGR 1270 H6
1700 LMGR 1290 H1
21800 SDCo 1135 B3
2900 SDCo 1136 A7
20000 SDCo 1152 D2
1000 SDGO 1269 B5
E Washington St
100 VSTA 1087 H6
W Washington St
1600 SDGO 1268 H6
Washingtonia Dr
600 SNMS 1129 A3
Wasp Wy
2600 SDGO 1288 C1
Water Lily Dr
1400 CHLV 1311 G2
Water Lily Wy
1900 CHLV 1311 G2
Water St
5600 LMSA 1251 C7
- SDGO 1268 G6
1000 SDGO 1289 B5
Water View Ct
8300 SDCo 1290 J5
Water View Ln
600 SDCo 1290 J5
Water Wy
3600 OCSD 1107 C3
Waterbury Ct
1300 SNMS 1128 B3
Waterbury Dr
2000 CHLV 1311 D4
Waterbury Wy
2700 CRLB 1106 J3

Watercourse Dr
6800 CRLB 1126 J5
Watercrest Ct
3300 SDCo 1311 A1
Watercrest Dr
5600 SDCo 1311 A1
Waterfall Pl
6200 SDGO 1249 J7
Waterford Dr
3300 OCSD 1086 J7
Waterford Ln
- SDGO 1189 B2
Watergum Tr
9900 SNTE 1231 D4
Waterhill Rd
11700 SDCo 1231 J4
Waterhouse Glen
900 ESCN 1109 J7
Wateridge Cir
10400 SDGO 1208 D6
Wateridge Vista Dr
10600 SDGO 1208 D6
Waterline Wy
2500 CHLV 1311 G4
Waterloo Av
700 ELCJ 1252 B6
Waterloo Wy
- SNMS 1128 H3
Waterman Av
1400 ELCN 6499 F4
1800 ELCN 6559 F1
Waterman Ct
900 ELCN 6499 F5
6700 SDGO 1248 J6
Waters End Dr
6900 CRLB 1126 J5
Waterside Dr
2100 CHLV 1311 E4
Waterton Rd
10800 SDGO 1209 H1
Watertown Ln
600 CHLV 1311 E3
Waterview Wy
5000 OCSD 1067 A6
Waterville Lake Rd
1000 CHLV 1311 F5
Waterville Rd
7800 SDGO 1351 F2
Waterwood Ct
2200 CHLV 1311 G6
Watkins Ct
11000 SDGO 1209 H1
Watson Pl
8900 SNTE 1251 A1
Watson Ranch Rd
8300 SDGO 1189 B3
Watson Wy
7200 LMSA 1270 F2
1700 SDCo 1108 A3
2300 VSTA 1108 A4
Watt Rd
24100 SDCo 1173 E3
Watt Wy
16100 SDCo 1173 E3
Wattle Dr
7000 SDGO 1290 G7
Watwood Rd
1500 LMGR 1290 F2
Wave Av
- CRLB 1106 F7
Wave Crest Ct
700 SDGO 1247 H7
Wave Ct
6000 SDGO 1290 D6
Waverly Av
5600 SDGO 1247 G3
Waverly Ct
3400 SDCo 1272 E6
Waverly Downs Ln
12100 SDGO 1170 B7
Waverly Ln
- SNMS 1128 F6
Waverly Pl
500 ESCN 1129 J2
Waverly Rd
4600 OCSD 1107 E3
Wawona Dr
3500 SDGO 1268 B7
Waxflower Ln
- SDCo 1027 J3
Waxie Wy
- SDGO 1229 E7
Waxwing Dr
1200 VSTA 1087 F4
Waxwing Ln
1200 CHLV 1330 G2
Wayfarer Dr
9600 LMSA 1251 C5
Wayfinders Ct
- CRLB 1127 B5
Wayland Grove Ct
13800 POWY 1190 F3
Wayne Av
900 CHLV 1311 C5
500 ELCJ 1251 J4
Wayne Hill
16000 SDGO 1169 B3
Wayne Ln
3100 SDGO 1248 D3
Waynecrest Ln
10000 SNTE 1231 D3

Waynes Wy
- SDCo 1152 C5
Wayside Av
1100 ELCJ 1251 G3
Weakley Rd
- CALX 6620 E6
Weather Vane Dr
600 SDCo 1078 J4
(See Page 1078)
Weatherby Av
2100 ESCN 1110 C7
Weatherhill Ct
- SDGO 1209 H2
Weatherhill Wy
- SDGO 1209 H1
Weatherly Rd
- CRLB 1127 C4
Weathers Pl
6400 SDGO 1208 G5
Weatherstone Ct
- SDGO 1208 E2
Weatherstone Wy
600 SNMS 1128 G6
Weathervane Av
2000 ESCN 1130 D1
Weathervane Pl
1700 ESCN 1130 C1
Weatherwood Ct
1700 SNMS 1128 C6
Weatherwood Pl
11600 SDGO 1210 A2
Weatherwood Ter
11100 SDGO 1210 A2
Weaver St
1200 SDGO 1290 C2
Weaverville St
- CHLV 1331 B2
Weaving Ln
17700 SDGO 1149 H7
Webb Rd
- SDGO 1288 A5
- SDGO 1289 C2
Webber Wy
1700 CHLV 1331 E2
Weber Creek Rd
- CHLV 1311 E6
Weber Ct
9300 SDCo 1271 B6
Webster Av
3000 SDGO 1289 E4
Webster Rd
300 ImCo 6319 E2
(See Page 6319)
Webster Wy
- ESCN 1110 F5
Wedgemere Ct
2700 ESCN 1110 E7
Wedgemere Rd
1800 ELCJ 1251 C5
Wedgewood
2000 OCSD 1086 J7
Wedgewood Av
2600 ESCN 1130 E1
Wedgewood Dr
100 SDGO 1290 H4
Wedgwood Pl
1800 CHLV 1331 F3
Weekend Villa Rd
1500 SDCo 1152 D2
Weeping Willow Rd
2700 CHLV 1312 A6
(See Page 1312)
3600 OCSD 1086 F1
Weeping Willow Wy
2100 SDCo 1027 H6
Weers St
1300 ELCJ 1251 D4
Weiser Av
7500 SDGO 1249 A6
Weiss Wy
- SDCo 1109 H4
Weisser Wy
400 CHLV 1330 C3
Weitzel St
400 OCSD 1086 A7
800 OCSD 1106 B1
S Weitzel St
200 OCSD 1086 B7
400 OCSD 1106 B1
Welch Pl
- CHLV 1331 A3
Welch Rd
- SDGO 1289 C2
Welcome St
1400 BRAW 6320 B1
(See Page 6320)
Welcome View
28600 SDCo 1089 C3
Welcome Wy
- SDCo 1173 J4
Weld Blvd
2100 ELCJ 1251 B1
Weldon Wy
2500 SDCo 1028 C6
Welk Highland Ct
- SDCo 1069 C7
Welk Highland Dr
29400 SDCo 1069 B7
29000 SDCo 1089 C1
Welk Highland Ln
29500 SDCo 1069 B7

Welk View Ct
9500 SDCo 1089 C1
Welk View Dr
- SDCo 1089 A1
Wellbourn St
3700 SDGO 1268 H6
Wellbrook St
1800 CHLV 1331 E1
Weller St
6800 SDGO 1228 F4
Welles St
- SDGO 1289 E7
Wellesley St
5300 LMSA 1270 G1
E Wellesley St
5400 LMSA 1270 G1
W Wellesley St
5300 LMSA 1270 G1
Wellesly Av
3200 SDGO 1228 D5
Wellesly Ct
6300 SDGO 1228 D5
Wellesly Pl
6600 SDGO 1228 C5
Welling Wy
200 SDGO 1290 F4
Wellington Hill Dr
13200 SDCo 1232 C7
Wellington Ln
1900 VSTA 1108 A4
Wellington St
3000 SDGO 1249 A5
Wellington Wy
7400 SDGO 1249 A5
Wellpot Pl
900 VSTA 1087 H4
Wells Av
200 ELCJ 1251 F5
Wells Fargo Trl
600 SDCo 1138 B5
(See Page 1138)
Wells St
2100 SDGO 1268 B7
Wellsona Ct
- SDGO 1209 F1
Wellspring St
2500 CRLB 1107 A6
Wellston Pt
4600 SDGO 1188 B4
Wellworth Pt
5000 SDGO 1188 D4
Welmas Rd
- SDCo 1029 G5
Welmer Pl
3200 SDGO 1228 C4
Welmer St
6600 SDGO 1228 D5
Welsh Rd
10900 SDGO 1209 D3
Welsh Wy
1300 SDCo 1172 G1
Welton Ln
13100 POWY 1190 G4
Welton St
500 CHLV 1330 B3
Wembley St
7200 SDGO 1250 A5
Wenatchee Dr
8200 SDCo 1231 G7
8200 SDCo 1251 G1
Wendela St
5300 OCSD 1087 E1
Wendell Cutting Ct
1300 ELCJ 1251 J3
Wendell St
4600 SDGO 1289 J1
Wendi Ct
- SDCo 1048 B4
Wendi St
5600 LMSA 1250 H7
Wendover Terr
13300 SDGO 1188 D4
Wendy Ln
1100 ESCN 1109 J7
Wenrich Dr
6100 SDGO 1250 C6
Wenrich Pl
5900 SDGO 1250 C6
Wensley Av
1900 ELCN 6499 E7
- ELCN 6500 A7
- ELCN 6559 D1
Wentworth Cir
900 VSTA 1108 A4
Wentworth Ct
3000 SDCo 1272 D5
Wentworth Dr
3300 SDCo 1272 E5
Wentworth Pl
- SNMS 1108 J4
Wentworth Wy
3300 SDCo 1272 D5
Werner St
7100 SDGO 1228 F4
Wernes St
2000 SDCo 1152 D7
Werris Creek Ln
14800 SDGO 1170 B7
Wescott Ct
8700 SDGO 1189 C1

Wesley Dr
- SDGO 1248 B3
Wesley Drive Cir
- SDGO 1248 B3
Wesley Pl
6600 SDGO 1270 E1
Wesley Wy
1600 VSTA 1107 G4
Wesleyan Pl
4000 SDGO 1269 G2
Wesmead St
5800 SDGO 1290 C5
Wessex St
18600 SDGO 1150 B5
West 07th St
- ENCT 1147 J7
West 08th St
- ENCT 1147 J6
West Airport Rd
1000 OCSD 1086 C5
West Av
1600 NATC 1309 H2
West Bluff Ct
600 ENCT 1147 E6
West Bluff Dr
500 ENCT 1147 E6
West Canyon Av
3300 SDGO 1249 F4
West Canyon Terr
9600 SDGO 1249 F5
West Cliff Ct
1800 CRLB 1106 H6
West Dr
2000 SDCo 1252 H4
1800 VSTA 1107 C1
West Fashion Valley
- SDGO 1268 J3
West Fork Rd
14100 SDCo 1030 E7
West Haven Dr
3700 CRLB 1106 H5
West Hills Pkwy
9300 SDGO 1230 H6
West Incense Cedar Ln
4200 SDCo 1156 E4
West Incense Cedar Rd
1000 SDCo 1156 D5
West Ln
- SDCo 1187 J1
400 SDCo 1252 H3
West Oak Glen Wy
31200 SDCo 1070 E2
West Point Av
7200 LMSA 1270 F3
West Point Dr
1500 CHLV 1330 J4
1800 CRLB 1106 H6
West Ranch Rd
900 SDCo 1128 B2
West Ranch St
4900 CRLB 1107 A6
West Rim Ct
9400 SDCo 1232 B4
West Rim Rd
12600 SDCo 1232 B4
West Roundup Cir
100 SNTE 1231 E5
West Side Rd
- SDCo 1154 F3
- SDCo 1174 C4
West St
3200 LMGR 1270 G6
500 OCSD 1106 B2
500 SDGO 1289 J5
West Star Rd
3200 SDCo 1078 H6
(See Page 1078)
West Village Dr
- SDCo 1252 F7
Westbourne St
300 SDGO 1247 E1
Westbridge Glen
3000 ESCN 1150 A2
Westbrook Av
7400 SDGO 1290 H7
Westbury Av
7900 SDGO 1209 A2
Westbury Rd
- SDCo 1088 E7
Westby St
400 CHLV 1330 B2
Westchester Av
10400 SDGO 1209 D4
Westcliff Dr
- SNMS 1128 F2
Westcliffe Pl
3200 SDGO 1268 C7
Westdale Ct
100 ELCJ 1251 C5
Westerly Ct
4700 OCSD 1087 D4
Western Av
- BRAW 6319 H4
(See Page 6319)
N Western Av
- BRAW 6259 H7
(See Page 6259)
S Western Av
500 BRAW 6319 H2
(See Page 6319)

Western Gailes Row
11200 SDGO 1189 J3
Western Springs Rd
3400 ENCT 1148 C4
Western St
3900 SDGO 1268 C4
Western Trails Dr
7900 SDCo 1252 A1
Westerra Ct
- SDGO 1228 C1
Westford Wy
- SDCo 1169 G2
Westgate Pl
3800 SDGO 1289 G1
Westgrove Rd
1600 SDCo 1272 B3
Westhill Ln
9300 SDCo 1231 H5
Westhill Rd
8900 SDCo 1231 H6
Westhill Ter
11500 SDCo 1231 H6
Westhill Vista
11600 SDCo 1231 H5
Westin Wy
1100 SNMS 1128 E6
Westinghouse St
1700 SDGO 1268 J1
E Westinghouse St
1700 SDGO 1268 J1
Westknoll Dr
5300 SDGO 1247 J3
Westknoll Ln
5300 SDGO 1247 J3
Westlake Dr
100 SNMS 1108 G7
Westlake St
500 ENCT 1147 D6
Westland Av
2100 SDGO 1289 F1
Westleigh Pl
6900 SDGO 1208 H4
Westling Ct
- POWY 1170 F3
Westly Ln
- SDGO 1210 C2
Westmark Wy
13200 POWY 1190 F4
Westminster Dr
1800 ENCT 1167 D2
Westminster Pl
1300 ESCN 1130 D2
Westminster Ter
5000 SDGO 1269 G2
Westmont Ct
400 CHLV 1311 A4
Westmont Dr
3100 SDCo 1048 D1
Westmore Cir
10900 SDGO 1209 B3
Westmore Ct
10900 SDGO 1209 B3
Westmore Ln
10900 SDGO 1209 A2
Westmore Pl
1400 OCSD 1087 E3
10900 SDGO 1209 B3
Westmore Rd
8900 SDGO 1209 C3
Westmorland St
- CHLV 1311 C7
Weston Cir
100 VSTA 1087 G3
Weston St
4600 SDCo 1271 E3
2300 SDGO 1270 E7
Westonhill Dr
10400 SDGO 1209 C3
Westover Pl
5000 SDGO 1290 A1
Westport Dr
4400 OCSD 1066 G7
Westport Ln
900 VSTA 1087 J7
Westport Rd
1200 SNMS 1128 B2
Westport St
2200 SDGO 1290 D7
Westport View Dr
5100 SDGO 1330 J7
Westport Wy
1200 SNMS 1128 B2
Westridge Dr
4700 OCSD 1087 D4
Westridge Ln
2100 SDCo 1088 A2
Westridge Pl
11600 SDCo 1231 H5
Westrose Wy
13000 SDCo 1090 D6
Westside Dr
7700 SDGO 1269 B1
Westvale Rd
9000 SDGO 1189 C2
Westview Ct
600 CHLV 1310 G5
2200 SDCo 1028 A6
Westview Dr
400 CHLV 1310 G5
4500 LMSA 1270 H3

73 INDEX
INDEX 73
Westview Pkwy
Windy Mtn Ln
SAN DIEGO CO.

San Diego County Street Index

STREET
Block City Map# Grid

Westview Pkwy
11700 SDGO 1209 E1
Westview Pl
600 CHLV 1310 G5
7100 LMGR 1270 F6
Westview Rd
15400 POWY 1171 B6
1800 SDCo 1028 A6
Westward Ct
- SDGO 1209 F2
Westward Ho Cir
1800 SDCo 1252 C3
Westway Dr
8400 SDGO 1227 H4
Westwind Dr
1200 ELCN 6559 G1
N Westwind Dr
300 ELCJ 1251 C5
S Westwind Dr
100 ELCJ 1251 C6
Westwood Cir
- SDGO 1209 E3
Westwood Dr
3200 CRLB 1106 G4
2000 VSTA 1107 C1
Westwood Pl
1400 ESCN 1109 E5
1400 OCSD 1087 E3
Westwood Rd
2000 VSTA 1107 C1
Westwood St
2300 SDGO 1310 C1
Wetherly St
7900 LMSA 1270 H4
Wethersfield Rd
9300 SNTE 1230 J5
Wexford St
10500 SDGO 1189 G7
Weymouth Wy
5200 OCSD 1066 J4
5200 OCSD 1067 A3
Whale Watch Wy
8300 SDGO 1227 J4
Whalen Lake Rd
- OCSD 1086 G1
Whalers
- SDGO 1331 A6
Whaley Av
1700 SDGO 1289 F2
Whaley St
500 OCSD 1106 C3
Wharton Rd
- SDGO 1268 E6
9400 SNTE 1231 B4
Wharton St
700 SDCo 1067 A1
Wheat Dr
- SDGO 1209 D6
- SDGO 1229 A1
Wheat St
3200 SDGO 1248 D3
Wheatland Pl
11200 SDGO 1210 H2
Wheatlands Av
10700 SNTE 1231 F5
Wheatlands Ct
9400 SNTE 1231 F5
Wheatlands Rd
9300 SNTE 1231 F5
Wheatley St
6900 SDGO 1248 J6
7300 SDGO 1249 A6
Wheaton St
5300 LMSA 1270 G1
Wheatstalk Ln
5900 SDCo 1311 B1
Wheatstone St
- SDGO 1248 G6
Wheatville St
- CHLV 1311 E6
Wheel Hub Pl
300 SDCo 1058 H6
(See Page 1058)
Wheeler St
2400 SDCo 1234 C6
Wheelhouse Dr
- SDGO 1330 J6
Wheeling Ln
3200 SDCo 1310 H1
Whelan Dr
7800 SDGO 1250 H4
Whelan Lake Rd
- OCSD 1086 F1
Whellock Wy
9500 SDGO 1189 E4
Whigham Pl
1600 SDCo 1252 B4
Whimbrel Ct
- SDCo 1127 B7
Whinchat St
2000 SDGO 1269 A1
Whip Dr
200 SDCo 1078 F1
(See Page 1078)
Whipple Av
7100 SDGO 1228 G4
Whipple Wy
4900 SDGO 1228 F4
Whippletree Ln
10800 SDCo 1271 G7
Whippoorwill Glen
300 ESCN 1109 G5
Whippoorwill Ln
4800 SDCo 1310 H1
Whiptail Ct
12100 SDCo 1212 B4
Whiptail Loop
- CRLB 1107 G7
- CRLB 1127 G1
Whirlwind Ln
- SDCo 1171 J2
Whirlybird Wy
5800 SDCo 1311 B1
Whisper Dr
1500 CHLV 1311 G7
Whisper Trace Rd
3200 SDCo 1068 D5
Whisper Wind Dr
2100 ENCT 1147 J6
Whisper Wind Ln
2100 ENCT 1147 J7
Whisper Wind Rd
- SDCo 1068 D5
Whispering Brook Dr
400 VSTA 1087 F3
Whispering Heights Ln
- SDGO 1208 G3
Whispering Highlands Dr
1200 ESCN 1130 F2
Whispering Hills Ln
- SDGO 1208 E2
Whispering Leaves Ln
9300 SNTE 1230 H6
Whispering Meadows Ln
13800 SDCo 1292 G3
(See Page 1292)
Whispering Oaks Dr
16300 SDCo 1171 G3
Whispering Oaks Ln
16800 SDCo 1171 G3
Whispering Palm Dr
1500 OCSD 1087 E2
Whispering Palms Lp
- CHLV 1311 H5
Whispering Pines Dr
1700 SDCo 1136 C5
Whispering Ridge Rd
14300 SDGO 1210 G1
Whispering Sage Ln
1800 SDCo 1152 F2
Whispering Trails Dr
- CHLV 1311 G3
Whispering Tree Ln
- POWY 1190 C5
Whispering Trl
9600 SDCo 1234 A3
Whispering Water Dr
1100 SNMS 1129 B2
Whispering Willow Dr
- SNTE 1231 C5
Whistler Rd
- SDGO 1287 J5
Whistling Ln
2200 CHLV 1331 H1
Whistling Straits Gl
200 ESCN 1109 H3
Whitaker Av
- CHLV 1330 H2
Whitby Glen
400 ESCN 1110 D6
Whitcomb Wy
10400 SDCo 1169 F3
White Alder Av
- CHLV 1311 J4
White Alder Ct
- SDCo 1169 C2
White Birch Dr
400 CHLV 1311 B3
10400 SDGO 1209 J3
1900 VSTA 1107 G5
White Butte Dr
14900 POWY 1190 J4
White Camarillo Ln
35300 SDCo 1028 J6
White Cap Ln
- OCSD 1085 J7
White Christmas Ct
7900 SDCo 1168 J2
White Emerald Dr
- SDGO 1188 D4
White Fox Run
200 SDCo 1028 B2
White Goose Rd
2400 SDCo 1297 G6
(See Page 1297)
White Hawk Rd
3100 ESCN 1110 F7
3100 ESCN 1130 F1
White Hickory Pl
1600 CHLV 1311 J7
White Horse Ct
1500 CHLV 1311 B3
White Horse Ln
200 SDCo 1047 F3
White Lilac Rd
4200 SDCo 998 G7
White Oak Ct
5200 OCSD 1087 E2
White Oak Dr
1800 SDCo 1254 A1
1900 SNMS 1128 B2
White Oak Ln
5400 SDGO 1188 E5
White Oak Pl
2500 ESCN 1110 D6
White Oak Wy
12400 POWY 1190 C6
White Owl Dr
2500 ENCT 1148 A7
White Pine Ct
2700 CHLV 1311 J7
2700 CHLV 1331 J1
White Pine Ln
10000 SNTE 1231 D2
White Pine Wy
4400 OCSD 1086 J2
White Pl
9500 LMSA 1251 B6
White Rd
- SDGO 1288 A7
White Rock Station Rd
- POWY 1170 F2
White Rose Ln
10400 SDCo 1169 G2
White Sage Ln
1500 SDGO 1289 G5
White Sage Pt
3200 SDCo 1318 B6
(See Page 1318)
White Sands Dr
- SNMS 1128 A3
White Star Ln
14200 SDCo 1070 F2
White Star Rd
- SDCo 1070 F2
White Vale Ln
15400 POWY 1170 J6
White Wing Dr
2400 SDCo 1294 E6
(See Page 1294)
White Wood Canyon
- POWY 1170 F1
Whitecap Dr
6900 CRLB 1126 J6
Whitecliff Dr
- SDGO 1227 J2
Whitefield Pl
7700 SDGO 1227 G6
Whitefish Ln
- OCSD 1086 G2
Whitehall Cir
10900 SDGO 1209 A3
Whitehall Rd
1700 ENCT 1147 A2
10800 SDGO 1209 A4
Whitehaven Wy
4900 SDGO 1268 F1
Whitehead Pl
8100 LMSA 1250 H7
Whitehills Rd
9900 SDCo 1232 C3
Whitehorn
- SDCo 1233 B3
Whiteport Ln
8800 SDGO 1251 A4
Whitesage Rd
500 SNMS 1128 G3
Whitesail St
- CRLB 1127 A4
Whitesands Ct
- CRLB 1107 B3
Whitestone Rd
1600 SDCo 1291 E2
Whitewater Dr
13400 POWY 1190 J4
Whitewater St
7000 CRLB 1126 J6
Whitewing Pl
- CHLV 1331 A1
Whitewood Ln
200 ENCT 1167 H1
Whitewood Pl
300 ENCT 1147 J6
Whitey Dr
1700 CRLB 1106 G7
Whiting Ct
700 SDGO 1247 H7
Whiting Woods Dr
1500 SDCo 1109 D1
Whitman St
2800 SDGO 1268 F4
Whitmore St
400 SDGO 1289 G4
Whitney Ct
6900 SDGO 1248 J6
Whitney Pl
- CRLB 1127 G2
Whitney Rd
- POWY 1190 G4
Whitney St
100 CHLV 1310 C7
600 CHLV 1330 A1
2800 SDGO 1248 J6
E Whitney St
- CHLV 1310 D6
Whitney Wy
- ELCN 6559 F2
Whitsett Dr
1300 ELCJ 1251 B3
Whittaker Ln
12200 SDCo 1232 A5
Whittier St
3300 SDGO 1268 C7
Whittman Wy
- CRLB 1127 A1
Wichita Av
600 ELCJ 1252 B6
Wicker Pl
1300 ESCN 1110 A6
Wickerbay Cove
- SDGO 1190 A7
Wickham Wy
2800 CRLB 1106 F3
Wickley Pl
4600 OCSD 1107 E3
Wicopee Pl
3300 SDGO 1248 D3
Widdecke Wy
- SDCo 1023 D2
Wide Oak Rd
1700 SDCo 1315 A3
(See Page 1315)
Wide Valley Ln
11400 SDGO 1209 J4
Widgeon Ln
900 CHLV 1330 C2
Widgeon Rd
29800 SDCo 1297 G5
(See Page 1297)
Wieber Av
- SDGO 1289 C2
Wiegand St
- ENCT 1148 B4
Wiegand Wy
- ENCT 1147 F6
Wieghorst Wy
12300 SDCo 1271 J4
Wienert Rd
- ImCo 6439 A2
Wigeon Pl
- CRLB 1127 D6
Wiggins Wy
900 ELCJ 1251 E7
Wight Wy
1800 SDCo 1252 A1
Wightman St
2400 SDGO 1269 C5
4900 SDGO 1270 A5
Wigwam Ct
8800 SNTE 1230 J5
Wikiup Rd
16200 SDCo 1173 F3
Wil-Ev Dr
600 SNMS 1108 J6
Wilajobi Wy
13800 SDCo 1191 F6
Wilbee Ct
2800 SDGO 1249 D6
Wilbur Av
1300 SDGO 1247 H5
2400 SDGO 1248 B4
Wilcox St
300 OCSD 1086 E5
3600 SDGO 1287 J3
Wild Acres Rd
1400 SDCo 1068 G5
Wild Blossom Terr
- SDGO 1208 E4
Wild Canary Ln
1100 ENCT 1147 J5
Wild Canyon Dr
- SNMS 1128 F6
Wild Canyon Ln
- ENCT 1147 J5
Wild Colt Pl
14700 SDCo 1273 A5
Wild Flower Ln
13100 POWY 1170 D4
Wild Flower Wy
8000 SDGO 1250 D3
Wild Grape Dr
9800 SDGO 1209 G5
Wild Holly Ln
15900 POWY 1170 E5
Wild Horse Creek
18500 POWY 1150 J6
Wild Horse Dr
- ImCo 6560 B6
Wild Horse Glen
9700 SDGO 1169 E3
Wild Horse Trl
100 SNTE 1231 E5
Wild Iris Ct
900 SNMS 1128 E5
Wild Iris Rd
2300 SDCo 1234 A5
Wild Lilac Cres
800 SNMS 1128 G2
Wild Lilac Trl
1800 SDCo 1136 D5
Wild Mustang Pl
14700 SDCo 1273 A5
Wild Oak Ln
3300 ESCN 1130 H2
Wild Oak Rd
900 CHLV 1310 J7
28900 SDCo 1237 C5
Wild Oats Ln
3600 SDCo 1311 B1
Wild Orchid Wy
10400 SDCo 1169 E2
Wild Rd
- SDCo 1029 C7
Wild Rose Ln
- IMPE 6499 D2
Wild Rose Rd
900 SDCo 1156 D5
Wild Stallion Pl
14700 SDCo 1273 A6
Wild West Pl
14400 SDCo 1272 J5
Wild Willow Hollow
20300 SDCo 1129 A7
Wildalier St
- CHLV 1330 H2
Wildbrook Pl
1900 CHLV 1311 E4
Wildcat Canyon Rd
15800 SDCo 1173 A5
14700 SDCo 1193 B2
(See Page 1193)
11700 SDCo 1212 E5
11000 SDCo 1232 C1
Wildcat Dr
- BRAW 6319 H3
(See Page 6319)
Wildcat Rd
- ImCo 6320 C3
(See Page 6320)
Wildcat Wy
- OCSD 1086 H4
Wilder Wy
- SDCo 1231 H5
Wilderness Rd
16500 POWY 1170 F3
Wilderness Wy
- ELCJ 1251 J5
Wilderthorn Ln
- SDCo 1251 J1
Wildflower Dr
- CRLB 1127 A4
- ENCT 1148 C5
1700 VSTA 1087 D7
Wildflower Ln
3700 SDCo 1028 E5
Wildflower Pl
600 ESCN 1109 F4
Wildflower Valley Dr
- ENCT 1148 C5
Wildflower Wy
13000 SDCo 1090 C5
Wildgrove Ln
14500 POWY 1170 H5
Wildhorse Ln
500 SNMS 1108 C6
Wildhorse Trail Wy
2600 CHLV 1311 J6
Wildlife Rd
10000 SDGO 1210 A4
Wildmeadow
- SDGO 1210 D2
Wildmeadow Pl
1400 ENCT 1147 G4
Wildrose Glen
3800 ESCN 1150 C3
Wildrose Terr
- CRLB 1127 B6
Wildrose Wy
- SDGO 1209 E3
Wildwind Dr
2800 SDCo 1272 C6
Wildwood Ct
- CHLV 1331 B1
Wildwood Dr
4900 OCSD 1087 C1
600 SDCo 1156 E1
Wildwood Glen Ln
23900 SDCo 1235 J5
Wildwood Ln
- SDCo 1254 F7
Wildwood Rd
3800 SDGO 1268 A7
Wiler Dr
800 CHLV 1310 G7
Wiley Ct
13600 POWY 1190 F3
Wiley Rd
- CHLV 1331 C5
Wilfred St
900 ELCJ 1251 G2
Wilgen Rd
22000 SDCo 1129 B4
Wilhite Ln
30600 SDCo 1070 G4
Wilkerson Ct
7800 SDGO 1249 A3
Wilkes Ln
15800 SDGO 1169 D4
Wilkes Rd
29900 SDCo 1069 G6
- SDCo 1089 H2
Wilkie Wy
100 SDCo 1252 J3
Wilkinson Dr
200 SNMS 1129 A1
Willa Wy
7900 SDGO 1250 H4
Willaman Dr
- SDCo 1068 D5
Willamette Av
4100 SDGO 1248 E2
Willapa Cove
- SDGO 1209 J1
Willard Av
- BRAW 6319 G4
(See Page 6319)
Willard St
3200 SDGO 1228 C5
Willet St
500 ELCJ 1251 G4
Willet Wy
- CRLB 1127 D7
William Av
1300 CHLV 1330 C4
William Pittenger Pl
300 SDCo 1027 J1
William Tell St
21800 SDCo 1135 B3
Williams Av
4900 LMSA 1270 G2
Williams Ln
1800 OCSD 1106 F2
Williams Ranch Rd
2700 SDCo 1135 F7
Williams Rd
37000 SDCo 1299 G2
(See Page 1299)
Williams Terr
3500 ENCT 1148 D3
Williams Valley Ct
29700 SDCo 1069 A5
Williams Wy
8600 SDGO 1229 B2
Williamsburg Ln
4700 LMSA 1270 G3
Williamston St
800 VSTA 1087 J5
Willie Baker Wy
10600 SDCo 1291 F1
Willie James Jones Av
200 SDGO 1290 A5
Willis Ct
400 ELCJ 1251 C5
Willis Rd
1900 ELCJ 1251 C5
Willits Rd
- SDCo 1253 G2
Willman Wy
5300 SDCo 1047 G7
Willoughby Rd
- ImCo 6620 B4
Willow Av
2100 OCSD 1086 C5
Willow Bend Dr
- ELCN 6559 J3
1500 SDCo 1272 F1
Willow Bend Pl
2600 SDCo 1272 F1
Willow Creek Cir
- CHLV 1311 F4
Willow Creek Dr
1400 VSTA 1088 B3
Willow Creek Pl
- SDCo 1130 H2
Willow Creek Rd
10100 SDGO 1209 F5
Willow Ct
- BRAW 6259 J6
(See Page 6259)
4200 NATC 1310 E5
10800 SDCo 1169 G3
Willow Dr
- ELCN 6559 H1
- SDCo 1232 D6
Willow Glen
700 ESCN 1130 C7
Willow Glen Dr
900 SDCo 1252 F7
2300 SDCo 1272 E3
Willow Glen Ln
- SDCo 1272 E3
Willow Glen Rd
- SDCo 998 C5
Willow Grove Av
9400 SNTE 1231 B6
Willow Grove Cir
9000 SNTE 1231 B6
Willow Grove Ct
9000 SNTE 1231 B6
Willow Grove Pl
100 ESCN 1110 F6
9000 SNTE 1231 C6
Willow Heights Rd
2900 SDCo 998 C7
Willow Ln
- SDCo 1089 B3
25700 SDCo 1109 E2
100 SDCo 1149 E3
1300 SDCo 1233 G6
1900 SDGO 1288 C1
Willow Meadow Pl
100 ESCN 1110 F7
Willow Oak Dr
2800 SDCo 1172 D5
Willow Park Rd
28600 SDCo 1089 E2
Willow Pl
- CRLB 1127 B4
Willow Pond Rd
- SNTE 1231 C5
Willow Ranch Rd
14000 POWY 1170 G6
Willow Ranch Trl
15400 POWY 1170 G6
Willow Rd
15000 SDCo 1212 H6
12700 SDCo 1232 B1
100 SDGO 1350 G4
Willow Rd Ext
- SDCo 1212 G7
- SDCo 1232 E1
Willow Ridge Dr
1900 VSTA 1107 F5
Willow Run Rd
13500 POWY 1170 F3
Willow St
- CHLV 1310 F3
3400 SDCo 1310 F2
2700 SDGO 1268 C7
1200 SDGO 1288 B2
Willow Ter
8600 SNTE 1231 C7
Willow Tree Ct
3400 OCSD 1086 D3
Willow Tree Ln
3100 ESCN 1110 F6
800 SDCo 1027 H4
Willow Trl
27700 SDCo 1089 F4
Willow View Ln
30800 SDCo 1070 E3
Willow Walk Rd
5200 OCSD 1067 B3
Willow Wood Glen
- ESCN 1109 D2
Willow Wy
- ELCJ 1251 J6
1800 VSTA 1107 G5
Willowbrook Ct
800 CHLV 1311 D5
1900 ELCJ 1252 C4
Willowbrook Dr
2500 OCSD 1087 F2
Willowbrook St
2300 ESCN 1129 E7
Willowbrook Wy
- ImCo 6560 D7
- SNTE 1231 B5
Willowcreek Ln
1000 SDCo 997 J7
Willowcrest Wy
400 CHLV 1310 F7
Willowgreen Ct
1400 ENCT 1147 G4
Willowgrove Av
8900 SNTE 1231 A6
Willowhaven Rd
1700 ENCT 1147 G4
Willowmere Ln
- SDGO 1208 E1
Willowood Ln
2000 ENCT 1147 H6
Willows Rd
4100 SDCo 1234 F6
- SDCo 1235 B4
Willows Wy
3800 NATC 1310 D3
Willowside Ln
3900 SDCo 1271 B4
Willowside Ter
1200 SDCo 1234 G6
Willowspring Ct
2100 ENCT 1147 J6
N Willowspring Dr
300 ENCT 1147 J6
S Willowspring Dr
500 ENCT 1147 G7
Willowspring Pl
2100 ENCT 1147 H6
Willowview Ct
1400 ENCT 1167 F1
Willowwood Dr
11200 SDGO 1169 J4
Wills Creek Rd
- SDGO 1209 J1
Wills Rd
- ImCo 6260 E3
(See Page 6260)
Willson Rd
1200 SDCo 1253 D3
Wilma Pl
1500 ESCN 1130 B4
Wilma St
2700 SDCo 1310 C2
Wilmington Av
12200 SDCo 1070 A7
Wilmington Dr
- CHLV 1311 H2
Wilmington Rd
11800 SDGO 1190 A2
Wilsey Wy
12200 POWY 1190 B2
Wilshire Av
3600 CRLB 1107 A4
Wilshire Dr
5300 SDGO 1269 G2
Wilshire Rd
1500 OCSD 1047 D7
100 OCSD 1067 C5
Wilshire Ter
3400 SDGO 1269 C6
Wilson Av
2500 CRLB 1106 F3
800 ELCJ 1251 E7
1600 ESCN 1110 B7
1400 NATC 1309 H2
4600 SDGO 1269 F4
Wilson Ct
- CALX 6620 J5
Wilson Pl
2100 ESCN 1110 C6
Wilson Rd
1300 SDCo 1153 A7
1600 SDCo 1173 A1
Wilson St
300 BRAW 6320 C1
(See Page 6320)
300 ELCN 6499 G6
5100 LMSA 1271 A1
Wilstone Av
1700 ENCT 1147 A2
Wilt Rd
1400 SDCo 1028 E4
Wilton Rd
1800 ENCT 1147 A2
Wilts Pl
5100 SDGO 1248 G1
Wiltsie Wy
4800 SDGO 1249 G2
Wilvinn Dr
8100 SNTE 1251 B1
Wimbelton Ln
- SDCo 1089 D3
Wimberly Sq
13000 SDGO 1189 H4
Winamar Av
300 SDGO 1247 E2
Winamar Pl
2000 ESCN 1129 G7
Winans Cove
7900 SDGO 1209 A1
Wincheck Rd
10500 SDGO 1209 G1
Winchester Ct
1200 VSTA 1087 E6
Winchester Dr
- ELCJ 1251 H5
Winchester Ln
300 IMPE 6439 F4
Winchester St
2000 OCSD 1086 C7
5500 SDGO 1310 C2
Winchester Wy
9900 SDCo 1232 D3
Wind Break Ct
3300 SDGO 1187 J5
Wind Break Rd
13100 SDGO 1187 J5
Wind Cave Pl
- CHLV 1311 H4
Wind Chime Dr
1400 CHLV 1331 E1
Wind Creek Rd
2900 SDCo 1253 J3
Wind Drift Dr
900 CRLB 1126 J4
Wind Flower Wy
300 OCSD 1086 J2
Wind Pl
4000 ESCN 1150 D4
Wind River
- OCSD 1086 J2
Wind River Rd
1100 CHLV 1331 B2
2500 SDCo 1272 C4
Wind Sock Wy
500 CRLB 1126 J7
Wind Star Wy
- CRLB 1127 A4
Wind Surf Wy
4700 SDGO 1330 H6
Wind Trail Wy
- CRLB 1107 B6
Windansea St
1300 OCSD 1087 B5
Windbrook Wy
- SDGO 1209 G2
Windchime Av
1400 CHLV 1331 D1
Windcrest Dr
800 CRLB 1126 J5
Windcrest Ln
11700 SDGO 1189 J2
Windemere St
10200 SDCo 1109 F2
Winder St
1700 SDGO 1268 H6
Windermere Dr
- SNMS 1128 C6
Windermere Point Wy
700 OCSD 1066 F7
Windfall Ter
4600 OCSD 1087 D3
Windfall Trl
700 SDCo 1138 B6
(See Page 1138)
Windflower Wy
900 SDGO 1288 A2
Windham Ct
8900 SDCo 1271 A7
Windimere Ct
700 SDGO 1247 H7
Winding Canyon Rd
14800 POWY 1170 J7
14800 POWY 1171 A7
Winding Creek Dr
6600 SDGO 1250 D3
Winding Fence Wy
2900 CHLV 1311 J2
Winding Oak Dr
1000 CHLV 1330 J1
Winding Ridge Dr
- SDGO 1209 G2
Winding Trl
5700 SDCo 1252 H1
Winding Wy
700 ENCT 1147 G5
Windingwalk St
1600 CHLV 1331 H1
Windingwalk Wy
2300 CHLV 1311 F7
Windjammer Cir
300 CHLV 1310 F5
Windjammer Wy
4800 CRLB 1106 H7
Windmill Dr
- SDCo 1251 J7
Windmill Pl
1500 CHLV 1331 A2
Windmill Ranch Rd
- ENCT 1148 A6
Windmill St
5200 OCSD 1087 D1
Windmill View Rd
2100 ELCJ 1251 B2
Windom Peak Wy
- SDGO 1190 A7
Windpiper Rd
16200 POWY 1170 G3
Windridge Cir
- SNMS 1128 F2
Windridge Dr
1300 SDCo 1251 J7
Windrift Wy
3500 OCSD 1107 G4
Windriver St
1800 SNMS 1128 F6
Windrose Cir
- CRLB 1127 A7
Windrose Ct
15800 SDGO 1169 H5
Windrose Wy
400 CHLV 1310 F5
15900 SDGO 1169 H5
Winds Ridge
- SDCo 1234 B6
Windsock St
8400 SDGO 1351 G1
Windsong Ln
1100 SDCo 1089 C7
1400 SDCo 1109 D1
Windsong Rd
- SDCo 1091 F5
7500 SDGO 1209 A3
Windsor Cir
600 CHLV 1310 E6
Windsor Creek Ct
900 ENCT 1167 E2
Windsor Ct
2700 CRLB 1107 A5
700 VSTA 1087 J6
Windsor Dr
7900 LMSA 1270 H3
5000 SDGO 1247 J4
Windsor Grey Wy
200 SDCo 1028 J6
Windsor Pl
700 ESCN 1129 F4
Windsor Rd
1400 ENCT 1167 E2
3500 OCSD 1107 F3
Windstone Glen
2800 ESCN 1110 E7
Windswept Ter
3600 SDGO 1187 J4
Windvane Ln
100 CRLB 1126 J6
Windward Dr
800 SDCo 1156 D1
Windward Ln
800 CRLB 1126 J5
Windward Ridge Wy
- SDGO 1208 G3
Windward St
6700 SDGO 1290 F6
Windward Wy
2500 CHLV 1311 G3
200 OCSD 1085 J7
400 OCSD 1086 A7
Windwood Wy
- SDCo 1272 C6
Windy Bluff Ln
- SDGO 1208 E4
Windy Heights Wy
- SDGO 1188 D5
Windy Hill Ter
900 ENCT 1167 E1
Windy Ln
3000 SDCo 1310 D4
300 VSTA 1087 F6
Windy Mtn Ln
13200 SDCo 1050 C7

74 INDEX
Windy Ridge Rd
INDEX 74
Zeta St
SAN DIEGO CO.

San Diego County Street Index

STREET
Block City Map# Grid

Windy Ridge Rd
7500 SDGO 1209 A1
Windy Ridge Wy
11500 SDGO 1209 A1
Windy Summit Pl
11400 SDGO 1169 J5
Windy Wy
500 CHLV 1311 E3
100 SNMS 1108 H6
Windyridge Glen
400 ESCN 1109 G6
Winecreek Ct
10200 SDCo 1169 E5
Winecreek Rd
16400 SDCo 1169 E5
- SDGO 1169 F6
Winecrest Rd
9900 SDCo 1169 E5
Winen Wy
9000 SDGO 1249 D6
Wineridge Pl
700 ESCN 1129 E4
15000 SDGO 1169 F6
Wineridge Rd
14700 SDGO 1169 F6
Winesprings Ct
15200 SDCo 1169 F6
Winesprings Dr
15900 SDCo 1169 F5
Winewood St
200 SDGO 1290 F3
Winfield Av
6000 LMSA 1251 A6
Wing Av
8000 ELCJ 1251 F2
Wing Flight Ct
7800 SDGO 1250 G4
Wing Span Dr
7900 SDGO 1250 G4
Wing St
3200 SDGO 1268 D5
Wingate St
4600 OCSD 1107 E3
Winged Foot Cir
- SDCo 1090 F4
Winged Foot Gn
2100 ESCN 1109 D4
Wingfoot Pl
1700 SDCo 1272 B5
Winland Hills Dr
5800 SDCo 1188 E1
Winlow St
3100 SDGO 1270 B6
Winn Ranch Rd
17900 SDCo 1156 G7
Winnebago Av
4600 SDGO 1248 F1
Winners Cir
5700 SDCo 1311 B2
Winnetka Dr
2800 SDCo 1310 H2
Winnett St
1600 SDGO 1290 D2
Winona Av
6600 SDGO 1250 A6
4700 SDGO 1270 A3
Winona Ct
2800 ImCo 6439 C5
5100 OCSD 1087 C1
Winrow Rd
1800 SDCo 1252 C3
Winship Ln
2300 SDGO 1288 G1
Winslow Rd
3500 OCSD 1107 E2
Winsome Dr
2200 ESCN 1129 G7
- ESCN 1149 G1
Winsome Pl
300 ENCT 1147 J5
Winsome Wy
2000 ENCT 1147 H6
Winstanley Wy
13400 SDGO 1188 C4
Winston Dr
700 SDGO 1290 A3
Winter Creek Ln
- SDCo 1070 G2
Winter Gardens Blvd
- SDCo 1231 J3
9700 SDCo 1232 A4
8100 SDCo 1251 J1
Winter Gardens Dr
12000 SDCo 1231 J7
12200 SDCo 1232 A7
12000 SDCo 1251 J1
Winter Haven Ln
2200 SDCo 1028 B7
Winter Haven Rd
900 SDCo 1027 H7
1300 SDCo 1028 A7
Winter Hunt Ln
- SDGO 1208 E2
Winter Ln
1500 CHLV 1312 B7
(See Page 1312)
1300 SDCo 1252 A1
Winter Rd
2400 OCSD 1087 D6
Winter View Ct
7900 SDCo 1251 J2
Winter View Pl
1200 SDCo 1251 J1
Wintercreek Pl
- SNTE 1231 B5
Wintercrest Dr
12000 SDCo 1231 J4
12100 SDCo 1232 A4
Wintergreen Dr
2700 CRLB 1106 G3
12100 SDCo 1232 A4
Wintergreen Glen
300 ESCN 1109 G6
Wintergreen Ln
2400 SDCo 1028 B6
Wintergreen Pl
400 SNMS 1109 C7
Winterhaven Ct
2300 SDCo 1028 B7
Winterhaven Rd
700 SDCo 1027 G7
Winterhawk Ln
200 ENCT 1167 J1
Winters Ct
300 SNMS 1108 J7
Winters Hill
3000 SDCo 1088 E7
Wintersweet St
1900 SDGO 1350 D3
Winterwarm Rd
1900 SDCo 1028 A7
1800 SDCo 1048 A1
Winterwarm Wy
2800 SDCo 1048 A1
Winterwood Ln
7500 SDGO 1209 A3
Winthrop Av
- CRLB 1107 A4
Winthrop St
5200 SDGO 1228 H7
Wire Mountain Rd
- SDCo 1085 H4
- SDCo 1086 A3
Wireless Wy
- SDGO 1208 E5
Wisconsin Av
200 ELCJ 1251 F5
6900 LMSA 1270 E1
600 OCSD 1106 B1
800 SDCo 1027 F3
E Wisconsin Av
1000 OCSD 1106 B1
Wise St
- CHLV 1330 J2
Wisecarver Ln
3600 SDCo 1274 C5
Wisecarver Truck Tr
- SDCo 1274 C7
Wishbone Wy
2900 ENCT 1148 B3
Wishing Star Dr
1500 CHLV 1311 H7
Wishing Star Wy
2400 CHLV 1311 H7
Wiskon Wy
32200 SDCo 1051 B6
Wispering Woods Ct
4600 SDGO 1188 B5
Wister Dr
9200 SDCo 1271 B1
Wisteria
- SDCo 1233 B3
Wisteria Av
- POWY 1190 F3
Wisteria Ct
- IMPE 6499 D2
1900 SDCo 1272 D2
Wisteria Dr
5100 OCSD 1107 E4
- SDCo 1128 G3
3300 SDGO 1268 C6
Wisteria Glen
1600 ESCN 1109 D6
Wisteria St
500 CHLV 1330 H3
Wisteria Wy
7200 CRLB 1127 B6
2300 NATC 1290 A6
Wistful Vista
7900 SNTE 1230 G7
Witch Creek Mtn Rd
27200 SDCo 1154 D1
Witham Rd
100 ENCT 1147 F7
Witherby St
400 OCSD 1106 B2
4400 SDGO 1268 G5
Witherspoon Wy
300 ELCJ 1251 B5
Witt Pl
12400 POWY 1190 C3
Witt Rd
12200 POWY 1190 B3
Wittman Wy
3100 SDGO 1350 F5
Wizard Wy
- SDCo 1071 B5
Woden St
1900 SDGO 1289 G7
Wohlford Dr
- ESCN 1110 E5
Wohlford St
5200 OCSD 1087 D1
Wolahi Rd
34300 SDCo 1176 C5
(See Page 1176)
Wolbert Pl
3400 SDGO 1289 F4
Wolf Canyon Loop
1900 CHLV 1331 E2
Wolf Point Ct
600 OCSD 1067 C7
Wolff Ct
5800 LMSA 1251 C7
Wolford Dr
400 SDCo 1290 J4
Wolfs Hill Rd
- CHLV 1311 E7
Wolfsdorf Wy
1600 CHLV 1331 E2
Wolfstar Ct
6100 SDGO 1228 G6
Wolverine Ter
- CRLB 1107 D7
Wolverine Wy
- SDGO 1189 B3
1700 VSTA 1088 B5
Wolviston Wy
1700 SDGO 1350 A2
Womack Ln
500 SDCo 1027 F3
Womble Rd
- SDGO 1268 D7
Womble St
- NATC 1309 F2
Womsi Ln
15400 SDCo 1050 J5
Womsi Rd
- SDCo 1050 J5
Wonder Ln
8000 SDCo 1252 A1
Wonder View Dr
2000 SDCo 1088 B2
Wonderful View Rd
- SDCo 1232 E5
Wood Dr
700 ENCT 1147 C3
Wood Duck Dr
10500 SDCo 1149 F7
Wood Ln
- SDCo 1071 A3
Wood St
5200 LMSA 1271 A1
Wood Valley Tr
- SDCo 1273 G5
Wood Worth Wy
- SDGO 1268 D7
Woodacre Dr
2300 OCSD 1106 H1
Woodbine Pl
1700 OCSD 1106 D2
Woodbine Wy
7600 SDGO 1290 G4
Woodbridge Rd
1700 ESCN 1109 D5
Woodbrook Ln
1700 SDCo 1027 G5
Woodburn St
1700 ELCJ 1251 H2
Woodbury Ct
2900 CRLB 1107 B4
Woodbury Pl
2100 ESCN 1109 G5
Woodchuck Pt
10400 SDGO 1209 J4
Woodcraft Wy
- SDGO 1209 G2
Woodcreek Pl
13200 POWY 1190 D2
Woodcreek Rd
900 SDCo 1027 H4
Woodcreek St
14200 POWY 1190 E2
Woodcrest Dr
300 SDCo 1027 F3
Woodcrest St
1400 CHLV 1311 B6
Wooddale Row
6000 SDGO 1248 B1
Wooden St
- NATC 1309 F1
- SDGO 1289 G7
Wooden Valley St
1300 CHLV 1311 E7
Woodfern Ln
1900 CRLB 1147 E3
Woodford Dr
2900 SDGO 1228 A6
Woodfords Pl
- CHLV 1331 C1
Woodgate Pl
13700 POWY 1190 F5
Woodglen Pl
2100 ESCN 1109 G5
Woodglen Ter
1400 CHLV 1311 A2
Woodglen Vista Dr
10300 SNTE 1231 D2
Woodglen Wy
1900 ELCJ 1251 C3
Woodgrove Dr
1000 ENCT 1167 E2
Woodhaven Dr
1300 OCSD 1087 D2
1000 SDCo 1290 J3
Woodhill St
1400 ELCJ 1252 A6
Woodhollow Ln
14100 POWY 1190 E2
Woodhouse Av
500 CHLV 1310 F6
Woodhue Ln
14600 POWY 1190 E1
Woodlake Dr
1000 ENCT 1167 E2
Woodland
2500 OCSD 1106 F2
Woodland Ct
4100 LMSA 1271 B4
1300 SNMS 1109 C6
Woodland Dr
4300 LMSA 1271 B3
300 SDCo 1108 B2
Woodland Glen
1900 ESCN 1110 B5
Woodland Heights Glen
- ESCN 1109 C3
Woodland Hills Dr
400 SDCo 1149 J1
Woodland Ln
300 SDCo 1252 H4
Woodland Pkwy
14000 POWY 1170 G4
800 SNMS 1109 C6
Woodland Rd
2500 SDCo 1136 D7
Woodland Valley Glen
1900 ESCN 1109 C4
Woodland Vista Dr
9600 SDCo 1232 D3
Woodland Wy
3400 CRLB 1106 F5
Woodlands Glen
- LMSA 1270 E5
Woodlands Ln
8500 SDGO 1228 A4
Woodlark Ct
1500 CHLV 1330 F5
Woodlark Ln
- CHLV 1330 F4
1700 SDCo 1027 G5
Woodlawn Av
200 CHLV 1309 J6
500 CHLV 1310 A7
700 CHLV 1330 A2
Woodlawn Dr
800 SDCo 1156 D1
9000 SDGO 1209 D4
Woodleaf Av
1300 CHLV 1331 C1
Woodley Pl
800 ENCT 1147 D4
Woodley Rd
- SDCo 1147 F4
Woodman St
1600 SDGO 1310 G1
S Woodman St
200 SDGO 1290 E4
Woodmeadow Ln
200 SDCo 1153 B5
Woodmont Pl
13100 POWY 1190 D2
Woodmont St
13100 POWY 1190 D2
Woodmoss Ct
2000 ENCT 1147 H5
Woodpark Dr
10000 SNTE 1231 E3
Woodpark Wy
400 OCSD 1086 F3
Woodpecker Wy
7900 SNTE 1230 H7
Woodpine Dr
1500 SDCo 1272 B4
Woodrail Dr
1200 VSTA 1087 G4
Woodridge Cir
2800 CRLB 1106 F3
Woodridge Wy
7500 SDGO 1290 G5
Woodrock Ln
15900 SDCo 1172 A4
Woodrose Av
10000 SNTE 1231 D3
Woodrow Av
900 SDGO 1290 F2
Woodruff Wy
9300 SNTE 1231 A5
Woodrun Pl
1600 SDCo 1272 B4
Woodrush Ct
11200 SDGO 1189 J2
Woodrush Ln
11200 SDGO 1189 J1
Woods Dr
- CHLV 1311 J3
500 SNMS 1109 C6
Woods Hill Ln
- SDCo 1153 C7
Woods Ln
100 SDCo 1234 J3
Woods Valley Ct
27100 SDCo 1090 E5
Woods Valley Rd
13800 SDCo 1090 E5
16100 SDCo 1091 C5
Woodset Ln
14700 POWY 1190 C1
Woodshadow Ln
100 ENCT 1147 H6
Woodshawn Dr
7100 SDGO 1290 F5
Woodside Av
12000 SDCo 1231 J4
12400 SDCo 1232 B3
11100 SNTE 1231 G5
N Woodside Av
10800 SNTE 1231 F5
Woodside Ct
- CHLV 1311 F3
Woodside Dr
1900 ELCN 6559 G2
Woodside Ln
800 ENCT 1147 J5
Woodside Pl
- ESCN 1109 F4
Woodside Terr
11500 SNTE 1231 H4
Woodside Wy
1000 SOLB 1187 G1
Woodson Crest Rd
- SDCo 1171 C3
Woodson Ct
- SDCo 1172 A2
N Woodson Ct
17200 SDCo 1171 F3
N Woodson Dr
16400 SDCo 1171 F3
S Woodson Dr
15900 SDCo 1171 E3
Woodson Ridge Rd
- SDCo 1171 B3
Woodson View Ln
17100 SDCo 1171 E3
Woodson View Rd
16200 POWY 1170 F4
Woodsong Ct
- SDCo 1089 A1
Woodsong Dr
- SDCo 1089 A1
Woodspring Dr
800 CHLV 1311 E4
Woodstock Pl
13700 SDCo 1090 E6
Woodstock St
4500 CRLB 1107 A4
Woodstork Ln
100 SDCo 1027 F5
Woodstream Pt
10800 SDGO 1210 A2
Woodthrush Ln
100 SDCo 1027 F5
Woodvale Dr
3800 CRLB 1106 H5
- SNTE 1230 J7
Woodview Dr
1200 OCSD 1087 C2
Woodview Pl
9500 SDGO 1249 E4
Woodville Av
- CHLV 1331 D1
Woodward Av
1300 ELCN 6499 F5
200 ESCN 1129 H2
Woodward Rd
- SDGO 1287 H4
Woodward St
400 SNMS 1108 J4
Woodway Ct
200 SDGO 1290 G5
Woodwayne Dr
10300 SNTE 1231 D3
Woodwind Dr
2100 ENCT 1147 J7
Woodwind Rd
2700 CRLB 1106 F3
Woodwind St
1600 CHLV 1331 D1
Woody Hills Dr
1700 SDCo 1272 B1
Woody Ln
13000 POWY 1190 G5
Woodyard Av
5000 LMSA 1270 G2
Wooster Dr
4000 OCSD 1087 B6
Worcester Glen
- ESCN 1110 D7
Worchester Pl
6900 SDGO 1208 H4
Worden Rd
- SDGO 1288 D1
Worden St
2600 SDGO 1268 C6
Works Pl
4700 SDGO 1269 E3
World Trade Dr
12300 SDGO 1170 B7
11800 SDGO 1190 A1
Worsch Dr
12400 SDGO 1188 B7
Worsch Wy
4100 SDGO 1188 B7
Worthing Av
10800 SDGO 1209 B3
Worthington Rd
500 IMPE 6439 C6
- ImCo 6439 H5
38700 SDCo 1320 A3
(See Page 1320)
Worthington St
600 SDCo 1290 J3
1000 SDGO 1290 J3
Wotan Dr
1000 ENCT 1167 F1
Wozencraft St
1000 CALX 6680 C2
Wrangler Ct
900 CHLV 1310 H3
Wranglers Dr
300 SDCo 1058 G6
(See Page 1058)
Wrelton Dr
600 SDGO 1247 G5
Wren Bluff Dr
9700 SDCo 1169 E4
Wren Glen
1100 ESCN 1109 E5
Wren Haven Wy
16800 SDCo 1169 F4
Wren St
1100 SDGO 1290 D2
- SNTE 1230 G7
Wren Wy
900 SNMS 1128 E2
Wright Av
- CORD 1288 G4
Wright Canyon Rd
24000 SDCo 1193 E4
(See Page 1193)
Wright Ct
- BRAW 6260 C7
(See Page 6260)
Wright Pl
1900 CRLB 1127 C3
Wright Rd
- CORD 1288 F5
Wright St
3500 SDGO 1268 G6
Wrightwood Rd
- SDCo 1068 D1
Wueste Rd
- CHLV 1312 A4
(See Page 1312)
1700 CHLV 1332 A1
(See Page 1332)
- SDGO 1332 A3
(See Page 1332)
Wulff St
1000 SNMS 1109 B5
Wunderlin Av
6000 SDGO 1290 C3
Wyandotte Av
2600 SDGO 1228 B7
2600 SDGO 1248 B1
Wyatt
- SDGO 1350 H2
Wyatt Ct
1400 SDGO 1350 H2
Wyatt Pl
1500 ELCJ 1251 D4
Wycliffe St
10000 SNTE 1231 D2
Wyconda Ln
4900 SDGO 1290 A6
Wyconda Wy
1300 SDGO 1290 A6
Wye St
14600 SDGO 1189 H1
Wyeport Rd
- SDCo 1172 A5
Wyeth Rd
- SDCo 1232 E5
Wykes St
500 CHLV 1330 B3
Wyman Wy
9600 SDCo 1271 C7
Wyndemere Ct
26200 SDCo 1109 G1
Wyndemere Ln
11000 SDCo 1109 G1
Wyndhaven Dr
13300 SDGO 1188 A5
Wyneland Rd
19400 SDCo 1151 B3
Wynell Ln
3000 LMGR 1270 J6
Wyngate Pt
13400 SDGO 1188 C4
Wynn St
1200 OCSD 1086 A5
Wynola Rd
- SDCo 1135 F5
1700 SDCo 1136 B3
100 SDCo 1172 D1
Wynwood Ct
- SDCo 1130 J3
Wyoming Av
4900 LMSA 1270 E1
Wystone Dr
1300 SDGO 1290 A6

X

Xana Wy
3100 CRLB 1127 J5
3100 CRLB 1128 A5
Xavier Av
800 CHLV 1311 C5
Xenophon St
3800 SDGO 1268 B6

Y

Yacon Cir
200 VSTA 1087 E7
Yacon St
300 VSTA 1087 E7
Yacoo Ct
13700 SDCo 1292 G2
(See Page 1292)
Yale Av
4300 LMSA 1270 F4
Yale Dr
3700 OCSD 1107 A2
Yale St
1600 CHLV 1311 C5
Yama St
2100 SDGO 1289 G7
Yankee Ct
2100 ESCN 1129 E6
Yankee Point Wy
800 OCSD 1066 F7
Yankton Dr
12900 POWY 1190 D4
Yanonali Av
1500 CHLV 1331 C2
Yaqui Dr
15300 SDCo 1176 E5
(See Page 1176)
Yaqui Pass Rd
3400 SDCo 1079 F7
(See Page 1079)
5900 SDCo 1119 B4
(See Page 1119)
Yaqui Rd
1400 SDCo 1058 G5
(See Page 1058)
Yarmouth Ct
700 SDGO 1247 H7
Yarrow Dr
6200 CRLB 1127 E3
Yarrow Wy
600 SNMS 1128 H3
Yaweh Ln
29400 SDCo 1317 H3
(See Page 1317)
Yazoo St
14400 SDGO 1189 H1
Ybarra Rd
3400 SDCo 1271 F6
Yearling Ct
5700 SDCo 1311 B2
Yearling Glen Rd
4800 SDGO 1208 B2
Yellow Pine Ct
- SDCo 1089 B2
Yellow Pine Pl
1600 CHLV 1311 J7
Yellow Rose Ln
10400 SDCo 1169 G2
Yellow Throat Rd
13800 POWY 1170 F5
Yellowstone Pl
9700 SNTE 1231 E4
Yellowstone Rd
- CHLV 1311 J6
Yerba Anita Dr
5500 SDGO 1269 J1
5300 SDGO 1270 A1
Yerba Anita Wy
5000 SDGO 1270 A2
Yerba Buena Dr
3300 SDCo 1028 D1
Yerba Ln
3500 CHLV 1310 G3
Yerba Santa Dr
4400 SDGO 1269 J1
5000 SDGO 1270 A2
Yerba Santa Rd
24000 SDCo 1315 J4
(See Page 1315)
Yerba Valley Rd
- SDCo 1212 D4
Yerba Valley Wy
- SDCo 1212 D3
Yerba Verde Dr
1200 ELCJ 1251 D3
Yermo Ct
16500 SDCo 1169 F4
Yesteryear Ln
- SDCo 1028 B2
Yettford Rd
1800 VSTA 1108 A3
Yew Ct
2100 CHLV 1331 H3
Yew Ln
- SDCo 1149 D4
Ymca Wy
100 SDCo 1289 J4
Ynez Path
3800 SDCo 1099 E2
(See Page 1099)
Ynez Pl
2700 CORD 1288 J7
Yodel Ln
2000 SDGO 1350 A1
Yokohama Ct
5800 SDGO 1250 E7
Yokum Ct
- SDCo 1027 E2
Yolanda Av
9400 SDGO 1249 F6
Yolanda Pl
2400 SDGO 1249 F6
Yolo Ct
8300 SDGO 1189 B6
Yonge St
3700 SDGO 1268 B6
Yorba Ct
1300 CHLV 1311 B6
Yorba Linda Ct
24200 SDCo 1173 E2
York Av
1300 ESCN 1110 A7
14200 POWY 1190 F2
York Ct
700 SDGO 1247 H7
York Dr
1800 SDCo 1108 B2
1100 VSTA 1108 B1
York Pl
1500 ESCN 1110 B7
York Rd
2700 CRLB 1106 J4
York View Cir
1700 SDCo 1108 C2
Yorkshire Av
5800 LMSA 1250 J7
Yorktown Dr
10200 SDGO 1249 G5
Yorktown St
- IMPB 1349 J2
Yosemite Dr
- CHLV 1311 H4
Yosemite St
4300 CRLB 1106 J5
3700 SDGO 1248 A7
3500 SDGO 1268 A1
Yost Cir
5200 SDGO 1247 J4
Yost Dr
1600 SDGO 1247 J4
Yost Pl
5200 SDGO 1247 J4
Young St
1300 ELCJ 1251 D4
Youngstown Wy
9200 SDGO 1208 F7
Yourell Av
1400 CRLB 1106 E3
Yourman Rd
700 CALX 6620 F4
- ImCo 6560 F4
- ImCo 6620 F2
Ysabel Creek Rd
- SDGO 1131 B7
- SDGO 1151 B1
Ysidro Dr
24300 SDCo 1173 F1
Yuba Dr
- CHLV 1311 D5
Yucatan Wy
1600 SDCo 1027 F5
Yucca Av
3300 SDGO 1248 D3
Yucca Dr
1900 ELCN 6559 E1
3200 SDCo 1156 E1
2500 SDCo 1297 E4
(See Page 1297)
Yucca Hill Rd
2200 SDCo 1253 J1
Yucca Rd
1700 OCSD 1106 F1
500 SDCo 1028 D3
- SDCo 1213 A6
Yucca Ridge Ln
700 SDCo 1109 B2
Yucca St
- IMPE 6499 D3
14000 SDCo 1272 H7
14000 SDCo 1292 H1
(See Page 1292)
Yucca Ter
3200 SDCo 1028 D3
Yucca Trl
28400 SDCo 1089 F2
Yucca Wy
3500 SDCo 1028 D2
Yuki Ln
4300 CRLB 1106 G6
Yukon St
14400 SDGO 1189 H1
Yukon Wy
- POWY 1190 D5
Yuma Av
4900 OCSD 1067 B7
4700 OCSD 1087 B1
Yuma Glen
1000 ESCN 1109 F6
Yuma Rd
34600 SDCo 1176 D4
(See Page 1176)
Yuma St
5700 SDGO 1268 G3
Yvette Wy
3700 CRLB 1106 F5
Yvonne St
2800 OCSD 1087 D7

Z

Z St
25800 SDCo 1109 E2
3500 SDGO 1289 F6
Zabel Ct
8800 SDCo 1271 A5
Zabyn St
2200 OCSD 1106 E1
Zach Canyon Pl
1400 CHLV 1331 B2
Zachary Glen
- ESCN 1110 B5
Zada Ln
300 VSTA 1088 A6
Zagala Ct
11000 SDGO 1250 A2
Zamora Ct
1600 CHLV 1331 E2
Zamora Wy
2200 CRLB 1127 G7
4600 OCSD 1107 F4
Zane Ct
6700 SDGO 1248 J6
Zanja Pl
24700 SDCo 1173 G2
Zanzibar Ct
700 SDGO 1247 H7
Zanzibar Rd
- ELCJ 1251 J5
Zapata Av
10000 SDGO 1209 B2
Zapata St
11300 SDGO 1209 C2
E Zapata St
- CALX 6620 G6
Zapo St
1900 DLMR 1187 G4
Zarina Lake Dr
38500 SDCo 1320 A4
(See Page 1320)
Zarina Ln
400 ENCT 1147 G5
Zarza Corte
- CHLV 1311 A7
Zaslavsky Pl
- SDGO 1169 D3
Zealand Wy
8100 LMGR 1270 H7
Zebrina Pl
6900 CRLB 1127 E6
Zed St
3900 SDGO 1248 E4
Zeigler Ct
15700 SDCo 1173 J4
Zeijl Ln
8500 SDCo 1232 A7
Zeil Pl
5400 SDGO 1270 B5
Zeilin St
500 SDCo 1067 A1
Zeiss St
1400 OCSD 1086 B5
Zelda Av
4600 LMSA 1270 F3
Zeller St
1700 SDGO 1290 E1
Zember Ct
- VSTA 1108 A2
Zemco Dr
7500 LMGR 1290 G2
Zemke Av
13700 SDGO 1189 D3
Zena Dr
6400 SDCo 1270 D5
Zenako Ct
6000 SDGO 1228 E5
Zenako St
3900 SDGO 1228 E6
Zencaro Av
8800 SDGO 1249 C6
Zenith Ln
4200 OCSD 1107 C2
Zenith St
400 CHLV 1330 C5
Zenor Ln
10500 SDCo 1169 F2
Zenos Wy
4800 OCSD 1107 F6
Zephyr Av
1500 ELCJ 1252 B2
Zepplin Av
- SDGO 1229 E2
Zermatt Ln
3600 SDCo 1150 D2
Zero Rd
6400 SDGO 1270 D6
Zest Ct
500 SDGO 1290 G6
Zest St
7200 SDGO 1290 G6
Zeta St
8400 LMSA 1250 J7

STREET Block City Map# Grid

Zezere Dr
400 OCSD 1086 J4
Ziga Dr
- SDCo 1071 A7
Zilliox Ln
600 SNMS 1108 J6
Zimmer Cove
5000 SDGO 1188 D5
Zinfandel Ter
500 CHLV 1311 D3
Zinfandel Wy
- SNMS 1109 A3
Zinnia Ct
6600 CRLB 1126 J5
4300 SDGO 1330 G7
Zinnia Hills Pl
13500 SDGO 1188 F4
Zion Av
4400 SDGO 1249 H6
4900 SDGO 1250 A6
Zion Ct
300 SDCo 1153 A6
Zips Wy
11000 SDCo 1069 F1
Zirbel Ct
11900 SDGO 1210 B1
Zirbel Wy
11300 SDGO 1210 B1
Zircon St
- IMPE 6439 C7
5600 SDGO 1290 B2
Zlatibor Ranch Rd
- ESCN 1130 C5
Zlatibor Ranch Terr
- ESCN 1130 C5
Zodiac St
6700 CRLB 1127 G6
Zodiak Av
- SDGO 1209 F7
Zoe St
3800 SDGO 1248 E5
Zola Glen
1800 ESCN 1109 F6
Zola St
3700 SDGO 1268 B6
Zolder Ct
2000 SDCo 1272 C4
Zolderdo Rd
11400 SDCo 1271 H4
Zona Gale Rd
- ENCT 1147 E6
Zoo Dr
2900 SDGO 1269 C7
Zoo Pl
1900 SDGO 1269 C7
2100 SDGO 1289 C1
W Zoo Rd
- SDGO 1130 H6
Zora St
5900 LMSA 1250 G6
Zorita Ct
11200 SDGO 1250 A2
Zoro Wy
1600 SDGO 1349 J2
Zorzal Ct
- BRAW 6320 C3
(See Page 6320)
Zozoa Ct
- BRAW 6320 C2
(See Page 6320)
Zubaron Ln
7000 CRLB 1127 G7
Zulu Wy
2600 SDGO 1290 F7
2600 SDGO 1310 F1
Zumaque
18700 SDCo 1168 G3
Zumbrota Rd
3200 SDCo 1234 D4
Zuni Dr
400 DLMR 1187 F4
Zuni Trl
1600 SDCo 1099 E2
(See Page 1099)
Zura Wy
6200 SDGO 1270 C2
Zurich Dr
1200 SDGO 1350 A1
Zutano Ln
1500 SDCo 998 B6

#

1st Av
- CHLV 1310 C4
1300 CHLV 1330 E4
4000 SDGO 1269 A5
2500 SDGO 1289 A1
1st Pl
19600 SDCo 1149 E2
1st St
500 BRAW 6319 H1
(See Page 6319)
800 CALX 6680 H2
- CORD 1288 F4
1400 CORD 1289 A5
800 ELCN 6499 J7
1200 ENCT 1167 C1
600 IMPB 1329 E7
300 IMPE 6439 E7
1300 OCSD 1086 B7
- SDCo 998 J3
2000 SDCo 1136 B6
800 SDCo 1152 J5
- SDCo 1271 F7
- SDGO 1229 F5
1400 SNMS 1128 D1
8800 SNTE 1231 E6
E 1st St
600 NATC 1289 H7
2400 NATC 1290 A6
N 1st St
100 ELCJ 1251 H5
1200 SDCo 1251 H3
S 1st St
- BRAW 6319 H4
(See Page 6319)
400 ELCJ 1251 H6
2nd Av
1000 CHLV 1330 D3
3200 SDGO 1269 A7
1700 SDGO 1289 A2
E 2nd Av
100 ESCN 1129 J3
800 ESCN 1130 A2
N 2nd Av
- CHLV 1310 B4
W 2nd Av
800 ESCN 1129 H3
2nd Pl
19500 SDCo 1149 E2
2nd St
300 BRAW 6319 J2
(See Page 6319)
600 CALX 6680 H2
- CORD 1288 F4
- ELCN 6499 J6
1700 ELCN 6559 J1
100 ENCT 1147 B6
1100 ENCT 1167 C1
700 IMPB 1329 F7
300 IMPE 6439 E6
- ImCo 6560 A7
- SDCo 998 H4
34900 SDCo 1029 J4
- SDCo 1066 B2
1900 SDCo 1136 B7
100 SDCo 1152 H5
10900 SDCo 1231 F3
- SDCo 1271 F7
- SDGO 1308 A1
10600 SNTE 1231 E3
E 2nd St
600 NATC 1289 H7
2400 NATC 1290 B6
N 2nd St
1200 ELCJ 1251 J3
1600 SDCo 1251 J2
S 2nd St
700 ELCJ 1251 J7
- ELCN 6559 J2
W 2nd St
- CALX 6680 E2
3rd Av
200 CHLV 1310 B5
1300 CHLV 1330 D4
4000 SDGO 1269 A5
2400 SDGO 1289 A1
E 3rd Av
700 ESCN 1130 A2
W 3rd Av
700 ESCN 1129 H3
3rd Pl
20100 SDCo 1149 E3
3rd St
- BRAW 6319 J1
(See Page 6319)
- CALX 6680 F2
- CORD 1288 F4
300 CORD 1289 A6
900 ELCN 6499 J5
1700 ELCN 6559 J1
100 ENCT 1147 B6
900 ENCT 1167 B1
1000 IMPB 1329 F7
1000 IMPB 1349 F1
600 IMPE 6439 E6
- ImCo 6560 B7
4500 LMSA 1270 J3
- SDCo 1066 B2
2000 SDCo 1136 B7
900 SDCo 1152 J6
- SDCo 1291 F1
8900 SNTE 1231 E6
E 3rd St
200 NATC 1289 H7
2300 NATC 1290 B6
- NATC 1309 H1
N 3rd St
500 ELCJ 1252 A4
S 3rd St
600 ELCJ 1252 A6
4s Commons Dr
10500 SDCo 1169 F3
4s Ranch Pkwy
16500 SDCo 1169 E3
4th Av
400 CHLV 1310 B7
1000 CHLV 1330 C3
4000 SDGO 1269 A5
1300 SDGO 1289 A2
E 4th Av
100 ESCN 1129 J3
1000 ESCN 1130 B2
N 4th Av
- CHLV 1310 A4
W 4th Av
700 ESCN 1129 H4
4th Pl
20100 SDCo 1149 E3
4th St
- CALX 6680 F2
- CORD 1288 F5
200 DLMR 1187 F6
900 ELCN 6499 H5
- ELCN 6559 H1
100 ENCT 1147 B6
2300 ENCT 1167 J1
800 IMPB 1329 F7
1000 IMPB 1349 F1
300 IMPE 6439 E6
4400 LMSA 1270 J3
- NATC 1309 G1
- SDCo 1066 C1
2000 SDCo 1136 B7
300 SDCo 1152 H5
- SDCo 1291 F1
8900 SNTE 1231 E6
E 4th St
600 NATC 1289 H7
1700 NATC 1290 A7
200 NATC 1309 H1
N 4th St
- CORD 1288 F4
200 ELCJ 1252 B5
900 SDCo 1252 B4
5th Av
- CHLV 1310 A5
1100 CHLV 1330 C3
4000 SDGO 1269 A5
900 SDGO 1289 A3
E 5th Av
200 ESCN 1129 J3
1000 ESCN 1130 B2
N 5th Av
- CHLV 1310 A4
W 5th Av
800 ESCN 1129 H4
5th Pl
19800 SDCo 1149 D4
5th St
- BRAW 6259 J7
(See Page 6259)
300 BRAW 6319 J1
(See Page 6319)
400 CALX 6680 F2
400 CORD 1288 H6
- DLMR 1187 G6
500 ELCN 6499 H5
1500 ELCN 6559 H1
100 ENCT 1147 B6
2400 ENCT 1167 J1
500 IMPB 1329 F6
1100 IMPB 1349 F2
300 IMPE 6439 E6
3200 NATC 1290 C6
12300 POWY 1190 C3
- SDCo 998 H5
- SDCo 1066 C1
- SDCo 1085 H4
2000 SDCo 1136 B7
100 SDCo 1152 H5
- SDCo 1291 F1
E 5th St
- CALX 6680 J2
600 NATC 1289 H7
1700 NATC 1290 A7
200 NATC 1309 H1
06th Ln
- SDGO 1228 A2
6th Av
4200 SDGO 1269 A5
1400 SDGO 1289 B2
E 6th Av
400 ESCN 1130 A3
W 6th Av
600 ESCN 1129 H4
6th Ex St
4000 SDGO 1269 B5
6th Pl
20000 SDCo 1149 D4
6th St
100 BRAW 6319 J2
(See Page 6319)
100 CALX 6680 F2
400 CORD 1288 H6
100 DLMR 1187 F6
1100 ELCN 6499 H5
- ELCN 6559 H2
400 IMPE 6439 E6
- ImCo 6560 B7
- SDCo 1066 C1
- SDCo 1085 H4
100 SDCo 1152 H5
- SDCo 1271 G7
- SDCo 1291 F1
- SDGO 1229 F5
E 6th St
1300 NATC 1289 J7
2300 NATC 1290 A7
- NATC 1309 H1
7th Av
3900 SDGO 1269 B5
1400 SDGO 1289 B2
E 7th Av
100 ESCN 1130 A3
W 7th Av
200 ESCN 1129 J3
7th Pl
19900 SDCo 1149 D3
7th St
- BRAW 6259 J7
(See Page 6259)
- BRAW 6319 J1
(See Page 6319)
100 CALX 6680 F1
100 CHLV 1330 C6
500 CORD 1288 H6
100 DLMR 1187 F6
2100 ELCN 6499 G4
2100 ELCN 6559 H2
2300 ENCT 1147 J7
500 IMPB 1329 G6
1100 IMPB 1349 G1
300 IMPE 6439 E6
- ImCo 6560 B7
- SDCo 1066 C1
100 SDCo 1152 G5
- SDCo 1291 F1
E 7th St
1400 NATC 1289 J7
3400 NATC 1290 C6
100 NATC 1309 H1
8th Av
3900 SDGO 1269 B5
1500 SDGO 1289 B2
E 8th Av
300 ESCN 1130 A3
W 8th Av
800 ESCN 1129 J4
8th Dr
1900 SDGO 1289 B2
8th Pl
19400 SDCo 1149 D4
8th St
300 BRAW 6319 J2
(See Page 6319)
- CALX 6680 F1
400 CORD 1288 H6
400 DLMR 1187 G5
1700 ELCN 6499 G3
1500 ELCN 6559 G2
2300 ENCT 1147 J7
500 IMPB 1329 G6
1400 IMPB 1349 G2
200 OCSD 1085 J7
1000 OCSD 1086 A6
- SDCo 998 J5
- SDCo 999 A5
- SDCo 1066 C1
- SDCo 1085 H4
100 SDCo 1152 G5
- SDCo 1291 F1
3600 SNMS 1108 D7
E 8th St
1600 NATC 1290 A7
100 NATC 1309 H1
N 8th St
- BRAW 6320 A1
(See Page 6320)
W 8th St
300 NATC 1309 G1
9th Av
4200 SDGO 1269 B4
1400 SDGO 1289 B2
W 9th Av
1600 ESCN 1129 F4
100 ESCN 1130 A3
9th St
- BRAW 6319 J3
(See Page 6319)
- CALX 6680 F1
400 CORD 1288 G6
300 DLMR 1187 G5
- ELCN 6499 G6
- ELCN 6559 G2
2300 ENCT 1147 J6
2400 ENCT 1148 A6
500 IMPB 1329 G7
1300 IMPB 1349 G2
400 IMPE 6439 E6
- ImCo 6620 B1
3200 NATC 1290 C7
12300 POWY 1190 C4
- SDCo 1066 D1
- SDCo 1085 G4
100 SDCo 1152 G5
- SDCo 1291 F1
3500 SNMS 1108 C7
E 9th St
2200 NATC 1290 A7
100 NATC 1309 H1
1800 NATC 1310 A1
W 9th St
- NATC 1309 H1
10th Av
4300 SDGO 1269 B4
600 SDGO 1289 B3
E 10th Av
100 ESCN 1130 A3
N 10th Av
500 SDGO 1289 B4
W 10th Av
800 ESCN 1129 H4
10th St
400 CALX 6620 G7
- CALX 6680 F1
400 CORD 1288 G7
300 DLMR 1187 G5
500 ELCN 6499 G5
- ELCN 6559 G4
500 IMPB 1329 H7
1400 IMPB 1349 H2
300 IMPE 6439 E5
- ImCo 6620 B1
- NATC 1309 F2
- SDCo 1066 D1
- SDCo 1085 H4
100 SDCo 1152 G5
- SDCo 1291 F1
- SDGO 1229 G4
E 10th St
2800 NATC 1290 B7
2100 NATC 1310 A1
11th Av
1100 SDGO 1289 B3
E 11th Av
100 ESCN 1130 A4
N 11th Av
500 SDGO 1289 B4
W 11th Av
1900 ESCN 1129 F4
1300 SDCo 1129 H5
11th Pl
20300 SDCo 1149 E1
11th St
600 BRAW 6260 A7
(See Page 6260)
200 BRAW 6320 A1
(See Page 6320)
300 DLMR 1187 F5
- ELCN 6499 G4
- ELCN 6559 G2
2200 ENCT 1147 J6
500 IMPB 1329 H6
1000 IMPB 1349 H1
300 IMPE 6439 E5
- ImCo 6620 B1
- SDCo 1066 E1
- SDCo 1085 H4
100 SDCo 1152 G6
E 11th St
2800 NATC 1290 B7
- NATC 1309 H2
2100 NATC 1310 A1
W 11th St
- NATC 1309 F3
12th Av
1200 SDGO 1289 B3
N 12th Av
300 SDGO 1289 B4
W 12th Av
1000 ESCN 1129 H5
12th Pl
20200 SDCo 1149 E1
12th St
100 DLMR 1187 F5
1400 ELCN 6499 G4
2200 ENCT 1147 J5
- ENCT 1148 A5
800 IMPB 1329 H7
1400 IMPB 1349 H2
300 IMPE 6439 E5
500 NATC 1309 G2
- SDCo 1085 H3
300 SDCo 1152 G6
E 12th St
- NATC 1309 H2
2100 NATC 1310 A1
W 12th St
100 NATC 1309 H2
E 13th Av
100 ESCN 1130 A4
W 13th Av
1200 ESCN 1129 H5
13th St
500 BRAW 6260 B7
(See Page 6260)
- BRAW 6320 B2
(See Page 6320)
100 DLMR 1187 F5
2100 ENCT 1147 J5
1200 IMPB 1349 H1
- IMPE 6439 E5
- SDCo 1085 G3
200 SDCo 1152 F6
- SDGO 1229 G4
600 SDGO 1289 B3
500 SDGO 1329 H7
E 13th St
1000 NATC 1309 J1
2200 NATC 1310 B1
S 13th St
- SDGO 1289 B4
E 14th Av
100 ESCN 1130 A4
14th Pl
900 ESCN 1129 H5
14th St
400 BRAW 6320 B2
(See Page 6320)
300 DLMR 1187 F5
- ELCN 6499 F6
- ELCN 6559 G3
2100 ENCT 1148 A5
1200 IMPB 1349 J1
400 IMPE 6439 E5
- ImCo 6620 B1
100 SDCo 1152 F6
600 SDGO 1289 B3
900 SDGO 1329 J7
E 14th St
600 NATC 1309 J2
1500 NATC 1310 A1
W 14th St
700 NATC 1309 G2
E 15th Av
100 ESCN 1130 A4
W 15th Av
1100 ESCN 1129 H5
200 ESCN 1130 A5
15th St
400 DLMR 1187 F4
- IMPE 6439 F5
- SDCo 1047 A5
300 SDCo 1152 F6
600 SDGO 1289 C3
800 SDGO 1329 J7
1200 SDGO 1349 J1
E 15th St
- NATC 1309 H2
1400 NATC 1310 A1
W 15th St
700 NATC 1309 G2
W 16th Av
700 ESCN 1129 J5
16th St
600 BRAW 6260 B7
(See Page 6260)
600 BRAW 6320 B2
(See Page 6320)
- ELCN 6559 F2
200 SDCo 1152 F6
- SDGO 1229 G4
300 SDGO 1289 C4
900 SDGO 1329 J7
1100 SDGO 1349 J1
E 16th St
100 NATC 1309 H2
1400 NATC 1310 A1
S 16th St
900 SDGO 1289 C4
W 16th St
700 NATC 1309 G3
17th Av
300 ESCN 1130 B5
900 SDCo 1130 C4
17th St
600 BRAW 6320 B2
(See Page 6320)
1400 ELCN 6499 F4
3000 NATC 1310 C1
900 SDGO 1289 C3
1000 SDGO 1349 J1
E 17th St
- NATC 1309 H2
1600 NATC 1310 A1
S 17th St
100 SDGO 1289 C4
W 17th St
800 NATC 1309 G3
18th St
- BRAW 6320 B2
(See Page 6320)
100 DLMR 1187 F4
1100 ELCN 6499 E5
- ELCN 6559 F2
600 SDGO 1330 A6
E 18th St
- NATC 1309 J2
2800 NATC 1310 B1
W 18th St
800 NATC 1309 G3
19th St
100 DLMR 1187 F4
1100 ELCN 6499 E5
- ELCN 6559 F2
- SDCo 1027 B7
- SDCo 1047 A2
1000 SDGO 1289 C3
E 19th St
600 NATC 1309 J2
2400 NATC 1310 B1
S 19th St
100 SDGO 1289 C4
W 19th St
800 NATC 1309 G3
20th St
100 DLMR 1187 F4
300 SDGO 1289 C4
E 20th St
- NATC 1309 H3
1300 NATC 1310 A2
W 20th St
700 NATC 1309 G3
21st St
100 DLMR 1187 F4
1800 ELCN 6499 E6
1200 SDGO 1289 C3
E 21st St
- NATC 1309 H3
1000 NATC 1310 A2
W 21st St
400 NATC 1309 H3
22nd St
200 DLMR 1187 F3
100 ELCN 6499 E6
1500 ELCN 6559 E1
1700 NATC 1310 B2
1000 SDGO 1289 C3
E 22nd St
- NATC 1309 J3
2200 NATC 1310 B2
N 22nd St
200 SDGO 1289 C4
W 22nd St
700 NATC 1309 G3
23rd St
100 DLMR 1187 F3
100 ELCN 6499 E6
1600 ELCN 6559 E1
1100 SDGO 1289 C3
E 23rd St
1000 NATC 1310 A2
W 23rd St
700 NATC 1309 G3
24th St
100 DLMR 1187 F3
1500 ELCN 6559 E1
- SDGO 1208 A2
1100 SDGO 1289 C3
700 SDGO 1330 B7
E 24th St
200 NATC 1309 J3
2200 NATC 1310 B2
W 24th St
1600 NATC 1309 G4
25th St
200 DLMR 1187 F3
100 NATC 1309 H3
1100 SDGO 1289 D3
1100 SDGO 1350 B1
E 25th St
- NATC 1309 J3
W 25th St
800 NATC 1309 G4
26th St
200 DLMR 1187 F3
1100 SDGO 1289 D3
E 26th St
200 NATC 1309 J3
1000 NATC 1310 A3
S 26th St
1000 SDGO 1289 D6
W 26th St
- NATC 1309 H3
27th St
100 CHLV 1330 C5
200 DLMR 1187 F3
700 SDGO 1289 D3
800 SDGO 1330 C7
1300 SDGO 1350 C2
E 27th St
200 NATC 1309 J3
S 27th St
1100 SDGO 1289 D6
28th St
200 DLMR 1187 F3
3700 SDGO 1269 D6
1200 SDGO 1289 E3
E 28th St
600 NATC 1309 J3
1000 NATC 1310 A3
S 28th St
600 SDGO 1289 E5
W 28th St
1400 NATC 1309 G4
29th St
100 DLMR 1187 F3
3800 SDGO 1269 E5
900 SDGO 1289 E3
E 29th St
100 NATC 1309 J4
S 29th St
300 SDGO 1289 E5
30th Pl
700 SDGO 1289 E3
30th St
4500 SDGO 1269 E4
1200 SDGO 1289 E3
1300 SDGO 1350 D1
E 30th St
200 NATC 1309 J4
1400 NATC 1310 A3
S 30th St
300 SDGO 1289 E5
W 30th St
100 NATC 1309 H4
31st St
3600 SDGO 1269 E6
600 SDGO 1289 E3
E 31st St
- NATC 1309 J4
S 31st St
300 SDGO 1289 E5
32nd St
- NATC 1309 J4
4600 SDGO 1269 E3
600 SDGO 1289 F3
E 32nd St
2300 SDCo 1310 C3
S 32nd St
- SDGO 1289 F4
W 32nd St
1200 NATC 1309 G5
33rd Pl
4300 SDGO 1269 F4
33rd St
4800 SDGO 1269 F3
400 SDGO 1289 F3
S 33rd St
200 SDGO 1289 F4
W 33rd St
- NATC 1309 J4
34th St
4900 SDGO 1269 F3
800 SDGO 1289 F3
35th Pl
- SDGO 1269 F4
35th St
4800 SDGO 1269 F3
900 SDGO 1289 F3
S 35th St
200 SDGO 1289 F4
W 35th St
- NATC 1309 J5
36th St
4600 SDGO 1269 F3
200 SDGO 1289 G4
S 36th St
200 SDGO 1289 G4
37th St
4400 SDGO 1269 G4
S 37th St
300 SDGO 1289 G5
38th St
4600 SDGO 1269 G3
1000 SDGO 1289 G3
S 38th St
900 SDGO 1289 G5
39th St
4300 SDGO 1269 G4
800 SDGO 1289 G3
S 39th St
300 SDGO 1289 G5
40th St
4500 SDGO 1269 G4
600 SDGO 1289 G3
S 40th St
600 SDGO 1289 H5
41st St
4400 SDGO 1269 G4
600 SDGO 1289 H3
S 41st St
700 SDGO 1289 H5
42nd St
4600 SDGO 1269 H3
1000 SDGO 1289 H2
S 42nd St
500 SDGO 1289 H5
43rd St
4000 SDGO 1269 H5
400 SDGO 1289 H3
S 43rd St
700 SDGO 1289 H5
44th St
- SDCo 1289 J4
4400 SDGO 1269 H4
1100 SDGO 1289 H2
S 44th St
700 SDGO 1289 J5
45th St
4500 SDGO 1269 J4
400 SDGO 1289 J3
S 45th St
100 SDGO 1289 J4
46th St
4300 SDGO 1269 J4
1100 SDGO 1289 J2
S 46th St
200 SDGO 1289 J5
47th St
4500 SDGO 1269 J3
1600 SDGO 1289 J2
S 47th St
1000 SDGO 1289 J5
48th St
6000 SDGO 1249 J7
4500 SDGO 1269 J4
1800 SDGO 1289 J1
S 48th St
1200 SDGO 1290 A6
49th St
6300 SDGO 1250 A6
4700 SDGO 1270 A3
1800 SDGO 1290 A1
S 49th St
100 SDGO 1290 A5
50th St
6900 SDGO 1250 A5
4700 SDGO 1270 A3
1900 SDGO 1290 A1
S 50th St
1300 SDGO 1290 A6
51st St
6800 SDGO 1250 A5
4700 SDGO 1270 A3
700 SDGO 1290 A3
52nd Pl
5200 SDGO 1270 A5
52nd St
3200 SDGO 1270 B6
2300 SDGO 1290 A1
53rd St
3200 SDGO 1270 B6
300 SDGO 1290 B4
54th Pl
4200 SDGO 1270 B4
54th St
4500 SDGO 1270 B3
400 SDGO 1290 B3
55th Pl
5000 SDGO 1270 B2
55th St
5200 SDGO 1270 B2
200 SDGO 1290 B4
56th Pl
5500 SDGO 1290 B3
56th St
4500 SDGO 1270 B4
1000 SDGO 1290 B3
57th St
1000 SDGO 1290 B2
58th Pl
5700 SDGO 1270 B4
58th St
4200 SDGO 1270 C4
S 58th St
300 SDGO 1290 C4
59th St
4700 SDGO 1270 C3
500 SDGO 1290 C3
S 59th St
400 SDGO 1290 C5
60th St
4600 SDGO 1270 C3
- SDGO 1290 C3
61st St
500 SDGO 1290 C3
S 61st St
100 SDGO 1290 C4
62nd St
4600 SDGO 1270 C3
500 SDGO 1290 D3
63rd St
4500 SDGO 1270 D3
500 SDGO 1290 D3
64th St
4900 SDGO 1270 D2
500 SDGO 1290 D3
65th St
800 SDGO 1290 D3
S 65th St
400 SDGO 1290 D5
66th St
400 SDGO 1290 E3
S 66th St
100 SDGO 1290 E4
67th St
4700 SDGO 1270 E3
600 SDGO 1290 E3
68th St
4500 LMSA 1270 E3
4800 SDGO 1270 E2
800 SDGO 1290 E3
S 68th St
400 SDGO 1290 E3
69th Pl
4800 SDGO 1270 E2
69th St
2400 LMGR 1270 E7
4100 SDGO 1270 E4
800 SDGO 1290 E3
70th St
4400 LMSA 1270 E3
5100 SDGO 1270 E2
71st St
4400 LMSA 1270 F3
4900 SDGO 1270 F2
600 SDGO 1290 F3
72nd St
4900 SDGO 1270 F2
73rd St
4600 LMSA 1270 F3
4900 SDGO 1270 F2

San Diego County Points of Interest Index

SAN DIEGO CO.

San Diego County Points of Interest Index

SAN DIEGO CO.

Golf Courses   **San Diego County Points of Interest Index**   Libraries

SAN DIEGO CO.

SAN DIEGO CO.

Historic Sites

Hospitals

Law Enforcement

Libraries

San Diego County Points of Interest Index

SAN DIEGO CO.

SAN DIEGO CO.

Military Installations

Museums

Open Space

SAN DIEGO CO.

SAN DIEGO CO.

San Diego County Points of Interest Index

Parks & Recreation

San Diego County Points of Interest Index

Schools

SAN DIEGO CO.

San Diego County Points of Interest Index

FEATURE NAME Address City ZIP Code	MAP#	GRID
Arroyo Vista Charter School - 2491 School House Rd, CHLV, 91915	1311	H6
Aseltine School, 4027 Normal St, SDGO, 92103	1269	C5
Ashley Falls School, 13030 Ashley Falls Dr - SDGO, 92130	1188	D5
Audeo Charter School, 10170 Huennekens St - SDGO, 92121	1208	G5
Aurora High School, 641 Rockwood Av, CALX - 92231	6680	G1
Aviara Oaks Elementary School - 6900 Ambrosia Ln, CRLB, 92011	1127	D6
Aviara Oaks Middle School, 6880 Ambrosia Ln - CRLB, 92011	1127	D6
Avocado Elementary School - 3845 Avocado School Rd, SDCo, 91941	1271	G4
Avondale Elementary School, 8401 Stansbury St - SDCo, 91977	1290	J2
Baker Elementary School, 4041 T St, SDGO, 92113	1289	H5
Balboa City School, 525 Hawthorn St, SDGO, 92101	1289	A1
Bancroft Elementary School, 8805 Tyler St, SDCo - 91977	1271	A7
Banyan Tree - Mira Mesa - 9636 Tierra Grande, Number 200, SDGO, 92126	1209	E6
Barbara Worth Junior High School, 385 D St - BRAW, 92227 (See Page 6259)	6319	J1
Barnard Elementary School, 2930 Barnard St - SDGO, 92110	1268	C5
Barnett Elementary School, 23925 Couna Wy - SDCo, 92065	1173	E2
Bay Park Elementary School, 2433 Denver St - SDGO, 92110	1248	E7
Bayshore Preparatory School - 100 N Rancho Santa Fe Rd, SNMS, 92069	1128	E1
Bayside Elementary School, 490 Emory St, IMPB - 91932	1329	G6
Bayview Terrace Elementary School - 2445 Fogg St, SDGO, 92109	1248	C5
Bear Valley Middle School - 3003 Bear Valley Pkwy S, ESCN, 92025	1150	C1
Beaumont Elementary School, 550 Beaumont Dr - VSTA, 92084	1088	A7
Beautiful Saviour Lutheran Elementary School - 3030 Valley St, CRLB, 92008	1106	F4
Bella Mente Montessori Academy - 1737 W Vista Way, VSTA, 92083	1107	D1
Ben Hulse Elementary School, 303 S D St, IMPE - 92251	6439	E6
Benchley-Weinberger Elementary School - 6269 Twin Lake Dr, SDGO, 92119	1250	G5
Benito Juarez Elementary School - 2633 Melbourne Dr, SDGO, 92123	1249	E6
Benjamin Franklin Elementary School - 4481 Copeland Av, SDGO, 92116	1269	H4
Berean Christian Academy - 23663 Viejas Grade Rd, SDCo, 92126	1235	G2
Bernardo Elementary School - 1122 Mountain Heights Dr, ESCN, 92029	1149	H1
Bernardo Heights Middle School - 12990 Paseo Lucido, SDGO, 92128	1170	B6
Beta-Selam Academy, 6429 Imperial Av, SDGO - 92114	1290	D3
Beth Israel Day Jewish Elementary School - 2512 3rd Av, SDGO, 92103	1289	A1
Bethel Academy, 1200 East 8th St, NATC, 91950	1309	J1
Bethune Elementary School - 6835 Benjamin Holt Rd, SDGO, 92114	1290	E6
Beyer Elementary School, 2312 E Beyer Blvd - SDGO, 92173	1350	G4
Bird Rock Elementary School - 5371 La Jolla Hermosa Av, SDGO, 92037	1247	G4
Bishops Episcopal High School - 7607 La Jolla Blvd, SDGO, 92037	1227	E7
Black Mountain Middle School, 9353 Oviedo St - SDGO, 92129	1189	D3
Blanche Charles Elementary School - 1201 Kloke Av, CALX, 92231	6620	D7
Blessed Sacrament Parish School, 4551 56th St - SDGO, 92115	1270	B3
Blossom Valley Elementary School - 9863 Oakmont Ter, SDCo, 92021	1233	A3
Bobier Elementary School, 220 W Bobier Dr - VSTA, 92083	1087	G4
Bonita Country Day Elementary School - 625 Otay Lakes Rd, CHLV, 91913	1311	B4
Bonita Road Christian School, 73 E Bonita Rd - CHLV, 91910	1310	D5
Bonita Vista High School, 751 Otay Lakes Rd - CHLV, 91913	1311	C5
Bonita Vista Middle School, 650 Otay Lakes Rd - CHLV, 91910	1311	B5
Bonsall Elementary School, 31555 Old River Rd - SDCo, 92003	1068	A2
Bonsall High, 7350 W Lilac Rd, SDCo, 92003	1048	F7
Bonsall West Elementary School, 5050 El Mirlo Dr - OCSD, 92057	1067	B5
Borrego Springs Elementary School - 1315 Palm Canyon Dr, SDCo, 92004 (See Page 1058)	1079	C2
Borrego Springs High School, 2281 Diegueno Rd - SDCo, 92004 (See Page 1058)	1078	H1
Borrego Springs Middle School - 2281 Diegueno Rd, SDCo, 90024 (See Page 1058)	1078	H1
Bostonia Christian Elementary School - 211 S 3rd St, ELCJ, 92019	1252	A6
Bostonia Elementary School, 1390 Broadway - ELCJ, 92021	1252	A3
Boulder Oaks Elementary School - 2320 Tavern Rd, SDCo, 91901	1254	A1
Brawley Christian Academy, 430 N 2nd St, BRAW - 92227 (See Page 6259)	6319	J1
Brawley Union High School, 480 N Imperial Av - BRAW, 92227 (See Page 6259)	6319	J1
Breeze Hill Elementary School, 1111 Melrose Wy - VSTA, 92081	1107	F1
Brookshire International Academy - 3295 Market St, Ste 100, SDGO, 92110	1289	F3
Buena Vista Elementary School - 1330 Buena Vista Wy, CRLB, 92008	1106	E4
Burton C Tiffany Elementary School - 1691 Elmhurst St, CHLV, 91913	1311	C5
CPMA Middle Magnet School, 5095 Arvinels Av - SDGO, 92117	1228	G7
Cajon Park Elementary School - 10300 N Magnolia Av, SNTE, 92071	1231	E3
Cajon Valley Home, 1384 Broadway, ELCJ, 92021	1252	A3
Cajon Valley Middle School, 395 Ballantyne St - ELCJ, 92020	1251	G5
Cal Coast Academy, 11555 Clews Ranch Rd - DLMR, 92014	1188	C7
Calavera Hills Elementary School - 4100 Tamarack Av, SDGO, 92116	1107	B3
Calavera Hills Middle School, 4104 Tamarack Av - SDGO, 92111	1107	B3
Calexico High School, 1030 Encinas Av, CALX - 92231	6680	H1
Calexico Mission Academy, 601 E 1st St, CALX - 92231	6680	G2
Calvary Chapel of La Mesa Christian - 7525 El Cajon Blvd, LMSA, 91941	1270	G2
Calvary Christian Academy, 1771 E Palomar St - CHLV, 91913	1311	D7
Calvary Christian Elementary School - 885 E Vista Wy, VSTA, 92084	1087	J5
Calvary Christian High School, 885 E Vista Wy - VSTA, 92084	1087	J5
Calvin Christian Junior & High School - 2000 N Broadway, ESCN, 92026	1109	H5
Calvin Christian of Escondido Elem School - 1868 N Broadway, ESCN, 92026	1109	H5
Camarena (Enrique S.) Elementary School - 1650 Exploration Falls Dr, CHLV, 91915	1331	G1
Campo Elementary School - 1654 Buckman Springs Rd, SDCo, 91906(See Page 1296)	1317	H3
Canyon Crest Academy High School - 5951 E Village Center Loop Rd, SDGO, 92130	1188	F5
Canyon Ridge Christian Prep - 1200 Old Highway 395, SDCo, 92028	998	G6
Canyon View Elementary School - 9225 Adolphia St, SDGO, 92129	1189	D6
Capri Elementary School, 941 Capri Rd, ENCT - 92024	1147	C3
Cardiff Elementary School, 1888 Montgomery Av - ENCT, 92007	1167	D3
Carl Sandburg Elementary School - 11230 Avenida del Gato, SDGO, 92126	1209	B2
Carlsbad High School, 3557 Monroe St, CRLB - 92008	1106	G5
Carlsbad Village Academy, 1640 Magnolia Av - CRLB, 92008	1106	G5
Carlton Hills Christian Elementary School - 9735 Halberns Blvd, SNTE, 92071	1231	B4
Carlton Hills Elementary School, 9353 Pike Rd - SNTE, 92071	1231	B5
Carlton Oaks School, 9353 Wethersfield Rd, SNTE - 92071	1230	J6
Carmel Creek Elementary School - 4210 Carmel Center Rd, SDGO, 92130	1188	B6
Carmel Valley Middle School, 3800 Mykonos Ln - SDGO, 92130	1188	A6
Carmel del Mar Elementary School - 12345 Carmel Park Dr, SDGO, 92130	1188	A7
Carrillo Elementary School, 2875 Poinsettia Av - CRLB, 92009	1127	H3
Casa de Oro Elementary School - 10227 Ramona Dr, SDCo, 91977	1271	E5
Case Educational Program - 785 Grand Av, Ste 101, CRLB, 92008	1106	E5
Casita Ctr for Tech-Science & Math Elem Sch - 260 Cedar Rd, VSTA, 92083	1107	C1
Castle Park Elementary School, 25 Emerson St - CHLV, 91911	1330	E2
Castle Park High School, 1395 Hilltop Dr, CHLV - 91911	1330	F3
Castle Park Middle School, 160 Quintard St - CHLV, 91911	1330	E4
Cathedral Catholic High School - 5555 Del Mar Heights Rd, SDGO, 92130	1188	E4
Center City High School, 240 S Maple St, ESCN - 92025	1129	J3
Centers of Learning By the Sea, 950 Garland Dr - SDGO, 92154	1330	C7
Central Elementary School, 4063 Polk Av, SDGO - 92105	1269	G5
Central Elementary School, 1290 Ebony Av, IMPB - 91932	1349	H1
Central Elementary School, 122 W 4th Av, ESCN - 92025	1129	J3
Central Elementary School, 933 E Av, NATC, 91950	1309	J1
Central Union High School, 1001 W Brighton Av - ELCN, 92243	6499	G7
Cesar Chavez Elementary School, 1404 S 40th St - SDGO, 92113	1289	G6
Cesar Chavez Elementary School - 1251 E Zapata St, CALX, 92231	6620	J6
Cesar Chavez Middle, 202 Oleander Dr, OCSD - 92057	1087	A1
Chabad Hebrew Academy, 10785 Pomerado Rd - SDGO, 92131	1209	J5
Challenger Junior High School - 10810 Parkdale Av, SDGO, 92126	1209	A4
Challenges Community Day School - 707 Carey Rd, OCSD, 92058	1086	C6
Chaparral Elementary School, 17250 Tannin Dr - POWY, 92064	1170	D2
Chaparral High School, 1600 N Cuyamaca St - ELCJ, 92020	1251	D2
Charles A Lindbergh Elementary School - 4133 Mt Albertine Av, SDGO, 92111	1248	J3
Charles Cadman Elementary School - 4370 Kamloop Av, SDGO, 92117	1248	C2
Charter School of San Diego, 2245 San Diego Av - SDGO, 92110	1208	G5
Chase Avenue Elementary School - 195 E Chase Av, ELCJ, 92020	1251	F7
Chauncy I Jerabek Elementary School - 10050 Avenida Magnifica, SDGO, 92131	1210	A4
Cherokee Point Elementary School, 3735 38th St - SDGO, 92105	1269	G5
Chesterton Elementary School, 7335 Wheatley St - SDGO, 92111	1249	A6
Chet F Harritt Elementary School, 8120 Arlette St - SNTE, 92071	1230	J7
Children's Creative and Performing Arts - 3051 El Cajon Blvd, SDGO, 92104	1269	E4
Children's Paradise - El Norte - 986 W El Norte Pkwy, ESCN, 92026	1109	F6
Childrens Creative & Performing Arts Academy - 4431 Mt Herbert Av, SDGO, 92117	1248	F2
Childrens Creative & Performing Arts Academy - 6611 University Av, SDGO, 92115	1270	E4
Childrens School, 2225 Torrey Pines Ln, SDGO - 92037	1227	H6
Childrens Workshop School - 2255 Camino del Rio S, SDCo, 91916	1269	C3
Childs Primary School, The, 3811 Mt Acadia Blvd - ELCN, 92243	1248	H4
Chollas-Mead Elementary School, 4525 Market St - CALX, 92243	1289	J3
Christ Church Day Elementary School - 1114 9th St, CORD, 92118	1288	J7
Christ Community School, 585 W Orange Av - ELCN, 92243	6499	H7
Christ Cornerstone Lutheran Academy - 9028 Westmore Rd, SDGO, 92126	1209	D3
Christ Lutheran Elementary School - 7929 La Mesa Blvd, LMSA, 91941	1270	G2
Christa McAuliffe Elementary School - 3701 Kelton Dr, OCSD, 92056	1086	J7
Christian Academy of Chula Vista, 494 E St - CHLV, 91910	1310	A6
Christian Creative Learning Academy - 2920 Main St, LMGR, 91945	1270	G7
Christian Elementary School, 6747 Amherst St - SDGO, 92115	1270	E2
Christian Junior-Senior High School - 2100 Greenfield Dr, ELCJ, 92019	1252	D4
Christian Life Academy - 2081 Bear Valley Pkwy, Ste B220, ESCN, 92025	1130	D1
Chula Vista Christian Elementary School - 960 5th Av, CHLV, 91911	1330	B2
Chula Vista High School, 820 4th Av, CHLV, 91911	1330	B2
Chula Vista Hills Elementary School - 980 Buena Vista Wy, CHLV, 91910	1311	B6
Chula Vista Learning Comm Charter School - 590 K St, CHLV, 91911	1330	B2
Chula Vista Middle School, 415 5th Av, CHLV - 91910	1310	A7
Church of Nativity Elementary School - 6309 El Apajo, SDCo, 92067	1168	E6
City Arts Academy Charter School, 611 S 35th St - SDGO, 92113	1289	F5
City Heights Preparatory Charter - 3770 Altadena Av, SDGO, 92105	1270	A5
City Tree Elementary School, 320 Date St, SDGO - 92101	1289	A2
Clairemont High School, 4150 Ute Dr, SDGO - 92117	1248	E4
Classical Academy, 2950 Bear Valley Pkwy S - ESCN, 92025	1150	C1
Classical Academy High School - 144 Woodward Av, ESCN, 92025	1129	J2
Classical Academy Online - 4183 Avenida De La Plata, OCSD, 92056	1087	B5
Classical Academy Vista, 2585 Business Park Dr - VSTA, 92081	1107	J6
Classical Charter Academy Elementary School - 130 Woodward Av, ESCN, 92025	1129	H2
Clear View Charter School, 455 Windrose Wy - CHLV, 91910	1310	F5
Clover Flat Elementary School - 39639 Old Highway 80, SDCo, 91905	1300	D6
Coastal Academy Elementary School - 4183 Avenida de la Plata, OCSD, 92056	1087	B5
Coleman Tech Charter High School, 3540 Aero Ct - SDGO, 92123	1249	B4
College Preparatory Middle Middle - 5150 Jackson Dr, LMSA, 91942	1271	A1
Colonel Ed Fletcher Elementary School - 7666 Bobolink Wy, SDGO, 92123	1249	A7
Community Center For Academic Excellence - 616 East 8th St, NATC, 91950	1309	J1
Convenant Christian Elementary School - 505 E Naples St, CHLV, 91911	1330	G1
Conway Elementary School, 1325 Conway Dr - ESCN, 92027	1109	J6
Cook Education Center, 2255 Camino del Rio S - SDGO, 92108	1269	C3
Cornerstone Christian Elementary School - 13617 Midland Rd, POWY, 92064	1190	F3
Coronado High School, 650 D Av, CORD, 92118	1288	H6
Coronado Middle School, 550 F Av, CORD, 92118	1288	H6
Coronado Village Elementary School, 600 6th St - CORD, 92118	1288	H6
Cortez Hill Academy Charter High School - 201 A St, SDGO, 92101	1289	A2
Country Montessori School of Poway - 12642 Monte Vista Rd, POWY, 92064	1170	C6
Covenant Christian High School, 505 E Naples St - CHLV, 91911	1330	G1
Creekside Elementary School - 12362 Springhurst Dr, SDGO, 92128	1190	A6
Crest Elementary School, 2000 Suncrest Blvd - SDCo, 92021	1252	H3
Crestview Elementary School, 510 Sunset Dr - VSTA, 92081	1107	H1
Crown Point Elementary School - 4033 Ingraham St, SDGO, 92109	1248	A6

Schools

San Diego County Points of Interest Index

Schools

SAN DIEGO CO.

SAN DIEGO CO.

Schools

San Diego County Points of Interest Index

Schools

SAN DIEGO CO.

86 INDEX

INDEX **86**

Schools

San Diego County Points of Interest Index

Schools

SAN DIEGO CO.

SAN DIEGO CO.

San Diego County Points of Interest Index

FEATURE NAME Address City ZIP Code	MAP#	GRID
Pete W Ross Elementary School, 7470 Bagdad St - SDGO, 92111	1249	A3
Phil D Swing School, 245 W A St, BRAW, 92227 (See Page 6259)	6319	H1
Phoebe A Hearst Elementary School - 6230 Del Cerro Blvd, SDGO, 92120	1250	C7
Pilgrim Lutheran Elementary School, 497 E St - CHLV, 91910	1310	A5
Pine Glen Academy, 15519 Villa Sierra Rd, SDCo - 92082	1070	J5
Pine Valley Elementary School, 7454 Pine Blvd - SDCo, 91962	1237	C7
Pioneer Elementary School, 980 N Ash St, ESCN - 92027	1110	A7
Pivot Charter School - San Diego - 1030 La Bonita Dr, Ste 350, SNMS, 92078	1128	C3
Poinsettia Elementary School, 2445 Mica Rd - CRLB, 92009	1127	G4
Point Loma Senior High School - 2335 Chatsworth Blvd, SDGO, 92106	1268	C7
Pomerado Elementary School, 12321 9th St - POWY, 92064	1190	B4
Poway High School, 15500 Espola Rd, POWY - 92064	1170	G5
Preuss School-UCSD, 9500 Gilman Dr, SDGO - 92093	1228	B1
Promise Charter Elementary School, 730 45th St - SDGO, 92102	1289	J3
Prospect Avenue School, 9303 Prospect Av - SNTE, 92071	1231	B7
Quantum Academy, 420 N Falconer Rd, ESCN - 92027	1110	E6
Rainbow Advanced Institute for Lrn Charter - 5253 5th St, SDCo, 92028	998	J5
Ralph Dailard Elementary School, 6425 Cibola Rd - SDGO, 92120	1250	E4
Ramona Christian Academy - 23726 Gymkhana Rd, SDCo, 92065	1173	D1
Ramona Community School, 1010 Ramona Street - SDCo, 92065	1152	E6
Ramona Elementary School, 415 8th St, SDCo - 92065	1152	G6
Ramona Faith Academy, 320 3rd St, SDCo, 92065	1152	H5
Ramona High School, 1401 Hanson Ln, SDCo - 92065	1172	G1
Ramona Lutheran Elementary School - 520 16th St, SDCo, 92065	1152	F7
Rancho Bernardo High School - 13010 Paseo Lucido, SDGO, 92128	1170	B6
Rancho Buena Vista High School - 1601 Longhorn Dr, VSTA, 92081	1107	G4
Rancho Elementary School, 8845 Noeline Av - SDCo, 91977	1290	J4
Rancho Encinitas Academy, 910 Encinitas Blvd - ENCT, 92024	1147	E6
Rancho Minerva Middle School, 2245 Foothill Dr - VSTA, 92084	1088	C6
Rancho San Diego Elementary School - 12151 Calle Albara, SDCo, 92019	1272	A4
Rancho Santa Fe Elementary School - 5927 La Granada, SDCo, 92067	1168	D3
Rancho Santa Fe Middle School - 5927 La Granada, SDCo, 92067	1168	D3
Rancho de la Nacion Elementary School - 1830 E Division St, NATC, 91950	1290	A7
Rancho del Rey Middle School, 1174 E J St - CHLV, 91910	1311	A7
Ray Kroc Middle School, 5050 Conrad Av, SDGO - 92117	1228	G7
Reach Academy, 230 Jamacha Rd, ELCJ, 92019	1251	J5
Reformation Lutheran Elementary School - 4670 Mt Abernathy Av, SDGO, 92117	1248	J1
Regina Caeli Academy, 1185 Belmont Terrace - VSTA, 92084	1108	C1
Reidy Creek Elementary School - 2869 N Broadway, ESCN, 92026	1109	H3
Reynolds Elementary School, 4575 Douglas Dr - OCSD, 92057	1066	J6
Rhoades School for the Gifted - 141 S Rancho Santa Fe Rd, ENCT, 92024	1167	J1
Richland Elementary School, 910 Borden Rd - SNMS, 92069	1109	B5
Riley Elementary School, 5650 Mt Ackerly Dr - SDGO, 92111	1248	H4
Rincon Middle School, 925 Lehner Av, ESCN - 92026	1109	J5
Rio Seco Elementary School, 9545 Cuyamaca St - SNTE, 92071	1231	D4
Rios Elementary School, 14314 Rios Canyon Rd - SDCo, 92021	1232	G6
River Valley Charter High School, 9707 Marilla Dr - SDCo, 92040	1231	J4
Riverview Elementary School - 9308 Winter Gardens Blvd, SDCo, 92040	1231	J5
Robert E Lee Elementary School, 6196 Childs Av - SDGO, 92139	1310	D2
Robert Fulton Elementary School - 7055 Skyline Dr, SDGO, 92114	1290	F4
Robert L Mueller Elementary School, 715 I St - CHLV, 91910	1330	A1
Rock Academy School, The, 6866 Linda Vista Rd - SDGO, 92111	1268	H1
Rock Springs Elementary School - 1155 Deodar Rd, ESCN, 92026	1109	F7
Rockwood Elementary School - 1000 Rockwood Av, CALX, 92231	6680	G1
Rolando Elementary School, 6925 Tower St - LMSA, 91941	1270	E3
Rolando Park Elementary School - 6620 Marlowe Dr, SDGO, 92115	1270	D5
Rolling Hills Elementary School - 15255 Penasquitos Dr, SDGO, 92129	1169	H7
Roosevelt Middle School, 850 Sagewood Dr - OCSD, 92057	1087	C1
Rosa Parks Elementary School, 4510 Landis St - SDGO, 92105	1269	H5
Rose Elementary School, 906 N Rose St, ESCN - 92027	1110	B7
Rosebank Elementary School, 80 Flower St - CHLV, 91910	1310	C5
Royal Academy of, 32768 Via del Venado, SDCo - 92082	1049	E5
SIATech, 1325 Iris Av, IMPB, 91932	1349	J2
Sacred Heart Academy Elementary School - 4895 Saratoga Av, SDGO, 92107	1267	J6
Sacred Heart Parish Elementary School, 706 C Av - CORD, 92118	1288	J7
Sacred Heart School, 428 S Imperial Av, BRAW - 92227 (See Page 6259)	6319	J2
Sage Canyon Elementary School - 5290 Harvest Run Dr, SDGO, 92130	1208	D2
Sage Creek High School, 3900 Cannon Rd, CRLB - 92010	1107	C5
Saint Joseph Academy, 500 Las Flores Dr, SNMS - 92078	1108	C7
Salk Elementary School, 7825 Flanders Dr, SDGO - 92126	1209	A5
Salt Creek Elementary School, 1055 Hunte Pkwy - CHLV, 91914	1311	H4
Samuel FB Morse Senior High School - 6905 Skyline Dr, SDGO, 92114	1290	E5
San Altos Elementary School, 1750 Madera St - LMGR, 91945	1290	F1
San Diego Academy Elementary School - 2800 E 4th St, NATC, 91950	1290	B6
San Diego Academy High School, 2800 E 4th St - NATC, 91950	1290	B6
San Diego Cooperative Charter Elem School - 2850 6th Av, SDGO, 92103	1269	A7
San Diego Cooperative Charter School - 7260 Linda Vista Rd, SDGO, 92111	1248	J7
San Diego French American School - 6550 Soledad Mountain Rd, SDGO, 92037	1247	J1
San Diego High School, 1405 Park Blvd, SDGO - 92101	1289	B2
San Diego Jewish Academy - 11860 Carmel Creek Rd, SDGO, 92130	1208	B1
San Diego Jewish Academy Elementary School - 11860 Carmel Creek Rd, SDGO, 92130	1208	B1
San Diego Liberal Arts Academy - 11255 Redbud Ct, SDGO, 92127	1169	J5
San Diego MET School, 7250 Mesa College Dr - SDGO, 92111	1249	A5
San Diego Neighborhood Homeschools - 3548 Seagate Way, Ste 140, OCSD, 92056	1087	A5
San Diego Sch of Creative & Performing Arts - 2425 Dusk Dr, SDGO, 92139	1290	E7
San Dieguito High School, 800 Santa Fe Dr - ENCT, 92024	1167	E1
San Dieguito High School Academy - 710 Encinitas Blvd, ENCT, 92024	1147	E6
San Elijio Elementary School - 1615 Schoolhouse Wy, SNMS, 92078	1128	E6
San Elijio Middle School, 1600 Schoolhouse Wy - SNMS, 92078	1128	E6
San Luis Rey Elementary School - 3535 Hacienda Dr, OCSD, 92054	1086	F4
San Marcos Elementary School - 300 W San Marcos Blvd, SNMS, 92069	1108	G7
San Marcos High School - 1615 W San Marcos Blvd, SNMS, 92078	1128	C2
San Marcos Middle School, 650 W Mission Rd - SNMS, 92069	1108	G6
San Miguel Elementary School - 7059 San Miguel Av, LMGR, 91945	1270	F7
San Onofre Elementary School, 200 Pate Dr - SDCo, 92672	1023	E2
San Pasqual Academy - 17701 San Pasqual Valley Rd, SDCo, 92025	1131	F6
San Pasqual High School - 3300 Bear Valley Pkwy S, ESCN, 92025	1150	C2
San Pasqual Union Elementary School - 15305 Rockwood Rd, SDGO, 92027	1130	H4
San Rafael Elementary School - 1616 San Rafael Dr, SDCo, 92054	1085	J5
San Ysidro High School, 5353 Airway Rd, SDGO - 92154	1351	A2
San Ysidro Middle School, 4345 Otay Mesa Rd - SDGO, 92173	1350	G3
Sanderling Waldorf School, 1905 Magnolia Av - CRLB, 92008	1106	G5
Santa Fe Christian School Comm Elem School - 838 Academy Dr, SOLB, 92075	1167	G7
Santa Fe Christian School Community HS - 838 Academy Dr, SOLB, 92075	1167	G7
Santa Margarita Academy, 400 W Elder St, SDCo - 92028	1027	F3
Santa Margarita Elementary School, 1 Carnes Rd - SDCo, 92054	1086	A2
Santa Sophia Academy Elementary School - 9806 San Juan St, SDCo, 91977	1271	D4
Santana High School, 9915 N Magnolia Av, SNTE - 92071	1231	E4
Santee Alternative, 10250 El Nopal, SNTE, 92071	1231	E3
Santee Elementary School - 10445 Mission George Rd, SNTE, 92071	1231	E6
Santee Success Program, 10280 N Magnolia Av - SNTE, 92071	1231	E3
Sarah Anthony-Sierra Vista School - 2801 Meadow Lark Dr, SDGO, 92123	1249	B6
School of the Madeleine Elementary School - 1875 Illion St, SDGO, 92110	1268	F1
Scripps Elementary School - 11778 Cypress Canyon Rd, SDGO, 92131	1210	A1
Scripps Ranch High School, 10410 Treena St - SDGO, 92131	1209	F4
Sequoia Elementary School, 4690 Limerick Av - SDGO, 92117	1248	H1
Shadow Hills Elementary School - 8770 Harbison Canyon Rd, SDCo, 91901	1233	E6
Shiloh Christian Academy, 2770 Glebe Rd, LMGR - 91945	1270	F6
Shoal Creek Elementary School - 11775 Shoal Creek Dr, SDGO, 92128	1190	A3
Sierra Academy Of San Diego - 6460 Boulder Lake Av, SDGO, 92119	1250	H5
Sierra Madre Elementary School - 1605 W Mission Rd, SNMS, 92069	1108	E6
Sierra Vista High School, 325 E Bobier Dr, VSTA - 92084	1087	H4
Silver Gate Elementary School, 1499 Venice St - SDGO, 92107	1288	A1
Silver Strand Elementary School, 1350 Leyte Rd - CORD, 92118	1309	D6
Silver Wing Elementary School, 3730 Arey Dr - SDGO, 92154	1330	F7
Skyline Elementary School - 606 Lomas Santa Fe Dr, SOLB, 92075	1167	F6
Skyward Academy, 1745 Skimmer Ct, CRLB, 92011	1127	D5
Smythe Elementary School, 1880 Smythe Av - SDGO, 92173	1350	F2
Soille San Diego Hebrew Day Elem School - 3630 Afton Rd, SDGO, 92123	1249	C4
Sojourner Truth Learning Academy - 5825 Imperial Av, SDGO, 92114	1290	B4
Solana Highlands Elementary School - 3520 Long Run Dr, SDGO, 92130	1187	J5
Solana Pacific Elementary School - 3901 Townsgate Dr, SDGO, 92130	1188	A6
Solana Santa Fe Elementary School - 6570 El Apajo, SDCo, 92067	1168	F6
Solana Vista Elementary School - 780 Santa Victoria, SOLB, 92075	1167	G5
South Bay Christian Academy, 395 D St, CHLV - 91910	1310	A5
South Oceanside Elementary School - 1806 S Horne St, OCSD, 92054	1106	D3
Southern California Yeshiva High School - 3410 Mt Acadia Blvd, SDGO, 92111	1248	G5
Southport Christian Academy Elem School - 142 E 16th St, NATC, 91950	1309	H2
Southport Christian Academy High School - 142 E 16th St, NATC, 91950	1309	H2
Southwest High School, 2001 Ocotillo Dr, ELCN - 92243	6559	E1
Southwest Junior High School, 2710 Iris Av - SDGO, 92154	1350	C2
Southwest Senior High School, 1685 Hollister St - SDGO, 92154	1350	B2
Southwestern Christian Elementary School - 482 L St, CHLV, 91911	1330	B2
Spencer Valley Elementary - 4414 Highway 78 and 79, SDCo, 92070	1135	F4
Spring Valley Elementary School, 3845 Spring Dr - SDCo, 91977	1271	A5
Spring Valley Middle School, 3900 Conrad Dr - SDCo, 91977	1271	C4
Springall Academy, 6460 Boulder Lake Av, SDGO - 92119	1250	H5
St. Augustine High School, 3266 Nutmeg St - SDGO, 92104	1269	E7
St. Charles Borromeo Academy Elem School - 2808 Cadiz St, SDGO, 92110	1268	E6
St. Charles Elementary School, 929 18th St - SDGO, 92154	1330	A7
St. Columba Elementary School - 3327 Glencolum Dr, SDGO, 92123	1249	D5
St. Didacus Elementary School, 4630 34th St - SDGO, 92116	1269	F3
St. Francis of Assisi Elementary School - 525 W Vista Wy, VSTA, 92083	1087	G7
St. Gregory The Great Catholic - 15315 Stonebridge Pkwy, SDGO, 92131	1210	H1
St. James Academy Elementary School - 623 S Nardo Av, SOLB, 92075	1187	F1
St. John Elementary School, 1003 Encinitas Blvd - ENCT, 92024	1147	E7
St. John of the Cross Elementary School - 8175 Lemon Grove Wy, LMGR, 91945	1270	H5
St. Johns Episcopal Elementary School - 760 1st Av, CHLV, 91910	1330	D1
St. Jude Academy, 1228 S 38th St, SDGO, 92113	1289	G6
St. Kieran Elementary School, 1347 Camillo Wy - ELCJ, 92021	1252	A3
St. Lukes Lutheran Christian Day Elem School - 5150 Wilson St, LMSA, 91941	1271	A1
St. Martin of Tours Academy, 7708 El Cajon Blvd - LMSA, 91941	1270	G2
St. Mary Star of the Sea Elementary School - 515 Wisconsin Av, OCSD, 92054	1106	B1
St. Marys Catholic Elementary School - 700 S Waterman Av, ELCN, 92243	6499	E7
St. Marys Elementary School, 130 E 13th Av - ESCN, 92025	1130	A4
St. Michael Elementary School - 15542 Pomerado Rd, POWY, 92064	1170	C6
St. Michaels Academy, 2637 Homedale St, SDGO - 92139	1310	E1
St. Patricks Elementary School, 3820 Pio Pico Dr - CRLB, 92008	1106	F6
St. Patricks Elementary School, 3583 30th St - SDGO, 92104	1269	E6
St. Pauls Lutheran Elementary School - 1376 Felspar St, SDGO, 92109	1247	J6
St. Peters Catholic Elementary School - 450 S Stagecoach Ln, SDCo, 92028	1027	J3
St. Pius X Elementary School, 37 E Emerson St - CHLV, 91911	1330	E2
St. Ritas Elementary School, 5165 Imperial Av - SDGO, 92114	1290	A4
St. Rose of Lima School, 473 3rd Av, CHLV, 91910	1310	C7
St. Stephen Lutheran School, 1636 E Mission Rd - SDCo, 92028	1027	J1
St. Therese Academy Elementary School - 6046 Camino Rico, SDGO, 92120	1250	C6
St. Vincent de Paul Elementary School - 4061 Ibis St, SDGO, 92103	1268	J5

Schools

San Diego County Points of Interest Index

Subdivisions & Neighborhoods

Subdivisions & Neighborhoods

Visitor Information

SAN DIEGO CO.